Encyclopedia
of
Policy Studies

PUBLIC ADMINISTRATION AND PUBLIC POLICY

A Comprehensive Publication Program

Executive Editor

JACK RABIN
Professor of Public Administration and Public Policy
Division of Public Affairs
The Capital College
The Pennsylvania State University—Harrisburg
Middletown, Pennsylvania

ANNALS OF PUBLIC ADMINISTRATION

Encyclopedia
of
Policy Studies

Second Edition, Revised and Expanded

edited by

Stuart S. Nagel

Department of Political Science
University of Illinois
Urbana-Champaign, Illinois

Marcel Dekker, Inc.   **New York•Basel•Hong Kong**

Dedicated to the
Application of Political and Social Science to
Important Public Policy Problems

Library of Congress Cataloging-in-Publication Data

Encyclopedia of policy studies / edited by Stuart S. Nagel. -- 2nd.,
   rev. and expanded.
         p.   cm. -- (Public administration and public policy ; 53)
      Includes bibliographical references (p.   ) and index.
      ISBN 0-8247-9142-8
      1. Policy sciences.   I. Series.
   H97.E6   1994   93-44894
                                                                      CIP

The publisher offers discounts on this book when ordered in bulk quantities. For more information, write to Special Sales/Professional Marketing at the address below.

This book is printed on acid-free paper.

Marcel Dekker, Inc.
270 Madison Avenue, New York, New York   10016

Current printing (last digit):
10 9 8 7 6 5 4 3 2 1

PRINTED IN THE UNITED STATES OF AMERICA

Contents

Introduction to the Second Edition

This is the thoroughly revised Second Edition of the *Encyclopedia of Policy Studies*. Every chapter is new, although we have preserved the general organization.

We have also included the Introduction to the First Edition. It provides material that is still current on a high level of generality regarding (1) the general nature and background of policy studies, (2) institution of policy studies, (3) substance, process, and methods of policy studies, (4) the future of policy studies, and (5) the purpose and organization of the Encyclopedia.

The audiences toward which the Encyclopedia is directed are still basically the same. The Encyclopedia has been and should be of value to students and instructors in courses dealing with public policy studies. The Encyclopedia is relevant to doing research on numerous sub-fields and issues in policy studies. It is also relevant to practitioners involved in recommending, making, implementing, or evaluating public policy. Those people come from a variety of disciplinary backgrounds, countries, and government agencies.

This second edition differs from the first edition in various ways other than the fact that all the chapters are new. The chapters update the relevant public policies, experiences, theoretical perspectives, literature, evaluations, and other aspects of the chapters. They collectively provide a comprehensive description and analysis of the policy studies field.

The suggestions to the chapter authors generally recommended that they should show more attention to three aspects of policy studies that were not as well-emphasized in the first edition. We wanted more concern for cross-national analysis, including developing nations. We wanted more concern for inter-disciplinary analysis, including references to economics, sociology, psychology, law, natural science, and other fields. We also wanted more concern for the impact of policy studies research on governmental decision making.

Another important way in which this edition differs from the previous edition is the emphasis on evaluating alternative public policies as contrasted to merely describing them or discussing how they came into being.

In that regard, policy studies can be defined as the study of the nature, causes, and effects of alternative public policies. This new *Encyclopedia of Policy Studies* contains chapters that emphasize all three perspectives. Many of the chapters dealing with specific policy problems (1) describe the *nature* of the relevant public policies, (2) discuss the *causal* factors responsible for why some policies have been adopted and others rejected, and (3) seek to *evaluate* approaches to the problem in order to draw a conclusion as to what approach should be adopted.

Perhaps the most important, but least emphasized, approach within policy studies is the evaluative approach. Public policy evaluation can be defined as the process of determining which of various alternative public or governmental policies will most achieve a given set of goals in light of the relations between the policies and the goals.

That definition brings out the five key elements of policy evaluation:

1. Goals, including normative constraints and relative weights for the goals
2. Policies, programs, projects, decisions, options, means, or other alternatives that are available for achieving the goals
3. Relations between the policies and the goals, including relations that are established in intuition, authority, statistics, observation, deduction, guesses, or other means
4. Drawing a conclusion as to which policy or combination of policies is best to adopt in light of the goals, policies, and relations
5. What-if analysis designed to determine the effects on the tentative conclusions of making changes in the goals, policies, or relations

Goals are whatever effects one is seeking to achieve or avoid. Desired effects are benefits to be maximized. Undesired effects are costs to be minimized. In public policy analysis, there are six frequently mentioned goals: The three E's are generally associated with economics. They are (1) effectiveness, or the quantity of benefits achieved; (2) efficiency, or the cost at which the benefits are achieved; and (3) equity or the distribution of the benefits and the costs among persons, groups, or places. The three P's are generally associated with political science. They are (1) public participation, or the extent to which majority and minority elements of the public have a part in making the decisions; (2) predictability, or the extent to which the decisions are consistent with constitutional principles and reasonable expectations; and (3) procedural due process, or the extent to which those allegedly hurt by the decisions can seek meaningful redress or exoneration.

Policies can be referred to as laws, decisions, options, projects, programs, or other terms for alternatives. Public policies tend to be divided into those that have (1) a political science emphasis, such as foreign policy, defense policy, electoral policy, legislative reform, and civil liberties; (2) an economics emphasis, such as economic regulation, labor policy, communications, taxing and spending, and agricultural policy; (3) a sociology-psychology emphasis, such as poverty and welfare, minorities, criminal justice, education, and population policy; (4) an urban-regional planning emphasis, such as land use, transportation, and environmental protection; and (5) a natural science or engineering emphasis, such as technological innovation, health policy, energy policy, and biomedical policy.

The *relations* between policies and goals can be positive or negative, strong or weak, expressed in absolute or relative terms, and constant or exhibiting diminishing returns. Establishing relations is often the most difficult part of optimizing analysis, although difficulty also occurs in establishing the relative weights of the goals and in drawing conclusions from the goals, policies, and relations.

There are basically four forms for *drawing conclusions* from goals, policies, and relations as to which policy or combination is best depending on the nature of the problem. The four forms can be referred to as optimum choice, risk, level, and mix analysis. Optimum-choice analysis (or basic benefit-cost analysis) involves lump-sum alternatives that do not allow for adopting a fraction of an alternative or more than one of the same alternative. Optimum-risk analysis (or decision theory) also involves lump-sum alternatives, but whether they produce benefits (or costs) is contingent on the occurrence of one or more probabilistic or risky events. Optimum-level analysis involves a policy that can take many positions along a continuum, but one in which doing too much or too little is considered undesirable. Optimum-mix analysis (for allocation theory) involves multiple policies, places, activities, persons, or other entities to which a budget, time, or other scarce resources are to be allocated.

Other concepts that are often used to mean the same thing as public policy analysis include policy evaluation, policy studies, program evaluation, public management science, policy analysis, and policy science. One can make distinctions among those concepts as follows:

1. Policy evaluation emphasizes evaluating alternative public policies, as contrasted to describing them or explaining why they exist.
2. Policy studies includes describing policies, explaining their existence, and evaluating them.
3. Program evaluation emphasizes evaluating a specific program like a halfway house in Chicago in 1984, as contrasted to developing general principles of how to evaluate.
4. Public management science emphasizes decision making that is involved in implementing broader decisions, generally made by legislatures and agencies that have quasi-legislative authority.
5. Policy analysis emphasizes analytical methods, which can be quantitative or qualitative.
6. Policy science emphasizes quantitative methods.

Methods of public policy analysis refer to the following procedures:

1. How to draw a conclusion as to which policy to adopt from information on goals, policies, and relations
2. How to establish the relations between policies and goals
3. How to determine what policies are available for adoption and what goals are appropriate to consider

Some books on prescriptive theory and methodology by political scientists are given in the bibliography.

The policy studies field within political science had its origins in the turbulent 1960s. One might consider the establishment in 1971 of the Policy Studies Organization as the beginning of the formalizing of the field. One might also consider the First Edition of the *Encyclopedia of Policy Studies* as a preliminary or transitional codifying of the major ideas of the field in terms of general approaches and specific policy problems.

The Second Edition of the Encyclopedia is now a more firm codification of a maturing field of study. We anticipate that there will be a third edition sometime early in the 21st century. At that time, there will be more new material and new participants.

Until then, the editor and chapter authors hope that this edition will serve well to communicate the nature of the policy studies field. May the Encyclopedia both summarize and stimulate new and useful ideas regarding the relevance of political and social science to important public policy problems.

BIBLIOGRAPHY

Bowman, J., and Elliston, F. (Eds.) (1989). *Ethics, Government, and Public Policy*. Greenwood, West-port, CT.

Brewer, G., and deLeon, P. (1983). *The Foundations of Policy Analysis*. Dorsey Press, Homewood, IL.

Dahl, R., and Lindblom, C. (1953). *Politics, Economics, and Welfare: Planning and Politico-Economic Systems Resolved into Basic Social Processes*. Harper and Brothers, New York.

Dolbeare, K. (Ed.) (1975). *Public Policy Evaluation*. Sage, Beverly Hills, CA.

Dror, Y. (1971). *Design for Policy Sciences*. American Elsevier, New York.

Dunn, W. (1983). *Values, Ethics, and the Practice of Policy Analysis*. Lexington Books, Lexington, MA.

Dye, T. (1976). *Policy Analysis: What Governments Do, Why They Do It, and What Difference It Makes*. University of Alabama Press, Birmingham.

Fischer, F. (1980). *Politics, Values, and Public Policy: The Problem of Methodology*. Westview Press, Denver.

Fischer, F., and Forester, J. (Eds.) (1987). *Confronting Values in Policy Analysis: The Politics of Criteria*. Sage, Beverly Hills, CA.

Frohock, F. (1979). *Public Policy: Scope and Logic*. Prentice-Hall, Englewood Cliffs, NJ.

Goodin, R. (1982). *Political Theory and Public Policy*. University of Chicago Press, Chicago.

Gregg, P. (Ed.) (1976). *Problems of Theory in Policy Analysis*. Lexington-Heath, Lexington, MA.

Groth, A., and Wade, L. (Eds.) (1984). *Comparative Resource Allocation: Politics, Performance, and Policy Priorities*. Sage, Beverly Hills, CA.

Ingram, H., and Mann, D. (Eds.) (1980). *Why Policies Succeed or Fail*. Sage, Beverly Hills, CA.

Lasswell, H. (1971). *A Pre-View of Policy Sciences*. American Elsevier, New York.

Lowi, T., and Stone, A. (Eds.) (1978). *Nationalizing Government: Public Policies in America*. Sage, Beverly Hills, CA.

MacRae, D. (1976). *The Social Function of Social Science*. Yale University Press, New Haven, CT.

Nagel, S. (Ed.) (1990). *Policy Theory and Policy Evaluation*. Greenwood, Westport, CT.

Palumbo, D. (Ed.) (1987). *The Politics of Program Evaluation*. Sage, Beverly Hills, CA.

Palumbo, D., Fawcett, S., and Wright, P. (Eds.) (1981). *Evaluating and Optimizing Public Policy*. Lexington-Heath, Lexington, MA.

Raskin, M. (1986). *The Common Good: Its Politics, Policies and Philosophy*. Routledge and Kegan Paul, London.

Stone, D. (1988). *Policy Paradox and Political Reason*. Scott, Foresman/Little, Brown, Boston.

Whicker, M., and Moore, R. (1988). *Making America Competitive: Policies for a Global Future*. Praeger, New York.

Wildavsky, W. (1979). *Speaking Truth to Power: The Art and Craft of Policy Analysis*. Little, Brown, Boston.

Introduction to the First Edition

The purpose of this introduction to the *Encyclopedia of Policy Studies* is to describe briefly the general nature and background of policy studies, the institutions of the field, its substance/process/methods, its future, and the purpose/organization of this Encyclopedia.[1]

I. THE GENERAL NATURE AND BACKGROUND OF POLICY STUDIES

The field of policy studies can be broadly defined as the study of the nature, causes, and effects of alternative public policies for dealing with specific social problems. Some people in the field, such as Duncan MacRae and Yehezkel Dror, prefer to emphasize policy effects and the evaluation or optimization of these effects; others, such as Thomas Dye and Charles Jones, prefer to emphasize causal determinants and processes. Those who emphasize prescription, however, recognize that one cannot prescribe policies without an awareness of what policies are likely to be adopted and effectively implemented. Likewise, those who emphasize causes recognize that the effects of policies are often an important causal factor in shaping policies.

Policy studies is a field in itself and also an approach that is applicable to all fields of political science and all social science disciplines. Policy studies differs from what political scientists generally do in that most political scientists traditionally have not been concerned with specific policy problems such as environment, poverty, crime, and so on, although many now are. Policy studies also differs in its emphasis on the relations between policies and effects, whereas most political scientists have been concerned almost exclusively with government structures, processes, and behavior. Policy studies draws on the classical political science concern for controversial policy issues and normative evaluation. It also draws on the behavioral political science concern for using quantitative methods, although applied to policy problems. As such, policy studies tends to provide a kind of synthesis between classical and behavioral political science.

Although political science has played an important part in the development of policy studies, the field is truly interdisciplinary. Political science contributes a concern for the political and administrative feasibility aspects of alternative public policies. Economics contributes a concern for benefits, costs, and maximizing benefits minus costs, with an emphasis on deducing presc. iptive conclusions from given goals and intuitively or empirically accepted relations. Psychology emphasizes the relevance of rewards and punishments in motivating people, and it provides a research paradigm emphasizing pretests and posttests of experimental and control groups. Sociology is concerned with social problems, social classes, and social statistics. Anthropology, geography, and history provide broadening perspectives across places and times. Natural science contributes a concern for the physical and biological factors that are often important in such policy problems as energy and health. Mathematics provides quantitative tools for measuring, analyzing, and evaluating the effects of alternative public policies. Philosophy shows a special concern for the values toward which public policies are directed and the ultimate logic of policy analysis.

The field of policy studies and its orientation have changed tremendously since 1970, as indicated by the rapidly expanding list of relevant journals, organizations, articles, books, book series, convention papers, conference themes, courses, schools, grants, and academic and government job openings. What has caused these changes? One early stimulus was the general public's concern for civil rights, the war on poverty, peace, women's liberation, environmental protection, and other social problems of the late 1960s and early 1970s. The scholarly implementation of those concerns among academics was facilitated by the development of new statistical and mathematical methods, the spread of computer software, and the development of relevant interdisciplinary relations. The relative attractiveness of the government as an employer and research sponsor also increased, as the role of universities in employment and research funding decreased. A more recent stimulus has been the concern for obtaining more government output from reduced tax dollars. In that regard, government retrenchment has decreased government prosperity, but it has increased the prosperity of policy analysts.

II. INSTITUTIONS OF POLICY STUDIES

The basic institutions of an academic field include training programs, research centers, funding sources, publishing outlets, associations, and placement opportunities. *Training programs* associated with policy studies can be classified in various categories, but it is quite possible to put programs in more than one category. The categories include whether the program is emphasizing (1) graduate or undergraduate work, (2) training for government teaching, (3) multiple disciplines or one discipline, (4) methodology or substance, (5) classroom or field experience, (6) university budget money or grants and contracts, (7) policy processes or evaluation of policy alternatives, (8) federal or state and local, (9) cross-national or national, and (10) questioning general societal goals or accepting them. Perhaps the most distinguishing characteristic of various programs relevant to the interests of political scientists is whether they emphasize a political science approach, as in the Berkeley Graduate School of Public Affairs; an economics approach, as in the Harvard Kennedy School; or a social-psychological approach as in Northwestern's Evaluation Research Program. Those diverse orientations are increasingly coming together in recognition that each has a unique and valuable contribution to make. Political science emphasizes process and feasibility; economics emphasizes deduction and optimizing; and social psychology emphasizes experimentation and attitudes.

Many political science departments or universities could develop interdisciplinary training programs by simply cross-listing courses, faculty, and students. Benefits from developing a policy studies program include increased job opportunities, grants, program funding, intellectual stimulation, policy relevance, publishing opportunities, enrollment, faculty recruitment, and the opportunity to build on relevant departments and people. The incremental costs of a policy studies program are quite low given the existing people and facilities at nearly all universities. What may be especially needed is to get university administrators to show more recognition of the opportunities that exist if they can pull together some of their existing resources in a coherent policy studies training program.

Nongovernmental *research centers* in the policy studies field can be divided into those at universities (such as the Yale Institution for Social and Policy Studies or the UCLA Institute for Social Science Research) and those not at universities (such as Brookings, Abt Associates, Urban Institute, Mitre, and The American Enterprise Institute). Like training programs, research centers can also be classified in terms of quality, but that is much more difficult to do. There does seem to be some consensus that university research centers are good on general principles and creativity, but nonuniversity centers are generally better on following detailed specifications and meeting time constraints. What may be needed are more research centers that can draw upon academic creativity while still being effective in responding to government requests for proposals.

Funding sources in the policy studies field include both government agencies and private funding sources. Leading government sources with a broad orientation include the National Science Foundation (especially the Division of Applied Research and the Division of Policy Analysis) and the National Institutes of Mental Health. Virtually every government agency has the authority to issue a purchase order to buy research products relevant to the interests of the agency, including Defense, Energy, Housing and Urban Development (HUD), Health and Human Services (HHS), Justice, Agriculture, Transportation, Commerce, Labor, and Education. Leading private sources with broad orientation include the Ford Foundation (especially the National Affairs Division and the Committee on Public Policy), Rockefeller, and Russell Sage. Numerous private foundations have specialized interests in various policy problems, as indicated by the *Foundation Directory*.

On the matter of *publishing outlets*, there are a number of new journals in the field, including *Policy Analysis, Policy Sciences, Public Policy, Public Interest,* and the *Policy Studies Journal*. Although there is substantial overlap among those journals, each has a somewhat separate focus as reflected in their titles. *Policy Analysis* is concerned especially with the methodology of policy studies, with an emphasis on economic reasoning in program evaluation. *Policy Sciences* is also concerned especially with methodology, but with more emphasis on operations research, management science, and cross-national authors. *Public Policy* has focused more on substance than method, but its former political emphasis is moving toward economics. *Public Interest* is concerned mainly with substance and values, particularly from the perspective of nonmathematical sociology. The *Policy Studies Journal* tries to combine substance and method, although mainly with a political science or political orientation and a symposium format.

Other general policy-oriented scholarly journals include *Evaluation Quarterly*, the *Journal of the American Institute of Planners*, the *Journal of Legal Studies*, the *Journal of Political Economy*, the *Journal of Public Economics*, the *Journal of Social Issues*, the *Journal of Urban Analysis, Law and Contemporary Problems, Law and Society Review, Policy and Politics, Public Administration Review, Public Choice, Social Indicators Research, Social*

Policy, Social Problems, Society, Socio-Economic Planning Sciences, and *Urban Affairs Quarterly.* Disciplinary social science journals such as the *American Political Science Review* are increasingly publishing articles with a policy orientation. A number of scholarly publishers have established a book series or a set of books that deals with policy studies. These include Lexington, Sage, Ballinger, Duxbury, Elsevier, Goodyear, Marcel Dekker, Pergamon, Praeger, St. Martin's, and Academic Press. Some of the better-known series include the Sage Yearbooks in Politics and Public Policy, the Sage Policy Studies Review Annual, the Lexington-PSO series, and the Elsevier Policy Sciences Book Series.

There are now a number of new *associations* in the policy studies field. Like training programs and journals, they can be partly classified in terms of whether they are associated with political science, economics, or sociology-psychology. The Policy Studies Organization (founded in 1972) is associated especially with political science. The Association for Policy Analysis and Management (founded in 1979) is associated especially with economics, although so is the more mathematical Public Choice Society. The Evaluation Research Society (founded in 1977) represents especially psychology and sociology, and it is in the process of merging with the Evaluation Network and the Council for Applied Social Research. Psychologists and sociologists are also represented by units within the APA and ASA, namely, the Society for the Psychological Study of Social Issues and the Society for the Study of Social Problems. There may be a need for more interaction and coordination among these associations in order to promote more interdisciplinary projects such as joint symposia, publications, research, convention panels, legislative testimony, and other activities.

Placement opportunities include the training programs and research centers mentioned previously. For many academic fields, placement opportunities include private business. The counterpart in policy studies is mainly government agencies. They represent the heart of policy studies, since there would be no government policies without government agencies. In other words, they represent not only an outlet for placing students and placing ideas, but also a reciprocal source of ideas relevant to improving the work of the training programs and research centers. Some government agencies, however, are more actively involved in planning and evaluating alternative policies than are other agencies. Federal agencies are especially active, but state and local agencies are becoming more so with the passage of legislation requiring more evaluation and the need to stretch tighter budgets. Among federal agencies, the planning and evaluation units at HUD, HHS, Labor, and Defense are generally well regarded, along with the executive office agencies such as the Office of Management and Budget (OMB) and the Domestic Council. In doing policy evaluation, Congress has the help of the General Accounting Office, the Congressional Budget Office, the Office of Technology Assessment, and the Congressional Reference Service. A survey of political scientists in government mentioned the need for more policy research by academic political scientists, more exchange of information between academics and practitioners, and more training on how government agencies actually function.

III. SUBSTANCE, PROCESS, AND METHODS OF POLICY STUDIES

Core courses in policy studies programs generally cover substance, process, and methods. A key issue in discussing policy studies *substance* is determining the social problems that are important to policy studies training and research. The answer is generally those social problems to which governments devote a substantial amount of resources. That is a descriptive approach to clarifying policy studies substance. A prescriptive approach points to the social problems on which governments should devote a substantial amount of resources, regardless of whether they do or not. For example, is family policy a subject for active government involvement with regard to husband-wife relations and parent-child relations? Is religious policy such a subject, with regard to facilitating parochial schools, contributions to religious institutions, and some forms of religious behavior? Closely related is the question of the relative importance of different policy problems in a policy studies program. Another key issue in the realm of policy studies substance is how to classify substantive policy problems. One approach classifies problems in terms of the disciplines with which they are most often associated, including problems especially related to political science (e.g., civil liberties or defense), economics (e.g., economic regulation or taxing-spending), sociology-psychology (e.g., race relations or population), planning (e.g., land use or transportation), and physical or biological science (e.g., energy or health).

Key issues in discussing the policy *process* include the following:

1. Do policies get made more by rational analysis of the relations between alternative policies and goals, or by incremental trial and error?
2. In studying policy adoption and implementation, how much emphasis should be placed on process analysis, as contrasted to the determinants and effects of policy variation?
3. In policy studies training, how much emphasis should be placed on process, as contrasted to methods and substance?
4. To what extent does the process change when we talk about different substantive issues such as crime policy versus environmental policy?
5. How does the policy adoption and implementation process differ across levels of government, branches of government, and across nations?
6. To what extent should the process be an evaluative goal in itself with regard to such matters as public participation, fair procedure, openness, and predictability?
7. To what extent should policy analysts consider political and administrative feasibility in evaluating alternative policies?
8. What is a good policy process in terms of effectiveness, efficiency, and equity on such dimensions as federalism, separation of powers, judicial review, the two-party system, and majority rule with minority rights?

Some issues in discussing policy analysis *methods* include:

1. How is policy analysis similar to and different from business analysis?
2. How can policy analysts become more sensitive to social values and more questioning of goals when evaluating alternative policies?
3. How can one predict the effects of alternative policies, as contrasted to reacting to policies that have already been adopted?
4. How can one accept goals as given and attempt to determine what policies will maximize them, rather than accepting policies as given and merely attempt to determine what are their effects?
5. How may analysts be given a good grounding in social science research methods, including a concern for meaningful measurement, sampling, determination of relations, and causal analysis?
6. How may analysts be given a good grounding in both finite math and calculus-oriented marginal analysis?
7. How can we keep analysts from going overboard in seeking precision methods when less precise techniques give the same results, or from suffering the opportunity cost of not taking advantage of precision that might be easily available?

8. How can we get analysts to be more sensitive to the subject matter with which they are working, as contrasted to using mechanical quantification without thinking through the implications?
9. How can we get analysts to analyze questions that have relatively broad significance, rather than unduly narrowly focused questions?

IV. THE FUTURE OF POLICY STUDIES

The future direction of policy studies is likely to be toward more growth, or a stabilizing at a high level of academic and government activity. Growth is likely to continue, since the causal forces responsible are still continuing. Those causal forces include the public concern for important policy problems, although the nature of the problem keeps changing. In the late 1960s and early 1970s, the problems related to civil rights, poverty, Vietnam, women's liberation, and environmental protection. In the early 1980s they related more to inflation, energy, and the Middle East. The causal forces also include improved quantitative methods, increased attractiveness of government as a social science employer and research sponsor, and increased government concern for stretching scarce resources.

Deeper causal forces relate to factors that explain increased government involvement and growth over the last 80 years. Those factors are of three kinds. First, there are socioeconomic forces such as (1) the increased severity of world conflicts, (2) the growing importance of public education, (3) the growth of large interstate and multinational business, (4) the growth of big labor and other pressure groups that seek aid and require regulation, (5) increased urbanization and the resulting loss of self-sufficiency, (6) increased severity of periods of inflation and recession, (7) competition with foreign ideologies, and (8) the fact that regulation and government activity generate more regulation and activity. Second, there are certain enabling factors, such as (1) expanded sources of government revenue necessary for carrying on increased government programs, (2) improved managerial techniques for handling large-scale government operations, and (3) changing constitutional interpretations. Third is the ideological shift from a prevailing attitude favoring minimal government toward an attitude that government has many positive responsibilities.

Within the field of policy studies, one might predict more specific increases in the following:

1. Training programs (undergraduate and graduate, disciplinary and interdisciplinary, and academic-oriented and practitioner-oriented)
2. Policy research centers (university, governmental, and nonuniversity private)
3. Funding sources (government line agencies such as HHS, government research agencies such as the National Science Foundation, and private foundations such as the Ford Foundation)
4. Publishing outlets (both journals and book publishers)
5. Policy-oriented scholarly associations (disciplinary, interdisciplinary, professional, and problem-focused)

Within the social sciences, one might predict increases in the following:

1. The percentage of social scientists who identify with policy studies
2. Emphasis on policy evaluation and implementation rather than just explaining variation across decisions
3. Use of microeconomic reasoning, rather than just statistical data processing

4. Concern for a wider variety of policy problems
5. The concern across subfields within each social science discipline for the nature, causes, and effects of relevant public policies
6. Synthesis between the traditional philosophical concern for normative evaluation and the scientific or behavioral concern for quantitative analysis
7. Interaction between social science academics and practitioners in training programs and in government
8. Reaching out to other disciplines in view of the interdisciplinary nature of policy problems

In general, policy studies seems to be a boom industry as a subdiscipline, an interdiscipline, and a developing new discipline. Policy studies also seems to be providing some new vitality to political and social science, while political and social science provide the foundation for policy studies.

V. PURPOSE AND ORGANIZATION OF THE ENCYCLOPEDIA

The purpose of this Encyclopedia is to bring together a set of chapters that analyze the basic issues and references dealing with each major aspect of the field of policy studies. The aspects of the field can be organized into general approaches to policy studies and specific policy problems. The general approaches cover matters that cut across the specific problems. Each specific problem deals with an area of government activity in which there is a general consensus that government ought to be involved, but controversy as to what forms that involvement should take. The general approaches include stages in policy studies research such as basic conceptualizing, research methodology, and research utilization. The approaches also include stages in the policy process such as policy formation and implementation. At the general level, one might also be concerned with policy analysis across nations and across disciplines, and concerned with the special policy problems of different levels of government, including state and urban government.

A meaningful way of classifying specific policy problems is in terms of the scholarly discipline with which they are most often associated. All policy problems are inherently multidisciplinary. The disciplinary classification used in this Encyclopedia merely indicates what discipline tends to offer the most courses and journal articles on the policy problem from among the basic disciplines of political science, sociology, psychology, planning, natural science, and engineering. The problem of poverty, for example, clearly involves economic, political, psychological, and planning aspects, but it is classified under sociology because sociology and social work departments tend to offer more courses on the subject than do other departments. The disciplines of law and operations research are relevant to nearly all policy fields, since policy often manifests itself in laws, and since operations research provides general methodologies for arriving at means for maximizing given goals. Having a set of categories helps to make the Encyclopedia more organized, rather than an A-to-Z "laundry list" of policy approaches and problems. Using a disciplinary classification also brings out the fact that many disciplines are relevant to policy studies.

Problems with a political science emphasis include foreign policy, defense, electoral matters, legislative reform, and civil liberties. Problems with an economics emphasis include economic regulation, labor, consumer protection, communications, taxing/spending, and agriculture. Problems with a sociology-psychology emphasis include poverty, minorities, crime, education, and population. Problems with an urban and regional planning emphasis include housing, land use, transportation, and environmental protection. Problems with a natural science or engineering emphasis include science/technology policy, health, energy, and biomedical policy. For each of those 23 specific policy problems and each of the nine previously mentioned general approaches, an expert social scientist has been chosen to draft for the Encyclopedia a comprehensive survey of the subject. Contributors have been requested to emphasize the basic issues and references so as better to inform nonexperts as to the nature of each aspect of the policy studies field.

This work is referred to as an encyclopedia rather than as a handbook, partly because there is already a *Handbook of Policy Studies*, edited by Stuart Nagel and published by Lexington Books in 1980. That Handbook is a short summary of the professional aspects of the field, rather than an intensive analysis of general policy approaches and specific policy problems, as this Encyclopedia is. A more important reason for using the word "encyclopedia" is the fact that the word "handbook" is defined in the *American College Dictionary* as "a small book or treatise serving for guidance as in an occupation or study." This volume is not small and not just vocational. Rather it is large and broadly conceived from a scholarly perspective. The separate chapters, however, can be considered as modules in their respective fields, and the Encyclopedia also has considerable practical policy relevance. According to the *American College Dictionary*, the word "encyclopedia" does not necessarily involve an alphabetic arrangement, although that might often be the case. Literally, the word "encyclopedia" means taking a walk around a subject. That is the purpose of this Encyclopedia, namely, to provide a grand tour of the field of policy studies.

Many people deserve credit for the massive amount of work that went into developing this Encyclopedia. They include the 41 chapter authors or co-authors who have communicated their expert knowledge by drafting detailed chapters covering their specialties. Thanks are also owed to Marcel Dekker (as publisher of the Encyclopedia) and to Jack Rabin (as editor of the series) for having inspired this work. Credit is also due to the numerous authors of papers, articles, book chapters, and books that are referred to in these Encyclopedia chapters. Most of that literature has been written within the last 10 or so years. The policy studies field is young but is growing rapidly. It is hoped that this Encyclopedia will record well that past growth and help stimulate future growth regarding the applications of political and social science to important policy programs.

Stuart S. Nagel

NOTE

1. For further details on many of these subjects, see S. Nagel (1980), *The Policy Studies Handbook* (Lexington-Heath, Lexington, MA).

Contributors

Robert B. Albritton *Northern Illinois University, DeKalb, Illinois*

James Anderson *Texas A&M University, College Station, Texas*

Ralph Baker *Ball State University, Muncie, Indiana*

Robert H. Blank *University of Canterbury, Christchurch, New Zealand*

Christopher J. Bosso *Northeastern University, Boston, Massachusetts*

Robert W. Broyles *University of Oklahoma, Oklahoma City, Oklahoma*

Charles Bulmer *University of Alabama, Birmingham, Alabama*

Donald J. Calista *Marist College, Poughkeepsie, New York*

John Carmichael *University of Alabama, Birmingham, Alabama*

Fred S. Coombs *University of Illinois, Urbana-Champaign, Illinois*

Yehezkel Dror *The Hebrew University of Jerusalem, Jerusalem, Israel*

James A. Dunn, Jr. *Rutgers University, Camden, New Jersey*

David Falcone *University of Oklahoma, Oklahoma City, Oklahoma*

Peter Fisher *University of Iowa, Iowa City, Iowa*

Don F. Hadwiger *Iowa State University, Ames, Iowa*

Wynn Hjermstad *Urban Development, City of Lincoln, Lincoln, Nebraska*

Gerald L. Houseman *Indiana University, Fort Wayne, Indiana*

Valerie M. Hudson *Brigham Young University, Provo, Utah*

Richard S. Katz   *The Johns Hopkins University, Baltimore, Maryland*

Michael E. Kraft   *University of Wisconsin, Green Bay, Wisconsin*

Robert M. Lawrence   *Colorado State University, Fort Collins, Colorado*

George J. McCall   *University of Missouri, St. Louis, Missouri*

Fred Meyer   *Ball State University, Muncie, Indiana*

Stuart S. Nagel   *University of Illinois, Urbana-Champaign, Illinois*

Cheol H. Oh   *Arkansas State University, Jonesboro, Arkansas*

Marian Lief Palley   *University of Delaware, Newark, Delaware*

Marybeth Peterson   *U.S. Air Force Academy, Colorado Springs, Colorado*

Dianne M. Pinderhughes   *University of Illinois, Urbana-Champaign, Illinois*

Alan L. Porter   *Georgia Institute of Technology, Atlanta, Georgia*

Robert F. Rich   *University of Illinois, Urbana-Champaign, Illinois*

Leroy N. Rieselbach   *Indiana University, Bloomington, Indiana*

David Brian Robertson   *University of Missouri, St. Louis, Missouri*

Harrell R. Rodgers, Jr.   *University of Houston, Houston, Texas*

Frederick A. Rossini   *George Mason University, Fairfax, Virginia*

Warren J. Samuels   *Michigan State University, East Lansing, Michigan*

Steven R. Smith   *Duke University, Durham, North Carolina*

Christopher H. Sterling   *The George Washington University, Washington, DC*

Larry L. Wade   *University of California, Davis, California*

Geoffrey Wandesforde-Smith   *University of California, Davis, California*

Norman Wengert   *Colorado State University, Fort Collins, Colorado*

Louise G. White   *George Mason University, Fairfax, Virginia*

Linda Faye Williams   *University of Maryland, College Park, Maryland*

UNIT ONE
GENERAL APPROACHES TO POLICY STUDIES

Part A
CONCEPTUAL, METHODOLOGICAL, AND UTILIZATION STAGES IN POLICY ANALYSIS

1

Basic Concepts in Advanced Policy Sciences

Yehezkel Dror
The Hebrew University of Jerusalem, Jerusalem, Israel

The 21st century is sure to be a critical one for humanity as a whole and for many cultures, regions, and countries in particular. Driven by growing demographic imbalances, technological innovations, value transformation, and shifting geostrategic and geoeconomic maps, the 21st Century will be hyperturbulent, which will make deliberate efforts to influence the future through collective choice very difficult indeed. Policy-making practices that failed during the 20th century to address effectively relatively less exacting issues can hardly be expected to cope successfully with the supercomplex issues of the 21st century.

However, emerging problems, ranging from the dangers of fanaticism armed with biological weapons, to the moral and realpolitical contradictions between becoming "one world" and being loaded with extreme inequalities, pose urgent needs for high-quality innovative policy making. If these needs are not met, a dire future awaits humanity despite "end of history" delusions (Fukuyama, 1992; to be compared with the much superior Huntington, 1991). Hence, a paradigmatic shift in capacities to govern, so as to reduce the abyss between requirements and capacities, is imperative.

Adjusting governance capacities to the requirements of the 21st century necessitates major redesign of all levels and principles of governance (Dror, 1993a). This chapter addresses one facet of needed governance redesign; namely, generic prescriptive knowledge on policy making, which is *policy sciences*.

The idea of policy sciences is not new, having been proposed by Daniel Lerner and Harold Lasswell in 1951 (Lerner and Lasswell, 1951) and further developed during the years under different names, such as policy studies, or policy analysis (e.g., see Lasswell, 1971). But, however useful presently available policy-making knowledge may be, it is grossly inadequate for meeting the challenges of the 21st century. Hence, the need for a paradigmatic jump toward what I call "advanced policy sciences." Looked at in terms of the history of policy-making knowledge, we must move to a "third-generation" type of policy sciences, the first generation being constituted by 18th and 19th century policy-relevant studies (as presented, for instance, in Collini et al., 1983), and the second generation by contemporary policy studies, with important foundations being provided by classical and renaissance statecraft thinking.

This chapter presents some proposals for moving in the proposed direction in the form of a set of 25 main principles for advanced policy sciences, followed by some concluding observations on necessary institutional rearrangements and on the personal meanings of devoting oneself to advancing policy sciences and their applications. But, before presenting some basic concepts in advanced policy sciences through decomposition into principles, the overall conception of advanced policy sciences as statecraft professionalism, which directs my endeavor, must be clarified.

I. ADVANCED POLICY SCIENCES AS STATECRAFT PROFESSIONALISM

The traditional basis of statecraft is "practical intelligence" (Sternberg and Wagner, 1986), which is based on innate abilities and augmented by various forms of learning and tutorship, writings of the Mirror for Princes genre, and advisory structures. As demonstrated throughout history, this has been very inadequate a basis for guiding the fate of nations and other collective entities, with the exception of a minuscule minority of statecraft prodigies, on the availability of whom when needed most one cannot rely.

Taking into account the growing complexity of policy issues and the increasing costs of policy failures (King and Schneider, 1991; Zolo, 1992), notable improvements in statecraft are essential. Knowledge how better to choose grand policies and make critical choices is at the core of statecraft, whereas constituting the main subject of policy sciences. Therefore, I propose to view advanced policy sciences as statecraft professional, although not encompassing all of the facets of statecraft, with the aim of upgrading policy sciences being to contribute to the improvement of statecraft.

One implication of this view is that policy sciences are a modern extension of traditional interests in statecraft. Truly, study of classical writings in statecraft dealing with policy, in the sense of using power to achieve collective objectives (as contrasted with politics, as in dealing with gaining and keeping power), is a must for moving toward advanced policy sciences. Good starts are Machiavelli's *Discourses* and the *History of the Peloponnesian War* by Thucydides, followed by the many texts on statecraft (e.g., as surveyed in part in Fernandez-Santamaria, 1983). Good biographical studies of outstanding statecraft practitioners can also be very helpful (as illustrated by Planze, 1990).

The proposed view of advanced policy sciences as statecraft professionalism has multiple and, in part, radical implications, such as for providing senior policy makers with opportunities to study advanced policy sciences and motivating them to do so (Dror, 1993b). It also serves to redress some widespread errors on the nature of policy studies, such as viewing them mainly as applied social sciences (e.g., as wrongly perceived in Lindblom, 1990). But I leave such side issues to other opportunities, dedicating this chapter to the major task of exploring the principles of advanced policy sciences.

II. PRINCIPLES OF ADVANCED POLICY SCIENCES

Unavoidably, the concept of advanced policy sciences must be broken down to permit examination of its main ideas. I do so by distinguishing between 25 main principles, which add up to a set reflecting the main body of advanced policy sciences as a whole. References to some of the literature dealing with main principles can serve the interested reader to go deeper into what can only be hinted at within the confines of this chapter. Of course, advanced policy sciences builds on presently available knowledge in policy studies, familiarity with which, as presented in other chapters of this Encyclopedia and their references, should antecede entry into the exacting domains of advanced policy sciences.

A. Philosophy of Judgment and Action as the Foundation, Together with Cognitive Studies, Rather Than Philosophy of Science

The tendency to base prescriptive policy studies on philosophy of science and, concomitantly, on positivistic approaches, is in principle mistaken: science strives for truth, as defined from time to time by consensus in different disciplines. But the mission of advanced policy sciences is different though correlated; namely to improve decisions, in the sense of arriving at better ones than would otherwise be made. This task, as well as features such as time constraints imposed by the rhythm of decision making, put advanced policy sciences into the domain of philosophy of judgment, philosophy of action, (e.g. Moya, 1990) as well as practical reasoning (Raz, 1978), and also in some respect philosophy of the mind, but not philosophy of science. As far as possible, standards of science should be aimed at and methods of science should be utilized. But, fundamentally, advanced policy sciences is a "knowledge-rich pragmatic" (Sternberg, 1990: 5 and Chap. 5 pass.) rather than a "scientific" endeavor in the Anglo-American sense of that term (as distinct from the Continental European conception of science, which is much broader and includes the humanities).

Advanced policy sciences must fit methods to the wild nature of problems, aiming at "preferization," in the sense of reaching better decisions than would otherwise be the case rather than "optimization." To overcome the concern Wittgenstein (1953: 232) expresses when stating "the existence of the experimental method makes us think we have the means of solving the problems which trouble us; though problem and method pass one another by," advanced policy sciences accepts the adage of Maynard Keynes—"it is better to be roughly right than precisely wrong." Much reliance on hermeneutics and other "soft" approaches, such as thought experiments (Sorensen, 1992), is essential when dealing with murky conundrums, with verisimilitude serving as a main standard for acceptability.

Cognitive studies must be added to the foundations of advanced policy sciences, all the more so as they are ignored in most of mainstream policy studies. Dealing with information processing, perception, and thinking, in the broad senses of these terms including their emotional, volitional, and neurological as well as cultural bases, the salience of cognitive studies for advanced policy sciences is immense, together with overlapping concerns of philosophy of the mind.

Given such foundations, advanced policy sciences often takes the form of heuristic principles, qualitative protocols for policy reflection, and guidelines for ratiocination. It deals with reasoning and deliberation rather than with calculation; modeling, for instance, serving more as a metaphor than as an algorithm.

These characteristics of advanced policy sciences pose serious problems and dangers, such as too much subjectivism and lack of quality-control yardsticks. But, when the choice is between such problematic on one hand and lack of relevance to critical choices on the other, my suggestion is to move ahead with advanced policy sciences, with philosophy of action, and philosophy of judgment serving as main foundations.

B. Ultra-Rationality as a Grounding

Conventional notions of rationality, such as underlying economics and operational research as well as some schools of psychology of thinking, are inadequate as a grounding for advanced policy sciences. For instance, these notions ignore "rationality of irrationality," self-binding as a superior mode of rationality (Schelling, 1984; Elster, 1979), the usefulness under some circumstances of self-delusions (Martin, 1985), and so forth. Therefore, more complex and advanced notions of "ultra-rationality" are needed as a grounding for advanced policy sciences.

These include, for example, acceptance of different modes of reasoning, thinking, and imagining, as "rational" for various facets of advanced policy sciences rather than regarding "logic" as dominating. For instance, composition of realistic visions and development of bad scenarios to be avoided, as discussed below, involve creation of "alternative worlds," approaching the definition of the function of poets by Aristotle (cf. Bruner, 1986: Chap. 3).

Related is the need to overcome the tendency of most of policy sciences to assume rationality by actors. Logically, even a narrow conception of rationality should not inhibit recognition of "irrationality" as characterizing actors, together with appreciation of the cultural bindings of all notions of "reasonableness" and with avoidance of the tendency incorrectly to associate and even fuse the idea of "reasonable" with the notion of "rational." But, as a matter of fact, much of contemporary policy studies do assume rationality by actors, in part at least as a consequence of narrow notions of rationality and in part because available models work better with simple rationality assumptions, as in the theory of games. Also, because mainstream policy studies are deeply imbued with simple rationality assumptions, other models of behavior are hard to accommodate. Instead, advanced policy sciences should fully recognize various forms of nonrational and counterrational behavior as an important feature of reality.

C. Globalization

Despite some efforts to the contrary (e.g., Ganapathy et al., 1985), policy sciences are still in the main United States based in culture, in implicit as well as explicit values, in assumptions and in orthodoxies. Thus, underrating of situations that require revolutionary changes, assumptions that liberal democracy fit all conditions, trust in the basic goodness of human nature, mainly materialistic notions of human needs, culture-bound conceptions of "reasonableness," antirisk attitudes, overrating of market mechanism and underrating of the critical importance of the state, ignorance of societal architecture tasks and the need for guiding elites, and an underlying assumption of relative resources abundance—all illustrate some underpinnings coloring most of policy studies as a result of US influence. To these should be added ignorance of realities prevailing in most of the world and incapacity to comprehend value systems and policy orthodoxies radically different from those prevailing now in the Western world. A priori rejection of policy options that may be essential in some Third World countries, even though contradicting Western values, adds to the blind spots characterizing most of policy studies as a result of narrow cultural bases.

Hence, the need to globalize policy sciences, not in the sense of diffusing its present versions around the world, but of broadening and diversifying the cultural foundations and reality perceptions of advanced policy sciences. They must fit diverse conditions and different value systems, subject to overriding ethical imperatives accepted, or explicitly postulated, as binding humanity as a whole.

Globalization of policy sciences is essential not only to make it useful for most of humanity, such as concentrated in China and India, but also to increase the validity of advanced policy sciences for the West in general and the United States in particular by broadening perspectives, providing contrasts, and opening up policy vistas foreclosed by any monocultural setting.

D. Broad and Long-Range Estimates of the Dynamics of Situations

The images of the world on which policy making is predicated channelize most of policy thinking. Therefore, upgrading of these world images is a main step in improving policy making and a central task for advanced policy sciences.

Let me emphasize the constructivist approach assumed here, according to which policy worlds (note the plural!) are not and should not claim to be simple reflections of reality but constitute a complex construct of our minds and cultures directed at meeting the concerns and needs of policy making and reflecting some facets of "realities" but not representing reality as such.

Improvement of estimations as essential for upgrading policy making involves two levels: "meta-estimation," which deals with rules, symbols, concepts, schema, and theories to be applied in estimation, as illustrated by some of the principles of advanced policy sciences discussed in this chapter; and substantive estimates of main world features relevant to policy making, which unavoidably are based on explicit or implicit meta-estimations.

On the meta-estimation level, the main principle is to focus on the dynamics of situations rather than on static pictures. As choice is always concerned with the future, the past and present are relevant for estimations only as bases for an outlook into the future. This requires identification of the dynamics shaping the future so as to enable us, on the basis of the past and present plus the dynamics, to make some statements on evolutionary potential into the future. This requires a quite sharp break with much of estimation practice and literature, comparable to the jump in human thinking on numbers with the move toward "focusing attention upon the operation by which numbers are changed rather than upon the numbers themselves" (Barrow, 1992: 105).

Required are broad situational evaluations of the dynamics that encompass main policy domains; long-range appraisals, doing justice to social time, as explained soon; and special attention to discontinuities, trend changes, uncertainties, shifts (Toffler, 1990), jumps, and mutations. Declining curves, passing windows of opportunity, and surprise domains need particular care. Search for declining curves deserves emphasis because of their far-reaching implications for appropriate policy modalities, such as the need for large-scale innovative interventions rather than incremental decisions, as will be explained soon.

Adequate estimation of the dynamics of situations requires many changes in meta-estimation approaches, methods, and mapping, including ways of cognizing and interpreting turbulent and sometimes hyperturbulent realities, the development of appropriate frames of appreciations, changes in cognitive maps and attribution theories, and more. However, the persistence of security intelligence failures despite intense efforts to overcome them (Handel, 1989: part 2; Laqueur, 1985) raises serious doubts about realizing such essential breakthroughs unless significant improvements in intelligence and estimation capacities do take place, first on the meta-estimation and then, with their help, on the substantive estimation level, with constant interaction between those two.

Thus, to mentioned a fundamental meta-estimation failing resulting in many estimation errors, new facts, even if perceived, are given interpretations fitting past-produced world pictures and tacit presuppositions. But, as the world is changing rather than changes occurring in the world, to use a formulation coined by Ortega y Gasset (Dobson, 1989: 179), with much of the change being "discontinuous," "cascading," and "surprising," in the sense of contradicting culturally produced anticipations, presuppositions, and stipulations, upgrading of estimation qualities is difficult and depends, first of all, on improvements in meta-estimation capacities.

E. Thinking in Terms of Interaction with Dynamic Environments

Advanced policy sciences considers issues in terms of active interaction with very dynamic and, in part, reactive environments, as contrasted with the tendency often to underrate the transmutations and responses of contextual and target systems (very relevant is Wohlstetter, 1964). In dealing with dynamic and, in part, competitive and sometimes malevolent and intrusive environments, the appropriate mix between preadjustment, postadjustment, efforts to shape or at least to influence the environments, and self-isolation from the environments, should be carefully evaluated, as should be dialectic and nonlinear interaction sequences with cooperative, hostile, and also nonreactive dynamic environments.

Often relevant, though not to be overworked, is the concept of competitiveness, with the search for various blends of cooperative and conflictive policies and striving for various forms of net advantages, as in economic and security domains, but also in cultural ones. Application of concepts of competition to efforts to attract high-quality and scarce human resources illustrate their relevance beyond conventionally recognized domains. Albeit, in many policy domains, the frame of thinking of competition can be very misleading, with cooperation and solidarity being more appropriate. Therefore, a pluralism of conceptual frames is necessary for analyzing complex interaction situations.

F. Consideration in Terms of Rise and Decline of Nations and Success and Failure of Great Enterprises

Advanced policy sciences should use as its broadest frame of thinking historic and theoretical conjectures concerning the rise and decline of nations and regimes, the long-range impacts of revolutions, successful and failing development endeavor, and the fate of other "Great Enterprises" (in the sense of Wakeman, Jr., 1985).

This principle fully exposes the ambitious and demanding nature of advanced policy sciences. Our knowledge, for example, of the variables shaping the fate of nations, is rudimentary. An interesting body of literature dealing with different aspects of the subject is available (e.g., Eisenstadt, 1978; Hawrylyshyn, 1980; Kennedy, 1987; Kohr, 1957; Linz and Stepan, 1978; Olson, 1982; Porter, 1990; Tainter, 1988; Unger, 1987b), not to speak of the speculations by Edward Gibbons and Arnold J. Toynbee, which deserve critical study by advanced policy sciences maestros. But, to be frank, knowledge in this field consists at best of partial explanations, in the main of weak conjectures at the most, and often of not more than surmises and speculations. Thus, despite intense attention by outstanding scholars, the decline and fall (or, to look at the same phenomena differently, the long survival) of the Roman empire has not been satisfactorily explained (for a modern illustration of the very large literature on this subject, see MacMullen, 1990, as criticized in Hopkins, 1991). Still, without at least posing salient questions on the fate of Great Enterprises and penetrating somewhat into the causes of rise and decline—even if main variables are multiple, unknown, changing, and perhaps in part historically specific and also unknowable—advanced policy sciences has no hope of being relevant to primary concerns; namely, the fate of nations and other pivotal entities and the destiny of great, and sometimes heroic, endeavor.

G. Thinking-in-History, Without Being Bound by the Past

The meta-historical assumption underlying advanced policy sciences is that the future is non-necessitarian and underdetermined rather than overdetermined by the past (Gellner, 1988; Unger, 1987a). Put differently, the future is a product of dynamic combination and inter-action between necessity, contingency, chance, and choice. Accordingly, human activities, including policy making, enjoy in principle significant degrees of freedom with meaningful impact potentials on evolving realities (Dror, 1986: Chap. 4), up to radically molding some aspects of the future. Within this perspective, the mission of advanced policy sciences is to increase the actual capacity of humanity to influence the future for the better through col-lective choice processes.

Albeit, the past shapes and contains evolutionary potentials for the future (Hallpike, 1988). Furthermore, the past constitutes essential raw material for studying and trying to understand societal processes (very relevant is Skocpol, 1984, indicating needs and possibili-ties for "historical policy studies," as one of the essential bases for advanced policy sciences; but see Boudon, 1984) and serves as an essential context for comprehending the presence. If the aspiration of advanced policy sciences to help impact long stretches of time stream, up to reshaping trajectories of evolution in time, is added to the considerations, then thinking-in-history clearly emerges as a categoric must.

Borrowing terminology from the French *Annales* Historic School (e.g., Braudel, 1980), however, without accepting its theses discounting impact of human policies on fundamental realities, advanced policy sciences faces the fundamental contradiction between decision mak-ing located in human time, and in even shorter "political time" (a term that should be added to Braudel's categories), on one hand, and the necessity to take into account long lead times and impact cycles, together with the desire to influence phenomena in social time, on the other. To bridge this contradiction, thinking-in-history is essential in the sense of considering issues in terms of long-range processes, with all their uncertainties and mutations. To do so, a radical break with the nonhistoric, and often antihistoric, disposition of most of contem-porary policy studies is obligatory.

Much more is needed than some "applied history," which may indeed be very danger-ous, or the study of the history of particular policy issues however relevant, or relatively un-demanding mini–"thinking-in-time" (Neustadt and May, 1986, but see superior Chap. 14). Instead penetration into deep historic processes is required (e.g., Faber and Meier, 1978) however hard and in part impossible.

Thinking-in-history poses difficult meta-historic as well as methodological issues and involves multiple pitfalls and dangers, such as misuses of history (May, 1972), as already well discussed by Nietzsche (as explained in Kaufmann, 1974: 144 ff.). However, there is no hope of correctly understanding contemporary events and current processes and for impacting as aimed at on longer time spans if policy thinking is confined to thin slices of time, as is the rule in most policy-making and policy studies alike. Thinking-in-history, therefore, deserves all the more underlining as a must for advanced policy sciences.

However, a contrary danger must also be guarded against; namely, being captivated by history and historic thinking. Too much thinking in terms of the past may lead to ignorance of shifts making the present and future in important respects very different from the past, can produce nostalgic clinging to images of the past that have no real relevance for the future, tends to reinforce policy inertia and incrementalism, and does produce too narrow views of the feasibility of building futures very different from the past even though based on it. There-fore, thinking-in-history is essential, but must be combined with breaking out of the past as a policy cage.

H. Bad Avoidance Together with Good Achievement

Advanced policy sciences moves along two, partly distinct and partly overlapping and converging, lines: reducing the probability of worst and bad scenarios and upgrading the probability of desirable scenarios. This principle is important because (1) it is often easier to conceptualize and reach agreement on "bad" situations to be avoided than on "good" ones to be approximated; and (2) when viewed in terms of the history of human decision making, avoidance of some very bad situations would constitute a very significant improvement.

Reducing the likelihood of bad contingencies requires recognizing their possibility and specifying them in general form at least. This depends a lot on creativity up to poetic imagination, as already mentioned, which is anathema to "calculative" mainstream policy studies and beyond the capacity of its armanentarium.

Adding to difficulties is the distastefulness of bad contingencies to necessarily optimistic decision makers, as well as their high political sensitivity. But without developing and seriously considering bad contingencies, advanced policy sciences is grossly inadequate. Here, we confront one of the many tensions between advanced policy sciences and political organizations and also broader social and cultural propensities and needs. The psychological and political costs of considering very bad contingencies must be realized to understand barriers hindering better policy making and to enable the search for ways to make advanced policy sciences more usable by reducing such costs. Thus, work on very unpleasant scenarios should be done in closed compartments of central minds of governments and distribution of resulting studies must often be very confined.

I. Debugging

Policy making, and advanced policy sciences itself, are both prone to many pathologies, as illustrated by "motivated irrationality" (Pears, 1984), with strong feelings, hopes, and desires, as well as insidious dominant ideologies, often corrupting reasoning, as already well discussed by Francis Bacon in his treatments of "idols" and "phantasms."

To start with advanced policy sciences, self-awareness, maximum efforts to exit oneself, multicultural bases as mentioned, explicit counterreasoning, the use of diverse languages, as well as coopting decision psychologists and philosophers of judgment and mind into advanced policy sciences teams for observing and correcting policy reasoning all illustrate ways in which advanced policy sciences should and can counteract and contain some of its own error propensities.

Albeit, simplistic views must be avoided. Thus, in principle, advanced policy sciences should be "cold" as contrasted with the nature of politics as "hot." But emotions and advanced policy sciences are not always enemies, constituting also essential though dangerous partners. To illustrate this point, let me mention the function of emotions as stimuli to creativity. Therefore, sophisticated understanding of the often negative but sometimes positive (e.g., Sousa, 1987) functions of itense emotions in policy reasoning is needed.

Related are issues of advocacy uses of advanced policy sciences, justified by aggregation models with confrontation between different biases expected to upgrade overall policy making. But overdoses of advocacy combined with exaggerated trust in adversary processes may well undermine a more objective and partly value-neutral view of advanced policy sciences as an ideal to be approximated as much as humanly possible. It may also corrupt actual contributions of advanced policy sciences to policy making and reduce its acceptability by policy makers. Here again US culture and beliefs tend to overdominate much of contemporary policy sciences thinking.

Let me move on to the role of advanced policy sciences, suitably cleared of some of its own biases and error propensities in decision-making debugging. The importance of this task deserves underlining, leading to quite some revisions in the nature of advanced policy sciences and expansion of its essential knowledge bases.

Traditionally, efforts to upgrade policy quality are based on various notions of rationality to be approximated. But advanced policy sciences should in part adopt an additional approach; namely, counteracting and off-setting actual policy-making weaknesses and pathologies.

It follows that advanced policy sciences must include a good knowledge of actual decision-making processes, individual (e.g., Hogarth, 1990; Osherson and Smith, 1990, pass.) as well as organizational (e.g., March, 1988; Sims et al., 1986) and interorganizational (e.g., Maoz, 1990), with special attention to decision-making diseases (e.g., Hogwood and Peters, 1985) and decision-making errors of rulers (Hybel, 1990), undesirable irrationalities (e.g., Elster, 1983), information-processing inadequacies (e.g., Vertzberger, 1990), negative impacts of strain and stress (e.g., Janis and Mann, 1977), as well as adversity (Dror, 1986: Chap. 3), "groupthink" propensities (e.g., Janis, 1982; Hart, 1990), "mindlessness" (Langer, 1989), blindspots (Sorensen, 1989), up to "dominant ideologies" and their reality-blinding effects (Abercrombie et al., 1980), and many more, as in part already mentioned (e.g., May, 1972; Pears, 1984) and in part to be taken up later (e.g., Kahneman et al., 1982).

To further illustrate this point, let me mention the need in advanced policy sciences for suspicion about compromises. Compromises are morally often supported and regarded as a value by themselves, largely because of misunderstanding of the Greek "golden mean" rule and of the nature of "moderation" (Hartshorne, 1987). More important, compromises are, as a matter of fact, often politically essential for building and maintaining essential coalitions and consensus. However, compromises far beyond the requirements of minimum winning coalitions and maintenance of basic agreement are also widely misused as a convenient shortcut saving hard thinking and making politics easier. This is the case even if broad agreement is regarded as a democratic value by itself, which is debatable beyond some point if it prevents substantive value realization.

Compromise overrating is dangerous because, unless evaluated as separate options, compromise options often combine the worst features of a number of clear-cut alternatives and provide all decision partners with less of what they want and could get. Therefore, although recognizing the strength of procompromise factors and the unavoidability and desirability of a lot of compromising, still advanced policy sciences calls for careful evaluation of compromise options in conjunction with its debugging tasks.

J. Focus on Grand Policies

Advanced policy sciences should focus on overall policy trajectories, macropolicies, grand strategies, policy paradigms, and so forth. To put the matter in its most ambitious form: Advanced policy sciences deals with grand policies aiming at a significant impact on the future up to setting and changing national long-term directions of evolvement (cf. Kennedy, 1991).

The actual tendency in most of policy making is to move from ad hoc and limited decisions to aggregative implicit and de facto grand policies seldom considered as such, accompanied by declarations of intentions and hopes that have little action implications and even less lasting consequences. Hence, the importance of the mission of advanced policy sciences to focus on grand policies, including selection of policy modalities, as discussed below. Grand policies in turn provide guides, frames, directives, and settings for more limited decisions while being influenced and reshaped in part by the latter and operationally expressed through them.

Overall development strategies in less developed countries and industrial strategies for highly developed nations illustrate such needs, often eroded by detailed day-to-day decisions on one hand and improvisation on the other, with tactics often displacing grand-policy thinking. The limitations of mainstream policy studies, especially their appropriateness for considering mini-choices while being inadequate for grand-policy choices, further aggravate and legitimize the domination of tactics over strategy. Therefore, refocusing of policy sciences on grand policies constitutes all the more vital a principle.

K. Policy Modality Deliberation

In some circumstances, the preferable grand policy is to have none, but instead to proceed by incremental policy changes at most. This is the case when realities are on an ascending curve that can with a high probability be expected to continue. The reverse situation is posed when a domain is on a steep decline and approaches disaster, with the risks of very radical policy innovations being preferable to the certainty of failure in their absence.

To put the matter in more general terms, different conditions require quite distinct policy-making modalities. Thus, radical transformation endeavor, such as in the former Soviet Union and the Republic of South Africa, require very different policy modalities than do policies in more settled situations. And, under conditions of turbulence, fine policy tuning is a delusion and robust policies are needed.

Similarly, action portions need careful selection, in quantitative and qualitative measures, depending on critical mass and appropriate scales of intervention. Policy effectiveness is usually not linear, with different allotments being required to achieve various results under multiple conditions. In some cases, only large-scale efforts can bring about meaningful results (Schulman, 1980), whereas in others more than a little is waste and sometimes counterproductive.

Widespread pathologies in measuring out policy instrument quantum include both doing more of the same when the marginal utility of additional efforts is zero or negative and allocating small bits of effort to important issues when only a large allotment can be effective. Hence, the need in advanced policy sciences to consider nonlinear policy output functions and allocate policy instrument portions accordingly as part of policy modality choice.

A different policy modality choice considers the use of systematic planning, in its diverse forms, as a main mode of policy making in contrast to reliance on improvisation, up to crisis decision making, or on dispersed and also fragmented and piecemeal decision making. Related, though different, is the choice between more coordinated policies on one hand and reliance on focused selective-radical interventions to achieve desired results by shock effects and "locomotive-of-change" forces (Hirschman, 1986) on the other.

Another modality choice deals with allocation of policy-making tasks between different mixes of more decentralization and deconcentration versus more centralization and concentration, with the pure model of a market system and the pure model of a hierarchical command system serving as polar antipodes. Here, policy modality deliberation overlaps institutional concerns and meta–policy making, as discussed later.

As errors in policy modality spoil all of policy making conditioned by it, the urgency of engaging in explicit policy modality choice as a main principle of advanced policy sciences assumes immense importance.

L. Concentration on Critical Choices Within Coherent Perspectives

The idea of "critical choice" is well put in its purest form by a saying of the Confucian Hsün-tsu: "Yang Chu weeping at the crossroads said 'Isn't it here that you take a half step wrong and wake up a thousand miles astray'?" The idea of advanced policy sciences is epitomized by the mission of providing professional guidance for such choices, although often these are more diluted and constitute a lengthy and convulsed decision chain rather than a decision event.

Every nation and comparable entity faces a limited number of critical choices expected to have significant impact on the future up to fateful crossroads of history. Contrary to prevalent tendencies to concentrate on the urgent and current rather than the significant, advanced policy sciences tries to identify critical choices and allocates to them much of the available policy-improvement resources, such as organized brainpower and policy professionalism.

On a somewhat broader level, advanced policy sciences deals with the posing and conceptualization of policy issues on the basis of reality probing and reality evaluation. As the perception of issues tends to channelize solution efforts, this is a most important function that deserves much attention (e.g., Dery, 1984).

When significant policy domains are on a declining slope, critical choice opportunities must be created up to crisis instigation. In such situations, the search for options that provide critical choice possibilities is a main concern of advanced policy sciences. Converse situations are posed by "windows of opportunity," where critical possibilities are suddenly opening up for a limited time, including during crises. Contemporary policy studies grossly neglect such situations. Advanced policy sciences, in contrast, must be critical choice–occasion seeking, creating, and utilizing.

Concentration on critical choices, including their debugging (Janis, 1989) must be combined with coherent perspectives, which consider discrete decisions within an overall national and supranational view—taking care to balance disparate handling of specific choices with a congruent perspective. This is all the more essential because of the tendency both of policy-making practice and of much of policy studies to deal myopically with single decision items without considering decision sets as a whole. This does not imply a recommendation to try and engage in comprehensive planning, inter alia because of uncertainties and the preferability sometimes of shock interventions, or also from a coherent long-range perspective (as discussed in works of Albert O. Hirschman). But coherent perspectives are essential and should constitute a main characteristics of advanced policy sciences.

M. Futuribles and Grand Designs

Further to help and overcome the enslavement of policy making to current pressures and imminent adversities and in order to provide long-range compasses and dynamic goal directions for policy making, longer-range *futuribles*, in the sense of long-term comprehensive alternative possible futures (Jouvenel, 1967), up to "grand designs" and "umbrella concepts" (for this term, see United States Army Training and Doctrine Command, 1985). Often, realistic visions, as discussed later, are also needed to better link long-range policies to present decisions. Construction of scenarios backward in time, for example, from the *futuribles* or grand designs, to the present, is an essential advanced policy sciences method supplementing and counterbalancing the usual practice of thinking from the here and now into the future.

The evolution of the European Community and some parts of Dutch physical planning (Dutt and Costa, 1985) illustrate successful uses of advanced designs as a major policy compass. The Middle East illustrates a situation in which futuribles and grand designs are essential, the question being what possible futures can meet main decision criteria within a range of say 10 to 30 years. The problem of employment for growing populations in Mexico and India depicts another type of critical policy issue that cannot be effectively faced without construction of long-range alternative futures, grand designs, and realistic visions. Indeed, all radical societal transformation efforts need constructs of possible and desirable futures as a grounding for long-range policies and as a basis for societal architecture.

Here, grand policy analysis interfaces with a very different kind of activity; namely, utopian thinking—which has important functions to fulfill in providing bases for composition of realistic visions and inspirational ideals for societal choice (for a striking illustration from the history of Zionism and Israel, see Elboim-Dror, 1993). This illustrates the necessity of advanced policy sciences to input ideas from societal thinking as a whole, as discussed later.

N. Structure and Institution Concerned

A main feature of advanced policy sciences should be intense concern with structures and institutions—as resources and bases for policies and constraints upon them, as objects for policies, and as influenced by policies even if not aimed at. Policy reasoning in terms of societal architecture, constitution setting (also in the broad sense of that term as referring to societal structures; see Giddens, 1984), shaping of politics via institutions (March and Olsen, 1989), social and economic institution building, structural paths and their adjustment (North, 1990), and macro-organizational design and redesign, should be central to advanced policy sciences.

Structural and institutional factors are implied in all of policy making, are recognized as susceptible to unanticipated consequences and as often causing them (e.g. Boudon, 1982), and are often aimed at explicitly, such as in economic structural adjustment policies. But most of the policy sciences is not geared to take proper account of structures and institutions. Thus, to take widely aimed-at economic structural adjustments, even though having profound implications for political systems and for social structures as a whole, they are usually considered mainly in economic terms, with educational and locational aspects looked at as economic policy instruments and some auxiliary social policies being added as an afterthought at most (e.g., OECD, 1987; World Bank, 1990). This is a grave mistake that explains, in part at least, the counterproductive effects of many economic structural policies and their rejection by policy makers who sense their grievous omissions.

Conversely, when a policy focuses on specific institutions, policy making is often considered in a narrow perspective. Thus, political constitution writing is usually left to public law experts, with a sprinkling of political scientists, instead of being considered as institutional mega-architecture also requiring, in addition to a broad spectrum of traditional specialists, intense application of advanced policy sciences.

Law is a main form of policy, a major societal institution, and a main determinator of social institutions and human behavior. Therefore, a prescriptive theory of legislation should be closely related with advanced policy sciences, whereas in turn legislative theory should be based in part on advanced policy sciences. However, US and UK policy sciences literature tends to neglect the nature of legislation as policy making despite the obvious importance of laws and courts as main expressions and determinators of public policy and despite some very relevant work by some legal scholars interested in legislation theory, going back to Roscoe

Pound's view of legislation as social engineering. In contrast, most of Continental Europe tends to overemphasize the legal perspective and neglecting its obvious nature as an instrument and tool of policy making. A balanced theory of legislation meeting urgent requirements of advanced policy sciences is just in its beginnings (e.g., Hill, 1982, especially Chap. 1 and literature cited there).

The culmination of structure and institution considerations as a central concern for advanced policy sciences is reached when radical systems reforms are the main object of policy making. This is nowadays drastically the case in the Republic of South Africa, the former Soviet Union, the Eastern European countries, and, differently, in China; to a significant though lesser extent in many development countries; and in other but very significant ways in the European Community area.

These instances demonstrate the central position that radical system transformations occupy in contemporary policy making, which is sure to continue and expand in the 21st century. Hence, the crucial importance of structure and institution concern as urgently needed in advanced policy sciences up to advancement of reformcraft as a central and distinct theme (Dror, 1989).

O. Handling of Deep Complexity

Complexity is recognized as needing handling in mainstream policy studies, especially within the systems approach in its varieties (e.g., Checkland, 1981; Churchman, 1982; Miser and Quade, 1985, 1988). But much more is needed to handle "deep complexity," to go beyond surface views of complexity, to cognize its intricacies, and to do justice to its inmost features. Although some treatments try do take up some of the submerged features of complexity (e.g., Campanella, 1988; Pages, 1988), handling of deep complexity within policy sciences is just in its beginning. Thus, the implications for advanced policy sciences of more advanced notions of complexity, as developed, for instance, by Ilya Prigogine (Prigogine, 1980; Nicolis and Prigogine, 1989), have been scarcely taken up. Superficial application of fashionable concepts, such as chaos notions, may well do more harm than good by supplying slogans rather than profundity.

No overarching conceptions of complexity that meet the needs of advanced policy sciences are available. The very notion of deep complexity may in large parts be unspecifiable with presently available conceptual packages and imaginary, which lack, for example, guidelines, images, symbols, and concepts essential for constructing policy worlds in ways doing justice to salient complexities.

Here we may run into innate limits of the human brain. However, the limits can be pushed and much can and should be done to upgrade handling of deep uncertainty. Thus, a main rule for handling of deep uncertainty is to perceive, accept, and process contradictions. Following some trends in modern logic, advanced policy sciences must embrace and handle contradictions whether taking the form of dialectic processes and ironies of history, or of contradictory policy requirements, or of cognition of contradictions in estimations, and more.

Related is the need to accept and utilize counterintuitive dynamics, such as "micromotives and macrobehavior" (Schelling 1978), and to overcome the mental trapping of "common sense," as culturally conditioned (Geertz, 1983: Chap. 4). To put it bluntly: Common sense is no good for handling complexity, which often is counterintuitive. Concomitantly, simplification maxims of the Occam's razor type are not to be automatically adopted.

Less demanding is the recommendation to adopt multiple perspectives (Linstone et al., 1984), with main issues to be considered from diverse points of view both in terms of salient theories and models and in terms of types of actors. Tougher is the more advanced requirement to apply multiple disciplinary perspectives and a variety of disciplinary knowledge. Most inclusive of the ideas mentioned here for better handling of deep complexity is the necessity to apply a combination of different images, symbols, principles, frames, approaches, orientations, methods, methodologies, and tools. To put this principle metaphorically into the form of a modified law of requisite variety: Very complex approaches are essential for handling deep complexity (relevant is Mitroff et al., 1983).

This idea deserves emphasis and broadening: To try and achieve profundity in facing deep uncertainty, it is necessary to use multiple imagery, thinking modes, languages, and knowledge bases, reaching far beyond interdisciplinary and multiple perspectives. Required are a variety of reality encoding languages and symbols, alternative modes of knowledge making, different ways of thinking, and more.

A necessary preliminary base for moving in such directions is integration between numerical and qualitative literati and also artistic mind sets. Therefore, the tendency in most of policy sciences to emphasize quantitative approaches with neglect of "soft" ones must be reversed. At the same time, innumeracy (Paulos, 1988) is intolerable. What is needed is more than a combination between quantitative and qualitative as well as literati and also some artistic language use and reasoning capacities; namely their integration. To handle deep complexity, as well as satisfy other principles of advanced policy sciences, it is necessary to exercise professionalism in terms of hard data, and nonmetric scales, and the completely qualitative, and the "undefinable" other than by metaphor and by literary and also artistic imagery. Hence, the need to bridge and combine different cultures in advanced policy sciences, in particular so for adequately handling of deep uncertainty.

To end my discussion of this principle fittingly with a paradox, it may well be that what appears to be very complex in essence is relatively simple once the basic nature of underlying phenomena is revealed (Slobodkin, 1992). But reliably to recognize such "simplicity" hiding behind apparently very complex situations requires very high-quality penetration through "deep" complexity, thus posing a major challenge to advanced policy sciences.

P. Policy Gambling

In the face of pervasive uncertainty, much of it innate to societal and physical dynamics, decisions are in essence gambles. When uncertainties involve the very forms of alternative futures and the very dynamics of change, as they usually do, decisions are fuzzy gambles with unknowable and, in part, indeterminate payoff functions involving inter alia unavoidable proliferation of unexpected and often undesired consequences. When critical decisions are faced, nations have no choice but to "gamble with history" (Dror, 1990). Such a policy-gambling perspective, based on a view of dynamic realities as in significant part between probabilistics (e.g., Gigerenzer et al., 1989; Suppes, 1984), chaos (e.g., Gleick, 1987; Stewart, 1989) and indeterminacy is fundamental to advanced policy sciences.

Put differently, advanced policy sciences is grounded on a world view according to which, as mentioned, the future is shaped by some largely unknowable, and even more so unknown, dynamic and ultra-dynamic combination between necessity, contingency, chance, and choice. Advanced policy sciences deals with choice, which interacts with necessity, contingency, and chance in a variety of modes that in essence always constitute fuzzy gambling.

However intellectually obvious, the policy-gambling perspective has far-reaching and very disturbing implications, all the more so as it contradicts psychological, political, and cultural needs and propensities (e.g., Douglas and Wildavsky, 1982; Wildavsky, 1988; and, for an important classification, Thompson et al., 1990, especially pp. 62–65) and cannot be adequately handled intuitively (Arkes and Hammond, 1986: pass.; Kahneman et al., 1982).

Not only are essential features of policy gambling neglected in policy studies and falsified by most policy-making practices and traditions, but worse: Even better policy sciences texts and advanced professional practice often artificially reduce uncertainty by relying on the delusions of subjective probability.

To enable advanced policy sciences to handle correctly genuine uncertainties, significant methodological innovations are needed related to the view of the future as between necessity, contingency, chance, and choice. A new grammar of uncertainty and heuristic protocols is needed, with probabilistic terminology being expanded so as to include denominations for various kinds of uncertainty, surprise-propensity, ignorance, and indeterminacy, and the interrelations within such an expanded set of concepts must be worked out. The semiotic of uncertainty needs clearing up to reduce reliance on ambiguous terms and minimize the contradictory psychological connotations of interchangeable terminology. The logic of policy gambling should be clarified, with better differentiation between expectations and lottery values. Protocols for reducing uncertainty, based on the combinational use of diverse prediction approaches and methods, must be worked out, together with explication of their dependence on the past and consequent limits. Mapping of predictions, irreducible uncertainties, indeterminacy, chance-prone domains, and ignorance, needs much improvement—with special attention to communicating correct uncertainty maps to unwilling and underequipped decision makers. Doctrines for handling low-probability high-impact contingencies need development. And intense debugging must become the rule to reduce the many psychological biases and culturally motivated irrationalities characterizing human handling of uncertainty (for more detailed treatment of some of these proposals, see Dror, 1988).

The far-reaching implications of viewing choice as "fuzzy gambling" go beyond the need for additional methods and protocols and requiring restructure of large parts of policy studies that lead to significant changes in policy reasoning, and indeed policy intuiting, as a whole. When one takes into account that most of the other principles of advanced policy sciences depend on the policy-gambling perspective, because of increased uncertainties introduced by thinking-in-history, handling of deep complexity, and taking reacting environments more into account, for example, then the conclusion may well be that of all the ideas expounded in this chapter "policy gambling" is the single most radical and important principle.

Q. Value Analysis and Goal-Search Up to Realistic Vision Composition

The inclusion of value analysis and goal-search within advanced policy sciences further illustrates its multi-mode nature as well as its unique philosophical bases. It raises the fascinating problem how to improve a process from an external perspective without interfering with its internal axiomatic and axiological bases and justifications.

Socratic dialogues provide a classical illustration of possibilities to help legitimate value judges to clarify for themselves their value preferences through elicitation (Fischhoff, 1989). Other already-mentioned principles deal with this subject, such as the value bases of futuribles and the value principles of policy gambling. But much more can and should be done without usurping the roles of legitimate value judges, as themselves determined by values and ideologies.

For instance, the field for value judgment can be structured, with explication of underlying exchange rates, time preferences, and lottery values; professed values can be critically examined to evaluate their nature as real values or as instrumental means that have become dogmatized; many value issue can be analyzed in ways helpful to their understanding and application (e.g., to pick four very different policy-relevant illustrations, Rawls, 1971; Walzer,

1977; Gibbard, 1990; Sen, 1992); broad value and goal sets can serve as checklists for evaluation of policy options; value and goal consistencies can be verified; alternatives can be better sensitivity tested to value preferences, with resulting delimitation of essential value judgment; value and goal futures can be explored; value taxonomies can be constructed, moving from absolute values to decision criteria; and more.

Work on "tragic choice" (Calabresi and Bobbitt, 1978) and on unresolved conflict (Levi, 1986) illustrate some ideas available in the literature (as further expanded in Hechter et al., in publication), in addition to underpinnings provided by analytic philosophy, some schools of ethics, theology, political philosophy, and also parts of anthropology and semiotic. But within policy sciences, the subject is very neglected and also distorted (despite Fischer, 1980) and suffers from a surplus of advocacy and scarcity of relatively value-insensitive methodologies. Although some rigorous methodologies for handling some value-analysis issues do exist (e.g., Borcherding et al., 1990: pass.; Keeney and Raiffa, 1976), these have a narrow domain of applicability. Very little is available in contemporary policy studies that can help with value judgment and goal-search when complex bundles of dynamically changing and contradiction-loaded intergenerational comparisons, tragic choices, and intricate fuzzy gambles are faced—adding an additional factor resulting in "fragility of goodness" (Nussbaum, 1986) in policy making. Hence, the magnitude of this principle as an essential area of advanced policy sciences.

Further to illustrate possibilities, let me take the domain of goal costing as a relatively well-developed method but one extremely underutilized in practice while also in need of further advancement. However qualitative in part, historic-thinking based, uncertainty saturated, and innovation encouraging, advanced policy sciences must consider relations between objective and resources in the broadest sense of those terms, with attention to the need to allocate priorities in using scarce resources. Therefore, advanced policy sciences should be associated with costing and budgeting and with progress toward new modes of multi-year output-oriented budgeting. Failures of planning-programming-budgeting systems, zero budgeting, and similar attempts demonstrate difficulties. But unless advanced policy sciences is tied in to resources-allocation decisions, its chances of influencing actual policy making for the better are much reduced. Therefore, budgeting reforms must be considered within advanced policy sciences, especially in relation to feasibility mapping, value analysis, goal-search, and priority setting.

The subject of value analysis again exposes the main tensions between political reasoning and advanced policy sciences. Value analysis requires value and goal explication and value sensitivity testing of options, as indeed demanded by nearly all schools of ethics. But politics often requires values to be opaque and hidden and sensitivities to be camouflaged so as to reduce conflict and ease coalition building and maintenance. Similarly, value judgment and goal-search improvement require priority setting, which is anathema to most of politics.

Advanced policy sciences, as already indicated, goes beyond the search for more effectiveness, in the sense of better realizing given values, and moving on into the domain of goal-search. Although operating within "hypergoods" (Taylor, 1989: especially 63–73) accepted within one's culture and society and respecting the prerogative of legitimate value judges in selecting main substantive values, advanced policy sciences aspires to make essential contributions to goal-search, such as by considering value futures as a potential fact, developing new value options, and stimulating goal innovativeness by legitimate value judges.

A penetrating way to engage in goal-search, in conjunction with other advanced policy sciences principles such as development of futuribles and grand designs and with application of a variety of value analysis methods, is the composition of realistic visions, as already mentioned—for choice by legitimate value judges and, perhaps, citizen as a whole (as proposed in Jouvenel, 1967) and with their participation. Open-ended realistic visions constitute essential policy compasses, especially in societies engaging in active self-transformation. Such visions in turn are highly value sensitive and border on utopian composition, as already mentioned, posing main value analysis and goal-search tasks up to value and goal invention for advanced policy sciences.

R. Learning and Changing One's Mind

Steep and sophisticated learning curves, based on environment monitoring, on feedback, on social experimentation, on knowledge production and accumulation, and so forth, are essential, all the more so because of the features of policy gambling and their undermining of simplistic learning modes. Designing and building carefully designed learning as a continuous process into policy options and into advanced policy sciences itself is therefore essential. Here advanced policy sciences moves into upgrading of the adaptive capacities of organizations (Greene, 1982) up to crisis-management upgrading, as discussed later on.

In another terminology, sociocybernetics constitutes a frame for advanced policy sciences. Whether focusing on control and evolution of self-steering systems (Geyer and Zouwen, 1986), on governmental learning impediment removal (Etheredge, 1985), on learning how to learn (Michael, 1973), or on handling of turbulence and complexity (Campanella, 1988), adequate learning approaches must be built into advanced policy sciences, with all their institutional implications.

On another level, essential is a capacity to change one's mind on the individual and organizational levels. This leads to a view of advanced policy sciences as in part a belief-revising process (Harman, 1986), with application of the open-mind concept (Rokeach, 1960). Related are needs for a mix between short-range and long-range memories and their upbuilding as essential for policy learning on one side and a capacity to forget as not less essential for learning, especially under rapidly changing conditions, on the other.

The real crux of learning and changing one's mind is the requirement for iconoclasm and for overcoming deep substrata of tacit presuppositions, stipulations, and entrenchments up to breaking out of vicious spirals of policy recursion and, most difficult of all, exiting some features of dominant culture. Fundamental learning, as necessary within advanced policy sciences, depends on iconoclasm in respect both to explicit and especially implicit policy paradigms, policy orthodoxies, policy presuppositions, policy axioms, and dominant policy culture features. Advanced policy sciences must think of the unthinkable—say it, write about it, and sometimes recommend it.

This is always very hard and becomes impossible near the corridors of power, where doubts about accepted policy assumptions are not welcome and where hot emotional involvement inhibits exiting oneself as essential for changing one's mind. The closing down of the Central Policy Review Staff in the UK in 1983, after it came up with some politically costly iconoclastic innovations (Blackstone and Plowden, 1988: Chap. 9) demonstrates the difficulty of tolerating iconoclasm near the centers of decision making. Governmental think tank structures kept at arms-length from central minds of governments, but still functionally parts of policy making, can help. But much of the needed iconoclasm should take place in societal policy contemplation enclaves and in independent policy R&D organizations, with governmental policy making adopting parts of it, as suggested later on.

S. Innovation and Creativity

In contrast to analytical approaches proper, which concentrate on screening of alternatives and that dominate most of regular policy sciences, advanced policy sciences emphasizes innovation—which is all the more needed when available alternatives are unsatisfactory, often because of raising aspirations or changing situations, as is increasingly the case. What is frequently required is moving onto a different curve rather than optimizing on an existing one (cf. Wohlstetter, 1964: 106), involving inter alia adoption of fresh policy-appreciation frames (Vickers, 1965).

But this again is a painful process confronting both frozen mind sets on the individual and organizational levels and interest networks, as well as cultural blinders, on the societal level. Therefore, advanced policy sciences frequently evokes a lot of hostility and may depend on conditions permitting what Schumpeter (1952) called, in a different context, constructive destruction (very relevant is Olson, 1982).

Recognition of the pressing need for more policy creativity raises very vexing questions, such as: Are any design methods available to support the creativity principles of advanced policy sciences? Is policy creativity in the main a matter of institutional structures and cultures? Is policy creativity in essence a matter of finding creative persons whether they have a professional background in advanced policy sciences or not? Has policy creativity little to do with such specified variables, depending on diffuse sociocultural processes or idiosyncratic and little-understood personality features?

Existing knowledge does not provide answers to such questions. A main recommendation, therefore, is to put issues of policy creativity with priority on the advanced policy sciences research agenda, including reprocessing of relevant work, such as on policy entrepreneurs and policy innovators (e.g., Casson, 1982; Lewis, 1980; Merritt and Merritt, 1985; Polsby, 1984), and initiation of new studies. But it must be admitted that as long as the psychology of creativity is underdeveloped, to put it mildly, upgrading of policy creativity involves operating a black box.

Still, within this pragmatic limit, a great degree of action based on experience and prototheories can be taken to upgrade policy innovativeness, such as broadening cultural perspectives, as already suggested; careful literature search for ideas and extensive study of comparative experiences in other countries, which is amazingly often neglected; diversifying staff in terms of disciplinary background and personality type, with efforts to include creative persons even if they are otherwise troublesome and artistic personalities; and, as discussed later on, careful monitoring of societal policy thinking.

Another recommendation that seems well supported by available experiences is to advance special think-tank–type policy research and development (R&D) organizations that may not assure policy creativity but does increase its probability (Dror, 1984).

Issues of policy innovation and creativity illustrate tensions and antinomies between different policy sciences conceptions and requirements, which are hard to bridge. Thus, analysis in the narrower sense of screening of alternatives is critical, morphological, and involves convergent thinking, whereas policy creativity is related to quite different characteristics, such as divergent thinking up to poetic and artistic alternative worlds that produce imagination. Analysis and option invention presuppose, therefore, quite different modes of thinking and reasoning and require diverse states of mind, personalities, and institutional bases.

These and other contradictory needs of advanced policy sciences in turn reinforce the already-presented meta-principle that only a complex system of thinking can handle complex problems—raising many issues for advanced policy sciences structure such as training, staffing, and underlying disciplines that require intense attention.

T. Addressing Crises Decisions

Crises, in the sense of unexpected, and often unexpectable, events, filled with uncertainties that require a quick response that may have important consequences, are endemic to the turbulent change processes characterizing the foreseeable future. Therefore, crises decisions constitute an important mode of policy making, which must be addressed by advanced policy sciences. This is all the more important when simple conceptions of crisis management as aiming at restoration of status quo ante are rejected, both as impossible and as neglecting singular opportunities; and even more so when crisis instigation is recognized as sometimes a preferable policy-making modality.

To improve unavoidable crisis improvisation it must, paradoxically, be grounded in deep policy thinking. Unless main policy issues are considered in depth before a crisis occurs, policy-thinking infrastructures essential for guiding crisis decisions are lacking. Unforeseeable crises require a lot of time-compressed policy deliberation involving much improvisation. But if relevant issues have been studied before the crisis occurs, crisis improvisation stands a much better chance of achieving desired long-range objectives.

This view entails a number of implications for crisis management as a distinct field of study, practice, and professionalization (e.g., see Comfort, 1988; Lagadec, 1990, 1991; Rosenthal et al., 1989, and their bibliographies) and for advanced policy sciences. Although crisis management improvement should be based to a large extent on advanced policy sciences, advanced policy sciences should consider crises possibilities, develop compressed-time policy consideration methods and tools, and concern itself with designing and improving crisis decision systems. Concomitantly, the necessity to improve deep policy thinking, in part with the help of advanced policy sciences, to handle and utilize unexpected and unexpectable crises should be recognized and diffused throughout policy making.

U. Politics Sophisticated but Segregated

Relationships between advanced policy sciences with politics raise very troublesome moral, personal, and professional problems. Morally these problems involve appropriate codes of professional conduct and, in particular, the question whom to serve and when to exit or whistle. Personally, they involve deep frustrations, as already noted by Goethe, with policy professionals often asking themselves whether they should not themselves strive for political power that will enable them, so they think, to implement good policy advice rather than waste it on obtuse clients. Professionally, the question is how far and in what ways to take political realities, goals and values into account as core considerations within advanced policy sciences.

Leaving the moral and personal issues for later, let me make four comments on handling of politics within advanced policy sciences:

1. Political realities should be taken as a constraint, but not in a too narrow and rigid way (Dror, 1988). In part at least, advanced policy sciences should regard statesmanship (and stateswomanship) as the craft of making the necessary possible as opposed to a view of politics as the art of the possible in conservative a way.

2. Advanced policy sciences must understand the politics of its own activities, including the many contradictions between political needs and reasoning on one side and the basic world view and mission of advanced policy sciences on the other. Some such contradictions have already been mentioned, such as between value clarification versus goal ambiguity, and the political costs of iconoclasm. Others can be added, such as the desirability of having many and novel policy options for policy upgrading versus the frequent political convenience of incrementalism. The power-map implications of locating advanced policy sciences activities near top decision makers add to the picture of difficult relations between "policy" and "politics" and their implications for the acceptability of policy sciences inputs in the labyrinths of power. Such and other political costs of giving more weight to policy sciences knowledge in policy-making realities should be taken into account within advanced policy sciences and ef-

forts must be made to reduce them; for example, by designing preferable alternatives and packaging policies. Also advanced policy sciences should make contributions to political feasibility enlargement, such as by political reforms. Advanced policy sciences must recognize its political costs, alert its clients to the policy errors resulting from giving in to political constraints beyond the essential, and building up its credibility.

3. Advanced policy sciences should avoid dealing with purely political advice directed at power gaining, power upbuilding, and power maintaining. Similarly, the political uses and misuses of advanced policy sciences need clarification and resistance, and policy sciences professionals should not participate as such in the political controversies beyond the confines of their professional competence.

4. Summing up the above points and enlarging upon them: Advanced policy sciences must be sophisticated politically but keep itself segregated (though not isolated) from politics. Political sophistication implies a good understanding of the realities of politics, including its inmost tiers, within a dynamic frame doing justice to the variability of politics, its cultural bases, and its dynamics, as well as its dependence on accidental features, individual top decision makers, and unpredictable exogenous events. However, such political sophistication must be combined with segregation from politics, in the sense of observing a border between power-oriented political advice and policy-focused professionalism. Rulers are entitled to both types of help and advanced policy sciences must understand the nature, bases, and importance of the first one, but the two should be kept distinct.

V. Fruitful Interface with Policy Contemplation as a Diffuse Societal Process

Quite different in rationale is the principle to upgrade fruitful interface with policy contemplation as a diffuse societal, intellectual, cultural, and political process. As already mentioned, some advanced policy sciences principles, such as iconoclasm and innovation, depend on broad societal processes in which free societies and democracies enjoy a distinct advantage. This is the case with many additional principles of advanced policy sciences.

Wild alternatives, counterfactual assumptions, hermeneutic contemplation, value invention and utopian thinking, social critique, social inventions, and similar products of various societal strata, such as free-floating intellectuals and university academics as well as politicians, ideologues, various inventors and also grass-root activists, constitute essential inputs into advanced policy sciences. Far from being hostile to them, advanced policy sciences seeks insights, ideas, and approaches throughout society while preserving its specific identity and mission as a distinct professional component of societal problem-handling capacities.

W. Meta-Policy Making Concerns

Meta-policy making, in the sense of policy making on policy making, including structures, processes, personnel, and guiding principles (Dror, 1983, pass.), has already been touched on at several times previously. Advanced policy sciences faces here a dilemma: Upgrading policy quality through application of approaches and methods depends on suitable structures, professionals, and indeed cultures. Thus, policy paradigm iconoclasm requires independent think tanks; segregation from politics with opportunities to provide input into policy making depends on the existence of professional advanced policy sciences enclaves near the corridors of power but not fully integrated into the political entourage of rulers; and relating advanced policy sciences to specific crisis decisions requires highly developed and run-in crisis management systems. But some division of labor is essential, with a distinction to be drawn between, for example, constitution writing, governance reform, organization design, decision process management on one side and advanced policy sciences on the other.

Much overlap and cross-fertilization is vital: Advanced policy sciences is necessarily concerned with many issues of institution design and process reform, as already discussed, whereas disciplines concentrating on constitution writing, governance reforms, and so forth, need quite a few advanced policy sciences components. Team work can help and is essential for main meta-policy–making projects, as are individuals combining advanced policy sciences professionalism with overarching professionalism in governance upgrading as a whole.

However, design, reform, and upgrading of policy-making systems in a narrower sense constitute core issues for advanced policy sciences and is a major subject in urgent need of work as a main issue of redesigning governance for the 21st century.

X. Policy-Inputting Orientation

Although I reject a mainly policy-debate oriented perception of advanced policy sciences (for a different view, see Majone, 1989), still the difficulties in translating complex studies into forms accessible to busy and often nonprofessional decision makers and inputting them into policy making without undue oversimplification must be faced. In this sense, inputting orientation is a main principle for advanced policy sciences that aims not at selling conclusions by appeal to interests and emotions but at providing decision makers with an opportunity to avail themselves of professional policy thinking by correctly understanding it and its implications.

A first requirement it to have access to main decision makers and those who serve as their mind keepers and mind shapers. Assuming access exists, the main problem is how to present complex policy considerations in ways fitting information-processing capacities and interests of top-level decision makers so as to present the gist of the policy study, to debunk decision making, and to contribute to upgrading of policy reasoning as a whole.

It is impossible to present advanced policy sciences studies, including, for instance, explorations of deep complexity and mapping of diverse uncertainties, in simple prose language, short conventional position papers, and attractive oral briefings without dangerous oversimplifications and also falsifications. Instead, required are novel multidimensional analysis display modes that fully utilize the potentials of modern knowledge presentation technologies and employ dynamic graphics to help cognition, understanding, and insight (for some relevant ideas, see Tufte, 1983, 1990; novel technical possibilities inherent in modern computer programs are discussed in Dror and Lafore, 1990).

The scarcity of suitable briefing and display facilities in nearly all of the 32 offices of rulers that I have examined, with serious weaknesses even in what are regarded as very advanced display facilities, such as in defense operations centers (e.g., in presenting and analyzing uncertainties and complexity), indicate the scope of innovations needed on inputting advanced policy sciences studies into actual policy making.

Thus, novel types of decision-support systems fitting the needs of top-level decision making (what I call DSSR, or decision support systems for rulers) are essential for upgrading interface between advanced policy sciences studies and the centers of power. But more fundamental changes are required to overcome widespread preliteracy, innumeracy, and hostility to sophisticated policy-professional inputs pervading much of higher politics.

Here, a limit to the potentials of advanced policy sciences as an approach to improving policy making is reached as long as it is upgraded without related changes in other core components of policy making, including the qualifications of top decision makers and characteristics of policy-making culture. But this leads us into domains beyond the scope of this chapter.

Y. Reflexiveness

The last recommended principle of advanced policy sciences is to be reflexive; that is, to be self-conscious, self-critical, and self-transforming. This is what this chapter is all about: Advanced policy sciences should achieve a quantum jump and can do so, but in order to move in the recommended direction, more attention to the nature and mission of advanced policy sciences, more skepticism on the present state of the art of policy studies, and intense efforts at self-transformation must characterize policy sciences aspiring to advance itself.

III. INSTITUTIONAL IMPLICATIONS

The above 25 advanced policy sciences principles do not exhaust the subject. But I hope my message is clear: Even if ambitions are restrained to notions analogous to "minimum rationality" (Cherniak, 1986), the proposed conception of advanced policy sciences is very demanding intellectually as well as applicatively.

Some considerations ease the task: Progress with the proposed principles is a matter of degrees. And an adequate level of advanced policy sciences can be achieved as an aggregative product of interactive networks, with none of the components by itself fully realizing all of the principles. But still, the postulated specifications are very demanding when compared with most of the policy studies realities.

Nevertheless, I think that the proffered conception of advanced policy sciences is neither an exercise in pure exhortation nor a revised platonic idea of knowledge for rulers (though I admit by nova-platonic view that rigorous training of decision staffs and decision makers is essential). Progress in the direction of advanced policy sciences, hand-in-hand with advancement of other policy-relevant disciplines, is not only necessary and useful but also possible on the basis of the present state of the art and available ideas.

To move ahead, a number of institutional innovations are needed. Let me just mention briefly three main ones so as to further amplify the portrait of advanced policy sciences.

Professional university programs in advanced policy sciences based on public policy schools but different in important respects are a must. Let me share with the readers my continuous sense of shock at the fact that 4 to 5 years of university studies entitle a person to a graduate degree in policy analysis certifying to professional expertise, whereas to become a medical doctor, one must engage in 7 years of university studies and apprenticeship, to be followed by 3 years of advanced training before becoming a specialist—and I would not entrust my health beyond routine problems to such a physician before he or she accumulates years of experience. Is it that handling of policy issues is easier than health problems and that the body of knowledge on policy problems is more solid and easy to teach? Or is it more a matter of delusion that "common sense" can take care of most problems and a little smattering of some techniques provides whatever more may be needed?

To start to become a professional in advanced policy sciences, as espoused in this chapter, a rigorous 7-year university program, to be followed by a multi-year internship in outstanding think tanks is a minimum. The curriculum of the 7-year study program must cover all of the present policy studies learning, knowledge related to the 25 principles of advanced policy sciences presented in this chapter, professional training on application of knowledge to a multiplicity of policy domains, and some additional elements such as a professional code of ethics.

Advanced policy sciences can neither develop nor make actual contributions to policy making without two additional types of institutions, which exist in rudimentary form but require much maturation. The first such institutions are think tanks, in the sense of policy R&D organizations, as best represented by the RAND Corporation and differently by the Brookings Institution. To advance policy sciences and apply it to critical choices, think tanks require quite to breakthroughs (Dror, 1984). They must become really interdisciplinary, much more diverse in their frames and thinking and methodologies, and their role in policy making must be revised and better protected so as to maintain thinking freedom together with opportunities to input ideas, analyses, and recommendations into top-level choice processes (as well as public deliberation, relations between these two modes of contributing to policy making, and in-between ones, to be carefully designed, so as to preserve credibility, integrity, and confidentiality).

To really make advanced policy sciences, as well as other types of policy knowledge, relevant to critical choices, institutionalization of professional staffs for top-level decision makers is essential. Although high-level decision makers have staffs, these are usually more politics oriented, monodisciplinary, overinvolved in bureaucratic politics, and nonprofessional in policy studies. An already-mentioned comparative study of mine of 32 offices of heads of governments (Dror, in progress) showed that only in single cases were policy sciences professionals included in the staffs, and this was by accident rather than design.

Given the present state of policy studies, there may be good reasons for not basing them on high-level decision staffs. But assuming progress toward advanced policy sciences takes place, utilization of useful knowledge in high-level decision making depends on building up policy sciences staffs in the labyrinths of power, with a division of labor between the necessarily limited advice that such staffs can render and policy R&D organizations working more in depth. However, designing and maintaining well-functioning policy sciences staffs for rulers is a difficult task (Blackstone and Plowden, 1988; Dror, 1987; Dror, in progress), which itself is a main subject for advanced policy sciences R&D.

These are only some highlights from the broad subject of institutional conditions and implications of advanced policy sciences, but they indicate the linkage between advancing and utilizing policy sciences and required institutional changes.

Let me conclude and complement the exploration of advanced policy sciences by looking at it from an additional angle; namely, policy sciences as a life mission.

IV. POLICY SCIENCES AS A LIFE MISSION

It is clear by now that the proposed notion of "advanced policy science" is a very demanding one for its practitioners (and clients). The effort demanded from all of us aspiring policy scientists is manifestly justified in terms of the importance, and indeed essentiality, of policy sciences for the future of humanity. But I think there is more to a personal commitment to policy sciences. Climbing on the shoulders of Max Weber's famous essays on *Science as a Vocation* (1917) and *Politics as a Vocation* (1919) (the best annotated edition is Mommsen and Schluchter, 1992), let me conclude this chapter by offering some thoughts on policy sciences as a life mission (for a longer treatment of this theme, see Dror, 1993c), which will also serve to add some facets to the idea of advanced policy sciences.

1. Policy Sciences "Professionalism"

Choosing policy sciences as one's life mission involves becoming a policy sciences professional. The prime feature of "professionalism" is "knowledge in action" (Schon, 1983), which I reformulate in the context of policy sciences professionalism as the capacity and routine of building bridges between abstract knowledge and concrete issues. The essence of professionalism is practice based on deep knowledge. Although scientists focus on the production of knowledge and technicians or artisans concentrate on practice, the professional must be conversant with both science and practice, his or her own specialty being the transformation of science and other types of systematic knowledge into action, together with the development of action-relevant knowledge, with reality serving both as the target and as a learning laboratory.

To this essence of policy sciences professionalism, three features must be added: a code of professional ethics; an attitude of "clinical concern" and of being "cold" in the midst of emotional irrationality and hot power competition; and a good dose of skepticism, with strong suspicion of "the obvious" and common sense up to iconoclasm.

The code of professional ethics must deal with the questions for whom to work, when to exit and whistle, and how to avoid conflicts of interest. Policy professionals must remain cold about highly emotional issues and not be swayed by power struggles; otherwise their professional judgment becomes corrupted and they become politicians or prophets rather than policy professionals.

Related is the requirement of skepticism, first in the weaker form of being doubtful about "obvious" solutions and "common sense" answers, policy sciences professionals, going beyond what meets the eyes to counterintuitive and un–common-sense perspectives. In the stronger sense, the skeptical facets of policy sciences professionalism leads to iconoclasm, with readiness to "speak truth to power" and to deconstruct cherished policy orthodoxies.

2. Self-Identity

Based on the history of Western thought leading to the perception of this-worldly activities in terms of a "calling," and Max Weber's secularization of this conception (Goldman, 1988), as well as on Confucian notions of the role of advisors to rulers (e.g., Wright and Twitchett, 1962), my contention is that policy professionalism can, and often should, be engaged in as a life mission and provide an existential meaning to life in terms of moral significance, internal rewards, and personal challenge.

The primary internal rewards of policy sciences professionalism as a life mission is, as indicated, the knowledge that one is participating in a high-value activity directed at increasing human welfare, including facing evil (Kekes, 1990); namely, public policy making. Secondary, but very important, existential pleasures (cf. Florman, 1976) intrinsic in policy professionalism are triple: braving the scientific riddle of trying to know and understand policy-making actuality; facing the intellectual and moral challenges of prescriptive thinking; and the satisfactions of participating in impacting on reality by applying one's knowledge and skills to recalcitrant materials. The broad scope of relevant knowledge and the diversity of situations with which one is working multiply these intrinsic rewards, with nothing related to collective choice being outside the purview of the advanced policy sciences professional.

However, the territories of advanced policy sciences professionalism are also loaded with bitter fruits. Often even the best application of the most advanced knowledge will not provide satisfactory answers to policy quandaries. And when a good policy option is identified, political clients will frequently close their mind to it. As well put by a frustrated policy proto-professional in the Ottoman Empire in 1596:

> Listen to me, elder brother, for I've experienced this! The wail of pipe and drum is a great headache. Is not the state of wisdom enough for you, Ali? Why should lowly people humiliate you? (Fleischer, 1986: 229–230).

Therefore, policy sciences professionalism is a recommended life mission only for those of us who really feel "called" to it and who are fitted by temperament and self-reshaping to find fulfillment in this activity while accepting stoically its frustrations.

3. Policy Sciences Competence

The observations on university studies in advanced policy sciences indicate the investments one must make in order to build up required competence. It is incumbant upon us to be "workaholics" as a moral duty and as the only way to build up the expertise implied in our desire and claim to be policy sciences professionals. Constant broad readings, permanent learning from observing and doing, active efforts to broaden our experience by laboring in different cultures, incessant processing of our tacit knowledge into an explicit one that can, and should, be shared with others in accumulative a way while persistently, conscientiously, and meticulously applying our knowledge to vexing issues—these should keep us busy day and night, year after year. So that when the time comes to evaluate what we did with our life we can say with some justification that we tried to live up to the demands of policy sciences professionalism as a mission.

REFERENCES

Abercrombie, N., Hill, S., and Turner, B. S. (1980). *The Dominant Ideology Thesis*. Allen and Unwin, London.

Arkes, H. R., and Hammond, K. R. (Eds.). (1986). *Judgment and Decisionmaking: An Interdisciplinary Reader*. Cambridge University Press, Cambridge, UK.

Barrow, J. D. (1992). *Pi in the Sky: Counting, Thinking, and Being*. Clarendon Press, Oxford, UK.

Blackstone, T., and Plowden, W. (1988). *Inside the Think Tank: Advising the Cabinet, 1971–1983*. Heinemann, London.

Borcherding, K., Larichev, O. I., and Messick, D. M. (Eds.). (1990). *Contemporary Issues in Decision Making*. Elsevier, Amsterdam.

Boudon, R. (1982). *The Unintended Consequences of Social Action*. Macmillan, London.

—— (1984). *Theories of Social Change*. Polity Press, Cambridge, UK.

Braudel, F. (1980). *On History*. University of Chicago Press, Chicago.

Bruner, J. (1986). *Actual Minds, Possible Worlds*. Harvard University Press, Cambridge, MA.

Calabresi, G., and Bobbitt, P. (1978). *Tragic Choice: The Conflicts Society Confronts in the Allocation of Tragically Scarce Resource*. Norton, New York.

Campanella, M. (Ed.). (1988). *Between Rationality and Cognition: Policy-Making Under Conditions of Uncertainty, Complexity, and Turbulence*. Albert Meynier, Torino, Italy.

Casson, M. (1982). *The Entrepreneur: An Economic Theory*. Barnes & Noble, Totowa, NJ.

Checkland, P. (1981). *Systems Thinking, Systems Practice*. John Wiley, Chichester, UK.

Cherniak, C. (1986). *Minimal Rationality*. MIT Press, Cambridge, MA.

Churchman, W. C. (1982). *The Systems Approach: Revised and Updates*. Dell, New York.

Collini, S., Winch, D., and Burrow, J. (1983). *That Noble Science of Politics: A Study in Nineteenth-century Intellectual History*. Cambridge University Press, Cambridge, UK.

Comfort, L. K. (Ed.). (1988). *Managing Disaster: Strategies and Policy Perspectives*. Duke University Press, Durham, NC.

Cooper, D. E. (1990). *Existentialism: A Reconstruction*. Blackwell, Oxford, UK.

Dery, D. (1984). *Problem Definition in Policy Analysis*. University Press of Kansas, Lawrence.

Dobson, A. (1989). *An Introduction to the Politics and Philosophy of Jose Ortega y Gasset*. Cambridge University Press, Cambridge, UK.

Douglas, M., and Wildavsky, A. (1982). *Risk and Culture: An Essay on the Selection of Technical and Environmental Dangers*. University of California Press, Berkeley.

Dror, Y. (1983). *Public Policymaking Reexamined*. Supplemented ed. Transaction, New Brunswick, NJ.
—— (1984). Required breakthroughs in think tanks. *Policy Sciences* 16: 199–225.
—— (1986). *Policymaking Under Adversity*. Transaction, New Brunswick, NJ. Paperback 1988.
—— (1987). Conclusions. In *Advising the Rulers*. W. Plowden (ed.). Blackwell, Oxford, UK.
—— (1988). Uncertainty: Coping with It and with Political Feasibility. In *Handbook of Systems Sciences: Craft Issues and Procedural Choices*. H. J. Miser and E. S. Quade (Eds.). North-Holland, New York, pp. 247–281.
—— (1989). Memo for system-reforming rulers. *Futures* 21: 334–343.
—— (1990). Fateful decisions as fuzzy gambles with history. *Jerusalem Journal of International Relations* 12: 1–12.
—— (1993a). *Governance for the 21st Century: A Report of the Club of Rome*. In publication.
—— (1993b). School for rulers. In *A Systems-Based Approach to Policymaking*. K. B. De Green (Ed.). Kluwen Academic Publishers, New York, Chap. 5.
—— (1993c). Policy professionalism as a vocational calling. *Policy Studies Journal*. In publication.
—— (in progress). *Staffs for Rulers*.
Dror, A., and Lafore, R. (1990). *OS/2 Presentation Manager: Programming Primer*. Osborne McGraw-Hill, Berkeley, CA.
Dutt, A. K., and Costa, F. J. (Eds.). (1985). *Public Planning in The Netherlands*. Oxford University Press, Oxford, UK.
Eisenstadt, N. S. (1978). *Revolution and the Transformation of Societies*. Free Press, New York.
Elboim-Dror, R. (1993). *Yesterdays Tomorrow*: Vol. I. *Zionist Utopias*; Vol. II. *An Anthology of Zionist Utopies*. Yad Izhak Ben-Zvi Institute and Bialik Institute, Jerusalem (English version in progress).
Elster, J. (1979). *Ulysses and the Sirens: Studies in Rationality and Irrationality*. Cambridge University Press, Cambridge, UK.
—— (1983). *Sour Grapes: Studies in the Subversion of Rationality*. Cambridge University Press, Cambridge, UK.
Etheredge, L. S. (1985). *Can Governments Learn? American Foreign Policy and Central American Revolutions*. Pergamon Press, New York.
Faber, K.-G., and Meier, C. (Eds.). (1978). *Theory der Geschichte*: Vol. 2. *Historische Prozesse*. Deutscher Taschenbuch Verlag, Munich.
Fernandez-Santamaria, J. A. (1983). *Reason of State and Statecraft in Spanish Political Thought, 1595–1640*. University Press of America, New York.
Fischer, F. (1980). *Politics, Values, and Public Policy: The Problem of Methodology*. Westview Press, Boulder, CO.
Fischhoff, B. (1989). Value elicitation: Is there anything in there. In publication.
Fleischer, C. H. (1986). *Bureaucrat and Intellectual in the Ottoman Empire: The Historian Mustafa Ali (1541–1600)*. Princeton University Press, Princeton, NJ.
Florman, S. C. (1976). *The Existential Pleasures of Engineering*. St. Martin's Press, New York.
Fukuyama, F. (1992). *The End of History and the Last Man*. Free Press, New York.
Ganapathy, R. S., Ganesh, S. R., Maru, R. M., Paul, S., and Rao, R. M. (Eds.). (1985). *Public Policy and Policy Analysis in India*. Sage, New Delhi.
Geertz, C. (1983). *Local Knowledge: Further Essays in Interpretive Anthropology*. Basic Books, New York.
Gellner, E. (1988). *Plough, Sword and Book: The Structural of Human History*. University of Chicago Press, Chicago.
Geyer, F., and Zouwen, J. Van D., et al. (1986). *Sociocybernetic Paradoxes*, Sage, London.
Gibbard, A. (1990). *Wise Choices, Apt Feelings: A Theory of Normative Judgment*. Harvard University Press, Cambridge, MA.
Giddens, A. (1984). *The Constitution of Society: Outline of the Theory of Structuration*. Cambridge University Press, Cambridge, UK.
Gigerenzer, G., et al. (1989). *The Empire of Chance: How Probability Changed Science and Everyday Life*. Cambridge University Press, Cambridge, UK.
Gleick, J. 1987). *Chaos: Making a New Science*. Viking, New York.

Goldman, H. (1988). *Max Weber and Thomas Mann*: *Calling and the Shaping of the Self*. University of California Press, Berkeley.

Greene, K. B. De. (1982). *The Adaptive Organization*: *Anticipation and Management of Crisis*. Wiley, New York.

Hallpike, C. R. (1988). *The Principles of Social Evolution*. Clarendon, Oxford, UK.

Handel, Michael I. (1989). *War, Strategy and Intelligence*. Frank Cass, London.

Harman, G. (1986). *Change in View*: *Principles of Reasoning*. MIT Press, Cambridge, MA.

Hart, P. 'T. (1990). *Groupthink in Government*: *A Study of Small Groups and Policy Failure*. Swets & Zeitlinger, Amsterdam.

Hartshorne, C. (1987). *Wisdom as Moderation*: *A Philosophy of the Middle Way*. State Unive;rsity of New York Press, Albany.

Hawrylyshyn, B. (1980). *Road Maps to the Future*: *Towards More Effective Societies*. A Report to the Club of Rome. Pergamon, New York.

Hechter, M., Cooper, L., and Nadel, L. (Eds.). *Values*. Stanford University Press, Stanford, CA. In publication.

Hill, H. (1982). *Einfuehrung in die Gesetzgebunglehre*. C. F. Mueller, Heidelberg.

Hirschman, A. (1986). *Rival Views of Market Societies*. Viking, New York.

Hogarth, R. M. (Ed.). (1990). *Insights in Decision Making*: *A Tribute to Hillel J. Einhorn*. University of Chicago Press, Chicago.

Hogwood, B. W., and Peters, G. B. (1985). *The Pathology of Public Policy*. Oxford University Press, Oxford, UK.

Hopkins, K. (1991). The greed that was Rome. *The Times Literary Supplement*, No. 4582, January 25: 24.

Huntington, S. P. (1991). *The Third Wave*: *Democratization in the Late Twentieth Century*. University of Oklahoma Press, Norman.

Hybel, A. R. (1990). *How Leaders Reason*: *US Intervention in the Caribbean Basin and Latin America*. Blackwell, Oxford, UK.

Janis, I. L. (1982). *Groupthink*: *Psychological Studies of Policy Decisions and Fiascoes*. Rev. ed. Houghton Mifflin, Boston.

—— (1989). *Crucial Decisions*. Free Press, New York.

Janis, I. L., and Mann, L. (1977). *Decisionmaking*: *A Psychological Analysis of Conflict, Choice, and Commitment*. Free Press, New York.

Jouvenel, B. de (1967). *The Art of Conjecture*. Basic Books, New York.

Kahneman, D., Slovic, P., and Tversky, A. (Eds.). (1982). *Judgment Under Uncertainty*: *Heuristics and Biases*. Cambridge University Press, Cambridge, UK.

Kaufmann, W. (1974). *Nietzsche*: *Philosopher, Psychologist, Antichrist*. Princeton University Press, Princeton, NJ.

Keeney, R. L., and Raiffa, H. (1976). *Decisions with Multiple Objectives*: *Preferences and Value Trade-offs*. Wiley, New York.

Kekes, J. (1990). *Facing Evil*. Princeton University Press, Princeton, NJ.

Kennedy, P. (1987). *The Rise and Fall of the Great Powers*: *Economic Change and Military Conflict from 1500 to 2000*. Random House, New York.

—— (Ed.). (1991). *Grand Strategies in War and Peace*. Yale University Press, New Haven, CT.

King, A., and Schneider, B. (1991). *The First Global Revolution*: *A Report by the Council of The Club of Rome*. Simon and Schuster, London.

Kohr, L. (1957). *The Breakdown of Nations*. Routledge & Kegan Paul, London.

Lagadec, P. (1990). *States of Emergency*: *Technological Failures and Societal Destabilization*. Butterworth-Heinemann, London.

—— (1991). *La Gestion Des Crises*: *Outils de reflexion à l'usage des decideurs*. McGraw-Hill, Paris.

Langer, E. J. (1989). *Mindfulness*. Addison-Wesley, Reading, MA.

Lasswell, H. (1971). *A Pre-view of Policy Sciences*. Elsevier, New York.

Laqueur, W. (1985). *A World of Secrets*: *The Uses and Limits of Intelligence*. Basic Books, New York.

Lerner, D., and Lasswell, H. D. (Eds.). (1951). *The Policy Sciences: Recent Developments in Scope and Method*. Stanford University Press, Stanford, CA.

Levi, I. (1986). *Hard Choices: Decision Making Under Unresolved Conflict*. Cambridge University Press, Cambridge, UK.

Lewis, E. (1980). *Public Entrepreneurship: Towards a Theory of Bureaucratic Political Power—The Organizational Lives of Hyman Rickover, J. Edgar Hoover and Robert Moses*. Indiana University Press, Bloomington.

Lindblom, C. E. (1990). *Inquiry and Change: The Troubled Attempt to Understand and Shape Society*. Yale University Press, New Haven, CT.

Linstone, H. A., et al. (1984). *Multiple Perspectives for Decisionmaking: Bridging the Gap Between Sciences and Action*. Elsevier, New York.

Linz, J. J., and Stepan, A. (Eds.). (1978). *The Breakdown of Democratic Regimes*. Johns Hopkins University Press, Baltimore.

MacMullen, R. (1990). *Corruption and the Decline of Rome*. Yale University Press, New Haven, CT.

Majone, G. (1989). *Evidence, Argument, and Persuasion in the Policy Process*. Yale University Press, New Haven, CT.

Maoz, Z. (1990). *National Choices and International Processes*. Cambridge University Press, Cambridge, UK.

March, J. G. (1988). *Decisions and Organizations*. Blackwell, Oxford, UK.

March, J., and Olsen, J. (1989). *Rediscovering Institutions: The Organizational Basis of Politics*. Free Press, New York.

Martin, M. W. (Ed.). (1985). *Self-Deception and Self-Understanding: New Essays in Philosophy and Psychology*. University Press of Kansas, Lawrence.

May, E. R. (1972). *"Lessons" of the Past: The Uses and Misuses of History in American Foreign Policy*. Oxford University Press, New York.

Merritt, R. L., and Merritt, A. J. (Eds.). (1985). *Innovation in the Public Sector*. Sage, Beverly Hills, CA.

Michael, D. N. (1973). *On Learning to Plan—and Planning to Learn*. Jossey Bass, San Francisco.

Miser, H. J., and Quade, E. S. (Eds.). (1985). *Handbook of Systems Analysis: Overview of Uses, Procedures, Applications, And Practice*. North-Holland, New York.

—— (Eds.). (1988). *Handbook of Systems Analysis: Craft Issues and Procedural Choices*. North-Holland, New York.

Mitroff, I. I., Quinton, H., and Mason, R. O. (1983). Beyond Contradictions and Consistency: A Design for a Dialectic Policy System. *Theory and Decisions* 15: 107–120.

Mommsen, W. J., and Schluchter, W. (Ed.). (1992). *Wissenschaft als Beruf/Politik als Beruf, Max Weber Gesamtausgabe*, Vol. 17. J.C.B. Mohr, Tübingen, Germany.

Moya, C. J. (1990). *The Philosophy of Action*. Blackwell, Oxford, UK.

Nicolis, G., and Prigogine, I. (1989). *Exploring Complexity: An Introduction*. Freeman, New York.

Neustadt, R. E., and May, E. R. (1986). *Thinking in Time: The Uses of History for Decision Makers*. Free Press, New York.

North, D. C. (1990). *Institutions, Institutional Change and Economic Performance*. Cambridge University Press, Cambridge, UK.

Nussbaum, M. C. (1986). *The Fragility of Goodness: Luck and Ethics in Greek Tragedy and Philosophy*. Cambridge University Press, Cambridge, UK.

OECD. (1987). *Structural Adjustment and Economic Performance*. OECD, Paris.

Olson, M. (1982). *The Rise and Decline of Nations: Economic Growth, Stagflation, and Social Rigidities*. Yale University Press, New Haven, CT.

Osherson, D. N., and Smith, E. E. (Eds.). (1990). *Thinking—An Invitation to Cognitive Science*, Vol. 3. MIT Press, Cambridge, MA.

Pages, H. (1988). *The Dreams of Reason: The Computer and the Rise of the Sciences of Complexity*. Simon & Schuster, New York.

Paulos, J. A. (1988). *Innumeracy: Mathematical Illiteracy and Its Consequences*. Hill and Wang, New York.

Pears, D. (1984). *Motivated Irrationality*. Clarendon Press, Oxford, UK.

Planze, O. (1990). *Bismarck and the Development of Germany* (3 vols.). Princeton University Press, Princeton, NJ.

Polsby, N. W. (1984). *Political Innovation in America*: *The Politics of Policy Initiation*. Yale University Press, New Haven, CT.

Porter, M. E. (1990). *The Competitive Advantage of Nations*. Free Press, New York.

Prigogine, I. (1980). *From Being to Becoming*: *Time and Complexity in the Physical Sciences*. Freeman, New York.

Rawls, J. (1971). *A Theory of Justice*. Harvard University Press, Cambridge, MA.

Raz, J. (Ed.). (1978). *Practical Reasoning*. Oxford University Press, Oxford, UK.

Rokeach, M. (1960). *Open and Closed Mind*. Basic Books, New York.

Rosenthal, U., Charles, M. T., and Hart, P. 'T. (Eds.). (1989). *Coping With Crisis*: *The Management of Disasters, Riots and Terrorism*. Thomas, Springfield, IL.

Schelling, T. C. (1978). *Micromotives and Macrobehavior*. Norton, New York.

—— (1984). *Choice and Consequence*: *Perspectives of an Errant Economist*. Harvard University Press, Cambridge, MA.

Schon, D. A. (1983). *The Reflective Practitioner*: *How Professionals Think in Action*. Basic Books, New York.

Schulman, P. R. (1980). *Large-Scale Policymaking*. Elsevier, New York.

Schumpeter, J. (1952). *Capitalism, Socialism and Democracy*. Allen & Unwin, London.

Sen, A. (1992). *Inequality Reexamined*. Harvard University Press, Cambridge, MA, and Russell Sage Foundation, New York.

Sims, H. P. Jr., and Gioia, D. A., et al. (1986). *The Thinking Organization*: *Dynamics of Organizational Social Cognition*. Jossey Bass, San Francisco.

Skocpol, T. (Ed.). (1984). *Vision and Methods in Historical Sociology*. Cambridge University Press, Cambridge, UK.

Slobodkin, L. B. (1992). *Simplicity and Complexity in Games of the Intellect*. Harvard University Press, Cambridge, MA.

Sorensen, R. A. *Blindspots*. (1988). Clarendon Press, Oxford, UK.

—— (1992). *Thought Experiments*. Oxford University Press, Oxford, UK.

Sousa, R. de (1987). *The Rationality of Emotion*. MIT Press, Cambridge, MA.

Sternberg, R. J. (Ed.). (1990). *Wisdom*: *Its Nature, Origins, and Development*. Cambridge University Press, Cambridge, UK.

Sternberg, R. J., and Wagner, R. K. (Eds.). (1986). *Practical Intelligence*: *Nature and Origins of Competence in the Everyday World*. Cambridge University Press, Cambridge, UK.

Stewart, I. (1989). *Does God Play Dice? The Mathematics of Chaos*. Blackwell, Cambridge, MA.

Suppes, P. (1984). *Probabilistic Metaphysics*. Blackwell, Oxford, UK.

Tainter, J. A. (1988). *The Collapse of Complex Societies*. Cambridge University Press, Cambridge, UK.

Taylor, C. (1989). *Sources of The Self*: *The Making of the Modern Identity*. Harvard University Press, Cambridge, MA.

Thompson, M., Ellis, R., and Wildavsky, A. (1990). *Cultural Theory*. Westview, Boulder, CO.

Toffler, A. (1990). *Power Shift*: *Knowledge, Wealth and Violence at the Edge of the 21st Century*. Bantam, New York.

Tufte, E. R. (1983). *The Visual Display of Quantitative Information*. Graphics Press, Cheshire, CT.

—— (1990). *Envisioning Information*. Graphics Press, Cheshire, CT.

Unger, R. M. (1987a). *Part I of Politics, a Work in Constructive Social Theory*: *False Necessity—Anti-Necessitarian Social Theory in the Service of Radical Democracy*. Cambridge University Press, Cambridge, UK.

—— (1987b). *Variations on Themes of Politics, a Work in Constructive Social Theory*: *Plasticity into Power—Comparative-Historical Studies on the Institutional Conditions of Economic and Military Success*. Cambridge University Press, Cambridge, UK.

United States Training and Doctrine Command (1985). *Army 21 Interim Operational Concept*. US Training and Doctrine Command, Fort Monroe, VI.

Vertzberger, Y. Y. (1990). *The World in Their Minds*: *Information Processing, Cognition, and Perception in Foreign Policy Decisionmaking*. Stanford University Press, Stanford, CT.

Vickers, G. (1965). *The Art of Judgment*: *A Theory of Policymaking*. Chapman and Hull, London.

Wakeman, Jr., F. (1985). *The Great Enterprise*: *The Manchu Reconstruction of Imperial Order in Seventeenth-Century China* (2 vols.). University of California Press, Berkeley.

Walzer, M. (1977). *Just and Unjust Wars*: *A Moral Argument With Historical Illustrations*. Basic Books, New York.

Wildavsky, A. (1988). *Searching for Safety*. Transaction, New Brunswick, NJ.

Wittgenstein, L. (1953). *Philosophical Investigations*. Macmillan, New York.

Wohlstetter, A. (1964). Sciences and design of conflict systems. In *Sciences for Military Decisions*. E. S. Quade (Ed.). Rand McNally, Chicago.

World Bank (1990). *The Economy of the USSR*: *Summary and Recommendations*. The World Bank, Washington, DC.

Wright, A. F., and Twitchett, D. (Eds.). (1962). *Confucian Personalities*. Stanford University Press, Stanford, CA.

Zolo, D. (1992). *Democracy and Complexity*: *A Realistic Approach*. Polity Press, Cambridge, UK.

2
Systematic Policy Evaluation

Stuart S. Nagel
University of Illinois, Urbana-Champaign, Illinois

I. EVALUATION ELEMENTS

The basic elements in systematic policy evaluation are (1) goals to be achieved; (2) alternatives available for achieving them; (3) relations between goals and alternatives; (4) tentative conclusions as to which alternative, combination, or allocation is best; and (5) what-if analysis designed to show the effects on the tentative conclusions of changing the inputs. The inputs are the goals, alternatives, and relations. The outputs are the tentative conclusions and the what-if analysis.

These are elements rather than steps. They occur in a cyclical fashion rather than sequentially. Trying to develop some goals leads to ideas for alternatives, which in turn leads to ideas for more goals and vice versa. Drawing tentative conclusions also leads to rephrasing the inputs and vice versa.

The material that follows discusses the evaluation elements in detail, followed by a discussion of various methodological problems such as how to deal with (1) multiple dimensions on multiple goals; (2) multiple alternatives that are too many to determine the effects of each one; (3) multiple missing information, especially as to how the alternatives relate to the goals; (4) the need for simplicity in drawing and presenting conclusions in spite of all the multiplicity; and (5) the use of what-if analysis for dealing with multiple and possibly conflicting constraints, as well as other methodological problems.

A. Goals to Be Achieved

As for policy analysis goals, the subject deals with the relative importance of such basic concepts as efficiency (or benefits/costs); profitability (benefits minus costs); effectiveness (benefits regardless of costs); equity (the distribution of benefits or costs); detriments (negative social indicators like crime); and marginal rate of return (change-in-benefits/change-in-costs). Seeking to clarify these basic concepts raises some interesting questions, for example:

1. Which is better, a good benefit/cost ratio or a good benefits/costs difference?
2. Which is better, a one-unit increase in efficiency or a one-unit increase in effectiveness?
3. Which is more efficient, a city with 100 crimes and $50 in anticrime expenditures or a city with 200 crimes and $25 in anticrime expenditures?
4. Which is better, a project with a good benefit/cost ratio or a project with a good ratio of change-in-benefits to change-in-costs?

The subject matter goes into further detail on the matter of equity as a policy goal. It defines equity in terms of providing people, groups, and places with a minimum level of income, education, freedom from crime, or other things of value that a government or society can allocate. The subject is also concerned with measuring degrees of equity or inequity, using equity as a criterion for choosing among policies, and the problems of tradeoffs between equity and other goals, such as efficiency or freedom.

The subject deals with supplementing the basic substantive goals with process goals. These emphasize public participation, predictability of decisions, and procedures that facilitate proving one is deserving of benefits or innocent of wrongdoing. These goals are referred to as the three Ps—participation, predictability, and procedure. They are especially associated with political science in contrast to the three Es—effectiveness, efficiency, and equity—which are especially associated with economics. These process matters may often be goals in themselves; for example, society and policy makers are often willing to sacrifice some effectiveness, efficiency, and equity in order to provide for more participation, predictability, and procedural due process as ends in themselves. In this context, *equity* and *equality* are nearly synonymous, and *productivity* can refer to either effectiveness or efficiency. Likewise, *public participation* is a synonym for democracy or political freedom, which includes both majority rule and the right of minorities to try to convert the majority.

The subject of policy analysis goals emphasizes how goals of freedom of speech and religion, equality of treatment, fair criminal procedure, and basic economic security can be justified in terms of their social consequences. These consequences include higher standards of living, psychological well-being, and both effectiveness and efficiency in achieving general societal goals. The subject also emphasizes that freedom can help secure equality for individuals who might otherwise be deprived, and that a satisfactory level of equality tends to generate an atmosphere that allows more freedom. Particularly important is the idea of justifying minority rights that relate to political freedom, equity, and fair procedure in terms of how they benefit the majority and the total society.

B. Alternative Policies

As for policy-analysis means, these issues consist of:

1. Using positive and negative incentives
2. Decreasing discretionary abuses while preserving flexibility
3. Balancing public and private sector implementation
4. Structuring government for greater goal achievement

We are not, for example, specifically interested in whether the energy shortage might be resolved better by emphasizing nuclear or solar energy. We are, however, concerned with the general problem of providing incentives, including incentives for encouraging energy conservation and innovation. We are also concerned with decreasing the abuses of discretionary power (including the power of energy regulators) by providing clear guidelines or other controls. In addition, we are concerned with the controversy of public versus private ownership both in the energy field and in other fields. Likewise, energy policy is influenced by basic government structures, but so are all policy problems. There is less general agreement on goal-achieving means than on goals themselves, but we try to find aspects of the opposing arguments in which a compromise or agreement is more likely to be found. *Goal-achieving means* refers to both formation and implementation of policy but with an emphasis on implementation.

An important means issue is the use of positive and negative incentives in order to encourage socially desired behavior, especially behavior that will increase societal productivity. In recent years, there has been an increasing advocacy of the use of positive incentives. For example, liberals advocate decreasing criminal behavior by providing would-be burglars and muggers with the incentive of legitimate job opportunities. Such positive incentives probably keep middle-class people from committing crimes more than does the fear of serving time in jail. Likewise, conservatives recommend a system that provides business firms with tax incentives in order to encourage greater productivity and the hiring of unemployed minority workers rather than a system that orders business firms to comply with various regulations. Both groups recognize that society probably can get better compliance through rewards than punishments.

When it comes to discretionary abuses, one often thinks of decision makers who have wide discretion for holding arrested persons in jail pending trial or for holding defendants in prison after conviction. Both liberals and conservatives agree that such discretion is often abused and should be subjected to more effective control, although not necessarily for the same reasons. Liberals tend to believe that pretrial decision making results in too many people being held in jail, contrary to the presumption of innocence. Conservatives tend to think pretrial decision making results in too few people being held in jail, contrary to the desire to prevent crimes by those who are out on bail. When it comes to sentencing, liberals want the discretion of judges and parole boards decreased because they believe the discretion is used discriminatorily. Conservatives often want to decrease such discretion because they find it is used too leniently.

A controversial implementation issue is the extent to which various societal functions should be carried out by government or by private enterprise. Both sides, operating in a democratic context, tend to agree on such goals as the need for achieving more gross national product, freedom and popular control, opportunity, and security and initiative. However, they generally disagree on whether the public sector or the private sector is more capable of achieving these goals. The degree of disagreement may be lessening, however, as socialist advocates recognize the value of using the marketplace to aid in determining prices and production quantities and the value of competitive income incentives to stimulate productivity and innovation. Likewise, the capitalist advocates recognize increasingly the value of more national economic planning, especially in dealing with inflation and unemployment and with taxation and subsidy incentives for productivity and innovation. There may be a trend toward more responsiveness of the economy to consumers and workers regardless of whether the government-economy relation is socialistic or capitalistic.

How to structure government for greater goal achievement raises a particularly important set of issues for political science. These issues relate to fundamental governmental structures in terms of the relations between:

1. The national government and the states, provinces, and cities
2. The chief executive and the legislature
3. The courts as constitutional guardians and the executive-legislative branches of government

4. The political parties vis-à-vis each other
5. The government and the people in terms of majority rule and minority rights to try to convert the majority

Among political and social scientists, there is increasing concern about how these structural issues relate to societal productivity. There is an increasing trend toward giving more power to the national government and the executive branch to cope with policy problems. At the same time, the courts have imposed new constraints on civil liberties and have expanded majority rule by widening the franchise. Structural issues tend to be influenced by who is occupying the structure, but there is underlying agreement on many aspects of these issues among both liberals and conservatives.

C. Relations Between Goals and Alternatives

1. The Use of 1 to 5 Scales and Multidimensionality

To deal with multidimensionality in the past, we have advocated working with incremental differences, weighted raw scores, and part/whole percentages. All now seem inferior to 1 to 5 scales as being unnecessarily complex. We looked at about five different objections that could be made to 1 to 5 scales and showed how easily they could be overcome.

One very simple objection is that the scale only provides for 5 notches, which is not very sophisticated. The answer is that it provides for an infinite number of notches because one could specify an infinite number of decimals between the numbers 1 and 5.

1. It is very common to talk about scores of 4.5, 3.5, 2.5, and 1.5.
2. It is also common to say that some relation is just slightly better than nothing and let us give it a 3.1, or that it is slightly worse than nothing and give it a 2.9.
3. The bicycles problem in Beijing illustrates how one could meaningfully have many degrees, starting out with 1 to 5 and then coming up with alternatives that fit between the other alternatives and likewise fit between the scores.

Another point was how to translate scores that are not on a 1 to 5 scale into 1 to 5 scale scores, such as gross national product figures that were about $100, $400, $300, and $250.

1. The first step is to decide what number on a 1-5 scale the lowest dollar amount corresponds to. We said it was about 3.5, meaning somewhere between nothing and a mild increase.
2. The second step is to decide what number on a 1 to 5 scale corresponds to the highest number. That, we said, was about a 4.5; it was not perfect, which a 5 implies, but it was better than just a mild increase.
3. We can then translate any of the other numbers and preserve the relative ratios by using high school algebra interpolation. We could reduce that to a formula instead of a diagram. In terms of symbols, maybe we would not want to use X and Y, but instead use A and B. It is just a matter of solving for A_2 in the diagram, where A_2 equals the formula given. A_2 is the translated value expressed on a 1 to 5 scale.

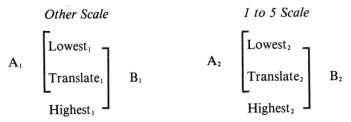

$A_1/B_1 = A_2/B_2$
$A_2 = (A_1) (B_2)/B_1$
$Translate_2 = Lowest_2 + A_2$

The point was made that maybe a 1 to 5 scale fails to take into consideration diminishing returns because an increase from 4 to 5 is only a 25% increase and an increase from 1 to 2 is a 100% increase.

1. One answer is that from a 1 to a 2 is a doubling or halving on the negative side of the scale, and changing from a 4 to a 5 is a doubling or a halving on the positive side of the scale.
2. If the 1 to 5 scale is all positive, which is not the way we normally do it, then it would be appropriate to make use of percentages.

The point was also made that a 1 to 5 scale for purposes of choosing does not have the same meaning as it does for purposes of allocating. That is true. We should translate the 1 to 5 scale back into $-2, -1, 0, +1$, and $+2$ in order to take into consideration that a 1, 2, and 3 on a 1 to 5 scale are really negative numbers or zeroes. We would not want to allocate anything to an alternative that has a negative or zero relation with the composite goal or the overall total. Negative scores are only relevant for allocation purposes. For choosing purposes, the threshold gap is the same regardless whether the zero point is below 1 or is at 3. On negative goals, we avoid them by phrasing the goal in a positive way. That is more of a problem with regard to the 1 to 3 weighting system than it is the 1 to 5 relation scoring.

2. Missing Information

There is much less likely to be any missing information when we use a 1 to 5 scale. That kind of scale is so easy to use that it would be hard for an individual to say that they are so in the dark they do not know whether there is a positive or negative relation. If they do know that it is a positive relation, then they have eliminated three of the five possible scores.

Then all they have to decide is whether the positive relation is a mild one or a strong one. That should be rather easy to answer as contrasted to specifying exactly how many units are involved.

The threshold analysis provides an excellent check on what would happen if we were wrong in saying that it is mild rather than strong or strong rather than mild. One can quickly see that the same bottom line would still hold with either a score of 4 or a score of 5. Thus, for all practical purposes, there is no missing information. If a 4 produces a different bottom line than a 5 produces, then one does have to decide which number makes more sense. That is a lot easier than having to decide exactly what the number should be in every cell in the matrix. This narrows it down to just one cell and to one pair of numbers rather than an infinite number of possibilities.

D. Drawing Evaluative Conclusions

1. The Overall Goal

Principle 1. The overall goal in optimizing analysis is to maximize benefits minus costs, or the satisfaction from the good effects of adopting a policy minus the dissatisfaction from the bad effects.

Minimizing costs subject to a safety net or minimum benefit constraint was an alternative popular with the Reagan administration. That kind of alternative, however, produces undesirable results. For example, if there is a 50-unit minimum benefit constraint, then project A that costs less than project B will be favored over project B if project A produces more than 50 benefit units even though project B may produce many more benefit units and thus be much more profitable. Likewise, maximizing benefits subject to a maximum cost constraint also produces undesirable results. For example, if there is a 60-unit maximum cost constraint, then project A will still be favored over project B if project B exceeds the 60-unit cost constraint even though project B may be much more profitable.

Picking projects because they have high benefit/cost ratios can also produce undesirable results. The results will not be undesirable if the project that is highest on B-C is also highest on B-C. That will happen if the costs or benefits for both projects are the same. If one project is better on benefits but worse on costs, as is often the case, then that project may be higher on B-C but lower on B-C. Business people judge projects and firms on income minus expenses, not on income divided by expenses. The project with the better B/C ratio is likely to have unspent funds, which might be spendable elsewhere. If doing so brings in enough additional profit, then the combination of project A plus the additional project C may be better than project B because the combination of the two is more profitable, not because project A had a higher B/C ratio than project B. Like the other alternatives to maximizing benefits minus costs, the B/C ratio is often resorted to rather than coming to grips with the problem of subtracting monetary costs from nonmonetary benefits.

2. The Basic Methodology

Principle 2. List the benefits minus costs for each alternative, and then pick the alternative that is highest on B-C, or find a shortcut or indirect method for arriving at the same result.

The ideal way in theory to arrive at the policy or combination of policies that maximizes benefits minus costs is to determine the benefits minus costs for each policy and choose the policy that scores the highest. In practice, that approach may not work where (1) the benefits are nonmonetary and the costs are monetary, which may make the subtraction process meaningless; (2) some or all of the benefits, the costs, and/or the weights of the goals may be unknown; (3) the number of alternatives may be huge, as where one is allocating a large number of resource units to a substantial number of activities, places, or persons; or (4) the relations between each policy and each benefit or cost may be highly complex. These four conditions are the basis of the four objections to optimizing analysis applied to law or to almost any subject matter.

E. What-If Analysis

In policy evaluation, sensitivity analysis is a useful source of information about goals, policies, and relations when authority, statistics, and deduction do not provide clear answers regarding them. Sensitivity or threshold analysis enables one to determine how much room for error there is in weighting the goals, listing out the policies, or measuring the relations. Often, the controversy over precision in these matters is wasted because, within the range in which the controversy occurs, the overall conclusion as to which policy or combination is best is still the same. Sensitivity analysis also enables the policy evaluator to convert difficult questions about goals, policies, and relations into relatively easy questions, such as, Is a given weight, policy, or relation above or below some threshold? rather than, What is the exact weight, policy score, or relation?

How to dispose of criminal cases provides an example of applying sensitivity analysis when the goals and their relative weights are unclear. There are basically two ways to dispose of criminal cases; namely, through trials and guilty pleas. The main goals for deciding which type of disposition is better are (1) the respect for the legal system that each method generates and (2) the time consumption that each method incurs. If trials receive a score of 6 on a 1 to 10 respect scale in a public opinion survey and pleas receive a score of 2, then trials get a percentage score of 6/8, or 75%, and pleas get a score of 2/8, or 25%. If trials average 120 days and pleas average 30 days from complaint to disposition, then trials get a percentage score of 120/150, or 80%, and pleas get a score of 30/150, or 20%. If the two goals are weighted equally, then trials are the loser because they have a benefit score of 75% and a cost score of 80%, whereas pleas have a benefit score of 25% and a cost score of 20%. It is difficult to determine how much weight respect should be given relative to time consumption. However, one does not have to make that determination. All one has to do is note that the threshold equation in which the benefits minus the costs of trials equals the benefits minus the costs of pleas is 75% (W) − 80% = 25% (W) − 20%, where W is the relative weight of respect versus time consumption. Solving for W yields a threshold value of W* = 1.20. Therefore, if we can agree that respect is worth more than 1.20 times saving days, then trials are the better method of disposition; it is unnecessary to decide the relative value of their importance. One (or both) of the two scores on each of the two goals of 6, 2, 120, 30, could also be converted into a letter in the threshold equation to be solved in order to determine its threshold value.

In using sensitivity analysis to determine a set of feasible policies, we have to distinguish between a method that will provide a set of policies from which we can choose rather than a method designed to arrive at an optimum policy. All four sources of information can be used to arrive at either feasible policies or an optimum policy. In the context of this chapter, however, we are referring to methods for determining the goals, policies, and relations from which an optimizing conclusion can be drawn. Legislative redistricting provides a good example of where a variation on sensitivity or threshold analysis can be used to narrow the policies but not to arrive at an optimum policy. In the redistricting of a state legislature by grouping counties, precincts, or other units together, millions of policies are possible because every grouping or pattern is a different policy. A frequently used method for dealing with such a huge number of policies is to (1) start with the status quo districting, (2) move a unit out of the first district into the second district, and then (3) compare the new pattern with the original pattern. If the new pattern is an improvement over the previous pattern, then it becomes the new threshold above which the next pattern has to improve. After going through many rounds, the last pattern left can be declared the winner even though it may not be the optimum. Sensitivity or threshold analysis is closely related to the concept of satisficing. This concept involves going through as many rounds of moving units from one district to another until we arrive at a pattern that satisfies whatever constraints we have to abide by.

Sensitivity analysis can be used to help determine the relations between policies and goals. In many instances, the same conclusion will be reached as to the best policy regardless of the magnitude of the relation between the policy and the goal as long as the relation is known to be higher or lower than a given level. In 1970, for example, the 250 legal services programs of the Office of Economic Opportunity were evaluated by teams of lawyers and representatives of the poor. Each program was scored according to its overall satisfaction (S). In addition, the percentage of time and money that each program spent on case handling and on law reform was determined. These percentages were then multiplied by the program budget and divided by the number of clients in order to obtain a figure for case-handling dollars per client ($C) and law-reform dollars per client ($L) for each program. With these data, the relation between S and $C and then the relation between S and $L across the programs could be determined. The first relation is −0.03 by way of a linear regression analysis and the second relation is +0.34. A linear relation was used contrary to the principle of diminishing returns because the feasible allocations were narrowly confined. The programs were expected to spend 80 to 90% on case handling and 10 to 20% on law reform. Within that range, substantial diminishing returns does not have an opportunity to occur. The analysis generates controversy over whether the case-handling relation is truly negative. For allocation purposes, however, it makes no difference. One would optimally allocate as much money as possible to law reform and as little as possible to case-handling within the constraints as long as the case-handling relation fell below +0.34—and even if it were +0.20 or +0.30.

II. METHODOLOGICAL OBSTACLES TO OVERCOME

The essence of decision-aiding software is that it is designed to process a set of

1. Goals to be achieved
2. Alternatives for achieving them
3. Relations between goals and alternatives

in order to choose the best alternative, combination, or resource allocation in light of the goals, alternatives, and relations.

   Some of the main benefits of systematic policy evaluation and/or decision-aiding software are in accurately and quickly handling five key methodological problems in decision making. They are

1. Multiple dimensions on multiple goals. This is the apples and oranges program.
2. Multiple missing information.
3. Multiple alternatives that are too many to be able to determine the effects of each one.
4. Multiple and possibly conflicting constraints.
5. The need for simplicity in drawing and presenting conclusions in spite of all that multiplicity.[1]

A. Adding Apples and Oranges

Decision-making problems often involve multiple goals measured on a variety of different dimensions, such as miles, hours, dollars, 1 to 5 attitude scales, yes-no dichotomies, and so forth.

   Some of the ways in which multiple dimensions are handled include

1. Multiply the apples by two if you like each apple twice as much as each orange. Then everything will be expressed in orange units.
2. Ask whether the gain in apples from choosing one alternative is worth more or less than the gain in oranges from choosing a second alternative.
3. Convert the apple units into percentages by dividing the raw scores on the apple goal by the sum of the apples, and convert the orange units into percentages by dividing the raw scores on the oranges goal by the sum of the oranges.

   These methods become clearer with the concrete illustrative example of choosing between two affirmative action programs for a medical school. One program produces a lot of minority students but treats few patients. The other program produces a few minority students but treats many patients. The example is shown in Table 1.[2]

B. Missing Information

We often do not know relation scores of each alternative on each goal, and we often do not know the relative weights of the goals.

Table 1 Four Methods for Dealing with Multidimensional Tradeoffs

Policy	Raw score increments		Part/whole percentaging (%)			
	Students trained (S)	Patients treated (P)	Students trained (w = 1)	Patients treated (w = 2)	Unweighted sum	Weighted sum
Policy A (X₁)	30	10	60	36	96	132
Policy B (X₂)	20	18	40	64	104	168
Total (whole)	50	28	100	100	200	300
Difference (increment)	$+ 10S \gg - 8P?$					
Threshold			W60 + 36 = W40 + 64		W* = 1.40	

Policy	Paired-comparison monetizing			Weighted raw scores		
	Students trained $Y = (S)^{0.92}$	Patients treated $Y = (P)^{0.90}$	Sum	Students (expressed in terms of patients) W = 2	Patients	Sum
Policy A (X₁)	$22.85	$ 7.94	$30.79	60	10	70
Policy B (X₂)	$15.74	$13.48	$29.22	40	18	58
Total	$38.59	$21.42	$60.01	100	28	128
Threshold				W30 + 10 = W20 + 18		W* = 0.80

1. Incremental analysis has the advantage of simplicity, especially where there are only a few policies and goals. It is also applicable to variables that are nonquantitative. It involves a minimum of transforming of the raw data. It reduces the value judgment to determining whether the incremental gain of one policy is preferred over the incremental gain of a second policy.
2. Percentaging analysis has the advantage of being applicable where there are many policies and goals. It reduces the value judgment to determining the relative weight of the goals.
3. Paired-comparison monetizing tends to consider all the values of the relevant decision makers, although their values are not disaggregated into separate components. Working with monetized variables may also be more comfortable for many people. Paired-comparison monetizing reduces the value judgments to determining at what point a set of non-monetary benefits is equal to a quantity of dollars.
4. Weighted raw scores have the advantage of being relatively easy to apply where all the goals have tangible units like students or patients, rather than intangible units like scores on a 1 to 9 attitude scale, where part/whole percentaging tends to be easier to handle.

The key way in which missing information is handled is to allow the user to determine quickly and accurately the effects of inserting various values for the missing information. More specific techniques include

1. What-if analysis: The computer shows what would happen if we make changes in the goals, alternatives, and/or relations.
2. Threshold analysis: The computer shows for each relation-score and goal-weight the value that would cause a tie between the second-place alternative and the first place alternative.
3. Convergence analysis: The computer shows for each goal weight at what magnitude the goal tends to dominate the other goals such that nothing is to be gained by increasing the weight further.

4. Best-worst analysis: The computer shows what the conclusion would be using values that most favor a given alternative, and then values that least favor a given alternative. The two conclusions are then averaged.

These methods become clearer with the concrete illustrative example of deciding between nuclear energy and solar energy in light of their long-term value and cost, as is shown in Table 2.[3]

C. Allocating Resources

Decision-aiding software can help in allocating resources, as contrasted to the generally easier problem of just finding a best alternative or combination.

A good way of allocating resources is to convert into percentages the raw merit scores of the objects to which the resources are to be allocated. One can then apply the percentages to the grand total available to be allocated. A good way to convert the raw scores into percentages is by dividing them by their total within the same goal in order to get part/whole percentages. Those percentages can then be summed across the goals using a weighted sum where the goals have different weights.

Table 3A shows how the P/G% software can be used in an allocation problem where the bottom line consists of allocation percentages. The alternative methods shown are trials and plea bargains. Additional alternatives could be added such as diversions or dismissals. The goals shown are to reduce delay and to increase respect for the legal system. Additional

Table 2. Threshold Values, Insensitivity Ranges, and Change Slopes

Goals / Policies	Long-term value (Y_1)	Low cost (Y_2)	Weighted sum
Nuclear (X_a)	a_1 $\quad$ +1 4 (3 to ∞)	A_2 $\quad$ +1 3 (2 to ∞)	7
Solar (X_b)	b_1 $\quad$ −1 5 (−∞ to 6)	b_2 $\quad$ −1 1 (−∞ to 2)	6
Weights	W_1 $\quad$ −1 1 (−∞ 2)	W_2 $\quad$ +2 1 (0.5 to ∞)	

1. The symbol in the upper left-hand corner of each cell shows (1) the identifying symbol of each relation, with the letter indicating the goal; (2) the identifying symbol of each weight, with the subscript indicating the goal to which the weight refers.
2. The number in the middle of each cell shows (1) the value of the relation on a 1 to 5 scale; (2) the value of the weight, with the least important goal having a weight of 1.
3. The number in the upper right-hand corner of each cell shows by how much the gap changes between the two alternatives being compared if the input increases by one unit.
4. The number in parentheses in each cell is the threshold value for each input. At that value, there will be a tie in the weighted sum of the two alternatives being compared.
5. The range in parentheses in each cell is the insensitivity range. That range shows how far down and up each input can go without affecting which alternative is the winner.

Table 3. Allocating Cases to Methods of Resolving

A. The raw data

	Delay (days)	Respect (0–10 scale)
Trials	120	6
Pleas	30	2
	150	8

B. The transformed raw data

	Speed (1/days)	Respect (−5–+5)
Trials	1/120 or 0.00833	+1
Pleas	1/30 or 0.03333	−3
	5/120 or 0.04166	−2

C. The part/whole percentages

	Speed P/W%	Respect P/W%	Aggregate P/W%	Allocation %
Trials	20	100	120	60
Pleas	80	0	80	40
	100	100	200	100

D. The weighted P/W%s

	Speed (w = 1)	Respect (w = 2)	Aggregate P/W%	Allocation %
Trials	20	200	220	73
Pleas	80	0	80	27
	100	200	300	100

1. The raw data are hypothetical but realistic. The object is to decide on the optimum allocation of cases to trials versus pleas in light of the facts that (1) trials receive a score of 120 days on delay and pleas 30 days, and (2) trials receive a score of 6 on respect and pleas a score of 2.
2. Transforming the raw data involves (1) calculating the reciprocals for the raw score of the negative goals of delay; (2) recalculating the raw scores on respect using a scale that shows absolute zero. If N equals absolute zero, then subtract N from each of the original raw scores. For example, on a 0 to 10 scale, the number 5 (or below) might be absolute zero.
3. Calculating the correct part/whole percentages involves (1) calculating the part/whole on the inverted negative goal; (2) giving zero% to any alternative that has a negative raw score, then calculating the part/whole percentages for the other alternatives.
4. Calculating the allocation percentages involves (1) multiplying the part/whole percentages in each column by the relative weight of the goal to which the column pertains; (2) summing the weighted part/whole percentages across each alternative; (3) dividing those aggregate percentages by the sum of the weights. The results are the allocation percentages for each alternative or budget category.

goals could be added such as reducing expense and increasing the probability of innocent defendants being acquitted.

The raw data show that the average trial in our hypothetical court system takes 120 days and the average plea bargain takes 30 days from arrest to disposition. The data also show that the trial's alternative receives a respect score of 6 on a 0 to 10 scale in a rough survey of attorneys and pleas receives a score of only a 2. It would not be meaningful to add 120 days to a respect score of 6 to get an overall score for trials because (1) delay is measured in days and respect is measured on a 0 to 10 scale, which necessitates a common measure in order to be able to add these scores; (2) delay is a negative goal where high scores are undesirable; and (3) a score of 2 on respect may be a negative score such that each additional plea bargain decreases respect for the system.

To deal with those problems, we do the following:

1. The delay scores are converted into part/whole percentages by dividing each score by the sum of the delay column but after inverting for the negative goal.
2. The inversion is done by working with the reciprocals of the delay scores. That means working with 1/120 and 1/30 rather than 120 and 30. Doing so preserves the fact that trials are four times as bad as pleas on the goal of delay, whereas making pleas score higher than the trials score. We are then working with speed rather than delay as a goal. Speed should be given a weight of $+1$ if delay has previously been given a weight of -1.
3. The respect scores are also converted into part/whole percentages by dividing each score by the sum of the respect column but after adjusting for the fact that pleas may have a negative score.
4. That means determining the value of a true zero on the 0 to 10 scale and subtracting that value from the 0 to 10 scores. Thus, if a 5 is the separation point between positive scores and negative scores, then a 6 is the equivalent of a $+1$ and a 2 is the equivalent of a -3. Those transformed numbers are shown in Table 3B.

Table 3C converts the transformed data into part/whole percentages. Pleas is given 0% on respect because one would not want to allocate anything more than the minimum possible if pleas has a negative score and if more respect were the only criterion. We can now add across the percentages and obtain an aggregate percentage of 120% for trials and 80% for pleas. We then divide by 2 to bring the sum of those percentages down to 100% because we cannot allocate more than 100%.

Table 3D takes into consideration that respect is considered to be twice as important as speed. That means multiplying the percentages in the respect column by 2. The new aggregate percentages are then 220 and 80%. We then divide by 3 or the sum of the weights to obtain the allocation percentages of 73 and 27%. Not all allocation problems involve multiple dimensions, negative goals, or negative scores. If, however, one can follow the allocation analysis of Table 3, then one can deal with simpler allocation problems.[4]

D. Adjusting for Constraints

Decision-aiding software can help in dealing with constraints that require minimums or maximums on the alternatives or the goals or other conditions that must be met regardless of how high the scores are of an alternative on the goals.

The main ways in which constraints are handled are

1. The constraints can be met *before* one allocates scarce resources or determines the relation scores. Doing so tends to result in giving an alternative more than it is entitled where

it only deserves the minimum. That result cannot occur if adjustments are made *after* allocating so as to bring alternatives up to their minimums.

2. The best way of resolving conflicting constraints is to expand the total benefits available or reduce the total costs to be imposed so that all the constraints can be satisfied simultaneously. If that is not possible, then resolve conflicting constraints by developing compromises that satisfy each constraint in proportion to its importance. Other less desirable alternatives involve partially satisfying all constraints equally or fully satisfying certain constraints in the order of their priority.

Adjusting for constraints is illustrated with the same problem as allocating a budget to police and courts in light of crime reduction and fair procedure. The constraints specify minimum amounts to the police and the courts, but those minimums may add to more than the total budget available.

A good way to adjust to satisfy the equity constraints with two, three, and four budget categories is as follows:

1. With two budget categories, suppose category A is below its minimum and category B is above its minimum. After allocating in proportion to their aggregate scores, then give category A its minimum. Give the rest of the total budget to category B.
2. With three budget categories, suppose A is below its minimum and B and C are above their minimums. Then give A its minimum. Divide the rest of the total budget between B and C in proportion to their aggregate scores, as in Table 4.
3. With four or more budget categories, one can reason by analogy to the three-category situation. No matter how many budget categories are below their minimums in the initial optimizing, give them their minimums and then remove them from further allocating. The remainder of the total budget then gets divided proportionately among the other budget categories.[5]

E. Simplicity of Analysis

Decision-aiding software that is based on multi-criteria decision-making (MCDM) can greatly simplify the analysis of a variety of decision-aiding programs that have traditionally used more complicated and often less valid methods, such as arrow diagrams, payoff matrices, decision trees, optimum level curves, indifference curves, functional curves, and multiobjective programming. The essence of MCDM software is that it works with a table, matrix, or spreadsheet with alternatives on the rows, evaluative criteria on the columns, relation scores in the cells, and a summation column at the right showing the overall score or allocation percent of each alternative.

A good illustration of the simplicity of MCDM and P/G% software is the decision whether to take away or leave an abused child with the child's family. Table 5 shows the problem analyzed with a traditional payoff matrix, and Table 5B shows the problem analyzed with a P/G% spreadsheet table. Both approaches show the alternatives on the rows. The payoff matrix shows contingent events and possibly their probabilities on the columns, whereas the P/G% approach shows goals and their relative weights on the columns. The payoff matrix shows relative payoffs in the cells, whereas the P/G% approach shows relation scores on a 1 to 5 scale in the cells between the alternatives and the goals. The payoff matrix shows benefits minus costs on the right side with each element discounted by the probability of its occurring, whereas the P/G% approach shows the weighted summation scores for each alternative at the right side.

Table 4. Data for Illustrating Equity Constraints and Adjustments to Satisfy Them

Allocation criteria / Budget categories	Raw scores		Transformed scores			Allocation results				
				Allocation percentages (%)		Optimum allocations ($)		Minimums ($)	Adjusted allocations ($)	
	Crime reduction (1)	Fair procedure (2)	Aggregate scores (3)	2-way (4a)	3-way (4b)	2-way (5a)	3-way (5b)	(6)	2-way (7a)	3-way (7b)
Police	2.00	1.00	3.00	43	39	214	195	240	240 (min)	240 (min)
Courts	1.00	3.00	4.00 / 7.00	57	51	286	255	80	260 (100% of 260)	218 (84% of 260)
Corrections	0.50	0.25	0.75	NA	10	NA	50	40	NA	42 (16% of 260)
Totals			7.75	100	100	500	500	360	500	500

1. Optimizing can be done first, and then adjustments are made to satisfy the constraints if they have not been satisfied already In other words, if we optimally allocate without considering the minimums, we obtain what is shown in column 5a (for two budget categories) and column 5b (for three budget categories). If we then consider the minimums, we obtain what is shown in columns 7a and 7b.
2. There is $500 available to be allocated this year. There was $450 available to be allocated last year.
3. The minimums in column 6 are equal to 80% of last year's budget. Last year, the police received $300, the courts received $100, and corrections received $50.
4. The numbers in columns 1 and 2 are based on a rough survey of a small sample of some people who are knowledgeable about the criminal justice system.
5. The formulas for the numbers in the other columns are:

   $(3) = (1) + (2)$ $(4a) = (3)/7.00$ $(4b) = (3)/7.75$ $(5a) = (4a) (\$500)$ $(5b) = (4b) (\$500)$
   $(6) = 80\%$ of last year's allocation

6. The best way to make the adjusted allocations of 7a and 7b is to give any budget category its minimum (from column 6). If its optimum (from column 5a or 5b) falls below its minimum, then divide the residue among the other budget categories in proportion to their aggregate scores (from column 3).

Abbreviation: NA, not applicable.

Both approaches are applied to the same empirical situation in Table 5. The payoff matrix tends to lead to a decision to take the child away because the probability of severe abuse is likely to be greater than the threshold probability. The P/G% approach leads to a closer decision because it emphasizes multiple criteria of avoiding abuse, preserving family love, and saving the taxpayer cost. One could argue that those three criteria are taken into consideration in the relative payoffs in the cells of the payoff matrix. However, by lumping all three criteria together, their separate existences and sensitivity values get overwhelmed by the criterion of avoiding abuse. The payoff matrix may thus lead to results that are less valid in terms of the decision maker's goals than the P/G% approach.

Table 5. Comparing a Payoff Matrix with P/G% on Decision Making Under Conditions of Risk (e.g., Deciding Whether to Take Away or Leave an Abused Child)

A. The payoff matrix

	Severe subsequent abuse		
	Would not occur	Would occur	
Take away	(a) − 50	(b) + 100	Benefits − Costs
Leave	(c) + 50	(d) − 100	$(P)(100) - (1 - P)(50)$

B. The P/G% approach

	Avoid abuse (w = 2)	Preserve family love (w = 1)	Save taxpayer cost (w = 1)	Weighted sum
Take away	4	2	2	12
Leave	2	4	4	12

1. The cell entries in Table 5A are arrived at by asking the decision makers the following questions:
   a. Of the four possible occurrences, which ones are desirable (marked plus) and which ones are undesirable (marked minus)?
   b. Of the undesirable occurrences, which one is the most undesirable (marked minus 100)?
   c. How much more undesirable is the most undesirable occurrence in comparison to the less undesirable occurrence (marked minus 50 to show that cell d is twice as bad as cell a)?
2. With that information, one can determine the threshold probability as follows:
   a. At the threshold, the discounted benefits equal the discounted costs (i.e., $100 P = 50$ minus $50 P$).
   b. The solution for P in that equation is $P^* = d/(a + d)$ or $P^* = 100/(50 + 100) = 0.33$.
   c. That means that if the probability is greater than 0.33, there will be severe subsequent abuse, then the child should be taken away.
3. The scoring of each alternative in Table 5B on each criterion is on a 1 to 5 scale, where 5 = highly conducive to the goal, 4 = mildly conducive, 3 = neither conducive nor adverse, 2 = mildly adverse to the goal, and 1 = highly adverse. Decimal scores can be given between these numbers where appropriate.
4. Avoiding abuse is considered to be twice as important as preserving whatever family love might exist or saving taxpayer cost.
5. By considering multiple criteria rather than emphasizing the probability of severe subsequent abuse, the decision is much closer and more dependent on the specific facts or scores on the first two criteria than on a general threshold probability.
6. If the criteria are given equal weight, then leaving the child wins by 10 points to 8 points. The threshold or tie-causing values of the weights are 2, 0, and 0. The threshold values of the relation scores are then 6, 4, 4, 0, 2, and 2, reading across the matrix. There will be a tie if any of those values are substituted for any weight or relation score when each goal is started with a weight of 1.

The advantages of the P/G% approach over a payoff matrix include

1. P/G% can explicitly consider any number of criteria such as the three shown above.
2. P/G% can explicitly consider any number of alternatives such as, take away to an institution, take away to a foster home, take away to a relative's home, leave with counseling, or leave without family counseling.
3. Being able to consider multiple criteria and multiple alternatives makes the P/G% approach more validly in conformity with reality and not just a simplistic abstraction.

4. P/G% is also simpler with its 1 to 5 scales, weighted criteria, computerized threshold analysis, and logical way of analyzing a problem in terms of alternatives, criteria, and relations.[6]

F. Some Conclusions

As mentioned in the beginning of this section, the main benefits of the decision-aiding software and/or systematic policy evaluation are its accuracy and speed in handling the five key methodological problems in evaluation analysis. To fully appreciate the relevance of the software, it is necessary to actually use it. We can, however, briefly describe how the software applies to each problem.

Multiple Dimensions on Multiple Goals

1. In comparing any two alternatives, one can show for each goal the incremental gain of the better alternative over the other alternative. This can be more easily done by putting the goals on the rows and the two alternatives on the columns because the software subtracts across the rows. One can then pick the alternative that has the more desired set of increments.
2. One can specify the importance of each goal relative to the least important goal. Those weights can consider both importance and the nature of the measurement units where raw scores are used.
3. The software is capable of working with the relations either as raw scores or part/whole percentages by exercising an option on the data management menu.

Missing Information

1. The software can do what-if analysis by allowing the user to change any of the inputs and quickly see how those changes affect the bottom-line conclusion.
2. The main menu gives the user an option to do a threshold analysis or a convergence analysis to determine the critical values for relation scores or goal weights, above which one alternative would be better and below which another alternative would be better.
3. In specifying the criteria, one can divide each criterion into a best version and a worst version, such as the best possible cost on each alternative and the worst possible cost. The computer can then show the overall best score, the overall worst score, and the midpoint for each alternative.
4. The software can also draw indifference curves or threshold curves showing the combination of scores on two or more variables that would lead to a tie between any two alternatives.

Allocating Resources

1. The user can specify the grand total available to be allocated. The program will multiply that grand total by the allocation percentages for each alternative or budget category.
2. The allocation percentages are calculated by obtaining an overall score for each alternative and then dividing each overall score by the sum of the scores in order to obtain part/whole allocation percentages.
3. The program can transform the raw scores by determining their reciprocals where negative goals are involved or by subtracting the value of absolute zero from each raw score where negative scores are involved. Those transformations may, however, be easier to do with a calculator and then just enter the results into the data matrix.

Adjusting for Constraints

1. The user can enter minimum constraints for each alternative, and the program can guarantee they will be met in whatever allocation is done. A better approach though would be to optimize ignoring the constraints and then make adjustments for any alternative or criterion that violates its minimum or maximum.
2. The ease of doing what-if analysis facilitates resolving conflicting constraints and conflicting decision makers by enabling both sides or a mediator to try different alternatives, criteria, weights, constraints, relations, and other inputs until a mutually satisfying solution is found.

Simplicity

1. The essence of the software is the idea of putting alternatives on the rows of a spreadsheet matrix, criteria and weights on the columns, relations in the cells, and overall scores for the alternatives in the right-hand column.
2. That system is in conformity with a great deal of systematic decision making, as indicated by the popularity of spreadsheet software, payoff matrices, decision trees, and other formats that can be reduced to a decision matrix.

This kind of evaluation analysis could be done with pencil and paper or even implicitly in one's mind. The analysis is, however, substantially facilitated by the availability of the software and microcomputers. The software encourages thinking more explicitly about evaluation problems without confining the user to quantitatively measured variables. It facilitates creativity by allowing changes to be so easily made. We may be at the advent of new ways of thinking about program evaluation, policy analysis, and decision making to the benefit of the decision makers and those who are affected by their decisions.[7]

NOTES

1. For further details on optimizing in terms of goals, policies, relations and conclusions, see S. Nagel, *Public Policy: Goals, Means, and Methods*, St. Martin's, New York, 1984; and E. Quade, *Analysis for Public Decisions*, North-Holland, Amsterdam, 1982. These two books could be referred to for any of the eight principles. The Nagel book uses numerous legal examples. Other books that take an optimizing perspective toward law include R. Posner, *Economic Analysis of Law*, Little, Brown, Boston, 1977; and G. Tullock, *The Logic of the Law*, Basic Books, New York, 1971.
2. On dealing with nonmonetary benefits and costs, see M. Thompson, *Benefit-Cost Analysis for Program Evaluation*, Sage, Beverly Hills, CA, 1980; and E. Gramlich, *Benefit-Cost Analysis of Government Programs*, Prentice-Hall, Englewood Cliffs, NJ, 1981; although those authors may overemphasize monetizing nonmonetary variables rather than working with them in their original form or close to it. Also see S. Nagel, "Nonmonetary Variables in Benefit-Cost Evaluation," *Evaluation Review* 7: 37–64, 1983; and S. Nagel, "Economic Transformations of Nonmonetary Benefits in Program Evaluation," in J. Catterall (ed.), *Economic Evaluation of Public Programs*, Jossey-Bass, San Francisco, 1985.
3. On dealing with missing information without having to gather additional information, see M. Thompson, *Decision Analysis for Program Evaluation*, Ballinger, Cambridge, MA, 1982; and C. Harris, *The Break-Even Handbook*, Prentice-Hall, Englewood Cliffs, NJ, 1978. Also see S. Nagel, "Dealing with Unknown Variables in Policy/Program Evaluation," *Evaluation and Program Planning* 6: 7–18, 1983; and S. Nagel, "New Varieties of Sensitivity Analysis," *Evaluation Review* 9: 772–779, 1985.
4. On diverse methods for dealing with the multiplicity of alternatives in allocation problems, see P. Kotler, *Marketing Decision Making: A Model Building Approach*, Holt, New York, 1971 (calculus

and statistical analysis); C. McMillan, *Mathematical Programming*: *An Introduction to the Design and Application of Optimal Decision Machines*, Wiley, New York, 1970 (reiterative guessing and operations research); and S. Nagel, *Policy Evaluation*: *Making Optimum Decisions*, Praeger, New York, 1982 (variations on part/whole percentaging in Chapters 10–13). Also see S. Nagel, "Optimally Allocating Federal Money to Cities," *Public Budgeting and Finance* 5: 39–50, 1985.

5. On dealing with constraints in public policy analysis in general, see S. Nagel, *Public Policy*: *Goals, Means, and Methods*, St. Martin's, New York, 1984, especially the chapters on equity, effectiveness, human rights, discretion, economic structure, government structure, political feasibility, and ethical constraints. On quantitative constraints in allocation problems, see S. Nagel, "Allocation Logic," in *Policy Evaluation*: *Making Optimum Decisions*, Praeger, New York, 1982, where the problem of allocating to police, courts, and corrections is also discussed.

6. On the matter of simplicity in drawing and presenting conclusions in evaluation analysis see S. Nagel, "Comparing Multi-Criteria Decision Making and P/G% with Traditional Optimizing," in Yoshikazu Sawaragi (ed.), *Multiple-Criteria Decision Making*, Springer-Verlag, Berlin, 1987; and S. Nagel, "Simplifying Basic Methods," in *Public Policy*: *Goals, Means, and Methods*, St. Martin's, New York, 1984. On the subject of taking away abused children, G. Cooper, et al., "Neglect," in *Law and Poverty*: *Cases and Materials*, West, St. Paul, MN, 1973.

7. On policy/goal percentaging and the P/G% software, see B. Radcliff, "Multi-Criteria Decision Making: A Survey of Software," *Social Science Microcomputer Review* 4: 38–55, 1986; S. Nagel, "P/G% Analysis: An Evaluating-Aiding Program," *Evaluation Review* 9: 209–214, 1985; and S. Nagel, "A Microcomputer Program for Dealing with Evaluation Problems," *Evaluation and Program Planning* 9: 159–168, 1987. On the applicability of P/G% to all five analytic problems, see S. Nagel, *Evaluation Analysis with Microcomputers*, JAI Press, Greenwich, CT, 1988.

3
Decision-Aiding Software and Super-Optimum Solutions

Stuart S. Nagel
University of Illinois, Urbana-Champaign, Illinois

I. DECISION-AIDING SOFTWARE

A. Definitions

The essence of decision-aiding software in a public policy context is the ability of the software to process a set of societal goals to be achieved, alternative public policies for achieving them and relations between goals and alternatives in order to arrive at a best alternative, combination, allocation, or predictive decision rule.

Any software can be helpful in making decisions such as information retrieval software like Westlaw and Lexis that provide relevant citations and excerpts. Even office-practice software such as word processing, file management, and bookkeeping software can be helpful in making decisions by providing relevant reports. To qualify as decision-aiding software, though, the software should deal with the five essential elements of alternatives, criteria, relations, tentative conclusions, and what-if analysis either for prescribing what decisions ought to be reached or for predicting what decisions will be reached.

B. Benefits, Costs, and Trends

The potential benefits of decision-aiding software depend to some extent on the particular kind of software, but there are a number of cross-cutting benefits (as well as costs) worth mentioning. Such software encourages policy people to be more explicit about goals they are seeking to achieve, alternatives available for achieving them, and relations between goals and alternatives. This more structured form of thinking is a benefit to the public policy profession (even if it creates greater dilemmas in problem solving) because it stimulates the policy analyst's creativity in searching for more imaginative solutions. In addition, this process can be helpful in dealing with missing information by indicating how high a damage award, settlement offer, or other input has to be in order to bring a tentative second-place alternative up to first place. Such information can ease policy decision making by identifying whether a numerical value has a threshold, breakeven, or other critical value. This software can also simplify policy decision making by aiding in making choices in complex situations that allow for combinations of alternatives. It does so by asking the user to supply only enough information to deal with the problem and then delivering only enough information for the user to make a decision.

A cost involved in using decision-aiding software is the need to learn how to use it. However, that cost is dropping as the software becomes more user-friendly and the instruction manuals are improved. A possible implicit cost is the temptation this software might create for some users to rely exclusively on the computer without injecting any substantial knowledge of their own. However, most such software demands substantial input from the user in order to function. On balance, the benefits of decision-aiding software do seem to outweigh the costs substantially, especially if the software is considered to be a supplement to rather than a substitute for traditional methods.

A number of trends indicate that the time is ripe for policy analysts, policy makers, and policy scholars to adopt decision-aiding software. This software has been applied to all fields of law and to all types of policy skills, including counseling clients, negotiating with the opposition, advocating a position before a government agency, generalizing from a set of facts or doctrine, evaluating alternative policies, and deciding the best order in which to process cases. This increased use is coupled with an increasing mention of decision-aiding software in both practitioner and scholarly law journals, as well as increased publication of entire books devoted to this subject. Finally, the software industry is continuing to produce new products devoted to this market.

C. Types and Examples

There are at least seven different kinds of decision-aiding software. Those categories include decision trees, linear programming, statistical software, spreadsheets, rule-based software, multi-criteria decision-making, substantive software, and idea generators.

1. Rule-Based Software

Rule-based software contains a set of rules for dealing with a narrow or broad field of policy. The user gives the computer a set of facts and it applies the rules to the facts in order to determine which alternative decision is likely to be decided. Such software is sometimes referred to as artificial intelligence (AI) or expert systems, but the other forms of decision-aiding software also have characteristics associated with AI and expert systems. Rule-based software for prediction or prescribing decisions could include Teknowledge, Expert87, ExSys, ESCA-DSS, MicroExpert, Ashton-Tate, and Texas Instruments. For a good comparative review of rule-based expert systems software, see C. Grafton and A. Permaloff, Expert System Development Programs and Their Alternatives, *Social Science Microcomputer Review*, 4: 165–180, 1986. Rule-based software that is specifically related to governmental rules include Judith, DataLex, Rubric, Hypo, Lex, Default, Oblog-2, Esplex, and LexVision. Many of those law-related programs are described in *Proceedings of the First International Conference on Artificial Intelligence and Law*, Northeastern University, 1987.

2. Decision Tree Software

Decision tree software makes decisions under conditions of risk such as whether to go to trial or accept a settlement. A decision tree is usually pictured as looking like a tree on its side with branches and subbranches. The branches generally represent alternative possibilities that depend on the occurrence or nonoccurrence of probabilistic events. Decision tree software includes the Arborist, SuperTree, Clarence, Ondine, StrataTree, and RiskCalc. For an analysis of decision tree software applied to dispute resolution, see M. Raker, The Application of Decision Analysis and Computer Modeling to the Settlement of Complex Litigation, *Symposium on Computer Models and Modeling for Negotiation Management*, Cambridge, MA, Massachusetts Institute of Technology, 1987; and Nagel, Microcomputers, Risk Analysis, and Litigation Strategy, *Akron Law Review* 19: 35–80, 1985.

3. Linear Programming Software

Linear programming software allocates money, time, people, or other scarce resources to activities, places, tasks, or other objects to which the resources are to be allocated. In terms of form rather than function, linear programming involves maximizing or minimizing an objective function or algebraic expression subject to constraints generally in the form of inequalities like greater than or less than. Linear programming and related software includes Erikson-Hall, Lee-Shim, IFPS, Holden-Day, LP Master, Burns-Austin, LP Professional, and Vino-Gino-Lindo. A good comparative analysis of linear programming and related packages is R. Sharda, et al., Mathematical Programming Software for Microcomputers, in S. Gass, et al. (eds.), *Impacts of Microcomputers on Operations Research*, Amsterdam, North-Holland, 1986.

4. Statistical Software

Statistical software predicts how a future case is likely to be decided regarding liability, damages, guilt, sentence, or other judgment in light of past cases or expert opinions. Statistical software generally involves calculating averages or predictive equations in which decisions or other outcomes are related to legal or factual inputs. Statistical software include StatPal, Hall-Adelman, ABC, Stat, EpiStat, PsychoStats, Crosstats, Chao, SPSS, SAS, BDM, StatFast, and StatPac. A good comparative analysis of statistics packages is D. Lezotte, Statistical Software for Micro-computers, in S. Gass, et al. (eds.), *Impacts of Microcomputers on Operations Research*, Amsterdam, North-Holland, 1986.

5. Spreadsheet-Based Software

Spreadsheet-based software can align alternatives in rows, criteria in columns, relations in cells, overall scores for each alternative in a column at the far right. It has the capability for determining what it would take to bring a second-place or other-place alternative up to first place. Spreadsheet software (especially if based on Lotus 1-2-3) includes Best Choice, What's Best, 1-2-Tree, Minitab, 1-2-3 Breakeven, PG Lotus, and GoalSeeker. For an analysis of some aspects of decision-aiding spreadsheet software, see D. Bammi and L. Padelford, Using Spreadsheets for Decision Analysis, in S. Gass, *Impacts of Microcomputers on Operations Research*, Amsterdam, North-Holland, 1986. Also see S. Nagel, Using Spreadsheets to Choose Among Alternatives, in *Decision-Aiding Software: Skills, Obstacles, and Applications,* London, PSO-Macmillan, 1990. The category of spreadsheet software emphasizes form rather than purpose since the spreadsheet form can be used to do rule-based expert systems, decision trees, linear programming, statistical analysis, or for other purposes. In that sense, decision-aiding software can be classified as spreadsheet based if the screens emphasize rows and columns but as non–spreadsheet based if the screens emphasize lists of questions or rules, tree branching diagrams, equations, or parameters, as is done with most but not all rule-based, decision tree, linear programming, and statistical software, respectively. Most people find the spreadsheet format to be much easier to work with.

6. Multi-Criteria Decision-Making Software

Other decision-aiding software that does not fit into the above categories but that does process alternatives, criteria, and relations to arrive at a precription evaluation or a prediction explanation. This software is often referred to as multi-criteria decision-making (MCDM) software because it emphasizes multiple criteria, although it may also work with multiple alternatives. The miscellaneous MCDM software includes such names as Lightyear, Confidence Factor, Decision Analyst, Expert Choice, Prefcalc, DecAid, Electre, Policy PC, P/G%, DecisionMaker, Decision, PG Plato, Seriatim, Decision Making, Decide, Pairs, MASS, MOLP, MAUD, and MIDAS. For comparisons of MCDM software, see P. Humphreys and A. Wisudha, *Methods and Tools for Structuring and Analyzing Decision Problems*, London School of Economics and Political Science, 1987; B. Radcliff, Multi-Criteria Decision Making: A Survey of Software, *Social Science Microcomputer Review* 4: 38–55, 1986; B. Golden, et al., Decision Insight Systems for Microcomputers, in S. Gass, *Impacts of Microcomputers on Operations Research*, Amsterdam, North-Holland, 1986. Some of the software fits into more than one category, such as Best Choice or P/G%, which can perform the functions in all six categories, although it is mainly classified as spreadsheet-based software. The category of MCDM software emphasizes the multiple nature of the inputs rather than the purpose of the software or its form. More traditional decision-aiding software works with single goals or objective functions such as monetary profit and frequently just a single alternative where the question is should it be adopted or not.

7. Software that Generates Alternatives, Goals, and Relations

There is also software that is useful for generating alternatives, goals, or relations but that does not process those elements in order to draw a conclusion. Software that can help in generating alternatives includes the Idea Generator, the Brainstormer, and Trigger. Software that helps generate relations such as the probability of an alternative achieving a goal includes SPAT. Statistical software can also sometimes be used for generating relations, such as regression coefficients or average scores of an alternative on a criterion.

Useful comparative evaluations of the different kinds of decision-aiding software can be found in the published articles and chapters that are cited above. Other relevant literature compares methodologies rather than software packages. That literature includes C.-L. Hwang and K. Yoon, *Multiple Attribute Decision Making*: *Methods and Applications*, Berlin, Springer-Verlag, 1981; H. Brightman, *Problem Solving*: *A Logical and Creative Approach*, Georgia State University, Atlanta, 1980; and S. Nagel, *Evaluation Analysis with Microcomputers*, JAI Press, Greenwich, CT, 1989. The category that is most versatile and user-friendly is probably the spreadsheet category, especially variations on Lotus 1-2-3. It can do most kinds of risk analysis, allocation analysis, and prediction analysis easier than decision tree, linear programming routines, or a statistical package.

D. Relations with the Policy Studies Organization (PSO)

Decision-aiding software is not only relevant to decision making in the policy studies field, but it has also been especially relevant to some of the activities of the Policy Studies Organization (PSO). It is a key feature that attracts people to the training workshops that the PSO has sponsored at various annual meetings of the American Political Science Association, the American Society for Public Administration, the Association for Public Policy Analysis and Management, the American Evaluation Association, and the American Bar Association.

It is also a key feature in the training workshops that PSO has sponsored as part of its international activities such as workshops at meetings of the International Political Science

Association, the International Association of Schools and Institutes of Administration, and the United Nations. That also includes such overseas universities as the University of the Philippines, People's University of China, the University of Zagreb in Croatia, the Free University in Berlin, and the University of Nairobi.

Decision-aiding software has also been a key feature in various government agencies commissioning the Policy Studies Organization to conduct workshops for policy analysts and policy makers within the agencies. That includes the Office of Personnel Management, the Congressional Budget Office, the Central Intelligence Agency, and the Department of Defense.

A number of books in the Policy Studies Organization Series of Macmillan, Greenwood, JAI, and Nelson Hall deal with decision-aiding software. The books are edited or authored by the PSO publications coordinator. All royalties go to PSO. The books include *Decision-Aiding Software: Skills, Obstacles, and Applications* (Macmillan, 1990), *Public Administration and Decision-Aiding Software* (Greenwood, 1990), *Developing Nations and Super-Optimum Solutions Analysis* (Nelson Hall, 1990), and *Applications of Decision-Aiding Software* (Macmillan, 1991).

The Policy Studies Organization probably maintains the most comprehensive software exchange specializing in policy-relevant methodology and substance, more so than any organization, university, or other software exchange or archive. PSO receives frequent requests for information, documentation, and software from government agencies, universities, and individuals interested in policy studies.

Members and nonmembers of the PSO who are interested in learning more about policy-relevant decision-aiding software and any of the above workshops or publications should write to the Policy Studies Organization, 361 Lincoln Hall, University of Illinois, Urbana, IL 61801.

II. SUPER-OPTIMIZING ANALYSIS IN GENERAL

A. Basic Definitions

Super-optimizing analysis refers to dealing with public policy problems by finding an alternative that enables conservatives, liberals, and other major viewpoints to all come out ahead of their best initial expectations simultaneously.

Super-optimum solutions (SOSs) in public controversies involve solutions that exceed the best expectations of liberals and conservatives simultaneously. We are primarily concerned with public or governmental controversies and not controversies among private individuals such as marriage, consumer, employment, or other such disputes. We are, however, interested in controversies over what statutes, judicial precedents, or administrative regulations should be adopted governing marriage, consumer, employment, or other such relations.

An optimum solution is one that is best on a list of alternatives in achieving a set of goals. A SOS is one that is simultaneously best on two separate sets of goals. One set is a liberal set and the second set is a conservative set. Both sets may share many or all of the same goals, but they are likely to differ in terms of the relative weights they give to the same goals.

B. A Minimum-Wage Example

For example, in the minimum-wage controversy, both liberals and conservatives endorse the goal of paying a decent wage and the goal of not overpaying to the point where some workers are unnecessarily laid off because their employers cannot afford the new higher minimum.

Liberals, however, give relatively high weight to the first goal and relatively low but positive weight to the second goal, and vice versa for conservatives.

The liberal alternative in the minimum wage controversy might be $4.40 an hour and the conservative alternative might be $4.20 an hour. The liberal alternative would thus score higher on the "decent wage" goal and the conservative alternative lower. On the goal of "avoiding overpayment," the liberal alternative would score lower and the conservative alternative higher. This real data would thus provide a classic tradeoff controversy.

The object in this example is to find a solution that is simultaneously better from a liberal perspective than $4.40 an hour and better from a conservative perspective than $4.20 an hour. One such (SOS) would be to provide for a minimum wage supplement by the government of 22 cents an hour to each unemployed person who is hired. The worker would receive $4.41 an hour but the employer would pay only $4.19 an hour.

The liberal-labor interests would be getting more than their best expectation of $4.40 an hour, and the conservative-business interests would be paying less than their best expectation of $4.20 an hour. The government and taxpayers would be benefitting by virtue of (1) the money saved from otherwise providing public aid to unemployed people; (2) the money added to the gross national product that provides income to others, increases taxes, and an increased base on which to grow in subsequent years; (3) better role models for the children of people who would otherwise be unemployed; and (4) an upgrading of skills if qualifying for the wage subsidy means business has to provide on-the-job training and workers have to participate.

C. SOSs Contrasted with Other Types of Solutions

Solutions to public controversies can be classified in various ways. First there are SOSs in which all sides come out ahead of their initial best expectations, as mentioned above. At the opposite extreme is a supermalimum solution in which all sides come out worse than their worst initial expectations. That can be the case in a mutually destructive war, labor strike, or highly expensive litigation.

Pareto optimum solutions in which nobody comes out worse off and at least one side comes out better off. This is not a very favorable solution compared with a SOS. A Pareto malimum solution would be one in which nobody is better off and at least one side is worse off.

A win-lose solution where what one side wins the other side loses. The net effects is zero when the losses are subtracted from the gains. This is the typical litigation dispute when one ignores the litigation costs.

A lose-lose solution where both sides are worse off then they were before the dispute began. This may often be the typical litigation dispute, or close to it when one includes litigation costs. Those costs are often so high that the so-called winner is also a loser. That is also often the case in labor-management disputes that result in a strike, and even more so in international disputes that result in going to war.

The so-called win-win solution. At first glance, this sounds like a solution where everybody comes out ahead. What it typically refers to though is an illusion since the parties are only coming out ahead relative to their worst expectations. In this sense, the plaintiff is a winner no matter what the settlement is because the plaintiff could have won nothing if liability had been rejected at trial. Likewise, the defendant is a winner no matter what the settlement is because the defendant could have lost everything the plaintiff was asking for if liability had been established at trial. The parties are only fooling themselves in the same sense that someone who is obviously a loser tells himself or herself that he or she won because he or she could have done worse.

D. General Ways of Arriving at SOSs

Having a third-party benefactor like this is one of many ways of arriving at SOSs. Other ways include (1) expanding the resources available, (2) setting realistically higher goals than what was previously considered the best, (3) having big benefits for one side but only small costs for the other side, (4) combining alternatives that are not mutually exclusive, (5) removing or decreasing the source of the conflict, and (6) developing a package of alternatives that would satisfy both liberal and conservative goals.

One procedure for arriving at SOSs is to think in terms of what is in the conservative alternative that liberals might like. And likewise, what is in the liberal alternative that conservatives might like. Then think whether it is possible to make a new alternative that will emphasize those two aspects. Another technique is to emphasize the opposite. It involves saying what is in a conservative alternative that liberals especially dislike. What is in the liberal alternative that conservatives especially dislike. Then think about making a new alternative that eliminates those two aspects.

A variation on that is to add new goals. The usual procedure starts with the conservative goals as givens in light of how they justify their current best alternative, and it starts with the liberal goals as givens in light of how they justify their current best alternative. This technique says to think about the goals conservatives tend to endorse that are not currently involved in the controversy, but that could be brought in to justify a new alternative. Likewise, what goals do liberals tend to endorse that are not currently involved in the controversy, but that could also be brought in. For this technique, a good example is the free-speech controversy where liberals want virtually unrestricted free speech in order to stimulate creativity and conservatives want restrictions on free speech in order to have more order in the legal system. However, liberals also like due process, equal protection, and right to privacy. That raises questions as to whether it might be permissible to restrict free speech in order to satisfy those constitutional rights, where the restrictions are not so great, but the jeopardy of those other rights might be great. Likewise, conservatives like policies that are good for business. They might therefore readily endorse permissive free speech that relates to advertising, to trying to convince workers that they should not join unions, or that relates to lobbying.

One problem with SOSs is that they look so good that they may cause some people to think they might be some kind of trap. An example is the Camp David Accords. That example is a classic superoptimum solution where Israel, Egypt, the United States, and everybody involved came out ahead of their original best expectations. According to the *New York Times* for March 26, 1989, however, Israeli intelligence at least at first opposed Anwar Sadat's visit to Israel and the Camp David Accords until close to the signing on the grounds that it all sounded so good, it must be a trap. The Israeli intelligence thought that Israel was being set up for a variation on the Yom Kippur war whereby Israel got into big trouble by relaxing its guard because of the holidays. They viewed this as an attempt to get them to relax their guard again, and then any minute the attack would begin. They were on a more intense alert at the time of the Camp David negotiations than they were at any other time during Israel's history. This nicely illustrates how SOSs can easily be viewed by people as a trap because they look so good that they are unbelievable. Traditional solutions are not so likely to be viewed as traps, and they are taken more at their face value, which is generally not much.

E. Relations to Decision-Aiding Software

Super-optimizing is an approach to public policy analysis. Policy analysis or policy evaluation can be defined as processing a set of goals to be achieved, alternatives available for achieving them, and relations between goals and alternatives in order to arrive at a best alternative, combination, allocation, or predictive decision rule. Policy analysis can be facilitated by decision-aiding software. Such software involves showing goals on the columns of a table, alternatives on the rows, and relations as words or numbers in the cells. The overall totals can be shown on a column in the far right, with an analysis that can quickly show how the totals would change if there were changes in the goals, alternatives, relations, or other inputs.

That kind of decision-aiding software also facilitates the finding of superoptimum solutions. It can quickly determine the liberal and conservative totals for each alternative. It can quickly test to see if a proposed SOS does score better than the best liberal and conservative alternatives using the liberal and conservative weights. Such software also facilitates finding SOS solutions by enabling one to work with many alternatives and many criteria simultaneously. Each side can thereby give on some criteria that are not so important to it and receive on other criteria in order to arrive at solutions where both sides come out ahead of their initial best expectations.

Some of the key literature on decision-aiding software includes P. Humphreys and A. Wisudha, *Methods and Tools for Structuring and Analyzing Decision Problems*, London School of Economics and Political Science, 1987; S. Gass, et al. (eds.), *Impacts of Microcomputers on Operations Research*, North-Holland, Amsterdam, 1986; and S. Nagel, *Evaluation Analysis with Microcomputers*, JAI Press, Greenwich, CT, 1989.

F. Relations to Dispute Resolution and Growth Economics

Another stream of inspiration has come from people in the field of mediation and alternative dispute resolution. Some of that key literature includes L. Susskind and J. Cruikshank, *Breaking the Impasse*: *Consensual Approaches to Resolving Disputes*, Basic Books, New York, 1987; S. Goldberg, et al. (eds.), *Dispute Resolution*, Little, Brown, Boston, 1984; and S. Nagel and M. Mills, Microcomputers, P/G%, and Dispute Resolution, *Ohio State Journal on Dispute Resolution* 2: 187–223, 1987.

Still another stream of inspiration has come from people who are expansionist thinkers. This includes the conservative economist Arthur Laffer and the liberal economist Robert Reich. They both have in common a belief that policy problems can be resolved by expanding the total pie of resources or other things of value available to be distributed to the disputants. The expansion can come from well-placed subsidies and tax breaks with strings attached to increase national productivity. That kind of thinking can apply to disputes involving blacks-whites, rich-poor, men-women, North-South, urban-rural, and other categories of societal disputants. Some of that key literature includes I. Magaziner and R. Reich, *Minding America's Business*: *The Decline and Rise of the American Economy*, Harcourt, Brace, New York, 1982; and P. Roberts, *The Supply Side Revolution*, Harvard University Press, Cambridge, MA, 1984.

When the idea of SOSs was first proposed in the 1980s, people thought it was some kind of funny trick to think one could arrive at solutions to public policy problems that could exceed the best expectations of both liberals and conservatives simultaneously. Since then, the ideas have been presented in numerous workshops where skeptical and sometimes even cynical participants would divide into groups to try to develop SOS solutions to problems within their subject-matter interests. They found that by opening their minds to the possibilities and by following some simple procedures, they could succeed in arriving at reasonable SOS solutions. It is hoped that this research will contribute in the long run to decreasing the glamour and excitement of SOSs by making such solutions almost a matter of routine thinking. There is joy in creating new ideas, but there is more joy in seeing one's new ideas become commonplace.

G. Role of SOSs in PSO Activities

One way in which superoptimizing has become involved in PSO activities is by way of the training workshops for U.S. government agencies and the government agencies of developing nations. All PSO members are invited to volunteer to serve as instructors in related policy analysis short courses to be conducted in developing nations, with transportation expenses covered by the U.S. Peace Corps.

Another way SOS analysis relates to PSO is through the edited and authored PSO books, including the forthcoming volume entitled *Applications of Super-Optimizing Analysis*. All PSO members are invited to submit manuscripts for possible inclusion in that book.

A third way in which SOS analysis has become relevant to PSO is in the decision making of the PSO that emphasizes finding alternatives for dealing with internal disputes in which all major viewpoints can come out ahead of their best initial expectations. That approach has been used in determining who the new editors might be for the *Policy Studies Journal* and the *Policy Studies Review*.

It also is the approach that has been used in bringing together diverse viewpoints toward expanding the total pie of PSO so that there can simultaneously be more nonsymposium articles and more symposium articles instead of emphasizing tradeoffs between the two. The same applies to having (1) more political science and more interdisciplinary activities simultaneously, (2) more American government and more international activities, and (3) more theoretical generalizing and more practical impact on policy makers and policy appliers.

III. THE CHINA POPULATION PROBLEM AS AN IN-DEPTH EXAMPLE

The term *super-optimizing* refers to a new and useful form of public policy evaluation. It seeks to find solutions to policy problems whereby conservatives, liberals, and other major viewpoints can all come out ahead of their best initial expectations simultaneously.

Any or all of the Agency for International Development (A.I.D.) evaluation priority areas could be used for *illustrative purposes*. Given the short space available in the *A.I.D. Evaluation News*, it would probably be better to do a more in-depth analysis of one of the eight priority areas. The problem of population planning can serve as an illustration, including population planning in China where the problem may be more severe and difficult than in any other nation.

Table 1 is a SOS table and it shows goals to be achieved in the columns, alternatives available for achieving them in the rows, and indicators of relations between goals and alternatives in the cells. It also shows neutral, liberal, and conservative totals in the columns at the right. Those totals reflect neutral, liberal, and conservative weights for the goals. This is a simplified SOS table. It only involves two goals and four alternatives. Other SOS tables may involve more goals and more alternatives.

A. Alternatives, Goals, and Relations as Inputs

The basic *alternatives* are listed in the rows. They are labeled conservative and liberal in the contemporary Chinese policy context. The conservative alternative is to try to enforce a strict one-child policy on family size. The liberal alternative is to be completely flexible on family size. The compromise position between conservative and liberal freedom is to have a de facto

Table 1. Super-Optimizing Analysis Applied to the China Excess Population Problem

Criteria / Alternatives	C Goal Small families	L Goal Reproductive freedom	N Total (neutral weights)	L Total (liberal weights)	C Total (conservative weights)
C Alternative Strict one-child policy	4	2	12	10	14*
L Alternative Flexible on family size	2	4	12	14*	10
N Alternative One child with exceptions allowed	3	3	12	12	12
S Alternative Remove causes of excess children	5	5	20	20**	20**

1. Relevant causes of excess children in the China population context include
   a. The need for adult children to care for their elderly parents, which could be better handled through social security and/or jobs for the elderly.
   b. The need for extra children to allow for child mortality, which could be better handled through better child health care.
   c. The need for male children in view of their greater value, which could be better handled through providing more opportunities for females.
   d. The lack of concern for the cost of sending children to college, which could be better handled through a more vigorous program of recruiting rural children to college.
2. It is not a super-optimum solution to provide monetary rewards and penalties in this context because
   a. The monetary rewards for having fewer children enable a family to then have more children.
   b. The monetary punishments for having more children stimulate a family to have still more children to provide offsetting income.
   c. The monetary rewards and punishments are made meaningless by the simultaneous policies which are increasing prosperity in rural China.
*Indicates the leading alternative on the column before considering the SOS alternative.
**Indicates an alternatives that is the leading alternative on both the liberal and conservative columns after considering the SOS alternative.

modified one-child policy. Exceptions might include sometimes allowing a second child if the first is a daughter or allowing a second child among rural but not urban people.

One of the key *goals* is small families given the tremendous burden on the Chinese economy and government services of a billion people reproducing at a rate greater than about one child per family. Even one child per family would mean substantial short-run population growth. This would occur because people are living longer in China. If one simplifies the arithmetic by saying that if the 500 million males marry the 500 million females and have one child apiece within the next few years, then the population goes from 1 billion to 1.5 billion. That increase of half a billion is more people than every country of the world currently has with the exception of China and India. The second key goal is reproductive freedom. Even the conservatives recognize that interfering with reproductive freedom causes much antagonism toward the government. Thus both goals are endorsed by both conservatives and liberals in China, but Chinese conservatives place relatively more emphasis on small families, and Chinese liberals place relatively more emphasis on reproductive freedom.

The *relation* between each alternative and each goal is shown using a 1 to 5 scale. A 5 means highly conducive to the goal, 4 means mildly conducive, 3 means neither conducive nor adverse, 2 means mildly adverse, and 1 means highly adverse to the goal. We have here a classic tradeoff. A strict one-child policy is good on small families but bad on reproductive freedom. Flexibility on family size is good on reproductive freedom but bad on small families. The compromise alternative is to be middling on both like compromises in general. This compromise is better than the worst on both small families and reproductive freedom. It is clearly not better than exceeding the best expectations on both goals simultaneously.

B. Irrelevant Tax Breaks and Subsidies

In many public policy problems, the SOS involves well-placed subsidies and tax breaks. Well-placed *tax breaks* are meaningless in a communist society. Under communism, people do not do much direct tax-paying (especially income taxes) the way they do in Western societies. Instead the government is supported by paying people less than they are worth in their government jobs. The difference is a hidden tax. Ironically, this fits well the Marxist idea of surplus value exploitation of labor. It is an easy form of tax to collect, but it does not allow for the use of tax breaks as incentives.

China has tried subsidizing small families by giving *monetary rewards* to those who have small families and monetary punishments to those who do not have them. The effect has been almost the opposite of the government's intent. The subsidies to small families have in many instances increased their income so they can now afford to have more children. Having a monetary punishment or reduced salary may even motivate parents to have an additional child to help bring in more income to offset the reduced salary. Also, moving simultaneously toward a more prosperous free market (especially in farm products) has enabled many rural people to now have more children and not be bothered by the withdrawal of subsidies or other monetary punishments.

Well-targeted tax breaks and subsidies may not work so well for Chinese population planning, but they are improvements over what had previously been tried. In the 1970s, ideology still played a big part in Chinese policy evaluation. That meant consulting Marx and Mao in order to find solutions. Marxist ideology, however, gave conflicting recommendations. On the one hand Marx said that Malthusian population planning was designed to keep the working class from expanding and taking over. On the other hand, the capitalists supposedly wanted lots of workers in order to have a reserve army of the unemployed as a threat to use against aggressive unionists and other workers. In the early 1980s, the move away from ideology toward technocracy resulted in an overemphasis on developing birth control techniques, as if having effective birth control devices would automatically reduce population without any incentives to adopt them.

C. Getting at the Causes

A SOS would make more sense for dealing with the China population problem. It should provide small families and reproductive freedom simultaneously. Doing so may require looking to the *causes* of having additional children and then trying to remove or lessen those causes.

One cause is a need to have children who will support parents in their *old age*. Adopting a more effective social security system helps eliminate or lessen that cause. China, however, cannot presently afford an expensive social security system. As a meaningful substitute, Chinese public policy is seeking to provide more job opportunities for the elderly, especially in rural areas. Doing so will lessen their need to have large families in order to be supported in their old age.

Another cause is having additional children as backup because the *death rate* is relatively high among rural Chinese children prior to age 5. Various forms of pediatric public health can make a big difference. This includes giving shots and using effective remedies to prevent life-jeopardizing infant diarrhea and dehydration.

A third cause is the widespread feeling that female children are worthless in terms of bringing honor to the family. One therefore keeps trying until at least one son is born. That cause can be substantially lessened by the new moves in China toward greater *opportunities for females* to become lawyers, doctors, and enter other prestigious occupations. In China, women's liberation has facilitated birth control, whereas in the United States birth control has done more to facilitate women's liberation.

A fourth cause for larger families in rural China (as compared with urban China and elsewhere) is the fact that urban parents are more likely to limit their families in order to be able to afford *college educations* for all their children. The probability of going to college has generally been much lower in rural areas. Thus a fourth element in the package of policies to remove causes of too many children is to have a more affirmative action program to encourage rural children to go to college.

D. Side Benefits and Facilitators

This four-part package has super-optimum characteristics because it can reduce family size, thereby pleasing conservatives, and it can preserve reproductive freedom, thereby pleasing liberals. It also has the super-optimum characteristic of increasing *national productivity* while simultaneously decreasing the expense of having so many people to feed, house, and cloth. It increases national productivity by making better use of the skills of older people, women, and rural people. Other developing nations can also learn from China's experiences with those matters.

One can apply this kind of analysis to the other seven priority problems in the A.I.D. evaluation agenda. Finding SOS solutions is facilitated by the use of spreadsheet-based *decision-aiding software*. It allows one to work simultaneously with many goals, alternatives, and relations. That includes missing information and goals that are measured in multiple ways. Such software also allows for what-if analysis to see how the tentative conclusions change as a result of changes in the inputs.

Super-optimum solutions are also facilitated by having *checklists* based on generalizing from previous examples. Such checklists and examples can be found in the growing literature on super-optimizing. That literature includes win-win dispute resolution, growth economics, and non–zero-sum games. For further details, see Super-Optimizing Analysis and Developmental Policy, in S. Nagel, *Global Policy Studies: International Interaction Toward Improving Public Policy*, New York, St. Martin's Press, and London, Macmillan, 1991; and on Improving Public Policy Toward and Within Developing Countries, in Nagel, *Public Administration and Decision-Aiding Software: Improving Procedure and Substance*, Westport, Conn., Greenwood Press, 1990.

IV. THE SOS PROCESS

Super-optimum solutions are alternatives to public policy problems that can enable conservatives, liberals, and other major viewpoints to all come out ahead of their best initial expectations simultaneously. The purpose of this section is to clarify how to generate, adopt, implement, and facilitate such solutions.

A. Generating SOSs

There are approximately eight different ways of arriving at SOSs. They consist of the following:

1. *Expanding the resources* available. An example might include well-placed subsidies and tax breaks that would increase national productivity and thus increase the gross national product and income. Doing so would enable the tax revenue to the government to increase even if the tax rate decreases. That would provide for a lowering of taxes instead of trying to choose between liberal and conservative ways of raising them. It would also provide for increasing both domestic and defense expenditures instead of having to choose between the two.

2. *Setting higher goals* than what was previously considered the best while still preserving realism. An example might include the Hong Kong labor shortage with unemployment at only 1%. Hong Kong is faced with the seeming dilemma of having to choose between foregoing profits (by not being able to fill orders owing to lack of labor) and opening the floodgates to mainland Chinese and Vietnamese (in order to obtain more labor). A SOS might involve adding to the labor force by way of the elderly, the disabled, and mothers of preschool children. Also by providing more and better jobs for those who are seasonally employed, part-time employed, full-time employed but looking for a second job, and full-time employed but not working up to their productive capacity.

3. Situations where one side can receive *big benefits but the other side incurs only small costs.* An example is in litigation where the defendant gives products that it makes. The products may have high market value to the plaintiff but low variable or incremental cost to the defendant because the defendant has already manufactured the products or can quickly do so.

4. Situations involving a *third-party benefactor* that is usually a government agency. An example is government food stamps that allow the poor to obtain food at low prices, whereas farmers receive high prices when they submit the food stamps they have received for reimbursement. Another example is rent supplements that allow the poor to pay low rents, but landlords receive even higher rents than they would otherwise expect.

5. *Combining alternatives* that are not mutually exclusive. An example is combining government-salaried legal-aid attorneys with volunteer attorneys. Doing so could give the best of both the public sector and private sector approach to legal services for the poor. Another example is combining (1) tax-supported higher education plus democratic admission standards with (2) contributions from alumni and tuition plus merit standards. Doing so results in universities that are better than pure government ownership or pure private enterprise.

6. Removing or *decreasing the source of the conflict* between liberals and conservatives rather than trying to synthesize their separate proposals. An example would be concentrating on having a highly effective and acceptable birth control program to satisfy both the proponents and opponents of abortion because abortions would then seldom be needed. Another example would be concentrating on a highly effective murder-reduction program to satisfy both the proponents and opponents of capital punishment. Such a murder-reduction program might emphasize gun control, drug medication, and reduction of violence socialization.

7. Developing a *package of alternatives* that would satisfy both liberal and conservative goals. An example is pretrial release where liberals want more arrested defendants released prior to trial and conservatives want a higher rate of appearances in court without having committed a crime while released. The package that increases the achievement of both goals includes better screening, reporting in, notification, and prosecution of no-shows, as well as reduction of delay between arrest and trial.

8. *Redefining the problem* so as to clarify the shared goals that both the liberals and conservatives are seeking. In that sense, an SOS solution is one that produces increases in the goals favored by conservatives and also in the goals favored by liberals, which are normally thought of as inherently involving a tradeoff situation. A good example is the problem of jury size in which conservatives want smaller juries so as to make it easier to convict the guilty. Liberals want larger juries to make it more difficult to convict the innocent. An SOS solution might redefine the problem to be how to simultaneously increase the probability of convicting the guilt and decrease the probability of convicting the innocent. In other words, how to make juries more accurate on both convicting the guilty and acquitting the innocent. Allowing note taking by jurors and requiring accessible videotaping may do much more for each of those goals than a complete victory for either side on the almost irrelevant problem of jury size.

B. Adopting SOSs

Merely arriving at a suggested policy that is capable of enabling conservatives, liberals, and other major viewpoints to all come out ahead of their best expectations simultaneously does not guarantee that the policy will be adopted or that it will be successfully implemented even if it is adopted.

Since SOS policies enable all sides to be better off than their best expectations, one would think that merely developing such policies would get them adopted. There are, however, at least four factors that can interfere with successful adoption. One should watch for their presence and one should plan accordingly in order to deal with these factors.

1. Upping the Ante

Suppose one side says we must have a minimum of 500 units and the other side says we will not pay 1 unit more than 400 units. Suppose further, an SOS solution is developed to enable the first side to obtain 501 units and the second side to only have to pay 399 units. One would think such a solution would be instantly adopted. The first side might, however, say that it has now changed its mind and wants 600 units after seeing how easy it is to get 501 units. To deal with such a problem and many other SOS situations, it is helpful to have a third-party mediator (or one or both of the parties) make clear that if the initial demands are more than satisfied, the dispute should be considered resolved. It should also be made clear that if the gap widens from an original gap of 500 versus 400 to 600 versus 400, then it may be impossible to provide an SOS solution because the cost to one of the parties or a third party may become too great.

2. Satisfying the Mediator

Mediators and representatives of the conflicting parties or viewpoints can often be helpful in developing SOSs because they are trusted by each side more than the other side is trusted. However, an SOS solution might sometimes be developed that does not get adopted because the mediator or the representative of one side or the other needs some satisfaction other than knowing that both sides are pleased. This can be the situation where each side is represented by one or more lawyers who want to be paid substantially for their services. The agreement may involve one side getting something that is worth 501 units to it, with the other side paying something that is worth only 399 units to it. An example is where the second side gives products that it makes. The lawyer may not be happy with receiving one third of the 501 units, and may therefore discourage such an SOS settlement unless adequate provision is made for covering the lawyer's fees. That can be done by the receiving side agreeing to convert some of the 501 units into cash to pay the lawyer or obtaining cash from other sources available to the receiving side. This problem does need to be explicitly recognized because the lawyer may otherwise have a conscious or subconscious tendency to disrupt the settlement for reasons that are supposedly for the client's benefit.

3. The Revenge Factor

This can occur where the receiving side in the above example is pleased to receive 501 units but is displeased that the giving side is only paying 399 units, as measured by the giving side's benefit/cost assessment. It can also occur where the giving side is pleased to have to give only 399 units but is displeased that the receiving side is getting 501 units, as measured by the receiving side's benefit/cost assessment. Under those circumstances, it helps to have a third-party mediator emphasize to each side how well off it is even beyond its initial best expectations. There may be some special circumstances where it is necessary for the other side to suffer in order to provide specific deterrence to him or her or general deterrence to discourage others from engaging in similar undesirable behavior. In noncriminal situations, a revenge factor may be the equivalent of cutting off one's opportunity to greatly benefit in order to spite the other side as well as oneself.

4. Suspicion that a Trap Is Involved

If one side demands a minimum of 500 units and the other side says we will give you 501 units, it is reasonable for the receiving side to be suspicious that there is a trap or catch involved. Again, a third-party mediator (or the giving side that wants adoption) can present the SOS solution in such a way that both sides can see the results are mutually beneficial and that it makes sense to accept them. This kind of suspicion is likely to be reduced if from the start all sides are instructed or directed toward finding a SOS. That kind of orientation not only lessens suspicion, but it also becomes a self-fulfilling prophecy that leads to finding SOSs.

5. Vested Jobs or Property

A big problem in replacing a traditional compromise with an SOS is that there may already be vested jobs or property in the previous decision that need to be taken into consideration. An example is that both conservatives and liberals strongly endorse rent supplements over public housing projects. Conservatives do so partly because rent supplements represent a marketplace solution to housing for the poor. Liberals do so partly because rent supplements facilitate integration along economic and racial lines. The rent supplement program has, however, not replaced public housing. A big part of the explanation is the vested jobs and property in the previous solution. Public housing was previously supported by liberals as a form of equitable socialism. It has been tolerated by conservatives as an approach to housing for the poor that would not involve integration at a time when integration was less acceptable. Neither of those original purposes have much explanatory value for the retention of public housing over a rent supplements program but the existence of vested jobs and property does.

The key question is not what explains why the SOS has not been fully adopted, but rather what to do about that kind of interfering factor. The traditional compromise approach is a variation on grandfathering or a tolerated zoning use. Such a solution means that no new public housing projects are built but the old ones are allowed to deteriorate. It also means that people holding jobs under the old system are allowed to retain them but a minimum of replacement occurs when the former jobholders die, retire, or resign. An SOS that relies more on well-placed subsidies would phase out the property as quickly as possible rather than wait for natural obsolescence. A fast phase-out though would not mean a wasteful dynamiting of the public housing projects as was done with the Pruitt-Igoe Homes in St. Louis, Missouri. Instead, the projects could be made available along with appropriate subsidies for use as factories, warehouses, or other buildings as part of an inner city Enterprise Zone Project, which is an SOS in itself. The jobholders could also be provided with well-placed subsidies for retraining, buying small businesses, or other alternative activities that fit their skills. This problem of what to do about vested jobs and property comes up in many SOS situations, such as tariff reduction that can be highly mutually beneficial internationally. Adequate provision needs to be made for people and property that have a vested interest in the previous, less beneficial activities.

C. Implementing SOSs

One would think that arriving and adopting an SOS would produce mutually beneficial results. That is not necessarily the case. An SOS may be arrived at using the checklist of seven approaches previously mentioned or other approaches. The solution may be successfully adopted by a legislature, court, administrative agency, business firm, or other entity after overcoming the four factors mentioned above that sometimes interfere with successful adoption. Yet, the SOS may fail to achieve its mutually beneficial results for at least the following five reasons.

1. No Strings Attached

Super-optimum solutions to public policy problems often involve subsidies or tax breaks, such as the 30% across-the-board tax break given by the Reagan administration in the early 1980s. This was meant to be an SOS that would so stimulate the economy that the gross national product (GNP) would increase and thereby provide more money for government spending at lower tax rates than before the 30% tax break. It would enable an SOS increase in government spending and a reduction in taxes simultaneously without adding to the deficit. The idea was arrived at by supply-side economists and adopted by Congress. It failed in practice because there were no strings attached to the tax breaks to provide for any retooling of the economy that would have resulted in the productivity increases needed to increase the GNP. Instead, the money went disproportionately to real estate, luxury goods, and high executive salaries.

2. Insufficient Funding

The Enterprise Zone idea of the Reagan administration was well conceived and adopted with bipartisan enthusiasm. It also had strings attached by way of offering subsidies to business firms only if they would partly locate in inner city neighborhoods. Doing so would provide employment opportunities that would reduce welfare expenditures and antisocial behavior, whereas improving role models, productivity, multiplier effects, and tax-paying by people who otherwise would be heavy tax recipients. The program failed in practice mainly because the amount of money was not enough to do much attracting of business firms to inner city neighborhoods and relaxing regulatory legislation was not acceptable as a substitute by Congress.

3. Competent Personnel

The housing programs of the Reagan administration had many strings attached (at least on the books) regarding the kind of housing that should be provided by private contractors. There was also big money available. The program could have been an SOS program in the sense of exceeding the best expectations of landlords, tenants, and the general public. A key reason the program failed was that it was placed in the hands of people who were largely political appointees rather than specialized, experienced civil servants. The contracts as a result tended to be awarded too much on the basis of partisan considerations and campaign contributions rather than on the basis of merit.

4. Proper Sequencing of Events

The subsidy for developing an electric car embodied in the 1972 Air Pollution Act is an example of Democratic legislation that was well intended, successfully adopted, well funded, competently administered, and had detailed specifications for what would constitute an acceptable electric car. As of 1992, it has produced no significant results. If an electric car had been developed, we would have less expensive and better-quality transportation simultaneously, especially in terms of air pollution as well as energy independence. A key explanation for the failure of the legislation is that it did not provide for a step-by-step incremental development of an electric car through a series of numerous grants to try out various component ideas. Instead, the legislation provided for a massive reward after a whole electric car had been developed at high-cost, high-risk expense to private-sector individuals. The reward was to be that the government would replace its internal combustion automobile fleet with those electric cars. What was thought of as a well-placed subsidy failed to take into consideration the numerous implementation problems that had to be provided for along the way.

5. Imaginative Personnel

Point 3 above refers to competent personnel, which means people in that context who will comply with federal rules concerning nonpartisan government procurement. Avoiding fraud and corruption is a minimum regarding qualified personnel. More imagination than that is needed in order to implement SOSs successfully, as well as to develop them in the first place. For example, even if the National Science Foundation (NSF) were given large sums of money to award grants to develop components for an electric car, the implementation of that well-placed subsidy might still fail. The reason might be that the NSF would rely on peer review to determine who should get those grants for developing innovative ideas. Peer review probably works well for funding conventional research. If one wants to develop breakthrough unconventional ideas, however, then review by well-credentialed people in the field may result in an undue rejection of ideas that they find disturbing to what they are accustomed to in their conventional wisdom. It may be necessary to resort to nonpeer review in the sense of including imaginative humanities people and social scientists to evaluate the proposals from physicists, chemists, and engineers who are likely to submit the grant proposals. Innovation and implementation of an SOS is too important in terms of its implications and opportunities to be left to the subject-matter experts.[1]

D. Facilitating SOSs

A SOS is not going to occur unless it is generated, adopted, and implemented. Those are among the essential prerequisites. In addition to those prerequisites, there are also facilitators that are not essential but that can be greatly helpful in bringing about SOSs. They include such concepts as (1) competitive politics, (2) competitive business, (3) well-targeted subsidies, (4) childhood socialization, (5) national productivity, (6) better policy analysis, (7) innovative risk-taking, (8) sensitivity to opportunities, (9) optimistic pessimism, and (10) higher societal goals.

1. Competitive Political Parties

This is a key facilitator because the out-party is constantly trying to develop policies (including possibly SOS policies) in order to become the in-party. The in-party is also busy developing new policies in order to stay the in-party. New policies are developed largely as a result of changing domestic and international conditions not just for the sake of newness. Without the stimulus of an out-party, the in-party would have substantially less incentive to be innovative. More important, without the possibility of becoming the in-party, the out-party would lose its incentive to be innovative. More innovation generally comes from the out-party than the in-party (all other factors held constant), including the possibility of SOS innovations.

2. Competitive Business Firms

Competition among political parties may be essential for facilitating SOS public policy. Competition among business firms may be essential for facilitating a prosperous economy and a prosperous world through international business competition. Numerous examples can be given of nations that failed to advance and collapsed largely owing to a one-party system, such as the former Soviet Union. Likewise, numerous examples can be given of business firms that failed to advance and virtually collapsed largely because of lack of substantial competition such as the American steel industry. The American automobile industry has not collapsed, but it did fail to develop small cars, cars that resist style changes, safer cars, less expensive cars, and more durable cars in comparison with the international competition that was not taken seriously until almost too late.

3. Well-Targeted Subsidies and Tax Breaks

In the context of SOSs, this tends to mean subsidies and tax breaks that increase national productivity and international competitiveness. Such subsidies and tax breaks are the opposite of handouts that provide a disincentive to increased productivity on the part of either welfare recipients or big business. Good targeting in this regard especially refers to upgrading skills and stimulating technological innovation and diffusion. A dollar invested in those kinds of subsidies is likely to pay off many times over without necessarily having to wait very long for the results.

4. Childhood Socialization

In the SOS context, this refers to creating a frame of mind that causes adults to do what is socially desired because the alternative is virtually unthinkable. This can be contrasted with a less effective emphasis on deterrence whereby socially desired behavior is achieved through threats and bribes. Examples include childhood socialization to reduce adult behavior that is violent, alcoholic, drug addictive, and hostile toward constitutional rights.

5. Increased National Productivity

All these facilitators are important. Economists might rightfully consider increased national productivity to be especially important. It leads to an increased gross national product or national income, which means an increased tax base to which the tax rate is applied. If increased productivity increases the tax base, then tax rates can be lowered and still produce more tax money for well-targeted subsidies that produce further increases in national productivity. Those increases, however, are not an end in themselves. The increased national income can facilitate finding and implementing SOSs that relate to employment, inflation, agriculture, labor, business, poverty, discrimination, education, families, the environment, housing, transportation, energy, health, technological innovation, government structures, government processes, world peace, international trade, and every other public policy field. In other words, with more money and resources available, SOSs are facilitated but they often draw upon creativity that is associated with doing much better on relevant goals with constant or decreasing resources.

6. Better Policy Analysis Methods and Institutions

Super-optimum solutions are likely to be facilitated by policy analysis methods that deal with multiple goals, multiple alternatives, missing information, spreadsheet-based decision-aiding software and a concern for successful adoption and implementation. Better policy analysis institutions refer to training, research, funding, publishing, and networking associations. Those institutions can be part of the activities of universities, government agencies, and independent institutes in the private sector. The extent to which those policy institutions deal with super-optimizing analysis will make them even more relevant to facilitating SOSs.

7. Innovative Risk Taking

This is an important SOS facilitator because many SOSs involve technological fixes. In order to develop those new technologies, many people usually had to risk substantial amounts of money, time, effort, and other resources. There may have been a strong possibility that it would have all been wasted. An SOS society needs more people who are willing to take such chances. Classic examples include Marie Curie and Irène Joliet-Curie who sacrificed about 30 years of work plus their health to develop radium and thus radioactivity, which is part of the basis for nuclear energy. Thomas Edison frequently not only risked his resources but his whole reputation by announcing inventions before he had developed them in order to give himself an ego risk as a stimulus to quickly inventing what he falsely said he had already done.

8. Sensitivity to Opportunity Costs

This means either through socialization or an appropriate incentive structure trying to get decision makers to be more sensitive to the mistake of failing to try out a new idea that might work wonders as contrasted to being so sensitive to sins of comission rather than omission. Both wrongs are undesirable. One can, however, say that a police officer who wrongly beats a suspect is doing less harm to society than a president who wrongly fails to adopt a new health care program that could save numerous lives or a new education program that could greatly improve productivity and the quality of life. A person who is sensitive to opportunity costs tends to say, "Nothing ventured, nothing gained," whereas an insensitive person tends to say, "Nothing ventured, nothing lost." We need more of the former in order to facilitate the generating, adopting, and implementing of SOSs.

9. An SOS Combination of Pessimism and Optimism

This does not mean a balance or a compromise between being pessimistic and being optimistic. It means being 100% pessimistic or close to it regarding how bad things are and how much worse they are going to get unless we actively do something about it, including developing SOSs. It simultaneously means being 100% optimistic or close to it regarding how good things can get in the future if we do vigorously work at it including developing SOSs. This is in contrast to those who say the present is wonderful and needs little improvement. It is also in contrast to those who say the present may be wonderful or not so wonderful but some invisible hands or automatic forces of Adam Smith, Karl Marx, or God will automatically improve the future.

10. Constantly Seeking Higher Goals

This list is in random order. Some of the items overlap or interact, but it is better to overlap than leave gaps in this context. It is appropriate perhaps to have the last facilitator relate to constantly seeking higher goals. Traditional goal seeking leads to compromises. Worse, it can lead to one side trying to win 100% and the other side losing 100%, but the war, strike, litigation, or other negative dispute resolution leads to both sides losing close to 100%. Obviously seeking higher goals is more likely to result in higher goal achievement than seeking lower goals, including SOS goal achievement. The counterargument that is sometimes made is that higher goals lead to frustration because of the gap between goals and achievement. There may be more frustration in fully achieving low goals that provide a low quality of life when others are doing better. High societal goal seeking (including SOSs) is facilitated by all of the above factors, but it is a factor in itself because high goal seeking tends to become a self-fulfilling prophecy.

Note

For further details on super-optimum solutions, see S. Nagel, "Super-Optimum Mediation in Rule-Making Controversies," *Journal of Management Science and Policy Analysis* 6: 70–78, 1989; "Super-Optimum Solutions in Public Controversies," *Future Research Quarterly* 5; and S. Nagel and M. Mills, *Developing Nations and Super-Optimum Policy Analysis*, Chicago, Nelson-Hall, 1991. For further details on successful adoption and implementation of SOS solutions, see S. Nagel, *Policy Analysis Methods, Process, and Super-Optimum Solutions*, University of Michigan Press, Ann Arbor, 1992; and S. Nagel and M. Mills, "Arriving at Super-Optimum Solutions for Greater Productivity," in M. Holzer (Ed.), *Handbook of Public Productivity*, Marcel Dekker, New York, 1991. An earlier article in the *Policy Studies Journal* discussed basic concepts associated with super-optimum solutions as background to this article: See S. Nagel, "Super-Optimizing Analysis in Policy Studies," *Policy Studies Journal* 8: 507–513, 1990.

4

The Utilization of Policy Research

Robert F. Rich
University of Illinois, Urbana-Champaign, Illinois

Cheol H. Oh
Arkansas State University, Jonesboro, Arkansas

Although it has been an issue of long-standing concern (Lynd, 1939), during the 1960s, the perceived lack of utilization of social research results became an issue of direct relevance for managers of public service programs and for those responsible for the funding of research and development activities. During the recent prolonged economic downturn, the need to use scarce resources effectively and efficiently has become increasingly acute. In this context, concepts and strategies of knowledge utilization have a much greater salience than they might have had in the last 3 decades (Backer, 1991; Rich, 1991). Thirty years ago, policy research was undertaken with the intention that it have immediate and direct use in improving the quality of social and economic programming. In practice, however, some types of policy research information were seen as "generally not exerting significant influence on program decisions" (Weiss, 1972b: 10–11).

The limited success of large-scale government intervention, from the New Deal to the New Frontier and the Great Society (Aaron, 1978), presented a dilemma for program managers: Could they rely on the social sciences to guide their work? Is social science information qualitative or quantitative relevant to the needs of public-sector officials? Is social science information available to potential users? More importantly, how can the effects of information on governmental decisions be conceptualized and measured? Blue ribbon commissions (e.g., the National Academy of Sciences' Panel on Federal Investment in Social R&D, the Brim Commission, the Commission on Federal Paperwork) have concentrated on problems of translating research into action as well as on problems of "over-" and "underutilization" of social science-related information.

Within the scientific community, some researchers responded to this perceived underutilization by recommending that the social sciences be less involved in such applied activities as program evaluation (Zusman, 1976). Others began studying the process of applying research information to public policy (Halpert, 1966; Lippitt, 1965; Nagi, 1965; Sadofsky, 1966;

Watson and Glaser, 1965). Results of these studies suggest that the utilization of research may in fact be substantial, although diffuse, indirect, and difficult to track (Cohen, 1977; Innes, 1990; Knorr, 1977; Nelson, et al., 1987; Oh, 1992; Patton et al., 1975; Pollard, 1987; Rich, 1975, 1977, 1991; Schneider, 1986; Weiss, 1977b, 1980).

In this chapter, we (1) present a historical perspective on knowledge use and its societal applications; (2) analyze how various classes of theories relate to knowledge utilization; (3) critically review the literature regarding the process of applying policy research to public policy making; and (4) point to critical issues of concern for researchers and practitioners involved in this field.

I. KNOWLEDGE UTILIZATION: A HISTORICAL PERSPECTIVE

A. Roots of Policy Research

Historians and philosophers generally believe that the advancement of society/civilization is related directly to the advancement of knowledge and the way in which knowledge is used by members of society. The fundamental basis for societal actions comes from what is "known"—known because it is accepted as valid/true by society as a whole.

This belief that knowledge is central to the advancement of the individual in society antedates our own Anglo-American culture. In ancient Greece, a higher level of education was deemed necessary for a successful career in a democratic government. This type of education included training in humanistic studies, the arts, and public speaking (Rich, 1979).

In most Western countries, this conception was extended to the training of civil servants, who were assumed to be highly educated and, even, learned individuals. At a minimum, the civil servant was thought to be a generalist capable of making informed judgments on a wide variety of topics/issues.

As the demands made on bureaucrats increased and as public-sector decision making became increasingly complex, expectations changed. Generalists were transformed into specialists or learned to rely on policy analysts to provide the "scientific basis" for decision making.

It has only been since World War II, however, that those responsible for public policy have come to view policy analysis as a subset of scientific research subject to the laws, procedures, and potential for "certainty" of scientific methodology. Indeed, the field called policy sciences evolved in this period. More recently, since the 1960s we have begun to view science policy and social policy as inextricably linked, with social policy amenable to the laws of scientific inquiry and with science policy having a direct and fundamental influence on the quality of our lives.

B. Use of Policy Research in Organizations

Although policy research can be seen as having many different functions over time, it has one timeless and unique feature: it is expected to aid directly in the policy-making process. The results of policy research are meant to "provide feedback which can be used for program development . . .[as] part of a cycle of planning, implementing, observing, and correcting" (Rapp, 1969).

The dynamic nature of the organizational system warrants a brief discussion here on the concept of systemic "change." The concern in the field of utilization is in following the impact of research information through modes of change within a system. Such a conscious and systematic study of the change process may be seen as the foundation of efforts at planned change: the "conscious, deliberate, and collaborative effort to improve the operations of a human system, whether it be self-system, social system, or cultural system, through the utilization of scientific knowledge" (Bennis et al., 1969: 4).

The investigation of the phenomena of utilization from an empirical perspective has been dominated by individuals concerned with planned change (Havelock, 1972; Havelock and Lingwood, 1973; Larsen, 1980; Lippitt, 1965; Rogers, 1962; Zaltman, 1979). These individuals have focused on the process of diffusion and have assumed that their analyses of specific innovations could be applied more broadly to utilization (Larsen, 1980). Consequently, "the term innovation [has become] central to [the] knowledge utilization phenomena" (Zaltman, 1979).

C. Utilization: The Search for a Definition

Those involved in studying the research utilization process—applied social researchers, practitioners, and policy makers—with quite different disciplinary biases and professional needs, have employed a variety of concepts and units of analysis in their search for factors that influence utilization. Thus, when more than one discipline is examined, we often find a great diversity of seemingly conflicting research in terms of definitions of utilization as well as factors seen to influence it. As a result, the extent of utilization depends largely on how the term *utilization* is conceptualized and measured (Caplan et al., 1975).

To quote Patton (1978:24), in the context of evaluation research in his search for a utilization definition:

> Most of the literature on evaluation research never explicitly defines utilization. But there is an implicit definition: utilization occurs when there is an immediate, concrete, and observable effect on specific decisions and program activities resulting directly from evaluation research findings. This definition stems from the stated purpose of evaluation research, which is to gather data that can be used to make judgments about program effectiveness. If such data is gathered, then a judgment ought to follow. That judgment leads somewhat directly to concrete action and specific decisions.

Employing this definition, many researchers have concluded that applied research is underutilized (Agarwala-Rogers, 1977; Bruce, 1972; Cox, 1976; May, 1975; Parsell, 1966; Sadofsky, 1966; Schulberg and Baker, 1968; Weiss, 1971, 1972b, 1972c).

Recently, a less pessimistic outlook on utilization has emerged. As Cohen (1977: 527) has stated:

> A decision maker who decided to pursue some course of action that is inconsistent with evaluation findings may still be employing the research if it provided some input for his/her decision. . . . It seems unrealistic for an evaluator to expect his/her findings to be automatically converted into policy (i.e., implemented). However, it does not seem unrealistic to expect evaluation research findings to have some bearing on . . . policy decisions.

Knorr (1977: 180) also found that utilization may be indirect and diffuse:

> Utilization does not follow the pattern of technical implementation of results established in the natural or technological sciences. Rather the main area of utilization consists of an indirect (bound to undergo further decision processes), diffuse (taken into account to various degrees and at different positions), difficult to localize utilization responsibility (distributed over various decision levels), and possibly delayed discursive processing of

the result in the stage of program development and decision preparation. The low visibility of this kind of utilization and the far too high expectations contribute to the popularity of the thesis that little utilization takes place. Its plausibility should be reexamined in the light of the present data and arguments.

Clearly, utilization, as seen in this perspective by Patton, Knorr, Cohen, Weiss, and Rich, is different from the adoption of technologies as seen by those concerned with planned change. *Use* in this case is not as clearly defined, and it does not have the direct, concrete, documentable application that the planned-change field can and does claim.

Beyond the traditions represented by Zaltman and Knorr, there are other perspectives on how to conceptualize and measure utilization within a policy context.

The economist would advise us to examine the "value" of knowledge. As Machlup (1979) notes: "Readers acquainted with theories of value, especially in economics, will remember that 'use value' has long been a favorite expression. . . ." Generally, the economic approach has been one of measuring the tangible or intangible good of a use or application of knowledge. They have also been concerned with questions of who pays and who benefits from a use of knowledge.

The sociologist, social psychologist, and information scientist have focused on the relationship between social and psychological structures. "The success of social science can be measured by the extent to which it expands the boundaries between our private orbits of direct experience and the social and psychological structures that shape them from a distance" (Gregg et al., 1979). Social structures are seen as being reflected in the ways in which social problems are defined by researchers and policy makers. "The nature of problems—and the question of the social processes that structure them"—are particularly important from this point of view (Holzner and Fisher, 1979). Here social structures are examined through citation analysis and through coding procedures that assess problem definitions—including whether the author concentrates on "person"-centered, "milieu"-centered, or "system"-centered characteristics (Gregg et al., 1979). Recent studies have suggested that utilization is a complex phenomenon, not a unitary concept, and have pointed out its multiple dimensions. According to this view, the partial use, premature use, nonuse, and abuse/misuse of information need to be included in studies of knowledge utilization (Dunn, 1980; Larsen, 1981; Weiss and Bucuvalas, 1981). As Mandell and Sauter (1984: 151) succinctly point out:

> These revised views imply that no single measure of use is likely to be broad enough to be able to detect the entire range of ways in which social science research is used. Rather, *multiple measures* [our emphasis] of use are required in order to avoid overlooking important uses of social science research.

II. THEORIES OF KNOWLEDGE USE IN ORGANIZATIONS

Although there have been some studies on various purposes of knowledge utilization (Quadrel and Rich, 1989; Weiss, 1977) there is no exact theory of knowledge utilization. As Rich (1991: 322) contends, "within academic circles, the field is not viewed as one in which theory building has taken place; theory with respect to knowledge utilization is not well developed." Although there is no exact theory with respect to knowledge utilization in organizations, theories in other areas can assist us in understanding the phenomena in question. In fact, many social theories posit that information/knowledge plays an important role in explaining cognitive, social, and political-economic behavior. Each approach has put forward a conception of what types of information are important, what significance they have in explaining bureaucratic behavior, and how they are used. An examination of each of these theories permits one to analyze many different meanings of knowledge and knowledge utilization.

A. Weberian Approaches to Organizational Behavior

In explaining how organizations work and prosper, information/knowledge has been assumed to play an important role. In this case, information takes the form of the expertise of public officials.

The bureaucratic literature of the Weberian tradition identifies expertise as the primary source of bureaucratic power. "Weber contends that the power of executive officials is rooted in the technical or professional skills that distinguish administrators from amateur politicians. Bureaucratic power thus reflects the technological revolution and the growing influence of specialized knowledge in modern civilization" (Rourke, 1972).

Weber conceives of several distinct types of significant knowledge:

Training and skills that an individual brings to the bureaucracy—in other words, between-the-ears kinds of knowledge
That which confers the ability to produce and process information
That which confers the ability to apply information to problem-solving situations (a very general skill)

Having specified these different conceptions of knowledge, the Weberians go on to point out that expertise has served on the foundation for an independent/autonomous position of bureaucratic power.

Since bureaucracies began to develop a position of independent power and authority they have devoted some of their attention to securing and maintaining their own autonomy, which is often called organizational interests. This notion of organizational interest is especially important for our analysis of knowledge utilization in organizations because it lies at the foundation of bureaucratic power. This proposition sets the stage for understanding how organizations process and use information. As long as a bureaucracy has a monopoly on the technical skills, expertise, and other forms of information it provides to decision makers, its position is not contested and it is protected. Given this situation, one of the bureaucratic responses is an attempt to create an artificial monopoly through the use of secrecy. Along these lines, Weber (1968) suggests:

> This superiority of the professional insider every bureaucracy seeks to further increase through the means of keeping secret its knowledge and incentives. Bureaucratic administration always tends to exclude the public to hide his knowledge and action from criticism as well as it can.

A large element of how knowledge is used or not used is the strong preference among career officials to defer to expertise:

> Their own involvement and influence depend in large part on other officials deferring to their expertise. To challenge the expertise of another career group is to risk retaliation. Thus, Foreign Service Officers have been extremely reluctant to challenge the military on strategic questions or to challenge Treasury officials on economic matters (Halperin, 1974).

Officials defer to expertise in the expectation that they will be likewise deferred to in what is considered to be their specialty.

In the case of bureaucratic theory, it is clear that the judgment of what constitutes "meaningful knowledge is more closely related to questions of values and insulation of power than it is to science or the objective, technical quality of information. *The usefulness of information has more to do with the characteristics of the person who possesses it (i.e., an expert) than it does with the substance of the message that is being conveyed.*

According to bureaucratic theory, therefore, it seems clear that:

1. Information is essential to the power and prestige of bureaucratic organizations.
2. The desire to protect organizational interest affects information produced in bureaucracies and types of information disseminated to other bureaucratic agencies and the public.
3. There is a tendency to search for very limited information and to rely on the inventory of information already developed within the bureaucracy. Therefore, information from external sources is less likely to be consulted.
4. The trustworthiness and the credibility of information sources are essential for use of information. Therefore, the use of information happens when information confirms the policy position or interest held by policy makers.

B. Classic Approaches to Organizational Behavior

The most frequently discussed construct/model of human behavior in organizations is the "rational actor mode" (Allison, 1971). The rational actor is engaged in the process of "optimizing." The optimizing stragegy advocates selecting the course of action with the highest payoff. This strategy requires estimating the comparative value of every viable act in terms of expected benefits and costs.

All rational actor theories call for systematic canvassing of possible alternatives, for a systematic analysis of the consequences of each alternative in light of the values/goals that one wants to maximize, and for possible choices to be guided by this analysis (Braybrooke and Lindblom, 1963). There is some disagreement among those writing about rationality, but all writers/scholars seem to agree that comprehensive and prospective analysis is essential. "Comprehensiveness is often seen as logically necessary for rational choices; in fact, rational choice comes close to being defined as a choice that, *inter alia*, responds to a comprehensive consideration of all relevant variables" (Braybrooke and Lindblom, 1963).

The limitations of rationality as a method of problem solving have been thoroughly indexed in the literature. Herbert Simon (1976) has pointed out that human beings rarely adopt this decision-making approach. "Part of the problem is that determining all the possible favorable or unfavorable consequences of all the feasible courses of action would require the decision maker to process so much information that impossible demands would be made on his resources and mental capabilities" (quoted in Janis and Mann, 1977).

Others argue that one can certainly be rational without engaging in a comprehensive search through all relevant and available information resources (Downs, 1967). Eulau et al. (1970) argue that highly accurate, reliable, and complete information resources are not ipso facto conducive to rational decision making in a representative democracy. "On the contrary, from the societal perspective, it may actually be so costly as not to be a rational instrument of government at all."

In other words, the rational actor theory has the following conceptions of knowledge and knowledge use:

1. All relevant information will be searched and used in human decision-making processes— in this case, types of knowledge or information are not differentiated.

2. It is assumed that the human mind is capable of processing all sources of available knowledge.
3. It is assumed that all relevant sources of available knowledge should be applied to a given problem.
4. "Use" is loosely defined in terms of considering all available sources of knowledge in weighing alternative courses of action. Presumably, the available knowledge will dictate the action ultimately taken.

C. Psychosocial Approaches to Organizational Behavior

Psychosocial theories teach us that the

> psychological nature of the interactions between . . . two parties is of paramount importance. . . . We are saying that in order for effective knowledge utilization to occur a rather complex set of psychological and social relationships is needed. We ignore considerations of psychology at the expense of endlessly repeating our misunderstandings of ourselves and others (Mitroff and Mitroff, 1979).

In essence, we have learned that as far as knowledge utilization is concerned, we should be focusing on "between-the-ears" processes and complex social relations that influence how information will be processed and used.

Because of the limitations of the rational actor model, decision makers are prone to adopt suboptimizing solutions (Miller and Starr, 1967). According to March and Simon (1958), the decision maker *satisfices* rather than maximizes: He looks for the course of action that is "good enough" and that meets a minimal set of requirements.

Simon (1976) argues that the *satisficing* approach best describes decision making because it reflects the limitations and constraints placed on human beings in organizations. Decision makers can be characterized as being subject to "bounded or limited rationality," which makes them prone to gross simplifications when dealing with complex decision-making problems.

Simon's work has been very influential in offering an alternative to the rational actor model. He argues rather forcibly that the satisficing approach best fits the limited information processing capabilities of human beings (Janis and Mann, 1977).

> Man's limited ability to foresee further consequences and to obtain information about the variety of available alternatives inclines him to settle for a barely "acceptable" course of action that is better than the way things are now. He is not inclined to collect information about the complicated factors that might affect the outcome of his choice, to estimate probabilities, or to work out preferred orderings from many different alternatives. He is content to rely on a drastically simplified model of the buzzing, blooming confusion that constitutes the real world (Simon, 1976); (discussed in Janis and Mann, 1977).

Social theorists have come to accept the power of the satisficing approach (Etzioni, 1968; Johnson, 1974; Miller and Starr, 1967; Young, 1966). Cyert and March (1963) point out that policy decisions are likely to be made on the basis of short-term acceptability within an organization.

The satisficing theories make it clear that

Use is limited to the most relevant information as opposed to all of the information.
Relevant use is self-defined in terms of the needs of the decision makers.
Use is loosely defined—there is no particular differentiation between types of use or types of information. Unlike theories where there is a distinction between types of information

(e.g., cost/benefit theories), the satisficing theories give us only a very loose conception of information and types of utilization.

Psychosocial theories make an important contribution to our understanding of what constitutes usable knowledge and of the need for conceptualizations of the definitions of utilization. In these theories, we are reminded that information is processed through the mind, and that psychological/cognitive processes are essential to understanding different conceptions of use and different forms of information.

D. Contextual Approaches to Organizational Behavior

Other approaches to organizational theory attempt to understand the organization in terms of its broader cultural and political-economic environment (Meld, 1974; Scott, 1966). Bennis and Slater (1968), for example, have approached the reality of fluctuating environmental demands on organizations by suggesting that an organization is composed of temporary task-oriented (rather than rule-oriented) groups, being formed and re-formed to respond to the organizational need of the moment. Such task forces would gather individuals with the skills necessary to meet an environmental challenge and would disband when the need abated. This approach acknowledges the impact of, and the need for, flexible responses to a dynamic environment, and is applicable to a wide variety of regulatory, funding, community, or professional demands. However, there is a question as to the durability of the solutions of such temporary task forces once disbanded; preexisting patterns of organizational response may tend to reemerge once the crisis is over (Katz and Kahn, 1978: 283).

Another contextual approach to organizational theory may be found in the field of economics. As Pugh (1966: 247) puts it:

> The facts that all organizations operate in an economic environment and the success or failure of many is judged on economic terms mean that the study of the context and the performance of organizations must rely primarily on economic concepts.

In this view, the organization is seen as an "active participant in economic decisions rather than as a passive resultant of market forces" (Pugh, 1966: 246). These contextual approaches then, in their recognition of extra organizational influences, add to other attempts at explaining organizational behavior.

Whereas the classic and psychosocial approaches discussed above involve the flow of objective information through the program's formal structure and subjective intrapsychic/interpersonal dynamics, respectively, contextual variables involve the less proximal and manipulable arena of program context. For Meld (1974: 453),

> choices that involve public versus private benefits are generally acknowledged to be political. However, when program choices affect different groups in the population differentially—in taxes, benefits, services, and so on—is not public policy also being made? Are not different political values being assigned to the various groups? The issue then is political—an issue of "who wins, who loses?" in the collection and distribution of resources. It is not a question of analysis and evaluation. Planners often make such decisions on the basis of negotiation, rather than on the basis of research data.

Cohen (1977; 139) agrees, stating that "decision-making, of course, is a euphemism for the allocation of resources—money, position, authority, etc. Thus, to the extent that information is an instrument, basis, or excuse for changing power relationships within or among institutions, [organizational research] is a political activity." The relevant context for program operation and policy research utilization includes two components: (1) *administration*, involving program enabling and regulatory legislation, as well as funding sources; and (2) *culture*, involving the program's community and clients, and the professional "culture" or values of program policy makers and staff as well as of the policy research enterprise itself.

Administrative policy making in large part depends on political and economic value judgments by policy makers. When the stakes are high (Cohen, 1977), research procedure and findings are apt to be subject to political manipulation (Cook et al., 1980; Meld, 1974; Weiss, 1972d) reflecting the perceived feasibility of utilizing findings (Cook et al., 1980; Weiss, 1972b, 1972c) as seen by policy makers, funders, and politicians subject to the pressures of competing influences (Weiss, 1973, 1975). The political uses of research, which, like the psychosocial reactions of program staff, serve to maintain program existence (Weiss, 1972b), include (1) commissioning a study to delay undesirable policy making, (2) providing ammunition to gain support for a successful program, (3) ducking responsibility by using evidence to make a decision for a policy maker, (4) discrediting opposition, (5) gaining prestige and improved public relations through the commissioning of a blue ribbon panel of researchers, and (6) fulfilling mandated program grant requirements and justifying budget requests (Weiss, 1972a, 1977b). In addition, the fact that funding for policy research is often controlled by the agency or program in question further implicates the role of economic context in the policy research endeavor (Suchman, 1967).

The cultural context of community groups and service consumers also may influence the use of policy research and its findings. Information regarding a study and its findings may be withheld from the public or manipulated by policy makers (Stufflebeam, 1974; Weiss, 1972c) in light of the community's response to a popular program negatively assessed, the need to withhold certain treatments for the sake of an experiment, or the need for program support and voluntary cooperation of clients in research procedures (Suchman, 1967). In fact, research findings may be used by consumer groups to support their own interest in a program (Weiss, 1972a); in particular through the use of media attention (Riecken and Boruch, 1974).

Finally, it must be noted that the professional values of the program policy makers and program staff and of the research "community" represent yet another cultural context of the policy research endeavor. Researchers, because of their professional backgrounds and often nonprogram institutional bases (Schatzman and Strauss, 1973), enter the research field with biases and values that, practically speaking, constitute a political stance implicitly endorsing certain program goals, research methods, or policy outcomes (Stufflebeam, 1974; Weiss, 1973, 1975). At times, these professional orientations differ from values and ideological doctrines of the program policy maker or staff, and conflicts resulting in the lack of utilization of policy research findings may ensue (Berk and Rossi, 1976; Caplan, 1979; Caplan and Rich, 1976; Rich, 1977; Suchman, 1967; Weiss, 1972c).

The contextually constrained nature of the policy research system does not, however, imply a hopelessly subjective and unscientific course of events. A researcher's "knowledge of community structure and function . . . may provide for a substantive contribution . . . as great, and perhaps even more telling than his methodological skills in conducting [policy] research" (Suchman, 1967: 166). The acceptance of the influence of political values on research utilization (Argyris, 1971) may lead to their employment in methodology that takes values and biases into scientific account (Berk and Rossi, 1976; Guttentag, 1973; Riecken and Boruch, 1974; Scriven, 1976).

E. Communication-Related Approaches to Organizational Behavior: The "Two Communities" Metaphor

Although we do not consider the "two communities" metaphor to be a distinct organizational theory (Dunn, 1980), it has been treated as such in much of the knowledge utilization literature. As a result, we are treating it here as a separate approach to theory, although it would be more appropriately conceived of under the contextual approaches to organizational behavior.

Communication-related studies of knowledge utilization begin with the assumption that there is a "great divide" (Weiss, 1978) between the culture of science and that of government and that this gap serves to explain the process of knowledge utilization. In the broadest sense, knowledge utilization had been thought by many—many studies based on this approach to be a problem of *linkage*: building links between the knowledge production and knowledge utilization processes (Havelock, 1969). The nature of the linkages or mechanisms of knowledge transfer advocated depends to a great extent on one's diagnosis of the problem.

Many sociologists and communication scientists have expressed the belief that there is a "gap" between the culture of science and the culture of government. The problem is to bridge this gap so that greater and more effective utilization of science and technological information can follow (Rich, 1979). The nature of the problem is often assumed to be one of "communication failure or lack of organized effort to systematically introduce social science knowledge in usable form where it will most likely be used" (Caplan, 1979).

Others have observed that the problem may be one of "breaking down the hostility between researchers, program managers, federal policy makers, and third-party users" (National Research Council, 1978). In this case, the gap that exists, and the bridge that must be built, may be functions of politics (the rules and procedures of the public problem-solving process). Another way of conceptualizing this issue is in terms of the bureaucratic problems associated with the interactions among knowledge production and utilization processes (Caplan and Rich, 1976; Rich, 1977). In this perspective, the problems has to do with overcoming or finding ways to bypass standard operating procedures. According to this view, one could effect change in the knowledge utilization process by influencing regular or traditional bureaucratic rules and procedures. The "bridge" in this case would be in gaining an increased understanding of how bureaucracies work and how their standard operating procedures affect the production and utilization of knowledge.

A "gap" may also reflect alternative or competing incentives or reward systems (Lingwood, 1979). Program managers are rewarded for providing concrete results; in many cases, they are responsible for program implementation and must focus on the nuts and bolts of how to do it. They may, indeed, appreciate research much as a connoisseur appreciates good food; it may likewise be viewed as a luxury. Researchers and research administrators, on the other hand, often hold the same values as the academic or scientific community, who reward the productivity of scholarship for the sake of scholarship. Neither set of values is better, more rational, or intrinsically "correct." The 1978 National Research Council Study Project, entitled *The Federal Investment in Knowledge of Social Problems*, stated: "we noted considerable tension between program officials, who feel that they receive little help from research, and research administrators, who are weary of anti-intellectual program managers and their demands for how-to-do-it manuals" (p. 44). The nature of the need for constructing a bridge in this case seems to be related to educating officials who "have a limited understanding of how new information can foster innovation and change" (p. 53). Presumably, this education would be in the nature of rewards and incentives, as well as in the politics of problem solving in the public sector.

III. THE LITERATURE ON INFORMATION USE: WAYS OF VIEWING UTILIZATION

This chapter argues that utilization is a process and not simply a goal to be attained at one point in time but a series of less than discrete "events" varying over time and area of application that are dependent on the type of information in question. We realize that all information is not the same. In daily life, we regularly employ information gathered during schooling and professional training, from colleagues and friends, from the media, and from other more diffuse sources of information in our environment; these are the foundations of the data and facts we all store in our brains. "Mundane" types of information (Machlup, 1980) join with more particularly organizational sources of information (e.g., policy analyses, demonstration project and evaluation research results, financing models, cost-efficiency studies, and structural and demographic statistics) to comprise the spectrum of types of information potentially used by a policy maker. In the realm of organizational decision making, it is generally assumed that the possession of information distinguishes the "expert" as "knower" from the policy maker as "user" of information. However, these varying types of information are generally not distinguished from each other in the research utilization literature; when they are, there is generally no attempt made to place the type of information studied for use on a reference classification of types of information. It seems apparent that different types of information will be used in different ways, and that the literature leaves this source of potential variance in utilization largely untapped, much to the detriment of a theory of policy research utilization.

We may also conceive of these sources of information as being differentially utilized depending on the information needs of the user. Certainly, a budget director in need of information relating to financing decisions, for example, might very well underutilize demonstration project results. This is not to say that another type of use—for example, a director of services—would not utilize such information if appropriate to specific problem-solving needs. Thus, the needs of the user in specific areas of application are important to understanding and assessing information utilization, and they may be seen as another perspective on variation in use largely ignored in the utilization research literature.

There have been exceptions to this lack of a framework. In terms of information use, one approach has been to distinguish between "instrumental" (immediate and directly observable) and "conceptual" (potentially having delayed and diffused impact, and therefore less readily observable) types of information use in policy making (Caplan et al., 1975; Knorr, 1977; Rich, 1975; Weiss, 1977a).

The problem addressed by this approach to types of use (and in need of more attention in the realm of types of users and information) becomes one of specification. If we agree that all forms of information and types of use are not the same (nor equally important for varying policy problem-solving needs), then we must begin to specify typologies of information and use, and the conditions and circumstances under which various types of information will be employed for varying types of use.

A review of the literature on knowledge utilization reveals a dearth of studies employing these crucial distinctions in their research designs. Even in those studies that (though not employing an information typology) clearly delineate the type of information being investigated, we still find a lack of *precision* in specifications of levels and types of use and delineations of decision-making contexts (Larsen, 1980).

In an attempt to specify the relationships among types of information, types of institutional problem-solving needs, and types of use, we will review selection utilization literature, explicating ways of thinking about use through an ordering scheme based on concrete approaches to the assessment of use. To reiterate: In reviewing studies of utilization, we have looked for both breadth of scope in specifying forms of information that in varying situations will result in different types of use, as well as precision of measurement of use.

Although we concentrate here primarily on survey research, we do recognize the influence of other, more qualitative methods. Social framework analyses (Coleman, 1980; Nelkin, 1979; Rich, 1979), intellectual histories (Lindblom and Cohen, 1979; Pollak, 1980), and case studies (Deitchman, 1976; Horowitz, 1967), for example, have each made their unique contribution to our understanding of the use of information in society.

By far the most common way of viewing policy research utilization has been through the use of survey methods. In these investigations, structured observations, interviews, and questionnaires are the primary tools; often used in conjunction with relevant documents and research reports to obtain a fuller picture of the research utilization process.

A. Structured Observations

When used in a structured manner (i.e., with predetermined categories within which to place observations), observational methods can offer precision of measurement as well as a breadth of specification unbiased by respondent self-report. However, with this mode of inquiry, we find the potential for biases based on a loss of objectivity on the part of the researcher. In a field situation entailing direct observation, researchers may tend to identify with subjects under study. Furthermore, blind spots may develop as the investigator becomes accustomed to more common or subtle organizational behaviors. A structured checklist of observations to be made and categories within which to code observed behaviors may be helpful in this regard (Larsen, 1980; Selltiz et al., 1959). Another bias, which may be more difficult to control, can be introduced through reactivity of the subject to the phenomenon of being observed. However, this reactivity often fades after familiarity is established, and in any event is a problem shared with most other methods of inquiry. A further means of avoiding subject reactivity would be to observe subjects unobtrusively, or entirely without their awareness; however, with research on policy makers in public organizations such stealth would be impractical and quite likely unethical as well.

The literature on structured observational methods as applied to utilization research in public service organizations is just beginning to emerge. One innovative example may be found in an unpublished doctoral dissertation (Daillak, 1981) growing out of Alkin's work on the utilization of educational evaluation (Alkin et al., 1979). Daillak followed educational evaluators over a 6-month period, sitting in on meetings, making structured observations, and conducting postmeeting in-depth interviews. Daillak's study offered a detailed, first-hand analysis of evaluator styles and holds promise as an alternative mode of investigating the policy-making process.

An exciting example of the potential for precision of structured observations and of the analytical power of a design that clearly specifies several types and levels of variables may be found in Larsen and Werner's (1981) study, "Measuring Utilization of Mental Health Program Consultation." In this work, trained observers carefully recorded data regarding recommendations and suggestions made during 39 2-day mental health program consultations. Characteristics of the recommendations measured and a large number of consultation characteristics were rated. Use was conceptualized as occurring on both the individual suggestion level (N = 788) and on the level of the consultation as a whole (N = 39) and was measured on a 7-point scale ranging from several degrees of utilization, through simple interest in an idea, to several degrees of nonutilization. Measurements were taken at 4-month and 8-month follow-up sessions after consultation.

Although the sample of consultations in this study appears to have been self-selected by community mental health centers specifying an interest in expert consultation on program change, and the levels of use were self-reported through follow-up interviews, Larsen and Werner's (1981) use of structured observations highlights the potential for precision of this approach in the specification of variables important to the research utilization process.

B. Sample Surveys

In an attempt to identify instances of empirically based social science knowledge influencing policy decisions, Caplan and co-workers (Caplan, 1977; Caplan et al., 1975) conducted interviews with 204 federal-level officials. This landmark study presented a foundation for understanding and how and why social science informatin is used at the national level. However, the types of use and forms of research were broadly conceived; thus, it was not possible to differentiate among various types of applications. Furthermore, the study is biased in focusing on empirically grounded sources of social science information and on utilization for which the respondent had to recall specific details of the study (including the name of the investigator).

Knorr (1977) provides another example of the application of survey methods to discern utilization. In a study conducted in Austria (offering one of the few cross-cultural validations of the research utilization phenomena), Knorr interviewed 70 federal and municipal decision makers and sent questionnaires to 628 social scientists. In this instance, several different policy areas were investigated, four functions of social science knowledge were identified, and subjective and objective forms of data were distinguished. Knorr concludes that instrumental utilization does occur (albeit with legitimating or motivating purposes) more often than had been suspected, but that such use may be indirect, diffuse, difficult to localize, and subject to delayed discursive processing (i.e., symbolic uses) rather than straightforward and easily measurable.

Although most research has held forms of information or types of utilization constant, some research has attempted systematically to sample user situations. Some of the earliest attempts to assess research utilization in this manner may be found in the work of Ronald G. Havelock and his associates at the Center for Research on Utilization of Scientific Knowledge at the University of Michigan's Institute for Social Research (Havelock, 1973; Havelock and Mann, 1968). Havelock selected a stratified national sample of school districts and administered a questionnaire asking for information on various uses of resources and on characteristics of school districts that might relate to their utilization of innovations (including research and ideas).

Patton et al. (1975) also employed a stratified sampling technique to select 20 evaluations randomly from five strata based on "nature of program." Three levels of respondents were interviewed for each of the 20 evaluations studied. In this research, however, utilization was still broadly defined, and the form of information (evaluation) was held essentially constant.

In a study of information behavior in German complex organizations, Badura and Waltz (1980) clearly specify types of information, user characteristics and situations, and characteristics related to the utilization of social science knowledge. The researchers used a stratified sample based on "organizational culture" of more than 400 law graduates, scientists, and engineers, and behavioral and social scientists selected from eight private-sector firms and four policy-related departments of the federal government. Types of information were specified as (1) economic, (2) scientific-technical, (3) legal, (4) linguistic, and (5) social scientific. Although Badura and Waltz take care to specify the variables under consideration, their dependent measures are of attitudes toward and perceived need for social science knowledge.

As a result, they measure attitudes (potentially) related to the utilization of social science knowledge and not utilization behavior itself. A further difficulty with Badura and Waltz's dependent measure is one shared with most survey research—that is, the self-report nature of questionnaire measurement. However, although self-reported behaviors are subject to many of the same potentials for distortion as are self-reported attitudes, self-reported behaviors are more readily subject to objective verification (through the archival record) than are self-reports of attitude or behavioral intent.

An example of a study that considers all three dimensions under scrutiny here (form of information, type of use, and user situation or need) can be found in a recent Weiss and Bucuvalas (1977) project measuring characteristics of social science research deemed useful for policy making. Weiss and Bucuvalas selected a stratified sample of 250 federal, state, and local mental health policy makers and applied social researchers. The respondents were instructed to assess 50 abstracts of studies selected for representativeness as to type of study, sampling characteristics, and clarity of results. The abstracts were varied systematically on the basis of manipulability of major explanatory variables, administrative feasibility of the implications, and degree of congruence with prevailing beliefs in the mental health field. Finally, respondents were interviewed and asked to rate the abstracts based on 2 questions regarding usefulness and 29 descriptive characteristics related to the types of purposes the study results might serve. By systematically varying forms of information and policy maker's situation, and by measuring use on the basis of several measures, the Weiss and Bucuvalas (1977) study comes close to capturing the variation inherent in the utilization process. However, it is not clear whether the measures of potential utility or usefulness would be the same as actual utilization. Weiss and Bucuvalas are asking what respondents *would do* if confronted with a given study—not what they *actually have done*.

In a study of utilization in mental health policy research currently in progress, Rich attempts to overcome these difficulties by approaching each of these sources of variation in utilization. A stratified sample of federal- and state-level mental health policy makers responded to questionnaires and structured personal interviews. Area of application was varied based on service-oriented versus financial policy need. Form of information was varied based on service-oriented information (program evaluation, demonstration project results, statistical data, and expert advice) or finance-oriented information (cost-efficiency studies, financing models, statistical data, and expert advice). Type of use was varied across both area of application and form of information, and attempts were made to assess the effect of various nonresearch extraneous factors for each type of information in both the service-oriented and finance areas of application. Preliminary results indicate different levels of use for different types of information depending on the characteristics of the policy maker and on the type of institutional need for problem-solving information.

C. Time-Series Analyses

This last study brings us to an additional source of variance in the utilization process; that is, differences in the level of utilization over time. Traditionally, utilization research has been conducted in the information science tradition; that is, research information is conceived of as "input" and utilization as "output" (in terms of research-based policy). Generally, a direct one-to-one correspondence between input and output is assumed. In attempting to investigate a less straightforward relationship between information and utilization, formidable methodological difficulties present themselves. First, bits of knowledge tend to accumulate and congeal to a point where it is difficult to discern discrete, identifiable inputs. Second, because the process of making policy decisions is multiply determined, it is often impossible to trace the specific knowledge bases for specific decisions even in cases where the population of bits of applicable knowledge may be discretely identified (Caplan and Rich, 1976). That much having been said, and keeping in mind the distortions of self-reporting techniques that plague most survey research, attempts have been made to trace degrees of utilization seen over time.

In Rich's (1975, 1977, 1981) study of the National Opinion Research Center's Continuous National Survey, which looked at the utilization process over time, the phenomena of delayed use and of "waves of utilization" were identified. Generally, during the first wave of measurement, "instrumental" (or concrete and directly identifiable) use was seen to a greater extent than was "conceptual" (or diffuse and less straightforwardly identifiable) use. During the second wave, the reverse was found to be true, with conceptual uses outnumbering instrumental uses. The first wave, which included many of the uses intended to collecting the data, seemed to occur from the point of the receipt of the information through approximately 3 months thereafter and was oriented toward information inputs with policy-action implications. The second wave of use generally occurred from 3 to 6 months after the information was received and was oriented toward information inputs offering understanding of the policy context within which decision making took place. In addition to its other advantages, this research points to the importance of studying types of use over time if one is to attain a clear picture of the utilization process. (Results of Rich's current project, when available, will offer another set of data illuminating the process of policy research utilization over time.)

Although the survey studies reviewed above deal to varying extents with issues of *specification* and *precision*, they all share, at least in part, sources of bias related to self-report (e.g., self-definition, memory, and social desirability distortions), which limit the validity of conclusions drawn. Experimental designs ultimately offer a powerful research tool. Currently, however, practical difficulties limit the broad applicability of experimental methods to the real-world settings essential for research on the process of policy research utilization. As a result, we may look toward other methods, based on more objectively measurable data, which might reduce some of the threats to validity encountered when information is collected indirectly or secondhand.

D. Citation Analyses

A more precisely quantifiable method of assessing the impact of knowledge, and one that is not subject to respondent reactivity (although still subject to researcher selection bias), is that of social framework analysis based on citation analysis. Taking samples of the literature from the years 1936, 1956, and 1976, Gregg et al. (1979) read and coded 698 articles in six social problem areas taken from a wide variety of both pure and applied journals. More than 80 pieces of information were coded for each article, including type of journal, type of article, independent variables, causal attributions, relevance to theory or practice, and type of theory or practice under consideration. Each article was further analyzed on the basis of a more particular coding of the independent variables, causal attributions, and patterns of attributions studied. Results indicated complex relations among the causal attributions and among the attributional patterns that characterized each article. The data also revealed significant differences when examined by problem area, type of article, and type of journal. In addition, the authors discussed the role of political and nonscientific factors in social science and extrapolated from their data to predict future trends for the development of the social science.

Of particular significance to the present methodological discussion is the power of this research method for specifying (with the precision of measurement offered by the citation analyses) complex interactions among forms of information and types of use (as seen through the journal analyses). In this study, we do not, however, find "user situations" assessed. Furthermore, this research method was applied by Gregg and associates on the broadest of social science "cultural" levels. The potential clearly exists, however, for the specification of types of social science research users, and the application of the method to the assessment of institutional use of research reports.

E. A Note on Experimental Designs

The specification of information, situation, and use and the precision with which they are measured are crucial to the development of utilization studies. However, through the control of extraneous influences and the purposive manipulation of "treatments," experiential and quasi-experimental research designs offer the potential elimination of certain threats to validity and reliability, thereby increasing the logical certainty with which we can answer the sorts of questions we have been asking here (Campbell and Stanley, 1966). Whereas the field of utilization research has not developed to the point where true experiments have been tried on a systematic basis, there have been preliminary attempts to utilize experimental and quasi-experimental techniques to isolate and assess influences on knowledge use. A well-developed example of the potential for experimental investigation of research utilization is given by a recent Pelz and Horsley (1981) study. The investigators measured outcome of a research utilization program designed to "disseminate current research findings and facilitate organizational modifications required for sound implementation in nursing departments of a sample of Michigan hospitals." Under stratification by size of hospitals within geographical and institutional clusters, hospitals were randomly assigned to 13 "treatment" and 15 comparison groups. Type of treatment was specified as to presence or absence of an innovation team (IT) (or of an "artificial" IT for the control situations) at the hospital. Variation in situation was controlled for through the use of the stratified random sampling employed. Levels of use were specified through five direct and five indirect measures of research utilization as a result of the IT training program intervention. In addition, observations were made at three times: prior to intervention, 1 year postintervention, and, in one-half of the treatment groups, 2 years postintervention. On average, the results of the direct measures indicated that the IT intervention was more effective than either non-IT or artificial IT groups, with gains decreasing over the next year.

Although the geographical and institution stratification categories did not play a role in Pelz and Horsley's (1981) analysis of effects, this study does specify type of intervention to be utilized and type and degree of utilization over time. The sophistication of this design, however, offers a most promising direction for further research.

Again, the point of relevance for our present purposes is that experimental designs *can* be employed in the study of the research utilization process with attendant increases in the logical certainty of findings obtained.

IV. CRITICAL ISSUES IN THE FIELD OF KNOWLEDGE UTILIZATION

Even a cursory review of the literature on information acquisition, dissemination, and utilization/impact in decision making generally reveals that in spite of the efforts to explain the gap between the perceived need to use information in decision making and the ability to supply this "need" into "practice," the literature has some serious problems (see Backer, 1991; Caplan, 1979; Caplan et al., 1975; Ciarlo, 1980; Dunn, 1980; Innes, 1990; Oh, 1992; Pollard, 1987; Rich, 1979, 1981, 1991; Weiss, 1977; Weiss and Bucuvalas, 1980; Wingens, 1990).

First, the literature on information utilization has a conceptual problem; namely, the implicit assumption that use of information makes a difference in decision making (about a similar point of view, see Nagel, 1984; Nelson et al., 1987; Pollard, 1987; Shrivastava, 1985). This assumption implies that use of information is implicitly or explicitly conceived of as having a simultaneous effect on decision making. Past studies have focused either too much or not enough on the utilization aspect of information processing in organizations. Consequently, they do not pay serious attention to the impact dimension of information processing in decision making. However, in many cases, assumptions have been confused with facts and assertions confused with empirical proof (Innes, 1990). Information influences decision making without necessarily being actively used. Therefore, the assumption needs to be tested in terms of theoretical rigor and empirical validity. As Rich (1983) suggested, use of information needs to be investigated methodologically as an independent or intervening variable (i.e., use for what) rather than as a "dependent variable (i.e., use as the end of information processing in decision making)," which has been the main focus of past studies. Once placed in historical and theoretical perspective, a broad range of dependent variables (i.e., impact) and independent variables (i.e., types or sources of information, need for information, and policy area of application) begins to emerge. Levington and Hughes (1981), for example, distinguished utilization from impact. Utilization is conceptualized as an individual-level phenomenon and impact as a macro-level variable, referring to changes (either subtle or dramatic) that social science research causes in overall decisions (about a similar point of view, see Berg and Theodo, 1980; Useem and Dimaggio, 1978). Although the distinction made by Levington and Hughes (1981) is helpful, a considerable variety among the measures of impact still exists. Therefore, unless the diversity among different measures of impact is properly recognized and specified, employing multiple, different measures of impact is likely to hinder rather than facilitate the development of a systematic understanding of use of information and its impact (Mandell and Sauter, 1984).

Second, information processing in decision making is a complex phenomenon involving environmental, organizational, and individual components in addition to specific characteristics of information; i.e., sources, content, or quantity of information received by decision makers (Becker, 1991; Nelson, 1981). However, most of the past studies generally lack a comprehensive conceptual framework embracing such factors in a systematic way (Backer, 1991; Innes, 1990; Kelly and Kranzberg, 1978). The authors of past studies often picked up a set of variables that they thought were significant for their studies with little consideration of other factors from a comprehensive position based on substantive theories. As Rich (1981: 14) correctly states, "instead of trying to understand the overall problem solving situation and assessing where utilization fits in, we are focusing on an artificial utilization process which assumes that *all of the other factors can be held constant*" [our emphasis]. The lack of a conceptual framework embracing multiple levels of reality has led researchers to much conjecture about information utilization/impact with little theoretical basis and, subsequently, little systematic empirical investigation (Bozeman and Bretschneider, 1986). A study of information acquisition, dissemination, and utilization/impact ignoring such factors and based on a simple paradigm is likely to be counterproductive and may actually contribute to the abuse of information (Larsen, 1981; Oh, 1992).

What remains to be specified is the relative contribution of each of the variables of theoretical importance to the process of information utilization in decision making. To gauge the role of each variable and the causal relationships among the variables, it is necessary to build a comprehensive conceptual framework. Although there have been a few attempts to understand comprehensively how information is used in the decision-making process (Bardura and Waltz, 1980; Weiss and Bucuvalas, 1977, 1980), we can still find some methodological difficulties in these studies; that is, the dependent variable is a measure of attitude toward, or perceived need for social science research rather than utilization behavior itself, and dealing with potential use of information rather than an actual situation.

Third, the amount of empirical research on information acquisition, dissemination, and utilization/impact is distressingly small (Backer, 1991; Ciarlo, 1979; Conner, 1981; Larsen, 1981; Oh, 1992). As Barber emphatically and correctly states, "the predominant present view of the sociology of knowledge is of a separate, philosophical, ideological . . . and nonresearchable field" (recited in Landecker, 1982: 73). Of the limited empirical studies, most deal with utilization in terms of a simple description of respondents' answers to specific questions. Or a simple explanation of the variance in the dependent variable (i.e., use of information) is used by largely relying on regression methods (Caplan, 1979; Caplan et al., 1975; Havelock, 1973; Larsen and Werner, 1981; Patton et al., 1975; and Bolas, 1982). This mode of inquiry has been, however, made without investigating the causal linkages among the variables involved in the process of information *acquisition*, *dissemination*, and *utilization/impact* by decision makers (Mandell and Sauter, 1984). For example, although it is clear that some types of information are preferred over others (i.e., statistical data are more utilized than policy evaluation), little is known about why these choices are being made. By understanding causal linkages among the factors involved, we will be able to demonstrate a complex and rich picture about the direct, indirect, and/or spurious influence that variables may have on the use of information and its impact. Thus, what we need to do, as Huberman (1987) points out, is no longer to attempt exploratory studies but rather use explanatory and/or confirmatory studies. A well-developed example of causal modeling concerning the process of information utilization and its impact is a recent study by Oh (1992). On the basis of a comprehensive theoretical framework and sophisticated statistical methods, Oh examines empirically the causal relationships among the factors involved in the process of information utilization and its impact in governmental decision making.

Fourth, we also need to specify clearly what it is we are attempting to utilize. We feel that studies of knowledge utilization have been unnecessarily burdened with narrow conceptions and measures of utilization: The assumption seems to be that when speaking of the use of information, one is naturally referring to "new knowledge," as opposed to what is already known and stored in the human brain; "new knowledge" usually refers to empirically grounded information as opposed to "intuition," "hunches," "traditions," or many other forms of information.

Distinctions need, however, to be drawn among general organizational information, research-based information, innovative programs and technologies, and policy makers' intuitions in order to describe more accurately use of information in actual decision making. In addition, the variety of users of information (i.e., legislative, administrative, and community, as well as administrative and service-oriented users) and the various contexts within which utilization occurs need to be examined. For example, past studies pay little attention to the effect that differences in policy areas may have on use of information and its impact. We may agree on a set of explanatory variables but not agree that they are equally important across different policy areas. Effects of the differences between policy areas may provide a new theoretical clue to our understanding of the phenomena in question.

Finally, we need to be more sensitive to the problems of distinguishing between instances where utilization of social science information should be facilitated and instances where one may want to counsel deliberate nonutilization of the available studies. Not all utilization is good, and not all nonutilization is harmful. It is tautological to maintain that information is used. The crucial point seems to lie in identifying the policy-related information that will benefit society and then to develop the mechanisms that will facilitate its effective application.

V. CONCLUSIONS

This chapter has attempted to place selected literature on utilization of policy research into a broad historical context. The interests of individuals and society in the application of knowledge/science/information to meet human needs dates back to the Ancient Greeks. Moreover, the use of information in social problem solving is a critical component recognized in almost every major social, economic, and political theory. It is clear that the creation, diffusion, and use of information plays a significant role in explaining individual and organizational behavior.

Although much empirical or theoretical work has been done in the area of knowledge utilization, there appear to be serious conceptual and methodological problems that need to be resolved.

More importantly, as a cursory review of past studies demonstrates, it seems clear that there is no exact theory with respect to knowledge utilization in organizations. This is mainly because scholars have only put forward partial and incomplete theories. Taken together, they do not constitute an overall theory. Although there are some theories in other areas related to the phenomena in question, we can still find some difficulties in them (Oh, 1992).

For one thing, the role of information is merely implied or assumed. This suggests that past theories (especially rational actor theories) do not explicitly deal with information as an independent agenda of research with its own implication; rather it is treated as an instrumental tool for some other main concern (i.e., securing rationality of human behavior).

For another thing, even when the use of information is treated as the main concern of a study, technically as the dependent variable (i.e., the two-communities metaphor), a narrow range of explanatory variables often causes a serious problem. Most empirical studies are based on one or two schools of thought without considering other important theories. As a result, past theories provide only a partial explanation of knowledge utilization in organizations.

Future studies need to synthesize the scattered or partial theoretical constructs into an integrated theoretical system. As Rich (1991) argues, variables of all the models will be needed in building a comprehensive theory of knowledge utilization in organizations.

Further work is also needed in the area of measurement. Different measures of use (i.e., subjective versus objective measures, or multiple dimensions of use) should be compared with assess the utility in capturing the phenomenon being studied. Replications should be undertaken to test the validity of the measures. The field of knowledge utilization offers an open agenda with many unanswered questions. Once some closure is reached on the measurement issues, it should be possible to advance toward a systematic theory of knowledge roduction, dissemination, and utilization in organizations.

REFERENCES

Aaron, H. J. (1978). *Politics and the Professors*. The Brookings Institution, Washington, DC.

Agarwala-Rogers, R. (1977). Why is evaluation research not utilized? In *Evaluation Studies Review Annual*, vol. 2. M. Guttentag (Ed.). Sage, Beverly Hills, CA.

Alkin, M. C., Daillak, R., and White, P. (1979). *Using Evaluations: Does Evaluation Make A Difference?* Sage, Beverly Hills, CA.

Allison, G. T. (1971). *Essence of Decision: Explaining the Cuban Missile Crisis*. Little, Brown, Boston.

Argyris, C. (1971). Creating effective research relationships in organizations. In *Readings in Evaluation Research*. F. G. Caro (Ed.). Russell Sage Foundation, New York.

Backer, Thomas (1991). Knowledge utilization: The third wave. *Knowledge* 12.

Badura, B., and Waltz, M. (1980). Information behavior in the German Federal Government: The case of the social sciences. *Knowledge: Creation, Diffusion, Utilization* 1(3): 351–279.

Beckhard, R. (1975). Strategies for large system change. *Sloan Management Review* 16(Winter): 43–55.

Bennis, W. G., and Slater, P.E. (1968). *The Temporary Society*. Harper & Row, New York.

Bennis, W. G., Benne, K. D., and Chin, R. (1969). *The Planning of Change*. Holt, New York.

Berg, W. G., and Theodo, R. (1977). Policy research: Belief and doubts. *Policy Analysis* 3.

Berk, R. Z., and Rossi, P. H. (1976). Doing good or worse: Evaluation research politically re-examined. In *Evaluation Studies Review Annual*, vol. 1. G. V. Glass (Ed.). Sage, Beverly Hills, CA.

Bozeman, B., and Bretschneider, S. (1986). Public management information and system: Theory and practice. *Public Administration Review* (Special Issue).

Braybrook, D., and Lindblom, C. E. (1963). *A Strategy for Decision*. Free Press, New York.

Bruce, R. G. (1972). What goes wrong with evaluation and how to prevent it. *Human Needs* 1: 10–11.

Bulmer, M. (1981). Applied social research: A reformulation of "applied" and "enlightenment" models. *Knowledge* 3.

Campbell, D. T., and Stanley, J. C. (1966). *Experimental and Quasi-experimental Designs for Research*. Rand McNally, Chicago.

Caplan, N. (1977). A minimal set of conditions necessary for the utilization of social science knowledge in policy formulation at the national level. In *Using Social Research in Public Policy Making*. C. H. Weiss (Ed.). Lexington Books, Lexington, MA.

—— (1979). The two communities theory. *American Behavioral Scientist* 22: 459–470.

Caplan, N., and Rich, R. F. (1976). Open and closed knowledge inquiry systems: The process and consequences of bureaucratization of information policy at the national level. Presented at the Meeting of the OECD Conference on Dissemination of Economic and Social Development Research Results, Bogota, Colombia.

Caplan, N., Morrison, A., and Stambaugh, R. J. (1975). *The Use of Social Science Knowledge in Policy Decisions at the National Level*. Institute for Social Research, Ann Arbor, MI.

Ciarlo, James A. (Ed.) (1981). *Utilizing Evaluation*. Sage, Beverly Hills, CA.

Cohen, L. H. (1977). Factors affecting the utilization of mental health evaluation research findings. *Professional Psychology* Nov.: 526–534.

Coleman, J. S. (1980). The structure of society and the nature of social research. *Knowledge, Creation, Diffusion, Utilization* 1(3): 333–350.

Cook, T. D., Levinson-Rose, J., and Pollard, W. E. (1980). The misutilization of evaluation research: Some pitfalls of definition. *Knowledge: Creation, Diffusion, Utilization* 1(4): 477–498.

Cox, G. B. (1976). Managerial style: Implications for the utilization of program evaluation information. Paper read at the 84th annual American Psychological Association convention, Washington, DC.

Cyert, R. M., and March, J. G. *A Behavioral Theory of the Firm*. Prentice-Hall, Englewood Cliffs, NJ.

Diallak, R. (1981). *A Field Study of Evaluators At Work* (CSE Report No. 154). Center for the Study of Evaluation, Los Angeles.

Deitchman, S. J. (1976). *The Best-Laid Schemes: A Tale of Social Research and Bureaucracy*. MIT Press, Cambridge, MA.

Downs, A. (1967). *Inside Bureaucracy*. Little, Brown, Boston.

Dunn, W. E. (1980). The two-communities metaphor and models of knowledge use: An exploratory case survey. Knowledge: *Creation, Diffusion, Utilization* 1(4): 515-536.

Etzioni, A. (1968). *The Active Society.* Free Press, New York.

Eulau, H., Sackman, N., and Nien, M. (1970). *Information Utility.* AFIPS Press, Montvale, NJ.

Glaser, E. M., and Backer, T. E. (1977). Innovation redefined: Durability and local adaption. *Evaluation* 4: 131-135.

Gregg, G., Preston, T., Geist, A., and Caplan, N. (1979). The caravan rolls on: Forty years of social problem research. *Knowledge: Creation, Diffusion, Utilization* 1(1): 31-61.

Guttentag, M. (1973). Subjectivity and its use in evaluation research. *Evaluation* 1(2): 60-65.

Halperin, M. (1974). *Bureaucratic Politics and Foreign Policy.* Brookings Institution, Washington, DC.

Halpert, H. P. (1966). Communications as a basic tool in promoting utilization of research findings. *Community Mental Health Journal* 2(3): 231-236.

Havelock, R. G. (1969). *Planning for Innovation Through Dissemination and Utilization of Knowledge.* Institute of Social Research, Ann Arbor, MI.

—— (1972). *Training for Change Agents.* Institute for Social Research, Ann Arbor, MI.

—— (1973). Resource linkage in innovative educational and problem solving: Ideal vs. actual. *Journal of Research and Development in Education* 6: 76-87.

Havelock, R. G., and Lingwood, D. A. (1973). *R & D Utilization Strategies and Functions: An Analytical Comparison of Four Systems.* Institute for Social Research, Ann Arbor, MI.

Havelock, R. G., and Mann, F. C. (1968). *Research and Development Laboratory Management Knowledge Utilization Study.* Institute for Social Research, Ann Arbor, MI.

Holzner, B., and Fisher, E. (1979). Knowledge in use: Considerations in the sociology of knowledge application. *Knowledge: Creation, Diffusion, Utilization* 1(2): 219-244.

Horowitz, I. L. (1967). *The Rise and Fall of Project Camelot: Studies in the Relationship between Social Science and Practical Politics.* MIT Press, Cambridge, MA.

Innes, J. E. (1990). *Knowledge and Public Policy.* Transaction, New Brunswick, N.J.

Janis, I. L., and Mann, L. (1977). *Decision-Making.* Free Press, New York.

Johnson, R. J. (1974). Conflict avoidance through acceptable decisions. *Human Relations* 27: 71-82.

Katz, D., and Kahn, R. L. (1978). *The Social Psychology of Organizations,* 2nd ed. Wiley, New York.

Kelly, P., and Kranzberg, M. (Ed.) (1978). *Technological Innovation: A Critical Review of Current Knowledge.* San Francisco Press, San Francisco.

Knorr, D. (1977). Policymakers' use of social science knowledge: Symbolic or instrumental? In *Using Social Research in Public Policy Making.* C. H. Weiss (Ed.). Lexington Books, Lexington, MA.

Larsen, J. K. (1980). Knowledge utilization: What is it? *Knowledge: Creation, Diffusion, Utilization* 1(3): 421-442.

—— (1981). Knowledge utilization: Current issues. In *The Knowledge Cycle.* R. F. Rich (Ed.). Sage, Beverly Hills, CA.

Larsen, J. K., and Werner, P. D. (1981). Measuring utilization of mental health program consultation. In *Utilizing Evaluation: Concepts and Measurement Techniques.* J. A. Ciarlo (Ed.). Sage, Beverly Hills, CA.

Lehman, S. (1975). Psychology, ecology and community: A setting for evaluation research. In *Handbook of Evaluation Research,* vol. 1. E. Struening and M. Guttentag (Eds.). Sage, Beverly Hills, CA.

Levigton, L. C., and Hughes, E. F. X. (1981). Research on the utilization of evaluation. *Evaluation Review* 5.

Lindblom, C., and Cohen, D. (1979). *Usable Knowledge.* Yale University Press, New Haven, CT.

Lingwood, D. A. (1979). Producing usable knowledge. *American Behavioral Scientist* 22: 339-362.

Lippitt, R. (1965). The use of social research to improve social practice. *American Journal of Orthopsychiatry* 35: 663-669.

Lynd, R. (1939). *Knowledge for What?* Princeton University Press, Princeton, NJ.

Malchlup, F. (1979). Uses, values, and benefits of knowledge. *Knowledge: Creation, Diffusion, Utilization* 1(1): 62-81.

—— (1980). *Knowledge and Knowledge Production.* Princeton University Press, Princeton, NJ.

Mandell, M. B., and Sauter, V. L. (1984). Approaches to the study of information utilization in public agencies. *Knowledge* 6.

March, J. G., and Simon, H. (1958). *Organizations.* Wiley, New York.

May, J. (1975). Symposium: The policy uses of research. *Inquiry* 12(3): 228–233.

Meld, M. B. (1974). The politics of evaluation of social programs. *Social Work* July: 448–455.

Miller, D. W., and Starr, M. K. (1967). *The Structure of Human Decisions.* Prentice-Hall, Englewood Cliffs, NJ.

Mitroff, I., and Mitroff, D. (1979). Interpersonal communication for knowledge utilization. *Knowledge: Creation, Diffusion, Utilization* 1(2): 203–217.

Nagel, Stuart (1984). *Public Policy: Goals, Means, and Methods,* St. Martin's Press, New York.

Nagi, S. (1965). The practitioner as a partner in research. *Rehabilitation Record* (July/Aug): 1–4.

National Research Council (1978). Study project on social research and development. *The Federal Investment in Knowledge of Social Problems,* vol. 1. D. E. Stokes (Chairman). National Academy of Sciences, Washington, DC.

Nelkin, D. (1979). Scientific knowledge, public policy, and democracy. *Knowledge: Creation, Diffusion, Utilization* 1(1): 106–122.

Nelson, S. D. (1981). Knowledge creation. In *The Knowledge Cycle.* R. F. Rich (Ed.). Sage, Beverly Hills, CA.

Oh, C. H. (1992). *Policy Information and Policy Making in Governmental Bureaucracies: A Causal Modeling of Processes and Impacts.* Unpublished doctoral dissertation, University of Illinois, Urbana.

Parsell, A. P. (1966). *Dynamic Evaluation: The Systems Approach to Action Research* (Report No. SP-2423, Systems Development Corporation, Santa Monica, CA). Paper presented at the 61st Annual Meeting of the American Sociological Society, Miami, Florida.

Patton, M. Q. (1978). *Utilization-Focused Evaluation.* Sage, Beverly Hills, CA.

Patton, M. Q., Grimes, P. S., Guthrie, K. M., Brennan, N. J., French, B. D., and Blyth, D. A. (1975). *In Search of Impact: An Analysis of the Utilization of Federal Health Evaluation Research.* Minnesota Center for Social Research, University of Minnesota, Minneapolis.

Pelz, D. C., and Horsley, J. A. (1981). Measuring utilization of nursing research. In *Utilization Evaluation: Concepts and Measurement Techniques.* J. A. Ciarlo (Ed.). Sage, Beverly Hills, CA.

Pollak, M. (1980). Paul F. Lazarsfield: A sociological biography. *Knowledge: Creation, Diffusion, Utilization* 2(2): 157–177.

Pollard, W. E. (1987). Decision making and the use of evaluation research. *American Behavioral Scientist* 30.

Pugh, D. S. (1966). Modern organizational theory: A psychological and sociological study. *Psychological Bulletin* 66(4): 235–251.

Quadrel, M. J., and Rich, R. F. (1989). Information selection in the house of representatives. *Knowledge* 11.

Rapp, M. L. (1969). *Evaluation as Feedback in the Program Development Cycle.* Rand Corporation, Santa Monica, CA.

Rein, M., and White, S. H. (1977). Policy research. *Policy Analysis* 3.

Rich, R. F. (1975). *An Investigation of Information Gathering and Handling in Seven Federal Bureaucracies: A Case Study of the Continuous National Survey.* Unpublished doctoral dissertation, University of Chicago, Chicago.

—— (1977). Uses of social science information by federal bureaucrats: Knowledge for action vs. knowledge for understanding. In *Using Social Research in Public Policy Making.* C. H. Weiss (Ed.). Lexington Books, Lexington, MA.

—— (1979). The pursuit of knowledge. *Knowledge: Creation, Diffusion, Utilization* 1(1): 6–30.

—— (1981). *Social Science Information and Public Policy Making.* Jossey Bass, San Francisco.

—— (1991). Knowledge, creation, diffusion, and utilization. *Knowledge* 12.

Rich, R. F., and Goldsmith, N. M. (1983). The utilization of policy research. In *Encyclopedia of Policy Studies.* S. S. Nagle (Ed.). Marcel Dekker, New York.

Riecken, H. W., and Boruch, R. F. (1974). *Social Experimentation*: *A Method For Planning and Evaluating Social Intervention*. Academic Press, New York.

Rogers, E. M. (1963). *Diffusion of Innovations*. Free Press, New York.

Rourke, F. (1972). *Bureaucratic Power in National Politics*. Little, Brown, Boston.

Sadofsky, S. (1966). Utilization of evaluation results: Feedback into the action program. In *Learning in Action*. J. L. Schmelzer (Ed.). U.S. Government Printing Office, Washington, DC.

Schatzman, L., and Strauss, A. L. (1973). *Field Research*: *Strategies for a Natural Sociology*. Prentice-Hall, Englewood Cliffs, NJ.

Schneider, A. L. (1986). The evaluation of a policy orientation for evaluation research. *Public Administration Review* (July/August).

Schulberg, H. C., and Baker, F. (1968). Program evaluation models and the implementation of research findings. *American Journal of Public Health* 58: 1248–1255.

Scott, W. R. (1966). Some implications of organization theory for research on health services. *Milbank Memorial Fund Quarterly* 44(Oct., Pt. 2): 35–64.

Scriven, M. (1976). Evaluation bias and its control. In *Evaluation Studies Review Annual*, vol. 1. G. V. Glass (Ed.). Sage, Beverly Hills, CA.

Seashore, S. E., and Bowers, D. G. (1970). Durability of organizational change. *American Psychologist* 25: 227–233.

Selltiz, C., Jahoda, M., Deutsch, M., and Cook, S. W. (1959). *Research Methods in Social Relations*, Rev. ed. Holt, New York.

Shrivastava, P. (1985). Knowledge systems for strategic decision making. *Journal of Applied Behavioral Science* 2.

Simon, H. A. (1976). *Administrative Behavior*: *A Study of Decision-Making Processes in Administrative Organizations*, 3rd ed. Free Press, New York.

Stufflebeam, D. L. (1974). An administrative checklist for reviewing evaluation plans. Personal communication.

Suchman, E. A. (Ed.) (1967). *Evaluation Research*. Russell Sage Foundation, New York.

Useem, M., and Dimaggio, P. (1978). An example of evaluation research as a cottage industry. *Sociological Methods and Research* 7.

Van de Vall, M., and Bolas, C. (1982). Using social policy research for reducing social problems. *Journal of Applied Behavioral Science* 18.

Watson, G., and Glaser, E. M. (1965). What we have learned about planning for change. *Management Review* 54(Nov.): 34–36.

Webber, D. J. (1987). Legislators' use of policy information. *American Behavioral Scientist* 30.

Weber, M. (1968). *Economy and Society*. G. Roth and C. Wittich (Eds.). Bedminster, New York.

Weiss, C. H. (1971). *Organizational Constraints on Evaluation Research* (Report of Contract HSM-42-69-82, NIMH, 6/71). Bureau of Applied Social Research, New York. (Also published in condensed form as Between the cup and the lip. *Evaluation* 1(2): 49–55.)

—— (1972a). Introduction. *Evaluation Research*: *Methods for Assessing Program Effectiveness*. Prentice-Hall, Englewood Cliffs, NJ.

—— (1972b). Evaluating educational and social action programs: A treeful of owls. In *Evaluating Action Programs*: *Readings in Social Action and Education*. C. H. Weiss (Ed.). Allyn & Bacon, Boston.

—— (1972c). Utilization of evaluation: Toward comparative study. In *Evaluation Action Programs*: *Readings in Social Action and Education*. C. H. Weiss (Ed.). Allyn & Bacon, Boston.

—— (1972d). The politicization of evaluation research. *Journal of Social Issues* 26(4): 57–68.

—— (1973). Where politics and evaluation research meet. *Evaluation* 1(3): 37–45.

—— (1975). Evaluation research in the political context. In *Handbook of Evaluation Research*. E. L. Struening and M. Guttentag (Eds.). Sage, Beverly Hills, CA.

—— (1977a). Research for policy's sake: The enlightenment function of social research. *Policy Analysis* 3: 531–545.

—— (1977b). Introduction. In *Using Social Research in Public Policy Making*. C. H. Weiss (Ed.). Lexington Books, Lexington, MA.

—— (1978). Many meanings of research utilization. Unpublished manuscript.

Weiss, C. H., and Bucuvalas, M. J. (1980). *Social Science Research and Decision Making*. Columbia University Press, New York.

Wingens, M. (1990). Toward a general utilization theory. *Knowledge* 12.

Young, S. (1966). *Management: A Systems Analysis*. Scott Forsman, Glenview, IL.

Zaltman, G. (1979). Knowledge utilization as planned social change. *Knowledge: Creation, Diffusion, Utilization* 1(1): 82–105.

Zusman, J. (1976). Can program evaluation be saved from its enthusiasts? *American Journal of Psychiatry* 133: 1300–1305.

Part B
STAGES IN POLICY FORMATION AND IMPLEMENTATION

5
The Practice and Study of Policy Formation

Christopher J. Bosso
Northeastern University, Boston, Massachusetts

I. REGIME POLITICS, REGIME POLITICAL SCIENCE

Reflecting on the state of American political science, Lowi (1992:1) argues that "every regime tends to produce a politics consonant with itself; therefore every regime tends to produce a political science consonant with itself. Consonance between the state and political science is a problem worthy of the attention of every political scientist." The same can be said about the study of policy formation, which as an approach consciously or not always seems to shift with the political winds. From its origins in wartime operations research through the early 1970s, the literature on policy formation reflected, indeed, provided the rationale for, a relatively nonideological and even nonpartisan tilt toward activist governance in the United States and other advanced industrial societies. These decades marked the apogee of scholarly and governmental faith in "scientific" approaches to policy analysis, and, as a result, of a field known as "policy sciences" or "policy studies." The Policy Studies Organization itself was founded in 1971. Programs in policy analysis sprouted within graduate schools of all types, and everybody professed the need to apply "proper" analytic techniques to the conceptually separate stages of policy formation and program evaluation. In fact, implementation was lamented widely as a "missing link" in the policy process (Palumbo and Calista, 1990).

That omission was rectified by the early 1980s as government reacted to skyrocketing budgets and restive taxpayers by turning sharply away from policy innovation and expansive policy agendas. Scholars worried darkly of system overload and the policy literature as a whole began to exhibit keener attention to adjusting existing statutory and regulatory policy to the hard lessons learned in "bringing truth to power" (Wildavsky, 1979). Much of the earlier optimism about and enthusiasm for policy formation had dimmed as did, it seemed, the general vibrancy of the policy literature. The action instead lay in implementation, a shift with profound impacts inasmuch as that literature's mantra about "feasibility" endowed great legitimacy on cost-benefit and other economics-infused approaches. Most of this literature of course proved in a rather narrow sense that programs almost never work, and probably should never be tried to begin with. Such conclusions meshed well with (or were produced by) potent conservative asssaults on decades of government activism in more than one regime. To read much of the literature on policy formation during this time is to conclude: Nothing worked. Small wonder that Jones began the 1984 edition of his *Introduction to the Study of Public Policy* with a chapter entitled simply, "The Causes of Policy Failure Are, at Root, Political."

In the 1990s the study of policy formation and the making of public policy both are going through fundamental rethinking. Most of the classic literature on policy formation had emerged decades earlier, in an era of relatively healthy budgets and nonideological governance, but by the 1990s the picture was of widespread austerity and sharp ideological conflict about the proper spheres of government action. What new programs emerged in the late 1980s seemed to contain a goodly share of largely symbolic outputs; for example, legislation on plant closings (Portz, 1991) and workfare (Palumbo and Calista, 1990), each enacted in the heat of the 1988 presidential election. Others, because of legal budgetary restrictions, required proponents to cannibalize other programs, move financing off-budget, or, increasingly, simply pass off the costs of mandates to other units or levels of government. Add to these conditions unsettled electorates and the strength of organized interests defending entrenched programs, and the picture was of general policy stalemate and flaccid support for programs with weak or unpopular constituencies. This picture was not confined to the United States, nor even to advanced industrial societies, as the experiences of nations ranging from Sweden to Zimbabwe attest.

The current scholarship on policy formation has reacted to these conditions by going back to *prepolicy* or, at least, *predecision* dynamics. "Having been discovered, dissected, and declared no longer missing from policy action," observed May (1991a, 187), "implementation appears to be on the wane as a focal point for those seeking broader lessons for improving public policies. Much of the current literature about public policy formation is now centered on conceptual aspects of problem attribution and construction of alternative policies." In this vein, the study of policy formation has begun to settle out along two distinct but interlinked dimensions. The first is *agenda-setting*, concerned with how problems are—or are not—defined as in the legitimate purview of government and do—or do not—get onto the formal policy agenda. With ever-more crowded agendas, but also apparently enervated governmental capacity or will, what few problems actually become priorities is no longer solely an academic question. The literature on agendas certainly is not new (e.g., Schattschneider, 1960; Edelman, 1964), but it is blossoming at a time of acute ideological competition over the very purpose of government.

The second dimension is tied to agenda-setting, but focuses more on what has come to be called *policy design*. This construct requires, among other things, "a model of the structural logic of policy; a model of individual decision makers whose behavior impinges upon policy; and a model of the contexts within which decisions relevant policy are made" (Schneider and Ingram, 1990: 78). This last point is particularly important, because it turns the study of policy formation away from some of its less restrained efforts to "control" for contextual factors. "Regardless of definition," May (1991a-188–189) adds, "an important perspective of those writing about policy design is the *emphasis on matching content of a given policy to the political context in which the policy is formulated and implemented*" (emphasis supplied). Context matters, and it is not entirely manipulable.

More than that, the policy design perspective reflects not only the crowdedness of the contemporary agenda for action but, also, its stunningly universal austerity. Governments ranging from the new republics of the former Soviet Union to local governments in California grapple with aging physical infrastructures, tight budgets, and, perhaps also universal, citizenries far less willing to accede to the agendas and spending wishes of those who govern. Policy design as an angle of vision in many ways is an effort—part scholarly, part ideological, perhaps—to return the study of policy formation to basic questions about what works, what does not and why, without discarding any option a priori because of ideological or theoretical bias. In many ways it is a back-to-basics movement spawned by frustrations over what had become a rather truncated set of policy options. In shifting the focus *back* to policy formation, argue Linder and Peters (1990: 54), "the range of available design choices expands from those limited by existing capabilities and supportive climate in prospective implementing organizations to the full armamentarium of government's policy instruments." In this regard, students of policy formation who ignore the nature of public problems, the contexts surrounding policy formation, and, perhaps most critical, the centrality of ideas, also probably forget that to study public policymaking is to study, in the words of Lowi (1992: 5) "an *un*natural universe that requires judgment and evaluation." If our theories and methods do in fact mirror the real world, we are long overdue for radical rethinking.

II. THE CROWDED AGENDA OF GOVERNMENT IN THE 1990s

Political conflict is not like an intercollegiate debate in which the opponents agree in advance on a definition of the issues. As a matter of fact, *the definition of the alternatives is the supreme instrument of power* [our emphasis]. He who determines what politics is about runs the country, because the definition of alternatives is the choice of conflicts, and the choice of conflicts allocates power. (Schattschneider, 1960: 68).

The dynamics by which problems get atop the agenda of action, and where alternatives are defined by and for policy makers, powerfully shape policy formation in any political system. This is true especially in an American context of weak party cohesion, relatively permeable governing institutions, and the evolution (or degeneration) of much of politics into uncompromising catfights over values and ideas. Yet the United States seems increasingly unexceptional in this regard, as one is reminded in looking at the tremors induced by instantaneous global telecommunications.

How these conditions bode generally for policy formation in any single system, much less across systems, is as yet unclear. It *can* be asserted with some confidence that any government's capacity to maintain some sort of reasonable control over its own agenda for action is more problematic than ever, particularly when the issues at hand (e.g., AIDS) increasingly transcend ever-evanescent national boundaries. The specter of uncontrollability suggested in the previous sentence is intentional, both with respect to policymaking and the study of policy formation. The rapidity with which issues cascade through societies and political systems, and the ever-more apparent interconnections among a great many supposedly separate issues, can make formal agendas *seem* random and temporary, even as we know that they also are shaped by core societal values, institutional and legal constraints, and, in no small way, by history. The interaction effects produced between the turbulence of issues and the relatively greater constancy of other contexts are not as yet fully appreciated, but one gets a partial inkling of the future in such policy-shaping events as the media-saturated 1984 Ethiopian (see Bosso, 1989) or 1992 Somalian famines, the live pictures from Baghdad and Jerusalem during the 1991 Persian Gulf conflict, or, far less dramatically, the 1992 Earth Summit in Rio de Janeiro. In each case, more than one national government altered at least its public rhetoric in the face of (or for fear of creating) a global public spectacle. The phenomenon of course is not confined to the world stage, as any local city councillor can attest about the effects of the television cameras when it comes time to pass decisions on controversial issues.

To study policy formation is to study problems. The question of agendas thus is central, and can be divided into three prime avenues for inquiry: the perceived nature of problems; the institutional contours through which problems (and possible solutions) flow; and, finally, the key interactions between perceived problems and institutional venues, mediated by strategic elites, that in no small part shape agendas and policy choices.

A. On Problems

Jones and Matthes (1983: 119) argue that "much of what government does represents efforts to deal with contradictory and conflictual definitions of and solutions to society's problems." Not all problems are alike, of course. More accurately, not all problems are *perceived* to be alike by policymakers, attentive interests, or the mass public. We can list below just a few variables that influence greatly how problems are perceived:

- mass versus elite issue saliency (Schattschneider, 1960)
- novelty of problem (Downs, 1972)
- perceived distribution of costs and benefits (Wilson, 1972)
- technical/social/economic/political complexity (Nelkin and Pollack, 1982)
- images of those affected (Rochefort, 1986; Baumgartner and Jones, 1990a)
- manipulability of images (Cobb and Elder, 1972; Baumgartner, 1989)
- values about the proper role of government, etc. (Mucciaroni, 1991)

To a great degree, perceptions about a problem and the probability of its "solution" depends on whether there is consensus that some goal is good or, more central, that it is a legitimate matter for government intervention. For example, the often-posed "moon-ghetto" conundrum—"If we can put a man on the moon why can't we solve the problems of the ghetto?"—stems from vast differences in societal consensus about the goals themselves. Going to the moon was an easy goal to spell out because success or failure could be judged rather cleanly (getting there and returning safely), the goal meshed with prevailing social values (for example, technological innovation, the frontier spirit, competing with the Soviets), and, as Nelson (1977: 14) argues, it "had the advantage of not threatening significant interests and of promising something to several." Curing poverty, however, is a far less consensual goal, if only because those who see poverty as a personal failing understandably resist spending money on the "undeserving." Nor can one design an antipoverty program without generating some unpopular impacts on others, such as the working class, if the program is perceived to threaten their own relative social status.

Even supposing consensus on goals, there is no guarantee about agreement on *means*. Returning to the moon-ghetto metaphor, in many ways the space program was a simple engineering problem (albeit one of great *technical* complexity), where most involved agreed roughly about how to get to the moon and back safely. Problems whose solutions might require redistribution (Ripley and Franklin, 1984) or, at least, the perceived imposition of disproportionate costs (Wilson, 1972), however, hardly are the same as those that seem more distributive or positive-sum. Going to the moon was a problem with consensual goals and positive-sum solutions. Solving poverty has neither advantage.

A rough typology along the dimensions of agreement on goals and means gives a sense that *types of problems* truly matter (Bosso, 1987). Some problems are relatively "simple" not in and of themselves but because there exists wide consensus on ends *and* means—we know where we want to go and agree more or less about how to get there. A good example is Project Head Start, a remnant of Lyndon Johnson's Great Society which even conservatives can support. After all, giving underprivileged children a chance to excell in school—the helping hand, not the handout—echoes deeply rooted societal values about equality of opportunity, and generally is not perceived as coming at the expense of other goals or interests. The popularity of Head Start, that everyone wants to be included, is a sure sign that the program is at least a political success.

Problems on which there is a general agreement on goals but conflict over means are what we might call "technical" problems. For example, few policymakers or citizens traditionally have questioned the value of economic growth. Instead, the battle always seems to be over whether government should boost spending, restrict itself to manipulating the money supply, cut taxes, pursue some combination of these approaches—or do nothing at all and let the invisible hand of the market take over. The options pursued may be affected greatly by values or broad ideology, but one certainly can influence the choice of policy instruments by showing that one at least in theory works better than the others, as was the case with supply-side economics in the early 1980s.

For a third type of program the conflict is largely over goals, while debates about the choice of means recede into the background. In this vein, the problems are more "morally complex" than anything else. For example, the most ardent opponents of abortion care little whether science ever "proves" the moment of fetal viability, or if use of the RU486 pill legally would constitute an abortion. For them the issue simply is the taking of life, a matter of religious, ethical or moral beliefs, not the efficacy of any particular technique. Whether a society imposes the death penalty also depends little on the methods of execution chosen, although making the methods of execution more "humane" certainly can affect public acceptance of capital punishment. Instead, the focus is on a normative debate over whether it is right for the state to exact such a punishment. These are moral issues, not easily solved by "rational" analysis, although they can become less salient or divisive because of technological or societal changes. Abortion, for example, might disappear as a major societal issue if advances in birth control technology make the need for most abortions moot.

Not surprisingly, the problems of greatest intractability are those with no consensus on either goals *or* means, as Bosso (1987: xiii) suggests with the battle over the U.S. government's policy on chemical pesticides:

> With respect to pesticides, it is almost impossible to find agreement on ends because the ends themselves often are clearly incompatible: environmentalists may seek to rid the earth of pesticides at any cost; chemical firms may seek to maximize profits; farmers want inexpensive and effective pesticides to maintain high crop yields at lower costs; public health officials want to eradicate disease. Consumers . . . want cheap food, which might lead them to support the wide use of pesticides, but they also fear the possibly carcinogenic effects of pesticides residues in that food or in the environment.

Contemporary governance increasingly confronts such quandaries. For policy maker and scholar alike, such problems contain arrays of interconnections, both among their constituent parts and, more troublesome, with other problems. Transboundary problems like acid rain bedevil policy makers, who must decide *which* problem in any bundle of interrelated problems is the most important. They also must estimate out how addressing that problem will affect the others. Finally, because some might throw up their hands at the complexities lain before them, they must calculate the costs of doing nothing at all.

With this in mind, the question of problems and agendas, and about the choices that confront policy makers, ultimately may come down to broader values and societal priorities. As Stone (1988: 7) argues, "the essence of policy making in political communities" is "the struggle over ideas." She continues:

> Ideas are the medium of exchange and a mode of influence even more powerful than money and votes and guns. . . . Ideas are at the center of all political conflict. Policy making, in turn, is a constant struggle over the criteria for classification, the boundaries of categories, and the definition of ideals that guide the way people behave.

"Policy makers are not faced with a given problem," wrote Lindblom (1966: 13), "they have to identify and formulate the problem." This is the guts of politics, a constant struggle among interests to get their respective problems onto the agenda of action, or, alternately, seeking with equal ardor to keep some matters out of the public realm. Such conflicts come in many guises: some problems seemingly never get onto the agenda of government action because prevailing social values, ideologies, or norms keep them off almost without debate. For others a pluralist conception of interested publics pushing for access onto the agenda seems the appropriate description of reality. Regardless which image holds in any particular situation, agenda formation is a process shaped by conflict.

B. Institutions and Agenda Setting

To acknowledge this last point also is to admit that the formal system of institutions and procedures within which problem definition and agenda-setting take place hardly is a neutral arena. Indeed, perhaps more noticeable than in any other facet of the study of policy formation generally is the reaffirmation of the importance of formal institutions, rules, procedures, and organizational hierarchies. The renewed interest in institutions within policy studies is a welcome reminder, at least for (and from) political scientists, that even the most "rational" human behavior takes place within contexts, some of them more sharply defined and enduring than others.

The formal superstructure of a system of governance powerfully shapes how problems are at least drawn to and dealt with by government. Writes Schattschneider (1960: 71):

> A conclusive way of checking the rise of conflict is simply to provide no arena for it or to create no public agency with power to do anything about it. There are an incredible number of devices for checking the development of conflict within the system. . . . All forms of political organization have a bias in favor of the exploitation of some kinds of conflict and the suppression of others because *organization is the mobilization of bias.* Some issues are organized into politics and others are organized out.

In a critique of Kingdon's (1984) pathbreaking work on agenda formation, Mucciaroni (1991: 10) argues that the literature frequently fails to appreciate the impacts on agendas generated by system sturcture. "Political institutions are structures with perhaps the greatest impact on policy," says Mucciaroni. "[They] make up the topography, the banks and riverbeds that channel and shape participants' behavior." And yet, as Schattschneider (1960: 72) argued, "One difficulty scholars have experienced in interpreting American politics has always been that the grand strategy of politics has concerned itself first of all with the structure of institutions. The function of institutions is to channel conflict; institutions do not treat all forms of conflict impartially." Studies of agenda setting focus generally on *nonstructural* variables—strategic elites, policy "streams," and so on—all of which probably are critical at the mid- and micro-levels of analysis, the levels of particular decision processes, formal governmental agendas, individual elites. But far less is discussed about the macro level, the "topography" of the system itself. Scholars acknowledge, usually in passing, that system structure has independent impacts *of some kind* (see Kingdon, 1984: 81), but there is remarkably little straightforward discussion about how features like genuine federalism, true separation of institutional power, distinctive means and staggered terms of selection have had *independent* impacts on the ways issues flow into and are dealt with by government in the United States.

Some scholars have addressed these matters more recently. Baumgartner (1989: 196) argues that all political elites practice Schattschneider's strategies of "socializing" and "privatizing" conflict regardless of institutional structures, yet, as he shows in comparing United States and French nuclear power policy making, precisely *how* respective elites do so is constrained by the system itself:

> The complicated institutional structures of the United States and the autonomy of a number of governmental authorities allowed opponents many opportunities to shift the venue of the debate to one where they could be successful. In France, on the other hand, a determined set of governmental agencies use a streamlined set of institutions and procedures in order to keep consideration of nuclear power restricted to a small set of experts with a shared interest in the growth of the program.

Systems of governance *do* have shapes—fixed points, boundaries, doorways, and so forth— and to recognize a system's shape also is to know something about the patterns of policymaking *possible* within that system. Looking at policy formation this ways allows the scholar to turn away from reductionism and toward a renewed effort to ask superficially simple questions about the macro-effects of any system of governance. The roles played by strategic elites, organized interests, political parties, and other actors without doubt are critical in agenda setting, and policy formation generally, but *only* as conditioned or structured by the biases of the system itself. Much of the literature on agenda setting talks about "access" as if institutions were mere gates, albeit with sentient gatekeepers. Yet, by virtue of constitutionally-mandated function, fundamental design, and legal jurisdiction, formal institutions do shape the way that issues get onto the agenda for action and are addressed (if only rhetorically) by policy makers. Policy entrepeneurs may shop for appropriate and opportune venues, and elites may define issues, but this freedom is constrained at least in part by the system's topography. Although Baumgartner and Jones (1990: 4) argue rightly that "there are no immutable rules which determine which institution in society will be granted jurisdiction over particular issues," there are nonetheless patterns influenced by formal rules and structures. What follows are but a few examples:

1. Degree of Centralized Governing Authority

A distinguishing feature of the U.S. system is its constitutional apportionment of true governing authority among a national government and an array of less powerful, but equally distinct, subnational bodies, each dealing with issues and problems within its particular jurisdiction. The effects of this particular structural feature on agendas—for example, how many or what types of issues never get to the national government in the first place, or, perhaps, not for a long while—still are not well understood. The British scholar H. G. Nicholas (1981: 21) reminds us that the U.S. Constitution "gives the federal government very little power to oblige the states to take positive action when they have a mind not to. . . . The overwhelming mass of American law is state-originated and state enforced without interference by the agencies of the federal government." Problems thus may percolate up to the national government only when they will not or cannot be addressed adequately by the various states. This picture is a bit simplified as past decades have witnessed tremendous blurring of jurisdictional lines and the creation of innumerable sectors of vertical linkages among federal, state and local officials based on program and problem realms, but the constitutional bifurcation of power remains, powerfully shaping issue dynamics. Variations in formal systems of governance among the various American states also provide a particularly rich medium of institutional niches and channels through which issues may bounce long before they become national agenda items. The tax revolt that marked so much of the politics of the 1980s began with California's Proposition 13 in no small way because that state's lenient initiative process provided a readier mechanism for translating majoritarian impulses into public policy than any found in many other states, or in the U.S. Constitution. Starting on the West Coast, the tax rebellion leapfrogged from state to state depending usually on the availability and stringency of state initiative and petition laws, before hitting Washington in more diffuse but still palpable ways.

Seen as a whole, the friction created by conflict among semi-autonomous states, added to tensions between the states and the national government, makes the process by which issues get to the national government more *dissipative* in the United States as compared to a more unitary system, where policy decisions radiate from the central government and where, by necessity, all issues must go for resolution. Federalism is a topography of many distinct (and surely not serial) sluicegates into which issues can be siphoned off before they build up the velocity necessary to reach the national government. This structural arrangement preserves a higher degree of localism in agendas than one might find in more unitary systems, and of course creates tremendous obstacles to rapid changes in national policy—just as the framers of the Constitution in many ways intended.

2. Separation of Institutional Powers

Another obvious question is how the tripartite division of functions embedded in the U.S. Constitution affects how issues are drawn to and dealt with by the national government. It is a systemic centrifuge of divided institutional power and fractionated representation that, in concert with federalism, is directed ultimately at dissipating spasms of majoritarian issue saliency before they produce rapid and potentially destabilizing national change. On the other hand, that same system, particularly through a legislature based on geographical representation, readily grants to smaller, more narrowly configured constitutuency interests a great deal of access—the basis of pluralist politics and theory. With this in mind, it may be no surprise, as Mucciaroni (1991: 11) suggests, that a Kingdon model of agenda setting—with its focus on the converging "streams" of ideas, actors, and political contexts—may be useful most "for describing policy-making in the United States, where the institutional structure is fragmented and permeable, where participation is particularistic and fluid, and coalitions are often temporary and ad hoc." How it applies to more centripetal or less articulated political systems, particularly those marked by strong party government or hegemonic bureaucracies, is far less certain.

3. Institutionally Induced Rhythms

The American system also provides a rather unique (even peculiar) *periodicity* to its issue dynamics via its constitutional provision for staggered-but-set terms of office and totally separate means of election. These create predictable "windows" (to use Kingdom's [1984] term) that, upon their opening, provide powerful if momentary avenues for agenda setting. The rigidity of the system also means, however, that legislators and, particularly, executives alike have much less control over their agendas than might those where incumbents can call elections or where the selection of one set of officials can influence powerfully that of the other. The opportunities for agenda influence where governments have more control over the spacing and timing of elections gives one a sense of possibly distinctive patterns in American issue dynamics.

4. Institutionally-Induced Instability

Finally, the robust constitutional array of checks and balances also means that these institutions—particularly Congress and the presidency—actively vie for primacy over agenda setting and problem definition in ways rare in other national systems of governance. For example, as Harrison and Hoberg (1991: 6) find in comparing regulatory styles in the United States and Canada, "conflict between legislative and executive branches in the U.S. often publicizes the regulatory agenda. In contrast, Canadian regulatory agencies and ministers exercise greater discretion with respect to publicizing their agenda." The tensions among the three separate and largely autonomous branches thus makes for highly fluid issue dynamics, particularly if viewed from the mid-level perspectives of congressional committees and executive agencies, or from the micro-level perspectives of individual decision makers. In the absence of strong, cohesive parties, the conflict between the executive and a bicameral legislature along—particularly with splits across partisan lines—makes predicting issue dynamics in the American system rather problematic.

With respect to its overall effects on agenda setting, the American system of governance is *both* absorptive and highly dissipative. Its competing centers of authority and many avenues for issue representation provide for more niches into which demands can go, a permeability that in many ways gives the system its resiliency and legitimacy. On the other hand, most issues are never dealt with by the national government because they are sluiced off either by other centers (e.g., the states) or bounce around almost indefinitely among the levels of federalism or the branches of the national government. The system's very design militates against a broadly arrayed issue (e.g., national health care) even getting serious attention within the national government unless societal or political perturbations are powerful enough to "boost" the issue with sufficient velocity to overcome the system's innate centrifuge. Seen from overhead, the U.S. system is incredibly bumpy and creates tremendous turbulence; friction that dissipates energy not unlike the ways in which the many eddies and channels of rock-filled streams slow the flow of water. In such ways, majoritarian impulses are chopped and channeled and major change is harder to achieve. Institutional design, seen from this perspective, shapes policy formation.

C. Images, Venues, Strategic Actors—And Politics

Although the nature of problems and the institutional superstructure of any system greatly shape the ways that issues get onto the agenda for action and, once there, how they are dealt with by policy makers, such "pre-decision" factors certainly are not deterministic. Politics, motivated by simple self-interest, shared ideals, values, or whatever, still matters in propelling problems through and past the obstacles that keep the agenda for action from getting overloaded. Someone has to care passionately if a perceived problem is to be something more—the *intensity* factor pluralists long have pointed to as a factor explaining why some groups succeed and others do not.

Some of the factors that propel problems onto the agenda for action obviously are exogenous: natural catastrophes, unanticipated human events (e.g., the 1990 Iraqi invasion of Kuwait), and technological or ecological changes, such as the legal implications of biotechnical research (Cobb and Elder, 1972: 84). And, of course, the pervasive and instantaneous nature of global communications allows events to dominate agendas ever more starkly and immediately, such as when images of famine in Africa or alleged atrocities in Bosnia stir mass publics and impel leaders into action. The telecommunications-imposed coziness of the global order may allow leaders far less latitude over their agendas than they might recognize, a condition some already are calling the "CNN curve" after the Cable News Network that has done so much to alter global news coverage and viewership. On the other hand, the rapidity with which news stories change might make externally induced agendas rather fluid. Mass publics whipsawed by shifting images might well be more easily placated by highly public but essentially symbolic responses.

Beyond these external factors, however, are the intense interests and strategic actors whose support for or hostility to issues matters most immediately in structuring the formal agenda for action. The opportunities for agenda influence, and the positions of leverage necessary for and available to potential actors of course vary across systems: ideologically cohesive parties (e.g., Israel, Jamaica); national or, even, subnational elites who control major voting blocs (e.g., India); strong bureaucratic (e.g., France), ruling party (e.g., Cuba), religious (e.g., Iran), or military (e.g., Nigeria) elites; hegemonic economic interests of whatever kind (e.g., the drug cartel in Colombia). In the United States the picture is of many actors and interests competing for access and influence from an abundance of strategic positions. Given the features of the formal system and the diversity within the nation itself, it is no wonder that studies of agenda formation in the United States tend to take as their points of departure the pluralist image of competition among organized interests, both in and out of government.

"In a system like the U.S.," argues MIlward (1991: 3), "there are many different access points and one institution or jurisdiction rarely controls a given policy domain. *Policy communities* serve to knit this fragmented system of governance together." Whether such a community is depicted as a "subgovernment" (Freeman, 1955), "issue network" (Heclo, 1978), or 'advocacy coalition' (Sabatier, 1988), within each there are assumed to exist "actors from a variety of public and private organizations at all levels of government who share a set of basic beliefs (policy goals plus causal and other perceptions) and who seek to manipulate the rules of various government institutions in order to achieve those goals over time" (Sabatier, 1991: 279). This depiction in many respects remands the discussion to Schattschneider's (1960: 3) classic assessment, "At the nub of politics are, first, the way in which the public participate in the spread of conflict, and second, the processes by which the unstable relation of the public to the conflict is controlled." Political conflict is, to repeat, a tension between those seeking to expand (or socialize) participation in a debate and those working to minimize (or privatize) participation. "Public policies are made through the interaction of the images which are used to explain them and the institutions which are able to claim jurisdiction over them." Baumgartner and Jones (1989: 1) argue. "Policy makers attempt to manipulate both of these factors in order to achieve their programmatic goals." However stated, struggle is over *both* the definition of issues and control over the processes and arenas within which decisions are made. Having formal jurisdiction is not enough.

Several recent longitudinal studies of policy formation bear out this point forcefully. Bosso (1987: 256), examining 40 years of U.S. federal policy toward chemical pesticides, concludes that perhaps "the most powerful change in the pesticides policy case was its being redefined as an environmental matter; *loss of the power to define the issue* was probably the most critical factor causing the decline of the pesticides subgovernment" [our emphasis]. Mucciaroni (1990: 266), in a lengthy study of postwar federal employment policy, argues cogently that

Of the three factors (interests, institutions, and ideas), none had a more substantial and direct impact on charting the direction and framing the content of employment policy than ideas. . . . Institutions may have blocked certain alternatives, shaped the packaging of programs, influenced the timing of changes, and led to implementation failures. The political activities of organized interests (or lack of them) may have influenced the level and distribution of program benefits and circumscribed the role of employment programs in the economy. But it was the subjective predispositions that policy makers brought to their task and their receptivity to the ideas of experts and reformers that had the greatest influence on the substance of policy.

Such case studies are given critical empirical support in important comparative work by Baumgartner and Jones (1990a, 1990b), who look at several policy areas (smoking, pesticides, nuclear power) over time and conclude that "failure to control the images associated with a policy can lead to loss of control over the policy itself, even when it appears to be firmly within the institutional jurisdiction of influential groups all of whom favor the current direction of public policy. Control over issue definition is key to policy formation.

These studies also unearth strikingly similar long-term issue dynamics. In most cases, policies were formulated originally under conditions of relatively limited participation and mostly positive public perceptions of the issue's image. The result is subgovernment dominance, an irony in that most of these policy areas studies began with the late 1940s and early 1950s, when pluralism emerged as the guiding paradigm of American politics and political science. What follows are efforts by defenders of the status quo to manipulate both the image of the policy area and the venues for policy formation, particularly as more and ever-diverse interests both in and outside government recognize a stake in and, thus, demand to take part in (or be part of) decision making for what becomes an increasingly controversial issue. In each case, and usually in the early 1970s, the subgovernment defending the status quo crumbles or becomes distended, and in its place emerges a broader, more permeable, and far more inchoate "sloppy hexagon" (Jones, 1979), "issue network" (Heclo, 1987), "policy community" (Milward, 1991), or "advocacy coalition" (Sabatier, 1988). This relentless socialization of conflict eventually produces great policy fluidity and, even, stalemate, at least until the next time there occurs an imbalance among public perceptions and the array of interests (see Baumgartner and Jones, 1990a; Bosso, 1987; Hoberg, 1992; Jones, 1975; Mucciaroni, 1990). Whether it be the "intrusion" of environmental perspectives into the debate over pesticides, of health views in the cases of smoking or nuclear power, or the battle over core values on an array of social policies, whoever best manipulates the image of an issue has an edge in the battle over the agenda for action and, as a result, an advantage in policy formation.

Finally, these studies share a focus on configurations of shared policy or issue interests, not on mass behavior, the rough structure of the economy, class or other elite backgrounds, individual leaders, or any single institution. As Sabatier (1991: 269) argues clearly, "one of the clearest conclusions to emerge from the policy literature is that understanding the policy process requires looking at the intergovernmental policy community or subsystem—composed of bureaucrats, legislative personnel, interest group leaders, researchers, and specialist reporters within a substantive policy area—as the basic unit of study." This perspective has practical and normative implications. In tracing policy configurations these longitudinal studies of policy formation conclude that, at least in the United States, the nature of the policy agenda and, thus, the direction of public policy, usually is in greater flux than one might assume by looking at class structure, ideologies, or institutions alone. There is change amidst seeming stability. As Baumgartner and Jones (1990a: 24) suggest

Pluralism, then, is not invariably conservative. The existence of multiple venues certainly makes it difficult to rout the old order. But it also allows new policy ideas to find niches within which to flourish. Because powerful economic interests cannot normally dominate all venues, they can lose control of the policy image that protects them if they do not also control policy images. As images change, so does the possibility for dramatic policy change contrary to the will of those previously favored by governmental arrangements.

How much this assessment pertains to other political systems is as yet unclear, largely because of the relative scarcity of good longitudinal policy studies, especially across systems (but see Baumgartner, 1989; Lundqvist, 1980). A cursory look at other advanced industrial systems, at least, suggests that much of the same kinds of issue-based dynamics take place, although in forms congruent with a system's particular structural characteristics and underlying social values (Vogel, 1986). In any case, the primacy of agenda setting in policy formation is more evident than ever.

III. POLICY DESIGN AND THE CHOICE OF INSTRUMENTS

Formulation is the least analytically developed stage in the conventional policy-making process model; knowledge of its dynamics is limited to actual experience or to case study accounts. As yet, we do not have the degree of understanding about how governments fashion remedies that we do about how they choose problems to address, or have those problems thrust upon them. (Linder and Peters, 1990b: 104–105)

Having stressed the importance of agendas and issue definition, we acknowledge that these dynamics are only parts of the broader policy formation equation. The remainder involves designing specific formal policy *outputs*—statutes, programs, regulations, and so forth—that can generate the necessary and sufficient clearance from those who influence decision making (e.g., legislatures, executives, bureaucrats, and, even, citizens) and, one hopes, actually attack the problem. The implementation literature of the 1970s and early 1980s greatly improved our understanding of why policies sometimes fail, but, as Palumbo and Calista (1990: 4–6) point out, much of this scholarship too frequently erred in assuming (1) policies almost *always* fail, if only because costs and benefits were defined so narrowly and instrumentally that "success" was unlikely; (2) implementation, like administration, was somehow both conceptually and operationally separate from other aspects of policymaking, such as obtaining political support; (3) definitions of implementation as an activity in and of itself usually were narrow and technical, focussing almost exclusively on the delivery systems of "nonpolitical" bureaucratic agencies; and finally (4) problem definitions and policy designs usually are clear and unambiguous, thus program failure results inherently from misdirected or poor implementation. But, as Palumbo and Calista (1990: 5) say about this last point, "problem definition and policy design are *political activities* [our emphasis], and therefore, they are products of conflict that results in bargaining and compromise." Formation and implementation cannot be thought of as separate activities.

The literature on policy design to emerge in the mid-1980s begins from this point of reference, and has, as May (1991a: 188) writes, an overall "emphasis on matching content of a given policy to the political context in which the policy is formulated and implemented." Those writing in this vein in many ways want to reorient the scholarship on policy formation back to the acknowledgement that the *initial design* of formal policy outputs matters, and that the policy studies have precious little understanding about the actual efficacy of various kinds of formal outputs, particularly across policies or nations. More important, this approach seeks to address directly the reality that every choice of "policy instrument" reflects, and therefore must take into account, broader societal, economic, technical, and political contexts both among decision makers and those for whom policy outputs are intended. Effective policies, say Schneider and Ingram (1990: 77), "must motivate individuals to engage in policy-preferred behavior." A more elegant definition of effectiveness is yet to be found.

A. The Elements of Design

Keeping in mind this goal of creating effective policy outputs, any theory of policy design contains elements that address the (1) the nature of problems, goals, and, outcomes—what is to be achieved and why; (2) the nature of target populations—who is to be affected; (3) rules that specify what target populations and the agents of policy implementation can and cannot do; and (4) the tools or incentives embedded in policy outputs that will make it likelier that goals will be achieved. Much of the discussion that follows is adapted from Schneider and Ingram (1990: 80–88).

1. Problems, Goals, and Outputs

We already have spent a great deal of time discussing the nature of problems and the definition of alternatives, but beyond these dynamics is the actual expression, through formal policy outputs, of what decision makers *want* to achieve. Yet policies too often contain multiple goals, either explicit or implicit, which themselves also "change over time and change in relation to perceptions of what is possible to achieve" (Schneider and Ingram, 1990: 83), so implementation is part of a hopefully iterative process of policy learning. Any valid theory of design thus must be able, at minimum, to explain how differences in the nature of goals and policy outputs will lead directly to, or at least make more likely, distinct policy outcomes.

2. Target Populations

The behavior of target populations powerfully affects policy success or failure, and thus the contours of policy design. In crafting a policy designed to deter drug abuse, or sexual practices linked to the spread of AIDS, the choice of policy instruments will vary tremendously according to whether target populations are educated, affluent, and generally healthy or, by contrast, uneducated, poor, and generally unserved by the health system. The former are likelier to respond sufficiently to the availability of information connecting behavior to outcomes, and to the implications that continued behavior might well jeopardize their lives; the latter probably will need an array of additional social services (e.g., health care, jobs) to reinforce any message, no matter how potent normatively.

Any study of policy design, particularly in democratic political systems, thus must take into account "*policy participation*," which refers to "the decisions and actions of direct and indirect target populations that impinge upon achievements of policy goals" (Schneider and Ingram, 1990: 84). Such participation can be assessed along several dimensions, keeping in mind that the nature of the problem and of the target groups still play major roles in the choices made:

a. *Voluntary Utilization of Available Opportunities Versus Induced Compliance with Directives.* Policies designed according to the former can be oriented more to providing information to individuals (e.g., locations and operating hours of recycling centers), and thus are easier to design and implement (not to mention less expensive), while those requiring compliance probably will focus more on sanctions (e.g., higher waste disposal costs for nonrecyclers). In the latter case, policy participation is likely to be more conflictual, and success more problematic.

b. *Society Versus the Individual.*   The perceived nature of the goods will affect policy participation. Outputs might be public goods (e.g., pollution abatement) where policy makers need to educate citizens and spread out risk, or merely may distribute particularistic benefits (e.g., social security checks) requiring little of the individual save political support should benefits get threatened. Simple distributive policy outputs thus are far easier to design and implement than any attempting to deal with public goods and their attendant "free rider" problems (see Bosso, 1987; Ripley and Franklin, 1984).

c. *Coproduction Versus Counterproduction.*   The first concept refers to voluntary "decisions and actions taken by citizens in response to policy initiatives that constitute or facilitate the achievement of policy goals," the latter as "decisions and actions taken by citizens in response to policy initiatives that thwart achievement of policy goals" (Schneider and Ingram, 1990: 85–86). This dimension may involve, for example, whether individuals during a drought respond to pleas to conserve water or, in line with perfectly (if narrowly) self-interested behavior, they take advantage of the situation by continuing wasteful practices in the assumption that even more water will be available if everyone *else* conserves. The latter type of behavior—or a priori assumptions that such responses will dominate—obviously would impel far more coercive policy outputs.

d. *Parallel Production Versus Parallel Counterproduction.*   This final dimension refers to when citizens act independently, without directives, and their actions promote or thwart the achievement of policy goals. People who pick up litter or conserve water because it seems like "the right thing to do" can be said to engage in parallel production; those who litter or waste water obviously are acting counterproductively, even though there may be no policy directing them *not* to act in these ways. This dimension, not surprisingly, concerns such factors as levels of education, societal norms, culture, ideologies, and values (i.e., "Driving my car whenever, wherever, and for as long as I like is my right as an American") and designing policies to undo years of accepted (or ignored) behavior obviously is rather problematic.

    "Policy designs are more likely to be successful," say Schneider and Ingram (1990: 86), "if they include targets who are connected in logical ways to desired ends, *and* who can be motivated to engage in the policy participation that is needed." In this sense, and fortunately for most modern democracies, citizens generally are willing to act in ways that boost the likelihood of policy success. They generally obey the law, respond to appeals of what they regard as legitimate authority, take advantage of opportunities to maximize their own well-being, and even display notions about a public good. Political culture, public values, a polity's history, and the degree to which citizens regard government and the law as legitimate, all matter, although how much and in what particular mix remains a question.

    We also should note, in this regard, that the level of government and the nature of policy agents—those responsible for implementation—also must be factored into the equation. "Whereas most national politics is about principles, regulations, and funding," argue Bolland, et al. (1991:16), "politics at the local level tends more directly to concern people and their needs." National policy makers can argue that principles are important (e.g., whether a city has a responsibility for its homeless population), but for "street level bureaucrats" like social workers or police officers the "targets" of public policy have names and faces. Policies guided by grand ideals or ideologies that fail to take into account elemental human factors probably will be regarded as misdirected, even cruel, by those in the front lines, and the success of a policy will undermined accordingly.

3. Policy Rules

Policy rules "tell targets and agents what they must (or may) do, or what they must not do, when to do it, and how it should be done" (Schneider and Ingram, 1990: 86). Policy participation in this line of thought is affected by rules governing *timing* of action, how quickly compliance is supposed to occur, and those that control "feedback about effects"—how quickly evaluation of program success or failure is supposed to happen. Rules mandating speedy implementation and almost instantaneous evaluation, such as in crises, obviously structure a far different participatory role among both agents and target populations than do those where implementation proceeds in phases and where measuring results can take years (see, e.g., Ripley and Franklin, 1984).

B. Tools: The Choice of Policy Instruments

A line of inquiry in its own right is to understand and, perhaps, prescribe the choices of tools used by government to address perceived problems. Schneider and Ingram (1990: 87) define tools as "explicit or implicit incentives and other means imbedded in the policy that increase the probability of agents and targets taking actions in concert with policy objectives." Policies can only work through people, both as the agents of implementation and the target populations, so the choice of tools hinges on assumptions about human motivations. Schneider and Ingram examine the behavioral assumptions within policy tools by looking at dimensions based on strategies the tools employ to elicit the desired policy participation. In each case the choice of tools requires some assessment of the type of policy participation needed and, more important, of how target populations will react to policy proposals.

1. Authority

This dimension refers to reliance on the inherent power of the state, and the expertise that resides within its hierarchical arrangements. Policy instruments based on authority can include those aimed at enhancing citizen belief in the justice of the law and the legitimacy of the state, both of which can induce compliance. However, as Schneider and Ingram (1990: 4; see also Bolland, et al., 1991) argue, "tools that rely upon authority are not likely to work as expected when there are strong cross-cutting factors, such as those exerted by powerful and influential interest groups on local-level officials who are attempting to implement federal policy guidelines." The record of federal intervention in local implementation of civil rights laws comes to mind as an example of what happens when moral appeals alone do not work.

2. Incentives

In this dimension government employs payoffs, either positive or negative, to induce desired behavior. Reliance on incentives assumes that individuals will respond, which is not necessarily the case when issues involve core values (e.g., opposition to sex education in the schools) or when people truly cannot overcome entrenched behavior. Using tangible, direct payoffs might be the easiest way to induce desired behavior (e.g., cash subsidies to lower grain production), but such incentives may not always be available.

3. Capacity Building

This dimension involves providing knowledge, information, or resources to enable individuals or groups to take the actions needed, or it simply can involve removing obstructions to action. It also may presume norms that support an activist citizenry. The data provisions in the 1986 Emergency Planning and Community Right to Know Act, for example, enable communities to know what kinds of chemical emissions are being generated by local businesses. Such data on possible health threats are credited for giving grassroots activists the capacity to mobilize citizens who might not be active in politics or even consider themselves environmentalists.

4. *Symbolic and Hortatory*

Such instruments aim to change individual perceptions through manipulation of symbols or policy "rationales," or through public relations campaigns, among other mechanisms. Exhortations during World War II to buy Liberty Bonds worked because of shared beliefs about aiding the war effort. Discussions about problem definition fits into this dimension, particularly insofar that mass media are instrumental vehicles for altering perceptions of events, issues, or problems. Policy makers facing austere budgets or entrenched opposition to substantive outputs can always resort to public appeals or the manipulation of symbols to achieve a degree of desired behavior, although the longer-term efficacy of such approaches is somewhat in doubt.

5. *Learning*

Such tools "provide mechanisms for gaining feedback about the effects of previous actions, or reactions of others to the results of previous actions" (Schneider and Ingram, 1990: 95). Using surveys to gauge public responses to policy directions, and making changes in policies as a result of the survey data, might be considered one such tool.

6. *Policy Design Without Publics*

May (1991a: 191–192) adds another dimension to this interplay of target groups, contexts, and instrument choice when he asks how the relative presence or absence of an issue "public" or "publics" affects the overall equation. Most of the literature on policy formation in the United States, at least, falls in the tradition of pluralist conceptions of politics, and thus looks almost entirely at policies *with* publics. In such cases, and in line with key pluralist tenets, policy options "are fashioned and choices are made in policy worlds comprised of multiple publics with competing interests and differential resources." At the other end of the continuum, however, are policies shaped in the absence of strongly interested publics and within almost apolitical policy environments. Says May (1991a: 194):

> Publics surrounding the issue are neither extensive nor a source of major conflict. Issue networks or policy communities are only weakly developed. Belief systems concerning problems and solutions are tentative and dominated by technocratic expert opinions. Relevant policy discussions take place in the backwaters of political institutions.

The possibilities available to policy makers in such a case obviously differ greatly from an issue context of salient public conflict, strong partisanship, and highly visible decision dynamics.

However, issues and thus policymaking dynamics are not fixed in stone. An issue without an apparent public can evolve with time into one marked by "normal" politics, at least as practiced in the United States. See, for example, Bosso (1987) on the evolution of pesticides policy; Weingast (1980) or Baumgartner and Jones (1990a) on perceptions about nuclear power. The point is that such differences pose distinct design and implementation challenges. Designing and implementing policies addressed to discernible and competing publics requires balancing acts, with policymakers worrying both about structuring interest representation and building sufficient coalitions of political support. The picture is of classic pluralist conflict, with outputs legitimized as the good policy if only they survived the gauntlet. But for policies without publics May (1991a: 198) says, "problems are ill-defined, responses uncertain, and the political environment unlikely to be a severe constraint." Policy under such contexts is likely to be made by experts guided by their own, probably narrower, conceptions of the public good, and, while there are fewer obvious constraints to implementation, policies are likelier to fail for sheer lack of public support, rather than any active opposition. As May suggests, the broader policy environment must be taken into account in discussing policy design, choice of instruments, or implementation.

C. Tools and National Contexts

Finally, a key question to be addressed is whether the policy design literature—indeed, the policy literature as a whole—is overly nation-specific. Theories of policy design cannot help but be constrained by the same contexts that constrain policymaking (Linder and Peters, 1990b: 104). Howlett (1991: 15), after assessing prevailing theoretical approaches to policy design in American, British, and Canadian policy studies, finds that none are close to being the "general theories" that transcend national boundaries or styles of policy making. Given the assumptions embedded in the policy design approach, he adds, this apparent lack of transportability is "a direct result of the fact that, as all of the analysts have pointed out, instrument choice *is* context bound. As such, it can never exist as a separate theory of political life, but must exist as part of a more general theory of national public policy making."

Howlett concludes that a fruitful avenue lies in the expanding on the notion of "national styles" of policymaking explored previously by such works as Lundqvist (1980) and Kelman (1981) on the United States and Sweden; Nelkin and Pollack (1982) on France and West Germany; Richardson, et al. (1982) on Western Europe broadly; Harrison and Hoberg (1991) on the United States and Canada; and Vogel (1986) on the United States and Great Britain. The relative aridity of comparative policy studies might be reversed with a renewed appreciation for the relative *distinctiveness* of national policy styles amidst problem-induced similarities. For example, as Vogel (1986: 250) points out in comparing the United States and Britain on environmental policy, "the relative formalism of the American regulatory system—its reliance on clearly defined rules and standards—reflects the inadequacy of informal mechanisms of social control within a highly individualistic culture . . ." The United States *is* different, but so is Canada, Kenya, and Argentina. While to compare is first and foremost to seek out similarities—ideally, generalizeable statements that apply across problem types and systems—it is also to admit to a sensitivity for the unique. Thus, there may be no single model, no grand theory of policy design, but there are nonetheless plenty of common problems, instruments, and to some degree, policy styles. Much more comparatively focussed empirical and conceptual work needs to be done to flesh out the relationships between national (and subnational) policy styles and the selection of policy instruments, but also needed are more solid case studies upon which good mid-level theories can be built. Particularly useful would more comparative versions of the kinds of longitudinal case studies that have begun to shed new light on how problems, policies, and policy communities evolve. Even as the world seems gripped by change, what change looks like is not at all clear.

IV. POLICY FORMATION IN A TURBULENT WORLD

Rosenau (1990) argues persuasively that the world is entering into an age of unparalleled "turbulence" with respect to the interactions among nation-states, subnational and cross-national institutions and nongovernmental organizations, and publics. Citizens everywhere are more informed, and more sophisticated, if only because of the effects of telecommunications technology, travel, and an ever-interdependent global economy. These same exogenous variables have eroded the hegemony of any nation-state, even over its own citizens, while nongovernmental organizations (e.g., Greenpeace) operate freely as global entities. The picture is of a "hyper-pluralistic" and "multicentric" world, where interactions (e.g., among American environmental groups, the United Nations, transnational corporations, and Brazil over saving Amazonian rain forests) are more interconnected, more fluid, less predictable, and, most apparent to the average citizen, disturbingly fast paced. Says Rosenau (1990: 8):

> Unlike conventional diplomatic or organizational situations, which evolve in the context of formal procedures, cautious bargaining, and bureaucratic intertia, those beset by turbulent conditions develop rapidly as the repercussions of the various participants' actions cascade through their networks of interdependence. Sustained by the complexity and dynamism of diverse actors whose goals and activities are inextricably linked to each other, and facilitated by technologies that transmit information almost instantaneously, turbulent conditions tend to be marked by quick responses, insistent demands, temporary coalitions, and policy reversals, all of which propel the course of events swiftly if erratically along the fault lines of conflict and cooperation.

Perturbations taking place in such a world cascade with maddening rapidity through societies and political systems, and straining the fabric of the one and the formal processes of the other. The real world also challenges our constructs about policy formation in two ways. First, it makes even more useful as a focal point Sabatier's notion of advocacy coalitions, because the very idea denotes networks of alliances based on specific problems and issues, narrowly focused and ever fluid dynamics that mirror what probably is happening. The focus for the student of public formation should be on such coalitions and, ideally, in a comparative perspective.

The second point to be made concerns the traditional linearity of the study of public policy processes. We always understood that stage models were *meant* as heuristics, that the real world seemed sloppier and more random than our models ever could convey. Yet too often those subtle caveats were forgotten or ignored in a physics/economics-induced search for grand unified theories of causality. The nature of such theories certainly clashed with gut feelings that the real world was a lot less linear and mechanistic than the models could handle. The physical and natural sciences themselves are themselves turning away from models and toward the far more dynamic conceptions of nonlinear systems, such as chaos theory, if only because such approaches better explain *change* in a world characterized by flux, not stable equilibria.

Chaos theory is beginning to be applied within the social sciences, and the conceptual implications, at least, are profound. For example, among the key tenets of chaos theory is the notion of "sensitive dependence on initial conditions," the realization that relatively small changes in original conditions can have profound systemic impacts. In this vein, as Cobb and Elder (1972), among many, long have pointed out, relatively small technological or societal pertubations can have massive effects on issue dynamics, and thus on policy formation. A single private citizen using a portable videocamera to record a case of apparent police brutality in Los Angeles can produce "shock waves" that reverberate throughout the society (even the world) and which can themselves affect policies at several levels of government. Applying the same concept to the American system of government, we can see how macrolevel relationships among the three branches also can be affected powerfully by relatively microscopic changes in initial conditions—such as a single senatorial election—because such pertubations are amplified by the struggle among the branches. All this probably looks a lot less chaotic as we focus away from the macro-level of analysis and toward more mid-level (e.g., committee jurisdictions) and micro-level (e.g., lesiglative districts) issue dynamics, which can seem very stable even as the macro picture gets incredibly messy. The point is that such a world of interconnected components and constant flux looks a lot different, but truer to form, than those created through models that assume equilibrium as normalcy.

In many ways, the healthiest trend is the admission, albeit a grudging one for many, that policy making is not engineering and the study of policy formation cannot be a laboratory science. In policy making contexts do matter, citizens do not always act according to narrow economic self-interest, and decisions are made on the basis of incomplete or biased information. Worse, at least for the elegance of our models, such "irrational" factors as ideas, values, and passions do have impacts. After all, politics is about values, not just "interests." As Nelson (1977: 14) reminds us, "The questions of what values, and whose values, ultimately are to count inherently must be answered through political process, not rational analysis alone."

REFERENCES

Bachrach, P., and Baratz, M. (1970). *Power and Poverty: Theory and Practice.* Oxford University Press, New York.

Baumgartner, F. R. (1989). *Conflict and Rhetoric in French Policymaking.* University of Pittsburgh Press, Pittsburgh.

Baumgartner, F. R., and Jones, B. D. (1989). Shifting images and venues of a public issue: Explaining the demise of nuclear power in the United States. Paper presented at the Annual Meeting of the American Political Science Association, 1989, Atlanta, Georgia.

—— (1990). Attention and valence in agenda-setting. Paper presented at the Annual Meeting of the Southern Political Science Association, Atlanta, Georgia.

Bolland, J. M., Hoefer, R. M., and Wilson, J. V. (1991). The Multiple Faces of Agenda-Setting. Paper presented at the 1991 Annual Meeting of the American Political Science Association, Washington, DC.

Bosso, C. J. (1987). *Pesticides and Politics: The Life Cycle of a Public Issue.* University of Pittsburgh Press, Pittsburgh.

—— (1989). Setting the Public Agenda: Mass Media and the Ethiopian Famine. In M. Margolis and G. Mauser (Eds.). *Manipulating Public Opinion: Essays on Public Opinion as a Dependent Variable.* Brooks-Cole, Monterey, Calif., pp. 153–174.

Cobb, R. W., and Elder, C. D. (1972). *Participation in American Politics: The Dynamics of Agenda-Building.* Allyn & Bacon, Boston.

Downs, A. (1972). Up and down with ecology: The issue-attention cycle. *Public Interest* 28: 38–50.

Edelman, M. (1964). *The Symbolic Uses of Politics.* University of Illinois Press, Urbana.

Freeman, J. L. (1955). *The Political Process.* Random House, New York.

Gleick, J. (1987). *Chaos: Making a New Science.* Penguin Books, New York.

Harrison, K., and Hoberg, G. (1991). Setting the environmental agenda in Canada and the United States: The cases of dioxin and radon. *Canadian Journal of Political Science* 24 (1): 3–27.

Heclo, H. (1978). Issue networks and the executive establishment. In *The New American Political System.* A. King (Ed.). American Enterprise Institute, Washington, DC, pp. 87–124.

Hoberg, G. (1992). *Pluralism by Design: Environmental Policy and the American Regulatory State.* Praeger, New York.

Howlett, M. (1991). Policy instruments, policy styles, and policy implementation: National approaches to theories of instrument choice. *Policy Studies Journal* 19(Spring): 1–21.

Jensen, R. V. (1987). Classical chaos. *American Scientist* 75: 168–181.

Jones, C. O. (1975). *Clean Air: The Policies and Politics of Air Pollution Control.* University of Pittsburgh Press, Pittsburgh.

—— (1979). American politics and the organization of energy decision making. *Annual Review of Energy* 4: 99–110.

Jones, C. O., and Matthes, D. (1983). Policy formation. In *Encyclopedia of Policy Studies*. S. S. Nagel (Ed.). Marcel Dekker, New York, pp. 117–142.

Kelman, S. (1981). *Regulating America, Regulating Sweden: A Comparative Study of Occupational Safety and Health Policy*. MIT Press, Cambridge, MA.

Kingdon, J. (1984). *Ideas, Alternatives, and Public Policies*. Little, Brown, Boston.

Lindblom, C. (1966). *The Policymaking Process*. Prentice-Hall, Englewood Cliffs, NJ.

Linder, S. H., and Peters, B. G. (1990a). Research perspectives on the design of public policy: Implementation, formulation, and design. In *Implementation and the Policy Process: Opening Up the Black Box*. D. J. Palumbo and D. J. Calista (Eds.). Greenwood Press, Westport, CT, pp. 51–66.

—— (1990b). The design of instruments for public policy. In *Policy Theory and Policy Evaluation: Concepts, Knowledge, Causes, and Norms*. S. S. Nagel (Ed.). Greenwood Press, Westport, CT, pp. 104–119.

Lowi, T. J. (1992). The state of political science: How we became what we study. *American Political Science Review* 86(March): 1–7.

Lundqvist, L. J. (1980). *The Hare and the Tortoise: Clean Air Policies in the United States and Sweden*. University of Michigan Press, Ann Arbor.

May, P. J. (1991a). Reconsidering policy design: Policies and publics. *Journal of Public Policy* 11: 187–206.

—— (1991b). Policy learning and policy failure. Paper presented at the Annual Meeting of the American Political Science Association, Washington, DC.

Milward, H. B. (1991). Ideas, agendas and public policy. *Policy Currents* 1(January): 2–3.

Milward, H. B., and Laird, W. (1990). Where does policy come from? Paper presented at the Annual Meeting of the Western Political Science Association, Newport Beach, CA.

Mucciaroni, G. (1991). A Critique of the Garbage Can Model of Policy-Making. Mimeograph.

—— (1991). *The Political Failure of Employment Policy, 1945–1982*. University of Pittsburgh Press, Pittsburgh.

Nagel, S. S. (1988). Projecting trends in public policy. Paper presented at the Annual Meeting of the American Political Science Association, Washington, DC.

Nelkin, D., and Pollack, M. (1982). *The Atom Besieged: Antinuclear Movements in France and Germany*. MIT Press, Cambridge, MA.

Nelson, R. R. (1977). *The Moon and the Ghetto: An Essay on Public Policy Analysis*. Norton, New York.

Nicholas, H. G. (1980). *The Nature of American Politics*. Oxford University Press, New York.

O'Brien, D. (1986). *Storm Center: The Supreme Court in American Politics*. Norton, New York.

Paehlke, R. (1989). *Environmentalism and the Future of Progressive Politics*. Yale University Press, New York, CT.

Palumbo, D. J., and Calista, D. J. (1990). Opening up the black box: Implementation and the policy process. In *Implementation and the Policy Process: Opening Up the Black Box*. D. J. Palumbo and D. J. Calista (Eds.). Greenwood Press, Westport, CT, pp. 3–17.

Portney, K. E. (1986). *Approaching Public Policy Analysis*. Prentice-Hall, Englewood Cliffs, NJ.

Portz, J. (1990). *The Politics of Plant Closings*. Kansas University Press, Lawrence.

Richardson, J. (Ed.) (1982). *Policy Styles in Western Europe*. Allen and Unwin, London.

Ringquist, E. (1992). Reason, scientific certainty, and strategically crafted argument: Alternative theories of public policy in water development. Presented at the 1992 Annual Meeting of the Western Political Science Association, San Francisco.

Ripley, R. B. (1985). *Policy Analysis in Political Science*. Nelson-Hall, Chicago.

Rochefort, D. A. (1986). *American Social Welfare Policy: Dynamics of Formulation and Change*. Westview Press, Boulder, CO.

Sabatier, P. (1988). An advocacy coalition framework of policy change and the role of policy-oriented learning therein. *Policy Sciences* 21(Fall): 129–68.

—— (1991). Public Policy: Toward better theories of the policy process, in *Political Science*: *Looking to the Future*, vol. II, W. Crotty (Ed.). Northwestern University, Evanston, Ill.

Schattschneider, E. E. (1960). *The Semi-Sovereign People*: *A Realist's View of Democracy in America*. Dryden Press, Hinsdale, IL.

Schneider, A. L., and Ingram, H. (1990). Policy design: Elements, premises, and strategies. In *Policy Theory and Policy Evaluation*: *Concepts, Knowledge, Causes, and Norms*. S. S. Nagel (Ed.). Greenwood Press, Westport, CT, pp. 77–101.

Stone, D. A. (1988). *Policy Paradox and Political Reason*. Scott, Foresman, Glenview, IL.

Thaysen, U., Davidson, R. H., and Livingston, R. G. (1991). *The U.S. Congress and the German Bundestag*. Westview Press, Boulder, CO.

Truman, D. B. (1964). *The Governmental Process*: *Political Interests and Public Opinion*. Knopf, New York.

Vogel, D. (1986). *National Styles of Regulation*: *Environmental Policy in Great Britain and the United States*. Cornell University Press, Ithaca, NY.

Wilson, J. Q. (1973). *Political Organizations*. Basic Books, New York.

Winter, S. (1990). Integrating implementation research. In *Implementation and the Policy Process*: *Opening Up the Black Box*. D. J. Palumbo and D. J. Calista (Eds.). Greenwood Press, Westport, CT, pp. 20–38.

6
Policy Implementation

Donald J. Calista
Marist College, Poughkeepsie, New York

The field of implementation research is reconstructing itself. Following 20 years of empirical studies—mostly of the case variety—implementation researchers are generating propositions and hypotheses from which explanatory models, even theories, are emerging. These are no small feats. The much "older" field of policy formation is no better off. In fact, it has been implementation anomalies that have compelled the entire field of policy intervention to examine its own assumptions (Hofferbert, 1990). Implementation is now far from being the missing link in policy-making research (Hargrove, 1975). It is now integral to the field of policy intervention, including recognizing its influence on policy formation. A central theme of this chapter, therefore, relates implementation research to issues being examined across the field of policy intervention.

This chapter outlines how implementation research affects the larger field of policy intervention. First, the subfield of implementation will be identified and defined. Second, the contributions of implementation research will be reviewed. These discussions will serve a joint purpose. They will demonstrate how the outcomes of implementation research provide the underpinnings for emerging theoretical directions in policy intervention. Correspondingly, implications of theory building for practitioners, exemplified by both politicians and administrators, will be noted. The exploration will also assess how well emerging theories overcome certain weaknesses exhibited by implementation research. The candidate implementation theory must be robust, that is, inclusive, in order to contribute to a theory of policy intervention (Yin, 1982). Accordingly, a credible theory must be capable of coupling a cluster of embryonic implementation elements into higher-order policy intervention statements (Ostrom, 1989). A theory's credibility will also increase the more its propositions translate into hypotheses that are falsifiable.[1]

I. DEFINING THE FIELD

A. Faithful Adherence, Ambiguity, and Legalistic Implementation

It seems obvious to say that implementation represents the faithful fulfillment of policy intentions by public servants. Most early research accepts intentions at face value (VanHorn, 1979); implementation becomes believable through its adherence to policy intentions (Sabatier and Mazmanian, 1979). Researchers fully acknowledge, however, that policy outputs result from compromises hammered out in fragmented and dispersed decisionmaking environments, often characterized by conflicts over basic political purposes (Radin, 1977; Sharpe, 1985). Despite the apparency of this highly permeable situation, implementation is generally held accountable for policy failures. Faithful fulfillment of intentions gets confounded because, as the earliest research reveals, implementation must create "joint actions" out of previously unrelated actors and agencies—not always committed to constructing common outcomes (Pressman and Wildavsky, 1973). Similarly, discrepancies appear in outcomes because bureaucrats doing the implementing may restrain themselves from embracing policy intentions fully (Bullock, 1981). If bureaucrats seem to be writing their own implementation agendas, however, this does not simply mean self-aggrandizement is occurring.

Policy intentions often overlook the demands of implementation (Smith, 1973). Bureaucrats face uncertainties in coping with the everyday, and sometimes hostile, requirements of their jobs (Lipsky, 1971). Across the broad range of rehabilitative services, for example, bureaucrats are usually dealing with intractable clients (Nelson, 1977; Hargrove and Glidewell, 1990). Additionally, bureaucrats must frequently contend with ambiguous policy intentions; this situation leaves little alternative than to create intentions through implementation (Lipsky, 1978). Bureaucrats will also adjust policy intentions that either ignore or dismiss existing program processes (Derthick, 1972; Rosenbaum, 1979). These findings demonstrate that policy intervention must account for the complexities of implementation. Implementation research, however, has often found such complexity troublesome. It serves as a rationale to call for constricting policy intentions. Generally, this means tightening up the legal specifications of policy intentions (Larson, 1980; Sabatier and Mazmanian, 1981). Applying statutory constraints to define implementation has been revived recently (Ingram and Schneider, 1990). This view treats complexity less problematically. Writing "smart" statutes means learning from the implementation literature that different policies and programs require appropriate amounts of bureaucratic discretion.

Not all researchers make the legal perspective their prime concern (Ham and Hill, 1984; Thompson, 1984). In a much-cited work, Rein and Rabinowitz (1978) suggest that distinctive political and organizational influences need to be more fully captured by implementation research. They underscore the importance of recognizing that implementation must frequently rescue ambiguous policy purposes. They propose integrating implementation into a more general theoretical policy framework. Although this promise remains relatively unfulfilled, it has inhibited the legal orientation from dominating implementation research fully. Indeed, few now doubt implementation's transformational character as a source for emergent theories of policy intervention (Goggin, et al., 1990).

B. Implementation in Multiorganizational Settings

Transformation has two major features. Both derive from the multiorganizational relationships that manifest themselves throughout implementation (Scharpf, 1978). These relationships structure implementation. First, transformation in implementation appears because multiorganizational relationships are usually self-ordering constructs. They are rarely complete, although subunits can easily be distinguished by their purposes and boundaries (Scharpf, 1989). These relationships cut across public and private organizations whose commonality stems from proximity to policy arenas. These multiorganizational relationships form the core of a policy community (Heclo, 1978). Second, transformation also happens because a policy community continues to give these multiorganizational relationships a political character. Never completely satisfied with outcomes, policy communities will try to recreate them at different junctures of the policy process (Loomis, 1986). Policy communities, in other words, remain as politically active in forming policy intentions as they are in defining implementation. What distinguishes the politics of policy intention from implementation is that multiorganizational dynamics vary accordingly. That is, political mobilization in policy intentions revolves around the organizational characteristics of legislative committees (Weingast and Marshall, 1988), whereas for implementation, organizational relationships center on agency activities (Hult, 1987). Implementation research, however, often finds that political mobilization upsets intentions by producing the so-called unwitting outcomes of policy making (Linder and Peters, 1989a).

The frequency by which such outcomes appear leads to raising a fundamental issue about the public sector (Love and Sederberg, 1987). The issue is whether programs are meant to succeed—or fail (Moe, 1990). Policy makers are not simply miscreants; they are reality testers, who seek to protect favored programs from political redirection (or reduction) in implementation. That is, to minimize the influence of enemies, public agencies form subsets of highly bounded intro- and interorganizational relationships. These relationships become quite resistant to change. Such self-protection, which aims at repelling excisions from detractors, sometimes also resists entreaties from friends (Bardach, 1977). In effect, public agencies acquire survival rationales over and above whatever commitments are necessary to fulfill policy intentions (Radin, 1977). Furthermore, implementation produces perverse outcomes because policy intentions are neither solely initiated nor owned by government actions. Intentions are both shared and monitored across a wide spectrum of advocates and adversaries within policy communities (Heckathorn and Maser, 1990). These communities will need to measure their successes (or failures) against programs seeking to lock in present gains and fend against future incursions (Dunleavy, 1991). As a result, the most prevalent finding in implementation research is that outcomes are either disappointing or unwitting (Dethrick, 1990).

Some observers express concern that this situation threatens democratic principles (Linder and Peters, 1990; Lowi, 1979). At issue is whether focusing on feasibility in implementation reduces the desirability of intentions to secondary status. In effect, a reversal occurs in the policy process with desirability suffering at the hands of feasibility. The aspirations of a democratic polity loses out to meeting implementation requirements, usually associated with satisfying the idiosyncracies of agencies and bureaucrats. The dichotomy is a false one. Implementation does not simply supersede desirable goals with feasible ones. Implementation captures desirable (even if ill-formed) intentions that have gone astray; indeed, implementation protects earlier desirable intentions against sways in political fortunes. Desirable policy intentions may themselves be questionable in a variety of ways. Undesirability appears as intentions do not serve democratic purposes (Calista, 1986b). Desirable intentions may also contain the seeds of their own unsuccessful implementation when (1) resources are inadequate (Palumbo and Calista, 1990); (2) instruments are misjudged (Brodkin, 1986; Murphy, 1973); (3) initiatives miscalculated (Goggin, 1987); or, more telling, (4) when policy intentions deliberately handicap implementation that could upset prevailing social and political compacts (Benson, 1971). Correspondingly, formulating desirable intentions may simply remain elusive. Universal health care as desirable social policy continues to fall short of adoption in the United States because its formulation remains politically unreconciled; this, despite its advocacy ever since Theodore Roosevelt's presidency (1901–1909) (Rhodes, 1992).

II. THE INSTITUTIONAL CONTEXTS OF IMPLEMENTATION

Implementation of policy intentions occurs independent of whether deliberative—or desirable—choices are prescribed (Ham and Hill, 1984). While it is commonly agreed that preventive health care is highly desirable, both personally and fiscally, disadvantaged people do without it—an estimated 15% of the American population are uninsured (*New York Times*, 4 Dec., 1992: 1). The resulting outcomes are impacting numerous populations long before conventionally conceived policy formation unfolds (Brown, 1991). This situation belies conceiving of the entire process of policy intervention as following sequences or stages. A sequential framework assumes a temporality that ignores preexisting implementation conditions (Porter and Olsen, 1976). Implementation occurs before policies are viewed as problematic or worth correcting. For example, in voting rights before 1965 and in the environment before 1970, policies existed, although implemented primarily through states and localities. As public attention shifted to a national arena, culminating in federal legislation, the formative process appears to be one of policy redesign more than design (Buck, 1991). Redesign calls for challenging tacit assumptions held by policy communities however unformed. Redesign mobilizes the underlying multiorganizational relationships by focusing their attention on choices of policy instruments previously unheralded or unavailable (Bobrow and Dryzek, 1987). As policy redesign acquires both regularity and legitimacy, institutional contexts become more visible. Implementation becomes manifest as latent institutional relationships take shape to satisfy different decisional requirements.

There are four institutional contexts that define implementation, as noted in Figure 1. It is fruitful to discuss them in two ways: (1) in relation to their distinctive qualities and (2) in their creation of an overall implementation structure (Hjern and Porter, 1981).

The contextual proposal derives from two prior works—Hofferbert (1974) and Sabatier (1991). Both are models of policy intervention. Essentially, Hofferbert displays policy intervention primarily in political subsystems terms. Implementation largely flows from the directives of formation. Sabatier extrapolates from this model by stressing the interactive quality of major variables and by offering an institutional basis for analyzing policy intervention. This model highlights three decisional requirements around which three institutional choice levels are organized—constitutional, collective, and operational. These distinctions follow conventional understandings. Although implementation (which appears isolated at the operational level) forms feedback connections with the other levels, this limits its importance. Its activation occurs as responses to other levels. Correspondingly, viewing policy making as a series of levels reinforces the temporal bias in policy analysis. Without questioning the integrity of this model for policy intervention, modifying it leads to a better understanding of implementation. A more robust model of implementation will require that the three "levels" be expanded to four components. The expanded model, in effect, summarizes what has been learned from the implementation literature; notably, that implementation is not only an institutional phenomenon, it is also influenced by distinct contexts. The proposal views implementation unfolding within each of the other contexts—not simply interacting with them as an isolated phenomenon.

An examination of the expanded implementation model follows. Each of the four institutional choice contexts—the constitutional, collective, operational, and distributional—is

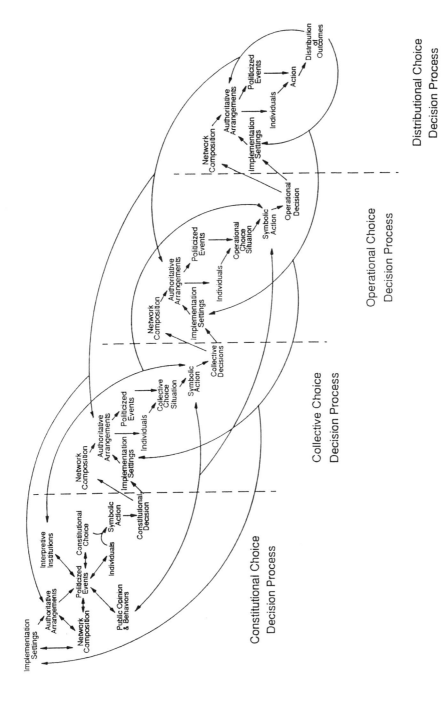

Figure 1. Institutional basis for policy implementation. [Adapted from Hofferbert (1974) and Sabatier (1991).]

discussed. This is followed by an analysis of the conflicts exhibited by each context. These conflicts derive from satisfying decisional requirements within each context. Overall, the robustness of the model arises because the same criterion variables appear within each context. Thus, the three endogenous and exogenous variables reiterate across contexts. The endogenous variables are network composition, authoritative arrangements, and implementation setting. The exogenous variables are public opinion and behavior, interpretive institutions, and individuals. Although these variables iterate across contexts, their mobilization occurs through politicized events that vary contextually. In sum, the expanded model proposes that implementation unfolds in institutional contexts.

A. The Four Institutional Contexts of Implementation

The institutional basis of implementation can be highlighted in three ways. First, institutional relationships are contextual by nature. This conceptualization avoids lapsing into a temporal understanding of implementation. A second characteristic of the model extends Sabatier's (1991) systemic notion. Contexts are not only highly interactive, the major variables iterate throughout them. Residuals of the same variables appear in all contexts, although the preeminence of the underlyfing multiorganizational relationships defining each context differs. Two factors influence such preeminence in each context. First, preeminence of multiorganizational relationships within each context depends on their decision-making focal point. For example, choices within constitutional contexts are broadly legal, whereas in distributional contexts, choices are narrowly interpretive and often idiosyncratic. Second, the ensuing decision-making processes yield stabilized rules and procedures that reflect multiorganizational preeminence across contexts. Because of their relative positioning, within the collective choice context, for example, congressional staff of committee chairs acquire preeminence over regular committee members (Rieselbach, 1986). Correspondingly, in the operational context, their counterparts influence outcomes in state capitals (Carlucci, 1989). Taken together, the demands of each decisional focal point and the appearance of rules and regulations give institutional contexts their identity (Ritti and Silver, 1986). Enhanced communication across institutional identities occurs as major variables reiterate within each context. (These variables will be discussed subsequently.)

The third feature of the revised model is its centerpiece. As noted, the model proposes four implementation contexts. In keeping with its source (Sabatier, 1991), the proposal includes constitutional and collective choice contexts—the former focuses on legal conventions and the latter statutory mandates. It is empirically unacceptable to collapse all the remaining implementation transactions into a solitary operational context. The operational context satisfies two decisional requirements, each reflecting different multiorganizational relationships. One set of decisions concerns the more typical interfaces of intergovernmental implementation structures (O'Toole and Montjoy, 1984); such decision making focuses on producing guidelines and strategies. These processes stand alone as an operational context. The other context is distributional and centers principally on managing the delivery of services. Separating the operational from the distributional context acknowledges critical differences in their decisional requirements. These contexts are, however, quite interactive. Participants will often be invited to work out their differences by legislative committees in the collective choice context. This migration across contexts captures another feature of the proposed implementation model. As each context interacts with a common set of criterion variables, implementation essentially becomes a reticulistic process (Klijn and Teisman, 1991). Put differently, although distinct decisional requirements define their orientations, institutional contexts are open systems (Checkland, 1981) that provide easy access for policy communities to move across them. The four contexts can now be discussed more fully.

The constitutional context is not limited by the limitations of legal constraints. It cross-cuts other contexts. That is, the tenability of constitutional actions will depend on how well the legacies and behaviors of courts command compliance from other contexts. Although their rhetoric often appears in symbolic terms, constitutional contexts more sharply delineate the interfaces between policy formation and implementation. This sharpness not only arises when court appointments are made but also when executive appointments are reviewed. Questioning of appointees now concentrates on anticipating how they will implement policies as much as it does on reviewing their character; anxieties are revealed in attempts to tie past behaviors to future actions, especially for judges (Shefter, 1992). The second context, collective choice, involves legislative and executive institutions; in a federal system, especially, its structural conditions are often seen as impediments to establishing clarified outcomes (Toonen, 1985). Decisions are usually highly compromised. Participants are reluctant to relinquish a degree of freedom—that translates into accepting ambiguity—and suggests losing future control. The next context, the operational, connects across numerous jurisdictions and governments—including quasi- and nongovernmental bodies; its decisions are often loose agglomerations of formal and informal pronouncements. Finally, a distributional context seems simple to describe, although it is most complex decisionally. It coordinates the outputs of other contexts and converts them to actions aimed at target populations. Complexity arises because decisional environments do not lead to uniform outcomes; decisions will vary, for example, as agencies and agents in the periphery will influence policy outcomes in accord with local laws and customs. In a federal system, this dispersion of distributional decision points leads to uneven policy implementation. The distributional context is singularly complex. Its transformational dilemma is to satisfy the demands of other contexts as it meets its own requirements to create uniform outcomes.

B. Institutional Contexts and Implementation Conflicts

As policy choices move across institutional contexts, implementation becomes a cumulative process. Cumulativeness occurs, however, without any necessity for clarification of a policy's origin or of its goal-directedness. Although participants in different contexts are familiar with one another's decisional requirements, gaining consistent cooperation across contexts remains implementation's great weakness. Not only do contexts, in effect, hold one another hostage (Stoker, 1991), but differences in how policies acquire their salience within each context will vary accordingly (Ripley and Franklin, 1986). As different conflicts are more likely to surface in one context than another, policy implementation can easily disaggregate. Discussion of conflict within each context is, therefore, important; it reveals why incohesiveness is an implementation weakness.

Within the constitutional context, a highly discussed conflict centers on the difficulties a president encounters in altering existing naval rules despite the gravity of a situation. In the 1962 Cuban missile crisis, the naval high command refused to alter its blockade protocols to help President Kennedy avert misinterpretation by oncoming Russian warships (Allison, 1971). Until this situation arose, the president tacitly agreed to blockade rules. This agreement fell apart within the constitutional context. Naval commanders could not justify making an exception in this double-edged game of chicken. Implementation conflicts within the constitutional context, though highly charged, are often more symbolic than real and will usually turn on the believability of who's in charge. Typically, this constitutional conflict occurred largely in a legal framework; conceivably, finalization of the issue could have required court intervention. Although the legitimacy of presidential authority went untested in other contexts, the delay in naval capitulation appeared to uphold its authority for junior officers. Appeasement is important for what it signifies. Deference must be paid to other contexts to win their endorsement for effective implementation.

Conflicts within the other institutional contexts are not as clear-cut as suggested by the constitutional context. This partly occurs because the hold of legal precedent is less unyielding in these settings. Conflicts tend to be, therefore, both recurrent and recursive: Outcomes remain unsettled and participants reappear regularly. Reticulism especially mediates across the collective choice and operational contexts (O'Toole and Montjoy, 1984). Agreement between these two contexts depends more on gaining cooperation than compliance. As a result, their decisions are more often blurred than not. Conflicts, however, have one common feature. The targets for the actions of the collective choice and operational contexts are principally located within the distributional context—on the whole, both contexts seek to redesign already-existing distributional outcomes. A major confounding feature of implementation appears at this juncture. Conflicts within the collective choice and operational contexts must often settle disputes between the same branches or jurisdictions of government. Conflicts appear because subunits of federal and state agencies seek opposing goals for the same policies (Dethrick, 1990; Pressman and Wildavsky, 1973). Within the collective context, for example, federal legislation concerning improving educational opportunities for poor children was left open-ended in anticipation of the complexity in adopting innovative programs. For the operational context, this opportunity allowed school districts to legislate their own requirements. It took some years to develop greater regularity in the face of reported variations between federal, state, and local executive branches (Berman and McLaughlin, 1976). Quite commonly, implementation conflicts within the operational context occur because executives and legislators disagree on the value of specific programs or agencies. For example, programs slated for reduction or recision by executives will seek out legislative "fixers" to ensure their continuance (Bardach, 1977).

Conflicts within the distributional level have been the traditional focus for implementation research. These conflicts obviously involve how action is ultimately either controlled or delivered (Radin, 1977). Conflicts not only arise within the distributional context but also between it and other contexts, usually with operational and collective choice contexts. Incidents of conflict are regularly reported in the media as other contexts react to the decisiveness of outcomes by distributional contexts. (Definitiveness, of course, does not carry with it any compulsion for consistency.) To protect against infringements by distributional context participants, legislators will invoke their own prerogatives. A state legislative committee, for example, reverses changes in a curriculum introduced by a state education department that would have given local schools more freedom from its oversight (*New York Times*, 22 Nov., 1992: 15). Distributional contexts also face internecine conflicts not only because of their proximity to target populations. Conflicts abound because their decisions must accommodate highly pluralistic political environments. For example, when a city education department replaces a decentralized school district board that refused to implement curriculum changes, it responds to the weight of public opinion and quickly reinstitutes the board (*New York Times*, 22, 24, 26 Nov., 1992: 1).

Contextual conflicts reveal one notable feature about implementation. Implementation is a gradualist phenomenon. Its outcomes result from aggregated choices occurring within and between organizational roles and interorganizational relationships (Stoker, 1991). Roles and relationships are always constrained by how tractable policy aggregation has become across institutional contexts. Consequently, outcomes will appear slowly and unevenly. Gradualism takes at least three forms. Policy choices either *evolve* (Majone and Wildavsky, 1978) as earlier challenges are absorbed through existing roles and relationships, or they *adapt* (Berman, 1980) as clarification of policy intentions and limitations of policy organizational situations become rectified, or they *drift* as shifts in political preferences materialize in institutional contexts and priorities are restructured (Rein and Rabinowitz, 1978). With few exceptions (Benson, 1971; Nelson, 1977), these three accommodationist views of implementation capture implementation as a gradualist phenomenon (Goggin et al., 1990). Central to the gradualist character of implementation is the conditioning provided by interactions between endogenous and exogenous variables.

C. Endogenous Variables: Networks, Authorities, and Implementation Settings

There are three endogenous variables: authoritative arrangements, network composition, and implementation setting. In the broadest sense, they form the elements of a policy community. This community is really plural in that some organizational relationships will cut across different institutional contexts. That is, these communities coalesce the various multiorganizational relationships that give form to each institutional context (Scharpf, 1978). Although the interactions among endogenous variables are determined by the decisional focus within each context, the institutional approach confirms that implmenetation moves across all contexts. This is most visible for the first endogenous variable considered—authoritative arrangements. The source of authoritative arrangements is fairly straightforward. Within each institutional context rule-making structures emerge to create compliance either directly from its own target populations or indirectly from those of other contexts. For example, a constitutional decision ordinarily assumes compliance by other agencies and governments across jurisdictions. The constitutional context, however, is actively involved in implementation. At times, courts reach down to initiate their own actions, as has occurred for certain civil rights (Kincaid, 1988). Nor are courts completely at the mercy of other agencies to gain compliance. The line between formulator and implementor simetimes gets blurred. Judges become implementors when courts directly supervise a situation; that is, by becoming its master, as has been done for school districts, prisons, and institutions for the mentally handicapped (Horowitz, 1977). Judges also become implementors when conflicts between other institutional contexts cannot be reconciled; this takes place occasionally by making 11th-hour decisions—by determining whether to allow a dated abortion-inducing pill into the country (*New York Times*, 15 Oct., 1992: 1) or by repeatedly having to decide on the death penalty.

Within the collective choice context, authoritative arrangements reveal that executives and legislators are also implementors. Ordinarily, they prescribe conditions for others to follow; notably for operational and distributional contexts. Executives and legislators, however, spend an inordinate amount of their time pursuing constituent casework. Estimates indicate legislators spend one quarter of their time on casework (Gellhorn, 1966). Executives do likewise through ombudsmen (Caiden, 1983). Legislators become implementors when they appoint special prosecutors who essentially bypass existing agencies in other contexts. During the Reagan administration, Congress (i.e., the House Judiciary Committee) virtually administered the 250 offices of the Legal Services Corporation because the president wanted to eliminate them (Ginsberg and Shefter, 1990). Although executives can take advantage of their unique position to dominate center stage in authoritative arrangements, some evidence suggests that, at the federal level, Congress has become more visible in agenda writing (Weingast and Marshall, 1988). In sum, authoritative actors within each context familiarize themselves with implementation because they cannot escape its demands.

The second endogenous variable, network composition, brings together multiorganizational relationships that converge on varying policy issues or existing programs. Networks embrace organizations and individuals whose membership arises from both public and private sector claimants of vested interest (DiMaggio and Powell, 1983). Networks overlap across contexts; members of the same interest group will make claims to various levels of government across contexts. Receptivity to these claims sometimes heightens because no agency can ensure, for example, that decisions by political appointees in the constitutional context will always be endorsed by bureaucrats in the distributional context (Knott and Miller, 1987). Network composition is also a function of whether the decisional demands are concentrated at the center or the periphery of government. Despite differences in those demands, network relationships achieve consistency by continually reaffirming their attachments and commitments to patterns of decision making.

Consistency also stems from the intermediary role played by the third endogenous variable. As bargaining arenas emerge between authorities and networks, implementation settings mediate their differences. Implementation settings generate orderliness to multiorganizational relationships within institutional contexts. Within the collective choice context, for example, legislative committees construct stable decision-making orders composed largely of adopting flexible rules and procedures, on one hand, and spreading (sub)committee chairs judiciously, but widely, on the other (Weingast and Marshall, 1988). These relational orders are always evolving as bargaining occurs between endogenous (and exogenous) variables. A major outcome is that legislative subcommittees form highly integrated relationships both with their counterpart agencies connected through authoritative arrangements and with helpful interests identified through network composition. The resulting situation resembles an iron triangle. Instead, there are as many iron triangles as there are institutional contexts. Implementation settings, in brief, create subgovernance structures that support decision-making activities. In highly decentralized and fragmented political systems, especially, governance structures partialize the legitimacy required to sustain implementation outcomes shared by varying institutional contexts (March and Olsen, 1989). Put differently, implementation settings augment the legitimacy of networks and authorities through the creation of memories and practices that distinguish one context from another. Implementation settings also give meaning to actions taken across institutional contexts. They create frameworks within which contexts establish their identities. As such, implementation settings become independent variables—a quality that will be elaborated subsequently.

D. Exogenous Variables: Public Opinion, Interpretive Institutions, and Individuals

There are three exogenous variables: public opinion and behaviors, interpretive institutions, and individuals. Institutional contexts never take public opinion for granted. Legislators especially are vulnerable to constituent dissatisfaction in locally important issues. Despite their high rate of reelection, incumbent legislators do not want to be numbered among the few who get turned out (Moore, 1992). Publics can also "unelect" entire agencies through ballot propositions (*New York Times*, 7 Dec., 1992: 1). Community characteristics will play a significant role in shaping the nature of public opinion and behaviors. Community characteristics often lead legislators to become both policy entrepeneurs within collective contexts or program fixers within operational contexts (Kingdon, 1984). The second exogenous variable, interpretive institutions, mainly includes analysts and journalists—both broadly defined. Analysts are of two types: those who walk a thin line between objectivity and subjectivity— commonly academics—and others who are outright spokespersons for advocacy groups— commonly think tankers (Calista, 1986a). In their reporting, journalists, too, are as much investigative as they are advocative. The third exogenous variable, individuals, does not lend itself to easy analysis. Taken together with interpretive institution participants, individuals are at the center of advocacy groups (Sabatier, 1988).

Obviously, individuals can play varied roles within any of the institutional contexts. Individuals in leadership positions—endogenously or exogenously—will generally dominate decisions within each context. There are many nameless (publicly, at least) leaders within the operational and distributional contexts—identified by their connection to authoritative arrangements or network composition—who influence implementation. Entrepreneurs appear among agencies in the distributional context too (Elmore, 1989). More visibly, legislators seek the public's attention by serving as committee chairs. In addition, legislative preference takes the form of adopting favored programs as "pets" (Bardach, 1977). Often, these pets will reflect constituent community characteristics (Kingdon, 1984). So honored, the life of implementors within distributional contexts, especially, will be considerably eased.

E. Implications of the Four Institutional Contexts

Employing an institutional framework has major implications for implementation research. Overall, the framework challenges the traditional separation of formation and implementation. Two major findings of implementation research support that challenge. First, acquiescing to a unidirectional movement from formation to implementation disguises a fundamental reality; policy platforms preexist their formation. Implementation sets the stage for policy formation. Yet, the existence of problematic policy arenas does not ensure that policies will be redressed (Sabatier, 1991). Implementation remains highly discordant for abortion and welfare policies (Rhodes, 1992). One result is to continue to blur the distinction between implementation and formation. Stated differently, in the absence of a more affirming stamp cast by constitutional or collective contexts, operational and distributional contexts create policy implementation structures that give the apparency of wholeness to formation. In sum, policy redesign defines itself against prevailing implementation.

It is now clear why implementation settings are independent variables. Policy actions originate in implementation settings within institutional contexts. Implementation settings become proxies for governance structures that mediate prevailing multiorganizational relationships among authoritative arrangements and network composition. Effectively, the politics of networks and authorities are reduced to dependent variables within governance structures (Hofferbert, 1990). Figure 1 reflects this situation by showing implementation setting as a triggering variable.

The second major implication of the institutional framework stems from recognizing the influence of implementation settings across institutional contexts. As institutional contexts are reticulistic (Scharpf, 1978), they cannot make decisions by ignoring other contexts. Institutional memory moves across contexts and inhibits such disregard. Memory, however, cuts both ways. It recalls prior failures to gain cooperation to implement policy, and, equally important, it reckons how the impacts of unintended actions will be interpreted by other institutional contexts (Yanow, 1990). The Supreme Court, in making the 1954 *Brown* v. *Board of Education* decision, implicitly understood the riveting demands that would be placed on other institutional contexts. In ruling to end school segregation, however, the Court did not seek immediacy, nor a 1- or 2-year (or any) time frame. The obvious nonenforceability of these alternate implementations to end segregation—long-embedded across institutional contexts, including its own—constrained the Court to say "with all deliberate speed." No ruling could uniformly eliminate the sources of segregation that inhere in institutional contexts—especially for authoritative arrangements—that cross 50 states and more than 15,000 school districts. Fundamentally, this landmark ruling accepted that implementation bargaining is inevitable in a highly pluralized form of policy making. This implies, however, that constitutional contexts cannot command compliance over policies that democratic polities want to undo or to leave unresolved. Such polities express dissatisfaction with constitutional compliance by concentrating their bargaining on implementation settings in other institutional contexts (Ostrom, 1991). In time, segregated schools reappeared (National Commission, 1983).

III. MODELS OF INSTRUMENTAL RATIONALITY AND IMPLEMENTATION

Implementation research does not assimilate such findings easily. Flawed outcomes are usually attributed to the systemic effects of the dispersal of power across institutional contexts. The result is reduced consensus in both posing and solving problems (Feldman, 1989). Limitations in problem definition stem from the methodological orientation of implementation research toward instrumental rationality (Fox, 1990). This orientation assumes that causal relationships can be both logically and empirically explicated. Implementation research exhibits this orientation most fully in the tendency to display relationships in systems terms (Sabatier and Mazmanian, 1981). Adoption of the systems view, however, confines implementation research to a narrow understanding of multiorganizational dimensions (Moe, 1991). Implementation research has been slow in accepting the independent effects of those dimensions in determining policy intentions and outcomes: "The assumption [is] that the administrative arrangements for . . . programs are everywhere alike or easily indicated, so that all which [is] left to account for variation in outcomes [are] 'political' influences or the 'controlled' program characteristics" (Hjern, 1987: 4). This assumption leads to affirming that programmed bureaucracies are modal organizations for the public sector (Hult and Walcott, 1991).

The systems view supports this presumption of instrumental rationality. Systems' inherent artificiality incorporates that any set of related variables can be guided by a basic ordering principle (Checkland, 1981). Whole units, in effect, cannot be discerned outside of representation as subunits or subsystems. Implementation research translates the principle of hierarchical ordering among subsystems into confirming that bureaucratic hierarchies can satisfy both equitability and efficiency (Barrett and Hill, 1984). Only a few researchers call for relaxing the bureaucratic assumption to enhance implementation (Molnar and Rogers, 1982; Thompson, 1982). Generally, programmed bureaucracies are favored because of the Weberian promise that routinization minimizes favoritism in serving the public interest. The corresponding promise is that adherence to specialization ensures efficiency among bureaucracies. Specialization makes monitoring bureaucrats easier. Commitment to a hierarchic mode by implementation research persists even when it uncovers many cases of failed policy outcomes. Recommendations for organizational improvements are narrowly circumscribed and directed at practitioners not policy makers per se (O'Toole, 1986). Implementation failure is usually attributed to the presence of bureaucratic politics (Murphy, 1971; Nakamura and Pinderhughes, 1981). Implementation research hardly questions whether the underlying routinization and specialization of programmed bureaucracies may be the source of disquieting politics (Palumbo and Calista, 1990).

A. The Behavioral Model

Implementation research generally views politics as reducing the capacity of democratic polities to ensure public interest (Linder and Peters, 1990a). Implementation restricts assertion of the public interest—that is, by transferring democratic politics to bureaucratic structures. There is near universal acceptance that bureaucratic politics in implementation cannot serve the normative purposes of democratic politics (Lowi, 1972). Rarely are public sector organizations considered capable of contributing to democratic purposes without controlling for their discretionary powers (Nelson, 1977). Further, the methodological dependence of implementation research on instrumental rationality and systems encourages treating bureaucratic politics as leading to suboptimal—if not perverse—outcomes (Echeverri-Gent, 1992). Acceptance of both these views also supports the expectation of suboptimality in another profound way. Implementation research employs two models of politics that confirms this expectation. Whether it is the cognitive limitations of the behavioral model, on one hand, or the myopia of subsystems in the incremental model, on the other, both models expect implementation to be self-limiting (Fox, 1990). As will become apparent in a subsequent discussion of alternative theoretical models, suboptimality need not be so corrosive in implementation.

The behavioral model mostly reflects the work of the Carnegie-Mellon school (Moe, 1990). Individuals intend to be rational but are boundedly so. Their circumscribed cognitive capacity—for instantaneous retrieval of all previously stored information—compels individuals to confine their actions to behavioral formulas. Individuals follow routines, habits, and protocols that become proxies for rational decisions. Accordingly, organizations will be forced to lower their collective optimality and concede to outcomes that are satisficing (Browning et al., 1984). Common references to support the suboptimality of organizations in implementation research appear as limits to cognition of organization members (March and Simon, 1958); distortions that control communications (Katz and Kahn, 1966); resistance to innovation (Downs, 1967); and difficulties to sustain organizational commitments (Weick, 1969). For implementation research, however, these restraints are not simply self-limiting. They presuppose the necessity of adopting bureaucratic controls to ensure accountability to the public will (Burke, 1990; Chase, 1979). Acceptance of command organizations remains unquestioned even when policies call for variations in implementing bureaucratic discretion (Ingram, 1990). Conditioned by their suboptimality, public bureaucracies are reduced to being continuous problem solvers (Kelman, 1984). Continuous problem solving appears demanding but is quite confining. For one, it directs implementation research simply to suggest marginal improvements to correct flawed outcomes (O'Toole, 1986). More consequentially, continuous problem solving leaves the underlying policy cores unexamined (Benson and Weitzel, 1985). These drawbacks diminish the potential of implementation research to contribute to a theory of policy intervention.

B. Incrementalism, Implementation, and Endowments

Discouragement from examining policy cores in implementation research also stems from its employment of the incremental model of politics (Elmore, 1989). The principal tenet of incrementalism is that political choice occurs at the margins of policy subsystems in that they are charged with implementing already-solved social problems (Lindblom, 1959). Policy subsystems are circumscribed by their capacity to make limited adjustments, to restrict comparisons, and to take small steps (Berman, 1980). Suboptimality manifests itself in institutional contexts as enduring relationships and commitments are unlikely to be disturbed. Minimally, implementation research relies on the incremental model to show how agencies bargain to prevent themselves from falling behind (Dunleavy, 1990). As the science of stable choices, incrementalism focuses on demonstrating how policy choices aggregate intermittently; that is, through non-coordinated mutual adjustments. The bounds of acceptable policy choices appear by muddling through between the streams of efficiency and equitability. It is incrementalism's focus on discovering choices in the margin that restricts its usefulness to implementation research. Incrementalism is ill-equipped to raising the knottier problems associated with the distribution of political endowments (March and Olsen, 1990).[2]

Incrementalism discourages implementation from redressing deficiencies in political endowments. Despite the limitations of incrementalism, from its inception, implementation research retains a prime concern for the integrity of policy choices. This stage has been set by Pressman and Wildavsky's (1973) discovery of numerous and intractable decision points involved in employment training: They found opposing advocacy groups, varying elites, uncooperating agencies, and competing jurisdictions interlocked to deflect policy intentions. Not only is no one in charge, no one seems to be at fault. That is, a match exists between legislators in the collective choice context not risking purposefulness by unambiguously defining employability and bureaucrats in the distributional context not risking receptivity by zealously embracing every innovation. Target unemployed groups were left only slightly better off in finding work than when the program began. Neither complete failure nor success, the problem of employment training had, at least, not escaped the policy agenda. On one hand, incrementalism leads implementation research to accept that a policy of employability does not aim at recreating political endowments, yet, on the other hand, incrementalism explains how certain training goals become implemented as policy outcomes across institutional contexts. Implementation research typically characterizes this situation as evolutionary (Majone and Wildavsky, 1979). Similar outcomes are common for other redistributive policies (Berman, 1978; Murphy, 1973). Both incremental and behavioral models of politics, in sum, do not easily embrace consideration of core endowment issues. Much like its adherence to the underlying research methodologies of instrumental rationality and systems, the adoption of these two models of politics by implementation research narrows its contribution to an overall theory of policy intervention (Goggin et al., 1990). Challenges to this situation are now creating opportunities for theory building that address endowment issues.

IV. MAJOR APPROACHES TO STUDYING IMPLEMENTATION

Before considering the promise of any theoretical breakthrough, three issues must be addressed. These issues are highly visible within implementation research. They are (1) distinguishing between formation and implementation; (2) determining whose perspective represents the focal point of implementation research; and (3) recognizing the value of program evaluation.

A. Policy Formation, Implementation, Vagueness, and Reconciliation

Analytically, it is easier to distinguish among participants in the policy-making process by separating policy formation from implementation (Sabatier and Mazmanian, 1983). It is equally important to consider why the distinction has been questioned. A distinction gets blurred for two important reasons. One is the overwhelming evidence of the significance of implementation in determining policy outcomes (Nakamura and Smallwood, 1980), and the other is the realization that implementation independently affects formation (Marvel, 1982;

Thompson, 1982; Weimer, 1983). No longer is it possible to say "absent" bureaucratic politics policy is what formulators say it is or that "present" bureaucratic politics policy is what implementors make it. Instead, policies are continuously designed and redesigned because desirable policies are rarely self-evident (Wildavsky, 1979).

Although it is correct to affirm that the promulgation of statutes is necessary for policy formation, this is not sufficient for policy implementation. As the earlier discussion of institutional contexts indicates, implementation informs formation. Implementation settings are the necessary focal points for multiorganizational bargaining. Within each institutional context, these settings mediate decision making between networks and authorities. The implementation setting within the collective choice context, for example, aims at gaining both cooperation and compliance from two target populations. One population lies within the bounds of the operational context; collective choice processes will be influenced by the awareness of the need to have its regulations and guidelines complemented by the operational context. The collective choice context also will respond to the successes and failures of the distributional context. Over time, the collective choice context—no different from other contexts—becomes more closely identified with the implementation requirements of its prime relationships. When collective choice agenda setters ask, for example, what will fly? (Kingdon, 1984), they have self-consciously become implementors. The phenomenological basis of their actions contributes to the development of a contextual institutional memory (Hjern, 1987). Memories are residuals of normalized implementation relationships within which policy outcomes unfold. Memories allow one context to anticipate how other contexts will respond to its decisions. They can also discern what will antagonize other contexts—an action often taken to express dissatisfaction over failure to dominate policy implementation (Hult, 1987). As outcomes aggregate within these highly reticulistic environments, it is therefore not surprising that implementation exemplifies vagueness. Vagueness is especially characteristic of the collective choice context's statutory relationship to implementation. Two kinds of vagueness prevail.

One is the well-known reluctance among legislators to avoid taking unnecessary risks. Specifying statutory intentions often gets turned over to operational or distributional contexts. Ostensibly, legislators want to ensure reelection by reducing their exposure to what might be viewed as extreme positions (Ginsberg and Shefter, 1990). Second, vagueness occurs because policy instruments will sometimes lack conviction or resources to facilitate compliance. Outcomes, as a result, often become unwittingly implemented due to the inoperability of instruments (Wamsley, 1985). Implementation research can only partially redeem this situation by invoking the accommodationist explanation; that is, of policy evolution (Browne and Wildavsky, 1984) or of adaptation (Berman, 1978). More commonly, policy implementation drifts (Rein and Rabinowitz, 1978). Most notably for redistributive—and somewhat less for regulatory—policies, this situation is not trivial. In these arenas, vagueness reveals the ideological resistances of democratic polities to address issues of political endowments. Vagueness gets reflected in policy intentions ill-disposed to reconcile discrepancies in political endowments (Osberg, 1984). To create opportunities for effective implementation, a policy's design must satisfy issues of political reconciliation. Irreconciliation has two consequences for implementation. One, irreconciliation is likely to reduce the importance of the constitutional and collective choice contexts in determining policy intentions. The operational—and the distributional—contexts will enlarge their scope by creating intentions through adaptations in the delivery of outcomes. Second, implementation politics, then, becomes a by-product of unreconciled policy intentions that fail to address questions of endowment. Even if some desirable outcomes appear (Feldman, 1989), irreconciliation invariably creates inconsistencies in implementation.

A reciprocity emerges, then, between vagueness in policy formation and inconsistency in implementation. Since vagueness is most evident in the highly politicized arenas of health, education, and welfare, inconsistencies in implementation proliferate (Goggin, 1987). Vagueness reinforces permeability in implementation. Both operational and distributional contexts will tolerate variability in implementing policies differently across governmental jurisdictions. Typically, there are as many "policies" affecting redistributive programs as there are states, counties, and cities that implement them. For example, monthly welfare payments, for a family of three people in Ohio are $520 and $662 in neighboring Wisconsin (Kettl, 1991). Differences in the fiscal capacities of states may partially explain the discrepancy (Goggin et al., 1990), but the situation reveals how attenuated redistributive policy making can become. In the absence of reconciliation, certain basic policy questions never seem to go away. That is, if the inability to deal with reconciliation only begs the endowment question, this also makes it difficult to distinguish precisely between formation and implementation.

B. From Whose Perspective?

In the implementation literature, the reconciliation question usually gets overshadowed by another irresolution. Despite its being nearly uniformly deplored (O'Toole, 1986), the literature divides itself between two perspectives. Referred to as a "top-down," this more widespread centrist view portrays itself as inherently democratic; it identifies with the faithfulness by which implementation adheres to the intentions of elected officials (Sabatier, 1986). The other view is a "bottom-up" perspective. It accepts the conditions faced by bureaucracies and bureaucrats as more compelling in shaping policy outcomes; implementation creates outcomes conforming to the everyday experiences of agencies and agents (Lipsky, 1978). Although raising the question—from whose perspective?—reinforces the divide, the two views must be addressed.

1. The Top-Down Perspective

The top-down view takes its cue from the presumption that optimal implementation principally emanates from clearly stated statutes or mandates (Sabatier, 1986). Presumably, implementation can then capture policy intentions more fully. The top-down view is normative; it presumes an exclusivity in that statutes incorporate desirable policy intentions that deserve fulfillment. Normativeness also expresses itself in the temporal assumption that policy intentions precede implementation. Despite its normativeness, the top-down view represents the ideal type for implementation research. Six major assumptions inform this view.

Primarily, the definitiveness of a statute structures effective implementation. As a corollary, a law's ability to enhance implementation will be affected by how explicit it employs a causal theory to define policy intentions. The top-down view, however, refers to policy formation as having "resolved" political issues not "reconciled" them (Sabatier and Mazmanian, 1979). Second, the explicitness of the causal theory also calls for legislation providing appropriate jurisdictional reach as well as contributing sufficient levers (resources and tools) to address a policy's underlying causes. Third, at the point of delivery, well-suited legal constraints are required to structure compliance by implementors and client groups. The assumption is that bureaucrats and clients should be disempowered from establishing their own priorities. Nonetheless, the view holds that implementation must be supported by a receptive legal environment. Fourth, however skilled and committed implementors need to be, they can also be expected to behave self-interestedly. Fifth, to gain the necessary cooperation of implementors, incentives from both executives and legislators are needed to sustain their support. Similarly, gaining interest-group involvement is important to effective implementation (Ripley and Franklin, 1986). Finally, the top-down view offers a disclaimer that implementation cannot withstand traumatic socioeconomic changes without throwing itself off course (Sabatier, 1986).

The schema assumedly achieves greater credibility by viewing implementation from a longitudinal perspective. It considers a 3- to 5-year wait for research as too premature; a 10-year lapse is preferable. The longer time frame allows for:

> . . . the focus on legally-mandated objectives [that] encourage[s] scholars to carefully distinguish the objectives contained in the legal documents from both the political rhetoric surrounding policy formation and the tendency of critics to evaluate a program on the basis of what could be mistakenly perceived to be its objectives (Sabatier, 1986: 28).

As programs age, presumably, they come closer to their intentions. The evidence is not so convincing; two well-known cases are presented. Both involve education, one occurs in England and the other in the United States. At issue in the British Open University case is whether it sacrificed an earlier objective of seeking out working-class applicants by later adopting a "first-come, first served" purpose (Cerych and Sabatier, 1986). The longer-run view, however, eludes measurement in two ways. First, there is no reason to accept that a policy gains integrity when it dismisses its founding "rhetoric." Whether the policy could have been adopted without it, no one knows, although it seems unlikely. To get the legislation passed, initially highlighting attracting working-class talent sounds very appealing. Through "policy succession" (Wildavsky, 1979), however, other programs emerge and create alternative educational opportunities, which reduce the need to implement earlier intentions. The second problem with employing the long-term research is that over time, implementors, not formulators, determine what "intentions" become. Once ensconced, academics could easily be convincing about preserving historic quality standards and be equally dismissive of undermining them by fulfilling affirmative action goals. This case, in short, involves a typical "camel's nose" implementation. That is, narrower intentions minimized the objections from existing academic institutions; subsequently, broadened intentions reduced the liability of counting on sole support from an undependable clientele.

Another case defending the top-down view through the usefulness of longer-term research has important implications for implementation research. Similar to the British example, it exhibits a failure to redistribute educational endowments because the underlying issues remain politically unreconciled. The situation illustrates one of the benchmark programs in implementation research—the Elementary and Secondary Education Act of 1965 in the United States (Berman and McLaughlin, 1976). The prime purpose of the act is ". . . to provide financial assistance to local educational agencies serving areas with concentrations of children from low-income families and to expand and improve their educational programs by various means" (Kirst and Jung, 1982: 124). Earlier studies found the program deficient: ". . . bringing about very little change because of ambiguous objectives, dubious casual theories, resistance of implementing officials, and the inability of proponents to organize at the local level" (Sabatier, 1986: 38). Unfortunately, this interpretation of an earlier research study is faulty. That study focused on throughputs; that is, how the money was spent and not on program outputs or outcomes. True, in 1966, about 5.5 million children were eligible and 8.2 million participated. In 1978, however, 9 million were eligible and 6 million participated. This fallout occurred because funding declined—even the eligible 60% who participated in 1978 received less dollars, both in absolute and adjusted dollars (Kirst and Jung, 1982: 128-29). Taking issue with how dollars are spent pales compared with whether implementation creates any improvements for participants—a finding necessary to determine effectiveness. Improvements have been doubtful. Recent achievement score statistics for minorities (not only the poor among them) indicate that they fall below whites by an entire standard deviation (Chubb and Hansek, 1990).[3]

Unhappily, the longer time frame dealt a double blow to disadvantaged children: Funds decreased and scores declined. The evidence presented by longitudinal research to support the top-down view undermines its own legitimacy. In both cases, the longer wait reveals more of what a policy settles for and less of clarifying intentions by closely controlling implementation. Generally, employing the longer-term view fails to focus on the effectiveness of outcomes: "neither proper indicators nor adequate discounting strategies to value the different effects have been developed" (Hellstern, 1985: 307). The worthiness of the top-down in explicating policy intentions appears little helped by longitudinal research. In sum, if initial problem definition remains elusive, problems also change over time—both these conditions require seeking alternative explanations for policy implementation.

2. The Bottom-Up Perspective

The bottom-up perspective emphasizes the criticalness of how outcomes are delivered. It asserts that policy intentions are not fully developed until they are negotiated. Unlike the top-down view, its analytical orientation is largely phenomenological and multiorganizational. Ostensibly, the bottom-up view questions whether policy making can ever be controlled from the top-down; at least not without some participation from the bottom. Critics of the bottom-up view say this questions the tenability of a democratic polity (Linder and Peters, 1990a). That is, a bottom-up view presumably replaces the desirability of policy intentions with the feasibility of policy outcomes. Yet, it is the top-down view that hazards the desirability of intentions by concentrating on summing up political preferences rather than on allocating endowments. In effect, the top-down perspective avoids issues involving the reconciliation of endowments, especially relating to redistribution policies (Ham and Hill, 1984). The bottom-up view establishes its normative identity with democratic politics differently. Democratic politics can be enhanced by expanding the mediating role played by implementation (Hjern, 1987). Within its contextualized environment, implementation need not make bureaucrats enemies of the public interest (Wamsley, 1985).

Although policy analysts have long been familiar with the way bureaucrats negotiate their powers of discretion (Kaufmann, 1960), not until Lipsky (1971) conceptualized street-level bureaucrats did the significance of bottom-up policy making take hold (Wildavsky, 1979). Three major findings of the bottom-up view need mentioning: (1) the domination of bureaucratic influence over policy in the distributional context (Murphy, 1971); (2) the validation of multiorganizational relationships that transform intentions into outcomes (Hjern and Potter, 1981); and (3) the contribution of implementation bargaining to create desirable intentions (Elmore, 1985).

These three findings have been captured in the concept of an implementation structure (Hjern and Porter, 1981). An implementation structure is a coordinative mechanism that is both stable and fluid. Its stability comes from the presence of programmatic (policy) orientations that pull together both public and private organizations to sort out their various priorities and to determine outcomes. The fluidity of implementation is twofold. Fluidity stems from the bargaining that occurs over seeking and distributing resources and from internal (and external) demands to incorporate new or to alter ongoing programs. The concept remains an appealing bottom-up view, although its application has been limited (Wittrock, 1985). It has only been marginally employed in certain European settings (Sabatier, 1986).

Although it correctly identifies that multiorganizational relationships represent the proper unit of analysis for implementation studies, it is hard to grasp how the whole of an implementation structure exhibits itself; that is, outside of various multiorganizational meeting points. Two reasons explain this methodological problem.

The first methodological weakness is the assumption that an implementation structure negotiates outcomes through a single or unitary context. This problem stems from ignoring the significant differences that institutional contexts exert on implementation (Goggin et al., 1991). Depending on whether bargaining, for example, surfaces in a constitutional compared with a distributional context, implementation issues will vary. (There are different decisional requirements between presidents calling on the National Guard to break industrial labor strikes and police calling for back-up to make drug arrests.) A second methodological drawback relates to a limited ability to address conflicts across contexts. For one, intergovernmental conflicts within the operational context will have different impacts on other contexts depending on whether political appointees are of the same party (Bullock, 1981). Innovation to one appointee becomes forbearance to another (Hult, 1987). Broadening the concept of an implementation structure, however, to respond to varying institutional contexts can enhance its analytical value and add to its conceptual contribution to the bottom-up view.

This potential begins by recognizing that each institutional context embodies its own implementation setting. These settings negotiate multorganizational relationships that emanate from authorities and networks and create institutional identities by defining decision rules and procedures. Contexts develop familiarity with implementation in two ways. One is through the generation of governance structures that implementation settings largely sustain. Familiarity with implementation also occurs as contexts must cooperate and comply with each other's actions. These conditions give credence to implementation being both a gradualist and cumulative process. At the same time, it is not inconsistent to say—as observers who are receptive to the bottom-up view assert—that the distributional context makes principal claim on delivering policy outcomes (Browne and Wildavsky, 1979; Thompson, 1982).

The significance of the distributional contexts arises because of its proximity to what is conventionally referred to as target populations or clients. This proximity allows distributional implementors to officiate over forming policy through the unique qualities of bureaucracies. There are four such qualities. First, bureaucrats must continuously interpret the success of their existing interventions. This occurs in relation either to external standards (both legal and professional) or to organizational objectives (both formal and informal). Second, street-level bureaucrats maintain a degree of independence even as they continue to meet constraints on their behaviors from legislative, adjudicative, regulative, or administrative sources. These constraints will face negotiation because of the dependence of other contexts on bureaucrats to implement outcomes favorably. Third, street-level bureaucrats establish a policy's legitimacy by coordinating service delivery with other organizations—governmental and nongovernmental. Street-level bureaucrats, in turn, are able to coopt client groups to act on their behalf from regulatory (Kaufmann, 1971) to redistributional policies (Brodkin, 1986). For the fourth reason, street-level bureaucrats are in a unique position to evaluate whether conditions they face in service delivery should be communicated both horizontally to co-workers and vertically to managers. Conversely, how much should be revealed about their own (often covert) accommodations to shape service delivery—usually in response to coping with intractable clients (Lipsky, 1978). If these explanations demonstrate that bureaucrats become preeminent in controlling policy outcomes, they also reverse the typical expectations of relationships between principals and agents (Moe, 1991). Bureaucratic decision making makes principals out of agents (Wamsley, 1985). Bureaucrats, in sum, gain power because they decide to whom and how much they should communicate.

3. Bridging the Perspectives: Reversible Logic

The most comprehensive expression of a bottom-up perspective comes from Richard Elmore. His work focuses on how participants create common purposes out of essentially multiple goal environments; that is, policy participants know more about where they think they want to be than how to get there. Policy outcomes are derived from participants exchanging proposals about policy implementation that lead them to create policy intentions. Policy making, in effect, becomes a process of backward mapping (Elmore, 1982). Later, Elmore (1985) employs the concept of reversible logic to explain how participants exchange implementation information to negotiate policy intentions. In essence, policy formation and implementation are not mutually exclusive. Backward mapping captures where participants (including target populations) want to be; indeed, goal clarification among participants emerges from the process. Cooperation becomes necessary because participants want to prevent others from putting roadblocks in their way. Therefore, they acquire a vested interest in learning about where others want to go. The process resembles an ends-causing-means logic except that means commonly derive from incompatible ends. Participants make three assumptions about the process: They possess (1) a normative view of what should be done and with what policy instruments, (2) an empirically based view of their potential for success, and (3) an evaluation of the impingements manifested by other participants. No one has the "whole" view of how to implement outcomes successfully. What surfaces is how participant preference orders coalesce across institutional contexts even though their sources may differ.

Reversible logic complements backward mapping: "Faced with a problem, policymakers frame solutions using the elements over which *they* exercise the greatest control. The content of policy at any given level of the system is a function of the implements people control at that level and the effects they are trying to produce at other levels" (1985: 37). Implements include resources and information that participants command as well as knowledge about what instruments appear to serve them best. In other words, in the absence of steering mechanisms, political and practitioner participants, especially, judge their success by how far they can push the implements they control. Although participants have incentives to increase their control over one another, they are limited by the scope of the implements at their disposal. Participants are also hampered by their identification in the contextual landscape.

Although participants in the policy process subject one another to varying forms of oversight, policy systems are notoriously freewheeling. One of the most centrist regimes, the French, with its elite corps of analysts and administrators, cannot escape an incompleteness that typifies all policy systems. This system, "characterized by its closure," gains wholeness only through the integration of fragmented policies orchestrated by a relatively concentrated ruling elite (Jobert, 1989). Donzelot (1985) notes that ". . . it was not easy to reconcile democratic principles and the market in France until institutional tools were invented to build up social policies consistent with the development of the market: Insurance on the one hand; public service on the other" (in Jobert, 1989: 378). Reversible logic defines that participants interact largely through a process of trial and error; that is, until policy instruments ultimately come to terms with political culture (Hofferbert, 1990).

In a fragmented political system, reversible logic confers regularity across the entire system of policy intervention. It also stabilizes institutional contexts that otherwise lack steering mechanisms. As reversible logic maps policy outcomes across these contexts, such pluricentrist systems (Klijn and Teisman, 1991) presuppose the adoption of compromised policy intentions

(Linder and Peters, 1989b). Compromise in institutional contexts results, however, from resolutions (not reconciliations) among advocacy coalitions (Sabatier, 1988). As Elmore suggests: "people at different political and administrative levels may or may not recognize that they operate in a system of interlocking parochial solutions" (1985: 38). The major signals in such a system do not necessarily emanate from the central government; the periphery can be equally activist. Authoritative arrangements, in other words, may have different ideological pulls between the center and the periphery. Economic development initiatives, for example, have recently emerged among the disparate states as the federal government ignores (nondefense) industrial policy (Osborne, 1990).

In pluricentrist systems, implementation appears to be neither top-down nor bottom-up. More likely it is from the "middle-out," which suggests balancing occurs across institutional contexts. These contexts involve participation in different implementation settings that intensify the democratic character of the overall policy system. Moving away from a dichotomized top-down and bottom-up perspective will provide more opportunity to develop an enriched theory of policy intervention.

4. Focus and Criteria of Program Evaluation

A key element in theory building will benefit from the growing relationship between implementation and program evaluation (Brewer, 1984). Traditionally, program evaluation focused on a relatively straightforward input and output model (Weiss, 1972). This approach coincided with the long-held view that separated formation from implementation. In effect, evaluation studies ignored the "black-box" of program throughputs (Palumbo and Calista, 1990). These studies were unconcerned with such issues as how program goals became distorted or whether perceptions of affected individuals differed (Hellstern, 1985). Evaluation studies now take on a broader view of causal relationships. They accept that program goals may not become apparent until implementation occurs (Bickman, 1987). This receptivity to the transforming capacity of throughputs has led program evaluation to enter the more subjective area of assessing the appropriateness of program goals—as reflected in policy resources and instruments (Lipsey and Pollard, 1989).

By focusing on examining policy assumptions, evaluation research redefines the problem of dealing with the implementation of unintended consequences. These consequences are no longer simply attributed to the distortions of administration (Cook and Shadish, 1986) or used to judge a program's success or failure (Love and Sederberg, 1987). Instead, evaluation research now attempts to discover whether program theory is well founded (Chen and Rossi, 1989). That is, consequences might be unintended if causes other than inadequate implementation have been eliminated; a related issue is whether the evaluation design itself satisfies the requirements of program theory. Poor evaluation design may erroneously conclude that a program is failing when it is not (Winter, 1990).

Program evaluation can contribute to implementation research in numerous ways. One major way concerns the extent of implementation. This involves its context: (1) whether the elements adopted by a program are reaching and serving the right clients or target groups and (2) whether the resources are adequate to serve them. That is, who and how many clients or groups are experiencing a program's services. Context also requires specifying program theory to determine satisfaction levels of potential demand. This approach gains from determining the costs and benefits of certain policies (Luft, 1976). Costs and benefits are represented by comparison of alternative calculations for different satisfaction levels of program goals retrospectively and prospectively. Context additionally includes assessments of whether program benefits require instrument correctives to satisfy program goals (Carlucci, 1990).

Finally, the influence on program evaluation of organizational processes is now significant (Scheirer, 1987). Implementation research needs to take more cognizance of the difficulties faced by program evaluation in determining organizational goal fulfillment (Bickman, 1989).

Programs can be evaluated at macro- and microlevels of implementation. Macroimplementation includes interorganizational and intergovernmental elements involved in goal fulfillment. Implementation of environmental controls, for example, concerns varying governmental agencies and jurisdictions in addition to private sector bodies (Jenkins-Smith, 1991). Microimplementation embraces the more familiar focal agency which carries out program goals. Macroimplementation reveals the difficulty of gaining agreement over what (or whose) program objectives are to be fulfilled (Feldman, 1989). Macrolevel program evaluation focuses on the interpretive aspects of implementation—how perceptions mesh and compliance occurs (Nagel, 1990). Policy objectives display themselves as both formation and implementation unfold and aggregate. Program outcomes, then, represent a confluence of actions among parties who may only superficially agree about mutual objectives. Generally, criteria or standards against which to measure success or failure at the macrolevel are absent. This challenge to program evaluation has been significant and not unrecognized in implementation research (Linder and Peters, 1989a).

The measurement problem is less pronounced for microimplementation. The adaptive approach largely prevails (Berman, 1980). Adaptation manifests itself to the degree that (1) goal statements are ambiguous; (2) program specifications are unclear; (3) participants are numerous; (4) causal theory is unconvincing, and (5) political environments are conflictual. Program evaluation must take account of adaptations as these conditions differentially appear across institutional contexts. Adaptation often occurs in perverse ways too. Implementing school programs for handicapped children resulted in great variation in the prioritization of goals and in the methods to achieve them (Weatherley and Lipsky, 1977). Environmental regulators must account for the creative ways corporations will seek out friendly court jurisdictions to delay compliance (Sabatier, 1988). More positively, evaluating how program's adapt to different locations has become a source of communicating succesful outcomes to other sites (Palumbo and Olivario, 1989). In some policy areas, however, this promise of transfer remains disappointing. Welfare training and work programs across the states exhibit some successes but mostly failures (Lurie, 1992), and predictably so (Palumbo and Calista, 1990). Success in redistribution programs can only be enhanced when articulation of program theory at the microlevel becomes reconcilable with the political assumptions of macrolevel policy goals (Kershaw and Fair, 1975).

Although implementation research has been long on pointing out program flaws at the microlevel, it has been short on calling for redefining policy intentions at the macrolevel. In his review of the literature, O'Toole (1986: 191) reports that there is "not much" in the way of questioning underlying policy intentions. Nor is there much cumulative learning within the field (Goggin et al., 1990). These impediments reflect on the models of research discussed earlier. First, recommendations for policy improvements fall in line with an incremental bias: Marginal improvements are offered for practitioners rather than policy makers per se. Second, the literature is overwhelmingly informed by case studies that heightens the behavioral aspects of implementation, especially in relation to bargaining (Loomis, 1986; Williams, 1982). Cumulation has been restrained because studies fail to challenge each other's conclusions with reconfigured hypotheses (Goodwin and Moen, 1981). The overall result is inconsistent recommendations. What troubles some studies about the lack of legislative specification (Browning et al., 1981) fails to concern others (Ham and Hill, 1984). Bureaucratic politics becomes both an extension (Bryner, 1981) and an interruption (Van Horn, 1979) of democratic conflict resolution. Such inconsistencies expose the limited range of most implementation research that focuses more on solving problems than on defining them. This failing avoids scrutinizing core policy issues more closely.

Some attempts at developing an inclusive theory of policy intervention still depict implementation as being on a different, hence lower, level than formation (Sabatier, 1991). These views remain under the sway of the top-down perspective and its underlying orientation toward incremental and behavioral research methodologies (Fox, 1990). Although the top-down view has produced more follow-up studies than the bottom-up view (Sabatier, 1986), it remains unconvincing. The top-down view has been unable to counter the overwhelming empirical evidence supporting the bottom-up view of implementation (Palumbo and Calista, 1990). Some expectation exists that an institutional view of implementation can integrate the two views (March and Olsen, 1989). The contextual framework discussed in this essay should ease that theory-building effort.

V. IMPLEMENTATION THEORY BUILDING

The lapses that exist in communicating research results and in accumulating related findings are major shortcomings of the implementation field. These problems do not stem from a lack of a sound body of empirical knowledge (Hofferbert, 1990). This situation reflects deficiencies in theory building. There appears to be an inability to propose a set of assumptions from which a testable set of hypotheses could be advanced (Goggin et al., 1990). This framework need not satisfy all the refinements of experimental design or normal science (Yanow, 1990). Any theory, however, must be capable of capturing implementation's institutional basis. In addition, this inclusive theory must enjoy having its propositions falsified. Two proposals will be discussed. Together, they will contribute to implementation research entering a renewed period of activity. Some prior case studies might benefit from secondary testing of their hypotheses.

A. A Theory of Policy Instruments

The first theory bases itself on the instruments of government, the tools authoritative decision makers employ—from persuasion to coercion—to affect policy choices. Unlike prior theories focusing on instruments (Hood, 1984), Linder and Peters (1989b) initially disclaim they are staking out a normative position, although they conclude with one. Their perspective centers on the cognition of actors adopting policy instruments: who chooses them, their meaning, and their subsequent ". . . interaction with organizational and systemic factors" (Linder and Peters, 1989b: 36). The perspective is a "subjectivist interpretation" of "how instruments are viewed by actors inside and outside government who make choices about them . . . and . . . the criteria used by these actors to judge the suitability of instruments for addressing policy problems" (Linder and Peters, 1989b: 36). The scope of this perspective goes beyond limiting itself to elected policy makers.

Essentially, it seeks to overcome the measurement problems that confound dense social and political policy environments. Better measurements can be gotten by uncovering the way decision makers perceive and express their cognitive policy maps. Moreover, although policy situations are unique, it is the organization in which the decision occurs that best explains instrument choice. Thus, the object is to develop an understanding of policy instruments by ". . . the manner in which they are conceptualized by the individuals who must make policy decisions, and contextualized to meet the demands of particular situations" (Linder and Peters,

1989b: 41). The proposal contains a set of three exogenous factors (systemic, organizational, and problem-specific variables) and one endogenous factor (individual variables) that influence choice among policy instruments. Instruments can be understood by their attributes ranging from complexity of operation to precision of targeting; the instruments include both market (tax break) and nonmarket (probation) choices.

Linder and Peters later present (1992) a fourfold typology to differentiate among policy-makers' perceptions of instruments. The four categories range from traditional decision makers who see clear distinctions between instruments, to more open-ended observers of policy design who favor contingent, phenomenological, and critical theory orientations. In the first category of perceptions, instrumentalists, there are mostly policy makers, but some scholars, who endorse a "select, few instruments to which they ascribe all power. . . ." (Linder and Peters, 1992: 5). These can be applied effectively to most situations. Instruments are not contextualized. Derived from instrumental rationality, this perspective leaves "little room for 'politics' " (Linder and Peters, 1992: 5). Next come the proceduralists. They do not favor particular instruments. Tools are not universal in their effectiveness. They need to be located in problem sets. Instruments are by-products of political conditions that need to be anticipated and accommodated situationally. Proceduralists highlight the importance of implementation; notably, from the bottom-up perspective. The third view, the contingentists, however, emphasize the performance criteria of instruments. These are determined by a goodness of fit between the criteria defining tools and contexts. This view reflects the inherent systems bias of political science. Last, and opposite, constitutivists are after the underlying meaning of policy instruments; they stress the importance of individual actors' values and perceptions. Tools are only imperfectably knowable. Policies are sound reconstructions in which both tools and contexts will vary according to their source. Linder and Peter (1992) identify with the latter as reflecting the current intellectual climate in political science.

Conceivably, knowledge of how decision makers perceive instruments allows for greater consistency in measuring them across formation and implementation. The subjectivist view can focus attention on the authenticity of policy debates by displaying decision makers' perceptions. This can occur because the subjectivist view accords greater voice to advocacy positions (Sabatier, 1988). Put differently, as decision makers are located by perceptual category, this might reflect the salience of issues; say, as reflected in constituent interests. Categorization can also discern whether some instruments are either being avoided or perhaps not intended for successful implementation (Benson, 1971). Accordingly, the strength of this perspective will revolve around whether categories can address issues of reconciling political endowments for major policy arenas. The question: How completely do policy intentions embrace political reconciliations that will allow implementation to redistribute endowments? That potential strength, however, reveals weaknesses.

Weakness derives from treating implementation too passively. A subjectivist reconstruction of policy instruments does not necessarily improve the scope of their aim. Nor does understanding perceptions precondition settlement of profound political issues. Moreover, the desirability of policy instruments may be unable to reconcile opposing societal values; notably, between market presumptions and democratic principles. Implementation research should avoid repeating its history—rediscovering that irreconciliation turns desirable instruments into infeasible outcomes. Questions of successful implementation need to consider whether policy instruments are capable of achieving political reconciliation. Unreconciled redistributive issues, however, condemn policy instruments to partial (and predictable) implementation failures, at least.

Those failures can be better understood by analyzing the relationships between the desirability of policy instruments and the possibility of political reconciliation. Essentially, this understanding requires constructing a dialogue among institutional contexts. First, the desirability of instruments cannot be separated from acceptance of their tenability in causal relationships. This is so because relationships become stabilized as steady-state solutions—even after the occurrence of repeated failures.[4] Solutions reflect the core of both institutional memory and learning. The highly interactive character of these institutional processes underscores how much their reticulistic nature shapes choice of policy instruments. That is, the perceptions of instruments needs to be located within embedded institutional processes (Jobert, 1988). Because institutional contexts negotiate their identities through implementation settings, a theory of policy instruments could gain greater coherence by incorporating how these identities shape perceptual preferences. For one, a theory can derive from the creation of a clearer empirical base on which preference orders are being articulated. For another, it can achieve greater depth by explaining how these preference orders relate to the likelihood of generating political reconciliation.

B. Transaction Costs, Public Choice, and Implementation

The missing link in American policy analysis is no longer the separation of formation from implementation (Hargrove, 1975). Now missing is a more fundamental linkage for which theory must account; namely, what are the dimensions of political reconciliation that reflect endowment discrepancies between market demands and democratic policy choices. A theory of policy intervention must be capable of analyzing the conditions of reconciliation with the market, not simply to explain the existence of the public sector as a default of market failures (Moe, 1991). Theory must be capable of systematically demonstrating trade-offs between varying market and nonmarket alternatives. It must elucidate how implementation of endowments is to be achieved. One framework attracts attention because it satisfies those requirements. The framework bases itself on the costs of transactions and derives from the field of economics. Before describing it, some preliminary remarks are in order. Political scientists fear acceptance of this framework subjects their field to contamination (if not subsumption) as it would endanger its central focus—the authoritative allocation of values (Bryson, 1984). This reaction can be mollified by making two points about the transaction costs view (Williamson, 1985). One is that the current state of implementation research has exhausted what political science offers it, especially in understanding the multiorganizational relationships in differing institutional contexts. Second, in economics, the transactions approach enjoys (suffers from) similar criticisms as it does in political science (Moe, 1991). Suspicions also exist because the transaction costs view shifts the focus of economics away from markets and toward firms (Lazonick, 1991). This so-called market failures approach reverses the basic assumptions of economics—firms not markets are efficiency maximizers that lower the costs of doing business. Under certain conditions, usually associated with the economics of scale of large modern enterprises, firms are better able to absorb the costs of markets; thereby, lowering the prices of goods and services. The question remains, however, whether any conceptual symmetry aligns public with private goods and services.

What joins the two fields in their potential use of transaction costs theory is its institutionalist orientation—to uncover what organizations do: to discover why they emerge, survive, and fail. That is, transaction costs view focuses on the wellsprings of economy, not economics per se: It seeks to determine how organizational decision making creates an institutional basis for capitalism (Williamson, 1985). In political science, similar issues are raised about institutional contexts at every juncture of policy intervention—not only for implementation. At the least, transaction costs theory will be able to provide insights into the organizational and interorganizational dimensions of implementation that political science has been unable to do for itself (Moe, 1990). Neither contamination nor subsumption will occur. The opportunity should not be lost to show how a transaction costs approach could unify a theory of policy intervention.

This possibility will not be easy to accept. Extending transaction costs economics to policy intervention can become more palatable, however, by relating it to the more familiar discipline-based public choice theory (Johnson, 1991; Shepsle, 1989). One empirical hurdle must be overcome to increase acceptance of the value of transaction costs. This requires recognizing that distinguishing between public-private sector organizations is a falsifiable proposition. This appears when organizational (and interorganizational) structures are viewed in relation to the production of collective goods and services. The proposition is: "Any presumption that social reality exists in two separable domains isolated from one another would be an obvious conceptual error" (Ostrom, 1989: 869). The postulate is falsifiable by observing that quasimarkets exist in the public sector through its ability to purchase goods and services: "quasimarkets are distinguishable from private markets because *collectivities* are the purchasing units, *not individuals*" (Ostrom, 1989: 872; our emphasis). In other words, ". . . collective organizations capable of taxing and regulating patterns of use are also necessary for the consumption of goods" (Ostrom, 1989: 872). Public sector organizations lose their distinction: "so long as multiple vendors are available, competitive options provide alternatives to an exclusive reliance on bureaucratic principles or organization in the public sector" (Ostrom, 1989: 872). That exclusivity was forcefully challenged in Salamon's (1981) finding that most federal government spending occurs through the creation of a "third sector" of quasi-non-governmental agencies, and private markets. In sum, "contestable quasimarket arrangements are feasible in the public sector" (Ostrom, 1989: 872).

A major difficulty in accepting the validity of the quasimarket proposition comes from focusing attention on the internal structure of an organization. Further, Ostrom (1989: 872) notes that, "the problem is why do quasimarkets and other patterns of interorganizational arrangements arise in the public sector?" Public organizations are collectivities ". . . largely concerned with problems of organizing consumption functions in a public economy" (Ostrom, 1989: 872). Put differently, neither the public choice nor transaction costs ecnomics theory endorses a wholesale expropriation of neoclassical economics to political science. Indeed, they are critical of it.

As Ostrom (1989: 872) clearly articulates, the inappropriateness of received neoclassical economics to the public sector is axiomatic:

> The neoclassical model of perfectly competitive markets does *not* provide appropriate assumptions for reasoning about public economics that have reference to the types of goods and services that are subject to the jointness of use or consumption, or to failure of exclusion, and other attributes that contribute to market weaknesses and market failures.

Indeed, the critique of neoclassical economics does not stop with its inability to account for public sector variables. Neoclassical economics cannot explain private markets where collectivities dominate in the exchange of goods and services (Lazonick, 1991). The falsifiability of the first postulate can be substantiated:

> If we shift attention away from the buying and selling among participants in the market to the milieu in which this buying and selling occurs, we would then find that markets

are themselves subject to joint use by buyers and sellers. Exclusion from the market itself does not prevail in "free" markets. The conditions of market organization have the characteristics of collective goods in contrast to buying and selling that occurs within markets (Ostrom, 1989: 873).

The first postulate can now be stated more inclusively: The distinctions between public and private multiorganizational arrangements are reducible to comparable collective goods dimensions.

The clarification of the first postulate opens the way to applying a transaction costs framework across the entire field of policy intervention. Its assumptions about neoclassical economics parallel those of public choice. Minimally, transaction costs can serve as an incipient theory of policy implementation because it relates the exchange of collective goods to multiorganizational settings; this will enhance its usefulness for policy intervention. Its core concepts, in other words, cut across both public and private organizational dimensions that define policy arenas (Calista, 1987a). This means that a transactional approach also displays how private markets replace public organizations when the latter incur implementation failures (Wolf, 1988). What is needed is an application framework that analytically incorporates these dual failures—of (private) markets and (public) bureaucracies—that avoids making false distinctions between policy instrumentation and implementation. Bryson and Ring (1990) provide this framework.

C. New Institutionalism and Policy Implementation

This framework restates the basic postulate by effectively putting the public and private sectors on the same empirical ground. That is, Bryson and Ring (1990) suggest that the public sector can measure its existence by how well it overcomes a "rebuttable presumption." This presumption stems from Schultze's (1979) argument: Simply because the modern state has adopted incremental welfare economics to address human and social problems does not mean it is superior to market-based solutions. Absent rebuttal, private markets are superior. Policy interventions cannot presume that by replacing private markets with public bureaucracies they are more capable of implementing even equitable outcomes. Such replacement may eliminate implementing equitable solutions already available as marketlike or quasimarket alternatives (Rushefsky, 1984). For example, by using incentives (negative income tax) rather than continuing welfare transfer payments—commonly considered both inequitable and inefficient—social welfare organizations can achieve greater equitability through efficient market alternatives (Kershaw and Fair, 1975).

1. The Rebuttable Presumption's Governing Principles

Bryson and Ring (1990) employ the rebuttable presumption as a basis to create an inclusive range of policy instruments. What is insightful about this approach is that markets and hierarchies are not treated as opposites. Instead, markets lie somewhere between self-service and government service solutions. Within this range are numerous quasimarket and market-correcting alternatives. The first step in policy intervention then is to discover whether instruments can survive the rebuttable presumption; at least in efficiency and equitability terms. Implementation plays a critical role in this process.

The rebuttable presumption can be operationalized by applying four governing principles to instrument adoption and implementation. First, instruments should be specified and detailed enough to account for market failure in policy formation and, equally important, for implementation: ". . . the failures to which the intervention itself is prone" (Bryson and Ring, 1990: 206). This dual accounting of instruments opens the way for considering the multiorganizational basis for implementation. Accounting for these relationships, however, does not compel policy intervention to favor the feasibility of implementation over the desirability of intentions. Second, the market's limited focus on efficiency need not be condemning. Its scope can be broadened to include public policy choices of justice and liberty. To these ends, organizational issues become critical to adjusting known implementation failures by choosing other desirable, and even more appealing, instruments. In sum, what presumably begins as an inherent economic concern for efficiency ends by not excluding instruments congenial to the public sector.

The third and fourth governing principles informing the rebuttable presumption are interrelated. Adoption of the presumption allows for switching instruments. Such triggering capacity also complements the decisional rules associated with the transactional approach. The final governing principle is the rebuttable presumption's inclusivity of policy instruments. It does not exclude employing market or nonmarket instruments. Transaction costs economics also contains this capability. For both, inclusivity is determined by lowering the costs of exchanges.

2. *Contracts, Governance Structures, and Reversible Logic*

Transaction costs economics indicates an exchange occurs: ". . . when a good or service is transferred across a technologically separable interface" (Williamson, 1981: 1544). A transfer implies some form of an agreement is occurring—usually taking the form of a contract (explicit or implicit) that subjects the parties to performance criteria. Contracts create a governance structure in which the costs of monitoring agreements are mutually, although not always equally, borne. Parties engage in two forms of contracting. One is *ex ante* that accounts for the transactions involved in ". . . planning, drafting, negotiating, and safeguarding the agreement" (Bryson and Ring, 1990: 212). The other contract is *ex post*. It covers the subsequent costs included in monitoring and correcting misalignments, setting up and running governance structures, and bonding secure commitments (Bryson and Ring, 1990: 212). Markets lose their superiority as *ex ante* and *ex post* costs can be absorbed more efficiently through different organizational forms. In relation to policy intervention, this loss occurs when the rebuttable presumption of market failure can be satisfied. This serves as a signal to evaluate policy instruments that are likely to satisfy both governing principles while minimizing transaction costs.

This search across a transactional frontier for alternative instruments can be fused with an expanded version of Elmore's (1985) concept of reversible logic. This concept is important because it is at the core of theory building in implementation research. In essence, it states that full knowledge of a policy instrument can only occur through a process of discovery. Instruments are only conceptual (perceptual) representations until praxis absorbs them as actual implementations. That is, policies are formulated in each institutional context as parties employ reversible logic by engaging in a process of forward and backward mapping. In effect, "a good bargaining strategy provides a way of maximizing one's own interests, but [it] also provides a way of anticipating the actions of others" (Elmore, 1985: 38). Thus, each institutional context recreates: "a policy [that] is both an authoritative statement of what *should* happen and a calculated judgment about what *will* happen" (Elmore, 1985: 38). This process of recreation reveals the prevalence of normative assumptions that distinguish interests in the public sector. This recreation of what should and will happen in bargaining strategies also captures the relation of reversible logic to transaction costs. The relationship stems from the application of similar concepts. Equivalence exists between reversible logic's maximizing of one's interests and anticipating another's actions; that is, with opportunism and bounded rationality in transaction costs.

3. Transactional Resources and Costs

Human beings are, respectively, both prone to self-interest with guile and suffer from limited cognition. Absent complete knowledge, humans can neither trust other parties nor process information fully. These transactional problems create asymmetries that lead parties to experience information impactedness. Taken together, these problems trigger transaction failures. They heighten uncertainties that increase costs on all transactions; these costs, in turn, create nontrivial losses as the search for improving governance structures unfolds. Governance structures require agreements between parties that allow them to cooperate with one another. What is messy about public sector structures is that their underlying agreements will be rewritten within each institutional context. Continuing the contractual metaphor also highlights how implementation settings create contextual governance structures between authoritative arrangements and network composition. Contracts ". . . define conditions under which individuals agree to be constrained—coerced, in effect" (Heckathorn and Maser, 1991). Neither constraint nor coercion can occur, however, without the willingness of parties to cooperate (to some degree) with one another (Stoker, 1991). Cooperation becomes easily interrupted in public policy making; these interruptions are the principal transaction costs associated with acquiring and processing information. To reduce these liabilities, implementation settings compel authorities and networks to incur costs by expending transactional resources (Heckathorn and Maser, 1990).

Transactional resources are expended in three ways. One, parties face bargaining and decision costs as it is difficult to discern the desirability of all alternatives. When "parochial solutions" are exchanged, it is not self-evident among parties ". . . which alternatives are inequitable" (Heckathorn and Maser, 1990: 1105). Similarly, parties are subject to search costs as they puzzle over the feasibility of alternatives. This question of what will work is often indistinguishable from how much will alternative costs. In effect, what will work is not simply a matter of feasibility but desirability when implementation costs are considered. There are also monitoring costs. These costs are highly unpredictable as there is a compounding effect of gaining compliance as policies move between and within institutional contexts. Neither judges nor street-level bureaucrats, for example, can fully account for their own compliance costs, which increase as they factor in the other's costs. It is the compounding effects of such compliance costs that leads to implementation failures (Ostrom, 1990). Such policy failures occur for defense (Melman, 1988) no less than for welfare (Brodkin, 1986).

As monitoring costs lead to implementation failures (Hult and Walcott, 1991), transaction costs come full circle. Its basic elements are falsifiable for both private and public sectors in that it specifies why markets and hierarchies fail. This is especially important for public sector policy implementation. That is, implementation failure in the public sector does not simply mean that the rebuttable presumption signals a return to markets (Wolf, 1988). Failure also creates alternative hierarchies, usually of the decentralized format, that are more likely to limit the liabilities of opportunism and bounded rationality (Rainey, 1990). In terms of reversible logic, maximizing one's interests or anticipating another's solutions can also stimulate the search for alternative mapping options. Extrapolating from such searches counters the view that employment of reversible logic could lead to, ". . . endlessly fine-tuning a wrong instrument" (Linder and Peters, 1990b: 309). Nonetheless, the monitoring costs associated with a search can suboptimize implementation outcomes. Reversible logic involves cumulative learning across institutional contexts that reduces suboptimality because, ". . . policies must have sufficient flexibility to allow for the difference between what should *and* what will happen (Elmore, 1985: 38–39; our emphasis). When such flexibility to implement hierarchical alternatives diminishes, however, the rebuttable presumption can no longer defend against market failure and transaction costs rise.

4. *Decision Rules and Implementing School Reform*

Transaction costs essentially concerns displaying how well the economics of efficiency can be satisfied. Yet, this does not exclude consideration of decision rules that can involve transaction costs in political debates and inform public policy interventions (Moe, 1991). Indeed, a transactions framework can embrace a much broader set of policy instruments precisely because its organizational orientation has generic application. Its decision rules are capable of asking *how much* efficiency, equity, or liberty are desirable and of learning *how well* those conditions are being satisfied by various organizational arrangements. Broadly conceived, application of transactional decision rules opens the way to consider the legal, economic, and social implications of adopting and implementing public policy instruments.

This application becomes of central importance in evaluating public school reform (Bryson and Ring, 1990). As an alternative to the use of "captive" instruments of government service, educational choice of schools would be governed by both subsidy and resultion—by providing vouchers. These policy instruments create quasimarkets of collective buyers of goods in that schools are selected without regard to residence. These quasimarkets allow schools to decentralize organizational decision making that lowers transaction costs significantly. This occurs as decentralized school units, coupled with the encouragement of curricular innovations, can satisfy transactional decision rules more fully. There are seven decision rules.

Applying them to school choice demonstrates how well they address both market and public sector issues. First, since school performance follows buyers, this limits the opportunism characteristic of captive situations. Second, small number problems are diminished as competition among schools invites newcomers. Third, uncertainty initially encourages bounded rationality and information impactedness to appear, although time allows informal and formal evaluations to reduce their effects. Fourth, some successful schools might limit nonexcludability and jointness of consumption. In districts that implement choice, however, all the schools reach the same high-water marks, which eases fears that liberty and justice are ill-served (Chubb and Moe, 1990). At the microlevel of implementation, one of the scarcest public goods, personal security, improves (*New York Times*, 16 Sept., 1992: 1). Fifth, some regulations can occur to ensure nondiscrimination of various types and to compensate for families disadvantaged by certain asset-specific investments. Sixth, asset specificity also implies developing greater reliance on decentralizing decision making (including client satisfactions) that maximizes on human rather than bureaucratic capital. Seventh, and highly critical to its implementation success, a voucher system can treat issues of equity, liberty, and justice. Regulations can underscore the need to ensure that choice precedes coercion. Application of these decision rules suggests that the desirability of school choice becomes enhanced by anticipating the pitfalls of implementation. School choice effectively becomes a bottom-up formulation. Correspondingly, the strength of the transactions approach lies not only in its ability to show the superiority of one policy instrument over another. As important, by satisfying its decision rules, transaction costs reveals the strengths and weaknesses of an entire range of instruments that can account for adopting policy choices.

VI. CONCLUSION: DEVELOPING CREDIBLE THEORY

A. Addressing the Shortcomings of Received Theory

A credible framework must address the shortcomings of the two major received theories. Both the behavioral and incremental frameworks are flawed not because they assume that various cognitive limitations constrain decision making; in this, they are even partially joined by the assumptions of transaction costs and reversible logic. The two models are unproductive because they endorse suboptimality in implementation by accepting programmed bureaucracies as modal public sector organizations. These organizations hardly pass efficiency tests (Rainey, 1992), much less foster equitability which gets muddled as embedded policies leave endowment issues largely unreconciled (March and Olsen, 1989). The underlying instrumental rationality—and systems bias—of these models self-limits the scope of what public organizations can fulfill; ironically, usually defended in the name of efficiency and equitability—often, collapsed simply as accountability. Public policy instruments are, therefore, invariably viewed as being blunted by implementation because multiorganizational relationships, in these models, are constrained by the trappings of conventional bureaucracies (Echeverri-Gent, 1992). This situation is most troublesome in implementing endowments as both the behavioral and incremental models do not make political reconciliation a condition of policy adoption. Implementation falters, however, as irreconciliations create an inordinate need to raise monitoring costs across all institutional contexts (Heckathorn and Maser, 1990).

The transaction costs approach addresses these shortcomings convincingly. Instead of bounded rationality limiting the scope of organizational arrangements, it becomes a platform to lower transaction costs. By fostering the discovery of alternatives, transaction costs turns to decentralized organizations as offering greater flexibility; decision making disperses itself to subunits empowered to achieve greater efficiency. The focus on efficiency does not exclude consideration of public interest goals as well (Bryson, 1984; Calista, 1987b). Transaction costs can readily expose inefficiencies. It can also disclose the costs of implementing inequitable alternatives. Inequitability fuses with the inefficient use of resources, especially when political irreconciliation undermines implementation. Furthermore, the link between transaction costs with reversible logic and the rebuttable presumption complements its capacity of locating lapses in political reconciliation.

B. Integrating Policy Formation and Implementation

Credible theory must integrate policy formation and implementation. Transaction costs joins formation and implementation by applying the same decision rules to their determination. These rules take hold whether policy instruments are supporting either markets or hierarchies. The rebuttal presumption puts public sector implementation on constant alert as to the costs of transactional resources. Transaction costs decision rules expose inefficiencies when monitoring reduces available resources; thereby, raising the cost of implementing policy instruments. When those costs become prohibitive, reversible logic negotiates solutions by refining existing instruments or reasserting market choices.

Adopting the transaction costs framework broadens the base of policy choices. Its search for organizational optimality avoids adherence to a top-down view of implementation (Sabatier, 1986). The top-down view tacitly assumes an organizational one-best way that inhibits implementation from refining policy instruments or from correcting hierarchies (Hjern, 1987). Movement away from the top-down view also will reduce the normative attachment that lingers for the dichotomy between politics and administration. Reducing that distinction advances the application of transaction costs for implementation research in another important way. The transactions assumption is that the more organizations increase their dependence on their members, the more incentives for trust will grow (Moe, 1990). This corollary postulate (associated with asset specificity) remains virtually unexplored across all the subfields of policy intervention (Calista, 1987a). Secondary analyses of implementation research receptive to this postulate could have powerful implications for policy intervention (Martin, 1983; Molnar and Rogers, 1982; Thompson, 1982).

C. An Incipient Theory of Policy Implementation

Correspondingly, credible theory must employ common elements to penetrate all institutional contexts—otherwise its contribution to a more encompassing theory of policy intervention deteriorates. The proposed institutional framework provides a comprehensive way to accept transaction costs elements to analyze implementation. These elements must form the basis for the testing of falsifiable hypotheses. Decision rules identified by transaction costs allow for the falsifiability of a mix of market and hierarchical policy instruments. That is, the major elements of bounded rationality, opportunism, and asset specificity can be falsified when satisfying them fails to reduce the suboptimality of outcomes—an analytical attribute unequalled by other models.

As indicated, transaction costs benefits from adopting the basic assumptions of both the rebuttable presumption and reversible logic. In essence, incorporating the rebuttable presumption and reversible logic reduces the uncertainties (and costs) of imperfect information associated with the key elements of transaction costs. Determining the integrity of policy instruments will center on learning how transactional resources are being expended and for what purposes. The results provide the constant on which implementation drives policy choices. Formulating choices will also be shaped by whether the requirements of the rebuttable presumption are being satisfied at the same time that reversible logic demonstrates that the alternatives are no less parochial. Together, the decision rules of transaction costs, the requirements of the rebuttable presumption, and the processes of reversible logic can lead to an incipient theory of implementation. This theory draws on conjoining their basic assumptions to measure how policy instruments are deployed in implementation—and to derive alternatives. Testing the theory can occur in implementation settings across institutional context. Minimally, the institutional framework, with its iteration of contextual variables, allows the theory to determine why policy alternatives are being ignored. This focus is especially important in relation to political reconciliation of endowments. Gains made by application of the institutional and transactional frameworks can have great impact on the entire field of policy intervention.

NOTES

1. Nearly all of the subsequent discussion deals with implementation in the United States. Though researchers are cited who conducted studies in other countries, the distinctiveness of the American situation receives primary attention. This largely occurs because of the inverse relationship that appears to exist between knowledge of policy structures, including implementation, and the presence of political reconciliation over major issues in the United States. The present period appears to be an unusually crowded one for addressing critical policy issues for the United States—or not.

2. One exemplar of noncoordinated policy implementation has become a central feature of American society; namely, suburbanization. Although it hardly exists in some coherent statement of a major

governmental intent, suburbanization became a significant outgrowth of numerous programs of government outlays and rebates. Although the explicit desire to undermine the urban core of American life could not be attributed to any of these programs, the outcomes speak for themselves. Through such well-endowed programs as the Federal Highway Fund, Veterans Administration loans and subsidies, and home loan and tax rebates, suburbanization implemented itself. These programs had enormous appeal, although they are all disaggregated in their intentions and implementation (Baer, 1975).

3. A recent study found severe flaws with this program and recommends its abandonment in favor of others that employ greater performance criteria for their renewal (*New York Times*, 11 Dec., 1992: 24).

4. Equally problematic in the subjectivist typology is the absence of defining postulates or principles that can capture both formation and implementation. Common elements are needed to display policy instruments more inclusively. It is not enough to say, for example, that the subjectivist view opens itself to a variety of explanatory principles. A typology with any theoretical potential must introduce elements that can generate hypotheses that, in turn, are subject to refutation. What happens in a situation in which the same instrument is introduced under different conditions but keeps yielding opposite implementation results? Does this implementation merely show the slow pace of learning? Or, does this render the instrument meaningless empirically, although its perception remains meaningful politically—even after repeated failures? Such reversals occurred for implementing capital gains tax policies between 1976 and 1987. They were raised in 1976 and 1987 and lowered in 1978, 1981, and 1984 (Minarik, 1992). The apparent object (perception) of this instrument is to affect the behavior of savings and investment, especially among the wealthy. Its outcomes are believed to be highly predictable—raising these taxes diminishes and lowering them increases capital investments. Yet this market form of implementation consistently had opposite results. As an instrument, it is neither a tax break nor a tax penalty. Even if perceived to be a penalty, the inconsistent outcomes cannot be attributed to the perverse behaviors of wealthy individuals. Perceptions of an instrument, in other words, may not confer integrity upon it. The typology weakens in the absence of operating principles that can gauge the value of an instrument by systematically comparing it to others.

REFERENCES

Alison, G. (1971). *Essence of Decisionmaking: Explaining the Cuban Missile Crisis.* Little, Brown, Boston.

Baer, W. C. (1975). On the making of a perfect and beautiful social program. *Public Interest* 39: 80-98.

Bardach, E. (1977). *The Implementation Game.* MIT Press, Cambridge, MA.

Barrett, S., and Hill, M. (1984). Policy, bargaining and structure in implementation theory: Towards an integrated perspective. *Policy and Politics* 12: 219-240.

Benson, J. K. (1971). Militant ideologies and organization contexts: The war on poverty and the ideology of "black power." *The Sociological Review* 12: 328-339.

Benson, J. K., and Weitzel, C. J. (1985). Social structure and social praxis in interorganizational policy analysis. In *Policy Implementation in Federal and Unitary Systems.* K. Hanf and T. A. J. Toonen (Eds.). Martinus Nijhoff, Dordrecht, The Netherlands.

Berman, P. (1980). Thinking about programmed adaptative implementation: Matching strategies to situations. In *Why Policies Succeed and Fail.* H. M. Ingram and D. E. Mann (Eds.). Sage, Beverly Hills, CA.

Berman, P., and McLaughlin, M. (1976). Implementation of educational innovation. *Educational Forum* 40: 347-370.

Beyer, J. M., and Trice, H. M. (1982). The utilization process: A conceptual framework and synthesis of empirical findings. *Administrative Science Quarterly* 27: 591-622.

Bickman, L. (1987). The functions of program theory. In *Using Program Theory in Evaluation.* L. Bickman (Ed.). Jossey-Bass, San Francisco.

—— (1989). Barriers to the use of program theory. *Evaluation and Program Planning* 12:387-390.

Bobrow, D. B., and Dryzek, J. S. (1987). *Policy Analysis by Design*. University of Pittsburgh, Pittsburgh, PA.

Brewer, M. B. (1984). Evaluation: Past and present. In *The University Edition of the Handbook of Evaluation Research*. Sage, Beverly Hills, CA.

Brodkin, E. Z. (1986). *The False Promise of Administrative Reform*. Temple University Press, Philadelphia.

Brown, L. D. (1991). *Health Policy and the Disadvantaged*. Duke University Press, Durham, NC.

Browne, A., and Wildavsky, A. (1984). Implementation as mutual adaptation. In *Implementation*. J. L. Pressman and A. Wildavsky (Eds.). University of California Press, Berkeley.

Browning, R. P., Marshall, D. R., and Tabb, D. H. (1981). Implementation and political change: Sources of local variations in federal social programs. In *Effective Policy Implementation*. D. A. Mazmanian and P. A. Sabatier (Eds.). Heath, Lexington, MA.

—— (1984). *Protest Is Not Enough*. University of California Press, Berkeley, CA.

Bryner, G. (1981). Congress, courts, and agencies: Equal employment and the limits of policy implementation. *Political Science Quarterly* 96: 411–430.

Bryson, J. M. (1984). The policy process and organizational form. *Policy Studies Journal* 12: 445–463.

Bryson, J. M., and Ring, P. S. (1990). A transaction-based approach to policy intervention. *Policy Sciences* 23: 205–229.

Buck, S. J. (1991). *Understanding Environmental Administration and Law*. Island Press, Washington, D.C.

Bullock, C. S., III (1981). Implementation of equal opportunity programs. In *Effective Policy Implementation*. D. A. Mazmanian and P. A. Sabatier (Eds.). Heath, Lexington, MA.

Burke, J. P. (1990). Policy implementation and the responsible exercise of discretion. In *Implementation and the Policy Process*. D. J. Palumbo and D. J. Calista (Eds.). Greenwood, Westport, CT.

Caiden, G. (1983). *International Handbook of the Ombudsmen: Country Surveys*. Greenwood, Westport, CT.

Calista, D. J. (1986a). On the orthodoxy and tentativeness of reform. In *Bureaucratic and Governmental Reform*. D. J. Calista (Ed.). JAI Press, Greenwich, CT.

—— (1986b). Linking policy intention and policy implementation: The role of the organization in the integration of human services. *Administration & Society* 18: 263–286.

—— (1987a). Transaction costs analysis as a theory of public sector implementation. *Policy Studies Journal* 15: 461–480.

—— (1987b). Resolving public sector implementation paradoxes through transaction costs analysis: Theory and application. *Policy Studies Review* 7: 232–245.

Carlucci, C. P. (1989). The role of the legislative analyst in policymaking. *Journal of Management Science & Policy Analysis* 7: 20–34.

—— (1990). Acquisition: The missing link in the implementation of technology. In *Implementation and the Policy Process*, D. J. Palumbo and D. J. Calista (Eds.). Greenwood, Westport, CT.

Cerych, L., and Sabatier, P. A. (1986). *Great Expectations and Mixed Performance: The Implementation of European Higher Education Reforms*. Trentham Books, Stove-on-Trent, UK.

Chase, G. (1979). Implementing a human services program. *Public Policy* 27: 385–435.

Checkland, P. (1981). *Systems Thinking, Systems Practice*. Wiley, Chichester, UK.

Chen, H-T., and Rossi, P. H. (1989). Issues in the theory-driven perspective. *Evaluation and Program Planning* 12: 299–306.

Chubb, J. E., and Hansek, E. A. (1990). Reforming educational reform. In *Setting National Priorities*. H. J. Aaron (Ed.). Brookings, Washington, D.C.

Chubb, J. E., and Moe, T. M. (1990). *Politics, Markets, and America's Schools*. Brookings, Washington, D.C.

Cook, T. D., and Shadish, W. (1986). Program evaluation: The worldly science. *Annual Review of Psychology* 37: 193–232.

Davies, T., and Mason, C. (1982). Gazing up at the bottoms: Problems of minimal response in the implementation of manpower policy. *European Journal of Political Research* 10:145–157.

Derthick, M. (1972). *New Towns In Town*. The Urban Institute, Washington, D.C.

—— (1990). *Agency Under Stress: The Social Security Administration*. Brookings Institution, Washington, D.C.

DiMaggio, P. J., and Powell, W. (1983). The iron cage revisited: Institutional isomorphism and collective rationality in organizational fields. *American Sociological Review* 48: 147–160.

Downs, A. (1967). *Inside Bureaucracy*. Little, Brown, Boston, MA.

Dunleavy, P. (1990). *Democracy, Bureaucracy and Public Choice*. Prentice-Hall, New York.

Echeverri-Gent, J. (1992). Between autonomy and capture: Embedding implementing agencies in their societal environment. *Policy Studies Journal* 20: 342–64.

Elmore, R. F. (1982). Backward mapping: Implementation research and policy decisions. In *Studying Implementation*. W. Williams (Ed.). Chatham House, Chatham, NJ.

—— (1985). Forward and backward mapping: Reversible logic in the analysis of public policy. In *Policy Implementation in Federal and Unitary Systems*. K. Hanf and T. A. J. Toonen (Eds.). Martinus Nijhoff, Dordrecht, The Netherlands.

—— (1989). Gordon Chase meets Robert Moses: Notes on the politics of public management. *Journal of Management Science & Policy Analysis* 6: 79–90.

Feldman, M. S. (1989). *Order Without Design*. Stanford University Press, Stanford, CA.

Fox, C. J. (1990). Implementation research: Why and how to transcend positivist methodologies. In *Implementation and the Policy Process*. D. J. Palumbo and D. J. Calista (Eds.). Greenwood, Westport, CT.

Gellhorn, W. (1966). *When Americans Complain*. Harvard University Press, Cambridge, MA.

Ginsberg, B., and Shefter, M. (1990). *Politics by Other Means*. Basic Books, New York.

Goggin, M. (1987). *Policy Design and the Politics of Implementation*. University of Tennessee, Knoxville, KY.

Goggin, M., Bowman, A., Lester, J. P., and O'Toole, L. J. Jr. (1990). *Implementation Theory and Practice: Toward a Third Generation*. Scott, Foresman, Glenview, IL.

Goodwin, L., and Moen, P. (1981). The evolution and implementation of family welfare policy. In *Effective Policy Implementation*. P. A. Sabatier and D. A. Mazmanian (Eds.). Heath, Lexington, MA.

Ham, C., and Hill, M. (1984). *The Policy Process in the Modern Capitalist State*. St. Martin's, New York.

Hargrove, E. C. (1975). *The Missing Link*. Urban Institute, Washington, D.C.

Hargrove, E. C., and Glidewell, J. G. (1990). *Impossible Jobs in Public Management*. University of Kansas Press, KN.

Heckathorn, D. D., and Maser, S. (1990). The contractual architecture of public policy: A critical reconstruction of Lowi's typology. *Journal of Politics* 52: 1101–1123.

Heclo, H. (1968). Issue networks and the executive establishment. In *The New American Political System*. A. King (Ed.). American Enterprise Institute, Washington, D.C.

Hellstern, G. M. (1985). Assessing evaluation research. In *Guidance, Control, and Evaluation in the Public Sector*. F. X. Kaufmann et al. (Eds.). deGruyter, Berlin.

Hjern, B. (1987). Policy analysis: An implementation approach. Paper read at the meetings of the American Political Science Association, Palmer House, Chicago, IL, Sept. 3–6.

Hjern, B., and Porter, D. D. (1981). Implementation structures: A new unit of administrative analysis. *Organization Studies* 2/3: 211–227.

Hofferbert, R. I. (1974). *The Study of Public Policy*. Bobbs-Merrill, Indianapolis, IN.

—— (1990). *The Reach and Grasp of Policy Analysis*. University of Alabama Press, Tuscaloosa, AL.

Hood, Christopher. (1984). *The Tools of Government*. Macmillan, New York.

Horowitz, D. L. (1977). Courts as guardians of the public interest. *Public Administration Review* 37: 148–154.

Hult, K. (1987). *Agency Merger and Bureaucratic Redesign*. University of Pittsburg Press, Pittsburgh, PA.

Hult, K., and Walcott, C. (1991). *Governing Public Organizations: Politics, Structures, and Institutional Design*. Brooks, Cole, Pacific Grove, CA.

Ingram, H. (1990). Implementation: A review and suggested framework. In *Public Administration: The State of the Discipline*. Chatham House, Chatham, NJ.

Ingram, H., and Schneider, A. (1990). Improving implementation through framing smarter statutes. *Journal of Public Policy* 10: 67–88.

Jenkins-Smith, H. C. (1991). Alternative theories of the policy process: Reflections on research strategy for the study of nuclear waste policy. *PS: Political Science and Politics* 24: 157–166.

Jobert, B. (1989). The normative frameworks of public policy. *Political Studies* 37: 376–86.

Johnson, D. B. (1991). *Public Choice.* Mayfield, Mountain View, CA.

Katz, D., and Kahn, R. L. (1966). *The Social Psychology of Organizations.* Wiley, New York.

Kaufmann, H. (1960). *The Forest Ranger.* Johns Hopkins Press, Baltimore, MD.

Kelman, S. (1984). Using implementation research to solve implementation problems: The case of energy emergency assistance. *Journal of Policy Analysis and Management* 4: 75–91.

Kershaw, D., and Fair, J. (1975). *The New Jersey Income Maintenance Experiments.* Academic Press, New York.

Kettl, D. F. (1991). *Deficit Politics.* Macmillan, New York.

Kincaid, J. (1988). The new judicial federalism. *The Journal of State Government* 61: 163–169.

Kingdon, J. W. (1984). *Agendas, Alternatives, and Public Policies.* Little, Brown, Boston.

Kirst, M., and Jung, R. (1982). The utility of a longitudinal approach in assessing implementation: Title I, ESEA. In *Studying Implementation.* W. Williams (Ed.). Chatham House, Chatham, NJ.

Klijn, E. H., and Teisman, G. R. (1991). Effective policy making in a multi-actor setting: Networks and steering. In *Autopoeisis and Configuration Theory: New Approaches to Societal Steering.* R. J. In't Veld, L. Schaap, C. J. A. M. Termeer, J. J. W. Van Twist (Eds.). Kluwer, Dordrecht, The Netherlands.

Knott, J. H., and Miller, G. M. (1987). *Reforming Bureaucracy: The Politics of Institutional Choice.* Prentice-Hall, Englewood Cliffs, NJ.

Larson, J. S. (1980). *Why Government Programs Fail: Improving Policy Implementation.* Praeger, New York.

Lazonick, W. (1991). *Business Organization and the Myth of the Market Economy.* Cambridge University Press, New York.

Lindblom, C. (1959). The science of muddling through. *Public Administration* 19: 79–88.

Linder, S. H., and Peters, G. (1989a). Implementation as a guide to policy formulation: A question of "when" rather than "whether." *International Review of Administrative Sciences* 55:631–52.

—— (1989b). Instruments of government: Perceptions and contexts. *Journal of Public Policy* 9: 35–58.

—— (1990a). Research perspectives on the design of public policy: Implementation, formulation, and design. In *Implementation and the Policy Process.* D. J. Palumbo and D. J. Calista (Eds.). Greenwood, New York.

—— (1990b). Policy formulation and the challenge of conscious design. *Evaluation and Program Planning* 13: 303–311.

—— (1992). The study of policy instruments. *Policy Currents* 2: 1, 4–7.

Lipsky, M. (1971). Street-level bureaucracy and the analysis of urban reform. *Urban Affairs Quarterly* 6: 391–409.

—— (1978). Standing the study of implementation on its head. In *American Politics and Public Policy.* W. D. Burnham and M. W. Weinberg (Eds.). MIT Press, Cambridge, MA.

Loomis, B. A. (1986). Coalitions of interests: Building bridges in a balkanized state. In *Interest Group Politics*, 2d ed. A. J. Cigler and B. A. Loomis (Eds.). Congressional Quarterly Press, Washington, D.C.

Love, J., and Sederberg, P. C. (1987). Euphony and cacophony in policy implementation. *Policy Studies Review* 7: 155–74.

Lowi, T. J. (1972). Four systems of policy choice. *Public Administration Review* 32: 298–310.

—— (1979). *The End of Liberalism*, 2nd ed. Norton, New York.

Luft, H. (1976). Benefit cost analysis and public policy implementation. *Public Policy* 24: 437–462.

Lurie, I. (1992). Evaluation of the Family Security Act. Working paper. State University at Albany Press, Albany, NY.

Majone, G., and Wildavsky, A. (1978). Implementation as evolution. In *Policy Studies Annual Review*, vol. 2. H. E. Freeman (Ed.). Sage, Beverly Hills, CA.

March, J. G., and Olsen, J. P. (1989). *Rediscovering Institutions.* Free Press, New York.

March, J. G., and Simon, H. A. (1958). *Organizations.* Wiley, New York.

Martin, S. (1983). *Managing Without Managers: Alternative Work Arrangements in Public Organizations.* Sage, Beverly Hills, CA.

Marvel, M. K. (1982). Implementation and safety regulation: Variations in federal and state administration under OSHA. *Administration & Society* 14: 15–33.

Melman, S. (1988). *The Demilitarized Society.* Harvest House, Montreal, Canada.

Minarik, J. J. (1992). Capital gains taxation, growth, and fairness. *Contemporary Policy Issues* 10: 16–25.

Moe, T. M. (1990). The politics of structural choice: Toward a theory of public bureaucracy. In *Organization Theory: From Chester Barnard to the Present and Beyond.* O. E. Williamson (Ed.). Oxford University Press, New York.

—— (1991). Politics and the theory of organization. *The Journal of Law, Economics & Organization* 7(special issue): 106–129.

Molnar, J. J., and Rogers. (1982). Interorganizational coordination in environmental management: Process, strategy, and objectives. In *Environmental Policy Implementation.* D. E. Mann (Ed.). Heath, Lexington, MA.

Moore, W. J. (1992). So long, Mr. Smith. *Natural Journal* 24: 2052–56.

Murphy, J. T. (1971). Title I of ESEA: The politics of implementing federal education reform. *Harvard Educational Review* 41: 35–63.

—— (1973). The education bureaucracies implement novel policy: The politics of Title I of ESEA, 1965–1972. In *Policy and Politics in America.* A. P. Sindler (Ed.). Little, Brown, Boston.

Nagel, S. S. (1990). Bridging theory and practice in policy/program evaluation. *Evaluation and Program Planning* 13: 275–283.

Nakamura, R. T., and Pinderhughes, D. M. (1981). Changing Anacostia: Definition and implementation. In *Implementing Public Policy.* D. J. Palumbo and M. A. Harder (Eds.). Heath, Lexington, MA.

Nakamura, R. T., and Smallwood, F. (1980). *The Politics of Policy Implementation.* St. Martin's, New York.

National Commission on Excellence in Education. (1983). *A Nation at Risk: The Imperative of Educational Reform.* Washington, D.C.

Nelson, R. R. (1977). *The Moon and the Ghetto.* Norton, New York.

New York Times. (1992). September 16:1; October 15:1; November 22:1; 24:1; 26:1; December 4:1; 7:1.

Osberg, L. (1984). *Economic Inequality in the United States.* Sharpe, Armonk, NY.

Osborne, D. (1990). *Laboratories of Democracy.* Harvard University Press, Cambridge, MA.

Ostrom, V. (1989). Some developments in the study of market choice, public choice, and institutional choice. In *Handbook of Public Administration.* J. Rabin, W. D. Hildredth, and G. J. Miller (Eds.). Marcel Dekker, New York.

—— (1991). *The Meaning of American Federalism.* Institute for Contemporary Studies, San Francisco, CA.

O'Toole, L. J. Jr. (1986). Policy recommendations for multi-actor implementation: An assessment for the field. *Journal of Public Policy* 6: 181–210.

O'Toole, L. J. Jr., and R. S. Montjoy (1984). Interorganizational policy implementation: A theoretical perspective. *Public Administration Review* 44: 491–503.

Palumbo, D. J., and Calista, D. J. (1990). Opening up the black box: Implementation and the policy process. In *Implementation and the Policy Process.* D. J. Palumbo and D. J. Calista (Eds.). Greenwood, Westport, CT.

Palumbo, D. J., and Oliverio, A. (1989). Implementation theory and the theory-driven approach to validity. *Evaluation and Program Planning* 12: 337–344.

Porter, D. O., and Olsen, E. A. (1976). Some critical issues in government centralization and decentralization. *Public Administration Review* 36: 72–84.

Pressman, J. L., and Wildavsky, A. (1973). *Implementation*. University of California Press, Berkeley.
—— (1984). *Implementation*. University of California Press, Berkeley, CA.
Radin, B. (1977). *Implementation, Change, and the Federal Bureaucracy: School Desegregation Policy in HEW, 1964-1968*. Teachers College Press, Columbia University, New York.
Rainey, G. W. Jr. (1990). Implementation and managerial creativity: A study of the development of client-centered units in human services programs. In *Implementation and the Policy Process*. D. J. Palumbo and D. J. Calista (Eds.). Greenwood, Westport, CT.
Rainey, H. G. (1992). *Understanding and Managing Public Organizations*. Jossey-Bass, San Francisco.
Rakove, M. (1975). *Don't Make No Waves; Don't Back No Losers*. Indiana University Press, Bloomington, IN.
Rein, M., and Rabinowitz, F. (1978). Implementation: A theoretical perspective. In *American Politics and Public Policy*. W. D. Burnham and M. W. Weinberg (Eds.). MIT Press, Cambridge, MA.
Rhodes, Robert P. (1992). *Healthcare Politics, Policy, and Distributive Justice*. State University of New York Press, Albany.
Rieselbach, L. (1986). Reforming Congress: Philosophy, politics, problems, prospects. In *Bureaucratic and Governmental Reform*. D. J. Calista (Ed.). JAI Press, Greenwich, CT.
Ripley, R. B., and Franklin, G. A. (1986). *Policy Implementation and Bureaucracy*, 2nd ed. Dorsey, Chicago.
Ritti, R., and Silver, J. H. (1986). Early processes of institutionalism: The dramaturgy of exchange in interorganizational relations. *Administrative Science Quarterly* 27: 259-287.
Rosenbaum, N. (1981). Statutory structure and policy implementation: The case of wetlands regulation. In *Effective Policy Implementation*. D. A. Mazmanian and P. A. Sabatier (Eds.). Heath, Lexington, MA.
Rushefsky, M. E. (1984). Implementation and market reform. In *Public Policy Implementation*. G. C. Edwards, III (Ed.). JAI Press, Greenwich, CT.
Sabatier, P. A. (1986). Top-down and bottom-up approaches to implementation research: A critical analysis and suggested synthesis. *Journal of Public Policy* 6: 21-48.
—— (1988). An advocacy coalition framework of policy change and the role of policy-oriented learning therein. *Journal of Public Policy* 6: 21-48.
—— (1991). Toward better theories of the policy process. *PS: Political Science and Politics* 24: 147-156.
Sabatier, P. A., and Mazmanian, D. A. (1979). The conditions of effective implementation. *Policy Analysis* 5: 481-504.
—— (1981). The implementation of public policy: A framework of analysis. In *Effective Policy Implementation*. D. A. Mazmanian and P. A. Sabatier (Eds.). Heath, Lexington, MA.
—— (1983). Policy implementation. In *Encyclopedia of Policy Studies*. S. S. Nagel (Ed.). Marcel Dekker, New York.
Salamon, L. (1981). Rethinking public management: Third party government action. *Public Policy* 29: 255-275.
Scharpf, F. (1978). Interorganizational policy studies: Issues, concepts, and perspectives. In *Interorganizational Policy Making*. K. Hanf and F. W. Scharpf (Eds.). Sage, London.
Scharpf, F. W. (1989). Decision rules, decision styles and policy choices. *Journal of Theoretical Politics* 1: 149-176.
Scheirer, M. A. (1987). Program theory and implementation theory: Implications for evaluators. In *Using Program Theory in Evaluation*. Jossey-Bass, San Francisco.
Schultze, C. (1979). *The Public Use of Private Interest*. The Brookings Institute, Washington, D.C.
Sharpe, L. J. (1985). Central coordination and the policy network. *Political Studies* 33: 361-381.
Shefter, M. (1992). Institutional conflict over presidental appointments. *PS: Political Science & Politics* 25: 4.
Shepsle, K. A. (1989). Studying institutions: Some lessons from the rational choice approach. *Journal of Theoretical Politics* 1: 131-148.
Smith, T. B. (1973). The policy implementation process. *Policy Sciences* 4: 197-209.

Stoker, R. P. (1991). *Reluctant Partners*: *Implementing Federal Policy*. University of Pittsburgh Press, Pittsburgh, PA.

Thompson, F. J. (1982). Bureaucratic discretion and the National Health Service Corps. *Political Science Quarterly* 97: 427–445.

—— (1984). Policy implementation and overhead control. In *Public Policy Implementation*. G. C. Edwards, III (Ed.). JAI Press, Greenwich, CT.

Toonen, T. A. J. (1985). Implementation research and institutional design: The quest for structure. In *Policy Implementation in Federal and Unitary Systems*. K. Hanf and T. A. J. Toonen (Eds.). Martinus Nijhoff, Dordrecht, The Netherlands.

Van Horn, C. E. (1979). *Policy Implementation in the Federal System*: *National Goals, Local Implementors*. Heath, Lexington, MA.

Wamsley, G. L. (1985). The agency perspective: Public administrators as agential leaders. In *Refounding Public Administration*. G. L. Wamsley et al. (Eds.). Sage, Newbury Park, CA.

Weatherley, R., and Lipsky, M. (1977). Street-level bureaucrats and institutional innovation: Implementing special education reform. *Harvard Educational Review* 47: 171–197.

Weick, K. (1976). Educational organizations as loosely-coupled systems. *Administration Science Quarterly* 21: 1–9.

Weimer, D. L. (1983). Problems of expedited implementation: The strategic petroleum reserve. *Journal of Public Policy* 3:169–190.

Weingast, B. R., and Marshall, W. J. (1988). The industrial organization of Congress; or, why legislatures, like firms, are not organized like markets. *Journal of Political Economy* 96: 132–163.

Weiss, C. H. (1972). *Evaluation Research*: *Methods of Assessing Program Effectiveness*. Prentice-Hall, Englewood Cliffs, NJ.

Wildavsky, A. (1979). *Speaking Truth to Power*. Little, Brown, Boston, MA.

Williams, W. (1982). The study of implementation: An overview. In *Studying Implementation*. W. Williams (Ed.). Chatham House, Chatham, NJ.

Williamson, O. E. (1981). The economics of organization: Origins, evolution, attributes. *The Journal of Economic Literature* 19: 1537–1568.

—— (1985). *The Institutions of Capitalism*. Free Press, New York.

Winter, Soren. (1990). Integrating implementation research. In *Implementation and the Policy Process*. D. J. Palumbo and D. J. Calista (Eds.). Greenwood, Westport, CT.

Wittrock, B. (1985). Beyond organizational design: Contextuality and the political theory of public policy. In *Policy Implementation in Federal and Unitary Systems*. K. Hauf and T. A. J. Toonen (Eds.). Martinus Nijhoff, Dordrecht, The Netherlands.

Wolf, Charles Jr. (1988). *Markets or Governments*: *Choosing Between Imperfect Alternatives*. MIT Press, Cambridge, MA.

Yanow, D. (1990). Tackling the epistemological issues in implementation research. In *Implementation and the Policy Process*. D. J. Palumbo and D. J. Calista (Eds.). Greenwood, Westport, CT.

Yin, R. K. (1982). Studying the implementation of public programs. In *Studying Implementation*. W. Williams (Ed.). Chatham House, Chatham, NJ.

Part C
POLICY ANALYSIS ACROSS NATIONS AND ACROSS DISCIPLINES

7

Comparing Policies Across Nations and Over Time

Robert B. Albritton
Northern Illinois University, DeKalb, Illinois

I. APPLICATIONS OF COMPARATIVE METHOD: GENERALIZATIONS ACROSS TIME AND SPACE

The history of policy development is marked by unanticipated consequences resulting from insufficient appreciation of large-scale system dynamics that characterize policy systems. Forrester (1971) explains these unforseen outcomes by demonstrating that macrolevel conceptual and technical changes often produce little in the way of significant policy effects; but even incremental shifts may set in motion complex social interactions with dramatic, unintended consequences. Because scientific evaluation and testing of alternatives at the system level are generally far too expensive and risky, policy formulation often is guided either by a "science of muddling through" (Lindblom, 1969) or by relying on experiences of other nations as "policy laboratories" for information as to probable outcomes of innovation and experimentation.

Comparisons of successes and failures in other nations thus can be invaluable resources for policy development. Guidance in developing income security policies and, more recently, health care policies in the United States has come from German experiences with income security programs in the 19th century and contemporary structures of the Canadian health care system. New political and economic structures within the European Community are now requiring member nations to choose from a wide range of collective strategies in monetary and social policy, as well as trade policy and national defense. Faced with these prospects, regimes can benefit from experiences of other nations by applying comparative methods to policy analysis.

As Ashford (1983) notes, developments in the field of comparative policy studies virtually always reflect corresponding developments in the general field of comparative political and social inquiry and in parallel developments within other social sciences. By definition, a "comparative" approach to policy studies involves more than one unit of analysis and implies comparisons across systems. Analysis of policy approaches within a single society is not, in this sense, comparative research. As attention to public policy grows, however, the literature is still most often represented by case studies of specific policy areas and limited to individual nations. Focusing almost exclusively on intrasystemic activity as the source of policy characteristics, they rely on a conceptualization of policies as highly idiosyncratic processes in which unique characteristics of nations determine outputs and outcomes (Ashford et al., 1978).

Because of inherent limitations in generalizing from unique conditions of time and space, case studies focusing on a single nation are truly comparative only as a very rough frame of reference for policy makers. If an analysis focuses on a nation or nations other than the United States, it is not strictly "comparative" unless, for example, attention to the Canadian health care system represents a form of comparative policy inquiry suggesting alternative approaches to health care coverage and cost containment relative to the United States.

A. Analysis of Single Systems

In their most productive form, idiosyncratic approaches (or case studies) represent more than simply "descriptive" theory. In order to "explain" policy, they may be based on a premise that any "case," limited to a single geographical area or a unique time frame, embodies a set of general theoretical propositions that informs the analysis. Thus, a case study becomes a "confirming" or "falsifying" illustration of what more general theory predicts over a range of observations (Przeworski and Teune, 1971).

Despite its limitations, the literature in comparative policy studies is, generally, of this type. In its best light, it represents a need to balance the dominance of American scholars in addressing policy issues by demonstrating contributions to policy development in other systems. Another contribution is that of balancing the "parochialism" of applied policy studies that define issues and interests narrowly with regard to national perspectives or specific policy areas (Heidenheimer et al., 1983: vii).

Two alternative frameworks address these issues. One emphasizes the unique set of national circumstances that contribute to a particular policy within a common framework of analysis: a history of policy development, specific methods and strategies of government intervention, the ability of a policy to achieve policy objectives or to address social goals, and a survey of problems and issues for the future (Ashford, 1990; Bolotin, 1989; DeSario, 1989). The other examines specific policy arenas emphasizing the variety of policy perspectives and choices, policy instruments, constraints, and outcomes (Hiedenheimer et al., 1983).

There is significant debate, however, over the utility of analytical frameworks in which successes or failures of specific nations may not have applications beyond national boundaries. The premise that policy structures and outcomes are "products of a particular national history, culture, and political and economic ideology" (Bolotin, 1989: xiv) is a limiting one for theoretical development in the policy field. This "idiographic" approach—that social science findings are peculiar products of unique social systems—in its less extreme form, is sometimes cast as an "area studies" approach, suggesting that regional similarities limit generalizations about policy to specific areas or regions of the world.

In fact, proponents of idiographic approaches often recognize their limitations for developing general policy theory. Even the most detailed and enlightened description of water resources development in Bhutan may not be relevant as a model for similar projects in other nations, especially other regions of the world. To the extent that "comparable" cases can be derived from studies of diverse systems, such as Poland, Indonesia, and the United States, analyses of single systems may be useful as a criterion for policy innovation and development elsewhere. But progress toward knowledge that can serve as a guide to policy development in nations requires more generalized statements about the range of phenomena surrounding policy structures, implementation, and outcomes than is possible in idiographic approaches.

B. Cross-National Analysis

Scholars interested in the theoretical development of public policy studies are often committed to approaches that stress analysis across systems. Borrowing from developments in comparative political studies, they argue that the goal of comparative policy studies is "to substitute names of variables for the names of social systems" (Prezyworski and Teune, 1971).

The argument that general theory can be developed from observations across units of analysis is based on analogies drawn from the natural sciences. If one wishes to determine the causes of boiling water, for example, scientists might examine the heat required to bring water to a boil in France, Zambia, Nepal, and the Philippines. They would probably discover that the average boiling point of water is quite different in each of these nations. They would not, however, argue that these differences are a result of unique national histories or cultures—nor, for that matter, unique national boundaries or terrain. Rather they would look for factors that determine the boiling point of water independently of unique conditions of time and space. They would, of course, substitute measures of atmospheric pressure (or at least altitude) as the variable representing France, Zambia, Nepal, and the Philippines and would treat these entities only as units of the analysis.

In this sense, comparative approaches may be more "nomothetic" (or "lawlike") in developing generalizations that transcend characteristics of specific social systems. Przyworski and Teune illustrate the character of comparative approaches by noting the fact that better-paid workers in Germany and Sweden are likely to be class conscious, whereas in the United Kingdom, the United States, and Australia, less well-paid workers are more class conscious (1971: 28–29). At one level, this finding is a historical generalization confined to spatiotemporal parameters; another approach holds that the relationship between workers and class consciousness across nations depend on other factors (variables) not yet identified. In other words, the bridge between historical observation and general theory is the substitution of variable names for proper names of social systems in the course of comparative research. One important implication of this approach is that both spatial and temporal characteristics, that is, unique national characteristics, become residuals in explaining structures and outcomes of public policy across nations and over time.

Studies of this type often take the form of most similar systems or most different systems designs and are a staple for area studies approaches. An example of a most similar systems design might compare policies among Scandinavian countries. The premise is that these countries share economic, cultural, and political characteristics to such a degree that factors held in common are "controlled" and have, presumably, zero impact on corresponding public policies. Differences in policy development then can be analyzed as a result of factors independent of broad system characteristics. Often, a strategy based on this approach is to compare Anglo-American countries, that is, countries with common cultural and legal traditions, with systems of continental Europe (Alford, 1967).

A most different systems design emphasizes subsystem characteristics, such as impacts of education on individual political participation. System characteristics—national cultural or political traits—presumably have no distinctive impacts. In this design, more than one level of analysis is possible—units of analysis at the subsystem level may be individuals, regions, or some other geographical unit.

The focus of this design is on relationships of variables, such as education and politics, rather than on national characteristics. The selection of observations across nations makes the analysis comparative, but because national characteristics are treated as having little significance, they are not necessarily explicit. General theoretical propositions are assumed to be valid across systems regardless of system effects. If this assumption turns out to be false, references to system characteristics need to be incorporated specifically into the analysis (Przeworski and Teune, 1971: 39).

The development of general policy theory often takes these assumptions a step further by requiring a focus on relationships among variables across multiple units of analysis. The level of interest is in systemic activity that produces systemic effects. The most productive approaches involve cross-national comparisons at the national level in which hypotheses concerning relationships between policy structures and outcomes can be analyzed using nations as the unit of analysis but focusing on relationships among variables specified by theory (Jackman, 1985; Wilensky, 1975).

There are, of course, exceptions to this strategy. Highly useful theoretical development can result from examining policies at subsystem levels—cities or provinces, for example—still in a comparative context. It is important for the researcher to be aware of implications of the approaches mentioned above in subsystemic analysis. Analysis of subsystemic units, whether they be regions, other geographical units, or individuals, involves either a most similar systems, a most different systems, or a cross-subsystems approach. This implies that any variation observed may be a reflection of system-level factors a priori excluded from the analysis.

Przeworski and Teune (1971: 28–29) show how system-level factors may affect interpretations obtained from simpler models in comparative analysis. Referring to Almond and Verba's 1963 study, *The Civil Culture: Political Attitudes and Democracy in Five Nations*, they reinterpret relative rankings of nations on feelings of relative freedom to discuss politics in five countries. By controlling for relative levels of education in each country, they show that the original rankings—United States, Great Britain, Germany, Italy, and Mexico—are reconstituted as: Great Britain, Mexico, United States, Germany, and Italy. Although units of analysis are individuals, the data are influenced by the relative ability of these individuals to obtain education in their respective countries, implying that access to education overrides concepts such as "nation," "culture," or "society" as explanations of this indicator of political efficacy. As a result, assumptions that freedom to discuss politics is a function of "Mexican" or "American" traits must be modified to reflect a more general level of theory focusing on levels of educational attainment. Furthermore, the impacts of education on political efficacy (holding other factors constant) should hold across all nations and over time. Cross-national policy studies rely on this logic and extend it to policy systems.

C. Analysis Over Time

A focus on national and regional comparisons, however, often overlooks dynamic dimensions of public policy that require comparisons within nations over time. The logic of longitudinal analysis is highly useful for policy applications because it lends itself more readily to cause-effect interpretation. Although temporal priority does not rule out alternative explanations of policy effects, an association of policy interventions with corresponding changes in outcomes represents a highly plausible connection between policy strategies and their outcomes.

Superficially, longitudinal analysis is similar to historical treatments common to case study approaches. As one scholar has put it: ". . . the general point that all public policies have a history and are in a large part determined by that history cannot be reasonably refuted" (Peters, 1972: 227). What is often absent in strictly case study approaches, however, is an ability to abstract common properties of the policy process—the dynamics of policy systems.

Comparisons of nations over time focus attention to dimensions of policy represented by stability and change, constraints, and the impacts of historical events, such as war or recession. The dynamics of change—incremental to discontinuous—may vary across policy types even more than across nations. Rose et al. (1976) use longitudinal perspectives for calling attention to these dynamic dimensions of public policies. In the process, they show that the ability of policy scholars to generalize on the basis of idiographic time periods may be misleading as a result of changing relationships within policy systems.

Observed relations among variables may be modified as a result of linear progressions, policy cycles, and even discontinuities (Rose et al.: 20). In other words, fundamental policy structures, represented as causal relationships from a static or cross-sectional analysis, may change over time as a function of policy dynamics (Peters, 1976). This implies that any generalizations based on limited time frames, especially in early periods of policy formulation, are fraught with risks for projecting future policy behavior. From this perspective, the risks of idiographical policy analysis and the need for general theories that are neither space bound nor time bound are even more obvious.

Weaknesses of time-bound and space-bound approaches have pressed scholars into model development that combines the two perspectives in "pooled data" analysis permitting simultaneous treatment of variance across nations and over time (Stimson, 1985). At the present time, methodological difficulties with this approach limit its utility for developing reliable models of policy processes. Analysis of data across nations and over time are most successful when the data are "long and thin" (long in the temporal dimension, but with fewer units of analysis) or "short and fat" (20 or more nations, but less than 10 temporal observations for each nation). Results from large-scale analyses of pooled data require information on statistical problems, such as heteroscedasticity from variation of measurement on the cross-sectional components while, at the same time, controlling for serial correlation in the temporal dimension. Despite these problems, pooled data analysis is the method that most closely conforms to the logic of general theory development in comparative policy studies (Crepaz, 1992).

II. MEASUREMENT ISSUES IN COMPARATIVE POLICY ANALYSIS

Nations vary dramatically in their approaches to government over a variety of areas. Some nations choose unitary systems over federal systems in the exercise of sovereignty; some choose to separate the exercise of government authority between a president and the legislative branch, whereas others rely on parliamentary systems alone. Some do not even pretend to democratic forms of government.

Governments also vary widely in their approaches to public policy. The utility of comparative analysis is based on assumptions that economic policies or welfare services are undertaken differently in different nations or at different times—past and present. The fact that nations differ in their government priorities and their definitions of who is poor, who requires public support and health care, or what is the effective balance between economic and social needs makes comparative policy analysis a useful exercise in estimating what specific government interventions are likely to achieve.

Whenever one endeavors to make international comparisons, it is necessary to choose the appropriate dimensions of analysis. Most studies—whether case studies or cross-national— emphasize at least three areas: (1) socioeconomic and political backgrounds, (2) resources available to government, and (3) government expenditures. Each of these areas poses special problems for comparative analysis and requires special strategies for measuring appropriate indicators.

A. Socioeconomic Environments

Nations vary most widely in population size. Although the point may seem self-evident, many of the dimensions on which scholars wish to evaluate nations are simply functions of gross population size. China, for example, has a higher gross national product (GNP) than many European nations, but one does not think of the Chinese people as having a higher standard of living than, say, the Belgians. This is because measures of national productivity or consumption are largely a function of the number of people in a nation. In fact, many indicators, such as numbers of poor persons, numbers of unemployed persons, and even numbers of crimes committed are all functions of the number of people in a population. In other words, the more people, the more cases there are of a particular behavior or status. Most analysts choose indicators for comparisons that represent the *relative* status of societies regardless of population size. They do this by controlling for population size, so that comparisons are made on a per capita basis or a measure of incidence, such as numbers in a given category per 100,000 population.

There are important cautions, however, for analysis of data aggregated in this manner. Per capita indicators are often highly skewed by deviant cases. A phenomenal rise in per capita income of a village in India may be a function of the development of a shrimp-fishing industry that benefits only three entrepeneurs involved in holding the business. If per capita income is interpreted as an indicator of general resources available to the population, in this case, the indicator would miss the mark. A measure of *median* income would more clearly reflect the actual status of the population on this category of measurement. Attention to even more sensitive indicators of policy distribution (some scholars adapt the Gini index) are often advisable, depending on emphases of the analysis.

B. National Resources

Most scholars acknowledge that national resources have considerable impacts on the nature of policies adopted by various nations (Groth et al., 1984). One of the best examples is the fact that policies of income security—social security systems—or environmental preservation do not appear as important priorities until more basic issues of economic development have been resolved. The development of income security policies in association with higher levels of economic development has limited studies in this area to industrialized nations, as in the OECD and Eastern Europe. However, analytical frameworks developed in a primarily European context surely contain highly important implications for social programs in newly industrialized countries (NICs) as nations arrive at this stage of development.

National policies limiting the cutting of forests are significant issues in most countries of the world. Comparisons of these policies among nations, however, pose inherent difficulties as a result of differences of scale in national resources. Although reductions in forest areas are significant policy issues in both Brazil and Thailand, for example, significantly smaller reductions in forested areas of Thailand may have more dramatic consequences than larger amounts of forest cutting in Brazil. This outcome is a result of the much larger forest resources of the Amazon basin in Brazil. In terms of data, this means that a much larger quantity of tree cutting will represent a much lower percentage reduction of Brazilian forests. The use of acreage reductions in square kilometers versus percentages of total forested area have very different implications. In this and other policy areas, researchers must exercise great care in matching configurations of the data with conceptual frameworks in order to achieve appropriate results of the analysis.

C. National Expenditures

Reliance on indicators of national expenditures also poses problems for analysis. Not least of these is the fact that different types of expenditures are recorded in widely different categories. The United States, for example, treats military pensions and veterans hospitals as social expenditures; many of the public works expenditures in the former USSR were allocated to the military budget. Clearly, these expenditures are not strictly comparable. Many of these differences have been mitigated for OECD nations, which have attempted to standardize national expenditures. Independent researchers have made efforts to analyze military and civilian expenditures in other nations in order to construct comparable data (Sivard, 1985; Taylor and Hudson, 1972). These data are generally regarded as more reliable than nationally reported data and most comparative research relies heavily on these sources. The overall effect of data disparities, however, has been to confine much comparative public policy analysis to industrially developed nations where the data are presumed to be comparable.

The major problems associated with analysis of public expenditures involve the development of comparable scales of measurement. Although data standardized in U.S. dollars are easily obtained, the actual value of national currencies in terms of purchasing power represents a data problem that has not been resolved to any satisfactory degree. Longitudinal analysis is an asset in analyzing expenditure data because they may be analyzed in units of national currency. In longitudinal studies, however, inflation becomes a factor that requires control, usually by transforming expenditure data into constant currency units. (An excellent primer on this problem is the discussion of comparability of budget items in Pryor, 1968, Appendix A.)

Proportions of national expenditures, such as military or social welfare spending, are often treated as indicating relative commitments by governments to specific policy areas. In general, the use of comparative data in this way has been productive. Problems arise, however, in considering this indicator over time. One problem is the "asymtotic" limits implied by the fact that the proportion of expenditure allocations in any given area cannot exceed 100% nor fall below 0%. The asymtotic effect is that the higher the proportion of expenditures in any given area, the lower will be the relative proportionate increase over time.

Consider expenditures in two nations in which social welfare expenditures constitute 50% and 10%, respectively, of national expenditures of $1 billion. A $100 million increase in one nation represents only a 20% relative increase in national spending, whereas the same increase in the second nation means a 100% increase. In addition, asymtotic effects occur as a result of the inability of government programs to utilize ever higher proportions of the budget at the upper end and of the difficulties of program termination at the lower end. In fact, the nation with higher proportions of social welfare spending may be involved in greater spending effort even with lower proportionate increases.

Most studies control for aggregate size of national economies by using ratios of spending for a particular policy as a proportion of GNP or of total public expenditures. Ratio measures of this type can become tautological when increases in one category "necessarily entail decreases in other categories" (Hayes, 1975: 27). In this area, as in others, care must be taken to conform indicators to conceptual frameworks of analysis and to meet validity requirements that are appropriate for any explanatory research.

D. Data Sources

Although United Nations' publications provide data on most nations of the world, some scholars regard these data as suspect. The suspicion arises from the fact that these data are self-reported and that nations have significant economic and other stakes in what these data show. Stories abound from scholars who claim to have been present while data were literally "invented" for reporting to the United Nations by bureaucrats in nations that had significant needs for technical assistance from the United Nations or World Bank loans.

In some nations, caution in the use of data sources is well advised. Data purporting to represent Burma, Liberia, Sudan, Somalia, or even the Georgian Republic pose considerable problems of comparability because of instability or governmental information controls in these countries. Opening of nations to outside scrutiny by the World Bank and other agencies that insist on developing reasonably reliable indicators have made these data sources more acceptable for comparative policy studies. When researchers exercise appropriate care in selecting a set of nations for comparative analysis, data from the same source are often reliable and consistent indicators of relative national positions on indicators of interest. One point worth mentioning is that cross-national comparisons of these data do not, in general, cast aspersions on the nations subject to analysis because the focus is on policy variables rather than the nations involved.

Bearing in mind reservations noted above, major data sources that cover virtually all nations are the United Nations' *Statistical Yearbook of the United Nations*, the OECD's *National Accounts Statistics*, and the International Monetary Fund's *International Financial Statistics*. Scholars may also rely on more specialized publications such as the WHO, *World Health Statistics* (WHO), *Demographic Yearbook* (United Nations), *Labor Force Statistics* (OECD), and *Balance of Payments Yearbook* (International Monetary Fund) for more policy-specific data, as well as a wide range of other publications by these organizations. Despite reservations, these data sources have proven to be sufficiently reliable in providing construct-valid indicators to warrant their use in comparative studies.

III. THEORETICAL FRAMEWORKS IN COMPARATIVE POLICY STUDIES

Most theoretical frameworks for policy studies rely heavily on analysis of systems. Easton's (1965) general framework has been attractive, even necessary, for policy studies because of its emphasis on outputs in characterizing political systems. Attention to outputs as a focus of political analysis directs attention to policies as a central component of what governments do. This innovation in the study of linkages between systems characteristics and results of government activity provides the basis for integrating descriptive studies of policy-related government activity into a more analytical theoretical framework.

Easton's work also emphasizes the interdependence of inputs and outputs. If inputs across systems or over time remain the same but outputs vary significantly, there is an implicit assumption that policy differences are responsible for this variance. Similarly, if inputs vary dramatically but outputs (or outcomes) are remarkably similar, the result is considered attributable to variations in policy activity. More commonly, the framework of analysis considers variations in outputs as a function of variable inputs and then looks for other sources of explanation in policy structures or processes to account for further variation.

Inputs are conceptualized as a variety of social and economic conditions or resources that characterize a national entity or other unit of analysis. Outputs are represented as acts of government, such as budgets and spending, or as social outcomes, such as health, education, or even distributional qualities of national populations on general indicators of well-being, such as income and safety. The nexus is the set of political and policy structures—levels of democratic governance, political participation, centralization of governmental authority, and the ideologies or governing principles on which nations differ. There are theories linking initial social and economic conditions to political and policy structures (Lipset, 1959); some linking structures to outputs (Pryor, 1968); and still others that examine the impact of policies on outcomes controlling for initial levels of resources (Peters and Hennessey, 1975; Pryor, 1968).

Specializations focusing on comparative public policy developed primarily during the 1970s and 1980s (Ashford, 1983: 176). Two substantive areas characterize the literature. A consideration of each of these areas—economic policy and social welfare policy—represent general developments in theory and method in the field during the last two decades. In addition, a virtual cottage industry has developed in theories of consociatiational democracy or "corporatism" (Schmitter, 1974). This latter area also requires attention because of its prominent place in comparative policy theory.

A. Economic Policy

One of the most critical policy decisions in any society is the choice of economic systems. Contending ideologies within nations (as much as between nations) have focused considerable attention to comparisons of economic outcomes in "socialist" and "capitalist" systems. At stake are answers to questions as to the appropriate role of government in market and nonmarket transactions, the role of central planning, and appropriate paths to economic growth. Comparative analysis of this fundamental policy choice has important implications for Marxist theory, as well as for developmental perspectives, such as W.W. Rostow's notion of "stages of growth."

In the real world of actual economies and behaviors, distinctions drawn by ideological frameworks become less apparent. Pryor shows the difficulty in correlating features of economies with economic development. Part of the problem lies in defining what is meant by "capitalism" and "socialism." If the distinction is the level of "governmental" or "public" participation, for example, some "socialist" countries, such as the former Yugoslavia, have lower degrees of governmental ownership than certain "capitalist" countries such as Austria or Finland (1985: 20). Pryor also shows that data appropriate for examining the relative degree of government involvement, such as the proportion of the population employed in government enterprises, suggest that most "real" economic systems are "mixed" economies to a greater or lesser degree. Publicly owned utilities and garbage collection by local governments in the United States qualify as somewhat more than zero on the scale of government employment in economic enterprises. Finally, Pryor shows that although income extremes appear greater in more market-oriented economies, income inequalities are roughly similar in socialist, centrally administered economies of Eastern Europe and those of the West.

Perhaps the most productive work on economic policy has been the analysis of public expenditures across nations and over time. Budgets and budgeted expenditures are important as indicators of policy priorities on which nations differ. Relative expenditures for national security, social welfare, or economic development represent a diverse range of policy choices, which are affected by relative levels of economic resources, to be sure, but are clear outputs of policy system activity.

Two expenditure aggregates that have received considerable attention are public consumption expenditures for military purposes and those for social welfare (income security health, and education). Relative ratios of these categories of expenditures to GNP reflect very different orientations of public policy. Pressures of the cold war lead to the highest ratios for the United States and the Soviet Union, nations with very different orientations to market structures of the economy. As it turns out, emphases on military spending have little to do with specific characteristics of economic systems or, additionally, with measures of per capita income. Nor are there significant differences in these ratios among NATO or Warsaw Pact alliances and militarily neutral nations (Pryor, 1968: 91-93).

Economic system variables do play a significant role in accounting for the ratio of public consumption expenditures to the GNP in education, research and development, and nonmilitary external security (Pryor, 1968: 284). More centrally planned economies commit higher proportions of GNP to education than their more market-oriented counterparts. The lack of significant differences between centrally planned and more market-oriented economies in allocating public consumption expenditures, however, implies that variation *among* nations with similar economic systems is more important than variation *between* systems; nor does the level of economic development seem to play a large role in determining these options (Pryor, 1968: 285). The implication of the latter point is that neither rich nor poor nations (on a per capita basis) differ markedly in their relative allocations for military or social welfare expenditures.

Analyses of expenditures over time, however, imply something quite different. Perhaps the most important result of time series perspectives is the finding that as incomes rise, the ratio of public consumption expenditures rises. Pryor (1968: 288-91) observes that these increases occur primarily during the transition from rural-agricultural to urban-manufacturing societies, but that there are upward limits to these trends. One limit may be purely artifactual—nations with low levels of expenditures will show the fastest increases. Another relates to increasing resistance to higher levels of taxation necessary to attain even higher levels of social welfare expenditures—a supply-demand hypothesis.

Attention to budgets and spending has spawned considerable interest in substitution effects among public policy areas such as defense, welfare, health, and education. The literature in this area analyzes policy decisions and priorities concerning the allocation of scarce public resources and illustrates the variety of substantive and methodological issues that arise in the use of expenditure data. Previous work emphasizes trade-offs between national defense and public welfare policies, or "guns versus butter." Fluctuations in budgetary composition between these items in the United States indicate that there is no inherent stability in relationships between the welfare state and "military Keynesianism" (DeGrass, 1983).

Studies of substitution effects between military and other forms of public expenditures are mixed in their conclusions. Russett (1969) found significant reductions in civilian public consumption associated with military spending, but, responding to criticism that his analysis overemphasized impacts of World War II, he later reported no significant effects (1982). This finding coincided with other studies (Caputo, 1975; Pryor, 1968) that, in some cases, showed positive relationships among education, health care, and military spending. By contrast, Wilensky found significant negative relationships between military spending and welfare performance during the early 1950s in response to cold war pressures on military budgets (1974).

Pryor (1968: 122-123) suggests that relationships between military and civilian public spending are quite different over time from those based solely on cross-sectional analysis. Domke et al. (1983) examined this assumption for the United States, the United Kingdom, France, and the Federal Republic of Germany and came to mixed answers based on how the data were treated in a time-series analysis (including three-stage least squares). Dabelko and McCormick's study (1977) implies that findings of no significant trade-offs between military spending and other spending items may be a product of concentrating on Western, industrial nations. Ames and Goff (1975) and Hayes (1975) find significant negative relationships between defense and education spending in Latin American nations from 1948 to 1968.

These conflicting and puzzling results are largely a function of specific elements of the research designs involved. Clearly, the selection of different sets of nations produces different results, but studies that employ cross-sectional designs also lead to quite different findings from those employing time-series analysis. Cross-sectional studies are inappropriate in at least two respects. Theoretically, they are insensitive to historical events that have impacts on public policy; technically, they cannot respond to *changes* in overall spending levels. Whether countries exhibit different priorities in their budgets at any single point in time does not represent the underlying dynamic of policy choices involved in decisions to trade "guns" for "butter." Substitution effects can be considered more effectively by examining spending patterns over time.

Studies that rely on ratio measures tend to find stronger trade-offs between defense and public welfare spending than do those that focus on rates of change. Theoretically, the former analyses ignore the dominant view of budgeting as "an incremental process in which the previous year's allocations are rarely renegotiated, a view supported by study of budgetary decisionmaking in several countries" (Eichenberg, 1983). Technically, the uses of percent change in trade-off studies involve serious ratio problems that "can lead to statistical results that appear to indicate the presence of trade-offs between budgetary categories when none exist" (Berry, 1986). Researchers in this area should consult Berry (1986), Gist (1982), and Sirisimphand (1987) for creative approaches to the construction of budgetary indicators.

Finally, studies that rely on bivariate regression in ordinary least-squares models are highly subject to specification error when relevant variables are omitted, as they are in this method. Strong tradeoff effects often disappear when control variables are introduced into the model. Similarly, those studies that use time-series regression without correcting for serial correlation tend to find relatively stronger trade-offs between defense and public welfare spending as compared with those studies that control for common time-series effects. As some scholars suggest, valid tests of budgetary trade-offs are possible only in "more complex model(s) than the single equations that have typically dominated research" (Domke et al.: 25).

B. Social Welfare Policy

By far, the most highly developed theoretical area of comparative policy studies is that of social welfare policy. Early developments in this area focused on outcomes hypothesized to be issues of democratic, capitalist systems—those associated with social equality in developing welfare states (Cutright, 1967; Hewitt, 1977; Jackman, 1975). Hibbs' (1977) study of impacts of political alignments on macroeconomic outcomes offered considerable advances in methods employed in cross-national studies. Peters' (1972) analysis of welfare state developments in European nations focused attention to dynamics of social policy structures and away from the dominant emphasis on ideological systems.

Arnold J. Heidenheimer and Hugh Heclo are responsible for bringing comparative social welfare policy studies to new substantive levels by involving European researchers in the Social Policy Research Group of the Council for European Studies. Heidenheimer's aquaintance with the Study Group on Historical Indicators of Western European Democracies and Stein Rokkan inspired the first major classroom primer on comparative policy studies (1976). Even more significant, however, was their collaboration with Peter Flora in a project on the development of welfare states in Europe and America.

Although it belongs to a previous decade, comparative policy theory has scarcely advanced beyond this work. It represents what were, at the time, state of the art uses of data and methods in testing critical hypotheses about the development of welfare states. Perspectives of Europeans, who were less obsessed with the "socialist-capitalist debate" than many American colleagues, furthered attention to social forces that appeared more relevant in the European context. The result was a step-level advance of general theory in comparing social policy systems.

Research analyzing a wide variety of social policies across nations and over time has led to repeated confirmation of several hypotheses that now constitute a significant body of general knowledge in this area. One of the most important findings is the role of historical context for explaining levels of welfare policy development. Social insurance, for example, appears to have developed more rapidly under authoritarian regimes, in the European context, than in parliamentary democracies. *Within* democratic regimes, however, social insurance is associated with higher levels of political mobilization (Flora and Alber, 1981: 72).

These surprising findings become more intelligible in the context of more complex analysis. On one hand, they imply that more authoritiarian regimes *with developed bureaucracies* (and, therefore, administrative capacity) found innovation and experimentation with structures of social supports an important political thrust for wooing allegiances of mass populations against rising demands from a growing middle class. This development suggests both attention to bureaucracies as an engine of social policy and an explanation for lagging growth of social insurance programs in more democratic nations (Flora and Albers, 1981: 43–44). On the other hand, the findings suggest that in more democratic systems, there are inherent contradictions over the role of government in providing liberty, equality, and security (Heclo, 1981: 393; Kohl, 1981: 327).

The importance of historical context suggests three important approaches for understanding the underpinnings of social policy. First, there are different phases of development for social policy, which Heclo calls "experimentation," "consolidation," and "expansion" (1981: 384–394). The dynamics, that is, the determinants, of system development differ in important respects depending on the stage of overall policy development. Second, the development and expansion of policy is due largely to incremental growth mechanisms within the context of institutional systems (Heclo, 1981: 383; Heidenheimer et al., 1983; Wilensky, 1975). Finally, the values of "liberal" democracy are often at odds with more egalitarian values, so that political democracy does not necessarily lead to parallel developments in social policy systems. In fact, there comes a point at which the relative equality of citizens in affluent socieities undermines political commitment essential for sustaining social policy. These factors associated with historical context make the development of theoretical models of comparative policy systems more than a simple task. The possibility also exists for changes occurring in social welfare states in which dominant perceptions of existing social welfare policies are that they are too costly, ineffective, and promoting excessive government power.

Studies also confirm the importance of socioeconomic development and political mobilization as necessary conditions for social welfare development (Hiedenheimer et al., 1983: 69; Peters, 1972). Nations clearly require a minimal or threshhold level of economic development before turning attention to distributive issues such as income support. The fact that virtually all industrialized nations have long surpassed this threshhold explains why industrialization and urbanization appear to have little impact on welfare policies in European countries in the East or West. The hypothesis linking social and economic development to social welfare activity requires greater attention to periods in which nations are in the "experimental" stage, as in the newly industrialized nations of Asia.

By contrast, evidence consistently supports the importance of political mobilization in the development of social welfare systems. One of the most consistent contributors to the growth of social insurance is the rise of organized labor (Peters, 1972), although labor mobilization can have conflicting results when other political interests are involved (Heidenheimer et al., 1983: 219–220).

Impacts of the welfare state on societies represent yet another theme of the literature. Scholars such as Wilensky and Turner (1987) view orientations of regimes to the economy as being indistinguishable from concerns of the welfare state. This implies that one characteristic of social policy is active labor market policies to decrease unemployment (Crepaz, 1992: 152).

The effects of state activism in these areas is in dispute. Some scholars find evidence that leftist governments support policies that reduce unemployment at the cost of inflation, whereas conservative governments offer more concerted attacks on inflation, allowing unemployment to rise (Beck, 1982; Hibbs, 1977; Schmidt, 1982). Economists often argue that the growth of welfare states has produced decidedly negative impacts on the ability of markets to sustain economic growth (Korpi, 1985). One scholar summarizes this literature by suggesting that "the rate of unemployment increases as capitalism is softened by welfare state interventions, and it falls as the welfare state is weakened" (Schmidt, 1982: 240). Other scholars, however, argue that rising unemployment is associated with relative economic openness, a process associated with lower levels of government intervention in the economy (Crepaz, 1992).

C. Corporatist Structures and the Welfare State

One of the major theoretical developments in comparative public policy has been the collaboration of industry, commerce, labor, and other interests through systems known as "corporatism." The literature generally defines the concept as concensual bargaining among interest groups under the auspices of government in ways that blur distinctions between public and private sectors and between social and general economic policy. A model of this arrangement is the Austrian social partnership among economic sectors in which social and economic policy is negotiated among chambers of commerce, industry, agriculture, and labor. The role of parliament is confined to ratification and support of bargains obtained through this process (Lehmbruch, 1982). By contrast, other nations, like the United States, rely on bargaining of interests almost solely within the political process, which focuses interest-group conflict on legislatures and bureaucracies (Lowi, 1979).

The key feature of corporatism is that governments specifically incorporate organized interests into the process of policy formulation and implementation, thereby displacing direct policy leadership to organized private interests. Choices of corporatist versus laissez faire strategies represent macropolicy decisions that determine the course of social and economic policy, so that the two areas become highly interdependent (some would say virtually indistinguishable). At this level of analysis, one could say that corporatist theory includes the most important dimensions on which policies differ across nations and over time.

The literature is mixed in its revue of corporatist policy. Early evaluations of the contributions of corporatism to economic and social policy proved highly favorable when compared with pluralist systems, in attributing high levels of economic growth, low unemployment, and low inflation rates to corporatist strategies (Cameron, 1978, 1984; Hicks, 1988; Lange and Garrett, 1985; Schmidt, 1982; Wilensky and Turner, 1987). More recent considerations have a less sanguine interpretation (Cameron, 1988; Olson, 1982; Weede, 1984, 1986), arguing that corporatism has a negative net impact on economic growth.

The later analyses have been criticized for ignoring three essential issues in the debate: (1) the principal purpose of corporatist strategies is to reduce social conflict and attain political concensus and, therefore, should be evaluated only for their contributions in this area (Lijphart and Crepaz, 1991; Panitch, 1979; Wilensky and Turner: 48; Williamson, 1989:

151); (2) because economic openness and, therefore, vulnerability of small countries is the key to understanding development and success of corporatist strategies, the theory is less relevant to the world-dominant economies (Katzenstein, 1987: 203-23; Williamson, 1989: 151); (3) the rise of neoconservative governments during the 1980s interferred with effectiveness of consociational strategies to intervene successfully in national economies and are responsible for the rise in unemployment during that era (Crepaz, 1992).

In fact, Crepaz (1992) found significant *reductions* in unemployment associated with corporatist strategies, comparing nations across three policy eras, 1960-1990. These strategies produced equally significant impacts on reducing inflation, lending credence to the argument that corporatism "has not lost its capacity for societal guidance. . . . [nor] . . . its effectiveness to provide lower inflation and unemployment rates" (pp. 161). At the same time, Crepaz found some association with higher degrees of labor peace, although strike activity was more associated with social democratic governments (p. 162).

On the negative side, Crepaz (1992) found that corporatism appears to have lost its vitality as an engine of economic growth (p. 161). Because corporatist states are associated with strong welfare states, there is an inference that maintenance of social welfare systems has detrimental effects on economic performance. Governmental outlays, for example, are negatively related to economic growth (p. 162).

One of the most disturbing findings in the literature is a general pattern of decline in economic development associated with more highly developed welfare states. Here, the literature is puzzling. On one hand, there is evidence for the argument put forward by neoclassical economists that tax levels in welfare states have become so high that investment incentives have declined. One hypothesis (noted above) argues that welfare states are associated with higher levels of unemployment (Schmidt, 1982: 240).

The problem with this argument is that "government outlays," often used as a surrogate for the welfare state also include military spending, so that economic declines associated with this indicator may derive from sources other than the welfare state. Crepaz' (1992) analysis, however, suggests two other significant sources of unemployment—economic openness and a dummy variable indicating the decade of the 1980s. The former, combined with a finding that corporatism significantly reduces unemployment, argues for corporatist structures as a bulwark against adverse international economic climates (Katzenstein, 1983, 1985). The latter, contrasted with the decades of the 1960s and 1970s, suggests important shifts in the international economic environment with negative impacts spread across the 18 OECD nations included in the study (p. 151).

Although concensus on these points seems somewhat far off, theories of corporatism have attracted considerable interest as models for governments in newly industrialized nations. As such, they are guides to experiments linking social and economic development to democratic progress. Their importance, to date, is the indication that policy-making structures are highly significant for understanding specific policy development and implementation. Clearly, these structures are essential information in explaining the type and effectiveness of policies governments choose to adopt.

IV. SUMMARY AND CONCLUSIONS

Comparative policy studies have progressed significantly as a major theoretical specialization over the last decade. Building theory in the areas of social welfare, health, and other activities on a cross-national basis has been a significant development in the disciplines of political science and economics and, to some degree, in sociology. At this level, much of the analysis has been confined to developing hypotheses and testing Marxist versus laissez faire theories of the state. The results of this activity have required significant revisions both in the Marxist view of social reality and in the adequacy of market economies to provide necessary supports for the survival of democratic systems.

The general inference that must be drawn from these analyses is that sea changes in general environments have occurred, within specified time frames, that are comparable with, if not more significant than, national structures as sources of economic outcomes, such as unemployment and inflation. The implication is that comparisons of policy activity *across* nations neglects underlying dynamics of cause and effect that are products of *temporal* dimensions of public policy processes. Unfortunately, this means that cross-sectionally dominant models cannot be expected to represent the dynamics of policy systems. Unless the temporal dimension is included, a statistically based model is underspecified, in the sense that important variables are omitted from the analysis.

Temporal dynamics are often the subject of theory building in the case of social welfare systems (Flora et al., 1981; Peters, 1972; Rose, 1976). The importance of policy history noted above, however, provides only a rough surrogate for dynamics of the processes involved. A major problem is the unavailability of data before now-developed nations became industrialized, meaning that variance is limited in answering very fundamental questions about policy development in the social welfare area. Is the general finding that later-developing social welfare states institutionalize at higher levels of political development and socioeconomic mobilization (Flora and Albers, 1981: 63) a function of political opposition within more democratic societies or of unidentified variables within the policy process? Without information on developments within newly formed welfare states, these questions will remain largely unanswered. Yet, the level of current research suggests clear expectations for patterns of social policy development among emerging industrial states that will serve well as hypotheses for future analysis.

Crepaz' (1992) finding that impacts of corporatism are quite different in various time periods is important in its implications for general policy theory. First, it reinforces Peters' (1976) earlier conclusion that static analysis of a cross-section of nations will produce different outcomes depending on the time frame involved. Second, it suggests that abrupt changes in model contours associated with different time periods will create problems in specifying dynamics of policy systems. Clearly, policy dynamics are observable only in frameworks that encompass both spatial and temporal dimensions and the discontinuities that are a fundamental component of the latter. A significant task for the future of comparative policy studies lies in developing the more complex methodologies necessary to permit the capture of both dimensions within a single model.

Perhaps one reason that idiographic approaches are still prominent in policy studies is the responsiveness of this mode of analysis to a growing need in both public and private agencies for policy advice. The ideological debates represented by general theoretical perspectives noted above constitute arcane approaches to policy for persons directly involved in policy decisions. This is not to say that some understanding of general structures would not be helpful for appreciating the social dynamics that determine whether policies succeed or fail. For decision-makers, however, a more immediate need is to grasp probable cause-effect relationships implied in quite a different level of policy decisions. Applied policy analysis thus is more likely to resort to reductionist modes of analysis—which is what case studies are.

How does one begin to bridge the chasm between disciplinary and applied needs of comparative policy studies? It is peculiar that there has been little follow-up to studies over a decade old that call attention to administration and implementation as important focuses of comparative study (Rose, 1973; Peters, 1976, 1978). The consistent finding that the most prominent support for the welfare state (indeed, for all public programs) is the degree of bureaucratic development leaves begging the question of what characteristics of administrative action are most likely to further policy goals. Interactions between bureaucratic representatives of governments and the ublic is but one avenue of investigation that could benefit from comparative policy perspectives. Clearly, there are lessons to be learned from experiences of nations in their implementation of policies on an incremental versus a discontinuous basis.

As Ashford (1983) noted over a decade ago, very general social theories may have little or no bearing on institutional relationships and policy processes of countries in question. One reason is that few political or administrative actors are self-conscious about the norms or ideologies that are supposed to guide them. Most of them are pragmatic in their approach to policy development and see themselves as technicians responding to popular concensus—at least within their constituency. The actual preference orderings within that concensus may have a great deal more to do with the behaviors of institutions than more abstract social theories. The very successes of the welfare state change the concensual agenda to issues of a postindustrial society rather than one in which Marxist or laissez faire agendas predominate. Comparative policy studies still require the building, and then the integrating, of "islands of theory" necessary for understanding the complexities and dynamics of policy systems across nations and over time.

REFERENCES

Alford, R. R. (1967). Party and society. In *Studies in Comparative Politics*. F. J. Munger (Ed.). Thomas Crowell, New York.

Almond, G. A., and Verba, S. (1963). *The Civic Culture*: *Political Attitudes and Democracy in Five Nations*. University Press, Princeton, NJ.

Ames, B., and Goff, E. (1975). Education and defense expenditures in Latin America: 1948-1968. In *Comparative Public Policy*. C. Liske, W. Loehr, and J. McCamant (Eds.). Sage, Beverly Hills, CA.

Ashford, D. E. (1983). Comparing policies across nations and cultures. In *Encyclopedia of Policy Studies*. S. S. Nagel (Ed.). Marcel Dekker, New York.

—— (Ed.)(1990). *Discretionary Politics*: *Intergovernmental Social Transfers in Eight Countries*. JAI Press, London.

Ashford, D. E., Katzenstein, P. J., and Pempel, T. J. (1978). *Comparing Public Policies*: *A Cross-National Bibliography*. Sage, Beverly Hills, CA.

Beck, N. (1982). Parties, administrations, and American macroeconomic outcomes. *American Political Science Review* 76: 83-93.

Berry, W. (1986). Testing budgetary theories with budgetary data: Assessing the risks. *American Journal of Political Science* 30: 620-634.

Bolotin, F. N. (Ed.) (1989). *Education and Environment*. Greenwood Press, New York.

Cameron, D. (1978). The expansion of the public economy: A comparative analysis. *American Political Science Review* 73: 1243-1261.

Cameron, D. R. (1988). Distributional coalitions and other sources of economic stagnation: On Olson's *Rise and Decline of Nations*. *International Organization* 42: 561-605.

Caputo, D. (1975). New perspectives on the public policy implications of defense and welfare expenditures in four modern democracies: 1950-1970. *Policy Science* 6: 423-426.

Crepaz, M. M. L. (1992). Corporatism in decline? An empirical analysis of the impact of corporatism on macroeconomic performance and industrial disputes in 18 industrialized countries. *Comparative Political Studies* 25: 139-168.

Cutright, P. (1967). Inequality: A cross-national analysis. *American Sociological Review* 32: 562–578.

Dabelko, K., and McCormick, J. M. (1977). Opportunity costs of defense: Some cross-national evidence. *Journal of Peace Research* 14: 145–154.

DeGrass, R. W., Jr. (1983). *Military Expansion and Economic Decline*. Council on Economic Priorities, New York.

DeSario, J. P. (Ed.) (1989). *Health and Social Welfare*. Greenwood Press, New York.

Domke, W., Eichenberg, R., and Kelleher, C. (1983). The illusion of choice: Defense and welfare in advanced indust;rial democracies, 1964–1978. *American Political Science Review* 77: 19–35.

Easton, D. (1965). *A Systems Analysis of Political Life*. Wiley, New York.

Eichenberg, R. C. (1983). The expenditure and revenue effects of defense spending in the Federal Republic of Germany. *Policy Science* 16: 391–412.

Flora, P., and Alber, J. (1981). Modernization, democratization, and the development of welfare states in Western Europe. In *The Development of Welfare States in Europe and America*. P. Flora and A. J. Heidenheimer (Eds.). Transaction Books, New Brunswick, NJ.

Flora, P., and Heidenheimer, A. J. (1981). *The Development of Welfare States in Europe and America*. Transaction Books, New Brunswick, NJ.

Forrester, J. (1971). Counter-intuitive behavior of social systems. *Technology Review* January.

Gist, J. R. (1982). Stability and competition in budget theories. *American Political Science Review* 27: 327–358.

Groth, A. J., and Wade, L. L. (Eds.) (1984). *Comparative Resource Allocation*. Sage, Beverly Hills, CA.

Hayes, M. D. (1975). Policy consequences of military participation in politics: An analysis of tradeoffs in Brazilian federal expenditures. In *Comparative Public Policy*. C. Liuske, W. Loehr, and J. McCamant (Eds.). Sage, Beverly Hills, CA.

Heclo, H. (1981). Toward a new welfare state? In *The Development of Welfare States in Europe and America*. P. Flora and A. J. Heidenheimer (Eds.). Transaction Books, New Brunswick, NJ.

Heidenheimer, A. J., Heclo, H., and Adams, C. T. (1976). *Comparative Public Policy: The Politics of Social Choice in Europe and America*. St. Martin's Press, New York.

—— (1983). *Comparative Public Policy: The Politics of Social Choice in Europe and America*. 2nd ed. St. Martin's Press, New York.

—— (1990). *Comparative Public Policy: The Politics of Social Choice in Europe and America*. 3rd ed. St. Martin's Press, New York.

Hewitt, C. (1977). The effect of political democracy and social democracy on equality in industrial societies: A cross-national comparison. *American Sociological Review* 42: 450–464.

Hibbs, D. A., Jr. (1977). Political parties and macroeconomic policy. *American Political Science Review* 71: 467–887.

Hicks, A. (1988). Social democratic corporatism and economic growth. *Journal of Politics* 50: 677–704.

Jackman, R. W. (1985). Cross-national statistical research and the study of comparative politics. *American Political Science Review* 29: 161–182.

Katzenstein, P. J. (1983). The small European states in the international economy: Economic dependence and corporatist politics. In *The Antinomies of Interdependence: National Welfare and the International Division of Labour*. J. G. Ruggie (Ed.). Columbia University Press, New York.

—— (1985). *Small States in World Markets: Industrial Policy in Europe*. Cornell University Press, Ithaca, NY.

Korpi, W. (1985). Economic growth and the welfare state: A comparative study of 18 OECD countries. *Labour and Society* 10: 195–209.

Lange, P., and Garrett, G. (1985). The politics of growth: Strategic interaction and economic performance in the advanced industrial democracies, 1974–1980. *Journal of Politics* 49: 257–274.

Lehmbruch, G. (1982). Introduction: Neo-corporatism in comparative perspective. In *Patterns of Corporatist Policy-Making*. G. Lehmbruch and P. C. Schmitter (Eds.). Sage, London.

Lijphart, A., and Crepaz, M. (1991). Corporatism and concensus in eighteen countries. *British Journal of Political Science* 21: 235–246.

Lindblom, C. (1969). The science of "muddling through." *Public Administration Review* 19: 79–88.

Lipset, S. M. (1959). Some social requisites of democracy: Economic development and political legitimacy. *American Political Science Review* 53: 69–105.

Lowi, T. J. (1979). *The End of Liberalism.* 2nd ed. Norton: New York.

Olson, M. (1982). *The Rise and Decline of Nations.* Yale University Press, New Haven, CT.

Panitch, L. (1979). The development of corporatism in liberal democracies. In *Trends Toward Corporatist Intermediation.* P. Schmitter and G. Lehmbruch (eds.). Sage, London.

Peters, B. G. (1978). *The Politics of Bureaucracy.* Longman, New York.

—— (1976). Social change, political change, and public policy: A test of a model. In *The Dynamics of Public Policy.* R. Rose (Ed.). Sage, Beverly Hills, CA.

—— (1972). Economic and political effects on the development of social expenditures in France, Sweden, and the United Kingdom. *Midwest Journal of Political Science* 16: 225–239.

Peters, B. G., and Hennessey, T. M. (1975). Political development and public policy in Sweden, 1865–1967. In *Comparative Public Policy.* C. Liske, W. Koehr, and J. McCamant (Eds.). Sage, Beverly Hills, CA.

Pryor, F. L. (1968). *Public Expenditures in Communist and Capitalist Nations.* Irwin, Homewood, IL.

—— (1985). *A Guidebook to the Comparative Study of Economic Systems.* Prentice-Hall, Englewood Cliffs, NJ.

Przeworski, A., and Teune, H. (1971). *The Logic of Comparative Social Inquiry.* Wiley-Interscience, New York.

Rose, R. A. (1973). Models of governing. *Comparative Politics* 5.

—— (Ed.) (1976). *The Dynamics of Public Policy.* Sage, Beverly Hills, CA.

Russett, B. M. (1969). Who pays for defense? *American Political Science Review* 63: 412–426.

—— (1982). Defense expenditures and national well-being. *American Political Science Review* 76: 767–777.

Schmidt, M. G. (1982). The role of parties in shaping macroeconomic policy. In *The Impact of Parties.* F. G. Castles (Ed.). Sage, London.

Schmitter, P. (1974). Still the century of corporatism? *Review of Politics* 36: 85–131.

Sirisumphand, T. (1987). Public Policy Choices: Trade-Offs Between National Defense and Economic Development Expenditures in Developing Countries. Unpublished Dissertation, Northern Illinois University, Chicago.

Sivard, R. L. (1985). *World Military and Social Expenditures: 1985.* World Priorities, Washington, D.C.

Stimson, J. A. (1985). Regression in time and space: A statistical essay. *American Journal of Political Science* 29: 914–947.

Taylor, C. L., and Hudson, M. (1972). *World Handbook of Political and Social Indicators.* Yale University Press, New Haven, CT.

Weede, E. (1984). Democracy, creeping socialism, and ideological socialism in rent-seeking societies. *Public Choice* 44: 349–366.

—— (1986). Sectoral reallocation, distributional coalitions and the welfare state as determinants of economic growth rates in industrialized democracies. *European Journal of Political Research* 14: 501–519.

Wilensky, H. (1975). *The Welfare State and Equality: Structural and Ideological Roots of Public Expenditures.* University of California Press, Berkeley, CA.

Wilensky, H. L., and Turner, L. (1987). *Democratic Corporatism and Policy Linkages.* Institute of International Studies, University of California, Berkeley, CA.

Williamson, P. J. (1989). *Corporatism in Perspective.* Sage, London.

8
Developing Nations and Public Policy

Stuart S. Nagel
University of Illinois, Urbana-Champaign, Illinois

I. IMPROVING PUBLIC POLICY TOWARD AND WITHIN DEVELOPING COUNTRIES

The purpose of this chapter is to discuss various public policy suggestions for improving aid to developing countries mainly on the part of the United States but also on the part of other developed countries. The emphasis is on aid in the form of ideas, which possibly will be communicated through university training activities. The chapter also is concerned with improving public policy within developing countries, especially regarding the use of incentives for encouraging socially desired behavior and regarding various fundamental rights that lead to more productive development.[1]

The suggestions of this chapter were partly stimulated as a result of touring Kenya, Malawi, Zambia, Brazil, Panama, Okinawa, and other places over the last few years. Especially helpful were conversations with leaders of the legal profession in various developing countries (such as the Malawi and Zambia Law Associations) and also leading public administrators (partly by way of the International Association for Schools and Institutes of Administration). Relevant places also include underdeveloped regions of developed countries such as the Delta region of Mississippi, the Negev Desert of Israel, and rural areas of western European countries.

All the suggestions involve communicating ideas to relevant people in developing countries. The communication can occur through on-site or in-class training programs conducted by universities. The emphasis builds on the Vista and Peace Corps idea that giving a person a fish provides food for a day, but teaching a person how to fish may provide food for life. The emphasis here is on the idea that teaching people how to choose among fishing, commercial activities, manufacturing, and other economic activities may provide much more than food in terms of the quality of one's life. On a still higher level, the emphasis is on teaching people how to choose among any kind of alternatives for achieving given goals.[2]

Another underlying theme is that the United States, other industrialized countries, and the United Nations can do more for developing countries by sharing information relevant to dealing with important policy problems than they can through military alliances or material aid. The policy problems are global in nature since they are shared by many countries. Also, many countries can cooperate to their own benefit in dealing with the problems. The more prosperous the underdeveloped countries, the more they will be able to buy products from the industrialized countries and from each other, and the more they will have good products to sell.[3]

Before getting into the specific social problems, one should note that public policy has the potential for encouraging socially desired behavior by working through five different related approaches. They are:

1. Increasing the benefits of doing right
2. Decreasing the costs of doing right
3. Increasing the costs of doing wrong
4. Decreasing the benefits of doing wrong
5. Increasing the probability that the benefits and costs will occur

This checklist logically leads to such questions as who are the doers, and what benefits and costs are involved. The answers depend on the specific subject matters, as discussed in this chapter.[4]

To aid in the analysis of the public policy ideas, a set of spreadsheet tables are presented based on multi-criteria decision-making (MCDM) for a sample of relevant policy problems. In this context, multi-criteria decision-making (MCDM) refers to processing a set of societal goals to be achieved, policy alternatives available for achieving them, and relations between goals and policies in order to choose or explain the best alternative, combination, allocation, or predictive decision rule.

The spreadsheet format involves putting goals on the columns, policy alternatives on the rows, relations in the cells, overall scores for each alternative at the far right, and the capability of determining what it would take to bring a second-place or other-place alternative up to first place. In this chapter, those spreadsheets relate to energy, pollution, unemployment-inflation, business-consumer relations, ethnic relations, majority rule, and free speech.[5]

II. TECHNOLOGY-RELATED IDEAS

A. Building on Biological Science

Developing countries could benefit from more use of soybeans to provide needed *protein* at relatively low cost in comparison to alternative sources of protein. Soybeans can also be converted to a variety of desired synthetic food products such as hamburgers, although the conversion costs still need to be reduced.

Better use of American corn-growing and *agricultural* techniques with regard to hybrid seed corn, herbicides, pesticides, and inexpensive fertilizers. This includes plowing under the stalks after the harvest to provide good natural fertilizer rather than burning the stalks or letting them decompose in the air.

High-leverage, low-cost *medical care* that saves the lives of children. This includes preventive medicine and measures for poliomyelites, infant dehydration, malaria, leprosy, yellow fever, and nutritional diseases. Saving children greatly wins friends, although it needs to be accompanied by birth control to have less children to save and by job opportunities for when the children become adults.

B. Building on Physical Science

More need for *electrification*, including at least one electrical outlet per village. Perhaps ideas could be learned from the U.S. Rural Electrification Administration.

More use of *synthetic fuels* made from agricultural products such as gasohol, ethanol, and oil substitutes. Developing countries can learn from the experiences of Brazil and American corn farmers during the oil crisis. Synthetic fuels may cost more to make than oil on the world market, but developing countries need the foreign exchange for other things, and they have the raw agricultural materials for oil substitutes.

More use of collectively used satellite dishes to receive *television* programs that originate in other countries. Some television can be highly educational, especially given the lack of books and other educational outlets.[6]

C. Using Incentives

A key problem among engineering-related problems is how to encourage the development of new *energy* sources and the conservation of existing energy. Relevant incentives include:

1. Increasing the benefits of doing right by tax reductions for adopting energy-saving devices like improved insulation, special thermostats, and coal-burning furnaces. Offering government purchase guarantees as an incentive to develop a feasible electrical car.
2. Decreasing costs of doing right by providing subsidies to municipal governments in order to reduce their costs of energy-relevant enforcement of housing and building codes.
3. Increasing the costs of doing wrong by publicizing the gasoline consumption qualities of different cars. Also charging vehicle taxes in proportion to gasoline consumption.
4. Decreasing the prestige benefits of driving gas-guzzling cars by making small-car driving a manifestation of patriotism.
5. Compiling data on the characteristics of alternative energy sources and energy-saving devices so as to allocate better the rewards, penalties, and other incentives.

Energy policy is mainly a physical science problem. The key biological science problem in public policy is how to encourage better *health care* on the part of both providers and recipients. This is an especially important problem in developing societies where there is generally more concern for biological survival than in more developed societies. Relevant incentives might include:

1. Health-care providers can be subsidized to provide low-cost care on a mass basis. Recipients can be given cash incentives to submit to vaccinations and birth control.
2. The cost to health-care insurers can be reduced per insured person by requiring universal public participation.
3. The cost of wrongdoing can be increased by requiring higher health-care insurance premiums for people who are at fault in having bad health records such as smokers or those who have excessive cholesterol rates.
4. Sometimes infant formulas are diluted in developing countries in order to make the formula go further. That would not be a benefit if there were no need for it as a result of adequate provision of infant milk and food supplements.
5. There is a need for better record keeping concerning the quantity, quality, and prices of the health-care providers and concerning the health of individuals so that public policy can better target the positive and negative incentives.

The problem of encouraging technological innovation is an especially important problem because *technological innovation* has large multiplier effects by virtue of its spillover into providing job opportunities, better products and workplaces, less expensive housing, anti-pollution devices, and other high-technology ways of dealing with social problems. Applying the checklist here might involve noting:

1. Government subsidies may be especially important for technological innovation because private capital may not be available in sufficient quantities and may not be so willing to wait for risky returns.
2. There are wasteful costs in reinventing the wheel, which means public policy should strive to inform those who can benefit from new technologies as to what is available.
3. Penalties can be imposed on firms that do not modernize such as automobile manufacturers or steel mills. The penalties can at least consist of not being provided with bail-out money or tariffs if they are threatened by more modern competition.
4. As for decreasing the benefits of doing wrong by not adopting new innovations, there are few benefits with the exception of not having to adapt or retool.
5. There is a need for more coordination in the allocation of subsidy benefits and tax incentives for technological innovation that may necessitate having a coordinating agency like the Japanese Ministry for International Trade and Investment.

As for *environmental* protection, that is an area in which there has been substantial experimentation with a variety of incentives. They include:

1. Providing tax incentives designed to encourage adopting pollution-reduction devices by business firms and municipal agencies. Tax incentives can include pollution taxes that are levied in proportion to the amount of polluting done.
2. Subsidies designed to reduce the cost of expensive retro-fitting and new facilities.
3. Penalties for wrongdoing other than fines, such as publicizing brand-name wrongdoers, facilitating damage suits by people suffering environmental injuries, the withdrawal of benefits, and (as a last resort) injunctions that close polluting firms.
4. Confiscating the profits made as a result of not introducing required pollution controls.
5. Better pollution-monitoring systems and bounties for reporting pollution violations plus enforcement agencies that do nothing but pollution enforcement.

C. A Policy Analysis Table on Energy Policy

Table 1 is a policy analysis table showing alternative energy policies on the rows, goals to be achieved on the columns, relations between the alternatives and the goals in the cells, and overall totals for each alternative at the far right. An emphasis on nuclear energy and oil is considered relatively conservative at least in terms of American public policy. An emphasis on solar energy and synthetic fuels is considered relatively liberal. An emphasis on coal and a mixture of energy sources is considered to be a somewhat neutral position ideologically.

The super-optimum solution where all major viewpoints can come out ahead involves a sequential combination with oil best on the short-term track, coal and synthetic fuels on the intermediate track, and solar and nuclear on the long-term track at least in terms of the American context, although not necessarily for any specific developing country.

The alternatives are scored on the goals using a 1 to 5 scale, where a 5 means highly conducive to the goal in a relative sense, a 4 means mildly conducive, a 3 means neither conducive nor adverse, a 2 means mildly adverse, and a 1 means highly adverse. The goals are weighted on a 1 to 3 scale, where a 3 means high importance, a 2 means middling importance, and a 1 means low but positive importance. The neutral total gives all goals middling importance. The liberal total gives liberal goals high importance, neutral goals middling importance, and conservative goals low importance. The conservative total gives conservative goals high im-

Table 1. Evaluating Energy Policy Alternatives

Criteria / Alternatives	C Goal +Energy business	C Goal Business use of energy	N Goal −Tax cost	N Goal Technologic feasibility short run	N Goal Technologic feasibility long run	L Goal Environmt, safety, and IR	L Goal Consumer interest and equity	N Total (Neutral weights)	L Total (Liberal weights)	C Total (Conservative weights)
C Alternative Nuclear & oil	4	2	2.5	3.5	3	2	2	38	36	40
L Alternative Solar & synthetic fuels	2	3	2.5	2.5	3.5	4	3	41	43*	39
N Alternative Coal & mixture	3	3	3	2.5	3	3	3	41	41	41
sos Alternative Sequential combination, well-placed subsidies	5	5	2	3.5	5	5	5	61	61**	61**

1. One should note that each policy has subpolicies that are not shown here such as (1) nuclear can be divided into uranium (the most common form), plutonium, and hydrogen; (2) oil can be divided into known deposits and unknown deposits; (3) coal can be divided into high polluting (the most common form) and low polluting; (4) synthetic fuels can be divided into natural (like oil shale) and artificial (like garbage); (5) solar can be divided into small-scale and large-scale.
2. One should note the big drawback for each energy source that are (1) nuclear lacks sufficient safety, especially nuclear wastes; (2) oils lack long-term value; (3) coal is bad on pollution; (4) synthetic fuels have high ongoing costs; (5) solar has high start-up costs for large-scale operations.
3. The choices can be best viewed in terms of three tracks that are (1) oil is best on the short-term track; (2) coal and synthetic fuels make the most sense on the intermediate track, with a need for developing more economic synthetic fuels; (3) solar and nuclear make the most sense on the long-term track, but there is need for developing safer nuclear energy and for research on implementing large-scale solar energy.
4. See notes to Table 2 for meaning of the symbols.

portance, neutral goals middling importance, and liberal goals low importance. Other symbols in these tables are defined in the footnotes to Table 1.

III. ECONOMICS-RELATED IDEAS

A. Building on Economic Science

More help is needed to developing countries on how to make better use of mass *labor*. This may be the main resource that most developing countries have. Perhaps studies could be made of how China has used mass labor to build roads, schools, and other projects with relatively little mechanical equipment and relying heavily on local raw materials. The projects created have much more value than the workers have been paid, although the workers receive a living wage. The surplus value can then be used as a form of savings for capital investment.

The use of more *cooperative* farming whereby equipment can be efficiently shared by way of machine tractor stations. The former Soviet Union has pioneered in that regard, but the machine tractor stations could be used in developing countries by farmers who own or at least sell their crops rather than by collectivized farmers. The stations could dispense knowledge as well as equipment like American county agents.

More emphasis on increasing the national income through a program of active governmental incentives, including *subsidies and tax breaks*. That has worked well in Japan, South Korea, Taiwan, Hong Kong, and Singapore. It combines the ideas of supply-side economics and industrial policy.[7]

B. Using Incentives

At the macroeconomics level, public policy is primarily concerned with decreasing *unemployment and inflation* or increasing employment opportunities and price stability. Devices such as manipulation of the money supply or taxing-spending differences are not so meaningful if unemployment and inflation are increasing simultaneously. An economy can also become distorted by trying to order business firms not to justifiably raise prices or by trying to order unemployed workers into certain jobs. An incentives approach might include such devices as:

1. Tax incentives to business firms and labor unions for keeping prices and wages down. Also monetary incentives to employers to hire the unemployed and monetary incentives to the unemployed to accept training and jobs.
2. Decreasing the costs of finding jobs and workers through better information systems.
3. Increasing the costs of violating price-wage guidelines and work incentives by withdrawing benefits and (in rare cases) by fines and other negative penalties.
4. Confiscating the benefits of price-wage violations by special taxes on the gains.
5. More accurate information on prices, wages, and unemployment in order to allocate the benefits and costs more effectively.

At the microeconomics level, public policy is concerned with relations between business and *consumers, labor*, and other business firms. Those subjects have been traditionally dealt with through economic regulation as manifested in such U.S. government agencies as the Federal Trade Commission, the National Labor Relations Board, and the Anti-Trust Division of the Department of Justice. An incentives approach might be substantially more effective in either a developed country or a developing country, including such devices as:

1. Providing tax incentives to business firms to develop better relations with consumers, labor, and other businesses.

2. Decreasing the costs of such activities by providing appropriate government subsidies.
3. Increasing the penalties where the lives or safety of people is jeopardized, as with dangerous products and working conditions.
4. Confiscating the gains that come from violating guidelines concerning consumer protection, worker protection, and the protection of a competitive environment.
5. Hotline systems for facilitating the reporting of wrongdoing, and award systems for encouraging the reporting of rightdoing.

C. The Right to Basic Economic Security

The right to basic economic security is a relatively modern right at least in the American context. It is embodied in statutes rather than in the Constitution. To the extent it is provided, however, there can constitutionally be no arbitrary classifications of recipients, or the equal-treatment right will be violated. Likewise, there can be no deprivation of government economic benefits unless the recipient is provided with due process to give him an opportunity to show the illegality of the deprivation.

Relevant statutes in American law include (1) the National Labor Relations Act of 1935, which provides the right to join labor unions that can aid in providing economic security; (2) the Fair Labor Standards Act of 1938, which provides for the right to a minimum wage, maximum hours, safe working conditions, and freedom from child labor; (3) the Social Security Act of 1935, which provides for aid to the aged, disabled, unemployed, and to dependent children; and (4) the Employment Act of 1946, which declared that the American people have the right to expect the federal government to provide maximum employment, production, and purchasing power.

Sometimes critics of these rights talk in terms of a conflict between freedom and economic security. On the contrary though, freedom of speech was very important in revealing the harm that was being done to society by the absence of these economic rights. Likewise basic economic security is necessary to make freedom of speech meaningful because those lacking economic security are generally not in a financial position to take advantage of expensive forms of communication, and economic insecurity also makes one less tolerant of deviant ideas and less adaptable to social change except change that will mean personal economic benefits. There is clearly a close relationship between economic security and equal treatment with regard to race relations because (1) being black and being poor are positively correlated, and because (2) those who discriminate often do so out of economic insecurity, and (3) being poor makes one more subject to discrimination.

An important general effect of increased economic security is to lessen economic anxieties that workers might have. Such anxieties can interfere with morale and efficiency and thereby lower the gross national product. Too much security, however, might cause a worker to lessen attempts to improve himself or herself.

All four of the key New Deal statutes mentioned above have had important specific consequences for American society, just as related statutes have in other countries. Statistics show a substantial increase in union membership subsequent to the passage of the National Labor Relations Act, and a substantial decrease in strikes for union recognition as contrasted to strikes for more favorable contract terms. Other statistical studies have shown that unions do produce higher wages, shorter hours, and safer conditions at least for union members.

For nonunion members, the Fair Labor Standards Act has provided similar, although lower, benefits. These economic effects have directly benefited a large segment of the population and indirectly benefited the total economy, particularly by virtue of the more efficient use of capital and labor that raising the price of labor has encouraged, and also by the economic stimulus stemming from increased purchasing power to the extent wages have increased more than prices. Strengthening unions has also had political effects by increasing the likelihood that legislation will be passed favoring union interests.

The Social Security Act has encouraged earlier retirement for the aged and, therefore, earlier advancement for the young. The aid to dependent children provisions have spawned a tremendous bureaucratic apparatus, and in that regard may soon be replaced by the Family Assistance Bill of 1971.

The Employment Act has not eliminated unemployment or price inflation, but its encouragement of greater government spending and lower taxes in time of unemployment and the reverse in time of inflation (combined with other governmental regulatory devices) has dampened the business cycle to some extent. Provisions in the Social Security Act that provide payments to the unemployed, dependent children, and the retired also help to level-off business cycles because these payments increase in times of recession and decrease in times of prosperity.

D. Deciding Among Alternative Relations Between the Public and Private Sectors

1. Noninvolvement of Government

Noninvolvement of government works best when the industry is highly competitive and competition is likely to achieve socially desired behavior. This is especially so regarding the pricing of products because competition can bring prices down. This is not so regarding such matters as environmental protection, occupational health and safety, or equal employment opportunity. In fact, competition is likely to hurt the achievement of those societal goals. If competition is high, business firms may cut back on antipollution, safety devices, and affirmative action programs because they may involve extra expense which the firms cannot afford.

Sometimes competition is not furthered by noninvolvement because the formerly competing firms may conspire to fix prices or may engage in mergers that result in too few firms to be competitive. Under those circumstances, antitrust litigation or regulation may be needed to supplement noninvolvement in order to promote competition for the benefit of consumers. The firms may also benefit from competition by virtue of increased sales due to lower prices, but especially by virtue of the stimulus it provides to innovation, including innovations that increase profits.

2. Subsidies

Subsidies are important when society wants business firms to provide unprofitable services to the poor, as with subsidies to the energy industry in the form of energy purchase supplements, or to the housing industry in the form of rent supplements. Subsidies may also be needed when innovation is too expensive for private industry to undertake, as with communications satellites, the development of nuclear energy, and the development of the airplane industry. The fields that were mentioned as not being especially relevant to competition could be handled by subsidies such as pollution, workplace safety, and equal opportunity. That might meet with political opposition on the grounds that business firms should not be subsidized to do the right thing. Such subsidies would be analogous to paying them not to commit crimes. It might be noted that subsidies in the form of tax foregoing are more politically acceptable than subsidies in the form of outright cash gifts, with low interest loans being in between.

3. Litigation

Litigation may help individuals to obtain compensation for negligence and occasional intential wrongdoing. It is not very effective in changing the behavior of business firms unless it becomes very expensive to them. Otherwise, the expense of paying damages may be substantially less than the expense of changing their behavior. By bringing a class action involving a great many injured people, litigation awards can become quite expensive. The reason litigation has been more important in promoting safer cars than safer airplanes is because an unsafe airplane that crashes generates a big news story that decreases consumer purchases of that airline's services. An unsafe car does not generate big news, but a few million-dollar damage suits can do so. Litigation can also be more effective if the legislatures or courts establish rules of strict liability or no-fault liability. The plaintiff then merely has to show that the defendant's product was a factor in the accident and not prove that the defendant acted negligently. Antitrust litigation is a special form of litigation separate from personal injury litigation, but it is often highly effective in changing behavior by restoring competition.

4. Regulation

Regulation is most meaningful where there are serious problems present and competition, subsidies, or litigation do not seem so meaningful. This is the case where we are interested in preventing serious accidents before they occur rather than compensating people or bankrupting an airline afterwards. Thus, we flatly prohibit certain unsafe practices regarding pilots, airplanes, toxic chemicals, and drunk driving. Regulation is also especially appropriate where there are scarce resources to be allocated, such as food rations in wartime, prime channels on radio or TV, or possibly gasoline during an energy shortage. The alternative would be to allow the highest bidder to have the food, prime channels, or gasoline that society might consider to be an inequitable solution. Regulation is also important when certain forms of business behavior are socially desired, but the marketplace provides no income-receiving or expense-avoiding incentives to behave accordingly, and society does not want to buy the behavior through subsidies.

5. Government Ownership

The main explanation or justification for government ownership in a basically free-enterprise society is that there are certain services that society wants to have performed and private enterprise finds them too unprofitable to provide. That includes much of the Amtrak passenger service, a post office system that delivers mail to every rural location at the same low price, and city public transportation. The alternative would be heavy subsidies of the private sector that would probably cost the taxpayer more than providing the service through government ownership or government employees, as is also the case with legal services for the poor.

A second big explanation and justification for government ownership is that the activity could be very profitable to some parts of the private sector, but that other parts of the private sector do not want to be preyed on. This is the case with government ownership of roads where conservative private businesses want government ownership rather than pay tolls to other business people in order to transport their goods. Likewise, the privately owned airlines seem to prefer government-owned airports rather than pay higher fees to privately owned airports in order to receive safety and other services that they now receive at government-owned airports.

A third explanation for government ownership is that the private sector firms or firms may be perceived as guilty or likely to become guilty of monopolistic abuses requiring a government takeover to prevent rather than use antitrust action that may be considered less efficient. This explanation has been a key factor in government ownership of such supposedly natural monopolies as telephone, electricity, water, and other such companies. Monopolistic abuses can relate to consumers, workers, stockholders, and government relations. Consumer abuses can include overcharging, poor quality, unsafe products, and inequitable services. So-called natural monopolies are, however, being increasingly seen as capable of some control

Table 2. Evaluating Policies for Dealing with Unemployment and Inflation

Criteria Alternatives	B1 L Goal – Unemployment to 3%	B2 C Goal – Inflation to 3%	EQ L Goal – Distribution of inflation & unemploymt.	F C Goal Free enterprise	N Total (Neutral weights)	L Total (Liberal weights)	C Total (Conservative weights)
C Alternative Do Nothing	3	3	2	4	24	22	26
C Alternative – Money + Interest	2	4	3	3	24	22	26
C Alternative – Spending + Taxes	2	4	3	3	24	22	26
C Alternative – Taxes – Domestic spend	4	4	3	3	28	28	28*
L Alternative + Money – Interest	4	2	3	3	24	26	22
L Alternative + Spending – Taxes	4	2	3	3	24	26	22

L Alternative							
Job creation	4	4	4	1	26	29	23
Price control						*	
L Alternative							
Tax breaks & subsidies	4	4	3	3	28	28	28
−Defense spending							
N Alternative							
Combine	3.5	3.5	3	3	26	26	26
sos Alternative							
Strings attach.							
Big subsidies	5	5	5	4	38	39**	37**
Objective allocation							

1. Symbols in these tables include: C = Conservative, L = Liberal, N = Neutral, S = Super-Optimum, #1 = Group 1, and #2 = Group 2.
2. The 1–5 scores showing relations between alternatives and goals have the following meanings: 5 = the alternative is highly conducive to the goal, 4 = mildly conducive, 3 = neither conducive nor adverse, 2 = mildly adverse, 1 = highly adverse.
3. The 1–3 scores showing the relative weights or multipliers for each goal have the following meanings: 3 = this goal has relatively high importance to a certain ideological group, 2 = relatively middling importance, and 1 = relatively low but positive importance.
4. A single asterisk shows the winning alternative on this column before considering the super-optimum alternative. A double asterisk shows the alternative that simultaneously does better than the conservative alternative, on the conservative totals, and better than the liberal alternatives on the liberal totals.

through competition, as with telephone companies and now electricity services as new forms of competition become technologically possible, for distant electric companies to supply electricity through remote systems.

E. A Policy Analysis Table on Unemployment-Inflation

Table 2 is a policy analysis table showing alternative ways of dealing with unemployment and inflation on the rows, goals to be achieved on the columns, relations between alternatives and goals in the cells, and overall totals at the far right. There are four relatively conservative alternatives consisting of (1) doing nothing, (2) decreasing the money supply and increasing interest rates that is especially designed to fight inflation, (3) decreasing government spending and increasing taxes at least in theory, and (4) decreasing tax rates (across the board or with selective tax breaks) and decreasing domestic spending, as in Reaganomics or supply-side economics.

There are four relatively liberal alternatives consisting of (1) increasing the money supply and decreasing interest rates that is especially designed to fight unemployment; (2) increasing government spending and decreasing taxes; (3) creating jobs, especially government jobs, to fight unemployment and imposing price controls to fight inflation; and (4) tax breaks and subsidies accompanied by a decrease in defense spending as part of liberal industrial policy. The neutral or compromise position tends to emphasize an eclectic, compromise combination.

The super-optimum solution where all major positions come out ahead emphasizes well-placed tax breaks, subsidies, and government loans with (1) strings attached to increase national productivity, (2) enough money to have a substantial impact, and (3) reasonably objective implementation by skilled professionals.

IV. SOCIOLOGY-RELATED IDEAS

A. Building on Sociological Science

There is a need for better planning for the *movement from rural* areas to urban areas. Such movement is inevitable as rural areas need less farmers owing to more efficient farming. Such movement could learn from the experiences of other countries, including the U.S. Rural Rehabilitation Service.

More help on techniques for crash programs to raise *literacy*, including literacy in English or other international languages. The successful experiences of other countries in that regard can be helpful, including Cuba and Israel. Literacy and other educational programs are high leverage in building human capital.

More emphasis on increasing the national income in order to reduce *poverty* and less emphasis on redistribution of existing income. If a country is 90% poor and 10% rich, spreading the wealth of the 10% may result in the country being 100% poor because spreading that wealth makes so little difference and decreases investment incentives. A developed country that is 10% poor and 90% rich can wipe out poverty by spreading some of the wealth to the poor, but even a developed country would be better off seeking to increase its national income so as to raise living standards for virtually everybody.[8]

B. Using Incentives

In the realm of social problems, poverty may be the most serious one for both developing and developed countries. That problem, however, is closely related to the macroeconomic problem of providing job opportunities briefly discussed above. Other key social problems include crime and ethnic group relations. On the matter of *crime*, the incentives approach might involve doing things like the following:

1. The main benefit of complying with the law should be that doing so gives one access to opportunities that are cut off to law violators. That means legitimate career opportunities must be provided to those who would otherwise turn to crime.
2. One cost of doing right may be a loss of prestige among youthful gang members who consider criminal behavior an indicator of toughness. There is a need for working to redirect such peer group values so that toughness can be displayed in more constructive ways.
3. The costs of doing wrong can include negative incentives of longer prison sentences, but it may be more meaningful to emphasize the withdrawal of career opportunities which would otherwise be present.
4. Provisions should be made for facilitating the confiscating of the property gains of criminal wrongdoing, and decreasing the vulnerability of the targets of crime to lessen the benefits obtained.
5. The probability of arrest and conviction can be increased partly through more professionalism among law enforcement personnel.

On the matter of *relations among races*, religions, and other ethnic groups, the incentives approach can encourage more equitable treatment on the basis of individual merit through such means as:

1. Tax incentives to employers, schools, landlords, and others who deal with racial minorities to more actively seek out well-qualified minority members.
2. Decreasing the costs of such affirmative action by having better information systems directed toward both the suppliers of opportunities and toward the minority members who are interested in advancing themselves.
3. Increased penalties for racial discrimination, including the publicizing of the convicted discriminators as a deterrence to others.
4. Confiscating gains from discriminating in the payment of wages or the provision of housing.
5. Periodic reporting of affirmative action activities so that benefits and penalties can be appropriately allocated.

The *housing* field is one of inadequate provision of decent housing for the poor and the lower middle class. Incentives to lessen the social problem might include:

1. Tax incentives and subsidies to building contractors to construct more housing, especially for low-income tenants or owners. On the demand rather than supply side, there may be a need for rent supplements to enable low-income tenants to afford what is available.
2. One of the costs of renting to poor people may be the extra maintenance expense, which could be reduced by educating tenants in property maintenance and by giving them more of a stake in the housing through equity arrangements, or at least representation in the decision making.
3. Increasing the costs of wrongdoing could include penalties imposed on landlords who do not provide housing that satisfies minimum decency levels, and also penalties imposed on tenants who are destructive or negligent.
4. Confiscating gains from discriminating in the payment of wages or the provision of housing by having them pay rebates, or having their property subject to attachment to cover the benefits they have wrongfully received.
5. Encouraging tenants to report both good and bad behavior on the part of landlords, and encouraging tenants to report vandalism on the part of fellow tenants and others.

C. **Equality of Treatment Across Groups**

Equal treatment under the law in the American context mainly relates to prohibitions on ethnic group discrimination, particularly discrimination against blacks. Discrimination refers to denying someone, because of his or her race, various opportunities for which they would otherwise be qualified. Discrimination can take many forms, including (1) governmental discrimination with regard to criminal procedure, school access, and voting; or (2) private discrimination with regard to housing, public accommodations, and employment. A form of discrimination exists when the dominant group forces segregation or involuntary separation on the minority group, but not when minority group members voluntarily choose to live together or to be distinctive. What are the effects of discrimination on the total society, particularly the dominant racial group, not just the group discriminated against?

Discrimination probably has a substantial effect on decreasing the gross national product by failing to make full use of the actual and potential skills that blacks have. Long-established discrimination by the building trade unions is a good example. Likewise, housing discrimination may prevent qualified blacks from living near suburban job openings to which they might otherwise lack meaningful access. Past school discrimination and inferior black school facilities might greatly lessen the chances that potential black professionals will achieve their potentiality.

Another kind of societal economic effect comes from segregated school and housing facilities. Segregated school systems may involve duplicate costs like the special Texas black law school or the Tennessee black medical school that were established with only a few students to avoid integrating white southern universities, although these two schools may have recently become economically viable institutions. Segregated housing patterns combined with employment discrimination can lead to ghetto slums with their disproportionately high costs for police, fire protection, and welfare recipients. These unnecessarily high costs of segregation should especially trouble conservative taxpayers.

Discrimination against a minority group frequently has a depressive effect on weaker members of the majority group. Thus, low wages paid to blacks tend to keep down the wages of whites in occupations that blacks might enter. Black strike-breaking labor can also deter more aggressiveness on the part of white unions. Likewise, depressed standards of police behavior in dealing with blacks are sometimes hard to change when the police deal with whites, especially poor whites.

Psychologically speaking, discrimination against blacks can create a false sense of superiority on the part of some whites. This may partly account for the lack of education and occupational ambition of many white southerners who have their race to fall back on to compensate for their lack of education and job status. Discrimination can also cause guilt feelings and anxieties on the part of whites, especially if their behavior and attitudes toward blacks conflict with democratic ideals that are preached in their society; thereby, creating the American Dilemma. Discrimination can, of course, have severe psychologically disturbing effects on blacks, but the emphasis in this impact analysis is on the effects on the total society in general and the majority whites in particular.

With regard to American foreign and military policy, domestic discrimination decreases the ability of the United States to win influence in Africa, Asia, and Latin America. Domestic discrimination may also decrease the morale of blacks in the armed forces, especially in a war against nonwhite people, and it may increase interracial friction within the armed forces as indicated by numerous clashes in the late 1960s.

An especially important effect of discrimination is the antagonism and hatred that it generates on the part of blacks toward whites. Such emotional incidents can spark into intro-ghetto riots and possibly eventually into interneighborhood riots. Discrimination also divides whites themselves between those who advocate faster removal of discriminatory barriers and those who advocate retention or slower removal. This intrawhite hostility sometimes manifests itself in student and other youthful protest activities.

Miscellaneous effects of discrimination include the loss of new manufacturing developments by discriminatory communities, which business executives consider to have an undesirable environment for raising their families. Discrimination by reducing black income can also reduce black consumer purchasing power, thereby hurting white business concerns. Finally, the presence of discrimination often deters nondiscriminatory behavior on the part of whites who do not want to discriminate, but who feel compelled to comply with what they perceive to be the dominant viewpoint unless the dominant viewpoint is made illegal by antidiscrimination legislation.

In addition to mentioning various phenomena that behavioral scientists tend to agree are effects of discrimination, some alleged effects that have no scientific acceptance should also be mentioned. For example, the absence of discrimination may indeed lead to increased intermarriage. No accepted biological study, however, has shown that the children of a racially mixed marriage are in any sense biologically defective. In fact, by lessening the skin-color purity of the races, there may be a lessening of friction between the races. In addition, the children of a racially mixed marriage are likely to have access to more societal opportunities than children with a wholly black background.

It is sometimes alleged that integrating schools will have the effect of lowering the learning level of white students without necessarily raising the level of black students. The Coleman Report, however, tends to show that economic class integration or racial integration along class lines (i.e., poor blacks with middle-class whites, poor whites with middle class blacks, poor blacks with middle class blacks, or poor whites with middle class whites) does not generally lower the learning level of middle-class children, but does raise the learning level of the poorer children.

Some whites in more frank moments correctly allege that their jobs would be in jeopardy if discrimination barriers were dropped. In this regard, dropping discrimination against blacks is like dropping tariff discrimination against foreign products. It might mean a temporary relocation of marginal less-efficient persons, but the total national economy benefits from the lowered consumer prices and from the more efficient use of its labor. Likewise, in the long run, removing inefficient racial discrimination can raise the gross national product, decrease governmental costs attributable to slums and duplicative facilities, increase depressed wages, make for more efficient geographical allocation of industry, and increase consumer purchasing power, as have been previously mentioned.

Although this discussion of equal protection under the law has emphasized racial discrimination, many of the same social consequences described would apply to much of the discrimination which is based on sex, religion, ancestral nationality, economic class, or other characteristics that usually lack sufficient correlation with ability to be meaningful criteria for allocating employment and other social opportunities.

D. Policy Analysis Table on Race Relations Policy

Table 3 is a policy analysis table showing alternative ways of dealing with race relations on the rows, goals on the columns, relations between alternatives and goals in the cells, and overall totals at the far right. The conservative alternative is to have no affirmative action in hiring or educational admissions but outlaw discrimination. The liberal alternative is to allow for preferential hiring of minorities. The neutral or compromise alternative as adopted by the U.S. Supreme Court is to allow for temporary preferential hiring where firms or government agencies had previously been guilty of racism until a balance is provided.

Table 3. Evaluating Policies Toward Race Relations

Alternatives	B1 C Goal + Economy	C N Goal − Tax costs	EQ L Goal Equity	N Total (Neutral weights)	L Total (Liberal weights)	C Total (Conservative weights)
C Alternative No affirmative action, but outlaw discrim. No pref. hiring	3.5	3	2	17	15.5	18.5
L Alternative Preferential hiring	3.5	3	2	17	15.5	18.5
N Alternative Affirmative action & temp. pref. hiring	4	3	2	18	16*	20*
sos Alternative Upgrade skills in K-12, OJT, & OIC	5	2	4	22	21**	23**

1. ? = Race relations is also an issue on which liberals and conservatives tend to take a more joint position rather than a more divisive position unlike traditional economic controversies.
2. Discrimination in this context means requiring or allowing a white with a score of 40 to be preferred over a black with a score of 60, where 50 is the minimum score for one who is qualified, or where both are qualified but the white is preferred even though the black applicant is substantially more qualified.
3. Affirmative action in this context means only hiring blacks who are qualified by actively seeking out qualified blacks through (1) advertising, (2) locating one's physical plant, (3) removing requirements that are racially correlated, but not correlated with job performance, and (4) providing on-the-job training for all but especially to overcome lack of training by blacks.
4. Preferential hiring means only hiring blacks who are qualified, but preferring qualified blacks over moderately less qualified whites, generally as a temporary measure to offset prior discrimination.

The super-optimum solution where everyone comes out ahead is to emphasize the upgrading of skills of minority members so that they can qualify for better job opportunities without needing preferential hiring. The upgrading of skills can occur as part of elementary-secondary education (K-12), on-the-job training (OJT), and special opportunities industrialization centers that train functionally illiterate people in such basic skills as the completing of employment applications (Opportunities Industrialization Center).

V. POLITICAL SCIENCE-RELATED IDEAS

A. Building on Political Science

There is a need for more use of systematic public *policy analysis* in choosing among alternative public policies. Here the developing countries can learn from methods taught at public policy schools such as Harvard, Princeton, Berkeley, Michigan, Minnesota, Texas, Pittsburgh. They can also benefit from the more practical textbooks used in such courses.

In seeking to win friends and influence, there should be more concentration on professors of *political science and law* in the univerisities of developing countries because they train the future leaders of those countries. Also, more concentration on reaching public administrators and lawyers because they are among the present leaders in developing countries.

More identification of the United States and developed countries with freedom of speech, fair procedure in criminal proceedings, and equal treatment under the law. This should include active encouragement of those basic *human rights* because they generate respect for the law and increased national productivity in developing countries.

More *international coordination* by the United States and other developed countries in providing more systematic aid. This means coordination by way of such international associations as the United Nations, the specialized international organizations, the European Economic Community, and various regional associations. The coordination should also involve more input from developing countries as to how the scarce resources of the developed countries might be put to better use.[9]

B. Using Incentives

Perhaps the most basic problem for a developing country or area is to encourage *good government* in the sense of competent, dedicated people and in the sense of stimulating innovative, useful ideas for dealing with social problems. Using the five-part checklist, public policy can encourage competency and diversity by such means as:

1. Increasing the compensation of meritorious government workers
2. Decreasing the communication costs of people with innovative ideas by providing them with access to mass media
3. Increasing the possibility of removal or demotion from government for those who do not satisfy competency standards
4. Confiscating the gains of people in government who corruptly benefit from wrongdoing
5. Decreasing the risks of whistleblowers who report wrongdoing and providing bonuses for those who report rightdoing.

The realm of political science is sometimes divided into internal and external government problems. External or *foreign policy* tends to be dominated by problems of how to encourage peaceful interaction on the part of other countries, especially neighboring countries. Relevant public policy incentives in that regard might include:

1. Increasing the benefits of mutual trade by developing agreements to benefit from each others specialties
2. Decreasing the costs of mutual trade by lowering barriers in the form of tariffs, quotas, complicated customs arrangements, and other restrictions
3. Increasing the cost of wrongdoing by developing internationally imposed penalties
4. Decreasing the benefits of wrongdoing by emphasizing that aggressive interaction will result in the acquisition of nothing of value by virtue of policies that provide for destruction of oil wells and other resources if necessary
5. Detection systems to determine that wrongdoing is occurring or is being prepared for.

C. Democracy as Majority Rule and Minority Rights

Democracy as defined above includes both majority rule and minority rights to try to convert the majority to minority viewpoints. As for the majority rule element, there are a number of points that can be made in favor of *majority rule* as being conducive to societal productivity, such as:

1. People almost genetically have a desire to exert control over their destinies. Democracy gives them at least the feeling that they are playing some part in controlling the government. Democracy thereby tends to make people feel happier in that regard; assuming all other things are held constant.

2. The more people who participate in government and politics, the greater is the leadership pool and the innovation potential. Thus, if an individual with valuable ideas and leadership qualities is in one of the disenfranchised groups in a society that does not enfranchise virtually all adult groups, then that person's abilities may not be put to good use.

3. A democratic form of government is more efficient because if it is not, it can be more easily voted out of office. A government that is not subject to being removed by majority rule may be less likely to improve itself. It may only change by shifting office holders through the equivalent of palace revolutions, but not change in terms of basic principles.

4. A democratic government in the hands of the people more quickly finds out about complaints, and it can thus better remedy the source of those complaints. By remedying those complaints and thereby obtaining more popular support, society is likely to have a more productive population than one that feels antagonistic toward the government and society.

5. Democratic governments tend to rely on an educated citizenry in order to function well, but they also tend to encourage citizens to become more politically enlightened by providing citizens with learning experiences through participating in governmental activities, especially on the local level.

6. Democracies are sometimes criticized because they move more slowly in making decisions by virtue of their governmental structures that require more approval by representatives of the people. That delay may, however, be more than justified if the decisions reached are more effective and efficient than they otherwise would be.

7. Democracies are also sometimes criticized because majoritarian rule can mean a lot of authority to those who are lacking in expert knowledge, a favorable orientation toward new ideas, or lacking in an attitude toward being especially productive. That may be a largely irrelevant point, though, if the leadership does tend to be reasonably knowledgeable, receptive toward innovation, and oriented toward societal productivity.

As for the minority rights element of democracy, there are a number of points that can be made in favor of *minority rights* to convert the majority as being conducive to societal productivity, such as:

1. In matters of science, the free circulation of popular, unpopular, and extremely unpopular ideas allows the truth to have a better chance of getting accepted. A dramatic example of where a dictatorial society was severely hurt by restricting freedom of scientific speech was Nazi Germany with regard to the development of nuclear weapons. In the 1930s, Einstein physics was looked upon by Hitler as Jewish physics and not to be encouraged. As a result, Nazi Germany lost time in the development of nuclear energy and weapons. In the meantime, Einstein helped convince President Roosevelt to develop the atomic weapons that helped the United States win World War II. That was a high opportunity cost for Nazi Germany to pay. A dramatic example of where a dictatorial socialistic society was severely hurt by restricting freedom of scientific speech was Communist Russia with regard to development of hybrid grains. In the 1950s, Mendelian genetics was looked upon by Stalin as Catholic biology and not to be encouraged. As a result, the Soviet Union encouraged an approach of growing crops that emphasized providing a good environment more than good genes. Environmentalism was in conformity with Stalin's interpretation of Marxism. Those were the years in which the Soviet Union fell from being a breadbasket of Europe to an importer of foreign grains to the substantial detriment of its economy and its international trade, from which it still may not have fully recovered.

2. In matters of policy rather than science, freedom of speech allows the most effective means to achieve given ends to have a better chance of getting adopted. A dramatic example of that from within the United States is the prohibition on advocating the aboliton of slavery, which existed in the South in the 1800s prior to the Civil War. Those restrictions on that

minority viewpoint may have helped delay the conversion of the southern economy from a slave economy to a free economy, and that delay may have facilitated the occurrence of the Civil War. More important, the legacy of prolonged slavery was probably a key factor in holding back the south for many years after the Civil War. Even now, the legacy of prolonged slavery may be a key factor responsible for at least some of the race relations problems of the United States. The occurrence of slavery is highly correlated with having a relatively unproductive, inefficient economy that provides little incentive for introducing modern labor-saving technology that can greatly raise standards of living. The poorest parts of the world are those that practice slavery, serfdom, peonage, and related forms of human bondage, and that generally place restrictions on advocating alternative economic systems.

3. Freedom of speech also provides a check on leadership that is corrupt, inefficient, and not complying with the legal system. The U.S. Supreme Court has recognized in some of its opinions that freedom of speech may be the most important right in the Bill of Rights. Without it, the other rights are less meaningful if one cannot inform others that the rights are being violated. Even the dictatorial Soviet Union at the height of the Stalin era encouraged people to speak out against corrupt and inefficient leadership, at least at the lower and middle leadership levels so long as the basic principles of communism were not attacked. The government had provided a subsidized periodical called *Krokodile* that carries articles and reports critical of bureaucrats who were not properly carrying out 5-year plans and other Soviet policies.

4. Free speech is indirectly responsible for higher standards of living to the extent that free speech promotes scientific discovery and dissemination, more effective means toward given societal goals, and more efficient governmental personnel. Some of the positive correlation is also due to the reciprocal fact that higher standards of living create a more tolerant middle class which allows still more freedom of speech.

5. Some critics of free speech argue that it leads to political instability and revolution. The empirical data tend to show just the opposite relation. This relation is partly attributable to the fact that free speech facilitates nonviolent change, particularly by providing more peaceful outlets through which potential revolutionaries can make themselves heard and win converts without resorting to revolution. The positive relation between free speech and nonviolent change is also partly attributable to the fact that free speech and nonviolent change are partly co-effects of having a large tolerant middle class. The correlation between permissiveness and stability is, however, not as high as the correlation between permissiveness and modernity.

D. A Policy Analysis Table on Free Speech Policy

Table 4 is a policy analysis table showing alternative ways of dealing with freedom of speech on the rows, goals on the columns, relations between alternatives and goals in the cells, and overall totals at the far right. The conservative alternative involves restricted free speech. The liberal alternative involves virtually unrestricted free speech. The neutral or compromise alternative as adopted by the U.S. Supreme Court involves some restrictions where conflicting constitutional rights are involved, such as (1) restrictions on campaign spending under the equal treatment clause, (2) restrictions on newspaper reporting of pending trials under the due process clause, and (3) restrictions on defaming nonpublic figures as part of one's right to privacy.

The super-optimum solution emphasizes (1) free speech for business, including the right to advertise low prices and better quality than one's competitors; (2) free speech for labor, including the right to recruit union members and publicize management wrongdoing; (3) gov-

Table 4. Evaluating Ways of Handling Freedom of Speech

Criteria / Alternatives	B1 C Goal Government stability	B2 L Goal + Creative ideas	B3 L Goal + Construct. criticism of government	B4 N Goal + DP, EP, & privacy	C N Goal − Tax costs	F N Goal Political or constitution. feasibility	N Total (Neutral weights)	L Total (Liberal weights)	C Total (Conservative weights)
C Alternative Restricted free speech	2	2	2	3	3	2	28	30	26
L Alternative Unrestricted free speech	2	4	4	2	3	2	34	40	28
N Alternative Some restrictions for EP, DP, and privacy	3	3	3	4	3	3	38	41*	35*
sos Alternative Free speech for business and labor, w/access	4	5	5	3	2	3	44	50**	38**

1. The neutral position does well on both the liberal totals and conservative totals, better than a more liberal or conservative position. This may be so because free speech is not an issue that divides liberals and conservatives the way economic issues do.

2. A policy that involves government funding and facilities for minority viewpoints would facilitate creative ideas and constructive criticism of government, but it seems politically unfeasible since the Supreme Court does not require it and a majoritarian Congress is not so likely to appropriate funds. The closest provision is probably requiring radio and TV stations to give minority parties free time when the major parties receive free time, and likewise with federal presidential funding provided that the minority parties are substantial.

3. Unlimited free speech would allow invasions of privacy, prejudicial pretrial publicity, and unlimited campaign expenditures, which neither the courts nor Congress endorse. Those rights of privacy, due process, and minimum equality in political campaigning are the fundamental rights which allow free speech limitations under Policy 3.

4. Examples of limitations under Policy 1 include pornography, libel, false pretenses, and advocacy that leads to physical harm. All those free speech exceptions have been substantially limited over the last 20 or so years.

ernment-subsidized access to mass media such as equal free TV time for political candidates and requirements that cable TV owners make time available for minority interest groups; and (4) more education and socialization at the elementary-secondary levels regarding the value of free speech for both conservative and liberal viewpoints.

VI. IDEAS BASED ON CHINA IN JUNE 1989

The points previously mentioned were generated from trips to Africa, Latin America, and Asia prior to visiting China in May and June of 1989. The following points were specially stimulated by that visit:

1. Developing countries have an even greater need for *systematic policy analysis* and governmental decision making than developed countries do. The United States could make many governmental mistakes over the next generation and still be a prosperous country. Developing countries, however, operate too close to the borderline of chaos, regarding their available resources, to be able to afford serious mistakes.
2. There is a need for *pragmatic experimentation.* All developing countries should not follow exactly the same model. They need to experiment in different parts of the country and different segments of the economy. That experimentation especially includes alternative ways of relating the government to the economy in terms of the marketplace, subsidies, tax breaks, regulation, and government ownership.
3. There is an especially strong need for putting resources into *educational development.* The introduction of new technologies is not so meaningful if the population does not have a sufficient educational level to be able to make good use of those technologies.
4. There is a need for encouraging innovative ideas relevant to more effective, efficient, and equitable development. This means encouraging a *pluralistic society* in terms of a free marketplace in ideas, especially academic freedom, freedom of the press, freedom of assembly, and multiple interest groups, as well as more than one political party.
5. *Competition* can be a useful stimulus regardless of whether it is competition between government-owned enterprises, private enterprises, or both. Competition can also be a useful stimulus in encouraging useful ideas in the academic world and elsewhere.
6. There is a need for *higher goals*, rather than being content with merely surviving or doing better than last year, so long as the goals are not totally unrealistic. Partly achieving high goals may result in more accomplishment than completely achieving low goals.
7. There is a need for thinking more in terms of public policy solutions where *all sides can come out ahead* rather than thinking in terms of tradeoffs and conflicts between classes, ethnic groups, age groups, the sexes, educational levels, and other social divisions.
8. There is a need for more use of *positive incentives* like subsidies and tax breaks but with strings attached. Those incentives should be designed to generate socially desired behavior, especially to increase national productivity. This can be contrasted to providing support for inefficient economic activities or support for those with powerful connections.
9. There is a need for more *professional training* in political science, public administration, and public policy analysis as contrasted to governmental decision making that is based on ideological considerations and personal connections.
10. There is a need for more participation by developing countries in international associations and other forms of *international interaction* so as to stimulate learning from each other.
11. The United States needs to play a stronger role in the use of its subsidies, tax breaks, and incentives to *encourage other countries* to adopt systems that are more pluralistic and less authoritarian and that are more pragmatic and less ideological.

12. Members of the Policy Studies Organization and others who have knowledge about policy evaluation methods should seek to share their ideas with scholars and governmental people from developing countries in *mutually beneficial interactions.*[10]

VII. CONCLUSIONS

One could conclude this discussion of improving public policy toward and within developing countries partly by summarizing the improvements that have been suggested. They involve building on knowledge and ideas developed in such fields as biology, physical science, economics, sociology, and political science. The improvements emphasize the importance of basic economic security, equality of treatment across groups, and democracy in terms of majority rule and minority rights. They also emphasize the use of incentives for encouraging socially desired behavior, especially positive incentives that involve increasing the benefits and decreasing the costs of rightdoing.

One could also conclude partly by saying something about what seem to be the trends on some of these dimensions. There are at least four major trends on which there is likely to be substantial agreement as to their presence and possibly their desirability. Those trends include:

1. Developing countries are almost by definition moving toward higher technology, industrialization, and urbanization. The key reason is because those developments have the potential for a high standard of living and a better quality of life.
2. Movement from economic systems that emphasize socialistic or capitalistic ownership of the means of production and distribution to a more pragmatic economic system, allowing for private sector activities subject to control through marketplace competition, subsidies, tax breaks, litigation, regulation, and the possibility or example of government ownership.
3. More equality of opportunity regarding groups differentiated in terms of race, religion, ancestral nationality, gender, economic class, age, education, urbanism, and other characteristics.
4. Movement from political systems emphasizing a strong individual, a single party, and one ideology to a more pluralistic political system.

One could also conclude by talking in terms of the kinds of attitudes that are most likely to bring about those trends and a better quality of life for people in developing countries. In that regard, there are three kinds of optimists and three kinds of pessimists.

The optimists include:

1. The stultifying optimist who says things are fine now and will be fine in the future
2. The inspirational optimist who says things are miserable now, but could be fine in the future if we or the relevant people work at it
3. The middling optimist who says things are neither fine nor miserable now, but there is room for improvement, and that working to bring about the improvements may have some effect

The pessimists include:

4. The pessimist who says things are miserable now, and they will be miserable in the future regardless what we or the relevant people do
5. The pessimist who says things are good now, but they are going to be horrible in the future
6. The middling pessimist who is middling about how good or bad things presently are, but who by definition sees the future as being bad

Of those six attitudes, the attitude most conducive to progress in developing countries is the second category. The first and third categories are not sufficiently inspirational because they tend to be too satisfied with things as they are. The fourth, fifth, and sixth categories are not sufficiently inspirational because they are too pessimistic as to what the future holds. We could also have a seventh category that combines the inspirational optimist in believing things are miserable but could be greatly improved with hard work, but that people lack the ability or willingness to do the hard work. This is more of a pessimistic category than an optimistic one.

A key element in building developing countries (or improving developed countries) is a favorable attitude toward how much influence one thinks people have over the future. Those who believe that the future is determined by supernatural forces, fate, or other forces beyond human control are, in effect, a detriment to progressive social change. So are those who believe in the potential of human efficacy but are pessimistic about the potential being exercised.

One of the most important ways of achieving the kind of cultural attitude associated with category 2 is to have successes on the technological, economic, sociological, and political fronts. It is hoped that this chapter will help stimulate other ideas regarding the improving of those public policies toward and within developing countries.

NOTES

1. For further details, see such books as E. Stockwell and K. Laidlaw, *Third World Development: Problems and Prospects* (Chicago: Nelson-Hall, 1981); J. Lewis and V. Kallab (eds.), *Development Strategies Reconsidered* (New Brunswick, N.J.: Transaction Books, 1986; W. McCord and A. McCord, *Paths to Progress: Bread and Freedom in Developing Societies* (New York: Norton, 1986); and F. Lazin et al. (eds.), *Developing Areas, Universities, and Public Policy* (London: Macmillan, 1988).

2. On the nature of choosing among policy alternatives, see E. Quade, *Analysis for Public Decisions* (Amsterdam: Elsevier-North Holland, 1989); D. MacRae and J. Wilde, *Policy Analysis for Public Decisions* (Lanham, Md.: University Press of America, 1979); and S. Nagel, *Public Policy: Goals, Means, and Methods* (New York: St. Martin's, 1984).

3. On global policy studies, see M. Soroos, *Beyond Sovereignty: The Challenge of Global Policy* (Columbia, S.C.: University of South Carolina Press, 1986); L. Brown et al., *State of the World* (New York: Norton, 1988), *Issues Before the 43rd General Assembly of the United Nations* (Lexington, Mass.: Lexington-Heath, 1989); and S. Nagel and M. Soroos (eds.), *Global Policy Studies* (London: Macmillan, 1990).

4. On the use of incentives for encouraging socially desired behavior, see D. Goulet, *Incentives for Development: The Key to Equity* (New York: New Horizons Press, 1989); L. Salamon (ed.), *Beyond Privatization: The Tools of Government Action* (Washington, D.C.: Urban Institute Press, 1989); B. Mitnick, *The Political Economy of Regulation: Creating, Designing, and Removing Regulatory Forms* (New York: Columbia University Press, 1980).

5. On multi-criteria decision-making, see C.-L. Hwang and K. Yoon, *Multiple Attribute Decision Making: Methods and Applications* (Berlin: Springer-Verlag, 1981); and M. Zeleny, *Multiple Criteria Decision Making* (New York: McGraw-Hill, 1982). On spreadsheet analysis applied to decision making, see O. Carroll, *Decision Power with Supersheets* (Homewood, Illinois: Dow Jones-Irwin, 1986); and J. Holt, *Cases and Applications in Lotus 1-2-3* (Homewood, Illinois: Irwin, 1988).

6. On the public policy problems that are closely related to biological science, physical science, and technology including food, health care, energy, technological innovation, and environmental protection among developing and developed countries, see W. Browne and D. Hadwiger (eds.), *World Food Policies: Toward Agricultural Interdependence* (Boulder, Colorado: Lynne Reinner, 1986); R. Straetz, M. Lieberman, and A. Sardell (eds.), *Critical Issues in Health Policy* (Lexington-Heath, 1981); R. Lawrence and M. Heisler (eds.), *International Energy Policy* (Lexington-Heath, 1980); D. Roessner

(ed.), *Government Innovation Policy: Design, Implementation, Evaluation* (London: Macmillan, 1988); and P. Downing and K. Hanf (eds.), *International Comparisons in Implementing Pollution Laws* (Amsterdam: Kluwer-Nijhoff, 1983).

7. On the public policy problems that are closely related to economic science, including unemployment-inflation, consumer protection, labor relations, social security, and public-private relations among developing and developed countries, see B. Gross and Alfred Pfaller (eds.), "Unemployment: A Global Challenge" (*Annals of the American Academy of Political and Social Science*, 492: 1–236, 1987); M. Nadel (ed.), *Consumer Protection Policy* (Policy Studies Review, 2: 417–550, 1983); C. Bulmer and J. Carmichael (eds.), *Employment and Labor-Relations Policy* (Lexington-Heath, 1980); N. Cutler (ed.), "Aging and Public Policy" (*Policy Studies Journal*, 13: 111–204, 1984); and D. Thompson (ed.), *The Private Exercise of Public Functions* (New York: Associated Faculty Press, 1985).

8. On the public policy problems that are closely related to sociological science including poverty, crime, race relations, housing, and education, among developing and developed countries, see H. Rodgers (ed.), *Public Policy and Social Institutions* (Greenwich, Ct.: JAI Press, 1984); J. Gardiner and M. Mulkey (eds.), *Crime and Criminal Justice: Issues in Public Policy Analysis* (Lexington, Mass.: Lexington-Heath, 1975); M. Palley and M. Preston (eds.), *Race, Sex, and Policy Problems* (Lexington, Mass.: Lexington-Heath, 1979); R. Montgomery and D. Marshall (eds.), *Housing Policy for the 1980s* (Lexington, Mass.: Lexington-Heath, 1980).

9. On the public policy problems that are closely related to political science including governmental reform, international relations, democracy, and free speech among developing and developed countries, see D. Calista (ed.), *Bureaucratic and Governmental Reform* (Greenwich, Conn.: JAI Press, 1986); E. Kolodziej and R. Karkavy (eds.), *Security Policies of Developing Countries* (Lexington, Mass.: Lexington-Heath, 1982); J. DeSario and S. Langton (eds.), *Citizen Participation in Public Decision Making* (Westport, Conn.: Greenwood, 1987); and D. Cingranelli (ed.), *Human Rights: Theory and Measurement* (London: Macmillan, 1988).

10. For further details on some of the above ideas, see S. Nagel, *Higher Goals for America: Doing Better than the Best* (Lanham, Md.: University Press of America, 1989). This book could have just as easily been called "Higher Goals for China" or more broadly "Higher Goals for Public Policy." The specific and cross-cutting policy problems that it deals with are virtually universal. Other books also deal with national goals to be achieved and policies for achieving them on a high enough level of generality to be applicable across nations. They include I. Sawhill (ed.), *Challenge to Leadership: Economic and Social Issues for the Next Decade* (Washington, D.C.: Urban Institute, 1988); M. Raskin, *The Common Good: Its Politics, Policies and Philosophy* (Boston: Routledge and Kegan Paul, 1986); C. Heatherly and B. Pines (eds.), *Mandate for Leadership: Policy Strategies for the 1990s* (Washington, D.C.: Heritage Foundation, 1989); and M. Green and M. Pinsky (eds.), *America's Transition: Blueprints for the 1990s* (New York: Democracy Project, 1989).

9
Policy Analysis Across Academic Disciplines

George J. McCall
University of Missouri—St. Louis, St. Louis, Missouri

Nagel (1992: 499) considers that "policy analysis can be broadly defined as the study of the nature, causes and effects of alternative public policies. All fields of scientific knowledge, but especially the social sciences, are relevant to such a study." Indeed, various reviews (Dror, 1971; Nagel, 1975) make a strong case for the policy relevance of perhaps the majority of fields listed in the catalogue of any major university. From among the professional schools of such a university, the schools of management (public or business administration), social work, urban planning, law, engineering, and medicine are reasonably viewed as being more or less policy relevant. From within the core college of liberal arts and sciences, a wide range of fields is considered policy relevant. Central are the social and behavioral sciences, particularly political science, economics, sociology, psychology, anthropology, and geography. Less centrally relevant are some of the natural sciences: mathematics, biology, chemistry, and physics. From among the humanities, history (as a sometimes social science) is most frequently cited, and a strong case is made for the policy relevance of philosophy.

What sort of study *is* policy analysis, and how does it relate to all these other fields of learning? This chapter seeks to analyze the rather catholic character of policy analysis in order to sort out the distinctive contributions made to it across a wide variety of academic fields. The first section considers the nature of disciplines and sets out a rudimentary framework of disciplinary relations. The second, third, and fourth sections, respectively, examine multidisciplinary, pluridisciplinary, and interdisciplinary conceptions of policy analysis.

Portions of this chapter have appeared in McCall and Weber (1983, 1984).

I. DISCIPLINES AND THEIR RELATIONS

A. The Nature of Scientific Disciplines

In classic terms, disciplines are branches of knowledge:

> The term *discipline* signifies the tools, methods, procedures, exempla, concepts, and theories that account coherently for a set of objects or subjects. Over time they are shaped and reshaped by external contingencies and internal intellectual demands. In this manner a discipline comes to organize and concentrate experience into a particular "world view" (Klein, 1990: 104).

The modern view (Dunn, 1980; Holzner and Marx, 1979; Kuhn, 1970) tends to equate disciplines with distinctive "epistemic communities," networks of scholars who share, if not a common paradigm, at least fundamental criteria for knowledge. Indeed, it is these communities who put the "discipline" into their respective fields:

> Taken together, related claims within a specific material field put limits on the kinds of questions practitioners ask about their material, the methods and concepts they use, the answers they believe, and their criteria for truth and validity. There is, in short, a certain particularity about the images of reality in a given discipline (Klein, 1990: 104).

Any scientific discipline contains the potential for developing any of three somewhat distinct foci—academic (or discipline) research, applied research, and/or practice (Weber and McCall, 1978a). *Discipline research* is that research designed to advance knowledge within an academic discipline and addressed to the members of that discipline (Coleman, 1972). *Applied research* is that research undertaken for application to some practical purpose beyond the academic concerns of a discipline (Lazarsfeld and Reitz, 1975). (Applied research thus includes, but is not exhausted by, *policy research*: research designed as a guide to social action in specific policies and addressed to an audience of political actors [Coleman, 1972].) *Practice*, on the other hand, is the provision of a more or less esoteric service—advice and/or action—to an individual or organizational client (Rebach and Bruhn, 1991; Specht, 1988).

The simple distinctions among these three potential foci of any scientific discipline cast important light on the differing relations to policy analysis of those fields that are professions (in which practice is the central activity) and those that are academic disciplines (in which discipline research is central). Both theory and research differ characteristically between these opposing models for organizing a science. Disciplines endeavor to develop *theories of fact*; professions strive to develop *theories of practice* (Schon, 1983), which define for the client desirable and undesirable conditions in relation to putative techniques for manipulating such conditions (e.g., the disease model in medicine). In either case, applied research (including policy research) is only a secondary focus. However, in a professional field, knowledge is pursued (i.e., research is undertaken) in order to improve practice; applied research is therefore rewarded by one's peers, a situation not to be found within a discipline. It is for this reason, among others (Hughes, 1963b), that academic disciplines with substantial segments engaged in applied research or practice—such as psychology, sociology, and political science—experience considerable internal strain toward the "professionalization" of their fields (Almond, 1990; Bash, 1984; Nelson, 1987).

B. Relations Among Disciplines

On the classic view of disciplines, as branches of knowledge, relations among disciplines are primarily taxonomic—connecting fields on the basis of "family resemblance" and partially shared lines of intellectual descent. On the more modern view, relations among disciplines are constituted through specific scientific interactions that somehow involve members of more than one epistemic community. These interactions include acts of research (e.g., reading, citing, reviewing, consulting, co-publishing, co-authoring, collaborating) and of instruction.

The disciplinarity of scientific interactions depends not only on the number of epistemic communities represented but also the symmetry and the degree of synthesis involved. Apart from the monodisciplinary case, most scientific interactions fail to achieve (or seriously attempt) any significant synthesis; the respective contributions of participants are simply juxtaposed, in an external and additive fashion. When such additive interactions involve representatives of two or more disciplines, they may be considered either *multidisciplinary* (if selection of the disciplines is merely ad hoc) or *pluridisciplinary* (if selection of the disciplines rests on some genuine elective affinity).

Of course, some interactions are indeed synthesizing, in result or intent. When such integrative interactions involve representatives of precisely two disciplines, they may be termed either *cross-disciplinary* (if the integration is asymmetrical) or *interdisciplinary* (if symmetrical). Those symmetrically integrative scientific interactions that involve more than two disciplines may be called *transdisciplinary*.

In these terms, the disciplinarity of a particular area of study—say, policy analysis—would depend on the relative frequency of the foregoing modes of scientific interaction. Of course, systematic data of this sort are not actually available, so that disciplinarity labels are applied only impressionistically (even wishfully).

II. MULTIDISCIPLINARY CONCEPTIONS: THE POLICY-RELEVANT SCIENCES

Along these lines, some commentators view policy analysis as merely a *topical area*, one touched upon by intellectuals of all sorts, from humanists (Mooney and Stuber, 1977) to ichthyologists like Rachel Carson, often in magnificent isolation from the contributions of other fields. Such isolation is not so much a matter of principle, like Comte's practice of "cerebral hygiene," but rather one of "pluralistic ignorance." The effect, nevertheless, is the merely additive and external juxtaposition of disciplinary contributions from across this broad spectrum.

The character of this additive mix does vary over time (Jann, 1991), with disciplines waxing and waning in popularity. During the 1960s, when "planning" was the catch phrase, social work and urban planning figured much more prominently than today. During the 1970s, when "analysis" was the buzzword, systems engineering, economics, and sociology contributed more heavily. During the 1980s, when "management" was the key phrase, the field of management science attained prominence.

Such shifts within the additive mix are driven not only by fashion dynamics within the policy field but also by dynamics internal to the various disciplines and professions. At any point in time, that is, the contributions made to policy analysis by the various fields of learning differ rather widely, in accordance not only with their varying interests but also significantly with their inner constitutions.

A. Academic Disciplines

A field of learning is a discipline to the extent that it offers "a single order of phenomena which, when observed and/or manipulated in a systematic way, yield a body of consistent theory" (Hughes, 1963a). A discipline is, in this sense, a science rather than an art.

Scientists, in the purest case, do not have clients. They discover, systematize, and communicate knowledge about some order of phenomena. They will be guided by faith that the society at large and in the long run will benefit from continued increase of knowledge about nature; but the various actions of the scientist, *qua* scientist, are undertaken because they add to knowledge, not because of any immediate benefit to any individual or group which may be considered its client (Hughes, 1952: 441).

Discipline research, in this mode, is the core activity within such academic disciplines. Not being undertaken for purposes of any application, discipline research is rarely applicable to improving policy making even though it is not infrequently policy relevant (Davis, 1975) in the sense of being addressed to a matter of general social concern. Instead, the policy fruits of discipline research are to be found largely in its fueling effects on the professions and on applied research (including policy research) conducted by members of the same or another discipline.

Applied research, within a discipline, is very much an ancillary and rather poorly rewarded activity. Policy research efforts, as a type of disciplinary applied research, are generally policy relevant but only sometimes applicable (Demerath et al., 1975; Dror, 1971; Scott and Shore, 1979).

Complex policy problems tend to be formulated quite narrowly to fit within the domain of a single discipline and to be analyzed only through the limiting (and sometimes distorting) lens of its own theoretical framework. Policy recommendations, then, tend to be restricted to policy instruments natural to the discipline; policy research within a discipline tends to lack an adequate appreciation of the necessity for social invention and experimentation and for the search for plausible points of policy leverage.

Disciplinary frameworks lack any established criteria for evaluating the significance of various policy issues or problems, and thus disciplinary policy research is characteristically vulnerable to issue fads and fashions and to over- or underreaction (including sensationalism). Such frameworks also generally fail to provide any perspective on the political realities of policy making, so that disciplinary policy researchers are often led to either utter naivete or profound cynicism in their development of policy recommendations.

Disciplinary policy research lacks the requisite flexibility in work arrangements to permit timely research response, and its norms of methodological perfectionism constitute a further obstacle to timely completion of policy studies. It tends also to ignore limitations on available policy resources and the consequent need for comparative cost-benefit analysis of policy alternatives.

It is scarcely surprising, then, that many research-based policy recommendations from the academic disciplines prove impractical or useless, if not actually counterproductive.

Such limitations on the applicability of disciplinary policy research are perhaps least unexpected in the case of the *natural sciences* because the order of phenomena with which they are distinctively familiar is radically different from the intricate social dynamics of policy making. The policy-relevant contributions of the physical science and life science disciplines are mainly substantive in relation to specific policy problems such as energy development or environmental protection. Many branches of applied mathematics—particularly statistics— provide both fundamental theoretical models (Greenberger et al., 1976; Kraemer et al., 1987) and research tools (Fairley and Mosteller, 1977) to a wide variety of the policy sciences.

Philosophy represents a somewhat oblique case because it does not purport to be an empirical science and members of this discipline undertake very little applied research. Yet philosophy, as the "mother discipline," exerts considerable influence on the core policy sciences. Its contributions effectively straddle those of the natural and the social sciences. Logic, as one branch of philosophy, closely parallels applied mathematics, in contributing fundamental theoretical models and research tools (e.g., axiomatic systems, rules of inference). Of special relevance is the recent work in modal logic on possible worlds, importantly underlying "futures analysis." Analytic philosophy is of considerable value in the clarification of fundamental concepts in all the policy-relevant disciplines, and the philosophy of science has made great strides in the "postpositivist" era. In the realm of social philosophy, normative philosophical analysis provides useful prescriptive principles. The field of ethics, revitalized by the work on justice stimulated by Rawls (1971), has substantial bearing on policy analysis (Callahan and Jennings, 1983; Tong, 1986), as does legal philosophy (Golding, 1975).

More than either philosophy or the natural sciences, the *social sciences*—as disciplines oriented toward the understanding of society and social behavior—both expect and are expected to prove useful in the improvement of policy making (Shotland and Mark, 1985). Although policy research remains very much an ancillary activity within these disciplines, it is an increasingly common and debated activity (e.g., van de Vall and Bolas, 1980).

A number of favorable trends in applied social science are often cited in these debates. First, more explicitly policy-oriented methodologies have been developed, such as social indicators and social reporting, evaluation research, and social experimentation. Second, new applied roles have emerged (Rebach and Bruhn, 1991), including advocacy roles (Weber and McCall, 1978b). Third, greater attention is devoted to social change and anticipated consequences. Fourth, more research is being conducted on policy making (including the role of scientists in this process) and on specific policies. And finally, applied social science is said to have exerted crucial substantive influence on some important policy recommendations and decisions (e.g., regarding pornography, riots, and desegregation).

Other commentators, however, find very limited progress made by applied social science research in the policy realm, particularly at the national level (Bulmer, 1982; Dror, 1971; McCall, 1984; Scott and Shore, 1979; Weiss, 1991; Wittrock, 1991). These commentators find that a very large proportion of applied social science studies fail to derive any policy action implications whatsoever. Furthermore, they find the purported cases of national policy input to be more illusory than real. In the first place, these inputs have been much more into policy recommendations (e.g., of presidential commissions) than into enacted policies. Second, most of these recommendations have been rejected by policy makers as being impractical or politically infeasible.

> Various reasons have been given for the irrelevance of much of the work done for policy. . . . One is that it tends to be too piecemeal, specialized and partial in scope to ever be applicable to policy-making. . . . A second reason is that the research has implications that are so far-reaching and revolutionary as to virtually assure inaction (Scott and Shore, 1971: 29).

And finally, even where social science research is reputed to have influenced enacted policy (e.g., the Supreme Court desegregation rulings), it is contended that the research merely supported decisions arrived at on other grounds. In short, policy research within the social science disciplines is seen as still suffering all the limitations of discipline-based research in general, as reviewed above.

These revealing criticisms, though quite generally applicable, tend to obscure key differences within this group of disciplines (McCall and Weber, 1984). For example, these disciplines vary rather sharply in their domains of interest (i.e., the single orders of phenomena with which they are concerned). In some cases, the domain is relatively restricted; economics and political science deal only with economic systems and political systems, respectively, and geography deals only with spatial distributions. In other cases, the domain is relatively encompassing, dealing in some ways with the entire sweep of society and of human behavior (e.g., sociology, anthropology, history, psychology).

These disciplines vary also in the nature of their theoretical frameworks. Some (such as economics and some branches of political science) deal in normative theory, whereas others confine themselves to explanatory theory. (Even the latter fields, however, contain within their theoretical frameworks distinctive value premises and normative principles, such as anthropology's commitment to cultural relativism. MacRae [1976] provides an insightful analysis of the distinctive "ethic" respectively characteristic of economics, of political science, of psychology, and of sociology.) Whether normative or explanatory, the theoretical framework of a discipline represents a distinctive intellectual perspective, resting on interrelated concepts, assumptions, and working principles of analysis.

Closely associated with these, of course, are distinctive modes of inquiry, or research methods, tailored to the types of data of interest. Some disciplines, such as history and anthropology, rely predominantly on qualitative data and analysis. But even between the relatively quantitative disciplines, the mix of particular quantitative methods used varies characteristically.

Among the several social sciences, the disciplines of sociology, anthropology, and history are comparatively holistic in their respective approaches to social life. That is, each is fundamentally system-oriented invoking the centrality of macroscopic sociocultural phenomena to any understanding of ordinary human affairs. Such views impart considerable hard-headed realism concerning the likely effectiveness of social change interventions and tend to provide few practicable suggestions for specific policy directions in resolving social problems.

1. Sociology

Of these holistic disciplines, sociology is the most nomothetic or generalizing in intent and is therefore the most self-consciously "scientific" (in respect of methodological rigor) and, thus, also the most quantitatively oriented. For each of these reasons, sociology is more often turned to for policy analysis than is anthropology or history.

Sociology is centrally interested in social structure—patterns of social interaction that are selective, recurrent, regularized, and regulated by various social controls (Blau, 1977). Its theoretical framework includes a variety of explanatory models (Marsden and Lin, 1982): static models (organizing a number of variables to account for structural characteristics), process models (explaining changes in variables within a social structure), and change models (explaining changes of a structure itself). Because all such models tend to presume substantial multiple causation, sociology pioneered in the survey research method and in the social science application of multivariate statistical analysis procedures, particularly in the form of "path analysis" and related procedures for the causal modeling of nonexperimental (or "correlational") data (Blalock, 1971).

Apart from the policy-analysis utility of social structural models and methodologies for understanding stasis and change, the policy relevance of sociology derives chiefly from its special disciplinary interests in social problems, deviant behavior, criminology, and demography (Reiss, 1984). Policy research in sociology (Demerath et al., 1975; Freeman et al., 1983; Innes, 1990) is almost entirely descriptive rather than prescriptive, and has heavily concentrated on policy process (particularly on the formulation, implementation, and effects stages) rather than on policy content. However, such research has been of limited applicability (Scott and Shore, 1979) owing in good part to the structural emphasis of the sociological framework, directing attention to variables scarcely amenable to manipulation through practical policies (Davis, 1975; Lazarsfeld and Reitz, 1975).

2. Anthropology

Anthropology, too, is fundamentally holistic in its view of human life. Although sharing sociology's interest in social structure, anthropology places greatest emphasis on cultural factors; for example, human/environment relations studied as "social ecology" by sociologists are studied as "cultural ecology" by anthropologists.

This central interest of anthropology in the range of cultural variations has been highly consequential for the policy relevance of the discipline (van Willigen, 1986). First of all, it has led anthropologists to focus on the study of relatively exotic peoples, most of whom are largely beyond the policy purview of Western nation-states. Second, the enshrinement of culture has fostered the disciplinary ethic of "cultural relativism" and the corollary general policy position that social change interventions should permit and encourage preservation of cultures. Third, this value placed on particular cultures has engendered significant tension within anthropology between its nomothetic interests (e.g., ethnology) and its more idiographic concerns (e.g., ethnography); this tension, in turn, has constrained the development of a rigorous methodology for cultural anthropology.

Yet, anthropology has in fact made distinctive contributions to policy making (van Willigen et al., 1989) through its latter-day focus on interethnic problems in urbanized societies, with particular attention to cultural barriers to effective and equitable service programming. Ethnographic field work methods have recently achieved some popularity among program evaluators (Patton, 1990), and anthropology also is evolving new, more quantitative methodologies for policy analysis (Harding and Livesay, 1984).

3. History

Although the discipline of history generally also pursues a holistic approach to human life, its adherents are sharply divided as to whether that discipline is indeed a social science. More idiographic even than anthropology, history has developed little in the way of a generalizing conceptual framework analogous to that of ethnology. Similarly, the methodological principles of historiography have not developed codified research practice and procedures comparable to those of ethnography, and quantitative history has not developed as steadily as quantitative anthropology. Still, excellently researched historical analyses—of great intellectual and evidential rigor—are not uncommon, and the very eclecticism of the historian's idiographic causal analyses is often advantageous.

Whether or not a "science," history brings to policy analysis (1) a distinctive knowledge, understanding, and acceptance of social change; and (2) a distinctive basis for forecasting societal developments. These contributions to policy making have, themselves, a substantial history and a promising future (Stearns, 1984). Military history has long influenced policy makers, and applied history (Schroder, 1980) dates back to 1912 in the United States but acquired real momentum through the disciplinary takeover by the subfield of social history (Rothman and Wheeler, 1981).

4. Psychology

At a pole opposite from holism are those social sciences that adopt an individualistic approach to human life, reducing macroscopic sociocultural phenomena to the aggregate of individual actions. At the extreme, a discipline such as psychology has been so fundamentally "person-centered" that many scholars have questioned whether it can be meaningfully considered a "social" science. Paradoxically, however, the average American citizen asked to name the social sciences would tend to rank psychology in first place. The very person-centered quality of psychology renders it less foreign—more immediately relevant—to the direct experience of most citizens and is highly compatible with the philosophical tenets of classical democratic theory. Psychology's prevailing diagnostic model of social problems—an "individual-deficit" model—carries clear and practicable policy implications that have been highly influential to a point where some backlash against a "therapeutic society" is now becoming evident. Not coincidentally, perhaps, the discipline of psychology is showing signs of increasing focus on person/environment interactions, rendering it a more "social" science and fostering the development of distinctive tools for policy analysis (Kasschau et al., 1985; Reppucci and Kirk, 1984).

The professionalization of psychology has gone further than any of the other liberal arts fields (Hughes, 1952), but perhaps only clinical psychology (Kiesler, 1985) merits designation as a profession. The earliest applied research of some policy relevance in social psychology was Lewinian group dynamics and behavior change (Marrow, 1969); more recent has been the development of community psychology (Orford, 1992), which takes the community as its client. Some psychological applied research (Janis, 1989; Suedfeld and Tetlock, 1992) has examined factors in the behavior of decision makers as individuals. Perhaps the most significant psychological contribution to policy research, however, has been the development of the methodology of planned social experimentation and quasiexperimental design (Cook and Campbell, 1979).

5. Economics

Like psychology, the discipline of economics (Whitley, 1986) seeks to reduce macroscopic sociocultural phenomena to the perceptions, motivations, and actions of individuals. But far more explicitly than psychology, economics transcends its interest in individual characteristics to explain aggregate patterns of action on both the small and the large scale (Amacher, 1984). Indeed, in the area of national economic policy this influence has been so great that Western economies can be said to have been restructured to fit the theories and methodologies of economists. Encouraged by this success (Nelson, 1987), economists have broken out of their traditional segmental concern with the economic sector alone and are applying their approach to an ever-widening range of policy problems (Amacher et al., 1976). Such expansion of applications may sharply test the limits of economic concepts and methods (Weimer, 1991), and in any case has provoked from other social scientists a growing skepticism about the soundness of the economic approach to policy analysis (Radnitzky and Bernholz, 1987).

6. Geography

The discipline of geography is concerned with the "man-land" relationship, particularly the spatial distribution of human populations and social functions. In the United States, however, these central topics were significantly preempted by human ecology and demography (as specializations within sociology). At the core of the theoretical framework of geography lie location theory (a rational choice model of optimum location of social functions, drawing heavily on economics) and the concept of the urban hierarchy (differentiating levels of human settlements and the varying service zones these serve). Modern geography is substantially quantitative, relying heavily on census data, mapping, and household survey research.

Geography was quite late in affording attention to social problems of any kind even though human ecologists of the Chicago School of Sociology had been undertaking spatial analysis of a wide variety of social problems since very early in this century. Applied research in American geography (Knox, 1987) dates only from the 1930s, and it was not until the late 1960s that the quest for policy relevance emerged, spawning a considerable body of work on the spatial dimensions of social justice (Kodras and Jones, 1990; Taylor, 1985) and, to a lesser extent, on environmental impact studies (O'Loughlin, 1975).

7. Political Science

Of all the social science disciplines, political science is the most inextricably linked to the study of public policy. Policy making is ultimately a political matter, and politics is the special domain of political science. It should not be surprising, then, if political science proves to be the most eclectic of the disciplines (Almond, 1990), drawing on all the others for concepts and methods useful to an understanding of the segmental phenomenon of political life. Like the holistic disciplines, parts of political science examine entire political systems as social organizations enacting distinctive political cultures, whereas other parts closely resemble the work of historians. Like the individualistic disciplines, political science after World War II took a decidedly behavioristic tack only now receding (Graham and Carey, 1972), although social choice models akin to those of economists are emerging as a major focus within political science today (Mueller, 1979). Again like economics, prescriptive policy analyses are not an uncommon mode of work for political scientists. But however much influenced by the other social science disciplines, political science brings to policy analysis a distinctive awareness of power and other political realities constraining the process of policy development and implementation (Nagel, 1984).

B. Learned Professions

The situation in professional fields is complementary to that in the academic disciplines: problems are client-derived, the core theories are prescriptive theories of practice, and applied research is importantly rewarded by peers. Why, then, have not the existing policy-relevant professions essentially subsumed the area of policy analysis?

One general reason is their one-sided emphasis on prescriptive studies to the relative neglect of descriptive studies. Since the core of any professional field of learning is its theory of practice, and such theories of practice are inherently prescriptive in nature, it is scarcely coincidental that the primary contributions of these fields to policy analysis have been prescriptive studies of policy content and process.

A second general reason has to do with the domains of validity of these theories of practice; a matter that is in turn closely related to the nature of the clients of the existing policy-relevant professions. The fact is that these clients are (at best) *managers* rather than policy makers; not surprisingly, therefore, the existing theories of practice are really theories for improving *managerial decision making* rather than for improving policy making (cf. Dror, 1971).

1. Management Science

The field of management (or administrative science, considered to include both public administration and business administration) strives to identify and apply generic "management principles" based on analysis of administrative processes, dynamics, and activities within a wide range of large-scale organizations. Its clients are to be found within the ranks of top-level and middle management in business firms and bureaucracies rather than within the policy-making ranks of those organizations. At the theoretical core of the field lies a concern for improved decision making (Simon, 1977), a concern grounded in social psychology but relying centrally on the information and decision sciences (including operations research, systems analysis, managerial economics, and systems engineering).

Perhaps the greatest contribution of the field of management to policy analysis (Dror, 1971) is its proclivity for a "systems approach" to problems, stressing the complex interrelatedness among a large number of conditions and events, and emphasizing the impossibility of judging the desirability of a single intervention without examining its ramifications in the operations of the entire system. Application of this approach to any concrete decision problem depends on the availability of some adequate model of the system permitting the (at least probabilistic) prediction of system effects through simulation. Such models are generally either mathematical models or computer programs; particularly important have been linear and dynamic programming, network analysis, game theory, and decision analysis. Recently, the utter dependence of the systems approach on strictly quantitative data and models has eased somewhat, incorporating such developments as gaming and the Delphi method.

The potential applicability to policy making of this management approach has been clearly recognized (e.g., Oman et al., 1992; Radnor, 1971; White, 1983). Others, however, doubt that such an approach is usefully transferrable from managerial decision making to policy making, citing a variety of limitations in the existing practice of mangement (Dror, 1971, 1986; Lynn, 1987). Indeed, improvement of managerial decisions, when the governing policies are in need of formulation or reformulation, may even be counterproductive, leading to more efficient pursuit of the wrong objective.

2. *Urban Planning*

A not dissimilar emphasis on a systems approach together with quantitative modeling techniques characterizes the profession of urban planning, whose clients, too, tend to be managerial decision makers—in municipal and metropolitan governments. When the term *planning* began to acquire a pejorative connotation during the "red scare" hysteria of the 1920s, the originally substantial social ameliorationism of this field was abandoned in favor of a narrower and safer centering on the arrangement and regulation of land use and land occupancy (Hubin, 1971). During this period, city planning became more closely associated with natural science fields (e.g., chemistry, physics, engineering, architecture) than with the social sciences.

It was not until about 1960 that this trend began to reverse itself and the field of city planning reconverged with social planning [a specialization within social work] to form the more comprehensive field of urban planning (Frieden and Morris, 1968). This broader approach, acquiring momentum through the twin forces of the war on poverty and the civil rights movement, rested on several related criteria: A decent modern environment includes not only physical comfort and work, but education, services, and social relationships that open opportunity for all; physical elements are not sufficient to establish the urban environment, and social measures are not powerful enough either; change that occurs by chance is not necessarily suitable for human needs.

Unlike the field of management, urban planning during the 1960s became quite concerned over the possibility of technocratic dictation—the substitution of technical for political decision making in the reshaping of urban America (Frieden and Morris, 1968; Gans, 1968). A great deal of professional debate developed regarding who is, or should be, the planner's client, and the concept of advocacy planning emerged as one device for reconciling professional practice with representative democracy (Davidoff, 1965; Davidoff and Davidoff, 1978). The strains of post-technocratic planning theory, and its relations to policy analysis, are closely examined in Friedman (1987).

3. *Social Work*

The domain of social work is *social welfare*, primarily "those programs implementing access to benefits, entitlements and services by other than market criteria" (Kahn, 1975). According to Meyer (1968: 495), "the objectives of social work are to help individuals, families, communities, and groups of persons who are socially disadvantaged and to contribute to the creation of conditions that will enhance social functioning and prevent breakdown."

The three principal divisions of social work practice (Specht, 1988) are case work, group work, and community organization, and are differentiated most clearly on the basis of type of client served—individuals, groups, and associations, respectively. Ancillary activities include social welfare administration and planning, social welfare research, and social action.

It is through the ancillary activity of social welfare administration and planning that the field of social work attains its principal policy relevance (Kahn, 1973). Social planning includes not only "welfare planning" (in the sense of allocative decisions regarding transfer payments within the social sector, akin to welfare economics) but also service coordination within the bewildering system of agencies for distributing social services (and is thus concerned with the resulting problems of discontinuity, fragmentation, inundation, access, procurement, and resource competition) (Weil, 1985). Once again, the clients of this professional activity are primarily agency administrators engaged in managerial decision making rather than policy makers.

Since these clients are themselves social service providers, it is not surprising that (in comparison with the field of management) social planning is less concerned to maximize economic efficiency at the possible expense of such social welfare principles as human dignity, social justice, and the good life (Heffernan, 1992). Similarly, as a branch of social work, social planning is much more intimately grounded in sociology and psychology than in the rationalistic and utilitarian models of microeconomics, mathematics, and engineering.

4. Law

Since laws constitute one very significant instrument of public policy, it is to be expected that the legal profession is of considerable policy relevance. Lawyers play unique roles both in the making and interpretation of law and in the advocacy of clients (individuals, government agencies, corporations, voluntary associations, and occasionally social categories or classes) within legal arenas. The legal profession greatly influences statute formulation through its disproportionate representation among legislators, and quite directly controls the process of case law (Horowitz, 1977). Legal advocacy has provided to the other fields the prototype of the advocacy model of practice and has contributed much to policy making, particularly within the area of public-interest legal practice (Patner, 1978).

However, neither the methodology of legal research (Sigler and Beede, 1977) nor the methodology of legal practice (Hart and McNaughton, 1971) is scientific in character, thus greatly limiting the profession's contribution to policy analysis. Legal research is primarily documentary analysis aimed at clarifying the historical development, overt intent, and subsequent legal interpretations of particular public policies (Sigler and Beede, 1977). Advocacy practice in the legal profession remains largely a rhetorical art (despite some use of social scientists in jury selection and in expert testimony). Similarly, the practice modality of legislative drafting remains oriented to developing legal language that is acceptable to legislatures and courts rather than specifically framed to achieve complex public policy goals.

In any case, the effectiveness of law making as a policy instrument is rather sharply limited. Effecting social change through laws involves overcoming a large component of inertial resistance (Mathieson, 1980); one interest group may prevail in the arena of formulation, whereas a countervailing interest group may win out in the arena of enforcement: "Law, by building in a possibility for defense, builds in the possibility of evasion" (Mayhew, 1971: 80).

5. Engineering

If law holds forth the attractive possibility of a "legal quick fix" of many policy problems, engineering (Perrucci and Gerstl, 1969) offers the comparably attractive and elusive prospect of a "technological fix"—the development and application of some new material product or process designed to solve a policy problem (e.g., the universal use of metal detectors in airports in response to the skyjacking problem). Although the benefits of technology are unquestionable, technological responses to policy problems—being more readily implementable than basic social reforms—too often fail (Ellul, 1965) for overlooking fundamental social causes, undesirable side effects (generating new problems while solving an earlier one), or the likelihood of technological countermeasures. (In fact, the example of antiskyjacking metal detectors can be seen to have displayed each of these flaws.)

The contributions of civil engineering to policy science by way of urban planning have already been noted, as have those of systems engineering through the management sciences (indeed, in the wake of the space program cutbacks during the 1960s, many systems engineers found employment in management consultation and in policy planning and evaluation firms). Not at all facetiously, it may be said that the greatest contribution of engineering to policy analysis surely stems from electronic engineering—in the form of computers, making possible highly elaborate manipulations of very large masses of policy-relevant data.

On the other side, perhaps the greatest disservice of engineering to policy analysis has been the dangerously misleading but ever-popular idea that policy science can be to the social sciences what engineering is to the natural sciences. Engineering rests on a base of ancient pragmatic knowledge, can take for granted a continuous flow of relevant basic and applied scientific research, operates on tangible and tractable material objects, and can utilize a clar-cut organizational model for research/development/testing/production. None of these conditions applies to policy science (Dror, 1971; Lazarsfeld and Reitz, 1975).

6. Medicine

Even more than in the field of law, the clients of medical practice tend to be ordinary individual citizens, with the major exception of the specialization of public health (or community medicine). Indeed, public health practice has always been closely linked with governmental activity, relying heavily on public law and public agencies of health care as instrumentalities.

Although the policy concerns of this branch of medicine are concerned mainly with health policy, this concern has traditionally been quite broadly construed, as including sufficient and acceptable supplies of food and water, control of physical environmental hazards, prevention and control of epidemic and endemic diseases, wide provision of health care services, and the relief of physical and social disability (Burton et al., 1980; Rosen, 1968). Since midcentury, social disability has been taken to include mental health problems of individual adjustment to the stresses of social living (Brown, 1985). Thus the concerns of public health closely resemble those of urban planning and social work, although its practice modalities rest more heavily on medical research and technology.

Medicine naturally offers medical-model diagnoses of social problems (Conrad and Schneider, 1978) and, like engineering, too often offers the prospect of a technological fix to policy issues and problems—for example, methadone maintenance as a solution to heroin addiction, or tranquilizers as a solution to mental illness. On the other hand, epidemiological methods (Mausner and Kramer, 1985) have proved powerful in analyzing the incidence and prevalence of all sorts of troublesome conditions, not necessarily medical.

III. PLURIDISCIPLINARY CONCEPTIONS: THE POLICY SCIENCES

In many scientific interactions—research projects, conferences, academic programs—selection of the participating disciplines is not entirely ad hoc (i.e., multidisciplinary) but rather rests on some felt notion of common interest, natural alliance, or elective affinity. Such interactions, again, are styled pluridisciplinary.

The pluridisciplinary view of policy analysis welcomes the contributions made by all the policy-relevant sciences but conceives a core set of "policy sciences" (Lerner and Lasswell, 1951) to enjoy in common a distinctive, intrinsic relevance to policy.

Which are the policy sciences? Among proponents of this view there exists considerable overlap, but no consensus, in the sets of disciplines identified. One plausible criterion (McCall and Weber, 1983) for including a field of learning in the policy sciences is that policy analysis constitute at least half of all its applied research output. By this criterion (although hard data do not exist) perhaps only the social science disciplines (sociology, cultural anthropology, history, psychology, economics, geography, political science) and the professional fields of management sciences, urban planning, social work, public health, and law would qualify as policy sciences.

IV. INTERDISCIPLINARY CONCEPTIONS: POLICY SCIENCE

In some scientific interactions, contributions by representatives of different disciplines are not merely juxtaposed but are in some way integrated. Such scholarly integration may be only instrumental in character or truly synoptic (Klein, 1990).

The simplest form of instrumental integration is *borrowing* of methods or concepts. Because borrowing tends to be an asymmetric interaction, it most often constitutes a *cross-disciplinary* interaction. Interactions of this cross-disciplinary sort are common between policy-relevant sciences, particularly from the academic disciplines to the professional fields. Indeed, the policy-relevant contributions of the physical science and life science disciplines are almost entirely indirect—in a sort of two-step flow, through the professions of engineering, urban planning, and medicine—as a consequence of discipline and applied (nonpolicy) research efforts generating knowledge and providing a basis for new technologies.

Methods and tools are most readily and frequently borrowed, especially from mathematics and economics. But also widely borrowed are survey methods (from sociology), ethnographic methods (from anthropology), experimental methods (from psychology), mapping methods (from geography), and historical methods.

Conceptual and substantive borrowing tends to be more domain-restricted but is still quite significant, particularly by the professional fields. For example, sociology contributes heavily to the professions of social work, management science (through organizational theory and research), urban planning (through human ecology and demography), law (through criminology and the sociology of law), and medicine (through medical sociology). Similarly, political science has long enjoyed an intimate, though ever-changing, association with the field of management (through that branch known as public administration), with urban planning (based on their common interest in municipal regulations), and with law (concerning the procedural aspects of government).

A second form of instrumental integration is *joint problem-solving*, where representatives of different fields work together in a limited and concrete project, like developing a regional earthquake-preparedness plan. This sort of "problem interdisciplinarity" (Huerkamp et al., 1981)—strictly instrumental, undertaken without any intention of seeking conceptual unification of knowledge—is encountered frequently in the ambit of policy research.

However, many proponents of the interdisciplinary conception of policy analysis have envisioned not merely such instrumental forms of sharing among the policy-relevant sciences but also genuine synthesis.

The simplest form of such synoptic interdisciplinarity is a substantially increased consistency of subject matters and methods; we speak of "interdisciplinarity of neighboring disciplines" (Huerkamp et al., 1981) when disciplines have approached each other to the extent that an overlapping area is created (Campbell, 1969). Each of them continues to contribute, but no one of them has concepts and methods adequate to establish hegemony over the area. "Policy science" may designate just such an area of convergence or overlap, comparable to gerontology or sociolinguistics.

More synoptic than continuing overlap of this sort is the emergence of a true hybrid—a new branch of knowledge, an "interdiscipline," like biochemistry or geophysics. Might policy science be one such hybrid interdiscipline? Perhaps so (Charlesworth, 1972; Dror, 1983, 1986; Hawkesworth, 1988), yet few scholars would seriously contend that interactions among the core policy sciences have created a new body of laws comprising the structure of a self-standing academic discipline.

A third synoptic possibility (Jantsch, 1970; Miller, 1982), is that policy science—like general systems theory, structuralism, Marxism, phenomenology, sociobiology, and futures research (Wasniowski, 1983)—represents a *transdisciplinary approach*. According to Klein (1990), "Transdisciplinary approaches are conceptual frameworks that transcend the narrow scope of disciplinary world views, metaphorically encompassing the several parts of material handled separately by specialized disciplines."

Fundamentally different from all these conceptions is the view, increasingly entertained (Anton, 1984; deLeon, 1981; Meltsner, 1979), that policy science is actually a *profession*, drawing upon (but not competing with) a variety of academic disciplines. Graduate programs in public policy are certainly organized along the lines of professional schools—providing little integrative coursework while emphasizing mastery of tools, the study of cases, and practical internship (Jann, 1991). At the heart of any profession lies a theory of practice which defines for clients what is problematic about their situations; Hogwood and Peters (1985) effectively suggest one in their metaphorically medical model of what can go wrong with the body politic. Descriptive accounts of the actual work of professional policy analysts are provided by Feldman (1989) and Hofferbert (1990).

V. CONCLUSIONS

This review demonstrates that *policy analysis*, the study of the nature, causes, and/or consequences of public policies, is an activity engaged in to varying degrees by a very wide range of fields of learning.

How do these activities differ across fields? Professional fields, organized around theories of practice, tend to emphasize prescriptive studies of policy content and process, whereas academic disciplines, organized around theories of fact, more frequently engage in descriptive studies. Consequently, *policy research*, as that type of applied research aimed at influencing policy makers, is found to be more prevalent within professional fields than within academic disciplines. Among the social sciences, the individualistic disciplines undertake more policy research than do the holistic disciplines.

How do the policy-analysis activities of one field relate to those of other fields? Often, they merely accumulate in hodge-podge juxtaposition. In both the multidisciplinary (policy-relevant sciences) view and the pluridisciplinary (policy sciences) view of policy analysis, such relations are considered the modal case. In contrast, a variety of interdisciplinary (policy science) views emphasize the frequency of instrumentally or synoptically integrative interactions across fields. The most persuasive of the interdisciplinary views holds that *policy science*, as a field of learning devoted to the scientific improvement of policy making, is best conceptualized as an emergent profession that might profitably draw pertinent facts, concepts, principles, theories, and methods from many academic disciplines (especially economics, political science, sociology, anthropology, and psychology) and from a number of related professions (especially management, urban planning, social work, and law).

REFERENCES

Almond, G. (1990). *A Disciple Divided: Schools and Sects in Political Science.* Sage, Beverly Hills, CA.
Amacher, R. C. (1984). Economics and public policy. In *Social Science and Public Policy: The Roles of Academic Disciplines in Policy Analysis.* G. J. McCall and G. H. Weber (Eds.). Associated Faculty Press, Port Washington, NY, pp. 159–179.

Amacher, R. C., Tollison, R. D., and Willett, T. D. (Eds.) (1976). *The Economic Approach to Public Policy.* Cornell University Press, Ithaca, NY.

Anton, T. J. (1984). Policy sciences and social sciences: Reflections from an editor's chair. In *Social Science and Public Policy: The Roles of Academic Disciplines in Policy Analysis.* G. J. McCall and G. H. Weber (Eds.). Associated Faculty Press, Port Washington, NY, pp. 201–214.

Bash, H. H. (1984). Sociology as discipline and as profession: A sociological scratch for every social itch? *International Journal of Sociology and Social Policy* 4: 15–28.

Blalock, H. M. (Ed.) (1971). *Causal Models in the Social Sciences.* Aldine, Chicago.

Blau, P. M. (1977). *Inequality and Heterogeneity: A Primitive Theory of Social Structure.* Free Press, New York.

Brown, P. (Ed.) (1985). *Mental Health Care and Social Policy.* Routledge & Kegan Paul, Boston.

Burton, L. E., Smith, H. H., and Nichols, A. W. (1980). *Public Health and Community Medicine,* 3rd ed. Williams & Wilkins, Baltimore.

Callahan, D., and Jennings, B. (Eds.) (1983). *Ethics, the Social Sciences, and Policy Analysis.* Plenum, New York.

Campbell, D. T. (1969). Ethnocentrism of disciplines and the fish-scale model of omniscience. In *Interdisciplinary Relationships in the Social Sciences.* M. Sherif and C. Sherif (Eds.), Aldine, Chicago, pp. 328–348.

Charlesworth, J. (Ed.) (1972). *Integration of the Social Sciences Through Policy Analysis.* American Academy of Political and Social Science, Philadelphia.

Coleman, J. S. (1972). *Policy Research in the Social Sciences.* General Learning Press, Morristown, NJ.

Conrad, P., and Schneider, J. W. (1978). *Deviance and Medicalization.* Mosby, St. Louis.

Cook, T. D., and Campbell, D. T. (1979). *Quasi-Experimentation: Design and Analysis Issues for Field Settings.* Rand McNally, Chicago.

Davidoff, P. (1965). Advocacy and pluralism in planning. *Journal of the American Institute of Planners* 31: 12–21.

Davidoff, P., and Davidoff, L. (1978). Advocacy and urban planning. In *Social Scientists as Advocates: Views from the Applied Disciplines.* G. H. Weber and G. J. McCall (Eds.). Sage, Beverly Hills, CA, pp. 99–120.

Davis, J. A. (1975). On the remarkable absence of nonacademic implications in academic research: An example from ethnic studies. In *Social Policy and Sociology.* N. J. Demerath, O. Larsen, and K. F. Schuessler (Eds.). Academic Press, New York, pp. 233–241.

deLeon, P. (1981). Policy sciences: The discipline and the profession. *Policy Sciences* 13: 1–7.

Demerath, N. J., Larsen, O., and Shuessler, K. F. (Eds.) (1975). *Social Policy and Sociology.* Academic Press, New York.

Dror, Y. (1971). *Design for Policy Sciences.* Elsevier, New York.

—— (1983). Basic concepts in policy studies. In *Encyclopedia of Policy Studies.* S. S. Nagel (Ed.). Marcel Dekker, New York, pp. 3–10.

—— (1986). *Policymaking Under Adversity.* Transaction Books, New Brunswick, NJ.

Dunn, W. N. (1980). The two-communities metaphor and models of knowledge use. *Knowledge: Creation, Diffusion, Utilization* 1: 515–536.

Ellul, J. (1965). *The Technological Society.* Knopf, New York.

Fairley, W., and Mosteller, F. (Eds.) (1975). *Statistics and Public Policy.* Addison-Wesley, Reading, MA.

Feldman, M. S. (1989). *Order Without Design: Information Production and Policy Making.* Stanford University Press, Stanford, CA.

Freeman, H. E., Dynes, R. R., Rossi, P. H., and Whyte, W. F. (Eds.) (1983). *Applied Sociology.* Jossey-Bass, San Francisco.

Frieden, B. J., and Morris, R. (Eds.) (1968). *Urban Planning and Social Policy.* Basic Books, New York.

Friedman, J. (1987). *Planning in the Public Domain.* Princeton University Press, Princeton, NJ.

Gans, H. J. (1968). *People and Plans.* Basic Books, New York.

Golding, M. R. (1975). Legal philosophy and policy studies. In *Policy Studies and the Social Sciences.* S. S. Nagel (Ed.). Lexington Books, Lexington, MA, pp. 201–207.

Graham, G. J., and Carey, G. W. (1972). *The Post-Behavioral Era*: *Perspectives on Political Science*. McKay, New York.

Greenberger, M., Crenson, M., and Crissey, B. (Eds.) (1976). *Models in the Policy Process*. Russell Sage Foundation, New York.

Harding, J. R., and Livesay, J. M. (1984). Anthropology and public policy. In *Social Science and Public Policy*: *The Roles of Academic Disciplines in Policy Analysis*. G. J. McCall and G. H. Weber (Eds.). Associated Faculty Press, Port Washington, NY, pp. 51–90.

Hart, H. M., and McNaughton, J. T. (1971). Some aspects of evidence and inference in the law. In *Evidence and Inference*. D. Lerner (Ed.). Free Press, New York, pp. 48–72.

Hawkesworth, M. E. (1988). *Theoretical Issues in Policy Analysis*. State University of New York Press, Albany.

Heffernan, W. J. (1992). *Social Welfare Policy*. Longman, London.

Hofferbert, R. I. (1990). *The Reach and Grasp of Policy Analysis*: *Comparative Views of the Craft*. University of Alabama Press, Tuscaloosa.

Hogwood, B. W., and Peters, B. G. (1985). *The Pathology of Public Policy*. Clarendon Press, Oxford, England.

Holzner, B., and Marx, J. M. (1979). *Knowledge Application*: *The Knowledge System in Society*. Allyn and Bacon, Boston.

Horowitz, D. L. (1977). *The Courts and Social Policy*. Brookings Institute, Washington, DC.

Hubin, D. (1971). The people who work at solving social problems. In *Handbook on the Study of Social Problems*. E. O. Smigel (Ed.). Rand McNally, Chicago, pp. 508–546.

Huerkamp, C. (1981). Criteria of interdisciplinarity. In *Center for Interdisciplinary Research, the University of Bielefeld*: *Annual Report 1978 and Supplement 1978–1981*. Center for Interdisciplinary Research, Bielefeld, Germany.

Hughes, E. C. (1952). Psychology: Science or profession? *The American Psychologist* 7: 441–443.

—— (1963a). Is education a discipline? In *The Discipline of Education*. J. Walton and J. L. Kuethe (Eds.). University of Wisconsin Press, Madison, pp.

—— (1963b). Professions. *Daedalus* 92: 655–668.

Innes, J. E. (1990). *Knowledge and Public Policy*: *The Search for Meaningful Indicators*, 2nd ed. Transaction, New Brunswick, NJ.

Janis, I. L. (1989). *Crucial Decisions*: *Leadership in Policymaking and Crisis Management*. Free Press, New York.

Jann, W. (1991). From policy analysis to policy management? An outside look at public-policy training in the United States. In *Social Sciences and Modern States*: *National Experiences and Theoretical Crossroads*. P. Wagner, C. H. Weiss, B. Wittrock, and H. Wollman (Eds.). Cambridge University Press, Cambridge, MA, pp. 110–130.

Jantsch, E. (1970). Interdisciplinary and Transdisciplinary University: A Systems Approach to Education and Innovation, *Policy Sciences* 1: 403–428.

Jones, E. (1975). Law, political science, and policy studies. In *Policy Studies and the Social Sciences*. S. S. Nagel (Ed.). Lexington Books, Lexington, MA, pp. 241–247.

Kahn, A. J. (1973). *Social Policy and Social Services*. Random House, New York.

—— (1975). Social work and policy studies. In *Policy Studies and the Social Sciences*. S. S. Nagel (Ed.). Lexington Books, Lexington, MA, pp. 57–61.

Kasschau, R. A., Rehm, L. P., and Ullman, L. P. (Eds.) (1985). *Psychology Research, Public Policy, and Practice*: *Toward a Productive Partnership*. Praeger, New York.

Kiesler, C. A. (1985). Clinical research and public policy. In *Psychology Research, Public Policy, and Practice*: *Toward a Productive Partnership*. R. A. Kasschau, L. P. Rehm, and L. P. Ullman (Eds.). Praeger, New York, pp. 194–206.

Klein, J. T. (1990). *Interdisciplinarity*: *History, Theory, and Practice*. Wayne State University Press, Detroit.

Kodras, J. E., and Jones, J. P., III (Eds.) (1990). *Geographic Dimensions of United States Social Policy*. Edward Arnold, London.

Knox, P. L. (1987). Planning and applied geography. *Progress in Human Geography* 11: 541–548.

Kraemer, K. L., Dickhoven, S., Tierney, S. F., and King, J. L. (1987). *Datawars*: *The Politics of Modeling in Federal Policymaking*. Columbia University Press, New York.

Kuhn, T. S. (1970). *The Structure of Scientific Revolutions*, 2nd ed. University of Chicago Press, Chicago.

Ladd, J. (1975). Policy studies and ethics. In *Policy Studies and the Social Sciences*. S. S. Nagel (Ed.). Lexington Books, Lexington, MA, pp. 177–184.

Lasswell, H. D. (1971). *A Pre-View of Policy Sciences*. Elsevier, New York.

Lazarsfeld, P. F., and Reitz, J. (1975). *An Introduction to Applied Sociology*. Elsevier, New York.

Lerner, D., and Lasswell, H. D. (Eds.) (1951). *The Policy Sciences*. Stanford University Press, Stanford, CA.

Lynn, L. E. (1987). *Managing Public Policy*. Little, Brown, Boston.

MacRae, D. (1976). *The Social Function of Social Science*. Yale University Press, New Haven, CT.

Marrow, A. J. (1969). *The Practical Theorist*: *The Life and Works of Kurt Lewin*. Basic Books, New York.

Marsden, P. V., and Lin, N. (Eds.) (1982). *Social Structure and Network Analysis*. Sage, Beverly Hills, CA.

Mathieson, T. (1980). *Law, Society, and Political Action*. Academic Press, London.

Mausner, J. S., and Kramer, S. (1985). *Epidemiology*. Saunders, Philadelphia.

Mayhew, L. H. (1971). Social planning, social control and the law. In *Handbook on the Study of Social Problems*. E. O. Smigel (Ed.). Rand McNally, Chicago, pp. 479–507.

McCall, G. J. (1984). Social science and social problem solving: An analytic introduction. In *Social Science and Public Policy*: *The Roles of Academic Disciplines in Policy Analysis*. G. J. McCall and G. H. Weber (Eds.). Associated Faculty Press, Port Washington, NY, pp. 3–18.

McCall, G. J., and Weber, G. H. (1983). Policy analysis across academic disciplines. In *Encyclopedia of Policy Studies*. S. S. Nagel (Ed.). Marcel Dekker, New York, pp. 201–221.

—— (Eds.) (1984). *Social Science and Public Policy*: *The Roles of Academic Disciplines in Policy Analysis*. Associated Faculty Press, Port Washington, NY.

Meltsner, A. J. (1979). Creating a policy analysis profession. In *Improving Policy Analysis*. S. S. Nagel (Ed.). Sage, Beverly Hills, CA, pp. 235–249.

Meyer, H. J. (1968). Social work. In *International Encyclopedia of the Social Sciences*. D. L. Sills (Ed.). Macmillan and Free Press, New York, 14: 495–506.

Miller, R. C. (1982). Varieties of interdisciplinary approaches in the social sciences. *Issues in Integrative Studies* 1: 1–37.

Mooney, M., and Stuber, F. (Eds.) (1977). *Small Comforts for Hard Times*: *Humanists on Public Policy*. Columbia University Press, New York.

Mueller, D. C. (1979). *Public Choice*. Cambridge University Press, Cambridge, England.

Nagel, S. S. (Ed.) (1975). *Policy Studies and the Social Sciences*. Lexington Books, Lexington, MA.

—— (Ed.) (1983). *Encyclopedia of Policy Studies*. Marcel Dekker, New York.

—— (1984). Political science and public policy. In *Social Science and Public Policy*: *The Roles of Academic Disciplines in Policy Analysis*. G. J. McCall and G. H. Weber (Eds.). Associated Faculty Press, Port Washington, NY, pp. 180–200.

—— (1992). Policy studies across social science substance. *Policy Studies Journal* 20: 499–502.

Nelson, R. H. (1987). The economics profession and the making of public policy. *Journal of Economic Literature* 25: 49–91.

O'Loughlin, J. (1975). Geographic contributions to policy studies. In *Policy Studies and the Social Sciences*. S. S. Nagel (Ed.). Lexington Books, Lexington, MA, pp. 163–173.

Oman, R. C., Damours, S. L., Smith, T. A., and Uscher, A. R. (1992). *Management Analysis in Public Organizations*: *History, Concepts, and Techniques*. Quorum Books, New York.

Orford, J. (1992). *Community Psychology*: *Theory and Practice*. Wiley, New York.

Patner, M. (1978). Advocacy and the public interest lawyer. In *Social Scientists as Advocates*: *Views from the Applied Disciplines*. G. H. Weber and G. J. McCall (Eds.). Sage, Beverly Hills, CA, pp. 49–66.

Patton, M. Q. (1990). *Qualitative Evaluation and Research Methods*, 2nd ed. Sage, Beverly Hills, CA.

Radnitzky, G., and Bernholz, P. (1987). *Economic Imperialism*: *The Economic Method Applied Outside the Field of Economics*. Paragon House, New York.

Radnor, M. (1971). Management sciences and the policy sciences. *Policy Sciences* 2: 447–456.

Rawls, J. (1971). *A Theory of Justice*. Belknap, Cambridge, MA.

Rebach, H. M., and Bruhn, J. G. (Eds.) (1991). *Handbook of Clinical Sociology.* Plenum, New York.

Reiss, A. J., Jr. (1984). Sociology and public policy. In *Social Science and Public Policy: The Roles of Academic Disciplines in Policy Analysis.* G. J. McCall and G. H. Weber (Eds.). Associated Faculty Press, Port Washington, NY, pp. 19–50.

Reppucci, N. D., and Kirk, R. H. (1984). Psychology and public policy. In *Social Science and Public Policy: The Roles of Academic Disciplines in Policy Analysis.* G. J. McCall and G. H. Weber (Eds.). Associated Faculty Press, Port Washington, NY, pp. 129–158.

Rosen, G. (1968). Public health. In *International Encyclopedia of the Social Sciences.* D. L. Sills (Ed.). Macmillan and Free Press, New York, 13: 164–170.

Rothman, D., and Wheeler, S. (1981). *Social History and Social Policy.* Academic Press, New York.

Schon, D. A. (1983). *The Reflective Practitioner: How Professionals Think in Action.* Basic Books, New York.

Schroeder, A. M. (1980). Applied history: An early form of public history. *Public Works Historical Society Newsletter* 17: 3–4.

Scott, R. A., and Shore, A. R. (1979). *Why Sociology Does Not Apply: A Study of the Use of Sociology in Public Policy.* Elsevier, New York.

Shotland, R. L., and Mark, M. M. (Eds.) (1985). *Social Science and Social Policy.* Sage, Beverly Hills, California.

Sigler, J., and Beede, B. (1977). *The Legal Sources of Public Policy.* Lexington Books, Lexington, MA.

Simon, H. A. (1977). *The New Science of Management Decision,* rev. ed. Prentice-Hall, Englewood Cliffs, NJ.

Specht, H. (1988). *New Directions for Social Work Practice.* Prentice-Hall, Englewood Cliffs, NJ.

Stearns, P. N. (1984). History and public policy. In *Social Science and Public Policy: The Roles of Academic Disciplines in Policy Analysis.* G. J. McCall and G. H. Weber (Eds.). Associated Faculty Press, Port Washington, NY, pp. 91–128.

Suedfeld, P., and Tetlock, P. E. (Eds.) (1992). *Psychology and Social Policy.* Hemisphere, New York.

Taylor, P. J. (1985). *Political Geography.* Longman, London.

Tong, R. (1986). *Ethics in Policy Analysis.* Prentice-Hall, Englewood Cliffs, NJ.

van de Vall, M., and Bolas, C. (1980). Applied social discipline research or social policy research: The emergence of a professional paradigm in sociological research. *The American Sociologist* 15: 128–137.

van Willigen, J. (1986). *Applied Anthropology: An Introduction.* Bergin & Garvey, South Hadley, MA.

van Willigen, J., Rylko-Bauer, B., and McElroy, A. (1989). *Making Our Research Useful.* Westview Press, Boulder, CO.

Wagner, P., Weiss, C. H., Wittrock, B., and Wollman, H. (1991). *Social Sciences and Modern States: National Experiences and Theoretical Crossroads.* Cambridge University Press, Cambridge,

Wasniowski, R. (1983). Futures research as a framework for transdisciplinary research. In *Managing Interdisciplinary Research.* S. R. Epton, R. L. Payne, and A. W. Pearson (Eds.). Wiley, New York, pp. 266–278.

Weber, G. H., and McCall, G. J. (1978a). Applied sociology: Issues and questions. Paper presented to Southwestern Sociological Association, Houston, TX.

—— (1978b). *Social Scientists as Advocates: Views from the Applied Disciplines.* Sage, Beverly Hills, CA.

Weil, M. (1985). *Case Management in Human Service Practice.* Jossey-Bass, San Francisco.

Weimer, D. L. (Ed.) (1991). *Policy Analysis and Economics: Developments, Tensions, Prospects.* Kluwer, Boston.

Weiss, C. H. (1991). Policy research: Data, ideas, or arguments? In *Social Sciences and Modern States: National Experiences and Theoretical Crossroads.* P. Wagner, C. H. Weiss, B. Wittrock, and H. Wollman (Eds.). Cambridge University Press, Cambridge, England, pp. 307–332.

White, J. J. (1983). Policy analysis and management science. In *Encyclopedia of Policy Studies.* S. S. Nagel (Ed.). Marcel Dekker, New York, pp. 11–41.

Whitley, R. (1986). The structure and context of economics as a scientific field. *Research in the History of Economic Thought and Methodology* 4: 179–209.

Wittrock, B. (1991). Social knowledge and public policy: Eight models of interaction. In *Social Sciences and Modern States: National Experiences and Theoretical Crossroads.* P. Wagner, C. H. Weiss, B. Wittrock, and H. Wollman (Eds.). Cambridge University Press, Cambridge, England, pp. 333–353.

Part D
POLICY PROBLEMS ON VARIOUS GOVERNMENT LEVELS

10

The States in the Federal System

David Brian Robertson

University of Missouri–St. Louis, St. Louis, Missouri

I. WHY STUDY THE STATES' ROLE IN PUBLIC POLICY?

A federal system, by definition, endows both the national and the state governments with the authority to make public policy. Struggles to define the boundaries of national and state authority pervade American politics because political opponents expect these different levels of government to resolve conflicts in different ways.

The way the boundaries of state and national authority are drawn helps some interests and harms others by expanding or limiting the scope of conflict (Schattschneider, 1960: 1–10). When different levels of government implement solutions to similar public problems, different sets of interests shape policy outcomes. Thus, federalism's effect on the scope of political conflict has constituted perhaps the most critical determinant of outcomes on issues as central to American politics as slavery, the regulation of commerce and labor, social welfare, and individual rights.

Indeed, one cannot identify an important government program that has not involved battles over the role of the federal government versus the states and localities. The history of intergovernmental relations in the United States reveals that debates about the level of government that should control public policy nearly always conceal fundamental disagreements about the very substance of policy itself.

In the 1960s, for example, opponents of civil rights protections used the claim of "states' rights" to try to prevent national control of civil rights issues. When federal courts ordered the desegregation of the University of Mississippi in 1962, Governor Ross Barnett appeared on statewide television to declare, "Mississippi, as a Sovereign state, has the right . . . to determine what the Federal Constitution has reserved for it," and that it would not comply. In phone conversations with U.S. Attorney General Robert Kennedy during the crisis, Barnett told Kennedy that the issue boiled down to "whether Mississippi can run its institutions or the federal government is going to run things." When Kennedy reminded Barnett, "you are a part of the United States," Barnett responded, "I don't know whether we are or not," and suggested that violence might ensue. The dispute over enrolling an African-American student at "Ole Miss" eventually resulted in a riot in which two died, dozens were injured, and federal troops occupied the campus (Navasky, 1971: 159–242).

In the 1980s, opponents of nuclear power used strikingly similar arguments to prevent the national control of nuclear plant safety rules and the start-up of nuclear power plants. When the Reagan administration announced that it would permit the Shoreham nuclear power plant on Long Island to open without the involvement of state and local officials in safety tests, liberal Democrats objected that such a procedure would violate "states' rights." Representative Edward Markey (D, Massachusetts) complained that federal officials had conspired against state and local officials and that the Nuclear Regulatory Commission appeared "to be on the verge of declaring open warfare against the states on this issue" (U.S. Congress, 1986: 240–241).

In both cases, the expressed concern about states' rights belied a desire to control policy outcomes. Although the opponents of a national law nominally opposed federal enforcement, they knew that if the issue were left to the states, they could exercise much more influence over the outcome. Groups that decisively influence policy at the state and local level often exercise much less influence in national policy making. Both Governor Barnett and Representative Markey sought to narrow the scope of conflict to the state level, where they and their allies could more easily control the outcome. Both Attorney General Kennedy and Reagan administration Energy Department officials sought to broaden the scope of conflict to the national level to maintain control and prevent their opponents from wresting it away.

One of the enduring consequences of the American federal structure is that policy conflicts tend to turn as much on jurisdictional questions as on the merits of policy alternatives. Understanding public policy in a federal republic requires an understanding of the states' policy role, the relationship of the states to the national government, and the nature of the political battles that turn on these issues.

II. THE EVOLVING ROLE OF THE STATES IN AMERICAN PUBLIC POLICY

A. The Constitutional Framework

The authors of the U.S. Constitution found it both undesirable and politically impossible to reduce drastically the states' role in policy making. The delegates to the constitutional convention of 1787 granted the states significant autonomy in the new political system in order to ensure that the required number of state legislatures would ratify the new government plan. Convention debates turned on ways to strengthen national institutions to achieve national security and commercial stability while reassuring the states that they would not lose their independence. Despite abundant assurances to this effect, the special state conventions narrowly voted to ratify the constitution in Massachusetts, New York, Virginia, and Rhode Island.

The Constitution is thus artfully ambiguous about the policy role of the states. Ratification required the subsequent adoption of a Bill of Rights, including the Tenth Amendment specifying, "The powers not delegated to the United States by the Constitution, nor prohibited by it to the States, are reserved to the States respectively, or to the people." At the same time, Article I, Section 10 of the Constitution prohibited the states from some policy actions, such as abrogating contracts, imposing tariffs, or making treaties. Constitutional clauses that permitted Congress "To make all laws which shall be necessary and proper" (Article I, Section 8) for executing national power and that established national laws as "the supreme Law of the Land" (Article VI) soon were interpreted as conveying "implied" powers to the national government potentially much more expansive than those expressed in the Constitution (see Goldwin and Schambra, 1986). However, the national government did not exercise these powers, and the Jacksonian Democrats in effect rejected an active national government role in most domestic affairs.

The states soon filled the domestic policy vacuum in the United States. As the chief architects of American contract and property law, states established the foundations of American capitalism. From 1789 until the 1930s, they served as the front-line managers of social change in the United States.

Thus, states have governed much of the daily life of American citizens. States rather than the national government have provided the details of business law, including laws about commercial relations and contracts, business creation and incorporation, occupational and professional standards, the sale of securities, and unfair transactions and practices. Slave codes, "Jim Crow" segregation, and early civil rights legislation all appeared at the state level. States have taken the primary responsibility for environmental management through laws controlling land use, mineral and water rights, and public health regulation. They have been the dominant providers of highways, welfare, health, natural resources management, corrections, and education. They have established many laws that govern individual financial relationships, including estate and inheritance laws. States dominate the criminal justice system. States created, maintained, and regulated local governments, and they are the primary architects of sales taxes and rules for property taxes. Finally, states have largely controlled laws about moral conduct, including alcohol and drugs, marriage, divorce, abortion, and sexual conduct (Reeves, 1985: 22–23).

Equally important, states have managed the conduct of politics. States are the chief source of electoral laws, including registration requirements, selection procedures for party candidates, and ballot access. These laws, in part, have maintained the American two-party system. States' business and trade union regulations affect the balance of power between these fundamental interests. States' regulations affect the political strategies of pressure groups. Local police and state militias have provided the first line of defense against domestic political violence.

B. Dual Federalism: 1789-1933

Until the 1930s, the strict separation of national and state policy responsibilities—characterized as "dual federalism"—was viewed widely as both descriptively accurate and desirable (for a detailed discussion of models of intergovernmental relations in the U.S., see Wright, 1988; see also O'Toole, 1993). For example, in *Barron* vs. *Baltimore* (1833), the Supreme court held that the Bill of Rights limited the powers of the federal government but not those of the states. Much of the conflict about public policy since the 1930s has turned on altering this strict separation in particular policy areas.

But by no means were national and state policy responsibilities separated as simply as "dual" federalism implies. Elazar (1962) demonstrated that although the ideology of dual federalism dominated political thought in intergovernmental relations up to the New Deal, governments commonly violated these principles in practice. For example, Congress promoted national expansion through a massive program of internal improvements. The creation of the Corps of Engineers (1802) and Albert Gallatin's 1808 proposal for a multimillion dollar national subsidy for internal improvements showed that the national government could aspire to leadership in domestic policy even during the presidency of a "states' rights" president such as Thomas Jefferson (Goodrich, 1948).

In the mid-19th century, federal grants to the states grew to substantial proportions. Between 1833 and 1866, the federal government gave 4.5 million acres of public lands to the states for canal construction, 3.5 million acres for roads, and 1.7 million acres for river improvements. From 1850 to 1872, the U.S. government gave another 131 million acres of federal lands to the states and to railroad companies for the construction of the national railway system (Bruchey, 1988: 36–37).

Despite the obviously cooperative nature of the federal system, the doctrine of dual federalism affected a wide range of important government decisions. In 1854, President Franklin Pierce vetoed congressional legislation that would have provided land grants to the states for the purpose of establishing institutions for the mentally ill. Pierce held that the Constitution granted no authority to permit the federal government to become "the great almoner of charity in the United States" (Pierce, 1975).

In the late 19th century, the courts used the dual federalism doctrine selectively to achieve desired policy outcomes. When the national government attempted to exert national control over business, the federal courts frequently ruled that such efforts violated national authority and illegally invaded states' prerogatives. The U.S. Supreme Court decided that the Sherman Anti-Trust Act of 1890, a law enacted to control monopolies, did not allow the federal government to prevent a monopoly in sugar refining on the grounds that manufacturing is not interstate commerce but rather an intrastate matter (*U.S.* v. *E.C. Knight Co.*, 1895). The Court invalidated both a national child labor prohibition and then a prohibitory tax on child labor on similar grounds (Commons, 1918, 1935: 440–442, 694–695).

Beyond some regulation of interstate commerce (in the form of railroad regulation, the Federal Reserve system, and a few other activities), the national government's capacity to affect domestic policy remained latent as the nation industrialized. By the early decades of the 20th century, federal revenues and spending per capita were considerably smaller than those of the states (Table 1). Only immense, federally directed mobilization for World War I brought the national and state governments to parity. As the nation returned to normalcy in the 1920s, the federal role gradually shrank. By the outset of the Depression, state and local government spending constituted two thirds of all government expenditures in the United States.

Grants-in-aid provided the only vehicle for the federal government to involve itself in domestic policy areas traditionally managed by the states. The federal income tax provided a way to fund cash grants to the states for specific social and economic purposes. Courts that struck down national laws upheld grants as constitutionally acceptable. The Federal Road Act of 1916 provided federal grants to state highway departments for the purpose of building and improving rural roads. The Vocational Education Act of 1917 authorized the federal

Table 1. Per Capita Government Revenues and Expenditures, 1902–1932

Year	Revenues ($)		Direct expenditures ($)	
	federal	state	federal	state
1902	6.48	10.86	7.14	12.80
1913	6.81	16.55	9.85	21.23
1922	30.63	36.49	33.04	47.41
1932	14.51	49.33	31.88	62.15

Source: U.S. Census Bureau, 1969: 31–32.

government to help pay teachers' salaries and other costs of state vocational education institutions. Because grants-in-aid permitted the states to control important choices about the use of federal funds (such as maintaining segregation), the states and their national representatives in Congress found them ideal for increasing federal action while retaining state power. Such grants-in-aid programs remained small throughout the 1920s, amounting to $163 million in 1931, with 83% of the total sum devoted to highway grants. But they set the precedent for the design and administration of social programs adopted during the New Deal: the states would receive federal dollars, and use their own personnel and administrative structures to carry out the programs (Break, 1981: 44).

By the time that the national government took a more active part in domestic affairs, the states occupied the domestic field. States had firmly entrenched programs involving long-established financial commitments and long-standing institutional ties. Thus, the states became the cornerstone for—and sometimes the chief obstacle to—many of the national domestic initiatives after 1933.

C. Cooperative Federalism: 1933-1961

The international depression of the 1930s caused unprecedented and irresistible needs for federal government action. The Depression so badly damaged the economy that demands to help overwhelmed private charities, cities, and states.

States provided only limited help for individual victims and for economically shattered cities. The states entered the Depression heavily indebted from the roads, schools, and other public construction projects of the 1920s. The gasoline and other tax revenues that fueled this construction evaporated as highway tourism and commerce ground to a halt. The states cut spending as revenues dropped. States slashed budgets for public works, from $1.35 billion in 1928, to $630 million in 1932 and $290 million in the first 8 months of 1933. With private construction at a near standstill, these cuts swelled the ranks of the jobless. Although 43 states enacted legislation to fund emergency unemployment relief between 1931 and 1935, only 8 of the 48 states provided any money for relief at the beginning of the New Deal (Patterson, 1969: 39–40; Geddes, 1937: 91–92).

With notable exceptions, such as New York, Pennsylvania, Wisconsin, and Minnesota, state governments lacked the ability and political will to assist the large cities, where the Depression took its greatest toll. State constitutions had been written for a rural, agricultural society that required minimal governance. Rural amateurs populated most state legislatures, which met briefly every other year and lacked professional staff. State constitutions normally required balanced budgets, which forced the states to reduce spending just as needs increased. Sparsely populated rural counties consistently outnumbered and outvoted city interests in the state legislatures. Like their legislatures, most governors remained philosophically conservative, being more attuned to rural than to urban constituencies (Patterson, 1969: 20–44).

Few who listened to Franklin Roosevelt's presidential campaign speeches in 1932 would have imagined that his administration would transform the federal government permanently into an active partner in domestic policy. Yet the New Deal marked a decisive turning point in government activism and in the relative fiscal role of the national and state governments (Table 2). Fueled by anti-Depression measures in the 1930s and large social insurance and military expenditures since then, federal direct spending permanently overtook state and local spending. Federal civilian employment also grew, from 581,000 employees in 1933 to just over 1 million by mid-1940, to 2 million by 1950, and has remained between 2.8 and 3.2 million since the late 1960s. By the late 1980s, state and local governments employed more than four times the number of federal civilian employees.

Table 2. Per Capita Government Revenues and Expenditures, 1936–1990

Year	Tax revenues ($)		Direct expenditures ($)	
	Federal	State	Federal	State
1936	30.29	52.28	63.90	59.63
1940	36.92	59.11	67.33	69.85
1950	231.96	104.91	249.95	150.22
1960	427.81	200.66	426.26	288.21
1970–71	665.57	460.47	729.30	730.52
1980–81	1,790.86	1,079.31	2,757.22	1,798.52
1989–90	2,542.19	2,016.88	4,029.69	3,356.46

Sources: U.S. Census Bureau, 1969: 30–31; U.S. Census Bureau, 1979: 31–37; U.S. Census Bureau, 1992: 3.

This federal growth fostered unprecedented state and local policy action. The New Deal institutionalized a cooperative federalism in which the national government encouraged state and local policy activism through grants-in-aid. Table 2 shows a substantial and generally growing disparity between revenues and expenditures at the subnational level since the 1930s. Because state and local governments generally must operate with balanced budgets and cannot borrow on the scale of the federal government, federal grants largely have funded the gap between spending and revenues at the state and local levels. At the federal level, the gap between spending and revenue indicates that the federal government incurred larger debts, especially in the 1980s.

This grants strategy partly reflected President Roosevelt's own preferences, and partly reflected the political opportunities and constraints that he faced on taking office. Roosevelt tended to heed the advice of experts who recommended federal-state cooperation. Experts who had drafted the laws of the progressive states also drafted key New Deal proposals. They recommended policies in which the states retained significant policy control (Witte, 1963). In this view, the national government would establish some policy standards, whereas the states would determine eligibility, benefit levels, and other rules, would provide the day-to-day administration, and would share program costs.

Politically, the grants strategy proved as much a necessity as a virtue. New Dealers understood that Congress and the Supreme Court would resist purely national programs. Four of the Court's nine justices were economic conservatives, who were willing to use the Court to prevent the national government from interfering with private business. At the same time, the Court's liberals, led by Justice Brandeis, refused to permit the New Deal to go too far toward centralizing government. It struck down many of the New Deal's efforts to use the commerce power to govern sectors of the economy (notably the National Industrial Recovery Act). By late 1935, federal judges in lower courts had issued 1600 orders to prevent federal officials from carrying out acts of Congress (Ikenberry and Skocpol, 1987: 407–411). Although the court grew more tolerant of New Deal programs after Roosevelt's landslide reelection in 1936, by then much of the New Deal legislation had institutionalized the administrative autonomy of state governments, partially in an effort to satisfy the Court.

Cooperative federalism through grants also aimed to mollify Congress, where many members opposed uniform national programs or effective federal oversight of program operations. Southern congressmen worried that the Social Security Act would improve conditions for blacks in the South by raising wages, thus undermining white dominance in that region. Ultimately, Congress produced compromises that removed some of the minimal federal requirements proposed by the administration. For example, changes in the Social Security Act increased the states' authority to fix the level of unemployment insurance and welfare benefits (Leuchtenburg, 1963: 39).

Thus, cooperative federalism became the path of least resistance for policy activism during the New Deal and beyond. Nearly all the new domestic programs that Congress approved in the 1950s through the 1970s involved grants. The 1949 Housing and Urban Development Act provided grants-in-aid to local urban renewal authorities and public housing authorities. The Urban Renewal program gave local urban renewal administrators authority to select sites, contractors, and development plans. The 1956 National Defense Highway Act was implemented through grants-in-aid to state highway departments (Freedman, 1969). The Water Pollution Control Act of 1956 provided grants to the states for sewerage-treatment construction (Jennings, 1969).

By the 1960s, grants generated little controversy in their own right. Instead, political disputes about grants turned on which constituency they would serve and which federal rules they would impose on the state and local governments.

III. GRANTS EXPANSION AND BENEFITS COALITIONS IN THE 1960s AND 1970s

A. Creative Federalism

During the 1960s, federal officials purposefully attempted to alter intergovernmental relationships. Presidents Kennedy and Johnson presented aggressive agendas for the expansion of the national government, and both used federal police powers and budgets to achieve their goals. They envisioned the national government as catalyst for reforming and energizing state, local, and private institutions.

Responding to the Johnson administration's leadership, Congress authorized 219 new grants between 1964 and 1966, including the major social commitments of the Great Society. The Economic Opportunity Act of 1964 financed new educational and job training programs for the poor. The Medicaid program of 1965 directed grants to the states to manage a new system for medical care for those eligible for Aid to Families with Dependent Children and other state-run assistance programs. Other grant programs funded education (the Elementary and Secondary Education Act of 1965) and police (the Safe Streets and Crime Control Act of 1968). Long-established grant programs, such as vocational rehabilitation and vocational education, were expanded to provide services for the mentally and physically handicapped. New authorizations expanded and targeted the 1949 Housing Act more closely to the needy. The administration proposed an innovative plan to create "model cities" (Palmer, 1984: 6–15).

These programs departed from previous patterns in American intergovernmental policy in four ways. First, nearly all of the social legislation enacted between 1964 and 1968 specifically addressed the issues of poverty, race, and equality of opportunity. The Civil Rights Act of 1964 struck down Jim Crow laws and prohibited employment discrimination. The Voting Rights Act of 1965 overrode discriminatory state election laws and provided for federal registrars in many southern states. Existing programs, such as the U.S. Employment Service and Federal Housing Administration home loans, were directed to make special provisions for minority clients.

Table 3 shows the effect of these changed priorities. In 1960, federal highway and other transportation grants constituted over 40% of federal grants expenditure. Between 1960 and 1970, education, training, employment, social services, and health grants eclipsed highway and other transportation spending as a share of federal grants expenditure. Together these

Table 3. Changes in the Composition of Federal Grants Outlays, 1960–1995

	% of grants outlays by function				
	1960	1970	1980	1990	1995[a]
Natural resources and environment	2%	2%	6%	3%	2%
Agriculture	3	3	1	1	1
Transportation	43	19	14	14	10
Community and regional development	2	7	7	4	2
Education, training, employment, and social services	7	27	24	17	13
Health	3	16	17	32	50
Income security	38	24	20	26	21
General government	2	2	9	2	1
Other functions	–	1	1	1	1
Total	100	100	100	100	100

[a]Estimate.
Source: U.S.OMB, 1992: 438.

categories still constitute about 40% of federal grants expenditure a generation after the Great Society, although the rapidly rising costs of health care have made Medicaid the chief engine of growth in these categories.

Second, the New Frontier and the Great Society sought to bypass existing state institutions and to establish direct connections between the federal government and local actors sympathetic to their national purposes. Both the War on Poverty and the Model Cities programs channeled funds to community-based organizations established to increase the participation of lower-income residents and to put these programs beyond the control of local power brokers (Palmer, 1984: 15–17). The War on Poverty's "community action programs" promised "maximum feasible participation" for the poor in determining how antipoverty funds would be spent (Congressional Quarterly, 1969: 746, 749).

Third, with the notable exception of Medicaid, most of the Great Society programs relied on *project* grants. Before the 1960s, Congress had written the larger grant programs as *formula* grants, which distributed funds to eligible recipients on the basis of statutory criteria and permitted little administrative discretion. Project grants required potential recipients to propose a project (such as a specific job training contract) to the federal agency in charge of administering grants for that purpose. Project grants placed potential recipients in competition with one another, which made it easier for federal bureaucracies to dictate the use of the funds. Of 219 grant programs added between 1962 and the end of 1966, 173 (or 4 out of 5) were project grants. In 1964, project grants accounted for one quarter of grants spending, but they accounted for one half by 1969 (ACIR, 1973: 25; Haider, 1974: 55).

Finally, the national government increased the number of mandates or conditions under which state and local governments received grants. The 1964 Civil Rights Act created a significant new instrument to achieve national standards in grants programs, which made discrimination in the administration of any federal grants program illegal—a so-called *crosscutting* requirement that applied to all federal grants-in-aid (ACIR, 1973: 71). Another method for strengthening the hand of federal administrators was the *crossover* sanction, which added new objectives to existing grants (e.g., the control of billboards as a condition for receiving highway grant funds). The number of federal requirements attached as a condition of federal aid increased from 4 in 1960 to 1034 in 1978 (Walker, 1981: 193–196). Finally, the federal government preempted the rights of states in certain areas, beginning with the Water Pollution Control Act of 1965, which permitted the Secretary of Health, Education, and Welfare to set water pollution standards for a state if existing standards were found to be inadequate (ACIR, 1973: 70–88).

B. The Great Society's Legacy in the Politics of Grants

By the end of the 1960s, the political stakes and conflicts involved in the intergovernmental grants system had intensified irreversibly. Federal grants spending rose to a peak in 1978 (Fig. 1). Grants spending increased during Democratic administrations (1933–1953, 1961–1969, 1977–1981) and Republican administrations (1953–1961, 1969–1977) alike. Midway through the Carter administration, grants spending began to drop, a trend that accelerated during the early Reagan years. Spending on grants leveled off in the mid-1980s and began to increase again during the Bush administration.

With so much money at stake, political battles turned on the question of who would control these moneys and on what terms. The very existence of these grants reflected and stimulated the growth of strong "benefits coalitions" (Anton, 1989) of interest groups focused on a particular public program. Benefits coalitions include those federal, state, and local public officials, as well as legislators, interest groups, issue experts, and others who benefit from the program. For example, a coalition including governors, mayors, county leaders, U.S. Department of Labor officials, community organizations, trade union groups, and the National Alliance of Business lobbied for expanded federal job training funds in the late 1960s and early 1970s. The resulting expansion of these programs in the Comprehensive Employment and Training Act of 1973 provided benefits to members of all these groups.

Public sector interest groups and Congress provided the most formidable political support for the explosive growth of grants in the 1960s and 1970s. Public sector interest groups representing cities (the United States Conference of Mayors and the National League of Cities), the National Association of Countries, and the National Governors' Association all enjoyed access to the executive branch and to Congress (Haider, 1974: 1–41). The decline of

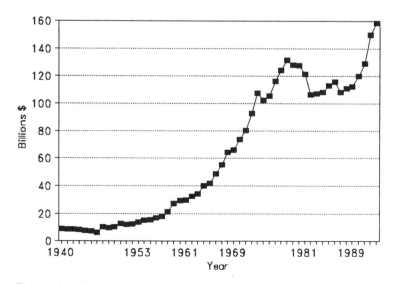

Figure 1. Grants to state and local governments.

strong local political parties fueled this direct action by muting the influence of party leaders in Washington (Conlan, 1986: 104). Grants provided additional funds to these governments and ensured that they would retain some control over program implementation.

Allocation formulas and conditions attached to grants divided these groups from each other. Big city mayors and community-based groups, as a natural part of the Democratic coalition, favored need-based grant formulas, direct federal-local funding, and federal oversight. States and counties (particularly suburban counties) favored fewer strings and population-based formulas, and were more representative of Republican constituents than were the large cities.

As participants in a decentralized institution, members of Congress focused on distributive policies that ensured maximum federal benefits and maximum local discretion over the use of money. Grants programs that emerged from Congress tended to be "widely distributed to encourage universal support," and were usually "distributed evenly among political jurisdictions," whether or not a state or district was capable of financing the program in question from its own resources (Arnold, 1981: 268). Thus, grant programs almost invariably passed the House of Representatives and the Senate by overwhelming margins, with an average majority of more than two thirds in each Congress since the early 1950s. Republicans joined Democrats to form bipartisan majorities for the programs (Chubb, 1985: 281–286).

C. The Nixon Administration's New Federalism

Post–World War II Republican presidential candidates implicitly accepted government activism but attacked excessive national bureaucracy. Richard Nixon argued early in his presidency that "a third of a century of centralizing power and responsibility in Washington has produced a bureaucratic monstrosity, cumbersome, unresponsive, ineffective." President Nixon sought to decentralize policy authority with a "New Federalism in which power, funds and responsibility will flow from Washington to the States and the people" (Nixon, 1969; see Conlan, 1988). Nixon proposed to implement this policy through revenue sharing and block grants.

Revenue sharing exemplified the Nixon grants strategy in its purest form. The State and Local Fiscal Assistance Act of 1972 attempted to divorce federal money from federal influence with unrestricted grants distributed on the basis of a formula. One third of the funds went directly to state governments, whereas the rest went to general purpose local governments such as counties, cities, and villages. Nixon's general revenue sharing proposal attracted little support when he introduced it as a $1 billion measure in 1969. When the proposed "shared revenue" was increased to $5 billion in 1971, the intergovernmental lobby responded more favorably. Lobbying by governors, mayors, state and local administrators, and the intergovernmental groups representing them helped to win its Congressional enactment (Brown, 1984: 73–74).

At the same time, Nixon proposed to replace many existing grants with block grants (originally termed "special" revenue sharing). Originally, the Nixon administration sought to merge 129 categorical grants into six block grants for urban community development, job training, law enforcement, education, transportation, and rural community development. These grants would consolidate several related categorical grants into a single grant over which state and local officials could exercise wide discretion within the bounds of the program's purpose. Formulas would replace project awards in determining state and local funding. One such block grant, the Comprehensive Employment Training Act of 1973, consolidated 17 of 64 job-training programs into one program. The Community Development Block Grant (CDBG) of 1974 brought together urban renewal, Model Cities, and five other programs (Brown, 1984: 87–92).

In most programs, Nixon successfully fought for enhanced state and local policy discretion. These changes tended to shift the grants-in-aid system away from the Democrats' urban constituency and toward the Republican constituency in suburban and rural areas and in Sunbelt states. In 1968, 62% of all federal grants for cities went to large cities with more than half a million residents. By 1975, only 44% went to large cities (Palmer, 1984: 36).

But the Nixon administration did not achieve the degree of decentralization it desired. Democrats in Congress resisted the complete delegation of policy authority to the executive branch and to state and local governments, and it approved only two of the original six block grants that Nixon proposed. By 1975, over three quarters of the federal grants continued to be distributed through categorical rather than block grants (U.S. OMB, 1987: H-25). Moreover, each of the new grants programs included more requirements and regulations than Nixon had envisioned. The National Environmental Policy Act of 1969, the Educational Rights and Privacy Act of 1974, and several laws prohibiting discrimination on the basis of sex, age, and the handicapped each added new crosscutting requirements to all federal grants (ACIR, 1984: 74–87).

These reforms left social policy more disorganized than ever. They increased the size of the grants system for which Washington nominally was responsible, but reduced federal control over policy. By the late 1970s, the problems of the grants system had grown to profound proportions. Through the grants system, the national government began to serve as a sort of social policy "bank," writing checks that state and local governments could cash and spend. One study conducted in the late 1970s found that "considerably less than one tenth of the federal budget is allotted to domestic activities that the federal government performs itself" (Mosher, 1980).

National domestic policy in many areas became increasingly fragmented, complex, and difficult to manage (Ingram, 1975). The grants strategy added state and local governments and a host of other participants to each stage in the policy process. Administrators in the national agencies faced the impossible task of managing billions of dollars by proxy. For example, the Economic Development Administration provided millions of dollars in project grants in an effort to develop economic opportunities for minorities in Oakland, California. After years of effort, the grants resulted in only a handful of permanent jobs for minorities. The failures of this effort literally became a textbook example of the difficulties of grants management (Pressman and Wildavsky, 1973). Such problems consumed national policy makers, provided ammunition for critics opposed to the programs, and stripped legitimacy from national efforts. Many concluded that government had simply become "overloaded" (Rose and Peters, 1978).

Partly because of the political backlash against previous Democratic programs and partly because of his background as a former state governor, President Carter approached federal power with ambivalence. During the Carter presidency federal expenditures for grants programs peaked in 1978 and leveled off (see Fig. 1). Like President Ford, he cut back revenue sharing and allowed inflation to reduce its value further. In some cases, the Carter administration added new restrictions and regulations to grant programs, and "targeted" them more specifically to Democratic constituencies in older cities of the Midwest and Northeast.

IV. FEDERALISM AS A POLICY BATTLEGROUND IN THE 1980s AND THE 1990s

A. The Reagan Administration's New Federalism

President Reagan clearly broke with the postwar consensus on grants activism. He attacked government activism itself. Like Nixon, Reagan promised a New Federalism that would return power to the states; "in a single stroke," he promised, "we will be accomplishing a realignment that will end cumbersome administration and spiraling costs at the Federal level" (Reagan, 1981a). In a speech to the National Conference of State Legislatures, he argued that

> . . . today the Federal government takes too much taxes from the people, too much authority from the States, too much liberty with the Constitution . . . the steady flow of power and tax dollars to Washington has something to do with the fact that things don't seem to work anymore. The Federal government is overloaded, musclebound, if you will, having assumed more responsibilities than it can properly manage . . . the Federal Government is so far removed from the people that Members of Congress spend less time legislating than cutting through bureaucratic redtape for their constituents (Reagan, 1981b).

Executive order 12612 codified the administration's federalism principles, stating that state administrative discretion should be maximized and federal preemption minimized (*Federal Register*, 1987; see also Conlan, 1988).

In contrast to the "new federalism" of the Nixon years, the Reagan administration aimed to cut grants-in-aid substantially. Reagan's original budget changes, embodied in the 1981 Omnibus Budget Reconciliation Act (OBRA) of 1981, eliminated $8 billion and 140 grants programs from Carter's proposal for that year. The 1981 budget cut federal grants by 13%—a cut twice as large as the overall national budget reduction of that year. The 1982 budget consolidated 76 separate categorical grants into 9 block grants in the areas of health, social services, education, and community development, and cut funding for these grants by 20%; leaving states with the option of ending these services or paying for them out of state revenues (Peterson, 1984: 244-245). Federal grants-in-aid expenditures in constant dollars dropped significantly for the first time since 1946 (Fig. 1).

Congress resisted further cuts after 1981. Grant spending in terms of real dollars remained substantially below the levels of the late 1970s until the Bush administration. Ironically, the limited funds for grants did not restrain the growth in grants programs, which increased from 400 in 1982 to 492 in late 1988 (Walker, 1991: 109–111). However, the large federal budget deficit ruled out the possibility of new federal grants-in-aid initiatives on the scale of those enacted between 1961 and 1978.

The increased grants spending of the late 1980s differed from that of the 1960s and 1970s. Entitlements, notably Medicaid, account for much of the growth in grants spending in recent years. Between fiscal years 1981 and 1992, payments to individuals via grants to state and local governments increased from $49 billion to $93 billion in constant 1987 dollars, an *increase* of 90%. Other forms of grants decreased from $72.5 billion to $56.9 billion in constant 1987 dollars, a *decrease* of 22% (U.S. OMB, 1992b: 165).

The Reagan administration also enhanced the conservative features of grants. The new block grants entailed very few regulations. The percentage of federal funds contributed in most grants was reduced, which required grant recipients to contribute a larger share of the cost. It was hoped that a higher matching requirement would reduce local government activism in areas previously stimulated when the national government paid most of the bill (Hansen, 1983: 440). States received a larger share of grants and more authority over program expenditures. Whereas 24.2% of state and local aid bypassed the states at the beginning of the Reagan administration, only 14.5% bypassed the states at the end of Reagan's term (Walker, 1991: 112).

The Reagan administration's tax policies also affected the intergovernmental system. Reductions in the highest federal income tax brackets made the federal income tax deduction for state and local taxes less valuable for many constituents, which strengthened the opposition to state and local taxes. The administration proposed dropping these deductions completely but accepted the 1986 Tax Reform Act without that provision. During the 1980s and 1990s, the White House acceded to a number of excise taxes that encroached on the traditional tax bases of the states. A North Carolina study concluded that, by increasing excise taxes on gasoline, tobacco, and alcohol in 1990, the federal government would collect $109 million from those sources in the state between 1991 and 1995, thus limiting the amount that the state could tax those same sources (Lemov, 1992: 24).

B. Regulatory and Judicial Federalism Since 1981

Although the Reagan administration philosophically supported deregulation of state and local government, in practice it often increased such regulation. Divided government offers a partial explanation. The Reagan administration was remarkably pragmatic about acceding to compromises with Congress that extended such rules. Congress passed and Reagan signed 92 statutes authorizing or expanding existing rules preempting state and local policy authority. Reagan vetoed only 2 bills involving preemption, and signed 10 bills providing for preemption relief for states and localities. Together with such mandates as direct legal requirements imposed on state and local governments and crosscutting requirements that apply to all grants-in-aid programs across the board, intergovernmental regulation increased substantially in the 1980s.

Many of these regulations imposed significant new costs on state and local government while as federal grants to these governments (excluding aid to individuals) declined 26% in constant dollars during the decade. For example, the Safe Water Drinking Act Amendments of 1986 imposed an estimated $2 to $3 billion annually on public water suppliers, and the Asbestos Hazard Emergency Response Act of 1986 imposed an estimated $3.15 billion over 30 years for removal of hazardous asbestos from schools (Conlan, 1991).

In other cases, the Reagan administration extended federal regulations in response to business preferences. Business often preferred federal to state regulation. Although business leaders endorsed decentralization in principle, they insisted on federal regulation when states, in response to federal deregulation, enacted more diverse and sometimes more stringent regulations. An industry official put it bluntly by observing, "I would rather deal with one federal gorilla than 50 state monkeys" (Moore, 1990).

Clearly, the administration favored national over state rules for industries where states implemented strict regulations. In the mid-1980s, the administration supported a federal product liability law that would preempt the power of states to enact stricter liability standards on the grounds that such state laws would unduly burden interstate commerce. The White House generally favored total preemption to free the banking, communications, and transportation industries from state interference. The Bus Regulatory Reform Act of 1982 prohibited state and local governments from regulating that industry. The Surface Transportation Assistance Act of 1982 guaranteed nationwide interstate highway access for tandem trailers by prohibiting states from regulating truck weights and lengths. The Cable Communications Policy Act of 1984 made local denial of a franchise renewal for an existing cable company very difficult, even when the company sharply increased its fees (Zimmerman, 1991).

Judicial decisions by increasingly conservative federal courts also reflected a selective use of federalism recalling the judicial selectivity of the early years of the century. Reagan elevated William Rehnquist to the position of Chief Justice of the Supreme Court in part because of Rehnquist's strong philosophical defenses of state sovereignty. However, a study of Rehnquist's decisions in nonunanimous Supreme Court reviews of state supreme court decisions during the Burger court showed his bias toward conservative outcomes rather than federalism. In cases where the state court decided in a conservative direction, he voted to reverse in 12% of the cases and to affirm the decision in 88% of the cases. When a liberal state court decision was at issue, he voted to affirm in 25% of the cases and to reverse in 75%. This pattern was particularly pronounced in civil liberties and criminal justice cases (Davis, 1992). The Court permitted states to impose substantial restrictions on abortion in *Webster* v. *Reproductive Health Services* (1989) and in *Planned Parenthood* v. *Casey* (1992). At the same time, the Court's decision in *Richmond* v. *Croson* (1989) struck down set-aside programs for minority contractors in 36 states and 200 local governments.

C. Federalism in the Bush Administration

The Bush administration continued most of the policies of the Reagan years. It proposed several block grant and decentralization plans. In March, 1990, Transportation Secretary Samuel Skinner suggested the turnover of 750,000 miles of the federally aided highway system to the states. In his 1991 State of the Union address, President Bush mentioned nearly $22 billion in education, environmental, social services, and law enforcement grants that could be returned to state and local governments. One of the largest of these turnovers was the $3.1 billion Community Development Block Grant program, the last remaining direct link between the cities and the federal government. The Senate Budget Committee projected that the Bush proposal would reduce federal aid by over $27 billion over 5 years. On these grounds, some compared the Bush plan with the Reagan proposal of 1982 and characterized both as a "Trojan horse," intended more to cut spending than to devolve authority (Pagano et al., 1991).

The Bush administration's fiscal 1993 budget plan presented a less ambitious $14 billion block grant proposal that included 12 education programs (constituting $2.3 billion in 1992 outlays), environmental construction grants ($2.2 billion), social services block grant ($2.8 billion), and administrative expenses in Medicaid, Aid to Families with Dependent Children, and food stamps (a total of $5.5 billion) (U.S. Executive Office of the President, 1992: 417). Though a more modest proposal than the previous suggestions, this plan elicited little support in the presidential election year.

At the same time, the ever-increasing federal budget deficit continued to affect intergovernmental relations profoundly. The Budget Enforcement Act of 1991 added a significant constraint to grants funding. It grouped all domestic programs in a single category and imposed a ceiling on costs for the category; thus putting grants-in-aid programs in competition with all other domestic priorities (Pagano et al., 1991).

Like his predecessor, Bush acceded to new laws that extended federal mandates affecting state and local governments. Several programs significantly increased in federal mandates to state and local governments. The Clean Air Act Amendments of 1990 strengthened penalties on states that did not meet federal implementation standards and timetables. States were required to expand Medicaid, first to all children in poverty up to the age of 6, and then in the fiscal year 1991 budget to all children in poverty up to the age of 18. The Americans with Disabilities Act required that public transportation and facilities be made accessible to the handicapped (Conlan, 1991: 46–48).

V. THE RESURGENCE OF THE STATES

In the 1980s, authors began to describe a "resurgence of the states." State governments took an active role to fill the policy vacuum left by the Reagan administration's partial withdrawal from the intergovernmental system (Bowman and Kearney, 1986). States creatively juggled funds to postpone or prevent the 1981 cuts from taking as severe a toll on public programs as the cuts implied. Many of the states demonstrated surprisingly budgetary resilience in the wake of federal budget cuts in the 1980s. Aggregate state education spending increased by 62% between 1978 and 1983, a period of often severe fiscal stress in state government (Bowman and Kearney, 1986: 214). Many states restored, or at least absorbed, some of the deep cuts in social program grants effected in 1981 (Nathan et al., 1987).

By the end of the 1980s, states still dominated the direct provision of public services in the United States. Table 4 compares federal with state and local spending on several such devices in 1977 (near the peak of federal grants expenditure) and in 1989 at the conclusion of the Reagan presidency. Table 4 controls for inflation and population growth by expressing this spending in terms of percentage of personal income. State and local governments continue to dominate spending for such services as education, public welfare, public hospital and services funding, corrections, highways, and sewerage and solid waste, whereas they spend as much as the federal government on housing and community development. Note that health and welfare spending do not include federal Social Security and Medicare expenditures (7.3% of personal income in 1989), and that general direct expenditures exclude federal grants to the states). Although federal direct expenditures were much larger than those of state and local governments in 1977, the gap narrowed in the 1980s. The two levels of government spent very nearly the same amount when interest payments on general debt are taken into account.

Although the states have continued to shoulder the responsibility for a large share of the nation's domestic policy, it became conventional wisdom in mid-century that the states were antiquated, amateurish, parochial, and often corrupt relics whose policy role was in eclipse and would soon evaporate completely. Most reformers believed that the federal government could manage policy more effectively than the state governments, with the exception of a few progressive states with highly professionalized administrators and legislatures. They argued that its size allowed the federal government to develop superior expertise and to achieve economies of scale that enabled it to achieve levels of professionalization, planning, comprehensiveness, and fairness that the states could not hope to match (see, e.g., Sanford, 1967). The vivid memory of state impotence in the face of the Depression and the resistance of southern state leaders to the civil rights revolution fortified this image.

Table 4. Federal, State, and Local Direct Expenditures as a Percent of Personal Income, 1977 and 1989

	Federal		State and Local	
	1977	1989	1977	1989
Education	0.5%	0.4%	6.4%	6.0%
Public welfare	0.9	0.7	2.1	2.2
Hospitals	0.2	0.2	1.1	1.1
Health	0.2	0.2	0.3	0.5
Corrections	–	–	0.3	0.5
Highways	–	–	1.4	1.3
Natural resources, parks and recreation	1.1	1.3	0.3	0.3
Housing and community development	0.1	0.3	0.2	0.3
Sewerage/solid waste	–	–	0.6	0.6
Total general direct expenditures	19.6	20.8	17.1	17.4
Interest on general debt	2.1	4.0	0.7	1.1
Total general direct expenditures minus interest payments on general debt	17.5	16.8	16.4	16.3

Source: ACIR, 1991: 124–125, 130–131.

Conventional wisdom about the states changed in the 1980s. Arguments about political overload at the national level were accepted not only by conservatives but also by many proponents of active and effective government. According to Kirlin (1984: 182–187), even if the federal government could deliver services efficiently, too much reliance on the distant national government harms government legitimacy.

Many, including liberals (Rivlin, 1992) as well as conservatives, view the shift toward more state policy responsibility as a positive development for three reasons. They argue that states are more responsive to citizens than is the federal government, (2) are more efficient policy managers than is the federal government, and (3) can serve as "laboratories of democracy" (Osborne, 1990), where governmental innovation can be tested and perfected. The evidence for each of these claims is mixed.

A. State Responsiveness

The argument that states could respond better to citizens than the federal government dates to the nation's founding. Madison argued in *The Federalist* (1961: nos. 46, 51) that state governments would protect against the exercise of arbitrary power by the national government because "the first and most natural attachment of the people will be to the governments of their respective states." In the 1980s, both conservatives in the Reagan administration (Domestic Policy Council, 1986) and some moderate and liberal policy analysts (Osborne, 1990; Schmidt, 1989) revived these arguments. For example, the Reagan administration's Executive Order 12612 comments that "the States uniquely possess the constitutional authority, the resources, and the competence to discern the sentiments of the people and to govern accordingly" (41685).

However, Madison (1961: no. 10) also suggested that single interests could more easily capture and dominate smaller political jurisdictions such as states. Evidence suggests that limits and biases restrict state government responsiveness. A smaller proportion of citizens participate in state and local than in national elections. State laws limit the emergence of alternatives to the two party system. Citizens with substantially higher incomes and status than average disproportionately vote in state initiatives and referenda (Magelby, 1984: 86, 104). Legislative processes in the states seem to offer special access to highly organized interests. In particular, business often seems to dominate state policy making, and corporate lobbying at the state level appears to have increased dramatically in the 1980s; an indication of the growing importance of state laws to business (Ambrosius and Welch, 1988; Moore, 1987; Zeigler, 1983).

The 1980s and 1990s demonstrate these biases, as well as considerable efforts to counter them. By the end of the Reagan administration, many of the states were implementing strict new regulations on insurance access, antitrust, corporate takeovers and plant closing, and consumer and environmental protection (Labaton, 1988). In some cases, a number of states took steps to protect traditionally powerless citizens, such as public housing residents, from the effects of federal cutbacks (Gold, 1989). Although the federal government did little to reform campaign finance, Minnesota and other states acted to do so. Increasingly conservative federal courts were counterbalanced by courts in many states that redoubled efforts to protect civil rights and civil liberties.

Ironically, many state officials support a more active federal role on the grounds that a stronger federal presence increases their responsiveness to average citizens. For example, many welcomed tough federal sanctions and the "hammer" provisions of the 1990 Clean Air Act because the threat of such federally imposed implementation plans increased their leverage with polluters. State and local officials could warn polluters that a failure to accommodate them would result in more intrusive and expensive regulations imposed by Washington (Conlan, 1991: 47).

B. State Effectiveness and Capacity

Changes in the fiscal and administrative capacity of state governments in the 1960s and 1970s enabled proponents of decentralization to argue that the states had become more trustworthy and as capable of effective program management as the federal government. Governors enjoy longer terms, greater veto, appointment, and reorganization powers and larger and more professional staffs. Like presidents at the national level, governors have become an energizing force in state government (Kaplan and O'Brien, 1991; Osborne, 1990; Sabato, 1983).

Other institutions of state government also have improved dramatically in the last 30 years. Legislatures have all been reapportioned to represent city and suburban populations as well as rural legislative districts. State legislators became more professional, with higher pay and benefits. Both legislatures and executives have access to larger, more professionalized staffs. State civil servants and judges also became more competent and professional (Reeves, 1985: 76, 122, 139–140, 180).

A substantial remaining constraint on state effort involves resources and effort disparities among the states. The gap between the revenue-generating capacity of the poorest and richest states remained wide in the late 1980s. The Advisory Commission on Intergovernmental Relations (ACIR) has developed a measure of tax capacity that combines property, retail sales, income, minerals, and other taxes. This index shows how different the states' abilities to raise money would be if all applied an identical set of tax rates. By 1988, Mississippi had only 65% of the taxable resources of the average state (among the 48 contiguous states); South Dakota, Alabama, Arkansas, South Carolina, West Virginia, Idaho, and Utah all enjoyed less than 80% of the average state tax capacity. At the same time, such states as Connecticut (143% of the average tax base), Nevada, Delaware, New Jersey, and Wyoming (each with more than 120% of the average) had substantial ability to raises funds for public services (ACIR, 1990: 144–145). Although federal grants-in-aid were sometimes justified on the grounds that they would reduce such disparities, they did not do so in the aggregate. Federal grants-in-aid increased the amount of funds available to each state, but they have not significantly reduced interstate resource disparities (Arnold, 1981: 268).

An enhanced fiscal capacity does not necessarily lead to generous policies; it only creates the possibility of doing so. In energy-rich states such as Texas, higher energy prices in the 1970s did not move historically conservative state governments to more policy effort. According to the ACIR, tax effort—that is, how much a state actually taxes those sources of revenue available to it—ranged even more widely than tax capacity in 1988, from New Hampshire at the low end of the contiguous states (62% of that of the average state) to New York at the high end (over 151%) (ACIR, 1990: 144–145).

Some of the state-level reforms have created new barriers to policy activism. Most states permit a governor to veto portions of legislation (including individual appropriations) rather than an entire law or a budget. Although this "item" veto is sometimes used to cut "pork barrel" legislation, and evidence suggests that the line item veto has a relatively modest effect on state spending, the line item veto is a one-way tool: it reduces effort but does not increase budgets or redirect spending.

Populist backlash against government also has inhibited state capacity during this period. California's 1978 enactment of a tax limitation initiative, Proposition 13, lead to a series of tax revolts in states across the nation. The tax limitation movement of the late 1970s and early 1980s tended to increase differences between the efforts of rich and poor states.

Several of the states that limited revenue growth, such as Missouri, Texas, and Utah, already had low (and regressive) tax systems (Hansen, 1983: 441–449).

The term-limitation movement of the early 1990s reflects the concern that state government has developed excessive capacity and that state legislators are too immune to electoral defeat. These laws limit the number of terms that state legislators can serve in office, and sometimes (as in California) cut legislative staff and benefits. In 1990, California, Oklahoma, and Colorado imposed term limits on their state legislatures, with the California measure requiring substantial cuts in legislative staff. In 1992, 14 states enacted term-limitation measures.

Voters in the United States have added an additional complicating factor in government capacity by splitting their ballots between party candidates for executive and legislative posts. The result is divided government, with one party in control of the governorship and the other in control of at least one (and usually two) houses in the state legislature. Over half the states had such a divided government in 1991. Governors elected as independents served in Alaska and Connecticut (Pagano et al., 1991).

C. Interstate Competition

Some of the concerns about state policy responsiveness and effectiveness manifest a deeper problem: competition among the states for business investment. The American states constitute the world's largest free-trade zone. No tariffs or other barriers counterbalance incentives for business to relocate to jurisdictions with lower taxes and less intrusive regulations. States thus face a strong incentive to resist excessive deviation from the practices of other states, particularly states with "business climates" (the mix of corporate taxes, regulations, subsidies, and services) more favorable to potentially mobile or expanding businesses.

Thus, it is widely perceived that a concern for "business climate" pervades state-level policy decisions (Ambrosius and Welch, 1988; Kenyon and Kincaid, 1991; Lowry, 1992; Walker, 1971: 366; Wilson, 1985: 41–42, 134–135). This incentive persists despite the mixed evidence that business climate actually affects economic growth, resources, and jobs (Kenyon, 1991; Plaut and Pluta, 1983) because states that are insufficiently friendly to business risk the loss of both tax payments and jobs. Political challengers and business leaders often blame incumbent office holders for the loss. Business executives exploit these arguments in negotiations over laws and regulations.

Thus, state and local governments resist offering stricter regulations and more attractive social benefits than other jurisdictions if such benefits require higher taxes or attract potentially dependent new residents who seek the benefits (Peterson and Rom, 1989; Robertson and Judd, 1989). Traditionally, interstate competition has put many states in the position of entering into a bidding war to provide "supply-side" incentives such as tax benefits and subsidies to lure new business into their jurisdiction boundaries or prevent established businesses from leaving (Eisinger, 1988). In the 1970s, political leaders in all parts of the country ascribed the Sunbelt's prosperity to its perceived political conservatism and aggressive recruitment of northern business. Public officials in northern industrialized states warned that they were losing jobs and industry to states with lower taxes, fewer services, and fewer protections for unions (Goodman, 1979).

Many conservatives viewed this competition as very positive. Public choice theorists believed that such markets for different mixes of taxes and public services would maximize consumer choice and impose considerable discipline on the public sector (Ostrom, 1991). The Reagan administration's Domestic Policy Council hoped that devolution would limit the expansion of state government capacity because under these circumstances "Ill-conceived public policy over the long-run leads to an exodus of business and talented individuals; the State's tax base erodes and its infrastructure deteriorates" so that states have very strong incentives "to rectify misguided public policy in order to maintain fiscal health and to enhance their appeal to potential residents" (Domestic Policy Council, 1986: 55–56). Thus, the Reagan administration believed that such interstate competition would help realize conservative goals.

Many observers contended that interstate competition intensified in the Reagan-Bush years, although the evidence is mixed (Kenyon, 1991). Even in the wake of tax revolts and budgets strapped by the recession of the early 1980s, the states continued to expand these supply-side economic development policies. State economic development officials concluded that "the commitment of state funds is substantial, and even the states at the lower end of the expenditure scale tend to make economic development a high priority, as measured by the proportion of available resources committed to this purpose" (NASDA, 1983: 3). The executive director of the Advisory Commission on Intergovernmental Relations could not remember a time when state officials expressed so much interest in attracting and retaining business investment. Although he conceded that the acute concern about business climate caused some increased investment in infrastructure and in education, it more frequently caused state leaders to pursue conservative tax policies (Shannon, 1986: 173–178).

Although some observers found evidence that interest in traditional supply-side policies to lure business investment had begun to wane in the mid- to late 1980s (Eisinger, 1988), the evidence is inconclusive. In the late 1980s and early 1990s, states entered into bidding wars for high-visibility facilities such as the United Airlines maintenance hub and the McDonnell Douglas MD-12 commercial airliner plant. Continuing efforts by some states to "raid" others' businesses made interstate competition acutely important during the recession of the early 1990s. For example, Connecticut's fiscal and political turmoil motivated Maryland officials to offer a cash bonus for every employee that a Connecticut company would relocate to Maryland. Several states maintained records on the leases of companies in Connecticut in the hope of enticing these companies to move when their leases expired (Johnson, 1992; see also Brinkley, 1992).

Whether or not interstate competition actually intensified during the 1980s, it imposed significant limits on the willingness of officials to use government as an active tool for regulating business or redistributing resources because so much of that responsibility devolved to the states in the 1980s. Interstate competition does not determine that states pursue conservative policies, but it creates a strong tendency to do so. Interstate economic competition sets important constraints on state policy innovation.

Interstate competition also reduces the pursuit of equity and income redistribution by states. The Tax Reform Act of 1986 increased interjurisdictional tax competition by reducing the tax rate on the federal income tax and thus the value of the state and local tax deduction. From 1985 to 1989, 19 states lowered their top tax rate, and three raised it. Although some states have made their tax structures more progressive in the 1990s, others have broadened the sales tax base, and such states as Texas were considering a value added tax (VAT), which generally is a regressive tax (Lemov, 1992: 26). A study by the Advisory Commission on Intergovernmental Relations concluded that interjurisdictional tax competition contributed to the decreased reliance on ability-to-pay taxes in the 1980s and 1990s (Kenyon, 1991: 37–38, 63).

D. States as Policy Laboratories

For liberals as well as conservatives, one of the strongest arguments for the return of powers to the states was state policy experimentation. An innovative state could serve as a policy "laboratory" in which innovative experiments could be tried out, improved, and then copied by other states. Before the New Deal, political progressives such as Supreme Court Justice Louis Brandeis often argued that American federalism permitted progressive states such as

Wisconsin and New York to serve as "social laboratories" that developed effective remedies for public problems later adapted by other states and often by the federal government (*New State Ice Co.* v. *Liebmann*, 1932).

The concept of states as social laboratories remains alluring today, and it is used to counterbalance the charge that the states are inherently conservative. Eisinger (1988) argued that states were replacing supply-side economic development strategies with new "demand-side" economic development policies that promoted high-skilled, high-wage work forces and homegrown businesses.

Stating that "the science of government is the science of experiment," the Reagan Domestic Policy Council (1986: 52–55) strongly argued this position. "The important point," said the Domestic Policy Council, "is that the States, as laboratories for testing public policies, can experiment with novel, risky, even exotic, approaches to their problems without threatening the nation as a whole." It identified many examples of state innovation that it admired, including educational reforms, "no-fault" automobile insurance laws, deregulation, and changes to labor relations, welfare, and criminal sentencing law.

Indeed, states developed innovative policies in a striking number of areas in the 1980s. California's environmental legislation serves as a model for regulating natural resources within a state, and other states have emulated its air pollution, coastline protection, and other programs. Missouri's early childhood education program attracted international interest. The failure of national health care to move forward on the national agenda prompted many states to expand health care access through pooled insurance plans and the extension of Medicaid. Massachusetts' guarantee of health insurance to all its citizens in 1988 was discussed as a prototype for national legislation.

However, given the constraints of state capacity and interstate economic competition, more states experiment with politically neutral or conservative programs than with redistributive ones. The states have an incentive to enact programs that appear to be cost effective in the short term that do not involve extensive redistribution and that have a positive or neutral effect on business climate. State innovations that meet these criteria tend to spread rapidly and universally. Innovations that do not meet these criteria spread slowly, incompletely, and sometimes are reversed (Robertson and Judd, 1989).

There are many examples of the latter in American history. Plant closing prenotification and public health insurance provide examples from the late 1980s. With industrial dislocation on the rise in the 1960s and 1970s, many industrialized democracies required employers to notify their workers in advance of a move or shutdown. Although 40 states considered some form of plant-closing legislation between 1982 and 1986, only three (Wisconsin, Maine, and Hawaii) enacted mandatory notification laws before the national legislation was approved in 1988 (Eisinger, 1988).

Massachusetts' highly touted plan for universal health insurance foundered in the recession of the early 1990s. By 1991, the new state governor called for repeal of the requirement that all businesses provide health insurance to employees because it would put the state's economy at a competitive disadvantage. Only Hawaii, whose geography and economic base made it far more difficult for businesses to relocate, was pursuing seriously universal health insurance on the Massachusetts model during the early 1990s (Eckholm, 1991).

Laws that improve the business climate or the budget position of the states tend to be received more quickly and widely. Right-to-work laws, which outlaw the "union" shop (requiring workers to join a union as a condition of employment) and enhance a state's business climate ranking, exemplify such a policy. The Taft-Hartley Act of 1947 permitted states to enact these laws. In the late 1980s, over 20 states had done so (though battles over repealing or enacting these laws mainly resulted in stalemates in the 1970s and 1980s).

Under conditions of fiscal stress in the late 1980s, states again began to experiment with creative ways to reduce welfare loads. For example, Wisconsin proposed a two-tiered welfare system that would pay newcomers to the state 25% less than long-time residents. Wisconsin and other states experimented with "Learnfare" to reduce Aid to Families with Dependent Children payments if a child fails to meet school attendance requirements. The Bush administration publicized such experiments as models for other states (U.S. OMB, 1992a: 418–420), although it did not allow Oregon to experiment with a triage policy to limit the expansion of health care costs in 1992.

The U.S. government usually must act as a catalyst to encourage the diffusion of state experiments. Before the Social Security Act, only nine states had merit systems covering welfare administrators. The federal social security law prompted all the rest to do so by 1940 (Gray, 1973; Welch and Thompson, 1980). The "grants strategy" of the 1960s and 1970s aimed to expand the range of policy experimentation and the degrees of freedom enjoyed by the states. As revenue shrinks and fiscal problems mount, state policy experimentation can be expected to narrow considerably.

VI. THE FISCAL CRISIS OF THE STATES

A. Growing Fiscal Problems in the 1980s

By the late 1980s, the combination of demographic change, economic restructuring, and increased federal mandates increasingly strained the budgets of many states. An array of problems such as decaying infrastructure, inadequate access to health care, homelessness, and increasing medical and education costs in the 1980s led to a growing backlog of unmet needs at the end of the decade. After a period of decline, the states also confronted rising school enrollments through the decade of the 1990s.

Although federal grants and economic growth helped to bring about state budget surpluses in the 1970s, recessions in the mid-1970s and early 1980s worsened state budgetary balances significantly. In the late 1980s, efforts, capital spending combined with recession, drove states to their worst financial imbalance crises since the late 1960s (U.S. OMB, 1992a: 441).

The states' relatively inelastic fiscal systems made their mounting fiscal problems worse. As a group, the states heavily rely on relatively inelastic taxes that result in substantial drops in revenue when the economy slumps. Although states now rely more heavily on relative elastic income taxes than they did in the 1950s, state income taxes became less elastic in the 1980s. Moreover, many states came to rely more heavily on excise taxes, the least elastic form of tax, during the 1980s. State budget-balancing requirements require cuts as revenues decline, which further worsened the economic situation within the states. New restrictions on revenue growth enacted after California's Proposition 13 also tended to worsen the effect of the downturn.

Federal policies in the 1980s further compounded the problems. First, cuts in grants required states to squeeze out additional resources to provide for programs and services. Second, by transferring policy responsibility to the states, the federal government transferred some domestic taxing and spending from the relatively elastic federal system to the relatively inelastic state and local stream. Third, the 1986 federal tax reform limited state and local governments' ability to leverage funds through bond sales. Fourth, specific mandates—particularly for Medicaid and corrections—crowded other spending priorities at the state level.

Increasing federal requirements, along with rapidly rising health-care costs, caused states to increase the share of Medicaid in their budgets from 9% in 1980 to 14% in 1990. In that year, the states spent $32.4 billion on the program. State officials expected state Medicaid spending to grow by about 15% a year through the 1990s (Conlan, 1991: 48: Lemov, 1992).

Federal courts have ordered states to increase capital and operating budgets for prisons and other correctional facilities. In 1990, prison systems in over 80% of the states were operating under court order. In addition, states' mandatory sentencing laws have increased the national prison population. State spending on corrections has increased 10-fold in less than a generation, from $2.1 billion in 1972 to $21.2 billion in 1989. State officials expected corrections costs to grow by about 10% a year through the 1990s (Hansen, 1991: 159; Lemov, 1992).

B. Economic Downturn and the States

Under these circumstances, protracted recession created a fiscal crisis in many states unprecedented since the 1930s. The collapse of the housing boom and defense cutbacks began to hurt the economies of New England as early as 1989. By 1990, the entire U.S. economy slumped, and recovery remained unusually anemic through 1992. Some economists believed the word *recession* inadequately captured the serious structural problems in the American economy, including severe debt problems for corporations, individuals, and the federal government.

Cuts in the defense industry were altering the economic structure of many states. Analysts expected Connecticut to lose 2.3% of its jobs owing to defense cutbacks between 1991 and 1997. Virginia would lose over 1.5% of its jobs, and California, Missouri, Arizona, and Massachusetts would lose over 1% each (Passell, 1992).

As manufacturing, construction, retail sales, and other business activity slowed, states' tax collections fell, whereas demands increased for unemployment, welfare, and other benefits increased. State revenue collections declined by at least $10 billion annually. The national Conference of State Legislatures reported in 1991 that 30 states expected a combined deficit of $30 billion for the 1992 fiscal year (Gold, 1992).

Such states as California, Maine, New Hampshire, Rhode Island, and Connecticut raised revenues in 1991 only to find their budgets severely out of balance in 1992. In 1991, 9 states cut basic welfare benefits, and another 31 states froze them (Roberts, 1992). Yet as the economy remained sluggish, delayed spending only increased demands for social services. An official of a public sector interest group told a Congressional committee that

> Although it may seem inappropriate to raise taxes or cut services during a recession, many states may have to revisit both alternatives in 1992. . . . Over the half the states report that expenditures for entitlement programs, education, or both are exceeding original appropriations—or would if they had not already been cut since fiscal year 1992 began (U.S. Congress, 1992: 77–81).

Steven Gold, director of the Center of the Study of the States, concluded that continuing fiscal stress at the state level was virtually inevitable into the mid-1990s (Lemov, 1992).

Some believed that California's problems foreshadowed the difficulties that other states would share. California's fiscal crisis attracted national attention in the summer of 1992. With an unemployment rate of nearly 9%, a declining defense sector, growing demands for services for newly arriving immigrants, and bills for natural disasters, including earthquakes and drought, the state's tax increase of 1991 failed to prevent a multibillion dollar shortfall in 1992. After a protracted standoff between a Republican governor and Democratic legislature (during which the state issued $3 billion in IOUs), California cut $6 billion in spending for education, health, welfare, and local governments. The state anticipated another $5 billion deficit in 1993 (Armstrong and Mitchell, 1992).

VII. TOWARD THE NEXT CENTURY

The budget crisis of the early 1990s dramatically exemplifies the intense politics that American federalism generates. Political opponents battle over the rules of national and state policy because the rules inevitably work to the advantage of some and the detriment of others by expanding or limiting the scope of conflict.

Two fundamental issues in particular—the extent of state discretion and the extent of interstate inequality—shape the results of these conflicts over federalism. First, if state economic, civil rights, welfare, education, or environmental policies are permitted to vary extensively, they are likely to do so. Because state economic structures, natural resources, cultures, and traditions vary enormously, policy outcomes also are likely to vary extensively. If the states enjoy no policy discretion, they must conform to standards set by a central authority. Some interests will favor state policy discretion because the resulting policy variation benefits them and harms their opponents. Some will oppose state policy discretion for the same reason. Both sides argue over the principles of federalism in order to control the scope and therefore the outcome of their conflict.

Second, if the states differ significantly in wealth and potential tax revenues, their policy choices will resemble those of businesses in competition. The most exposed and marginal competitors will cut costs in every way possible to remain solvent. In the private sector, such competition leads marginal firms to lower wages, to permit unsafe working conditions, and to engage in a variety of undesirable business practices called "unfair competition." Among states, this competition pressures marginal (i.e., poor) states to minimize taxes and services at levels that may endanger or impoverish their citizens. In both cases, their better-off competitors feel pressured to follow suit. In the absence of limits to their discretion, they more or less do so. A policy system so arranged may limit improvements in responsiveness and performance above a level necessary to prevent a political backlash.

These issues underlie the politics of federalism in the United States. The struggle to nationalize policy, and the counterstruggle to protect state's rights or to decentralize choice, always is conducted with a view to likely outcomes. Debates about which level of government is more responsive, effective, or innovative serve as much as weaponry for more fundamental clashes as they do to illuminate the value of federalism for realizing these values.

The American experience should be internationally instructive. The Canadian provinces, the former Soviet republics, and the nations of the European Community all confront the challenge of balancing independence and unity, unequal outcomes and guaranteed rights, jurisdictional competition, and common goals. At a global level, the world's nations also are struggling to find a common body of rules for governing the quality of the oceans, the air, and the ozone layer without excessively advantaging certain nations and harming others. The political conflicts over American federalism portend the discovery of a deep fault line in politics worldwide in the 21st century.

ACKNOWLEDGMENTS

Thanks to Tyler Fitch and Dennis R. Judd for helpful comments on the manuscript. The author acknowledges the support of the Public Policy Research Centers at the University of Missouri—St. Louis.

REFERENCES

ACIR (Advisory Commission on Intergovernmental Relations) (1973). *Categorical Grants: Their Role and Design.* Report A-52. ACIR, Washington, DC.

—— (1984). *Regulatory Federalism: Policy, Process, Impact and Reform*. Report A-95. ACIR, Washington, DC.

—— (1990). *1988 State Fiscal Capacity and Effort*. Report M-170. ACIR, Washington, DC.

—— (1991). *Significant Features of Fiscal Federalism, 1991*. Vol. 2: Revenues and Expenditures. ACIR, Washington, DC.

Ambrosius, M. M., and Welch, S. (1988). State Legislators' Perceptions of Business and Labor Interests. *Legislative Studies Quarterly* 13: 199–209.

Anton, T. J. (1989). *American Federalism and Public Policy: How the System Works*. Random House, New York.

Armstrong, L., and Mitchell, R. (1992). We haven't hit bottom—And won't until 1993. *Business Week* September 14: 27.

Arnold, R. D. (1981). The local roots of domestic policy. In *The New Congress*. T. E. Mann and N. J. Ornstein (Eds.). American Enterprise Institute, Washington, DC.

Bowman, A. O'M., and Kearney, R. (1986). *The Resurgence of the States*. Prentice-Hall, Englewood Cliffs, NJ.

Break, G. F. (1981). Fiscal Federalism in the United States: The First 200 Years, Evolution and Outlook. In *The Future of Federalism in the 1980s*. ACIR Report M-126. ACIR, Washington, DC.

Brinkley, J. (1992). Searching for New Jobs, Many States Steal Them. *New York Times* November 25: 1.

Brown, L. D. (1984). The Politics of Devolution in Nixon's New Federalism. In *The Changing Politics of Federal Grants*. L. D. Brown, J. W. Fossett, and K. T. Palmer (Eds.). Brookings Institution, Washington, DC.

Bruchey, S. (1988). *The Wealth of the Nation: An Economic History of the United States*. Harper & Row, New York.

Chubb, J. E. (1985). Federalism and the Bias for Centralization. In J. E. Chubb and P. E. Peterson (Eds.), *The New Direction in American Politics*. Brookings Institution, Washington, DC.

Clark, T. B., Iglehart, J. K., and Lilley, W., III (1972). The new federalism I: Return of power to states and cities looms as the theme of Nixon's second-term domestic policy. *National Journal* December 16: 1908–1912.

Commons, J. R. (1918, 1935). *History of Labor in the United States* (4 vols.). Macmillan, New York.

Conlan, T. J. (1988). *New Federalism: Intergovernmental Reform from Nixon to Reagan*. Brookings Institution, Washington, DC.

—— (1986). Congress and the Contemporary Intergovernmental System. In *American Intergovernmental Relations Today: Perspectives and Controversies*. R. J. Dilger (Ed.). Prentice-Hall, Englewood Cliffs, NJ.

—— (1991). And the beat goes on: Intergovernmental mandates and preemption in an era of deregulation. *Publius* 21: 43–57.

CQ (Congressional Quarterly) (1969). *Congress and the Nation, 1945–1964*. Congressional Quarterly, Washington, DC.

Davis, S. (1992). Rehnquist and state courts: Federalism revisited. *Western Political Quarterly* 45: 773–782.

Domestic Policy Council (Working Group on Federalism of the Domestic Policy Council, Executive Office of the President) (1986). The Status of Federalism in America. Unpublished mimeo, November.

Eckholm, E. (1991). Health care plan falters in Massachusetts slump. *New York Times* April 11: 1.

Eisinger, P. K. (1988). *The Rise of the Entrepreneurial State: State and Local Economic Development Policy in the United States*. University of Wisconsin Press, Madison.

Elazar, D. S. (1962). *The American Partnership: Intergovernmental Co-operation in the Nineteenth Century United States*. University of Chicago Press, IL.

Federal Register (1987). Executive Order 12612, Federalism. 52 (October 30): 41685–41688.

Freedman, L. (1969). *Public Housing: The Politics of Poverty*. Holt, New York.

Geddes, A. E. (1937). *Trends in Relief Expenditures, 1910–1935*, Works Progress Administration Research Monograph 10, Government Printing Office, Washington, DC.

Gold, A. R. (1989). States working to avert evictions of multitudes in subsidized housing. *New York Times* March 15: 14.

Gold, S. D. (1992). The federal role in fiscal stress. *Publius* 22: 33–47.

Goldwin, R. A., and Schambra, W. A. (Eds.) (1988). *How Federal is the Constitution?* American Enterprise Institute, Washington, DC.

Goodman, R. (1979). *The Last Entrepreneurs: America's Regional Wars for Jobs and Dollars*. South End Press, Boston.

Goodrich, C. (1948). National Planning of Internal Improvements. *Political Science Quarterly* 63: 16–44.

Gray, V. (1973). Innovation in the states: A diffusion study. *American Political Science Review* 68: 1174–1185.

Haider, D. H. (1974). *When Governments Come to Washington: Governors, Mayors, and Intergovernmental Lobbying*. Free Press, New York.

Hansen, S. B. (1983). Extraction: The Politics of State Taxation. In *Politics in the American States: A Comparative Analysis*, 4th ed. V. Gray, H. Jacob, and K. N. Vines (Eds.). Little, Brown, Boston.

—— (1991). Balancing Budgets in a Recession. *Publius* 21: 155–168.

Ikenberry, C. J., and Skocpol, T. (1987). Expanding Social Benefits: The Role of Society Security. *Political Science Quarterly* 102: 389–416.

Ingram, H. M. (1977). Policy Implementation Through Bargaining: The Case of Federal Grants-in-Aid. *Public Policy* 25: 499–526.

Jennings, M. K. (1969). Legislative Politics and Water Pollution Control, 1956–1961. In *Congress and Urban Problems*. F. N. Cleaveland (Ed.). Brookings Institution, Washington, DC.

Johnson, K. (1992). States see Connecticut business as ripe for picking. *New York Times* April 21, 1.

Kaplan, M., and O'Brien, S. (1991). *The Governors and the New Federalism*. Westview, Boulder, CO.

Kenyon, D. A. (1991). *Interjurisdictional Tax and Policy Competition: Good or Bad for the Federal System?* Advisory Commission on Intergovernmental Relations, Washington, DC.

Kenyon, D. A., and Kincaid, J. (Eds.) (1991). *Competition Among State and Local Governments: Efficiency and Equity in American Federalism*. Urban Institute Press, Washington, DC.

Kolbert, E. (1989). Albany needs $800 million, but who's going to raise taxes? *New York Times* January 22, E6.

Labaton, S. (1988). States March into the Breach. *New York Times* December 18: C4.

Lemov, P. (1992). The decade of red ink. *Governing* 5(August): 22–26.

Leuchtenburg, W. E. (1963). *Franklin D. Roosevelt and the New Deal, 1932–1940*. Harper & Row, New York.

Lowry, W. R. (1992). *The Dimensions of Federalism: State Governments and Pollution Control Policies*. Duke University Press, Durham, NC.

Madison, J. (1961). *The Federalist Papers*. C. Rossiter (Ed.). Mentor, New York.

Magleby, D. C. (1984). *Direct Legislation: Voting on Ballot Propositions in the United States*. Johns Hopkins University Press, Baltimore, MD.

Moore, W. J. (1987). Have smarts, will travel. *National Journal* (November 28): 3020–3024.

—— (1990). Stopping the States. *National Journal* July 21: 1758.

Mosher, F. C. (1980). The Changing Responsibilities and Tactics of the Federal Government. *Public Administration Review* 40: 541–548.

Navasky, V. (1971). *Kennedy Justice*. Atheneum, New York.

NASDA (National Association of State Development Agencies, et al.) (1983). *Directory of Incentives for Business Investment and Development in the United States: A State-By-State Guide*. Urban Institute Press, Washington, DC.

Nathan, R. P., Doolittle, F. C., and Associates (1987). *Reagan and the States*. Princeton University Press, NJ.

Nixon, R. M. (1969). Address to the Nation on Domestic Programs, August 8, *Public Papers of . . . President Richard M. Nixon, 1969*, Government Printing Office, Washington, DC: 637–645.

Osborne, D. (1990). *Laboratories of Democracy: A New Breed of Governors Creates Models for National Growth*. Cambridge, MA: Harvard Business School Press.

Ostrom, V. (1991). *The Meaning of American Federalism*: *Constituting a Self-Governing Society*. Institute for Contemporary Studies, San Francisco.

O'Toole, L. J. (Ed.) (1993). *American Intergovernmental Relations*, 2nd ed. CQ Press, Washington, DC.

Pagano, M. A., Bowman, A. O'M., and Kincaid, J. (1991). The state of American federalism, 1990–1991, *Publius* 21: 1–26.

Palmer, K. T. (1984). The Evolution of Grant Policies. In *The Changing Politics of Federal Grants*. L. D. Brown, J. W. Fossett, and K. T. Palmer (Eds.). Brookings Institution, Washington, DC.

Passell, P. (1992). The Peace Dividend's Collateral Damage. *New York Times* September 13, E3.

Patterson, J. T. (1969). *The New Deal and the States*: *Federalism in Transition*. Princeton University Press, NJ.

Peterson, G. E. (1984). Federalism and the States: An Experiment in Decentralization. In Palmer, J. L. and Sawhill, E. V. (Eds.). *The Reagan Record*: *An Assessment of America's Changing Domestic Priorities*, Ballinger, Cambridge, MA.

Peterson, P. E., and Rom, M. C. (1990). *Welfare Magnets*: *A New Case for National Standards*. Brookings, Washington, DC.

Pierce, F. (1975). Veto Message, May 3, 1854. In *Social Welfare*: *A History of American Response to Need*. J. Axinn and H. Levin (Eds.). Dodd, Mead, New York.

Plaut, T. R., and Pluta, J. E. (1983). Business Climate, Taxes and Expenditures, and State Industrial Growth in the United States. *Southern Economic Journal* 50: 99–119.

Pressman, J. L., and Wildavsky, A. (1973). *Implementation*. University of California Press, Berkeley.

Reagan, R. (1981a). Inaugural Address, January 23. In Weekly *Compilation of Presidential Documents*, January 26.

—— (1981b). National Conference of State Legislatures: Remarks at the Annual Convention in Atlanta, Georgia, July 30, 1981. In *Weekly Compilation of Presidential Documents*, August 3.

Reeves, M. M. (1985). *The Question of State Government Capability*. ACIR, Washington, DC.

Rivlin, A. M. (1992). *Reviving the American Dream*. Brookings, Washington, DC.

Robertson, D. B., and Judd, D. R. (1989). *The Development of American Public Policy*: *The Structure of Policy Restraint*. Scott, Foresman/Little, Brown, Boston.

Roberts, S. (1992). The Push for Curbs on Welfare. *New York Times* February 3: B12.

Rose, R., and Peters, B. G. (1978). *Can Government Go Bankrupt?* Basic Books, New York.

Sabato, L. (1983). *Goodbye to Good-time Charlie*: *The American Governorship Transformed*, 2nd ed. CQ Press, Washington, DC.

Sanford, T. (1967). *Storm Over the States*. McGraw-Hill, New York.

Schattschneider, E. E. (1960). *The SemiSovereign People*. Dryden, Hinsdale, IL.

Schmidt, D. (1989). *Citizen Lawmakers*: *The Ballot Initiative Revolution*. Temple University Press, Philadelphia.

Shannon, J. (1986). Federal and State-Local Spenders Go Their Separate Ways. In *American Intergovernmental Relations Today*: *Perspectives and Controversies*. R. J. Dilger (Ed.). Prentice-Hall, Englewood Cliffs, NJ.

U.S. Census Bureau (1969). *Historical Statistics on Government Finances and Employment*. 1967 Census of Governments, vol. 6, Topical Studies, no. 5. Government Printing Office, Washington, DC.

—— (1979). *Historical Statistics on Government Finances and Employment*. 1977 Census of Governments, vol. 6, Topical Studies, no. 4. Government Printing Office, Washington, DC.

—— (1992). *Governmental Finances*: *1989–90*, GF-90-5. Government Printing Office, Washington, DC.

U.S. Congress (Subcommittee on Energy Conservation of the Committee on Energy and Commerce, U.S. House of Representatives) (1986). *FEMA and Nuclear Powerplant Safety*, Hearing, November 15, 1985 and April 22, 1986, Government Printing Office, Washington, DC.

—— (Committee on the Budget, House of Representatives) (1992). *Federal Budget Impact on State and Local Governments*, Hearing, February 11, 1992, Government Printing Office, Washington, DC.

U.S. OMB (Office of Management and Budget) (1987). Federal Aid to State and Local Governments. *Special Analysis, Budget of the United States Government, Fiscal Year 1988*. Government Printing Office, Washington, DC.

—— (1992a). *Budget of the United States Government, Fiscal Year 1993*. Government Printing Office, Washington, DC.

—— *(1992b)*. *Budget of the United States Government, Fiscal Year 1993, Supplement*. Government Printing Office, Washington, DC.

Walker, D. B. (1981). *Toward a Functioning Federalism*. Winthrop, Cambridge, MA.

—— (1991). American federalism: From Johnson to Bush. Publius 21: 105–119.

Walker, J. L. (1971). Innovation in State Politics. In *Politics in the American States: A Comparative Analysis*. H. Jacob and K. N. Vines (Eds.). Little, Brown, Boston.

Welch, S., and Thompson, K. (1980). Impact of federal incentives on state policy innovation. *American Journal of Political Science* 24: 715–729.

Wilson, G. K. (1985). *Business and Politics: A Comparative Introduction*. Chatham House, Chatham, NJ.

Witte, E. E. (1963). *The Development of the Social Security Act*. University of Wisconsin Press, Madison.

Wright, D. S. (1988). *Understanding Intergovernmental Relations*, 3rd ed. Brooks/Cole, Pacific Grove, CA.

Zeigler, L. H. (1983). Interest Groups in the States. In *Politics in the American States: A Comparative Analysis*, 4th ed. V. Gray, H. Jacob, and K. N. Vines (Eds.). Little, Brown, Boston.

Zimmerman, J. F. (1991). Federal preemption under Reagan's new federalism. *Publius* 21: 7–28.

11
Urban Policy

Linda Faye Williams
University of Maryland, College Park, Maryland
Dianne M. Pinderhughes
University of Illinois, Urbana–Champaign, Illinois

Within a 2-week period during the spring of 1992, two well-publicized events highlighted the urgency of solving America's urban problems: a protracted riot in Los Angeles, broadcast live on television, following the verdict in the Rodney King police brutality case[1], and a massive water main leak that flooded Chicago's central business district[2] bringing nearly all downtown businesses to a soggy halt. With damage estimates of up to 7 billion dollars, the riots were first and foremost a crisis of people, and with damage estimates of higher than 1 billion dollars, the water main leak was first and foremost a crisis of place; but both were vivid demonstrations of how quickly unmet needs for prevention can become the disasters those needs foretold. Both were striking warnings of just how and where urban America as community and locality is collapsing, decaying, crumbling, and crashing. Both were momentous alarms blazoning the need for new urban policy.

This chapter focuses on conditions in and policies for cities. It addresses questions of urban need, issues related to the effects of past and current policies on urban areas, and the definition of possible future urban policy. The vast majority (75.2% in 1990) of the U.S. population lives in urban areas; almost half (48.3% in 1990) live in very large places (metropolitan areas with more than 1 million persons). It is the policies that have influenced the lives of this urban half—circumstances in the biggest cities and suburbs—that are the premier focus here.

Several themes are developed below. The first is that local governments are substantially different from both state and national governments; cities are much more limited in what they can do. Juridically and substantively dependent on higher levels of government, the place of cities in the national and global political economies determines to a very large extent the policy choices they make (Peterson, 1981). Although local governments are on the front-line of service delivery, urban authorities and citizens simply do not control what needs changing—for example, the rate of growth and nature of the demand for labor or such characteristics of the industries in which an individual is employed as profit rates, technology, unionization, and the industry's relationship to government. Indeed, cities more starkly than other arenas of American politics have been the terrain of social control that has had less to do with policy making devoted to substantive problem solving than with channeling and controlling discontent and potential rebellion (Katznelson, 1981). In short, urban politics is a politics of dependency, and thus urban problems simply cannot be resolved by urban governments alone.

A second theme faults those higher levels of government that do command more of the resources needed for change (particularly the federal) for failure to act in a responsible manner. Federal urban policy since World War II, and especially during the 1960s and beyond, has been driven more by urban political crises than a measured comprehensive and preventative approach. The federal government has never even developed an appropriate administrative mechanism to develop an urban policy or policies. The one agency devoted to urban issues, the Department of Housing and Urban Development (HUD), has never been able to live up to its role and mission of coordinating an interagency urban policy effort. As a result, the federal government has responded with mainly urban *programs* (piecemeal legislation and regulations directed toward specific crises and situations) than with urban *policy* (a comprehensive approach or integrated plan based on the realization that diverse urban problems arise out of complex interrelated realities and require appreciating urban consequences of seemingly nonurban programs). Often, the result of a program-specific approach in the absence of understanding how one governmental intervention can have unforeseen and unintentional consequences on other factors has resulted in not only the failure to solve problems at hand, but even worsening them. For example, the production partially stimulated by federally supported highways and federally provided house insurance fostered the outmigration of affluent persons from the cities and to the suburbs and often ended up generating undesirable vibrations such as increased neighborhood blight, housing abandonment, and declining tax bases in central cities that dramatically affected the entire complex web of urban society.[3]

A third theme flows from the constant confusion of urban programs with racial and poverty programs. This confusion is, of course, understandable to a large degree given two important post–World War II developments. The first is the massive demographical change that occurred in U.S. central cities and transformed many of the nation's biggest cities into the primary home for people of color (African-Americans, Latinos, and Asians), especially those with low incomes and limited job skills. The second is the reality that for the most part from John F. Kennedy's New Frontier to Lyndon B. Johnson's Great Society to Richard M. Nixon's New Federalism to Jimmy Carter's New Partnership, the nation's efforts to define strategic policy initiatives that addressed the problems or ills of cities, particularly distressed cities, were an outgrowth of the civil rights and antipoverty movements of blacks in the 1960s. Yet, although the demand for racial equality and justice and the drive to renew U.S. cities have occurred from decade to decade almost simultaneously, urban policy and racial policy should not be mistaken to be one and the same thing. For one thing, although there is a direct connection between race, ethnicity, poverty, and central city residence, even today the nation's central cities taken as a whole remain majority white in their population composition. For another, and more importantly, treating problems of people of color and problems of cities as one obscures the racism and injustice of nonurban areas even as it delimits the statement of the urban problems by ignoring issues of design, land use, infrastructure, and variety of city (e.g., the radically different problems in predominantly black versus predominantly white cities). Finally, as long as racism exists, treating urban problems as synonymous with racial problems helps to erode support for the kind of demands necessary to rebuild cities in general.

The fourth theme flows from the first three. Given the dependency of urban governments and the confusion that has dominated federal urban programs, it is hardly surprising that most big cities today are characterized by extreme need and severe distress. Even those cities whose fiscal health looks relatively good are characterized by deferred human and physical capital investment, higher tax rates, and lower urban service levels. While urban resources are scarce, problems are not. Almost any policy arena (employment, housing, education, poverty, transportation, environment, substance abuse, infrastructure, crime, health care, and race relations) reveals alarming statistics vis-à-vis the welfare of U.S. cities.

In sum, urban politics is dependent politics and successful urban policy requies a federal solution; the federal solution requires a holistic approach to the myriad of problems felt perhaps first in urban areas but ultimately throughout the nation; and until such an approach is forthcoming, increasing distress will characterize the future of U.S. cities.

To develop these themes, we first discuss the dependent structure of urban governments and policies. Then historical efforts at creating federal urban policies are evaluated, followed by examination of broad indicators of urban need and distress and urban problems in two key areas of concern are examined. Next, some recent efforts from city halls as well as citizen and nonprofit groups to current federal efforts in response to urban ills are also evaluated. The chapter closes with a discussion of the need for change in urban policy in the immediate future.

I. THE DEPENDENT STATUS OF URBAN GOVERNMENTS AND POLICY

Big-city mayors in particular and urban elected officials and administrators in general are often heavily criticized for failing to remedy a host of deficiencies (from fiscal stress to crime to poverty) in their cities. To be sure, some of these criticisms are well deserved, but all too often analysts approach the discussion of urban governance and urban policy as if they were not embedded in a larger political economy influencing, if not determining, what local governments can do and the policy choices available for them to make. A fuller understanding of urban policy and more accurate evaluation of the efforts of urban officials, however, requires that first and foremost one must recognize that cities are not nation-states; they are limited in what they can do (Peterson, 1981).

Urban governments and urban policy are dependent in two glaring ways. One way is constitutional: urban governments in the United States are juridically dependent on state governments. Another way is evolutionary: Urban policies are more often than not outgrowths of problems caused by national and global economic trends over which localities have little or no control.

A. Federalism and the Juridical Dependence of Cities

The more than 83,000 local governments in the United States face important constitutional limits in the nation's federal system. Legally subordinate to both of their larger partners in American federalism, local governments do not possess even the constitutional protections afforded the states vis-à-vis the federal government. Not only were local governments never mentioned in the U.S. Constitution, the legal roots for urban constitutional dependency were further clarified in Dillon's Rule promulgated in 1868. In that ruling, Judge John F. Dillon formalized the now familiar constitutional dependency of local government, arguing that states, as the creators of local governments, can destroy them at will and that local governments have no authority other than that granted by the state. As legal creatures of state government, local governments historically have not possessed standing to sue and to air complaints against their state even when a state action may appear to violate state constitutional or statutory provisions.[4]

One means of loosening state control of local governments, however, is to adopt home rule, a constitutional option for cities established by about 30 states. Within certain boundaries established by the state, home rule provides the residents of local jurisdictions with varying degrees of autonomy to shape their form of government. Still, "historically state courts have ruled that even home-rule states have preemptive rights over their local governments and that local governments cannot take action contrary to the interests of the state" (Pagano, 1990: 101).

The legal dependency of urban and other local governments on state governments places many limitations on the policies and practices urban governments may choose to pursue. For example, the state constitutional and statutory restrictions on local governments' taxing and spending authority that exist in the vast majority of states (43 in 1989) means that in practice a city cannot decide to improve its fiscal health by radically raising property taxes or taxing suburban commuters who work within the city without state government approval (Gold and Fabaricius, 1989). Meanwhile, mandates issued by state governments can require local governments to assume new program responsibilities—or augment existing ones—or to meet state-defined minimum standards without guaranteed reimbursement, often irrespective of local priorities or local fiscal capacity (Pagano, 1990). In short, the juridical dependency of cities can limit a local government's ability to raise revenues to pay for the initiatives its citizens need while commanding this one and the same local government to assume programs that might not be the city's chosen priority and that it might be unable to afford.

B. Economic Trends and the Substantive Dependence of Cities

Juridical dependence is only one manifestation of the broader substantive dependence of cities. As far back as 1970, Mayor Richard Hatcher of Gary, Indiana, pointed to the problem:

> I am mayor of a city of roughly 90,000 black people but we do not control the possibilities of jobs for them or money for their schools, or state funded social services. These things are in the hands of the U.S. Steel Corporation, the county department of welfare, the state of Indiana, and the federal government. . . . The resources are not available to the cities to do the job that needs doing (Allen, 1970: 111).

Since 1970, the dependent situation of cities as the locus of countless problems they did not cause and over which they have few or any resources to resolve has grown. Demographical changes (the vast growth of people of color and/or poor people migrating to big cities not only from rural America but from the Third World), for instance, depend heavily on "push" factors over which the receiving cities have virtually no control. The increasing mechanization and concentration of southern agriculture and the state of Third World economies obviously have had much more to do with the movement of poor people to big cities than any causes that could be controlled in the city have had (Katznelson, 1981). Similarly, urban authorities and citizens could hardly control the characteristics of the national economy (including its rate of growth, its place in the global economy, nor federal investments that influence growth, trade, and technology) that are the root causes of severe urban problems such as unemployment and underemployment.

The advent of the era of global capitalism has weakened still further the city's ability to control relevant resources. Facilitated by a series of technological revolutions in transportation (reducing shipping costs in relation to both bulk and value-added) and communications (making world financial markets a reality and worldwide command and control immeasurably faster and easier than ever before), the emergence of global capitalism has meant that firms can move anywhere they have the slightest cost advantage in labor costs and production conditions on a world scale. This development has strengthened the hand of business in dealing with urban governments. As long as businesses were captives of local markets and consumers, unable to move freely as tax burdens shifted, they were propelled into active political involvement and sought to be guardians of local government's treasury, but they nonetheless lacked the clear and unambiguous upper hand vis-à-vis local political elites they have today. With an enhanced ability to separate physically various stages in the production process (e.g., research and development, skilled machining and fabrication, semiskilled assembly, administration, and services) and to move production in general from central city to suburb to southern and western regions to abroad, global capital is in a vastly improved condition to either relocate or demand changes in urban policy (e.g., direct and enlarged outlays for infrastructure and for subsidies to potential investors) that benefit business as opposed to (or at the very least more than) other groups.

Financial institutions play significant roles in the changing balance of power between urban governments and business interests. Holding large amounts of local government debt, the larger regional banks can choose to exert decisive pressure on public budgets by refusing to extend further credit when the fiscal capacities of local units of government appear to finance capital to be imprudently extended. Thus, the decline of the relative control and autonomy of urban governments under global capitalism is linked in fundamental ways to the internationalization of production that is characteristic of this era. Urban policies are largely reflective rather than determinative of these economic developments because urban governments are only ''relatively autonomous'' (Ross and Trachte, 1990: 67–87; Smith, 1988).

In short, the dependent situation of U.S. cities has worsened. Particularly, the relevant economic factors have become less rather than more susceptible to local government control, and this trend has been most pronounced in the older cities of the Northeast and Midwest, but as declining economic fortunes in cities such as Los Angeles and Atlanta demonstrate, it is also true of western and southern cities.

II. THE HISTORY OF FEDERAL URBAN POLICY

It should be clear that although the dependent situation of U.S. cities has grown, it hardly constitutes a *new* situation. ''On the contrary. At least from the moment of early industrialization, American cities have been the repositories of social problems over which they have lacked control'' (Katznelson, 1981: 110). Recognizing this, from the critical antebellum period to the present, higher levels of government have, sometimes more and other times less, sought to help cities. This section evaluates these efforts.

A. Urban Policy Through World War II

For much of its history, the U.S. national government provided little in the way of financial assistance to local governments either directly or through the states. Instead, the national government left urban problems and urban policies to the states. By and large, states left these problems and policies to local governments: municipalities and, sometimes, counties (Kaplan and James: 1990). In particular, to the extent that redistributive programs existed prior to the New Deal, cities were their locus. In understanding why big-city governments were more likely than higher levels of government to undertake redistributive programs in this era, it is important to understand that the big-city Democratic machines that dominated urban politics in the 19th and early 20th centuries constantly faced redistributional pressures from below. It is also important to appreciate how big-city economies were more susceptible than at present to local redistributional politics. Unlike in the current era discussed above when the growth of national and global markets and electronic technologies has given capital a distinct upper hand vis-à-vis local political elites, in the late 19th and early 20th centuries, much of the urban economy was local. Business owners were captives of local markets and customers because they were unable to move freely as tax burdens shifted. To be sure, capital tied to national markets was less interested than small businesses in local politics during this earlier period, but even national businesses could be incorporated into local redistributional schemes. This was especially true for those national businesses that were geographically immobile and thus subject to pressures from local governments. For example, needing terminal space in a particular big city in order to transfer freight to other big cities, the country's major railroads often were compelled to support higher local taxes used to pay for redistributionary programs. The higher cost of machine-era local welfare states were then passed on by the railroad companies to their customers.

In the pre–New Deal context, then, cities were more, not less, responsive than the federal government to urban needs and problems requiring redistributive policy. For example, until the 1930s, local governments had the major responsibility for welfare and education policies designed to help the urban poor. State and national governments, especially when controlled by the Republicans or reform Democrats, were the biggest obstacles to local redistribution. (Erie, 1988).

Changes initiated during the progressive era (civil service reform, the personal voter registration system, direct primaries, and the official ballot — all heavily supported by upper-middle-class reformers as means of eroding party strength) and accelerated during the New Deal period (the birth of the U.S. welfare state) gradually insulated city governments from redistributional pressures and moved urban political issues within the "allocational" and "distributional" parameters that Paul Peterson's model of urban policy now takes as an unchanging datum (Peterson, 1981).

Thus, it was the Great Depression that brought the first major national attention to urban problems. In the crucible of economic despair, local political elites and newly mobilized lower-class claimants in the 1930s generated political forces that made the federal government expand its role. To meet the crisis of the Great Depression, the national government used Congress' constitutional authority "to lay and collect taxes [and] to pay the debts and provide for the common defense and general welfare of the United States" in order to expand its role (United States Constitution, Article I, Section 8). The New Deal thus introduced the idea that the national government could play an active role in bettering people's lives (Thomas, 1990). As a result, in the mid and late 1930s, Washington responded to the erosion of urban tax bases and the widespread hardship of the era with a surge of support for local public works, unemployment relief, and public housing programs. Federal aid to local governments rose from $10 million in 1932 to $278 million in 1940 (Kaplan and James, 1990).

Although World War II brought a sharp reduction in aid to local government, at least a modest level of federal assistance to cities was reestablished after the war as the federal government enacted legislation to support airport construction (1946), urban renewal (1949), urban planning (1954), and education in areas affected by military installations (1950). In essense, since the U.S. Supreme Court confirmed an affirmative role for the national government to play in improving the lives of average citizens in the 1939 decision of *United States v. Butler*, the federal government has "been engaged in the more or less conscious attempt to restructure the nation's political system" in order to solve the problems of cities (Long, 1978). Hence, since the New Deal, every presidential administration has had at least something (expressed or implicit) of a national urban policy.

Urban initiatives during the New Deal and the immediate post–World War II period (the Franklin Roosevelt, Harry Truman, and Dwight Eisenhower administrations), however, were related more to pump priming—getting the national economy working again—than they were to specific strategies to help cities in trouble. It is only more recently (the 1960s) that states and the federal government sought to fashion much more of an explicit urban policy; for example, assuming a substantial portion of responsibilities for welfare, housing subsidies, health care, and school spending in cities. From roughly 1960 to 1978, the number of federal grants directed at cities and their problems increased dramatically and, as a result, federal aid became an important source of money for many urban budgets for the first time. Conversely, the period since 1978 has been characterized by a steady retrenchment. It is these two periods (the 1960s expansion and post-1978 contraction) that are the focus of the remainder of this section.

B. Urban Policy in the 1960s and 1970s

Two different theoretical frameworks and practical tendencies have characterized urban policy since 1960. During the expansionary phase (1960 to 1978), "welfare state liberalism" (Smith, 1988) was the guiding theoretical outlook. In a nutshell, from this view urban land use and urban problems are the result of autonomous economic forces that are bearers of significant market imperfections. The good society (and by corollary its premier authoritative decision maker, the national government) should correct or adjust for these market imperfections through compensatory programs such as tax incentives for job creation, manpower training/retraining programs, social welfare programs, livable minimum wage laws, relatively generous unemployment compensation policies, as well as providing tax incentives to businesses to locate in hard-pressed areas of urban society.

This welfare state liberalism outlook was driven by real-life conflicts enveloping U.S. cities in the 1960s. When large numbers of displaced and chronically impoverished people of color migrated to the cities at the very time manufacturing, commerce, and affluent classes were fleeing the older central cities and moving to the suburbs and southern rim, the cities became the site of rebellion. From the nonviolent civil rights protests of the late 1950s and early 1960s, the rebellions grew into the violent riots of the mid and late 1960s. The demands of the impoverished in turn helped to trigger greater demands by other groups, such as municipal employees. As mayors struggled to appease these insurgent urban groups with jobs, benefits, and services, they turned to the national government for more and more help.

During the Kennedy and Johnson administrations, the principal method used to respond to these demands was the enactment of over 400 categorical programs for particular urban ills. "New initiatives were begun in many areas, including community action programs (1964), mass transportation (1964), manpower development and training (1964), neighborhood youth programs (1964), elementary and secondary education assistance (1965), basic water and sewer facilities (1965), community health services (1965), and law enforcement assistance (1968)"

(Kaplan and James, 1990: 226–227). These programs created a mixture of federal initiatives, agencies, guidelines, mandates, and federal-local relationships that affected cities and that, when pieced together, added up to sometimes consistent and sometimes inconsistent urban policies. Some efforts, for example, were directed at expanding the housing supply available to low-income families and individuals but some led to reducing the housing options open to the same households. Some federal strategies were directed at improving residential neighborhoods, but some federal aid programs generated the weakening of city neighborhoods. Perhaps part of the problem was that few federal grant programs were (nor are) directed exclusively at local governments, and of the money directed at local governments, only a small portion was received by large cities and could, therefore, properly be classified as part of the nation's urban policy (Kaplan and James, 1990).

Yet, although analyses related to impact suggest at times contrary results, it is clear that some people and some areas benefitted. The poor were provided with better access to health, housing, food, and select social services in many areas. Civil rights legislation secured increased opportunities for many people of color to gain access to improved education and jobs. Distressed central cities were granted more resources to respond to the needs of their low-income residents (Kaplan and James, 1990). Overall, the share of the national product channeled into the public sector rose dramatically in the 1960s, and the largest part of that increase was due to mounting municipal and state sector budgets (Piven and Cloward, 1977).

Part of the problem in assessing exactly how well these programs worked flows from the difficulty of decoupling program effects from the effects of the general level of economic prosperity that characterized the era. What is manifest, however, is that the healthy economy *and* the programs together help cut the overall poverty rate nearly in half (from 18.5% of families in urban areas in 1959 to 8.8% by 1974) and poverty among the elderly even more. Even the critics of President Johnson's War on Poverty, or direct aid to cities, or the Great Society in general usually have conceded that to denounce programs like Medicare, Head Start and aid to Women, Infants, and Children (WIC) would deny the suffering of tens of millions who would have found it difficult to survive without the help. In addition, it is important to note that these programs helped cities to stay afloat not only fiscally but politically. In essence, so long as the cities were in turmoil, these programs composed the political price enacted by insurgents in order to restore order (Piven and Cloward, 1977).

By the early 1970s, urban strife had subsided considerably. A degree of political stability had been restored partially as a key result of the federal concessions granted in the 1960s. But despite the anecdotes and statistics relating the positive effect of federal efforts during the early and mid 1960s, many scholars and political leaders looking at the diverse and multiple federal programs flowing into and/or used by cities and groups living in cities suggested that the nation could do better. They noted the absence of coordination, the varied inconsistencies between and among federal initiatives, and the limited impacts caused by bureaucratic complexities.[5]

Toward providing a more coordinated, cohesive, and comprehensive national strategy and simultaneously providing more flexibility to cities to respond to their own perceptions of their problems, Congress, in the early 1970s, began to convert categorical into block grants in key functional areas even as it asked HUD to prepare a biennial comprehensive urban policy report that would accommodate the then-anticipated tremendous growth of urban America and the related emptying out of rural areas. Both the Nixon-Ford and the Carter administrations, following this congressional mandate, attempted to define comprehensive urban policies.

As far as comprehension went, the Nixon and Ford efforts proved to be limited ones. Nixon's biennial reports were long on analysis of demographical trends and their likely impact on metropolitan areas and cities and short on hard recommendations. The urban policies of the early and mid 1970s still had to be defined from an examination of the collective actions of the Nixon and Ford administrations and not from any written, cohesive, or comprehensive urban policy statement (Kaplan and James, 1990). Where the Nixon-Ford programs were effectual was in decentralizing urban policy in a way that curtailed or eliminated the Great Society programs in favor of new revenue-sharing or block grant programs.

Block grants increased the general support for urban areas significantly. Between 1970 and 1978 there was a fourfold real increase in direct federal aid—from 3.7 to 15.7 million in 1984 dollars, and federal aid composed more and more of total city revenues—from 7.1% of the own-source resources of city governments in 1970 to 25.8% of own-source resources in 1978 (Fossett, 1983). Whatever else the boom in federal aid in the 1970s meant, however, the new revenue-sharing formulas decreased the targeting of federal funds into the worse-off cities and parts of cities and slowly redirected funding away from them and to richer cities, suburbs, and towns. Moreover, within each locality, some of the monies that had previously provided jobs and services in poor communities were spent to fund police services and reduce taxes (Piven and Cloward, 1977). Mayors, regardless of their race, had a political stake in reducing taxes even when their cities could not afford to do so, for tax cutting became a premier tool for pleasing business and wedding middle class constitutents to their electoral coalitions.

Given Nixon and Ford's failures to provide a comprehensive urban policy, Carter promised that his administration would be the first to develop one. Although the commitment and effort were admirable, what actually resulted was a set of programs that targeted limited federal dollars to distressed cities that by and large were losing their more affluent population. Strategies were directed at buttressing local economies, improving local neighborhoods, increasing job opportunities within cities, and improving local services. Finally, the policy sought to enlight neighborhood movements and other, primarily business, elements of the private sector in the partnership.

To be sure, the Partnership for Urban America as the program was called was bold in the context of what had happened in the United States before. Yet, this place-based program was far from comprehensive (Kaplan and James, 1990). One immediate problem with Carter's urban policy was its lack of prioritization—and without prioritization, clearly there was no coherent, general urban policy—even of the scope of that created by Johnson's Great Society.

Meanwhile, at the local level, changes were underway that undercut federal efforts, especially in the context of the persistent recession and rampant inflation that characterized the late 1970s and caused a sharp reduction in the standard of living of most depressed groups. As the impact of the long-term trends that were undercutting the manufacturing base of older cities came to be felt simultaneously with ebbing political turmoil, unemployment rates rose and municipal budgets based mostly on revenues earned through sales and income taxes declined.

The situation thus became ready for a mobilization of national and local business interests to bring big-city expenditures into line with revenues by cutting the costs of insurgent politics in the cities. The trigger for the mobilization of business interests was the threat of a default by New York City in 1975. Although the city did not default, the very threat made it possible to impose entirely new definitions of the urban fiscal situation on the populations of big cities across the nation.

In the face of the default, business sectors became highly vocal as they moved to restructure urban policies. On the one hand, they insisted on slashes in the payrolls, wages, and benefits of municipal employees as well as deep cuts in services to neighborhoods. On the other hand, they insisted that to bolster city revenues, states and municipalities would be required to make new and larger concessions to business: reduced taxes, enlarged subsidies, and relaxed regulation in matters such as environmental pollution. In the context of a self-conscious active mobilization on the part of business interests, many insurgent interest groups became confused and quiescent witnesses to the newly emerging municipal politics in which they had been active participants only shortly earlier.

In actuality, the processes underlying the fiscal crisis of the cities had been underway for at least two decades. In the years after World War II, the manufacturing base of many older cities weakened. The decline in central city manufacturing had a number of causes. In part, it resulted from the movement of both older plants and new capital to the South and abroad in search of cheaper labor. In part, it was the result of the movement of plants to the suburban ring, where labor costs were not necessarily cheaper but where federal investments in highways, housing, and other service systems reduced the cost of doing business in various other ways. In part, it was the result of the pattern of federal investments in defense and space exploration that bypassed the older manufacturing cities for the new cities of the South and West. These trends were intertwined with the flight of commerce and of the more affluent classes from the older central cities to the suburban rings and to the southern rim of the nation (Piven and Cloward, 1977). As these developments exacerbated, the plight particularly of the older cities of the Northeast and Midwest worsened during the Reagan-Bush years.

C. Urban Policy in the 1980s

In general, federal policy in the 1980s all but ignored the "urban problem." The most important direct urban aid programs—the Comprehensive Employment Training Act (CETA) and Local Public Works, for example—disappeared by the early 1980s, and general revenue sharing was soon to follow. Overall, a significant decline in urban-related expenditures occurred during the Reagan and Bush years. Distressed cities found their share of federal spending decreasing in the 1980s relative to the nation as a whole and to economically healthy cities (Cuciti, 1990). Direct aid to cities was cut especially as the Reagan administration redirected grants to the states. The most important factor contributing to this retrenchment was the budgetary squeeze that the federal government found itself in starting in the late 1970s. With the tax cuts of 1981, the Reagan administration's defense build-up, and the 1981 to 1982 recession, the squeeze was transformed into the crushing force of $200 billion annual deficits. The more money consumed by federal debt payments, the less money available for satisfying national housing, educational, and infrastructure needs.

The battle to reduce these deficits revealed that discretionary domestic spending, of which nonentitlement grants to state and local governments make up a significant portion, was not high on the Reagan administration's list of budgetary priorities. On an inflation-adjusted basis, grants for community and regional development was cut by two thirds, and those for education, training, and social services fell by 45%. Moreover, the most distressed cities were assaulted in yet another way: As the Reagan administration redirected money from the domestic agenda to the military one, the Sunbelt regions (Atlantic, Gulf, and Pacific cities) that had disproportionately supported Reagan in his elections benefited, whereas the most distressed cities (where more Democratic interests and constituencies were found) were defunded. These cities found themselves in the 1980s with decreasing federal subsidies for their ailing infrastructures, mass transit systems, social welfare programs, and neighborhood development programs. Meanwhile the administration's tax expenditure approach only served to accelerate corporate disinvestment from many declining industrial cities to new and more profitable forms of investment like real estate and more "flexible" points of production where the political power of workers was weaker (Phillips, 1990).

By the end of Bush's administration in 1992, federal aid to cities per capita had been cut by 60%, leading to the first nominal dollar reduction in federal aid in decades. For certain cities, and particularly some of those in the declining regions of the nation, the losses were very great.[6] As the United States approaches the 21st century, the specter of the federal budget deficit continues to preclude any expansion of aid to cities.

These developments have had an unhealthy impact on the status of urban policy and the single department expected to focus on urban affairs as well as local politics. For example, HUD, always the weakest of the cabinet departments, was savaged both ideologically and pragmatically during the Reagan-Bush years. Ideologically, the Reagan-Bush administrations left no room for a national role in urban affairs except for a small number of sharply restricted block grants and a vague (and for the most part never implemented) concept of enterprise zones. Even these programs were to funnel through the states, with mayors increasingly cut out of the process. Programmatically, HUD program after HUD program was dismantled. Between 1980 and 1987, HUD's budget fell 57%, the largest cut of any federal department. The authorization for federally assisted housing dropped from $27 billion to $1.5 billion. Community Development Block Grants were cut from $3.7 to $2.6 billion and Urban Development Action Grants (UDAGs) from $675 million to $20 million (Bahl et al., 1990). These reductions took place in an era when the proportion of U.S. homeowners declined, the number of homeless increased, the quantity and quality of rental stock decreased, and the long-standing shortage of public housing intensified. Overall, by 1987 HUD's appropriations had dropped from 7% of the total federal budget in 1978 to less than 1%. Departmental personnel fell from 17,000 in 1975 to a little over 12,000 in 1985—a decrease of 29% (National League of Cities, 1987).

In this context, the response of most city halls, whatever the color of their chief executives, was to avoid further fiscal problems by passing them on in the forms of deferred human and physical capital investment, higher tax rates, and lower urban service levels (Bahl, 1987). When combined with big cities' recapitalization schemes through decreasing tax abatements, the impact of these developments on people of color in cities was clear. Services to neighborhoods were reduced; much more so in impoverished neighborhoods than in more affluent ones. Municipal workers were laid off in large numbers, and the overwhelming impact of these layoffs were felt first by the people of color who were first hired during the turmoil of the 1960s (Mollenkopf, 1990). For many of the unemployed, welfare eventually became the only possible recourse, a fact that lent the growing welfare eligibility restrictions a special cruelty.

Finally, and much to the point of the structural constraints of federal fiscal conservatism on big-city politics, blacks and Latinos were assaulted in another way as well. Retrenchment in federal urban spending combined with financial and business leaders' growing control over municipal budget decisions through the creation of committees of businessmen and bankers such as New York's Big MAC, Atlanta's CAP, and Detroit's NDC supplanted the elected political stratum in making economic decisions. These developments thus deprived people of color of the limited influence in urban politics ordinarily wielded by the vote. Such gains in "minority political incorporation" as blacks and Latinos made since 1967 were clearly of little consequence in resisting the slashing of municipal budgets when both federal aid was cut back sharply *and* bankers and businessmen were, for all practical purposes, making budget decisions. Enlarging fiscal discrepancies in municipal budgets made the substantive dependency of cities acute and the vulnerability of elected officials blatant (Piven and Cloward, 1977).

D. Some Conclusions About Past Urban Policy in the United States

Beginning in the 1930s, the federal government asserted it had a role in improving the quality of life in American cities, and especially since 1960, every presidential administration has expressed concern over the health of U.S. cities, particularly older central cities. Both the New Frontier and the Great Society of the Kennedy-Johnson years initiated programs such as the War on Poverty, Model Cities, and urban renewal, aimed in part at the urban poor and in part at deteriorating urban neighborhoods. New federalism, Nixon-style, while generating a shift in the relative locus of aid funds to reflect its nonurban constituencies, increased the absolute volume of federal funds flowing into urban areas. President Carter promised the nation a comprehensive urban policy. His administration delivered something less—a set of federal programs and a cluster of activities tilted toward responding to the assumed ills of distressed central cities. Presidents Reagan and Bush linked their perceptions of city problems to the failure of the broader economy to provide cities with taxes and jobs. According to Reagan and Bush, improved economic performance would benefit most, if not all, cities. As a result, their administrations downplayed urban policy and program development initiatives.

The multiple and diverse social commitments of the Kennedy-Johnson administrations, the short-lived attempt to conceive of a comprehensive urban policy during the Carter administration, and even Nixon and Ford's revenue sharing were all laudable in the light of the minimal urban concerns of the Reagan and Bush administrations. Yet, the most sustainable conclusion is that in the end, urban problems have continued to grow, since no administration has been able or willing to develop and articulate a comprehensive set of related goals and strategies concerning cities—goals and strategies that would specifically govern programs, budgets, and subsequent performance evaluations. Since the 1930s, urban initiatives have been driven more by events—political pressures, protests, riots, and the often changing perceptions of city problems of different agencies, congressional committees, and the presidents themselves than by any broad-based set of comprehensive and preventative policies. The piecemeal program of federal policy toward the cities, the lack of coordination between the federal and local governments in the policy-making process, and the crisis-driven nature of urban policy making at all levels of government have sometimes generated almost as many problems as solutions in cities.

III. URBAN NEEDS AND URBAN PROBLEMS IN CONTEMPORARY RELIEF

That federal nor state and local urban policies have made significant progress in radically improving the plight of the largest cities in the United States is easily demonstrated by the mushrooming nature of urban problems and needs in a host of policy areas. Obviously, we cannot discuss the full list or trace out all the areas of urban policy needs in one chapter. Instead, we shall illustrate the general contemporary pattern of need by briefly focusing on two important urban policy areas: education and poverty. No claim is made here that these are the most two important or even pressing urban policy areas. Clearly, housing, crime, infrastructure, fiscal crisis, environmental pollution, transportation, and race relations are equal competitors. Education and poverty are chosen simply owing to the sheer amount of attention given these problems in the last decade and because both dramatically illustrate escalating urban needs and the inability of urban governments left to their own devices to solve urban problems.

A. Urban Education – Compulsory Inequality

Few policy areas more dramatically demonstrate the central themes of this chapter than urban education. The problems of the nation's urban schools are a microcosm of the results of cities' juridical and substantive dependency, the failure of higher levels of government to act, the confusion of urban policy with racial policy, and concomitant dualism in need and distress.

For example, it is well known that vast disparity characterizes the budgets of urban school districts. Those districts with the greatest needs (school districts where reading levels are lowest and poverty is highest) are precisely the school districts with the least funding (Kozol, 1991: 58). As Kozol points out, American children are required to attend schools—and schools in their own district. Yet, although the state requires attendance, it does not require equity; effectively this adds up to requiring inequality.

> For example, the average high school class of 30 children in Chicago received approximately $90,000 less each year than would have been spent on them if they were pupils of the highest spending of the city's Northern suburbs. When relative student needs are factored into the discussion, the disparities in funding are even more enormous. . . . Equity, after all, does not mean simply equal funding. Equal funding for unequal needs is not equality. The need is greater in central cities; and its children, if they are to have approximately equal opportunities need more than the children who attend suburban schools. Seen in this light, inequity in funding is startling. (Kozol, 1991: 54).

The reasons behind unequal funding of urban schools are equally well understood. Public education in the United States is funded by an arcane machinery. Most public schools in the United States depend for their initial funding on a tax on local property. Although state contributions (intended to make up for local wealth disparities) represent almost half of local school expenditures and the federal government contributes a small amount (approximately 6% of total school expenditures), these sources are insufficient in rendering equity given the decisive impact of the property tax in shaping inequality. Although very poor communities in cities tend to place a high premium on education and tax themselves at higher rates than do very affluent communities, they still end up with far less money for each child in school as a direct result of the different taxable values of houses and local industries in the respective communities.

Moreover, a variety of federal policies act to increase the gulf between the poorest central city schools and the richest suburban ones. For instance, because the property tax is counted as a tax deduction by the federal government, homeowners in a wealthy suburb get back a substantial portion of the money that they spend to fund their children's schools— effectively a federal subsidy for unequal education. Homeowners in poor districts get this subsidy as well, but, because their total tax is less, the subsidy is less. The mortgage interest that homeowners pay is also treated as a tax deduction—in effect, a second federal subsidy. These "subsidies" are large. In 1984, property tax deductions granted by the federal government were $9 billion. An additional $23 billion in mortgage-interest deductions were provided to homeowners: a total of some $32 billion. Federal grants to local schools, in contrast, totaled only $7 billion, and only part of this was earmarked for low-income districts (Kozol, 1991: 55).

As a result, total yearly spending—local funds combined with state assistance and the small amount that comes from the federal government—ranges today in a state like New York from $2,100 on a child in the poorest district to above $15,000 in the richest (Kozol, 1991: 83). The system, writes John Coons, "bears the appearance of calculated unfairness" (Coons, Klune and Sugarman, 1970: 41).

Beyond inequities of funding for schools, big cities face the added problem that an overly large portion of their limited tax revenues must be diverted to meet nonschool costs that wealthy suburbs and small towns do not face, or only on a far more modest scale.

> Police expenditures are higher in crime-ridden cities than in most suburban towns. Fire department costs are also higher where dilapidated housing, often with substandard wiring, and arson-for-profit are familiar problems. Public health expenditures are also higher where poor people cannot pay for private hospitals. All of these expenditures compete with those for public schools. So the districts that face the toughest challenges are also likely to be those that have the fewest funds to meet their children's needs. (Kozol, 1991: 54).

In short, it is well known that equalizing the funding of public education requires a national solution. Yet, the financing of public schools became more rather than less a predominantly local governance affair during the 1980s. Indeed, the web of policy support for young children that characterized the adoption of the Elementary and Secondary Education Act of 1965 at the federal level and the increasing state role in the funding of education during the 1960s and early 1970s dissipated since the mid 1970s. As far as the federal government went, two interpretations dominated the 1980s: (1) education was an individual or local responsibility; and (2) problems in urban schools were too great to solve and concomitantly investing additional money was a waste. In the end, federal and state policy makers refused to launch new initiatives in urban areas, leaving urban school districts to care for the students that remained. Moreover, deep cuts were made in past programs. For example, student grants were converted to student loans, and federal aid to education both at public schools and on the job was one of the few places where government spending was actually cut nominally. By 1993, analysts concluded that no sector of public spending was cut more than urban education in the recession of the early 1990s (*Washington Post*, February 1, 1993).

As Thurow (1992) pointed out, part of the problem is that increasingly every level of government in passing on the responsibility of financing the U.S. education system. Not only has the federal government become more rather than less unwilling to fund urban public schools, local and state governments appear unwilling to pay the costs for first-class schools as well. States and localities tend to conclude that they have little to gain by increasing the funding of schools, since less than half the population has children in school at any one time; that students will leave home and use their skills in different geographical regions of the country; that the high taxes necessary to pay for good schools would be politically unpopular (and they believe at least that they might drive industrial firms away); and that firms would locate next door and free ride on their well-educated work force. Given these views, local governments' response is let someone else make the necessary investments.

So unwilling was any level of government to take responsibility for funding public education that in 1993 in a middle-sized city in Michigan with mostly white students, schools closed for summer vacation in late March rather than in early June. Citizens nor local, state, or federal governments came to the Michigan school district's rescue with the funds needed to keep the system open. As Thurow (1992) concludes, when it comes to education investments, individual rationality (let someone else do it) produces collective irrationality (it does not get done).

Other problems abound in urban education. Beyond the massive problems in the elementary and secondary school systems is the failure to create any public-sector education program for postsecondary training for those who do not attend college. In fact, the United States is unique among industrialized nations in that it does not have an organized postsecondary education system for non–college bound high-school graduates. Whereas other nations spend heavily in postsecondary skills of the non–college bound (two to six times as much as the United States spends), the United States has no systematic plan for training and retraining of workers for increasing productivity in the new jobs generated by the technological revolution. Unlike German high-school graduates, who have the apprenticeship system or Japanese high-school graduates, who have lifetime employment guarantees, or the French high-school graduates, who find training and retraining as a result of France's 1% sales tax imposed on firms who do not train, urban high-school graduates in the United States have few means to acquire the skills needed in newer industries (Thurow, 1992). Concomitantly, urban unemployment increases.

Other problems involve racial dimensions. For instance, problems in K–12 education (Kindergarten through high school) as well as in postsecondary education are disproportionately felt in big central cities heavily populated by people of color. Thus, understandably much of the literature on urban needs focuses on demographics showing the "isolation" of blacks, especially in central city public schools (Wilson, 1987). For example, in 1980, the public school systems of U.S. central cities served 19% of all the white public school students, 48% of Latino public school students, and 56% of all the black public school students; indeed recent projections indicate that by the mid 1990s, just 7 of the nation's 25 largest city school systems will have white enrollments greater than 30% (Ornstein, 1987). It is this development that leads most of the literature on urban education to focus on its racial dimensions—the low reading scores, high dropout rates, poor motivation, and poor teachers of African-Americans especially. For example, authors such as Newman et al. (1990) concentrate on the racial demographics of urban public school systems; Orfield (1985) focuses on the need to desegregate public schools; and Peterson (1976, 1983) directs attention to the often fractious racial politics involving community control of school districts.

Yet, it is nevertheless apparent that too much of the literature on urban education demonstrates a tendency to synonymize the terms *black* and *urban* in ways that fail to supply ample directions for effective reform. First, despite the plethora of studies focusing on the racial dimensions of urban education problems, most fail to make even passing reference to continuing racism and segregation (rather than "isolation" as a mere accidental outgrowth of inexorable neutral market processes). Hence, the literature's insights on resolving racial problems in urban education are limited.

Second, although (as pointed out above) it is unquestionably true and important that public schools in large central cities are highly populated by people of color, it is nonetheless also evident that international comparisons demonstrate that all of the nation's schools (public and private are faring poorly in educating American children. For example, recent international comparisons of student achievement among nations as diverse as Columbia, Ireland, Korea, Canada, Spain, the United Kingdom, Japan, and the United States have concluded unanimously that American children had the lowest scores in mathematics and the second lowest in science (Haerkl, 1988; Hiebowitsh, 1989; Rossier, 1990; Verstegen, 1992).

Numerous outstanding national reports, including the Institute for Educational Leadership study, *Dropouts in America* (Hahn and Danzberger, 1987); the Committee for Economic Development study, *Children in Need* (Research and Policy Committee, 1987); the National Governor's Association report, *Making America Work* (1987); the Hudson Institute's report, *Workforce 2000* (Johnston and Packer, 1987); the W. T. Grant Foundation report, *The Forgotten Half* (1988), and the U.S. Education Department's *America 2000* (1991), have documented the need for change and provided directions. These studies suggest that although a large racial gap in education enrollment, dropout rates, and achievement test scores is still extremely problematic, the problem of the declining quality of education in the United States goes well beyond race. In addition to ending urban school funding inequity, a condition placing children with the greatest needs in precisely the worse schools, these studies tend to point out that many bargains must be struck between diverse sectors if the United States is to improve its schools. Taxpayers should agree to bring the wages of schoolteachers up to the levels found in Germany or Japan. Owing to widening opportunities for women in the labor market, long gone are the days when a captive female staff will provide the skills required at low wages. If the United States wants a quality education for its youth, it must begin to pay for it.

The teachers' end of the bargain would be to agree to a world-scale work effort and efficiency. As in other nations with leading educational systems, the U.S. school day would be lengthened by a couple of hours per day in high school and the school year would be at least 220 days long rather than 175 to 180 days. In addition to working longer, teachers would commit themselves to bringing nonclassroom administrative costs down to the levels found in Germany or Japan. In most of the U.S. big-city schools, fewer than half the employees are teachers; the nation could fund most of the improvements in teacher salaries out of cuts in administrative work. This would reverse the present trend of the best teachers moving into administration in order to earn higher salaries (Thurow, 1992).

Part of the bargain, as well, would require parents and teachers to join hands in forcing children to work harder at home. For example, international comparisons show that Japanese students do five times as many hours of homework per week as their U.S. peers. U.S. students read only one third as much as those in Switzerland (Haerkl, 1988).

The community end of the bargain would be to stop expecting schools to do everything. The school's prime responsibility is to educate not become parents. Wars on crime, drugs, teenage pregnancy—as necessary as they are—should be established elsewhere. In addition, the reforms in financing education should include a requirement for business firms to pay more taxes to train workers—for example, through a system similar to the corporate tax for this purpose in France or through expanding social security to include training for the young (Thurow, 1992).

In short, the problem for urban education policy is not the lack of information or studies. The problem is generating action in a system with 15,000 plus independent school boards whose incentives lie in other directions. Meanwhile, the quality of education in U.S. cities increasingly suffers with a devastating impact on young people. Clearly urban education is an area where federal policy makers desperately need to rethink their position vis-à-vis urban children and once again become players in the effort to design an effective policy response.

B. Urban Poverty—A Worsening Phenomenon

Before turning to poverty in cities per se, it is useful to dispel a number of common myths about the urban-poverty-race mix: Two thirds of poor people are white (66.5% in 1991; blacks composed 28.7% of the poor). The majority of poor people do not receive welfare in the sense of cash assistance (56.4% of poor families received no cash assistance in 1991), so poverty is far from synonymous with welfare. Only a minority of the poor (21% in 1991) live in the highly concentrated poverty areas of inner cities. The majority of poor family householders are high-school graduates *not* high-school dropouts (53.2% of poor family householders were high-school graduates in 1991). Most poor people are not "lazy bums" who do not wish to work (three fourths of the nation's poor in 1991 were either children under 18 years old (40.2%), elderly (10.8%), or working adults (24.3%)) (Edelman, 1990: 93; U.S. Bureau of the Census, 1992: vii–xxiv). Finally, in actuality the geographical map of poverty in the United States is bimodal: disproportionate numbers of the poor in rural areas and in central cities and fewer (albeit not a trivial number) in the suburbs. Persistent poverty is similarly bimodal, being concentrated in rural areas and in inner cities—with rural poverty being worst of all (Edelman, 1990).

Yet, since the 1960s the vast majority of attention to poverty has gone to urban poverty. Central cities, with 20.2% of their total populations and 32.5% of their children forced to live on incomes below the poverty line in 1991 compared with 9.6% of the total populations and 14.7% of the children in suburbs, have garnered the bulk of study (U.S. Bureau of the Census, 1992: 40–41). Studies amply demonstrate that urban poverty is the glue that binds most, if not every, other urban policy areas together. For instance, as discussed above, poor children suffer the worse schools; and the proportion of people who are poor declines with rising educational levels (U.S. Bureau of the Census, 1992: 70–73). Similarly (and obviously), poor people are the most likely to be unemployed, underemployed, and/or working in occupations and industries that pay low wages (U.S. Bureau of the Census, 1992: 80, 89). The poor are disproportionately likely to live in female-headed families—for example, in 1991, 46.5% of all female-headed households were poor households compared with 9.6% of married-couple families (U.S. Bureau of the Census, 1992: 40). The poor have both more health problems and are more likely to live without health insurance. While 14.1% of all Americans were not covered by any form of health insurance, 28.6% of all poor Americans were not covered in 1991 (U.S. Bureau of the Census, 1992: xviii). The poor are more likely to live in substandard housing and pay a higher proportion of their income for rent. The most abject of all the poor are homeless and their ranks rise daily (Edelman, 1990). The poor are also more likely to live in areas with environmental problems—from air and water pollution to being the sites of the most toxic waste dumps (Brown and Jacobsen, 1987; Rosenbaum, 1991). They live in neighborhoods with less well-developed transportation systems and more infrastructure problems in general (Pagano, 1990); and they are more likely to be both the victims and perpetrators of crime (Department of Justice, 1986). In short, it is in the discussion of urban poverty that one finds the complex mix of problems that plague cities.

Thus, no discussion of urban needs can proceed fruitfully without a discussion of the growth of poverty in U.S. cities since the mid 1970s. Since 1973, urban poverty has grown both in absolute magnitude and proportion and changed in its composition. In 1991, there were 35.7 million officially poor people in the United States, representing 14.2% of the population. Slightly more than 15 million poor people lived in central cities. These numbers represent a turnaround from the progress the nation made from 1959, the year it started keeping the statistics, until 1973. In 1959, 22.4% of Americans were poor. In 1973, the nation reached its all-time low of 11.1%, then held about steady until 1978, and then started to climb again (U.S. Bureau of the Census, 1992: 2). People of color in cities, especially, remain poor—37.1% of Latinos and 40.6% of African-Americans living in central cities were poor in 1991 (U.S.

Bureau of the Census, 1992: 39). But the even more shocking numbers involve the relationship between family structure and poverty. Children in female-headed families were poor at a rate of 55.5% in 1991. Children in Latina-headed families were poor at a rate of 68.6%, and 68.2% of the black children in female-headed families were poor.

Urban poverty in the 1980s was different in remarkable and important ways from its composition in the 1960s and earlier. First, the elderly used to be disproportionately poor and are now, as a group, less poor than the population as a whole. The indexing of social security and the enacement of the Supplemental Security Income (SSI) program in the early 1970s have added up to an enormous social-policy success for the urban elderly (although elderly women and people of color remain disproportionately poor).

Second, children as a group are now much poorer than the rest of the urban population. This is in large part due to the increased incidence of female-headed families, which has spelled economic disaster for millions of women and children. The jobs-skills mismatch that characterizes the urban labor market has intensified this problem (Kasarda, 1985). On the one hand, economic restructuring has meant the attraction of administrative services, corporate headquarters, and information technologies demanding a high-skilled labor force to cities, whereas the only other jobs growing are exceptionally low-wage service jobs. Whereas urban labor markets once offered opportunities of vertical mobility; today's urban labor market is cemented in horizontal layers. On the one end are the high-paying skilled services still disproportionately likely to be performed by middle-class white men and at the other end are those who perform the clerical support work, clean the offices, prepare and serve the foods, and carry out the garbage for the top sector—with little or no mobility in between (Berry, 1985). The increasing number of low-wage jobs for the semiskilled and unskilled and the continuing barriers women confront in getting good jobs mean that working women with children and no husband are more likely to be poor than they used to be. Further, welfare benefits (Aid to Families with Dependent Children and food stamps) have been steadily deteriorating in real terms for two decades (approximately 40% since 1970), so that transfer payments do not lift families who are unable to work out of poverty. Not surprisingly, therefore, the poor are getting poorer. About 40% of the poor, or 14.1 million people, now live on incomes below half the poverty line. (In 1978, the comparable proportion was 31.5 percent). For a family of four, this means existing on less than $7000 a year, and for a family of three on less than $5500 a year (U.S. Census Bureau: 1992: 148).

Third, the weakness in the U.S. economy that has persisted since 1973 has brought an increase in the number of families in which someone works full-time but is unable to earn enough to get the family out of poverty and a corresponding increase in the numbers of those who work part time because they cannot find full-time work and are in poverty as a consequence. Moreover, the new jobs created since the mid 1970s are not nearly as good as the ones they are replacing. Over half the new jobs created between 1975 and 1985, for example, offered wages in the lowest third of the wage structure (Edelman, 1990: 90). The working poor are a much clearer target for policy attention in the 1990s than was the case two decades ago.

Rising poverty places numerous tensions on city governments. First, increasing poverty means increasing demands for services—even as city governments' tax bases erode. Second, as riots in Los Angeles demonstrated in 1992, rising poverty means a combustible mix likely to explode at any time. Despite advances in voting rights and participation, the poor are still an alienated lot from city hall; as the civil rights leader Martin Luther King once observed, riots are the voice of the powerless. And third, and most important, poverty means a desperately low quality of life for a substantial proportion of the urban population.

After a hiatus of concern about the urban poor after the 1960s, the good news of the 1980s was that poverty made its way back onto the national agenda; the bad news was that a conservative consensus developed that stigmatized the poor and produced policies that worsened rather than improved their plight.

The conservative administrations of Ronald Reagan and George Bush, guided by a plethora of conservative authors from Robert Nozick (1974) to George Gilder (1981) to Charles Murray (1984) to Lawrence Mead (1986) and others, argued that welfare dependency, not poverty, was the real problem. Mead summarized the issue the way the Reagan-Bush administrations saw it when he wrote that in today's economy, few adults who work steadily full-time will remain poor. According to Mead, opportunity was available for nearly all and that anyone could make it who stayed on the job rather than abstaining from work and falling prey to the temptations of welfare. The main question as conservatives saw it was how to get nonworking people to seek and take jobs in order to become self-sufficient rather than to continue to languish on welfare. Thus, the Reagan administration repeatedly attempted to persuade Congress to reduce welfare spending and to restrict eligibility for welfare programs, actions resting on the reasoning that these programs caused dependency.

Although it was conservatives that first embraced the "urban underclass" construct as a way of attacking welfare, by the mid 1980s, liberals had been nearly completely drawn under its umbrella. The most important book on urban poverty written by a liberal in the 1980s was undoubtedly William Julius Wilson's *The Truly Disadvantaged* (1987). Although Wilson posited that "the problem of joblessness should be a top-priority item in any policy discussion focusing on enhancing the status" of the urban poor, and he called for "a macroeconomic policy designed to promote both economic growth and a tight labor market," and for extending benefits through universal programs (what he calls a "hidden agenda," of which a universal family or child allowance, common in other Western democracies would be enacted), many of his ideas were expressed so vaguely and his argument sufficiently incoherent and lacking rigor that his book was quickly appropriated by right-wing forces, who sought to move from "the war on poverty to the war on welfare" (Katz, 1989). In addition, by failing to examine how post policy—that is political choices, not simply the inexorable working of the market—had produced the plight of the so-called urban underclass *and* by confusing policies designed to counter racial and gender discrimination with poverty programs (e.g., affirmative action), Wilson's work has thus far produced only modest guidance for decisionmakers at any level of government. Moreover, neither Wilson's nor any of the other works on the so-called "urban underclass" ever provided more than a vague heterogeneous definition of the group. By lumping together welfare mothers, the long-term unemployed, and those engaged in street crime, Wilson and other liberals made it hopelessly impossible to devise a policy solution. After all, how could one and the same policy solve the problem of so diverse a group with so many differing causal factors behind their growth; could the *same policy* really be expected to solve the problems of a welfare mother and her children *and* transform muggers, robbers, and murderers into productive citizens?

By failing to grapple with these issues, Wilson and most other liberal analysts of the poor in the 1980s, regardless of their intentions, did more to advance the conservative onslaught against programs designed to help the poor than to produce better ones. By the early 1990s, liberal policy analyses of urban poverty had degenerated into being nearly indistinguishable from conservative ones. For example, Jencks (1992) even resurfaced once discarded and certainly unsubstantiated arguments about genetic differences in intelligence and propensity for criminal activity to discuss the determinants of the plight of the black urban poor.

In short, the policy consensus that developed in the 1980s among scholars and the public alike from left to right was that (1) assistance programs themselves contributed to rising unemployment and dependency by reducing the incentives to work; (2) welfare "as we know it" must end; and (3) some form of workfare/jobfare must take its place. This climate of opinion, in turn, led political leaders at all levels, and in both political parties, to call for reform in the nation's social policy, and particularly its welfare system.

Republican leaders proposed reforms that would require recipients to work or at least to train for work. Democrats joined Republicans to endorse the idea that individuals could rise out of poverty and become self-supporting through employment. Democrats, especially Democratic mayors, differed only in their contention that reaching this goal would require employment incentives. These would take the form, for example, of day-care allowances, health insurance, and the enforcement of child assistance payments from absent parents.

Party leaders eventually compromised in 1988 and enacted the Family Support Act. This Act established the Job Opportunities and Basic Skills Training Program (JOBS), often known as workfare. Workfare provided that able-bodied recipients of welfare, except those with small children, would eventually remain eligible for assistance only if they met certain work requirements. Recipients would have to participate in training programs or other activities designed to prepare them for employment or gain actual work experience through community programs. Once they had gotten jobs, public assistance would continue to give child care and health insurance benefits for a year to those whose jobs did not provide such services. Proponents of reform believed that by requiring nonworking people to "act responsibly," and by increasing the economic incentives for them to do so, workfare would move welfare recipients into employment enabling them to become sufficiently self-supporting so as eventually to be weaned off welfare (Schwarz and Volgy, 1992).

The view that public assistance should aid the able-bodied of working age only temporarily, until employment becomes available and enables them to care for themselves, was so popular by 1992 that every presidential candidate who addressed the issues of urban poverty campaigned on it. The candidate elected, Bill Clinton, in fact promised to limit welfare recipients to 2 years of eligibility; after that recipients would be forced to find jobs. The irony was that the U.S. economy was not only producing fewer and fewer jobs for the unskilled and semiskilled, but that even white-collar jobs were on the decline—the victim not only of the recession of the early 1990s but of the electronic revolution. Thus, while politicians of all parties agreed on moving people off of welfare and into jobs, there simply were no jobs—and no amount of short-term education or training appeared likely to solve the problem. Nor did such political rhetoric adequately address the plight of the very large number of nonelderly poor adults already working when they can but who remain poor. In 1991, 2.1 million worked full time and were unable to lift their families out of poverty. Another 7.1 million worked part time or only part of the year, often because they were unable to find full-time work or unable to accept it owing to lack of adequate available child care. The minimum wage produced $8840 for the whole year. The poverty line in 1991 was $13,924 for a family of four and $10,860 for a family of three. Clearly a minimum-wage job in a family with only one adult worker would not lift a family out of poverty.

In additon, the Clinton administration's promise of increased expenditures for day care, health care, or public sector job creation as necessary components of moving the poor into jobs met head-on with the need to reduce an ever-fattening federal budget deficit. Hence, as the Clinton administration began, much seemed Pollyana-like in discussions of the urban poor whether they were called underclass or something else. Meanwhile, the Los Angeles riots, which many concluded were much more of a class than race riot, demonstrated the urgency of answers. In short, as Schwarz and Volgy (1992) concluded:

> The problem is that the belief that all can be self-sufficient through work does not reflect reality. Whether the economy is experiencing substantial growth or not, millions of fully employed Americans cannot meet their families' basic needs, and millions more work hard, sometime in more than one job because they are unable to find year round full-time employment. In fact about 40 percent of all year round full-time workers in this nation cannot have the kind of family sometimes described as the American ideal—two parents and two children with one parent gainfully employed and the other at home—and simultaneously escape poverty. The painful truth is that there is no shortcut to overcoming the dearth of steady, decent-paying jobs in America. . . . When a shortage of steady, decent-paying jobs exists on this scale, governmental programs that aim to enable people to become self-supporting will have difficulty succeeding.

These problems were not simply ones of U.S. cities nor the U.S. as a whole. Poverty in Third World cities, always phenomenal, was being caught up with in the West. Every advanced Western industrial economy is plagued by high unemployment, low economic growth, and high deficits. Economic restructuring on a world scale replete with changes in international competition and standing and capital crises were causing problems for some nations, regions, metropolitan areas, and central cities. Economic restructuring within each capitalist nation was leading to uneven development where some areas flourish and others fail—leaving poverty high in the latter areas.

But in the United States, problems grew more severe not only because of economic change but also governmental action. At the federal level, not only were budgetary priorities turned toward retrenching help for the poor, but the escalating military expenditures that replaced spending on human resources were made in ways that benefitted the flourishing regions and cities with more Republican constituencies. In sum, changing urban and regional development patterns and the problems for the urban poor that spin off from these development patterns were the long-term result of social actions taken by both economic and political actors operating within a complex and changing matrix of relations between global and national political-economic forces and national and local social-political processes.

IV. CONCLUSIONS: CURRENT STRATEGIES AND PROSPECTS FOR REFORM

Evidence from the previous section covering only two urban needs (education and poverty) shows that the impetus for new urban policies rises from mounting problems in cities, not from evanescent political concerns. Although past policies proved fragile and short-lived, the distress that gave rise to them has proven to have staying power. If the plight of cities continues to be ignored, one could only reasonably expect a resurgence of the urban crisis of social movements sometime during the decade of the 1990s driven by an expanding poor population, a continuing housing shortfall, increasingly poor schools, and a persuasive almost uncontrollable urban culture full of alienation and its manifestations in escalating drugs, gangs, and crime tensions.

At this juncture, urban policy in the nation's history is up for grabs. At the federal level, demographic and economic trends are working against a resurgence of federal fiscal assistance to large cities. The fraction of the population living in large cities continues to decline. The relative economic position of the large urban centers also has continued to slide. As a result of these trends, the political clout of urban areas has eroded considerably since the mid 1960s, leaving them without the capacity to mount a successful legislative effort to expand federal aid to cities (Reischauer, 1990: 234). So unsuccessful have big-city mayors become in working through conventional electoral-representative routes that they were driven in the summer of 1992 to lead a national street protest in Washington, D.C.

Meanwhile, city governments, left to their own devices, are trying to ameliorate present conditions by and large through competing with each other, especially through offering tax incentives and subsidies to corporations. Typical local strategies for attracting and retaining translocal capital investment include a competitive and a structural strategy. The competitive strategy seeks to attract the remaining manufacturing potential of a region to a given jurisdiction. The structural strategy seeks to abet the transformation of urban economies toward characteristic retail and service sector agglomerations. Both have taken the form of private-public partnerships (Ross and Trachte, 1990).

Contemporary partnerships come in many varieties. Coalitions of business leaders have been organized, sometimes including prominent public officials, to generate local economic growth. Redevelopment authorities have been created that give selected private developers rights and responsibilities traditionally vested in the public sector, such as land clearance, administration of governmental grants, and approval of public subsidies. In the name of public-private partnership, public officials have provided an array of subsidies in efforts to stimulate private business development. Every state has issued industrial revenue bonds—tax-exempt bonds that make loans available to selected private businesses at below-market rates. Tax increment finance districts have been declared in several cities where public investments are made in selected areas, and the increased tax revenues generated by appreciating property values are retained in those areas for designated periods. Some states have established enterprise zones in which various regulations are waived or taxes are reduced. Urban Development Action Grants (UDAGs), whereby the federal government offers what amounts to seed funding for cities to leverage private investment for depressed areas, have financed several developments in many cities. Subsidies for training have been provided. Tax abatements and even cash grants have been offered in an effort to attract and retain private businesses. Partnerships have been organized around single projects and also as a part of ongoing redevelopment efforts. Community organizations have sometimes been invited to join. In virtually all cases, however, the traditionally unequal relationship between the private and public sectors has prevailed (Ross and Trachte, 1990: 3–4).

In short, both the competitive and structural strategic modes require local governments to subsidize in-migrant capital through a variety of tax, capital provision, and infrastructural schemes. Both require that local governments transform the political terrain in ways that will be perceived by potential investors as creating a propitious environment for new economic activity. Both have limitations in the context of global capitalism.

To be sure, several city governments are experimenting with new and potentially more beneficial forms of private-public partnerships. These new concepts of partnership include not only greater public control of the redevelopment process but almost more equitable distribution of benefits and burdens in local partnership activities. These concepts are exemplified by three important trends:

1. Strategic and demographical planning of economic development. Several cities have recognized that throwing incentives at developers may not be the most rational approach to urban economic development and have begun to insist on a more active public planning

presence in redevelopment policy—for example, funding the development of neighborhood organizations to engage in strategic planning.

2. Linkage policies. In return for lucrative development rights, primarily in downtown areas, cities require developers to contribute to special funds to meet community needs in such areas as housing, job training, public transportation, and child care.

3. Community economic development. The development of community development corporations (CDCs). Targeting their efforts on low-income areas, CDCs engage in hard and soft development activities; constructing or rehabilitating housing, starting small businesses, providing child care, or offering skills training. The goal of every CDC is the immediate relief of severe economic, social, and physical distress—and eventually, wider regeneration of the community. CDCs have received most of their funding from local and state agencies, as well as from private foundations such as the Ford Foundation. Increasingly, however, some private corporations and banks have become investors in CDC projects (Squires, 1991).

Although these strategies pose new hope, it is unlikely that they will be enough to succeed given the very real upper hand capital has compared with labor in the context of the new mobility of global capitalism in which corporations are freer than ever before to move to anywhere they have even the slightest cost advantage. What remains needed is a national (and perhaps increasingly even an internationally coordinated) approach.

Thus, beyond a firm understanding of city problems and the causes of city problems; beyond a firm grasp of economic, population, and social trends that vitally affect cities; beyond firm knowledge about which programs have worked and which have failed in the past and why; and beyond an overarching philosophy to guide the development of urban policy (Reischauer, 1990) in the context of global economic restructuring, what is needed is agreement that people in cities and their problems are a priority for all levels of government—even given budgetary constraints—because massive aid must be provided if the nation is to solve its urban problems. Coordinating strategies between diverse federal agencies with their disparate roles, missions, and client groups as well as between regions and cities; and finally developing the political will to help cities (especially among those affluent whites who have moved out to their own incorporated areas) is a task that only the federal government can undertake.

For instance, because cities' tax policies are in competition with each other, individual cities will not adjust their tax policy radically in accordance with needs of people or infrastructure. As a result, not only will people continue to be impoverished, but bridges will continue to collapse, urban infrastructures will decay, crumble, and crash; the sky will continue to fall. Only the federal government can impose uniform tax rates across all taxpayers and cities—they should step in (Reischauer, 1990).

At the level of the citizenry as a whole, Americans need to realize once again that they are all connected to the nation's cities. Since at least the industrial revolution, the United States has relied on the economic growth that her cities spurred. Today, even as American metropolises grow grayer and more decayed, from within them continue to come the economic growth, the art and culture, and the great diversity of people and opinion that combined are the lifeblood of the nation. Those who live in rural America depend on the city for its products. Those who live in suburban America depend on the city for the jobs to which so many of them travel into the city each day and the entertainment still countless others travel to frequently. When the last historic U.S. city is left to crumble, the death of the nation will not be far behind.

NOTES

1. On March 3, 1991, four Los Angeles policemen were videotaped beating Rodney King, an African-American while 17 other police officers watched. "Shown over and over on television, the amateur videotape became the most visible police use of force in this country's history and put the issue of police brutality on the national agenda" (*New York Times*, April 30, 1992). The four police officers in the videotape faced charges of assault and other criminal violations. A jury composed of 11 whites and one Latino, however, acquitted all four officers of assault on April 29, 1992. The jury concluded that the policemen had not broken any laws when they clubbed 56 times and kicked the mostly prone motorist. What appeared to most Americans of all races as a clear case of police brutality and injustice according to public opinion polls was the catalyst for a riot of poor blacks, Latinos, and whites in South Central Los Angeles resulting in the deaths of more than 50 persons. Several other big and medium-sized cities as diverse as Eugene, Oregon, Minneapolis, Minnesota, Madison, Wisconsin, and Atlanta, Georgia, also erupted in violence in the fractious aftermath. For examples of poll data, see *New York Times*, May 11, 1992: A1, 7, and *Newsweek*, May 11, 1992: 14–17.

   In the spring of 1993, the four police officers were charged under federal statutes with violating King's civil rights. A federal jury convicted two of the officers (Stacey Koon and Lawrence Powell) of civil rights violations and acquitted two other officers on April 17, 1993. The verdict at least partially vindicated "the 20-20 vision of everyone who had seen King's civil rights mutilated on videotape." For story of second verdict and its aftermath, see *Newsweek*, April 26, 1993: 21–31.

2. In April 1991, a quarter billion gallons of murky Chicago River water gushed into a nearly 60-mile network of turn-of-the-century freight tunnels under the Loop closing downtown businesses for days. A top city official had known about the leak but, acting for a cash-strapped government, had delayed repairs costing only about $50,000. Weakened infrastructure could cause similar disasters across the country. For example, New York City, where many water lines were laid before 1890, has more than 600 water main breaks a year; historic sections of Boston and Washington, D.C., sit atop sewer lines predating 1912; and even younger cities, such as Stockton, California, are struggling as demand often pushes pressure in sewer pipes to 140% of capacity. Meanwhile, according to the U.S. Conference of Mayors, more than 7000 public works projects are on hold because cities cannot finance them. See *Newsweek*, April 27, 1992: 22–27.

3. For a discussion of the differences between decisions, programs, policies, and social movements, see H. Heclo (1974: 1–16) and D. P. Moynihan (1970).

4. Only in the past decade have some state courts begun to grant local governments rights to challenge their state in courts. "The implications of these events are extraordinary in light of the century-old Dillon's rule" (Pagano, 1990: 101).

5. By choosing to deal directly with hundreds of localities, the federal government guaranteed bureaucratic complexity and lots of red tape. Different local governments have different functional responsibilities, internal structures, politics, and taxing authority. In some areas, the urban problems that concerned federal policy makers were exacerbated, if not caused, by various restraints state laws placed on cities. Examples of this include the limited annexation authority that most large cities had and their inability to tax workers in the city who commuted from the suburbs. In addition, few urban problems respected local jurisdictional boundaries. Thus, the recipient of a federal grant often had only a piece of the problem within its area of responsibility. Trying to get around these problems, the national government tried to design programs in excruciating detail to try to anticipate every circumstance that might arise. This created a system characterized by red tape and regulation under which recipients were forced to submit plans, preproposals, proposals, and progress reports. Federal bureaucrats were charged with reviewing these submissions at every stage, thus maximizing the opportunity for conflict and contention. In the end, neither federal grant givers nor local recipients were happy. The latter chafed under the red tape, excessive regulations, and delays imposed by the national government. The former were overwhelmed by the work load and stung by the criticism they received from what were supposed to be grateful beneficiaries. In addition, the growing import of federal-local fiscal relations caused strains with the state governments. Some cities were

accused of being more attuned to the wishes and priorities of the national government than to those of the state capitals. Some states, partially as a reaction to these new strains, slacked off their own efforts to deal with the problems of their big cities. For discussion, see Kaplan and James (1990).

6. Big-city governments had become greatly dependent on federal assistance in the 1970s. For example, Baltimore, Buffalo, Cleveland, and Detroit, to name only four of the nation's most distressed cities, all received at least 40 cents in direct federal aid for every dollar raised from own-sources in 1977. Thus, the sharp cutback in federal assistance left their economies in disastrous peril. For discussion, see Bahl, Dimcombe, and Shulman (1990).

REFERENCES

Allen, R. L. (1970). *Black Awakening in Capitalist America.* Anchor Doubleday, Garden City, NY.

Bahl, R. (1987). The New Urban Fiscal Economics. In *State and Local Finance in the Era of New Federalism.* M. E. Bell (Ed.). JAI Press, Greenwich, CT, pp. 77–114.

Bahl, R., Duncombe, W., and Shulman, W. (1990). The new anatomy of urban fiscal problems. In *The Future of National Urban Policy.* M. Kaplan and F. James (Eds.). Duke University, Durham, NC, pp. 32–59.

Berry, B. J. (1985). Islands of Renewal in Seas of Decay. In *The New Urban Reality.* P. E. Peterson (Ed.). Brookings Institution, Washington, D.C.

Brown, L. R., and Jacobsen, J. L. (1987). *The Future of Urbanization: Facing the Econological and Economic Constraints.* Worldwatch Institute, Washington, D.C.

Coons, J. E., Clune III, W. H. and Sugarman, S. D. (1970). *Private Wealth and Public Education.* Harvard University Press, Cambridge, MA.

Cuciti, P. (1990). A nonurban policy: Recent public policy shifts affecting cities. In *The Future of National Urban Policy.* M. Kaplan and F. James (Eds.). Duke University, Durham, NC, pp. 235–252.

Department of Justice (1991). *Crime in the United States.* Department of Justice, Washington, D.C., p. 16.

Edelman, P. (1990). Urban Poverty: Where Do We Go from Here? In *The Future of National Urban Policy.* M. Kaplan and F. James (Eds.). Duke University, Durham, NC, pp. 89–100.

Erie, S. P. (1988). *Rainbow's End: Irish-Americans and the Dilemmas of Urban Machine Politics, 1840–1985.* University of California Press, Berkeley, CA.

Fossett, J. W. (1983). *Federal Aid to Big Cities: The Politics of Dependence.* U.S. Government Printing Office, Washington, D.C.

Gilder, G. (1981). *Wealth and Poverty.* Basic Books, New York.

Gold, S. D., and Fabaricius, M. A. (1989). *How States Limit City and County Property Taxes and Spending.* National Conference of State Legislatures, Denver.

Haerkl, E. H. (1988). National assessment of education progress in the USA: Achievement, changes in achievement, and between-state comparisons. *International Journal of Education Research* 12: 671–699.

Hahn, A., Danzberger, J., and Lefkowitz, B. (1987). *Dropouts in America: Enough is Known for Action.* Institute for Educational Leadership, Washington, D.C.

Heclo, H. (1974). *Modern Social Politics in Britain and Sweden: From Relief to Income Maintenance.* Yale University Press, New Haven, CT, pp. 1–16.

Hiebowitsh, P. S. (1989). International comparisons and U.S. school reform. *The Education Digest* 55: 23–29.

Jencks, C. (1992). *Rethinking Social Policy.* Harvard University Press, Cambridge, MA.

Johnston, W. B., and Packer, A. E. (1987). *Workforce 2000: Work and Workers for the Twenty-First Century.* The Hudson Institute, Indianapolis, IN.

Kaplan, M., and James, F. (Eds.) (1990). *The Future of National Urban Policy.* Duke University Press, Durham, NC.

Kasarda, J. D. (1985). Urban Change and Minority Opportunities. In *The New Urban Reality.* P. E. Peterson (Ed.). Brookings Institution, Washington, D.C.

Katz, M. B. (1989). *The Undeserving Poor: From the War on Poverty to the War on Welfare.* Pantheon Books, New York.

Katznelson, I. (1981). *City Trenches: Urban Politics and the Patterning of Class in the United States*. Pantheon Books, New York, p. 110.

Kozol, J. (1991). *Savage Inequalities: Children in America's Schools*. HarperCollins, New York.

Long, N. E. (1978). Federalism and perverse incentives: What is needed for a workable theory or reorganization for cities. *Publius: The Journal of Federalism* 8: 77.

Mead, L. (1986). *Beyond Entitlement: The Social Obligations of Citizenship*. Free Press, New York.

Mollenkopf, J. (1991). New York City: The great anomaly. In *Racial Politics in American Cities*. R. P. Browning, D. R. Marshall, and D. H. Tabb (Eds.). Longman, New York, pp. 114–141.

Moynihan, D. P. (1970). Policy vs. program in the '70s. *The Public Interest* 20: 414.

Murray, C. (1984). *Losing Ground: American Society Policy 1950–1980*. Basic Books, New York.

National Governors' Association. (1987). *Bringing Down the Barriers*. Washington, D.C.

National League of Cities (1987). *City Fiscal Conditions in 1987*, a Research Report of the National League of Cities.

New York Times, "King Video Shown Around the World," April 30, 1992, A1.

New York Times, "Rodney King Verdict: Poll Finds Disapproval," May 11, 1992, A1.

Newman, F., Palaich, R., and Wilensky, R. (1990). Reengaging State and Federal Policymakers in the Problems of Urban Education. In *The Future of National Urban Policy*. M. Kaplan and F. James (Eds.). Duke University Press, Durham, NC, pp. 61–88.

Nozick, R. (1974). *Anarchy, State, and Utopia*. Basic Books, New York.

Orfield, G. (1985). Ghettoization and its alternatives. In *The New Urban Reality*. P. E. Peterson (Ed.). Brookings, Washington, D.C., pp. 161–193.

Ornstein, A. (1987). Urban Demographics for the 1980s: Educational Implications. *Education and Urban Society* 16: 477–496.

Pagano, M. A. (1990). State-local relations in the 1990s. *Annals* 509: 94–106.

Peterson, P. E. (1976). *School Politics: Chicago Style*. University of Chicago Press, Chicago.

—— (1981). *City Limits*. University of Chicago Press, Chicago, pp. 3–4.

—— (1983). Urban politics and changing schools: A competitive view. In *Schools in Cities: Consensus and Conflict in American Educational History*. R. K. Goodenow and D. Ravitch (Eds.). Holmes and Meier, New York, pp. 229–247.

Phillips, K. (1990). *The Politics of Rich and Poor*, Random House, New York.

Piven, F. F., and Cloward, R. (1977). *Poor People's Movements: Why They Succeed, How They Fail*. Pantheon Books, New York.

Reischauer, R. D. (1990). The rise and fall of national urban policy: The fiscal dimension. In *The Future of National Urban Policy*. M. Kaplan and F. James (Eds.). Duke University Press, Durham, NC, pp. 225–234.

Research and Policy Committee of the Committee for Economic Development (1987). *Children in Need—Investment Strategies for the Educationally Disadvantaged*. Committee for Economic Development, Washington, D.C.

Rosenbaum, W. A. (1991). *Environmental Politics and Policy*. Congressional Quarterly, Washington, D.C.

Rossier, M. (1990). International comparisons in science classrooms. *Studies in Science Education* 18: 87–114.

Ross, R. J., and Trachte, K. C. (1990). *Global Capitalism: The New Leviathan*. State University of New York Press, Albany.

Schwarz, J. E., and Volgy, T. J. (1992). *The Forgotten Americans: Thirty Million Working Poor in the Land of Opportunity*. W. W. Norton, New York.

The Siege of L.A. *Newsweek*, May 11, 1992, p. 30.

Smith, M. P. (1988). *City, State and Market: The Political Economy of Urban Society*. Basil Blackwell, New York.

Squires, G. (1991). *Unequal Partnerships*. University of Chicago, Chicago.

Thomas, R. D. (1990). National-local relations and the city's dilemma. *Annals* 509: 106–17.

Thurow, L. (1992). *Head to Head: The Coming Economic Battle Among Japan, Europe and America.* Morrow, New York.

U.S. Bureau of the Census (1992). Current Population Reports, Series P-60, no. 180. *Money Income of Households, Families and Persons in the United States: 1991.* U.S. Government Printing Office, Washington, D.C.

U.S. Education Department (1991). *America 2000: An Education Strategy Sourcebook.* Government Printing Office, Washington, D.C.

Verstegen, D. (1992). International comparisons of educational spending: A review and analysis of reports. *Journal of Education Finance* 17: 257–271.

Washington Post (February 1, 1993). Economists View Public Sector Spending. A1, D4.

Wilson, W. J. (1987). *The Truly Disadvantaged: The Inner City, the Underclass, and Public Policy.* University of Chicago Press, Chicago.

W. T. Grant Foundation Commission on Work, Family and Citizenship (1988). *The Forgotten Half: Non-College Youth in America.* W. T. Grant Foundation, Washington, D.C.

UNIT TWO
SPECIFIC POLICY PROBLEMS

Part E
PROBLEMS WITH A POLITICAL SCIENCE EMPHASIS

12
Foreign Policy Analysis

Valerie M. Hudson
Brigham Young University, Provo, Utah

The origins, evolution, decline, and renaissance of the field of foreign policy analysis is an exciting story in social science. If written only 5 or 6 years ago, this chapter would have struggled to mask the sense of stagnation that pervaded the field. Now no such whitewash is needed. Foreign policy analysis is once again at the forefront of theoretical and methodological progression in international relations. The largest research section in the International Studies Association is the Foreign Policy Analysis Section; the Association also has had four consecutive presidents whose research field is foreign policy analysis. Classes in foreign policy analysis are being added to curricula of universities; articles in the tradition of foreign policy analysis are making their way into high-profile journals in international relations. These events are as much a function of the changing world system as they are of the hard work of foreign policy analysts in pushing back the frontier of their field.

What is foreign policy analysis? Where did it come from? Where is it going? This chapter attempts to answer these questions, whereas pointing out the most salient or exemplary contributions to the literature. Please note that this chapter is not meant to be an exhaustive catalogue of every work touching on the subject of foreign policy. Rather it serves to define and set forth the core of the foreign policy analysis research agenda.

I. THE EVOLUTION OF FOREIGN POLICY ANALYSIS

A. Genesis

Although it can be claimed that the study of foreign policy is as old as the study of interstate relations, foreign policy analysis as a coherent research field distinct from other fields in international relations did not exist before World War II. This is not to say that foreign policy analysis does not examine relevant works that predate its emergence as a field (please refer to the list of References), but rather that a rationale for interest in certain of these works and not others began to appear with the emergence of the field. The roots of foreign policy analysis are to be found in the Realist tradition that held intellectual sway in the wake of World War II. Thinking about how the world should be—so characteristic of the years after World War I (Carr, 1939)—gave way to serious reflection on how the world was and what made it tick. Scientific investigation of international affairs seemed called for so that world events would not be surprising or unforeseen. Science would offer the control that philosophy or religion could not. Although a simplification, this is one way to describe the realism/scientism nexus that culminated in the behavioralist movement in the study of international affairs. (The influence of behavioralism, of course, was felt in all the social sciences.)

Interestingly, behavioralism in international affairs bifurcated in parallel with what was happening in the other social sciences. The two disciplines that took behavioralism to heart and carried it furthest, although along very different lines, were economics and psychology. Hallmarks of scientism, such as controlled experimentation, quantification and aggregation of cases, analysis by statisticomathematical techniques, and strict replication of results, are still part and parcel of these social science disciplines. What they are interested in explaining is at one level the same—human behavior. At another level, they are motivated by two different sets of explanatory concerns: economics is motivated by a desire to explain human behavior in general; psychology is motivated by a desire to explain human behavior in specific. Although economics starts with the individual classically rational human being, the goal is explanation of a much larger aggregate of such classically rational human beings. Although psychology may start with broad generalizations about human psychology, the goal is the specific application of these generalizations to a particular human in a particular set of circumstances. Neither orientation is right or wrong—they are just different.

Behavioralism in international relations experienced a similar split within the field itself. Some took what I would call the economics route to understanding nation-state behavior; others took the psychology route to understanding nation-state behavior. The first group—those who for lack of a better term might be called QIPers (with QIP standing for quantitative international politics, although their descendants might be better known as rational choice modelers)—desired to strip the subject of international relations down to its essential characteristics, relate those characteristics via statistical or mathematical equations, and analyze how closely they could fit these equations to nation-state behavior. If the fit was fairly good, explanation was said to obtain. The most famous example of this approach was the relatively short-lived but extremely influential school of arms race modelers, who, building upon the work of Richardson (1960a, 1960b), used differential equations to simulate the build-up of arms between two hostile nations (see, e.g., Caspary, 1967; Wallace, 1979; Zinnes, 1976). Here, as in economics, the goal is to be able to black box most of the detail distinguishing one nation-state from another. In this way, a generalized theory of nation-state behavior is possible.

Indeed, some controversy has raged in international relations over this very point: consider the following exchange by Kenneth Waltz and Robert Keohane (both belonging to the neorealist economic–style school):

> I essayed an international-political theory and not a domestic one. . . . The behavior and practice of states and of statesmen are omitted from international-political theory not because of their unimportance but because their exclusion from the systems structure requires a distinct theory dealing with the politics and policies of states. I see something problematic about this only for those who think that domestic and international politics must be combined in one theory. . . . The theoretical separation of domestic

and international politics need not bother us unduly. Economists get along quite well with separate theories of markets and firms. Students of international politics will do well to concentrate on separate theories of internal and external politics until someone figures a way to unite them. (Waltz, 1986: 339–340)

And Keohane (1986: 23–24) stated:

A number of economists are discontented with the disjunction between our knowledge of firms' behavior and orthodox microeconomics theory. . . . One of the issues highlighted by the debate between Waltz and his critics is precisely how serious is the disjunction between the assumptions of our systemic theory and what we know about unit-level behavior. Some of us seek eventually to build an integrated theory of world politics, linking the domestic and international levels of analysis, rather than being content with unit-level and system-level theories that are inconsistent with one another. Insofar as this is our goal, we should hesitate before following the neoclassical economists into what may be an intellectual dead-end.

The alternative is to view what is inside the black box to be of the most theoretical interest—this would be the analogue of psychology. Again, this is not a "better" choice, it is a different choice. Just as economic-style analysis of nation-state behavior has its advantages and drawbacks, so too does a more psychological-style analysis of foreign policy. The psychological, or what I would like to term the cognitive approach to foreign policy studies, seeks to unpack the black box of foreign policy decision making. Although not discounting the aggregate or systems explanations of foreign policy making, it suggests that such explanations cannot account for the wide diversity of behavior we see within the same international system. Nor, and this is especially relevant at this point in history, can such explanations account for system change. For that type of understanding, we need to examine the particularities of nation-states—we need to examine the levels *below* that of the nation-state.

As can be anticipated, this will add a lot of detail to our analysis. The upside of this is that we can explain (and perhaps even predict) in a much more specific fashion what nations do under what circumstances. The downside of this is that elegant and parsimonious theories that can be embodied in differential equations will prove elusive. This has been very troubling for the field of foreign policy analysis, as we shall see. Having adopted "high" and "scientific" standards of behavioralism, it was difficult for foreign policy analysts to apply these to what often turned out to be masses of messy, nonquantifiable data. More on this challenge later.

What levels lie below that of the nation-state? In a nutshell, human agents, singly or in groups. One could examine societal groups, such as farmers, intellectual elites, businessmen, religious organizations, political action groups, and so forth. One could examine political parties and the voters who support them. Within the government, one could examine bureaucracies and organizations. Or one could examine interorganizational groups, such as standing or ad hoc committees. Also, one could examine heads of state and their immediate circle of advisors. Overlaying all of these groups, one could examine broader national idiosyncracies such as culture, society, and history. One could examine internal economic conditions as these interface with external economic realities. All in all, the information that helps us answer the question as to why nations act as they do would be included in the field of foreign policy analysis. To borrow a felicitous phrase from Putnam (1988), nations do what they do because they are playing a "two-level game"; they are resolving the matrix of power internal to their nation and resolving the matrix of power external to their nation at the very same time. Who the players are, what their interests are, what their backgrounds are, what their capabilities are, what their perceptions are, what they stand to gain and from whom, and what they stand to lose and to whom, and how this all relates in the players' minds to the situation at hand and how they choose at last to make their decisions and whether any of this can be generalized to other cases constitute the core research inquiries of foreign policy analysis. The field has never been faulted for lack of theoretical ambition.

Two early works provided the conceptual and methodological spin that gave foreign policy analysis its distinctive approach. The first, by Richard Snyder, H. W. Bruck, and Burton Sapin (1954) is entitled *Decision-Making as an Approach to the Study of International Politics* (also see Snyder et al., 1963). The second, by James N. Rosenau (written in 1964 and published in 1966) is a book chapter entitled, "Pre-theories and Theories of Foreign Policy." The seminal influence of these works on the field that ultimately emerged cannot be overstated. Indeed, several of the major players who helped to construct the field in the 1960s and early 1970s knew both Richard Snyder and James Rosenau personally, either as their students or as their colleagues. Foreign policy analysis began, like many other research fields, as an "invisible college" (Crane, 1972; the early evidence of this can be found in the Michigan State conferences put together by Edward Azar and the later Inter-University Consortium of Comparative Foreign Policy).

In my opinion, Snyder's work offered a refreshing break from the geopolitical perspective of much traditional realist analysis of the postwar era (indeed, even of the prewar era). The chess metaphor was all too ingrained: the Soviet Union did X because it was in their national interest, so the United States did Y to protect its national interests from the effects of X, whereupon the Soviets reacted with Z to protect its interests from the effects of Y, and so on. The Snyder approach broke apart the monolithic view of nation-states: "the United States" could mean the President, it could mean the Secretary of Defense, it could mean the whole Defense Department, it could mean the Congress. Indeed, all of these entities could be doing things at once—and not all of these things might logically go together. Furthermore, the "national interest," that hoary chestnut, might not exist—it might be more productive to talk of the various players' interests, not all of which might coincide, and not all of which could be coherently related to anything resembling an objective national interest.

The Snyder book built on and contributed to the work that characterized the beginning of the "cognitive revolution" in the social sciences. To me, it asserts that if humans cannot be said to be classically rational, then nation-states, which after all are but shorthand for collectivities of human decision makers, cannot be expected to act in a classically rational fashion either. If so, we had better figure out how they really *do* make decisions, or else we will never be able to explain or predict their behavior. These findings came pouring in from all of the social sciences—psychology, economics, sociology, anthropology. They even gave rise to new and interdisciplinary fields of study, such as organizational behavior. Humans satisfice instead of optimize (Simon, 1985). They never possess and never seek perfect information. They seem incapable of considering more than two or three alternatives at any given time. They process information strangely under stress. Ulterior agendas, such as the need for group consensus or the desire to protect or extend "turf," undermine a rational catalogueing of expected costs and benefits, and emotional and ideological motivations similarly undercut a rational cost/benefit analysis. A situation can be interpreted in a myriad of ways, with such interpretation being dependent on the historical precedents used, the personalities and experiences of the humans interpreting the situation, and so forth (see Purkitt, 1991; and Kahneman et al., 1982, for excellent overviews of these types of findings). Collectivities of humans multiply the complexity of the decision calculus in logarithmic fashion (e.g., Arrow's paradox).

If Snyder's work inspired several generations to look "below" the nation-state level of analysis, and to focus on the foreign policy *decision* as the point of inquiry, Rosenau's work (1966) insisted on a systematic and scientific approach hinging on the method of comparing nations to the end of coming up with cross-nationally and longitudinally applicable generalizations about nation-state behavior. There is a now famous matrix in Rosenau's "pretheories" chapter that shows how eight types of nations (permutations of large/small size, developed/underdeveloped economy, and open/closed system of government) are influenced to a greater or lesser extent by different levels of foreign policy analysis. So, for example, small, underdeveloped, closed nations may be much more affected by variables at the individual level of analysis (i.e., the personality of the head of state) than might large, developed, open nations, which might be much more sensitive to societal pressure and pressure because of their perceived role in the international system. Purportedly such differences would exist regardless of the identities of the nations involved or the time period examined. Furthermore, it was clear that Rosenau encouraged a scientific confirmation or disconfirmation of these hypotheses through empirical testing. Could replicable studies with hefty N sizes be created to extend the scientific study of foreign policy? The major assumption here is that nations and their behaviors are comparable in some meaningful sense. Last, Rosenau explicitly rejected the notion that explanation at only one level of analysis was sufficient to comprehend the diversity of nation-state behavior. Explanations that *integrated* insights from several levels of analysis would prove to be the most satisfactory and the most capable of prediction.

The astute reader can already foresee some of the storm clouds on the horizon from adopting these two works as a conceptual and methodological starting point for a field of research. These difficulties will surface in a very stark way later in the evolution of foreign policy analysis. For now, let us see what the first flowering of foreign policy analysis, which was called comparative foreign policy, brought.

B. Comparative Foreign Policy

I was not part of the first generation of comparative foreign policy researchers, but sometimes I wish I had been. True, I see many of the shortcomings of the work of that generation, yet those were halcyon days, when comparative foreign policy seemed of infinite potential, when no problem seemed intractable. To talk to some of those in that generation, it seemed their goal was nothing less than a grand unified theory of all foreign policy behavior for all nations for all time. Some set of master equations would link all the relevant variables, independent and dependent, together, and when correlated with massive data bases providing values for these variables, would yield r-squares approaching 1.0. It was ambitious, perhaps overly so; it was visionary, perhaps naively so, but the sheer enormity of the tast called forth immense efforts in data collection, theory building, and methodological innovation that have few parallels in international relations. Ah, to be young and in comparative foreign policy in the late 1960s and early 1970s!

1. Data Collection

To realize their vision, CFPers (those in the field of comparative foreign policy) needed data, and lots of it, for many countries over many years. They needed data about that which they wanted to explain—foreign policy—and data about that which they felt would explain it. In general, this resulted in two distinct data collection efforts.

Before CFPers could collect data on foreign policy, they needed to conceptualize what they meant by that term. What was foreign policy? How did it differ from domestic policy?

Who was a legitimate foreign policy actor? How were foreign policy goals related to foreign policy behavior? Could you infer goals from behavior? Were foreign policies comparable, and if so, how? Indeed, an entire edited volume resulted from the work of one of the projects on this score (see Callahan et al., 1982). Borrowing from the psychological literature, it was felt that foreign policy was a subset of social behavior (more particularly, a subset of behaviors we call influence attempts), which could be described by the answers to the following question: Who does what to whom, how?

Taking this approach, it becomes clearer how foreign policy could be conceptualized. Foreign policy is an influence attempt characterized by the fact that either the recipient or the channel of the influence attempt is an entity external to the initiator of the attempt. (For a much fuller discussion of this entire point and those that follow, see Hermann, 1981, the predecessor to this chapter in the first edition of this book.) If we stipulate that we are interested in cases in which the initiators of influence attempts are nation-states or collectivities of nation-states (which most CFPers did—there were a few exceptions), then it follows that the attempt must be made by the legitimate authorities of the nation-state to influence or to use as a means of influence entities outside of the nation-state's political jurisdiction.

Furthermore, if we can describe the influence attempt as an action or behavior (who does what to whom, how?), then it is apparent that the true dependent variable in comparative foreign policy is foreign policy *behavior*, the tangible artifact of foreign *policy*. By this is meant that foreign policy is the course of action chosen on the basis of the decision makers' goals in respect to a certain situation. The implementation of that choice, which choice is by and large unobservable, is the foreign policy behavior, which behavior is by and large observable. The only recourse of the researcher interested in foreign policy is to infer it from foreign policy behavior (though this can be problematic, as Snyder and others have shown).

Taking this approach, the concept of a foreign policy "event" becomes a natural next step. If foreign policy behavior is your dependent variable, and if these behaviors are viewed as a series of influence attempts, then what you need for dependent variable data is a list of all influence attempts by nation-states to or using foreign entities. What would this list look like? It would look like a series of international events. Where would you get these international events? From newspapers, chronologies, government cable traffic, and so forth. Thus was spawned the great events data collection projects, which were funded primarily by the government (the National Science Foundation [NSF] or the Defense Department: Andriole and Hopple [1981] estimate that over $5 million was spent by the federal government on events data over the period 1967–1981). Many undergraduate and graduate international relations students of that era were employed to comb through these sources and pull out international events, code them according to elaborate coding rules found in hefty coding manuals, have their coding periodically checked for intercoder reliability, and punch the coding up on computer cards. The acronyms and initialisms of these projects live on; some because the data are still being collected (by private concerns or under the auspices of the DDIR [Data Development for International Research] Project, which is funded by the NSF) and others because the data they did collect are still useful as a testing ground for hypotheses: WEIS (the World Event/Interaction Survey), COPDAB (the Conflict and Peace Data Bank), CREON (Comparative Research on the Events of Nations), DON (the Dimensionality of Nations Project), and so on.

What did the students code the events for? After all, the events as they stood in the newspapers or chronologies were not directly comparable. How do you compare a diplomatic visit with a war? The formula who does what to whom, how? was the template for much of the coding. In each of the events data sets, an actor, a date, and a recipient or target is given.

The actor is the initiator of the influence attempt, the recipient or target is the subject of the influence attempt. The rest of the coding depends on the project—WEIS has, appropriately enough, a "WEIS code" that corresponds to 63 categories of behavior; e.g., "warn," "threaten," "embargo," and so forth. There is some attempt to scale these according to whether they are hostile or friendly actions, although it is not clear that an ordinal scale (much less an interval scale) can be created from what are, after all, nominal categories. COPDAB has an ordinal "COPDAB scale," ranging from 1 to 15, that describes behavior that is more or less friendly (from merging voluntarily into one country to all-out war). There has been some attempt to transform this scale into an interval measure through a modified Delphi technique. CREON has a very elaborate coding scheme, in which there can be multiple recipients, in which "channels" of influence are also identified, and in which there are numerous foreign policy behavior "attributes," instead of only one scale, along which behaviors can be compared. For example, in CREON, there is affect, commitment, instrumentality, independence of action, issue area, and so on. *Affect* refers to the direction and intensity of expressed friendliness or hostility. *Commitment* refers to the degree to which the actor has committed resources or made explicit pledges regarding future behavior. *Instrumentality* refers to what tools of implementation were used—diplomatic, economic, military, and so forth. *Independence of action* describes whether the influence attempt was an initiative or a reaction and whether it was multilateral or bilateral in nature. *Issue area* refers to the substantive problem the event concerns. Thus, in CREON, there are several dimensions along which foreign policy behaviors can be compared and contrasted and numerous possible categories of behavior that can be assembled from the individual pieces proffered by the attributes (see Dixon and Hermann, 1984).

Data collection on the independent variables was completely dependent on the theoretical perspective of the researcher. Some chose data readily available from existing compilations— from Arthur Banks' *Cross-Polity Survey*, or the periodic *World Handbook of Political and Social Indicators*, or United Nations, World Bank, or Arms Control and Disarmament Agency data books. This was generally hard, quantified data that was easily susceptible to statistical and mathematical manipulation. Others went out and collected their own data—most still insisted the data be at at least the ordinal level of measurement precision. The numbers of independent variables were sometimes staggering. DON had hundreds of variables; CREON had over 300. Again, all were computer coded and in readiness for correlation with the coded events data.

2. Theory Building

As the data were readied, theory building, which would allow for analysis of the data, was underway. Let the reader not read into this that the two enterprises were proceeding hand in hand in some logical and coherent fashion. Sometimes this was the case (see East et al., 1978, in connection with Callahan et al., 1982); sometimes the most influential theories were constructed by people wholly unconnected with the events data movement. The following categorization represents my understanding of the major theoretical breakthroughs during the heyday of comparative foreign policy. (This categorization is heavily influenced by the predecessor chapter in the first edition of this book, whose author, Charles F. Hermann, was also my primary mentor. Please also see the wonderful essay by Gerner, 1988. A historically interesting piece of these early years is a compilation of "findings" in comparative foreign policy put together by McGowan and Shapiro, 1973.)

Individual Characteristics.   The field of political psychology has grown tremendously over the past two decades, and its insights have enlightened comparative foreign policy. It was felt that under certain scope conditions—high stress or uncertainty, high decision-making power of the head of state, and so on—that the personal characteristics of the individual leader would become very important in understanding the foreign policy behavior of the nation. Early efforts at a systematic study of leader personality effects include work on the concept of the "operational code," an idea originating with Leites (1951) and refined and extended by George (1969), Johnson (1977), Holsti (1977), Walker (1977), and others. Defining an operational code involves identifying the core political beliefs of the leader about the inevitability of conflict in the world, the leader's estimation of his or her own power to change events, and so on, as well as an exploration of the preferred means of pursuing goals that the leader adopts, such as confrontation or conciliation. Other researchers have plowed similar fields with studies of leader motivations (Barber, 1972; Cottam, 1977; Hermann, 1980; McClelland, 1985; Winter, 1973); cognitive maps (Bonham and Shapiro, 1973; Axelrod, 1976); cognitive style (Hermann, 1980; Suedfeld and Tetlock, 1975); background characteristics (Beck et al., 1973; de Rivera, 1968; Stewart, 1977), perception (Etheredge, 1978; Jervis, 1976), and foreign policy orientation (Hermann, 1984). Good edited collections include Hermann (1977) and Falkowski (1979).

Small Group Dynamics.   Some of the most exciting work during this period centered on the effect of making foreign policy decisions in small groups. Social psychologists had explored the unique dynamics of such a decision setting before, but never in relation to foreign policy decision making, where the stakes may be much higher. The most important work, of course, is that of Janis (1972) whose path-breaking volume, *Victims of Groupthink*, began an entire research tradition. In that volume, and using studies drawn specifically from the realm of foreign policy, Janis shows convincingly that the motivation to maintain group consensus can cause deterioration in the decision-making standards of small groups. The empirical research of Leana (1975), Semmel (1982), Semmel and Minix (1979), Tetlock (1979), and others extended this tradition using aggregate analysis as well as case studies. Hermann (1978) has also done considerable research into group foreign policy decision making, in which he sees groupthink as one possible outcome of several. Depending on the characteristics of the group (size, role of leader, rules for decision, autonomy of group participants), specific predictions about the outcome of the deliberations can be made based on knowledge of the structure and the process of the group.

Bureaucratic Politics.   The 1970s also saw the emergence of a research agenda focusing on the influence of bureaucratic and organizational processes on foreign policy making. Presaged by the work of Richard Snyder, this research showed how the idiosyncracies of organizational life can come to eclipse more "rational" foreign policy making. Bureaucracies put their own survival at the top of their list of priorities, and this survival is measured by relative influence vis-à-vis other organizations ("turf"), by the organization's budget, and by the morale of its personnel. The organization will jealously guard and seek to increase its capabilities, as well as to perserve undiluted what it feels to be its "essence" or "mission." Large bureaucracies also develop standard operating procedures that aloow them to react to any situation despite the organization's inherent unwieldiness. These standard operating procedures can sometimes be the undoing of more creative and innovative solutions to foreign policy decision makers operating at a level above the organization. Nonetheless, it is almost always organizations and bureaucracies that implement the decisions of these higher-ups. The interface between goals and implementation is directly confronted at this point, and there may be much slippage due to the incompatibility of the perspectives of these different types of actors. Although the articulation of this research agenda can be found in works such as

Huntington (1960), Hilsman (1967), Neustadt (1970), and Schilling et al. (1962), probably the most often cited works are Allison (1971) and Halperin (1974). (Additional works co-authored by Halperin include Allison and Halperin [1972] and Halperin and Kanter [1973].) Allison (see Allison and Halperin, 1972) offers three different "cuts" at explaining one case—the Cuban Missile Crisis of 1962. He shows that the rational actor model of foreign policy does not suffice to explain the perplexities of the case at hand, and to unravel those perplexities, one must look at organizational process on both sides (the American and Soviet sides), and at the interorganizational struggles that took place within the respective governments at that time. Halperin (1974) is an extremely detailed amalgam of generalizations about bureaucracies accompanied by unforgettable examples from American foreign policy making of the 1950s, 1960s, and 1970s. This type of research was given added impetus by the circumstances of the Vietnam War, which was popularly seen as a war run amok in part because of the imperatives of bureaucratic empire building.

National and Societal Influences.   Of all the research of comparative foreign policy at this time, explanations at the level of the society or the nation seem least compelling in retrospect. Many revolve around the question of what types of nations are likely to become involved in war (see East, 1978; East and Hermann, 1974; Kean and McGowan, 1973; Rummel, 1972, 1977, 1979; Salmore and Salmore, 1978). Are large nations more likely to go to war than small nations? Are rich nations more likely to go to war than poor nations? Given the possibility of numerous perturbing variables, it is no wonder that this approach was never very fruitful. Efforts more specifically tied to economic factors operating within the society, such as Lenin's theory of imperialism or Choucri and North's notion of lateral pressure (1975), appeared more persuasive but still seemed to amount to the international equivalent of them's that got shall get, them's that not shall lose. (Although for an intriguing exception, see Richardson and Kegley, 1980.) Research on the operation and effectiveness of various societal groups (including voters) in relation to various types of governments was in its infancy at this point in time, although some notable works such as those of Chittick (1970), Dahl (1973), Dallin (1969), Deutsch et al. (1967), Hellman (1969), and Ogata (1977) were produced. Societal character, or a nation's socialization process, was also a subject of research (see e.g., Bobrow et al., 1979; Broderson, 1961; Hess, 1963; Merelman, 1969; Renshon, 1977). The notion of a "national role conception," which defined and set expectations for nation-state behavior according to the propositions of role theory, was elucidated during this period as well (Holsti, 1970).

System Effects.   Although more a part of mainstream international relations research at this time than part of comparative foreign policy, the results of theoretical work on the effects of the international system on foreign policy behavior of nations was useful to CFPers. Although one CFPer (see East, 1978) dealt explicitly with system effects of foreign policy behavior, most research was done outside of the invisible college. The effects of system type, as elucidated by Kaplan (1957, 1972), may depend on the number of poles in the system, the distribution of power among the poles, and the rules of the system game that permit its maintenance. This structure may then determine to a large extent the range of permissible foreign policy behavior of nations. The work of Waltz (1954, 1978) was extremely influential (and still is) in its description of the effects of an anarchical world system on the behavior of its member states. Rosecrance (1963), Hoffman (1961), Singer et al. (1972), and others also endeavored to trace the effects of system structure on resulting behavior, especially the relative incidence of war. Although significant and insightful, comparative foreign policy did not emphasize (although it also did not dismiss) this type of explanation, but rather it pointed out that variation in behavior during the time when a certain system is maintained cannot be explained by reference to system structure because the structure has not changed. Thus, explanation of that variation must be found at lower levels of analysis, where variation in the independent variables can be identified.

Integrated Analyses. To a hard-core CFPer, the ultimate aim was an integrated explanation of foreign policy behavior that tied together explanatory variables at all relevant levels of analysis. Unsurprisingly, these were few and far between. (An interesting exception not discussed here is the initial pedagogical, later research-oriented computer simulations of Guetzkow and his students [Guetzkow, 1963].) The four most ambitious efforts in CFP were those of Brecher (1972) and his associates, of the IBA Project (Wilkenfeld et al., 1980), of DON (Rummel, 1972, 1977), and of the CREON Project (East et al., 1978). These efforts were, in my opinion, inspired by the work of James Rosenau to one extent or another (DON the least, CREON the most). The explanatory systems included independent variables at all or nearly all levels of anlaysis, they were linked by propositions to properties or types of foreign policy behavior, and at least three of the four attempted to confirm or disconfirm by aggregate empirical analysis those propositions. To make a long story short (although I heartily encourage readers to investigate these works themselves, as they are fascinating), the empirical results were mixed. After all that effort and data collection and proposition construction and statistical manipulation, the r-squares were not very high! As well imagined, this was most distressing to the field of comparative foreign policy, and this ushered in a period of dismay and disenchantment.

C. Decline of Comparative Foreign Policy

A period of critical self-reflection began in the late 1970s and continued until the late 1980s. The very term *Comparative Foreign Policy* acquired connotations of old-fashioned naivete. Membership in the Comparative Foreign Policy Section of the International Studies Association plummeted. Those who had been near (but not at) the heart of comparative foreign policy studies began to publically vivisect it. Those at the heart of the research agenda, whereas never forsaking it, began to search for new directions. Theoretical, methodological, and empirical advances are very hard to find in the literature of this period. Criticism, sympathetic or not, is easy to find during this time (see, e.g., Ashley, 1976, 1987; Caporaso et al., 1987; East, 1987; Hermann and Peacock, 1987; Kegley, 1980; Munton, 1976; Smith, 1987). At one point, in exasperation, Kegley (1980: 12) chides, "CFP risks being labelled a cult of methodological flagellomaniacs."

To be blunt, this period of criticism from within and without was much needed and a very healthy development. Comparative foreign policy could not have continued as it had to that point. There were too many problems and inconsistencies in its approach, which needed to be sorted out before any future progress could be made. The stumbling blocks that I see include the following.

1. The tension between the desire for a hard science–like grand unified theory and the assumption that parsimony is not the right avenue to take if one really wants to explain and predict foreign policy behavior. Snyder (1954) and Rosenau (1964) are at best uneasy bedfellows in this regard, and basing a field of inquiry on these works will inevitably bring this inconsistency to light. Which do we really want: richly detailed, comprehensively researched explanations of a few cases, or overarching, fairly abstract, not comprehensively researched explanation of thousands of events? You can see the problem in desiring richly detailed, comprehensively researched explanations of thousands of events—it ain't going to happen in your

lifetime or mine! But the original CFPers rejected the case study approach as being unscientific and too much like the soft, anecdotal research of the "traditionalists" (Kegley, 1980). CFPers wanted to be behavioralists and to be scientific, and a hallmark of this was aggregate empirical testing of cross-nationally applicable generalizations across large N sizes. At the same time, they were committed to unpacking the black box of decision making, so the lists of explanatory variables they found to be useful grew longer and longer, and their disdain for the parsimonious "chess-match" approach to understanding foreign policy grew in lock step with their research findings. In retrospect, it was clear that push had to come to shove at some point. To which goal were CFPers more wedded? It began to prove impossible to be the servant of two masters.

2. A second concern was over the relative importance of being "policy relevant." CFP events data projects had originally sold the government on the notion that CFP would be policy relevant. To that end, events data were used to try and set up "early warning systems" that would alert policy makers to crises in the making around the world (as if policy makers do not also read the newspapers from which events data come!). Computer-aided tools with strange acronyms began to appear—EWAMS (Early Warning and Monitoring System), CASCON (Computer-Aided Systems for Handling Information on Local Conflicts), CACIS (Computer-Aided Conflict Information System), XAIDS (Crisis Management Executive Decision Aids) (see Andriole and Hopple, 1981). These never amounted to anything more than an intellectual exercise because the events themselves can be had from other sources—it was the theory that explained and predicted them that would be of use, and that theorizing was stuck at the level of globally applicable but specifically vacuous bivariate hypotheses such as "large nations participate more in international interactions than small nations." There was a fundamental disjunction between the goal of being able to say something predictive about a specific nation at a specific time in a specific sets of circumstances (which would be very policy relevant, but which might turn you into a—shudder—country expert) and the goal of grand unified theory (which was not very policy relevant, but which qualified you as a scientist and generalist—indeed, most hard-core CFP types and their students never developed a regional expertise, as did most of their peers in international relations). Which goal was more important?

3. There was a chasm between the methods used to construct and test the theory and the subject matter of the theory. The chain of reasoning seemed to go like this: If you want to be scientific, you must empirically test your theories. Adequate empirical testing of theories implies testing over large N sizes to ensure validity and reliability of results. Large N size testing necessitates quantification of data, so that large amounts of data may be processed using statistical or mathematical techniques. Therefore, CFP should construct and test its theories using quantified data and statistical and/or mathematical techniques of data manipulation. Obviously, something is missing in this reasoning: An examination of what would be appropriate in light of the nature of the subject matter—foreign policy decision making. Are the variables useful in understanding foreign policy behavior also usefully quantified? Are the ways in which factors are integrated in the minds of human decision makers expressable in statistical or mathematical equations? Are the dynamics of evolving perceptions and constant feedback to and modification thereof captured adequately by numbers and equations? Are regression techniques the best way to determine if one's theory matches one's data given the nature of the subject? Are our preferred techniques helping us to achieve our theoretical goals or preventing us from ever achieving them? This methodological crisis caused some to abandon the field as forever sterile. For others, the crisis sparked a search for methods that were more appropriate. In either case, during the crisis, little in the way of recognizable CFP

research was written or published, although a lot of hard mental effort was in fact taking place at several key universities around the country.

D. Rebirth: Foreign Policy Analysis

A happy coincidence of two evolutionary milestones in the field of international relations formed the basis for a rebirth of CFP under the new and less connotation-laden name of foreign policy analysis. These turning points were the end of the Cold Ware era and the adoption of new theoretical aims with correspondingly different methods by those who had practiced CFP.

The significance of the first can be seen when remembering the larger landscape of the field of international relations during the time of CFP's decline. What was in ascendance? A very economic-type macrolevel analysis of nation-state behavior. Neorealism and its critics and rational choice modeling dominated the theoretical arena, and discussion of this type of research constituted the bulk of course syllabi devoted to international relations theory. This type of analysis suffered a great blow by its inability to predict or even adequately explain the collapse of the Soviet Union. It is impossible to explain this system change on the basis of systems-level variables. Our intuitive understanding of the collapse involves variables at levels more conducive to psychology-type analysis—to foreign policy analysis. Thus, works written about the fall of the Warsaw Pact include factors such as the personalities of Gorbachev, Havel, and Walesa; the activities of transnational groups such as the Lutheran Church and the Green movement; the struggles between various domestic political players, such as the military, the Communist Party, the bureaucracies, and so forth; the role of economics and societal needs in sparking the desire for change. In short, the most cogent explanations of the fall of the Iron Curtain are those written from the standpoint of foreign policy analysis. This is a most felicitous occurrence, since economic-style analysis proved more efficient and hence more attractive during the Cold War period. It is not unfair to say that the renaissance of foreign policy analysis might never have occurred in the absence of this change in world events, which brought vividly to light the shortcomings of its theoretical rival.

This renaissance, in turn, could not have happened if researchers in foreign policy analysis had not resolved to some degree the problems that caused comparative foreign policy's decline. This resolution hinged on making some tough choices that entailed the abandonment of part of the core of the comparative foreign policy approach. Left behind were (1) the aim of a grand unified theory and (2) the methodological strictures imposed by the requirement of aggregate empirical testing.

In 1980, Kegley presaged the necessity of the first choice:

> To succeed partially is not to fail completely . . . goals [should be] downgraded to better fit capacities. . . . This prescribes reduction in the level of generality sought, so that more contextually-qualified, circumstantially-bounded, and temporally/spatially-specified propositions are tested. More of the peculiar, unique, and particular can be captured at a reduced level of abstraction and generality (Kegley, 1980: 12, 19).

Kegley's advice to reduce the level of abstraction, to come down from the rarefied air of grand theory to "middle-range" theory, and to capture more of the particular at the expense of being able to say something about everything was right on target. Foreign policy analysis was hobbled by what proved to be an outmoded view of what constituted a truly "scientific" approach. Abandoning this theoretical goal allowed other, healthier choices to be made: Policy relevance could be recaptured, and detailed analysis could now be legitimately performed (it was now okay to be a country expert!). Do not read into this that foreign policy analysis does not still embrace scientific desiderata—it certainly retains many of the standards that it began with, such as empirical falsifiability, systematic and comprehensive treatment of variables, the need for reliable and valid operationalization of independent and dependent variables, replicability of studies, the provision of scope conditions for all propositions, the desirability of generalizing from specific cases to potentially cross-nationally applicable statements, and the will to be rigorous in all stages of theorizing and testing.

Liberation from the perceived need to engage in aggregate empirical testing as the highest form of theoretical substantiation was long overdue, but nonetheless welcome. Now foreign policy analysts search for and use methods that allow them to utilize data at any level of measurement precision—from nominal to ratio—and to combine data at different levels of measurement precision. Texts relating to foreign policy making have become as important sources of data as any statistical yearbooks had been. Ways of combining information that simulate the actual cognitive and decision-making processes of policy makers are being explored. Intriguing operational measures are constructed to allow for maximum interpretation of a situation that may be close to unobservable. The case study—in more systematic form (e.g., process tracing)—has made a big comeback in foreign policy analysis, and the knowledge of country experts is actively being solicited for input in helping to analyze these cases (Richardson, 1987). An interesting and theoretically significant consequence of this development is that there has been a shift away from the "event" to the "decision" or "decision opportunity" as the appropriate unit of analysis in many foreign policy studies.

To illustrate these developments, as well as to show the range of new efforts in foreign policy analysis, I will modify the sixfold typology elucidated before. (I also refer the reader to the Hermann et al.'s [1987] volume *New Directions in the Study of Foreign Policy*, the purpose of which was to point the way out of the period of decline and does a fairly good job on that score; also see Gerner [1992].)

1. Cognitive Studies

The field of political psychology has grown immensely in recent years. The International Society of Political Psychology was formed, and the journals *Political Psychology* and *The Journal of Psychohistory*, among others, have been launched. Many of the members of the Foreign Policy Analysis Section of the International Studies Association (the former name of the section was, of course, the Comparative Foreign Policy Section) are also members of the ISPP. The volume *Political Psychology*, edited by Margaret G. Hermann (an original member of the CFP group!), was published in 1986, and is a survey of the diverse theoretical thrusts of modern political psychology. The ISPP has also started an annual summer workshop to train graduate students and academics in political psychology, and at a few universities, it is now possible to get a graduate degree in political psychology.

There has been much work in political psychology focusing on foreign policy effects, perhaps because of the great influence of Margaret G. Hermann on that field, perhaps because elite decision making in government is most clearly seen in certain cases of foreign policy (see Sylvan and Chan, 1984). Some of this work emanates from psychologists and some of it is the product of foreign policy analysis scholars. As I see it, the primary research areas (which all overlap one another) include (1) leader personality and perception studies, (2) cultural/societal differences in decision making, (3) small group dynamics, (4) computational modeling and natural language processing, and (5) role theory. Overarching these areas is a concern with how to study a decision—that is, what information is needed in order to set up a meaningful case study and in what form the information should be (see Anderson, 1987).

Interestingly, one of the most promising research areas of the 1970s—organizational/bureaucratic structure and process—has not expanded as one would have anticipated.

Leader personality and perception studies remains one of the most active research areas. Margaret G. Hermann continued to elaborate her set of foreign policy orientations for heads of state and to collect data for additional leaders. She extended her framework by developing hypotheses regarding the likely advisory groups to be preferred by certain leader types, the likely style of conflict resolution to be found within those groups, and so forth (see Hermann, 1987, in publication). Walker (1990) elaborated further on his work regarding on the concept of operational code and, along with others such as Bonham (Shapiro et al., 1988) and Maoz (Maoz and Shayer, 1987), continued development of cognitive maps of leaders (Walker and Watson, 1992). Analysis of the personalities of individual leaders can also be found in the work of Berrington (1989), Burke and Greenstein (1990), Glad (1989), and Post (1991). A welcome innovation has been the explicit comparison of different types of explanatory frameworks by applying them to understanding the same lader. This comparison allows for an inspection of the relative strengths and weaknesses of the various frameworks (see Snare, 1992; Winter et al., 1991). An overview edited volume on PP/FP (political psychology with reference to foreign policy) has also recently appeared (Singer and Hudson, 1992) and Yaacov Vertzberger has put out an impressive compilation of research findings (Vertzberger, 1990). Image analysis has also seen some significant growth (Cottam, 1986; Herrmann, 1985, 1986).

The examination of cultural and social differences with respect to decision making is beginning to blossom (Pye, 1986; Sampson, 1987). Notions of understanding and causal linkage may be different for different cultures (Motokawa, 1989). Conflict-resolution techniques seem to be different as well (Cushman and King, 1985; Gaenslen, 1989). The structures and processes of policy making also appear to be stamped by one's cultural and societal norms (Holland, 1984; Lampton, 1986; Leung, 1987; Willerton, 1987). As a result, there has been renewed interest in the topic of comparative political socialization and political learning (Etheredge, 1985; Merelman, 1986; Voss and Dorsey, 1992).

This area of research overlaps the next, the study of small group dynamics. Different group structures and norms may lead to different group processes, which in turn may lead to different foreign policy decisions. The exploration of these various permutations has occupied many scholars in foreign policy analysis (Dyson and Purkitt, 1986; Gaenslen, 1992; Kaplan and Miller, 1987; Orbovich and Molnar, 1992; Purkitt, 1992; Thompson et al., 1988). Of special interest has been the revisitation, critique, and refinement of Janis' concept of groupthink (Gaenslen, 1992; Herek et al., 1987, 1989; McCauley, 1989; Ripley, 1989; 't Hart, 1990).

A new research area in cognitive studies relating to foreign policy has arisen because of the aforementioned search for new methods to express what was unexpressable in statistical and mathematical terms. Often referred to as artificial intelligence-type studies in international relations, this term subsumes two different threads of research: computational modeling and natural language processing (Hudson, 1991, is a good overview edited volume, with the Schrodt, 1991, chapter being a recommended starting point). The former attempts to simulate the decision making of foreign policy elites, with inputs corresponding to the information the elites would likely receive, the processor representing the cognitive make-up of the elites, and the outputs corresponding to foreign policy actions. This has been an excellent laboratory for putting to empirical test some of the propositions gleaned from the broader study of PP/FP. Illustrative works in this regard include Ensign and Phillips (1991), Hudson (1991), Job and Johnson (1991), Orbovich and Molnar (1992), Mefford (1991), and Donald Sylvan et al. (1991). The second strand of theory construction, natural language processing, is less interested in foreign policy outputs than in discovering how language and precedent and background help to create a vision of reality in the mind of policy makers. That is, how do policy makers *construct* the world around them through language? Textual analysis is the methodological key to such works, and good examples include Alker et al. (1991), Banerjee (1991), Boynton (1991), Mallery (1991), and David Sylvan et al. (1991).

The last major area of theoretical and empirical study is that of role theory. Although work on roles specifically relating to foreign policy was rather sparse in the early days—consisting mainly of K. J. Holsti's pioneering article in 1970—in the second stage of foreign policy analysis, this has become a much more robust and promising field of inquiry. The efforts of Walker have been most prominent in moving the field forward, and Walker came out with a hefty edited volume in 1987 representing some of the many new directions the field was taking. New doctoral dissertations and theses utilizing role theory—a sure sign of new growth—are appearing as well (Breuning, in publication; Seeger, 1992).

2. Societal Group Influence on Foreign Policy

A new wave of theorizing has begun to explore how autonomous the state is in relation to other groups within the society. The chess-match approach to understanding international relations assumed for the more part that the state was very autonomous in foreign affairs—even when the state was democratic and therefore accountable to its citizens. This assumption served fairly well until its limitations were revealed with the fall of communism in the Eastern bloc nations. Obviously, there were societal limits on state autonomy. The work of Evans et al. (1985), Levy (1988), Lamborn and Mumme (1989), Mastanduno et al. (1989), and Putnam (1988) define some interesting aspects of this question. Of key interest are the scope conditions under which societal (and transnational) groups are more or less influential, the methodology by which one may trace the influence of these groups on foreign policy decision making by the government, and the exploration of the nexus between regime type and regime response to societal group activity. The overview essay of Muller and Risse-Kappen (1993) is an excellent point of departure for readers interested in this research. The cumulative work of Joe D. Hagan in this research area deserves special attention: Not only has he provided an explanatory framework with important organizing concepts, but he has collected a vast amount of data on societal group behavior in various nations and has attempted to test his propositions empirically using that data (Hagan, 1987, is a good introduction to his work). Very recent research spanning the spectrum of assumptions about state autonomy (from very autonomous to almost no autonomy) are represented in the edited volume *The Limits of State Autonomy*: *Societal Group Influence on Foreign Policy Formulation* (Skidmore and Hudson, 1993).

3. Integrative Explanatory Frameworks

Foreign policy analysis has not abandoned the goal of eventually integrating explanations found at various levels of analysis to come up with a more complete understanding of foreign policy behavior. However, the ways in which that integration is envisioned to take place has changed substantially from the days of Comparative foreign policy, when multiple regression and path analysis seemed the solution. Interestingly, it is the CREON Project, which was part of the original group of CFP efforts, that has pushed back the frontier the most in this regard. Indeed, it is the best example of cutting-edge integrative research, probably because it is the only self-consciously integrative effort I know of. Back in 1978, when East et al.'s volume *Why Nations Act* appeared, their analysis of foreign policy behavior spanned the gamut from personal characteristics of political leaders to systems effects. In the final chapter, the only way they saw to integrate this research was by statistical means. This proved to be a dead end. They lost all of the richness and detail that they had individually labored so hard to capture at each level of analysis.

CREON II, as the new effort has come to be called, leaves such a circumscribed vision of integration behind. Having already formulated propositions linking each independent variable to some variation on the dependent variable (foreign policy behavior), they have sought to combine, through a decision-tree structure, each possible variation in a decision situation. As this effort has progressed, key meta-variables have emerged that locate major branch departures in these trees. For example, from the combined work of Margaret G. Hermann on personal characteristics of heads of state, Charles F. Hermann on the structure and process of foreign policy decision making groups, and Joe D. Hagan on the conflict resolution processes of multiple autonomous actor regimes has come the concept of "decision unit." There are three types of decision units, and the determination of the type in a particular instance also tells you which of the independent variable clusters will be the most important. This echoes, but is a much more sophisticated version, of the original Rosenau approach (1966).

Using rules agreed upon by the researchers, if a decision unit is classified as a *predominant leader decision unit*, then variables relating to the head of state and his or her interaction with advisors and his or her style of processing information about the situation at hand will be most important. If it is a *single group decision unit*, then theoretical literature about small group structures and processes, groupthink, and coalition building will acquire importance. If it is a *multiple autonomous actor decision unit*, then literature and propositions about bargaining and conflict resolution will be most salient. Once the decision unit, and therefore the most important theoretical literature about decision making is highlighted, inputs about the particulars of the situation at hand are provided, and general outputs corresponding to statements about the values of foreign policy behavior attributes can be made; sometimes generally, sometimes specifically. (Works to consult include Hagen et al., 1982; Hermann and Hermann, 1989; Hermann et al., 1987; Hudson, 1991; and Stewart et al., 1989.)

The much awaited edited volume *Leaders, Groups, and Coalitions: How Decision United Shape Foreign Policy* (Hermann et al., in publication) also is methodologically path breaking in that after laying out the cross-national explanatory framework of decision units, the editors have solicited the assistance of country experts to apply the decision-tree structures to individual nations in the hopes of explaining those nations' foreign policy behaviors. Here we see an example of a creative approach welding the desideratum of cross-national applicability with the recognition that country expertise is invaluable in providing the detailed insight necessary to determine if these frameworks have any validity with regard to specific cases. The case study method is guided by the nomological explanatory framework. Traditionalism and behavioralism can coexist after all and strengthen one another in the process.

Most striking about CREON II is the cumulativeness of it all. Their frameworks, data, and methods have been painstakingly built and modified over the years so they all mesh together to produce explanation. This is unique not only in foreign policy analysis, but I would venture to say in most of what constitutes social science as well.

II. ASSESSMENT OF THE FIELD

Although the reader by now rightly suspects that my assessment of the field of foreign policy analysis is likely to be positive, I would like to begin this assessment by pointing out what I feel are the shortcomings of the field. Despite its new and refreshing character, there are still some notable flies in the ointment.

On a substantive level, given the importance of economic interdependence in world affairs, why do we not see more attempts to link economic factors to foreign policy behavior?

When this is done, it usually occurs as a secondary insight. Why are there not more works bridging the fields of foreign policy analysis and international political economy? Caporaso et al. (1987) and Moon (1987) have laid the case out in persuasive fashion—why has so little progress on this score taken place since then?

On a methodological level, I find two areas of greatest disappointment. One is that despite broad recognition that foreign policy behavior does not take place in a vacuum, that it is not profitably viewed as snapshots but rather as a moving picture, why have we still been unable to capture the dynamic element of foreign policy? Most often we limit ourselves to the starting point of one international actor, from whose perspective the decision will be made. Is it possible to free ourselves from that limit while still using the decision as the key dependent variable? Even within the strictures of examining one actor at a time, we still are unable to capture the flow and feedback of series of decisions that overlap, modify, and extend one another. We must break through this methodological barrier if we are to progress.

The second methodological problem is also knotty. At the cutting edge of integrative explanations, such as CREON II (and by the way, why are not there more concerted and cumulative efforts of this type?), there reaches a point at which the independent variables overdetermine the dependent variables. That is, if you have 75 independent variables, each of which can take on an average of five values each, can you calculate how many combinations of the variables and their values one could end up with? Now, try to link all of those combinations to change on four or five dependent variables, each of which can take on an average of five values apiece. There is more variation in the independent variables than can possibly be expressed at the level of variation in the dependent variables. This is a very big problem. In a sense, you know more than is useful to know. Either you do not need to examine all of those independent variables (just try to find a foreign policy scholar who will agree to drop consideration of independent variables), or you had better come up with a more detailed conceptualization of the dependent variable. I predict this will stymie the progress of CREON II and hinder its testing unless addressed in short order.

A last point, more ethical than theoretical or methodological, was first brought to my attention when I attended the 1985 conference on new directions in the study of foreign policy in Columbus, Ohio, which led to Hermann et al.'s (1987) book. Each of us was assigned to read, critique, and publicly review the essay of another of the participants. I was assigned to read the paper by Gregory Raymond entitled "Evaluation: A Neglected Task for the Comparative Study of Foreign Policy." Being a recently minted Ph.D. in the CFP/FPA tradition, I was taken aback to discover that throughout my graduate training I had not once considered how my expertise in foreign policy decision making might help me or might obligate me to *evaluate* the policies in question. CFP/FPA has a bad habit left over from the behavioral revolution—value neutrality. We study foreign policy, but we never venture to say whether we feel it is good or bad, right or wrong, effective or ineffective. The closest I have seen are studies on the quality of the decision-making process: Did they survey all the options?, Did they bring in outside experts?, and so forth (e.g., Janis, 1972). I call on my fellow scholars in foreign policy analysis to give serious consideration to our responsibility as experts to evaluate the substance of what we study.

In conclusion, although this chapter has not touched on all work relevant to foreign policy, and has certainly displayed an ethnocentric, American viewpoint of the field, I have tried to describe the evolution of the heart of what I understand to be foreign policy analysis. It is a fascinating hybrid bloom, with a noteworthy pedigree. Furthermore, it has demonstrated its hardiness and adaptability by reemerging from a period of theoretical decline stronger and more robust than ever. The changes in aims and methods that needed to be made were sometimes painful and sometimes large in scale, but the important point is that they were in fact made. The new world system offers a great opportunity for the study of foreign policy change (Hermann, 1990). Foreign policy analysis, if it continues in its theoretical and methodological innovation—and I believe it will—is best situated to exploit fully that opportunity and to help provide answers to some of the most pressing puzzles in international relations at this moment in history. It is an exciting time to be involved in foreign policy analysis, and I hope this chapter will encourage you to investigate the field more fully.

REFERENCES

Alker, H., Duffy, G., Hurwitz, R., and Mallery, J. (1991). Text modeling for international politics: A tourist's guide to RELATUS. In *Artificial Intelligence and International Policits*. V. M. Hudson and C. O. Boulder (Eds.). Westview Press, Boulder, CO, pp. 97–126.

Allison, G. (1971). *Essence of Decision*: *Explaining the Cuban Missile Crisis*. Little, Brown, Boston.

Allison, G., and Halperin, M. (1972). Bureaucratic politics: A paradigm and some policy implications. *World Politics* 24: 40–79.

Anderson, P. (1987). What do decision-makers do when they make a foreign policy decision? The implications for the comparative study of foreign policy. In *New Directions in the Study of Foreign Policy*. C. F. Hermann, C. W. Kegley, and J. N. Rosenau (Eds.). Allen & Unwin, Boston, pp. 285–308.

Andriole, S. J., and Hopple, G. W. (1981). The rise and fall of events data: Thoughts on an incomplete journey from basic research to applied use in the U.S. Department of Defense. U.S. Department of Defense, Washington, D.C., unpublished paper.

Ashley, R. K. (1976). Noticing pre-paradigmatic progress. In *In Search of Global Patterns*. J. N. Rosenau (Ed.). The Free Press, New York.

—— (1987). Foreign policy as political performance. *International Studies Notes* 13(2): 51–54.

Banerjee, S. (1991). Reproduction of perception and decision in the early cold war. In *Artificial Intelligence and International Politics*. V. M. Hudson (Ed.). Westview Press, Boulder, CO, pp. 310–326.

Barber, J. D. (1972). *The Presidential Character*: *Predicting Performance in the White House*. Prentice-Hall, Englewood Cliffs, NJ.

Beck, C., et al. (1973). *Comparative Communist Political Leadership*. McKay, New York.

Berrington, H. (1989). When does personality makes a difference? Lord Cherwell and the area bombing of Germany. *International Political Science Review* 10: 9–34.

Bobrow, D. B., Chan, S., and Kringen, J. A. (1979). *Understanding Foreign Policy Decisions*. The Free Press, New York.

Boynton, G. R. (1991). The expertise of the Senate Foreign Relations Committee. In *Artificial Intelligence and International Politics*. V. M. Hudson (Ed.). Westview Press, Boulder, CO, pp. 291–309.

Brecher, M. (1972). *The Foreign Policy System of Israel*. Yale University Press, New Haven, CT.

Breuning, M. *National Role Conceptions and Dutch Foreign Policy Behavior*. Doctoral Dissertation, Ohio State University. In publication.

Broderson, A. (1961). National character: An old problem re-examined. In *International Politics and Foreign Policy*. J. N. Rosenau (Ed.). Free Press of Glencoe, Glencoe, pp. 300–308.

Burke, J. P., and Greenstein, F. I. (1990). *How Presidents Test Reality*: *Decisions on Vietnam, 1954 and 1965*. Russell Sage Foundation, New York.

Callahan, P., Brady, L., and Hermann, M. G. (Eds.) (1982). *Describing Foreign Policy Behavior*. Sage, Beverly Hills, CA.

Caporaso, J. A., Hermann, C. F., Kegley, C. W., et al. (1987). The comparative study of foreign policy: Perspectives on the future. *International Studies Notes* 13(2): 32–46.

Carr, E. H. (1939). *The Twenty-Years' Crisis, 1919–39*: *An Introduction to the Study of International Relations*. Macmillan, London.

Caspary, W. R. (1967). Richardson's models of arms races: Description, critique, and an alternative model. *International Studies Quarterly* XI (March): 63–88.

Chittick, W. O. (1970). *State Department, Press, and Pressure Groups*. Wiley, New York.

Choucri, N., and North, R. (1975). *Nations in Conflict*. Freeman Press, New York.

Cottam, M. L. (1986). *Foreign Policy Decision-Making*: *The Influence of Cognition*. Westview Press, Boulder, CO.

Cottam, R. W. (1977). *Foreign Policy Motivation*: *A General Theory and a Case Study*. University of Pittsburgh Press, Pittsburgh, PA.

Crane, D. (1972). *Invisible Colleges*. University of Chicago Press, Chicago.

Cushman, D., and King, S. (1985). National and organizational culture in conflict resolution. In *Communication, Culture, and Organizational Process*. W. Gudykunst, L. Stewert, and S. Ting-Toomey (Eds.). Sage, Beverly Hills, CA, pp. 114–133.

Dahl, R. (Ed.) (1973). *Regimes and Oppositions*. Yale University Press, New Haven, CT.

Dallin, A. (1969). Soviet foreign policy and domestic politics: A framework for analysis. In *The Conduct of Soviet Foreign Policy*. E. Hoffman and F. Fleron (Eds.). Aldine-Atherton, Chicago, pp. 36–49.

deRivera, J. (1968). *The Psychological Dimension of Foreign Policy*. Merrill, Westerville, OH.

Deutsch, K. W., Edinger, L. J., Macridis, R. C., and Merritt, R. L. (1967). *France, Germany, and the Western Alliance*. Charles Scribner's Sons, New York.

Dixon, W. J., and Hermann, C. F. (1984). The structure of foreign policy: From conceptualization to observation. Paper presented at the 25th annual meeting of the International Studies Association, Atlanta, GA, March 27–31.

Dyson, J. W., and Purkitt, H. (1986). Review of experimental small group research. In *The Political Behavior Annual*. S. Long (Ed.). Westview Press, Boulder, CO, pp. 1:71–101.

East, M. A. (1978). National attributes and foreign policy. In *Why Nations Act*. M. A. East, S. A. Salmore, and C. F. Hermann (Eds.). Sage, Beverly Hills, CA, pp. 123–142.

—— (1987). The comparative study of foreign policy: We're not there yet, but. . . . *International Studies Notes* 13(2): 31.

East, M. A., and Hermann, C. F. (1974). Do nation-types account for foreign policy behavior? In *Comparing Foreign Policies*. J. N. Rosenau (Ed.). Wiley, New York, pp. 269–303.

East, M. A., Salmore, S. A., and Hermann, C. F. (Eds.) (1978). *Why Nations Act*. Sage, Beverly Hills, CA.

Ensign, M., and Phillips, W. (1991). Decision making and development: A "glass box" approach to representation. In *Artificial Intelligence and International Politics*. V. M. Hudson (Ed.). Westview Press, Boulder, CO, pp. 274–290.

Etheredge, L. S. (1978). *A World of Men*: *The Private Sources of American Foreign Policy*. MIT Press, Cambridge, MA.

Etheredge, L. (1985). *Can Governments Learn? American Foreign Policy and Central American Revolutions*. Pergamon Press, New York.

Evans, P., Rueschmeyer, D., and Skocpol, T. (1985). *Bringing the State Back*. Cambridge University Press, Cambridge, England.

Falkowski, L. S. (1979). *Psychological Models in International Politics*. Westview Press, Boulder, CO.

Gaenslen, F. (1989). On the consequences of consensual decision making: "Rational choice" in comparative perspective. University of Vermont.

Gaenslen, F. (1992). Decision making groups. In *Political Psychology and Foreign Policy*. E. Singer and V. M. Hudson (Eds.). Westview Press, Boulder, CO, pp. 165–194.

George, A. L. (1969). The "operational code": A neglected approach to the study of political leaders and decision-making. *International Studies Quarterly* 13: 190–222.

Gerner, D. J. (1988). Foreign policy analysis: Renaissance, routine, or rubbish? In *Political Science*: *Looking to the Future*. W. Crotty (Ed.). Northwestern University Press, Evanston, IL.

—— (1992). Foreign policy analysis: Exhilarating eclecticism, intriguing enigmas. *International Studies Notes* 18(4):

Glad, B. (1989). Personality, political, and group process variables in foreign policy decision-making: Jimmy Carter's handling of the Iranian hostage crisis. *International Political Science Review* 10: 35–61.

Guetzkow, H. (1963). A use of simulation in the study of inter-nation relations. In *Simulation in International Relations*: *Developments for Research and Teaching*. H. Guetzkow et al. (Eds.). Prentice-Hall, Englewood Cliffs, NJ.

Hagan, J. D. (1987). Regimes, political oppositions, and the comparative analysis of foreign policy. In *New Directions in the Study of Foreign Policy*. C. F. Hermann, W. Kegley, and J. N. Rosenau (Eds.). Allen & Unwin, Boston, pp. 339–365.

Hagan, J. D., Hermann, M. G., and Hermann, C. F. (1982). How decision unites shapes foreign policy behavior. Paper presented at the annual meeting of the International Studies Association, Cincinnati, OH.

Halperin, M. (1974). *Bureaucratic Politics and Foreign Policy*. Brookings Institution, Washington, D.C.

Halperin, M., and Kanter, A. (1973). The bureaucratic perspective: A preliminary framework. In *Readings in American Foreign Policy*. M. Halperin and A. Kanter (Eds.). Little, Brown, Boston.

Hellman, D. (1969). *Japanese Foreign Policy and Domestic Politics*. University of California Press, Berkeley.

Herek, G. M., Janis, I. L., and Huth, P. (1987). Decision making during international crises: Is quality of process related to outcome? *Journal of Conflict Resolution* 312: 203–226.

—— (1989). Quality of decision making during the Cuban missile crisis: Major errors in Welch's reassessment. *Journal of Conflict Resolution* 333: 446–459.

Hermann, C. F. (1978). Decision structure and process influences on foreign policy. In *Why Nations Act*. M. A. East, S. A. Salmore, and C. F. Hermann (Eds.). Sage, Beverly Hills, CA, pp. 69–102.

—— (1981). Foreign policy. In *Encyclopedia of Policy Studies*. S. S. Nagel (Ed.). Marcel Dekker, New York, pp. 269–298.

—— (1990). Changing course: When governments choose to redirect foreign policy. *International Studies Quarterly* 34(1): 3–22.

Hermann, C. F., Kegley, C. W., and Rosenau, J. N. (Eds.) (1987). *New Directions in the Study of Foreign Policy*. Allen & Unwin, Boston.

Hermann, C. F., and Peacock, G. (1987). The evolution and future of theoretical research in the comparative study of foreign policy. In *New Directions in the Study of Foreign Policy*. C. F. Hermann, C. W. Kegley, and J. N. Rosenau (Eds.). Allen & Unwin, Boston.

Hermann, M. G. (Ed.) (1977). *A Psychological Examination of Political Leaders*. The Free Press, New York.

—— (1980). Explaining foreign policy behavior using personal characteristics of political leaders. *International Studies Quarterly* 24: 7–46.

—— (1984). Personality and foreign policy decision-making: A study of 53 heads of government. In *Foreign Policy Decision-Making*: *Perceptions, Cognition, and Artificial Intelligence*. D. A. Sylvan and S. Chan (Eds.). Praeger, New York, pp. 53–80.

—— (Ed.) (1986). *Political Psychology*. Jossey-Bass, San Francisco.

—— (1987). Assessing the foreign policy orientations of sub-saharan African leaders. In *Role Theory and Foreign Policy Analysis*. S. G. Walker (Ed.). Duke University Press, Durham, NC, pp. 161–198.

——. The inputs and the outputs: What precipitates a decision and the nature of the decision. In *Leaders, Groups, and Coalitions*: *How Decision Units Shape Foreign Policy*. M. G. Hermann, C. F. Hermann, and J. D. Hagan (Eds.). In publication.

Hermann, M. G., and Hermann, C. F. (1989). Who makes foreign policy decisions and how: An empirical inquiry. *International Studies Quarterly* 33(4): 361–388.

Hermann, M. G., Hermann, C. F., and Hagan, J. D. (1987). How decision units shape foreign policy behavior. In *New Directions in the Study of Foreign Policy*. C. F. Hermann, C. W. Kegley, and J. N. Rosenau (Eds.). Allen & Unwin, Boston, pp. 309–338.

—— (Eds.). *Leaders, Groups, and Coalitions*: *How Decision Units Shape Foreign Policy*. In publication.

Herrmann, R. K. (1985). *Perceptions and Behavior in Soviet Foreign Policy*. University of Pittsburgh Press, Pittsburgh, PA.

—— (1986). The power of perceptions in foreign policy decision making: Do views of the Soviet Union determine the policy choices of American leaders? *American Journal of Political Science* 30(4): 841–875.

Hess, R. (1963). The socialization of attitudes toward political authority: Some cross-national comparisons. *International Social Science Journal* 15:542–559.

Hilsman, R. (1967). *To Move a Nation*. Doubleday, New York.

Hoffman, S. (1961). International systems and international law. In *The State of War: Essays on the Theory and Practice of International Politics*. Praeger, New York.

Holland, H. (1984). *Managing Diplomacy*. Hoover Institution Press; Stanford.

Holsti, K. J. (1970). National role conceptions in the study of foreign policy. *International Studies Quarterly* 14:233–309.

Holsti, O. R. (1977). The "operational code" as an approach to the analysis of belief systems. Final report to the National Science Foundation, Grant SOC75-15-368, Duke University, Durham, NC.

Hudson, V. M. (Ed.) (1991). *Artificial Intelligence and International Politics*. Westview Press, Boulder. CO.

—— (1991). Scripting international power dramas: A model of situational predisposition. In *Artificial and International Politics*. V. M. Hudson (Ed.). Westview Press, Boulder, CO, pp. 194–220.

Huntington, S. P. (1960). Strategic planning and the political process. *Foreign Affairs* 38(2): 285–299.

Janis, I. (1972). *Victims of Groupthink*. Houghton Mifflin, Boston.

Jervis, R. (1976). *Perception and Misperception in International Politics*. Princeton University Press, Princeton, NJ.

Job, B. L., and Johnson D. (1991). UNCLESAM: The application of a rule-based model of U.S. foreign policy making. In *Artificial Intelligence and International Politics*. V. M. Hudson (Ed.). Westview Press, Boulder, CO, pp. 221–244.

Johnson, L. K. (1977). Operational codes and the prediction of leadership behavior: Frank Church at mid-career. In *A Psychological Examination of Political Leaders*. M. G. Hermann (Eds.). The Free Press, New York.

Kahneman, D., Slovic, P., and Tversky, A. (Eds.). (1982). *Judgment Under Uncertainty: Heuristics and Biases*. Cambridge University Press, Cambridge, England.

Kaplan, M. (1957). *System and Process in International Politics*. Wiley, New York.

—— (1972). Variants on six models of the international system. In *International Politics and Foreign Policy*. J. N. Rosenau, Free Press of Glencoe, Glencoe, pp. 291–303.

Kaplan, M. F., and Miller, C. E. (1987). Group decision making and normative versus informational influence: Effects of type of issue and assigned decision rule. *Journal of Personality and Social Psychology* 53:306–313.

Kean, J. G., and McGowan, P. J. (1973). National attributes and foreign policy participation: A path analysis. In *Sage International Yearbook of Foreign Policy Studies*. Vol. I. P. J. McGowan (Ed.). Beverly Hills, CA, pp. 219–252.

Kegley, C. W. (1980). The comparative study of foreign policy: Paradigm lost? Institute of International Studies, Essay Series #10, University of South Carolina.

Keohane, R. (1986). Realism, neorealism, and the study of world politics. In *Neorealism and Its Critics*. R. Keohane (Ed.). Columbia University Press, New York.

Lamborn, A. C., and Mumme, S. P., (1989). *Statecraft, Domestic Politics and Foreign Policy Making: The EL Chamizal Dispute*. Westview Press, Boulder, CO.

Lampton, D. M. (1986). *Paths to Power: Elite Mobility in Contemporary China*. Michigan Monographs in Chinese Studies, vol. 55. University of Michigan, Ann Arbor, MI.

Leana, C. R. (1975). A partial test of Janis' groupthink model: Effects of group cohesiveness and leader behavior on defective decision-making. *Journal of Management* 111:5–17.

Leites, N. (1951). *The Operational Code of the Politburo*. McGraw-Hill, New York.

Leung, K. (1987). Some determinants of reactions to procedural models for conflict resolution: A cross-national study. *Journal of Personality and Social Psychology* 53: 898–908.

Levy, J. (1988). Domestic politics and war. *Journal of Interdisciplinary History* 18(4):653–674.

Mallery, J. (1991). Semantic content analysis. In *Artifical Intelligence and International Politics*. V. M. Hudson (Ed.). Westview Press, Boulder, CO, pp. 347–385.

Maoz, Z., and Shayer, A. (1987). The structure of peace and war argumentation: Israeli prime ministers versus the Knesset. *Political Psychology* 8(4): 575–602.

Mastanduno, M., Lake, D., and Ikenberry, J. (1989). Toward a realist theory of state action. *International Studies Quarterly* 33(4): 457–474.

McCauley, C. (1989). The nature of social influence in groupthink: Compliance and internalization. *Journal of Personality and Social Psychology* 572: 250–260.

McClelland, D. C. (1985). *Human Motivation*. Scott, Foresman, Glenview, IL.

McGowan, P., and Shapiro, H. B. (1973). *The Comparative Study of Foreign Policy: A Survey of Scientific Findings*. Sage, Beverly Hills, CA.

Mefford, D. (1991). Steps toward artificial intelligence: Rule-based, case-based, and explanation-based models of politics. In *Artificial Intelligence and International Politics*. V. M. Hudson, Westview Press, Boulder, CA, pp. 56–96.

Merelman, R. M. (1969). The development of political ideology: A framework for the analysis of political socialization. *American Political Science Review* 69:21–31.

—— (1986). Revitalizing political socialization. In *Political Psychology*. M. G. Hermann (Ed.). Jossey-Bass, San Francisco, pp. 279–319.

Moon, B. (1987). Political economy approaches to the comparative study of foreign policy. In *New Directions in the Study of Foreign Policy*. C. F. Hermann, C. W. Kegley, and J. N. Rosenau (Eds.). Allen & Unwin, Boston, pp. 33–52.

Motokawa, T. (1989). Sushi science and hamburger science. *Perspectives in Biology and Medicine* 32 (4): 489–504.

Muller, H., and Risse-Kappen, T. From the outside in and the inside out: International relations, domestic politics, and foreign policy. In *The Limits of State Autonomy*: *Societal Groups and Foreign Policy Formulation*. D. Skidmore and V. M. Hudson (Eds.). Westview Press, Boulder, CO.

Munton, D. (1976). Comparative foreign policy: Fads, fantasies, orthodoxies, and perversities. In *In Search of Global Patterns*. J. N. Rosenau (Ed.). The Free Press, New York.

Neustadt, R. E. (1970). *Alliance Politics*. Columbia University Press, New York.

Ogata, S. (1977). The business community and Japanese foreign policy. In *The Foreign Policy of Modern Japan*. A. Scalapino (Ed.). University of California Press, CA, pp. 175–203.

Orbovich, C., and Molnar, R. (1992). Modeling foreign policy advisory processes. In *Political Psychology and Foreign Policy*. E. Singer and V. M. Hudson (Ed.). Westview Press, Boulder, CO, pp. 195–218.

Post, J. (1991). Saddam Hussein of Iraq: A political psychology profile. *Political Psychology* 12(1): 279–289.

Purkitt, H. (1991). Artificial intelligence and intuitive foreign policy decision-makers viewed as limited information processors: Some conceptual issues and practical concerns for the future. In *Artificial Intelligence and International Politics*. V. M. Hudson (Ed.). Westview Press, Boulder, CO, pp. 35–55.

—— (1992). Political decision making in small groups: The Cuban missile crisis revisited—One more time. In *Political Psychology and Foreign Policy*. E. Singer and V. M. Hudson (Ed.). Westview Press, Boulder, CO, pp. 219–245.

Putnam, R. (1988). Diplomacy and domestic politics: The logic of two-level games. *International Organization* 42(3): 427–60.

Pye, L. (1986). Political psychology in Asia. In *Political Psychology*. M. G. Hermann (Ed.). Jossey-Bass, San Francisco, pp. 467–486.

Raymond, G. (1987). Evaluation: An neglected task for the comparative study of foreign policy. In *New Directions in the Study of Foreign Policy*. C. F. Hermann, C. W. Kegley, and J. N. Rosenau (Eds.). Allen & Unwin, Boston, pp. 96–110.

Renshon, S. A. (Ed.) (1977). *Handbook of Political Socialization.* The Free Press, New York.

Richardson, L. F. (1960a). *Arms and Insecurity: A Mathematical Study of the Causes and Origins of War.* Boxwood Press, Pittsburgh, PA.

Richardson, L. F. (1960b). *Statistics of Deadly Quarrels.* Boxwood Press, Pittsburgh, PA.

Richardson, N. R. (1987). Dyadic Case Studies in the Comparative Study of Foreign Policy Behavior. In *New Directions in the Study of Foreign Policy.* C. F. Hermann, C. W. Kegley, and J. N. Rosenau (Eds.). Allen & Unwin, Boston.

Richardson, N., and Kegley, C. W. (1980). Trade dependence and foreign policy compliance. *International Studies Quarterly* 24:191–222.

Ripley, B. (1989). Kennedy, Johnson, and groupthink: A theoretical reassessment. Paper presented at the annual meeting of the American Political Science Association, Atlanta, GA, August 31–September 3.

Rosecrance, R. (1963). *Action and Reaction in World Politics.* Little, Brown, Boston.

Rosenau, J. N. (1966). Pre-theories and theories of foreign policy. In *Approaches to Comparative and International Politics.* R. Barry Farrell (Ed.). Northwestern University Press, Evanston, IL.

Rummel, R. J. (1977). *Field Theory Evolving.* Sage, Beverly Hills, CA.

—— (1972). *The Dimensionality of Nations Project.* Sage, Beverly Hills, CA.

—— (1979). *National Attributes and Behavior.* Sage, Beverly Hills, CA.

Salmore, B. G., and Salmore, S. A. (1978). Political regimes and foreign policy. In *Why Nations Act.* M. A. East, S. A. Salmore, and C. F. Hermann, Sage, Beverly Hills, CA, pp. 103–122.

Sampson, M. (1987). Cultural influences on foreign policy. In *New Directions in the Study of Foreign Policy.* Allen & Unwin, Boston, pp. 384–408.

Schilling, W. R., Hammond, P. Y., and Snyder, G. H. (1962). *Strategy, Politics, and Defense Budgets.* Columbia University Press, New York.

Schrodt, P. (1991). Artificial intelligence and international relations: An overview. In *Artificial Intelligence and International Politics.* V. M. Hudson (Ed.). Westview Press, Boulder, CO, pp. 9–34.

Seeger, J. (1992). *Towards a Theory of Foreign Policy Analysis Based on National Role Conceptions: An AI/IR Approach.* Master's Thesis, Brigham Young University.

Semmel, A. K. (1982). Small group dynamics in foreign policy-making. In *Biopolitics, Political Psychology, and International Politics.* G. W. Hopple (Ed.). St. Martin's Press, New York, pp. 94–113.

Semmel, A. K., and Minix, D. (1979). Small group dynamics and foreign policy decision-making: An experimental approach. In *Psychological Models in International Politics.* L. S. Falkowski (Ed.). Westview Press, Boulder, CA, pp. 251–287.

Shapiro, M., Bonham, M., and Heradsveit, D. (1988). A discursive practices approach to collective decision-making. *International Studies Quarterly* 32: 397–420.

Simon, H. (1985). Human nature in politics: The dialogue of psychology with political science. *American Political Science Review* 79:293–304.

Singer, E., and Hudson, V. M. (1992). *Political Psychology and Foreign Policy.* Westview Press, Boulder, CO.

Singer, J. D., Bremer, S., and Stuckey, J. (1972). Capability distribution, uncertainty, and major power war, 1820–1965. In *Peace, War, and Numbers.* B. M. Russett (Ed.). Sage, Beverly Hills, CA.

Skidmore, D. and Hudson, V. M. (Eds.). *The Limits of State Autonomy: Societal Groups and Foreign Policy Formulation.* Westview Press. In publication.

Smith, S. (1987). CFP: A theoretical ctitique. *International Studies Notes* 13(2): 47–48.

Snare, C. (1992). Applying personality theory to foreign policy behavior: Evaluating three methods of assessment. In *Political Psychology and Foreign Policy.* E. Singer and V. M. Hudson (eds.). Westview Press, Boulder, CO, pp. 103–134.

Snyder, R. C., Bruck, H. W., and Sapin, B. (1954). *Decision-Making as an Approach to the Study of International Politics.* Foreign Policy Analysis Project Series, No. 3, Princeton University, Princeton, NJ.

—— (Eds.) (1963). *Foreign Policy Decision-Making.* The Free Press Rosenau, New York, 1966.

Stewart, L. (1977). Birth order and political leadership. In *A Psychological Examination of Political Leaders.* M. G. Hermann (Ed.). The Free Press, New York, pp. 206–236.

Stewart, P. D., Hermann, M. G., and Hermann, C. F. (1989). Modeling the 1973 Soviet decision to support Egypt. *American Political Science Review* 83(1): 35–59.

Sylvan, D., Majeski, S., and Milliken, J. (1991). Theoretical categories and data construction in computational models of foreign policy. In *Artificial Intelligence and International Politics*. V. M. Hudson (Ed.). Westview Press, Boulder, CO, pp. 327–346.

Sylvan, D. A., and Chan, S. (Eds.) (1984). *Foreign Policy Decision-Making: Perception, Cognition, and Artificial Intelligence*. Praeger, New York.

Sylvan, D., Goel, A., and Chandrasekaran, B. (1991). Modeling foreign policy decision making as knowledge-based reasoning. In *Artificial Intelligence and International Politics*. V. M. Hudson (Ed.). Westview Press, Boulder, CO, pp. 245–273.

Tetlock, P. E. (1979). Identifying victims of groupthink from public statements of decision-makers. *Journal of Personality and Social Psychology* 378: 1314–1324.

't Hart, P. (1990). *Groupthink in Government*. Swets and Zeitlinger, Amsterdam.

Thompson, L., Mannix E. A., and Bazerman, M. H. (1988). Group negotiation: Effects of decision rule, agenda, and aspiration. *Journal of Personality and Social Psychology* 54:86–95.

Vertzberger, Yaacov (1990). *The World in Their Minds*. Stanford University Press, Stanford, CA.

Voss, J. and Dorsey, E. (1992). Perception and international relations: An overview. In *Political Psychology and Foreign Policy*. E. Singer and V. M. Hudson (Ed.). Westview Press, Boulder, CO, pp. 3–30.

Walker, S. G. (1977). The interface between beliefs and behavior: Henry A. Kissinger's operational code and the Vietnam War. *Journal of Conflict Resolution* 21: 129–168.

—— (Ed.) (1987). *Role Theory and Foreign Policy Analysis*. Duke University Press, Durham, NC.

—— (1990). The evolution of operational code analysis. *Political Psychology* 11:403–418.

Walker, S. G., and Watson, G. L. (1992). The cognitive maps of British leaders, 1938–39: The case of Chamberlain-in-cabinet. In *Political Psychology and Foreign Policy*. E. Singer and V. M. Hudson, Westview Press, Boulder, CO, pp. 31–58.

Wallace, M. D. (1979). Arms races and escalation. *Journal of conflict resolution* 23 (March): 3–16.

Waltz, K. (1954). *Man, the State, and War*. Columbia University Press, New York.

—— (1986). Reflections on *theory of international politics*: A response to my critics. In *Neorealism and Its Critics*. R. Keohane, Columbia University Press, New York.

—— (1978). *Theory of International Politics*. Addison-Wesley, Reading, MA.

Wilkenfeld, J., Hopple, G. W., Rossa, P. J., and Andriole, S. J. (1980). *Foreign Policy Behavior*. Sage, Beverly Hills, CA.

Winter, D. G. (1973). *The Power Motive*. The Free Press, New York.

Winter, D. G., Hermann, M. G., Weintraub, W., and Walker, S. G. (1991). The personalities of Bush and Gorbachev measured at a distance: Procedures, portraits, and policy. *Political Psychology* 12(2): 215–245.

Zinnes, D. (1976). *Contemporary Research in International Relations*. The Free Press, New York.

13
International Security and the National Policy Maker

Marybeth Peterson
U.S. Air Force Academy, Colorado Springs, Colorado

I. THE PROBLEMS OF SECURITY IN THE POST-COLD WAR INTERNATIONAL SYSTEM

Participants in the international system face two simultaneous challenges: reevaluating the theoretical concepts that have guided their selection of specific security policies and resolving urgent contemporary problems of international and national security that confront the post-cold war world. These tasks are particularly difficult because the issues that dominate the current security agenda must be settled within an evolving security framework, the ultimate outcome of which is itself a primary security issue.

A. Scope of the Chapter

This chapter surveys security studies as a field of policy analysis dedicated to the solution of contemporary security problems of the international system. The chapter is divided into two separate surveys. The first section focuses on the problem of security as it has evolved through the cold war to the post–cold war world. The second part is a survey of contemporary security problems with which the post cold war international system is presently dealing.

The concept of security itself is today very much debated, and, accordingly, the field of security studies is also at issue.[1] The purpose of this chapter is to explore the evolving nature of security while remaining fixed on the relevance of this evolution for the policy maker. The intent is not to take sides in the ongoing debate, but to offer a clear and coherent outline of the field while presenting the major issues of security policy as they appear today. The goal of this survey is to create a "handbook" for security policy makers to use as a tool in the development of a framework in which policy decisions about using force and threats between social communities can be made.

B. A Broad Conception of Security

The traditional definition of security policy refers to the use of force and threats to get what one wants in the international arena. This conceptualization considers coercive force as the only relevant means for the achievement of security. Increasingly, though, this conceptualization is being recognized as having significant limitations and security policy is being extended to include the achievement of security ends using noncoercive means as well.

The classic realist approach to security focuses on the nation-state. This perspective emphasizes the concept of national power and the importance that nation-states attach to the acquisition of power as the primary factor determining how much influence one state can wield over rival states in the international system. Hans Morgenthau was the primary advocate of the "realist" school of international politics in the 1950s and his work, *Politics Among Nations*, stressed the accumulation of national power as the driving force of national behavior (Morgenthau, 1985).

Morgenthau's argument has since been extended by so-called neorealists, led by Kenneth Waltz, who argue that the anarchical nature of the international system based on the nation-state necessarily induces states to seek power, especially military power, to preserve and to perpetuate the system through a balance of power system (Waltz, 1979). Morgenthau and his followers have been termed "realists" because they describe national behavior not in terms of what states should do but in terms of how they actually behave. The scholars from the realist school accepted the international system as they found it and have attempted to construct a theory that works with the forces driving international behavior instead of a theory that is contrary to the incentives that motivate states to act.

1. *Balance of Power Theory and the Maintenance of Order in the International System*

Hedley Bull is another member of Morgenthau's realist school. Bull carries Morgenthau's argument farther and argues that the basis for order in the international system is the establishment of a society of states. This society not only preserves the system and the individual states comprising it, but it also fosters peace, international order, and economic development. Implicit in Bull's concept of a society of states is the presence of codes of behavior that have developed over time to govern state behavior which are not totally dependent on a Hobbesian view of the human race.[2]

This is an extension of the balance of power theory subscribed to by the classic realists who argue that the preservation of order has been achieved throughout the history of the states system because states have balanced each other when one among them amassed preponderant amounts of national power. This school explains the security policy of the great powers in terms of their priority on preserving a balance of power among them.

As one state accumulates a certain level of military force and capability, its eye is constantly scanning the coincident accumulations of power among national rivals. States, then, must decide whether the challenge to the balance of power made by other states is worth the outlay of national resources and decide what it would take to "balance" the threatening international actor.[3]

The post–World War II international environment has witnessed specific instances of such power balancing in the efforts of the United States and the former Soviet Union to maintain a balance of nuclear forces throughout the cold war era and in related attempts to balance the East-West fronts between NATO and the Warsaw Pact. Bull characterized the modern-day phenomenon of mutual nuclear deterrence as a special case of balance of power theory in which each state strived to acquire sufficient nuclear power to deter a nuclear attack on the part of the other while simultaneously convincing their nuclear rival that they had the will and capability to retaliate against a nuclear attack.[4]

The difficulty of formulating accurate threat perceptions based solely on assessments of rival states' power has been highlighted by scholars who have tried to emphasize the psychological component of states' perceptions. Robert Jervis, Richard Lebow, and Janice Stein have undertaken empirical case studies of contemporary interstate relationships focusing on the factors that determine the success or failure of states' attempts to deter other states (Jervis, et al., 1985). Their argument is that since assessments of rival states' power or deterrent capability involves an assessment of underlying psychological relationships between states and the decisions of decision makers within them, then emotions, perceptions, and calculations relevant to this assessment should not be ignored.

Balance of power theorists have also been challenged and complemented by those who contend that a balance of satisfactions between rival states is a more accurate description of international behavior than pure power politics. Historian Paul Schroeder's reexamination of 19th century European diplomacy concludes that stability was maintained in the international system by managing the conflicting demands within it (Schroeder, 1989). The satisfactions of both the great and lesser powers were satisfied by balancing the right to pursue ascendancy within the system with the recognition of the legitimate interests and rights of threatened states. Schroeder's view is consistent with Bull's analysis of the evolution of a society of states with its expectation of minimum standards of international behavior that surpassed the Hobbesian world of pure power politics.

Schroeder argued that states recognized the ability of preserving the balance of satisfactions system that successfully accommodated the conflicting needs of its members. Such an approach, as applied to the contemporary international system, suggests the usefulness of broadening the security agenda to include the management of problems that threaten the political equilibrium of the system.

It is clear, then, that classic notions of security are being challenged in the contemporary era. Some argue that the concept of security should be recast to recognize the role of perceptions, whereas others contend that notions of security should reflect the reality of the balancing of satisfactions that has characterized the international system throughout its history. Such a reframing of the concept of security, the reformers argue, would lead to a more accurate explanation of the behavior that has characterized the international system in the cold war while also offering the best hope for resolving the growing demands and competing satisfactions that characterize the post–cold war era[5] (Kanet and Kolodziej, 1991).

2. The Case for Expanding the International Security Agenda

Although the focus of policy makers is likely to remain fixed on interstate conflicts to include the study of specific policies that states should adopt in order to prepare for, prevent, or engage in war (Walt, 1991), increasingly, this classic approach, based on realist assumptions to explain constancy or change in security regimes, is being challenged as insufficient. Many analysts are arguing that an approach that is narrowly focused on the use of military force as a means of pursuing the national interests of states neglects other critical dimensions of security, including economic development and welfare and shared notions among people and states of legitimacy and the responsiveness of security regimes to their political wants and values.

Again, the contemporary security policy maker is reminded of Schroeder's contention that security regimes should focus on balancing satisfactions among nations and also of Bull's argument that social order depends on the achievement of three universal goals of social life: security against violence, the assurance that promises made will be kept, and security from the usurpation of possessions.[6] Security analysts are increasingly recognizing the implications of instability within national societies as threats to the maintenance of order between them.

Indeed, in his April 1992 *Arms Control* article, Edward Kolodziej explained the demise of the cold war and the collapse of the Soviet Union through an analysis that posited that welfare determinants, political reassurances, and the responsiveness of regimes to demands for greater national self-expression and democratization, as well as the protection of human rights, were critical dimensions of the Soviet Union's security problem.

Kolodziej (1992) argues that the cold war can be explained not only as a balance of terror based on the recognition of the cost of deviating from respecting the realities of mutual assured destruction but also as an era in which the superior ability of the West to meet its welfare needs and the West's open political system placed pressure on the Soviet Union for economic and political reform leading ultimately to its reorientation toward a market economy and the advent of its process of democratization.

Barry Buzan has also explored the concept of the state and its relationship to the concept of security. Buzan (1991: 60) argues that classic notions of the state as the composite of central institutions and a separate phenomenon from the society that it governs are too restrictive. Traditional international relations interpretations of state behavior being dependent on the systemic structure of the international system are also too restrictive in Buzan's view. Buzan calls for a comprehensive management of security problems based on a broadened interpretation of state behavior that takes into consideration the domestic characteristics of states.

Buzan modifies the analysis of theorists such as Kenneth Waltz, who regard states as like units whose security needs should be focused on the relationship of the state to its external environment. Instead, Buzan argues that states vary more than in their status as powers— they vary also in terms of their social-political cohesion. These variances in the ability of the state to be secure within itself determines whether or not states are classified as "strong" or "weak" states and the range of their security problems.

Weak states are distinguished by the attention that they are forced to pay to domestically generated threats to security because of their inability to create a domestic and political consensus within the state. Strong states, conversely, are characterized by the presence of strong and stable institutions that have earned the legitimacy of the population, a clearly defined territory, and a national security effort focused primarily on protecting the state from external threats (Buzan, 1991: 96–107). According to this view, the domestic characteristics of a state should determine its approach to its national security, and these characteristics vary from state to state.

Both Kolodziej and Buzan, then, support an expansion of the post–cold war security agenda that considers the varying abilities of states to regulate civil strife within them, the potential for states to pose security threats to their own citizens, and organizational factors of individual states that enhance or impede their ability to manage their national security effort. They represent growing support in the field of security studies for the inclusion of dimensions of security that go beyond the standard notion that only the study of the coercive use of threats is relevant for policy makers entrusted with formulating policies that ensure the security of their nations.

Additionally, the link between economics and security is being emphasized. Paul Kennedy's study of collapsing empires argues that the overextension of military power and the resultant outlays in military spending to support it ultimately lead to the collapse of overall economic performance and the ability of powers to sustain their "greatness" (Kennedy, 1987).

Judith Reppy's survey on the economics of national security supports Kennedy's study with the assertion that at some level, expenditure for the military can weaken a nation rather than strengthen it because the economic costs outweigh whatever benefit is gained from the military forces (Reppy, 1989). Reppy acknowledges that states have legitimate social welfare goals in addition to meeting national security requirements but does not go so far as to include these goals as part of the national security problem.

Political economist Robert Gilpin also argues that the competing imperatives of the market and the state lead to the inevitable politicization of economic issues that has profound security implications for the state. There is an inherent tension between the logic of the market that seeks to locate economic activities where they are most productive and the logic of the state that tries to control this process in order to accumulate capital, and, consequently, national power (Gilpin, 1987). The state must manage these competing imperatives in order to achieve both continued economic growth that will enable it to meet the demands of its population and the proper degree of intervention with market forces to ensure that its security requirements are met.

The relevance of political economy for security issues is that the interdependence of national economies has led to the realization that the state can be used to affect economic outcomes. Economic power and the health of the economic and technological base of a society are consequently being regarded as determinants of national power along with military power[7] (Pleshakov, 1991).

C. Remapping the Cold War Agenda

Repeated evidence of the Soviet Union's intent to expand its power across Europe as borne out in the presence of large numbers of Soviet forces in central Europe, the sovietization of Eastern Europe, and the 1948 Berlin crisis galvanized the West into countering the expansion of Soviet power with its countervailing build-up of military strength. The West's response was primarily embodied in the North Atlantic Treaty Organization (NATO) (Rubinstein, 1980). The next four decades was characterized by confrontation between the two new superpowers carried out primarily in the European theater. Regional conflicts also contributed to the superpower rivalry in that their outcomes shifted the East-West balance and affected each side's effort to gain supremacy over the socioeconomic and ideological system of the other.[8]

Recent scholarship, however, has questioned this standard interpretation of cold war behavior based on the West's containment of the Soviet desire to expand its empire. Soviet scholar Michael MccGwire argues that the Soviet conventional arms build-up that began in the 1970s was undertaken in order to prevent the occurrence of nuclear war. In this view, the primary motivation of Soviet strategists was to ensure the survival of the Soviet state by building up its forces in such a way that the USSR could fight and prevail in a sustained conventional war (MccGwire, 1987).

Additionally, Raymond Garthoff argued that the Soviet and American perceptions of the concept of deterrence throughout the cold war era were fundamentally different. Whereas the Americans relied on deterrence to prevent an attack on the West by the Soviet Union and as a means of preventing Soviet expansionism, the Soviets had viewed the build-up of military power as a means of deterring the West from initiating a war against the Soviets (Garthoff, 1987).

Deterrence as a theoretical construct and its requisite acquisition of huge quantities of nuclear weapons by both superpowers was adopted by both rivals as the primary component of cold war governance and as a reliable basis for the achievement of their mutual goals of long-term global ascendancy short of war.[9] American strategic thinkers recognized that the imperative governing the employment of military force in the nuclear era was the prevention of all-out war (Brodie, 1959).

Deterrence theory was developed in civilian think tanks by analysts who employed the rationality of game theory. Deterrence theorists assumed that in such cases where the contemplated attack looked unrewarding because of the credibility of the deterrer's threat, rational challengers of the status quo would refrain from undertaking aggressive behavior (Schelling, 1960). The results of this approach were the strategies of massive retaliation and its follow-on strategy of flexible response. The aim was to prevent aggressive Soviet behavior while also diminishing the potential of conflicts escalating into all-out nuclear war.

Strategic studies in this era focused on developing and critiquing deterrence theory. Some argued that an unwillingness to believe that deterrence could fail resulted in the lack of an actual war-fighting strategy (Gray, 1984; Kahn, 1971). Others contended that deterrence theory failed in empirical case studies (George and Smoke, 1974), whereas still others argued that the fundamental assumptions of rationality that deterrence theory depended on were extremely flawed (Jervis, et al., 1985).[10]

Despite the criticisms of the central assumptions of deterrence theory, superpower conflict was managed through the gradual development of a mutual understanding regarding which issues threatened the core values of the respective powers. These interests were protected and the overall peace maintained because each side was deterred by the other's threats of violent reaction in the form of nuclear weapons.

The cold war strategy of the superpowers was based on an underlying hostile and aggressive relationship that no longer characterizes relations between the United States and the former Soviet Union. Hence, a post–cold war strategy must be developed that reflects the current perception of threats on either side. The cold war security regime also performed essential functions that maintained the stability of the international system. These included containing the German problem by means of the division of Germany, limiting nationalist aspirations of NATO members and the Warsaw Pact, and the containment of disunity within both the Western and Eastern alliances (Kolodziej, 1992).

These functions have not yet been transferred to a post–cold war security regime capable of guaranteeing the stability of Europe and of other regions whose conflicts were contained by the cold war security regime. The collapse of the bipolar system has left in its wake both the challenge of "mopping up" the issues that used to separate the East and the West as well as the management of a whole new collection of issues that represent distinctive challenges to the stability of Europe and the international security system as a whole. These issues are the subject of part two of this chapter.

II. CONTEMPORARY POLICY PROBLEMS

A. Prospects for Stability in the Post-Cold War World

The two primary threats to regional and international peace that remain in Europe from the cold war era are being contained through the processes of continued European integration and arms control negotiations. These threats are the weapons that remain in the former Soviet Union and the possibility of an ascendant Germany. Additional threats stem from the inability to contain nationality conflicts in the region and the destabilizing effects of continued nuclear proliferation in the international system.

By allowing noncommunist governments to come to power in its Eastern European satellites, accepting the unification of Germany within NATO, signing the Conventional Forces in Europe Treaty (CFE) in 1990 and the Strategic Arms Reduction Treaty (START) in 1991, many obstacles are now in place to limit the potential of Russia reimposing its dominance in Central Europe or threatening Western Europe with invasion.[11]

Similarly, Germany has cast its lot with the process of European integration, realizing that adjusting to the demands of its European neighbors to limit its behavior in the international environment allows Germany to capitalize on its economic strength while also checking any tendency toward future expansion.[12] It seems, then, that the possibility of Western Europe reverting to its pre–World War II condition of pursuing separate nationalist foreign and defense policies that periodically pitted them against each other is not likely to recur in a post–cold war Europe that continues to pursue European integration.

However, not all analysts are optimistic about the prospects for stability in the post–cold war world. Stanley Hoffmann represents a school of analysts who contend that the cold war security system was based on flawed principles that will not serve the international community well in the post–cold war international environment. He cites two primary sources of international insecurity that are insufficiently addressed in a system of world politics that assumes that states monopolize the international system and are not constrained by the world capitalist economy. These sources of insecurity are the inequality among states, which is worsening because of the economic disparities that the capitalist world system generates, and the danger of nationalism, which is replacing the collapsed ideology of communism as the primary threat to the security of states, and which may be accompanied by religious revivalism.[13]

Hoffman's analysis is particularly worrisome to the post–cold war international system because it is based on the argument that the theoretical framework that seemed to satisfy policy makers in the cold war era does not fit the conditions of the present international environment. He argues that the principle of state sovereignty is inadequate because the world economy does not allow individual states to act with autonomy, and also because it may sanction atrocities within a nation-state's territory in violation of internationally accepted standards of human rights with the result of internal matters of states spilling over into the agenda of international politics.[14]

Hoffmann argues further that although many long-term threats to security have been resolved owing to the end of the cold war, stability will continue to elude the international system. International security organizations and individual governments are unable to achieve both the national resolve and consensus needed to create effective post–cold war security institutions. The cost required to rehabilitate Eastern Europe and the former Soviet Union while also narrowing the gap in national wealth that separates the North from the South and that contain the seeds of the problems of international politics found in famine, mass migration, and national instability is prohibitive.[15]

John Mearsheimer agrees with Hoffmann that nationalism is the single greatest threat to peace (Mearsheimer, 1990). Like Hoffmann, Mearsheimer also points to the inequalities among states as a primary source of insecurity in the international system. Mearsheimer, though, is concerned with relative disparities of power in the increasingly multipolar system, which he argues are a key determinant of instability. He laments the end of the cold war because it provided order in an anarchic security environment. According to Mearsheimer, bipolarity, balanced military power, and nuclear weapons ensured the stability of the cold war system.

Although a self-described realist, Mearsheimer is resistant to accept the forces operating in the international system today as he finds them. Both Hoffmann and Mearsheimer harbor pessimistic outlooks for the prospects of stability in the post–cold war world. Hoffmann's view, however, is rooted in a recognition of a changing reality where economic interdependence and latent nationalism infringes on the sovereignty of states and leads to more instability in the international system. Mearsheimer, however, subordinates internal values such as economic interdependence and democratization to the interstate struggles that states experience. For Mearsheimer, the stability of the system depends on its structure. Consequently, he reasons that multipolar systemic configurations are inferior to bipolar ones because a multipolar system is inherently more unstable.

The international security agenda has clearly changed from its old emphasis on managing the competitive bipolar relationship of two ideologically diametrically opposed hegemonic superpowers to dealing with the problems left by the collapse of one and the relative decline of the other's ability to influence international events. The policy agenda has fundamentally shifted away from the containment of the USSR as a superpower. The path has been cleared for the development of more widely accepted norms of international behavior and the collaborative solution of the concrete security problems that now crowd the international security policy agenda.[16]

These concrete issues run the gamut of security challenges and include the familiar problems of arms control and disarmament accords, and their verifications, as well as the new quagmires of the containment of coercive and expansionist nationalism, the dismantling of the former Soviet bloc's military machine, the control of nuclear proliferation, and the redesign and reprioritization of international organizations and security regimes to formulate and implement collective security and collective defense policies.

B. Arms Control

Schelling and Halperin offer the classic definition of arms control: "All forms of military cooperation between potential enemies in the interest of reducing the likelihood of war, its scope and violence if it occurs, and the political and economic costs of being prepared for it."[17] This conception of arms control applies today to conflicts around the globe. Arms control, however, does not necessarily imply disarmament. The goal of disarmament is the eventual elimination of all weapons, whereas the goal of arms control has been to ensure that a mutually stable deterrent relationship between the rival parties is maintained.

Schelling and Halperin argue further that the essential feature of arms control is the recognition of the common interest and the possibility of reciprocation and cooperation between the military establishments of potential enemies.[18] The theoretical basis of arms control has been the management of the strategic military relationship between the superpowers, with a specific focus on removing the incentives for either side to launch a preemptive first strike.[19]

There is an inherent paradox underlying the concept of arms control in that rival parties must be convinced to give up positions adopted in order to get their way in the international system. However, excessive reliance on so much violence in order to get one's way in the international system makes it impossible to ever carry out the threats (Schelling, 1960).

Stability is achieved through a negotiating process that is sensitive to the destabilizing effects of certain classes of weapons as well as the destabilizing effect of quantitative imbalances of weapons in the bilateral superpower relationship. Of particular concern is removing the incentive for a preemptive attack that is caused when one side perceives the other's retaliatory forces to be vulnerable to attack. Measures that reduce the likelihood of achieving surprise, which make targeted weapons less vulnerable to attack, and that reduce the perception that a "preventive war" is in the best interests of the attacking party are all objectives of arms control.[20]

Arms control had been the centerpiece of East-West relations during the cold war, but some have argued that with the absence of political differences, arms control has become a marginal element in East-West relations.[21] However, reaching arms control agreements with the successor states of the former Soviet Union and solving the practical problems of the transportation and disposal of arms throughout the Commonwealth of Independent States (CIS), along with the problematic exercise of creating a post–cold war security regime in Europe among the prevalent less than stable conditions, tempers the optimistic analysis of some that arms control is only a "left-over" increasingly less relevant policy issue for the current era.

Opportunities for consensus on arms control issues improved dramatically with the emergence of a post-Soviet regime willing to cooperate with the West. Previously, lack of consensus on fundamental underlying ideological differences rendered arms control largely ineffective. Arms control was used as another tool of diplomacy to manage the superpower relationship, but its effectiveness was constrained because of the competitiveness of superpower relations.

The demise of the cold war has made many of these long-standing differences moot. Indeed, competition shifted so swiftly to cooperation that the international community has witnessed the phenomenon of a series of successfully negotiated accords at the end of the cold war. These include the Intermediate-Range Nuclear Forces (INF) Treaty, the Conventional Forces in Europe (CFE) Treaty, and the Strategic Arms Reduction Talks (START) Treaty.

Clearly, the arms control relationship between the United States and the former Soviet Union has improved. But, questions surrounding the practical implementation of these recent agreements has led to the appearance of new policy issues such as the need to provide financial and technical assistance to these financially strapped Soviet successor states in order to secure the safe transport of nuclear weapons to depots where they will be stored and ultimately destroyed.[22]

Traditional approaches to East-West relations have been replaced with new concepts of security based on mutually beneficial political arrangements, deep reductions in arms, and the continuation of only the minimum amount of military forces required for credible mutual deterrence (Trofimenko, 1990). The tailoring of military forces is particularly problematic. Reducing force structures without a clear idea of what specific military threats confront either individual states or the regional security organizations of which they are a part is a challenge confronting national security policy makers today. Policy makers are confronted with determining how much is enough to fulfill their needs for reasonable sufficiency in an era when the required degree of military preparedness is uncertain.

C. Arms Transfers and Production in the Post–Cold War Environment

Additionally, it can be argued that the spread of weapons increases the probability of war— especially if weapons proliferate to unstable regions of the world already engaged in conflict.

The introduction of great quantities of more technologically advanced weapons into these regions may change the character of war and encourage greater violence as a means of settling disputes (Blacker and Duffy, 1984).

Edward Laurence defines "arms transfers" or "arms trade" as the acquisition and maintenance of national security by states through the acquisition of military capabilities. Laurence argues that the phenomenon can best be studied by observing the commodities that are traded in the international system for the purpose of enhancing the military power of the recipient nation.[23] The specific dimensions of the concept include the dollar value and mode of payment of the transfer, the quantity of arms transferred, the quality and military utility of the transfer, the type of training and support services that accompany the transfer, and the mode of production of the transfer.[24]

Michael Klare traces the evolution of U.S. arms transfers policy over the past several decades and concludes that the United States has become too reliant on arms sales as its main instrument of achieving security objectives abroad. He points to the lack of restraint in burgeoning arms sales and cautions that such transfers are likely to be counterproductive to the national security interests of the suppliers as highly armed clients rely on their arsenals as usable instruments of power that may be employed whenever national interests dictate.[25]

The situation is exacerbated further by the collapse of the "bipolar" system that contained conflict in the developing world by mandating that states align with the rival superpowers. The post–cold war era, by contrast, features an armed developing world with individual states free to pursue self-defined national agendas uninhibited by the restraining hand of either the East or the West.[26]

Laurence's analysis supports the view that the international arms transfer regime has changed markedly over the past decade and enters the post–cold war era fundamentally transformed in many respects. The evaporation of the communist threat and the subsequent reduction in forces in both the East and the West has put pressure on the arms industries of the former superpowers to export. But the concurrent decline of the international economy and the high debts of developing states has dampened the demand of many recipients of arms transfers.

Additionally, the downsizing of forces is taking place within the domestic context of limited fiscal resources and the constraining effect of competing social demands for the scarce economic resources of states. The question of arms transfers places states starved for hard currency in a dilemma because many of them, such as the successor states of the Soviet Union, rely on arms exports for the continuation of indigenous defense industries and to earn hard currency. Klare (1984) additionally cautions against arms sales to states with large debt because the diversion of national resources to arms purchases is likely to impede development and support repressive regimes.

The nature of the participants in the international arms system has changed, so that the predominance of nation-states as the main actors in the system has been lessened with the rising influence of defense firms. Additionally, the international arms transfer system is characterized by a greater level of illegal arms transfers, such as those that surfaced regarding the arming of Iraq, and by a proliferation of suppliers other than the major industrial countries.[27]

The evolution of the international arms transfer regime has many consequences for the behavior of the actors within it. First, major arms suppliers are no longer able to control the outbreak of conflict or control the conflict once it begins by using arms as an instrument of policy. Second, recipient states are now able to acquire a significant degree of military capability to threaten the major states in the system. The arming of Iraq is a case in point. Third, arms transfers have become less significant as a means of influencing other actors in the international system but have become a legitimate means of adding to the coffers of nation-states who export them.

These incentives in the international system to support weak domestic economies through the export of arms throughout the world have caused many to consider the need to control arms transfers to be the new central agenda item in arms control (Ferguson, 1991). The international community has recognized the need to develop multilateral measures to prevent developing states from acquiring ballistic missiles and nuclear technology as well as the need to develop measures that punish actors within the system that violate its norm of behavior.[28]

1. The Dilemma of the Soviet Successor States

The next decade is certain to feature attempts to deter the successor states of the Soviet Union from selling off the assets of the Soviet armed forces now scattered across most of the separate states. The trend begun in the Gorbachev era to reduce the export of arms along with procurement demands to outfit Soviet forces are being reversed in several post-Soviet republics. These exports are occurring within the context of unstable domestic environments that have been unable to put into place export regulations that prevent the unsanctioned sale of state assets by former Communist Party and military officials who have gained access to them (Almquist and Bacon, 1992).

D. Regional Competition and Security Regimes

Although the East-West arms control regime has benefited from the switch to cooperative methods of negotiating, many regions are still practicing a competitive approach to arms control owing to the continued presence of fundamental underlying differences between adversaries. Some international security theorists are calling for a distinction between cooperative and competitive approaches to arms control.[29] The variety of relationships between the possessors of arms in the international system call for a variety of approaches toward negotiating force structures that will be stabilizing.

The traditional East-West efforts to conduct arms control were rooted in the competitive approach that had as its objective the stabilization of the balance of military forces of two political adversaries. The competitive approach was aimed at controlling the traditional security dilemma, which is characterized by one state's pursuit of security in the form of a military build-up, only to find itself left insecure because of the reactive build-up of its adversary in response to the first initiative. The cooperative approach is used by states with compatible security and political interests who realize that actions that increase the security of other states can also enhance their own security.[30]

Competitive approaches to arms control can potentially be applied to regions still plagued by endemic conflict such as the Middle East, South Asia, the Korean Peninsula, Pakistan, and India, which have exchanged lists of nuclear sites, and eventually, the Balkan states, which are currently engrossed in violent warfare. Policy makers involved in cooperative efforts will be prevalent in regions recovering from decades of adversarial relationships. The process of forging agreements that emphasize confidence-building measures such as ensuring the transparency, or lack of secrecy, of military activities and capabilities, and cooperation in on-site verification inspections will continue.[31]

1. Regional Security Regimes

Additionally, issues regarding the future of regional alliance systems and their associated security organizations are crowding the international security agenda. The diffusion of threats and the increasing degree of incompatibility of members of regional security systems contemplating expansion of membership bodes poorly for the effectiveness of regional security systems. International security policy makers must weigh the strengths and functions of existing security organizations while discerning the proper mix of authority among them in the future.

2. Example of Europe

The creation of supranational European institutions in the cold war era led to the gradual incorporation of European economic life into the framework of the European Community (EC) and the organization of European defense into NATO, and increasingly, the Western European Union (WEU) as well as the Conference on Security and Cooperation in Europe (CSCE).[32] In the post–cold war era the process of economic, security, and political integration has been interrupted by forces from the East that demaqnd incorporation in European economic and security regimes. The post–cold war European security regime is consequently crowded with the coexistence of NATO, the WEU as a security arm of the EC, and the CSCE. Each has a distinct security emphasis and membership.[33]

For example, NATO has served the function of organizing the US–Western European security relationship through the coordination of defense policies accompanied by decades of joint military operations. The WEU is experiencing a revival of sorts after decades of existing solely as a paper organization. Many Europeans who favor an independent European security organization support the development of the WEU into the military arm of the European Community (EC). Meanwhile, the former members of the Warsaw Pact in Europe are searching for participation in a security regime to alleviate the threat of national ethnic unrest and general instability in the region.

The shifting defense environment has blurred the roles security organizations formed in the cold war era. International security policy makers must sort out the security arrangements presently available to them and decide on their respective roles. Some are calling for an arrangement that does not exclusively choose among the organizations but supports an interlocking relationship among them that capitalizes on the comparative advantages of each and would allow for a variety of responses depending on the particular crisis.[34]

E. A New Look at Deterrence and Stability

The diminishment of the Soviet threat has called into question the continued relevance of the concept of deterrence. Mutual nuclear deterrence has been the centerpiece of U.S. and Soviet military strategy since each side became dependent on nuclear weapons as the main repository of national military power. But, the transformation of the political relationships between the world's nuclear powers has led to a reassessment of deterrence theory that has driven the potential employment of nuclear arsenals since their arrival.

One major area of activity that has already been explored is arms control. Agreement must be reached on what levels of nuclear weapons should be maintained to ensure that the deterrent effect between nuclear powers is maintained and the stability of the international system remains.[35] Initial significant drawdowns were agreed to by Presidents Bush and Gorbachev under START I. While the process of ratification was underway, the Soviet Union broke into four independent nuclear powers—Russia, Ukraine, Kazakhstan, and Belarus—all of which will have to be brought on board in order for the agreement to be effected. The cooperation of Ukraine, which has been resistant to abiding by its START I commitments to remove all nuclear weapons from its territory, is essential to the success of START II. START

II is essentially a numerical amendment to START I negotiated between Presidents Yeltsin and Bush that will draw down the nuclear forces of both sides to levels between 3000 and 3500 nuclear warheads when fully implemented, but it assumes that the conditions agreed to in START I will carry over into the amended treaty.[36]

A related issue is how the role of the lesser nuclear powers will be changed with the significant drawdowns promised by the superpowers through such agreements as START. Their influence is likely to become greater in an international system where there is less of a discrepancy between their quantities of nuclear weapons and those of the superpowers. Britain and France do not favor any substantial reductions in their nuclear forces and argue any reductions will reduce the deterrent value of their small forces. France will, however, cut its strategic nuclear submarine force from six to four and gradually phase out its Mirage IV and IRBM (intermediate range ballistic missiles) nuclear systems.[37] China also is resistant to disarmament efforts and has stated that such measures will not be considered until the major powers' nuclear arsenals have scaled down to its level.[38]

There is also a growing similarity in the political character of all nuclear powers (with the exception of China) that may lead to the development of general strategies of deterrence based on prudent consideration of what is necessary to maintain a condition of stability between nuclear powers in general as opposed to the old view that deterrence was designed to control the policy of adversaries.[39]

The post–cold war environment has seen a shift in all of the major dimensions of deterrence. Primary among these is the object of deterrence itself. Arguably, the object remains the nuclear forces of the Russian Federation, but the threats of both an all-out conventional attack on the territory of Western Europe is no longer worrisome because the political will for such aggression has dissipated, Russia has lost its Eastern European allies, and the progress of arms control has codified the conventional balance of forces to include the withdrawal of heavy armor and forces of an offensive nature in Europe so that major conventional armaments in the Soviet successor states west of the Urals will be reduced to one third their 1988 levels when the CFE is fully implemented.[40]

A corollary to this development is the reduced need for a nuclear umbrella extended to European allies in order to compensate for an inferior conventional weapons position vis-a-vis the Soviets in Europe. The loss of an advantage in conventional forces weakens the logic of nuclear escalation because neither side is either threatened by the conventional superiority of the other or determined to augment conventional superiority with nuclear weapons.[41] There is a consensus that nuclear deterrence is becoming increasingly less relevant. The contention is that peace between the superpowers will reduce the preoccupation with violence among them and remove nuclear deterrence from its centerpiece position in strategic thought (Betts, 1991).

There is also agreement, however, that as long as nuclear weapons exist, "existential deterrence" will be necessary. These analysts contend that the potential for proliferation within the post–cold war international system in general and the uncertainty of long-term stability of command and control within the former Soviet Union only complicates the deterrence agenda. They argue that if nuclear proliferation occurs to any extent in the post–cold war world, the reliability of command and control will be undermined simply because of the increased number of nuclear "triggers" that need to be managed.[42]

Finally, there is the ongoing debate among deterrence theorists about the logic of deterrence theory itself regardless of the recent changes in the international system. This debate pits those who are convinced of the compelling logic of threatening to retaliate against an aggressor's act of violence against those who have come to the conclusion that the defects of deterrence theory render it an unusable theory that should be abandoned given its potential to be the conceptual force behind the destruction of civilization.[43]

F. Proliferation in the Post-Cold War World

1. Nonproliferation Issues

Many analysts regard the proliferation of nuclear weapons as the greatest threat to international security in the post-cold war era. Although no states have officially joined the United States, Russia, Britain, and France in the nuclear weapons club since China did in 1964, it is widely believed that Israel, South Africa, Pakistan, and India are de facto members. The spread of nuclear weapons to the developing world is particularly troublesome because many of these states are located in highly volatile regions that have been characterized by conflict.[44]

The post-cold war world must deal with the specific problem of the proliferation of nuclear technology in the wake of the collapse of the Soviet Union. Developing international security safeguards that address the issue of the Soviet "brain drain" is yet another task that international security policy makers must undertake to contain the potential nuclear proliferation that could take place in the absence of such controls (Potter, 1992).

Not all scholars agree that the proliferation of nuclear weapons is a dangerous phenomenon. Waltz (1981) argues that the spread of nuclear weapons could stabilize regional conflicts in the same manner that conflict between the superpowers was avoided owing to the presence of nuclear weapons.

Van Evera (1990) echoes Waltz' support for proliferation with the position that nuclear weapons allow lesser states that possess them to stand up to powers with greater resources. The threat of escalation to nuclear war deters significant challenges to the lesser state's security. According to this view, nuclear proliferation should be regarded as a net benefit to peace. Whatever dangers that are inherent in proliferation, Van Evera contends, can be managed by the existing nuclear powers by guaranteeing the security of non-nuclear states and using force to prevent the acquisition of nuclear weapons in those states where proliferation is not acceptable.

Additionally, Reiss (1988) argues that states capable of building nuclear arsenals have deliberately decided against doing so because they have determined that the threat of developing nuclear arms or of detonating weapons that have been developed will bring them more benefits than carrying their nuclear programs to completion. According to this view, the international system rewards behavior that supports the containment of the spread of nuclear weapons with rewards that are in the best interests of potential nuclear proliferators who comply with the standards set by the existing nuclear powers.

2. Strengthening the Nonproliferation Regime

Most states, however, do not subscribe to the view that proliferation is a positive force in the international system. Consequently, since the onset of nuclear weapons, measures have been proposed and adopted to reduce the security threats inherent in the acquisition of nuclear weapons by more states. The centerpiece of the nonproliferation regime is the 1968 Nuclear-Nonproliferation Treaty (NPT), which declares that the further spread of nuclear weapons is not in the security interests of the states that comprise the international system; and it provides for verification of the pledges that its signatories make (Scheinman, 1987).

The organizational core of the nonproliferation regime is the International Atomic Energy Agency (IAEA), which is responsible for implementing international safeguards.[45] A issue being debated is whether or not the IAEA should be given greater authority to ensure that safeguards for the nonproliferation of nuclear weapons and nuclear weapons technology is ensured in the post–cold war era. Safeguards are a set of measures designed to create confidence that states are complying with specific nonproliferation obligations.[46] As such, safeguards are technical means of verifying compliance with legal obligations.

The IAEA was created in 1956 to promote peaceful uses of nuclear energy and to monitor the miliary applications of nuclear technology. Its track record throughout the nuclear age has been remarkably good, but the discovery of Iraq's clandestine nuclear weapons program in the aftermath of the Persian Gulf War has resulted in greater support for the implementation of measures that would strengthen the IAEA.[47]

An agreement between the state and the IAEA is required in order for the state to be subject to safeguards. Additionally, states enter into agreement with the IAEA at varying levels of commitment to comply with nuclear nonproliferation. Categories of states range from non-nuclear states who have made binding nonproliferation commitments, to states who have not made binding nonproliferation commitments, to nuclear states agreeing to accept monitoring to ensure the safety of their peaceful programs.[48]

Specifically, the IAEA focuses on ensuring the material accountancy of nuclear materials, measures that reduce the barriers to access of weapons programs, and on-site inspections.[49] However, the IAEA is limited to inspecting only "declared" facilities. The Iraqis were able to circumvent the IAEA by conducting their activity in undeclared facilities. Expansion of IAEA authority to include on-site inspection of "suspect" facilities as well would allow the IAEA to follow-up on available intelligence information acquired through national technical means such as was available through US intelligence in the case of Iraq and expose clandestine programs earlier.[50]

The IAEA can also play a crucial role in ensuring that nuclear weapons have been removed from the territory of the Soviet successor states and ensuring that fissile material is placed under international safeguards.[51] To the extent the former Soviet Union's peaceful nuclear program continues, the IAEA also can verify that materials are not being transferred to the pursuit of military projects.[52]

Broadening the IAEA's access to information, unrestricted access to any suspect location, and the right to turn to the United Nations Security Council in the event of refused access, along with sufficient funding of IAEA programs could greatly enhance its effectiveness and contribute to the construction of a worldwide nonproliferation regime.[53]

Another measure within the nonproliferation regime focuses on placing controls on the suppliers of nuclear weapons technology and resources. The 1987 Missile Technology Control Regime (MTCR) is aimed at limiting the risks of nuclear proliferation by controlling transfers that would contribute to nuclear weapon delivery systems other than manned aircraft. Those who adhere to the MTCR guidelines limit their exports of missiles able to carry 500 kilograms over an area of 300 kilometers.[54]

The MTCR attempts to address the instability inherent in the introduction of ballistic missile technology to conflict-ridden regions.[55] However, states in the developing world are resistant to MTCR because it limits the transfer of technology that could benefit development in general, and because it specifically limits transfers of ballistic missiles necessary for the launching of satellites and the development of a civilian space program.[56]

3. Chemical and Biological Weapons Regimes

Another issue on the international security agenda is the control of the proliferation of chemical and biological weapons (CBW). The threat of states actually using chemical and biological weapons became real in the 1980s when the use of CBW by Iraq was verified in the war between Iran and Iraq. These weapons are particularly difficult to control because they are inexpensive to produce and easy to conceal.

Four measures dominate the agenda for the control of chemical and biological weapons: (1) export controls on the materials and technology needed to produce CBW, (2) sanctions against companies that supply such materials or technology, (3) assistance to groups or states affected by the use of CBW, and (4) arms control agreements that restrict the use of CBW and contain regional confidence-building measures.[57]

Export controls are focused on making it more difficult for potential or known proliferators to import the materials needed to support their chemical and biological weapons programs. Specific controls have been placed on precursor chemicals needed to make chemical agents as well as on the technology related to their production. Foremost among multilateral export control efforts has been the Australia Group, which is made up of 15 Western industrialized countries that have adopted guidelines to control both the production of chemical and biological agents.[58]

Sanctions are directed against both countries that actually use chemical and biological weapons and suppliers, including individual firms, who enable them. The intent of sanctions is to produce disincentives against the use of chemical and biological weapons for countries that already have them and to deter countries contemplating the development of such programs.[59]

Assistance can be provided to the victims of chemical and biological weapons in both the anticipation of their use and in the actual event of chemical or biological attack. Assistance can include the development of defensive programs against such attacks as well as the provision of humanitarian and medical aid.[60] Finally, the restriction of chemical and biological weapons through arms control agreements is an essential step toward nonproliferation of these weapons.

The centerpiece of the CBW nonproliferation strategy is the Chemical Weapons Convention (CWC). The CWC bans the production and stockpiling of all chemical weapons, prohibits the production of chemicals that could lead to the development of chemical weapons, and monitors the production and use of all other chemical agents known to be used in the development of chemical weapons.[61]

Concluded in September of 1992, more than 120 nations have thus far joined the convention since its signing in Paris in January 1993. Most countries believed to have chemical weapons signed the pact with the exception of some Arab countries and Iraq—a known violator of the treaty's provisions.[62] Responsibility for verifying the agreement will fall to the IAEA. Inspections of both declared and suspected facilities will be carried out. There are also provisions for sanctions against states who violate the terms of the agreement and assistance to states attacked with chemical weapons.[63]

Problems in the actual implementation of the treaty stem from the difficulty of monitoring the chemical industry, which can legitimately produce civilian products with the same materials that contribute to the production of chemical and biological weapons. Additionally, states that fear that they may become victims of chemical weapons complain that assistance measures that are voluntarily funded are not adequate (Feinstein, 1992).

G. Verification Issues in the Post-Cold War Environment

Grin and Van Der Graaf (1990) define verification as: "the process, pursued by one or several parties, of determining on basis of data acquired by own means or supplied by the verified party or parties to which extent the behavior of the latter is consistent with the measures agreed upon in the treaty.'' The position of the West throughout the cold war era was that arms control agreements that cannot be properly verified should not be negotiated. The Soviets, on the other hand, regarded verification provisions as transgressions against the conduct of their internal affairs and distrusted proposals that would allow for on-site inspections (van der Graaf, 1992).

The Intermediate-Range Nuclear Forces (INF) Treaty signed by President Ronald Reagan and Soviet leader Mikhail Gorbachev in December 1987 is significant in the evolution of "effective'' verification because it is the first arms control agreement to contain highly intrusive provisions for verification.[64] Measures such as on-site inspections are necessary, Krepon argues, if long-term reductions in arms are to be realized. Arms control agreements that feature reductions rather than the banning of particular weapons must rely on such intrusive measures to ensure compliance among the signatories.

The cooperative environment of the post–cold war era is conducive to the achievement of further strides in verification. New opportunities exist for the inclusion of far-reaching varification regimes within arms control agreements. The START Treaty and the Chemical Weapons Convention both contain extensive on-site inspection provisions.[65] The willingness of states to allow more intrusive verification measures has substantially raised the confidence of those concerned about the viability of arms control treaties. This is particularly true among developing states with minimal independent national technical means for verification in the absence of on-site inspections.

The possibility of more extensive verification provisions has resulted in more demanding standards of verification that may even allow for the detection of acts on the part of the monitored party that go beyond the specific limits of the treaty but are regarded as militarily significant to the monitoring party.[66] The specific verification agenda includes the possibility of distinguishing between cooperative and adversarial verification. Verification regimes could be constructed based on a graduated system of implementing rigorous verification provisions included in treaties depending on the degree of compliance or noncompliance detected.

Such a system could help alleviate the expensive costs of verification in instances when verification regimes may be too rigorous for a particularly cooperative phase of relations between the states that are parties to the agreement. In this way, during eras when former adversaries are demonstrably consistently complying with the verification regime, the unnecessary burden of continuously employing all authorized means to verify compliance can be lessened.

H. Multilateral Approaches to Regime Creation

1. Collective Security in the Post–Cold War Era

The redesign and reprioritization of international organizations and security regimes in order to formulate, implement, and enforce collective security and collective defense policies is a crucial undertaking currently evolving in the international system. International security policy makers must decide which conditions are sufficient for intervention into the affairs of other states. The collapse of the cold war has created a favorable atmosphere for the resurgence of militant nationalism around the globe.

2. The United Nations and Peacekeeping

The withdrawal of ideological criteria for the support of UN policies due to the convergence of social democratic principles among its primary members has opened up new possibilities for the UN to fulfill its originally intended role as an instrument of keeping peace in the international system (Stiles and MacDonald, 1992).

The end of the cold war and the recession of the Soviet Union and the United States into the background of regional conflict mediation has left a vacuum in the international system for the United Nations to assume a wider role in the mediation of regional conflicts. Paul Diehl argues that collective enforcement, peacekeeping, and peacemaking are the various responses to regional conflict that the UN will take in the post–cold war world.[67]

Diehl concludes that although the end of the cold war has widened some of the parameters of UN action, significant limitations remain that will prevent the UN from undertaking a major enforcement role in regional conflicts.[68] Primary among these is the nature of the UN itself as an organization of sovereign states that are resistant to any measures that would transfer national sovereignty to an organization that might pursue actions contrary to the national intersts of its individual members.

Diehl predicts that two conditions must be present for effective UN intervention to occur. First, it must be possible to declare an aggressor in the conflict easily. Second, there must be a major international actor willing to organize the effort within the framework of the UN. Under such conditions, then, conflicts that are of greatest interest to the major actors of the international system will receive priority within the UN as well.[69]

Harleman (1992) offers another option for the UN in the post–cold war era — peace building. By peace building, he means greater participation on the part of the UN in disarmament activities. He advocates peace building as part of an overall effort that puts more stock in preventing conflict than international security policy makers have traditionally invested.

Although international security policy makers have increasingly turned to the UN since the Soviet Union's cooperation fostered a new era of collegiality within it, it is becoming clear that the UN is neither structurally prepared nor militarily able to accomplish the expanded array of tasks that the international community is considering assigning to it. Although the UN-based coalition formed to sanction and carry out the Persian Gulf War is frequently pointed out as evidence of the UN's ability to be an enforcement agency for the international system, the Persian Gulf effort was little more than the multinational cooperation of states loosely coalesced (Mackinlay and Chopra, 1992).

True multilateralism—the subordination of control of soveriegn armed forces to a centralized community authorized to act by the international community—has yet to materialize in the post–cold war international system. International security policy makers must decide what role should be assigned to the UN and develop specific policies to ensure that the UN is able to execute the role given to it.

III. CONCLUSIONS

A review of the international security agenda points to a significantly increased workload for international security policy makers in the aftermath of the cold war. Although the use of military force and the principles of deterrence will remain as building blocks of the international security regime, nonmilitary aspects of security are growing and becoming increasingly relevant. The changing nature of the threat from superpower conflict to unrestrained outbreaks of nationalist unrest calls for the inclusion of additional tools and new approaches to the resolution and management of the forces that currently threaten the members of the international system.

NOTES

1. For discussions on the debate over where the field of security studies is headed, see Walt, S. M. (1991). The renaissance of security studies. *International Studies Quarterly* 35: 211–239, along with a rebuttal by Kolodziej, E. A. (1992). Renaissance in security studies? Caveat lector! *International Studies Quarterly* 36: 421–438. Also see Kolodziej, E. A. (1992). What is Security and Security Studies? *Arms Control* 13(1): 1–31. Also see Lynn-Jones, S. M., and Nye, J. S. (1988). International security studies: A report on a conference on the state of the field. *International Security* 12(4): 5–27; and Chipman, J. (1992). The future of strategic studies. *Survival* 34(1): 109–131.
2. Bull, H. (1977). *The Anarchical Society*. Columbia University Press, New York, Chap. 1.
3. Ibid., p. 111.
4. Ibid., p. 123.
5. For a characterization of the cold war era as a balancing of satisfactions among the superpowers, see Kanet, R. E., and Kolodziej, E. A. (Eds.) (1991). *The Cold War as Cooperation*. John Hopkins Press, Baltimore.
6. Bull, H. (1977). *The Anarchical Society*. Columbia University Press, New York.
7. Pleshakov, K. (1991). Our national interests in the transitional period. *International Affairs* 11: 12–20. Pleshakov argues that the failure of the Soviet Union to resolve the threats to the unity of the state posed by its domestic agenda has led to a radical transformation of the national interest in Russia, so that security interests are dominated by the tasks of democratization and moving to the market economy.
8. Mortimer, E. (1992). European security after the cold war. *Adelphi Papers* 271: 35.
9. For a review of the development of deterrence theory, see Freedman, L. (1989). *Evolution of Nuclear Strategy*. St. Martin's Press, New York.
10. Two key studies on the main figures of the strategic community responsible for the evolution of deterrence theory are Herken, G. (1985). *Counsels of War*. Knopf, New York; and Kaplan, F. (1983). *Wizards of Armageddon*. Simon & Schuster, New York.
11. Mortimer, E. (1992). European security after the cold war. *Adelphi Papers* 271: 8.
12. Deporte, A. W. (1979). *Europe Between the Superpowers*. Yale University Press, New Haven, CT, p. 187. Also see Kolodziej, E. A. (1992). What is security and security studies? *Arms Control* 13(1): 13.
13. Hoffmann, S. (April 1992). Delusions of World Orders, *New York Review of Books*, p. 37.
14. Ibid.
15. Ibid., p. 40.
16. Chipman, J. (1992). The future of strategic studies. *Survival* 34(1): 114.
17. Schelling, T. C., and Halperin, M. H. (1961). *Strategy and Arms Control*. Twentieth Century Fund, New York, p. 2.
18. Ibid.
19. For a discussion on the impact of arms control on the stability of the nuclear relationship between the superpowers and the likelihood of preemptive strikes, see Talbott, S. (1979). *Endgame*. Harper & Row, New York, Chap. 10.
20. Schelling, T. C., and Halperin, M. H. (1961). *Strategy and Arms Control*. Twentieth Century Fund, New York, pp. 9–17.
21. Daalder, I. H. (1992). The future of arms control. *Survival* 34(1): 51.
22. Ibid., p. 54.
23. Laurence, E. J. (1992). *The International Arms Trade*. Lexington Books, New York, p. 3. For a summary of the field as well as an in-depth treatment of issues related to arms transfers, influence, leverage, and dependence, see Catrina, C. (1988). *Arms Transfers and Dependence*. Taylor and Francis, New York. For an analysis of US policy, see Klare, M. (1984). *American Arms Supermarket*. University of Texas Press, Austin. Data and analysis of arms transfers can be found in the Stockholm International Peace Research Institute's (SIPRI) *Yearbook of World Armaments and Disarmaments* published annually by Oxford University Press (1986–1992) and previously by MIT

Press. Also see *The Military Balance* published annually by the International Institute for Strategic Studies in London.

24. Laurence, E. J. (1992). *The International Arms Trade*. Lexington Books, New York, p. 17.
25. Klare, M. (1984). *American Arms Supermarket*. University of Texas Press, Austin, p. 238.
26. Ibid., pp. 14–15.
27. Laurence, E. J. (1992). *The International Arms Trade*. Lexington Books, New York, pp. 128–131.
28. Ibid., pp. 155–169.
29. Daalder, I. H. (1992). *Strategy and Arms Control*. Twentieth Century Fund, New York, p. 52.
30. Ibid., p. 51.
31. Also see Brams, S. J., and Kilgour, D. M. (1988). *Game Theory and National Security*, Blackwell, New York.
32. Mortimer, E. (1992). European security after the cold war. *Adelphi Papers* 271: 10. The Maastricht Treaty signed in December 1991 designated the WEU as the future security arm of the EC. The CSCE incorporates all the states of Europe and the former Soviet republics and is regarded as too large and diverse to serve as a policy-making body. For recent histories on the EC, see Hackett, C. (1990). *Cautious Revolution: The European Community Arrives*. Praeger, New York; and Lodge, J. (1990). *The European Community and the Challenge of the Future*. Pinter, London.
33. For a more in-depth treatment of European security institutions, see Hyde-Price, A. (1991). *European Security Beyond the Cold War*. Sage, Newbury, CA.
34. Chipman, J. (1992). The future of strategic studies. *Survival* 34(1): 121.
35. Quester, G. H. (1992). The future of nuclear deterrence. *Survival* 34(1): 74.
36. See transcript from Arms Control Association December 30, 1992 press conference on START II signing found in *Arms Control Today* 22(10): 3–9.
37. Memorandum on ''Les Choix Pour L'Equipment De Forces'' (December 1992), furnished by the French Embassy, Washington D.C.
38. Tempest, R. (1992). Yeltsin urges Britain, France, China arms cuts. *Los Angeles Times*, January 31, part A, p. 1, col. 6.
39. Quester calls this ''counterpower targeting''; see Quester, G. H. (1992). The future of nuclear deterrence. *Survival* 34(1): 80.
40. Dean, J., and R. W. Forsberg (1992). CFE and beyond: The future of conventional arms control. *International Security* 17(1): 93.
41. Quester, G. H. (1992). The future of nuclear deterrence. *Survival* 34(1): 84.
42. Ibid., pp. 82–88.
43. For an in-depth look at the debate on the viability of rational deterrence theory, see the Symposium in *World Politics* 61(2): 143–247.
44. Spector, L. (1987). *Going Nuclear*. Ballinger, Cambridge, MA, p. 4. Also see Spector, L. (1989). *The Undeclared Bomb: The Spread of Nuclear Weapons 1987–1988*. Harper Business, New York, along with Spector, L. (1991). *Nuclear Ambitions: The Spread of Nuclear Weapons 1989–1990*. Westview, Boulder, CO; and Spector, L., and Smith, J. P. (1992). *Nuclear Threshold: The Global Spread of Nuclear Weapons 1990–1991*. Westview, Boulder, CO.
45. See Scheinman, L. (1987). Resources for the Future. Washington D.C., for a thorough discussion of the IAEA and its role in the nonproliferation of nuclear weapons.
46. Blix, H. (1992). IAEA safeguards: New challenges. *Disarmament* 15(2): 40.
47. Keeny, S. M., and Panofsky, W. K. H. (1992). Controlling nuclear warheads and materials: Steps toward a comprehensive regime. *Arms Control Today* 22(1): 8.
48. Blix, H. (1992). IAEA safeguards: New challenges. *Disarmament* 15(2): 36–38.
49. Ibid., p. 39.
50. Keeny, S. M., and Panofsky, W. K. H. (1992). Controlling nuclear warheads and materials: Steps toward a comprehensive regime. *Arms Control Today* 22(1): 8.
51. Potter, W. C. (1992). Exports and experts: Proliferation risks from the new commonwealth. *Arms Control Today* Jan/Feb: 36.
52. Keeny, S. M., and Panofsky, W. K. H. (1992). Controlling nuclear warheads and materials: Steps toward a comprehensive regime. *Arms Control Today* 22(1): 8.

53. Blix, H. (1992). IAEA safeguards: New challenges. *Disarmament* 15(2): 44–46.
54. Missile Technology Control Regime, *The Arms Control Reporter*, p. 706.A.1., Jan 92.
55. Chipman, J. (1992). The future of strategic studies. *Survival* 34(1): 124.
56. Missile Technology Control Regime, *The Arms Control Reporter*, p. 706.A.1.
57. Harris, E. D. (1991). Towards a comprehensive strategy for halting chemical and biological weapons proliferation. *Arms Control* 12(2): 138.
58. Ibid., pp. 131–132.
59. Ibid., p. 134.
60. Ibid., p. 139.
61. Smith, R. K. (1991). The marginalization of superpower arms control. *Security Studies* 1(1): 49.
62. Waxman, S. (1993). Chemical arms pact picking up support. *The Altanta Journal and Constitution* January 14, 1993, sec. A, p. 7. See also special issue (1992), Chemical Weapons Convention. *Arms Control Today* 22(8).
63. Harris, E. D. (1991). Toward a comprehensive strategy for halting chemical and biological weapons proliferation. *Arms Control* 12(2): 150.
64. Krepon, M. (1988). *Verification and Compliance.* Ballinger, Cambridge, MA, p. vii.
65. For an extensive discussion of the role of on-site inspections in the verification regimes of arms control agreements, see Lewis A. Dunn's (1990) edited volume *Arms Control Verification and the New Role of On-Site Inspection.* Lexington Books, Lexington, MA.
66. McFate, P. B. (1992). Where do we go from here? Verifying future arms control agreements. *Washington Quarterly* 15(4): 77.
67. Diehl, P. F. (1992). International Actors: The United Nations—Collective enforcement, peacekeeping, and peacemaking. Paper presented to the Conference on Coping with Regional Conflict at the University of Illinois, Urbana, October 9–11, p. 3.
68. Ibid., p. 28.
69. Ibid., p. 7–10.

REFERENCES

Achen, C. H., and Snidal, D. (1989). Rational deterrence theory and comparative case studies. *World Politics* 61(2): 143–169.
Almquist, P., and Bacon, E. (1992). Arms exports in a post-Soviet market. *Arms Control Today* 22(6): 12–17.
Betts, R. K. (1991). The concept of deterrence in the postwar era. *Security Studies* 1(1): 25–36.
Blacker, C. D., and Duffy, G. (Eds.) (1984). *International Arms Control: Issues and Agreements.* Stanford University Press, Stanford, CA.
Blix, H. (1992). IAEA Safeguards: New Challenges. *Disarmament* 15(2): 33–47.
Brams, S. J., and Kilgour, D. M. (1988). *Game Theory and National Security.* Blackwell, New York.
Brodie, B. (1959). *Strategy in the Missile Age.* Princeton University Press, Princeton, NJ.
Bull, H. (1977). *The Anarchical Society.* Columbia University Press, New York.
Buzan, B. (1991). *People, States, and Fear*, 2nd ed., Lynne Reinner, Boulder, CO.
Catrina, C. (1988). *Arms Transfers and Dependence.* Taylor and Francis, New York.
Chipman, J. (1992). The future of strategic studies. *Survival* 34(1): 109–131.
Daalder, I. H. (1992). The future of arms control. *Survival* 34(1): 51–71.
Dean, J., and R. W. Forsberg (1992). CFE and beyond: The future of arms control. *International Security* 17(1): 76–109.
DePorte, A. W. (1979). *Europe Between the Superpowers.* Yale University Press, New Haven, CT.
Diel, P. F. (1992). International actors: The United Nations—Collective enforcement, peacekeeping, and peacemaking. Paper presented to the Conference on Coping with Regional Conflict at the University of Illinois, Urbana, October 9–11.
Dunn, L. A. (Ed.) (1990). *Arms Control Verification and the New Role of On-Site Inspection.* Lexington Books, Lexington, MA.

Feinstein, L. (1992). Geneva negotiators complete chemical weapons treaty. *Arms Control Today* 22(7): 24.

Ferguson, J. (1991). The changing arms control agenda: New meanings, new players. *Arms Control* 12(2): 191–210.

Freedman, L. (1989). *The Evolution of Nuclear Strategy.* St. Martin's Press, New York.

Garthoff, R. L. (1987). *Deterrence and the Revolution in Soviet Military Doctrine.* Brookings, Washington D.C.

George, A. L., and Smoke, R. (1974). *Deterrence in American Foreign Policy: Theory and Practice.* Columbia University Press, New York.

—— (1989). Deterrence and foreign policy. *World Politics* 61(2): 170–181.

Gilpin, R. (1987). *The Political Economy of International Relations.* Princeton University Press, Princeton, NJ.

Gray, C. (1984). Nuclear strategy: The case for a theory of victory. In *International Security in Strategy and Nuclear Deterrence.* S. E. Miller (Ed.). Princeton University Press, Princeton, NJ.

Grin, J., and van der Graaf, H. J. (1990). *Unconventional Approaches to Conventional Arms Control Verification.* St. Martin's Press, New York.

Hackett, C. (1990). *Cautious Revolution: The European Community Arrives.* Praeger, New York.

Harleman, C. (1992). Peace-keeping and disarmament in the peace-building process. *Disarmament* 15(3): 119–132.

Harris, E. D. (1991). Towards a comprehensive strategy for halting chemical and biological weapons proliferation. *Arms Control* 12(2): 129–160.

Herken, G. (1985). *Counsels of War.* Knopf, New York.

Hoffmann, S. (1992). Delusions of world order. *New York Review of Books* April: 36–43.

Hyde-Price, A. (1991). *European Security Beyond the Cold War*, Sage, Newbury, CA.

Jervis, R. (1989). Rational deterrence: Theory and evidence. *World Politics* 61(2): 183–208.

Jervis, R., Lebow, R. N., and Stein, J. G. (Eds.) (1985). *Psychology and Deterrence.* Johns Hopkins Press, Baltimore.

Kahn, H. (1971). *On Thermonuclear War.* Princeton University Press, Princeton, NJ.

Kanet, R. E., and Kolodziej, E. A. (Eds.) (1991). *The Cold War as Cooperation.* Johns Hopkins Press, Baltimore.

Kaplan, F. (1983). *Wizards of Armageddon.* Simon & Schuster, New York.

Keeny, S. M., and Panofsky, W. K. H. (1992). Controlling nuclear warheads and materials: Steps toward a comprehensive regime. *Arms Control Today* 22(1): 3–9.

Klare, M. T. (1984). *American Arms Supermarket.* University of Texas Press, Austin, TX.

Kennedy, P. (1987). *The Rise and Fall of the Great Powers.* Random House, New York.

Kolodziej, E. A. (1992a). Renaissance in security studies? Caveat lector! *International Studies Quarterly* 36: 421–438.

—— (1992b). What is security and security studies? *Arms Control* 13(1): 1–31.

Krepon, M. (1988). *Verification and Compliance.* Ballinger, Cambridge, MA.

Laurence, E. J. (1992). *The International Arms Trade.* Lexington Books, New York.

Lebow, R. N., and Stein, J. G. (1989). Rational deterrence theory: I think, therefore, I deter. *World Politics* 61(2): 208–224.

Lodge, J. (1990). *The European Community and the Challenge of the Future.* Pinter, London.

Lynn-Jones, S. M., and Nye, J. S. (1988). International security studies: A report on a conference on the state of the field. *International Security* 12(4): 5–27.

Mackinlay, J., and Chopra, J. (1992). Second generation multinational operations. *The Washington Quarterly* 15(3): 113–131.

MccGwire, M. (1987). *Military Objectives in Soviet Foreign Policy.* Brookings Institution, Washington D.C.

McFate, P. B. (1992). Where do we go from here? Verifying future arms control agreements. *Washington Quarterly* 15(4): 75–85.

Mearsheimer, J. J. (1990). Why we will soon miss the cold war. *Atlantic* 266(2): 35–50.

The Military Balance. Institute for Strategic Studies, London, published annually.

Missile Technology Control Regime (1992). *Arms Control Reporter* Jan.

Morgenthau, H. (1985). *Politics Among Nations. Knopf, New York.*

Mortimer, E. (1992). *European security after the cold war. Adelphi Papers* 271.

Pleshakov, K. (1991). Our national interests in the transitional period. *International Affairs* 11: 12–20.

Potter, W. C. (1992). Exports and experts: Proliferation risks from the new commonwealth. *Arms Control Today* 22(1): 32–37.

Quester, G. H. (1992). The future of nuclear deterrence. *Survival* 34(1): 74–88.

Reiss, M. (1988). *Without the Bomb*: *The Politics of Nonproliferation.* Columbia University Press, New York.

Reppy, J. (1989). On the economics of national security. In *Security and Arms Control.* E. A. Kolodziej and P. Morgan (Eds.). Greenwood Press, New York.

Rubinstein, A. Z. (1989). In *The Soviet Union in World Politics.* K. London (Ed.). Westview Press, Boulder, CO.

Scheinman, L. (1987). *The Nonproliferation Role of the International Atomic Energy Agency.* Resources for the Future, Washington D.C.

Schelling, T. C. (1960). *The Strategy of Conflict.* Galaxy Books, New York.

Schelling, T. C., and Halperin, M. H. (1961). *Strategy and Arms Control.* Twentieth Century Fund, New York.

Schroeder, P. W. (1989). The nineteenth century system: Balance of power or political equilibrium? *Review of International Studies* 15: 135–153.

Smith, R. K. (1991). The marginalization of superpower arms control. *Security Studies* 1(1): 37–53.

Spector, L. (1987). *Going Nuclear.* Ballinger, Cambridge, MA.

—— (1989). *The Undeclared Bomb*: *The Spread of Nuclear Weapons 1987–1988.* Harper Business, New York.

—— (1991). *Nuclear Ambitions*: *The Spread of Nuclear Weapons 1989–1990.* Westview, Boulder, CO.

Spector, L., and Smith, J. P. (1992). *Nuclear Threshold*: *The Global Spread of Nuclear Weapons 1990–1991.* Westview, Boulder, CO.

Stiles, K. W., and MacDonald, M. (1992). After consensus, what? Performance criteria for the UN in the post–cold war era. *Journal of Peace Research* 29(3): 299–311.

Talbott, S. (1979). *Endgame.* Harper & Row, New York.

Tempest, R. (1992). Yeltsin urges Britain, France, China arms cuts. *Los Angeles Times* January 31, part A, p. 1, col. 6.

Trofimenko, H. A. (1990). The end of the cold war, not history. *The Washington Quarterly* 13(2): 21–35.

Van der Graaf, H. J. (1990). Past Experiences with Verification. In *Unconventional Approaches to Conventional Arms Verification.* J. Grin and H. J. van der Graaf (Eds.). St. Martin's Press, New York.

Van Evera, S. (1990). Europe after the cold war. *International Security* 15(3): 7–57.

Walt, S. M. (1991). The renaissance of security studies. *International Studies Quarterly* 35: 211–239.

Waltz, K. N. (1979). *Theory of International Politics.* Addison-Wesley, Reading, MA.

—— (1981). The spread of nuclear weapons: More might be better. *Adelphia Papers* 171.

Waxman, S. (1993). Chemical arms pact picking up support. *The Atlanta Journal and Constitution,* January 14, sec. A, p. 7.

14
Electoral Policy

Richard S. Katz
The Johns Hopkins University, Baltimore, Maryland

I. APPROACHES TO ELECTORAL POLICY

The conduct of elections is one of the oldest and most continuously contested areas of policy. Aristotle, Cicero, leaders of the medieval Catholic church, Machiavelli, Peel, and Disraeli, to name only a few from previous centuries, were all concerned with the politics of election, as well as with electoral politics. In America, electoral reform was often a subject of debate in the colonial legislatures. Elections, or more properly lack of elections, provided a central focus for the American Revolution under the banner "no taxation without representation." Since independence, electoral policy has remained a lively issue; fully half the constitutional amendments ratified since the Bill of Rights have been concerned with the conduct of elections, as have large volumes of legislation and litigation. Securing equal electoral rights for blacks has been one of the central rallying cries of the move to dismantle apartheid in South Africa, and the introduction of contested elections was the first definitive step in the demise of communist rule in Central and Eastern Europe.

As a policy area, electoral policy has two interrelated but analytically separable focuses. One has stressed the centrality of elections to democracy. Although there is agreement neither on the relative importance of such democratic values as equality, personal development, popular participation, and popular sovereignty, and indeed even on their meanings, nor on such more procedural questions as who should be allowed to vote, how votes should be aggregated into lists of elected candidates, or what parties and candidates should be permitted to do in campaigns, those taking this approach evaluate electoral systems and proposed reforms in terms of function and process and on normative grounds without explicit attention to the particular policies likely to be adopted in other areas. From this point of view, policies adopted on the basis of appropriate elections would be desirable or legitimate because of the legitimacy of the electoral process.

The other approach to electoral policy reverses this statement, and evaluates elections in general and particular electoral policies on the basis of their likely impact in other fields. Changing the rules of the electoral game may make it more or less likely that a specific group will have its interests attended to by government, more or less likely that certain candidates or types of candidates will be elected, and more or less likely that identifiable resources, tactics, or decision criteria will be influential in determining the results (Finer, 1975). Thus, one might evaluate the direct primary based on the type of candidates it produces and its impact on party organizations (and the impact of that on government in general) rather than on the "democratic" grounds of direct popular participation.

These two approaches are related. Reforms that "democratize" elections are likely to have policy consequences in many fields. And because those who favor elections on democratic grounds usually also have an idea of what democratic policy is, this may lead to conflicts. On the other hand, in democratic societies, elections are the great legitimizers. There is something generally unacceptable about partisan manipulation of the electoral system. Thus, reforms actually designed to influence policy or alter the intergroup balance of power are likely to be defended on more high-minded grounds. Nonetheless, many electoral reforms have significant and sometimes counterproductive consequences because the connections between normative concerns and practical results have been ignored.

A. Functions of Elections

There are a number of criteria by which electoral policies may be evaluated (Rose and Mossawir, 1967). The first is often forgotten in its simplicity but exercises a controlling influence nonetheless. To be acceptable, any electoral process must produce a determinate winner. For example, systems requiring an absolute majority of the votes cast must provide for the possibility that with three or more candidates none will achieve a majority.[1]

In a democracy, elections confer legitimacy on those chosen to wield government power. Procedures such as plurality rather than majority elections may be criticized as illegitimately granting power to someone chosen by less than half the people. Similarly, it is often on this ground that parliamentary elections that fail to produce a clear majority party are criticized and because of its capacity to "manufacture" majorities that the US Electoral College is supported.[2]

Elections also are expected to impose popular control over the government. Exactly what this means is subject to debate. To some, popular control, or popular sovereignty, demands that the will of the people be translated into public policy. Elections give the people a choice among candidates standing for alternative policy programs; the winner thus has a mandate to carry a platform into effect and by so doing gives effect to the popular will. In the view of some, this requires that the electorate choose between exactly two disciplined political parties, one of which will necessarily achieve a majority and act to implement its program (Beer, 1969). At the other extreme, others suggest that this requires representation of the full range of public opinions in proportion to their popular support so that compromise and accommodation may be achieved in the legislative arena. Still others take a less active view of the role played by public opinion in policy making. Rather than prospectively determining the direction of policy, this view sees public opinion as retrospectively judging the result of government. Elections give the people the opportunity to turn out of office politicians whose stewardship of government has failed to produce acceptable results and impose constraints on politicians who might otherwise infringe on the people's rights and liberties (Dahl, 1956; Ranney, 1962).

Popularly imposed direction and restraint in mass societies are exercised through representatives rather than directly (with the partial and infrequently used exceptions of recall, initiative, and referendum[3]). The meaning of representation, however, is contested and how a particular electoral system is judged often depends on the meaning of representation preferred as well as on the nature of the groups that one believes ought to be represented. First, representation can be either direct or virtual. "Direct" representation involves a personal relationship between the constituent and the representative; one can be "directly" represented only by someone elected from one's own district. Virtual representation, on the other hand, requires only that there be a representative, whether from the constituent's district or not, who can speak for his or her interests (Pitkin, 1967). Thus, a black voter in New Jersey might be "virtually" represented by a black congressman from New York but would not be "directly" represented by him. Only multimember systems can provide direct representation for local minorities. Is virtual representation adequate?

Second, a representative can be expected simply to transmit the preferences of his or her constituents (delegate) or to exercise independent judgment in advancing their interests (trustee) (Wahlke et al., 1962). Moreover, in either case, the "constituents" can be understood as those who voted for the representative; all those who live in the representative's district; all those who supported the representative's party or who belong to his or her "group" regardless of where they live; or the entire citizenry.

A related question concerns whether it is, in fact, individual people who are to be represented in the first place. Traditionally, communities were represented as organic wholes. As democracy spread, the object of representation became people in their capacity as residents of communities. This style of representation is reflected in plurality and majority electoral systems. But there are other aspects to people that might also deserve representation. For example, people might be represented as holders of opinions or supporters of particular parties. This is the logic of proportional representation. Alternatively, they might be regarded as primarily members of specific occupational or economic strata (corporatist representation) or as members of distinct ethnic or racial groups. Attention to any one of these can alter one's evaluation of an electoral system.

Equality is yet another democratic virtue that elections may be expected both to reflect and to further. Until quite recently, this was often not the case either in theory—with multiple votes or votes in additional districts allowed on the basis of property or educational qualifications in several countries or more simply with large segments of the population excluded from voting at all—or in fact—with gross disparities in district populations. Now, and especially in the United States since the series of court decisions beginning with *Baker* v. *Carr*, equality has become more important in the evaluation of electoral systems.

Finally, elections may be valued because popular participation in public affairs is seen as a value in itself. Active involvement in government may be necessary to the citizen's intellectual and moral development. Patriotism and public spirit may be built from participation in public life (Bachrach, 1967). The development of community, which some claim is essential to the formation of a fully human personality, may require active participation in the management of public affairs (Barber, 1984). From the point of view of the rulers rather than the ruled, loyalty and voluntary compliance may be furthered by at least the illusion of participation (Ginsberg and Weissberg, 1978; Swearer, 1961). And if direct participation, either real or illusory, is impossible in societies with millions of voters, elections provide a more manageable substitute.

In addition to all of these, of course, one also wants elections to produce wise, just, and efficacious results: to choose worthy officeholders and good policies (Einaudi, 1954). The problem arises because in the real world, the desiderata may be incompatible with one another. The choice of electoral policy often reflects a choice among these competing values.

B. Impact on Other Policies

Electoral policy is also important because of its potential impact on all other policy fields. In democratic societies, basic decisions are made by individuals who have been elected by the people. Any policy that changes the identity of public office holders is likely to change the decisions made. Make it easier for politicians representing the poor to be elected, for example, by eliminating property qualifications for voting, and it becomes more likely that policies favoring the poor will be adopted. This influence can extend beyond those directly elected to the bureaucracy as well. Knowing that their actions are subject to review by those elected and that their departments are ultimately dependent on those elected, bureaucrats try to anticipate the reactions of their elected masters (Crossman, 1972). Thus, even in areas of secondary importance, election outcomes may have an impact as civil servants attempt to go along in order to get along.

Electoral policy can significantly alter the balance of power among competing interests either by altering the balance of their votes (as through suffrage expansion) or voting power (as through reapportionment of legislative seats) or by altering the importance of resources that they control. For example, campaign finance has been regulated in many countries with the intention of lessening the political influence of big contributors.

Even more generally, electoral policy can have a substantial impact on the whole policy-making process and the whole style of politics by determining the kinds of behavior that are likely to be rewarded with reelection (Mayhew, 1974). Some electoral systems (plurality election and especially the single transferrable vote) encourage localism and patronage, whereas others (large district proportional representation) encourage ideological politics (Katz, 1980). The electoral system can influence the number of political parties and hence the ease with which a majority is formed and the stability of government (Rae, 1971); by denying some interests legitimate representation, it may also encourage extraparliamentary activity such as demonstrations, strikes, or violence.

II. OPTIONS IN ELECTORAL POLICY

Electoral policy involves myriad decisions ranging from the obviously profound (whether to elect legislatures by proportional representation or simple plurality) through the apparently trivial but occasionally substantively important (where the ballots are to be counted) to the arcane technical (what weight paper is to be used for ballots). In general terms, however, these may be grouped into six major, albeit both arbitrary and partially overlapping, questions:

1. Electoral formula—By what rule are votes translated into lists of elected and defeated candidates.
2. Districting—How are seats apportioned among constituencies (if they are), and how are those constituencies themselves defined.
3. Nature of choice—What offices are filled by direct election (as opposed to indirect election, political appointment, or civil service procedures); how are voters asked to express their preferences, especially how is the ballot arranged; are voters allowed a choice among various candidates of a single party or presented with each party's nominees on a take-it-or-leave-it basis.

4. The electorate—Who may participate as a voter and under what conditions or restrictions.
5. Candidacy and campaigning—How does a party or candidate gain access to the ballot; what subsidies, supports, or other privileges are given to officially recognized candidates; what restrictions are placed on the activities of candidates and their supporters.
6. Integrity—What steps are taken to assure the enforcement of electoral regulations and the general honesty and fairness of the electoral process.

A. Electoral Formula

In detail, the range of possible electoral formulas is virtually without limit. In practice, however, the formulas in actual use can be divided into two major categories—candidate-oriented and list-oriented—each with a relatively manageable number of subtypes.

1. Candidate-Oriented Formulas

The most common of the candidate-oriented systems is *single-member plurality election* (SMP), which has been used to elect most members of Congress, most state governors, the British House of Commons, and the parliaments of most former British colonies (e.g., Canada, New Zealand, South Africa, India, Jamaica). The territory is divided into a number of districts (one district in the case of state governors), each of which elects one representative or other official. Each voter has a single vote that must be given to a single candidate. At the end of the polling, the votes for each candidate are counted and the one with the most votes wins regardless of how well other candidates may have done and regardless of how narrow the margin between the first- and second-ranked candidates.

More generally, SMP is only the simplest of a class of *plurality* formulas, distinguished by (1) the number of officials elected from each district, (2) the number of votes cast by each voter, and (3) whether a voter can give more than one vote to a single candidate. When each voter has as many votes as the number (greater than 1) of officials to be elected but may cast only one vote per candidate, the system is *multimember plurality election* (MMP), or in the limiting case of a single district for many representatives *at-large election*. MMP was used before 1885 to elect many members of the British House of Commons, and is used today to elect members of some state legislatures; at-large election is often used for local councils. When the voter has fewer votes than the number of seats to be filled, the system is *limited voting* (or in the extreme case of many members and a single vote, the *single nontransferable vote*, used to elect the Japanese House of Representatives), and when more than one vote may be given to a single candidate, the system is *cumulative voting*.

In contrast to MMP, limited vote and cumulative voting are both more favorable to minorities. For example, a party with 51% of the vote in a three-member MMP district would win all three seats. With voters limited to two votes, however, the party would need the solid (and coordinated) support of just over 60% of the voters to be assured of all three seats, whereas with cumulative voting, just over 75% of the voters would be required to guarantee a clean sweep. The comparison with three SMP districts is more complex because the outcome would depend not just on total votes but as well on the districts to which they were assigned. If districts were drawn to the minority's advantage, then, in theory, they could win one seat with 51% of the vote in one district and none in the other two (i.e., approximately 17% of the total); on the other hand, if their voters were dispersed evenly throughout the three districts, the result would be precisely the same as with MMP.

These examples all assume two parties, each with an optimal number of candidates so that votes are not unnecessarily dispersed. If there are more than two parties or excessive nominations, plurality elections can be won by candidates with only minority support. For example, in the 1987 British election, 279 of the 650 seats in the House of Commons were won with under 50% of the vote and 25 with under 40%. This problem is particularly vexing if a minority candidate wins only because of a schism in the natural majority party. Majority systems attempt to prevent this by requiring a candidate to achieve an absolute majority (50% + 1) of the votes to be elected.

The simplest majority system, analogous to SMP, is *single-member majority* (SMM), which is used for election to the French National Assembly and in several states in the American South. SMM works exactly like SMP except that a candidate must have at least 50% of the total vote in order to be elected. If no candidate achieves this quota, a second election is held, but this time either with candidacy restricted to the two candidates who headed the first poll (in which case, one must achieve a majority in the second round) or with the provision that the second round will be held under SMP. Instead of asking voters to select a single candidate and then holding a second election if none achieves an absolute majority, voters may be asked to rank all the candidates, with the understanding that if no candidate receives an absolute majority of the first preferences, the candidate with the fewest first preferences will be eliminated and the votes that candidate received will be distributed to the candidates ranked second on those ballots, and so forth until one candidate has an absolute majority. This *alternative vote* is used to elect the Australian House of Representatives.

When the alternative vote is applied to multimember constituencies, it is called the *single transferable vote* (STV). In this case, the required quota is not 50% + 1 (which obviously could be achieved by only one candidate), but the so-called Droop quota, equal to the number of votes divided by one more than the number of seats and then rounded up to the next highest integer. If M is the number of seats to be filled, this is the smallest number of votes that each of M candidates could achieve while assuring that no other candidate could have as many. (Note that 50% + 1 is the Droop quota for the case of $M = 1$, and so this is directly analogous to majority systems.) As with the alternative vote, voters rank all candidates and any candidate with a number of first preference votes equal to the quota is elected. If a candidate has more votes than the quota, surplus votes are transferred in proportion to the next available preference on that candidate's ballots; if no candidate has a surplus, the candidate with the fewest votes is eliminated and his or her ballots transferred, with the process continuing until the required number of candidates have reached the quota, or (given that votes may become nontransferable if not all candidates are ranked) all but the required number have been eliminated. STV is used to elect the parliaments of Ireland and Malta, as well as local school boards in New York City and the Cambridge, MA, city council.

Single-member systems tend to underrepresent, often dramatically, minorities whose strength is geographically dispersed. Although the theoretical limits suggested above of a party with 51% of the vote (or less in the case of multiparty races) winning all the seats, or a party with 26% of the vote winning a majority of the seats, are unlikely to occur, actual experience is sometimes only a little more encouraging. To cite two Canadian SMP examples: In one election in Prince Edward Island, the Conservative party won 42% of the vote but no seats, whereas in another election, the United Farmers of Alberta won 67% of the seats with less than 40% of the vote. The degree to which minorities are underrepresented depends on the way in which the districts are drawn, but SMP often approximates the "cube law" that the ratio of the two parties' shares of the seats will equal the cube of the ratio of their votes (Kendall and Stuart, 1950; Tufte, 1973). Moreover, this "mechanical" discrimination against minorities may underestimate the true handicap under which they suffer because their supporters, anticipating that votes cast for minor parties will be "wasted," may be "psychologically" led not to vote for them in the first place (Duverger, 1959). In this respect, SMP can be said to encourage two-party competition, and thus the likelihood that a single party will have an absolute majority of the seats in the legislature, albeit possibly based on a minority of the popular votes. On the other hand, SMP is the most advantageous system for minorities whose support is concentrated in a few districts in which they can achieve local pluralities.

As all this implies, SMP and MMP can be used to exclude racial or other minorities by dividing their votes among several districts or by creating large multimember districts in which local pluralities are submerged. This has been a particularly significant problem in the United States, with a number of reapportionment plans and at-large electoral systems overturned by the courts on the grounds that they "dilute" minority voting strength. Ordinarily, the required remedy has been redrawn single-member districts, in which a number of minority dominated districts are specifically created. More recently, the courts have also allowed the use of the "semiproportional" system of cumulative voting in cases in which the minority population is so dispersed as to make creation of minority districts infeasible (Engstrom, 1992).

In one sense, SMM and alternative vote reduce the minority handicap by making it possible for voters to support a minor candidate in the first round or with their first preferences without throwing their votes away altogether. More often, however, they benefit majorities because they allow a majority to fragment without paying the high electoral price exacted by SMP. Currently, for example, it is argued that SMM discriminates against blacks in the American South because it allows white voters to coalesce behind a single candidate, and thus prevent the election of a black who might achieve a plurality, but not an absolute majority, in the first round. In more ideologically based systems, SMM tends to discriminate against extreme parties. After an initial trial of strength in the first round of voting, parties often form alliances by withdrawing in complementary districts and instructing their supporters to vote for the remaining candidate of the alliance. In making such alliances, moderate parties are in a far stronger bargaining position because they have a choice of allies, whereas extreme parties typically do not. Moreover, once a deal is struck, the extreme party is more likely to deliver its supporters in the districts where it has withdrawn. This system has been used in France particularly to undermine the strength of the Communist Party (Campbell, 1965). STV avoids most of these problems (which some would regard as strengths). So long as votes are transferred within party, the partisan result will be the same as under Droop quota largest remainder PR (see below), and indeed the system is usually called PR or PR-STV in Britain and Ireland. Aside from specious arguments about its complexity, the most commonly raised criticism of STV is precisely its failure to limit the number of parties. On the other hand, although the Irish party system has shown some tendency to fragment under STV (the 1989 election left six parties plus four independents represented in the Dáil), Malta has developed a solid two-party system.

Finally, all candidate-oriented systems tend to emphasize the representation of communities as organic wholes. Especially in single-member systems, the candidate finally elected is expected to represent the interests of all residents of the constituency, including those who voted for other candidates and continue to support other parties. The relationship between constituent and representative is not mediated by party. Even under STV, there is a strong tendency for parties to distribute their nominations throughout the district and for candidates to divide the district into personal bailiwicks, thus preserving something of the territorial representation typical of single-member districts. There is also a marked tendency toward personalism and patronage in politics (Sacks, 1976).

2. List-Oriented Formulas

If the aim of elections is to produce a legislature that accurately reflects the distribution of opinions in society or to give each vote an equal marginal impact on the outcome regardless of where it is cast, all the candidate-oriented systems (with the limited exception of STV) have serious weakness. The alternative, used to elect most of the parliaments of Western Europe (the exceptions being France—SMM; the UK—SMP; and Ireland—STV), is to award seats to groups of candidates (party lists) in proportion to their popular support. The hallmark of these systems of *list-proportional representation* (PR) is that even if votes formally are cast for individual candidates, the allocation of seats among parties is based on the total numbers of votes received by each list rather than on the simple numbers of votes received by the candidates as individuals.

There are two families of PR systems (Carstairs, 1980). Under *largest remainder* systems, a quota is computed. Each list then receives one seat for every whole multiple of the quota contained in its total vote, with the remaining seats assigned to the lists with the largest remainders. Quotas in common use are the Hare quota (valid vote divided by number of seats to be filled); the Droop quota (valid vote divided by one more than the number of seats); and Imperiali quota (valid vote divided by two more than the number of seats). The larger the quota (Hare is largest), the more likely small parties are to gain representation. Under *highest average* systems, each list's total vote is divided by a series of numbers (d'Hondt: 1, 2, 3, ...; Ste. Laguë: 1, 3, 5, ...; modified Ste. Laguë: 1.4, 3, 5, ...) with seats awarded in order of the resulting quotients. Here, the higher the ratio between successive numbers in the series, the more favorable the outcome for small parties. The greatest influence on the representation of small parties, and on the proportionality of the result overall, however, is the number of members elected from each district; the fewer the districts (and consequently the more members elected from each district, ultimately with the entire country serving as a single district as in Israel and the Netherlands), the more proportional the result (Taagepera and Shugart, 1989).

With these two basic families, a number of additional wrinkles are possible. Proportionality can be increased while retaining a district system by distributing at the national level either supplementary seats or seats unassigned at the district level on the basis of whole quotas with regard to the national vote distribution (e.g., Sweden). In order to preserve high proportionality among significant parties while limiting fragmentation of the party system, a minimum threshold can be imposed before a party receives any seats (e.g., the German "5% clause") or before it may participate in a distribution of remainders or supplementary seats (e.g., Italy). Small parties (and fissiparous parties) can be aided through *apparentement*, under which the votes received by several tied lists are totaled before the initial distribution of seats is made.

One effect of PR is to lower the cost of exit from a party for dissatisfied minorities. Where in majority or STV systems a schism is likely to be costly, and where in plurality systems it would almost certainly result in severe losses, in PR systems a schism may be nearly costless. Conversely, PR seems to discourage alliances formed in the electoral arena. Instead, it encourages ideological competition in which similar parties maximize their apparent differences (Katz, 1980). The result is that where plurality systems encourage compromise early, and a choice by the voters among a sharply reduced set of "packaged" alternatives, PR offers the voters a wider choice but often with a less direct link between electoral outcomes and public policy (Katz, 1987; Milnor, 1969).

B. Apportionment and District Boundaries

In list PR systems with large districts, the actual district boundaries make little difference. Coupling a small province with a large one or transferring a small area from one district to another may disadvantage a few politicians, but with many members per district, it is easy to maintain proportionality between population and district representation by adjusting the number of deputies per district, and so long as this proportionality is maintained, actual boundaries will make little difference to the party balance.

In smaller districts, and particularly in single-member districts, however, constituency boundaries can be crucial. Here, there are two general classes of problems—malapportionment and gerrymandering. *Malapportionment* refers to significant disparities in the number of people represented by each deputy, a possibility that when systematic can lead to significant overrepresentation of some interests. *Gerrymandering* refers to the drawing of district lines for political advantage, even within the stricture of equal district populations (see Polsby, 1971).

Malapportionments can result either from failure to redistrict after shifts in population or from application of principles other than equality in the drawing of district lines. One of the most malapportioned legislatures was the British House of Commons before 1832. Each of the English counties (special provision was made for Scotland) had equal representation, whereas the boroughs were represented on the basis of their importance several hundred years before, with some "rotten boroughs" with no residents at all continuing to send members. Since 1832, although the British have recognized population as one important basis of representation, major disparities in district populations are allowed to exist in deference to other principles. Reflecting the notion of community representation, for example, local boundaries are respected. Where a district would otherwise be unmanageably large or difficult to travel (the Shetland and Orkney Islands), it is permitted to continue with below-average population. Scotland and Wales are systematically overrepresented. In 1983, the largest constituency (Isle of Wight) had 4.13 times the population of the smallest (Western Isles). Similar deference to "community of interest or . . . identity" and the need for "manageable geographic size," plus a requirement that the number of members assigned to each province never be reduced (Electoral Boundaries Readjustment Act, s. 13) reduced the disparity between largest and smallest districts in Canada from a ratio of 21:1 before 1964 to about 7.5:1 in 1984.

Although not as badly apportioned as the unreformed House of Commons, the trend in the pre-1960 United States was roughly what it had been in Britain. Although the Constitution requires periodic redistribution of congressional representation among the states, states would often adjust to the loss of a congressional seat by combining two adjoining districts or to a gain in Congress by dividing their most populous district. In 1960, for example, the largest congressional district in Texas had a population of 951,527, whereas the smallest had only 216,371. State legislatures were similarly malapportioned. In some cases, one house would represent counties rather than people. Even the "popular" houses often had not been reapportioned in many years. Also in 1960, more than half of the lower house of the legislature was elected by less than 20% of the voters in Connecticut, Delaware, Florida, Kansas, and Vermont. This led to a series of court challenges beginning with *Baker* v. *Carr* and *Reynolds* v. *Sims* that have imposed strict limits on allowable population disparities for congressional districts, districts for both houses of state legislatures, city and county councils, and so forth.

Reapportionments were (and are) often resisted for quite obvious reasons. In many cases, what is asked is that the current majority reduce its own representation. Given usual population trends, the effect of malapportionment has generally been to overrepresent rural interests. This is also the case when representation of communities or local government units is stressed. Although contrary to the norm of equality, this is sometimes defended on the ground that rural voters are particularly virtuous or worthy of representation because they embody the backbone and spirit of the country.

Changes in district boundaries are unsettling to existing party and personal campaign organizations. They may force incumbents to compete against one another in the new districts or reduce some incumbents' margins of victory. In any event, they add to electoral uncertainty. The requirement of equal population also forces local boundaries to be violated, which sacrifices community representation and leads to a crazy-quilt pattern of district boundaries. Two areas in the same state legislative district may be in different congressional districts and lead to complicated career patterns and campaign arrangements.

Gerrymanders differ from malapportionments in that they are conscious attempts to manipulate the results of elections by changing the district boundaries and can coexist with perfectly equal district sizes. Indeed, some observers believe that by making local government boundaries irrelevant to the district-drawing process, the "reapportionment revolution" simply made gerrymandering easier. Although the term is American, the process of gerrymandering is quite ancient, having been used, for example, in the Roman Republic. It is also usually associated with single-member plurality systems, but the Irish reapportionment before the 1977 election was an attempt to gerrymander in an STV system. Because, for example, a party with 51% of the vote would *ceteris paribus* expect to win two of three seats or two of four seats, whereas a party with 41% of the vote would still win two of four seats but only one of three, a party that manipulated district lines so as to create three member districts where it expected to win over 50% of the vote, but four member districts where it expected to win under 50%, could significantly distort the distribution of seats in its own favor (Mair, 1986).

Although gerrymanders can be aimed at the general advantage of a party, they can also be directed for or against particular individuals. In some cases, the results can be quite bizarre, as the California congressional district created in an attempt to defeat Paul McCloskey that was contiguous only at low tide. Another example is provided by Congressman Sam Stratton of New York, who had his district in Schenectady abolished. He then moved to Amsterdam, only to have that district abolished as well; ultimately, he was elected from Albany. There also can be bipartisan gerrymanders, in which incumbents of both parties conspire to protect their own seats.

Equal-sized districts say nothing about fairness with respect to parties. They also say nothing about the representation of minorities. Although gerrymanders designed to exclude minorities have been outlawed, those designed to ensure their representation have been approved. The problem is that what benefits one minority may harm another (see *United Jewish Organizations of Williamsburgh, Inc. v. Carey, LA*).

If districting decisions have great potential impact, then the way in which those decisions are made becomes important. In general terms, there are four basic models available. The simplest is not to (re)draw boundaries; either the whole country serves as a single district or else permanently fixed units, such as states or counties, serve as the districts, with the number of representatives allocated to each varied according to some fixed formula to reflect changes in population. Although these options are the most common in PR systems, they are not available in systems using SMP. In these systems, district boundaries traditionally were established by ordinary legislation. Although this reflects the ideal that political decisions ought to be made by politically accountable officials, it has the obvious disadvantage of putting those with the greatest personal incentive to gerrymander in charge of districting. To avoid this, a number of countries (e.g., the UK, Canada, Ireland, India) have established politically neutral (either nonparty or bipartisan) boundary commissions to reapportion parliamentary seats. Finally, it has been proposed that legislation should establish a fixed formula (setting, e.g., minimum standards for, or weights to be accorded to, criteria that are generally regarded as desirable such as population equality, compactness, and contiguity) by means of which districting plans could be compared. Under this procedure, anyone would be free to submit a districting plan, with the one judged best according to the formula to be implemented automatically.

C. Nature of Choice

Much of the above discussion has assumed, or at least has been consistent with the assumption that, elections are simply about the periodic choice of parliamentary representatives. This leaves unanswered a number of important questions concerning the nature of elections.

First, how many officials and of what types ought to be elected, and should they be elected directly or indirectly? On one hand, if popular involvement in government is a primary objective, then by multiplying the number of elective offices, one multiplies the number of opportunities for individual citizens to participate as candidates and ultimately as elected officials. Indeed, by creating pressure to fill offices, election may inspire more popular participation than would occur spontaneously in a direct democracy. On the other hand, when there are many directly elected officials, power and responsibility tend to be fragmented, so that even if the people are able to hold more officials personally accountable, they lose the ability to hold any individual or party collectively responsible for the overall management of public affairs. Moreover, one may ask whether officials whose impartiality is vital (i.e., judges) or whose functions are primarily technical ought to be chosen on the basis of unmediated popular appeal.

A related question is whether officials should be chosen by direct or indirect election. Although one tends to think of direct election as the more democratic, there are at least four reasons why one might prefer indirect election, at least for some offices. Most commonly in modern times, indirect election of one house of the national legislature is a reflection of a federal state; while one house represents the people, and is directly elected by them, the other house represents the federated governments, and so is chosen by them. Examples are the Bundesrat in West Germany, the U.S. Senate before 1913, and the parliamentary assembly of the European Economic Community (EEC) before 1979. A second justification, particularly relevant to the election of a head of state, is the desire to deny the person elected the legitimacy conferred by direct election. In parliamentary systems, this is important in that it assures that the prime minister (although himself or herself indirectly elected) rather than the president will be the effective head of government. In reverse, this was one of the arguments advanced by European integrationists in favor of direct election of the EEC parliament. Third, indirect election of cabinets and prime ministers (i.e., their selection by the parliament) allows flexibility for interparty negotiations and the possibility (not considered by everyone to be an advantage) that the terms of those negotiations, and thus the government, will be changed during the life of a parliament. As significantly, even if there is a bipolar system, and hence effectively direct choice of the prime minister by the people, parliamentary rather than direct election allows a prime minister who has lost the confidence of the people or his or her party to be replaced without waiting for a fixed term to expire. Finally, one might favor indirect election because of doubts about the ability of the people to make a wise choice. This was one argument in favor of the Electoral College in the United States—the people, unfamiliar with candidates from other states, might vote for demagogues, but they could be trusted to select local men of judgment to choose a president for them. As things have developed, the US Electoral College has been reduced to registering, in weighted form, the result of popular election, thus eliminating much of the indirectness of presidential elections.

Indirect election presents a number of problems, however. First, such systems tend to weight the votes of citizens differently depending on where they live. The US Electoral College, and even more the procedure of voting by states in the House of Representatives in case there is no majority in the Electoral College, is seen by some as favoring the least populous states. Others argue that the winner-take-all system by which the electors from each state (except Maine and Nebraska) are chosen has forced candidates to pay most attention to states with closely contested elections and a large number of electoral votes (Longley and Braun, 1972). No one, however, claims that all voters are treated equally. Second, by eliminating local minorities, indirect election tends to produce majorities where they might not otherwise exist; whether these "manufactured" majorities should count as a strength or a weakness of the US Electoral College or the British House of Commons in acting as an electoral college to chose a prime minister is a matter of debate. Finally, indirect election presents the problem of the "faithless elector." Although there have been occasional defections by individual US electors, these have never been significant. Defections have been more significant in the indirect election of the Italian president.

A second question is whether voters are given a choice among various candidates of each party, as opposed to being presented with each party's choice of candidate(s) on a "take-it-or-leave-it" basis. The latter is achieved in candidate-oriented systems if each party nominates only as many candidates as it can hope to win (i.e., one per district in SMP systems) and in list-oriented systems when each party submits an ordered list of candidates with the proviso that the seats it wins will be filled by the appropriate number of candidates from the top of the list. In either case, the party organization has real power. A candidate denied (re)nomination or assigned to an unfavorable position on the list has (to the extent that party preferences determine voting choices) no chance of (re)election regardless of the people's views.

The spector of a few party tyrants deciding among whom the people can choose has seemed antidemocratic to some reformers, who have insisted on greater popular involvement in the choice of candidates. In single-member systems, intraparty choice comes, if at all, when party nominees are selected because it is to a party's clear advantage to have only one candidate in the final election. In the United States, an intraparty choice is provided by the direct primary. In PR and STV systems, however, parties ordinarily nominate more candidates than they can elect. With STV, this automatically means that the choice of representatives from among each party's nominees is left to those who vote for its candidates. In PR systems, the party's voters may be allowed to influence or determine the order of election by use of a personal preference vote.

The simplest form of preference voting allows each voter to single out one (or more) of the candidates of the list for which he or she has just voted for personal support. Candidates from each list are then declared elected in the order of their personal voting strength. In this case, those of each party's voters who cast explicit personal preference votes completely determine the order in which candidates are elected, and preference voting may be a primary cause of parliamentary turnover (Katz, 1986; Katz and Bardi, 1980). In other systems, although a personal preference vote is permitted, the party is able to influence the order of election more substantially. Greatest control is given to the party when its list order prevails unless changed by a substantial percentage of its voters. Because only a minority of voters cast preference votes, this kind of preference voting is usually in fact illusory (Campbell, 1965; Pedersen, 1966).

One of the motivations for the direct primary and preference voting was to undermine the power of central party bosses. The illegitimacy of the smoke-filled room, coupled with a distaste for party discipline that punished a representative for preferring his or her constituents to his or her party leader, led some advocates of democracy to insist that the voters choose people as well as parties. In this attempt, the reformers were quite successful. Central party control has been undermined in systems with effective preference voting. This reform has had a variety of other effects, however, not all of which are necessarily desirable.

If preference voting has weakened a candidate's need for the support of a central party organization, it has not lessened the importance of organization in general. Instead, it has made candidates dependent on personal organizations that can be mobilized to ward off intraparty challenges as well as to fight a general election. Because the resources needed to maintain such an organization cannot be mobilized through the party, this often makes candidates dependent on special interests. The vitality of the party organization, and its ability to perform other functions such as mobilizing mass support, channeling demands, and coordinating government is sapped, as personal organizations become more important to candidates and the party less important. One frequent result is factionalism in the party; another is fragmentation (Katz, 1980; Mayhew, 1974; Thayer, 1969; Zariski, 1965).

Preference voting also has an impact on the type of candidate who is likely to be successful. For professional politicians, the most important thing in an election is to win and keep winning. This gives them a strong incentive, especially in single-member plurality systems, to choose candidates who will be attractive to the electorate as a whole and who will perform well in office so that the party will be returned to power at the next election. Moderate, capable, responsible, if perhaps uninspiring, candidates, and a balanced ticket are likely results. Individual voters, however, lack both the knowledge and the incentive to select this kind of candidate. In a primary, instead of supporting the candidate they think is best able to win the general election, knowledgeable voters choose the candidate they would most *like* to have win the general election. But because the distribution of opinion, and particularly of active and informed opinion, within a single party is likely to be far different from that of the general electorate, this may lead to extremist candidates. For most voters, intraparty voting, which is divorced from the anchoring cue of party labels, is a contest among relative unknowns. Any candidate who can grab their attention is likely to have a great advantage in securing their votes. This naturally gives an advantage to incumbents. It also encourages image builders, flashy campaigners, irresponsible promises, and demagoguery over quiet competence.

Although it is often assumed that elections merely record voter preferences, the format of the ballot may, in fact, play a significant role in determining what preferences the voters appear to express. In Norway and Sweden, for example, voters may indicate their selections on a plain sheet of paper. More commonly, they use ballots printed by the parties; but of course, each party's ballot lists its own candidates in the party's preferred order, which makes it difficult for voters to cast effective personal preference votes. In the United States before the 1890s, party-provided ballots were the norm, again each listing only its own candidates, thus making split-ticket voting relatively difficult (Rusk, 1970). Moreover, if party-printed ballots are of distinctive colors (as they often were in the United States), secrecy in voting may be made nugatory.

For list systems, the most significant ballot question concerns the ease with which the party list order can be changed. The Italian ballot, for example, does not list candidates' names, so to cast a preference vote the voter must remember the names or numbers of the candidates he or she wishes to support. In other systems, the local or party-preferred candidate may be given an advantageous position, or it may be made easier to cast a ballot maintaining than one changing the party's list order. An additional question, which applies to candidate-oriented systems as well, is the degree to which voting by illiterates is facilitated, as, for example, by including a pictorial symbol for each party as well as its printed name.

Because party is technically superfluous to the operation of candidate-oriented systems, the inclusion of party designations is an open question. When they are not included, one has a nonpartisan ballot. Until 1974, Britain used nonpartisan ballots in parliamentary elections. They continue to be used in some US local elections. Similarly, in multimember districts, should all of a party's candidates be listed together? In the Irish STV system, they are not, whereas in the Maltese STV system, they are. Grouping candidates by party has a strong impact on the level of interparty transfer votes under STV, whereas simply including party labels seems to have a more marginal influence on the level of party voting under SMP. A related question concerns the order in which candidates should be listed. Except where the party column format dictates otherwise, candidates may be listed alphabetically, randomly, or in rotation, either overall or within party. This is particularly important when there are many candidates and in STV systems especially with regard to transfer votes because candidates at the top of a list tend to do better than those at the bottom, who do better than those in the middle (Bain and Hecock, 1957; Mueller, 1970).

Where several offices are filled at each election, as is usually the case in the United States, these questions compound into the distinction between grid (party-line) and office block formats. In a party-line ballot, the names of the candidates are arranged in a grid, with party defining one dimension and office the other. Often there is a single box or lever to cast a straight party vote. An office block ballot, on the other hand, sorts the candidates only by office. The party-line ballot discourages split-ticket voting by making a straight ticket far easier to cast (Walker, 1966). It also tends to suggest that one "ought" to think of politics in partisan terms (Rusk, 1974). Either form of ballot, but especially grid ballots, also may put independents and third-party candidates at an obvious disadvantage by relegating them to the bottom of the ballot paper or voting machine.

As this suggests, most of these questions can be subsumed under a more general question—should elections be seen primarily as choices among organized parties or primarily as choices among individual candidates. In the former case, restricting direct election to a few key positions (and holding such elections simultaneously in order to maximize the likelihood that the party balance will be the same for all offices), allowing the party organization to control which individuals will be elected, and using a partisan grid ballot are most appropriate. In the latter case, however, maximizing the number of directly elected officials and freeing them from control of their parties through use of preference voting, staggered elections, and a nonpartisan or office block ballot would be more appropriate.

D. The Electorate

Although most modern democracies claim to have universal suffrage, in fact, no country allows everyone who wants to vote to do so. Historically, electorates were highly restricted and the question of who would be allowed to vote was quite contentious. As qualifications based on property holding, race, and gender were relaxed, the question of suffrage appeared to be resolved, only to reappear with regard to age and citizenship, along with related questions concerning barriers to voting such as registration requirements and monolingual versus multilingual ballots on one hand and compulsory voting on the other.

1. Suffrage

Although specific suffrage requirements vary enormously, most requirements themselves and their justifications can be grouped (with allowance for the fact that some requirements may be justified in more than one way) under three broad headings: those relating to community membership and having a personal stake in the outcome; those relating to competence; and those relating to autonomy.

The principal suffrage requirements bearing on community membership or having a stake in the outcome are those relating to citizenship and residency. Citizenship, as a formal statement of membership in the national political community, is nearly everywhere required for voting, but there are exceptions. In the 19th century, as many as 22 US states allowed voting by immigrants who had declared their intention to become citizens, whereas Uruguay allows foreigners with 15 years residency and the United Kingdom allows citizens of the Republic of Ireland to vote in national elections. Other countries, particularly in Europe, bar aliens from voting in national elections but allow those with several years residence to vote in local elections. Residence requirements aim to restrict voting to those with a settled stake in the community, and who may be expected still to be around to live with the consequences of their electoral decisions. They also aim to prevent flooding the polls with temporary "residents" trucked in solely to influence the result in a particular marginal district. Residency requirements have been reduced nearly everywhere on the grounds that to do otherwise violates the rights of the mobile (middle class) or transient (lower class, blacks in the United States, leftists in post-Franco Spain). In the United States, the Voting Rights Act permits states to require no more than 30 days residence in presidential elections; rather than maintain two registers, all but two states require no more than 30 days residence for any election; moreover, the "intensity" of residence required also has been reduced, so that in some states, a park bench qualifies as a legal place of residence. In other countries, requirements range from none at all (e.g., residence on the day the register is prepared or on the day the election is held) to at least the 3 years being required in the Northwest Territories of Canada, where temporary workers at mining sites might otherwise outnumber the permanent residents. As with residence, the argument that only those who pay the bills should determine how taxes are raised and spent was used to justify an array of income, property holding, and tax-paying requirements for suffrage; although these generally were abolished for national elections by the early years of the 20th century, they (or additional votes for property holders) survived rather longer both in the United States and elsewhere with regard to local elections and elections specifically authorizing the floating of bonds or the imposition of property taxes.

The criterion of competence was also used to justify property requirements on the assumption that property indicated judgment and/or intelligence. More typically, this criterion justifies the general (but not universal) exclusion of the mentally impaired, and it has also been used to exclude illiterates or those unable to communicate in the national language. Claims of incompetence have also been marshalled to justify exclusion of racial groups (e.g., blacks in the United States before the Fifteenth Amendment and in South Africa into the 1990s) and women (based on their supposed emotionalism and irrationality, or on the claim that there are separate spheres of life to which the two genders are differentially suited). Although women generally were enfranchised in the years immediately following one or the other of the two World Wars (the first country to allow women an equal vote was New Zealand in 1893), it was not until 1971 that Switzerland recognized women's right to vote in federal elections, and they are still barred from voting in some cantonal elections (e.g., in Appenzell Inner-rohden). Finally, the major exclusion based on competence is that of children. By 1950, there was general consensus that 21 was an appropriate age at which to allow the enfranchise, although many Latin American countries allowed 18-year olds to vote. Since then, the 18-year-old franchise has become the norm.

The criterion of autonomy can also justify the exclusion of the incompetent, of those on public relief, or married women, and of children (including grown children without their own households)—they cannot be taken to be independent of those upon whom they depend. It was also used by Blackstone to justify the exclusion "of persons who are in so mean a situation as to be esteemed to have no will of their own." Similarly, the Brazilian constitution of 1891 denied the vote to "Members of monastic orders, companies, congregations, or communities of whatever denomination, subject to a vow of obedience, rule, or statute which involves the renunciation of individual liberty."

2. *Registration of Voters and Other Barriers to Voting*

Advance preparation of a list of voters allows timely resolution of disputes over voter eligibility and was introduced to counter the wholesale corruption reputed to be typical of nineteenth-century elections (Mackenzie, 1958). The problem is that significant numbers of otherwise qualified voters may be denied the vote solely because they are not registered, and this may significantly influence the balance of political power (Kelley et al., 1967).

In most of the world, this problem is minimized by laying the burden of seeing that citizens are duly registered on the government. On the European continent, registration of voters is usually a side process in the general registration of citizens for identity cards, national insurance, and internal passports. In Britain, a postal canvass is conducted annually to produce a register for that year; although this register is nearly totally accurate when it is prepared, its accuracy decays through the year as people move, die, or come of age. The Canadians instead conduct a door-to-door canvass just before each parliamentary election. In the United States, however, the burden of registration is placed on the citizen. In the early days of registration, voters were often required to appear personally before every election. More recently, this has been widely replaced with permanent registration (voters remain registered so long as they vote at least once every 2 or 4 years) and frequently can be handled by mail. Nonetheless, registration ordinarily must still be performed well in advance of the elections, and only 73.8% of the voting-age population were registered in 1976, and registration requirements are generally regarded as among the principal reasons why voter turnout is lower in the United States than in any comparable country except Switzerland. This has led to some experiments with election-day registration, but this largely defeats the original purposes of registration: that is, to prevent fraud, to allow timely resolution of disputes, and to assure that voters are assigned to the correct districts.

Beyond making registration easier or automatic, a number of other practices affect the ease of voting and, hence, the ultimate level of participation. Among these are allowing postal or advance voting or transfer of constituencies by those who expect to be away from home on election day; keeping the polls open for long hours, either on a weekend or with election day as a holiday or, even more, for more than 1 day; and provision of multilingual ballots and other electoral documents. Italy, in fact, goes so far as to provide reduced rail fares to the border and free travel within the country for workers returning to their home communes to vote.

3. Compulsory Voting

In extreme form, a country can encourage turnout by making voting compulsory. In Europe, this is the case in Belgium, Greece, and Liechtenstein, as well as in three provinces of Austria and four cantons of Switzerland, and it was the case in the Netherlands until 1970. For all practical purposes, voting also is compulsory in Italy (although there are no criminal sanctions, the constitution describes voting as "a civic duty" and a nonvoter's identity papers are so stamped). Elsewhere, voting also is compulsory in Australia and much of Latin America. Often, exceptions are made for the very old (e.g., those over 70 in Greece), the very young (e.g., under 18 in the Philippines), those who live a great distance from the polls (e.g., more than 200 kilometers in Greece), and in the early days of women's suffrage in Latin America for women as well. Even though sanctions are rarely imposed, comparison of turnout before and after the introduction (or in the Dutch case, the repeal) of compulsory voting as well as cross-sectional statistical analyses suggest that this provision increases turnout by at least 10% (Blais and Carty, 1990).

Compulsory voting has both normative and political justifications. Normatively, many have argued that voting is a *duty* of citizenship rather than a *right*, and as with other duties (e.g., paying taxes or military service), citizens may be compelled to perform it. Politically, compulsory voting may increase the political weight of the poor, who generally have the lowest rates of turnout. Compulsory voting has also been introduced to prevent popular discontent from manifesting itself in massive rates of abstention. For example, it was argued that "in Paraguay mandatory voting [enabled] Stroessner to claim that he [was] a popularly elected, legitimate leader" (Ochoa, 1987). On the other hand, repeal of compulsory voting was supported by the major Dutch parties in the hope that those voting for splinter parties would instead stay home.

E. Candidacy and Campaigning

Regulation of candidacy and campaigning is forced by the conflict of values. The requirement that voters be given maximal choice conflicts with the need to simplify choice to a level at which it is manageable by voters and at which the result will not be so fragmented as to be meaningless. The liberal right to unfettered competition, far from assuring fairness, may perpetuate (and magnify) the advantages (like private wealth) that some candidates enjoy, to say nothing of the possibilities of bribery, deceit, and intimidation. As this implies, controls over candidacy and campaigning fall under two main headings: those concerning access to the ballot and those limiting the activities of candidates and their supporters. To these may then be added a third category of policies: those concerning the allocation of subsidies, media access, and other political "goods" given to candidates.

1. Ballot Access

One set of requirements for candidacy generally follows the requirements for voting only at a higher level (i.e., more property, higher age, longer residence), although in some cases, the requirements for candidacy were actually lower. For example, the minimum age for election in Denmark was 25 from 1866 through 1915, although for most of the period, the voting age was 30. Additionally, there may be bars on subversives (e.g., bars to communists in several US states or to anticonstitutional parties in Germany) or to officials of previous regimes.

A second set of requirements aims to eliminate frivolous candidacies. These generally are of two types. On one hand, candidates and/or parties may be required to demonstrate their popular support by presenting nominating petitions signed by a significant number of voters. This is most common in the United States, where the signatures of between 1% and 5% (depending on the state) of registered voters frequently are required for a candidate to appear on the ballot, but this also is the primary bar to frivolous candidacies in Denmark, which requires a party to have signatures equal to 1/175 of the votes cast in the previous election. In other countries, a monetary deposit that is lost if the candidate or party does not achieve a specified vote threshold discourages frivolous candidacies. For example, although British candidates require the signatures of only 10 voters to be nominated, they must also post a deposit of £500, which is forfeited by any candidate who fails to receive 5% of the vote. Although these requirements apply to new parties, many countries, including the United States, have provisions that guarantee a place on the ballot to parties that won a minimum percentage of the vote in the previous election. In the U.S. case, candidates (including incumbents) still must petition to appear on the primary ballot and so become eligible for the party's guaranteed position, whereas in other countries, the choice of candidates is an internal party decision that is made according to each party's own rules.

2. Supports and Subsidies

An additional reason for restricting access to the ballot is that many systems provide a range of valuable subsidies to recognized candidates. These may be of any or all of three basic kinds. The simplest is direct cash payment. The second is the direct provision of services (postal delivery of campaign propaganda, broadcasting time, meeting halls) either free or at reduced rate. Finally, there is indirect subsidy; for example, through tax deductions for political contributions or regulations compelling commercial broadcasters to make time available to candidates at below commercial rates. In this section, the primary focus is on the first two forms of public subvention, although the last may be significant in some cases.

With both direct cash subsidy and provision of services, the problem of allocation is important. Here there are two basic models: equality and proportionality. Each has its problems. Equality encourages candidacies inspired only by the subsidy (e.g., the 1986 British candidate of the "Connoisseur Wine Party" who used his publicly provided mailing to all voters in the constituency to promote his wine shop) as well as the possibility that parties will split so as to increase their total subsidy. Indeed, is it fair that two parties with 5% support each should between them receive twice the subsidy of a single party with 50% support? Moreover, adherence to the principle of equality in the allocation of broadcasting time may make coverage of some kinds of events, such as debates among the leading candidates, impossible. On the other side, however, proportionality tends to entrench the status quo by denying new movements the resources to make the appeals that would allow them to demonstrate their popularity.

The principle of equality is most likely to be used in the direct provision of services, with proportionality being more common in the allocation of broadcasting time and most common in the allocation of direct financial support. All of this, along with the possibility that the support to which subsidy is proportional might be assessed in more than one way, is illustrated by the United States. Although there are no direct services provided to candidates, broadcasting is indirectly subsidized by the requirement that time be sold to qualified candidates at the lowest commercial rate. This, along with the equal access provision of the Federal Communications Act, applies equally to all candidates. Financial support is given to presidential primary contenders in the form of matching grants; once a candidate has raised at least $5000 in contributions of $250 or less in each of 20 states, he or she becomes eligible for a dollar-for-dollar match of the first $250 per contributor in individual donations. Here the criterion is proportionality to small donations. Candidates in the presidential general election receive outright grants provided they accept overall spending limits. The full grant ($46.1 million in 1988) is given to the candidate of each major party; "major party" is defined as a party whose candidate received at least 25% of the vote in the previous election. Proportionately reduced grants are given to the candidates of minor parties (between 5 and 25% of the vote in the previous election), whereas candidates of new parties also receive proportionately reduced grants, but only if they win at least 5% of the vote and only after the election. In this case, the criterion is proportionality to vote. As this shows, another question is whether support is given before or after the election. Cash in advance is obviously more useful than a promise of reimbursement at a later date for all parties, but this is especially the case for new parties, which need to use the subsidy to generate the public support that will in turn justify the subsidy. Thus, systems of proportional subsidy, like the US or German system, that give subsidies in advance to the established parties but reimbursement after the fact for new or minor parties are doubly stacked in favor of the status quo.

3. Campaign and Finance Restrictions

Long before the question was raised of attempting to promote fairness in electoral competition by subsidizing candidates or parties, most countries had regulations intended to promote fairness by prohibiting or requiring various practices. These regulations can be divided first between those that relate to nonfinancial activities and those that relate particularly to campaign finance; the latter can then further be divided on one hand between those that focus on spending and those that focus on fund-raising or contributions, and on the other hand, between those that impose limits or other restrictions and those that merely require openness. In all of these, a crucial concern is the conflict between any regulation of campaign activity and the principle of free speech.

The least exceptionable regulations are those concerning complicity in overt fraud or undue pressure. Organizing "repeaters," making threats, or offering bribes are all generally prohibited. Electioneering within polling places is generally prohibited in the United States; in some other countries, electioneering may be prohibited everywhere on election day. More difficult are regulations on the content of campaign materials. It is quite common (e.g., the case in 42 US states) to require that any campaign literature includes the name of the printer, publisher, or other responsible party. Less common, and more controversial, are regulations that limit libelous, false, or otherwise misleading advertising. Near one extreme, British law prohibits "any false statement of fact in relation to the candidate's personal character or conduct . . . unless [the accuser] had reasonable grounds for believing, and did believe, the statements to be true" (Representation of the People Act, 1983, sec. 106); at the other extreme, in the United States, there is only the common law of libel, which as applied to public figures requires "actual malice" as demonstrated by proof that the statement was known to be false or made in reckless disregard of the truth. Moreover, the British law allows injunctive relief, whereas the American law allows only damages after the fact.

Although regulations of this kind are important in that widespread indulgence in the practices they prohibit would destroy the fairness of elections, and although their application in some particular cases is debatable (e.g., to hire a taxi to take a voter to the polls would be illegal in Britain but not in Maryland), the basic division between acts that are prohibited and those that are allowed makes these regulations relatively simple. Financial regulations, which set limits on activities (fund-raising and spending) that are in the abstract both necessary and acceptable, are more complicated. Nonetheless, they are also widely regarded as necessary. At the risk of only slight oversimplification, one may say that limits on campaign spending are intended to prevent candidates from buying elections, whereas limits on contributions are meant to prevent other individuals or groups from buying candidates.

A number of questions must be addressed in formulating rules limiting expenditures. First, to whom does the limitation apply? In general, list-oriented systems limit spending by parties, under which not only local organizations but also candidates as individuals are subsumed. Candidate-oriented systems, on the other hand, in part because their laws often do not take cognizance of parties, may limit only the spending of candidates and their direct agents, although as the Canadian case illustrates, the fiction that elections are not really contests among parties gradually is being abandoned. Failure to regulate spending by parties can seriously undermine the entire exercise, as the British example makes clear; in 1983, for example, the Labour and Conservative Parties spent more than three times as much as the total spending of their parliamentary candidates (Butler and Butler, 1986: 228, 248), yet only the latter was regulated. Difficult as the problem of party spending may be, however, the more intractable problem is spending on behalf of a candidate or party by supporters who are not formally connected to either. One possibility, used in Britain and New Zealand with regard to campaigning in favor of (or in opposition to) specific candidates, is to prohibit all spending unless authorized by the candidate/party (or his or her/its agent) and counted against the allowable total. In the United States, spending by candidates is unregulated except for presidential candidates who elect to accept federal funding. Spending by parties and other organizations on behalf of candidates generally are regulated as contributions. On the other hand, "independent expenditures," that is, those made without consultation with the candidate's organization, are excluded from the spending limits and reporting requirements that apply to direct expenditures.

Second, what is included as an expenditure subject to limitation? Among items often excluded are fees for attorneys and accountants required to comply with the law and personal expenses (hotels, meals) of the candidates. A related question, with widely variable answers, is how goods and services that are either donated or sold at below market value are to be accounted.

Third, should expenses that are not overtly directed at garnering votes but nonetheless have that effect be included as campaign expenses? In the United States, for example, "partybuilding" activities that are not directed toward the election of any particular candidate are unregulated, which gives rise to the category of "soft money." A related problem is the "nonpolitical" activity of incumbent officeholders. Members of Congress, for example, have an impressive array of facilities—free postage, district offices, television and radio studios, staff assistance—to help them communicate with and serve their constituents. Especially because the optimal kind of campaigning is that which appears to be selfless constituency service, one must ask at what point these activities ought to be limited if challengers are to have a fair opportunity to campaign.

Turning to restrictions on contributions, most regulations fall into two major categories— those limiting the acceptable source and those limiting the maximum size—of an acceptable contribution. The earliest regulations (e.g., 1907 in the United States and 1908 in Canada) dealt with the sources of contributions and generally were directed against business. These bans were later extended to include trade unions. Such contributions are permitted in Britain, however, and the rise of Political Action Committees in the United States has allowed for widespread union and business contributions, albeit not from the unions or corporations per se. Other groups sometimes prohibited from making political contributions are foreigners, state and semistate enterprises, and civil servants. Perhaps most restrictive is the Province of Quebec, which allows contributions only from qualified voters.

The first federal regulation of the *amount* of contributions was included in the Hatch Act of 1940, which imposed a limit of $5000 per year on individual contributions to a candidate or political committee and $3 million per year in total for any political committee. Because a single person could make $5000 contributions to each of several committees all supporting the same candidate, however, massive contributions remained legal. In 1974, general contribution limits were introduced, restricting both the individual and annual total contributions of individuals, political committees, and parties to the campaigns of candidates for federal office. Following the Lockhead scandal, Japan introduced a similar set of restrictions. Under the simpler circumstances of a party-oriented electoral system, Spain, in 1985, limited individual contributions to a party to 1 million pesetas.

Financial limitations may be supplemented by requirements of public disclosure. On one hand, such requirements may dissuade candidates from accepting questionable contributions (or from acting after the fact in a way that would lend credence to charges that the contributions were really bribes), whereas on the other hand, they allow voters to know which candidates are beholden to which interests. American federal candidates and committees, for example, are required to report the names and addresses of any donors contributing more than $200 in a year. In other cases, requirements that significant contributions be disclosed are a substitute for other limitations. Thus, when the Canada Elections Act of 1974 introduced a requirement that all contributions over Can$100 be reported, it repealed the bans on corporate and union contributions, as well as an earlier ban on contributions from Americans. Although several countries have reporting requirements of this general type, there are significant differences regarding the maximum size of a contribution that can be accepted without being individually disclosed. In some cases, such as Canada or Spain, even modest contributions must be reported, whereas in others, only quite sizable donations must be itemized (e.g., DM10,000 in Germany or ÖS100,000 in Austria).

In order to be effective, reports must be timely and sufficiently detailed to convey meaningful information. American law is particularly stringent with regard to timeliness, in that quarterly reports are required plus additional reports immediately before and after the election; in Canada and Australia, in contrast, candidates and parties have between 4 and 6 months to complete their reports. Obviously, if one objective of disclosure is to allow candidates to bring the behavior of their opponents to the public's attention as a campaign issue, only reports made available before the election will do. Even if this is impossible, reports filed well after public interest in an election has waned are likely to have a very limited deterrent effect. With regard to detail, the Italian requirement that only aggregate totals of private donations be reported makes the reports of much less use than those in which individual donations are itemized. On the other hand, in an era of computer-generated forms, US parties have discovered that one way to hide sensitive information is to bury it in mountains of detailed reports.

In addition to myriad problems of scope and enforcement, campaign regulations also apparently conflict with the principle of freedom of speech. The right to speak without access to the means of disseminating what is said (broadcasting facilities, printing presses, meeting halls) would be a pale right indeed. All of these cost money. To restrict the right to spend money for the dissemination of speech, and by extension to restrict the right to contribute money to a collective effort for the dissemination of speech, is effectively to restrict the right to speak itself. At the same time, the same argument suggests that unrestrained spending gives disproportionate freedom of speech to those with disproportionate financial resources. Although full freedom of speech would require that unlimited resources be available to speakers, effective freedom requires that all citizens be put on an equal footing, even if this involves re-straining the better endowed, lest some citizens be able to drown out the others. The United States, based on the guarantees in the Bill of Rights, has opted for the former view regarding spending limits, with the only limits being those voluntarily accepted in exchange for public subsidy, but the latter with regard to contributions (*Buckley* v. *Valleo*). In many other coun-tries, the "equal playing field" argument had held greater sway.

F. Integrity

Electoral victory is valuable because it confers not only office but legitimacy. For legitimacy to be conferred, however, requires that the election be perceived as fair. In part, this means having electoral rules that conform to socially accepted standards of fairness. Some might argue that a US president chosen by the House of Representatives after an Electoral College deadlock would lack legitimacy, notwithstanding that the procedure is enshrined in the Con-stitution, or indeed that parliaments elected by SMP or city councils elected at-large are nec-essarily illegitimate if legislative majorities are not reflective of electoral majorities. Similarly, the exclusion of nonwhites from South African elections meant that they conferred at best limited legitimacy either in the eyes of most of the population or internationally.

The other requirement of fairness is that the electoral rules be obeyed. No country is free of electoral frauds; cases of ballot box stuffing, for example, have been a regular feature of US politics since the eighteenth century. Nonetheless, in most Western countries, the basic integrity of the electoral system is taken for granted. The same is not the case in many new democracies, and so the twin problems of maintaining fairness and maintaining the percep-tion of fairness become more important.

The number of ways in which elections can be unfair is limitless, but three major classes of unfairness have been thought to infect many elections, particularly in the Third World: wholesale exclusion of potential voters from the polls, whether by legal means (e.g., the pre-1962 Chilean system, whereby voters could only register on 8 days each month, and then only during a 2-hour period) or by intimidation; the coercion of voters; and the tampering with, or ignoring of, the ballots in the determination of the result. Both the prevalence of these problems and the difficulty of demonstrating that they have been avoided to those whose level of trust in the regime is quite low have led to the widespread use of foreign teams of observers to attest to the fairness of the ultimate result.

III. POLICY MAKING

Electoral policy is preeminently political. What is at stake is the fundamental distribution of political power and office. The values at issue are not mere matters of taste but the basic norms of free democratic societies. The ramifications of electoral policy decisions extend to all areas of policy made by elected officials. This presents a serious paradox. On the one hand, elec-toral policy is too basic and too important to be made by officials who are not politically re-sponsible. On the other hand, however, can elected officials be trusted to make policy in an area that so vitally and immediately affects their own personal interests as incumbents as well as the partisan interests they were elected to represent?

With the exception of a few questions, such as the Federal Communication Commis-sion's jurisdiction over broadcasting, electoral policy in the United States is made by the legis-lative branch of government—usually Congress or the state legislature—although, as with many other policy areas, intervention by the courts is increasingly common. Until the 1960s, federal involvement in electoral policy was minimal. The Constitution established direct election of the House of Representatives and the Electoral College but left the method of selection to the states. Later, the Seventeenth Amendment mandated direct election of senators as well. Suffrage was likewise a state matter; all that was required was that suffrage for federal elections be no more restrictive than for elections of the more numerous house of the state legislature. Subsequent amendments required that the vote not be denied on the basis of race, sex, or age over 18, or on the basis of failure to pay a poll tax. The date of federal elections was also established by Congress. Court involvement was directed primarily against racial discrimination in the South.

Since 1964, Congress has taken a more active role in establishing electoral policy. In order to protect the rights of minorities, the Voting Rights Act of 1965 and subsequent amendments gave the attorney general substantial powers to review state actions affecting elections, including registration of voters, the actual conduct of the election, and reapportionment. Congress has also taken a more active role in regulating campaign finances. These rules are overseen by the Federal Election Commission. As this body establishes a case law tradition, it will become an increasingly important policy maker.

Most other policy questions are decided by the state legislatures. Nominating procedures and deadlines, registration requirements, and finance of nonfederal elections are all state matters. Most significantly, the drawing of district boundaries, for both state offices and for the House of Representatives, generally is done by the state legislature. Naturally, this makes control of the legislature in the years immediately following a census particularly important.

For the most part, court involvement, although pervasive, has been reactive, judging the constitutionality of both federal and state actions. Although some finance regulations have been overturned, the courts have generally allowed great leeway in regulating elections. One area of electoral policy in which the courts have been quite active, however, is legislative redistricting. Not only have they, through judicial review, established standards for population equality that must be met when state legislatures draw district lines, they have also imposed reapportionment plans of their own when the states failed to act. In doing this, the courts have imposed even more restrictions on themselves, in the name of avoiding politics, than they have imposed on the legislatures. Although states may adopt multimember districts, a court-ordered plan can only have single-member districts. Court-ordered plans must also conform more closely to strict population equality than legislatively devised plans (*Connor v. Finch*). This total attention to equal population means, of course, that other criteria are given little or no weight.

In an effort to avoid the conflict of interest inherent in allowing legislatures to draw the districts from which their own members will be elected, some countries have set up nonpartisan commissions. The British, for example, have constituency boundary commissions for England, Wales, Scotland, and Northern Ireland that periodically suggest modification of district lines. A similar plan is used in Canada. This requires a political culture in which boards of distinguished citizens can be expected to "rise above party politics." Whether such a system could be adopted in the United States is very doubtful. To date, although the Federal Election Commission has been bipartisan in the sense of having members from both parties, party-line votes have been significant.

IV. CONCLUSIONS

Partisan concerns are always central to electoral policy. Although electoral systems are openly adopted or supported precisely because they will aid one party over another only rarely, it is inescapable that the choice of an electoral system will aid some parties and hurt others. Reforms proposed and defended on the basis of lofty principles are often little more than attempts by those temporarily in power to ensure their continued advantage. This is not to say that normative concerns are irrelevant to electoral policy making even when viewed strictly from the viewpoint of the self-interest of policy makers. To win an election is valuable primarily because of the legitimacy it confers. Unless the electoral process is perceived by the vast majority of citizens to be fair, so that they ought to submit voluntarily to the decisions of those elected, electoral victory is worth very little.

If reforms are adopted either for partisan advantage or for normative reasons, one of history's clear lessons is that they can have unintended consequences. Rather than making parties more democratic, preference voting has often increased the power of oligarchs within the party or interest-group systems. Although US campaign finance reform has decreased the importance of individual wealthy contributors, it has made candidates more dependent on special interest groups with their political action committees and on media consultants and fund raisers. One key to understanding the likely impact of a reform is to ask how candidates seeking election can adapt themselves to it.

This points, in particular, to the importance of organization. Many reforms directed against parties have had precisely the opposite effect from that intended because organization allowed the party to adapt better than its less-organized opponents. Early registration schemes often aided the urban machines they were supposed to combat because the ward heeler got people to the registrar's office, whereas the reformers, relying on civic spirit, did not (McCormick, 1953). Preference voting had a different effect for the Italian Communist Party with a disciplined organization than it had for the Christian Democrats without one. Often reforms supported in the name of democracy and popular participation redound to the benefit of organized interests. In each case, it is not the reform itself but the way parties, politicians, interest groups, and voters adapt to it that determines the result.

V. ORGANIZATIONS AND ELECTORAL POLICY

A variety of organizations take an active part in the formulation and study of electoral policy. The Federal Election Commission, aside from being an active participant in the regulatory process, publishes valuable compendia of electoral law reforms and electoral case law at federal, state, and local levels. Also at the official level, the League of State Governments has periodically published studies of state electoral systems. Among private organizations, the National Municipal League (publisher of the *National Municipal Review*) and groups such as Common Cause, the Rainbow Lobby, the Coalition for Free and Open Elections, and the Ralph Nader groups have been active in pressing for "democratic" reforms such as finance control and for openness and probity in the conduct of elections. At the level of more scholarly organizations, both the Brookings Institution and the American Enterprise Institute have been leaders in electoral policy research. *Congressional Quarterly* has also published many reports on proposed electoral reforms. Organized research groups on electoral systems exist in both the American Political Science Association and the International Political Science Association.

In Europe, the Inter-Parliamentary Union has sponsored compilations of electoral practice in member countries (e.g., Herman and Mendel, 1976). The Commission of the European Communities has been active in sponsoring research into electoral systems, particularly with an eye to the establishment of an electoral system for the European parliament. An important research institute (the Centre d'Analyse Comparative des Systèmes Politiques) at the University of Paris has played a key role in the study of emerging electoral systems of Eastern Europe. As in the United States, there are as well many private groups sponsoring reforms. The best known of these is the British Proportional Representation Society, which advocates replacing the British single-member plurality system with STV; an analogous organization exists in Ireland to push for the replacement of STV by plurality election.

As democracy has spread, a number of organizations have grown up to offer support services for those establishing or reforming their electoral systems, as well as providing teams of outside observers. Prominent among these organizations have been the International Foundation for Electoral Systems in Washington, the Westminster Foundation for Democracy in London, and the Centro de Asesoria y Promocion Electoral in San José, Costa Rica.

NOTES

1. In majority electoral systems, this is a common occurrence in the first round of voting, so a procedure for dealing with it will be well institutionalized. Plurality systems, with no second round of voting and only infrequent ties, use more ad hoc procedures. Often ties are resolved by the drawing of lots. Especially in parliamentary elections, this may be acceptable because if a single seat changes hands, it will have little effect on such questions as cabinet formation. In Sweden for a time, however, the Riksdag was tied. It was then agreed among the parties that tie votes would be resolved by the toss of a coin, with the provision that no coin toss would be regarded as a vote of no confidence.
2. Whether a "manufactured" majority really confers legitimacy depends on the gullibility of the people. To the extent that plurality systems discourage votes for third parties, they probably do contribute to the legitimacy of the result. If a candidate with only 40 to 45% of the vote were to win a decisive majority in the US Electoral College, it is unlikely that the legitimacy of the election would be increased by the institutional creation of a majority, especially if, as is possible, one of the winner's opponents had more popular votes.
3. The use of the referendum is becoming more common in Europe, where it resolved the question of divorce in Italy, entry into the European Economic Community in Britain, Ireland, Norway, and Denmark, and devolution of power in Scotland and Wales. Especially in Britain, this has engendered significant debate over the appropriateness of direct public policy making without the mediation of parliament.

REFERENCES

Bachrach, P. (1967). *The Theory of Democratic Elitism.* Little, Brown, Boston.

Bain, H. M., and Hecock, D. S. (1957). *Ballot Position and Voter's Choice.* Wayne State University Press, Detroit.

Barber, B. R. (1984). *Strong Democracy.* University of California Press, Berkeley.

Beer, S. H. (1969). *British Politics in the Collectivist Age.* Vintage Books, New York.

Blais, A., and Carty, R. K. (1990). Does proportional representation foster voter turnout? *European Journal of Political Research* 18: 167–81.

Butler, D., and Butler, G. (1986). *British Political Facts 1900–1985.* Macmillan, Houndmills, Hants, UK.

Campbell, P. (1965). *French Electoral Systems.* Faber and Faber, London.

Carstairs, A. M. (1980). *A Short History of Electoral Systems in Western Europe.* Allen & Unwin, London.

Crossman, R. H. S. (1972). *The Myths of Cabinet Government.* Harvard University Press, Cambridge, MA.

Dahl, R. A. (1956). *A Preface to Democratic Theory.* University of Chicago Press, Chicago.

Duverger, M. (1959). *Political Parties.* Wiley, New York.

Einaudi, L. (1954). *Il buongoverno.* Editori Laterza, Bari.

Engstrom, R. L. (1992). Modified multi-seat electoral systems as remedies for minority vote dilution. *Stetson Law Review* 21: 743–70.

Finer, S. (1975). *Adversary Politics and Electoral Reform*. Anthony Wigram, London.

Ginsberg, B., and Weissberg, R. (1978). Elections and the mobilization of popular support. *American Journal of Political Science* 22: 31–55.

Herman V., and Mendel, F. (1976). *Parliaments of the World*. Macmillan, London.

Katz, R. S. (1980). *A Theory of Parties and Electoral Systems*. Johns Hopkins University Press, Baltimore.

—— (1986). Intrapary preference voting, In *Electoral Laws and Their Political Consequences*. B. Grofman and A. Lijphart (Eds.). Agathon, New York.

—— (1987). Party government and its alternatives. In *Party Governments*: *European and American Experiences*. R. S. Katz (Ed.). de Gruyter, Berlin.

Katz, R. S., and Bardi, L. (1980). Preference voting and turnover in Italian parliamentary elections. *American Journal of Political Science* 24: 97– 114.

Kelley, S., Ayers, R., and Bowen, W. (1967). Registration and voting: Putting first things first. *American Political Science Review* 61: 359–379.

Kendall, M. G., and Stuart, A. (1950). The law of the cubic proportion in election results. *British Journal of Sociology* 1: 183–196.

Longley, L. D., and Braun, A. G. (1972). *The Politics of Electoral College Reform*. Yale University Press, New Haven, CT.

Mackenzie, W. J. M. (1958). *Free Elections*. George Allen & Unwin, London.

Mair, P. (1986). Districting choices under the single-transferable vote. In *Electoral Laws and Their Political Consequences*. B. Grofman and A. Lijphart (Eds.). Agathon, New York.

Mayhew, D. R. (1974). *Congress: The Electoral Connection*. Yale University Press, New Haven, CT.

McCormick, R. P. (1953). *The History of Voting in New Jersey*. Rutgers University Press, New Brunswick, NJ.

Milnor, A. J. (1969). *Elections and Political Stability*. Little, Brown, Boston.

Mueller, J. E. (1970). Choosing among 133 candidates. *Public Opinion Quarterly* 34: 395–402.

Ochoa, E. C. (1987). The rapid expansion of voter participation in Latin America: Presidential elections, 1845-1986. In *Statistical Abstract of Latin America 25*. J. W. Wilkie and D. Lorey (Eds.). University of California at Los Angeles Latin American Center, Los Angeles.

Pedersen, M. W. (1966). Preferential voting in Denmark. *Scandinavian Political Studies* 1: 167–187.

Pitkin, H. (1967). *The Concept of Representation*. University of California Press, Berkeley.

Polsby, N. W. (1971). *Reapportionment in the 1970s*. University of California Press, Berkeley.

Rae, D. W. (1971). *The Political Consequences of Electoral Laws*. Yale University Press, New Haven, CT.

Ranney, A. (1962). *The Doctrine of Responsible Party Government*. University of Illinois Press, Urbana.

Rose, R., and Mossawir, H. (1967). Voting and elections: A functional analysis. *Political Studies* 15: 173–201.

Rusk, J. G. (1970). The effect of the Australian ballot reform on split ticket voting: 1876-1908. *American Political Science Review* 64: 1220–1238.

—— (1974). The American electoral universe: Speculation and evidence. *American Political Science Review* 78: 1028–1049.

Sacks, P. M. (1976). *The Donegal Mafia*. Yale University Press, New Haven, CT.

Swearer, H. (1961). The function of Soviet local elections. *Midwest Journal of Political Science* 5: 129–149.

Taagepera, R., and Shugart, M. S. (1989). *Seats & Votes*. Yale University Press, New Haven, CT.

Thayer, N. B. (1969). *How the Conservatives Rule Japan*. Princeton University Press, Princeton, NJ.

Tufte, E. R. (1973). The relationship between seats and votes in two-party systems. *American Political Science Review* 67: 540–554.

Walker, J. (1966). Ballot forms and voter fatigue: An analysis of the office block and party column ballots. *Midwest Journal of Political Science* 10: 448–463.

Zariski, R. (1965). Intra-party conflict in a dominant party: The experience of Italian Christian Democracy. *Journal of Politics* 27: 3–34.

15
Legislative Change, Reform, and Public Policy

Leroy N. Rieselbach
Indiana University, Bloomington, Indiana

Process profoundly influences policy. The structure of institutions, including legislatures, that produce policy will affect, perhaps decisively, the content of that policy. In consequence, those who care about programs will have a stake in the organizational features of the institutions that enact them; when dissatisfied with programmatic results, they may well seek to change the structures and processes in the hope of inducing different outcomes. Those who are unhappy, in short, will become "reformers," endeavoring to create a "more effective" institution that produces "better" policies.

Some such process has taken place since the late 1960s in American legislatures, particularly in the U.S. Congress.[1] Vietnam, Watergate, the "energy crisis" of the 1970s, and severe economic dislocations revealed the relative weakness of representative assemblies. Lawmakers, reacting to a variety of supposed shortcomings, adopted a series of wide-ranging changes in the legislative institution between 1970 and 1977. As the 1990s began, policy immobilism ("gridlock" as it became popularly known) and scandal revived interest in congressional reform. This chapter attempts to put these alterations in theoretical and historical context, to describe them briefly, and to assess their impact on congressional policy making.[2]

I. CHANGE, REFORM, AND POLICY: SOME DEFINITIONS

Reform, defined as *intentional efforts* to reshape institutional structures and processes, is only one, and perhaps not even the most important, source of organizational alteration. *Change*, more broadly conceived as *any shift*—intended or inadvertent, evolutionary or revolutionary—in basic institutional patterns or procedures, may occur more randomly and unobtrusively. In addition, the content of *public policy*, the values—money, power, symbolic preferment—that statutes or other organizational (here legislative) activities confer may reflect either reform or change, as defined, or both. Thus, change appears basic; a variety of causes may stimulate new forms of organization and action and lead to new institutional out-comes. In this light, reform is best seen as a type of change; an explicit effort to bring about preferable (and perhaps particular) results through specific structural or procedural altera-tions.

To sort out the causes and shape of change, including reform, and to assess the impact, if any, of change on the legislature's policy enactments is a complicated task, for as Rohde and Shepsle (1978) make clear, change may flow from a multiplicity of forces. For one thing, *events* outside the assembly may impinge directly on it. Domestic recession or international crisis may pose problems that highlight congressional deficiencies. Failure to meet such chal-lenges may goad reformers to seek to restructure the legislature. Such external developments may raise new issues, may induce *agenda change*, with which Congress may feel compelled to deal, and which require new institutional forms (Sinclair, 1982, 1989). Finally, *membership turnover* may bring new personnel with different backgrounds, experiences, and perspectives to the legislature; newcomers may operate the existing machinery in ways quite at variance with old routines or may seek to rebuild the legislative engine to produce more efficient per-formance (see Asher and Weisberg, 1978; Brady, 1988; Burstein, 1979; Clausen and Van Horn, 1977; Deckard, 1976). Alternatively, events may compel incumbents to reassess their views, leading to either policy change or reform efforts, or both. For example, the frustra-tions of the Vietnam-Watergate decade and the major infusion of new blood into Congress, particularly in the 1964 and 1974 elections, contributed directly to the period of major change of the early and mid-1970s (Cavanaugh, 1980; Loomis, 1988; Rohde et al., 1985). In short, events, agenda shifts, and new members, neither planned nor predictable, may contribute as much or more to legislative change than any self-conscious reform movement.

II. REFORM IN THEORY

Given the complexity of the change phenomenon, and the number of interests and individuals involved in large, bicameral legislatures, it is not surprising to find that reform, when it comes, is seldom guided by broad visions of a "better" state of affairs. Rather reformers have most frequently followed an incremental strategy, singling out prime targets—for example, the arbitrary power of committee chairpersons or the role of "unlimited debate" (filibuster)—and seeking to remove them, in piecemeal fashion, as barriers to a "more effective" legislature. Ad hoc, shifting coalitions of reformers act to modify structural failings as they perceive them; support for one set of changes implies nothing about backing other, subsequent sets. Reform, in toto, over any given period—as the history of congressional reform in the 1970s so abundantly illustrates—may well, and often does, consist of contradictory, incompatible elements.

A. Some Broad Perspectives on Legislatures

This is not to argue, however, that there are no sweeping visions of what Congress might be in the best of all possible political worlds. Indeed, Davidson et al. (1966: 15–36; see also Sal-oma, 1969: Chaps. 1–2) outline three such views of the national assembly.

1. The Executive Force Theory

Proponents of the executive force model (Burns, 1949, 1963; Clark, 1964) are pessimistic about congressional capacity to govern. They stress the need to solve pressing political, eco-nomic, and social problems and despair that the legislature can contribute meaningfully to policy formulation. The executive, by contrast, is likely to be the catalyst for progress; Congress, given its basic structures and processes, can only impede innovation. As a decentralized, fragmented institution, representing multiple interests, especially the rural, small town, "conservative" constituencies of Middle America, the legislature is incapable of acting decisively. It is better suited to oppose than to create and to react than to invent.

In consequence, if policy making is to meet the nation's needs, the president must be permitted to lead unobstructed by a recalcitrant Congress. Executive initiatives must pass and be implemented. Reform should reduce the legislative ability to frustrate presidential policy making. Independent sources of power—committees and subcommittees, for instance—should be curbed. Rules of procedure, which permit minorities to block action, require modification. In general, the path of presidential proposals through Congress needs to be smoothed substantially. This executive supremacy view, in sum, stresses presidential leadership and reduces Congress' role to legitimation, perhaps modification, and review after the fact (Huntington, 1973). The president proposes and the legislature disposes according to his wishes.

2. The Responsible Parties Model

An alternative avenue to escaping congressional obstructionism is through the use of disciplined, cohesive, "responsible" political parties. If the majority party, given its command of the legislative terrain as the chief organizational mechanism of the assembly, marched smartly and decisively forward in rank, its policy proposals would triumph at each and every stage of the lawmaking process. If, moreover, the president commanded the party troops, they would advance his (desirable and progressive) programs without risk of rear-guard delay or defeat.

Proponents of responsible parties (e.g., American Political Science Association, 1950; Bolling, 1965) promote reforms to enlist rank-and-file members of Congress in the partisan armies. In general, they would empower the respective party national committees to manage the electoral process. With the ability to control the nomination, using a legal monopoly of campaign finance, for example, the central committees could compel their elected representatives: To break ranks would, in effect, end the deserter's political career; the nomination would be given to a new, more loyal recruit. Inside Congress, the rules would be rewritten to ensure that disciplined majorities could more easily carry the legislative day. In sum, in the responsible parties' view, the president proposes and his loyal partisan army disposes consistently with his marching orders. Here, too, Congress would eschew policy making and emphasizing instead legitimizing and nonpolicy representational (e.g., constituent service) activities.

3. The "Literary" Theory

What appear as Congress' vices to the proponents of executive force and responsible parties models become virtues to adherents of the literary theory (Burnham, 1959). The latter pay homage to "constitutional tradition," to checks and balances, to separation of powers. In their view, Congress should restrain the power-seeking executive during both policy formulation and implementation. Policy departures should come slowly, only after careful deliberation that considers all alternatives, and only after a genuine national consensus emerges. Thus, a decentralized legislature, to which multiple interests have access, and that can act only cautiously, is highly desirable.

These virtues have been lost in the 20th century, the so-called age of executives, and reform is required to restore the status quo ante. To that end, literary theorists resist all centralizing mechanisms: They prefer an election system that protects legislators' independence; they fear disciplined political parties that might run roughshod over citizen sentiments; they distrust executive leadership in any form; and, most important, they are predisposed to congressional procedures that protect the power of individual legislators to speak, slow action, promote deliberation, and oversee the administration. Overall, they want Congress to propose *and* dispose—to make policy, to represent citizens, to police the bureaucracy—to countervail the executive. They seek to restore Congress to what they see as its rightful, legitimate place at the very center of the political process.

4. The Congressional Supremacy ("Whig") Model

The literary view shades off into a vision that stresses to an even greater extent the centrality of Congress. Legislative supremacists see Congress as "the first branch of government" (de Grazia, 1965, 1966b) and therefore the prime mover in national affairs. They favor all the reforms that the literary theorists advocate as well as other changes intended, in effect, to strip the chief executive of most major bases of authority. This "whig" view envisages a Congress that proposes and an administration, president and bureaucracy, that disposes in strict accordance with legislative desires. A supreme Congress will both make policy explicitly— on its own terms—and oversee the implementation of that policy.

Overall, then, there are broad visions of Congress, each of which entails is own particular set of structural and procedural reforms. Each view could, theoretically, provide a model against which to evaluate specific reform proposals: Does a given suggestion move the legislature, or is it likely to do so, toward a clearly stated objective? Central to such assessment is a general question about the obligation of government and a narrower issue relating to the role of Congress in policy making. Both executive force and responsible parties proponents stress action; government must find prompt and effective solutions to national problems. In stark contrast, the literary and congressional supremacy views focus on caution and consensus; policy initiatives should come slowly and after due deliberation leads to wide agreement that new programs are needed.

These considerations carry concomitant organizational requisites, which revolve around the centralization of Congress. Those who desire to foster active policy making, the executive force and responsible parties theorists, seek to subordinate Congress in a centralized set of structural arrangements. Dominant executives, sustained by an accommodating legislature, formulate and implement (presumably) innovative public policies. Those who prefer inaction look favorably on a decentralized legislature—with numerous, autonomous decision-making centers—that can move only after attending to many points of view and melding them into widely acceptable programs. In other words, the proexecutive visions seek to minimize independent congressional policy influence, whereas prolegislative views seek to maximize it.[3]

B. Evaluating Reform: Some Criteria

These visionaries paint more or less coherent pictures of what the legislature should be. Reformers, in practice, are less often moved by such comprehensiveness; they tend to be legislators who seek to alter their institution in ways that advance their own, relatively narrow causes (Jones, 1977a). Beginning in 1970, in response to a series of legislative "crises," they imposed a wide variety of changes on themselves without much conscious effort to justify them as integral parts of any far-reaching plan to create a Congress of clear design. Observers of these structural shifts have, nonetheless, discerned some central tendencies in them, which provide some criteria with which to categorize and assess these developments.

For instance, Davidson and Oleszek (1976) distinguish between *adaptation* and *consolidation*. The former consists of reforms intended to permit more efficacious, from the legislative vantage point, relationships with external actors—executives in particular, but also judges, interest-group clienteles, and citizens more generally. Consolidative reforms seek to relieve internal stresses to reduce tensions that occur within the assembly. Thus, frustrated career expectations of junior lawmakers led them to attack the entrenched (as they saw it) power structure of Congress to make legislative service more meaningful and satisfying for themselves.

Jones (1977b) proposes a more sophisticated category scheme. He distinguishes among the content of *reforms enacted* (do they affect the legislature's electoral arrangements, its internal procedures, its distribution of power, its analytical capacity, or its authority relative to external actors?); the *change accomplished* (in personnel, allocation of authority, in the legislative process itself, or in the actual output of Congress); the *functions served* by reforms (following Davidson and Oleszek, 1976, whether they reflect adaptation or consolidation); and the *institutional effects realized* by the reforms (the extent to which they move the assembly toward a legislative supremacy, executive force, or party responsibility model of Congress). Jones' ambitious integrative effort makes clear the extraordinary difficulties inherent in sorting out reformers' intentions, actions, and accomplishments.

A more practical way to assess reform is to focus on legislative purposes (Rieselbach, 1993). Some reforms (e.g., enhancing the ability of party leaders to centralize congressional operations and move programs ahead more effectively) seek to enhance legislative *responsibility* to make Congress better able to define, impose, and implement its own policy priorities. Others (e.g., "democratizing" the assembly through a more equitable allocation of authority) aim to promote legislative *responsiveness* to make the assembly more representative of citizen viewpoints. Still others (e.g., financial disclosure statutes) are intended to increase Congress' visibility to improve its *accountability* to the public.

In sum, such theorizing as exists about legislative reform does little more than raise some general, but pertinent, questions. The visionaries pose the central question: What sort of legislature is most desirable? Literary theorists and legislative supremacists envision Congress as a potent, if cautious, policy maker; executive force and responsible parties proponents prefer to keep Congress at the periphery of the policy process. The more pragmatic observers of reform present a series of subsidiary questions about specific reforms: At what *aspect*—internal structures or external relationships—of Congress is reform aimed? What is the extent of reform proposals? Is the intent realized? What is the overall effect of reform on the legislative institution? (For other efforts to pose equivalent questions, see Oleszek, 1977; Patterson, 1977; Rieselbach, 1975; and Sheppard, 1985). In the real world, the basic issue has been ignored, and the secondary questions answered only after the fact of reform. Change has occurred without much guidance from theory in any form.

III. REFORM IN REALITY

This is not to suggest, however, that reform has been implemented purposelessly. The conclusion is only that reform—and there was an exceptional period of reform in the 1970s that trailed off in the succeeding decade, but shows signs of resurfacing in the 1990s—has proceeded pragmatically and incrementally, being intended to deal directly with discrete matters, not to restructure the assembly in keeping with some grand design. Indeed, a singular combination of developments, beginning with the mid-1960s emergence of the anti–Vietnam War protests, produced a barrage of criticism of legislative performance and some extraordinary steps to remedy the exposed shortcomings. These steps were halting and taken in different and not always compatible directions, with little conscious thought about their long-run implications.[4]

Events and new members created conditions in which Congress considered reform seriously. The legislature's inability to influence the conduct of the Indochina conflict and its confrontation with the Nixon administration over impoundment, which revealed with extraordinary clarity the chaotic character of the congressional budgetary process (Ippolito, 1978; LeLoup, 1988; Wildavsky, 1988), made obvious the assembly's weakness relative to the executive branch. Simultaneously, the electoral process—in consequence of the Goldwater candidacy of 1964, the Nixon resignation (and the controversial pardon of the "disgraced" ex-president by his successor, Gerald Ford) in 1973-1974, and an increasing tide of retirements from Congress in the 1970s—brought a "new breed" of lawmaker to Capitol Hill. The newcomers recognized Congress' failings; they were younger, more policy oriented, more independent minded, and as a result less predisposed to adhere to the ordinary modus operandi. Moreover, many of these new members found it electorally advantageous to run "against" Congress (Fenno, 1975, 1978) and were thus prepared to make reform a major part of their personal agendas. Reform became possible under these propitious circumstances.

This singular combination of events and personnel turnover stirred up a wave of congressional self-evaluation and analysis; without these elements of basic change, it is doubtful that reform would have followed. In any case, Congress, goaded by the liberal Democratic Study Group (Stevens et al., 1974) adopted the Legislative Reorganization Act of 1970 (Kravitz, 1990). Congressional introspection grew apace thereafter. The House conducted three separate self-studies: The (Bolling) Select Committee on Committees in 1973-1974 (see Davidson and Oleszek, 1977; U.S. House, 1973, 1974); the (Obey) Commission on Administrative Review in 1977 (U.S. House, 1977a, 1977b); and another Select (Patterson) Committee on Committees during the 96th Congress (U.S. House, 1980). Not to be outdone, during the same period, the Senate launched the (Hughes) Commission on the Operation of the Senate (U.S. Senate, 1976a); a temporary Select (Stevenson) Committee to Study the Senate Committee System (Parris, 1979; U.S. Senate, 1976c); a study by two ex-members—James R. Pearson (R., Kansas) and Abraham Ribicoff (D., Connecticut) (Plattner, 1983); and a Temporary Select (Quayle) Committee to Study the Senate Committee System (Cohodas, 1984).[5] An extraordinarily varied welter of ideas emerged from these assessments; many were adopted (more were not!). For convenience, we identify three separate sets of reforms—for responsibility, responsiveness, and accountability—but in fact the proposals were implemented piecemeal and seriatim, without reference to broad theorizing or even to one another.

A. Reform for Responsibility: Restoring Congressional Policy Influence

1. Seeking External Influence

One major thrust of reform—to enhance congressional responsibility and therefore to make the legislature a more efficient and effective policy maker—followed two tracks: the first, in many ways the most visible and dramatic, aimed to shore up Congress' position relative to the executive. If the national legislature could impose its own policy preferences, even in the face of executive opposition, it would recapture its ability to act as a responsible policy maker. In fact, the argument, which "liberals" most commonly advanced, made sense only when a perhaps atypical conservative Republican president sat in the Oval Office. A reinvigorated Congress could indeed save the Great Society from decimation (Orfield, 1975), but in the long-run, an independent legislature would be more in keeping with the literary or whig theorists' views than with the policy goals of those who led the reform battles in the 1970s.

However, short-run considerations proved decisive. Congress moved against the president in 1973, passing the War Powers Resolution to circumscribe the commander in chief's authority to commit American military forces to combat, as in Korea and Indochina. The legislation, enacted over President Nixon's veto, gave Congress the ability to compel the executive to withdraw any troops sent into the field within 60 days (90 days under special conditions) (see Frank and Weisband, 1979; Holt, 1978; Pious, 1979).[6] In theory at least, the executive should cultivate congressional approval before committing troops or risk legislative reversal of his military leadership.

Budgetary reform constitutes a second congressional effort to enhance the legislature's authority. Acknowledging past failure to exercise effective control over federal expenditures, Congress adopted a major reform package: the Budget and Impoundment Control Act of 1974. The law created new budget committees in each chamber; provided them with a powerful analytic agency, the Congressional Budget Office, capable of competing with the Office of Management and Budget; and charged them with imposing fiscal discipline on an archaic budgetary process (Ellwood and Thurber, 1977a, 1977b; Finley, 1975; Havemann, 1978; Steinman, 1977). The new scheme aimed to let Congress produce a coherent, unified budget that compared revenues and expenditures, and did so on a fixed (though in practice flexible) timetable. The Act sought to enable Congress to centralize and coordinate its consideration of the budget, and thus to compete on even terms with the executive for fiscal supremacy. Tacked on to the budget reforms were major restrictions on the president's power to impound—to delay spending or to decline to spend entirely—funds that Congress had duly authorized and appropriated (Dodd and Schott, 1979: 133–135; Fisher, 1975: Chaps. 7–8; Munselle, 1978). Enacted specifically in response to Richard Nixon's aggressive, and often illegal, use of impoundment, these new provisions made it considerably more difficult for the president to control the flow of federal funds.[7]

The 1974 statute did not bring the swelling budget deficit under control, and the legislature, recognizing that the process was in dire distress, in 1985 passed a Balanced Budget and Emergency Deficit Control Act (popularly known as Gramm-Rudman-Hollings [GRH] after its three Senate sponsors). The GRH statute set maximum deficit limits and required mandatory cuts in spending if the deficit targets were not met. The act also revised budget procedures to enable, reformers hoped, Congress to meet the deficit goals and eventually bring the budget into balance in ways congenial to the legislature (on Gramm-Rudman-Hollings, see inter alia, Gilmour, 1990: Chap. 5; Shuman, 1988: Chap. 10; Thurber, 1991; and White and Wildavsky, 1989: Chap. 19). GRH did not work and Congress reversed course in 1990, when it enacted a Budget Enforcement Act that abandoned the effort to restrict the size of the deficit in favor of imposing spending ceilings ("caps") on government outlays and establishing another set of new budgetary procedures (Thurber, 1992). Congress has continued to cast about for ways to discipline its budget making and to impose its budgetary priorities even in the face of presidential opposition.

Third, on the institutional level, Congress moved to strengthen its informational resources. The legislature created new research agencies—the Congressional Budget Office and the Office of Technology Assessment, the latter to analyze the potential impact of various scientific programs. It has refurbished and revitalized old ones. The General Accounting Office has moved well beyond simply auditing the federal books to become a powerful agency for systematic policy analysis. The Congressional Research (formerly the Legislative Reference) Service of the Library of Congress is larger, more skilled, and well staffed; it produces serious research for congressional committees and individual members (on these developments, see Arieff, 1979; Thurber, 1981; U.S. Senate, 1976b). Congress also has sought to harness computers to legislative needs (Frantzich, 1979); numerous information systems help representatives know more about more issues. Staff resources—capable experts on individual and committee payrolls—have expanded enormously during the 1970s, providing members with specialists to assign to policy formulation and assessment (Fox and Hammond, 1977; Malbin, 1980). To the extent that useful and usable data flow from such innovations, Congress is able to counterpoise its programmatic preferences to those of the executive; it need no longer defer so readily to an administration presumed to possess superior information.

Finally, Congress began to assert, far more forcefully than previously, powers already established. The Legislative Reorganization Act of 1946 had formalized the legislature's obligation to oversee the executive branch; Congress was to exert "continuous watchfulness" over administrative agencies and bureaus (Harris, 1965; Ogul, 1976). Greater informational resources, coupled with an enlarged number of vantage points—particularly in subcommittees—stimulated an upsurge of congressional surveillance of the executive (Aberbach, 1990; Dodd and Schott, 1979: Chap. 6; Foreman, 1988; and Regens and Stein, 1979). Even the seemingly sacrosanct Central Intelligence Agency (CIA) came in for substantial scrutiny. Watergate revelations triggered major investigations of the CIA, which led directly to House and Senate creation of Intelligence Committees charged to oversee the intelligence community. In addition, a 1974 amendment to the foreign aid bill (the Hughes-Ryan amendment) required the CIA to report "covert operations" that it conducted, or had carried out on its behalf, to "the appropriate committees of the Congress."[8]

More generally applicable as a policy-control device is the legislative veto, which Congress came increasingly to employ in the 1970s. Though found in a variety of forms, the legislative, or congressional, veto reserved to Congress the opportunity to block executive actions—reorganizations, arms sales, agency regulations—within a specified time period.[9] Fundamentally, the veto permitted the legislature to prevent executives from acting, although they were authorized by law to do so, when some significant number of lawmakers disagreed with the substance of administrative policy (Bolton, 1977; Gilmour, 1980). Both the War Powers Resolution and the Impoundment title of the 1974 Budget Act contained congressional veto provisions, as did more than 150 other statutes, many enacted after 1975 (Cohen, 1980; Cooper, 1985; Craig, 1983; Dodd and Schott, 1979: 231–232). In 1983, the Supreme Court, in the case of *Immigration and Naturalization Service* v. *Chadha*, struck down the veto and ruled that it violated the separation of powers and "presentment" clauses of the Constitution. In practice, however, the decision has constricted but not eliminated the veto. Congress remains able through alternative procedures to block proposed executive actions; delegation to the executive may require the latter to send its regulatory proposals to Congress and, if the legislature does not vote to approve them, refrain from implementing them (Fisher, 1985; Franklin, 1986; Kaiser, 1984).

2. Centralizing Congressional Operations

If the first facet of the effort to improve congressional responsibility sought to redress a perceived imbalance between the legislature and the executive, the second—directed at centralizing legislative procedures—focused on the same end, at least to a limited extent. The House of Representatives, aware that its fragmented, decentralized decision-making structure impeded coherent policy formulation, took a few halting steps toward strengthening the capacity of the majority party to impose some discipline on its members and, thus, on the institution. These were consolidative reforms that made efforts to improve internal organization, enhancing responsibility, and making Congress a more effective policy maker. The long-run implications were scarcely considered, and indeed are difficult to fathom. If reforms create a centralized legislature that can impose its favored programs on a hostile president, they are compatible with the literary and congressional supremacy views. If, on the other hand, reforms permit presidential partisans to move his programs ahead without serious opposition, the new procedures would please the proponents of executive force and responsible party positions.

Specifically, the reforms adopted sought to enable the majority party, the Democrats, to move its legislative programs ahead more efficaciously. The party—the caucus and its leader, the Speaker—were made stronger, whereas the committees, the chief roadblocks to legislative responsibility, were in some ways brought to heel. (On these developments, see Jones, 1980; Dodd and Oppenheimer, 1977b; and the sources cited in note 2.) Party power was enlarged in several ways. The caucus met in December, before each new Congress, to organize. Its members claimed for themselves the right to pass on committee assignments and to approve committee chairpersons. The latter step undermined the hoary "seniority rule" (at least in principle) and, in fact, led to the ouster in 1975 of three elderly Southern oligarchs (Hinckley, 1976; on seniority generally, see Hinckley, 1970, and Ornstein and Rohde, 1975). Appropriations subcommittee chairs were also subject to caucus scrutiny. In addition, the caucus created a Steering and Policy Committee, and eventually empowered it to make committee assignments.

The Speaker also received additional authority. He or she was granted power to regulate the flow of legislation to committees: to make multiple or serial referrals, impose time limits on committee consideration, and create ad hoc (select) committees to facilitate coherent treatment of complex policy issues (Vogler, 1978). Informally, the Speaker has frequently set up "task forces," composed of friendly and supportive members, to solicit support for party policy initiatives (Garand and Clayton, 1986; Sinclair, 1981). The Speaker was also given a major voice in the new Steering and Policy Committee; in effect, more than half of the 35 members are the Speaker's appointees and, presumably, allies. Finally, the Speaker was empowered to nominate, subject to caucus approval, Democrats to serve on the Committee on Rules; selecting loyal party members has contributed to the firm yoking of that panel, which was a major obstacle to liberal legislation in the 1950s and 1960s, to the party leadership (Oppenheimer, 1978, 1980a).

A few other reforms, with implications for centralization, were adopted during the decade of the 1970s. The new budget process, noted previously, contains the seeds of centralization: If the new budget committees ever succeed in imposing control over the disparate standing committees and appropriations subcommittees, they will be poised to dictate the congressional budget. A series of rules changes, directed largely to eliminate dilatory tactics, were designed to ease the path of legislation by curtailing the minority's ability to subvert the majority. The most significant of these changes is the weakening of the Senate filibuster: The number of votes needed to end debate was reduced from two thirds of those present (64 or 65 under ordinary circumstances) to a constitutional three fifths majority (60 votes); the possibilities for a postcloture "filibuster by amendment" were largely eliminated by rules changes that mandated that the vote on final passage must come within 30 hours after cloture is invoked (see *Congressional Quarterly Weekly Report*, 1975: Cooper, 1979; Oppenheimer, 1985). In sum, stronger party leadership and limitations on minority power position the parties to centralize policy making to a greater degree than was the case in the prereform period.

B. Reform for Responsiveness: Decentralization and Democratization

Congressional reformers tended to view committees as the major locus of the legislature's difficulties. Liberals, mostly Democrats, and junior members of both parties viewed powerful panels with displeasure. The former found their policy preferences frustrated in committees where conservative southerners were safely ensconced in the chair and protected by the seniority rule. The latter felt deprived of the opportunity to participate fully: The chairperson, frequently in collaboration with the ranking minority member, dominated the committee's internal life. Strengthening the parties was one way to circumvent recalcitrant committee leaders, but the reformers, and their number increased in the 1970s as an unusually large contingent of newcomers was elected, were unwilling to pass up the opportunity to improve their own individual circumstances.

Thus, the reformers pushed successfully for a series of consolidative changes, which relieved the internal stresses that strong committees created. Because these alterations were decentralizing, opening positions of influence to many members previously powerless, the changes increased Congress' responsiveness; they established a legislative process more accessible to greater numbers of outside interests—citizens, organized groups, and governmental personnel. More basically, though the reformers seem to have given little conscious consideration to the matter, these decentralizing changes appear to be most compatible with the literary theory. By diffusing influence more widely, the alterations create conditions that exacerbate the problems in assembling majorities; a legislature that can integrate policy only with great difficulty, through complex bargaining and negotiating processes, is likely to act as neither a supreme policy formulator nor a pushover for powerful presidents. Rather, it will be most effective in blocking action by requiring compromise as the price of even modest policy departures.

Specifically, the reform movement undercut the dominant position of committee chairpersons, effectively devolving their authority to independent subcommittees (Smith and Deering, 1984). As noted, the effort to enhance the position of the political parties produced steps to curb the committee chairs, but only part of their power was assigned to the parties. More significantly, substantial portions were reallocated to the rank and file, mainly junior members. Such shifts were particularly pronounced in the House, where, first of all, members were limited to one subcommittee chair each. In addition, no individual could select a second subcommittee assignment until each full panel member had chosen one subcommittee position. Similar changes in the Senate effectively guaranteed that members of both chambers could secure a "piece of the action" in subcommittee earlier in their congressional careers (Congressional Quarterly, 1977: 743–794; and sources cited in note 2).

The House went further: The Democratic caucus, in 1973, adopted a series of changes, collectively known as the "subcommittee bill of rights," to protect the independence of subcommittees (Dodd and Oppenheimer, 1977b; Freed, 1975; Ornstein, 1975b; Rohde, 1974). The bill of rights required that subcommittees have fixed jurisdictions and that legislation on these subjects be referred automatically to them; it permitted subcommittees to meet at the pleasure of their members, to write their own rules, and to control their own budgets and staffs. Moreover, 2 years later, the caucus mandated that all committees with more than 20 members create a minimum of four subcommittees. The upshot of these changes has been to establish an "institutionalized" subcommittee system, with active, permanent, and independent panels (Davidson, 1981; Haeberle, 1978). Subcommittee members are strategically located to exert considerable influence over matters in its jurisdiction (though such areas may be quite narrow).

In sum, these changes have made the House more like the Senate (Foley, 1980; Ripley, 1969). Both chambers are decentralized: Committee chairpersons must, under threat of ouster, share their authority with full committee majorities and subcommittee leaders. In general, more people, operating from more secure power bases, now have the potential to shape legislative policy making.

C. Reform for External Consumption: Accountability

A final set of changes sought to counter an increasingly hostile public opinion. Along with all governmental institutions, and politicians generally, Congress fell into public disfavor in the 1960s and 1970s (Parker, 1977; Patterson and Caldeira, 1990). Although citizens had continuing confidence in their own members of Congress, they considered Congress collectively to be performing poorly (Cook, 1979; Parker and Davidson, 1979). To remedy this situation and restore public approbation, Congress imposed on its members a series of reforms, adaptive in character, designed to expose its operations to public scrutiny. To the extent that citizens (and voters) could discover what their representatives were doing, and satisfy themselves that these activities were ethically beyond suspicion, the populace could hold Congress accountable and accept the legislature's policy making as legitimate and untainted. The need to reassure a skeptical public stimulated these reforms; as usual, little if any consideration of their long-range impact was visible. In fact, if these accountability alterations have any effects, they are likely to promote the literary theory, at the margins at least. If the reforms, by making congressional politics more visible, place obstacles in the path of party leaders—"open" decisions openly arrived at will involve more participants and, in turn, weaken the power of any set, including the party apparatus (Froman and Ripley, 1965)— they will undercut the potential for executive force or party responsibility models. Conversely, if these reforms permit opponents of policy change to identify and exploit legislative "veto points," they make it more difficult for Congress to act, limiting the legislature to blocking or modifying policy initiatives, as the literary theorists prefer.

In any event, three broad programs, intended to expose members and congressional operations to the glare of publicity, were implemented in the 1970s. First, the Federal Election Campaign Act of 1971, as amended in 1974, 1976, and 1979, and as interpreted by the Supreme Court in *Buckley* v. *Valeo* (1976), established a congressional election system in which contributors' donations are limited and candidates' expenditures are not. What the latter spend, however, and the sources of these funds must be disclosed (Alexander, 1984; Congressional Quarterly, 1976: 544–557). In general, the laws both limit large gifts and record even more modest ones on the public record.

Second, both the House and Senate adopted codes of ethics, including financial disclosure provisions, designed to deter or expose conflicts of interest (Bullock, 1978). Members were required to report gifts they (and their employees) receive; their property holdings, their investments in securities, and their debts; and their income from all sources. Such disclosures should enable concerned citizens, or enterprising journalists, to discover to whom, if anyone, members of Congress are in any way financially beholden, and to assess the extent, if any, to which members' personal interests impinge on matters about which they must, as legislators, vote or otherwise become involved.

Finally, members of Congress concluded that they should carry on their internal operations in the "sunshine" (Bullock, 1978). The Legislative Reorganization Act of 1970 decreed that legislators vote publicly in committee and on the floor: Committee roll calls are to be recorded and made available; new requirements for recording votes reduce the possibility that members can avoid going "on the record," as individuals during debate and preliminary floor consideration of legislation (Kravitz, 1990; Ornstein and Rohde, 1974). The committee process was opened up as well: All sessions, including "markups" and conference committee meetings, are to be public unless a majority votes, in public, to close them. Although executive sessions on secret or controversial matters remain possible, the burden of proof now lies with those who would exclude outside observers.

When in the 1990s scandals involving the House Bank—in reality a check-cashing service for members—and the House Post Office as well as a public perception that legislators were a pampered elite, possessing numerous perquisites—a gym, free flowers, reserved parking spaces, and low-cost medical care, among others—kindled public hostility toward Congress, the legislature was quick to take action. The "perks" were eliminated or drastically reduced (Berger, 1992), and the House appointed a Director of Non-legislative and Financial Services to manage the chamber's internal affairs (Donovan and Kuntz, 1992). These developments suggest that citizens can find out not only what their representatives are doing but also whether the conduct is in any way ethically suspect. A satisfied citizenry, able to hold its legislators to account, should come once again to hold its national legislature in high regard.

IV. THE IMPACT OF REFORM ON POLICY

That substantial and significant legislative reform has occurred is incontrovertible; the problem, of course, is to assess the consequences that change and reform have wrought. Because reform has been undertaken in response to many influences—political and personal—and because it has not been guided by any broad, long-term, widely shared vision of desirable legislative structure, its effects seem inconsistent and uncertain. Indeed, because reformers promoted change for diverse reasons, some profess satisfaction while others remain unhappy and push for additional reform. The impact on the content of policy is especially difficult to decipher. Yet the available evidence suggests that the results of reform have been many and varied. Reformers' intentions have sometimes been realized, and sometimes not; on other occasions, quite unintended, and often undesirable, consequences seem to have followed from reform efforts. Congress is at once more responsible, more responsive, and more accountable, but not necessarily to the overall benefit of the legislature. And whatever the outcome, intended or otherwise, it may be impossible ever to ascertain definitively whether the reform or other factors—turnover and events—explain the observed results.[10]

A. Congressional Responsibility

1. The Challenge to the Executive

Nowhere is the difficulty in disentangling the effects of reform from those of more general change more visible than in the effort to evaluate the impact of the congressional challenge to the executive branch. The War Powers and Budget Acts passed during a period of popular discontent, rapid turnover in Congress, and a scandal-ridden and politically vulnerable presidency. There has been (fortunately!) no clear test of the war powers provisions, and the legislature has yet to establish a workable budget process.

Thus, the available evidence suggests that to date Congress has not used its newly claimed authority to impose its will on the executive, especially in the military realm (Fisher, 1991; Katzman, 1990). On numerous occasions, the president has felt obliged to report to Congress in compliance with the War Powers Resolution; but most military adventures (e.g., Gerald Ford's recapture of the ship *Mayaguez*, seized by Cambodia in 1975, or George Bush's "arrest" of General Manuel Noriega) were short-lived and were over before a decentralized Congress could formulate a meaningful response. On two occasions, however, Congress played a visible part with respect to sending armed forces abroad. In 1983, it forced Ronald Reagan to acknowledge his obligations under the War Powers Resolution and in return authorized dispatch of U.S. Marines to Lebanon for 18 months. On the eve of the 1991 Persian Gulf War, the legislature voted grudgingly, by a narrow 53 to 46 margin in the Senate, to permit George Bush to use force to end Iraqi occupation of Kuwait.

In reality, Congress has the opportunity to participate in military policy making only when troops remain in the field for substantial periods. In these circumstances, Congress *can* act decisively, ordering the troops home if it wishes, or by default, doing nothing and thus requiring the President to cease military operations. The issue, of course, is whether the legislature *will* act, imposing its preferences on the commander in chief, who will most certainly invoke the "national interest," the nation's prestige and honor, and the gravity of the situation. There is no cause to believe with certainty that members of Congress will, in such circumstances, be prepared to run the risk or assume the responsibility for overruling the chief executive.

More speculatively, the War Powers Act may be significant less after the fact of military involvement than as a prior deterrent to precipitous, or difficult to justify, armed intervention. Presidents can never be entirely certain that Congress will approve their actions, and they may calculate carefully about congressional response before commiting troops. For example, there was widespread speculation that the Ford administration was considering direct intervention, in 1974, in the civil war in Angola. The foreign policy committees of Congress, especially the Senate Foreign Relations panel, became increasingly concerned, given the perceived lessons of our Indochina involvement, that American commitment of money and military supplies might escalate into military support of our favored faction. Such forthright expression of concern may well have contributed to executive caution: No use of U.S. troops was ever publicly proposed.[11] Whether such actions truly constrain the President is difficult to determine; if they do, whether this is desirable depends on the observer's view of the president and/or the policy that military intervention would seek to pursue.

On balance, the president's position is likely to prevail. To be sure, Congress has flexed its institutional muscles frequently. On the one hand, Congress has imposed its preferences, at least negatively, on frequent occasions. It refused to ratify SALT II, the strategic arms limitations treaty with the former Soviet Union, and it has repeatedly delayed or blocked arms sales to various foreign governments by using the legislative veto. (For a full treatments of congressional-executive relations in foreign affairs, see Crabb and Holt, 1992; and Mann, 1990.) On the other hand, some signs point to a revival of legislative deference to executive international relations leadership. Heightened international tensions increase risk to the country, and incline legislators to accept the views of the professional military. For instance, Congress not only has failed to enact a comprehensive "charter" to control intelligence agencies but also has backed away from the Hughes-Ryan oversight provisions, moving to reduce the number of committees entitled to know what activities the CIA undertakes overseas. Similarly, domestic problems—recession or the "energy crisis," for example—with their obvious electoral implications, may require members to redirect their attention to the home front, leaving international matters to the executive.

During the Reagan administration, Congress repeatedly cut the defense budget below the president's request (but allowed it to rise dramatically above previous levels), imposed limits on production and deployment of the MX missile (but refused to eliminate the system entirely), and reallocated military assistance to foreign nations. The end of the cold war and the collapse of the Soviet Union gave Congress a chance to challenge the president, but the legislature proved cautious, preferring to make marginal, piecemeal cuts in military spending rather than producing a major "peace dividend" through substantial reductions.

In sum, although presidents can no longer count on customary congressional acquiescence to their foreign policy initiatives, the legislature's assertiveness may reflect less structural reform than more basic, evolutionary change: more members more willing, under the stimulus of political circumstances, to use basic legislative prerogatives to challenge the administration. Should membership and situations alter, the pattern of congressional deference or contention is likely to ebb and flow. Members' policy preferences and political purposes more than institutional reforms may be the decisive determinants of congressional challenges to the executive.

Assessment of the new budget process, as a token of legislative revival, yields a similarly cloudy picture: Reform interacts with other forms of change to produce unpredictable results. On the plus side, the 1974 Act clearly restored Congress' *potential* to assert legislative supremacy in financial affairs. When and if the legislators want to act decisively, they can use the new procedures to do so. In fact, between 1975 and 1979, Congress observed the form of the new scheme, but the process did not fundamentally alter spending priorities (between military and domestic programs) or staunch the flow of red ink (the deficit and the national debt continued to grow inexorably). In 1981, under Ronald Reagan, the more centralized budget process worked, at least in principle. The administration lowered taxes, cut domestic spending, and raised defense expenditures dramatically. The centralized congressional process produced a budget efficiently and on time, but it did not restore an independent congressional influence in financial matters. The legislature deferred to the executive.

After 1981, more normal budgetary politics reappeared, and Congress found itself unable to use the budget process to control the deficit. The Gramm-Rudman-Hollings law, adopted in 1985, did not work. Congress complied formally with its terms, using accounting sleight of hand to pass budget resolutions that, on paper, met the law's deficit reduction requirements; in reality, the legislators were unable or unwilling to abide by the self-imposed limits and continued to appropriate funds in excess of the budget targets.

The 1990 Budget Enforcement Act was no more successful. The reformers hoped that spending caps (fixed ceilings) for discretionary spending and "pay-as-you-go" financing (increased outlays in one area had to be offset by equivalent cuts elsewhere in the budget) would make it impossible for spending to exceed the fixed limit the act imposed, but despite their good intentions, the deficit for fiscal 1992 reached a record $290 billion. In sum, despite the quality of the Congressional Budget Office's analysis (Wildavsky, 1984) and Congress' capacity to look at the budget from a far broader perspective, a variety of substantial changes in the budget process have not worked to make the legislature a responsible budgeter. Congressional partisanship,[12] an unwillingness to cut popular domestic programs, and the sheer size of the deficit have conspired to overwhelm the budget process. Where there is no agreement on the substance of policy, tinkering with the rules will have little impact on budgetary outcomes.

With respect to impoundment, the Budget Act has had a clear and pronounced effect. The president is now considerably less able to regulate the flow of federal funds. Impoundment for policy purposes, as Richard Nixon practiced it, is now virtually impossible without legislative acquiescence, and the burden has been transferred to the executive to win that approval (Shuman, 1988). When Congress appropriates, it is far more probable that the funds will be spent. Yet the anti-impoundment provisions have had unintended consequences as well. Traditionally, impoundment was a useful, and noncontroversial, device that promoted efficient administration. Now, all matters, even the most routine deferrals, must be reported to Congress; members have complained that many hours are wasted on relatively trivial items, a concern that bureaucrats share (Pfiffner, 1977; Wildavsky, 1984).[13] Once again, it seems clear that reforms have enabled Congress to act and to win, if it has the determination to do so. Whether the legislature does, and what the long-term effect of such decisiveness will be, remain open questions.

With respect to the legislative veto, the Supreme Court decision in *INS* v. *Chadha* (1983) restricted an authority that Congress possesses but has been loath to use forcefully. Inaction is no longer sufficient to block executive action; the lawmakers, by majority vote, must now in most cases act positively to kill administrative rulings and their action is subject to a presidential veto (Cooper, 1985; Fisher, 1987; Franklin, 1986). Congress must treat veto-related issues as it would normal legislation and must spend considerable time and energy on them. The legislative veto survives, but in a form that reduces its overall effectiveness as a check on unbridled executive branch policy making.

Similar uncertainties appear about the results of the "information revolution." From one perspective, it is incontrovertible that members of Congress have substantially greater quantities of data than ever before. Enlarged staff resources, new agencies (Congressional Budget Office [CBO] and Office of Technology Assessment [OTA]), more effective old support facilities (General Accounting Office [GAO] and Congressional Research Service [CRS]), and increasing computer technology combine to expand enormously the congressional capacity to engage in serious analysis, which can sustain legislative alternatives to executive initiatives. These developments, however, are not necessarily an unmixed blessing.

For one thing, members of Congress may not have adequate incentives to seize these new opportunities. Fundamentally, in some, perhaps most, circumstances, senators and representatives are politicians rather than objective analysts. They may well be searching less for optimal policies than for programs that will serve their political purposes. They want ideas that will satisfy their constituents—voters and supporting interest groups. They need solutions that will survive the bargaining and compromising policy process of a decentralized legislature. Policy analysts who do not recognize the political needs of their principals will find their advice ignored. Where politics and analysis merge, the latter may be of considerable use to legislators; where they diverge, analysis is likely to receive low priority (on these matters, see Jones, 1976; Schick, 1976; Whiteman, 1985).

Moreover, information that these reforms make available may actually distract lawmakers from programmatic activities. Too much data, "information overload," may overwhelm members. They may not know how to cope with what is available to them and they may be increasingly inclined to look to staff for substantive guidance (Hammond, 1985; Malbin, 1980). Conversely, staff personnel who are prepared to be "entrepreneurs" rather than impartial "professionals" (Price, 1971) may come to play powerful policy roles. Dependence on the experts may undercut the members' ability to exercise genuinely independent policy judgments. Finally, there is an information management problem; members may spend more time and energy administering large staffs than they do using the data that their information resources supply. Although some offices now employ professional managers (Hammond, 1978), the risk remains that organizational confusion and chaos will intrude on legislators' ability to engage the substance of policy questions.

In sum, Congress in the 1990s is better equipped institutionally to challenge presidential policy leadership. The reforms it has adopted—the War Powers Act, the Budget Act, strengthened analytic capacity—have placed the national legislature in a strong position to define and fight for its own priorities. But capability and its use are not necessarily synonymous: Whether Congress will, in fact, employ its weapons against the executive depends equally on both member willingness to do so and events encouraging them to seize the initiative. What this suggests, of course, is that Congress can, but only sometimes will, be the more forceful policy advocate that reform has enabled it to be.

2. *Empowering the Leadership*

Congressional reformers not only sought to rearm the legislature against the executive, but also to improve responsibility through strengthening the political parties. More cohesive, centralized parties would be better able to move a program through Congress efficiently, to overcome the opportunities for delay and defeat built into a pluralistic institution. In reality, the legislators were unwilling to cede more than a modicum of their individual independence to party leaders, and the movement toward centralization has proven halting at best. The parties remain, on balance, dependent on the willingness of their partisans to support the leadership.

There have, however, been some party successes in the House. In the Senate, little effort was made to increase party power and members' freedom of action continues unencumbered (Sinclair, 1989; Smith, 1992). By contrast, in the House, the Democratic caucus has assumed and exercised the right to "hire and fire" committee chairs and has occasionally insisted on a party policy position. Party leaders, through the Steering and Policy Committee, have had some influence over committee assignments, and have gained some influence over the Rules and, to a lesser extent, Ways and Means Committees (Sinclair, 1992a; Strahan, 1990). The Speaker's enlarged bill referral power has been a mixed blessing. Although the Speaker can refer a bill to several committees at once and impose time limits on their consideration, multiple referral greatly exacerbates the problem of coordinating congressional activity, requiring more individual members to reach agreement before legislation is enacted (Davidson, 1989; Davidson and Oleszek, 1992).

Some observers (Davidson, 1992a; Rohde, 1991; Sinclair, 1992b) profess to see a "post-reform Congress," featuring strengthened political parties increasingly capable of centralizing legislative operations. They acknowledge that party leadership is "conditional" (Rohde, 1991), that renewed partisanship and party leadership depend more on rank-and-file members' need for and willingness to defer to the leaders than on the latter's ability to compel loyalty (see also Palazzolo, 1992). Nonetheless, in an age of austerity and divided government, some members have come to recognize the difficulties inherent in legislative decentralization and have deferred, reluctantly, to party leadership, especially with respect to budgetary policy (Davidson, 1988; Dodd and Oppenheimer, 1989). Party leaders, augmented by the chairs and ranking members of the important fiscal committees, have negotiated budgets at "summit" meetings with the administration. Even so, centralization—reflecting reform or member acquiescence—remains elusive, and without it policy-making responsibility remains a will-o'-the-wisp.

Finally, procedural reforms have produced only minimal effects; and entangled in broader changes, some of those have been unanticipated. Dilatory tactics are more difficult to use, and legislation is somewhat less likely to get enmeshed in parliamentary thickets in the House. Easing quorum call requirements, voting by machine, clustering votes, and permitting committees to meet more readily have expedited the flow of business, but these reforms have had little impact on the substance of policy. Neither have the revised Senate cloture procedures facilitated more rapid processing of bills. This is not because cloture has not been invoked; it has been used more successfully in recent years (see Congressional Quarterly, 1990: 1037–1039). Rather the norms governing the conduct of filibusters have changed markedly. Historically, unlimited debate was reserved for major matters, those about which an intense minority felt passionately (Wolfinger, 1971). At present, by contrast, any topic, however minor, seems fair game for extended debate, led by a handful of Senators, or on occasion a single member. Norm changes, condoning seemingly frivolous filibusters, have undercut the intended effect of rules reforms. Thus, the filibuster, conducted or merely threatened, continues to shape Senate floor action on much legislation. Minorities, and even individual senators, remain able to thwart leaders and to impede Congress' capacity to legislate responsibly.

B. Reform for Responsiveness

Basic to leadership failure to centralize congressional operations, even with its enlarged authority, is the devolution of influence, formerly lodged in full committees, to subcommittees. The reformers, especially the junior members within their ranks, chafed under the restrictions that the old committee regime imposed on them: an inability to participate fully in committee affairs, much less to contribute meaningfully to the policy content of committee legislation. The reformers' chief targets were the full committees that powerful, sometimes tyrannical, conservative chairs dominated. By lessening the power of the committee oligarchs, they hoped to make Congress more responsive. Thus, the reformers modified the seniority rule, limited the number of committee positions that any individual could hold, altered the committee assignment process, and devolved much committee power to subcommittees. Viewed narrowly, these reforms accomplished their purpose, but from a broader perspective their proponents may have won the battle but lost the war. Increased responsiveness may have slowed the legislative process by requiring more elaborate bargaining among more participants to reach agreement; it may have made congressional decision making more arduous and more prone to legislative gridlock.

With respect to seniority, the old order has been altered. Although only the House has deviated from the seniority rule, election has put committee chairs on notice that they retain their positions on sufferance of their committee and party colleagues. The threat of removal is credible—two chairs lost their jobs in 1985, another in 1991, and a fourth at the outset of the 103rd Congress—and chairs seem more inclined to vote with partisan majorities in consequence (Crook and Hibbing, 1985). In the reformed Congress, individual members have increased opportunities to compete for preferred committee assignments. The new rules in both parties in both chambers guarantee all members a major committee post. Yet members do not always succeed in winning the places they covet. There are not always enough committee seats to go around. Party leaders may intervene when seats on particularly important committees are at stake. Thus, members have greater opportunity to find congenial places in committee, but there is no certainty that they will succeed in doing so.

The major thrust of the committee reforms was to create and sustain independent subcommittees, and here the reformers have succeeded admirably (Deering, 1982; Hall and Evans, 1990; Smith and Deering, 1984: Chap. 4). The House moved a long way toward subcommittee government when it adopted the subcommittee bill of rights and passed new rules granting more members significant subcommittee positions. But power has not increased uniformly across all subcommittees; nor is it clear that subcommittee influence exceeds that of the full committees. Subcommittees have assumed greater significance in the House, but they are not automatically the prime movers in congressional policy making.

Still, the subcommittee reforms did enable junior members to advance rapidly to assume subcommittee chairs. The new chairpersons are more liberal, more "typical" Democrats, thus making committee leadership more representative of the entire party. More important, many subcommittees are independent and active: They hold more hearings and initiate consideration of more legislation; their leaders manage more legislation on the floor. They are often expert (with their own staffs) and they are protected from outside interference by guarantees of jurisdiction, control over their own rules, and adequate budgets. Party leaders seldom intervene in subcommittee affairs (Smith and Deering, 1984, 1990).[14]

But subcommittee independence is not autonomy. Subcommittee control of legislative business is restricted. They remain subordinate to the full committees, which ultimately report legislation to the floor. The full committees may challenge and reverse their more adventurous subcommittees (Smith and Deering, 1984: 161–162). In addition, subcommittees—particularly those that deal with pork barrel, constituency matters—are open to external, group influences and may find it necessary to defer to clientele interests. The broader range of policy-making participation that democratization has fostered has led nonmembers to take a greater interest in committee and subcommittee operations, which enlarges the range of opinions that subcommittees need to consider. In short, full committees, ordinary members of Congress, and outside groups constrain subcommittees.

Such subcommittee freedom suggests that structural change has produced more fragmentation than centralization. Party leaders cannot easily impose their preferences on independent subcommittees. In consequence, there are at present more individuals and power centers to deal with in coordinating congressional policy-making activities. Concomitantly, the legislature's ability to act at all, much less decisively, may have declined as a result of reform. A decentralized institution further fragmented, for whatever motives, may find it nearly impossible to integrate small increments of power sufficiently to produce meaningful policy innovations.

On balance, democratization has increased members' opportunity to participate in congressional deliberations at the expense of the full committees, but it has not done so uniformly or with consistent effects on legislative policy making. Because explicit structural reform coexists with a variety of other changes, all of which impinge differentially on the various elements of legislative organization, it is hardly surprising to discover that reform and change combine in numerous ways within different units of Congress. Fenno (1973) has made clear that congressional committees vary along a number of dimensions—members' personal goals, the environmental context within which the committee works, the panel's "strategic premises" (decision rules or norms), and its decision-making premises (specialization, partisanship, participation)—that together shape the policy decisions they make. In short, committees differ, and changes—events that alter environmental forces, the rise and fall of leaders, membership turnover, for example—have a differential impact on them.

The House Ways and Means Committee offers a clear instance of the ways these changes combine to produce unintended and negative consequences. Long a target of liberal hostility (or jealousy) during Wilbur Mills' lengthy and successful tenure as chairperson, the committee suffered the wrath of the reformers when circumstances were conducive, i.e., when Mills' personal problems left him, and his panel, vulnerable. Mills was, in effect, forced from the chair and Ways and Means was stripped of its committee assignment powers, required to create subcommittees, enlarged from 25 to 37 members, and deprived of some procedural protection (the "closed rule") for the legislation it reported. The upshot was that the new Ways and Means chair, Al Ullman (D., Oregon), failed to sustain the bipartisan consensus that had characterized the committee (Manley, 1970; Unekis and Rieselbach, 1984), the panel began to split along party lines (Parker and Parker, 1985; Unekis and Rieselbach, 1984), and it suffered a series of humiliating defeats on the floor (Oppenheimer, 1980b; Rudder, 1977, 1978).[15] Rudder (1978) concludes that Ways and Means' ability to carry its proposals on the floor was seriously impaired. In 1980, Ullman was defeated for reelection; Dan Rostenkowski (D., Illinois) acceded to the chair. The new leader, steeped in decentralized congressional politics, guided Ways and Means to some measure of restored influence. Strahan (1990) concludes that the reform has altered irrevocably the context within which the committee must operate, but that it has adapted under Rostenkowski and reclaimed a position of centrality, if not the dominance it exercised in the Mills era, in the fiscal politics of Congress.[16]

Planned reform and other elements of change mix in distinctive fashions to influence performance at the subcommittee level as well. Nowhere is the impact clearer than with respect to bicameralism. Reform and change moved the House some distance toward subcommittee government. The Senate, in sharp contrast, changed very little. New members, pursuing a new agenda with a new spirit of independence, promoted individualism in the House; in the Senate personal freedom of action had long been the rule. With numerous and desirable committee assignments, senators have less need to use subcommittees as a forum for influencing policy and little incentive to increase the authority of the subcommittees. The full committees continue to make the major decisions. Hard-pressed senators, short of time but not of influence in full committee and on the floor, have less need to strengthen and use subcommittees (Sinclair, 1989; Smith and Deering, 1990).

A final feature of the move toward responsiveness was to give members more staff assistance. Here reformers have also accomplished much of what they set out to do. Members' personal staffs have grown enormously; so have committee payrolls. In the Senate, each member is entitled to a staff aide for each committee assignment. These resources, coupled with research assistance from the enhanced congressional support agencies, give individual senators access to substantial data that they can use to support their programmatic preferences (Hammond, 1978). Presumably, these enlarged staff resources have improved congressional responsiveness.

On balance, insofar as the evidence permits generalization, the overall effect of congressional reallocation of internal authority appears to favor decentralization. Although party power has won an occasional dramatic victory, committee and subcommittee independence more often carries the day. Committees and subcommittees are distinctive units in an increasingly decentralized structure, and on the whole they have claimed and jealously guarded their authority. By multiplying the number of power centers involved in policy formulation, reform and change have both increased the need for complicated bargaining and compromise to reach policy agreement and made that agreement more difficult to attain.

The reformers' success in enhancing responsiveness, thus, has not been costless. Diffusion of power has damaged Congress' capacity to make policy effectively and efficiently; that is, to be responsible. In the House, the increased dependence on subcommittees has expanded the members' workload, and even with more staff help, they may have difficulty coping with the new demands on their time and energy (Malbin, 1980). Specialization and expertise in the House seem to have declined; fewer representatives—only those on a given subcommittee—may be well enough informed to deal decisively, as specialists, with particular policy issues. Fewer individuals take the lead in narrower policy domains, and as they leave Congress or move to other full or subcommittee positions, "institutional memory," the ability to relate current problems to past performance, may be damaged.

In addition, more subcommittees may make members more vulnerable to interest group representatives. Lawmakers with responsibility for particular programs are less numerous and thus more easily identifiable. Lobbyists know whom to approach and members may have incentives to enter into mutually beneficial, in a narrow sense, relationships with group representatives. The broader, national interest may get less attention in such circumstances. Finally, independent subcommittees add a new layer to an already decentralized decision-making process. To pass, programs must now clear subcommittee and full committee hurdles as well as survive an onslaught of floor amendments non–committee members propose (Smith, 1989). Committee and party leaders must consult more members, particularly because subcommittee jurisdictions are not always clearly defined and several panels may insist on considering the same piece of legislation. To deal with this organizational complexity takes time, and bills may be slowed if not sidetracked by the need to consider compromise and to construct coalitions among so many participants. Even assertive party leaders (e.g., Speaker Jim Wright [D., Texas] in the late 1980s) are unlikely to have the capacity to counteract member individualism and produce legislative responsibility.

In the Senate, the story is different, but the result is the same. Individualism has long been the hallmark of senatorial behavior, and reform has not undercut the individual members' freedom of action. Senators, like representatives, are able to pursue their policy predilections relatively unencumbered. For Congress as a whole, then, reform has enlarged the potential for responsiveness but at a cost in responsibility. By multiplying the number of power centers, reform and change have increased the need for elaborate bargaining and compromise to reach agreement and move congressional business ahead. These developments do not please those who prefer a more responsible Congress.

C. Reforms for Accountability: Restoring Public Approbation

On the face of it, reforms intended to permit the public to inform itself about congressional commitments and deliberations, and thus to hold members to account more easily, have attained their purposes. All three sets of reforms have opened legislators' accounts and activity to citizen, and media, scrutiny: The Federal Election Commission collects and disseminates candidates' campaign finance data; members file their financial disclosure information and the media publicize it (the number of millionaires in the Senate, for instance, makes good copy); the vast majority, more than 95%, of congressional subcommittee and full committee meetings are open sessions. Yet beneath the surface, the picture is more cloudy. Each set of reforms has seemingly produced one or more unforeseen, and undesirable, consequences. In addition, the House Bank and Post Office controversies of 1991–1992 have adversely affected popular sentiments about Congress (*Public Perspective*, 1992).

To start, there is little persuasive evidence that citizens pay greater attention to Congress than they did in the prereform era (Ferejohn, 1977; Mann, 1978; Tedin and Murray, 1979). Polls reveal that the electorate is not better informed about legislative action. Incumbents continue to win reelection with relative ease. In 1990, however, in the wake of Congress' difficulty in passing a budget, a number survived with reduced pluralities. In 1992, with the public allegedly fevered with anti-incumbent, anti-Congress passion, 88% (325 of 368) of the incumbents seeking reelection succeeded in retaining their seats.[17] As in 1990, however, many saw their margins sharply reduced.

Second, with committee proceedings and voting matters of public record, lawmakers can no longer hide behind closed doors and unrecorded votes; they must take care to protect their political futures. The presence of lobbyists and administrative officials at public sessions—where they can monitor members' behavior, offer texts of amendments, and notify their employers when and where to apply pressure—may make it more difficult for committees to act decisively. Increasingly, they have resorted to "executive" or "informal" sessions, held prior to official meetings, where members can talk freely and develop compromises without the intrusive presence of outsiders. Formal meetings may do little more than ratify agreements reached in private. The burgeoning term limit movement—seeking to limit legislators to no more than 12 years congressional service—aims primarily to make members less responsive to parochial interests and more attuned to the broader national interest (Benjamin and Malbin, 1992). Fourteen states passed term limit referenda in 1992, most by overwhelming margins.

Financial disclosure, which the House and Senate ethics codes mandate, has had limited visible effects. There has been little if any dimunition in the frequency of ethical problems. The Senate, for instance, reproved Mark Hatfield (R., Oregon) and David Durenberger (R., Minnesota) for financial irregularities and chastised the "Keating Five"—found to have used poor judgment or worse in attempting to influence regulators' treatment of a troubled savings and loan institution. The future may, however, may be more promising. Voters have not been particularly kind to legislators revealed as unethical. Members tarred in some way by scandal or conflict of interest have been prominent among the few incumbents defeated for reelection. "Abusers" of the House Bank were numerous among incumbent losers in 1992; voters also turned out Nicholas Mavroules (D., Massachusetts) after he was indicted on 19 counts of fraud and bribery.

Finally, campaign finance reform has led to paradoxical results (Magleby and Nelson, 1990; Nugent and Johannes, 1990). On one hand, the new election system—with limits on contributions, but none on expenditures, and with full disclosure provisions—has seemingly helped to entrench incumbents, especially in the House. Private groups, particularly the newly legitimized political action committees (PACs), have preferred contributing to incumbents, who hold powerful committee or party positions, to the riskier strategy of funding challengers who might someday hold prominent posts. Contribution limits appear to hinder hard pressed House challengers. Senate contests, by contrast, tend to be more competitive (Abramowitz and Segal, 1992; Westlye, 1991). Challengers are more visible and attractive, better able to solicit the funds they need, and, in consequence, to unseat the incumbent. To whatever degree incumbent electoral security reduces personnel turnover, accountability, however plausible in principle, will be inhibited. Old members espousing old points of view may continue to serve—even if they are out of touch, in policy terms, with their constituents—because they can fend off serious challenges.

On the other hand, public scrutiny—the combination of campaign finance and personal disclosure requirements—has made life more difficult for members of Congress. During the 1970s, record numbers—many relatively young, with substantial seniority and positions of prominence and power—chose to retire rather than risk the relentless exposure of their daily routines, and those of their families, to public scrutiny. Many found the rewards of legislative service not worth the long hours and the loss of privacy. The exodus, however, slowed appreciably in the 1980s (Moore and Hibbing, 1992), as members seemed prepared to endure the attention that their positions in Congress attracts. In 1992, however, redistricting and scandal induced 66 members to retire (and another 13 left the House to seek other office); combined with incumbent defeats, these decisions produced an infusion of 110 new members in the 103rd Congress.

In sum, the potential for citizen-informed accountability is real but unrealized. Although congressional activity is more accessible to citizens, the evidence suggests that sunshine reforms have had limited effects. In fact, visibility may contribute to legislative inertia. Ever aware that they are on display, members may conclude that inaction is the better part of valor. Rather than alienating constituents and groups whose electoral support is vital, they may avoid controversy and decline to act. By increasing the participation of external actors in congressional policy making, the accountability reforms may have made Congress not only more democratic but also more permeable—more open to outside pressures that reduce the institution's capacity to make effective public policy. Steps to increase accountability, like those to promote responsiveness, may have undercut congressional responsibility, to the regret of those who seek a more innovative and effective legislature.

V. CONCLUSIONS: WHAT HATH REFORM WROUGHT (OR WREAKED)?

This review of developments and consequences of an unprecedented period of reform makes clear, at the very least, that conscious effort to redesign legislatures is part of, and quite similar to, the general pattern of American politics. Both as a substantive issue and as a means to an end—a revised and presumably "better" policy process—reform is best understood as an integral element of an ongoing political system, characterized as much by unplanned change, or evolution, as by any revolutionary recasting of legislative institutions. This central fact goes far to explain both the nature of the reforms adopted and the consequences of those reforms for policy formation, enactment, and implementation.

As a subject of the legislative process, reform looks very much like most other policy domains. Legislators—motivated by power, policy, and reelection goals—are the prime movers for reform, and they tend to treat it, as a substantive issue, in much the same way as they deal with other matters. Reforms have been incremental not wholesale, individually modest not radical reactions to events and "crises," not products of comprehensive planning. Specifically, there was little talk of the relative merits of a Congress compatible with the executive force, literary, or legislative supremacy notions. To the contrary, members came to recognize their inability to cope with the dominant executive, to formulate successful programs, or to meet the public's ethical expectations. Citizen concerns complemented these member perceptions, leading the legislators to act, in response to internal and external pressures, as circumstances dictated. Policy failure in Vietnam—the product of executive leadership and legislative acquiescence—inspired the War Powers Act. Congressional ineffectiveness led lawmakers, both liberals and conservatives, to reform the budget process and induced Democrats to move to curb the committees. Given the opportunity that these developments offered, junior members, lacking in power, leaped in to reallocate authority not only to their party leaders but also to themselves. The dramatic decline in popular approbation for government in general, and Congress in particular, rooted in Watergate and legislative scandals, created the climate for campaign finance, financial disclosure, and "sunshine" reforms. Reforms, in short, were adaptive and consolidative, intended to enhance congressional responsibility, responsiveness, and accountability, but simultaneously were political, pragmatic, and more-or-less spontaneous responses to seemingly irresistable forces.

The fate of the reform impetus, when the conditions that precipitated it faded in intensity and receded into history, makes clear the incremental nature and ephemeral quality of reformism. After 1977, members seemed to feel that enough had been done. To be sure, some conditions demanded response. A loophole in the Senate filibuster rule, which permitted post-cloture "filibusters by amendment," was quickly closed in 1979. When ethical failings surfaced, the members moved rapidly to "censure," "denounce," or even expel their wayward colleagues. But on the whole, the reform spirit flagged. Policy "gridlock" and ethical failings revived interest in reform, especially with respect to accountability, as the 1990s opened, but it remains unclear what specific steps Congress will take. In the absence of numerous facilitating conditions—supportive members, the press of public opinion, the stimulus of national and international events—reform is likely to founder. Such conditions were present between 1970 and 1977, but faded rapidly thereafter; the tide of congressional reform ebbed with them. Whether the events of the late 1980s and early 1990s will turn the tide back toward serious reform remains problematic.

Whatever the outcome, as the 103rd Congress convenes, reform is very much in the air. The members themselves are focusing on accountability; they seek to reclaim the respect of the citizenry. They have cut back drastically on their perquisites of office and the House has appointed a professional administrator to manage its affairs. They are considering campaign finance reforms designed to eliminate or reduce the power of political action committee and "fat cat" "soft money" (unregulated large donations to party organizations) contributions, widely perceived to secure undesirable influence in the policymaking process.

Outside observers (Mann and Ornstein, 1992) look to enlarging congressional responsibility. Their proposals seek to expand the Speaker's ability to centralize legislative operations and to reduce decentralization so that party programs may move more easily. The Speaker would appoint a majority party Agenda Committee to define party positions, he would get the authority to remove committee and subcommittee chairs (subject to caucus approval), and he would be able to select members not on committees originating legislation to serve on conference committees. Conversely, committee jurisdictions would undergo realignment, committee size and the number of subcommittees would shrink, and members would be entitled to fewer assignments and less staff support. Individualistic members would be less able to resist partisan pressures. On the other hand, a movement is afoot to give the president a form of the line-item veto—so-called "enhanced rescission" authority—that would force Congress to vote to reject executive proposals to cancel duty enacted appropriations items. Ceding such power to the president would surely limit Congress' capacity to make its spending decisions prevail in the face of executive opposition. It is not clear how many, if any, of these reforms will pass, but it obvious that events and new members have forced the legislature to pay attention to a new series of reform proposals.

Like earlier reforms, these programs resemble other policy areas in terms of their incremental content and mode of adoption, and, also like previous efforts, it will not be surprising if their impact turns out to be uncertain and unpredictable. The numerous reforms adopted in Congress have often been incompatible with one another. Reformers have won some victories, attaining their goals; suffered some reverses, failing to achieve their purposes; and often discovered that their alterations have led to quite unexpected and frequently undesirable results. Indeed, such is the case with each set of reforms Congress enacted.

Specifically, Congress is most certainly positioned to oppose the president, but given the rapid change in membership and the shifting push of events, it is not clear that there will be steady pressure on the members to use their potentially powerful weapons. The ultimate consequences of the War Powers and Budget Acts, coupled with the increase in Congress' analytic capacity, remain impossible to predict. Similarly, structural change has produced a mixed pattern of results. New party and leadership powers are in place, but have only occasionally been employed decisively to promote partisan cohesion and, as a result, effective policy making. The legislature may, or may not, be a more responsible policy maker. Similarly, it is equally certain that it is easier to hold Congress accountable since the passage of campaign finance, financial disclosure, and public operations standards. More can be known about congressional deliberations, but there is no reason to believe that more actually is known, at least by ordinary citizens.

On balance, Congress has become more decentralized, more responsive to a multitude of forces inside and outside its halls, and as a result more hard pressed to formulate and enact coherent, responsible public policies. Structural change has enlarged the number of power centers, in particular House subcommittees, involved in policy making, and party power cannot readily mobilize them in support of programs that either challenge or sustain the president. Junior members have secured advantageous legislative terrain, but have used it differently in different committees (and subcommittees) and on different policy questions. "Sunshine" changes have left members visible and vulnerable to attentive publics, most often organized interests. More independent members, faced with more difficult policy choices—the "politics of scarcity" requires allocation of sacrifice rather than permitting dispensation of largesse—on issues that evoke great emotion—abortion and energy, for example—find it politically expedient to avoid risky actions. To do so, of course, is to duck controversy: to defer to others, to delay, or to obfuscate. In consequence, Congress often seems unwilling or unable to frame and fight for its policy preferences. Paradoxically, greater individual influence somehow sums to reduced institutional authority.

In short, Congress reforms itself in much the same way, and with much the same results, as it makes public policy on more substantive matters. In the absence of any overarching vision of what the legislature should be, reform, when it comes, is piecemeal and episodic, swept along by powerful tides of more general political change. As long as this situation persists, and there is scant reason to suspect that circumstances will alter, reform will remain an uncertain activity. Congress may well, for lack of a viable alternative, continue to "muddle through" as part of the characteristic and classic pattern of American politics and policy making. The altered Congress of the 1990s will differ, in unexpected and unpredictable ways, from the "reformed" legislature of the 1980s, which was unquestionably quite distinct from that of the 1960s. Given the uncertainty of change and reform, however, there is no guarantee that it will be "better."[18]

NOTES

1. The most dramatic instances of reform have occurred in Congress, although change has restructured state legislatures as well. Moreover, most systematic investigations of reform have focused on the national legislature; the literature on the states is fragmentary and inconclusive. Thus, attention here is limited to Congress.
2. For an overview of these events and their consequences, see Davidson et al., 1966; Dodd, 1977; Ornstein, 1976; Ornstein and Rohde, 1978; and Patterson, 1978. A number of collections (de Grazia, 1966a; Dodd and Oppenheimer, 1977a; Ornstein, 1974, 1975a; Rieselbach, 1977, 1978; and Welch and Peters, 1977) contain much useful material on these issues. For the more recent period, see Center for Responsive Politics, 1986; Davidson, 1992b; Polsby, 1990; Quirk, 1992; Rieselbach, 1993; Rohde, 1991: Chaps. 1–2; Sheppard, 1985; and Shepsle, 1989.
3. Huntington (1973: 7) captures the dilemma precisely: "If Congress legislates, it subordinates itself to the executive; if it refuses to legislate, it alienates itself from public opinion. Congress can assert its power or it can pass laws; but it cannot do both." Reforms, at least those guided by a broad view of Congress' place in national politics, make this choice explicitly.
4. Much writing on reform reflects this short-term focus (e.g., Clark, 1965; Committee for Economic Development, 1970; McInnis, 1966; New York City Bar Association, 1970; Twentieth Century Fund, 1974). So, too, does almost all testimony before congressional committees (see, inter alia, U.S. House, 1973).
5. In 1991, in reaction to popular discontent with its policy performance and its members' ethical behavior, Congress created a new Joint Committee on the Organization of Congress, chaired by Senator David Boren (D., Oklahoma) and Representative Lee Hamilton (D., Indiana), to assess the need for reform of the legislative process.
6. Congress apparently had so little faith in its capacity to oppose the President that it wrote the law in such a way that legislative *inaction* triggers the troop withdrawal. That is, although the chief executive can introduce forces into hostilities on his own initiative, he is obligated to withdraw them unless Congress acts positively—by declaring war or enacting some legislative authorization of the conflict—to approve the commitment.
7. As with the war powers procedures, the anti-impoundment provisions were written to permit Congress to get its way with a minimum of effort. To rescind, that is, cancel, appropriations, the president

must secure an approving resolution from both houses; inaction by either house obligates the chief executive to spend the money. To defer, that is, delay, expenditures is less difficult; a presidential request to defer is approved automatically unless either house votes a resolution of disapproval.

8. The committees were Foreign Relations in the Senate, Foreign Affairs in the House, and the Armed Services, Appropriations, and Intelligence panels in each chamber.

9. Both chambers, either house, or even a single committee—through requirements that an agency "come into agreement" with it before acting—were able to exercise the veto, usually by enacting resolutions of disapproval (although some statutes permitted inaction to indicate disapproval) within a specified (usually between 30 and 90 days) period. The one-house veto, providing for either House or Senate to block executive action, was controversial; all presidents have resisted it, as an unconstitutional derogation of the separation-of-powers principle. Until the *Chadha* case (see below), the courts steadfastly refused to resolve the issue (Bolton, 1977).

10. For an imaginative, but largely ignored, plea to treat "reforms as experiments," as hypotheses to be tested scientifically and abandoned if disconfirmed, see Campbell (1969).

11. Just to be certain, Congress added an amendment, by overwhelming margins in each chamber, to the Defense Department (DOD) appropriations bill forbidding the expenditure of funds for "any activities involving Angola directly or indirectly." Since CIA funds were hidden in the appropriation, this action effectively removed the legal basis for either overt or covert intervention in Angola.

12. Partisanship is a particular problem in the House. The Budget Committee differs dramatically from other committees: It restricts its members to three (originally two) terms of service; it represents other revenue-related committees (Appropriations, and Ways and Means) and the party leadership in its ranks. These unique membership requirements reflected marked disagreement about the substantive purposes of the new process. Some members hoped that more effective procedures would rationalize the legislative budgeting, but others sought to influence directly fiscal outcomes. Liberals expected the new process to provide more funds for social programs and less for defense; conservatives hoped for the reverse. The latter, in addition, were eager to see the Budget Committee control "backdoor spending," mostly for social welfare, that otherwise escaped legislative scrutiny. Given these expectations, committee assignments tend to go to liberal Democrats and conservative Republicans, leaving the panel polarized and volitile (Fisher, 1977; LeLoup, 1979). Partisanship has threatened the process, and the House has been hard pressed to comply with the Act, often passing the required budget resolutions by slender margins. The influence of the committee has ebbed and flowed—its centrality declined under the 1990 Budget Enforcement Act, which established spending ceilings that constrained the committee's freedom considerably—but its partisan cast has endured (Schick, 1990; White and Wildavsky, 1989; Wildavsky, 1988).

13. In addition, some critics have speculated that the law inadvertently gives the president the power to rescind funds, temporarily, for policy purposes, authority never previously acknowledged. That is, the chief executive can propose rescissions that effectively withhold funds for the 45 days until congressional inaction compels release of the monies.

14. Such sweeping generalizations, of course, disguise wide variations among subcommittees (see Evans, 1991; Malbin, 1978; Ornstein and Rohde, 1977; and Price, 1978).

15. For example, dissident member Democrats, abetted by a caucus decision to instruct the Rules Committee, reversed the committee on the floor and repealed the oil depletion allowance. More devastating still, the committee's major 1977 energy tax bill was destroyed by amendments on the floor, exposed under an open rule.

16. Even though Ways and Means reestablished its bona fides as a major force in fiscal politics after Rostenkowski assumed the chair, it could in no way dominate tax policy during the 1980s and suffered its share of defeats on the House floor (see Strahan, 1990: Chaps. 6–7).

17. Of these losses, nine were the inevitable result of redistricting that matched two sitting members in the same constituency.

18. It is, no doubt, risky to discount the effect of reform and change on congressional policy making. The legislature remains a representative institution. Where there is consensus in the country, Congress will reflect it; institutional structures and processes cannot deter its actions when a majority

of its members, for whatever motives, want to act. Where agreement is lacking, as it most often is, the sort of congressional politics projected here is likely to appear. On these divisive issues, recent change (whether evolutionary or reform-induced), especially increased decentralization and greater member independence, seems likely to make congressional action more difficult. Thus, the odds continue to favor instability and uncertainty in Congress' policy formulation; if such is the case, reform and change will have contributed significantly to the shape of legislative politics. (On the conditions that seem to facilitate innovative congressional policy making, see Rieselbach, 1986.)

REFERENCES

Aberbach, J. D. (1990). *Keeping a Watchful Eye*: *The Politics of Oversight*. Brookings Institution, Washington, D.C.

Abramowitz, A. I., and J. A. Segal. (1992). *Senate Elections*. University of Michigan Press, Ann Arbor.

Alexander, H. E. (1984). *Financing Politics*: *Money, Elections and Political Reform*, 3rd ed. CQ Press, Washington, D.C.

American Political Science Association, Committee on Political Parties (1950). *Toward a More Responsible Two-Party System*. Rinehart, New York.

Arieff, I. B. (1979). Growing staff system on hill forcing changes in Congress. *Congressional Quarterly Weekly Report* 37: 2631–3654.

Asher, H. B., and Weisberg, H. F. (1978). Voting change in Congress: Some dynamic perspectives on an evolutionary process. *American Journal of Political Science* 22: 391–425.

Benjamin, G., and M. J. Malbin (Eds.) (1992). *Limiting Legislative Terms*. CQ Press, Washington, D.C.

Berger, T. J. (1992). After the perk wars, what's left? *Roll Call* September 14, sec. B, pp. 40–42.

Bolling, R. (1965). *House Out of Order*. Dutton, New York.

Bolton, J. R. (1977). *The Legislative Veto*: *Unseparating the Powers*. American Enterprise Institute, Washington, D.C.

Brady, D. W. (1988). *Critical Elections and Congressional Policy Making*. Stanford University Press, Stanford, CA.

Bullock, C. S., III (1978). Congress in the sunshine. In *Legislative Reform*: *The Policy Impact*. L. N. Rieselbach (Ed.). Lexington Books, Lexington, MA, pp. 209–221.

Burnham, J. (1959). *Congress and the American Tradition*. Regnery, Chicago.

Burns, J. M. (1949). *Congress on Trial*. Harper, New York.

—— (1963). *The Deadlock of Democracy*. Prentice-Hall, Englewood Cliffs, NJ.

Burstein, P. (1979). Party balance, replacement of legislators, and federal government expenditures, 1941–1976. *Western Political Quarterly* 32: 203–208.

Campbell, D. T. (1969). Reforms as experiments. *American Psychologist* 24: 409–429.

Cavanagh, T. E. (1980). The deinstitutionalization of the House. Paper presented to the Everett McKinley Dirksen Congressional Leadership Research Center–Sam Rayburn Library Conference, Understanding Congressional Leadership: The State of the Art, Washington, D.C., June 10–11.

Center for Responsive Politics. (1986). *"Not for the Short Winded"*: *Congressional Reform, 1961–1986*. Center for Responsive Politics, Washington, D.C.

Clark, J. S. (1964). *Congress*: *The Sapless Branch*. Harper & Row, New York.

—— (Ed.) (1965). *Congressional Reform*: *Problems and Prospects*. Crowell, New York.

Clausen, A. R., and Van Horn, C. E. (1977). The congressional response to a decade of change, 1963–1972. *Journal of Politics* 39: 624–666.

Cohen, R. E. (1980). Congress steps up use of the legislative veto. *National Journal* 12: 1473–1477.

Cohodas, N. (1984). Panel proposes Senate committee changes. *Congressional Quarterly Weekly Report* 42: 3035.

Committee for Economic Development (1970). *Making Congress More Effective*. Committee for Economic Development, New York.

Congressional Quarterly (1976). *Guide to Congress*, 2nd ed. Congressional Quarterly, Washington, D.C.

—— (1977). *Congress and the Nation*, vol. IV. Congressional Quarterly, Washington, D.C.

—— (1990). *Congress and the Nation*, vol. VII. Congressional Quarterly, Washington, D.C.

Congressional Quarterly Weekly Report. (1975). Filibuster: Amendment Procedure 33: 2721-2722.

Cook, T. E. (1979). Legislature vs. legislator: A note on the paradox of congressional support. *Legislative Studies Quarterly* 4: 43-52.

Cooper, A. (1979). Senate limits post-cloture filibusters. *Congressional Quarterly Weekly Report* 37: 319-320.

Cooper, J. (1985). The legislative veto in the 1980s. In *Congress Reconsidered*, 3rd ed. L. C. Dodd and B. I. Oppenheimer (Eds.). CQ Press, Washington, D.C., pp. 364-389.

Crabb, C. V., Jr., and Holt, P. M. (1992). *Invitation to Struggle: Congress, the President, and Foreign Policy*, 4th ed. CQ Press, Washington, D.C.

Craig, B. H. (1983). *The Legislative Veto: Congressional Control of Regulation*. Westview Press, Boulder, CO.

Crook, S. B. and J. R. Hibbing (1985). Congressional reform and party discipline: The effects of changes in the seniority system on party loyalty in the U.S. House of Representatives. *British Journal of Political Science* 15: 207-226.

Davidson, R. H. (1981). Subcommittee government: New channels for policy. In *The New Congress*. T. E. Mann and N. J. Ornstein (Eds.). American Enterprise Institute, Washington, D.C., pp. 99-133.

—— (1988). The new centralization on Capitol Hill. *Review of Politics* 50: 345-364.

—— (1989). Multiple referral of legislation in the U.S. Senate. *Legislative Studies Quarterly* 14: 375-392.

—— (1992). The emergence of the postreform Congress. In *The Postreform Congress*. R. H. Davidson (Ed.). St. Martin's Press, New York, pp. 3-*123*.

—— (Ed.) (1992b). *The Postreform Congress*. St. Martin's Press, New York.

Davidson, R. H., Kovenock, D. M., and O'Leary, M. K. (1966). *Congress in Crisis: Politics and Congressional Reform*. Wadsworth, Belmont, CA.

Davidson, R. H., and Oleszek, W. J. (1976). Adaptation and consolidation: Structural innovation in the House of Representatives. *Legislative Studies Quarterly* 1: 37-65.

—— (1977). *Congress Against Itself*. Indiana University Press, Bloomington.

—— (1992a). From monopoly to management: Changing patterns of committee deliberation. In *The Postreform Congress*. R. H. Davidson (Ed.). St. Martin's Press, New York, pp. 129-141.

Deering, C. J. (1982). Decentralization in the U.S. House of Representatives: A note on bill management as a measure of subcommittee government. *Legislative Studies Quarterly* 7: 533-546.

de Grazia, A. (1965). *Republic in Crisis*. Federal Legal Publications, New York.

—— (Coordinator) (1966a). *Congress: The First Branch of Government*. American Enterprise Institute, Washington, D.C.

—— (1966b). Toward a new model of Congress. In *Congress: The First Branch of Government*. A. de Grazia (Coordinator). American Enterprise Institute, Washington, D.C., pp. 1-22.

Deckard, B. S. (1976). Political upheaval and congressional voting: The effects of the 1960's on voting patterns in the House of Representatives. *Journal of Politics* 38: 326-345.

Dodd, L. C. (1977). Congress and the quest for power. In *Congress Reconsidered*. L. C. Dodd and B. I. Oppenheimer (Eds.). Praeger, New York, pp. 269-307.

Dodd, L. C., and Oppenheimer, B. I. (Eds.) (1977a). *Congress Reconsidered*. Praeger, New York.

—— (1977b). The House in transition. In *Congress Reconsidered*. L. C. Dodd and B. I. Oppenheimer (Eds.). Praeger, New York, pp. 21-53.

—— (1989). Consolidating Power in the House: The rise of a new oligarchy. In *Congress Reconsidered*, 4th ed. L. C. Dodd and B. I. Oppenheimer (Eds.). CQ Press, Washington, D.C., pp. 39-64.

Dodd, L. C., and Schott, R. L. (1979). *Congress and the Administrative State*. Wiley, New York.

Donovan, B., and P. Kuntz . (1992). Retired army general hired to clean House. *Congressional Quarterly Weekly Report* 50: 3491-3492.

Ellwood, J. W., and Thurber, J. A. (1977a). The new congressional budget process: Its causes, consequences, and possible success. In *Legislative Reform and Public Policy*. S. Welch and J. G. Peters
(Eds.). Praeger, New York, pp. 82–97.

—— (1977b). The new congressional budget process: The hows and whys of House-Senate differences.
In *Congress Reconsidered*. L. C. Dodd and B. I. Oppenheimer (Eds.). Praeger, New York, pp.
163–192.

Evans, C. L. (1991). *Leadership in Committee: A Comparative Analysis of Leadership Behavior in the
U.S. Senate*. University of Michigan Press, Ann Arbor.

Fenno, R. F., Jr. (1973). *Congressmen in Committees*. Little, Brown, Boston.

—— (1975). If, as Ralph Nader says, Congress is "the broken branch," how come we love our congressmen so much? In *Congress in Change: Evolution and Reform*. N. J. Ornstein (Ed.). Praeger,
New York, pp. 277–287.

—— (1978). *Home Style: Representatives in Their Districts*. Little, Brown, Boston.

Ferejohn, J. A. (1977). On the decline of competition in congressional elections. *American Political
Science Review* 71: 166–176.

Finley, J. J. (1975). The 1974 congressional initiative in budget making. *Public Administration Review*
35: 270–278.

Fisher, L. (1975). *Presidential Spending Power*. Princeton University Press, Princeton, NJ.

—— (1977). Congressional budget reform: Committee conflicts. Paper presented to the Annual Meeting of the Midwest Political Science Association, Chicago, April 21–23.

—— (1985). Judicial misjudgments about the lawmaking process: The legislative veto case. *Public
Administration Review* 45: 705–711.

—— (1987). The administrative world of *Chadha* and *Bowsher*. *Public Administration Review* 47: 213–
219.

—— (1991). War powers: The need for collective judgment. In *Divided Democracy: Cooperation and
Conflict Between the President and Congress*. J. A. Thurber (Ed.). CQ Press, Washington, D.C.,
pp. 199–217.

Foley, M. (1980). *The New Senate: Liberal Influence on a Conservative Institution, 1959–1972*. Yale
University Press, New Haven, CT.

Foreman, C. H., Jr. (1988). *Signals from the Hill: Congressional Oversight and the Challenge of Social Regulation*. Yale University Press, New Haven, CT.

Fox, H. W., Jr., and Hammond, S. W. (1977). *Congressional Staffs: The Invisible Force in American
Lawmaking*. Free Press, New York.

Franck, T., and Weisband, E. (1979). *Foreign Policy by Congress*. Oxford University Press, New York.

Franklin, D. P. (1986). Why the legislative veto isn't dead. *Presidential Studies Quarterly* 16: 491–501.

Frantzich, S. E. (1979). Computerized information technology in the U.S. House of Representatives.
Legislative Studies Quarterly 4: 255–280.

Freed, B. F. (1975). House reforms enhance subcommittee power. *Congressional Quarterly Weekly
Report* 33: 2407–2412.

Froman, L. A., Jr., and Ripley, R. B. (1965). Conditions for party leadership: The case of the House
Democrats. *American Political Science Review* 59: 52–63.

Garand, J. C., and K. M. Clayton. (1986). Socialization to partisanship in the U.S. House: The Speaker's task force. *Legislative Studies Quarterly* 11: 409–428.

Gilmour, J. B. (1990). *Reconcilable Differences? Congress, the Budget Process, and the Deficit*. University of California Press, Berkeley.

Gilmour, R. S. (1980). The new congressional oversight and administrative leadership. Paper presented
to the Everett McKinley Dirksen Congressional Leadership Research Center-Sam Rayburn Library Conference, Understanding Congressional Leadership: The State of the Art, Washington,
D.C., June 10–11.

Haeberle, S. H. (1978). The institutionalization of the subcommittee in the U.S. House of Representatives. *Journal of Politics* 40: 1054–1065.

Hall, R. L., and C. L. Evans. (1990). The power of subcommittees. *Journal of Politics* 52: 335–355.

Hammond, S. W. (1978). Congressional change and reform: Staffing the Congress. In *Legislative Reform: The Policy Impact*. L. N. Rieselbach (Ed.). Lexington Books, Lexington, MA, pp. 183–193.

—— (1985). Legislative staffs. In *Handbook of Legislative Research*. G. Loewenberg, S. C. Patterson, and M. E. Jewell (Eds.). Harvard University Press, Cambridge, MA, pp. 273–319.

Harris, J. P. (1965). *Congressional Control of Administration*. Doubleday Anchor, Garden City, NY.

Havemann, J. (1978). *Congress and the Budget*. Indiana University Press, Bloomington.

Hinckley, B. (1970). *The Seniority System in Congress*. Indiana University Press, Bloomington.

—— (1976). Seniority, 1975: Old theories confront new facts. *British Journal of Political Science* 6: 383–399.

Holt, P. (1978). *The War Powers Resolution*. American Enterprise Institute, Washington, D.C.

Huntington, S. P. (1973). Congressional responses to the twentieth century. In *The Congress and America's Future*, 2nd ed. D. B. Truman (Ed.). Prentice-Hall, Englewood Cliffs, NJ, pp. 6–38.

Ippolito, D. S. (1978). *The Budget and National Politics*. Freeman, San Francisco.

Jones, C. O. (1976). Why Congress can't do policy analysis (or words to that effect). *Policy Analysis* 2: 251–264.

—— (1977a). Will reform change Congress? In *Congress Reconsidered*. L. C. Dodd and B. I. Oppenheimer (Eds.). Praeger, New York, pp. 247–260.

—— (1977b). How reform changes Congress. In *Legislative Reform and Public Policy*. S. Welch and J. G. Peters (Eds.). Praeger, New York, pp. 11–29.

—— (1980). House leadership in an age of reform. Paper presented to the Everett McKinley Dirksen Congressional Leadership Research Center–Sam Rayburn Library Conference, Understanding Congressional Leadership: The State of the Art. Washington, D.C., June 10–11.

Kaiser, F. M. (1984). Congressional control of executive actions in the aftermath of the *Chadha* decision. *Administrative Law Review* 36: 239–276.

Katzman, R. A. (1990). War powers: Toward a new accommodation. In *A Question of Balance: The President, the Congress, and Foreign Policy*. T. E. Mann (Ed.). Brookings Institution, Washington, D.C., pp. 35–69.

Kravitz, W. (1990). The advent of the modern Congress: The Legislative Reorganization Act of 1970. *Legislative Studies Quarterly* 15: 375–399.

LeLoup, L. T. (1988). *Budgetary Politics*, 4th Ed. King's Court Press, Brunswick, OH.

—— (1979). Process versus policy: The U.S. House Budget Committee. *Legislative Studies Quarterly* 4: 227–254.

Loomis, B. A. (1988). *The New American Politician: Ambition, Entrepreneurship, and the Changing Face of Political Life*. Basic Books, New York.

Malbin, M. J. (1978). The Bolling Committee revisited: Energy oversight on an investigative subcommittee. Paper presented to the Annual Meeting of the American Political Science Association, New York, August 31–September 3.

—— (1980). *Unelected Representatives: Congressional Staff and the Future of Representative Government*. Basic Books, New York.

Manley, J. F. (1970). *The Politics of Finance*. Little, Brown, Boston.

Magleby, D. B., and C. J. Nelson. (1990). *The Money Chase: Congressional Campaign Finance Reform*. Brookings Institution, Washington, D.C.

Mann, T. E. (1978). *Unsafe at Any Margin: Interpreting Congressional Elections*. American Enterprise Institute, Washington, D.C.

—— (Ed.) (1990). *A Question of Balance: The President, the Congress, and Foreign Policy*. Brookings Institution, Washington, D.C.

Mann, T. E., and N. J. Ornstein. (1992). *Renewing Congress: A First Report*. Brookings Institution, Washington, D.C.

McInnis, M. (Ed.) (1966). *We Propose: A Modern Congress*. McGraw-Hill, New York.

Moore, M. K., and J. R. Hibbing (1992). Is surving in Congress fun again? Voluntary retirements from the House since the 1970s. *American Journal of Political Science* 56: 824–828.

Munselle, W. G. (1978). Presidential impoundment and congressional reform. In *Legislative Reform*: *The Policy Impact*. L. N. Rieselbach (Ed.). Lexington Books, Lexington, MA, pp. 173–181.

New York City Bar Association (1970). *Congress and the Public Trust*. Atheneum, New York.

Nugent, M. L., and J. R. Johannes (Eds.) (1990). *Money, Elections, and Democracy*: *Reforming Congressional Campaign Finance*. Westview Press, Boulder, CO.

Ogul, M. S. (1976). *Congress Oversees the Bureaucracy*: *Studies in Legislative Supervision*. University of Pittsburgh Press, Pittsburgh, PA.

Oleszek, W. J. (1977). A perspective on congressional reform. In *Legislative Reform and Public Policy*. S. Welch and J. G. Peters (Eds.). Praeger, New York, pp. 3–10.

Oppenheimer, B. I. (1978). Policy implications of Rules Committee reforms. In *Legislative Reform*: *The Policy Impact*. L. N. Rieselbach (Ed.). Lexington Books, Lexington, MA, pp. 91–104.

—— (1980a). The changing relationship between House leadership and the Committee on Rules. Paper presented to the Everett McKinley Dirksen Congressional Leadership Research Center–Sam Rayburn Library Conference, Understanding Congressional Leadership: The State of the Art, Washington, D.C., June 10–11.

—— (1980b). Policy effects of U.S. House reform: Decentralization and the capacity to resolve energy issues. *Legislative Studies Quarterly* 5: 5–30.

—— (1985). Changing time constraints on Congress: Historical perspectives on the use of cloture. In *Congress Reconsidered*, 3rd ed. L. C. Dodd and B. I. Oppenheimer (Eds.). CQ Press, Washington, D.C., pp. 393–413.

Orfield, G. (1975). *Congressional Power*: *Congress and Social Change*. Harcourt Brace Jovanovich, New York.

Ornstein, N. J. (Ed.) (1974). Changing Congress: The committee system. *Annals of the American Academy of Political and Social Science* 411: 1–176.

—— (Ed.) (1975a). *Congress in Change*: *Evolution and Reform*. Praeger, New York.

—— (1975b). Causes and consequences of congressional change: Subcommittee reforms in the House of Representatives, 1970–1973. In *Congress in Change*: *Evolution and Reform*. N. J. Ornstein (Ed.). Praeger, New York, pp. 88–114.

—— (1976). The Democrats reform power in the House of Representatives, 1969–1975. In *America in the Seventies*. A. Sindler (Ed.). Little, Brown, Boston, pp. 1–48.

Ornstein, N. J., and Rohde, D. W. (1974). The strategy of reform: Recorded teller voting in the House of Representatives. Paper presented to the Annual Meeting of the Midwest Political Science Association, Chicago, April 25–27.

—— (1975). Seniority and future power in Congress. In *Congress in Change*: *Evolution and Reform*. N. J. Ornstein (Ed.). Praeger, New York, pp. 72–87.

—— (1977). Shifting forces, changing rules and political outcomes: The impact of congressional change on four House committees. In *New Perspectives on the House of Representatives*, 3rd ed. R. L. Peabody and N. W. Polsby (Eds.). Rand McNally, Chicago, pp. 186–269.

—— (1978). Political parties and congressional reform. In *Parties and Elections in an Anti-Party Age*. J. Fishel (Ed.). Indiana University Press, Bloomington, pp. 280–294.

Palazzolo, D. J. (1992). From decentralization to centralization: Members' changing expectations for House leaders. In *The Postreform Congress*. R. H. Davidson (Ed.). St. Martin's Press, New York, pp. 112–126.

Parker, G. R. (1977). Some themes in congressional unpopularity. *American Journal of Political Science* 21: 93–109.

Parker, G. R., and Davidson, R. H. (1979). Why do Americans love their congressmen so much more than their Congress? *Legislative Studies Quarterly* 4: 53–61.

Parker, G. R., and S. L. Parker. (1985). *Factions in House Committees*. University of Tennessee Press, Knoxville.

Parris, J. H. (1979). The Senate reorganizes its committees, 1977. *Political Science Quarterly* 94: 319–337.

Patterson, S. C. (1977). Conclusions: On the study of legislative reform. In *Legislative Reform and Public Policy*. S. Welch and J. G. Peters (Eds.). Praeger, New York, pp. 214–222.

—— (1978). The semi-sovereign Congress. In *The New American Political System*. A. King (Ed.). American Enterprise Institute, Washington, D.C., pp. 125–177.

Patterson, S. C., and G. A. Caldeira. (1990). Standing up for Congress: Variations in public esteem since the 1960s. *Legislative Studies Quarterly* 15: 25–47.

Pfiffner, J. P. (1977). Executive control and the congressional budget. Paper presented to the Annual Meeting of the Midwest Political Science Association, Chicago, April 21–23.

Pious, R. M. (1979). *The American Presidency*. Basic Books, New York.

Plattner, A. (1983). Report urges major changes in Senate structure, rules. *Congressional Quarterly Weekly Report* 41: 695–696.

Polsby, N. W. (1990). Political change and the contemporary character of Congress. In *The New American Political System*, 2nd version. A. King (Ed.). American Enterprise Institute, Washington, D.C., pp. 29–46.

Price, D. E. (1971). Professionals and "entrepreneurs": Staff orientations and policy making on three Senate committees. *Journal of Politics* 33: 316–336.

—— (1978). The impact of reform: The House Subcommittee on Oversight and Investigations. In *Legislative Reform*: *The Policy Impact*. L. N. Rieselbach (Ed.). Lexington Books, Lexington, MA, pp. 133–157.

Public Perspective. (1992). A public hearing on Congress. November/December, pp. 82–92.

Quirk, P. J. (1992). Structures and performance: An evaluation. In *The Postreform Congress*. R. H. Davidson (Ed.). St. Martin's Press, New York, pp. 303–324.

Regens, J. L., and Stein, R. M. (1979). Congressional oversight behavior: Components of committee-based activity. Paper presented to the Annual Meeting of the American Political Science Association, Washington, D.C., August 31–September 3.

Rieselbach, L. N. (1975). Congressional reform: Some policy implications. *Policy Studies Journal* 4: 180–188.

—— (Ed.) (1977). Symposium on legislative reform. *Policy Studies Journal* 5: 394–497.

—— (1993). *Congressional Reform*: *The Changing Modern Congress*. CQ Press, Washington, D.C.

—— (1986). Congress and policy change: Issues, answers, and prospects. In *Congress and Policy Change*. G. C. Wright, Jr., L. N. Rieselbach, and L. C. Dodd (Eds.). Agathon Press, New York, pp. 257–289.

—— (1993). *Congressional Reform*: *The Changing Modern Congress*. CQ Press, Washington, D.C.

Ripley, R. B. (1969). *Power in the Senate*. St. Martin's Press, New York.

Rohde, D. W. (1974). Committee reform in the House of Representatives and the subcommittee bill of rights. *Annals* 411: 39–47.

—— (1991). *Parties and Leaders in the Postreform House*. University of Chicago Press, Chicago.

Rohde, D. W., Ornstein, N. J., and Peabody, R. L. (1985). Political change and legislative norms in the United States Senate, 1957–1974. In *Studies of Congress*. Glenn R. Parker (Ed.). CQ Press, Washington, D.C., pp. 147–188.

Rohde, D. W., and Shepsle, K. A. (1978). Thinking about legislative reform. In *Legislative Reform*. *The Policy Impact*. L. N. Rieselbach (Ed.). Lexington Books, Lexington, MA, pp. 9–21.

Rudder, C. (1977). Committee reform and the revenue process. In *Congress Reconsidered*. L. C. Dodd and B. I. Oppenheimer (Eds.). Praeger, New York, pp. 117–139.

—— (1978). The policy impact of reform of the Committee on Ways and Means. In *Legislative Reform*: *The Policy Impact*. L. N. Rieselbach (Ed.). Lexington Books, Lexington, MA, pp. 73–89.

Saloma, J. S., III (1969). *Congress and the New Politics*. Little, Brown, Boston.

Schick, A. (1976). The supply and demand for analysis on Capitol Hill. *Policy Analysis* 2: 215–234.

—— (1990). *The Capacity to Budget*. Urban Institute, Washington, D.C.

Sheppard, B. D. (1985). *Rethinking Congressional Reform*: *The Reform Roots of the Special Interest Congress*. Schenkman Books, Cambridge, MA.

Shepsle, K. A. (1989). The changing textbook Congress. In *Can the Government Govern?* J. E. Chubb and P. E. Peterson (Eds.). Brookings Institution, Washington, D.C., pp. 238–266.

Shuman, H. E. (1988). *Politics and the Budget: The Struggle between the President and the Congress*, 2nd ed. Prentice-Hall, Englewood Cliffs, NJ.

Sinclair, B. D. (1981). The Speaker's task force in the post-reform House of Representatives. *American Political Science Review 75*: 397–410.

—— (1982). *Congressional Realignment, 1925–1978*. University of Texas Press, Austin.

—— (1989). *The Transformation of the U.S. Senate*. Johns Hopkins University Press, Baltimore.

—— (1992a). The emergence of strong leadership in the 1980s House of Representatives. *Journal of Politics 54*: 657–684.

—— (1992b). House majority party leadership in an era of legislative constraints. In *The Postreform Congress*. R. H. Davidson (Ed.). St. Martin's Press, New York, pp. 91–111.

Smith, S. S. (1989). *Call to Order: Floor Politics in the House and Senate*. Brookings Institution, Washington, D.C.

—— (1992). The Senate in the postreform era. In *The Postreform Congress*. R. H. Davidson (Ed.). St. Martin's Press, New York, pp. 169–191.

Smith, S. S., and C. J. Deering. (1984). *Committees in Congress*. CQ Press, Washington, D.C.

—— (1990). *Committees in Congress*, 2nd ed. CQ Press, Washington, D.C.

Steinman, M. (1977). Congressional budget reform: Prospects. In *Legislative Reform and Public Policy*. S. Welch and J. G. Peters (Eds.). Praeger, New York, pp. 73–81.

Stevens, A. G., Jr., Miller, A. H., and Mann, T. E. (1974). "Mobilization of liberal strength in the House, 1955–1970: The Democratic Study Group." *American Political Science Review 68*: 667–681.

Strahan, R. (1990). *New Ways and Means: Reform and Change in a Congressional Committee*. University of North Carolina Press, Chapel Hill.

Tedin, K. L., and Murray, R. W. (1979). Public awareness of congressional representatives: Recall versus recognition. *American Politics Quarterly 7*: 509–517.

Thurber, J. A. (1981). The evolving role and effectiveness of the congressional research agencies. In *The House at Work*. J. Cooper and G. C. Mackenzie (Eds.). University of Texas Press, Austin, pp. 292–315.

—— (1991). The impact of budget reform on presidential and congressional governance. In *Divided Democracy: Cooperation and Conflict Between the President and Congress*. J. A. Thurber (Ed.). CQ Press, Washington, D.C., pp. 145–170.

—— (1992). New Rules for an old game: Zero-sum budgeting in the postreform Congress. In *The Postreform Congress*. R. H. Davidson (Ed.). St. Martin's Press, New York, pp. 257–278.

Twentieth Century Fund (1974). *Openly Arrived At: Report of the Twentieth Century Fund Task Force on Broadcasting and the Legislature*. Twentieth Century Fund, New York.

Unekis, J. K., and Rieselbach, L. N. (1984). *Congressional Committee Politics*. Praeger, New York.

U.S. House of Representatives, Commission on Administrative Review (1977a). *Administrative Reorganization and Legislative Management*, 2 vols. U.S. Government Printing Office, Washington, D.C.

—— (1977b). *Final Report*, 2 vols. U.S. Government Printing Office, Washington, D.C.

U.S. House of Representatives, Select Committee on Committees (1973). *Hearings on the Subject of Committee Organization in the House*, 3 vols. U.S. Government Printing Office, Washington, D.C.

—— (1974). *Committee Reform Amendments of 1974*. U.S. Government Printing Office, Washington, D.C.

—— (1980). *Final Report*. U.S. Government Printing Office, Washington, D.C.

U.S. Senate, Commission on the Operation of the Senate (1976a). *Toward a Modern Senate: Final Report*. U.S. Government Printing Office, Washington, D.C.

—— (1976b). *Congressional Support Agencies: A Compilation of Papers*. U.S. Government Printing Office, Washington, D.C.

U.S. Senate, Temporary Select Committee to Study the Senate Committee System (1976c). *The Senate Committee System*. U.S. Government Printing Office, Washington, D.C.

Vogler, D. (1978). The rise of ad hoc committees in the House of Representatives: An application of new research perspectives. Paper presented to the Annual Meeting of the American Political Science Association, New York, August 31–September 3.

Welch, S., and Peters, J. G. (Eds.) (1977). *Legislative Reform and Public Policy*. Praeger, New York.

Westlye, M. C. (1991). *Senate Elections and Campaign Intensity*. Johns Hopkins University Press, Baltimore.

White, J., and A. Wildavsky. (1989). *The Deficit and the Public Interest*: *The Search for Responsible Budgeting in the 1980s*. University of California Press, Berkeley.

Whiteman, D. (1985). The fate of policy analysis in congressional decision making: Three types of use in committee. *Western Political Quarterly* 38: 294–311.

Wildavsky, A. (1984). *The Politics of the Budgetary Process*, 4th ed. Little, Brown, Boston.

—— (1988). *The New Politics of the Budgetary Process*. Scott, Foresman/Little Brown, Glenview, IL.

Wolfinger, R. E. (1971). Filibusters: Majority rule, presidential leadership, and Senate norms. In *Congressional Behavior*. N. W. Polsby (Ed.). Random House, New York, pp. 111–127.

16
Free Speech and Civil Liberties

Gerald L. Houseman
Indiana University, Fort Wayne, Indiana

The broad and varied institutions, instruments, and determinants of public policy on matters of civil liberties have in many ways created some practical obstacles for anyone who seeks to do an overview of this field. Most of the research conducted on civil liberties issues and concerns seek to simplify this task through concentration upon a specific focus—search and seizure issues, or gay rights, or perhaps affirmative action law enforcement—or through behavioral studies of public attitudes and actions that reflect such matters as levels of tolerance, awareness of human rights concerns, or perhaps voting intentions that are related to such issues.[1]

The task undertaken here, and which is seen as manageable within the context of the enormous literature and resources, is to chart the most important current and recent developments in light of broad social and political trends found in America and, to some extent, in the international community as well. These include (1) the end of the cold war and what this major event in both international and domestic politics means for civil liberties policies. It can be said at the outset that, contra some sets of public opinion data and some outright insularity revealed by public attitudes, this development will deepen our awareness of some of the comparative and international aspects of civil liberties policy just because new forces, such as multiculturalism, will tend to push us this way and because this is ultimately a matter of our own self-interest; (2) the end of 12 years of Republican rule and the arrival of the Clinton administration, which will surely effect some changes in both policy substance and policy emphasis; (3) technological developments, which are occurring at a seemingly ever-quickening pace and that pose some problems of response (and, indeed, of catching up) for virtually all areas of public policy; (4) economic change, which has always guided our national and constitutional law evolution; (5) the dialogues of civil liberties issues, which certainly have their continuities but are also subject to social and political developments and even to a penchant for trendiness[2]; and, finally, (6) methodological issues and developments, which seem to show that various approaches gain or lose currency over time for a variety of reasons.

Ideology sometimes impinges upon the latter, whether we wish to acknowledge this or not; and explicitly ideological goals and purposes most assuredly are found to often inform the work of erudite and careful legal and social science scholarship. This matter must also be addressed, although it should be regarded as a perennial of civil liberties policy rather than any kind of new development. It will take on great importance even in this avowedly pragmatic Clinton era on which we are embarking.

In addition, there are the perennial issues of constitutional law which, it is safe to say, can be relied on to appear in law reviews, social science journals, books, administrative decisions, and court decisions, among other places. As with ideology—and this is not always a separate matter from ideology—these outlooks and desires can be counted on to make their mark in the future as much as they have in the past.

I. THE END OF THE COLD WAR AND EMPHASES ON INTERNATIONAL AND COMPARATIVE ASPECTS OF CIVIL LIBERTIES POLICY MAKING

Neither social science nor the legal community nor even the great coteries of political journalists in the United States and around the world have managed to come to grips with the end of the cold war. This is understandable because the cold war lasted for half a century and its demise is a new and in many ways unexpected development. The cold war shaped our foreign and defense policies, our systems of budget and finance, our communications and socialization systems and institutions, our aid policies, domestic political attitudes toward such issues as health care and labor-management relations, and, most acutely, our law enforcement and civil liberties policies.

The end of the cold war and the end of the threat of Communism has been lamented quite often, both publicly and privately, by officials, commentators, and certain kinds of politicians. A good example of this kind of lament is found in an editorial in the London *Evening Standard* of early 1990 that outlined the solid fear that Communism inspired in the West, and then went on to say that few people realize the "enormously important role played by fear of Russia . . . in keeping America's feet on the ground."[3] The excesses of political liberalism were kept on a leash because of this; and, most appreciatively, the editorial states that

> The threat of aggressive Russian communism has been of incalculable value to the cause of Western civilization in the last 40 years, justifying conservative values and practices which would otherwise have been long ago eliminated by the dominant liberal *zeitgeist*.[4]

Congress member Vin Weber expressed a similar sentiment in a television interview during the 1992 presidential campaign. Such pronouncements are a longing look back at an issue that sometimes—if not always—worked, and that, in any event, was always serviceable to any aspiring politician of any particular party. One need only to observe that anti-Communism took on dominant proportions in the careers of people like Richard Nixon, Ronald Reagan, William F. Buckley, Jr., and almost the entire neoconservative movement, among many others.

It can now be assumed that loyalty-security issues and litigation that invariably posed problems for civil libertarians if not for the Bill of Rights and its free speech and political rights protections, will fade into the background, at least for a while. It should be remembered, all the same, that these have a way of returning over and over again throughout the nation's history, whether in the form of Alien and Sedition Acts, abuses that take place during times of national emergency or civil disorder, or as excuses for dealing with unpopular causes or minority groups. Consider for the moment the issue of gays in military service. One of the standard objections raised is on national security grounds, a point that appears to have little empirical or justifiable merit.

One way of keeping the bogey spirit alive, of course, is to find a replacement, and that search is presently being carried out. So far it is to no avail. When the word *Communism*, with its array of semiotic and indeed metaphysical powers, is compared with the present puny efforts—"political correctness," for example, or "L-word" liberalism—it can be seen that the new bogeys simply do not cut it. The search will have to go on.

The point is that myth dies hard. What are we to say, for example, about the mindset created by such events as the perjury conviction of Alger Hiss? If an eminent Russian historian and researcher is to be believed (and we can hardly be sure of any evidence like this), then Hiss, the high State Department official thought to have been treasonous and not merely a perjurer, was innocent. (In one sense, we should believe this finding because we have been quite ready to believe the Russians when they tell us they were really bad about things like Korean Air Lines Flight 007 and the many sins of Stalin and others.) But if this finding is true, then how do we place in historical context, not to mention civil liberties policy contexts, this singular event? The Hiss conviction, after all, was much of the solid meat of the argument that domestic Communism was indeed a threat in America and that it was surely necessary to establish grand inquiries in the Congress, in the Executive Branch, and certainly in the courts to deal with this severe problem. How should we view this legacy now? And how should we concern ourselves with many of the statutes, administrative rulings, and court decisions that are still on the books and that may well affect our future as precedents on such matters? We can leave to their own thoughts and devices those people for whom the Hiss conviction was a major motivating event, although we might try to sympathize with the effect such a jolt must have on their psyches.

There are many more effects on civil liberties policy that flow from the end of the cold war, however. It appears at times that the United States now seeks to be a more insular nation; one that is motivated by domestic rather than international concerns. The 1992 elections tended to underscore this current. Certainly some attitudes found in public-opinion polling appear to verify this trend. Attitudes toward nations that are trading partners have become more hostile. Attitudes toward immigration have moved toward policies that are restrictive. The economy, it is believed, needs to take on a civilian mold while defense concerns are downplayed. And such attitudes are probably related to the near-hysteria that was such an important part of the atmosphere during the 1990–1991 Gulf War, which saw attacks on Arab-Americans, more than an occasional espousal of antisemitism, and questions about the patriotism of the antiwar demonstrators and their supporters.

These attitudes are particularly unfortunate at this time because two opportunities are now being presented to civil liberties policy making in an international sense. The first is the general trend toward democracy and free systems found around the world and that is unmistakable. Nations that are lagging in terms of their development toward openness and tolerance—China, for example, or North Korea or Haiti or Serbia—are receiving great and concentrated attention from the international community. Amnesty International now wins as many headlines, or perhaps more, than the American Civil Liberites Union (ACLU) manages to obtain. The second opportunity is that accorded to researchers, who are probably in the best position they have enjoyed in a long time, to take advantage of the winds of change and freedom in order to turn the spotlight on causes, types, and concerens of civil liberties policy making in a great variety of spheres. The yield from comparative civil liberties policy research can be practical as well as substantial because there are important trends at work in the world that call for us to become aware and stay aware. The hard and determined drive of many governments to achieve a complete national identity card system, for example, may certainly bode ill for many peoples.[5] And new and sophisticated systems of political control, press censorship, and even torture show that international and comparative research can illuminate problems and dangers.

One last obvious point about the cold war's demise is that racial, ethnic, and religious tensions have been exacerbated by the rapid changes that have come in the wake of this development. And this requires attention to questions of intolerance and its causes, the matter of developing practical policy instruments for dealing with such crises, and, sadly, with the matter of genocide.

II. THE CLINTON ADMINISTRATION COMES TO POWER: A SEA CHANGE?

Sophisticated policy analysts and political scientists, among others, often like to focus on the eternal verities of politics and policy; and this particular disposition for "realism" supports a view that stresses the continuities rather than the changes wrought by electoral preferences. The talk that dwells on how Presidents Reagan and Carter were the same on this or that matter, despite differences in rhetoric, or about how bureaucratic propensities or solutions over a period of time tend to conform to certain parameters, can have the effect and often *does* have the effect of promoting cynicism about policy making and, most especially, about politicians and their staffs of decision makers. There is an irony at work here, for one of the canons of political science and policy studies that seems long established is that voting is a desirable civic activity because, it is assumed, it does make a difference, at least in the long run.

Civil liberties policy issues are at the cutting edge of such considerations, and a more or less trite observation will demonstrate this. How does one go about convincing the nonvoter that issue stances of the candidates and parties really are different and that a real choice is available? The most ready method at hand, it would appear from anecdotal evidence, is to contrast the types of Supreme Court and federal judgeship appointments that are likely to be made by a Clinton or a Bush, a Reagan or a Mondale. It is also quite easy to contrast positions in recent years on such policy issues as abortion, gay rights, affirmative action, or the Seventh Amendment issue of access to the courts (sometimes called the "crazy law suits" issue). Issues of womens' rights were particularly in evidence in 1992 in Senate and House campaigns, and they clearly affected the national campaign in the wake of the Clarence Thomas Supreme Court confirmation hearings of 1991.

Experience suggests that both axioms, continuity of policy as well as whether voting makes a difference, are flawed in various ways; but no matter. What does seem clear is that the Clinton years will see some changes in civil liberties policy making, probably on all of the matters cited above. A different set of political actors will be calling the shots, at least at the top of the system. In the subterranean spheres, such as the bureaucracy and the lower levels of the court system, not to mention the states, quite different initiatives may be expected.

III. TECHNOLOGICAL DEVELOPMENTS

One of the old saws found throughout the social sciences tells us that technology outpaces its responses, and this clearly seems to be the case today.

Advances in the use of fetal tissue for treating Parkinson's disease and other maladies can be contrasted with the rather absurd attempts of the Bush Administration to stymie such efforts. New and advanced birth control devices seem to show the way toward a technological solution to the abortion controversy.[6] Breakthroughs in consumer product development and in information processing may give the upper hand to this or that company or nation well before any tariff legislation, antitrust action, or civil liberties safeguards can be put into place. The question of whether we should be seeing the number that is calling us on the telephone will reach resolution long after this capability has been achieved. And the findings of astronomy, geology, and biology will continue to baffle and betray those who believe our planet is only 6000 years old and that the earth is at the center of the universe.

True as it is, however, this observation does not get us far. It is probably more useful to look at a political system that seems to have successfully mastered the use of technology for its own ends and that embodies technological sophistication as one of its chief characteristics. The United States? Yes, potentially; but the country that serves as the best paradigm for our approach is thoroughly modern Singapore. What we can learn from its example can inform us about the kinds of outlines that shape technology's major threats to civil liberties.

The casual visitor to this small city-state may become aware of some of its laws and restrictions by observing the ban on chewing gum or the red light cameras that help to ensure orderly traffic. One might even notice the severe penalties meted out for failure to flush public toilets or for littering. It is far more likely, however, that a tourist will simply notice that the shopping malls that dominate the landscape are thoroughly modern and pristine and perhaps that the subway is beautiful and runs on time.

It must be submitted, however, that this is a government that has managed to combine terrific economic growth and general prosperity with a soft kind of repression meant to ensure its perpetuity. There is no crude Stalin-like statism at work here. The press is controlled but is ordered not to be sychophantic, setting up a tightrope it may take some time for journalists to master. Political prisoners, of which there are few because most people choose to ignore politics, are tortured, but not in such a way as to leave marks on their bodies. They are dressed in thin pajamas and the room temperature is set very low. The foreign press also is subject to censorship, but it presents a slightly more technical problem because the government wants foreign periodicals available in the luxury hotels and other locations frequented by foreigners. In the dispute between Singapore and Dow Jones, the publisher of the *Asian Wall Street Journal* and the *Far Eastern Economic Review*, the authorities never sought to ban the publications from the country entirely. They simply insisted on low circulation numbers, perhaps only 400 copies altogether. Since Dow Jones was not interested in such a minimal business, it withdrew its publications altogether; and in response, the government simply printed up 400 copies of these publications—international copyright is not observed—and kept up appearances as it wished.[7] It can be seen that such strategies on torture and on the press may yield results many of us might not approve of, but the fact remains that these are comparatively soft measures and are less likely international targets of protest than the crudities of a North Korea or an Iran.

Technology takes on its most complete and durable form in Singapore, however, in the matter of the national identification card; for unlike those of any other nation, it eventually will be electronic, thus enabling authorities to find anyone at any time, to know who they are with, and probably to know what they are doing.

Orwellian? Yes, but this is perhaps the wave of the future. Singapore has its imitators. Nearby states, for example, are trying to set up their own national electronic ID systems, and one of the contractors researching and manufacturing this new product cheerfully told me that privacy is a thing of the past. But the purpose here is not to dwell on the identity card, but to think in practical and policy terms about the implications of a government and a society that are very successful, economically, and that, on a long list of matters, seems to have found modern and more effective ways to establish a kind of authoritarian omnipotence. As for the electronic identity card, it clearly represents some kind of wave of the future. It most certainly would have and, indeed, does have supporters in the United States and other democracies. Perhaps, indeed, privacy is a thing of the past.[8]

Singapore may seem far away from the shores of the United States, and in terms of physical distance, this perception is correct; but many of the motivations and forces that have animated events there are present in all societies. As Justice Brandeis pointed out in his famous dissent in *Olmstead* v. U.S. (1928), dangers to privacy and related liberties are often set into motion by bureaucratic mentalities that are essentially well-meaning.[9] It does not require very astute observation to see that the United States today has developed some severe problems, even though it is better off than most nations, in such areas as technological crime-fighting remedies, computer-measured work performance on a minute-by-minute basis, observations of workplace activities from remote positions, the amassing of credit and consumer information (which is now becoming incredibly sophisticated and nuanced), and quite intrusive forms of medical records keeping and information gathering, among other matters.

As for the perennial argument about whether technology liberates or oppresses us, the short answer surely has to be that it depends, after all, on particular circumstances and issues. In the meantime, it is safe to say, technological developments promise to continue to keep policy makers and ordinary citizens on their toes.

IV. ECONOMIC CHANGE AND THE EVOLUTION OF LAW

Economic change mandates much of the evolution of law, and it has been ever thus. The courts, and most especially the Supreme Court, of the late 19th and early 20th centuries are still the subject of scholarly debate on the issues of whether they advanced or retarded a humane level of economic development[10]; and a certain kind and amount of recent scholarship has continued to insist that the past 50 years have all been a mistake in the matter of interpreting property rights.[11] Although such topics and debates are likely to persist into the future, however, the economy of the United States and, most certainly, of the world are changing in basic ways.

It is not possible within the purview of this chapter to chart all of these trends, but listing a few of them is in order. Quite obviously, the major economic actors in the world, whether corporate or governmental, are involved in very tough trade rivalries. These are exacerbated by a general decline in world economic growth which has persisted since 1973 and has resulted in losing ground on living standards in both the economically advanced and Third World nations.[12] National economies, including the United States, are further squeezed by the loss of job opportunities wrought by industrial migration and downsizing.[13] And, most acutely, business firms are trying out new forms of organization that have the effect of limiting employment chances. One popular current model of the business firm, for example, is called "center and ring," among other names. In this model, the firm has an inner core and two outer rings. In the core are the permanent employees, a small and select band of perhaps talented but most certainly lucky people who enjoy some measures of job security and benefits. In the inner ring are the temporary employees, who are hired and discarded as needed. This is seen as the biggest of the groups, and it is possible that on occasion a member of this unfortunate group will be given a permanent role and graduate to the select circle. Finally, in the outer ring, are the consultants, who are to lend dynamism and good planning to the company as long as their advice is considered worthwhile.

Other trends operate similarly to limit employment possibilities. Among these are downsizing, the reduction of both the size of the firm and its work force, which results in early-retirement incentives and, in the happiest of cases, the loss of employment numbers through attrition; the weakening of unions, who admittedly may be involved in restrictive work practices from time to time but also provide a foundation of security for workers and potential workers; the sometimes wage-depressing effects of new free trade agreements; the financial crisis that now seems to be part and parcel of state and local government bureaucracies and educational establishments; and an almost constant but sometimes unmet need for retraining in certain industries and job skill areas. None of these trends are immutable; but it is clear that structural economic problems are going to cause pain for some time to come.

Against this hard backdrop, the policies of the Reagan and Bush years are seen by many observers, neutral and objective as well as partisan, to have resulted in a deliberate and sometimes catastrophic weakening of the safety nets that previous generations took for granted. Unemployment compensation is more difficult to obtain for many individuals because a wide variety of administrative guidelines have been made less flexible.[14] Welfare programs have felt similar pressures and in some locales have been cut in absolute terms. Nutrition, education, and other social services have also faced cuts or dismemberment. Health care reforms have been strongly resisted, and 35 million people have no health insurance even though a comprehensive and workable plan is in place in every other major industrialized nation and even though such a program was proposed by President Harry S. Truman way back in 1949.

In this climate, it has been difficult to argue for job rights, protections, or even sensibilities, and it will take some time to turn this situation around. Only in the areas of protection for women and minorities have there been solid gains in recent years, although these must be considered a great cause of social advancement and awareness. The fact remains, all the same, that the traditional "terminate-at-will" approach to employment relations is clearly dominant, undermining economic security for even the most conscientious of workers. The major exceptions to the terminate-at-will rule have been government employment, discrimination laws aimed at protecting women or minorities, and union contracts. The major justification for terminate-at-will, which might include rather petty reasons for letting an employee go, has been that the employee is always free to quit and that this somehow is a sword of Damocles over the employer. Obviously this argument has increasingly less relevance in today's economy (if it was ever justified), but it has made it possible for appellate courts to even uphold firing a worker for exercising his or her legitimate political rights while in an off-duty status.[15] Also pending at the moment, to cite another relevant example, is the case of a woman fired for smoking at home during her own leisure days and times.

The traditions of corporate privilege, by contrast, are changing in favor of these artificial persons. The word *privilege* is not used lightly here because this is in fact the status of incorporation in the laws of the 50 states and at the federal level as well. The classic rationale for this has been that corporations exist as a privilege, not as a right, because the practice of establishing limited liability for the owners should be seen as an extraordinary grant by the citizenry and its government.[16] But courts, and most especially the Supreme Court, have tended to push this important criterion of privilege into the background while finding that corporations do indeed hold rights that have heretofore been left unrecognized.[17] Labor unions and other countervailing organizations have been weakened both by policy dicta and by extra-legal activities during the past two decades or more, and stockholders' rights such as bringing up the matter of executive compensation at an annual meeting have been abrogated by a variety of Securities Exchange Commission rulings.

The net effects of these policy developments are bad enough if one is interested in a society that is just, free, and balanced between interests, but a further handicap for the American economy and polity may result from these developments; namely, the entrenchment of power and privilege may well prove to be a severe detriment when, as it surely will, the Clinton administration decides to undertake an industrial policy aimed at promoting employment and international competitiveness. Nearly all of the plans proffered on behalf of industrial policy schemes envision some changes in the corporate world in response to the new dynamics of the world economy, and such changes may well require the abridgment of some of the privileges of the past. It will be that much more a struggle to bring about changes because of the lop-sided schemes of civil liberaties policy of the past few years.

Economic change, then, shall continue to dictate civil liberties policy making just as it did in the 19th and early 20th centuries, as it did during the Great Depression and its aftermath, and as it surely has in the half century since the end of World War II.

V. THE DIALOG OF CIVIL LIBERTIES POLICY MAKING

Civil liberties issues are more than mere semantics; but it remains the case, all the same, that these issues can sometimes take on greater significance because of factors relating to the linguistic dynamics of words used to describe rights and the policies that surround them. The distinguished James Boyd White, for example, has spent much of his professional career dissecting the told and untold meanings of legal terms and argument.[18] More to the point, we know that debates on civil liberties issues become heated, at least in part, because the emotive content of the words involved — words like rights, duties, free speech, property, or cruel and unusual — tends to work against the construction of objective assessment or consensus building.

Recent scholarship has pointed out that "rights talk" based on the rather natural hyperindividualism found in American culture can and does have the effect of debasing consideration and discussion of civil liberties issues.[19] Most of us can agree that this occurs from time to time, and it can even take odd forms: for example, the hyperindividualistic terms and norms often used in debates and discussion on civil liberties policy making are applied, in toto, to debates involving group rights and group norms even though there are some logical problems with this. Such confusions animate much of the debate over issues such as affirmative action and other equal protection measures. In a similar vein, the rights talk that abounds in the writings of conservative property advocates such as Richard Epstein helps to add to confusions and certainly to emotive content.[20]

One should not expect resolution of such dialog difficulties in the foreseeable future; for the emotive content of civil liberties issues will ensure that this problem remains. We can remind ourselves, as this section of this chapter intends, that this is a perennial problem.

VI. METHODOLOGICAL ISSUES AND METHODOLOGICAL DEVELOPMENT

Some decades have passed since C. Herman Pritchett, Glendon Schubert, and others first took us down some sophisticated paths of measuring civil liberties policy making by looking at such areas as judicial behavior patterns, mathematical modeling, mass perceptions of civil liberties issues and their possible resolution, or perhaps police or prosecutorial norms and behavior; in other words, the study of law or law-related issues in a new and largely behavioral dimension. Any casual or regular reader of *Judicature, Law and Society* or perhaps the

Policy Studies Journal knows that the development of scholarship on civil liberties policy making has moved rather far over the past several decades, taking the study of law out of some of its more hidebound habits.

For a little more than a decade, the public choice movement has been making an impact on the social sciences; and, not surprisingly, public choice has been influential in legal studies.[21] Almost exclusively, however, public choice methodology has been limited to the traditional areas of common law decision making such as torts, contracts, or property.[22] At the heart of such concerns is the belief that market economics provides an unbeatable model of efficiency and fairness for the allocation of anything of material value and for the establishment of a fair hearing for all claimants in the legal arena. (It did not hurt the public choice cause, incidentally, when the distinguished Ronald Coase of the University of Chicago School of Law, author of the key foundation article for this approach, recently received a Nobel Prize in economics.)[23]

It almost goes without saying that public choice methods—critics might call it public choice doctrine[24]—do not readily appear to be applicable to issues of civil liberties policy making. This is because it is offensive to many to be asked to think that such foundations of a democratic system as free speech or a fair trial could be subject to the kinds of give-and-take pressures found in that ultimate paradigm of public choice, the free market. (Taking such offense of course begs such questions as the implications of the plea bargaining process or, say, the relationship between crime control budgets and the number of arrests made in a given community.) This offended viewpoint appears, on the face of it, to be valid because many, or even most, of us like to believe that freedom and its protections are immutable, eternal, and indivisible.

Whatever the case, public choice methods and approaches are advocated by scholars and, more to the point, are found in rulings from the federal appellate bench, among other places, in cases that may not be considered to be in the traditional civil liberties categories of policy making, but that nonetheless hold grave implications for human rights matters that are sometimes buried within the enactments, rulings, or court decisions in such areas as labor law, consumer protection, stockholders' protections, social welfare needs, or perhaps educational needs. And this helps to pinpoint the realization that one of the problems found in civil liberties policy making is that we tend to confine our attention to the traditional kinds of claims made under the Bill of Rights.[25]

Up to this moment, a very strong tendency of the public choice movement in law, often called the "law and economics" movement, has been support of politically and economically conservative causes and interests. This may abate in time as scholars of varied persuasions develop a greater impact on the movement. On what might be considered the other side of the ideological spectrum, although it should be pointed out that this is an attempt for a term of convenience more than precision, is found the Critical Legal Studies (CLS) movement, which sometimes likes to think of itself as revolutionary, at other times seems quite mundane, and at still other times is more confusing than anything else. Critical Legal Studies has had a strong impact at Harvard and several other law schools, very little impact among social scientists, and virtually no impact in society at large; but CLS does seem to be avoewedly determined to affect civil liberties policy making on the side of what it considers social justice, and this requires attention to such matters as academic freedom, the rights of women and minorities, and the rights of the working class.[26] These aims and their attendant policy goals are clearer than the deconstructionist methodology associated with CLS and its postmodernist roots.[27]

Sometimes overlooked or forgotten in discussions of approaches to civil liberties policy making is the traditional "fortress" approach adopted by the ACLU and some of the internationally based human rights organizations, such as Amnesty International. The "fortress" view is one that is grounded in frankly political strategies, but its philosophical roots are also important. The "fortress" view, which is simplicity itself, says that human rights are on the winning side in few times or places, historically or geographically, and that support for them requires constant vigilance, awareness of how popular majorities can be easily swayed to support antiliberties measures and postures, and, perhaps most important, that human rights sensibilities, in contrast to popular whims and sentiments, are gained slowly and quite methodically over time by careful, conscientious, and contemplative individuals. Because it is simplistic, the "fortress" view rarely finds its way, at least in its unvarnished and classic character, into the literature of civil liberties policy making. It may be seen as primarily political instead of scholarly in its purpose.

Such a distinction may be deceptive, however. We know from the foregoing and many other discussions that ideological roots play their role in both the scholarly and practical sides of civil liberties policy making at all levels and in all of the many civil liberties issues of contention. Bearing this in mind, it is certain that the future promises continued lively debate on both the substance and methods involved.

NOTES

1. Patterns of behavior which are fundamental to a civil liberties sensibility are set out in H. McCloskey and A. Brill, *Dimensions of Tolerance*: *What Americans Believe ABout Civil Liberties* (Russell Sage Foundation, New York, 1983).
2. J. B. White, *The Legal Imagination* (University of Chicago Press, Chicago, 1986).
3. Reprinted in the *International Herald Tribune*, February 27, 1990.
4. Ibid.
5. G. L. Houseman, *The Right of Mobility* (Kennikat Press, Port Washington, NY, 1979); but a much more cheerful view of ID systems is found in J. W. Eaton, *Card-Carrying Americans*: *Privacy, Security, and the National ID Card Debate* (Rowman and Littlefield, Totowa, NJ, 1986).
6. A great deal of speculation on resolution of the abortion issue centers upon RU-486 and other pills or devices which will obviate much of the need for abortion clinics.
7. *Silencing All Critics*: *Human Rights Violations in Singapore* (Asia Watch, New York, 1990).
8. Interview in the Far East, November, 1989.
9. P. Strum, *Louis D. Brandeis*: *Justice for the People* (Harvard University Press, Cambridge, MA, 1984).
10. M. C. Porter, "Lochner and Company: Revisionism Revisited," in *Liberty, Property and Government*: *Constitutional Interpretation Before the New Deal*, E. F. Paul and Howard Dickman (Eds.) (SUNY Press, Albany, NY, 1989, pp. 11–38).
11. A brief treatment setting out some of this view is R. A. Epstein, "Property, Speech, and the Politics of Distrust," in *The Bill of Rights in the Modern State*, G. R. Stone, R. A. Epstein, and C. R. Sunstein (Eds.) (University of Chicago Press, Chicago, 1992, pp. 41–90).
12. Many sources will supply this information, among them J. Kolko, *Restructuring the World Economy* (Pantheon, New York, 1988).
13. The basic economic explanation for this can be found, among other places, in W. A. Lewis, "Economic Development with Unlimited Supplies of Labour," *Manchester School of Economics* 22 (May, 1954): 139–181.
14. The attack on unemployment compensation began in earnest during the Thanksgiving weekend of 1982, when the Reagan administration announced that it would seek to tax unemployment compensation; this proposal with withdrawn shortly thereafter, but the administrative rulings since then have been restrictive at the federal level and in many of the states.

15. *Civil Liberties* 327(April): 8, 1979.
16. An extensive discussion of this appears in Chapter 3 in G. L. Houseman, *Questioning the Law in Corporate America*: *An Agenda for Reform* (Greenwood Press, Westport, 1993).
17. *First National Bank of Boston* v. *Bellotti*, 435 U.S. 465 (1978).
18. *The Legal Imagination*; also, the many other distinguished books written by White.
19. M. A. Glendon, *Rights Talk*: *The Impoverishment of Political Discourse* (The Free Press, New York, 1991).
20. R. A. Epstein, *Takings* (Harvard University Press, Cambridge, MA, 1985).
21. Richard A. Posner, *Economic Analysis of Law* (3rd ed.) (Little, Brown, Boston, 1986).
22. Ibid; also, see N. Furniss, "The Political Implications of the Public Choice-Property Rights School, *American Political Science Review* 72 (March, 1978): 399–410, and E. G. West, *Adam Smith and Modern Economics: From Market Behavior to Public Choice* (Edward Elgar, Worcester, England, 1990).
23. R. H. Coase, "The Problem of Social Cost," *Journal of Law and Economics* 3: 1–28, 1960.
24. See Chapter 7 of *Questioning the Law in Corporate America*.
25. Professor Martin Shapiro of the Boalt Hall (University of California—Berkeley) School of Law often makes the point in his lectures that profound civil liberties questions are embedded in these statutory and common law areas.
26. M. Kelman, *A Guide to Critical Legal Studies* (Harvard University Press, Cambridge, MA, 1987).
27. Ibid; *Critical Legal Studies* (Harvard Law Review Association, Cambridge, MA, 1986).

Part F
PROBLEMS WITH AN ECONOMIC EMPHASIS

17
Economic Regulation

James Anderson

Texas A&M University, College Station, Texas

The regulation of private economic activity is one of the primary tasks of governments in the United States. Some regulatory programs are focused on particular industries—railroads, broadcasting, and the stock markets are instances in point. Other regulatory programs cut across industry lines and deal with such functional areas as collective bargaining, environmental pollution, and competitive practices. As we will see, economic regulation has become more intensive and extensive through the course of the 20th century.

My concern in this chapter is essentially with the regulation of private economic activity by the national government. Other chapters in this book, such as those dealing with energy, transportation, labor, and environmental policies, are somewhat overlapping. There is no easy or clear-cut way to differentiate them from this chapter. It is perhaps sufficient to state that my lens is on business activity generally, whereas they focus on particular policy areas.

Several facets of economic regulation are scrutinized in this chapter. I open with a discussion of the nature of regulation and then move on to the development of the American regulatory state and the "expanse" of regulation that it entails. The second half of the chapter looks at some regulatory problems, the regulatory reform movement, and deregulation. Some generalizations about the future of the regulatory state are offered in conclusion.

I. THE NATURE OF REGULATION

What is regulation? In this chapter regulation should be taken to mean economic regulation, even when that adjective is not included. A well-known text on public policies states, "Regulation is what regulators do" (Shepard and Wilcox, 1979). A definition of that sort is catchy, perhaps, but it aids little in understanding. Shepard and Wilcox do go on to provide some amplification:

To regulate has at least three definitions. One is tough and unilateral: "to govern or direct according to rule." Another refers to compromise and smoothing over: "to reduce to order . . . to regularize." And another is superficial, perhaps empty: "to make regulation." Actual regulation varies among these, sometimes strict, sometime strict, sometimes trivial or even a tool of corporate interests.

The third definition is logically deduced from their statement, "Regulation is what regulators do." There is, however, nothing to be gained from belaboring this. Something better is needed.

Lawyers and economists often distinguish antitrust policy, which is intended to maintain competitive conditions in the economy, from regulation. What it is that differentiates these two categories of government action is not made clear. One is just left with the notion that there is a difference between government efforts to maintain competition and regulatory programs, such as regulation of railroads by the Interstate Commerce Commisssion (ICC). In an important sense there is. Antitrust law lays down some basic rules of the economic game—for examples, "Thou shalt not monopolize" and "Thou shalt not collude to restrain trade." Within this framework of rules, businesses are free to act and to compete or not compete as they choose. Regulation of railroads by the ICC went considerably further, however, and really involved the agency in the management of the railroads. Decisions to raise rates, to abandon service, to issue new securities, and other matters required ICC approval. Control of the railroads, in short, was more intensive and intrusive than antitrust, and ICC judgment could be substituted for railroad judgment.

In each of these instances, and in all of the others that are normally thought of as involving the economic regulation, the common element encountered is government action intended *to limit the discretion*, the freedom of action, of private individuals and companies engaged in some sort of economic activity. Some actions may be proscribed, others may be specified or required, and penalties or sanctions are authorized for violators (Stone, 1982: 10–11). Thus companies and labor unions are told that they cannot refuse to bargain collectively in good faith, whereas banks and other money lenders are required to provide borrowers with information on the actual costs of loans. Regulatory programs may, and do, differ significantly in extent or degree to which they restrict the discretion of the regulated parties, but the fact that in some way they have this effect is what puts them in the category of regulation.

A number of government actions that often carry the designation of "regulation" are not within the purview of this concept of regulation. These include agency rules or regulations specifying internal structures and procedures or operating practices, and Internal Revenue Service regulations, which are an aspect of public finance. Also excluded are managerial regulations, such as those relating to the use of public lands, that involve the government as a party to the transactions at issue. These matters are not what usually come to mind when one thinks of economic regulation.

In recent years, a line has been drawn between economic regulation and social regulation. In this formulation, economic regulation, which is said to have come first in point of time, involves control of rates, entry, and standards of service. The regulation of railroads and motor carriers is illustrative. In comparison, "the new style social regulation affects the conditions under which goods and services are produced and the physical characteristics of products that are manufactured" (Lilley and Miller, 1977: 51). Regulation of industrial pollution by the Environmental Protection Agency and product safety by the Consumer Product Safety Commission are instances of social regulation. Another writer avers, "Social regulation can generally be differentiated from economic regulation by the former's concern with harm to our physical (and sometimes moral and aesthetic) well-being, rather than harm to our wallets" (Reagan, 1987: 86). In practice, however the line between social and economic regulation is smudgy. Stone (1982: 41) contends that although there may be significant differences in the relevant statutes, both social and economic regulation are "designed to enhance the material enjoyment of life."

The regulatory tool kit contains a variety of instruments that can be authorized for use in the implementation of regulatory programs. Examination of the more important ones will further elaborate the nature of regulation.

A. Rule Making

Most regulatory agencies are authorized to make rules, which, following the Administrative Procedure Act (1946), can be defined as agency actions of "general applicability and future effect." Rules are usually intended to fill in the details of the law, given that Congress tends to legislate in general terms. Thus, the Occupational Safety and Health Administration (OSHA) is authorized to make and enforce rules to protect against industrial illnesses and accidents, the Federal Aviation Agency (FAA) to make rules governing airline safety, and the Federal Trade Commission (FTC) to make rules about unfair or deceptive practices. Rules, which have the same legal effect as laws enacted by Congress, comprise a major portion of the corpus of regulatory policy.

B. Adjudication

Agency adjudication involves the application of a statutory provision or a rule to a particular action or situation. The output of a successful adjudication (from the agency perspective) is an order or directive telling someone to do or not do something; thus the FTC may direct a company to "cease and desist" using a particular advertising claim because it is deceptive, or the ICC may direct a railroad to make reparation to a shipper who was charged an unreasonable rate. Agency adjudication is akin to action by the courts, whereas rule making is essentially legislative in style.

C. Price, Rate, and Profit Controls

Agencies may be authorized to control the rates or prices charged by companies. State public utility commissions can regulate the rates of return, or profit levels, of telephone, electric, gas, and other companies that come under their jurisdiction. The Federal Energy Regulatory Commission regulates rates charged by interstate electric power companies and the ICC continues to exercise some supervision over railroad and motor carriers rates. Overall, rate regulation by national agencies has declined in extent because of the deregulation movement (see further on). Through the Fair Labor Standards Act Congress has provided that employers engaged in interstate commerce or the production of goods or service therefore must pay no less than a minimum wage of $4.35 per hour.

D. Standard Setting and Enforcement

Many regulatory programs involve the setting of standards to govern economic or business behavior and their enforcement through inspection, monitoring, self-reporting by businesses, and related proceedings. Standards, which may be specified directly by Congress or by agencies exercising authority delegated to them, involve industrial health and safety, control of air and water pollution, motor vehicle safety, the wholesomeness of meat, and a multitude of other matters. Often a choice can be made between performance and specification or design standards, as in the instances of pollution control and motor vehicle safety. Thus a performance standard sets a goal for the reduction of a particular pollutant, with affected companies being left with discretion as to what means to use to attain the goal. In contrast, a design or specification standard might require the use of scrubbers to reduce smokestack emissions. Inspection—the examination of products, premises, accounts and records, and so on—is commonly done to determine whether there is compliance with standards. Persuasion, bargaining, threat of prosecution, and other efforts may be made to induce violators to come into compliance. Actual prosecution is typically the last resort. Those who call this "command and control" regulation convey a simplistic notion of what it entails.

E. Licensing

Licensing, which may also be called enabling action, is another common regulatory technique. Licenses are sometimes called "licenses," but they also can be named franchises, permits, certificates of convenience and necessity, or charters. Whatever its name, a license typically permits someone to do something that is otherwise prohibited, whether to drive a car, use the corporate form of business organization, operate a television broadcast station, or practice medicine. Licensing may be used to allocate scarce resources, such as in the case of television broadcast stations; to ensure a level of competence, as in the licensing of automobile drivers and doctors; or to reduce or limit competition, as in the case of commercial banks and many occupations. Several dozen different trades, professions, and occupations are licensed by the various states, with the number ranging from 10 to 45 in a given state. It is, as was noted, a very widespread form of regulation.

F. Prohibition of Undesirable Practices

Some practices or activities may be regarded as so undesirable, whether on moral, environmental, or other grounds, that they are simply and completely banned. Of course, where standards are involved, those who do not meet the standards set either cannot engage in the pertinent activity or are subject to penalties, but there is at least the possibility of participation. Such does not exist when an activity is prohibited or banned, such as the private sale of liquor, the use of certain pesticides, or the conduct of business in an areas zoned residential. The difference between standards and prohibition can be illustrated with banking regulation. There are standards for "sound" banking practices, such as those involving loans to officers, to which banks are required to comply. In contrast, many states ban the practice of branch banking. Here the foreclosure of activity is complete—no room at all is left for the exercise of private discretion.

G. Noncoercive Action

A variety of techniques that can be used to influence or shape the exercise of private economic discretion can be categorized as noncoercive in that legal penalties or sanctions are not attached to noncompliance. Examples include the use of mediation and nonciliation in the settlement of labor disputes, "moral suasion" by the Federal Reserve Board to influence bank lending practices, and the establishment by the U.S. Department of Agriculture of voluntary quality standards for many agricultural commodities. Both the Johnson and Carter administrations employed voluntary wage-price guideposts in their campaigns to hold down inflation. The effectiveness of such techniques depends on a "consensus of purpose," which often does not develop or persist.

H. Economic Incentives

The techniques thus far discussed are sometimes collectively designated as traditional or classic regulation (Breyer, 1982). In the last couple of decades, the use of taxation as an alternative form of regulation has frequently been advocated, particularly by economists. Thus it has been proposed (e.g., Kneese and Schultze, 1975) that instead of relying on standard setting and enforcement to control air and water pollution, taxation could be employed to better advantage. Thus, a tax or fee would be levied on each unit of a pollutant discharged into the environment that would be sufficient to make it economically attractive for polluters to reduce their discharges and thereby avoid paying some or all of the tax or fee. It is believed that this system would be more effective than traditional regulation because it would utilize the incentives of the marketplace to achieve a public purpose. Opposition to the use of economic incentives has come from persons who are committed to traditional regulatory patterns, who believe that taxation should only be used to raise revenue, or who envisage various administrative and political problems in using taxation for regulatory purposes.

To date, little actual use has been made of economic incentives (or taxation). An exception occurs under the Clean Air Act of 1990, which authorized an emissions trading system for the electric power industry. Companies will have their sulfur emissions restricted by allowances assigned to individual plants by the Environmental Protection Agency. Companies that find it economical to reduce emissions below their allotted level can sell their excess allowances to other companies with excess emissions. All of this is supposed to result in the efficient reduction of sulfur pollution to a specified overall level (*New York Times*, July 17, 1991). This use of emissions trading will provide an opportunity to see how practice squares with economic theory.

Before moving to the next section, it should be useful to use the private discretion criterion to compare regulation with two other forms of economic intervention; namely, government promotion and government ownership of business. Promotion involves governmental encouragement or assistance to private business activities, whether through cash subsidies, tax benefits, the provision of free data and information, guarantee of loans, or construction of facilities (e.g., airports and harbors). This is done to induce businesses to undertake or continue involvement in desired activities by enhancing their profitability or the likelihood thereof. Businesses retain much discretion as to whether to engage in the promoted activities, although there is an element of control involved, but it is control through the carrot rather than the stick (donkeys can be consulted to learn more about the comparative use of these techniques). To illustrate, assume government wants to bring about industrial plant modernization (to achieve what is sometimes called reindustrialization). This could be done by making investment tax credits available to those who modernize. Or the government could set plant modernization standards and penalize those who failed to meet them. Which of the two businesses would prefer and which is likely to be msot effective should be readily apparent.

The government might take the position, however, that private management is incapable of or unlikely to modernize a particular industry and decide that the only workable solution is to make it a government enterprise. If such were done, there would be no room left for the exercise of private managerial discretion; all would be governmentally determined. Although there are a variety of government enterprises in the United States, and many of them are more efficient than folklore would have it, there has been no strong urge to replace private enterprise with public enterprise. The Western European democracies rely considerably more on government enterprises than does the United States, especially in transportation and industrial production.

II. THE DEVELOPMENT OF THE REGULATORY STATE

Governments in the United States have always engaged in the regulation of private economic activity, although for the first century of our national history most regulations flowed from the various state governments. The experiences of three states are illustrative. The Handlins (1947) report that in the decades following the American Revolution, Massachusetts engaged in such regulatory activities as the setting of manufacturing standards, the licensing of lotteries, the licensing of mill sites (on condition that the millers agree to limits on their rates, among other things), and the setting of tolls charged by bridges and ferries licensed by the state. In Pennsylvania, Hartz (1948) found an extensive variety of regulatory programs, including regulation of creditor-debtor relations, control of liquor traffice, labor legislation, regulation of banks and insurance companies, and inspection and licensing programs.

> The inspection program included such articles as flour, fish, beef, pork, hogslard, flaxseed, butter, biscuits, harness and leather, tobacco, shingles, potash and pearlash, staves, heading and lumber, ground black-oak bark, pickled fish, spiritous liquors and gunpowder.

Licensing was applied to such occupations as "innkeepers, peddlers, retailers of foreign goods, liquor merchants, brokers of various kinds, wharfage pilots, and auctioneers" (Hartz, 1948). Missouri, a newer Western state, also was actively involved in the economy, including inspection and licensing programs, and labor regulation (Primm, 1954).

Throughout much of the 19th century, national regulatory activity was rather limited, being restricted to such matters as protective tariffs, supervision of trade with the Indian tribes, and steamboat inspection. In the years after the Civil War, as industrialization increased and the economy became more and more national in scope, pressures developed for the control of the railroads and large businesses ("trusts") spawned by the transformation of the economy. State regulation was first sought and, when this appeared ineffective or unavailable, attention turned to the national government. The enactment of the Interstate Commerce Act (1887) and the Sherman Act (1890) mark the beginning of a shift in political power and regulatory activity from the states to the national government. The 20th century has witnessed a tremendous expansion of national economic regulation.

Much of the growth in national regulatory activity has come in surges during the Progressive Era, the New Deal years, and the decade stretching from the mid-1960s to the mid-1970s. During the Progressive Era, railroad and antitrust regulation were strengthened, meat inspection and pure food and drug laws were adopted, the Federal Reserve System was created, and regulatory programs of benefit to agriculture were increased. By the end of the Progressive Era, regulation was established as the dominant method used by government in dealing with the economic problems of the new American industrial society. Musolf (1965) has provided an explanation for this occurrence:

> In ideological terms, regulation has drawn strength from the general belief that it is a halfway house between laissez faire and socialism. If the former became increasingly inappropriate as the Industrial Revolution continued, the latter appeared equally inappropriate in an economy largely based on vigorous private enterprise. Certainly regulation lacks the ideological appeal of the other two, but America has not been fertile soil for elaborate ideologies. Regulation permits, and even invites, the piecemeal, pragmatic approach to specific public policy problems that seems to fit the American temperament.

After a period of comparative quiescence during the 1920s, the pace of regulatory expansion increased markedly during the 1930s. The business community was in disarray and disfavor and the New Deal, dedicated to economic relief, recovery, and reform, produced a variety of major regulatory statutes. A partial listing includes the two Agriculture Adjustment Acts, the Securities Exchange Act, the Public Utility Holding Company Act, the National Labor Relations Act, the Robinson-Patman Act, the Motor Carrier Act, the Communication Act of 1934, the Civil Aeronautics Act, the Natural Gas Act, the Fair Labor Standards Act, and the Food, Drug and Cosmetics Act of 1938. Some of this New Deal regulatory legislation, such as the National Labor Relations Act and the Food, Drug and Cosmetics Act, was intended primarily to protect the interests of disadvantaged groups in society, such as workers and consumers. Other statutes, although containing a protective element, were designed to help promote economic recovery and the interests of particular economic groups by restricting competition among their members. Here the Motor Carrier Act and the Civil Aeronautics Act are illustrative. Many of the independent regulatory commissions were products of New Deal legislation. By the end of the 1930s, there was no doubt that, henceforth, a major role of the national government would be that of regulator of the economy.

The third major period of regulatory growth, overlaps the liberal Johnson and the conservative Nixon and Ford administrations. Indeed, as Table 1 indicates, more regulatory legislation was enacted under Nixon than Johnson. A pragmatic conservative and an astute politician, Nixon was willing to sign such legislation into law and, even when he did not favor it, claim some credit. Much of the legislation enacted during this third surge period was concerned with protecting the environment and safeguarding the health and economic interests of consumers and workers. The environmental movement and consumerism were at peak strength during these years.

There are some aspects of this surge in regulation that merit notice. First, a number of major new regulatory agencies were created, including the Environmental Protection Administration (EPA), Consumer Product Safety Commission, Occupational Safety and Health Administration (OSHA), and Commodity Futures Trading Commission. Most of these new agencies were organized along functional rather than industry lines, in contrast to practice during the New Deal years. Second, regulatory statutes came in two contrasting styles. Some were quite lengthy and detailed, such as the Clean Air Act of 1970 and the Employee Retirement Income Security Act. Others conferred broad substantive discretion on the administering agency. The Consumer Product Safety Act and the Occupational Safety and Health Act are in point. Detail, however, does not always preclude the exercise of agency discretion, nor do broad grants of discretionary authority necessarily enable agencies to act effectively or expeditiously in handling problems. Third, industries that previously had not had much direct experience with regulation now found it to be of major importance in their operations. The automobile and chemical industries, for example, came under substantial regulation by EPA, OSHA, and other agencies.

Many factors—political, social, economic, and philosophical—contributed to the emergence and expansion of the American regulatory state. One could attempt to handle the task of explaining its development ideographically, accounting for the adoption of first one major regulatory program and then another. Not only would this require much time and space, it would also be both tedious and redundant. More useful is a focus on the general causes of regulatory growth. Two explanatory schemes will be summarized here. One draws primarily upon Steiner's (1953) discussion of the underlying causes of regulation. The other is the economic theory of market failure.

Table 1. Federal Economic Regulatory Legislation 1966–1976

Year enacted	Title of statute
1966	Clean Water Restoration Act
	Fair Packaging and Labeling Act
	National Traffice and Motor Vehicle
	Child Protection Act
1967	Wholesome Meat Act
	Flammable Fabrics Amendments
	Air Quality Act
1968	Natural Gas Pipeline Safety Act
	Consumer Credit Protection Act
	Wholesome Poultry Products Act
	Radiation Control for Health and Safety Act
	Tire Research and Safety Act
1969	Air Quality Act Amendments
	Federal Coal Mine Health and Safety Act
	Child Protection and Toy Safety Act
1970	Clean Air Amendments
	Egg Products Inspection Act
	Occupational Safety and Health Act
	Poison Prevention Packaging Act
	Securities Investor Protection Act
	Economic Stabilization Act
	Fair Credit Reporting Act
1971	Economic Stabilization Act Amendments
	Federal Boat Safety Act
	Lead-Based Paint Poisoning Prevention Act
	Wholesome Fish and Fisheries Products Act
1972	Consumer Product Safety Act
	Motor Vehicle Information and Cost Savings Act
	Noise Control Act
	Equal Employment Opportunity Act
	Federal Environmental Pesticide Control Act
	Federal Water Pollution Control Act Amendments
	Ports and Waterways Safety Act
1973	Agriculture and Consumer Protection Act
	Emergency Petroleum Allocation Act
	Flood Disaster Protection Act
1974	Atomic Energy Act
	Commodity Futures Trading Commission Act
	Magnuson-Moss Warranty/FTC Improvement Act
	Council of Wage and Price Stability Act
	Employee Retirement Income Security Act
	Federal Energy Administration Act
	Transportation Safety Act
	Fair Labor Standards Act Amendments
	Safe Drinking Water Act
	Equal Credit Opportunity Act
	National Mobile Home Construction and Safety Standards Act
1975	Energy Policy and Conservation Act
	Securities Act Amendments

Table 1. Continued

Year enacted	Title of statute
1976	Railroad Revitalization and Regulatory Reform Act
	Consumer Leasing Act
	Medical Devices Act
	Antitrust Improvements Act
	Consumer Product Safety Commission Improvement Act
	U.S. Grain Standards Act
	Toxic Substances Control Act

A. Underlying Causes of Regulation

Just as no single factor or cause accounts for the general growth of government in modern societies, neither is there a satisfactory explanation of similar sort for the narrower task of explaining the expansion of economic regulation. (However, for an unsuccessful effort to do so, see Stigler, 1971.) The problem is still much too complex. Of more utility is Steiner's contention that there are several somewhat overlapping causes that underlay the growth of regulation. They include the following.

1. Technological Change and the Breakdown of Laissez Faire

The transformation of the United States from a rural agrarian society into an urban industrial society produced conditions that did not conform to laissez faire or minimal government assumptions. In a modern industrial society, for example, the pursuance of self-interest does not always lead to harmony, competition does not always prevail, and the market does not always provide security for those willing to work hard. People were (and are) often disinclined to accept the action of the market mechanism as the decider of their economic fate, especially when it becomes unpleasant. Moreover, people came to insist that social and ethical values as well as economic values should be reflected in the operation of the economy. Generally, the economy (the marketplace) was seen as a product of human activity, as something properly subject to control and improvement through government action when its results were thought unacceptable. Persons suffering economic distress or dislocation in the market have often sought governmental aid in dealing with their problems.

2. Problems of Resource Coordination

Government action has often been viewed as necessary to bring about more efficient coordination and utilization of resources. Consequently, regulatory programs often require the disclosure of information designed to improve individual economic decisions, as in the purchase of products or the borrowing of money, and to prevent fraud, deception, or chicanery. Macroeconomic controls—fiscal and monetary policies—are used by government in an attempt to ensure full utilization of the economy's resources and an absence or reduction of inflation. The Employment Act 1946 generally committed the national government to this course of action. Presidential administrations that do not satisfactorily handle this task are likely to suffer at election time.

3. Pressures to Resolve Group Conflicts

Economic activity has been a fertile source of conflicts in American society. Conflicts have developed between labor and management, big business and small business, bankers and bank depositors, farmers and the purchasers of farm commodities, buyers and sellers of stocks and bonds, and many others. The resolution or adjustment of group conflicts has variously involved efforts to equalize group power (the Wagner Act), to resolve conflicts that threaten the public interest (labor dispute settlement), to establish the "rules of the game" among groups (prohibition of unfair competition), and to protect the economically weak against the economically strong. The last item, says Steiner (1953), "has always been a function of government in the American code of political morality." The resolution of conflict, indeed, is a basic reason for the existence of government.

4. *The Socialization of Risk*

People have long been interested in shifting some or many of the risks of economic life from themselves to government. People have always been concerned with security. What has changed in the 20th century is not so much the desire for security as the way security is defined and the means for achieving it. Many economic risks once accepted as just, inevitable, or "acts of God" are now viewed as public problems. Much more reliance is now placed on government action to protect individuals against the economic hazards of old age, unemployment, industrial illness and accident, and low incomes. But the quest for security is not simply an individual concern. Many businesses have also successfully sought greater security through government action, whether in the form of protective tariffs to reduce foreign competition, restrictions on entry into businesses (such as commercial airlines and motor carriers) to reduce domestic competition, or subsidies and insurance to reduce the costs and risks of investment and entrepreneurship. What is it but a concern basically with security, a concern over the risks of competition, that caused many airline, motor carrier, and railroad officials to resist deregulation (albeit, perhaps, in the name of the need to maintain an adequate transportation system, the public interest, or some other higher goal)?

It must be stressed that these are *underlying* causes. They help explain why people often seek governmental assistance, regulatory programs in our case, to ameliorate perceived economic problems, and why there is often responsiveness by government to calls for intervention. They do not explain why in particular instances some succeed in this endeavor and others do not, why Congress established a Consumer Product Safety Commission but a few years later refused to authorize an Agency for Consumer Advocacy. Such discrete actions will depend upon the configuration of political forces that exist at a particular time and are focused on a given issue. To put it a different way, the quartet of underlying causes helps explain (if not necessarily justify) the shift of the national government's role from that of "night watchman" to that of active and pervasive regulator of economic activity. Is does not account for everything.

B. The Theory of Market Failure

A relatively recent economic construct, the theory of market failure has acquired considerable acceptance as a rationale for possible government intervention in the economy and as a critique of existing regulatory programs. In this scheme of things, the market is taken as the norm, as the best means for securing the efficient allocation of resources for a society and perhaps other values such as individual freedom and the minimalization of government power. Only when the market works improperly, that is, when it "fails," is there ostensibly a need for government intervention. Market failure can take a number of shapes.

One is in the case of "natural monopolies." In some instances, the economics of scale may be such that it is inefficient for more than one firm to supply a product such as electrical power. Consequently, a single firm is authorized to provide service for a given city or area. In the absence of regulation, the firm could restrict its output and charge prices above the "competitive level." Regulation in such instances is seen as necessary to protect consumers against the exercise of monopoly power and to help secure allocation efficiency by setting rates for the monopolists at a "competitive level."

Regulation may also be justified when there are third-party or spillover effects that are not reflected in the price of a product. Thus the costs of air and water pollution resulting from the operation of a factory may not be reflected in the prices consumers pay for its products. More of these products may be purchased then would be the case if their (higher) prices reflected the true costs of pollution. Regulation is then justified to ensure that the costs of pollution are not ignored. Another way to do this would be to levy a fee or tax on the discharge of pollutants by the factory. (Moreover, there is really no way to establish a market for clean air.)

Third, consumers may lack the information necessary for the market system to operate effectively. If they lack information on the quality of products, the true cost of interest, or the potential effectiveness of a drug, they will not be able to evaluate competing products effectively and make rational economic decisions. A misallocation of resources may again be the consequence. Government action here may be taken to ensure that buyers will have sufficient information or perhaps to reduce the costs of information that might conceivably be obtained by them acting alone. Market economists see this as the justification for truth-in-lending legislation. Others may see it as necessary to protect borrowers against deception.

Fourth, the government action may be necessary to maintain competition. Classic economics to the contrary, competition neither always prevails nor maintains itself. Many of those who prefer the market system to government regulation for allocation of resources and values see a need for antitrust action to maintain competitive conditions in the economy. Action may be necessary to block the development of monopolies, to break them up when they exist, or to prevent restrictions on competition, as through price-fixing agreements, bid rigging, and other forms of collusive behavior. Interestingly, price fixing is the most clear-cut and obvious violation of the Sherman Act's prohibition of restraints of trade; it is also the type of violation most frequently prosecuted by the Antitrust Division.

Although there many be additional forms of market failure, these should adequately illustrate the theory's application. Articles analyzing regulatory programs from this perspective appear with regularity in such outlets as the *Journal of Law and Economics*. Those for whom the market failures rationale is appealing—most economists, many lawyers, and others—take the stance that many current regulatory programs are unnecessary or undesirable, and that society would be better served by more reliance on the market.

Proponents of market failure theory sometimes employ it to "explain" the growth of regulation over the past century. Indeed, it is true that, perhaps with some contrivance, many regulatory programs can be shoe-horned into one or another of the categories of failure. If one looks carefully at the historical record, however, what is found is that regulatory programs were sought and justified, not in terms of market failure, but on the basis of such concerns as equity, the control of economic power, protection of the public interest, prevention of destructive or predatory competition, elimination of fraud and deception as unfair or unethical, and the need for social justice. Market failure theory rests largely on the normative premise that efficiency is the desideratum on which decisions on regulatory should be based. In actuality, many other values have much more importantly contributed to the historical expansion of the resultory state.

III. DIMENSIONS OF THE REGULATORY STATE

That the national government is now responsible for a vast amount of economic regulatory activity is beyond question. It is not an easy task, however, in limited space, to present a definitive view of the extent and variety of contemporary regulatory programs, let alone provide a good notion of their impact on economy and society. The best I can do is to provide an impressionistic sketch of some of its dimensions.

One way to provide a rough outline of the expanse or scrope of the regulatory state is to list, as is done in Table 2, the various national regulatory agencies. In developing the list I used the definition of a regulatory agency formulated by the Senate Committee on Government Operations (except for the appointments criterion). The definition reads:

> A Federal regulatory agency . . . is one which (1) has decision-making authority, (2) establishes standards or guidelines conferring benefits and imposing restrictions on business conduct, (3) operates principally in the sphere of domestic business activity, (4) has its head and/or members appointed by the President . . . subject to Senate confirmation . . . and (5) has its legal procedures generally governed by the Administrative Procedure Act.

The 44 agencies listed under the three categories in Table 2 include all of the major economic regulatory agencies and many of the lesser ones. Agencies such as the Bureau of Land Management in the Department of the Interior are not included because their regulationlike activities are tied into their management of public lands and property.

A regulatory agency's organization type has importance for its conduct of regulatory activity. Independent regulatory commissions are plural-headed, usually having either five or seven members who are appointed by the president with senatorial consent for fixed, staggered terms of office. No more than a majority of a commission's members can come from the same political party and they can be removed from office only for specified causes, usually stated as inefficiency, neglect of duties, or malfeasance in office. Decisions of the regulatory commissions are not subject to formal presidential review or approval. Executive bureaus' location within executive departments puts them in the presidential chain of command; their decisions are open to hierarchical review and coordination. Bureau chiefs are political appointees who serve at the pleasure of the executive. Independent agencies are so designated because they are located outside the executive departments. They do come under presidential supervision, which in practice is going to be much more thorough for the important Environmental Protection Agency then for the little-known National Credit Union Administration, which likely has very little presidential contact. Further on, some more of the implications of agency type will be touched on.

Regulatory policies differ greatly on the basis of such criteria as their purposes, the number of people or companies that come within their purview, control techniques, direct and indirect economic costs, and economic impact. Simply to lump them together under the broad heading of regulation glosses over such differences. A somewhat rudimentary classification scheme, which uses general purpose as a differentiating criterion, yields five categories of regulatory policy.

Competitive regulatory policies are concerned with maintaining competitive conditions in the economy, as by preventing monopolization and unreasonable restraints of trade. The Sherman Act, Clayton Act, Federal Trade Commission Act, and other antitrust laws are the primary components of this type of regulation. The maintenance of competition has long

Table 2. National Regulatory Agencies, 1992

Independent Regulatory Commission
  Commodity Futures Trading Commission
  Consumer Products Safety Commission
  Federal Communications Commission
  Federal Maritime Commission
  Federal Reserve Board
  Federal Trade Commission
  Interstate Commerce Commission
  National Labor Relations Board
  Nuclear Regulatory Commission
  Securities and Exchange Commission
Independent Agencies
  Environmental Protection Agency
  Equal Employment Opportunity Commission
  Federal Deposit Insurance Corporation
  Federal Mediation and Concilation Service
  National Transportation Safety Board
  National Mediation Board
  National Credit Union Administration
Bureaus in Executive Departments
  Agricultural Marketing Service (USDA)
  Agricultural Stabilization and Conservation Service (USDA)
  Animal and Plant Health Inspection Service (USDA)
  Antitrust Division (Justice)
  Bureau of Alcohol, Tobacco, and Firearms (Treasury)
  Bureau of Export Administration (COM)
  Drug Enforcement Administration (Justice)
  Economic Regulatory Administration (Energy)
  Federal Aviation Administration (DOT)
  Federal Grain Inspection Service (USDA)
  Federal Railroad Administration (DOT)
  Food and Drug Administration (HHS)
  Food Safety and Inspection Service (USDA)
  Mine Safety and Health Administration (DOL)
  National Highway Traffice Safety Administration (DOT)
  National Marine Fisheries Service (COM)
  Occupational Safety and Health Administration (DOL)
  Office of the Comptroller of the Currency (Treasury)
  Office of Federal Contract Compliance (DOL)
  Office of Interstate Land Sales Registration (HUD)
  Office of Surface Mining Reclamation and Enforcement (Interior)
  Office of Thrift Supervision (Treasury)
  Packers and Stockyards Administration (USDA)
  U.S. Customs Service (Treasury)
  U.S. Geological Survey (Interior)

been a cardinal goal of American regulatory policy. In the last few decades it has begun to catch on in other industrial countries.

Protective regulatory policies are intended to protect the public by preventing or eliminating the existence of activities and conditions variously regarded as unfair, unsafe, unhealthy, undesirable, or, for good measure, immoral. Illustrative are programs to reduce or prevent air and water pollution, unsafe and unhealthful workplaces, the sale of unsafe and ineffective drugs, the use of deceptive trade practices, the sale of unwholesome meat and poultry products, and the operation of unsafe commercial aircraft. Protective regulation may also require the disclosure of information to buyers and consumers, as on true interest rates for loans and credit, the nutritional content of food products, and on the actual coverage of product warranties.

Promotional regulatory policies serve to protect or benefit the interests of those who are ostensibly regulated. Often this involves programs that limit entry into businesses or occupation or lessen competition in some manner among those in the field. Some would call much of what is involved here "self-regulation." A good set of illustrations are state occupational licensing programs, which are frequently dominated by members of the licensed groups. There is also a good measure of self-regulation in agricultural marketing orders for milk, fruits, and vegetables, and some of it in agricultural price support programs. Other examples in this category are tariffs and other import-restriction programs, the Robinson-Patman Act (intended to lessen price competition for the benefit of small businesses), and "buy America" requirements for government purchasing.

Some regulatory policies, established for other purposes, may over time take on a promotional orientation. Railroad regulation by the ICC was initiated primarily to protect shipper interests. After enactment of the Transportation Act of 1920, which authorized the ICC power to set *minimum* railroad rates, among other things, regulation became more and more responsive to and promotive of the railroads' interests. The history of motor carrier regulation provides another example of this sort of regulatory metamorphosis.

Managerial regulatory policies, which can also be tagged as public utility–type programs, are usually but not always applied to natural monopolies—for example, electric power, gas, and telephone companies—where it is believed that competition will not function as an effective regulatory mechanism. Usually involving rate, entry, and service regulation, this type often injects regulating agencies into the making of basic managerial decisions. Control may also be exercised over financial and accounting practices. This pattern of regulation is the most restrictive in its impact on the exercise of private economic discretion. Once well illustrated by ICC regulation of railroads and motor carriers, deregulation has reduced their value as examples. A better current illustration is the regulation of household utility companies by state public service commissions. This type of regulation is usually centered on particular industries, as is promotional regulation. In comparison, protective and competitive regulation more often than not cut across industry lines in their concern with various business practices or economic activities.

Macroeconomic regulatory policies are intended to influence the overall operation of the economic system. Fiscal and monetary policies, and sometimes price and wage controls, are used to combat inflation and recession, and to encourage economic growth. The national government became fully committed to this sort of regulatory activity only after World War II. Although macroeconomic regulatory policies focus on the economy as a whole, with the partial exception of monetary policy, they are directed at the behavior of particular groups of persons—those whose taxes are raised or lowered, or those seeking to increase prices when restraints on prices are in effect, and so on. Monetary policy operates somewhat differently in that when, say, the money supply is tightened, no particular set of persons is the target. In the nature of things, however, some may find it more difficult to borrow money than others—small businesses may experience more difficulty than large businesses, for example, because of differing credit ratings. In one way or another, macroeconomic programs are intended to influence or control the exercise of private economic discretion.

Most regulatory policies can be fitted into one or another of these cateogires without great difficulty. Some programs, however, will overlap a couple of categories. Meat inspection can serve as an example. If the position is taken that the primary purpose of meat inspection by the Food Safety and Inspection Service is to protect consumers against unwholesome meat, and a good case for this can be made, then it becomes a protective regulatory program. But one might also contend, and not without some basis, that meat inspection is a promotional program in that, by increasing consumer confidence in the wholesomeness of meat, it encourages the purchase of larger quantities to the ultimate benefit of meat producers and processors. It should not be surprising in an area of activity so diverse and complex as economic regulation that some programs have multiple purposes or resist the easy assignment of pigeonholes.

A technique that is sometimes used to portray the growth in the volume of regulations issued by agencies, or reduction in that growth, involves comparison of the number of pages in the *Federal Register* for various years. Critics of regulation are especially prone to the use of this ploy. Thus one might learn that the size of the *Federal Register* expanded, as indeed it did, from approximately 20,000 pages in 1970 to 61,000 pages in 1978, for a growth rate of slightly over 300%. In actuality, however, this is at best a rough measure of the increase in regulations, and it really says nothing about their implementation. Only a fraction of the *Federal Register*'s pages are taken up by the final rules flowing from agencies. Many more pages are consumed by informational materials—notices of proposed rule makings, descriptions of agency procedures, statements explaining and justifying rules, and the like. A better measure of regulation growth is expansion of the *Code of Federal Regulations*. This bulky codification of agency rules increased in size by 40% between 1970 and 1978, which reflects substantial but less than spectacular growth. Even this cannot be taken as an indication that economic activity was 40% more controlled at the end of the period examined. Such a determination must depend on such matters as the nature and total number of regulations in place, the numbers of persons and companies within their jurisdiction, and the vigor and skill with which they were enforced.

Still, one can glean a useful impression of the present-day regulatory state from a longitudinal view of the *Federal Register*. The fluctuations of the total pages published annually in it since 1936 are graphically displayed in Figure 1. Along about 1970, or midway in the 20th centuries third surge in regulatory legislation, a major permanent expansion of the *Federal Register* occurred. Fluctuations continued, the number of pages in the Register were cutback under the Reagan administration, but it does not revert to anything approaching its pre–third surge size. This is what should be expected because ultimately it is legislation that drives the regulatory state, not agency preferences or election returns.

Further comprehension of the dimensions of the regulatory state can be obtained from other statistical sources. Both expenditures for national regulatory agencies and their number of personnel have grown substantially since 1970. Budgetary outlays (in 1982 dollars) for all regulatory agencies increased from $3.4 billion in 1970 to an estimated $9.1 billion in 1992, or by about threefold. This was considerably less than 1% of the national budget. Personnel employed by regulatory agencies grew in numbers from 71 thousand in 1970 to 122 thousand in 1992 (see Table 3). Three quarters of them are employed by agencies engaged in social regulation.

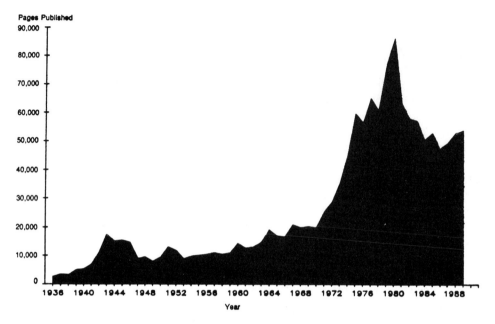

Figure 1. *Federal Register* analysis pages published, 1936–1989.
Source: Regulatory Program of the United States, 1991.

Collectively regulatory personnel account for around 4% of the national government's civilian employees. Nor are all of them involved in writing regulations, as is sometimes asserted. On the basis of these figures, regulation does not loom large within the government. If all of the regulatory agencies and their programs were abolished, this would have a negligible effect on the reduction of either the national budget (or the deficit) or the bureaucracy.

Table 3. A Measure of Regulatory Growth

	Staffing of federal regulatory agencies (fiscal years, full-time–equivalent employees)					
	1970	1975	1980	1985	1991	1992[a]
Social regulation	53,190	80,632	95,412	79,146	91,334	92,331
Consumer safety, health	41,463	51,287	55,176	45,063	52,340	52,552
Job safety, workplace	6,486	12,323	17,810	14,201	13,615	13,622
Energy	703	5,045	5,433	3,953	3,469	3,541
Environment	4,538	11,977	16,993	15,929	21,910	22,616
Economic regulation	18,043	22,689	26,258	22,817	28,670	30,075
Banking and finance	5,759	7,407	9,524	8,864	13,419	13,586
Other businesses	12,284	15,282	16,734	13,953	15,251	16,409
Total	71,233	103,321	121,670	101,953	120,004	122,406

[a]Based on Bush budget proposal.
Source: Washington University Center for the Study of American Business.

Arguably, the most important dimension of the regulatory state is its impact on society and the economy. Are people better off because of regulatory programs? Are workers more safe, consumers healthier and better informed, the environment cleaner and more aesthetically pleasing as a consequence of regulatory activity. What impact does regulation have on investment, productivity, and growth in the economy? What segments of the population benefit, and benefit the most, from regulatory programs? These are good questions for which satisfactory answers—that is, answers that are reasonably precise and broadly convincing—are in very short supply.

Efforts are occasionally made to estimate the costs and benefits of regulatory programs in financial terms. Thus the Office of Information and Regulatory Affairs (part of the Office of Management and Budget) estimated that costs of regulation on the economy in 1990 were somewhere in the $430 to $562 billion range (Victor, 1992). Numbers such as these, which are typically based on heroic assumptions, are of decidedly questionable value. But, assuming these are ballpark figures, what of the benefits of regulation? These are even more difficult to estimate and more often than not they are ignored. At this point, about all that can be reasonably said is that regulatory programs collectively are costly. They also carry with them many benefits. Whether they are worth the cost is as much or more a political than an economic judgment.

However one chooses to measure the size or extent of the regulatory state, there can be no doubt that it has expanded greatly during the second half of the 20th century. But it is also true that the increased volume of regulation that this entails has been imposed on a much larger, more diverse, more complex economy. If much private economic activity has been subjected to some sort of regulation, much opportunity also remains for the exercise of private economic discretion. How much is a fine topic for conjecture and debate and for systematic and rigorous inquiry.

IV. REGULATORY PROBLEMS

The implementation of regulatory programs has generated a substantial variety and volume of problems, complaints, and alleged failures. Everyone seems to have a favorite regulatory anecdote or two involving the misuse, abuse, nonuse, or overuse of regulatory power. Whether one finds a particular regulatory program to be necessary and effective likely depends on several matters—the nature and purposes of the program, the skill and zeal with which it is administered, the economic interests and ideological perspective of the person making judgment, and so on. Very few, if any, persons would say that all regulatory programs are either necessary, desirable, or reasonably well administered. So, too, would few persons consider economic regulation generally unnecessary and inappropriate. (Some of the more devout followers of the "Chicago school of economics" do seem to approach this position.) However, both the general supporters and general critics cite a variety of problems (or shortcomings, or failures) in the conduct of regulatory programs. In this section, some of these problems are surveyed in order to provide a perspective on regulatory performance as well as background for the next section on regulatory reform. None of the problems cited is relevant to all regulatory agencies or programs, nor are all relevant to a particular program or agency. Such is the case with generalizations. Some of the problems cited are more economical, others are either more political or administrative in nature.

Rate or price regulation is said to distort the operation of the market and to interfere with prices as the allocators of resources. Inefficiency is the result. Thus it was argued that the regulation of commercial airline rates by the Civil Aeronautics Board (CAB) kept passenger rates too high, thereby discouraging air travel, while stimulating competition among the airlines on the basis of frequency of flights, seating arrangements, fancy meals, and other "frills." Viewed from a market perspective, the consequence was misallocation of resources. In the instance of the regulation of the field price of natural gas by the Federal Power Commission (the forerunner of the Federal Energy Regulatory Commission), it was contended by opponents that prices were held too low, consequently encouraging excess consumption of gas while discouraging exploration and development of additional supplies. Gas shortages developed in the 1970's as a result. Not everyone, of course, agreed with this viewpoint. Generally, with the exception of public utilities, critics of rate and price regulation view reliance on the market as the best way of determining prices and bringing supply and demand into balance.

Whether intentionally or not, regulation on occasion may cause a reduction in competition. This is typically the case when there is limitation of entry of firms into an industry or persons into an occupation or profession. Examples include control of banking entry by the Office of Comptroller of the Currency and others and radio and television broadcast entry by the Federal Communications Commission. Price competition in the shipping industry has been dulled by the Federal Maritime Commission's regulation of foreign shipping rates. The Robinson-Patman Act (1936) was intended to lessen price competition, albeit in the guise of preventing price discrimination, between small businesses and their larger competitors (chain stores, discount houses, and so on) for the benefit of the former. Those who prefer competition tend to find such regulation objectionable. They reject the contention that regulation is needed to prevent "excessive competition." If undesirable competitive practices like "predatory pricing" should occur, these they say should be handled by such means as antitrust prosecution or private judicial action.

A reduction or delay in scientific and technological progress is another failing that can result from regulation. There have long been complaints that the licensing of new drugs by the Food and Drug Administration, under the requirement that they be proven safe and effective, has slowed the introduction of new drugs into the market (Asch, 1988; Peltzman, 1973). The Interstate Commerce Commission (ICC) was castigated for delaying the introduction of "big john" cars for grain transportation and "piggyback" cars for hauling truck trailers by the railroads. Concerned about the uncertainty and other problems such cars might cause in the railroad industry, the ICC delayed approving their use for several years (Kohlmeier, 1969).

A common complaint during the past couple of decades has been that many regulations, although perhaps of some societal benefit, entail costs that exceed their benefits. In short, regulations are sometimes characterized by an unfavorable cost/benefit ratio. It is commonplace to encounter industry groups and their supporters arguing that an air or water pollution control standard fashioned by the Environmental Protection Agency is defective because its costs (e.g., direct administrative costs, industry costs of compliance) will exceed the value of its benefits (e.g., reduced health hazards, aesthetic values). This assumes, of course, that the various costs and benefits or a regulation or program can be quantified with reasonable accuracy. Economists tend to be more confident of this then do environmentalists. In 1980, the U.S. Supreme Court held that a new and more stringent standard for benzene discharges set by the Occupational Safety and Health Administration exceeded its legal authority because the agency did not demonstrate that its benefits justified the additional costs that would be imposed on industry. The underlying contention of the cost/benefit argument is that if the costs of a regulation or regulatory program exceed its benefits, there is a net reduction in social welfare and, on this basis, the regulation should be eliminated. Economic efficiency is the underlying value here. An examination of the literature will indicate that far more attention has been paid to the costs than the benefits of regulation in such assessments. This in part reflects the ideological proclivities and economic interests of those involved.

Moving now to more political or administrative problems, a familiar feature of regulatory lore has been the contention that regulatory agencies are often "captured" by the groups they are to regulate, and regulation then becomes a means for promoting group interests rather than protecting the public interest. Or, to put it differently, the regulated control the regulators. Favorite examples include the "capture" of the ICC, the CAB, and the Federal Maritime Commission by the railroads, airlines, and shipping companies, respectively. Some would say that this happens because as agencies move through their life cycle (gestation, youth, maturity, and old age), they lose their vigor and more or less fall naturally into the clutches of the regulated industries that have intense and concentrated interests in regulation, whereas the interests of the public are limited and diffuse. There are also other explanations. Typically, however, one finds that neither the meaning of capture nor the process by which it is accomplished is very well or convincingly explained. And further, if the CAB and the ICC were the captives as alleged of the airlines and the railroads, why did these two agencies take initiatives in deregulation in the later 1970s that were strongly opposed by the regulated industries? If agencies appear to be too responsive to the interests of those they regulate, this is much more likely to be a function of their statutory mandates. Whether "captured" or not, it may well be that some agencies are too responsive to those whom they regulate, at least in the view of some persons and groups. But then they may be pushed in this direction by their authorizing statues, and by the exercise of official initiative and discretion.

Regulatory agencies are sometime assigned competing or overlapping jurisdictions, which can produce conflict or a lack of coordinations in their operations. Thus, railroad regulation may be implemented without sufficient concern for the impact that it may have on competing forms of transportation. This has given rise to recommendations that the various national transportation regulatory agencies be merged into a single agency (Ash Council, 1971). The Federal Reserve Board, Office of Comptroller of the Currency, Federal Deposit Insurance Corporation, and state banking agencies all share jurisdiction over banks. To avoid the requirements or disabilities of national policy, banks sometimes shift from national to state charters. Other problems also arise. Overlapping jurisdiction does not necessarily yield conflict or lack of coordination, however. In the area of antitrust, the Antitrust Division and the Federal Trade Commission have amicably shared the field for decades.

Economic regulation in the 20th century is predominantly administrative regulation. Judicial regulation, the enforcement of regulatory legislation primarily through court proceedings, has gone by the boards except in a few areas such as antitrust, where the courts still are important in applying and interpreting the law. Agencies often operate under broad statutory mandates that confer substantial discretion, and provide little explicit instruction on priorities, but impose many procedural requirements. As a consequence of these and other conditions, administrative regulation is sometimes characterized by such problems as slowness and delay in the completion of proceedings, cumbersome and complex procedures, inadequate information (as on the costs and benefits of proposed actions), and a lack of qualified personnel. Here I will focus on the issue of delay. A study by the Senate Committee on Governmental Affairs (1977b) reported that administrative agency proceedings averaged more than 19 months for licensing, 21 months for rate making, and 36 months for enforcement actions. In a survey for the committee of more than 1000 lawyers who practiced before eight major regulatory commissions, "undue delay" was most frequently cited as a major problem of federal regulation. The causes of delay include the volume of cases, complex procedural requirements, poor agency leadership and management, uncertainty, and efforts by affected private parties to put off final agency action. Slowness and delay are not confined to administrative regulation; it also appears in regulation involving the courts. A classic illustration involves the government's antitrust suit against the IBM Corporation, filed in January 1969, on the last day of the Johnson administration; in January of 1982, the case was still in the trial stage when the government decided to dismiss it on the ground that it was "without merit."

Finally, agencies are often accused of making unwise, ill-considered, or "bad" decisions. Such judgments may issue from persons who find particular agency actions to be inconvenient, inexpedient, or otherwise counter to their interests. In other instances, such judgments may be more impartial and based on the legal or substantive merits of the actions or due consideration of their societal effects. It would, for example, seem difficult to accuse a person of partiality for regarding the Occupational Safety and Health Administration rule prohibiting the use of ice in drinking water in workplaces as unnecessary, dumb, or something of that sort. The rule was a carryover from an earlier era, when there was a fear that the ice used to cool drinking water might be cut from polluted ponds. OSHA did repeal the rule (which was one of the consensus standards adopted soon after the agency was established) along with several hundred others in 1978.

V. REGULATORY REFORM

The reform urge is endemic in the American political system, and regulation has been the target of its full share of reform proposals and efforts. Several major attempts at reform have centered on the independent regulatory commissions. These were based on studies by the President's Committee on Administrative Management (1937), which is famous for its depiction of the regulatory commissions as "a 'headless fourth branch' of the Government, a haphazard deposit of irresponsible agencies and uncoordinated powers"; the Attorney General's Committee on Administrative Management; the two Hoover Commissions (1949, 1955), headed by ex-President Herbert Hoover; James M. Landis's Report on Regulatory Agencies to the President-Elect (1960); and the President's Advisory Council on Executive Organization (1971). Most of these studies recommended changes in regulatory commission organization and procedures. Little basic change in the commissions followed from these reports because of a lack of responsiveness by Congress to executive proposals for commission reform. Frequently referred to as "arms of Congress," the commissions are viewed by members (especially liberal Democrats) with affection and proprietary instincts. Reformers in recent decades have found other targets.

The 1970s were witness to a substantial widening of both the interest in and scope of regulatory reform. Presidents Gerald Ford and Jimmy Carter gave substantial and continuing interest to regulatory reform, popular interest in reform expanded, and many of the members of Congress, both liberal and conservative, came to manifest strong interest (beyond the ever-present rhetoric) in the operation and improvement of regulatory processes and policies. Collectively, all of this can fairly be described as a regulatory reform movement. It was not, however, a monolithic phenomenon. Rather reformers came in various patterns and hues. Following the lead of Professor David Welborn (1977), three orientations toward regulatory reform—traditionalist, populist, and restrictivist—can be identified and limned.

The *traditionalist* orientation long dominated thinking about economic regulation, viewing it for the most part as basically sound and necessary to control the exercise of private economic power. The basic structural change advocated by those with a traditionalist orientation was stronger presidential control and leadership of the regulatory agencies to overcome the diversity and lack of coordination in their activities. This would be done by shaping the general outlines of policy rather than by deep intervention in the details of policy making. Beyond that only limited changes were seen as necessary to make the regulatory system fully sound and effective. These included such actions as larger budgets, better personnel improved procedures, clarification of statutory authority, and better definitions of standards and improved internal agency organization and management. In a way, their view was that the problems of regulation can be corrected by more and better regulation.

Those with the *populist* orientation also accepted the necessity of economic regulation. They viewed corporate power with considerable suspicion and saw a need for more regulation to ensure that governmental power dominated over corporate power. Presently, however, their view was that, at the least, business had been able to use its political power to cause regulatory programs to be more responsive to business interests than to those of the public. To put it another way, regulation had failed because it did not adequately benefit the public; the cause of this failure was essentially political.

Persons who held the populist orientation believed that regulatory reform should be designed to ensure the existence of "pervasive and direct democracy in governmental and economic affairs" (Lazarus, 1974). There were two general routes to this goal. One was to reduce the influence of regulated interests by such means as limitations on *ex parte* contracts with agencies, strong conflict of interests rules, and restrictions on the employment of officials by regulated companies. The other route was to enhance the influence of the public in agency proceedings. This be done by such means as open meetings ("sunshine") requirements, creation of offices of consumer or public counsel within agencies, subsidization of public participation in agency proceedings, and permitting outside groups to petition agencies for regulatory action.

Persons with a *restrictivist* orientation had a basic dislike for administrative regulation, viewing much of it as unnecessary or a burdensome interference with the operation of the market. Business people, economists, and conservative were numerous in this category. Business people tended to view regulation as bothersome and as a limitation on profits. Economists saw it as something that more often than not restricted rather than promoted competition and interfered with the efficient allocation of resources. The restrictivists had several preferred reforms. One was the elimination of regulations that restrict competition, together with more reliance on antitrust action to prevent any misuse of economic power (Commission on Law and the Economy, 1979). Another was in the reliance on market or economic incentives (e.g., fees or taxes) rather than administrative regulation, which was stigmatized as "command and control" regulation, as in the area of environmental protection (Schultze, 1975). A third was to make more extensive use of the techniques of economic analysis, such as cost effectiveness and cost/benefit analysis, in making decisions on economic regulatory issues and in appraising the consequences of regulatory programs.

A general view of the adherents of these three regulatory orientations is conveyed by Welborn (1977):

> Each of the three major orientations to questions about regulation are represented in the regulatory reform process, including in the Congress. The strongest reflection of the traditionalist orientation is in the agencies themselves and among the regulated and their representatives. The restrictivist orientation is reflected by economists generally and by those institutions which they populate. In the government, these include the Council of Economic Advisers and the Council on Wage and Price Stability. It is also reflected in

significant ways in places such as the Antitrust Division of the Department of Justice, the Department of Transportation and the Federal Trade Commission . . . it [also] appeared in potent form at the presidential level during past years. The populist orientation, of course, is reflected in the main by public interest organizations such as those comprising the Nader group and Common Cause.

The regulatory reform movement achieved some notable successes in the late 1970s and early 1980s. Most dramatic, perhaps, was the enactment of a number of deregulatory statutes (see Table 4). Many persons come to believe, without accepting the whole philosophy of the restrictivists, that regulation could be made less burdensome if more reliance was placed on self-interest and competition for the control of economic activity.

The quest for deregulation was given major impetus by President Ford, who made deregulation a major goal of his short-lived administration, and who put it on the national policy agenda. Initially, it was easy to be somewhat cynical about deregulation and its prospects because it seemed to lack a convincing rationale. For not a few deregulation appeared to mean "get rid of the regulatory programs that I don't like but keep those that I favor." However, as deregulation narrowed in on the regulated industries, particularly transportation and finance, where regulation often involved limitations on competition, the deregulation campaign

Table 4. Deregulation Legislation

Railroad Revitalization and Regulatory Reform Act (1976). Railroads were permitted to set maximum rates at any level they chose when competition existed. Moreover, rates could be raised or lowered by 7 percent in either direction as long as they were not "predatory" and the railroad did not dominate the market involved. Rates could not be ruled too low by the ICC if they covered the variable costs of providing service.

Airline Deregulation Act (1978). This law provided for the phasing out of airline economic regulation. CAB authority over domestic airline routes ended in 1981 and its power over domestic rates, faires, mergers, and acquisitions expired in 1982. The CAB was abolished on January 1, 1985. (Safety regulation by the Federal Aviation agency continues.)

Staggers Rail Act (1978). The railroads were given yet greater freedom to raise and lower rates, and it became easier for them to discontinue unprofitable routes. Most of the authority railroads had to use rate bureaus to set rates jointly was eliminated.

Motor Carrier Reform Act (1980). Truckers were accorded greater flexibility in setting rates. It was made easier for new companies to enter the industry and terminated some of the industry's antitrust immunity in making rate arguments. Some restriction on trucking route authorizations and "piggyback" freight traffic were removed. Restrictions on hauling food were loosened.

Depository Institutions Deregulation Act (1980). This act authorized the removal of interest rate ceiling on savings and loan associations and banks. S&L's were permitted to issue credit cards, accept checking accounts, and become more like commercial banks. They were also given more freedom in making investments.

Garn-St Germain Depository Institutions Act (1982). The range of permissible investments or loads for S&L's was further expanded and they were accorded more freedom to compete with banks, which were also freed from some restrictions. For example, both were permitted to provide interest bearing NOW accounts and money market demand accounts.

Bus Regulatory Reform Act (1982). Applying to intercity buses, this legislation increased freedom of entry for new companies and eased the expansion or abandonment of services by existing companies. Although bus companies were given greater freedom to raise and lower rates, their ability to set rates jointly was restricted.

gained momentum. Economists and others had long been critical of many aspects of these programs. In their writings and testimonies before congressional committees, they provided both a justification for deregulation and an alternative to regulation for satisfactory industry control, particularly for the transportation area (Brown, 1989; Derthick and Quirk, 1985). Some of these programs were also criticized as contributing to inflation, which was a major public issue in the late 1970s.

The deregulatory campaigned pulled support from several sources—the Ford and Carter administrations, as already noted; many economists and others with a restrictivist orientation; officials at the ICC and CAB; consumer and public interest groups; and, in time, substantial majorities in Congress. Transportation regulatory programs, which had flowered during the New Deal years, or earlier in the case of the railroads, reflected the notion that rate controls and entry limitations were appropriate governmental responses to industry problems. Stringent control of the practices of financial institutions had long been thought as necessary to ensure their soundness and protect the interests of depositors. By the later 1970s, however, such regulatory philosophical had come under sharp assault and deregulation took on the aura of an idea whose time had come. As Wilson (1980) has suggested, ideas as well as interests can have important effects on the course of regulatory policy.

The regulatory reform movement also produced a number of other positive legislative responses. In line with the populist orientation, the Government in the Sunshine Act (1976) required plural-headed boards, commissions, and agencies to conduct their business in open public proceedings unless a majority of the members decided it would not be in the public interest and other requirements were met. The actual effect of this law is unclear (Heffron and Feeley, 1983). Some agencies, such as the Federal Trade Commission, were authorized to finance public participation in their rule-making proceedings in order to enhance fairness and information flow. New legislation that accorded with the traditionalist orientation included the Regulatory Flexibility Act and the Paperwork Reduction Act. Under the Regulatory Flexibility Act, agencies are supposed to give explicit consideration to the economic and paperwork impact of new rules on small businesses. The Paperwork Reduction Act, which grew out of a recommendation of the Commission on Federal Paperwork and was enthusiastically supported by the Carter administration, created an Office of Information and Regulatory Affairs (OIRA) in the Office of Management and Budget (OMB). OIRA was directed to establish a policy for federal statistical activities, to review and approve all agency requests for information from private sources, and to reduce the paperwork burden imposed by the government. Other non-legislative changes in line with the traditionalist orientation included increased, if episodic, congressional oversight of regulatory agencies, agency rationalization of enforcement programs, and changes designed to strengthen regulatory agency management.

Another important facet of regulatory reform was the development of stronger and more intensive presidential supervision of executive branch regulatory agencies. (The independent regulatory commissions, because of their peculiar legal position, have been exempted from this activity.) Beginning with the Nixon administration's Quality-of-Life review in the early 1970s, every president has sought to exercise greater control over regulatory agency rule making (Eads and Fix, 1984; Gerston et al., 1988). Efforts of this sort reached a climax in the Reagan administration.

In February 1981, President Reagan issued Executive Order 12291 providing for the review of proposed regulations. Although the order drew on the experiences of previous administrations, notably that of the Carter administration, it created a regulatory review process that much exceeded its predecessors in scope, stringency, and formality. Executive Order 12291 specified that all proposed rules issued by executive branch regulatory agencies had to be accompanied by a regulatory impact analysis (RIA) that assessed their estimated costs and expected benefits, including effects that oculd not be monetarily valued, unless such calculations were prohibited by law, as they were in some instances. Major regulations were defined as those which would impose annual costs of $100 million or more on the economy, which would lead to major cost or price increases, or which would have "significant adverse effects on competition, investment, productivity, innovation, or the ability of U.S.-based enterprises in domestic or export markets." OMB (in actuality OIRA) was authorized to supervise the evaluation process, to make final decisions on what were major rules, and to hold up the publication of proposed rules or the issuance of final rules until agency-OMB differences were resolved. OMB could also exempt major rules from review. The executive order further stated that rules could be issued only if their estimated benefits exceeded their estimated costs. If more than one alternative was available, the least costly one had to be used. Agencies bore the burden of proof that these standards were met. Cost/benefit analysis can yield useful information on the possible consequences of proposed rules. As provided in Executive Order 12291, however, cost/benefit analysis became a decision rule—a means for determining whether proposed regulations could be issued.

To the extent that it contributed to an improved rule-making process and better-designed regulations, the purpose of Executive Order 12291 was reform. The real concern of the Reagan administration, however, was not regulatory reform but regulatory relief; that is, reduction in the volume of regulatory activity, including the making of rules, and its impact on the economy. The executive order was part of a broader effort to cutback on regulation and to deregulate. Other administration actions included appointing persons with antiregulatory philosophies to agency leadership positions and reducing agencies' funding and personnel levels. Through its various efforts the Reagan administration did succeed in eliminating some regulations and in slowing down the promulgation of new regulations as Table 3 indicates. However, it did not have much success in the area of legislative deregulation.

Somewhere during the Reagan administration, the regulatory reform movement lost its way. Scores of bills intended to overhaul federal regulatory procedures were introduced in Congress during the late 1970s and early 1980s and the enactment of such legislation seemed a certainty. Only the "details" remained to be decided, but these can be of much importance. The Carter administration and some members of Congress were at loggerheads over the issue of legislative veto of proposed rules, for instance. The Reagan administration favored legislation along the lines of its Executive Order 12291, but there was considerable congressional opposition to this, particularly in the House. By early 1983, however, interest in regulatory reform had waned and the issue dropped off of the policy agenda.

The Bush administration continued in place the supervisory system created by Executive Orders 12291 and 12498. The latter executive order, issued by President Reagan in early 1985, required executive branch regulatory agencies to send their annual regulatory programs to OMB for approval and for inclusion in the administration's regulatory program (McGarity, 1991). President Bush added the Council on Competitiveness to the executive armamentarium. A cabinet-level interagency group, the Council was chaired by the vice president. Operating mostly through its staff, the Council acted to resolve differences between OIRA and the regulatory agencies. Its concern was customarily to reduce the stringency and compliance costs of proposed regulations in order to further economic development. The Council was abolished by the Clinton administration early in 1993.

VI. CONCLUSIONS

The regulatory state has weathered both the deregulation movement and the assaults of the Reagan administration, although its scope was pruned a bit and the output of regulations was somewhat reduced. Under the Bush administration, however, regulatory activity began to regain momentum. New regulatory statutes were enacted—the Clean Air Act of 1990, Americans with Disabilities Act, Oil Pollution Act, Nutrition Labeling and Education Act, and more. Some of the regulatory agencies—e.g., the Federal Trade Commission, Environmental Protection Agency, and Food and Drug Administration—became more active. These developments occurred despite the antiregulatory rhetoric emanating from President Bush and various members of his administration. Although Bush's administration attempted to counteract the rise in regulation, notably through a moratorium on new regulations, its efforts were first distracted by the 1992 presidential election campaign and then terminated when the administration suffered election defeat. The new Clinton administration portended a more favorable environment for regulatory activity.

For the foreseeable future, however, regulatory agencies will likely limp along on restricted resources that enable them to deal with only a portion of the matters within their jurisdiction. This has forever been the plight of regulatory reasons. Their activity and impact have typically been restrained through resource limitations. Thus, for instance, the EPA has not since 1981 received specific funding to enforce the Noise Control Act; its enforcement of the Safe Drinking Water Act also suffers from limited resources. Again, the Occupational Safety and Health Administration has resources sufficient to inspect annually only a minuscule percentage of the workplaces under its jurisdiction. Generally speaking, Congress has been more generous in supplying regulatory agencies with legal authority and more inclined to demand action from them than it has been forthcoming with resources and political support. Thus is the impact of regulatory programs tempered.

Historically the regulatory process in the United States has been predominantly adversarial in style. Kelman (1981) attributes this to the self-assertive nature of American values. Rival parties in interest—environmentalists and industrialists, labor unions and management, consumer groups and food processors—strongly, sometimes bitterly, contest to influence the decisions of regulatory officials. Each side stakes out its position and makes the strongest case possible for its point of view, leaving it to the agency to chose from among them. Administrative procedure supports this style. As Kelman (1981) notes

> The history of administrative procedure in the United States is one of imposition of adversary procedures on government agencies, conceived as a way to deal with objections to the very legitimacy of administrative decision making.

Such procedural requirements helped supply bureaucrats with the legitimacy that might have been gained, but was not, from being elected by the people or from acting in judicial fashion. The Administrative Procedure Act and other statutes ensure that regulatory agencies operate along adversarial lines.

In recent years, agencies have made some attempts to utilize more accommodationist proceedings. The EPA, for instance, has made some use of regulatory negotiation to develop regulations to implement some portions of the Clean Air Act of 1990. Thus, oil companies, clean-fuel manufacturers, environmental and consumer groups, automobile manufacturers, and state government officials negotiated a program to provide cleaner-burning gasoline to smog-ridden cities by 1995. Moreover, they agreed not to lobby against regulations implementing the program nor to challenge them in the courts (Weisskopf, 1991). The use of regulatory negotiation was both encouraged and formalized in 1990 when Congress adopted the Negotiated Rulemaking Act. Notwithstanding such developments, adversarial action will undoubtedly continue as the most common mode of administrative regulatory policy development.

Finally, some form of systematic presidential supervision of the regulatory agencies will continue beyond the Bush administration. This has become routinized, an expected and accepted presidential activity, if not one that is fully institutionalized. Regulation has become too important in scope and impact on the economy for the president largely to ignore, as it was before 1970. An important question involves the form such supervision should embody. Should it continue to involve detailed executive office intervention in rule-making proceedings, mostly with the intent of lessening the stringency or impact of regulations? I am unaware of any instances between 1970 and 1992 when presidential intervention in the regulatory process was intended to strengthen a proposed regulation, even during the Carter administration when executive officials often spoke of the need to improve the quality of regulations. If executive intervention is merely a means for attempting to impose a conservative ideology on the agencies, whatever the content of legislatively prescribed policy, or an opportunity for those who have lost out at the legislative and agency stages of the policy process to recoup their losses, then executive supervision loses much of its moral force and serves up a skewed vision of the public interest. Rather than detailed intervention, presidential action to provide tone and general policy direction to regulatory agencies, and the selection of responsive and competent agency leader, would appear a more appropriate strategy of presidential influence.

REFERENCES

Asch, P. (1988). *Consumer Safety Regulation*. Oxford University Press, New York.

Ash Council (The President's Advisory Council on Executive Organization) (1971). *A New Regulatory Framework*. U.S. Government Printing Office, Washington, DC.

Bernstein, M. (1955). *Regulating Business by Independent Commission*. Princeton University Press, Princeton, NJ.

Breyer, S. (1982). *Regulation and Its Reform*. Harvard University Press, Cambridge, MA.

Brown, A. (1989). *The Politics of Airline Deregulation*. University of Tennessee Press, Knoxville.

Commission on Law and the Economy (1979). *Federal Regulation: Roads to Reform*. American Bar Association, Washington, DC.

Derthick, M., and Quirk, P. J. (1985). *The Politics of Deregulation*. Brookings Institution, Washington, DC.

Eads, G. C., and Fix, M. (1984). *Relief or Reform? Reagan's Regulatory Dilemma*. Urban Institute Press, Washington, DC.

Gerston, L. N., Fraleigh, C., and Schwab, R. (1988). *The Deregulated Society*. Brooks/Cole, Pacific Grove, CA.

Handlin, O., and Handlin, M. F. (1947). *Commonwealth: A Study of the Role of Government in the American Economy: Massachusetts, 1774–1861*. New York University Press, New York.

Hartz, L. (1948). *Economic Policy and Democratic Thought: Pennsylvania 1776–1780*. Harvard University Press, Cambridge, MA.

Heffron, F., and McFeeley, N. (1983). *The Administrative Regulatory Process*. Longman, New York.

Kelman, S. (1981). *Regulating America, Regulating Sweden*. MIT Press, Cambridge, MA.

Kneese, A. V., and Schultze, C. L. (1975). *Pollution, Prices, and Public Policy*. Brookings Institution, Washington, DC.

Kohlmeier, L. (1969). *The Regulators*. Harper & Row, New York.

Lazarus, S. (1974). *The Genteel Populists*. Holt, Rinehart and Winston, New York.

Litan, R. E., and Nordhaus, W. S. (1983). *Reforming Federal Regulation*. Yale University Press, New Haven, CT.

Lowi, T. J. (1979). *The End of Liberalism*. Norton, New York.

McGarity, T. O. (1991). *Reinventing Rationality: The Role of Regulatory Analysis in the Federal Bureaucracy*. Cambridge University Press, New York.

Musolf, L. D. (1965). *Government and the Economy*. Scott, Foresman, Chicago.

Peltzman, S. (1973). An evaluation of consumer protection legislation: The 1962 drug amendments. *Journal of Political Economy* 81: 1067.

Primm, J. N. (1954). *Economic Policy in the Development of a Western State: Missouri 1820–1860.* Harvard University Press, Cambridge, MA.

Senate Committee on Governmental Affairs (1977a). *The Regulatory Appointments Process.* 85th Cong., 1st Sess. U.S. Government Printing Office, Washington, DC.

—— (1977b). *Delay in the Regulatory Process.* 95th Cong., 1st Sess. U.S. Government Printing Office, Washington, DC.

Schultze, C. (1977). *Public Use of Private Interest.* Brookings Institution, Washington, DC.

Shepard, W. G., and Wilcox, C. (1979). *Public Policies Toward Business.* Richard D. Irwin, Homewood, IL.

Siskind, F. B., and Shor, G. M. (1980). Regulations that get public approval. *Houston Chronicle*, August 21, 1980.

Steiner, G. A. (1953). *Government's Role in Economic Life.* McGraw-Hill, New York.

Stigler, G. J. (1971). The Theory of Economic Regulation. *Bell Journal of Economics and Management Science*, vol. 2.

Victor, K. (1992). Tale of the Red Tape. *National Journal*, vol. 24, March 21, pp. 684–687.

Weisskopf, M. (1991). An Unlikely Alliance on Cleaner Air. *Washington Post National Weekly*, Aug. 26–Sept. 1, p. 32.

Welborn, D. M. (1977). Taking stock of regulatory reform. Paper presented at the 1977 Annual Meeting of the American Political Science Association, Washington, DC.

Wilson, J. Q. (1980). *The Politics of Regulation.* Basic Books, New York.

18
Labor Policy

Charles Bulmer and John Carmichael
University of Alabama, Birmingham, Alabama

I. BACKGROUND

Government policy in support of the labor movement in the United States was slow to develop. In its modern form, government promotion of organized labor really began in 1935 with the passage by Congress of the National Labor Relations Act (Wagner Act). This act as amended by the Taft-Hartley Act in 1947 and the Landrum-Griffin Act in 1959 constitutes major legislation affecting labor.

The right of workers to join together in unions was recognized in the United States rather early. In 1842, a significant decision by the Supreme Court of Massachusetts, *Commonwealth v. Hunt*, declared that labor unions were not illegal per se; it was only when labor unions engaged in unlawful activity that their actions were proscribed. Although this was a decision by a single state court, it was generally accepted doctrine throughout the United States. Nevertheless, activities of labor organizations were hindered by such devices as civil suits against their leaders for damages, and in the latter part of the 19th century by the labor injunction. This latter weapon was most effective and was used with increasing frequency in the 20th century, attaining perhaps its most widespread use in the 1920s.

In 1890, the Sherman Act was passed by Congress. Aimed at controlling the growth of business trusts, the act was unclear with respect to its possible use against labor unions. The act declared that any combination or trust in restraint of trade was illegal. Certainly the intent of the drafters of the legislation was not to include labor unions in the prohibition; however, in 1908, in the "Danbury Hatters' Case," Loewe v. Lawlor, the U.S. Supreme Court ruled that a labor union did fall within the intent of the Act.

In 1914, Congress passed the Clayton Act, a comprehensive set of amendments to the Sherman Act. This legislation attempted to clarify some of the ambiguities of the Sherman Act, mainly by being more specific. With respect to labor, it purported to exempt unions from antitrust liability and attempted to circumscribe the situations in which injunctions could be used against labor unions. This endeavor was not successful; labor unions were the object of efforts by the federal courts, particularly in the 1920s, to limit their actions. Again, in 1932, Congress attempted to reduce the use of the injunction by, among other things, providing that the injunction could not be employed to prevent a strike by unions. This was the Norris–La Guardia Act, which also outlawed the "yellow-dog contract" whereby a worker agreed, as a condition of employment, not to join a union.

In 1933, during the first year of the Roosevelt administration, the National Industrial Recovery Act (NIRA) became law. Aimed mainly at bolstering business at a time of a nation-wide depression by encouraging business to establish "codes of fair competition," this legislation also contained Section 7(a), where guaranteed workers the right to join labor unions and to engage in collective bargaining with management. Also, the National Industrial Recovery Act provided that no employee could be required to join a company union as a condition of employment.

Nevertheless, company unions, dominated by management, grew rapidly in the 1930s and reflected an attempt by employers to thwart the growth of employee unions after the enactment of Section 7(a) of the National Industrial Recovery Act. Company unions increased in number, in 1933, by almost 200%. An estimated 70% of all employer-promoted unions in existence when the National Labor Relations Act (1935) was passed were formed after the enactment of Section 7(a) of the National Industrial Recovery Act.

Following passage of the National Industrial Recovery Act, President Roosevelt, in August 1933 by executive order, created the National Labor Board to handle labor disputes threatening suspension of work. This was done without express legislative authority. Although this was not the first governmentally sponsored labor board to mediate labor disputes, it marked the first time such a board had been created during a period of peace with application industrywide. (In 1918, a National War Labor Board was created and was in operation for 16 months. The Transportation Act of 1920 created a Railroad Labor Board consisting of representative of labor, industry, and the public. It had no enforcement powers but relied on public opinion to encourage compliance with its decisions. Its composition was similar to that of the Labor Board created in 1933. Railway workers had been the object of legislation specifically affecting them as early as 1916 when Congress, in the Adamson Act, limited their employment to an 8-hour day. Then in 1926, the Railway Labor Act created a U.S. Board of Mediation, whose purposes paralleled those of the Labor Board established in 1933.)

The National Labor Board (1933) were composed of three labor members, three employer representatives, and a seventh member, Senator Robert F. Wagner of New York, as chairman. (Senator Wagner was the author of the National Labor Relations Act of 1935.) The first task of the board was the handling of problems arising under Section 7(a) of the NIRA. The board, in a given case, attempted to determine the facts, define issues, and use its good offices to mediate a labor dispute.

If these attempts failed to resolve the dispute, measures to ensure compliance were available. The case could be referred to the Department of Justice and the Compliance Board of the National Recovery Administration. The Compliance Board might deprive an employer of the right to fly the "blue eagle" emblem, which would deny him or her the ability to sell goods to the government. The Department of Justice might prosecute, but the maximum fine for failure to comply was small ($500). The National Labor Board expired in 1934, but during its 1-year existence settled approximately 1000 threatened strikes.

After several months as chairman of the National Labor Board, Senator Wagner introduced in the Senate, in early 1934, a bill similar to the Wagner Act passed in 1935 and designed to create a new and more powerful Labor Board. Instead of passing this bill, however, Congress passed a joint resolution authorizing the president to establish one or more boards to investigate labor disputes under Section 7(a) of the National Industrial Recovery Act and conduct elections among employees to determine their representatives for collective bargaining.

Under authority of this resolution, President Roosevelt appointed the National Labor Relations Board, which commenced operation in July 1934 and continued in existence until August 1935, at which time the National Labor Relations Board, established by the National Labor Relations Act (Wagner Act), came into existence.

The first National Labor Relations Board (1934) served an important function in protecting labor's right to bargain collectively. It had the power to investigate and to order and conduct elections. The board had to depend largely on voluntary compliance, however, and lacked really effective enforcement powers. Perhaps one of the board's outstanding accomplishments was the building up of a group of informed and experienced personnel. The National Labor Relations Act of 1935 preserved the existing staff of the National Labor Relations Board and directed that it be transferred to the newly created board.

Senator Wagner of New York was largely responsible for passage of the Act in 1935, and it is interesting to note that support for this legislation by the Roosevelt administration initially was less than enthusiastic. Before the Senate passed the bill, President Roosevelt had, in fact, invited Senator Wagner to a White House conference where, in Roosevelt's presence, two senators tried to persuade Senator Wagner to withdraw the bill. Only after the Senate passed the bill, and before the House considered it, did Roosevelt endorse the bill.

II. DEVELOPMENT OF MODERN LABOR LAW

A. National Labor Relations Act (Wagner Act) (1935)

This new law restated the basic language of Section 7(a) of the National Industrial Recovery Act, which had just been declared unconstitutional in the Supreme Court decision, *Schechter* v. *United States* (1935). The Wagner Act, in Section 8, defined certain unfair labor practices on the part of employers. These included the refusal of an employer to bargain collectively with employees' representatives. The new Labor Board had stronger enforcement powers than its predecessor. If an employer refused to comply with an order of the National Labor Relations Board (NLRB), the act contained no criminal penalties but authorized the NLRB to file the record of the proceedings with a federal Circuit Court of Appeals. The court would decide, after hearing argument, whether, on the record, there was evidence to sustain the NLRB's order. If there was, the court would issue its own order affirming the NLRB's order.

Opposition to the Labor Board, and to the Wagner Act itself, was intense in some quarters. For example, a conservative organization, the National Lawyers Committee of the American Liberty League, asserted that the act was definitely unconstitutional:

Considering the Act in the light of our history, the established form of government and the decisions of our highest Court, we have no hesitancy in concluding that it is unconstitutional and that it constitutes a complete departure from our constitutional and traditional theories of government.

In addition to attacks on the constitutionality of the act, claims were made that the act was unfair. One criticism was directed at the fact that the Act forbade interference by employers with the employees' right to self-organization and collective bargaining but did not forbid coercion of employees by labor, nor, in fact, did the act define and prohibit any unfair practices by union organizers. The act was allegedly one sided and discriminated against the employer.

Without question, the Wagner Act was directed at strengthening labor's position relative to that of employers. (Not until the passage of the Taft-Hartley Act in 1947 were unfair labor practices on the part of unions defined and prohibited.) The argument of the proponents of the Act was that this was necessary to place labor in a more nearly equal position with employers for the purpose of bargaining.

Until the Supreme Court upheld the Wagner Act in 1937, a major part of the NLRB's efforts involved the fighting of injunction suits designed to prevent hearings. During this period of almost 2 years, nearly 100 injunction suits were filed to restrain the NLRB. Eventually, the Supreme Court ruled that the district courts did not have jurisdiction in the cases. Finally, the constitutionality of the act was upheld in a series of five cases decided by the Supreme Court i 1937, the most significant one being *National Labor Relations Board* v. *Jones and Laughlin Steel Corporation*. The NLRB determined that Jones and Laughlin had discharged some of its employees because of labor union activities, defined under Section 8 of the Wagner Act, as constituting an unfair labor practice. The company failed to comply with an order of the Board to reinstate the employees and was sued by the Board. The Supreme Court sustained the order of the Board and further declared that the Wagner Act was constitutional because cessation of operations by industrial strife at Jones and Laughlin would have a most serious effect on interstate commerce, on which the Act was based. This case had significance beyond its impact on labor relations because it was the first case declaring a major New Deal law constitutional; it was a turning point for the Supreme Court, which since that time has taken a much more liberal position on major issues affecting American society, including labor relations.

No more important labor act has been passed by Congress than the Wagner Act; two other acts of major importance to labor are the Taft-Hartley Act (1947) and the Landrum-Griffin Act (1959), both of which are amendments to the Wagner Act. It will be useful to consider the provisions of the Wagner Act in some greater detail.

Section 3 created the NLRB, originally composed of three members, subsequently increased to five, whose terms of office are for 5 years. Members are appointed by the president, must be confirmed by the Senate, and can be removed by the president only for "neglect of duty of malfeasance in office." This is consistent with the rule established by the Supreme Court in *Humphrey's Executor* v. *United States* (1953), wherein the Court declared that a member of a regulatory agency could be removed by the president only for good cause. Section 7 guaranteed the right of collective bargaining, in language identical to that in Section 7(a) of the NIRA, which was declared unconstitutional in 1935. Section 8 made it an unfair labor practice for an employer to interfere with employees' right to form unions, to dominate or interfere with the creation or administration of unions, to discriminate against employees seeking to join labor unions, to discharge or otherwise to discriminate against employees for filing unfair labor practice charges, and to refuse to engage in collective bargaining with union representatives.

Section 9 provided for the selection of the union to represent employees in a particular company. The union is determined by a majority vote of the employees; if a single employee so requests, the NLRB can conduct a representation election. The election may involve the selection of one union from among two or more unions, and the workers have the right to vote for no union.

Section 9(b) empowered the NLRB to determine the appropriate unit for collective bargaining purposes. This might be the employer unit, craft unit, plant unit, or some subdivision thereof. Although the Wagner Act did not specify how this determination was to be made, the NLRB developed certain guidelines. The Board decided that in determining the appropriate unit, no rigid rule is to be applied but each case is to be considered on its own merits. The Board considers the history of labor relations in the industry, the organization of the business in terms of function or geographic location, and the existing arrangements for employee representation. After the determination of the appropriate unit, the NLRB may order an election.

Under Section 10 of the act, if a charge of an unfair labor practice has been filed with the NLRB, the Board can conduct hearings to ascertain if such practice has occurred.

In spite of provisions in the Wagner Act granting the NLRB power to act to prevent unfair labor practices, the NLRB rendered relatively few decisions in its early history. In the first year, the NLRB issued only 56 decisions finding unfair labor practices and ordering employers to cease and desist and three decisions dismissing charges. In the second year, there were only 39 cease and desist orders and 8 dismissals.

In 1935, a deep cleavage occurred in the labor movement with the formation of the Committee for Industrial Organization (CIO). The formation of this new labor organization followed the vote at the American Federation of Labor (AFL) 1935 convention against unrestricted industrial unionism in the mass production industries. This was to give rise to conflict within the ranks of labor and was to result in problems for the NLRB that had not been anticipated.

Although the controversy between those favoring the craft unit and those favoring the industrial unit had been a bitter and recurrent one throughout the history of the American labor movement, the conflict became particularly acute after formation of the Committee for Industrial Organization. Prior to 1936, the American Federation of Labor had been one of the main champions of the government's attempt to foster self-organization among employees. During the first year of the NLRB's existence, the Board was not disturbed by conflicts between AFL and CIO unions. The conflict, however, became rather severe in 1936–1937.

Section 9(b) of the Wagner Act, as previously noted, authorized the Board to determine the appropriate unit. After the formation of the CIO, the craft unions of highly skilled workers were in danger of being included in larger units and being outvoted. The AFL considered the CIO a rebel organization. The NLRB, so far as it was concerned, was faced with the problem of striking a balance between two conflicting demands: freedom of employees to choose their bargaining representative and stability of labor relations in the plant. If the NLRB were to grant representation to every group seeking it, chaos might result. On the other hand, if it never permitted representation, the legitimate special interests of groups with particular skills might be submerged in a plantwide unit.

Rather early the NLRB developed the "Globe" doctrine to help it decide. In the Globe case, one union sought a single unit for all production and maintenance employees while two other unions sought to represent separately two small craft groups. After reviewing the collective bargaining history and nature of the employer's business, the NLRB concluded that either a single overall unit or three separate units might be appropriate, and that where the considerations were so evenly balanced, the determining factors should be the desire of the employees themselves. The NLRB permitted the two craft groups to vote for separate representation or to become part of the larger industrial unit.

The NLRB in 1938 was faced with opposition from employers and was seeking to mediate dissension within the ranks of organized labor. The AFL accused the NLRB of showing favoritism toward the CIO. In 1938, statistics, in fact, showed that since 1935 the CIO had won a much greater number of elections than had the AFL. The AFL appeared ready to join with business interests in an attempt to discredit, if not to destroy the Labor Board. President William Green of the AFL was quoted in the summer of 1938 as having said in a public speech, "We will mobilize all our political and economic strength in an uncompromising fight until the board is driven from power."

Newsweek magazine reported in 1938 that an attorney for the AFL was planning to file unfair practice charges against employers who dealt with CIO unions, even if the NLRB had certified the CIO as collective bargaining agent. Although it is extremely doubtful that any of the defined unfair labor practice charges in the Wagner Act would permit such a suit to be sustained, an attempt such as this demonstrates the dissatisfaction of the major labor organization width the NLRB. Opposition by the AFL continued in spite of the fact that in the previous year, 1937, the Supreme Court had declared the Wagner Act, and the NLRB that it created, constitutional. Although competition between the two major labor organizations continued, the rift was healed when, in 1955, the two groups reunited to form the combined AFL-CIO.

Perhaps the greatest criticism directed at the Wagner Act after its passage was the omission of any unfair labor practices on the part of unions. Labor proponents argued that the limitation of such practices, to apply only to employers, was an attempt to place labor in a more equal bargaining position with management because of organized labor's weakened position in 1935. However, business interests continued to charge unfair treatment, and the Taft-Hartley Act in 1947 defined a number of unfair labor practices to apply to unions; the NLRB was now required to consider unfair labor practice charges against unions as well as against employers. The Wagner Act did not prohibit a union from making an agreement with an employer for a closed shop, whereby an employee was required to join a union before he or she could be employed. This was considered particularly unfair by business interests and was finally proscribed by the Taft-Hartley Act.

B. Fair Labor Standard Act

In 1938, Congress passed another important labor act, the Fair Labor Standards Act. In many respects, it represented the culmination of efforts begun much earlier to prescribe minimum wages, maximum hours of employment, and to regulate child labor. The federal government, by presidential order or congressional enactment, had previously extended protection to workers on a selective basis by limiting hours of employment and requiring minimum wages. For example, as early as 1840, President Van Buren by executive order set a 10-hour work day for workers in navy yards. In 1907, Congress limited the hours of employment for railroad workers engaged in interstate transportation to 16 hours, and the Adamson Act in 1916 reduced the maximum number of hours to 8 for such workers. The Davis-Bacon Act of 1931 required the payment of minimum wages equal to the prevailing rate in the locality for contractors employed by the federal government performing work in excess of a stated dollar amount. The Public Contracts (Walsh-healey) Act (1936) provided the same basic minimum wage requirement for government contractors, with time and a half for overtime, and it further stipulated a 40-hour work week. This Act provided a model for the Fair Labor Standards Act, although the latter Act was much broader in coverage in that it applied to employers engaged in interstate commerce (with certain exempted occupations). These originally included agricultural and domestic workers and certain retail employees. Today, the only major exempted occupation is that of workers employed in agriculture.

The Fair Labor Standards Act also limits or prohibits child labor for those industries engaged in interstate commerce. Labor of children under 14 years of age is regulated or prohibited, and the Department of Labor may limit hours and conditions of employment for workers between the ages of 14 and 16. No person under the age of 18 may perform work designated hazardous. Efforts had previously been made to regulate or prohibit child labor when Congress in 1916 passed the Owen-Keating Act prohibiting the shipment in interstate commerce of goods produced by child labor, but this Act was struck down by the Supreme Court in *Hammer* v. *Dagenhart* (1918). Congress tried again in 1918 with the passage of a law placing a 10% federal tax on all goods produced by child labor, but in a 1922 decision, *Bailey* v. *Drexel Furniture Co.,* the Supreme Court struck down the law as involving an unconstitutional use of the taxing power. Then in 1924, Congress submitted to the states for ratification a constitutional amendment regulating child labor, but the amendment was never ratified by the necessary number of states. With the passage of the Fair Labor Standards Act the amendment was no longer needed. Child labor has ceased to be a real problem in labor relations.

C. Workmen's Compensation

Employers in all states must provide workmen's compensation insurance, secured either from the state or from private firms. States supervise the programs; coverage is limited, however, mainly to manufacturing. Furthermore, benefits have been inadequate and have not kept pace with inflation. A recent 2-year study by the National Commission on State Workmen's Compensation Laws indicates that a substantial number of workers are excluded and that two thirds of the states offer substandard benefits. A recent proposal has been introduced in Congress to provide federal standards. One of the major provisions is to extend coverage to all public and private employees not otherwise covered by statues. Another proposal would provide for adjustment of benefits to reflect rises in average wage rates. A third recommendation calls for the extension of coverage to all work-related injuries and occupational diseases. There are other possible standards that need to be considered.

D. Labor Management Relations Act (Taft-Hartley Act) (1947)

The Taft-Hartley Act of 1947 was passed in an attempt to reduce some of the imbalance in labor management relations that had been created by the passage of the National Labor Relations Act of 1935. The feeling in many quarters was that the 1935 law had created a disproportionate advantage for labor in order to encourage the growth of unions and the collective bargaining procedure. The strikes by John L. Lewis' coal miners during World War II and the postwar strikes by other workers convinced the public that something had to be done.

One of the main provisions of the Taft-Hartley Act provides for unfair labor practices on the part of the unions. The earlier Wagner Act had provided for unfair labor practices on the part of employers. These were included in Taft-Hartley, but in addition, six unfair labor practices on the part of the unions were defined. It became an unfair labor practice for labor leaders to restrain or coerce employees in organizing for collective bargaining. Second, it was an unfair labor practice for labor leaders to cause an employer to discriminate against an employee for not belonging to a union. A third unfair practice was for labor leaders to refuse to bargain collectively with the employer. Fourth, secondary boycotts were prohibited. Fifth, it was an unfair practice to require excessive initiation fees, and finally payment for work not performed was prohibited.

Other provisions of the Taft-Hartley Act outlawed practices such as the closed shop, although the union shop was still permitted. Unions were required to file affidavits that their officers were not communists. Employers were permitted to sue unions for breach of contract. The size of the National Labor Relations Board was increased from three to five members, with three members constituting a quorum. It is interesting to note that, in the early years of the act, in spite of the fears of labor, most of the unfair labor complaints were against the employer.

The provisions of the Taft-Hartley Act most strongly opposed by organized labor were the right-to-work section and the secondary boycott provision. A continuing debate in the labor-management field has been the right-to-work provision in the Taft-Hartley Act. Organized labor has sought its repeal since its passage in 1947. Title I, Section 14(h), of the Taft Hartley Act states:

> Nothing in this Act shall be construed as authorizing the execution or application of agreements requiring membership in a labor organization as a condition of employment in any State or Territory in which such execution or application is prohibited by State or Territorial Law.

About half of the states have adopted right-to-work laws as a result of which union membership cannot be required of workers as a condition of employment. The union shop, which requires workers to join the union once they have been employed, is thus prohibited in these states, although they would otherwise be permitted under Taft-Hartley.

Strong arguments can be advanced both in support of and against right-to-work laws. For example, nonmembers do not pay a part of the expense involved in supporting union activities, yet they benefit from the improved working conditions that union activity makes possible. It is only fair that those who benefit from the union's activity should pay their share of the costs of running the union. On the other hand, one could argue that compulsory union membership violates the individual's freedom of choice. If, after weighing the factors involved, an individual chooses not to join a labor union, he should not be forced to act against his or her own judgment. The right not to join an organization should be respected. Making union membership a condition of employment violates this basic individual right and is an intolerable infringement on individual freedom. Also, not allowing required membership in union states may encourage union leaders to be more responsive to membership views because members have the right to withdraw or withhold union membership.

The secondary boycott prohibition, Section 8 of the Taft-Hartley Act, has provided another area of controversy in the labor-management relations field. The main objective of Section 8 was to keep third parties from becoming unnecessarily involved in labor disputes that do not concern them. Unions are forbidden from instigating actions against employers who might be doing business with another employer with whom the union has a dispute. The object is to keep te disputes confined to the parties directly concerned.

Some labor union supporters argue that the prohibition of secondary boycotts limits the effectiveness of the tactics unions must necessarily use in dealing with employers and Section 8 should be modified or repealed altogether.

The problem has been particularly apparent in the construction industry. A major objective of organized labor has been the passage of legislation by Congress that would permit what is known as common-situs picketing. Common-situs picketing is not specifically prohibited in the Taft-Hartley Act, but decisions of the Supreme Court and the National Labor Relations Board have placed restrictions on it by construing common-situs picketing to fall within the prohibition of the language in Section 8(b)(4)(B) banning secondary boycotts. Common-situs picketing usually involves union picketing of an entire area—a construction site would be the most obvious situation—the objective of which is to stop all work activity in the entire area. In the case of a construction site all contractors, whether involved in the labor dispute or not, would become objects of the picketing and would consequently suffer even though they could do little to affect the settlement.

Perhaps no union objective has generated such controversy as common-situs picketing. In 1977, organized labor launched a major effort to get a common-situs picketing bill passed by Congress. The unions argued that they needed the right of common-situs picketing to protect the right of workers in industries that are not heavily unionized and in which employment is seasonal. In spite of a tremendous lobbying effort, the bill was defeated in early 1977 and common-situs picketing is still prohibited under Taft-Hartley.

Some of the other provisions of Taft-Hartley were modified by the Landrum-Griffin Act, which was passed in 1959.

E. Labor-Management Reporting and Disclosure Act (Landrum-Griffin Act) (1959)

The Landrum-Griffin Act grew out of the investigations of the McClellan Committee in the 1950s. The investigations revealed certain abuses in union practices, particularly the Teamsters Union. Irregularities in the handling of pension, health, and welfare funds appeared to be widespread, and the membership seemed to have little control over the organization that was supposed to be representing their interest. One of the major goals of the Landrum-Griffin Act was to provide for greater membership control of labor organizations and to promote "democracy" within labor unions.

The Act included what is known as the "bill of rights" for union members. These include the right of union members to participate in the running of the organization, to nominate and vote for officers in the union, the right to speak freely at and otherwise participate in union meetings, and to take an active part in the organization's activities.

The Act also attempts to protect the financial integrity of labor organizations by preventing some of the abuses revealed by the McClellan Committee investigations. The Act requires detailed annual financial reports that include sources of income, expenditures, and salaries of union officers. The Act also requires disclosure of loans to union employers and requires officers and employees of the union to file reports with the Secretary of Labor disclosing any financial activities that could create a conflict with their union responsibilities. The Landrum-Griffin Act was a major step in the direction of reforming labor organizations.

F. Occupational Safety and Health Act (1970)

The Occupational Safety and Health Act (OSHA) was passed by Congress in 1970. It was a landmark piece of legislation. The purpose of the Act, in its own language, was to provide a "place of employment that is free from recognized hazards that are causing or likely to cause death or serious physical harm to his [the employer's] employees." To enforce the act and to develop proper safety and health standards, a National Institute for Occupational Safety and Health was created by the legislation. The Agency was given broad powers to enforce the provisions of the legislation, including those requiring record keeping and allowing for inspections and investigations.

The legislation has been controversial ever since its passage. Some argue that the standards set by OSHA have been unrealistic and arbitrary and have not resulted in significant improvement in the work environment of the average American worker. The standards have been ineffective and are not the most efficient way to go about reducing accidents in most industries.

Although it has remained controversial, suggested changes in the approach to occupational safety and health have not received very much support.

G. Equal Employment Opportunity

Congress mandated equal employment opportunity in Title VII of the Civil Rights Act of 1964. The law forbids discrimination based on race, color, religion, sex, or national origin discrimination in employment practices by employers, employment agencies, or labor organizations. The Act also created the Equal Employment Opportunity Commission (EEOC) to administer its provisions. Under the 1964 Act, the commission had the responsibility of investigating charges of discrimination in employment practices, but it had virtually no enforcement authority. The EEOC had no authority to initiate action on its own and could intervene only if an individual filed a suit claiming unlawful discrimination. By 1972, the feeling was that the EEOC should be given some enforcement powers and authority to act in the area of unlawful discrimination. To accomplish these goals, the Equal Employment Opportunity Act of 1972 expanded the coverage of Title VII and provided the Equal Employment Opportunity Commission with powers to enforce fair employment practices.

Under the 1972 Act, the EEOC is empowered to receive charges of unlawful employment practices from aggrieved persons. The Commission then has the responsibility of notifying the parties concerned of the charges within 10 days after receiving them conducting an investigation to determine the validity of the alleged violations. If after the investigation, the Commission discovers that the allegations are probably true, the law requires that the Commission attempt to eliminate the offending practice by informal methods such as conference and persuasion. These informal procedures are kept private, and penalties are provided for individuals making any part of the informal process public. If these informal procedures do not produce results, no later than 120 days from the filing of the charge, the Commission is authorized to take direct action in the form of a civil suit with respect to the charge. Under the 1972 Act, the courts are instructed to hear cases involving unlawful employment practices at the earliest practicable date and "to cause such cases to be in every way expedited." In spite of the emphasis or concern with expediting the handling of complaints, the Commission has experienced serious problems with the processing of alleged unlawful practices. The greatest problem the commission has had is dealing with the volume of complaints that have arisen under the Act. The Commission has been as much as 2 years behind in the processing of complaints.

Labor organizations are covered under the provisions of the Civil Rights Act. Title VII defines a labor organization in language very similar to that used in the Landrum-Griffin Act. The language is broad enough to include independent unions, national unions, and international unions in the United States. To come under the provision of the act a union must be engaged in an industry affecting commerce. The union is considered to be in an industry affecting commerce if it maintains a hiring hall or office and obtains employees for employers or jobs for employees. A union also falls within the scope of the act if it has 15 or more members and is the certified bargaining agent for employees in an industry affecting commerce.

Under the Civil Rights Act affected unions are forbidden to deny union membership to any individual because of race, color, religion, sex, or national origin or to cause any individual to be deprived of employment opportunities or to cause, or even attempt to cause, an employer unlawfully to discriminate against an individual. Unions also are prohibited from retaliating against anyone who should bring a complaint under the Act.

Because of some of the problems related to enforcement, a move was undertaken at the federal level in 1978 to reorganize equal employment responsibilities and to streamline the procedures of the EEOC. In a major administrative reorganization, most of the responsibilities for equal employment enforcement was shifted from agencies such as the Department of Labor, the Civil Service Commission, and the Equal Employment Opportunity Coordinating Council to EEOC. The move thus consolidated equal employment policy in the one agency most concerned and suited to the task of enforcing the provision of the equal opportunity legislation. In addition, the EEOC has developed a "backlog charge processing system" that the commission hopes will help it reduce the severe backlog of complaints that has always plagued it in the past and enable it to permanently eliminate backlogs in the future. Also, a "rapid charge processing system" was established by all EEOC district offices in 1978 to negotiate settlements quickly by combining investigation, conciliation, and litigation activities into one process. The process consists primarily of promptly gathering evidence from all parties concerned as soon as a complaint is filed and then by face-to-face conference between the complainant and the accused attempting to resolve the dispute. If these and further attempts at resolution fail to bring about an agreement, the EEOC then files a suit in the federal courts if the evidence warrants such action.

The attempt to bring about equality of opportunity in the area of employment has not been totally effective. Only continued effort, particularly at the federal level, can achieve this elusive goal.

H. Affirmative Action

One of the most controversial subjects in the area of equal employment opportunity is what has come to be known as affirmative action. Affirmative action is based on the notion that because certain groups have been the victims of discriminatory actions in the past, practices that discriminate in favor of these same groups are now justified. They are justified because no other way is available to help disadvantaged groups overcome the effects of past discrimination. Affirmative action programs have been implemented in several areas; most particularly in the areas of education and employment practices. A variety of schemes have been developed to give special treatment to certain groups when considering admission to colleges and professional schools and, in the area of employment, special consideration has been given to disadvantaged groups overcome the effects of past discrimination. Affirmative action programs have been implemented in several areas, most particularly in the areas of education and employment practices. A variety of schemes have been developed to give special treatment to certain groups when considering admission to colleges and professional schools and, in the area of employment, special consideration has been given to disadvantaged groups in hiring and training policies. Either quotas have been established or preferential treatment has been given to individuals identified as members of a "disadvantaged" group. Conversely, individuals who are not members of recognized disadvantaged categories have, in effect, been discriminated against in order to accommodate the special treatment given to the recognized disadvantaged groups. How one discriminates in favor of certain individuals without discriminating against certain other individuals at the same time has not yet been discovered. Whether discrimination is justified in certain situations is at the heart of the issue. In any case, the discrimination that takes place in the context of affirmative action has caused considerable controversy and debate, which is not likely to be resolved in the near future.

In 1979, the Supreme Court had to deal with the issue of affirmative action in the area of employment practices. A white worker at Kaiser Aluminum Company sued the company, which had turned him down for a training program established by the company, but accepted two black employees with less seniority. The program had been set up with an equal number of slots for black and white workers. Brian Weber, the white worker, claimed that Kaiser was discriminating against white employees in violation of the 1964 Civil Rights Act. In a complex ruling, the Court ruled that programs such as the one at Kaiser were intended to correct the unfair practices of the past, were temporary in nature, and did not violate the intent of the Civil Rights Act. In spite of the decision in *Weber* v. *Kaiser Aluminum Company*, it is doubtful that the issue of what has been labeled by some as "reverse discrimination" has been settled.

The Supreme Court has shown some doubts about programs in which employees are shown to be adversely affected by government action solely because of their race. In 1984, the Court ruled that white firefighters could not be terminated in favor of black firefighters with less seniority solely because of their race. Also in 1989, in the *Richmond* v. *Crosen* case, the Court ruled that a minority set aside plan in Richmond, Virginia, which required that 30% of all city construction contracts go to "blacks, Spanish-speaking, Orientals, Indians, Eskimoes, or Aleuts," violated the Equal Protection Clause of the Fourteenth Amendment. However, the Supreme Court has not yet reached a decision requiring a completely color-blind standard.

I. Comparable Worth

1. The Fair Labor Standards

Act was amended to include a provision providing for equal pay for workers regardless of sex. Employees who were being paid at different rates for work that was roughly equivalent would have to be equalized unless the different were due to seniority or merit. Employers must pay women who are comparable in terms of seniority and merit at the same rates as men when they are performing similar job responsibilities.

The idea of equal pay for equivalent work is now being expanded to include the concept that job descriptions that include similar requirements such as education, apptitude, technical abilities, and such should be compensated at the same rates even though the specific tasks performed are not the same. Evidence indicates that job descriptions requiring similar training and ability levels held historically by women are compensated at lower rates than positions requiring similar skills and training held by men. The duties and the skills are equal but historically the compensation is not. Many feel that the differences in compensation levels between positions requiring similar skills in the result of the fact that positions held historically by women were compensated at a lower rate regardless of the skill and training levels required for the job position. The solution to this problem, it is felt, is to evaluate the requirements of positions traditionally held by women and determine their comparable worth in relation to job descriptions traditionally held by men. Where they are comparable, the rates of the historically female positions should be raised to those of the historically male-dominated positions.

The problem that some see with this idea of comparable worth is the difficulty of making the subjective judgments that would be required. For example, is a master carpenter's skills worth the same wage rate as an administrative assistant? Will such evaluation almost necessarily be arbituary. Some believe that the best way to determine the worth of different job skills is to allow market forces to determine what an employer is willing to pay for skills that are perhaps comparable but different. At the same time, the higher-paying descriptions should be kept equally open to all regardless of sex.

The United States Equal Employment Opportunity Commission has rejected the concept of comparable worth and declined to recommend wages for traditionally male and female jobs. The federal courts have also refused to rule that different wages in traditionally male and female occupations is evidence of sexual discrimination.

The issue of comparable worth is likely to be at the vanguard of job-related equal opportunity issues in the coming years.

J. Full-Employment Policy

The Humphrey-Hawkins Act, or Full Employment and Balanced Growth Act, provides for long-term economic planning designed to ensure full employment, which is defined as an adult unemployment rate of 3%. It requires coordination among the president, Congress, and the Federal Reserve System. It obliges the Federal Reserve System to submit annual reports to the president and Congress of its monetary policies and how they would help to achieve full employment. The president is required to submit as a part of his economic report 5-year plans that set annual goals for employment and unemployment as well as projections for production, real income, and prices. The Act, if fully implemented, moves the free market economy several steps closer to the planned economies of the socialist systems. The government would assume the decision role in determining not only levels of unemployment but also production levels, income levels, and price levels.

The Full Employment and Balanced Growth Act was enacted into law in 1978. It represents the first major attempt on the part of the Congress to deal with the issue of full employment since the passage of the Employment Act of 1946.

Following World War II, there was considerable concern about a possible return to the high levels of unemployment and depression that characterized the 1930s. The Employment Act of 1946 was designed to address this concern and to enlist the support of the government to achieve the goals of high employment and low unemployment. The Act did not provide for the achieving of full employment by direct intervention on the part of the government as employee of last resort. Rather the government was charged with the responsibility of creating the conditions under which maximum employment opportunities would be available for those actively seeking work.

In order to promote "maximum employment," the Employment Act created the Council of Economic Advisers and the Joint Economic Committee of Congress. The Act also required an Annual Economic Report of the president. Although the Employment Act of 1946 attempted to promote full employment, it did not mandate the use of federal resources to assure that goal. The legislation thus fell far short of the desires of those who believed full employment to be the highest economic priority of government.

Following the passage of the Employment Act of 1946, the issue of full employment ceased to be a matter of great national concern. The much feared return of the high levels of unemployment that characterized the Great Depression of the 1930s failed to materialize. Even though the economy experienced periods of recession in the postwar period, the unemployment rate averaged 4.7%, which was, not enough to cause serious national concern. It was not until the mid-1970s, when unemployment stayed around 7%, that serious interest in government policies designed to achieve full employment returned. The result was the enactment of the Humphrey-Hawkins Act, which for the first time in American history set specific goals in the area of unemployment to be achieved by government intervention in the economy and which makes the reduction of unemployment the top economic goal of the federal government.

The debate over economic priorities was not ended with the passage of the Humphrey-Hawkins Act. Some have questioned whether the government could effectively coordinate fiscal, monetary, and employment policies with the result of creating jobs and providing stable economic growth in the manner called for by the Humphrey-Hawkins Act. For others, the 5-year plans called for in the legislation are disturbingly reminiscent of the planned economies of the communist bloc. Is this sort of policy really compatible with a free market economy?

Perhaps the biggest question of all concerning the unemployment goals of the Humphrey-Hawkins Act is the effect such a policy would have on the nation's other major economic concern of the present era; namely, inflation. What will be the effect of government-provided or government-instigated programs designed to achieve full employment on an inflation rate that has shown an ever-increasing tendency to achieve double-digit levels? Can the problem of unemployment or the achieving of full employment ever be solved or realized as long as the economy continues to be battered by prices rising at a level that only a short time ago would have been unthinkable? Isn't a policy that demands that full employment be achieved regardless of the impact on the other major issues of the economy an illusion doomed to failure?

These concerns were particularly evident at the end of the Act's first year. The annual economic report from the president, required by the Act, which includes estimates for employment and unemployment, projected an unemployment goal of 6.2%, which was a rate 0% higher than the rate at the time the report was issued!

III. ORGANIZING THE PUBLIC SECTOR

A. Hatch Act Reform

Hatch Acts, passed by Congress in 1939 and 1940, prohibit partisan activity on the part of public employees and seek to insulate them from coercion by political incumbents. A 1967 study commissioned by Congress recommended removing some of the restrictions on political activities by public employees. In 1976, a bill was passed by Congress permitting government workers to participate in election campaigns and to run for office themselves. The bill was also designed to strengthen further the protection against coercion of employees and would have established an independent board to assist in accomplishing this goal. However, the bill was vetoed by President Ford, and Congress failed to muster the necessary votes to override.

The question remains: Does the Hatch Act, in its present form, limit the civil and political rights of public employees? Would repeal of certain provisions of the Act subject the public employee to political pressures?

B. Public Employee Unions

The process of unionizing public employees was a slow one. In the 1950s, public employees made up only about 5% of the total union membership in the United States. Today that percentage has doubled.

There are several different types of labor organizations that represent the interests of employees in the public sector. There are those organizations that limit their membership to public employees or to employees or to employees of quasi-public, nonprofit, charitable, or educational institutions. The most important of these is the American Federation of State, County, and Municipal Employees (AFSCME). This all-public union is a member of the AFL-CIO. The membership of the organization includes workers in almost every type of government function and in both state and local government, with the exception of teachers and fire fighters.

In addition to those organizations that limit their membership to public employees or those working for quasi-public institutions, the public-sector employees are also represented by unions that represent workers in the private sector. Indeed, these mixed organizations are the most common type of union representing public employees. The three largest unions of this type are the Service Employers International Union, the Laborer's International Union of North America, both members of the AFL-CIO, and the International Brotherhood of Teamsters, Chauffeurs, Warehousemen, and Helpers of America.

The Service Employees International Union represents primarily workers employed in maintenance, servicing, and security in both the public and the private sector. The Laborers' Union is made up of unskilled and semiskilled workers in the construction industry. The bulk of its members are in the private sector, but about 10% of the union is made up of public employees. Its main interest is the federal employee. The Teamsters have represented public employees of municipal, county, and state government, particularly in the street, sanitation, and highway departments.

In addition to these major organizations, there are many state and local employee associations representing public employees in different areas, including the Fraternal Order of Police and the International Conference of Police Associations. There are also many professional associations that have become collective bargaining agents for public professionals, such as the National Education Association and the American Nurses Association, which are two of the largest.

As a result of the organization efforts of the last decade, a majority of public employees are now represented by unions, workers associations, or professional associations. The degree of organization varies from one area and geographic region to another. The large cities of the Middle Atlantic, Pacific, and North Central states show higher levels of union activity among public employees. However, organization in all regions has been substantial.

IV. LABOR LAW REFORM

Organized labor has pressed for modification of the basic labor law designed mainly to make the existing legislation more effective. Basically, the changes would expedite the work of the National Labor Relations Board and apply sanctions against employers who refuse to comply with decisions of the Board. These changes were embodied in the Labor Reform Act of 1977, which passed the House of Representatives but failed in the Senate as a result of a filibuster.

Specifically, the Reform Act would accelerate the holding of elections to certify unions as bargaining representatives and disposition of cases involving unfair labor practice charges. The Board would be required to streamline its procedures, and the Reform Act provides incentives to employers not to hinder the process of union organization. In general, the Act would enhance the ability of unions to organize workers.

A substantial change in the law would impose deadlines on the Board to minimize delays in the calling of representation elections. This would be accomplished by amending Section 9(c) of the Wagner Act, which simply directs that a representation election be held without specifying any time limit. The amended Section 9(c) would require the Board to call an election within 7 days after the filing of a petition for the election and to conduct the election no more than 15 days after the petition is filed.

In order to further expedite the work of the Board, the Reform Act provides that the decision of an administrative law judge (formerly the hearing examiner), on motion of the successful party, be final in unfair labor practice cases unless the Board decides to take the case on appeal. A quorum of two members of the Board can make this decision. Obviously, this amendment of the existing law would strengthen the position of the administrative law judge and potentially expedite procedures of the Board by removing the necessity for review by the Board; however, there is a safeguard in that, if two members of the board, comprising a quorum, should decide that the case merits further consideration, the Board can consider the matter.

Arguably, the number of administrative law judges should be increased because more decisions of these judges would likely be final than before. Presumably more time would be required to dispose of the cases when the likelihood of appeal to the Board is diminished. This would place a greater burden on the administrative law judges.

Membership of the Labor Board would be increased from five to seven under the proposed reform law. It is anticipated that this expansion in membership would expedite the handling of cases. Under Section 3(b) of the present law, the Board is allowed to "delegate to any group of three or more members any or all of the powers which it may itself exercise." Under the present five-person Board, only one such group would be possible, and the workload potential of the Board is not increased. However, if the number is expanded to seven members, then the Board could divide itself into two working units and, conceivably, substantially speed up its handling of cases.

Critics of the proposed change in the law assert that by expanding the size of the Labor Board from five to seven members, the result would be to produce further delays because agreement of seven rather than five members would be required, and this would mean more discussion and consideration. However, the fact that the Board could now consider cases in panels of three, and would probably do so except in the most serious cases, should increase the ability of the Board to handle in a expeditious manner the cases that are appealed to it.

Under the present law, the Wagner Act (1935) as amended, Section 10(f) permits the filing of an appeal from an order of the Board to the federal Court of Appeals in the circuit wherein an alleged unfair labor practice occurred. In the Labor Reform Act of 1977, this section would have been amended to provide for an appeal within 30 days from final order of the Board; otherwise, the decision of the Board would be final.

The intent of the amendment would be to hasten a final decision of the matter by preventing extended periods of delay because theoretically the aggrieved party, at present, has an indefinite time in which to file the appeal. A potential problem exists, however, in that by requiring filing of an appeal within a short period of 30 days, the result may be an increase in appeals and more cases in the federal court. Once the appeal has been filed, the court would have to rule, and the time in which the final ruling takes place typically involves an extended period. If the number of appeals increases, the time period for a final ruling by the Court should increase as the case load of the Court becomes larger. Furthermore, under the present law, voluntary compliance with the Board's decision frequently takes place; speeding up the appeals process might obstruct the ability to secure such compliance, although there would still be the possibility of out-of-court settlements.

Section 10(1) of the present act relating to unfair labor practices would be amended to include within the category of cases receiving priority treatment by the Labor Board those in which an employee has been fired in violation of Section 8(a) (3) or 8(b) (2) during a representation election or after a union has been certified as representative for the employees but before the first collective bargaining agreement.

If the Board determines that the employer has discharged the worker because of membership in a union, then the Board must go to the federal District Court to obtain an injunction reinstating the employee. A further protection to the worker is the amendment of Section 10(c), in the new Act, providing for double wages during the period of discharge and until reinstatement. This new provision is designed to assure than an order of the Board reinstating an employee will be effective. The Board is required not to rely solely on its own enforcement powers but also to secure the added help of the federal court.

A major complaint of organized labor under the present law is that an employee who is illegally fired for engaging in union organization efforts is entitled only to the back pay that would have been received had the employee not been fired. The amount the employee received also is subject to reduction because any wages received during the period of illegal firing is deducted from the amount of back pay that would otherwise be received. In addition, the employer can raise objections to the amount of the settlement by claiming that the employee did not diligently seek comparable employment or exercised poor judgment in seeking other employment during the period of illegal firing. Section 10(x) of the present law would be amended to require "double the employee's wage rate" for the period of unemployment due to the unfair labor practice.

Also, if the employer refuses to bargain with the designated representative of the employees prior to the establishment of the first collective bargaining contract, the Board may award to the employees compensation for the delay in bargaining based on the difference between what they received during the period of delay and the average increase in "wages and other benefits" obtained by other workers at the time of the negotiation of the collective bargaining agreement, which is to be determined by statistical measures available to the Bureau of Labor Statistics.

Another proposed change, similar to the above, would require that employers who refused to engage in "good faith" collective bargaining pay wage rates equal to the average rates prevailing industrywide. These "wage settlements" would be imposed on such employers.

A modification of Section 10(c) of the Wagner Act would deny government contracts to employers failing to comply with a final order of the Board. A list would be prepared by the comptroller general and circulated to all government agencies. No government contracts would be awarded to these employers during a 3-year period. This is perhaps the most drastic sanction of any in the Reform Act, to secure compliance with orders of the Labor Board, and involves, in a sense, "blacklisting" of employers, a practice used by employers against workers seeking to join unions at an earlier time in labor history. This remedy could be viewed as an improper use of governmental power and might raise serious constitutional questions. Government procurement has grown tremendously in the 20th century and accounts for a significant portion of many companies' business. Furthermore, the effectiveness of this sanction might be questioned because a company, particularly if the government contract accounted for a small portion of its total output, might forego the contract rather than comply with an order of the board. Workers might be intimidated by fear of losing their jobs. A reduction in the number of workers required would occur, and ironically, the withholding of government contracts would reduce, rather than increase, protection to employees.

Complaints have been made by unions that their representatives do not have sufficient opportunity to solicit workers and that these organizers should be given an opportunity during the work day to do so. Employers have the opportunity to talk to their employees during working hours; unions would like to have "equal access." An amendment to Section 6 of the existing law would require this, but with the stipulation that organizing efforts be consistent with the maintenance of normal and orderly production. How this could be accomplished without disturbing production is subject question. An argument can be made that unions already enjoy an advantage after working hours, and that "equal access" would give undue advantage to unions.

Perhaps no labor bill has provoked as much controversy as the Labor Reform Act of 1977. Supporters of the bill contend that it is necessary to make their basic labor law effective, to provide strong incentives to employers, who otherwise would resist compliance, to accept decisions of the Labor Board. Some employers view the proposal with alarm and consider it essentially as an attempt of labor to increase union membership at a time of decline in union strength as a percentage of the total working force.

V. INTERNATIONAL LABOR AFFAIRS

Although international trade union conferences to discuss world economic problems affecting labor are taking place with increasing frequency, there is generally a wide gap between the convening of those meeting and meaningful international action taken as a result. One of the most serious problems for the trade unions in the industrially developed part of the world is the flight of multinational companies to low-wage countries with developing economies and lower living standards.

The obstacles to the realization of widespread international collective bargaining agreement are many. One of the main problems is the conflicts of interest among trade unions in different countries within the same industry. Labor organizations in developing economies have different priorities from those unions in advanced nations. They are more likely to make concessions in terms of wages and working conditions to try to entice multinational companies away from high-cost production areas. Because of this, the international trade union reaction to the global expansion of the multinational corporation has not brought forth a real international collective bargaining process. However, it has made for greater cohesion and cooperation among international labor organizations.

In the face of the worldwide expansion of the multinational corporations, many of which are based in the United States, the American unions have opposed the loss of jobs overseas, especially to areas of cheap labor, by putting pressure on the Congress to enact legislation to restrict cheap imports. The unions have also urged the revision of American tax laws that they believe encourage the multinationals to expand aboard.

Opponents reject this approach by calling it protectionism that would be retaliated against by foreign competitors. It would also violate existing trade arguments, it is charged, and cause even greater job losses in the export field and industry generally.

NOTES

There are many excellent sources. Among those useful for further information are the following: C. J. Morris (Ed.). *The Developing Labor Law: The Board, the Courts, and the National Labor Relations Act* (Bureau of National Affairs, Washington, DC, 1971); and A. K. McAdams. *Power and Politics in Labor Legislation* (Columbia University Press, New York, 1964). The latter is a thorough treatment of the legislative history of the Landrum-Griffin Act. Additional sources include P. Selznick, *Law, Society, and Industrial Justice* (Russell Sage Foundation, New York, 1969); and J. S. Williams, *Labor Relations and the Law* (Little, Brown, Boston, 1965). Williams' book covers the early history and development of labor law, concentrating on the process of collective bargaining. A recent book covering many substantive areas in labor policy is C. Bulmer and J. L. Carmichael, Jr. (Eds.), *Employment and Labor-Relations Policy* (D. C. Heath, Lexington, MA, 1980).

A very useful source is *Labor Relations and Social Problems*, a series published by the Bureau of National Affairs in the 1970s. For example, particularly useful is J. R. Grodin and D. H. Wollett, *Collective Bargaining in Public Employment* (Bureau of National Affairs, Washington, DC, 1975). Another volume in the Bureau of National Affairs' collection that would be appropriate is Bureau of National Affairs, *The Equal Employment Opportunity Act of 1972* (Bureau of National Affairs, Washington, DC, 1973).

For the early history of the labor movement and an analysis of major federal legislation, see R. Wykstra and E. Stevens, *Labor Law and Public Policy* (Odyssey Press, New York, 1970).

For specific information on the Labor Board, see F. McCulloch and T. Bornstein, *The National Labor Relations Board* (Praeger, New York, 1974).

On the subject of public employees, J. D. Douglas, R. D. Horton, T. W. Kheel, et al.: *Public Employee Unions: A Study of the Crisis in Public Sector Labor Relations* (Institute for Contemporary Studies, San Francisco, 1975) analyzes the nature of and suggests solutions for current problems in public labor relations.

Some excellent additional publications dealing with labor-management policy in a general way are the following: J. S. Auerbach, *American Labor: The Twentieth Century* (Bobbs Merrill, Indianapolis, IN, 1969); J. M. Backer, *Guaranteed Income for the Unemployed* (Johns Hopkins University Press, Baltimore, 1968); S. K. Bailey, *Congress Makes a Law: The Story Behind the Employment Act of 1946* (Columbia University Press, New York, 1950); W. G. Bowen (Ed.), *Labor and the National Economy* (Norton, New York, 1965); E. J. Burtt, Jr., *Labor Markets, Unions and Government Policies* (St. Martin Press, New York, 1963); F. R. Dulles, *Labor in America* (Thomas Y. Crowell, New York, 1966); J. E. Finley, *White Collar Union* (Octagon Books, New York, 1975); H. W. Metz, *Labor Policy of the Federal Government* (Brookings Institution, Washington, DC, 1945); H. P. Northrup and G. F. Bloom, *Government and Labor* (Richard D. Irwin, Homewood, IL, 1963); and J. G. Rayback, *A History of American Labor* (Macmillan, New York, 1966).

There are many sources that deal with specific policy areas in labor-management relations. Some of the better ones listed by area are listed in the references.

REFERENCES

I. Collective Bargaining

Beal, E. F. (1967). *The Practice of Collective Bargaining*. Richard D. Irwin, Homewood, IL.

Chamberlain, N. W. (1965). *Collective Bargaining*. McGraw-Hill, New York.

Cox, A. (1958). The duty to bargain in good faith. *Harvard Law Review* 71.

Davey, H. W. (1959). *New Dimensions in Collective Bargaining*. Harper & Row, New York.

DeMenil, G. (1971). *Bargaining: Monopoly Power Versus Union Power*. M.I.T. Press, Cambridge, MA.

Dunlop, J. T., and Chamberlain, N. W. (1967). *Frontiers of Collective Bargaining*. Bureau of National Affairs, Washington, DC.

Peck, C. J. (1972). *Cases and Materials on Negotiation*. Bureau of National Affairs, Washington, DC.

Prasow, P., and Peters, E. (1970). *Arbitration and Collective Bargaining: Conflict Resolution in Labor Relations*. McGraw-Hill, New York.

Sherman, H. L. (1972). *Unionization and Collective Bargaining*. Bureau of National Affairs, Washington, DC.

II. Democratization of Unions

Bureau of National Affairs (1959). *The Labor Reform Law*. Bureau of National Affairs, Washington, DC.

Dunsford, J. E., Alleyne, R. H., Morris, C. J. (1973). *Individuals and Unions*. Bureau of National Affairs, Washington, DC.

Getman, J. G., Anderson, J., and Silverstein, E. (1973). *Allocation of Power and Individual Rights*. Bureau of National Affairs, Washington, DC.

Slovenko, R. (Ed.) (1961). *Symposium on LMRDA*. Claitor's Bookstore Publishers, Baton Rouge, LA.

III. Equal Employment Opportunity

Becker, G. S. (1957). *The Economics of Discrimination*. University of Chicago Press, Chicago.

Bracey, J. H. Jr. (Ed.) (1971). *Black Workers and Organized Labor*. Wadsworth, Belmont, CA.

Bureau of National Affairs (1973). *The Equal Employment Act of 1972*. Bureau of National Affairs, Washington, DC.

Foner, P. S. (1974). *Organized Labor and the Black Worker*. Praeger, New York.

Greer, S. (1949). *Last Man In: Racial Access to Union Power*. The Free Press, New York.

Hughes, M. M. (1970). *The Sexual Barrier: Legal and Economic Aspects of Employment*. Hughes, Chicago.

Lamb, C. M. (May 1978). Administrative coordination in civil rights enforcement: A regional approach. *Vanderbilt Law Review* 31.

MacNabb, R. R. (1969). *Equal Employment Opportunity. Machinery and Allied Products Institute*, Chicago.

Norgren, Paul H., and Samuel E. Hill (1964). *Toward Fair Employment*. Columbia University Press, New York.

Peskin, D. B. (1971). *The Building Blocks of EEO*. World, New York.

Sindler, A. P. (1978). *Bakke, Defunis, and Minority Admissions*. Longman, New York.

Sovern, M. I. (1966). *Legal Restraints on Racial Discrimination in Employment*. Twentieth Century Fund, New York.

IV. Labor Economics

Addison, J. T. (1979). *The Market for Labor: An Analytical Treatment*. Goodyear, Pacific Palisades, CA.

Azvedo, R. E. (1978). *Labor Economics*. Gale Research Co., Detroit.

Barbash, J. (1972). *Trade Unions and National Economic Policy*. Johns Hopkins University Press, Baltimore.

Bloom, G. F., and Northrop, H. R. (1955). *Economics of Labor Relations*. Richard D. Irwin, Homewood, IL.

Blum, S. (1969). *Labor Economics*. Arno Press, New York.

Brown, E. H. P. (1962). *The Economics of Labor*. Yale University Press, New Haven, CT.

Douglas, P. H., Hitchcock, C. N., and Atkins, W. E. (1969). *The Worker in Modern Economic Society*. Arno Press, New York.

Fair, R. C. (1969). *The Short-Run Demand for Workers and Hours*. North-Holland, Amsterdam.

—— (1969). *Excess Labor and Aggregate Employment Functions*. Princeton University Press, Princeton, NJ.

Fisher, M. R. (1971). *The Economic Analysis of Labour*. Weidenfeld, and Nicolson, London, England.

Furniss, E. S. (1969). *Labor Problems*. Arno Press, New York.

Galenson, W. (1959). *Labor and Economic Development*. John Wiley & Sons, New York.

Ginzberg, E. (1976). *The Human Economy*. McGraw-Hill, New York.

Gitlow, A. L. (1957). *Labor Economics and Industrial Relations*. Richard D. Irwin, Homewood, IL.

Gupta, R. D. (1971). *Wage Flexibility and Full Employment*. Vikas, Delhi, India.

Heneman, H. G., and Yoder, D. (1965). *Labor Economics*. South-Western, Cincinnati, OH.

Kuhn, A. (1967). *Labor Institutions and Economics*. Harcourt, Brace, New York.

Lester, R. A. (1964). *Economics of Labor*. Macmillan, New York.

McConnell, C. R. (1970). *Perspectives on Wage Determinations: A Book of Readings*. McGraw-Hill, New York.

Moore, H. L. (1967). *Laws of Wages.* Augustus M. Kelly, Clifton, NJ.
Morgan, C. A. (1966). *Labor Economics.* Dorsey Press, Homewood, IL.
Perlman, S. (1968). *A Theory of the Labor Movement.* Augustus M. Kelly, Clifton, NJ.
Phelps, E. S., Alchian, A. A., Holt, C. C., et al. (1970). *Microeconomic Foundations of Employment and Inflation Theory.* Norton, New York.
Rees, A. (1973). *The Economics of Work and Pay.* Harper & Row, New York.
Reynolds, L. G. (1974). *Labor Economics and Labor Relations.* Prentice-Hall, Englewood Cliffs, NJ.

V. Occupational Safety and Health

Anderson, C. (1975). *OSHA and Accident Control Through Training.* Industrial Press, New York.
Bureau of National Affairs (1971). *The Job Safety and Health Act of 1970.* Bureau of National Affairs, Washington, DC.
Fellner, B. A., and Savelson, D. W. (1976). *Occupational Safety and Health Law and Practice.* Practicing Law Institute, New York.
McCulloch, F. W., and Bornstein, T. (1974). *The National Labor Relations Board.* Praeger, New York.
Morris, C. J. (Ed.) (1971). *The Developing Labor Law.* Bureau of National Affairs, Washington, DC.
Smith, R. Stewart. (1976). *The Occupational Safety and Health Act.* American Enterprise Institute, Washington, DC.

VI. Public Sector

Bakke, E. Wright. (July 1970). Reflections on the future of bargaining in the public sector. *Monthly Labor Review* 93, No. 7.
Bradley, P. D. (1959). *The Public Stake in Union Power.* University Press of Virginia, Charlottesville.
Chauhan, D. S. (1976). *Public Labor Relations: A Comparative State Study.* Sage, Beverly Hills, CA.
Chickering, A. L. (Ed.) (1976). *Public Employee Unions: A Study of the Crisis in Public Sector Labor Relations.* Institute for Contemporary Studies, San Francisco.
Cohen, S. (Jan. 1979). Does public employee unionism diminish democracy? *Industrial and Labor Relations Review* 32 No. 2.
Connery, R. A., and Farr, W. F. (1970). *Unionization of Municipal Employees.* Academy of Political Science, New York.
Godine, M. R. (1967). *The Labor Problem in the Public Service.* Russell and Russell, New York.
Grodin, J. R., and Wollett, D. H. (1975). *Collective Bargaining in Public Employment.* Bureau of National Affairs, Washington, DC.
Gunderson, M. (1975). *Collective Bargaining in the Essential and Public Service Sectors.* University of Toronto Press, Toronto, Canada.
Hamermesh, D. S. (Ed.) (1969). *Collective Bargaining for Public Employees.* HJ. W. Wilson, Bronx, NY.
Krendel, E. S., and Samoff, B. L. (1978). *Unionizing the Armed Forces.* University of Pennsylvania Press, Philadelphia.
Love, T., and Sulzner, G. (Feb. 1972). Political implications of public implications of public employee bargaining. Industrial Relations 11.
Marx, H. L., Jr. (Ed.) (1969). *Collective Bargaining for Public Employees.* H. W. Wilson, Bronx, NY.
McCarthy, C. F. (July 1970). Collective bargaining and the local chief executive. *Public Personnel Review.*
Murphy, R. J., and Sackman, M. (Eds.) (1970). *The Crisis in Public Employee Relations in the Decade of the Seventies.* Bureau of National Affairs, Washington, DC.
Nesbitt, M. B. (1976). *Labor Relations in the Federal Government Service.* Bureau of National Affairs, Washington, DC.
Schick, R. P., and Couturier, J. J. (1977). *The Public Interest in Government Labor Relations.* Ballinger, Cambridge, MA.

Stieber, J. (1971). *Public Employee Unionism: Structure, Growth, Policy.* Brookings Institution, Washington, DC.

Warner, K. O., and Hennessy, M. L. (1967). *Public Management at the Bargaining Table.* Public Personnel Association, Chicago.

Wellington, H. H., and Winter, R. K. (1971). *The Union and the Cities.* Brookings Institution, Washington, DC.

Wirtz, W. W. (1964). *Labor and the Public Interest.* Harper & Row, New York.

VII. International Labor Affairs

International Confederation of Free Trade Unions Handbook (1979). *Trade Unions and the Transnationals*, 12th World Congress, Mexico City.

International Confederation of Free Trade Unions (1985). *World Economic Review*, New York.

Northrop, H. B., and Rowan, R. L. (1979). Multinational collective bargaining attempts. In *Multinational Industrial Relations Series* No. 6, University of Pennsylvania, Philadelphia.

United Nations Center on Transnational Corporations (1983). *Transnational Corporations in World Development.* Third Survey, New York.

United Nations Center on Transnational Corporations (1985). *Trends and Issues in Foreign Direct Investments*, New York.

United Nations Economic and Social Council, Commission on Transnational Corporations (1986) Report of the Secretarist, New York.

United States Department of Commerce (1981). *Direct Investment Abroad in 1980.* U.S. Government Printing Office, Washington, DC.

19
Communication Policy

Christopher H. Sterling
The George Washington University, Washington, D.C.

I. INTRODUCTION

"Communication" policy includes two broad subject fields that until quite recently were distinct and separate. Well into the 1980s, researchers and policy makers both tended to focus on either mass communication/media (press and electronic media and sometimes film) or common carrier telecommunication (point-to-point voice, data, and related services)—but seldom both. As outlined here, changes in technology and regulatory ideology have driven the two regimes more closely together, although distinctions still exist.

As in other sectors of policy, communication policy in the United States involves private sector ownership and operation (e.g., broadcast stations, newspapers, American Telephone and Telegraph (AT&T), local telephone companies) and public sector regulation and control (federal and state—sometimes local). Imposition of the latter has varied greatly over time, reaching a peak in communications from the 1927 Radio Act through the 1982 breakup of AT&T. Further, communication policy has varied and sometimes conflicting domestic and international aspects, with the latter becoming of increasing importance in recent years.

Likewise, as with many other sectors, communication policy results from constant tension among its three defining aspects: legal and political controls; technical options and limitations; and economic opportunities and constraints. The strength of each of these vary over time and by circumstance, as will be evident below. Finally, it should be made clear at the outset that the United States has never had any single comprehensive communications policy. Rarely has there been widespread public-private sector agreement on how to integrate broadly changing technology, political aims, and economic constraints into a cohesive policy with clear direction and predictability. Rather policy has almost always focused on one aspect of the field at a time, and resulted from the constant give-and-take among government agencies and private sector lobbying.

This chapter briefly reviews the development of communication policies, discusses the major current "players" in the overlapping policy arenas, and introduces selected policy clusters of importance in the 1990s. Extensive references are designed to assist readers seeking more information than this very cursory overview can provide.

II. DEVELOPMENT OF COMMUNICATION POLICIES

A. Constitution, Press, and Posts to 1840

The first and most basic foundation of communication policy rests on two parts of the U.S. Constitution. Article I, Section 8 (1789) gives Congress the right to regulate commerce between and among the states and with foreign powers. This "commerce clause" forms the base of the federal regulatory structure that has developed over the past century. Two years later, with the passage of the first 10 amendments as the Bill of Rights, the First Amendment (1791) began to define/limit government policy on communication content. That Congress could make no law affecting freedom of speech or of the press expanded over two centuries of case law to restrict any level of government (federal, state, or local) from taking action against rights of free speech and free press. These two parts of the Constitution together provide the underpinning for all that follows.

Important early Supreme Court decisions helped to refine and make more specific what "freedom of the press" really meant (Chafee, 1941, 1946; Hixson, 1989; also see Chap. 16). As a general matter of policy, however, regulation of communication usually meant regulation of technology or economic structure as an indirect means of affecting performance (especially media content) without running afoul of First Amendment restrictions (Emord, 1991; Powe, 1991).

Postal legislation in the 19th century, the first concerted "communication policy" at the federal level, defined the right of government access to build "post roads" to ease ground transport of the mail (the Constitution had included in Article I, Section 8, the right to build post offices and post roads as a part of the federal government's role). The 1866 Post Roads Act expanded this to cover access for mail routes and telegraph lines, as well as necessary military transportation. (Postal policy, centered in the semigovernmental U.S. Postal Service created in 1971, is now primarily a matter of governmental organization and economics, although it has some broader communication implications as well; see Tierney, 1988).

Another aspect of communication policy evident from the earliest days, and one under continual technological pressure then and now, concerns protection of intellectual property, especially copyright. This is a highly specialized subject area that is not discussed here (see, however, Henn, 1991; OTA, 1986).

B. Wire Monopoly: 1840–1920

After postal matters, communication policy developed primarily around concerns about monopoly pricing of and conditions of service for telegraph service and later telephone service. For most of this period, however, federal and state regulation of wireline communication was nearly nonexistent.

1. Telegraph Precedent

After years of developmental work, artist and telegraph system inventor S. F. B. Morse persuaded Congress to appropriate $30,000 to build an experimental telegraph line from Washington, D.C., to Baltimore. Placed under operational authority of the postmaster general, the line began operation in 1844. Continuing deficits led Congress to sell the fledgling telegraph system to private owners in 1847.

Of minor importance at the time, this decision set American policy apart from that of most other countries where the post/telegraph (and eventually telephone) tradition of public control and operation remained largely intact to the 1990s. Instead, a U.S. policy of private ownership and operation within an arena defined by public (federal and state) regulation evolved. As the telegraph and later telephone industries developed in importance and economic clout, postal authorities tried to get Congress to support a federal buy-out of the private services—these arguments being raised almost annually after the 1850s (Burleson, 1914).

Early telegraph operations were characterized by a host of small firms competing to build lines and develop service. Civil War demands fed telegraph expansion, especially in northern states. Consolidation began as capital costs to expand telegraph systems rose sharply. In 1856, Western Union appeared, and by 1866 was able to absorb two large competitors to become a near-monopoly provider of service (Lindley, 1975; Thompson, 1947).

2. Telephone Follows Telegraph

Even more rapidly than had been the case with the telegraph, expansion of the telephone after 1880 quickly took the form of monopoly ownership and operation (Brock, 1981). American Telephone and Telegraph (AT&T), created in the early 1880s as a long-distance provider (though technology limited "distance" severely until 1915), was dominant until the original Bell patents expired in 1893 to 1894. AT&T then faced an avalanche of new, small start-up local operators with which it refused to interconnect.

Company President Theodore Vail established the structure and approach of AT&T that lasted for a half century—including its role as a regulated monopoly, although AT&T prices and sometimes poor service contributed to the rise of regulation on state and federal levels (see below). In the years prior to World War I, AT&T expanded its control of local telephone companies, purchased Western Union, and established coast-to-coast long-distance service in 1915.

3. Rise of Wireless Competition

Unlike wire telegraph and telephone, wireless, or radio, was the product of different inventors in several countries. Although American inventors played important roles, British, and especially Marconi, interests dominated the field through World War I. Wireless consisted through 1920 of large companies active in point-to-point applications of radio in competition with telegraph and telephone services and thousands of amateurs—predecessors of today's "ham" operators. During the World War I emergency, the U.S. Navy was able to pool patents of many companies and countries to make the finest transmitters and receivers in the world—and to point to the kind of cooperative approach over patent control that would be necessary after the war (Howeth, 1963; Sterling and Kittross, 1990).

In 1919, the General Electric Company formed the Radio Corporation of America (RCA) as an operating subsidiary in cooperation with other key radio patent holders, including AT&T and eventually Westinghouse. RCA took over the long-distance stations (and patents) of the American branch of the Marconi Company as well as those of former enemy Germany. Following the Navy's wartime precedent, RCA developed a complicated patent-pooling arrangement to allow continued manufacture of radio receivers and transmitters for long-distance point-to-point work and sharing of the proceeds by the various patent holders (Howeth, 1963; Kittross, 1977).

With the exception of a few visionaries, no one thought about radio's application to what we know as broadcasting. The first radio broadcast stations aired late in 1920, but the real boom came 2 years later when more than 500 stations took to the air—with only a few available frequencies and almost no regulation. Chaos resulted, leading to public (and fledgling broadcaster) demand for congressional legislation. That action was a long time in coming.

C. Steps Toward Regulation

1. Interstate Commerce Commission, Antitrust, and Public Utility Commissions

The first independent regulatory agency, the Interstate Commerce Commission (ICC), was established in 1887 to regulate railway rates and service. Designed to be an expert entity free of executive branch politics, the ICC was given tariff authority over wire communications in the Mann-Elkins Act of 1910. Although the agency took little interest in telecommunication, it set the pattern for such later communications-related agencies as the Federal Trade Commission (1914), Federal Radio Commission (1927), and Federal Communications Commission (1934).

New York and Wisconsin, driven by progressive politics, were the first to create state public utility commissions (PUCs), again established first to regulate railway service and tariffs. Soon other states followed suit, and PUCs (sometimes under different names) took on regulation of telegraph and telephone services and rates within their state borders. Generally speaking, state regulation of wire communication was weak until the 1980s, when the breakup of AT&T forced more regulatory authority down to the state level (McCaw, 1984).

2. Wireless Acts of 1910 and 1912

Initial legislation on telecommunications focused almost entirely on maritime applications of wireless. The Wireless Act of 1910 was a brief statute only requiring wireless operators on some ships in coastal and ocean transport. It did, however, establish the principle of requiring a federal license to access spectrum. It was expanded 2 years later, partially as a result of wireless' role in the *Titanic* sinking, to tighten requirements. (Although the *Titanic* was not the first merchant ship to use wireless to summon rescuers, the saving of 700 lives—and the horror of 1500 persons lost owing to both insufficient lifeboats and the fact that nearby ships were not then required to have a wireless operator on board for 24 hours a day—captured the world's press attention, as did the story of the ship's two brave Marconi operators, one of whom died in the disaster.) A separate act that same year, the Radio Act of 1912, is more important because until 1927 it provided the only statutory control over telecommunication. It established the Department of Commerce as the locus for granting licenses, but it gave the department no discretion in when or how to license applicants. Further, it was restricted to point-to-point applications of radio and could not foresee the very different demands of broadcasting. These limitations eventually led to the 1927 Radio Act (Sterling and Kittross, 1990).

3. 1913 "Kingsbury Commitment"

The federal government made three attempts to breakup AT&T, of which the first is forgotten and only the third was successful. Under Theodore Vail, the company in 1913 made a fundamental shift in its relationship with government authorities. After years of expansion (it had purchased Western Union in 1909) and distain for any threatened regulation, Vail agreed, in the form of a letter sent by a company vice president (Nathan Kingsbury) to the U.S. attorney general, to cease taking over small local telephone firms, to divest Western Union, and to interconnect with independently owned local companies. This "commitment" staved off a threatened antitrust action by the government and led to several decades of AT&T operation as a regulated (though ineffectively until 1934 if not later) monopoly service (AT&T, 1914).

4. Government Operation 1917–1920

During World War I, telegraph and telephone operations came under control of the Post Office Department, but they were returned to their respective owners after 1919 congressional hearings concluded that permanent government operation of telegraph, telephone, and wireless (operated during the war by the U.S. Navy) systems was not in the public interest (U.S. House, 1919; U.S. Senate, 1919). At no time since, even during the much larger Second World War, has even temporary government operation of telecommunications been a serious consideration, although provisions in the Communications Act of 1934 (see below) allow for such operation in case of national emergency.

D. Telecommunications Development 1920–1970

1. Radio Act of 1927 – the Federal Radio Commission

Limitations in the 1912 Radio Act, combined with the post-1920 development of radio broadcasting, slowly increased pressure on Congress to update and expand legislation to include broadcasting and allow regulatory discretion in station licensing. Several years passed as the broadcast industry pressured Congress to take action to reduce the electronic confusion, and Congress debated whether to set up another independent expert agency. This was finally resolved early in 1927 with a new Radio Act that created the Federal Radio Commission (FRC) (Davis, 1927; Schemeckebier, 1932; Rosen, 1980; Sterling and Kittross, 1990).

The new Act established the basis for federal regulation in telecommunication as "the public interest, convenience, or necessity" (PICON), a phrase drawn in part from earlier railway legislation. The FRC, a temporary body until it was made permanent in 1930, quickly set up the structure (still largely intact in the 1990s) to license AM broadcast stations, established a very limited amount of government oversight over programming and codified related regulations. It did not, however, have jurisdiction over wired systems, which remained under the ineffectual ICC, and regulation of wireless continued to be shared with the Department of Commerce in ways not often clear.

2. Communications Act of 1934 – the Federal Communications Commission

The creation of the Federal Communications Commission (FCC) by the 1934 Communications Act grew out of the limits of the 1927 Act and the FRC. As a part of his New Deal, Franklin Roosevelt asked Congress for a cohesive agency to centralize regulation of both wire and wireless telecommunication. The 1927 Act was absorbed into the larger and more inclusive legislation—still in force in the 1990s, although often modified since (Paglin, 1989). The FCC continued to operate under the same PICON framework and added two members (for a total of seven) to cover its new responsibilities. Regulation of broadcasting continued seamlessly from FRC practices and precedents (Rahn, 1984; Rose, 1940).

3. Regulating AT&T

As mandated by Congress in the 1934 Act, the new FCC began an intensive investigation of AT&T's operations—the first in-depth government assessment of the company's role and practices. The investigation led to a 1938 draft report recommending substantial changes in the company and far closer regulatory oversight and a more watered-down final report useful now for historical purposes—and as a precurser to the second federal attempt to break up the telephone monopoly (Danielian, 1939; FCC, 1939). No action was taken on the FCC investigation or its findings because of World War II. After the war, however, the FCC data formed the basis for the first full-fledged federal antitrust case against the company, which was filed in 1949. After years of paper proceedings, the case was settled with a consent decree in 1956 that left the firm intact, but limited it from entry into the data-processing field, and required licensing of all innovations from Bell Laboratories (U.S. House of Representatives, 1958, 1959).

FCC regulation of the company was informal into the 1960s. Generally, AT&T tariff filings were accepted and approved with few questions asked (Bolter et al., 1984). Well into the 1960s, to work on common carrier questions was considered a kind of regulatory Siberia for most FCC commissioners (Brock, 1981; *Fifty Years of Telecommunications Reports*, 1985). Only in 1965, when evidence of AT&T cross-subsidy from regulated to competitive services and other possibly unfair competitive practices came to light, did more formal "rate of return" oversight become the norm at the FCC.

4. Regulating Changing Technologies

Almost from its creation, the FCC faced the fundamental policy question of how best to integrate new and changing technologies into existing media and common carrier systems. FM radio and television broadcasting were in the experimental stage in the mid-1930s, and after considerable debate, primarily over spectrum allocations, they were approved for commercial service in 1941. Wartime civilian production controls severely limited their growth until 1945. On the other hand, the War's needs helped spur development of microwave technology, coaxial cable, and radar systems, as well as substantially increasing knowledge about the use of higher frequencies in the spectrum. The latter led to a 1945 reallocation of FM broadcasting to its present band (88–108 MHz), creating short-term chaos as transmitters and receivers were rendered obsolete, but allowing sufficient space for the service to expand in the new larger allocation after 1960 (Sterling and Kittross, 1990).

The FCC grappled regularly in the post–war years with how to increase diversity of media ownership—both how many stations a single owner could control nationally and control of stations within single markets. The concern was over both economic concentration and programming diversity. Eventually, newspaper control of broadcast stations in the same market was banned, and the limit on the number of stations that could be owned increased from 7 of each type (set in 1953) to 12 of each type (in early 1992, the FCC voted to increase radio ownership ceilings to 30 of each type). No limit was ever placed on the number of cable systems or subscribers any one entity could control, nor were newer technologies subject to any ownership oversight or restrictions. TV networks were banned from owning cable systems, and telephone companies could not own broadcast or cable outlets in their telephone service area (Compaine et al., 1982; Rucker, 1968).

The FCC's primary policy concern from 1945 through the early 1960s was on creating and then maintaining sufficient channels for a national system of broadcast television. A freeze on processing new TV station applications from 1948 to 1952 gave the commission time to develop a merged VHF and UHF allocation. The post-1952 UHF stations, however, could not cover the same area as competing VHF stations in the same market, and this "intermixture imbalance," and the resulting financial crisis for UHF broadcasters, dominated FCC policy as the agency sought ways to make its 1952 TV allocation decision work. After threatening wholesale shifting of on-air stations to "deintermix" VHF and UHF assignments—

assigning channels of only one type to a given market—the FCC persuaded Congress in 1962 to pass an "all channel" bill requiring TV sets to be able to receive both VHF and UHF bands. But the weaker UHF service had to await the 1980s and widespread availability of cable TV systems carrying its signals to achieve true parity with VHF (Kittross, 1979).

One other federal policy initiative concerned noncommercial broadcasting. Following publication of recommendations from the private-sector Carnegie Commission (1967), President Johnson pressed Congress to establish a Corporation for Public Broadcasting (U.S. Senate, 1967). The CPB, in turn, set up National Public Radio (NPR) and the Public Broadcasting Service (PBS) in 1968–69 to act as networks for their respective media. Subsequent years were rife with controversy and argument over how the system should operate—whether local stations or the new national entities should control funding and programming decisions (Blakely, 1979).

5. *Initiating Carrier Competition*

Though little noted at the time, the FCC and the federal courts from 1956 through 1969 issued a series of decisions that laid the groundwork for the substantial changes in common carrier regulation that would follow. These were not part of any concerted policy shift, but rather were incremental case-by-case changes that, taken together, created much of the basis for the radical structural changes in the industry in the 1980s. The 1956 *Hush-a-Phone* and 1968 *Carterfone* decisions began to deregulate the terminal equipment markets while the 1959 *Above 890* and 1969 *MCI* cases helped to open up telephone and data communication transmission markets to new entrants (Borchardt, 1970; Brock, 1981; Irwin, 1971).

6. *Presidential Policy Assessments*

Only rarely has communication policy reached the Presidential level (other than in personnel-appointment and budget-setting aspects). A little-remembered 1904 report to President Theodore Roosevelt was the first and determined that the Navy should have policy and operational control of government uses of wireless (Kittross, 1977, Vol. I). Much later, and then twice within 20 years, presidential-level task forces reviewed telecommunications to assess possible changes in U.S. policy and its administration. The 1951 "Truman Board," reporting at the height of the Korean War crisis, devoted much attention to national security needs and how best to organize the government to make the most of fast-changing technology (President's Communication Policy Board, 1952). One result was establishment of a telecommunication advisor in the office of the President. The "Rostow" task force, reporting in the midst of the Vietnam War in late 1968, took a broader view, assessing both media and common carrier communications and urging policies to expand educational television and the use of satellite communication, as well as upgrading the status and role of the presidential advisor (President's Task Force on Communication Policy, 1968). This led to the creation in 1970 of the Office of Telecommunications Policy as an expanded White House long-range policy agency (Will, 1978).

E. **Deregulation and Technological Progress 1970 to 1990**

1. *Competitive Entry in Common Carrier*

By the 1970s, the FCC was paying more attention to economic reasoning and began to develop a concerted and coordinated procompetition policy for the telephone industry. The *Specialized Common Carrier* (FCC, 1971b) and *Domestic Satellite* (FCC, 1972a; Magnant, 1977) decisions were the first comprehensive steps encouraging market entry by new carriers offering specialized services to business and government—but not yet individual—users. The commission focused on the growing impact of changing technology with two long-lasting proceedings, its three *Computer Inquiries* (FCC, 1971a, 1980, 1990b) and the *Competitive Common Carrier* inquiry (FCC, 1983). In the former, the FCC undertook the difficult job of defining what it could and would not regulate as the distinction between communication and data processing grew ever fuzzier. The second eventually determined that all carriers—save only "dominant" AT&T—would be subject to "streamlined" regulatory procedures (Frieden, 1981, 1987). The cumulative impact of these proceedings added pressure on AT&T as more competing companies offered a variety of new services—and protested AT&T's protected monopoly status (Brock, 1981; Faulhaber, 1988).

2. Divestiture of AT&T

This pressure from competing companies, combined with some nagging discomfort over the 1956 Final Judgment between the Justice Department and AT&T that had in the long run changed very little, expanding technological options, and growing evidence of anti-competitive activities of AT&T led to the third—and ultimately successful—government attempt to break up AT&T. Filed in November 1974, the case went to trial in 1981 and was settled out-of-court early in 1982. Facing a likely adverse verdict, AT&T agreed to divest all of its local operating companies, an agreement ratified in the so-called "Modified Final Judgment" issued in August 1982. After months of planning and considerable expense, the local operating companies were spun off into seven regional holding companies (RHCs, often called Regional Bell Operating Companies, or RBOCs) on January 1, 1984. AT&T reverted to its core long-distance market, retaining both manufacturing and research (Bell Laboratories) facilities (Sterling et al., 1986; Stone, 1989; Temin and Galambos, 1987). The decision radically changed the face of telecommunication policy, removing the single most important company from dominance of the local (and still monopoly) market, leaving it to face (and still dominate) a far more competitive long-distance and terminal equipment market. In an attempt to continue separation of monopoly-regulated local service from competitive market segments, the RBOCs were initially prevented from entering the telecommunication manufacturing, information (or value-added service), and long-distance service markets. An initial post–breakup review of the new telephone landscape by the supervising federal district court in 1987 led to only minimal change (Huber, 1987). By the early 1990s, under continuing pressure from the RBOCs seeking entry into the "forbidden markets," the information services ban had been removed and the other limitations seemed likely to fall (Cole, 1991; Sterling and Kasle, 1988).

3. Rise of Cable Television

The development of community antenna television (CATV), beginning in the late 1940s, is one of the best examples of regulatory change in communication—as well as of varied regulation at the federal, state, and local levels (Copple, 1991). Until the mid-1960s, cable TV was largely unregulated (local towns or counties "licensed" cable with monopoly franchises—because the systems needed to use public rights-of-way—often lasting 15 or 20 years) and serviced only a tiny minority of homes unable to receive TV signals off the air. Under pressure from television broadcasters concerned about potential competition, the FCC initiated regulation of microwave distribution of distant TV signals by cable systems in 1965 and by 1972 had issued so-called "definitive" regulations limiting cable service as an ancillary to broadcast television (FCC, 1972b; Berner, 1976; Le Duc, 1973). Enforcement of the resulting technical and program rules created a short-lived FCC bureau of 300 civil servants.

Over the next 5 years, much of this structure, enacted in part as a compromise among competing interests (broadcasters, cable system owners, and cities which franchised cable systems), came unstuck. Economic revisionism at the FCC combined with court review overturned many of the regulations, so that by 1980, most commission control had disappeared. A 1976 revision of the copyright act (effective in 1978) gave cable systems a blanket right to restransmit broadcast signals in return for paying a small portion of gross receipts to a Copyright Royalty Tribunal, which in turn paid those receipts out to program copyright holders. In 1984, Congress enacted the deregulatory Cable Act (which became a new Title VI in the Communications Act), largely preventing FCC or local franchise authority rate or program regulation of cable systems (Ferris et al., 1983).

Paced by this deregulatory trend and the post-1975 expansion of satellite-delivered national cable pay and advertiser-supported networks, cable had become the majority video service distributor for U.S. homes by the late 1980s (Garay, 1988). With this expanded role came rising public and political criticism of cable monthly subscriber fee increases and poor service—and pressure by cities and the public for renewed regulation. (Late in 1992, Congress passed strong legislation placing FCC controls over much of cable [see p. 470].)

4. Deregulation of Existing Services

Faced with its own decisions allowing entry by new competitors, the FCC was under continuous pressure after about 1970 to deregulate older media and common carrier providers to create more of a regulatory "level playing field." The pressure did lead to some changes in both economic and technical regulation for media and common carrier providers, although broadcasting and AT&T remained more heavily controlled than their respective competitors (Crandall and Flamm, 1989; Newburg, 1989).

After 1979, the commission abandoned many fairly minor economic and programming regulations and removed some minor technical requirements as well. The controversial "fairness doctrine"—which had since 1949 required licensees to offer an overall balance of viewpoints in programming on controversial issues of local public importance, a provision upheld by the *Red Lion* decision (Supreme Court, 1969; Geller, 1973; Rowan, 1984)—was abolished by a more conservative FCC in 1987 that argued that the increase in available outlets (stations, cable systems, and other services) made such a fairness requirement unnecessary. Critics argued the doctrine actually limited expression of ideas by scaring broadcasters off even dealing with such issues because so many choices and decisions would have to be faced (FCC, 1987).

Supported by affected industries, many economic rules dating from the early 1970s—when TV networks still dominated their local affiliates—remained in place 2 decades later despite an FCC desire to do away with their artificial shaping of competition. The "Prime Time Access Rule" limiting network control of primetime hours helped to create an industry of program syndicators who argued for the continued protection they felt the rule provided them. Networks were also denied the right to own program producers or to be financially in lucrative program syndication (Ginsburg et al., 1991). As their audience and income declined in the 1980s, networks pressed hard for the lifting of such economic limitations.

In common carrier, deregulation took an economic approach (Weinhaus and Oettinger, 1988). After years of debate, the FCC adopted in 1989–1990 a system of "price cap" rules to replace the "rate-of-return" regulation of telephone carrier revenues and prices. The new approach, borrowing from British experience, called for limits or caps on price increases while encouraging company efficiency by allowing carriers to retain revenues gained from streamlined operation (FCC, 1989, 1990a). The FCC also conducted three inquiries into the computer/

communications interface to determine what should be regulated and how. The third, concluding in the early 1990s, set up an "open network" approach to allow competitive access to the public switched network (Borrows and Graniere, 1991).

The commission also moved away from setting specific technical standards for new services in the 1980s, beginning with its decision to allow, but not to select, a specific AM stereo broadcasting system in 1982 (Besen and Johnson, 1986; Sterling, 1982). Economic thinking overrode engineering analysis as the commission argued it had no business deciding among competing providers and the "marketplace" (undefined) should make such selections. Facing the far more economically central high-definition television standards decision in the early 1990s, the FCC seemed likely to revert to its traditional practice of making a selection from industry-tested options. Increasingly, the commission looked on technological frontiers as places for regulation by means of economic and competitive pressures rather than government oversight (Egon, 1990; Elton, 1991; Wright, 1991).

Looking back on a century of developing communication policy (from the formation of the ICC), one can discern patterns in all the details. Until the Radio Act of 1912, Congress took no overall policy initiative in communication. Only with its Radio Act of 1927 did the legislature specify a "public interest" policy standard that controlled communications policy for some 60 years. Broadcasting and related services dominated commission and congressional time and effort into the 1970s. Only then did the fast-changing common carrier field and related technologies emerge as the larger policy concern (Pool, 1983, 1990). Beginning in that same decade, *de*regulation (based in considerable part on economic analysis) emerged as the dominant trend in communication as government on all levels withdrew from detailed oversight owing in part to budget pressure but also to economic thinking underpinning a concerted policy to let marketplace competition define available services and prices (Kahn, 1970–1971; Weinhaus and Oettinger, 1987; Wenders, 1987).

III. COMMUNICATION POLICY PLAYERS IN THE 1990s

As the American political system has grown more diffuse with more nontraditional parties taking part in recent years, and as communication issues have become more central in American life, three groupings of policy makers have become evident: government agencies (both federal and state); the private sector, including regulated industries; and international organizations. Each of these, in turn, has been subject to considerable splintering and specialization as the communications industries have expanded and grown more controversial.

A. Government Agencies

1. Congress

Under the Constitution, of course, Congress is to establish overall policy in this as in other sectors of the economy. Although congressional legislation punctuates the development of communications policy, that has been less true in recent years. The four traditional roles of Congress have changed in order of priority, at least in communication. Macropolicy legislation has largely given way to budget-determined (and thus often short-term) priorities. With few exceptions, congressional approval of executive appointments, as to the FCC (U.S. Senate, 1976), is now less important than the regular "oversight" hearings where congressmen vent their feelings and ideas and sometimes bend policy without more formal legislative action (Krasnow et al., 1982). Staff reports, sometimes based on such oversight, briefly become agenda-setting analyses, although few lead to specific congressional or agency action.

Congressional communications policy responsibility resides largely in the communication subcommittees of the commerce committees of both houses of government. Undergoing periodic name changes, the communications subcommittees hold hearings and recommend action to the parent committee. Other subcommittees with responsibilities in communication include copyright and antitrust concerns within the judiciary committees, technology standards in the science and technology committees, and post office and related concerns of post office committees of both houses. Government application of telecommunications is under the eye of the government operations committees. The growing concern about America's telecommunications trade imbalance has lent growing importance to the views of the Foreign Affairs Committees of both houses.

But as the active communication policy-making role of Congress seems to have diminished in recent years, the importance of newer congressionally related entities has increased.

2. Congressionally Related Agencies

Congress has considerable help in its setting of overall policy directions. The past 25 years have seen important policy roles played by such congressional bodies as the Office of Technology Assessment (set up in 1974) that issues one or more detailed communications-related studies a year, the General Accounting Office that reports on FCC and other entities several times a year, and others. These specialized research/investigative bodies aid ever-larger member and committee staffs to keep on top of increasingly complicated and controversial communications issues. They usually select research or investigative "targets" with guidance or outright mandates from related House and Senate committees.

Office of Technology Assessment studies are of considerable lasting value as they assume little background, are the result of substantial research in and out of government, are clearly organized and comprehensive in scope, and take no specific point of view. Each takes from 1 to 3 years to complete and is designed to meet specific requests from congressional committees (OTA, 1990, 1991).

3. Federal Communications Commission

Established by the Communications Act of 1934, the FCC is, after Congress, the single most important agency in U.S. communications policy making because only it can authorize (license) service providers. From that essential function grows considerable regulatory power, although it is often not fully used. Theoretically independent of both the president and Congress, the agency is in reality responsible to both. As with other specialized agencies, the FCC has been accused of being "in bed with" the very industries it regulates.

Because so much of its energy is consumed by service authorization, the FCC has historically not focused well on mid- to long-range policy. Creation of an Office of Telecommunication Policy in the executive office of the president in 1970 spurred formation of an Office of Plans and Policy (OPP) at the FCC. A small office (usually about a dozen professionals), OPP became a largely economic research shop in the 1980s, issuing research reports and suggesting policy initiatives, usually at the behest, or with the blessing, of the FCC chairman.

A small player in federal terms, the FCC in the early 1990s had a total staff of about 1800 and an annual budget of some $125 million. The professional staff includes attorneys (by far the largest single profession), engineers, accountants, and economists. Much of the routine license processing work is done by lower-ranking staff with such titles as "carrier analyst" and "applications examiner." The staff is divided into functional bureaus, of which the largest and most important are the three that authorize and regulate service: common carrier, mass media (broadcasting until 1981), and private radio. Its five commissioners (seven until 1982) are appointed by the president to serve 5-year terms and may be reappointed, although they average about 3.5 years of service before reentering the private sector. Nearly all are attorneys (FCC, 1935–date; Hilliard, 1991).

4. Federal Executive Agencies

Of the many executive branch agencies that have some communications concern, only a few stand out as consistently central in policy making. Chief among these is the National Telecommunications and Information Administration (NTIA) in the Department of Commerce. Established in 1978, and successor to the 1970 to 1978 Office of Telecommunications Policy, NTIA both advises and speaks for the administration on telecommunications matters. It is headed by an assistant secretary of commerce appointed by the president. In recent years, it has issued important policy reports on common carrier infrastructure, telecommunication trade policy, and spectrum management (NTIA, 1988, 1991a, 1991b). It makes numerous filings with the FCC to reflect administration policy. Further, the agency authorizes federal use of spectrum through the Interdepartmental Advisory Committee (IRAC), which it supports. IRAC, set up in 1922, is the oldest telecommunication policy body in the United States—it serves as a cooperative administrator of federal users of spectrum and coordinates spectrum assignments with the FCC.

Within the Department of State, the Bureau of International Communications and Information Policy (ICIP) was the focus of international policy deliberation, although division of authority with NTIA and the FCC in this regard is not totally clear and some turf battles have resulted. Folded into another bureau in 1993, ICIP still helps select most American delegations to International Telecommunication Union (ITU)–related meetings (see below).

5. Federal User/Procurement Agencies

The Departments of Defense (DoD) and Transportation (DoT) and the General Services Administration (GSA) are chiefly concerned with federal service and terminal equipment procurement, and in that way can often affect national policy. Concern for national security led DoD to play an active role in the 1949 and 1974 AT&T antitrust cases, trying in both cases to turn back attempts to break up AT&T with which DoD then had a close working relationship. DoD was successful in the 1949 case but was largely ignored in the 1974 proceeding as it was felt defense concerns could be incorporated within a restructured industry. The RBOC's formation of Bell Communication Research (Bellcore) is one result of DoD concern with adequate access to the nation's public switched network. Large procurement orders by the Army, Navy, and Air Force have direct impact on the pace of technical development in telecommunication and can assist (with research funding and orders) commercial applications of defense-applicable technology such as high-definition television.

The Department of Transportation is another large user of telecommunication—both the Federal Aviation Administration and the Coast Guard are heavy users of spectrum for specialized communications. The General Services Administration administers the controversial "FTS 2000" (federal telecommunication service), which is a contract service from AT&T and Sprint Communications. The largest federal contract outside of Defense, FTS became controversial when its price structure seemed to charge agencies more than like services in the open market (Bennington, 1989). The National Aeronautics and Space Administration (NASA) is both a user and provider in telecommunication, having charge of all launches from the Kennedy Space Center in Florida. Until a 1990 policy change, the NASA shuttle was the prime means of launching commercial communication satellites. When the agency determined it could only handle defense and scientific payloads, the decision led to a resurgence of the commercial launcher industry, which had been moribund for more than a decade owing to concentration on shuttle launches.

6. Justice and the Courts

The Department of Justice's Antitrust Division plays a central role in structuring the telecommunications industry because of its proceeding that led to the breakup of AT&T in 1984 and the division's continuing policy oversight of the aftermath of that divestiture. Antitrust also has oversight (sometimes strong and at other times weak depending on the administration in power) on both media and common carrier industry structure and ownership. Economic indicators such as the Herfindahl index of concentration are used to help determine whether or not government intervention (in the form of antitrust suits or lesser actions) is needed to correct marketplace imbalance.

Because of its jurisdiction over the AT&T divestiture's aftermath, the Federal District Court for the District of Columbia, and more specifically Judge Harold Greene of that court, have played a far larger role in communications policy than would normally be the case for any single judge. Greene has been referred to as the "czar" of American telecommunication because of his close and continued supervision of both AT&T and RBOC activity, growing out of the provisions of the MFJ. Critics have argued that Greene's role demonstrates the weakness of the fairly narrow antitrust laws when they are applied to major industry restructuring.

Partially because of this very concern, there have been several attempts by Congress to move the continuing divestiture aftermath proceedings to the FCC as the expert agency in communication. None has suceeded, partially owing to congressional concerns about how the heavily deregulatory FCC would handle the complicated issues but also because of the fear of the precedent of such a shift (moving a legal proceeding from the jurisdiction of the court to a regulatory agency) might create for future policy makers.

7. State Public Utility Commissions

Under the American federal system, policy in many sectors is made by a combination of federal and state agencies. State public utility commissions (PUCs), although sometimes known by different names (e.g., in Virginia, the PUC is called the State Corporation Commission), play a growing role in telecommunications policy. They have control (to the degree assigned either by a state's governor, or more likely, its legislature) over rates and conditions of service of carriers operating within their borders.

Prior to the 1984 breakup of AT&T, PUCs were perceived as a regulatory backwater in communication, with their staffs being undereducated on the nuances of communication issues and economics. That has rapidly changed in the past decade as RBOC operating companies, still defined along state lines as they were under AT&T administration, seek to provide new services, more flexible tariff structures to meet growing regional or local competition, and face demands (from PUCs or state legislatures) for so-called "lifeline" service (those basic dialtone services provided at rock-bottom rates for low-income users).

PUCs vary greatly in make-up, expertise, and political context. Some PUC commissioners are elected, whereas others are appointed. A few states, notably Nebraska, have largely deregulated telecommunication services and facilities within their borders, thus doing away with most of the PUC's former role. Others, such as those of California and New York, have a reputation for regulatory toughness and constantly dogging carriers to upgrade service while keeping rate increases to a minimum.

PUCs coordinate their activity through the National Association of Regulatory Utility Commissioners (NARUC), which in turn helps to sponsor the National Regulatory Research Institute (NRRI), which undertakes economic and policy research studies for member PUCs. NARUC conventions have often provided the forum for important policy statements by national industry or regulatory figures.

PUCs also coordinate their activities with the FCC, usually through appointed Joint Boards, governed by provisions of the Communications Act of 1934. Such Boards, which are made up of selected FCC and PUC commissioners (usually two or three of each), deal with specific issues which cross federal and state lines and make recommendations to the FCC. On rare occasions, the FCC will seek to preempt state action when it finds the national interest served by a single national policy rather than varied state approaches. In several cases, however, states have successfully overturned FCC attempts to override state perogatives (U.S. Supreme Court, 1986; U.S. Court of Appeals, 1990).

B. Private Sector Players

American communications policy making differs from that in most other nations owing to the often central part played by nongovernmental entities. Much of the technical and operational expertise in media and common carrier telecommunication lies in the private sector, and to bring that practical knowledge to bear in the policy process necessarily involves companies, trade associations, and other non–governmental participants—and their legal counsels (Domhoff, 1978).

1. Regulated Industries, Lobbiests, and Trade Associations

By far the strongest nongovernmental role in policy making is played by the communication businesses themselves. Long before government regulation existed, communication firms played an informal self-regulatory role. Even after the FCC was set up, communication companies continued to play central roles in determining how they should be regulated. AT&T, for example, made very effective use of the federal and state regulatory systems to maintain its monopoly role into the 1970s. In support of this lobbying, the company sponsored some of the best economic policy research and even published a respected journal, now the *Rand Journal of Economics.*

The rise of MCI in the 1970s, however, showed that the regulatory system could also be pressured to open a competitive wedge. For more than a decade after its formation in 1963, MCI spent far more on litigation and lobbying representation before the FCC and Congress than it did on provision of service (Kahaner, 1986).

Communication companies had almost constant need for legal representation after 1920, and fed the growth of the communications bar. Many law firms in Washington specialize in communication matters before the FCC and Congress (or have divisions that do so), and they have thus become an important locus of policy expertise.

Pioneer broadcasters were at the forefront of demands that Congress create a regulatory regime for their fledgling industry in the 1920s. The National Association of Broadcasters (NAB), formed in 1923 to fight music licensing agency (ASCAP) demands for radio payments for the use of licensed music, soon became an active lobbiest for regulation, and then against regulator decisions, a role it has played with varied success for 7 decades. As the broadcast industry grew larger and more varied, more specialized trade groups developed to serve those more specialized concerns. Likewise, the National Cable Television Association (NCTA) became by the 1950s the primary voice of the cable industry, and it had an enviable record of legislative and regulatory agency success by the late 1980s. The Electronics Industry Association (EIA) is the largest of several organizations representing manufacturers and participates in policy making with congressional testimony, FCC filings, statistical publications, and an active role in standard setting.

2. Foundations, Policy Groups, Think Tanks

A unique and varied role in communications policy making belongs to privately funded foundations and related policy study centers (Domhoff, 1978). Such groups can have substantial impact on public policies. The Ford Foundation, for example, is largely responsible for public television surviving the pre–federal funding era with more than $300 million in grants to help build stations and programming before 1976. The Carnegie Foundation supported two important studies of public television (1967, 1979), the first of which was instrumental in creating the national system of public television (the second, coming at a time the federal government was under severe financial pressure, had far less impact). The privately funded Aspen Institute for Humanistic Studies, founded in the late 1940s, was by the 1970s regularly sponsoring important policy workshops that combined industry, government, and academe on neutral ground. The Annenberg Foundation supports two graduate schools educating communication experts, as well as a Washington-based conference and workshop center. And the Markle Foundation left its prior path of funding medical research and became a primary funder of research and public broadcast programming in the late 1960s. In each of these cases, the initial funding came from private wealth applied to continuing philanthropy.

3. Media

Simply by keeping all participants current on the latest developments, as well as by providing some degree of institutional history, both the general and trade press play an important role in the policy-making process about which they report. Specialized trade papers (e.g., the weekly *Telecommunications Reports* on common carrier, weekly *Broadcasting & Cable* and *Television Digest* on electronic media, and *Communications Daily* newsletter on the whole field with a Washington and policy emphasis) help define the policy agenda by their coverage. Important general publications such as major daily newspapers (especially *The New York Times* and *Washington Post* in the communications field) not only keep the larger policy community informed of specific developments, but their pages are common sources for lobbying advertising efforts, especially that aimed at Congress.

4. Professionals and Their Organizations

That the United States is a society of joiners is evident in the many different organizations within which communication policy is debated and sometimes made. Communication attorneys, for example, come together in general (American Bar Association) and focused (Federal Communications Bar Association) groups that provide arenas for policy discussion and negotiation. The Practising Law Institute (New York) is one of several entities that hold regular and intensive legal training seminars to keep attorneys current on media and telecommunication issues. The published handbooks from these sessions are important collections of recent documents.

Telecommunications engineers play an active role in technical standard development and other aspects of policy making, usually through such associations as the Institute of Electrical and Electronic Engineers (IEEE), or Society of Motion Picture and Television Engineers (SMPTE). These large membership groups hold annual conventions and technical exhibitions that help measure the pulse of technical change. The groups and their individual members work through the private sector American National Standards Institute (ANSI) to develop agreed-upon standards for U.S. use cooperatively, and to forward proposals for potential worldwide standards to the Geneva, Switzerland–based International Standards Organization (ISO), as well as to the International Telecommunication Union (see below).

Unions (such as the International Brotherhood of Electrical Workers [IBEW]) play a more minor role in developing technical policy. The Communication Workers of America (CWA), on the other hand, has been a very vocal player in domestic policy, being concerned especially with trade policy impact on employment levels. The Radio Television News Directors Association, made up of broadcast station news chiefs, is an important player in First Amendment issues.

Academics play several communication policy roles: as educators, consultants, and often as participants (while on leave or between academic appointments). Mass communications, especially journalism, has been a college subject since the early years of this century. Broadcasting courses and then degrees were added in many schools even before World War II, although major growth came in the 1950s and after. Education about common carrier telecommunications was restricted to engineering until the 1970s when several interdisciplinary and management programs developed, usually on the graduate level. By the early 1990s, hundreds of institutions offered media education, and dozens dealt with telecommunication in more than an engineering fashion. The larger and more research-oriented of these institutions help train future policy personnel, offer conferences and workshops, issue publications, and provide research and consulting to both private and public entities.

More communication policy research has appeared in recent years, attesting to both increased interest in this field and better research methods. *Telecommunications Policy* began in England in 1976 as a quarterly research journal and now appears nine times annually with worldwide coverage. Other journals, usually quarterly, in law (e.g., *Federal Communications Law Journal*), economics, political science, and media (e.g., *Journal of Communication, Journal of Broadcasting and Electronic Media*) have increasingly featured policy-relevant communications research in recent years.

C. International Organizations

1. International Telecommunication Union

Of lasting and primary importance on the global level is the ITU, which began as a European telegraph convention in 1865, has been regularly restructured since (gaining its present title and adding concern with radio in 1932), and is now a part of the United Nations (Codding, 1952; ITU, 1965). Based in Geneva, Switzerland, with nearly all countries as members, the ITU provides common ground for negotiating technical standards, the use of frequency spectrum, and implementation of changing technology in the world's telecommunication links (Codding and Rutkowski, 1986). The ITU includes three important entities in which the world's countries cooperate on technical, financial, and sometimes operations matters.

The International Consultative Committee on Telegraph and Telephone (the abbreviation CCITT is based on the French-language order of the words in the name) and the International Consultative Committee on Radio (CCIR) are central to standards development. Working parties focusing on specific technologies or standards meet regularly, shaping recommendations for world administrative conferences on either radio (WARCs) or telegraph-telephone (WATTCs) that are held roughly every 4 years. The International Frequency Registration Board (IFRB), as its name suggests, keeps detailed track of who is using which spectrum assignment for what around the world. In the 1980s, the ITU stepped up its assistance to Third World members interested in developing telecommunication infrastructure.

All of these ITU entities have some impact on domestic U.S. policy making as they help create the worldwide context for domestic decision making. The United States generally agrees with ITU decisions and treaties, but it will on occasion take an exception to a decision that threatens to disrupt an established U.S. use of spectrum or technical standard.

Based on the work of a high-level committee of 21 experts who made 96 detailed recommendations and a resultant special plenipotentiary conference of all members held late in 1992, the ITU will be substantially reorganized in 1993. This will be the most important internal change in the organization in several decades. The existing CCIR, CCITT, and IFRB will give way to a new three-division structure built around technical standards, radio communication, and development assistance. Each of these divisions will have international advisory committees, and a World Administrative Radio Conference (WARC) will be held every other year.

2. Other United Nations' Entities

UNESCO, the UN Educational, Scientific, and Cultural Organization, was created in the late 1940s to pull together cooperative ventures in all three areas. It undertook important studies of worldwide media development from 1947 into the 1980s when it ran afoul of changing U.S. views of what the agency should and should not do. When UNESCO supported a "new world information order" to encourage Third World media development—but that some Western media saw as endangering freedom of news flow and free speech—the U.S. and Britain both left the organization. Based in Paris, UNESCO continues to focus on media applications in the 1990s (Preston et al., 1989).

The World Intellectual Property Organization (WIPO) is based in Rome and is concerned with protecting the rights of information creators across national borders. The UN General Assembly's Committee on Peaceful Uses of Outer Space (CPUS) has for many years been the focus of debate on such topics as whether countries have a right to prevent reception from direct broadcast satellites.

3. Intelsat

First set up as a temporary consortium in 1964, the International Telecommunications Satellite Organization, headquartered in Washington, DC, became a permanent treaty-based body in 1973. Comsat, the American signatory, controls 25% of the votes in Intelsat operations, a proportion based in large part on U.S. use—and thus funding—of the system. Until 1973, Comsat handled operations for the consortium as well. Intelsat operates an international satellite system that is owned by member countries and that began in 1965 with Intelsat I. By the early 1990s, the system had progressed to the far-greater capacity Intelsat VI and VII satellite series (Alper and Pelton, 1984; Snow, 1987).

Intelsat is one of the few world organizations headed by an American—the last three director generals have been U.S. nationals. Yet, ironically, the United States has been the source of considerable pressure on the international body with its insistence on the right of separate, commercial satellite systems to provide limited competition to Intelsat services.

IV. SELECTED POLICY ARENAS

Any discussion of specific policy areas in a field as multifaceted as communication is, by definition, arbitrary in the issues selected, their arrangement, and the conclusions drawn.

Given the increasing merging of "domestic" and "international" arenas, most policy issues have impact both here and abroad. Although this discussion is not inclusive, it does briefly describe some of the major economic/structural, technical, and individual rights issues of the early 1990s. No priority is suggested by the ordering used here.

A. Economic and Structural Questions

1. *Diversifying Media Ownership*

Questions of ownership have run consistently through communication policy in recent decades and show no sign of abating as a matter of considerable emotion, if not very much considered policy making. "Who shall own" communication media has generated considerable heat over the years. The controversy stems from the assumption – widely researched but not clearly proved one way or the other – that media ownership has impact on media content (e.g., minority ownership of a broadcast station will increase minority programming), and that generally speaking, diversity of ownership will provide diversity of content and point of view (Bagdikian, 1990; Compaine et al., 1982).

In the 1990s, the FCC appears to be developing several parallel policies for media ownership: (1) allowing more concentration in radio broadcasting; (2) moving more slowly on changes in television ownership; while at the same time (3) placing no ownership limits whatever on newer media services.

After limiting radio-TV station ownership to seven outlets of each type for some 30 years, the FCC raised the ceiling to 12 stations owing to the growing number of stations on the air and industry pressure. Early in 1992, as a compromise with those desiring no limits whatever on one side and congressional concern about excessive deregulation on the other, the commission raised radio ownership limits to 18 stations of each type (leaving TV at 12); presumably to promote radio by encouraging consolidation of larger more viable owners. At the same time, the FCC scrapped rules more than a half century old to allow common ownership of more than one radio station in the same market.

TV outlet ownership is more controversial as there are fewer stations (less than 1500 compared with more than 10,000 radio outlets), and until the 1980s, broadcast network dominance of this market – and most of the broadcast audience in prime time viewing hours – was substantial. The motion picture industry and others pressured the FCC and Congress not to allow further consolidation of TV stations. Only after considerable debate in the mid-1980s was the FCC able to increase TV station ownership ceilings to 12 outlets. The 1992 further deregulation of radio bypassed the TV issue entirely.

Cable television policy is being revised and strengthened as this is being written. Limited by few ownership controls, and substantially deregulated with regard to rates and service in 1984 legislation, cable systems had by the late 1980s angered subscribers with steady rate increases and sometimes marginal service. Congress passed strong *re*-regulatory cable legislation late in 1992 that greatly expanded FCC power and authority over cable subscriber rates and conditions of service – largely reversing 15 years of deregulation. The FCC received added budget and personnel in mid-1993 to implement the law's many complicated provisions. The FCC and Congress established some cross-media limits (e.g., no cable system ownership by national broadcast TV networks or local telephone companies) 2 decades ago, but only in 1993, under a mandate to act from Congress, did the FCC seriously propose limiting any single cable owner (to no more than 25% of all subscribers).

FCC introduction of newer technology-based players such as LPTV, MMDS, and DBS to compete with both broadcasting and cable is characterized by a total lack of ownership concern. Only being defined as this is being written is commission policy on allowing telephone carriers into the media field—typically dubbed "cable-telco" for the most immediate concern of common ownership of the two systems providing wire or cable into individual households (Brotman, 1990). At issue as well is a developing battle between two separate monpolies—daily newspapers and local telephone companies—over the papers' fears that electronic information service delivery could undermine much of the financial viability of printed media.

A substantial question facing any possible merger of the two services is the totally different regulatory traditions involved. Common carriers have been regulated as to rates and conditions of service, but not content, whereas media rates are unregulated, ownership diversity is debated, and content responsibility is assumed. How to merge those varied approaches is a fundamental issue barely approached thus far.

2. Developing Efficient Domestic Computer/Telecommunications Infrastructure

Common carrier policy was established with policy decisions of the 1980s: the breakup of AT&T; streamlined regulation for long-distance carriers other than AT&T; encouraging entry by new players in new fields; and continued close surveilance of the local monopoly Regional Bell Operating Companies (NTIA, 1991b; OTA, 1990).

FCC policy in the early 1990s focuses on implementation of two policies initiated in the previous decade: (1) completion of a tremendously expensive and detailed policy known as "open network architecture" (ONA), the concluding portion of its Third Computer Inquiry (Borrows and Graniere, 1991; FCC, 1990b); and (2) full implementation of its "price cap" initiative designed to protect users while encouraging greater carrier efficiency (FCC, 1989, 1990a).

An extensive NTIA study of the U.S. telecommunications infrastructure (NTIA, 1991) concluded that government regulatory intervention should be kept to an absolute minimum and applied only when market competition does not suffice to control prices and conditions of service. NTIA advocated competition in local exchange markets and a more advanced notion of "universal service" (see below).

3. Encouraging International Privatization

Until quite recently, the U.S. practice of having private sector operation of telecommunication facilities was all but unique in the world. Most countries ran postal and telecommunication services through a government entity—a "PTT" for Post-Telegraph-Telephone administration. Based on part on observation of long U.S. experience with private sector operation and our generally lower prices and more rapid technical innovation, on the clear success of British Telecom as an operator privatized in the 1980s, and in part on the sharply increasing cost of upgrading national networks, a rush to privatization is evident in the early 1990s in the former Soviet satellite countries of Eastern and Central Europe, Western Europe, and in Latin America (Hills, 1986; Tunstall and Palmer, 1990; Hills and Papathanassopoulos, 1991).

4. Increasing Trade in Telecommunication Equipment and Services

The growing U.S. imbalance of trade in telecommunication since 1982 threatens to dominate if not define U.S. policy on world telecommunication. At issue are questions of trade and nontrade barriers to telecommunication services and equipment trade, mutual access to markets, accusations of unfair pricing to gain market share, and cultural dominance by developed over developing nations.

The development of European economic integration in the early 1990s has been one focus of concern as the EEC may both raise barriers to imports of American communication services and become a stronger competitor in world markets. The main focus, however, is on perceptions of unfair trade practices in communication among other fields by the Japanese. Pressure from Congress (being pressured, in turn, by affected U.S. companies) for some kind of reciprocal trade arrangements with both Europe and Japan will likely continue to increase in the 1990s (NTIA, 1990).

5. *Applying Communication in Economic Development*

Here there are two related sets of policy concerns: the costs and impact of using telecommunication to assist Third World development; and the application of telecommunication in state, city, and rural development both here and elsewhere. On the former, much research has been done though there is considerable disagreement still on the cost effectiveness and varied roles of telecommunication and media services in hastening agricultural, industrial, social, and political development in Third World countries (Saunders et al., 1983). The basic policy issue in the 1990s is how much developed countries are willing to contribute, and whether those contributions are bilateral and related to broader foreign policy concerns, or multilateral through such neutral sources as the United Nations, World Bank, or other cooperative agencies. There is considerable confusion, however, on which means of communication to stress for which purposes—radio due to its ubiquity and lack of need for audience literacy, television for its visual impact (but higher cost), newspapers for their depth (but distribution problems outside of major cities), or telephones to tie distant places together by voice lines.

In the U.S., there has been increased focus in recent years on the need to better understand and plan for telecommunication applications in economic development in rural areas (OTA, 1991; Schmandt et al., 1991), in cities (Schmandt et al., 1990), and at the state level where telecommunication policy making is now generally more important in the aftermath of AT&T's divestiture (Schmandt et al., 1989; Teske, 1990). Cities and states are going through the same cycle as the federal level: whether or not to regulate, and if so, how much so as not to impede technical innovation? Generally, most communities and many states are opting to regulate to only a limited extent as long as competition exists in the market in question.

B. **Regulating Changing Technology**

1. *Choosing Technical Standards*

As the United States becomes more active in global export markets, U.S. companies and government agencies are playing a more active part in worldwide technical standard setting. Agreement on such standards greatly aids interconnectability of national networks and different kinds of services. Widespread agreement on standards can greatly ease trade across national borders, although as with color TV standards in the 1960s, political and economic priorities in one or more countries can lead to multiple standards where technological considerations alone would promote a single approach (Crane, 1979). To get that agreement on a single approach, the worldwide negotiation process can take years, which threatens a technology with obsolescence before it reaches final approval (Savage, 1989; Wallenstein, 1990).

Until 1982, the FCC usually mandated a technical standard chosen from among those tested by industry recommendations on the best standard. While the FCC experimented in the 1980s with so-called "marketplace" technical standards (where the FCC allowed a new service to begin but left determination of which standard or standards would be used to providers of that service—see Besen and Johnson, 1986), it appears likely that the huge market potential and risks of high-definition television (HDTV) require a return to more traditional approaches. The FCC should receive industry test results of a "grand alliance" of four formerly competing all-digital HDTV systems by early 1994. FCC blessing of those results should lead to the U.S. standard for future developments in television. Given the failure of marketplace standard-setting with AM stereo (few stations picked a system and in early 1993 Congress mandated the FCC to formally select one. It seems government's role in standard-setting is again secure.

2. Improving Spectrum Management

Allocation, allotment, and assignment of telecommunication services that use spectrum—spectrum management—is a slow process increasingly under pressure from users and critics who argue market mechanisms could increase efficiency of spectrum use over the traditional centralized government "block allocation" scheme used for decades (Levin, 1971). Market mechanisms such as auction, lease, or outright sale confer property rights on spectrum holders who will then, so the economic argument goes, make the most efficient technical and economic use of "their" space (NTIA, 1991a). Arguing against such a radical shift in spectrum management are traditional spectrum users, including broadcasters and other older services who feel more comfortable with the present system even with its delays. Further, some spectrum-based services such as those for health and public safety, cannot compete in a market-driven spectrum world. So compromises, including specified set-asides for such services, must be included in any spectrum marketplace experiment or full-fledged policy implementation.

More efficient spectrum management is central to development of many new technologies, for without access to sufficient spectrum, some of those new services, including many proposed personal communication services (PCS), can never get off the ground. And spectrum access nearly always means *re*allocation of spectrum from some other use to the new service, raising comparisons of equity, number of people served, and the like between newer services seeking spectrum and older services already holding allocations.

3. Introducing Competing Technology Systems

Ever since innovation of the telephone began to threaten telegraph services, regulators and operators alike have faced how to deal effectively with changing technology—allowing innovation and transition without excessive disruption of existing services. All the talk in the 1980s and 1990s about so-called "new technologies" is really a misnomer—we face a variety of competing ways of accomplishing the same end—usually transmitting entertainment—and must chose among them. Few are really new having developed over a period of years, often in varied forms. The policy question is who does the chosing—a government agency selecting one or more technologies for adoption or a competitive market? Increasingly in the United States, the answer has been the latter—often to the confusion of consumers such as those trying to decide what kind of home audio or video recording devices to purchase among a plethora of incompatible formats with variable capacities and functions.

A major policy debate in the early 1980s surrounded the proposed introduction of direct broadcast satellite (DBS) services. Although the FCC finally found in favor of the new service and reallocated spectrum accordingly by 1983, the first generation of such service never got off the ground. Only in the 1990s with improved technology (chiefly video compression allowing several TV channels per satellite transponder) and a consortium approach did it appear likely the United States would see DBS service. In Europe and in Japan, DBS services were operating by the late 1980s, offering greater choice to viewers over limited terrestrial networks. At the United Nations, in the meantime, diplomats have argued for more than 15 years over whether a country has the right to restrict incoming DBS signals.

Policy makers often intercede is in such international markets when different countries and economic systems are tied by similar telecommunication networks. The first undersea telegraph cables of the 1860s showed the way for such cooperation. A century later, there was widespread agreement on the value of Intelsat when the satellite consortium was first set up in 1964, and there was not much disagreement on details of its role when it became permanent 9 years later. But then the potential of competing satellite systems, at least for some "thick route" business voice and data needs, became evident and the United States in the mid-1980s departed from the views of most other countries in pushing for acceptance of these "separate systems." At the same time, technology in the form of fiber optic undersea cables, increased capacity on the North Atlantic, and later Pacific routes, giving users a choice beyond Intelsat. How the international organization will respond to these twin competitive thrusts is still not clear.

C. Protecting Individual Rights

1. *Increasing Access to Communication*

This is a set of interrelated questions that is central to the communication policy debate in the 1990s. There are at least three separate and specific kinds of access. First comes a concern for individual rights to some degree of "universal service," whether that be plain old telephone or something more exotic. Second is a more specific focus on ethnic minority access: ownership of and employment in communication and programming by communication media of interest to minority audiences. Third and most diffuse is the concern by developing nations that they not be left behind in the race to current technologies—most specifically their concern about access to the geostationary orbit when their needs so dictate.

Defining communication "universal service" (one way of assessing individual access) in this era of rapid change is a difficult thing to do. To some, the term denotes a basic minimal level of two-way communication, usually voice, to which all individuals should have access, even if public subsidy is necessary to meet that goal. To others, universal service suggests a wider aim—getting as many modern communication technology options before as many potential users as is economically viable. This view posits plain old telephone service only as a base on which to build. If the former view holds sway, policy makers risk creating a substantial class of "information poor" of those who cannot actively participate in an increasingly information-driven society. Such an information "gap" could have important social and economic impact by early in the coming century.

A similar gap, but with an ethnic emphasis, is the continuing result until and unless minorities are given a greater chance to play a proportionate role in both electronic media and telecommunication. Although the "melting pot" image no longer holds the sway it once did to describe U.S. integration of minorities into mainstream life, communications media remain central to the self-image of such groups. The FCC has established numerous means to increase minority ownership and employment levels in electronic media (Compaine et al., 1982), but in the 1990s, it has seemed at least uncomfortable with its proactive role.

Access on a global level usually means two very separate things: (1) access to information about local and world events—i.e., what industrial countries call the "free flow" of information, whereas developed nations fear "cultural imperialism" given their lack of control of major world news agencies and entertainment channels (Aronson and Cowhey, 1988; Preston et al., 1989); and (2) access to/control of the means of international communication—geostationary orbital arc positions, satellite transponders, undersea cables, international broadcast transmitters, and the like (Demac, 1986; Hudson, 1990; and Smith, 1991). The first case is partially one of sociopolitical definition (with strong economic overtones), whereas the second is an example of the high cost of modern communication channels and the "first-come, first-served" approach of industrial nations. These two issues are at the base of most communication policy debates within the ITU and its organs as well as the United Nations itself.

2. Protecting Individual Rights

This becomes more important as technology makes it easier to both invade one's privacy (an issue dealt with elsewhere in this volume) and to make use of others' intellectual property without paying for the privilege. Copyright, patent, and related legal regimes are under assault by fast-changing technology, especially computer-based digital options (OTA, 1986).

Although Congress last revised the basic copyright law in 1976, several revisions have already been made in it, and digital audio and video recording devices are behind further pressure for change. Balancing broad societal needs to improve and develop through use of information against an individual's right for return on his or her intellectual property has been a policy issue at least since the Constitution gave Congress the power to enact laws to protect such property. The 1990s are already seeing highly emotional debates over such things, exemplified in the argument over "colorized" motion pictures (those originally issued in black and white and turned into color by digital computer processes)—arguments about who owns the "new" version, can it be legally protected as a "new" creation, and whether there is even a right (moral or legal) to produce such a thing in the first place. In the 1970s, attempts were made to limit severely availability of consumer videocassette recorders by a motion picture industry fearful of illicit recording of their product. Instead, what has developed is a far larger means of distribution than traditional theatrical showings. But the case shows both the danger of "Luddite" thinking and the real problems newer technologies create for older industries. Balancing these conflicts will be a major policy focus in coming years.

V. CONCLUSIONS AND COMMENTS

A. The Interaction of Policy, Technology, and Economics

The history and current state of communication policy are both the result of the constantly changing interrelationship among political pressures, technical development, and economic constraints. At any given time, different things lead or push change—rarely are all three in balance. Initial regulation of telecommunication, for example, was due to political concerns over monopoly telegraph and telephone service rates. The 1930s FCC investigation of AT&T grew out of similar concerns. Technology, on the other hand, drove change when the rise of broadcasting in the 1920s upset existing regulations that had not forseen such a service. Technology again drove electronic media policy as FM and TV challenged AM broadcasting. The economic survival of UHF television and economic dominance of TV networks controlled other policy concerns from 1950 well into the 1970s. A last strong political push for traditional regulatory values dominated the 1960s to be replaced after 1970 or so with technology pushing change in common carrier (microwave- and satellite-driven new entry) and electronic media (cable and satellite delivery threatening the broadcast order). Since about 1980, economic issues have dominated policy making (the AT&T breakup and subsequent restructuring of common carrier and the conflicting economic arguments of older versus newer media services).

Another parallel way to view such changes is on their varied disciplinary approaches—lawyers in the ascendency during times of political dominance, economists when economic issues defined change, and (more rarely) engineers and their technical concerns when technology drove policy decisions. But really to understand changing currents in this field, one must look for the interaction or varied weighting of all three.

Further, it can not be overemphasized that in U.S. communication policy, there has only rarely been widespread agreement on, or support of, any single policy for any period of time. Rather, one of the things making this field both fascinating and frustrating at the same time is the very disagreement over central issues and trends that is so evident in regulatory hearings or proceedings. This has led time and again to incremental change and compromise, second guessing, and reconsideration as opposed to any lasting planning with long-range goals in mind.

B. Retreat of Government—Deregulation

Evident for the past 150 years ago has been constant indecision over which—if any—government agencies should play what communication policy role. Government as the authorizer/licenser of telecommunication services is the essential function likely to change little in coming years. On the other hand, the follow-on role of one or more government agencies as regulators of those authorized services has steadily declined in the past decade, and it shows signs of continuing to do so. The cost (and deficit) of government, changing political ideology that argues for less governmental intervention in business, and improving technology that opens up more competition have all contributed to this deregulatory trend. Each year, the resulting competitive marketplace takes over more of what had been bureaucratic perogative. It is still too soon to judge whether this trend is healthy in the long run for users as well as providers of service and hardware, but indications are that it is.

Ironically, and as with other policy sectors, it had taken years to build up a communication regulatory structure in the first place. It took the *Titanic* disaster to push Congress into an effective regulation of maritime communication in 1912, and a rising clamour over 6 years of broadcasting chaos before Congress finally created the FRC in 1927. The changing relationship of the federal government and AT&T also evolved over decades, with the comfortable and often informal relationship being threatened only with the late 1930s FCC investigation, the 1949 filing of what turned out to be a fruitless antitrust case, and the final breakup in the 1980s. As we move farther from the 1982 agreement to break up AT&T, that decision can be seen as a kind of high-water mark of government regulation—the ultimate end of a process begun late in the 19th century. Although there is still some partisan disagreement over the pace of deregulation in both media and common carrier fields, the overall trend seems irreversable.

Deregulation is driven as well by a recognition that policy making in this field is increasingly reactive rather than proactive, being driven as it is in large part by technical changes outside the sphere of government management or control. As government is unable to move as fast as technological change—and the economic pressures and opportunities such change generates—there is a widespread feeling that government should "get out of the way" and let the marketplace operate.

C. Central Role of Communication in a Changing World

All of this said and done, communication policy is important because communication media and services are increasingly central in all levels of public and private sector operations worldwide. The brief Gulf War of early 1991 was fought on living room TV screens worldwide just as the latest communication technology connected fast-moving air and ground forces in the fighting itself. Dramatic changes later that year in the former Soviet Union not only played on Western TV screens, but it can be argued that the glare of world publicity on the attempted hardline coup in July prevented a reversion to the old ways of dictatorship just as censorship of news coverage allowed a Chinese government to suppress the Tieneman Square Chinese student uprising of two summers before. These are but dramatic examples of how much we have grown to depend on communication channels of all kinds—and how "policy" decisions, now made more typically by private sector competitors rather than government agencies, regarding those channels have large impact on our daily lives.

NOTE

The literature in communication policy grows—and improves—continually. References here are purposely extensive to include the best English-language material as of publication of this book. To stay current, check reviews in such journals as *Telecommunication Policy*, and *Journal of Communication* as well as the bimonthly *Communication Booknotes*, which annually details U.S. government communications publications in its July-August issue, and the biennial annotated bibliographies issued by *Booknotes* (write: Center for Advanced Study in Telecommunication, Ohio State University, Columbus, OH 43210).

REFERENCES

Alper, J., and Pelton, J. N. (Eds.) (1984). *The Intelsat Global Satellite System*. American Association of Aeronautics and Astronautics, New York.

Aronson, J. A., and Cowhey, P. F. (1988). *When Countries Talk: International Trade in Telecommunications Services*. Ballinger Publishing, Cambridge, MA.

AT&T (1914). *1913 Annual Report*. American Telephone & Telegraph Co., New York, 1914, pp. 24–27.

Bagdikian, B. H. (1990). *The Media Monopoly*, 3rd ed. Beacon Press, Boston.

Barnett, S. R., Botein, M., and Noam, E. M. (1988). *Law of International Telecommunication in the United States*. Nomos Verlagsgesellschaft, Baden-Baden, Germany.

Bennington, B. J. (1989). *Beyond FTS2000: A Program for Change*. National Research Council, Washington, D.C.

Berner, R. (1976). *Constraints on the Regulatory Process: A Case Study of Regulation of Cable Television*. Ballinger, Cambridge, MA.

Besen, S. M., and Johnson, L. (1986). *Compatibility Standards, Competition and Innovation in the Broadcasting Industry*. Rand Corporation, Santa Monica, CA.

Blakely, R. J. (1979). *To Serve the Public Interest: Educational Broadcasting in the United States*. Syracuse University Press, Syracuse, NY.

Bolter, W., Duvall, J. R., Kelsey, F. J., and McConnaughey, J. W. (1984). *The Transition to Competition: Telecommunications Policy for the 1980s*. Prentice-Hall, Englewood Cliffs, NJ.

—— (1990). *Telecommunications Policy for the 1990s and Beyond*. M. E. Sharpe, Armonk, NY.

Borchardt, K. (1970). *Structure and Performance of the U.S. Communications Industry: Government Regulation and Company Planning*. Graduate School of Business Administration, Harvard University, Cambridge, MA.

Borrows, J. D., and Graniere, R. J. (1991). *An Open Network Architecture Primer for State Regulators*. National Regulatory Research Institute (NRRI 91-20), Columbus, OH.

Brock, G. W. (1981). *The Telecommunications Industry: The Dynamics of Market Structure*. Harvard University Press, Cambridge, MA.

Brotman, S. N. (Ed.) (1990). *Telephone Company and Cable Television Competition: Key Technical, Economic, Legal and Policy Issues*. Artech House, Norwood, MA.

Burleson, A. S., Postmaster General (1914). *Government Ownership of Electrical Means of Communication*. 63rd Cong, 2nd Sess., Senate Document No. 399. (Includes appendices detailing all prior Post Office attempts at regaining control of the telegraph and telephone—most of this document reprinted in Kittross, 1977, Vol. I).

Carnegie Commission on Educational Television (1967). *Public Television: A Program for Action.* Harper & Row, New York.

Chafee, Z. Jr. (1941). *Free Speech in the United States.* Harvard University Press, Cambridge, MA.

—— (1947). *Government and Mass Communications: A Report from the Commission on Freedom of the Press* (2 vols). University of Chicago Press, Chicago.

Codding, G. A., Jr. (1952). *The International Telecommunication Union: An Experiment in International Cooperation.* E. J. Brill (Ed.). Leiden, The Netherlands (reprinted by Arno Press, New York, 1972).

Codding, G. A., Jr., and Rutkowski, A. M. (1982). *The International Telecommunication Union in a Changing World.* Artech House, Boston.

Cole, B. G. (Ed.) (1991). *After the Break-Up: Assessing the New Post-AT&T Divestiture Era.* Columbia University Press, New York.

Compaine, B. R., Sterling, C. H., Guback, T., and Noble, J. K., Jr. (1982). *Who Owns the Media? Concentration of Ownership in the Mass Communications Industry*, 2nd ed. Knowledge Industry Publications, White Plains, NY.

Copple, R. F. (1991). Cable television and the allocation of regulatory power: A study of governmental demarcation and roles. *Fed. Comms. Law J. 44:* 1:1 (December).

Crandall, R. W., and Flamm, K. (Eds.) (1989). *Changing the Rules: Technological Change, International Competition and Regulation in Communications.* Brookings Institution, Washington, D.C.

Crane, R. J. (1979). *The Politics of International Standards: France and the Color TV War.* Ablex Publishing, Norwood, NJ.

Danielian, N. R. (1939). *AT&T: The Story of Industrial Conquest.* Vanguard Press, New York (reprinted by Arno Press, New York, 1974).

Davis, S. (1927). *The Law of Radio Communication.* McGraw-Hill, New York.

Demac, D. A. (Ed.) (1986). *Tracing New Orbits: Cooperation & Competition in Global Satellite Development.* Columbia University Press, New York.

Domhoff, G. W. (1978). *The Powers That Be: Processing of Ruling Class Domination in America.* Random House, New York.

Egan, B. L. (1991). *Information Superhighways: The Economics of Advanced Public Communication Networks.* Artech House, Norwood, MA.

Elton, M. C. J. (Ed.) (1991). *Integrated Broadband Networks: The Public Policy Issues.* North-Holland, Amsterdam.

Emord, J. W. (1991). *Freedom, Technology and the First Amendment.* Pacific Research Institute for Public Policy, San Francisco.

Faulhaber, G. R. (1987). *Telecommunications in Turmoil: Technology and Public Policy.* Ballinger Publishing, Cambridge, MA.

(FCC) Federal Communications Commission (1935–date). *Annual Report*, Government Printing Office, Washington, D.C.

—— (1939). *Investigation of the Telephone Industry in the United States.* 76th Cong., 1st Sess., House Document No. 340 (reprinted by Arno Press, New York, 1974).

—— (1959). *Allocation of Frequencies in the Bands Above 890 Mc.* (Docket 11866). 27 FCC 359.

—— (1971a). *Regulation and Policy Problems Presented by the Interdependence of Computer and Communications Services and Facilities.* (Docket 16979), 28 FCC 2d 267. (Computer Inquiry I).

—— (1971b). *Establishment of Policies and Procedures for Consideration of Applications to Provide Specialized Common Carrier Services...* (Docket 18920). Report and Order. 29 FCC 2d 870.

—— (1972a). *In the Matter of Establishment of Domestic Communications Satellite Facilities* (Docket 16495). Report and Order. 35 FCC 2d 844.

—— (1972b). *Cable Television Report and Order* (Dockets 18397, 18373, 18416, 18892, 18894), 36 FCC 2d 3.

—— (1980). *Amendment of Section 64.702 of the Commission's Rules and Regulations (Second Computer Inquiry).* (Dockets 20828, 80-189), 77 FCC 2d 364.

—— (1983). *Competitive Carrier Rule-Making: Fourth Report and Order.* (Docket 79-252) 95 FCC 2d 554.

—— (1987). *In Re Complaint of Syracuse Peace Council against Television Station TWVH...* Memorandum Opinion and Order, 2 FCC Record 5043.

—— (1989). *Policy and Rules Concerning Rates for Dominant Carriers.* (Docket CC87-313), Report and Order, 4 FCC Record 2873 ("price cap" for AT&T).

—— (1990a). *Policy and Rules Concerning Rates for Dominant Carriers* (Docket CC-87-313), Report and Order, 5 FCC Record 6786 ("price cap" for RBOCs).

—— (1990b). *Third Computer Inquiry* (Docket CC85-229), 5 FCC Record 3084.

Ferris, C. D., Lloyd, F. W., and Casey, T. J. (1983). *Cable Television Law* (3 vols). Matthew Bender, New York (updated twice annually).

Fifty Years of Telecommunications Reports (1985). Telecommunications Reports, Inc., Washington, D.C.

Frieden, R. (1981). The Computer Inquiries: Mapping the Communications/Information Processing Terrain, *Fed. Comms. Law J.* 33: 55–115.

—— (1987). The Third Computer Inquiry: A Deregulatory Dilemma, *Fed. Comms Law J.* 38: 383–410.

Garay, R. (1988). *Cable Television: A Reference Guide to Information.* Greenwood Press, Westport, CT.

Geller, H. (1973). *The Fairness Doctrine in Broadcasting: Problems and Suggested Courses of Action.* Rand Corporation, Santa Monica, CA.

Ginsburg, D. H., Boetin, M. H., and Director, M. D. (1991). *Regulation of the Electronic Mass Media: Law and Policy for Radio, Television, Cable and the New Video Technologies.* West Publishing, St. Paul, MN.

Henn, H. G. (1991). *Henn on Copyright Law: A Practitioner's Guide,* 3rd ed. Practising Law Institute, New York.

Herring, J. M., and Gross, G. C. (1936). *Telecommunications: Economics and Regulation.* McGraw-Hill, New York (reprinted by Arno Press, New York, 1974).

Hilliard, R. L. (1991). *The Federal Communications Commission: A Primer.* Focal Press, Stoneham, MA.

Hills, J. (1986). *Deregulating Telecoms: Competition and Control in the United States, Japan and Britain.* Quorum Books, Westport, CT.

—— , and Papathanassopoulos, S. (1991). *The Democracy Gap: The Politics of Information and Communication Technologies in the United States and Europe.* Greenwood Press, Westport, CT.

Hixon, R. (1989). *Mass Media and the Constitution: An Encyclopedia of Supreme Court Decisions.* Garland Press, New York.

Horwitz, R. B. (1989). *The Irony of Regulatory Reform: The Deregulation of American Telecommunications.* Oxford University Press, New York.

Howeth, L. S. (1963). *History of Communications-Electronics in the U.S. Navy.* Government Printing Office, Washington, D.C.

Huber, P. (1987). *The Geodesic Network: 1987 Report on Competition in the Telephone Industry.* Government Printing Office, Washington, D.C.

Hudson, H. E. (1990). *Communication Satellites: Their Development and Impact.* Free Press, New York.

Irwin, D. A. (1985–date). *Telecommunications Regulatory Monitor.* Phillips Publishing, Potomac, MD.

Irwin, M. R. (1971). *The Telecommunications Industry: Integration vs Competition.* Praeger, New York.

(ITU) International Telecommunication Union (1965). *From Semaphore to Satellite.* International Telecommunication Union, Geneva.

Kahaner, L. (1986). *On The Line: The Men of MCI—Who Took on AT&T, Risked Everything, and Won!* Warner Books, New York.

Kahn, A. E. (1970–1971). *The Economics of Regulation: Principles and Institutions* (2 vols.). John Wiley & Sons, New York.

Kahn, F. (Ed.) (1984). *Documents of American Broadcasting,* 4th ed. Prentice-Hall, Englewood Cliffs, NJ.

Kittross, J. M. (Ed.) (1977). *Documents in American Telecommunications Policy* (2 vols.). Arno Press, New York.

—— (1979). *Television Frequency Allocation Policy in the United States.* Arno Press, New York (facsimile publication of the author's 1960 dissertation, University of Illinois, Chicago).

—— (1980). *Administration of American Telecommunications Policy* (2 vols.). Arno Press, New York.

Krasnow, E. L., Longley, L. D., and Terry, H. A. (1982). *The Politics of Broadcast Regulation*, 3rd ed. St. Martin's Press, New York.

Le Duc, D. R. (1973). *Cable Television and the FCC*: *A Crisis in Media Control.* Temple University Press, Philadelphia.

Levin, H. J. (1971). *The Invisible Resource*: *Use and Regulation of the Radio Spectrum.* Johns Hopkins Press, Baltimore.

Lindley, L. G. (1975). *The Constitution Faces Technology*: *The Relationship of the National Government to the Telegraph, 1866-1884.* Arno Press, New York.

Magnant, R. S. (1977). *Domestic Satellite*: *An FCC Giant Step—Towards Competitive Telecommunications Policy.* Westview Press, Boulder, CO.

McCaw, T. K. (1984). *Prophets of Regulation*: *Charles Francis Adams, Louis D. Brandeis, James M. Landis and Alfred E. Kahn.* Harvard University Press, Cambridge, MA.

(NTIA) National Telecommunications and Information Administration (1988). *NTIA Telecom 2000*: *Charting the Course for a New Century.* NTIA Special Publication 88-21, Government Printing Office, Washington, D.C.

—— (1990). *U.S. Telecommunications in a Global Economy*: *Competitiveness at a Crossroads.* Government Printing Office, Washington, D.C.

—— (1991a). *U.S. Spectrum Management Policy*: *Agenda for the Future.* NTIA Special Publication 91-23, Government Printing Office, Washington, D.C.

—— (1991b). *Telecommunications in the Age of Information*: *The NTIA Infrastructure Report.* NTIA Special Publication 91-26, Government Printing Office, Washington, D.C.

Newberg, P. (Ed.) (1989). *New Directions in Telecommunications Policy* (2 vols.). Duke University Press, Durham, NC.

(OTA) Office of Technology Assessment, U.S. Congress (1986). *Intellectual Property Rights in an Age of Electronics and Information.* Government Printing Office, Washington, D.C.

—— (1990). *Critical Connections*: *Communication for the Future.* Government Printing Office, Washington, D.C.

—— (1991). *Rural America at the Crossroads*: *Networking for the Future.* Government Printing Office, Washington, D.C.

Paglin, M. (Ed.) (1989). *A Legislative History of the Communications Act of 1934.* Oxford University Press, New York.

Pool, I. deS. (1983). *Technologies of Freedom*: *On Free Speech in an Electronic Age.* Harvard University Press, Cambridge, MA.

—— , edited by Noam, E. A. (1990). *Technologies Without Boundaries*: *On Telecommunications in a Global Age.* Harvard University Press, Cambridge, MA.

Powe, L. A., Jr. (1991). *The Fourth Estate and the Constitution*: *Freedom of the Press in America.* University of California Press, Berkeley.

President's Communication Policy Board (1952). *Telecommunications*: *A Program for Progress.* Government Printing Office, Washington, D.C. (reprinted in Kittross, 1977, Vol. II).

President's Task Force on Communications Policy (1968). *Final Report.* Government Printing Office, Washington, D.C.

Preston, W. Jr., Herman, E. S., Schiller, H. I. (1989). *Hope & Folly*: *The United States and Unesco, 1945-1985.* University of Minnesota Press, Minneapolis.

Rose, C. B., Jr. (1940). *National Policy for Radio Broadcasting.* Harper, New York (reprinted by Arno Press, New York, 1971).

Rosen, P. T. (1980). *The Modern Stentors*: *Radio Broadcasters and the Federal Government, 1920-1934.* Greenwood Press, Westport, CT.

Rowan, F. (1984). *Broadcast Fairness*: *Doctrine, Practice, Prospects*. Longman, New York.

Rucker, B. W. (1968). *The First Freedom*. Southern Illinois University Press, Carbondale.

Saunders, R. J., Warford, J. J., and Wellenius, B. (1983). *Telecommunications and Economic Development*. Johns Hopkins University Press, Baltimore.

Savage, J. G. (1989). *The Politics of International Telecommunications Regulation*. Westview Press, Boulder, CO.

Schmandt, J., Williams, F., and Wilson, R. H. (1989). *Telecommunications Policy and Economic Development*: *The New State Role*. Praeger, New York.

—— (1990). *The New Urban Infrastructure*: *Cities and Telecommunications*. Praeger, New York.

—— (1991). *Telecommunications and Rural Development*: *A Study of Private and Public Sector Innovation*. Praeger, New York.

Schmeckebier, L. F. (1932). *The Federal Radio Commission*: *Its History, Activities and Organization*. Brookings Institution, Washington, D.C.

Smith M. L. (1991). *International Regulation of Satellite Communication*. Martinus Nijhoff, Dordrecht, The Netherlands.

Snow, M. S. (1987). *The International Telecommunications Satellite Organization*: *Economic and Institutional Challenges Facing an International Organization*. Nomos Verlagsgesellschaft, Baden-Baden, Germany.

Sterling, C. H. (1982). The FCC and Changing Technological Standards. *J. of Commun. 32*: 4: 137–147 (Fall).

—— (Ed.) (1984). *International Telecommunications and Information Policy*. Communications Press, Washington, D.C.

——, Kasle, J. F., and Glakas, K. (Eds.) (1986). *Decision to Divest*: *Key Documents in U.S. v. AT&T 1974–1984* (3 vols.). Communications Press, Washington, D.C.

——, and Kasle, J. F. (Eds.) (1988). *Decision to Divest*: *The First Review, 1985–88*. Communications Press, Washington, D.C.

——, and Kittross, J. M. (1990). *Stayed Tuned*: *A Concise History of American Broadcasting*, 2nd ed. Wadsworth Publishing, Belmont, CA.

Stone, A. (1989). *Wrong Number*: *The Breakup of AT&T*. Basic Books, New York.

Temin, P. and Galambos, L. (1987). *The Fall of the Bell System*: *A Study in Prices and Politics*. Cambridge University Press, New York.

Teske, P. E. (1990). *After Divestiture*: *the Political Economy of State Telecommunications Regulation*. State University of New York Press, Albany.

Thompson, R. L. (1947). *Wiring a Continent*: *The History of the Telegraph Industry in the United States, 1832–1866*. Princeton University Press, Princeton, NJ.

Tierney, J. T. (1988). *The U.S. Postal Service*: *Status and Prospects of a Public Enterprise*. Auburn House, Dover, MA.

Tunstall, J., and Palmer, M. (1990). *Liberating Communications*: *Policy Making in Britain and France*. Basil Blackwell, Oxford, England.

U.S. Court of Appeals (1990). *People of the State of California and the Public Utility Commission of the State of California* v. *Federal Communications Commission*. 905 F. 2d 1217, Ninth Circuit.

U.S. House of Representatives (1919) Committee on Merchant Marine and Fisheries. *Government Control of Radio Communication*: *Hearings on H.R. 13159*. 65th Cong, 4rd Sess.

—— (19587). Committee on the Judiciary, Antitrust Subcommittee. *Consent Decree Program of the Department of Justice*: *Hearings*. 85th Cong., 2nd Sess., Part II, Volumes 1-2-3, American Telephone and Telegraph Co.

—— (1959). *Report on Consent Decree Program of the Department of Justice*. 86th Cong., 1st Sess.

—— (1981). Committee on Energy and Commerce, Subcommittee on Telecommunications, Consumer Protection, and Finance. *Telecommunications in Transition*: *The Status of Competition in the Telecommunications Industry*. 97th Cong., 1st Sess., Committee Print 97-V.

U.S. Senate (1919) Committee on the Post Office and Post Roads. *Government Control of the Telegraph and Telephone System*: *Hearings on H.J. Res 368* (4 vols.). 65th Cong., 3rd Sess.

—— (1967) Subcommittee on Communications of the Committee on Commerce. *The Public Television Act of 1967*: *Hearings*. 90th Cong., 1st Sess.

—— (1976) Committee on Commerce. *Appointments to the Regulatory Agencies*: *the Federal Communications Commission and the Federal Trade Commission (1949–1974)*. 94th Cong., 2nd Sess., Committee Print.

U.S. Supreme Court (1969). *Red Lion Broadcasting Co.* v. *Federal Communications Commission*. 395 U.S. 367.

—— (1986). *Louisiana Public Service Commission* v. *Federal Communications Commission*. 476 U.S. 355.

Wallenstein, G. (1990). *Setting Global Telecommunication Standards*: *The Stakes, The Players & The Process*. Artech House, Norwood, MA.

Weinhaus, C. L. (1988). *Behind the Telephone Debates*. Ablex Publishing, Norwood, NJ.

Wenders, J. T. (1987). *The Economics of Telecommunications*: *Theory and Practice*. Ballinger Publishing, Cambridge, MA.

Will, T. E. (1978). *Telecommunications Structure and Management in the Executive Branch of Government, 1900–1970*. Westview Press, Boulder, CO.

Wright, B. (1991). *The Law of Electronic Commerce*: *EDI, Fax, and E-Mail*: *Technology, Proof, and Liability*. Little, Brown, Boston.

20
Taxing and Spending Policy

Peter Fisher
University of Iowa, Iowa City, Iowa

Warren J. Samuels
Michigan State University, East Lansing, Michigan

Larry L. Wade
University of California, Davis, California

I. TAXES

A. Fiscal Federalism and Tax Structure

Taxes are mandatory contributions extracted from individuals and firms by governments for public purposes. In 1989, 77% of the general revenue of federal, state, and local governments combined consisted of tax receipts. The remainder consists of charges for services, fines, interest, rent, and other miscellaneous revenues. Individual and corporate income taxes account for 89% of federal tax revenues; states rely primarily on sales and income taxes, whereas local governments derive most of their tax revenue from property taxes. Although states and localities collected about $469 billion in taxes in 1989, compared with $616 billion collected by the federal government, the federal government transferred $126 billion to states and localities. These intergovernmental payments, for such things as welfare, education, and highways, permitted states and localities to spend about $762 billion, nearly matching the federal government's direct general expenditure of $783 billion (Table 1).

The federal share of tax collections has been declining in recent decades. In 1957, the federal government accounted for 71% of tax revenues; this figure had declined to 61% by 1979 and to 57% in 1989. The states have accounted for most of the difference; the state share of tax revenues increased from 15% in 1957 to 26% in 1989. Despite these shifts, the relative importance of different kinds of taxes has changed little; the property tax has accounted for about 13% of total tax revenues throughout most of the period between 1957 and 1989; the percentage accounted for by sales taxes has hovered around 21%, whereas income taxes have generally accounted for 59% to 61% of tax revenues.

Tax revenues of all levels of government increased from about 25% of gross national product (GNP) in 1947 to 28% in 1967 and to 31% to 32% in the 1970s and 1980s. Taxes are

Table 1. Federal, State and Local Own-Source General Revenues, 1989 (Millions of Dollars)

	Individual income taxes	Corporate income taxes	Sales and excise taxes	Property taxes	Other revenues	Total
Federal	445,690	103,291	52,527		138,948	740,456
State	88,819	23,861	138,249		115,782	366,712
Local	8,988		27,767	137,107	119,446	293,308
Total	543,497	127,152	218,543	137,107	374,176	1,400,476

Source: U.S. Advisory Commission on Intergovernmental Relations, 1991, pp. 120, 134, 136.

low relative to gross domestic product (GDP) in the United States when compared with the other 22 OECD (Organization for Economic Cooperation and Development) countries, which include the nations of Western Europe plus Canada, Japan, New Zealand, and Australia. In 1988, U.S. taxes represented 30% of GDP; only in Turkey did taxes represent a smaller share. The average among the 23 countries was 34%; the figure exceeded 40% in Austria, Belgium, Denmark, France, Ireland, Luxembourg, The Netherlands, Norway, and Sweden (U.S. ACIR, 1991: 14).

The optimal mix of taxes in a federal system depends on a number of considerations, including stability of revenues, ease of administration and compliance, opportunities for tax avoidance, and effects on location decisions. The property tax has remained dominant at the local level because it is a relatively stable and predictable source of tax revenue compared with income and sales taxes, which tend to fluctuate with the business cycle; because it is relatively easy to administer at the local level, particularly compared with income taxes that require auditing that is beyond the capabilities of all but the largest cities; and because it is difficult to avoid the tax or to conceal the owner's property.

Where states have permitted localities to adopt local "option" taxes—usually sales or income taxes—they have generally required the locality to "piggyback" on the state tax. That is, the local sales tax is simply an additional rate applied to the state sales tax base and collected along with the state sales tax and then remitted by the state back to the locality. Local income taxes can be piggybacked by applying a surcharge—a percent of state income tax liability—on the state income tax return. Some local income taxes, however, are not taxes on comprehensive income at all but are rather a flat percent of wages and salaries only, so that the entire tax is collected by the employer through withholding. Local option piggyback taxes are a form of revenue sharing in that they provide localities the option of sharing the state's tax base, with receipts returned to the locality of origin and with the state assuming all administration and auditing responsibilities.

States and localities also are constrained by the potential effect of taxes on location decisions of individuals and firms. It is generally assumed that higher-income individuals, in particular, are quite mobile and so can avoid progressive taxes by moving to localities with lower tax burdens on high-income individuals. Attempts by localities, and to a lesser extent by states, to engage in substantial redistribution can be self-defeating. For this reason, economists are generally agreed that income redistribution is properly and effectively carried out only at the federal level. Recognition of this constraint, along with the greater income elasticity of an income tax, provided arguments for revenue sharing, whereby the federal government would return part of its income tax receipts to states and localities, or states would share income or sales tax revenues with cities, counties, and school districts.

Economists also agree that stabilization policy can only be effectively carried out at the federal level; state and local governments cannot shoulder responsibility for stimulating demand during recessions or controlling inflation because they must operate with balanced budgets and because stimulative or contractive policies would be largely ineffectual at the state level unless substantially all states adopted similar policies. The progressive income tax is uniquely suited to economic stabilization; during periods of growth, tax receipts increase more rapidly than GNP, so that the tax acts as a brake on inflation; during an economic downturn, income tax revenues fall more rapidly than income, thus helping to support more consumer spending and dampen the recession. State income taxes are generally less progressive than the federal and raise about one quarter of the revenue; thus, it is primarily the federal income tax that plays a role as an automatic stabilizer.

B. Tax Incidence

The initial impact of a tax is readily identified: income taxes are paid by individuals and corporations; sales taxes are collected by retailers and then remitted to the states; property taxes are paid by homeowners, farmers, and businesses owning real estate. But it is important to distinguish between the impact of a tax—who writes the check to the tax collector—and the incidence of a tax—who ultimately bears the burden. Incidence differs from impact because of tax shifting. Incidence is correctly measured as the effect of a tax on the distribution of real incomes among individuals. Taxes falling initially on businesses are ultimately borne by individuals—either stockholders or owners (in the form or reduced dividends or capital gains), employees (in the form of lower wages or reduced employment), owners of land or capital (in the form of reduced rent), or consumers (in the form of higher prices).

Taxes are shifted as a result of efforts by a taxed business or individual to change his or her behavior to avoid or reduce the tax burden. At one extreme, a poll tax or flat tax per person cannot be shifted at all. Taxes on income from work cannot easily be shifted; they can be reduced only by reducing work hours. Thus, the incidence of the individual income tax is generally regarded as falling on the individuals earning the income. A sales or excise tax can be more readily shifted the more elastic the supply and inelastic the demand for the taxed good or service. Where supplies are elastic, producers offer less of the taxed good (shifting resources into lesser taxed areas); this creates a relative scarcity and drives up the price. Thus consumers bear a large part of the burden in higher prices (and thus reduced real incomes). Where supply is inelastic, as in the case of land or of other long-lived capital fixed in location, the goods cannot easily or quickly be withdrawn from the taxed market so the burden must fall on the supplier.

As a general rule, the more specific or narrow the tax, the more consumers can avoid it. This is because the demand for a narrowly defined group of goods is likely to be relatively elastic; consumers can shift purchases to substitute goods to avoid paying an excise tax, for example. A general sales tax on all consumption, on the other hand, could be avoided only by reducing overall consumption and saving more. In practice, only about half of consumption spending is subject to sales taxation in most states. This is because two major categories of consumption are excluded from the base in every state: housing and health care (including prescription drugs). In addition, of the 45 states with a sales tax, 27 exempt food for home consumption and 32 exempt consumer electric and gas purchases (Fisher 1988: 168).

The incidence of taxation concerns vertical equity; vertical equity is measured by computing an individual's tax burden as a percentage of the individual's income. If the percentage burden is higher among high-income individuals than among lower-income individuals, the tax is progressive. If the percentage declines with income, it is regressive. A tax that takes an equal percentage from all income levels is proportional.

The federal individual income tax is quite progressive; the effective tax rate (taxes as a percent of income) ranges from about 1% for the poorest tenth of the population to about 5.5% for the middle fifth, and 12% for the richest tenth (Wallace et al., 1991). State and local income taxes are only mildly progressive by comparison. Federal payroll or social insurance taxes, on the other hand, are roughly proportional until the top 10% of the population is reached, at which point the tax becomes distinctly regressive. This is because the tax is a flat rate on earnings up to a certain level and zero after than.

In estimating the incidence of the general sales tax, it is assumed that the burden falls entirely on consumers in proportion to their consumption spending. The general sales tax is somewhat regressive overall because the lowest-income individuals consume nearly all of their income, whereas at the highest-income levels, a large share of income is saved and thus escapes sales taxation. Estimates for 1980 indicated that the average burden from sales and excise taxes across the United States amounted to over 17% of family income for the lowest-income class (under $5000) and about 7.5% for the next lowest class ($5000 to $10,000), falling to less than 1% of income for those with incomes in excess of $500,000 (Pechman 1985: 56). The state and federal excise taxes on gasoline contribute to this regressivity. The general sales taxes are regressive despite the exemptions noted above. Since these items are necessities, inclusion in the tax base would render the tax more regressive.

Incidence is most difficult to estimate in the case of taxes on flows of income from capital (corporate income taxes) or directly on the capital stock (real property taxes). To the extent that the tax causes a business to reduce business activity (lower investment, production or employment) the tax will be shifted. The "new view" of the incidence of corporate income taxes and of property taxes falling on commercial property (including rental housing), begins with the notion of the national average tax rate. The average tax on capital is thought to be borne by the owners of capital since it cannot be escaped by moving one's capital to another location or to another industry. The more comprehensive the tax base (all forms of capital in all locations), the more this principle will hold. Deviations from the national average tax rate, on the other hand, are shifted forward to consumers and backward to owners of land and to labor. As owners shift capital from high-tax to low-tax uses or locations in order to achieve a better after-tax return, they will create relative scarcities of capital in the high-tax places and surpluses in the low-tax areas. This will raise the prices of rental housing and commodities in high-tax places and lower prices in the low-tax areas. It also will raise the demand for resources (land and labor) in the low-tax areas and lower demand in the high-tax areas. The conclusion is that property tax differentials transfer real income from consumers, landowners, and workers in high-tax jurisdictions to their counterparts in low-tax localities.

Attempts to estimate empirically the incidence of the corporate income tax and the property tax on business realty (including rental housing and commercial, industrial, and farm realty) begin with some assumption about the share of the burden borne by capital and the share shifted forward to consumers or backward to factors of production (primarily labor). The portion borne by owners is distributed progressively because the ownership of property is concentrated among higher-income groups. The portion shifted to consumers is somewhat regressive, for the same reason that a general sales tax is regressive. Thus, the regressivity or progressivity of the corporate income and property taxes, and indeed of the tax system as a whole, depends importantly on the shifting assumptions made.

If the corporation income and property tax burdens are distributed entirely to property income, both taxes are quite progressive, the combined burden ranging from 1.5% to 2.0% of income for the lowest family income classes in 1980 to 15% to 19% of income at the highest income levels. If, on the other hand, corporation income tax burdens are distributed half to property income and half to consumption and property taxes are distributed to consumption, then both taxes are quite regressive at the lowest-income levels and roughly proportional or slightly progressive after that (Pechman 1985: 56).

Overall, the federal, state, and local tax systems in the United States does not have a dramatic effect on the distribution of income. Depending on the assumptions made, taxes overall are slightly progressive (ranging from 20% of income at the bottom to 27% at the top), or they are roughly proportional through most of the income distribution (25% of income) but somewhat regressive at the ends: rising at the bottom to 30% and falling at the top to 22% (Pechman 1985: 4). The effect of the tax system on the degree of inequality of the income distribution (as measured by the Gini coefficient or the Lorenz curve) was to change it only 1.0% to 2.5%. In contrast, the system of transfers (such as social security, food stamps, and Aid to Families with Dependent Children [AFDC]) shifted the distribution by 10% in the direction of greater equality (Pechman 1985: 5-6).

Horizontal equity is another important concept in the evaluation of tax policy. Horizontal equity is defined as equal treatment of equals. Individuals are usually considered equals for tax purposes if they have equal real incomes. Persons with the same income may be taxed differently depending on whether they own or rent a home or depending on whether their income consists of wages, capital gains, or social security. Full or partial exemption of certain kinds of transfers from income taxation (such as unemployment compensation or food stamp benefits) will make the tax more progressive overall, since it reduces the average tax burden on the poor, but will introduce horizontal inequities, since households with the same overall income will pay different amounts of taxes depending on the source of their income. To take another example, lower tax rates on capital gains will reduce progressivity, since capital gains accrue largely to those in the highest income brackets, and will also introduce horizontal inequities by treating capital income more lightly than labor income.

In the debate on the tax reform act of 1986, a major argument was that the elimination of tax preferences improved horizontal equity; since most of these preferences benefitted upper-income groups, a political deal was struck to offset the elimination of preferences with a reduction in the top tax rate. The result was an income tax that is fairer overall in terms of horizontal equity. Furthermore, it appears that the base-broadening provisions (inclusion of formerly preferential income in the base) were sufficiently progressive to more than offset the lowering of top rates. Estimates by Wallace et al. (1991) indicate that although the Tax Reform Act of 1986 did not change the effective rate for the lowest income decile of the population, it did lower the effective rate for the middle 80% of households while raising the effective rate slightly (from 11.5 to 11.8%) for the richest tenth of the households; furthermore, the effective rate for the richest 1.0% was increased from 13.3 to 14.0%.

The proper degree of progressivity in a tax system is ultimately a political question. Arguments in favor of progressivity have been made on utilitarian grounds: the principle of equal sacrifice requires that a larger contribution be made by those with more income, since a dollar of taxes represents a smaller sacrifice of utility the larger one's income. Related to this is the notion of taxing only discretionary income; most state and federal income taxes do exempt from taxation a minimum level of income on the grounds that some subsistence level should be protected from taxation. Even with a flat tax rate, an income tax with a sizable exemption is progressive.

Evaluations of taxes on the basis of vertical and horizontal equity are grounded in the notion that fairness is measured by ability to pay. Those with equal ability to pay should pay equal taxes; those with greater ability to pay should pay more taxes. A contrasting equity principle often appealed to in debates on tax policy is the notion of benefit taxation: a person's tax burden should be proportional to the benefits that person receives from government services. Such a principle precludes income redistribution through government, and instead proposes a marketlike principle for evaluating the financing of government services. The more a tax is like a price, the better. The benefit principle is appealed to primarily in justification of earmarked taxes; for example, excise taxes on gasoline and tires are placed in a trust fund earmarked for spending on streets and highways. Thus, in the aggregate, users of roads are paying for the roads, although the relation between particular individuals' road miles driven and taxes paid will be far from perfect. The benefit principle also is appealed to in arguments for city earnings taxes on suburban commuters, who benefit from city services, and in arguments against school property taxes on the elderly.

C. Taxes, Incentives, and Efficiency

Much of the debate on tax policy since the late 1970s has focused on the alleged efficiency effects of taxation. It has long been recognized that government, by taxing some kinds of goods and services or some kinds of capital or labor more heavily than others, creates incentives for individuals and firms to change their behavior. Such behavioral changes cause tax shifting and affect incidence, as discussed above, but also can have significant changes on the level and composition of GNP by causing resources to be used more or less productively. Federal income tax laws enacted in 1981 and 1982 contained numerous and substantial tax preferences for investment, such as the investment tax credit and more advantageous depreciation provisions. A lively debate ensued as to whether tax policy would spur investment and economic growth, or whether the tax preferences were introducing major distortions in the signals business investors were responding to, with the result that capital would be allocated less efficiently than if market prices alone guided investment decisions.

At the state and local levels, legislators and city councils began to use tax policy explicitly for economic development purposes on a wide scale in the 1970s and 1980s. Corporate income tax credits for investment or for job creation and local property tax abatements on new industrial plant and equipment became common weapons in the "war between the states" for jobs and tax base. The debate on the effectiveness of such policies in spurring local development and reducing unemployment has continued, with most earlier scholarship arguing that such policies were ineffectual at the local level and amounted to a zero sum game (merely redistributing jobs) at best at the national level. More recent work has called these conclusions into question (see Bartik, 1991).

Many economists would argue that the best tax system is a "neutral" one; that is, the tax should create no significant incentives for any economic actors to alter their choices of jobs, investment, or consumption in terms of quantity, composition, or location. Choices would then be made solely on the bases of "undistorted" market prices. Deviations from neutrality would be justified only if needed to correct a market imperfection; that is, only to off-set a distortion in market prices. Such Pigouvian taxes would, for example, raise the prices of commodities that cause pollution, so that their prices reflect more accurately the total so-cial costs of production. Others have argued that it is appropriate to use tax policy to accom-plish a wide range of public purposes, and that the presumption that market prices are "cor-rect" unless proven otherwise and that taxes represent distortion cannot be supported.

Tax preferences have recently been included in a more general concept of tax expendi-tures. The proliferation of special features of the tax codes at all levels of government aimed at stimulating or subsidizing or discouraging certain economic activities led to the notion of a tax expenditure: a government program that provides funding to a particular group or for a particular activity not through budgeted expenditures or grants but through the tax system. The notion of tax expenditures requires that one first define the basic tax; any deviation from the basic tax is then a tax expenditure. The property tax, for example, is ostensibly a tax on the market value at a point in time of all real property (land, buildings, machinery and fix-tures, inventory). A property tax exemption for manufacturing machinery or for new indus-trial buildings is thus a tax expenditure. An exemption for intangible property (such as stocks and bonds) is not a tax expenditure but is part of the definition of the basic tax.

The income tax purports to be a tax on all sources of income. Most economists would agree that income should be defined as the net flow of resources to a household that is poten-tially available to support consumption by that household. Stated another way, income is equal to actual consumption plus additions to net worth (which represent potential consump-tion). This is a measure of how "well off" the household is in terms of the material standard of living it can afford. Deductions for costs of earning income, then, are not tax expenditures in that the income tax is designed to tax the *net* income (i.e., consumption potential) of indiv-iduals. Expenditures for the tools of one's trade or for work uniforms are neither consump-tion nor saving, and so are properly deducted from one's wages to arrive at income for tax purposes. On the other hand, in-kind income such as food stamps or rent-free living space is consumption and is therefore part of income. Similarly, unrealized capital gains increase household net worth and thus represent additional potential consumption even though one has chosen not to realize the gains yet. The exclusions for in-kind income and unrealized cap-ital gains thus represent tax expenditures.

The federal government and approximately 15 states now conduct tax expenditure stu-dies on a regular basis. The rationale is that tax expenditures should be subject to the same annual scrutiny during the budget process as normal expenditure programs. Tax expenditures certainly violate the notion of tax neutrality; they explicitly untax certain preferred activities or sources of income and thus act as incentives for individuals to change their behavior. This does not mean that tax expenditures are bad policy. One does not expect government expendi-ture to be "neutral," so why should one expect tax expenditures to meet this standard? Tax expenditures can serve many of the same public purposes as budgeted programs. Nonethe-less, to the extent that tax expenditures tend to become permanent entitlements free from legislative and executive scrutiny, and free from the public limelight, there is good reason to believe that their use imparts a bias in government policy against programs that are funded through the budget process. Any program that must be delivered by governmental agencies and employees, for example, must be a budgeted one and must compete with other budgeted programs for resources that are diminished by the cumulative effects of prior tax expenditure provisions.

D. The Fiscal Behavior of Political Systems

In neoclassical economic theory, fiscal activities of governments required no special attention. Government was presumed to be one of many actors in the economy, purchasing goods and services in the stylized free market as a price taker in pursuit of maximizing a social welfare function (presumably the "public interest") established by rational policy makers. In the prewelfare, preregulatory, and pre-Keyensian state, disregarding the peculiar aspects of fiscal policy making was a serviceable oversight, and the assumptions of conventional theory were more or less adequate to describe the economy as whole. However, with the (global) intrusions by 20th century governments into the economy, the resulting growth of the public sector, the emergence in popular opinion that government is somehow "responsible" for the economy's performance via its fiscal and other management tools, and the acceptance by politicians of that responsibility, a nonpolitical economy theory had limited explanatory power. An understanding of taxing and spending policy (and all other areas of economic policy as well) now requires models of the economy that include the polity as a dominating variable affecting economic events.

In the standard framework, price competition functions as an important guide to social welfare, since it yields a Pareto optimal allocation of private goods when there are a sufficient number of buyers and sellers, identical products, uninhibited mobility of resources, and perfect knowledge in the market. Governmental activity can assist or disrupt the tendency toward Pareto optimality in many ways, not least in its decisions respecting taxes and expenditures. What has been learned is that these decisions are not always taken by "just another" participant in the market place, or as one performing a unique economic function (providing an optimal supply of public goods, securing some agreed upon degree of equity, and so forth) but often by decision makers who not only have the power to interfere with economic efficiency but often seemingly perverse incentives to do so either unwittingly or deliberately. Thus, in addition to its function in traditional theory, modern governments have frequent opportunities to set prices, allocate capital and labor, grant subsidies to voting and money blocs, reward one generation of citizens at the expense of others, disguise tax burdens and conceal expenditures, over- or undersupply public goods, and otherwise interfere with market efficiency. Understanding this, voters and interest groups often find it more convenient to seek dispensations and stability from government than to confront the hazards and uncertainties of the marketplace: place hunting and rent seeking as Toqueville observed, "attract more recruits than any other trade." In short, when government was about a few things, "politicking" over taxing and spending could be largely ignored in economic theory; now that it is about everything, a more comprehensive theory is required. This perplexing problem has presented economists and political scientists with the great challenge of building a new body of theory able to accommodate the behavior of the both economic and political actors. One important effort in this vein consists of public choice theory, which essentially presumes that the axioms of microeconomic can be extended fully into the political realm.

The assumptions of public choice are now familiar (Mueller, 1979), and they take the following general form. Rational, welfare-maximizing individuals possess scarce resources and insatiable wants, and occupy various, sometimes overlapping, roles in society as workers, investors, consumers of public and private goods, as voters, taxpayers, interest group members and leaders, incumbent and opposition politicians, bureaucrats, judges, and so on. Classic economic theory was deficient in regarding its actors as, for the most part, households and firms (and foreigners) without analyzing the political roles occupied by the same personalities as those who populate the marketplace. In public choice, behavioral tendencies in the political realm are precisely the same as in the economic one, with an importance difference: Decision rules and incentives can and do vary greatly across realms. One may ask: Could one expect the rules of, say, ordinary democratic politics, to produce allocations that are Pareto optimal as in the consummate market? If not, is there a way to compose rules that would? Conceptually, then, the task of public choice is twofold: first, as a positive matter, to state the rules of the political system that lead self-interested actors to their collective decisions, whatever their aftermath (especially respecting the economy); second, to seek rules regarding political decision making which, if adopted, would lead to more efficient outcomes, i.e., to an improvement in general welfare. The latter task has proved daunting at best, and the disturbing conclusion reached that Pereto optimal outcomes are rarely even conceptually possible in democratic politics. (One solution, Wicksellian unanimity in voting, has obvious practical limitation outside, e.g., the Quaker meeting, the United Nations Security Council, or the jury box.) It is true as a practical matter that fully competitive markets also are rare as empirical specimens. As a cultural creation, however, the competitive market can serve as an elegant policy guide in the maintenance or creation of "workable" or "acceptable" markets. This same is not true of democratic politics: It seems impossible to erect a theoretical body of rules and attributes that could function as a consistent guide to Pareto optimal decision making in nonmarket settings. In short, although behavioral rules may be consistent, the idealized market has no close normative analogue in the polity. There are many reasons why this is so.

In the first place, democratic polities are unavoidably representative in nature. Elected politicians, however sensitive to voter preferences, must (unlike actors in welfare economics) necessarily engage in intersubjective comparisons of welfare: They must participate in the making of policy binding on everyone, and everyone includes not only constituents whose preferences are known (although invariably heterogeneous), but those who have voted insincerely and those who have not voted (or communicated in other ways) at all. The heterogeneity of constituency opinion also requires a decision rule (often some form of majority) to resolve issues, and any rule chosen will often produce problems of aggregation/instability (e.g., Arrow's paradox; see Arrow, 1963) and the imposition of significant losses on minorities. Although an iterative process might, over time, yield more gains than losses to all individuals, there seems to be no consistent way to guarantee such an outcome. Logrolling ("help my folks today and I will help your's tomorrow"), the compensation of losers, and sensitivity to intensities (e.g., an apathetic majority yielding to an intense minority), the simultaneous consideration of taxes and expenditures and other policy guides might well enhance efficiency, but there is an ad hoc quality to such recommendations: It has not proved possible to specify with any precision—to present an equilibrium model—the institutional arrangements that would produce consistently "better" results. The failure of theory in this area is not the failure of theorists but arises from the nature of the political process itself. In the economy, individuals must, sooner or later, reveal their preferences if an exchange is to be made. This is not typically so in politics, where the same individuals are free to exaggerate, deny, or conceal their preferences altogether depending on the tactical situation. In collective choice, even when single-peaked preferences exist and aggregation problems are absent, majoritarian rules permit the median voter to maximize utility at the expense of all others.

To say, however, that the policy cannot be made even conceptually efficient is not to say that improvements in efficiency are impossible. In fact, there would seem to be many political practices that are particularly harmful of efficiency and that might well be reformed by introducing alternative rules and incentives. From a public choice perspective, the problem of reform is one of aligning the incentives that shape the self-interested behavior of decision makers (voters, interest groups, bureaucrats, politicians) in such a way that they are led, in their own interests, to advance the welfare of the community at large however it might be defined. In short, public choice seeks to understand how efficient political behavior can be rewarded.

This understanding requires some considerable knowledge of the fiscal behavior of the modern democratic political system (politics re the American fisc are treated in Kosters, 1992, and Ornstein and Makin, 1993). To oversimplify greatly, one may speak of two perspectives on that behavior. Some scholars emphasize what Mitchell (1983) has called the "supply" side, others the "demand" side, of fiscal policy. In the supply models (Atkinson, 1986; Bartlett, 1973; Levi, 1988; Niskanen, 1971; Tullock, 1965), society is required to accept the level and incidence of taxes and expenditures as they are determined by various more or less unaccountable elites. In spite of democratic forms, policy is an elite-driven process in which, to take one institutional example among many, low-visibility iron triangles consisting of obscure legislative subcommittees, rent-seeking interests, and monopolistic bureaucrats combine to exploit the larger public by focusing benefits and distributing costs (Tullock, 1989).

In the demand models (Downs, 1957, and Black, 1958, are classic statements), society— or more precisely, its constantly reassorting majorities—gets more or less what it prefers in the way of expenditures (e.g., public goods, welfare transfers, business subsidies), and the tax bill represents more or less what it is prepared to pay for them. Political parties, for example, are said to offer competing platforms that allow voters to choose the tax/expenditure program most congenial to their own interests. The median voter fares well, indeed maximizes, in such schemes. Or pressure groups—whose very existence is a surrogate for intensity of political concerns (Dahl, 1956)—gain access to policy makers and have some heed paid to their demands. Obviously, partisans of these grand perspectives have very different estimates respecting the fiscal habits of modern democracies.

There is still another and quite disturbing view that has as yet been insufficiently explored: Much fiscal policy in democracies may be set by a convergence of interests between elite supply-siders and democratic demand-siders who combine to exploit the future, acting as generational or intertemporal maximizers who set a debt-trap for an inarticulate posterity. Groucho Marx made the same point less formally: "Posterity! What have those clowns ever done for us?" International and domestic debt crises, now recurring themes in political economy, result from the debt-trap. It is axiomatic in political science that policy makers in democracies are more responsive and accountable to popular expectations and demands than in polities with other characteristics. Other things being equal, then, would not differences between "democratic" and "nondemocratic" polities lead to systematic variations in the efficiency of their fiscal policies and, if so, in what ways? Given the assumptions of contemporary public choice theory, rational, self-interested decision makers in democracies, unless constrained by institutional rules, have powerful incentives to discount the future "excessively," that is, more than purely economic calculations would suggest, and to take decisions that generate inefficient, perverse, and even destructive social outcomes in the longer term. Indeed, under conditions of direct majority rule, chronic instability in fiscal policy must obtain, since no allocative pattern produced by government will be acceptable to some relevant portion of society (the minority or "have-nots"). Under such fissiparous circumstances, economic efficiency and stability as policy objectives are unobtainable, since a faction of the current majority can always be bribed by the current minority to join it in forming a new majority and a new allocation of taxes and spending (Usher, 1981). This is why politicians can never get either tax or spending policy "just right": It is impossible in view of the preferences of constantly shifting majorities. Nor is greed necessary to produce this result; fear will do just as well. If faction A refuses the bribe, faction B will not, and A will be made worse off. A will accept the bribe to leave the old and join the new majority.

In the more complex case of representative democracy, where the incentive of elective office induces politicians to maximize popular support, the same result hypothetically ensues except that representatives may have instruments available (inflation, deficit spending, and so forth) by which they can seek to deter or delay social conflict and loss of support and office. These results flow from the vetoes of Olson's (1982) quarrelsome distributional coalitions and culminate in Thurow's (1980) zero-sum society. Following this reasoning, debt crises in democracies might well be viewed as the delayed consequences of fiscal illusions introduced by governments to avoid allocating short-term losses to highly mobilized publics. As Ames (1987: 33) concluded from his longitudinal study of Latin American fiscal behavior: "Before elections, spending rises as incumbents try to ensure electoral success, and after elections spending rises again if a new leader has attained the presidency." Unconstrained democracies become gigantic prisoners' dilemmas, temporary solutions to which might be sought in excessive debt (presuming there are lenders sufficiently unfamiliar with democratic tendencies). Another of Ames' conclusions (p. 32) is directly pertinent here: " . . . the pressure to spend must be intense, because leaders ignore whenever possible such economic warnings as falling international reserves and IMF agreements." But why precisely should democratic participants discount the future excessively?

The following logic underlies the hypothesis. Individuals engaged in collective choice have more stunted time horizons than when engaged in private choice. The individual in private choice may defer current consumption in order to reap increased benefits from investments in the future. However, the same individual when engaged in public policy making will be unwilling to wait for future returns because, as Brennan and Buchanan observe (1985: 82–96), of the "attenuation of individually identifiable rights or shares in the fruits of collective or governmental 'investment'." Current "guarantees" by government that the individual's future share will be protected are unpersuasive: After all, future distributions will likely be made by officials not currently in office and who are not bound by earlier "contracts." The recognition of this intertemporal problem by participants in the policy process means that public debt will be preferred to taxation by both citizens and governments over some range of public spending. Governments can borrow at or below market interest rates, which are lower than the discount rate. Even far-seeing individuals who would otherwise prefer a debt-free future and who have elected a fiscally prudent government must succumb to the debt-trap because to relinquish current benefits will not ensure against a future tax liability imposed by a future government less congenial to the current electorate's fiscal sensibilities. Such a future government could easily annul all the work of the current government. As Brennan and Buchanan note (p. 94), "There is simply no rational basis for an individual to support, to 'vote for,' fiscal prudence in the operation of ordinary democratic politics. Public debt will tend to be overextended relative to any plausible long-term arguments for the use of this fiscal instrument."

Of course, real democracies are always circumscribed at manipulating the fisc by at least some restraining rules, either formal or cultural, for which reason they are usually, but not invariably, more "responsible" than the pure case would suggest—in that case, tomorrow would be discounted entirely. Despite this qualification, it remains important to explore whether there is a predisposition in democracies to imprudent (economically if not politically) fiscal behavior such as the debt-trap. It is important to observe that the debt-trap hypothesis as heretofore stated involves an implicit comparison between two types, or better degrees, of democracy: that between constitutional democracies in which voters and public officials are disciplined by rules and norms limiting their capacity/incentives to discount the future (e.g., line-item vetoes, balanced budget requirements), and democracies lacking such inhibitions and therefore predisposed to chose "soft" over "hard" fiscal options. Thus, the debt-trap hypothesis, as it stands, is less than comprehensive, since it offers no predictions concerning fiscal choices in nondemocracies. (To be sure, if democratic attributes constitute a continuous function, there is no unambiguous hiatus to separate democratic from nondemocratic regimes, and one might expect that fiscal tendencies would vary also with those attributes.)

What fiscal behavior might be expected of political systems with few or no democratic attributes? In the limiting case, where the despot is utterly insulated from the underlying population, fiscal decisions are essentially unpredictable, and, in the manner of the Roman emperor Caligula, dependent only on the despot's idiosyncratic interests. Random and even wildly oscillating fiscal choices would seem as probably as stable ones in such systems (Tullock, 1987). Following the debacle of the Great Leap Forward in China, Mao remarked that his public investment scheme had failed to consider transportation requirements: "Coal and iron will not walk by themselves. . . . I did not anticipate this point" (quoted in Rhoads, 1985: 70). The populist dictator of Argentina, Juan Peron, explained his fiscal policy as follows: "Give to people, especially the workers, all that is possible. When it seems to you that you are giving them too much, give them more. You will see the results. Everyone will try to scare you with the specter of an economic collapse. But all of this is a lie" (quoted in Pothier, 1982: 186). In autocracies, the smothering of political life—repression of opposition, silencing of alternative voices, manipulation of opinion, prohibitions against overt social conflict, the secrecy surrounding fiscal question, and, withal, the lack of public accountability—produces policy unconstrained not only by formal rules but by society itself. Such political detachment yields personalistic policy and, not infrequently, arbitrary and abrupt policy departures that may or may not be consistent with, by long-term standards, intelligent economic policy.

In the case of economic policy by benevolent dictators, one might expect a temptation to select the short-term maximizing alternative—the soft option—posed by the Samaritan's dilemma (Buchanan, 1975): sympathetic decisions to alleviate acute contemporary distress; consequent acceptance of similar public/private time disparities as in unconstrained democracies; foregone investment opportunities and future benefits; and even greater misery in the long term. In less sensitive dictatorships, no fixed rule would seem to apply except that highly variable political motives presumably dominate economic ones. Although difficult to measure, the security of the regime would seem to be an important factor influencing its fiscal policy. As Ames (1987: 33) observed of Latin American authoritarian regimes: ". . . few governments are so secure that the budget is not a tool for increasing support. Military governments may opt for austerity once they feel safe, but in their first year in power, they cover their political bases by public spending."

In still other authoritarian settings, political leaders may be under the sway of technically proficient economists whose advice on fiscal and other economic policies are consistent with long-term economic development. Such regimes may, as in South Korea and Taiwan, be able to develop and sustain a prudent and coherent social welfare function for an extended period.

For such existential reasons, fiscal choices in nondemocracies cannot be predicted confidently by existing theory, and they are therefore good candidates for empirical scrutiny and theoretical attention by public choice and other scholars interested in the fiscal behavior of modern states. An enhanced understanding of the fiscal consequences of political regimes and processes and the implications of those consequences for the economy would, as a normative matter, assist greatly in the important task of institutional reform.

II. SPENDING

A. Public Expenditure: Growth and Structure

There has been a gradual but enormous cumulative increase in public expenditures during the past century. Public spending as a percentage of gross national product in the United States increased from under 7% in 1890 to 10% in 1929 and 35% in 1990. Per capita, in 1990 dollars, the increase was from under $100 in 1890 to $767 in 1929 and $7600 in 1990. That public expenditure growth may be a correlate of economic and political modernization is suggested by the following: The ratio of public spending to GNP in most, but not all, developed, non–Soviet bloc countries has reached the range of 40 ± 10%; in the less developed countries, the range is approximately 17 ± 5%.

Changes in the structure of public spending in the United States have been no less remarkable. Intergovernmentally, although state-local spending increased relatively somewhat more rapidly in recent decades, the relative size of federal spending has been reversed: In 1900, approximately two thirds of public expenditure was at the state-local level; in 1988, the federal share was 57%. On the state-local level, in 1900, local spending was seven times state spending; in 1988, state spending was 50% greater than local spending. In terms of spending programs, although substantially all have vastly increased both absolutely and as a percentage of GNP, social welfare and education spending (on all levels of government) has increased enormously, constituting now some two thirds of civilian expenditures in contrast to one third in the early 20th century. Total civilian expenditure, as a percentage of total expenditures, has been unstable but was 79.2% in 1902, 79.5% in 1977, and 82.9% in 1989, having seen, for example, 62% in 1960.

B. Approaches to Public Expenditure Analysis

Perceptions of the meaning and significance of public spending are profoundly influenced by attitudes toward the economic role of government, the nature and source of social problems, and conceptions of socioeconomic justice. Among public expenditure analysts, at least four principal approaches are followed. The Pigovian approach emphasizes government as a corrective instrument to remedy perceived market failures, such as externalities and instability, imbalances of economic power, and poverty. Beyond this, the Pigovian approach accepts reliance on private enterprise and markets. Such acceptance is even greater and more thorough among Paretians. They would minimize government intervention, sanctioning only full specification of property rights to permit market exchange. Whereas Pigovians tend to perceive underspending by government, Paretians see overspending. The Marxists generally see government spending as a facet of the instrumental use of government by the dominant business class, functioning to facilitate private, corporate capital accumulation and the ideological legitimation of the capitalist system (the latter in part through welfare programs), in the face of perceived problems and crises of various sorts (Miliband, 1969; O'Connor, 1973). The institutionalists are interested principally in identifying the actual processes and consequences of public expenditure (and other government activities), including (and in common with others, especially but not solely the Pigovians) analysis of alternative policy instruments and the relations among decision-making structure, policy, and performance (Samuels and

Schmid, 1980). Each approach tends in practice to be a kaleidoscopic mix of positive and normative analysis. Finally, the conduct of public expenditure analysis, and policy analysis generally, is influenced by perceptions as to the relative importance in policy making of technical considerations and subjective judgments (contrast Musgrave and Musgrave, 1980: 5, with Burkhead and Miner, 1971: 98–99).

Approaches to public expenditure evaluation can also be compared in terms of their approach to valuation of the outputs and activities of the public sector. The Pigovian and Paretian approaches are both grounded in an individualistic ethic that views all value as coming from the individual as consumer. This approach has been formalized in benefit cost analysis, which takes individual demand or willingness to pay for a good or service as the only measure of value. Individual demand, arising from autonomous preferences and conditioned by income, is treated as if it were a "first cause" with unimpeachable legitimacy. All effects of a project or policy, at least in concept, should be valued according to how much individuals in the aggregate would be willing to pay for them. This includes intangible effects such as environmental quality, the availability of wilderness, or reduced risk of exposure to carcinogens.

The institutionalists and others have pointed out the vacuousness of this approach to value—what is good is whatever the people say they want at the moment—and have emphasized that individuals are products of society and that preferences and demands, far from being independent, are culturally shaped and constantly in flux. A benefit-cost analysis of 19th century U.S. federal Indian policies, for example, would no doubt have concluded that the net public benefit was positive, if the economists of the time could have ascertained that those Europeans who wanted the Indian homelands would have been willing to pay more to have them than the Indians were willing to pay to keep their land and their culture. Institutionalists would argue that this is an extreme but logical and inevitable extension of the method of cost-benefit analysis, which denies the cultural and historical determination of preferences and demand, subsumes all motivation under the pursuit of individual self-interest and allows for no social process of valuation, and glosses over the profound effects of the distribution of income on willingness to pay.

C. Some Further Determinants of Public Expenditures

Although there are a number of intractable interpretive problems in reaching a meaningful understanding, including the respective weights, of the causes of the enormous increase in public expenditure in the 20th century, the causes themselves are generally straightforward, however often interconnected.

1. There is the greater prevalence and costliness of war. This includes consideration of such factors as national security, control of the domestic population, the inefficiencies of military procurement and related budgetary processes, the military-industrial complex, the vested interests of the military establishment, the needs of ideology and national identity, imperialism, and the greater capital intensiveness of modern warfare.
2. There has been a complex set of changes in both the value system and the balance of political power in Western society. The state has been increasingly responsive to a wider array of organized interests who have not hesitated to use the state to advance their objectives. Thus, the values of hitherto excluded groups have newly entered government decision making.

3. There has been a growing consciousness of the policy (artifact) character of government and other institutional arrangements and a consequent orientation toward intervention in the sense of changing the interests to which government has been providing its support.

4. There has been a great increase in perceived technical knowledge in the biological, physical, and social sciences. This has enhanced both the desire and the perceived ability to control individual and collective environments, adjustments, and evolution.

5. There has been enhanced, albeit still selective, perception of externality problems and public good production possibilities (see below).

6. Although in one sense government has become a more readily available process of collective choice, in another, it has become more evidently both an arena and instrument of power play among economic and social interests. Substantially all groups have seen in government an avenue for redistribution of opportunity, income, and wealth, in part through the redetermination of legal rules and private rights.

7. There are observable tendencies for government programs to be resistant to termination and instead to expand, in part through the efforts of cumulating beneficiaries.

8. There has been a perception of lessened private capacity in an increasingly urban, industrial, and interdependent society, coupled with growing concerns over the distribution of personal welfare in a hierarchical society.

9. The production of certain private goods, such as the automobile, has engendered the wide-ranging and expensive production of governmentally produced goods, such as roads and highways and traffic and other controls.

10. Budgetary decision making has been fractionalized in several respects: Decisions are made on several levels of government, in various committees of legislatures, and decisions as to taxation and expenditures are generally separated. In addition, only rarely has a deliberate decision been made by Congress as to its total budget; and many expenditure arrangements are reached through the trading of votes by legislatures.

11. There is a certain logic of politics that involves the offering of voters increased prospective rewards so as to secure votes, a process reinforced by budgetary deficits that lower the immediate tax price of public spending (Buchanan and Wagner, 1977).

12. Certain demographic changes seem to have produced expenditure consequences: urbanization, industrialization, and changes in the age distribution of the population.

More specific and elaborate analysis of the determinants of public expenditure has focused on such topics as budgetary processes, voting rules, political pluralism, coalitions, politics, bureaucracy, ideology, political symbolism, and so on. A century ago, Adolph Wagner reached, on empirical grounds, a "law of rising public expenditures" and speculated that (on what in modern terms is) an increasing percentage of GNP going to (or through) government was due to pressure for socioeconomic programs consequent to and dependent on the interaction between private and public sector growth. More recent empirical studies have (1) correlated total public spending growth with economic growth; population increase; technology producing increased income, urbanization, and industrialization; and value system changes (Fabricant, 1952); and (2) found variances in municipal spending due principally to community size, housing density, population age, and industrialization (Winfrey, 1973: 170–172; Wood, 1962).

The consequences of public spending have been felt throughout the economy, in part through transfer payments, government purchasing, and the capitalization of the costs and benefits affecting the value of both income-earning and non–income-earning property, as well as through employment, profit-making opportunities, and capital gains. Government spending is a major factor in the determination of the distributions of individual income and wealth but has not greatly affected the quintile or decile distribution patterns. It has been found, for example, that the combination of state-local taxation and expenditure has had a mildly equalizing affect on income distribution despite a regressive tax system (Peppard and Roberts, 1977: 86–87); but that although explicit grants have redistributed income toward the poor, implicit grants of various types have tended to greater inequality (Boulding and Pfaff, 1972: 2).

D. Public Expenditure Theory

Although the seminal and architectonic work of Musgrave (1959) established allocation, distribution, and stabilization as the three principal dimensions of public finance, inducing public expenditures, most subsequent work concentrated on the interrelated (Samuels and Schmid, 1981) concepts of externality and public goods in what amounts to an effort to understand interdependence among economic actors and the fundamentals of public expenditure policy. Although both bodies of theory (as well as grants theory) are of controversial applicability to questions of actual policy and neither attempts to penetrate the actual processes of public expenditure decision making, together they articulate the elements of public choice ultimately encountered therein.

1. Externalities

The broadest analysis is the institutionalist, although it is in the distinct minority within economics. Externalities are defined broadly to cover all impacts on second or third parties and are seen to arise ultimately from interdependence and to be reciprocal in character. Externalities are ubiquitous, inevitable, and a function of power structure, as are externality solutions, which also generate further externalities, including changes in power, opportunity sets, and costs and benefits. The externalities treated by public policy are typically perceived selectively, especially given the reciprocal nature of externalities: Polluter and pollutee are so related, given geographical relationships and technology, that pollution (the impact on the pollutee of the polluter's actions) is inextricably related to the inhibition on the polluter's actions if the pollutee is to be assured of clean air or water. In this view, the fundamental problem of externality policy is which, or whose, externality, or whose interest is to be sacrificed to another's. The institutionalist also has broad and open-ended definitions of injury (benefit) and evidence of injury.

Quite different approaches are taken by the Pigovian and Paretian variants of neoclassical economics. Both, however, perceive markets as the preeminent mode of internalization, differing on their normative (and to some extent positive) treatment of market failure, so-called. The Pigovian considers markets to work when marginal private and social costs (and benefits) are equated and to fail when marginal social costs exceed marginal private costs (thereby resulting in overproduction of the commodity in question because the producer— and ultimately the consumer—is not compelled to bear all the costs thereof) or when marginal social benefits exceed marginal private benefits (thereby resulting in underproduction). Thus, the Pigovian seems to open the door to governmental corrective action although the mere identification of an externality is not sufficient to warrant such action, an additional normative premise being required to justify further government action in the area.

The Pigovian and general neoclassical approach also distinguishes between so-called pecuniary and technological externalities, the former comprising uncompensated impacts seen as taking place and priced within the market, the latter impacts not priced through the market. Institutionalists question the coherence (and policy significance) of the distinction: Impacts are impacts and even technological externalities have price consequences (the pollutee's costs are priced through the market).

If the pecuniary-technological distinction narrows the scope of externalities suitable for theory and policy, the Paretian approach narrows it much further. The Paretian, emphasizing the capacity of markets to internalize when rights are fully defined so as to permit trade, distinguishes between Pareto-relevant and Pareto-irrelevant externalities, the former involving impacts that give rise to trade (e.g., the pollutee buying off the polluter) and the latter not so. Although the psychodynamics of the distinction is that Pareto-irrelevant externalities are (or should be) irrelevant for policy, thereby closing the door to government corrective action, generally speaking, the set of Pareto-irrelevant externalities is relatively coextensive with the set of Pigovian inequality-condition externalities (say, once rights are fully defined so as to maximize opportunities for trade), thus leaving open in principle the possibility of government corrective action going beyond formal rights specification. Thus, from an institutionalist perspective, in both cases the question remains as to which (whose) externalities, in a world of ubiquitous and inevitable externalities, are to be promoted and which (whose) inhibited.

Not all externality correction measures involve public spending, but their discussion generally comes within the ambit of public expenditure analysis. Among the available correction procedures are regulation (e.g., pollution standards), property rights, liability rules, taxation (of pollution) or subsidy (of pollution control equipment), government production financed through either or both user charges or general taxation, education, and mergers. Governments, in general, can attempt either to produce a desired performance result or to promote further private action, independent of specific results. Policy making and execution are made complicated, however, by, inter alia, the naivetes of ideological wishful thinking; the fact that different rights or liability systems will produce different transaction cost situations, so that choice of system is tantamount to choosing performance result; and the practice of preference masking coupled with the realities of free and forced riders—which reintroduces the problem of externality per se.

2. Public Goods

A somewhat different but not mutually exclusive set of insights is acquired through the theory of public goods, much of which is focused on the alternative variables by which public goods are defined. In contrast to the concept of private goods, in which individuals solely enjoy consumption, goods have a "public" quality insofar as provision for one individual may constitute provision for others who may not be excluded from its enjoyment either at all or only at some more or less substantial cost. This is the predominant conception and blends two separable definitional criteria: (1) joint supply, joint consumption, or provision with a zero marginal cost for an additional consumer; and (2) nonexclusion or costly exclusion. But there are still other definitional criteria, and one or more of these have been combined with either or both of the first two to provide a variety of taxonomies of public goods or spectra of private-public goods. These include nonappropriability, individual nonadjustment of quantity, transaction costs, indivisibility, increasing returns, and some notion of externality itself.

The term *toll goods* has sometimes been used to refer to public utility types of goods, the production of which is subject to indivisibilities and increasing returns. Where a large and indivisible initial investment in capital is required, production capacity is created that has the characteristics of joint consumption or zero marginal cost, particularly where marginal or operating costs are minimal. The situation resembles a public good in that, once the facility is built, additional users can be accommodated at zero or near-zero cost. Nonetheless, exclusion is entirely feasible. Some have referred to these as "congestible public goods," to denote the fact that, as use increases, the facility will approach or exceed capacity, at whch point additional use may have high marginal costs.

It is worth noting the relation between externalities and public goods. First of all, externalities may be benefits or costs—goods or bads—and parallel to public goods are public bads. Second, many externalities are in the nature of public goods or bads. For example, air pollution is available to additional consumers at zero marginal cost; that is, one person's consumption of foul air does not diminish the quantity of foul air available to others. Furthermore, exclusion from consumption would be as infeasible as exclusion from the breathing of clean healthy air. An externality, then, can be seen as an auxiliary public good or bad generated by the production or use of a commodity. Some have argued for the term *mixed goods*; an automobile, for example, is a good that provides direct transportation benefits to the user and external costs to others in the form of exhaust. The general practice of most economists and other analysts is to use public goods theory for the benefits or goods and externality theory for the costs or bads, although in principle, the theories are symmetrical.

E. Recent Tax-Spending Policy in Perspective

The experience of the Reagan-Bush administrations (1981 to 1992) provides opportunity to consider several fundamental points: (1) the conflicts within and therefore ambiguity of what constitutes "conservative" economic policy, and (2) the dependence of the effectiveness, or consequences, of a policy less on the ideology and specifics of policy and more on the kaleidoscopic conditions under which the policy is carried out.

The question of the nature of conservative economic policy can be analyzed in terms of, first, the propositions deemed historically by conservatives to constitute principles of conservative economic policy and, second, the schools of thought that were more or less in open conflict within the Reagan and Bush administrations, although especially in the first term of the former.

For at least a half century conservatives have articulated certain principles of economic policy: that the economy is, or can be, self-stabilizing; that market solutions are by definition optimal, so that market results should be accepted without question; that governmental macroeconomic supervision of the economy is both unnecessary and destabilizing; that government should not be used to redistribute income and wealth; that the level of government spending is too high and should be lowered; that the federal government should have a balanced budget; and that although the economy is fundamentally strong, government should avoid the creation of uncertainty and other problems through tinkering with the economy.

Although this is not the place to question the accuracy of such propositions, three points can be made. First, although often voicing these principles, *by these criteria* the Reagan-Bush administrations were substantially not conservative: The administrations had their own activist stabilization and other macroeconomic policies; they actively attempted to manipulate certain markets and generate certain market results, even independent of defense considerations; they used government to redistribute income and wealth toward the highest few percentages of households; they did not lower the level of government spending (nor perhaps—depending on how the data are counted—even its rate of increase); they failed to balance the budget, indeed had the greatest deficits in the history of the country, quadrupling the national debt; and the "Reagan-revolution" rhetoric about the economic role of government (and especially about government spending) arguably had considerable uncertainty-creating consequences in a society in which about one third of GNP derives from government purchases.

Second, if one accepts as an alternative specification of the objective of conservative economic policy the redistribution of after-tax and after-spending income to the highest income brackets, then these administrations were in fact conservative.

Third, contrary to the administrations' ostensible rejection of an "industrial policy," it can be argued that the ultimate agenda of the Strategic Defense Initiative (SDI, or Star Wars) included, in addition to certain military goals, the promotion of new technology constituting a new industrial base—including lasers, new materials (superconductors), fiberoptics, parallel processing computers, and so on; while simultaneously facilitating the decline of the old-line basic industries—including steel, automobiles, textiles, and chemicals.

Be all that as it may, the conclusion is inescapable that the principles of "conservative" economic policy are ambiguous at best.

Especially during the first term of the Reagon administration, and even more particularly during the first two years, three schools of economic thought each with manifest conservative status were in conflict. The *supply-siders* believed that cutting tax rates and receipts would increase saving, the rate of profit, and investment, and would thereby increase the rate of economic growth and employment and reduce inflation. Eventual conflict among supply-siders would center in part on whether the policy of tax reduction was to have been accompanied by spending reduction. Some insisted that it should be, whereas others said that increased revenues from lower tax rates applied to higher levels of GNP would have readily supported the existing level of government spending.

The *monetarists* were concerned only or largely with reducing inflation, and believed that monetary policy should control the rate of growth of the money supply (by which is meant the ability of commercial banks to make loans thereby increasing the money supply in the form of demand deposit balances).

The *budget balancers* desired to balance the federal budget, in part because this signified fiscal responsibility to them and in part because the absence of deficits would lessen both inflation and the pressure of government borrowing in money markets and on interest rates.

While this is not the place to evaluate the accuracy or coherence of these schools, suffice it to say that most professional economists do not believe that there is a supply-side economics independent of traditional aggregate demand income-expenditure theory. Supply-siders were apt to emphasize growth of investment and thereby the capacity to produce. But traditional Keynesian macroeconomics, although focused on the determination of annual income, nonetheless also inevitably encompassed an increase in the capacity to produce correlative with an increase in net investment, just as did so-called supply-side economics. Moreover, the notion that a tax cut can be "supply-side" is itself falacious. Supply-side might mean the reduction of costs; ineed, if it means anything distinctive, it should be that. But a tax cut is, if anything, demand-side, increasing disposable income and therefore engendering, under propitious conditions, additional spending. Calling the tax cut supply-side was a ruse (the famous "Trojan horse") to rationalize tax cuts to corporations and highest-level income receivers, who would presumably save more, which would supposedly lead to more investment. Instead the tax cut could have led, and to some extend did lead, to greater conspicuous consumption, a demand-side induced boost to the luxury goods sector of the economy (also see below). In any event, the Reagan administration pursued so-called supply-side tax cuts, which were expansionary, and applauded tight money policies by the Federal Reserve System, which were deflationary and contractionary—with supply-side economists very early perceiving that tight money, with its high interest rates, was having negative effects on expansion. So two of three eminently conservative policies were pursued. The clear losers were the advocates of the third, the budget balancers.

Now to the matter of the effectiveness of a policy being a function of circumstances. The administration desired to lower the inflation rate and lower the unemployment rate. Both of these eventually took place. Certainly, too, by mid-decade inflationary expectations no longer ruled economic decision making. Strikingly, however, both professional and lay opinion, say, as of 1980, would have predicted that a quadrupling of the national debt (probably seen as impossible under a conservative administration during peacetime) would likely be accompanied by a strong expansion, considerable inflation, and rising interest rates. In fact, the quadrupling of the national debt was accompanied by a recession and subsequent weak expansion, a substantial reduction in the inflation rate, and a substantial fall in nominal interest rates (although a slight rise in real interest rates because the inflation rate fell more rapidly than nominal interest rates).

Given the combination of expansionary fiscal policy and deflationary/contractionary monetary policy, several scenarios were possible depending on circumstances. These scenarios included:

1. The failure of saving to increase. Coupled with tight money, this could have meant the failure of investment to increase. Saving as a percentage of GNP during the 1980s was lower than during the preceding decades.
2. Increased saving directed into portfolio investment (e.g., stocks and bonds) rather than real investment (plant and equipment). This would have been contractionary.
3. Increased investment could have been strong, generating a significant expansion.
4. The investment-generated expansion could have turned into inflationary excess, perhaps reinforcing inflationary tendencies consequent to a government deficit.
5. If the reduction in taxes had been accompanied by significant cuts in government spending, the result could have been contractionary.
6. High(er) interest rates consequent to both tight money and increased private sector activity due to the tax cut (increased demand for money) could have raised interest rates, thereby crowding out more or less significant interest-sensitive private spending, and thereby weakening whatever expansion would otherwise have taken place.
7. Unemployment could have been predominantly structural rather than cyclical, unresponsive to deficit- and/or investment-generated expansion.
8. The dampening effects of the recession phase of an ordinary business cycle. As matters turned out, such a recession did take place, perhaps worsened by adverse impacts on expectations due to the uncertainty created for many businesses by the prospects of a Reagan "revolution" in the economic role of government. Moreover, a second recession followed at the end of the decade; and the average level of unemployment during the decade was significantly above that of earlier decades.

It seems clear that the Reagan animus against taxes convinced voters that taxes, or tax increases, were inherently undesirable. Coupled with pressures to maintain if not increase both defense spending and domestic entitlement spending—pressures generated in part by politician desires to spend more rather than less and in part by citizen desires for more rather than fewer particular benefits from government—the combination of tax cuts plus lower revenue due to the recession led to historically high and generally increasing deficits and to a breakdown of coherent decision making, including frequent budgetary impasses, in Congress.

1. Deficits and the National Debt

The quadrupling of the national debt between 1981 and 1992 took place during a conservative Republican administration ostensibly opposed to deficits in principle but that attempted to both downplay the significance of its own deficits (it never submitted a balanced budget to Congress) and yet continue to use the issue as a means of manipulating political psychology. Aside from politics per se, the principal concern over deficits and the growing national debt has been with regard to the macroeconomic health of the economy. And here economists continue to remain somewhat divided.

The mainstream of economists, influenced by Keynesian income-expenditure theory, believe that deficits to combat unemployment, and surpluses to counter inflation, represent in principle a powerful means of compensatory fiscal policy. These economists believe that, given an accommodating monetary policy, deficits can help promote growth of real income, output, and employment. These economists also believe that there is no necessary macroeconomic burden of an internally held debt. Both issuance and repayment, if any, of the debt, and interest payments represent internal transfers and not leakages from the domestic income flow. To the extent that the national debt is held by foreigners (about 15% is thought to be so held), the purchase of the debt by foreigners represents an injection into the income flow, whereas both repayment and interest on the debt represents leakages.

These economists also insist that government debt is qualitatively different from private debt. Neither debt need be retired; both can be refinanced. More important analytically, whereas individual repayment of debt and payment of interest on debt is lost to the individual, to the extent that the debt is internally held, neither payment is lost to the macroeconomy. Moreover, government has the power to tax, something which private economic actors do not have.

Furthermore, deficit spending is comparable with, and no more harmful than, debt undertaken by private businesses, provided that in both cases the debt is accompanied by the creation of real assets (a factory or highway).

The traditional conservative view in opposition to deficits considers them a manifestation of fiscal irresponsibility and raises a specter of national bankruptcy. The former view neglects the use of debt in the private sector as a matter of leveraged finance. The latter view perpetuates the flawed comparison with personal debt, which neglects the absence of domestic macroeconomic burden from an internally held debt and the power to tax.

A more sophisticated conservative view shares with the traditional conservative position the desire to use the issue of deficits and national debt as an argument to limit government spending. The sophisticated view tends to emphasize technical considerations. One is that deficits lower the tax-price of government spending, thereby inducing greater demand for government spending than would occur if taxes fully covered the cost of government spending. Others are inflation and higher interest rates presumably due to deficits. Still others include the inhibition of capital accumulation as financial resources are used to finance government spending rather than real investment (which assumes that the latter is an operative alternative to the former, which is not necessarily the case); and constraint on future fiscal-policy choices.

Given that the quadrupling of the national debt between 1981 and 1992 raised neither the rate of interest nor the rate of inflation (see above), it is clear that those possible consequences, at least, are at most problematic.

Two other subsidiary issues should be noted. One involves the possibility in principle of an interest-free national debt (or substantial component thereof). Given the money-creating power of commercial banks and the fractional reserves which the banks must maintain, the argument is that statutory provision could be made requiring banks to hold interest-free government bonds as reserves, thereby both creating a demand for the bonds and avoiding interest charges on that part of the money supply represented by deposit balances created by banks in the process of financing the national debt, a power effectively delegated to the banks by the government. (It should be noted in this connection that not all methods of financing the national debt involve monetization of the debt; that is, the creation of money in the process of financing the national debt.)

The other is the Ricardian equivalence theorem. On the assumption that citizens are rational economic actors (an oft-criticized assumption conventional among mainstream economists), there need not be any behavioral difference between financing current government spending by taxation or by issuing bonds to be repaid at a later date. The reasoning is that rational actors can discount to the present the value of taxes paid in the future (to cover bond interest and repayment) so that the presently felt tax-price need not only be the currently paid tax, such that in principle it makes no difference how the spending is financed.

Experience from the period 1981 to 1992 leads economists of all schools to conclude that one result of the deficit and national debt situation during the Reagan-Bush administrations has been the confusion which that situation cast on budgetary decision making, especially with regard to making spending decisions on the arguable merits of the projects themselves. No one seems to question the usefullness of deficits and national debt as a tool of selective political manipulation; indeed, the tension and confusion have been so great that some have given credence to the conspiracy theory that the enormous deficits were planned, so as to inhibit growth of government spending.

2. Government Budgets and the Cultural Life of a People

The budget of a government is an indication of the policy position of the relevant administration. The budget, including the ways in which monies are raised and spent, is also indicative of, or derivative from, the social, political, ideological, cultural, and economic conditions of a people at a particular point in its history. Both consensus and conflict are manifest in the budget of a government. Arguments over the budget of a government are arguments over larger issues, including the economic role of government, the operation of the legal-economic nexus from which emanates the selectively perceptive phenomena of private and public sectors, so-called, and the determination of whose interest is to count in the social reconstruction of legal-economic, and indeed, cultural reality.

REFERENCES

Ames, B. (1987). *Political Survival: Politicians and Public Policy in Latin America*. University of California Press, Berkeley.

Arrow, K. J. (1963). *Social Choice and Individual Values*. John Wiley & Sons, New York.

Atkison, R. (1986). *Government Against the People*. Compuprint Publishing, Tyne and Wear, UK.

Bartik, T. J. (1991). *Who Benefits from State and Local Economic Development Policies?* Upjohn Institute, Kalamazoo, MI.

Bartlett, R. (1973). *Economic Foundations of Political Power*. The Free Press, New York.

Black, D. (1958). *The Theory of Committees and Elections*. Cambridge University Press, Cambridge, England.

Boulding, K. E., and Pfaff, M. (Eds.) (1972). *Redistribution to the Rich and the Poor*. Wadsworth, Belmont, CA.

Brennan, G., and Buchanan, J. M. (1985). *The Reason of Rules: Constitutional Political Economy*. Cambridge University Press, Cambridge, England.

Buchanan, J. M. (1975). The samaritan's dilemma. In *Altruism, Morality and Economic Theory*. E. S. Phelps (Ed.). Russell Sage Foundation, New York.

Buchanan, J. M., and R. E. (1977). *Democracy in Deficit*. Academic Press, New York.

Burkhead, J., and Miner, J. (1971). *Public Expenditures*. Aldine, Chicago.

Dahl, R. (1956). *Preface to Democratic Theory*. University of Chicago Press, Chicago.

Downs, A. (1957). *An Economic Theory of Democracy*. Harper, New York.

Fabricant, S. (1952). *The Trend of Government Activity in the United States Since 1900*. National Bureau of Economic Research, New York.

Fisher, R. C. (1988). *State and Local Public Finance*. Scott Foresman, Glenview, IL.

Kosters, M. H. (Ed.) (1992). *Fiscal Politics and the Budget Enforcement Act*. American Enterprise Institute, Washington, D.C.

Levi, M. (1988). *Of Rule and Revenue*. University of California Press, Berkeley.

Miliband, R. (1969). *The State in Capitalist Society*. Basic Books, New York.

Mitchell, W. C. (1983). Fiscal behavior of the modern democratic state: Public choice perspectives and contributions. In *Political Economy: Recent Views*. L. L. Wade (Ed.). Kluwer-Nijhoff, Boston.

Mueller, D. (1979). *Public Choice*. Cambridge University Press, Cambridge, England.

Musgrave, R. (1959). *The Theory of Public Finance*. McGraw-Hill, New York.

Musgrave, R., and Musgrave, P. G. (1980). *Public Finance in Theory and Practice*, 3rd ed. McGraw-Hill, New York.

Niskanen, W. (1977). *Bureaucracy and Representative Government*. Aldine-Atherton, Chicago.

O'Connor, J. (1973). *The Fiscal Crisis of the State*. St. Martin's Press, New York.

Olson, M. (1982). *The Rise and Decline of Nations*. Yale University Press, New Haven, CT.

Ornstein, N. J., and Makin, J. H. (1993). *Debt and Taxes: Politics and Fiscal Policy in America*. American Enterprise Institute, Washington, D.C.

Pechman, J. A. (1985). *Who Paid the Taxes, 1966–85?* Brookings Institution, Washington, D.C.

Peppard, D. M., and Roberts, D. B. (1977). *Net Fiscal Incidence in Michigan: Who Pays and Who Benefits?* Division of Research, Graduate School of Business Administration, Michigan State University, East Lansing, MI.

Pothier, J. T. (1982). The political causes of Argentine inflation. In *The Politics of Inflation: A Comparative Analysis*. R. Medley (Ed.). Pergamon Press, New York.

Rhoads, S. E. (1985). *The Economist's View of the World*. Cambridge University Press, Cambridge, England.

Samuels, W. J. (1980). Towards positive public choice theory. *Review of Social Economy* 38: 55–64.

Samuels, W. J., and Schmid, A. A. (1981). Interdependence and impacts: Toward the integration of externality, public goods and grants theories. In *Taxing and Spending Policy*. W. J. Samuels and L. L. Wade (Eds.). Lexington Books, Lexington, MA.

Thurow, L. (1980). *The Zero-Sum Society*. Basic Books, New York.

Tullock, G. (1965). *The Politics of Bureaucracy*. Public Affairs Press, Washington, D.C.

—— (1987). *Autocracy*. Kluwer Academic Publishers, Boston.

—— (1989). *The Economics of Special Privilege and Rent-Seeking*. Kluwer Academic Publishers, Boston.

United States Advisory Commission on Intergovernmental Relations (ACIR) (1991). *Significant Features of Fiscal Federalism*: Vol 2, *Revenues and Expenditures, 1991*. United States Advisory Commission on Intergovernmental Relations, Washington, D.C.

Usher, D. (1981). *The Economic Prerequisites to Democracy*. Columbia University Press, New York.

Wade, L. L. (1980). The political theory of public finance. In *Taxing and Spending Policy*. W. J. Samuels and L. L. Wade (Eds.). D. C. Heath, Lexington, MA.

Wallace, S., Wasylenko, M., and Weiner, D. (1991). The distributional implications of the 1986 Tax Reform Act. *National Tax Journal* 44(2): 181–198.

Winfrey, J. C. (1973). *Public Finance*. Harper & Row, New York.

Wood, R. C. (1962). *1400 Governments*. Anchor, Garden City, NY.

SUGGESTED READING

Beck, M. (1981). *Government Spending*: *Trends and Issues*. Praeger, New York.

Borcherding, T. E. (1977). *Budgets and Bureaucrats*: *The Sources of Government Growth*. Duke University Press, Durham, NC.

Buchanan, J. M. (1967). *Public Finance and Democratic Process*. University of North Carolina Press, Chapel Hill.

Haveman, R. H., and Margois, J. (Eds.) (1983). *Public Expenditure and Policy Analysis*, 3rd ed. Houghton Mifflin, Boston.

Higgs, R. (1987). *Crisis and Leviathan*: *Critical Episodes in the Growth of American Government*. Oxford University Press, New York.

Oates, W. E. (1972). *Fiscal Federalism*. Harcourt Brace Jovanovich, New York.

Okun, A. M. (1975). *Equality and Efficiency*. Brookings Institution, Washington, D.C.

Page, B. I. (1983). *Who Gets What from Government*. University of California Press, Berkeley.

Peppard, D. M. (1976). Toward a radical theory of fiscal incidence. *Review of Radical Political Economics* 8: 1-16.

Samuels, W. J. (Ed.) (1989). *Fundamentals of the Economic Role of Government*. Greenwood Press, Westport, CT.

Schmid, A. A. (1987). *Property, Power and Public Choice*, 2nd ed. Praeger, New York.

—— (1987). *Benefit Cost Analysis*: *A Political Economy Approach*. Westview, Boulder, CO.

Taylor, C. Lewis (Ed.) (1983). *Why Governments Grow*: *Measuring Public Sector Size*. Sage, Beverly Hills, CA.

Wildavsky, A. (1979). *The Politics of the Budgetary Process*, 3rd ed. Little, Brown, Boston.

21
Agricultural Policy

Don F. Hadwiger
Iowa State University, Ames, Iowa

Wynn Hjermstad
Urban Development, City of Lincoln, Lincoln, Nebraska

I. INTRODUCTION

Modern agriculture is at the cutting edge of new physical and biological knowledge. Its emergent technologies may provide the means to save the world's natural ecology. Modern foods can provide adequate nutrition and a standard of hygiene that shields humans from many ancient diseases. Against the great scourges of humanity, modern agriculture resists hunger, disease, and pestilence—and also war, to the extent that wars are fought over scarce food, fiber, and energy.

Some nations have made great gains in agricultural modernization, as indicated by growth in per worker agricultural production. Others have not, and nowadays this difference in performance seems more a result of the way agriculture is organized than a result of variations in food needs or available natural resources. The organization of agricultural production and marketing is in turn shaped or legitimized by public policy and by the decision-making structures from which policy derives.

Which decision structures are most effective in increasing productivity? In general, these are the autonomous structures in which farm organizations and agricultural ministries are among the key players. Much less effective are the integrative structures in which presidents, cabinets, and national planning and fiscal agencies make policy for agriculture and for other sectors as well. Nations achieving high per worker productivity growth have usually made an early transition to an autonomous decision system for agriculture.

II. THE CONTRIBUTIONS OF AGRICULTURAL POLICY TO AGRICULTURAL MODERNIZATION

Governmental policies have been crucial for agricultural development, according to many observers. "Governments matter," concluded Latin American specialist F. Lamond Tullis

507

(Tullis and Holist, 1986: xi). Many studies have explained the large variations in agricultural growth among countries by citing the impact of public policies. As examples, U.S. agricultural growth has been attributed in part to public research extending over more than a century that produced annual returns in excess of 35% of investment (Ruttan, 1982: 242-244). French neocorporatist governments fashioned a role for agriculture as the designated earner of foreign exchange—"the green petrol of France" (Keeler, 1987: 90-91). Taiwan's rapid agricultural growth was stimulated first by the Japanese imperial government and then by the refugee Chinese Nationalist government (Puchala and Stavely, 1979). The Korean government achieved production increases by offering farmers a subsidized package of "green revolution" seeds and fertilizer, and also by protecting domestic markets for local producers (Lee et al., 1990).

Discussed below are various governmental measures that can facilitate the development of a productive and efficient agriculture.

A. A Difficult First Step in Developing Agriculture Is to Find and Motivate a Set of Production-Oriented Farmers

In Taiwan before World War II, the Japanese colonial government improved productivity by keeping the productive landholders and removing the others (Puchala and Staveley, 1979). The imperial Japanese in this instance exercised virtually absolute power and were single-minded in their goal of making Taiwan a breadbasket for Japan. National governments too have found the structures to develop a corps of modern farmers. Governments may, for example, provide an environment in which efficient farmers are self-selected. In numerous Third World countries, opportunities for agricultural profits have prompted a shift of control from feudal structures to innovative, profit-oriented farms. Indeed, achieving this transition has been a major goal or result of many national and international agricultural policies (Griffin, 1974: 46-53). In the United States, public research and extension agencies were created to encourage the "innovative" farmers, and later, price-support programs provided windfall profits to the more efficient farmers, who were inclined or even under pressure to reinvest these profits to enhance further their efficiency and scale of operation. The importance of policy in fostering these innovative farmers was shown when policy momentarily failed to provide them a predictable environment during the 1920s and again in the 1980s, in which periods some of the most efficient farmers failed to survive (Runge, 1987).

Governments have secured high productivity from small farmers, as in the case of Cote d'Ivoire cocoa producers, and in the small farm agriculture mandated by land reforms in Korea, Japan, and modern Taiwan. These small farmers usually have required relatively more public assistance in the form of research, training, credit, and higher prices per unit sold. The small farm sector on the whole has been less productive and less efficient than larger farms, especially in developing countries such as Mexico which have been inconsistent in offering production incentives, and which have not provided small farmers opportunities to reinvest their profits in expanding and modernizing their own enterprise (Sanderson, 1992).

B. Government Can Assure that Farmers Receive Incentive Prices

This can be done by creating market mechanisms and rules that yield farmers a commensurate share of the end product price; or, more controversially, by intervening directly to increase and stabilize commodity prices and income. A principal measure for supporting prices of basic commodities, particularly in developing countries with growing populations, is to regulate food imports to guarantee domestic producers a portion of the domestic market. Thus, many governments by offering high rice prices encouraged the transition from subsistence to commercial farming, as farmers sought higher yields from "green revolution" technologies. Major exporting countries were occasionally able to support a world or regional price for a major agricultural export, as the United States and Canada together supported the world wheat price during several post–World War II decades.

Governmental price intervention has been much criticized, in part from theoretical perspectives that challenge any form of market intervention and in part because some governmental policies have had apparently unfortunate results. For example, "stop and go" programs that offer big production incentives and then drop these once production is adequate have punished the innovative farmers in such different settings as the United States (Runge, 1987) and the Philippines (Bouis, 1982). As another result, domestic surpluses are often dumped abroad, destabilizing world prices and robbing other exporters of markets, although it is now recognized that surpluses can be used creatively in assistance to developing countries, as for example, in building rural infrastructures. Mexico, as another example, has used U.S. concessionary programs in such a way as to finance price supports for its own farmers. Finally, governments intervening to keep consumer prices low may bring about a long-term decline in agricultural productivity and efficiency.

C. Public Investment in Agricultural Research and Extension Education Has Produced Enormous Returns in Productivity in Virtually Every Agricultural Setting (Ruttan, 1982)

The "green revolution" multiplied crop yields using a triumvirate of chemical pesticides, organic fertilizers, and adapted plant varieties. Gene splicing and other biogenetics breakthroughs are creating more usable plant and animal food products while reducing dependence on chemicals, and genetic improvements may simplify machinery and management systems, putting them within the reach of small farmers in developing countries. There are now many synthetic foods (margarine being an early example) that are relatively cheap, convenient to prepare, and nutritious. Agricultural science continues to be a wellspring of agricultural development.

D. Infrastructures Including the Transportation Networks, Markets, Commodity Storage, Water, Electrical Power, and Credit Are Virtually Prerequisites for Modernizing Agriculture (Bonnen, 1992), and It Is Government that Charters, Finances, or Actually Builds Them

Private industry by comparison has been relatively slow to address rural (spatially dispersed) demands except with the benefit of government subsidy or to avert competition from public and cooperative institutions. A variety of public agencies, including international assistance agencies and local governments, have taken leadership in such improvements as road, airport, and canal construction.

III. PUBLIC POLICY PATHOLOGIES

Governmental policies do not inevitably produce growth. Indeed the absence of productivity growth in some systems has been attributed to governmental policies. For example, Eastern

Europe—once a major agricultural exporter—became burdened with collectivization and ensuing policies that resulted in negative growth (Wong and Ruttan, 1990: 31–35). On the South American continent, food shortages are due in part to governmental policies that failed to stimulate agricultural development (Tullis and Hollist, 1986: xvii–xviii). The Mexican government's attempt to hold down food prices (as a means of placating urban consumers) resulted in reduced production for domestic use; then Mexico's compensatory effort to regain food self-sufficiency proved ineffective and was soon abandoned (Spalding, 1981: 1249). According to a scholar of African agriculture, "Within any given African country, faltering agricultural production can be explained in large part by government policies that significantly reduce the incentives to agricultural producers" (Lofchie, 1986: 10).

The clear implication from dozens of studies is that governments can achieve agricultural growth, and contrariwise, some failures of agriculture can be attributed to ineffectual government. Indeed it appears that productivity grows or stagnates mainly in response to policy (and market) stimuli rather than mainly in response to the potentiality of the natural resource base or the degree of nutritional "need." Several countries or regions whose history and setting offer a limited agricultural endowment, such as Western Europe, Korea, and Taiwan, have experienced surprising agricultural growth since World War II, whereas production has lagged in resource-rich regions such as Eastern Europe (Nazarenko, 1993), Africa (Strycker and Baird, 1992), and Latin America (Tullis and Holist, 1986). Meanwhile in many regions with chronic food deficits (e.g., Africa and Latin America), production growth has been sluggish. Explanations for the large variations among nations in the rate of agricultural growth must be sought elsewhere, particularly in institutional differences, including the different modes of decision making.

IV. MULTIPLE GOALS OF AGRICULTURAL POLICY

Productivity growth through modernization is one among several goals that governments may seek for their agricultures. Some goals can be made compatible, including the following: agricultural modernization may abet urban industrialization, increase political support from rural sectors, and improve the health and safety of citizens. Some goals have proved on the whole more difficult to reconcile, including embodying a particular sociopolitical structure in agriculture such as family farms, a landed elite, or communal farms; using agriculture to sustain existing rural communities; or visualizing the farm as a way station for "marginalized" citizens. Yet to be reconciled with agricultural modernization are ecological and esthetic goals: preservation of the natural ecology and preserving the beauty of farm landscapes.

A. Agricultural Modernization and Industrial Development

Rapidly developing countries have understood that agricultural growth is closely related to overall economic development. Governments of developing countries are commonly confronted with an agenda of expanding food needs and food production opportunities, referred to here as imperatives for increased agricultural productivity.

1. *The "population explosion."* No direct remedy has been found for the rapid growth of population, especially in rural areas (although population-control policies in China and a few other Asian countries have apparently begun to produce results). To maintain political stability, nations seek to provide expanding human populations with sufficient, inexpensive food. Partly because some governments are reluctant to use foreign exchange earnings for purchase of food, the goal of food autarchy (or, at least, of maximizing food

self-sufficiency) is widely sought. However, even some nations with large positive trade balances such as Japan may seek food self-sufficiency in order to please farmer voters or to reassure the general population that food will always be available locally.

2. *The availability of technologies for increasing agricultural production.* To meet the food needs of their expanding populations, governments of developing countries have felt obliged to embrace new production technologies which increase food production but also tend to release a large part of the agricultural workforce for other economic activity.

3. *The need for creating industrial capital through agricultural productivity.* To provide employment for a growing workforce, including displaced farmers, governments may rely upon the exploitation of their natural resources which, on a global basis, are largely agricultural. For example, taxes on agricultural exports provide governmental revenues, and meanwhile these agricultural exports are also a source of foreign exchange earnings.

4. *Upgraded diets.* As the workforce becomes urban, population growth slows down; even so, the aggregate value of food consumption may continue to grow because increased per capita income leads to upgraded diets. The agricultural economy is transformed by moving to higher-value products such as meat and dairy products.

B. Health and Safety of Food

No revolution was less predictable than that in diets, and hardly any cultural force has been less insistent than consumer demands for healthy and safe food supplies. Only decades ago, dieticians asserted that food habits were intractable, because people preferred familiar foods, because familiar foods had status value, and because they were the only foods most family cooks knew how to prepare and, therefore, the only foods likely to be available locally.

However, the environment changed, which encouraged revisions in diets. New lifestyles required "fast food." New technologies and delivery systems provided convenience and variety, and consumer movements within industrializing nations have added the demand that food be healthy and safe. Consumers—and the producers who are subject to their boycotts—expect government to provide authoritative information as well as regulatory rules and inspection. The consumer movement in industrial countries has dictated new public research initiatives and new infrastructures; for example, favoring an "alternative agriculture" that presumably provides safer and more wholesome food because it is not so dependent on pesticides and organic fertilizers. Consumer groups also manifest intense but conflicting pressures with respect to politics governing the use and abuse of animals involved in human food production.

C. Creating a Supportive Political Constituency

The people who farm are often vital political actors, and the main objective of farm policy may be to placate or manipulate them. In the past, farmers have often been ignorant, traditionalist, and suservient, and therefore have often been undemanding and dependable supporters of the existing regime. Yet many revolutionary movements found their base in the countryside. As political systems have begun to practice electoral democracy, governments have learned that unhappy farmers may jump traces and join the opposition. So governments may feel obliged to bring farmers into a ruling coalition, as in Mexico and Japan, by providing avenues for participation such as cooperatives, farm organizations, or political party organs. Mexican farmers during recent centuries have played cyclical roles in politics, sometimes as manipulable peasants, then as vanguards of the revolution, and recently as a bloc of status quo supporters who are not, however, to be taken for granted.

In mature Western democracies, the agricultural sector is likely to have gained excellent access to decision centers in the executive, legislature, and parties through an agricultural lobby that has achieved autonomous control over farm policy even to the point where the government accepts escalating costs of agricultural programs.

In virtually all political systems, therefore, political considerations can supercede all other goals for farm policy. Policies designed to be "rational" in pursuit of goals must also be "politically feasible"—that is, perceived to be advantageous to those who govern.

D. Agriculture as Socio-Political Structure

Characteristically in centuries past, rural land ownership was the linchpin of aristocracies: A landed ruling class extracted wealth from agriculture that was used to finance an army, to manipulate governments and laws, and to placate the masses. The bloody French and Mexican revolutions, among others, were directed against such landed systems. Indeed the U.S. Civil War was fought in part over the issue as to whether a slaveholding aristocracy should maintain and extend its geographical domain or whether small freeholders should ultimately predominate. In recent years under the tutelage of occupying forces, Japan and Korea redistributed their landed estates to a new clientele of minifarmers; and the United States joined with the Taiwan's Kuomintang dictatorship to terminate landed estates in that little country (while seemingly unable to insist on such reforms in its own former colony—the Philippines—and in other settings where a landed class supported U.S. defense interests).

Agricultural systems have often been shaped in conformance with the utopian ideologies of rulers. U.S. President Thomas Jefferson's Republican party at one time implemented Jefferson's belief that only an agrarian society could embody the civic virtues needed to sustain a republic. Jefferson initiated land laws that would create a nation of small farmers. He purchased the Louisiana Territory to give these farmers more room, and his successors continued to clear the American continent for settlement by "pioneers." In the former Soviet Union, by contrast, independent farmers (kulaks) were eliminated in Stalin's greatest purge, which produced a collectivized and also compliant countryside.

When rural people were expected to implement the social theories of their rulers, they were also expected to become adequate producers. Indeed, the proponents of grand theories have usually assumed a complementarity between the goal of ideological correctness and the goal of increased productivity, as in the case of free market theorists who advocate virtual repeal of the price and/or production controls that are now in effect for most agricultural systems. Currently, a radical agricultural theory advanced by "animal rights" advocates is that animal products are an inefficient as well as a morally unacceptable source of food. At least one other major social theory for organizing agriculture has been tested and virtually abandoned: Communal agriculture as adopted by various Marxist regimes has generally proved so unproductive as to become an Achilles heel of Communist political systems. Unfortunately for farmers designated to test these various social and economic theories, they have often been expected to display heroism even to the extent of self-sacrifice.

Although agricultural producers have frequently been unwilling victims of ideology, some farm groups have turned such ideology to their advantage. In particular, the Jeffersonian vision of a small farm society has been continually resurrected in the United States to justify public subsidies for producers, many of whom are no longer "small."

E. Agriculture as a Mainstay of Rural Communities

Many rural communities, at some formative stage in their development, have been dependent on an agricultural economy, and it is often assumed that agriculture is or should continue to be a major source of support for these communities. Thus, there is intense controversy over whether "green revolution" agricultural technology necessarily requires farm enlargement and whether rural communities can be sustained within a setting of large-farm agriculture. For example, it has been argued that in rice-growing areas of southern India, "green revolution" technology involving improved seeds, chemical fertilizers, and irrigation favored larger farmers (Lappé and Collins, 1977: 121); on the other hand, research studies are cited that found that small farmers also were able to benefit from modern technology, and that their increased income led to economic growth in the surrounding villages (Hazell, 1992). Clearly there are technologically advanced, productive small farms, although as in Korea, Taiwan, and Japan, these may be dependent on strong governmental support in the form of subsidized inputs, supported prices, and laws preventing farm enlargement. In the United States and the European Community, labor-saving technology has thinned the agricultural workforce until it is hardly relevant even in many of the communities traditionally centered around farming.

F. Agriculture as a Way Station for "Marginalized" Citizens

Large numbers of the world's citizens have not been effectively absorbed into the world's modernizing economies. Contributing to this pool of "marginalized" persons is rapid population growth and reduction of labor in modernized agriculture. As a partial short-range remedy, governments have attempted to stop or reverse the outmigration from rural areas, for example, by seeking to place size limits on commercial farms, or by developing a dual agriculture consisting in part of commercial farms that serve the production needs of an industrializing society, and also consisting in part of an agricultural sector that continues to provide living space and subsistence for "marginalized" citizens. Such policies, however, may misuse scarce resources: Even modernized small-scale commercial agriculture usually requires subsidies and services that developing countries find it difficult to provide; and with respect to the "marginal" sector, neither can developing countries with expanding food needs find "excess" land and other natural resources to serve subsistence populations. Indeed, the enormous pressure on natural resources from both commercial enterprises and from subsistence farming populations, especially in Africa and in Central/South America, threatens irreversible ecological catastrophe. Agriculture/forestry must become both more efficient and more constrained if it is to be sustained for future, more populous generations.

G. Agriculture as an Environmental Threat

Although some developing countries must avoid depleting natural resources, industrial countries face major problems of dealing with agricultural wastes. Although the United States and other industrial countries have found ways to address the problems of urban waste, these countries are only now seriously confronting the greater and more complex problems resulting from the massive releases into the environment of animal wastes, agricultural chemicals, and eroding soil. Two decades ago, a first major response to modern agricultural pollution was to prohibit DDT and other wide-spectrum pesticides that were effective but persisted in the environment and were obliterating birds and other desired life forms. Simultaneously it was necessary to seek alternatives to the DDT family of pesticides through the development of more acceptable pesticides. Recently, alternative farming strategies have minimized the use of chemical fertilizers and pesticides. Using a new biotechnology, there is the prospect of building genetic invulnerability into both plants and animals, which could result in a "clean" as well as an efficient agriculture. In the meantime, environmentalists responding to a surfeit of agricultural pollution are insisting, with some acquiescence from producer groups, that environmental protection should have at least equal status with the goal of agricultural efficiency.

H. Agriculture as Landscape

It has recently been realized that the perceived "beauty" of many regions or countries is largely a manifestation of their agriculture, and governments of affluent countries are increasingly ready to preserve attractive agricultural landscapes. Subsidies may be given to existing farmers for practices such as providing woodlands and wetlands that create an interesting "biodiversity"; zones may be established in which the land can not be converted from agriculture. Thus, it is made clear to farmers in these settings that their income derives only in part from production and in part from their contribution to the ambience of the countryside.

V. MAKING DECISIONS ON AGRICULTURAL POLICY

Some common patterns emerge both with respect to the participants in agricultural policy decisions, and the structures in which decisions are made. (Information which follows is based on a panel study of agricultural policy making in 18 "first world" nations and 24 "third and fourth world" nations, described in part in Hadwiger, 1992.) Some of these patterns were most characteristic in developing countries, and some patterns emerged that seem transitional to patterns characteristic in developed countries.

A. Influential Actors

The ministry of agriculture is an influential policy maker within most governments (Table 1). Two other governmental officials, the president/prime minister and the minister of budget, are generally important but much less likely than the ministry of agriculture to exert an "outstanding, primary influence" over agricultural policy.

   However, several entities important within some countries are unimportant or virtually absent in others (see Table 1). Within the government these include the legislative branch, legislative committees, the national planning agency, and the Ministry of Business or Commerce; outside the government, farm organizations are regarded as prominent actors in some systems. Political parties are frequently important, although not usually primary influences. Other methods for mass participation are not universally influential, including elections, popular protests, and opinion polls. In some systems, individual leaders are thought to exert primary influence. Elite social classes are regarded as a primary influence in some agricultural decision-making systems. Another frequently mentioned primary influence is an international body—the European Economic Community (EEC) for its members, and international assistance agencies for some developing nations. In only a few systems are foreign governments considered important influences. Scholars as advisers appear to be virtually without any influence in some systems and only "somewhat influential" in others. Churches too lack much influence over agricultural policy.

   Between developed and developing countries there are major differences in the casts of participants, although the ministry of agriculture plays a major role in both groups of countries (see Table 2). Private entities including farm organizations and political parties are quite influential in developed countries. For developed countries that belong to the EEC, the international government has prime influence.

   For developing countries, primary influence over agricultural policy decisions is more likely to be located within the government, particularly in the office of the president or prime

Table 1. Agricultural Policy Actors (42 Nations)

Category of policy actors	Percentage of respondents choosing each influence			
	Primary influence	Influential	Somewhat influential	No influence
Ministry of Agriculture	74	21	4	1
Prime Minister or President[a]	39	34	16	11
Ministry of Budget	24	38	24	13
National farm organization	29	34	23	14
National legislature	21	30	26	23
Political parties	11	37	26	27
Subagency of Min. of Agriculture	19	27	13	42
Farm commodity organizations	11	35	26	29
International body (such as EC)	27	19	19	36
Farm Cooperatives	9	24	38	28
National planning bureaucracy	13	14	22	51
Legislative committee	14	14	28	44
Min. of business, ind., commerce	5	21	29	45
Elections	6	15	29	50
A national leader	9	9	4	78
Provincial governments	8	12	26	55
Elite social class	11	8	1	80
Trade organizations	2	14	45	38
Foreign governments	5	11	31	54
Popular or street protests	2	9	30	58
Military	2	5	11	83
Opinion polls	0	5	17	78
Churches	0	4	11	86
Scholars, universities	0	4	42	55

[a]In cases where both were named, the highest score was selected.
Source: Hadwiger, 1992.

minister. Also important mainly in developing countries are the ministries of budget, planning, and commerce. Other entities that are influential in some developing countries include provincial governments, social elites, and the military.

B. Structures of Agricultural Decision Making

Not only the cast of important actors but also the decision-making structures typically diverge sharply between developed and developing countries. Political literature offers numerous models for decision making, several of which are relevant to agricultural policy. These are categorized here, and discussed below, as *integrative* structures, found mainly in developing countries, and *autonomous* structures, found mainly in developed countries (Table 3). A few structures seem to enable transition from one category of decision structure to another. Table 3 also provides evidence that these decision structures are associated with the *pace* as well as the *degree* of agricultural modernization: Autonomous structures tend to have achieved better productivity growth per agricultural worker.

Three decision structures, discussed below, were prominent in agricultural policy. The *national bureaucratic*, centering on national planning agencies, was reported by more than

Table 2. Who Is Influential? Developed versus Developing Countries

	Developed		Developing	
	Prime[a]	Total[b]	Prime	Total
Ministry of Agriculture	80%	98%	70%	95%
President or Prime Minister	13	53	61	90
National farm organization	48	83	12	43
National Legislative Body	15	43	25	58
Ministry of Budget, Finance	10	45	37	80
Political party(ies)	18	58	4	37
Subagency of Min. of Agric.	15	40	20	51
Farm commodity organization	16	44	6	45
International body (inc. EEC)	48	66	8	26
Farm cooperatives	13	38	6	28
National Planning Agency	0	3	22	47
Legislative committees	23	33	6	24
Ministry of Industry, Commerce	3	13	6	41
National elections	8	26	4	16
Individual leaders	13	18	6	18
Provincial governments	6	6	12	30
Social elites	3	11	16	24
Business, trade organization(s)	0	15	4	16
Foreign governments	3	13	6	16
Popular protest	0	13	3	10
Military	0	0	4	12
Opinion polls	0	10	0	0
Church(es)	0	3	0	4
Scholars, universities	0	3	0	4

[a]Percentage of all respondents answering "primary or outstanding influence."
[b]Percentage of all respondents answering "primary or outstanding influence," plus those answering "influential."
 The remaining options were "somewhat influential" and "no apparent influence."
Source: Hadwiger, 1992.

half of the respondents for developing countries; the *associationalist* structure, centering on the farm organizations and ministry of agriculture, was reported by more than one fourth of respondents for developed countries; and the *macropolitical* structure, centering on political parties and the president/prime minister was to be found within both developed and developing nations (see Table 3).

C. Integrative Structures

In integrative models, major decisions are made by the same sets of decison makers who decide general government policies and who make decisions for other policy sectors in addition to agriculture. For example, in a *cabinet* government under a *parliamentary* system, "responsibility for directing policies of a country lies in the hands of a small group of senior politicians" (Robertson, 1985: 2). Another integrative model is *autocratic* government in which one person or dictatorial party exercises unchecked power (Scruton, 1982: 33). Within some rural societies an elite *social class* holds the offices of the government and the military establishment. Under still another integrative arrangement—a *national bureaucratic* decision struc-

Table 3.   Decision Structure and Output

Countries with these decision structures	Average growth in productivity per worker 1970–1985	Number of countries	
		All	Developing
Integrative			
Cabinet/Parliamentary	85%	6	3
Autocratic	− 10	1	1
National Bureaucratic	39	15	15
Class Rule	58	5	4
Neocorporatist	88	4	2
Macropolitical	64	12	8
International Dependent	16	7	7
Autonomous			
Subsystem coalition	98	4	0
Multinational Autonomous	144	6	0
Associationalist	110	14	3
Political Associationalist	102	9	3
Bureaucratic Associationalist	62	6	4
Decentralized	87	5	2
Pluralist	95	9	3
Participatory	81	7	5

Source: Hadwiger, 1992.

ture—the planning, budgetary, and commerce agencies become the principal economic decision makers, controlling all areas of economic policy through such instruments as centralized planning, spending, and personnel appointments.

Several integrative systems offer the means for transition to more autonomous decision making. One of these is *neocorporatism*, in which national governments have usually shaped a structure of "peak associations" to speak for major economic sectors: For example, the government might designate a national farm organization to represent agriculture. Although the government's initial intention is to achieve an integrated national policy through negotiation with and manipulation of the peak associations, these peak associations tend to become more responsive to their constituencies, introducing autonomy (Wilensky and Turner, 1987).

Another decision structure, the *macropolitical*, can be transitional in either direction. Macropolitical structures permit an expansion in the number of participants in a decision (Schattschneider, 1961; Redford, 1969), as, for example, when a national political party secures a mandate from voters on a subject that had previously been controlled by a few decision makers, whether these were government planners within an integrative structure or agricultural interests within an autonomous subgovernment.

Similarly transitional is a *participatory* structure, which involves grass roots action in the form of mass protest or riots. Participatory activities have been used by agricultural producers to unsettle the existing government, especially in rapidly industrializing countries such as Korea and Taiwan, and in the process to gain attention to producer complaints (Lee et al., 1990). A government faced with the prospect of continual grass roots protests may decide to encourage a decision structure such as those discussed below in which producer groups have an effective voice.

D. Autonomous Structures

In contrast with integrated policy making is the operation of "autonomous subsystems," which have been found to control policy making in some developed countries. In the EEC, agricultural policy decisions are made largely at the multinational level, and the "ultimate decision maker" on agriculture in the EEC is a Council composed of agricultural ministers from the member countries (Moyer and Josling, 1990: 37). These ministers are quite responsive to agricultural lobbies in their respective countries and to a confederation of European agricultural lobbies (COPA) (p. 43). This "fragmentation by subject" (p. 35) within the EEC has permitted agricultural interests to shape the Community Agricultural Program. This EEC decision system is referred to here as *multinational autonomous*.

Conceptualizations of U.S. agricultural policy making include several autonomous decision structures. One of these is the *subsystem coalition*, earlier conceptualized as an "iron triangle" to emphasize a well-knit, invulnerable three-part structure of congressional committee, farm organization, and relevant bureaucracy within the U.S. Department of Agriculture. Currently, subsystem coalitions are transitory and are somewhat open-ended, with transformations occurring over time and with shapes differing by issue. There remains a core of interacting players (Salisbury et al., 1987) whose strategy is to maintain autonomous control of decisions on agricultural policy.

A more embracing concept is that of *modernizing associationalism* (Hamilton, 1990), which was instrumental in the development of public agricultural research, and which also established an institutional and leadership network based on shared developmental values. Major actors under modernizing associationalism include the Department of Agriculture and the state-level agricultural research institutions, as well as the scientific associations and farm and commodity organizations (particularly the Farm Bureau), which were formed and/or nurtured by the public agencies, as a public/private partnership to support and direct agricultural research. As different from neocorporatism, these public agencies were not acting as agents of an integrative decision system. Rather, U.S. agriculture's associationalism evolved independently of presidents and governing parties, and this system valued and guarded its autonomy.

One may find a partial associational framework consisting only of coalitions of agricultural interest groups and political parties within the private sector (*political associationalist*) or consisting of coalitions of leaders within the ministry of agriculture and its subagencies (*political associationalist*). Either of these may be a first step in the development of an autonomous structure.

The subsystem coalition and the associationalist structure tend to be mutually reinforcing, particularly in their support for a strong and semi-independent ministry of agriculture, and in offering legitimacy and access to farm organizations serving as principal actors.

A more generalizable concept of autonomous decisionmaking is that of *pluralism*. Pluralism involves decision making by "minorities of specialized leaders" in which "no single elite dominates decision making in every substantive area" (Presthus, 1964: 10, 21). Again unlike neocorporatism, elites in a pluralistic system have organized themselves into multiple, competitive groups and organizations, all lacking specific government sponsorship (Schmitter, 1974: 95). However, elites do seek an advantaged relationship, or access, to principal decision makers. Politics within a pluralist system is always in transformation, with some elites attaining access while others are losing out. This concept of a multistructured, continually transforming system can be applied particularly to describe the succession of leadership in the development of U.S. rural infrastructures of transport, storage, credit, water, and electric power.

Another autonomous decision structure, intersecting those above, emphasizes the involvement of provincial and local entities. *Decentralization* has been particularly evident within U.S. agricultural research policy, in which regional commodity groups and state experiment stations exercise great influence. Much rural infrastructure development has been achieved through state and local leadership. Currently, decentralization is seen as an alternative to an integrative structure in developing countries which are confronting the shortcomings of their centralized bureaucracies.

VI. AUTONOMOUS STRUCTURES AS MODERNIZING AGENTS

In general, autonomous systems such as the associationalist system in U.S. agriculture are associated with large productivity per agricultural worker and also fast growth in productivity per worker. There are several possible explanations.

1. An autonomous system can focus for long periods on achieving the goal of increased productivity and income in agriculture, unlike centralized systems that may neglect that goal in order to deal with crises such as urban unrest, threatened invasion, unbalanced governmental budgets, and inflation.
2. Within an autonomous system, public research appears to be highly valued, and under pressure to produce results of immediate practical value.
3. The specialized decision makers within an autonomous system may be good judges and administrators of appropriate technologies and management systems.
4. The task of mobilizing the agricultural sector can be managed within an associationalist framework that allocates specialized tasks and reinforces norms of increased productivity and income.
5. Autonomous systems sustain a more functional marketplace—on the one hand being concerned with stability, and on the other hand generally facing the long run effects of competition among producers of the same commodity and among producers of substitutable products.

VII. POLITICAL SUPPORT FOR AUTONOMOUS STRUCTURES

Although autonomous structures tend to focus on generating income from production, other potential objectives of agricultural policy are given attention when they become obstacles to the passage of income programs, or alternatively, when agricultural interests form coalitions with supporters of other objectives. In the United States, for example, the decline in the number of rural voters and rural legislators has led autonomous decision makers to expand beyond the iron triangle of exclusive agricultural politics to a broader network of related interests. Specifically, agricultural coalition leaders seeking a majority of congressional votes in support of agricultural programs after 1969 found new support from urban legislators with a proposal that incorporated both a generous food stamp program and an adequate farm income support program (Hansen, 1991: 205–211). In farm bills of 1985 and 1990, the environmental consequences of agricultural activity began to be addressed (albeit reluctantly) in response to the prospect of potential support or opposition from a notably influential "environmental lobby."

In effect, agricultural politics within autonomous decision structures, proceeding under the narrow goal of seeking adequate farm income, has created an efficient industry but also has loosed other impacts (or externalities), some affecting or creating political constituencies surrounding which were ultimately mobilized. For example, agricultural surpluses resulting from production subsidies provided opportunities to increase international food aid and trade and also offered a rationale for extending food purchasing power to poor Americans through the food stamp program. Adverse impacts of agricultural modernization on rural society and on the natural ecology generated constituencies that could be appealed to for support of a multiobjective farm program. As a result, the pattern of rural decision making in autonomous structures changed to include a large network of participating interests. The task of coalition leadership evolved from one of disciplining and protecting agricultural interests among friendly congressional committees, agricultural agencies, and farm organizations to one of managing opportunistic and shifting coalitions.

VIII. THE CONTINUING EVOLUTION OF AGRICULTURAL DECISION MAKING

As countries move to agricultural modernization, one should expect that agricultural policy decision structures will become more autonomous but also more complex. Such structures have enabled countries to improve productivity and efficiency and to deal with many externalities resulting from agricultural modernization. One can not suggest, however, that the future of those decision structures is secure based on their achievements. Indeed, major antitheses have been generated from critiques of these structures based upon perspectives and priorities, notably from public choice theory (Olson, 1982), market economic theory (Sanderson, 1990), and from political theory as well (Lowi, 1969). Such critiques of autonomous political structures overlook virtues but also draw attention to flaws and potential obsolescence. In due time an even more creative synthesis of integrative and autonomous structures may emerge.

REFERENCES

Bonnen, J. T. (1992). Why is there no coherent U.S. rural policy? *Policy Studies Journal* 20: 190–201.

Bouis, H. E. (1982). *Rice Policy in the Philippines*. Doctoral Dissertation, Stanford University,

Griffin, K. (1974). *The Political Economy of Agrarian Change: An Essay on the Green Revolution*. Harvard University Press, Cambridge, MA.

Hadwiger, D. F. (1992). Who creates food abundance? A cross-national study of agricultural policy decision structures and their impact upon productivity in developing countries. *Food Policy* 12:337–348.

Hamilton, D. E. (1990). Building the associate state: The Department of Agriculture and American state-building. *Agricultural History* 64: 207–218.

Hansen, J. M. (1991). *Gaining Access: Congress and the Farm Lobby, 1919–1981*. University of Chicago Press, Chicago.

Hazell, P. B. (1992). *The Green Revolution Reconsidered: The Impact of High-Yielding Rice Varieties in South India*. The Johns Hopkins Press, Baltimore.

Keeler, J. T. S. (1987). *The Politics of Neocorporatism in France: Farmers, the State, and Agricultural Policy-Making in the Fifth Republic*. Oxford University Press, New York.

Lappé, F. M., and Collins, J. (1977). *Food First: Beyond the Myth of Scarcity*. Houghton Mifflin, Boston.

Lee, Y. S., Hadwiger, D. F., and Lee, C-B. (1990). Agricultural policymaking under international pressures, the case of Korea: A newly industrialized country. *Food Policy* 15: 418–433.

Lofchie, M. F. (1986). Africa's agricultural crisis: An overview. In *Africa's Agrarian Crisis: The Roots of Famine*, S. K. Commins, M. F. Lofchie, and R. Payne (Eds.). Lynne Rienner Publishers, Boulder, CO.

Moyer, H. W., and Josling, T. E. (1990). *Agricultural Policy Reform: Politics and Process in the EC and the USA*. Iowa State University Press, Ames.

Nazarenko, V. (1993). Potential trade impacts of policy reforms in the former Soviet Union. In *International Agricultural Trade and Market Development*, J. Helmuth and D. F. Hadwiger (Eds.). Greenwood, Westport, CT.

Olson, M. Jr. (1982). *The Rise and Decline of Nations: Economic Growth, Stagflation, and Social Rigidities*. Yale University Press, Princeton, NJ.

Presthus, R. (1964). *Men at the Top; A Study in Community Power*. Oxford University Press, New York.

Puchala, D., and Staveley, J. (1979). The political economy of Tiawanese agricultural development. In *Food, Politics, and Agricultural Development: Case Studies in the Public Policy of Rural Modernization*, R. F. Hopkins, D. J. Puchala, and R. B. Talbot (Eds.). Westview Press, Boulder, CO, pp. 107–132.

Redford, E. S. (1969). *Democracy in the Administrative State*. Oxford University Press, New York.

Reich, R. B. (1983). *The Next American Frontier*. Times Books, New York.

Robertson, D. (1985). *A Dictionary of Modern Politics*. Europa Publications, London.

Runge, C. F. (1987). Inefficiency and structural adjustment in American agriculture: Who will quit and why? In *Public Policy and Agricultural Technology: Adversity Despite Achievement*, D. F. Hadwiger, and W. P. Browne (Eds.). Macmillan Press, Houndsmills, UK, pp. 33–52.

Ruttan, V. W. (1982). *Agricultural Research Policy*. University of Minnesota Press, Minneapolis.

Salisbury, R. H., Heinz, J. P., Laumann, E. O., and Nelson, R. L. (1987). Who works with whom? Interest group alliances and opposition. *American Political Science Review* 81: 1217–1234.

Sanderson, F. (Ed.) (1990). *Agricultural Protectionism in the Industrialized World*. Resources for the Future, Washington, D.C.

Sanderson, S. (1992). Mexican public sector food policy under agricultural trade liberalization. *Policy Studies Journal* 20: 431–446.

Schattschneider, E. E. (1960). *The Semisovereign People: A Realist's View of Democracy in America*. Holt, Rinehart and Winston, New York.

Schmitter, P. C. (1974). Still the century of corporatism? *Review of Politics* 36: ???.

Scruton, R. (1982). *A Dictionary of Political Thought*. Harper & Row, New York.

Spalding, R. J. (1981). Structural barriers to food programming: Analysis of the Mexican food system. *World Development* 13: 1249–1262.

Stryker, J. F., and Baird, K. E. (1992). Trends in African agricultural trade policy: Causes and prognosis. *Policy Studies Journal* 20: 414–430.

Tullis, F. L., and Hollist, W. L. (Eds.) (1986). *Food, The State, and International Political Economy: Dilemmas of Developing Countries*. University of Nebraska Press, Lincoln.

Wilensky, H. L., and Turner, L. (1987). *Democratic Corporatism and Policy Linkages: The Interdependence of Industrial, Labor-Market, Income and Social Policies in Eight Countries*. Institute of International Studies, University of California, Berkeley.

Wong, L-F., and Ruttan, V. (1990). A comparative analysis of agricultural productivity trends in centrally planned economies. In *Soviet Agriculture: Comparative Perspectives*, K. R. Gray (Ed.). Iowa State University Press, Ames.

Part G
PROBLEMS WITH A SOCIOLOGY OR PSYCHOLOGY EMPHASIS

22
Poverty and Income Maintenance Programs

Harrell R. Rodgers, Jr.
University of Houston, Houston, Texas

I. INTRODUCTION

Poverty remains a world plague—a specter that haunts even the richest nations in the Western industrial world. The United States, still by many measures the richest of all the world's nations, continues to suffer acute poverty. Every region of the country, every major city, and every ethnic group is afflicted by poverty.

No official attempt was made to measure U.S. poverty until the mid-1960s. Backdating its standard, the Social Security Administration reported that some 40 million people in the United States lived in poverty in 1960 and 1961 (Table 1). After a decade of enhanced welfare support, the number of poor dropped to 24 million in 1971. The number and rate of poverty remained fairly stable throughout the 1970s, averaging 24.6 million between 1968 and 1978. Poverty increased substantially during the years of the Reagan presidency, averaging 32.9 million between 1981 and 1989 and increased to 35.7 million in the last year of the Bush administration.

Why has U.S. poverty remained at such a high level despite a complex and expensive set of welfare programs? The answer is complicated and controversial. Some welfare experts contend that the poverty count remains high because of measurement error—that is, the government simply overestimates poverty (Murray, 1984). A much larger group of scholars believe the poverty standard to be inadequate and unsophisticated but maintain that even the best-designed measure would reveal a very large number of U.S. poor. This same group of scholars blame the nation's high rate of poverty on such factors as a fatally flawed welfare system, a faltering economy, and inadequate public schools (Danziger and Weinberg, 1986; Cottingham and Ellwood, 1989; Ellwood, 1988).

This brief introduction suggest the topics that must be investigated to understand U.S. poverty, the nation's welfare programs and their impact, and recent attempts at welfare reform. In the sections that follow, the poor in the United States are analyzed, the controversy

Table 1. Poverty Schedule: Family of Four, 1959–91

Year	Standard ($)	Millions of poor	% of total population
1959	2,973	39.5	22.0
1960	3,022	39.9	22.0
1961	3,054	39.9	22.0
1962	3,089	38.6	21.0
1963	3,128	36.4	19.0
1964	3,169	36.1	19.0
1965	3,223	33.2	17.0
1966	3,317	30.4	16.0
1966[a]	3.317	28.5	15.0
1967	3,410	27.8	14.0
1968	3,553	25.4	13.0
1969	3,743	24.1	12.0
1970	3,968	25.4	13.0
1971	4,137	24.1	11.0
1972	4,275	25.4	12.0
1973	4,540	23.0	11.5
1974	5,038	24.3	12.0
1974[a]	5,038	24.3	11.5
1975	5,500	25.9	12.0
1976	5,815	25.0	12.0
1977	6,200	24.7	12.0
1978	6,662	24.7	11.4
1979	7,412	26.1	11.7
1980	8,414	29.3	13.0
1981	9,287	31.8	14.0
1982	9,862	34.4	15.0
1983	10,178	35.3	15.2
1984	10,609	33.7	14.4
1985	10,989	33.1	14.0
1986	11,203	32.4	13.6
1987	11,611	32.5	13.5
1988	12,091	31.7	13.0
1989	12,675	31.5	12.8
1990	13,359	33.6	13.5
1991	13,924	35.7	14.2

[a]Note: Revision in census calculations.
Source: Derived from U.S. Bureau of the Census, *Money Income and Poverty Status of Families in the United States*. Series P-60, various years.

over the measurement of poverty reviewed, the causes of poverty examined, and U.S. welfare programs and reforms analyzed and compared with European income maintenance programs and antipoverty strategies.

II. MEASURING POVERTY: THE AMERICAN APPROACH

How do we decide whether someone is poor? There are a variety of approaches used by nations. Most fundamentally, poverty may be defined in absolute or relative terms. An absolute standard attempts to define some basic set of resources necessary for survival. A relative standard attempts to define poverty in relationship to the median living standards of the society. A relative standard shows not only how many people do not live close to the average standards in a society, but it also provides insight into how evenly income is distributed among the population. In 1969, the President's Commission on Income Maintenance in the United States (8) concluded that:

> The community's decision as to what is "essential" is dictated in general by its social conscience. If society believes that people should not be permitted to die of starvation or exposure then it will define poverty as the lack of minimum food and shelter necessary to maintain life. . . . As society becomes more affluent it defines poverty as not only the lack of the components of a subsistence level of living, but also the lack of opportunity for persons with limited resources to achieve the quality of life enjoyed by persons with an average amount of resources. The definition of poverty progresses from one based on absolute standards to one based on relative standards.

The irony of the commission's reasoning is that although the United States is certainly an affluent nation, it still defines poverty in absolute subsistence terms, and it is the only major industrial nation to do so.

The first U.S. poverty standard was formulated by the Council of Economic Advisors (CEA) in 1964. This standard attempted to estimate the minimal income needs of a four-person family, using as a base an estimate of the cost of a nutritionally adequate diet for the family (Rodgers, 1978: 18). In 1965, the Social Security Administration (SSA) attempted to improve upon the CEA standard but decided to continue to base the standard on the estimated cost of an "adequate" diet for families of various sizes. Using an economy food budget formulated by the National Research Council, a poverty standard was computed for various family sizes. It was assumed that food costs represented 33% of the total income needs of families of three or more and 27% of the total income required by two-person households.

Table 2 shows the 1991 poverty standard for families and unrelated individuals. The poverty cutoffs consist of 48 thresholds that vary by family size, the presence of children under 18, and, in some cases, the age of the householder. The standard ranges from $6532 for a single, unrelated individual over 65 years of age to more than $30,000 for a family of nine or more with only one child under 18. If a householder or family of one of the specified types has a cash income that falls below the cutoff level, the family is classified as poor.

Table 1 shows the poverty threshold for a family of four backdated to 1959 and the total number of persons counted as poor by year using the government's standard. Until 1969, the yearly changes in the poverty standard reflect changes in the cost of the basic food budget. Since 1969 the standard has been adjusted yearly according to changes in the Consumer Price Index. Taken at face value, the SSA standard suggests that substantial progress was made toward reducing poverty in the 1960s and 1970s, with some reversals occurring in the 1980s and lasting through the early 1990s.

An analysis of the actual computation of the official poverty standard for one family size is illustrative. In 1991, the poverty threshold for a family of four was $13,924. This standard allows $3481 per person per year, or $9.54 per day, one third being the allocation for food ($3.18). The family could spend a total of $4.24 per meal for all four persons, or $89.04 per week on food. A budget for a four-person family would look like this:

$4641.33 for Food: $3.18 a day ($1.06 per meal) per person; $22.26 per week per person.
$4641.33 for Shelter: $386.78 a month for rent or mortgage for four persons.
$4641.33 for Necessities: $96.69 a month per person for clothing, furniture, transportation, health care, utilities, taxes, entertainment, and so forth.

Table 2. Poverty Thresholds in 1991 by Size of Family and Number of Related Children Under 18 Years

Size of family unit	Weighted average thresholds ($)	Related children under 18 years								
		0	1	2	3	4	5	6	7	8 or more
1 person (unrelated individual)	6,932									
under 65 years	7,086	7,086								
65 years and over	6,532	6,532								
Two persons	8,865									
householder under 65 years	9,165	9,120	9,388							
householder 65 years and over	8,241	8,233	9,532							
3 persons	10,860	10,654	10,963	10,973						
4 persons	13,924	14,048	14,278	13,812	13,860					
5 persons	16,456	16,941	17,188	16,662	16,254	16,006				
6 persons	18,587	19,486	19,563	19,160	18,773	18,199	17,859			
7 persons	21,058	22,421	22,561	22,078	21,742	21,115	20,384	19,582		
8 persons	23,605	25,076	25,297	24,842	24,443	23,877	23,158	22,410	22,220	
9 persons or more	27,942	30,165	30,311	29,908	29,569	29,014	28,249	27,558	27,386	26,331

Source: U.S. Bureau of the Census, *Poverty in the United States: 1991.* Series P-60, No. 181, p. A8.

The first thing one notices about the allowance is that it is modest. It would be very difficult for a family of four to scrape by on the humble sums allowed by the formula. It is highly doubtful that anyone could routinely prepare a nutritious meal for four persons for $4.24, or that a family of four could be fed adequately on $89.04 a week. The allowances for rent or mortgages and other necessities are also extremely low. The same is true, of course, for other family sizes. Notice in Table 2 that a single person over age 65 is allowed only $6532 a year—$544 a month for all expenses.

The government's official definition of poverty may also produce a false impression of the amount of progress that has been made in reducing poverty. The reason is that the poverty standard has not kept pace with the rate of growth in personal income. In 1959, the poverty standard for a four-person family was 53% of median family income. By the early 1990s, it averaged only about 38% of median family income. Much of the decline in the poverty count since 1959, therefore, may be the result of the increasing gap between the standard and median family income rather than from families actually escaping poverty. For example, in 1990, the official poverty threshold for a family of four was $13,359 a year. The median annual income for four-person families was $41,451. If half the median income was used as the poverty standard, the relative standard would have been $20,750—an increase in the poverty threshold for a family of four of more than 50%.

The impact of the failure of the standard to track median family income was noted by the Organization for Economic Co-operation and Development (OECD, 1976: 63) as far back as 1976.

> It is not surprising . . . that the percentage of the United States population that falls below the official poverty line has declined over the last decade or more. . . . As long as poverty is defined in absolute terms, economic growth is likely to be enough to eliminate much of it without special income maintenance programs. . . .

The official poverty standard has been criticized on many other grounds, including a food budget base that is too low, the assumption that food costs represent one third of a family's financial needs, the failure of the government to consider the impact of taxes on family take-home pay, and the exclusion of noncash assistance from the calculations.

As noted above, there are many other critical views of the official poverty standard, with some scholars believing that the standard is simply not very sophisticated, resulting sometimes in both overestimates and underestimates of poverty. In recent years, the Bureau of the Census has conducted some interesting research on the official poverty standard, adjusting it in a variety of ways. Table 3 shows the official poverty standard for 1990, along with a combination of revisions designed to deal with criticisms of the formula. Note that the standard is adjusted to reflect, among other items, taxes, noncash welfare benefits such as food stamps and Medicaid, and the net imputed return on the equity of an owned house. The calculations clearly show that regardless of the poverty formula used, a very large number of Americans are classified as poor. Under the most stringent definition (#15), in 1990 over 24 million Americans were poor. Even using the government's modest poverty standards, when all government cash and noncash transfers for the poor are taken into consideration (#14), over 27 million Americans fall below the poverty threshold.

As noted above, in most industrialized nations, poverty is defined in a relative rather than an absolute manner. A relative standard defines poverty not in terms of the basic resources required for subsistence but in relationship to the modal standards of living in a society. Townsend (1974: 15) describes the spirit of a relative standard:

Table 3. Number and Percent of Persons in Poverty by Definition of Income: 1990 (Total number of persons was 248,644,000 in 1990. Numbers in thousands)

	1990	
Definition of income	No. below poverty	Poverty rate
Income before taxes:		
1. Money income excluding capital gains (current measure)	33,585	13.5
2. Definition 1 less government cash transfers	50,944	20.5
3. Definition 2 plus capital gains	50,754	20.4
4. Definition 3 plus health insurance supplements to wage or salary income	49,423	19.9
Income after taxes:		
5. Definition 4 less Social Security payroll taxes	51,875	20.9
6. Definition 5 less federal income taxes (excluding the EITC)	52,367	21.1
7. Definition 6 plus the Earned Income Tax Credit (EITC)	51,285	20.6
8. Definition 7 less state income taxes	51,758	20.8
9. Definition 8 plus nonmeans-tested government cash transfers	36,526	14.7
10. Definition 9 plus the value of Medicare	35,463	14.3
11. Definition 10 plus the value of regular-price school lunches	35,450	14.3
12. Definition 11 plus means-tested government cash transfers	32,884	13.2
13. Definition 12 plus the value of Medicaid	30,945	12.4
14. Definition 13 plus the value of other means-tested government noncash transfers	27,279	11.0
15. Definition 14 plus net imputed return on equity in own home	24,406	9.8

Source: U.S. Bureau of the Census, *Measuring the Effect of Benefits and Taxes on Income and Poverty: 1990.* Series P-60, No. 176-RD, p. 5.

Individuals, families and groups in the population can be said to be in poverty when they lack the resources to obtain the type of diets, participate in activities and have the living conditions and amenities which are customary, or are at least widely encouraged or approved, in the societies to which they belong.

The typical method of formulating a relative definition is by pegging it to median income. The poor are defined as those who earn less than some percentage of the median income for their family size. The percentage is generally in the 50 to 66% range. As noted above, if this approach was adopted in the United States, it would substantially raise the poverty standard and the poverty count.

The measurement of poverty, then, is both complex and political. Poverty is not easy to measure, and reasonable and informed people can vary substantially in their judgments of how it should be gauged. Despite all the controversy, one fact is clear: Regardless of the measure used, a very large number of Americans live in poverty.

III. THE POOR

Knowing who the poor are provides insights into the causes of poverty and suggests the reforms necessary to alleviate it. In the United States, poverty exists in all regions of the nation, affects every racial and ethnic group, the young and the old, the employed and unemployed.

Table 4. Number, Poverty Rate, and Standard Errors of Persons, Families, and Unrelated Individuals Below the Poverty Level in 1991 (Numbers in thousands. Persons, families, and unrelated individuals as of March of the following years)

		1990			
		Below poverty level		Poverty rate	
Characteristic	Total	No.	Standard error	No.	Standard error
Persons (all persons)	251,179	35,708	537	14.2	0.2
Race and Hispanic origin[a]					
white	210,121	23,747	451	11.3	0.2
related children under 18	51,631	8,321	230	16.1	0.5
black	31,312	10,242	252	32.7	0.8
related children under 18	10,178	4,637	138	45.6	1.7
Hispanic origin[a]	22,068	6,339	203	28.7	0.9
related children under 18	7,473	2,977	116	39.8	1.8
Family status					
in families	212,716	27,143	478	12.8	0.2
householder	67,173	7,712	151	11.5	0.2
related children under 18	64,800	13,658	282	21.1	0.5
related children under 6 years	22,853	5,483	190	24.0	0.9
other family members	80,742	5,774	231	7.2	0.3
in unrelated subfamilies	1,624	791	87	48.7	5.9
reference person	669	321	27	47.9	4.8
children under 18	863	451	57	52.3	7.7
unrelated individual	36,839	7,773	152	21.1	0.4
male	17,395	3,012	87	17.3	0.5
female	19,445	4,762	113	24.5	0.6
Age					
under 15 years	55,936	12,514	267	22.4	0.5
15–24 years	34,416	5,947	134	17.3	0.4
25–44 years	82,064	9,160	172	11.2	0.2
45–54 years	27,023	2,167	86	8.0	0.3
55–59 years	10,620	1,019	60	9.6	0.6
60–64 years	10,530	1,120	63	10.6	0.6
65 years and over	30,590	3,781	110	12.4	0.4
Residence					
nonfarm	246,737	35,150	533	14.2	0.2
farm	4,442	557	100	12.5	2.3
in metropolitan areas	195,918	26,827	476	13.7	0.2
in central cities	75,912	15,314	369	20.2	0.5
outside central cities	120,007	11,513	323	9.6	0.3
outside metropolitan areas	55,261	8,881	349	16.1	0.7
Region					
Northeast	50,788	6,177	206	12.2	0.4
Midwest	60,371	7,989	268	13.2	0.5
South	85,891	13,783	358	16.0	0.4
West	54,129	7,759	275	14.3	0.5

Table 4. *Continues*

Table 4. Continued

Characteristic	Total	1990			
		Below poverty level		Poverty rate	
		No.	Standard error	No.	Standard error
Families					
Race and Hispanic Origin[a] of House-holder (All families)	67,173	7,712	151	11.5	0.2
Married-couple families	52,457	3,158	90	6.0	0.2
Male householder, no wife present	3,025	392	30	13.0	1.0
Female householder, no husband present	11,692	4,161	105	35.6	1.0
White families	57,224	5,022	117	8.8	0.2
Married-couple families	47,124	2,573	80	5.5	0.2
Male householder, no wife present	2,374	257	24	10.8	1.1
Female householder, no husband present	7,726	2,192	73	28.4	1.0
Black families	7,716	2,343	76	30.4	1.0
Married-couple families	3,631	399	30	11.0	0.9
Male householder, no wife present	504	109	16	21.7	3.4
Female householder, no husband present	3,582	1,834	67	51.2	2.1
Hispanic origin families[a]	5,177	1,372	57	26.5	1.2
Married-couple families	3,532	674	39	19.1	1.2
Male householder, no wife present	383	71	13	18.6	3.5
Female householder, no husband present	1,261	627	38	49.7	3.5

[a]Persons of Hispanic origin may be of any race.
Source: U.S. Bureau of the Census, *Poverty in the United States: 1991*. Series P-60, No. 181, p. 1.

Some persons, however, are much more likely to be poor than others. Table 4 provides an overview of the poor population in 1991. From a strictly numerical criterion, whites constitute by far the largest group among the poor. Over 66% of the poor were white, whereas 28.7% were black. Hispanics, who may be of any race, were 17.8% of the poor. Despite their numerical superiority, poverty is a less severe hazard for whites than for minorities. In 1991, only 11.3% of whites were poor, compared with 32.7% of blacks and 28.7% of Hispanics.

Other than race, another predictor of poverty is the sex of the family head (Garfinkel and McLanahan, 1986; McLanahan and Booth, 1989; Rodgers, 1990; Wojtkiewicz et al., 1990). By far the largest group of poor people in the United States is made up of single women and their children. Over half of all poor people in America live in households headed by a woman. Female-headed households suffer a rate of poverty that is almost six times greater than the rate for married-couple families. In 1991, only 6% of all married couple families lived in poverty compared with 35.6% of all female-headed families. Yet, female-headed families are the fastest growing household type in the nation. Between 1959 and 1991, the number of female-headed households with children tripled. In 1991, some 23% of all families with children were headed by women. This included 17.5% of white families, 27% of Hispanic, and 54% of all black families with children. Over half of all children living in these households lived in poverty, with particularly high rates for minority children (Rodgers, 1990: 3–16).

The poverty rate for female-headed families is the primary reason why poverty among U.S. children has increased dramatically over the last 15 years. Children in the United States suffer a rate of poverty that exceeds 20% (21.8% in 1991), and they are the poorest major age group in the United States. Where poverty is concerned, it is a great deal safer to be old than young in the United States (Birkhauser et al., 1988; Haveman et al., 1988; Smolensky, 1988).

Thus, poverty most acutely affects minorities, female-headed families, children—especially those in single-parent minority families), and minorities concentrated in poverty pockets of major cities.

IV. CAUSES OF POVERTY

The causes of poverty are contested and controversial. There are many theories and many disagreements (Danziger and Weinberg, 1986; Ellwood, 1989; Mead, 1986; Murray, 1984; Rodgers, 1990). There are also a few antecedents that most poverty researchers agree on. Almost everyone agrees that the economy plays a role. When unemployment rates are low and the economy is growing at a healthy rate, poverty declines. During the last decade, the unemployment rate has remained rather high, and millions of additional Americans have been involuntarily employed only part-time or in a very low-paying job. Additionally, over the last 15 years, the earning power of the average American has not kept pace with inflation. Thus, there is evidence that in the 1980s and early 1990s the historic relationship between economic growth and poverty has weakened. Blank et al. (1990) recently published data showing that the same rates of economic growth that substantially lowered poverty in the 1960s had a more modest impact in the 1980s. The reason the authors conclude is that although the economic expansion of the 1980s did lower employment, the wages earned by the employed poor were so low that they were left in poverty.

Another study (Children's Defense Fund, 1992) recently documented the dramatic decline in the incomes of young families with children. The study found that adjusted for inflation, the income of the average young family with children fell 32.1% between 1973 and 1990. In 1973, the average young family with children had $27,765 in income. By 1990, these families averaged $18,844 in real purchasing power. The study found that about half of the decline could be explained by the growth of single-parent families. The other half was the result of eroded wages and the decline in the value of government payments. The study found that the child poverty rate for young families in 1990 was a sobering 40%.

In addition to wage and assistance erosion, among poverty researchers there is a consensus that social welfare programs are poorly designed (Danziger and Weinberg, 1986; Ellwood, 1988; Rodgers, 1990). Although there is no consensus on reform, almost everyone agrees that current programs do not address the conditions that make people poor, and that they do not break the cycle of poverty. In fact, a large percentage of the poor do not even receive aid. Among the poor who do obtain aid, only a very small percentage receive enough assistance to push them above the poverty line. Equally serious, social welfare programs have not been substantially altered to respond to the most marked change in U.S. demographics in the last 25 years—the dramatic increase in families headed by women.

Last, there is widespread agreement that the public school system is not adequately preparing a large percentage of all students for either employment or higher education. The impact is significant. Only 3.1% of all college graduates over 25 were poor in 1991, as were 9.6% of high school graduates.

V. THE AMERICAN WELFARE SYSTEM

Compared with the other major Western industrial nations, the United States developed federal welfare programs late in its history, and it has evolved the least comprehensive welfare system. The United States developed welfare programs reluctantly, and primarily in response to two great 20th century upheavals—the Great Depression and the Civil Rights movement. The depth and reach of the Great Depression prompted a reluctant Congress to pass the Social Security Act of 1935, an Act designed to assist those who were outside the labor force. Five major titles of the Act established modest assistance programs for the aged, the unemployed, the blind and disabled, dependent children (ADC), and an insurance program for workers and their families (social security). The Social Security Act was a radical departure for the federal government. Prior to the Act, the states had fashioned some welfare programs, but these were the first to be run by the federal government (social security) or in partnership with the states (ADC).

The Civil Rights movement and the ghetto riots of the 1960s prompted Congress to amend some of the original titles and add several new programs to the Social Security Act. In 1964, the Food Stamp Program was established, but only 22 states initially opted to participate. In 1965, Congress established the Medicare and Medicaid programs. In 1971, Congress adopted national standards for the Food Stamp Program, which finally were adopted by all the states in 1974. The Supplemental Security Income (SSI) program was passed in 1972 and became effective in 1974.

Despite the significant new programs added in the 1960s and 1970s, and a series of important amendments to the original titles, the Social Security Act of 1935 imposed a design and philosophy on U.S. welfare programs that has remained basically unaltered. Three features of the Social Security Act have proven to be particularly important. First, benefits under the original titles were designed for only limited categories of the needy. Even as the programs expanded in the 1960s and 1970s, this feature remained. Second, some of the titles allowed the individual states to determine who would receive assistance and how much aid they would receive. For example, ADC was changed to Aid for Families and Dependent Children (AFDC) in 1950 and became the nation's primary assistance program for the impoverished. Today the percentage of the poor in each state who receive benefits and the amounts they receive vary greatly because of state controls and options. Last, the Act did not provide health insurance. By 1935, most other Western industrial nations already had universal health programs for their citizens. The United States and South Africa are the only major Western industrial nations without comprehensive health care for all citizens.

As will be detailed below, the U.S. welfare system of the 1990s is complex and expensive. Yet, the U.S. has the highest poverty rate by far of any of the Western industrial nations. Why? There are at least four major reasons why poverty has persisted and even expanded over the last 15 years. First, U.S. welfare programs are not designed to eradicate the conditions that make recipients poor. Welfare recipients, for example, might need job training, day care, or education to escape poverty, but only a very small percentage of recipients receive this type of assistance. Second, the vast majority of those who receive welfare assistance are given far too little to push them over the poverty threshold. Third, in inflation-adjusted terms, welfare expenditures have declined quite significantly over the last 15 years. Fourth, a large percentage of the poor receive no assistance because they do not fit into the categories of the poor who are deemed to be "legitimate" or "truly needy."

With this background, we can analyze in more depth the nation's major welfare programs. Table 5 provides an overview of the preeminent programs and shows the basis of eligibility for each program, source of funding, form of aid, and actual and projected expenditures for recent years. The programs divide into three types:

1. Social insurance programs such as social security, Medicare, and unemployment compensation. These are not welfare programs because recipients contribute to them during

Table 5. Federal and State Expenditures for Selected Social Welfare Programs (in billions of dollars)

Program	Basis of eligibility	Source of income	Form of aid	1980	1981	1982	1983	1984	1985	1986	1987	1988	1989	1990
			Social Insurance Programs											
Social Security	Age, disability, or death of parent or spouse; individual earnings	Federal payroll tax on employers and employees	Cash	103.5	145.0	154.1	138.3	166.9	180.1	194.3	205.6	216.4	229.6	295.6
Unemployment compensation	Unemployment	State and federal payroll tax on employers	Cash	18.3	19.6	23.8	25.3	16.1	18.3	18.5	19.2	18.3	19.5	19.7
Medicare	Age or disability	Federal payroll tax on employers and employees	Subsidized health insurance	35.0	39.1	50.4	56.9	62.5	72.2	75.9	79.9	83.6	94.5	105.0
			Cash Assistance Programs: Means-Tested											
Aid to Families with Dependent Children (AFDC)	Certain families with children	Federal, state, local revenues	Cash and service	12.5	7.9	8.0	13.8	14.5	15.2	16.0	16.6	17.0	17.4	19.1
Supplemental Security Income (SSI)	Age or disability	Federal State revenues	Cash	8.2	7.2	7.9	10.8	11.1	11.8	12.8	13.0	14.7	15.7	16.1

Table 5. *Continues*

Table 5. Continued

Program	Basis of eligibility	Source of income	Form of aid	In-kind Programs: Means Tested										
				1980	1981	1982	1983	1984	1985	1986	1987	1988	1989	1990
Medicaid	Persons eligible for AFDC and SSI & medically indigent	Federal, state, local revenues	Subsidized health service	23.3	17.1	17.4	33.4	33.9	37.5	41.0	45.1	54.3	60.9	72.2
Food stamps	Income	Federal revenues	Voucher	9.1	11.4	11.0	12.5	12.3	12.5	12.4	12.4	14.4	14.9	17.7
Public housing	Income	Federal, state, local	Subsidized housing	5.2		7.9	9.1	9.5	10.5	9.5	9.1	9.1	9.9	10.6
Child nutrition	Income	Federal	Free or reduced-price meals	4.8		3.0	5.0	5.2	4.3	4.5	4.5	4.7	4.9	5.1
Women, Infants, Children (WIC)	Mothers with low incomes	Federal	Vouchers			0.9	1.2	1.2	1.2	1.4	1.5	1.8	1.9	2.1

Source: Social Security Bulletin, Annual Statistical Supplement, 1992.

their working years and receive benefits related to contributions. These are the most expensive of all social welfare programs.
2. Cash-assistance programs such as AFDC and SSI. These programs are means-tested, with benefits going only to those who meet income and other qualifications. They are pure welfare programs designed for the poor.
3. In-Kind programs such as food stamps and other nutrition programs, housing assistance, and Medicaid, which provide a noncash service. These programs are also means-tested and often have non–income-related qualifications that must be met by recipients. These programs are also designed for the poor.

As Table 5 shows, social insurance programs are by far the most expensive, followed by in-kind programs, with cash assistance a distant third.

Before individually analyzing the major welfare programs, Table 6 provides an interesting overview of welfare program participation. Table 6 shows that some 21% of all Americans receive some type of means-tested public assistance. Married-couple families with no children under age 18 are the least likely to receive assistance (15.3%), whereas almost 69% of all female-headed families with children under age 18 are recipients of one or more types of assistance. Of those individuals living below the poverty level, some 72% receive assistance. Almost 94% of all poor female-headed families receive benefits from one or more programs compared with 44% of all poor unrelated individuals. Interestingly, even among that group of poor considered to be the most legitimately needy by U.S. society—female family heads and their children—only about 70% receive cash assistance, 77% obtain food stamps, and 36% live in subsidized housing. Only about 50% of poor people aged 65 and over receive assistance, along with only 44% of poor unrelated individuals. Thus, regardless of their characteristics, many of the poor are totally outside the welfare system.

A. Major Welfare Programs

1. Aid to Families with Dependent Children

The core cash-welfare program for the poor is AFDC. All states plus the District of Columbia, Puerto Rico, Guam, and the Virgin Islands administer AFDC programs (Danziger, 1990). Primarily, AFDC provides benefits to female-headed households with children under age 18. The father of the children is normally absent. In recent years, the AFDC program has provided benefits to about 11 million people a month, including over 7 million children. Average family benefits are about $375 a month, or $128 per recipient. There are no standard national benefits under the AFDC program. Benefits vary greatly by state, ranging from average monthly family payments of $598 and $589 in Alaska and California, respectively, to only $118 in Mississippi and $169 in Texas. Eight states, all southern, provide less than $200 a month.

Even in the most generous states, benefits are rather modest, and some states seem to make no serious attempt to aid their poor. In 30 states, benefits are less than 50% of the poverty level. Only in Alaska and Hawaii does the combined value of AFDC and food stamps boost the average family of four above the poverty level. In most other states, the combined value of AFDC and food stamps leaves recipient families far below the poverty level (Ways and Means, 1985: 197). Low-paying states also cover a smaller proportion of all their poor. Texas, for example, has in recent years provided AFDC to only a little over 20% of its poor children.

The federal government reimburses 50 to 78% of a state's AFDC costs depending on the per capita income of the state and pays, on average, about 54% of all AFDC costs. The

Table 6. Program Participation Status of Household, by Poverty Status of Persons in 1991 (Numbers in thousands)

Characteristics	Total	In household that received means-tested assistance		In household that received means-tested assistance excluding school lunches		In household that received means-tested cash assistance		In household that received food stamps		In household in which one or more persons covered by medicaid		Live in public or subsidized housing	
		No.	%	No.	%	No.	%	No.	%	No.	%	No.	%
All income levels													
Total	251,179	57,925	23.1	46,977	18.7	27,184	10.8	25,697	10.2	37,117	14.8	10,873	4.3
65 years and over	30,590	5,498	18.0	5,421	17.7	2,961	9.7	1,416	4.6	3,655	11.9	1,537	5.0
In families	212,716	50,746	23.9	40,138	18.9	23,354	11.0	22,552	10.6	32,401	15.2	8,689	4.1
Related children under 18 years	64,800	22,798	35.2	17,232	26.6	10,328	15.9	11,683	18.0	14,409	22.2	4,540	7.0
In married-couple families	169,557	28,799	17.0	20,969	12.4	9,916	5.8	9,367	5.5	15,993	9.4	2,718	1.6
Related children under 18 years	47,895	11,710	24.4	7,694	16.1	3,400	7.1	4,187	8.7	5,996	12.5	1,131	2.4
In families with female householder, no spouse present	34,790	19,260	55.4	17,021	48.9	12,138	34.9	12,172	35.0	14,610	42.0	5,725	16.5
Related children under 18 years	14,545	10,040	69.0	8,789	60.4	6,488	44.6	7,056	48.5	7,737	53.2	3,309	22.8
Unrelated individuals	36,839	6,279	17.0	6,111	16.6	3,247	8.8	2,644	7.2	4,050	11.0	2,127	5.8
Below poverty level													
Total	35,708	26,034	72.9	23,359	65.4	15,566	43.6	17,920	50.2	19,824	55.5	7,183	20.1
65 years and over	3,781	1,897	50.2	1,874	49.6	1,113	29.4	879	23.2	1,328	35.1	736	19.5
In families	27,143	22,027	81.2	19,462	71.7	13,090	48.2	15,711	57.9	16,871	62.2	5,989	22.1
Related children under 18 years	13,658	12,025	88.0	10,618	77.7	7,466	54.7	8,992	65.8	9,485	69.4	3,507	25.7
In married-couple families	12,156	8,703	71.6	7,126	58.6	3,550	29.2	5,255	43.2	5,617	46.2	1,361	11.2
Related children under 18 years	5,066	4,117	81.3	3,303	65.2	1,633	32.2	2,590	51.1	2,677	52.8	666	13.1
In families with female householder, no spouse present	13,824	12,436	90.0	11,575	83.7	9,057	65.5	9,914	71.7	10,586	76.6	4,509	32.6
Related children under 18 years	8,065	7,458	92.5	6,936	86.0	5,586	69.3	6,125	75.9	6,462	80.1	2,779	34.5
Unrelated individuals	7,773	3,396	43.7	3,346	43.0	2,019	26.0	1,801	23.2	2,421	31.1	1,146	14.7

Source: U.S. Bureau of the Census, *Poverty in the United States: 1991.* Series P-60, No. 181, p. xvii.

federal government sets maximum asset limits for recipients ($1000), which states may lower. Homes, the equity value of a car up to $1500 or a lower state limit, and some items of personal property are generally not counted.

Since the early 1980s, funding for AFDC has not kept up with inflation. The 1990 average recipient benefit of $128 was less than it was between 1967 and 1980. This decline represented the priorities of the Reagan and Bush administrations, both of which sought to lower social welfare expenditures while shifting funding to the military budget.

As the major cash-assistance program for the poor in the United States, AFDC is fundamentally flawed. The program plays no meaningful role in preventing poverty, nor does it solve the problems of the overwhelming majority of the families that come under its jurisdiction. Most families qualify for the program because of the creation of a female-headed family and receive benefits for less than 2 years (Bane and Elwood, 1983). The program provides these families with transitional benefits as they deal with a period of poverty. There is, however, a large group of families that remain on AFDC for very long periods. About half of all recipients of AFDC remain on the rolls for almost 7 years. Almost 25% of all the families receive benefits for 10 or more years (Ellwood, 1986).

Most long-term recipients of AFDC are young, never-married mothers. Ellwood (1986) found that: "The single most powerful predictor of durations, when all else is held constant, is marital status. Almost 40% of all women who have never been married when they receive AFDC will have total welfare time of 10 or more years, whereas less than 15% of the divorced women have such long welfare times. The estimated stay for never-married women averages 9.3 years compared with 4.9 years for divorced women (Ellwood, 1986)."

A major deficiency of AFDC is that it generally does nothing more for recipient families than allow them to subsist below the poverty level. This is true even of chronic, long-term recipients. Although the majority of mothers are now in the job market, AFDC mothers overwhelmingly remain at home—unemployed and underskilled. In a highly superficial and ineffective way, AFDC and a number of other social welfare programs emphasize employment. Recipients of AFDC, food stamps, and unemployment insurance, for example, must register for job-training programs and accept available employment or forfeit benefits. In practice, most welfare mothers are exempt because they have children under age 6, are caring for an ill person or are ill themselves, or have no access to child care or job training. The result is that most welfare mothers are unemployed and in need of education and job training.

Other major criticisms of AFDC include the lack of a clear set of policies designed to strengthen recipient families. In fact, there is some evidence that AFDC rules, which until recently, have excluded most households with a father, have discouraged mothers from marrying the father of their children and even in some instances induced fathers to leave their families so that their wives and children could obtain assistance (Ellwood and Bane, 1985: 1–3; Plotnick, 1989; Rank, 1989; Ross and Sawhill, 1975: 114–120).

Educational assistance to both adults and children in AFDC families is generally conceded to be inadequate. Head Start and a number of other programs specifically designed for disadvantaged children have established excellent reputations for assisting children, but inadequate funding has limited access to these programs to less than 20% of all children qualified by the income of their parents (Berrueta-Clement et al., 1984; Brown, 1977; Yavis, 1982). Most children and parents receiving AFDC are given no special educational assistance.

In summary, AFDC can be thought of as a rather expensive program designed only to provide modest assistance to people who presumably are only temporarily poor and who are expected to find their own route out of poverty. This is true despite a considerable body of evidence that shows a majority of AFDC recipients remain on the rolls for very long periods of time.

2. *The Food Stamp Program*

The Food Stamp Program provides coupons that can be redeemed at most retail stores for food. Starting out as a small pilot program in the early 1960s serving less than a half million people, by the early 1990s over 20 million Americans were receiving benefits. To qualify for stamps, a household must have disposable assets of less than $2000 (or $3000 if one member is age 60 or over) and net income below the poverty level for the family size. The face value of the coupons an individual or family receives depends on the size and income of the household. For example, the maximum allotment to a family of four in 1990 was $352. Since most families have some income, including benefits under SSI or AFDC, allotments are generally far below the maximum. In 1990, for example, the monthly average value of the coupons per family member was $52.

The Food Stamp allotment, unlike AFDC payments, increases with the cost of living. It is based on the current market cost of foods that meet the Department of Agriculture's nutritional standards. If increases are warranted by market changes, adjustments are made once a year. However, since overall funding for the program has been declining in real terms, assistance per poor recipient has not increased since 1975 (Social Security Administration, 1990: 100).

There is abundant evidence that the Food Stamp Program and other nutrition programs have had a very positive impact on the health of recipients (Kotz, 1979: 9; Ways and Means, 1985: 260). As positive as the impact of the Food Stamp Program has been, some problems still exist. First, some families still do not receive enough vouchers to purchase all the food they need. The modesty of AFDC benefits aggravates this problem. Second, many poor families find it difficult or impossible to obtain food stamps. Nationally only about half of those eligible for food stamps receive them. The factors that deter recipients are numerous. In rural areas, the poor often cannot apply because the food stamp center is too far away and hours of service may be limited. In both rural and urban areas, millions of low-income families cannot qualify because of income and asset limitations. Finally, food stamp regulations are enforced rigorously, requiring detailed documentation of income, family size, living expenses, and assets. Many of the poor find this qualification process too daunting.

3. *Medicaid*

Medicaid is a state-federal program, with varying benefits available to recipients of AFDC, SSI, a few other categories of poor women and children, and, at state discretion, some other medically needy persons. In practice, most recipients are enrolled in AFDC or SSI. Only a little over half the poor receive benefits under the program. For the beneficiaries, the federal government requires that certain basic medical services be provided. If a state will pay for these services to qualified beneficiaries, the federal government will share the costs. As with AFDC, the federal government pays 50 to 78% of the states' Medicaid costs depending on the per capita income of the state.

The basic services that the states must provide include inpatient hospital services; outpatient services; physician services; laboratory and x-ray services; skilled nursing-facility services for persons over age 21; early and periodic screening, diagnosis, and treatment of physical and mental defects in eligible people under age 21; family planning services and supplies; and nurse-midwife services. If the state wants to expand the list of basic services and include other needy groups, the federal government will also pay a proportion of these costs. As a matter of practice, all states pay for some services beyond the basics required by the federal government. A few states provide all the supplemental services, whereas others provide only a few.

There is no doubt that Medicaid has had a very positive impact on the health of the poor. Studies (Miller, 1975; Silver, 1978) show that the poor have considerably fewer untreated medical problems now than they had before the program went into effect. They also show that currently the poor see physicians about as often as nonpoor people. Thanks largely to Medicaid and various nutritional programs, infant mortality rates have dropped by more than half since the program was established. In 1965, there were 24.7 deaths per 1000 live births; in 1986 there were 10.4.

The most serious problem with Medicaid is that participation is largely dependent on a person or family being poor and qualified for participation in the AFDC or SSI program. Additionally, because of low payment rates, many physicians and medical facilities will not treat Medicaid patients.

4. Supplemental Security Income

The SSI program was passed by Congress in 1972 and went into effect in 1974. SSI was designed to replace or supplement state programs that were generally quite modest and inadequate. SSI is a guaranteed income program for the aged, disabled, and blind. It is the only welfare program that guarantees that qualified recipients will have a specified level of cash income each month. For example, in 1991, SSI guaranteed an eligible recipient $407 a month and an eligible couple $610. Benefits are adjusted each year for cost-of-living changes. States at their discretion may subsidize federal payments.

Since most of the aged, disabled, and blind have some income, SSI is primarily a supplement. In 1990, some 4.7 million persons received benefits under the program, with average monthly benefits of $278. Although SSI has certainly increased the financial security of its beneficiaries, even combined with food stamps, the benefits often leave the elderly to live below the poverty level.

5. Summary

Over the last 50 or so years, the United States has evolved a complex and costly set of welfare programs. The programs did not evolve from a master plan designed to prevent and alleviate poverty. Instead, a basic philosophy and approach that grew out of the Social Security Act of 1935 have been preserved, whereas the basic structure and set of programs have grown quite substantially through a whole series of amendments. Today, most scholars agree that the welfare programs, individually and collectively, do not mesh well and are not designed to prevent poverty or resolve the problems of the people who come under their jurisdiction. The programs ameliorate some of the most pressing problems of the poor yet leave them in poverty with fundamentally unmet needs. They may very well contribute to the breakup of families as well as discourage the formation of families. If there is anything that most scholars and reformers agree on, it is that no person or group of persons starting out from scratch would design a welfare system that looks anything like the system currently in place.

In 1988, Congress passed the Family Security Act. This legislation amended the AFDC program in some significant ways. The new legislation will be phased in over a 5-year period beginning in 1990. Below we will examine this act and assess its impact on the nation's approach to welfare policy and the poor.

B. The Western European Approach

The United States' approach to social welfare policy is fundamentally different from that of most other Western industrial countries (Furness and Mitchell, 1984). There are two major differences. First, most of the Western industrial countries emphasize prevention of social problems, including poverty, by means of such policies as national health systems, extensive housing programs, job training, vocational education, and child and family allowances. Second, there is a belief that problems are best prevented if the most important programs are universal. Thus, these countries are much less likely to use means tests for program eligibility. Universal programs are not only more effective in preventing social ills, they generally enjoy broader public support and do not carry the social stigma often associated with means-tested welfare programs.

Comparing U.S. social welfare programs for low-income families with those of Western Europe reveals how significantly these differences manifest themselves in public policy. The United States is the only major Western industrial country that (DeSario, 1989; Kahn, 1983; Kamerman, 1980):

1. Does not have a uniform cash-benefit program for poor families
2. Restricts cash-welfare benefits almost exclusively to single-parent families headed by women
3. Has designed its main cash-welfare program to discourage mothers from working
4. Has no statutory maternity benefits
5. Has no universal child-rearing benefits
6. Has no universal health care benefits (Kamerman, 1984).

Some of the implications of these differences are fairly obvious. In the United States:

1. The emphasis is on dealing with families and individuals only after they become poor or seriously ill.
2. Assistance is designed to be temporary, varies significantly by state, and is limited mostly to families headed by single women who must remain single to continue to receive help.
3. Little or nothing is done to move welfare mothers into the job market, and, in fact, most are discouraged from seeking work by loss of benefits and supportive services (e.g., child care).
4. Poor families can receive critical assistance (e.g., medical care) only if they stay on welfare.
5. Most employed women cannot have a child without suffering serious wage loss or even loss of their jobs.

The major impact of the differences in the U.S. and Western European approach is that our programs are less effective in both preventing and resolving problems of poverty. Some recent research by Smeeding (1992) is insightful. Smeeding (31) compared the American poverty rate with that of seven other countries. Using a standardized poverty definition and the most recent year when comparable data were available, Smeeding calculated the poverty rate for each of the following countries:

U.S. (1986)	13.3%
Canada (1987)	7.0%
Australia (1985)	6.7%
Sweden (1987)	4.3%
Germany (1984)	2.8%
Netherlands (1987)	3.4%

France (1984)   4.5%
U.K. (1986)   5.2%
Average   5.9%

The poverty rate in the United States was 2.3 times the average of the other nations. The United States is, in fact, the only nation with a double-digit rate of poverty. The poverty rate for the U.S. elderly was 3.8 times the average of the other nations, whereas the U.S. poverty rate for children was 2.8 times the average.

The question, of course, is why are the U.S. rates so high. Smeeding (1992) examined a number of potential explanations. Two obvious explanations—that the U.S. poor work less and stay on welfare longer—both proved to be untrue. The U.S. poor seem to work as hard (Smeeding and Rainwater), and their time on welfare tends to be shorter than for the Europeans (Duncan). Another possible explanation is that perhaps the United States starts with a higher rate of prebenefit poverty. Interestingly, the opposite is true. The pretax and transfer poverty rate in the United States is about 19.9% compared with an average of 22.4% for the European nations. Thus, the European nations start with a higher rate of poverty, but they do a much better job of reducing it through effective welfare programs. As Smeeding (33) points out, the European nations spend more on welfare, target it better, and design their programs to promote economic independence.

1. Family Allowances

How different are the European programs? Each country has designed its programs to meet the particular needs of its citizens and public philosophy, but, as noted above, some policy approaches are employed by almost all the nations. For example, every Western industrialized nation except the United States provides a package of cash and in-kind programs to supplement the income of families with children (Kahn, 1983). Many countries call this set of programs a "family benefit" package. A central component is the child or family allowance, which can be found in 67 countries (Haanes-Olsen, 1989: 20; Kamerman, 1984: 263). In most of them, including Canada, Belgium, and the Scandinavian countries, the allowances are universal and tax free to all families regardless of income or family structure.

2. Health Care

All advanced industrial countries in the West—with the exception of the United States—have a universal program of national health insurance or a national health system (Cairncross, 1988). These programs provide comprehensive health care to all citizens regardless of income, age, family structure, or employment status.

3. Maternity Benefits

Most of the industrial nations have programs that protect the jobs and income of women for a period of time before and after childbirth (Kahn, 1983; Kamerman, 1980). Maternity leaves are generally covered by the country's social insurance program. This approach assures that a woman will receive the assistance regardless of the wealth of her employer. There is no means test for the program, benefits are in cash, and they are usually wage related. In most cases, a woman receives at least 90% of her normal wage up to some cutoff point. Most countries set the leaves for 24 to 26 weeks.

4. Child Support

Because of an innovative new program, child support by an absent parent is much more certain in most European nations. Austria, France, Denmark, and Sweden, among others, now use an approach called "advance maintenance payments" (Kamerman, 1988). Under this program, all absent parents are taxed a certain proportion of their income each month. The proceeds are accumulated and used to provide a minimum monthly grant to all children with an absent parent. If the absent parent is unemployed or cannot be found or identified, the child or children still receive the minimum grant. In addition to the obvious fact that all children receive monthly benefits under this program, another attraction is that the program increases the chance that an absent parent will make regular payments. The program does so not by penalizing the parent, but by assessing a fair and regular rate. This keeps the absent parent from falling behind in child support payments.

5. Child Care

National attitudes about whether child care should be provided so that men and women can be both parents and employed vary considerably by nation. A few countries, especially in Scandinavia and France, have in recent years concluded that women should be given the support they need to be mothers and career employees at the same time (Kamerman, 1988). This decision reflects the existence of both a more liberal social philosophy and often a labor shortage. In these nations, parents, particularly women, are provided free or low-cost child care so that they can work or pursue education or job training.

6. Summary

The social welfare systems of the other major Western industrial societies differ from the U.S. system in several important respects. First, most of these countries provide a broader core of universal, non–means-tested assistance to all citizens. Second, the countries have programs specifically designed to assist families with children. These programs are either universal or provided to all middle- and low-income families. Third, none of the countries denies assistance to intact families or requires a lone parent to stay unemployed, single, or poor to qualify for, or remain qualified for, critical assistance such as housing or health care. Fourth, the cash-benefit programs are uniform for all poor families regardless of family structure.

Because of the benefits that citizens receive from programs such as national health insurance, family allowances, varied housing programs, and maternity leaves, fewer low-income families need income-tested cash-welfare assistance. The universal and other broadly provided assistance programs thus increase the security, independence, and presumably the dignity of low-income families, allowing them more options for work, training, and education.

In short, the social welfare programs of Western Europe are better designed than U.S. programs. And, as we have seen, they do a much better job of preventing and alleviating poverty.

C. Reforming The American Welfare System

1. The Family Support Act of 1988

In October 1988, Congress passed the Family Support Act (P.L. 100-485, 102 Stat.2343). Although modestly funded, limited in scope, and designed to be phased in over 5 years, it is the most significant revision in the U.S. welfare system in over 25 years. One of the most important implications of the act is a change in basic welfare philosophy. For example, the Family Support Act assumes that both parents should be responsible for the welfare of their children, and that the only escape from poverty for most families is supported employment. The goal is to reduce considerably the time that families remain dependent on AFDC. The amendments are designed to alter AFDC to require that family heads be provided with the education, confidence, and job skills required by the labor force. To make employment a viable option, the bill finances child care for enrolled mothers. The bill also emphasizes improving child support from absent parents.

The provisions of the bill are being phased in over fiscal years 1989 to 1993. With a modest 5-year cost of approximately $3.3 billion (Riggins, 1991: 9), the Act will be too modest to impact poverty greatly. The provisions of the bill, however, are progressive and responsive to much of the criticism of the current system, and thus lay a foundation for much more substantial reform of the nation's welfare effort. There are five major provisions of the bill.

Title I. Child Support and Paternity.   As of November 1990, all states were required to provide wage withholding of child support from the noncustodial parent in all cases where a custodial parent receives public assistance or in those cases in which the custodial parent has asked for assistance in collecting child support (Garfinkel and McLanahan, 1990). In 1994, states will be required to institute wage withholding of child support for almost all support orders. Child support awards will become more uniform as guidelines set the standards for all support orders (Garfinkel and Klawitter, 1990). These guidelines will be reviewed on a regular basis.

As of 1992, states will be penalized if they fail to establish paternity in a certain proportion of all cases of children born out of wedlock and receiving benefits. To help states locate missing parents, the bill provides access to both Internal Revenue Service (IRS) and unemployment compensation data. A new commission will recommend ways to collect child support from noncustodial parents residing in a different state.

Title II. Job Opportunities and Basic Skills Training Program (JOBS).   This title requires all states to establish a JOBS program (Blau and Robins, 1990). All single parents with children over age 3 (or lower at state option) will be required to participate, unless they are ill, incapacitated, or have some other valid reason for nonparticipation. States have a great deal of discretion in designing programs, but they will have to be approved by the Department of Health and Human Services at least every 2 years. The JOBS program had to be established in each state by October 1990 (all states met the deadline) and statewide by October 1992. Still because of financial limitations, the states will not be required to enroll even 20% of their AFDC recipients in JOBS until 1995.

For those enrolled in JOBS, the state agency in charge of AFDC must assess the needs and skills of all AFDC heads. From this consultation, an employability plan for each recipient will be developed specifying the steps heads will undertake and the supportive services the participant will receive. The state programs must include education, job training, job preparedness training, and job placement. Postsecondary education and other approved employment activities may also be offered. Parents under age 24 without a high school diploma will be required to participate in an educational program leading to graduation. Demonstration projects will be carried out in five states to determine the advisability of providing education, job training, and placement to noncustodial parents.

In an effort to reduce long-term welfare dependency, the bill requires the states to spend at least 55% of all JOBS funds on (1) families that have received assistance for more than 36 months during the preceding 5 years; (2) families in which the head is under age 24 and has not completed high school; and (3) families that will lose benefits within 2 years because of the age of their children.

Title III. Supportive Services.   The states are required to provide child care to participants engaged in education, employment, or job training. To help recipients stay in the workforce and leave the welfare roles, the state can assist in child care for up to 1 year. The cost of the care to the parent will be based on a sliding scale. Families leaving the AFDC ranks because of employment will be eligible for Medicaid coverage for up to 1 year.

Title IV. AFDC Amendments.   The bill requires all states to establish an AFDC-UP program. Until this law, only about half the states allowed families headed by an unemployed father to qualify for AFDC. The bill required all states to establish the program by October 1990, but states new to the program may at their option limit benefits to a minimum of 6 months a year. Most states opted for a full-year program. Regardless, Medicaid benefits have to be ongoing. In all two-parent AFDC-UP families, one parent must participate in JOBS training or work at least 16 hours per week.

Again to help parents find and keep employment, the bill allows expenditures of $175 (or $200 if the child is under age 2) for child care. The allowable expenditure for child care will not be counted as income in calculating AFDC benefits. States may require single parents who are minors to reside with their parents or another guardian.

Title V. Demonstration Projects.   The bill funds a rather wide range of innovative demonstration projects at the state level to determine how well various experimental programs alleviate problems or promote certain desirable outcomes. For example, $6 million over a 3-year period is allocated to encourage innovative training and education programs for poor children. The sum of $3 million was authorized to fund programs to train poor family heads to be child-care providers. Eight million dollars was provided to establish programs to improve noncustodial parents' access to their children. Other programs will provide counseling for high-risk teenagers and incentives to businesses to create jobs for AFDC recipients.

Impact of the Act.   As currently funded—about $3.3 billion over 5 years—the Family Support Act will not have a major impact on poverty. The program is funded far too modestly to impact a very large percentage of all AFDC recipients and it phases in rather slowly. Still, most poverty analysts would agree that it moves welfare reform in the right direction. The AFDC program will be mroe oriented toward helping the poor overcome barriers to self-support and limiting time on welfare. It will also have a preventive thrust because poor children will receive some of the assistance they need to become viable adults. The state demonstration projects may also provide some important insights into programmatic ways of helping the poor.

The Act also establishes the concept of a contract between the individual and society. The recipient and the state both have rights and obligations. Another tenet of the Act is that family stability should be encouraged, thus the requirement that all states establish an AFDC-UP program. The Act also attempts to better target benefits, especially training, on those recipients most likely to remain on welfare for long periods of time.

Although the Act failed to establish a national minimum for AFDC benefits, does not adequately help states establish the required child care facilities, and is perhaps too inflexible in many of its requirements, it is a substantial improvement in welfare policy. The strides made in this bill might lead to a more rational and effective welfare policy in the United States.

VI. CONCLUSIONS

Poverty is likely to be a serious problem in America for a long time to come. This is true for three basic reasons: First, the family type most prone to severe poverty—female-headed families—continues to increase quite substantially and will continue to grow as a proportion of all families over the next decade. Second, the nation's major welfare programs are seriously flawed, contributing materially to the continuation and growth of poverty. Third, the nation's economy is sluggish and lacks the type of competitive edge in the world economy that the country needs.

The Family Support Act of 1988 is a step in the right direction, but it is badly underfinanced and limited in scope. Thus, this Act is too modest to correct the major deficiencies of the U.S. welfare system. The Act does establish a more logical philosophy upon which to build a more effective welfare system, and may over time inform a much better designed set of welfare policies in the United States. The major industrial nations of the Western world have clearly demonstrated that well-designed social welfare programs can prevent and greatly reduce poverty.

As the Family Support Act lays the foundation for a better welfare system, the states and federal government can make contributions toward a solution in other ways. For example, the states could make a major contribution by assuring that public school students receive an academically sound education. Better academic programs and standards in the nation's public schools would increase the employment prospects of millions of young people. Additionally, job-training and job-placement programs can be designed to meet the needs of specific groups, such as minority teenagers and welfare mothers. The evidence clearly shows that teenagers, young adults, and welfare mothers are job oriented and that they benefit significantly from well-designed programs. The cost of substantially reducing unemployment among these critical groups is quite reasonable, especially when discounted by the cost of broken homes and increased crime and welfare dependency.

It is perhaps worth noting that the federal government has a proven record of reducing poverty when it decides to do so. In 1959, 35.2% of all Americans aged 65 and over lived in poverty. In 1991, the poverty rate for the aged was 12.4%. The rate dropped dramatically because expenditures for social security were raised and pegged to inflation, whereas most of the medical needs of the aged were covered by Medicare and Medicaid. The aged have learned the value of government assistance and are a well-organized lobby. In 1990, over 30% of the total federal budget consisted of expenditures for the aged. By contrast, less than 10% of the budget is devoted to low-income families with children. The consequences are clear and well documented.

REFERENCES

Bane, M. J., and Ellwood, D. T. (1983). *The Dynamics of Dependency: The Routes to Self-Sufficiency.* Urban Systems Research and Engineering, Cambridge, MA.

Berrueta-Clement, J. R., et al. (1984). *The Effects of the Perry Preschool Program on Youths Through Age 19.* High Scope Educational Research Foundation, Ypsilanti, MI.

Blank, R., Cutler, D. M., and Katz, L. F. (1992). *The Brookings Review* 21–22.

Blau, D. M., and Robins, P. K. (1990). Job search outcomes for the employed and unemployed. *Journal of Political Economy* 98(3) (June): 637–655.

Brown, B. (1977). Long-term gains from early intervention: An overview of current research. Paper presented at the 1977 Annual Meeting of the American Association for the Advancement of Sciences, Denver, CO.

Burkhauser, R. V., Holden, K. C., and Feaster, D. (1988). Incidence, timing, and events associated with poverty: A dynamic view of poverty in retirement. *Journal of Gerontology: Social Sciences* 43(2) (March): S46–S52.

Cairncross, F. (1988). European countries vary widely in health-care delivery systems. *Financier: The Journal of Private Sector Policy* 12: 10–13.

Children's Defense Fund (1992). Center for Labor Market Studies. Northeastern University, Chicago.

Committee on Ways and Means (1985). Children in Poverty. U.S. House of Representatives, 99th Congress, 1st Session. Government Printing Office, Washington, D.C.

Cottingham, P. H., and Ellwood, D. T. (Eds.) (1989). *Welfare Policy For the 1990s*. Harvard University Press, Cambridge, MA.

Danziger S. (1990). Antipoverty policies and child poverty. *Social Work Research and Abstracts* 26(4) (December): 17–24.

Danziger S., and Weinberg, D. H. (Eds.) (1986). *Fighting Poverty: What Works, What Doesn't*. Harvard University Press, Cambridge, MA.

DeSario, J. P. (Ed.) (1989). *International Public Policy Sourcebook*. Greenwood, Westport, CT.

Ellwood, D. T. (1986). *Targeting Would-Be Long-Term Recipients of AFDC*. Mathematica Policy Research, Princeton, NJ.

—— (1988). *Poor Support: Poverty In the American Family*. Basic Books, New York.

Ellwood, D. T., and BAne, M. J. (1985). The impact of AFDC on family structure and living arrangements. *Research in Labor Economics* 7: 137–149.

Furness, N., and Mitchell, N. (1984). Social welfare provisions in Western Europe: Current status and future possibilities. In *Public Policy and Social Institutions*. H. Rodgers (Ed.). JAI Press, Greenwich, CT.

Garfinkel, I., and Klawitter, M. M. (1990). The effect of routine income withholding of child support collections. *Journal of Policy Analysis and Management* 9(2) (Spring): 155–177.

Garfinkel, I., and McLanahan, S. (1990). The effects of the child support provisions of the Family Support Act of 1988 on child well-being. *Population Research and Policy Review* 9(3) (September): 205–234.

—— (1986). *Single Mothers and Their Children*. The Urban Institute, Washington, D.C.

Haanes-Olsen, L. (1989). Worldwide trends and developments in Social Security, 1985–87. *Social Security Bulletin* 52(2). Department of Health and Human Services, Washington, D.C.

Haveman, R., Wolfe, B., Finnie, R., and Wolffe, E. N. (1988). Disparities in well-being among U.S. children over two decades: 1962–83. In *The Vulnerable*. J. L. Palmer, T. Smeeding, and B. B. Torrey (Eds.). The Urban Institute Press, Washington, D.C.

Kahn, A. J. (1983). *Income Transfers for Families and Children: An Eight-Country Study*. Temple University Press, Philadelphia.

Kamerman, S. B. (1980). *Maternity and Parental Benefits and Leaves: An International Review*. Columbia University Press, New York.

—— (1984). Women, children and poverty: Public policies and female-headed families in industrialized countries. *Signs: Journal of Women in Culture and Society* 10(21): 249–271.

—— (1988). What Europe does for single-parent families. *Public Interest* 19(1) (Fall): 70–86.

Kotz, N. (1979). *Hunger in America: The Federal Response*. Field Foundation, New York.

McLanahan, S., and Booth, K. (1989). Mother-only families: Problems, prospects, and politics. *Journal of Marriage and Family* 51(3) (August): 557–580.

Mead, L. M. (1986). Beyond entitlement: The social obligations of citizenship. Free Press, New York.

Miller, A. C. (1975). Health care of children and youth in America. *American Journal of Public Health* 65(April: 353–358.

Murray, C. (1984). *Losing Ground: American Social Policy, 1950–1980*. Basic Books, New York.

(OED) Organization for Economic Co-operation and Development (1976). *Public Expenditure on Income Maintenance Programmes*. OECD, Paris.

Plotnick, R. D. (1989). Welfare and out-of-wedlock childbearing: Evidence from the 1980s. Discussion paper no. 876-89. Institute for Research on Poverty, Madison, WI.

President's Commission on Income Maintenance Programs (1969). *Poverty Admidst Plenty*. Government Printing Office, Washington, D.C.

Rank, M. R. (1989). Fertility among women on welfare: Incidence and determinants. *American Sociological Review* (April): 296–304.

Riggins, P. E. (1991). Welfare reform in the federal system. *Intergovernmental Perspective* (Spring): 7–12.

Robins, P. K. (1990). Federal financing of child care: Alternative approaches and economic implications. *Population Research and Policy Review* 9(1) (January): 65–90.

Rodgers, H. (1990). *Poor Women, Poor Families: The Economic Plight of America's Female-Headed Families*, 2nd ed. M. E. Sharpe, Armonk, New York.

Rodgers, H. (Ed.) (1988). *Beyond Welfare: New Approaches to the Problem of Poverty in America*. M.E. Sharpe, Armonk, New York.

—— (1978). Hiding versus ending poverty. *Politics and Society* 8: 253–266.

Ross, H. L., and Sawhill, I. (1975). *Time of Transition: The Growth of Families Headed by Women*. Urban Institute, Washington, D.C.

Silver, G. A. (1978). *Child Health: America's Future*. Aspens Systems, Germantown, ND.

Smeeding, T. M. (1992). Why the U.S. antipoverty system doesn't work very well. *Challenge* 12 (January/February): 30–35.

Smolensky, E., Danziger, S., Gottschalk, P. (1988). The declining significance of age in the United States: Trends in the well-being of children and the elderly since 1939. In *The Vulnerable*. J. L. Palmer, T. Smeeding, and B. B. Torrey (Eds.). The Urban Institute, Washington, D.C., pp. 29–54.

Townsend, P. (1974). Poverty as relative deprivation: Resources and style of living. In *Poverty, Inequality and Class Structure*. D. Wedderbuan (Ed.). Cambridge University Press, London, p. 15.

Wojkiewicz, R. A., McLanahan, S. S., and Garfinkel, I. (1990). The growth of families headed by women: 1950–1980. *Demography* 27(1) (February): 19–30.

Yavis, J. (1982). The Head Start Program—History, legislation, issues and funding—1964–1982. *Congressional Research Service Report No. 82-93 EPW* (May).

23
Minority Politics in the U.S.: African–Americans, Women, and the Policy Process

Marian Lief Palley
University of Delaware, Newark, Delaware

One could discuss at length the problems of African-Americans, Hispanic Americans, Asian-Americans, or Native Americans. In this chapter, however, it is impossible to address the issues of importance to each of these groups and then to discuss the issues of special significance to women. Therefore, inasmuch as women represent more than half of the population and African-Americans represent the largest "nonwhite" minority group in the United States today (more than 12% of the population), this chapter will consider only issues relating to women and African-Americans. More specifically, a brief discussion of the evolution of the contemporary African-American and women's rights movement is followed by an assessment of the response of the political system to some of the articulated demands of these two population cohorts. Next, the goals of the major rights organizations and their roles in their respective movements are considered. Finally, this chapter addresses several separate policy areas—employment opportunities, educational opportunities, and reproductive rights—and assesses why "rights" groups have succeeded or failed in their attempts to bring about change.

It is important to begin with a brief statement on the role of African-American and women's groups regarding change. Both the African-American and women's rights movements are presented as somewhat monolithic in their goals. Certainly the major goals of most of the groups within the respective movements are akin to each other. The groups desire improved status for the members of the secondary group they represent. There are, however, differences in strategies and tactics displayed by different groups, which are glossed over in the pages that follow. Furthermore, special attention is paid to the mainstream of the two movements, which operates "within" the political system; that is, fringe groups that may want to alter radically or topple existing institutions and replace them with new ones are not discussed. These "fringe" groups are arguably significant in that they act to legitimize the more mainstream groups. (Thus in the late 1960s, fear of the African-American [Black] Panthers seems to have made a more moderate Martin Luther King and his followers acceptable to many people.) However, at least at the present time, these groups are not deemed central enough in the context of contemporary politics to discuss in this short chapter. Finally, the differential impact of changes on different groups of African-Americans and women is considered.

I. THE SOCIAL CONDITIONS

The conditions that have led to the demands of women and African-Americans for changed status in society are well known to most Americans and thus will receive just a brief statement. Since the Civil War, the African-American population in the United States has had disproportionately fewer income opportunities, poorer educational opportunities, unequal employment opportunities, and has suffered other general discrimination based on race. Even when examining recent unemployment data, such disparities are clear. According to the Bureau of Labor Statistics, in 1990, African-American male unemployment was 11.8% and the comparable figure for white males was 4.8%. The figures for females were 10.8% (African-Americans) and 4.8% (whites) (January 1991). African-American youth unemployment has been over 40% for many years. Regarding education, in 1960, 42% of African-Americans and 66% of whites had completed high school. By 1982, the figures had changed dramatically—80% of African-Americans and 90% of whites were high school graduates. The college graduation statistics paint a somewhat less rosy figure. By 1986, 23% of the white population had graduated from college, whereas only 12% of the African-American population had completed a college education (Schiller, 1989).

It was in response to these kinds of conditions that the African-American civil rights movement was born in the early years of the 20th century. The movement expanded in the years following the 1954 Supreme Court decision in *Brown* v. *Board of Education of Topeka* (347 U.S. 483) as the gap between expectations and reality was not closed (Barker and McCoy, 1976; Walton, 1972).

Women as a group also have been the object of discrimination. Traditionally, women received ''second-class'' status in the political, economic, and religious realms (Palley, 1976; Ruether, 1974). More recently, they too have demanded changes in their roles in society as expectations have been broadened in response to improved educational opportunities, technological advances that have effected a transformation in the role of women as mothers and housekeepers, and increased participation in the labor force. Thus, from 1950 to 1970, female labor force participation almost doubled.

Educated women grew up encountering contradictions in their lives. They had achievement-oriented values that were often contradicted by the ''traditional'' female role. These women became the leadership cadre of the women's movement in the decades of the 1970s and 1980s. Some of the women activists of the 1960s responded to their secondary (i.e., subordinate) positions in the new left civil rights movements of the early 1960s and were instrumental in fashioning the early feminist organizations (Gelb and Palley, 1987).

Though one can draw together the experiences of African-Americans and women and note the history of discrimination for both groups, it is important to distinguish between their experiences. Whereas African-Americans are disproportionately members of the lower class in this nation, women have traditionally drawn their status from their fathers or their husbands. Thus, women are distributed more evenly than African-Americans across class groupings—although women are at greater risk of being in poverty than are men (Schiller, 1989). Also, women are a majority who are treated like a minority. Finally, the modern African-American rights movement is older than the modern women's rights movement, which is less than 30 years old—although women's groups such as the League of Women Voters and the Council of Jewish Women are not feminist organizations, they are older, well-established women's organizations (Costain, 1975).

To what extent has the political system been responsive to the demands of African-Americans and women? This is, of course, a very difficult question to answer. To the extent that the demands made by African-Americans and women to eliminate sexual and racial discrimination are being institutionalized, they have been successful. However, legislation, administrative guidelines, and judicial decisions have not eliminated all discrimination, although they have reduced the extent of discrimination in policy areas as disparate as education, employment, credit, housing, reproductive choice, and the awarding of government contracts (Palley and Preston, 1979).

The courts were particularly active in the areas of education and housing, although judicial appointments by Presidents Ronald Reagan and George Bush moved the courts away from their central position as remedy providers for minority groups. For example, in March 1992, the Supreme Court in its decision in *Freeman* v. *Potts* (No. 89-1290) gave hundreds of formerly segregated school districts the opportunity to return to local control after decades of operating under federal court supervision. The eight to zero decision allows school districts to be relieved a court supervision as they achieve racial equality in various facets of their operations (Greenhouse, 1992). Women have also felt the transformation of the membership on the federal bench. Thus in 1992, the Supreme Court in *Planned Parenthood* v. *Casey* (112 S.ct. 2791; 1992) continued to whittle away at the rights granted women in *Roe* v. *Wade* (4106 U.S. 179) by redefining conditions under which women could be granted or denied by the separate states the right to choose to terminate a pregnancy.

Despite government activities that purported to improve opportunities for African-Americans, education remains a problem. Inner city schools are still predominately African-American, and as far as housing is concerned, despite Supreme Court decisions that deem many discriminatory practices unconstitutional, the vast majority of African-Americans still live in segregated neighborhoods (either by necessity or choice). In 1980, the Joint Center for Political Studies reported (Friedman, 1980) that in 23 of 26 medium and large cities with African-American majorities, 16 ranked among the poorest cities in the nation; and nearly one half had experienced sharp population declines in the previous decade. Also, most of these cities had relatively old housing stock. Ten years later, the same conditions prevailed. Wilson (1991) observed that ". . . especially since 1970 . . . the number of [inner cities neighborhoods] with poverty rates that exceed 40 percent—a threshold definition of 'extreme poverty' neighborhoods—has risen precipitously."

In addition, women and African-Americans on the average still earn considerably less than white men. Also on the average, women college graduates can expect to have lower earning capacities than male high school dropouts; also, the average earnings gap between African-Americans and whites has narrowed only very slightly in the past 10 years. In 1989, the average African-American household brought in 63ᶜ for every dollar that went to a white household. This compares to 62ᶜ for every dollar for African-American households in 1979 (Barringer, 1992). It is the case too that women and African-Americans have disproportionate risks of being poor and that although there are more women doctors, lawyers, and other professionals than there were 10 or 20 years ago, the vast majority of women who hold low-skilled or nonskilled jobs are paid at rates lower than those paid to men who hold low-skilled or nonskilled jobs (Schiller, 1989). Thus beginning sanitation workers, who are working at low-skilled jobs, on the average earn more than waitresses. Put into starker perspective, these same sanitation workers on the average earn more than skilled women who are beginning secretaries (Evans and Nelson, 1989).

Finally, conflict among women and African-Americans can have the effect of lessening the impact of both groups. Consider for a moment the question of quotas and affirmative action. C. Douglas Ades, who was for many years a Chemical Bank vice president, was quoted as saying: "The women threw a monkey wrench into the affirmative action process—many were educated, well-to-do and militant, and when the barriers came down, they jumped in, head-to-head with African-Americans, and the women won." Gloria De Sole, Associate Director of Affirmative Action at the State University of New York at Albany, charged in response that the issue of white women taking jobs from African-Americans is a "red herring." "If we argue about who comes first, then the man has us fighting among ourselves. This is divisiveness in the extreme. It is also guilt-tripping" (*The New York Times*, August 12, 1980). This type of interchange is destructive since "the more groups you include, the more you reduce the opposition to all the protected classes" (*The New York Times*, August 12, 1980). Although these were observations from 1980, they still hold true in the 1990s.

One final point should be noted before proceeding to discuss the two rights movements and specific policy areas. Although the policy effects seem relatively limited to some observers, African-Americans and women have made significant headway in several areas. More African-Americans and women hold public office than at any other time in American history. In 1993, there were 47 women serving in the House of Representatives and 6 women in the Senate. There were 39 African-American members of the House of Representatives and 1 African-American senator. Also, more African-Americans and women are succeeding in the professions and business; and the verbalization of hostility against these groups seems to have lessened over time.

II. THE NATURE OF THE RIGHTS MOVEMENT

The manifest goals of both the African-American rights movement and the feminist movement are to improve life conditions for African-Americans and women, respectively. The different groups within each of the movements, of course, focus on different issues and utilize different tactics to try to achieve their goals.

The African-American groups that seem to be in the forefront of the African-American rights movement in the 1990s include the National Association for the Advancement of Colored People (NAACP), the National Urban League, People United to Save Humanity (PUSH), and the various local organizations that have sprung up in communities to address local problems and grievances. Also, the NAACP Legal Defense and Education Fund has been central to many of the gains made by African-Americans in the judicial process. The Legal Defense and Education Fund was responsible for many of the court battles regarding school integration, segregated housing, and affirmative action.

The women's movement has no group comparable to the NAACP in terms of membership. In fact, no one of the feminist groups is a mass membership organization akin to the NAACP, which lists its membership at about 450,000. The National Organization for Women (NOW) does not have as large a membership base as the NAACP (NOW's membership base varies but it is usually below 200,000), and the other membership groups in the women's movement—the National Women's Political Caucus (NWPC) and the National Abortion Rights Action League (NARAL) have smaller memberships than NOW. The other groups associated with the women's movement are essentially nonmembership organizations—such as the NOW Legal Defense and Education Fund, the Women's Rights Project, and the Reproductive Freedom Project, the Center for Women Policy Studies, the NOW Project on Equal Education Rights (PEER), to name a few of these groups. These are essentially leadership-based organizations. They are, however, all important group players in the women's movement (Gelb and Palley, 1987). Furthermore, not only are feminist organizations involved in trying to affect the goals of the women's movement, some of the traditional women's organizations, such as the League of Women Voters, the National Federation of Business and Professional Women, United Methodist Women, The National Council of Jewish Women all have supported the women's movement on specific issues at different times (Gelb and Palley, 1987).

Just as the African-American rights movement has grassroots organizations, so too does the women's movement. These groups tend to focus their attention on issues such as violence against women and children. These are the groups that often run local shelters for battered women and children.

The women's movement, given the proliferation of groups, does not have the visible leadership that the African-American movement has traditionally been able to maintain. Rather coalitions based on specific issues ebb and flow in the feminist community. There have been no charismatic leaders in the women's movement who have received the media attention that African-American leaders such as Jesse Jackson or in earlier years that Martin Luther King and Malcolm X received.

Most successful political efforts require coalition development among disparate groups. The feminist groups have developed coalition building to a "science," having learned to build issue-specific coalitions to gain support from some groups on specific issues where these groups might be hesitant to be supportive on other issues of importance to women. For example, there are labor groups that have been supportive of feminist positions regarding equal employment laws and educational regulation, but they disappear from feminist coalitions when abortion rights are being discussed. Similarly, the Catholic Church has been supportive of many of the agenda items important to the women's movement. They too are absent from the pro-choice coalition (Gelb and Palley, 1987). However, other groups have joined the choice coalition. For example, the American College of Obstetrics and Gynecology stands firmly for freedom of choice.

African-American civil rights groups have also learned to build coalitions. They too have been able to garner support from diverse groups on issues. Inasmuch as their organizations are mass based, however, they do not have to generate complicated intramovement coalitions as a first step as do the women's groups. On such issues as school desegregation, fair housing, voting rights and redistricting, and equal employment opportunity, African-Americans have been able to generate support from non–African-American organizations. Thus the American Civil Liberties Union (ACLU) has provided support for school desegregation cases and fair housing cases, and some labor unions have joined African-Americans in their quest for equal employment opportunity. As noted earlier, there are occasions when women and African-Americans join together in common causes. The Leadership Conference on Civil Rights, directed by Ralph Neas, has been a particularly effective vehicle for such cooperation.

To be effective in influencing the political process, "out" groups in particular need to build coalitions. There are other useful conditions that seem to affect the success rate of these organizations. Gelb and Palley (1987) suggest that there are four "rules" that influence whether "out" groups will succeed or fail in their various efforts to bring about change:

1. To be effective in American politics, groups must be perceived as legitimate.
2. In order to appear legitimate, groups will find it necessary to focus on incremental issues. In this regard, role-equity issues are less threatening than role-change issues.
3. In order to appear legitimate, groups will stress the provision of information and concentrate on mobilizing their allies. They will seek to avoid confrontation that comes from use of protest tactics. They will form policy networks, and they will be willing to define success in terms of "increments."
4. Like other conventional interest groups, emergent groups will engage in a struggle over the definition of the situation. This struggle will almost always involve the manipulation of symbols favorable to one's cause. At time, these symbols will be used to privatize conflict (e.g., by defining the issue as one involving just role equity).

In the remainder of this chapter, several problem areas for African-Americans and women are examined. Problems are defined, and then group demands and political/societal responses are discussed. The success or failure of the movements regarding these issues is considered within the four-point framework just outlined.

III. SOME MAJOR ISSUE AREAS

A. Employment Opportunities

In the Urban League's *The State of Black America, 1992*, it was confirmed that conditions for the majority of American African-Americans had not changed markedly in the past 20 years. Although family income of African-American married families through the $50,000 a year range tracks closely with that of white families, only half of African-American families are headed by intact couples compared with 83% of white families. In fact, median African-American family income has remained around 60% of white family income since 1969, and African-American poverty has stayed in the 30 to 35% range. When African-American families achieve middle-class status, it is usually on account of multiple family incomes. Moreover, the net worth of African-American families in 1988 was just $4606. This was 10% of the figure for white families.

Although income and employment opportunities for African-Americans do not appear in the aggregate to have improved, this is not in fact the reality. There have been major strides in opportunities for African-Americans and an increasing number of African-Americans who have joined the middle class. Some of the change can be attributed to government mandated programming that continued despite the opposition of the Reagan and Bush administrations.

One of the major routes to middle-class status for African-Americans, however, has been government service (Hacker, 1992). African-Americans are only 10% of the national work force, but they comprise 25% of postal clerks and 23% of corrections officers. More than a third of African-American scientists are employed by the government agencies. Also, 23% of the enlisted personnel in the military forces are African-American (Stanfield, 1992). In fact, Bennett Harrison, a professor of political economy at Carnegie Mellon University has observed the "the growth of the African-American middle class has got a lot to do with the federal government, not so much in [enforcement] of affirmative action, but in direct hiring" (Stanfield, 1992). Harrison finds this a bit troubling for the future of the African-American middle class in an era of cutbacks and retrenchment.

African-American business ownership has never been on par with white business ownership despite the availability of special programs and loan opportunities. According to the

U.S. Census Bureau, in 1987, African-Americans owned 3% of all firms in the United States. Firms owned by African-Americans had average receipts of $50,000 that year, whereas those owned by whites had average receipts of $189,000. In 1989, the Supreme Court in its decision in *Richmond* v. *J.A. Croson Co.* (488 U.S. 469) struck down a provision of a Richmond, Virginia, policy that provided that a portion of city contracts be set aside for minority owned businesses. This has led to a significant decline in such contracts.

African-American college graduates are not doing as well today as they were 10 years ago. The proportion of African-American college graduates earning more than $35,000 fell from 17% in 1979 to 13% in 1987. The figure for white college graduates was 26% at both points in time (Stanfield, 1992).

Wilson (1987) in his book *The Truly Disadvantaged* observed that the African-American urban underclass had doubled between 1970 and 1980. He attributes this upward trend to the working conditions and the living conditions in poor neighborhoods. There has been an increase in the number of female-headed households, a decline in employment opportunities for young men and declining earning capacities for poorly educated worker, and a shift of poor populations from rural to urban settings (Wilson, 1987). These conditions did not improve during the 12 years of the Reagan and Bush presidencies. In fact, these conditions deteriorated further despite the fact that the African-American middle class continued to thrive. There was, in Wilson's words, a two-class African-American society that had emerged. One final point should be noted at this time. Even though the Bush and Reagan administrations were not particularly helpful to African-Americans and their special concerns, African-Americans were sometimes appointed to high-visibility positions in government. Perhaps the best example of this was the selection of Clarence Thomas to be an associate justice on the Supreme Court.

It is appropriate to ask what government actions have been taken to try to redress the racial imbalance in employment opportunities. Prior to 1980 and the election of Ronald Reagan, there were some very visible federal efforts: the Civil Rights Act of 1964, affirmative action programs, the Equal Pay Act and the Equal Employment Opportunity Act (EEOC), to name just a few of the most visible responses. In addition, there is the Civil Rights Commission, which is empowered to oversee employment practices in both public and private sector units that receive federal dollars. Special monetary incentives are provided minority businesses by the Small Business Administration—although, as noted above, there is still a paucity of African-American–owned businesses in this country. Finally, manpower training programs have been established, albeit on a relatively small scale, to train poor, largely nonwhite people for jobs. These latter programs have often trained people for positions that do not materialize. This is a special problem during periods of rapid technological advance or high unemployment.

The case of women and the employment scene is somewhat different from the case of African-Americans, although both groups share disproportionately the poorest paid positions in the work force. Women entered the paid labor force in increasing numbers in the 1970s and 1980s. In 1970, their full-time workforce participation was 18%. By 1992, this figure had increased to almost 57% (*The Washington Post*, 1992). The averge earning capacity of women relative to men has improved slightly over the same period. In the 1970s and early 1980s, women earned on average 59¢ for every dollar earned by a man. By 1992, the comparable figure was about 70%. Women, like African-Americans, tend to be clustered in the poorest paid jobs. Despite affirmative action programs, the EEOA and the uneven activities of the Civil Rights Commission, women have made only marginal improvements in the employment area.

Just as African-Americans in the professions and business have advanced in the environment of racial and sexual opportunity of the past 20 years, so too have professional and business women. There are more women lawyers and doctors than ever before in American history. However, women are sometimes symbolic—as are African-Americans—in their presence in both public and nonpublic decision-making forums. Thus one can count on one's fingers the African-Americans and women who are CEOs of Fortune 500 companies. There are more African-Americans and women in elective office in 1993 than ever before. As noted above, there are 47 women representatives and 6 women senators as well as 39 African-American representatives and 1 African-American senator. Also, women and African-Americans are being elected as governors and big city mayors, and over 20% of all state legislators are now women.

Despite the pronouncements of concern by African-American and feminist leaders, very little has been done to alter the lives of the African-Americans and women who are most discriminated against. There are the vast majority in both groups who are not in business or the professions. These are the people who tend to be located in the poorest paying, often dead-ended employment positions. Often union training programs are opened up only reluctantly and narrowly to members of these two population cohorts. At other times, job are classified so that women in particular will not apply, and if they do apply and are given the positions, they will find it difficult to advance. For example, the U.S. Navy will not allow women to serve on submarines. However, advancement in the military has traditionally been tied to combat experience. Harassment too has often made moving into new employment areas very difficult, especially for women.

In the past 10 or 12 years, attention has been directed to issues of pay equity and comparable worth. Despite efforts to advance change for women such that the jobs they tend to hold will be paid at levels comparable to jobs men tend to hold with similar skill levels, educational background, and responsibility, to date, there has been little positive change for women in this area.

Inasmuch as the majority of employment opportunities in the United States are in the private sector, active government involvement is very difficult. Moreover, the records of government agencies in advancing African-Americans and women have not been outstanding. Thus it has been found that women who work in government perceive discrimination in their workplaces. In the federal government, women and African-Americans still tend to be clustered at the bottom of the pay scale. The federal government's compliance with its own policy pronouncements is weak. Women and African-Americans tend to be clustered in the lower pay ranks; white men tend to be clustered in the higher pay ranks (Gordon, 1991).

What can be done about these unequal employment opportunities raises an entirely different set of problems. The groups that represent women and African-Americans tend to represent middle-class women and African-Americans. They have not focused their attentions as strongly as they might on the problems of the less fortunate members of their race or sex. These groups have tended to focus more of their energies on the concerns of the middle and upper classes in their group cohorts. Thus access to professions for the educated has been a more central concern than working conditions for nonunion labor or, until quite recently, day care facilities for women who cannot afford home care for their children when they work at poorly paid jobs. This later concern, although spearheaded by the children's rights movement in the 1970s and 1980s, is now a central concern of women's groups. In part, this seems to be a function of increased middle-class workforce participation as more women of the baby-boom generation have children and remain in the active labor force.

B. Educational Opportunities

An area that has received considerable attention from both African-American and feminist groups is education. In recent years, the focus has been on desegregation (and especially busing, free choice, and vouchers), affirmative action programs, and for women in particular, equal opportunities in athletics.

Desegregation has continued to receive considerable attention from the African-American rights community since World War II. The first major success came when, in 1954, the NAACP Legal Defense and Education Fund argued successfully before the Supreme Court in *Brown* v. *Board of Education of Topeka* (347 U.S. 483) that "separate is not equal." In the years since this landmark decision, numerous other court decisions have mandated the desegregation of public schools. It is not clear, however, to what extent these court rulings have been successful in bringing about school integration or how one should define success in the context of an issue as sweeping as school desegregation.

As noted earlier, the vast majority of African-American children in many urban school districts attend predominately minority classes, and many urban school districts have largely nonwhite student bodies. These conditions reflect segregated housing patterns as well as "white flight" from desegregated school districts. "White flight" is usually accompanied by "African-American middle-class flight" out of the public schools. Thus the minority population that remains in the urban public schools tends to be disproportionately in need. In 1965, Congress enacted the Elementary and Secondary School Act. This law targets some federal funds to school districts with "problems." Insofar as these urban districts tend to be disproportionately servicing needy children, and these children are disproportionately nonwhite, some federal funds flow to these school districts. Also, many states have responded to the funding problems confronted by the largely nonwhite urban school districts by establishing formulas for the distribution of state funds that will work to the advantage of these districts.

There is a concern and awareness that inner city school children do not fare educationally as well as suburban children. Although not all inner-city children are African-American and not all suburban children are white, inner-city schools, as noted previously, are disproportionately African-American (and Hispanic). The National Assessment of Educational Progress (NAEP) has been collecting data on school-age children and their achievement since the early 1970s. Their data indicate that between 1971 and 1988, there has been a closing of the achievement gap between African-Americans and whites in basic reading skills. But there is still a racially defined achievement gap, with African-Americans scoring lower on the tests than whites. In mathematics, there is also a racially defined gap. Here too in the 10 years between the first tests (1978) and 1988, there has been a decline in the differences in achievement as measured by these examinations (Jencks, 1991). SAT scores also point out racial differences in scores, with whites generally outscoring African-Americans on all parts of the test (Stanfield, 1992).

When nonwhites live in integrated neighborhoods, they go to integrated schools. But given the small portion of the population that lives in racially mixed neighborhoods, this is not a major consideration.

Throughout the 1970s and 1980s, African-American groups have been concerned with the maintenance of affirmative action programs for African-American students for admission to college and to specialized professional programs. Similarly, they have focused their attention on the maintenance of desegregation through the use of free choice and busing and court supervision of school districts that were ordered to desegregate their schools. In 1992, the Supreme Court relaxed court supervision (see above for discussion of *Freeman* v. *Potts*) of school desegregation. As far as busing is concerned, middle-class flight from urban school districts has limited the success of efforts to integrate schools racially.

The attention that continues to be focused by African-American rights groups on postsecondary education and on school desegregation has been criticized by some African-Americans as evidence of the middle-class bias of the movement. As evidence of this, it is can be observed that the African-American rights community has not focused the same attention on the problems confronted by welfare mothers and their children and low-wage earners as they have on these other issues. Women also have been concerned with affirmative action programs. Just as these programs have either led to expanded opportunities for African-Americans or occurred simultaneously to these chances for African-Americans, so have opportunities for women improved in the era of affirmative action—although the extent of their successes can be questioned. More women attend professional schools and thus there are more female lawyers, doctors, and business executives. Unlike the African-American movement, women's groups have not addressed the issue of quotas. In fact, they have not endorsed quotas for women. (African-American rights groups did, in fact, back away from discussing quotas during the 1980s when the Reagan and Bush administrations manipulated the idea of quotas to mean that opportunity for African-Americans meant unemployment lines for whites.)

Women's groups never endorsed quotas because of the belief that if sex is eliminated as a criterion for selection such that women are given an equal chance with men, women would be accepted into academic programs without any "special" programs or designations. During the 1980s, sex as generally eliminated as a criterion for selection to academic programs, and women in fact were accepted in numbers that reflected their numbers in the applicant pools.

Rather the groups in the feminist community focused considerable energies on the implementation of Title IX of the Education Amendments of 1972, which required that educational opportunities for women be equal to those provided for men in institutions that received any federal funds. In particular, they focused their attention on achieving parity with men in school athletics (Gelb and Palley, 1987). Women are somewhat successful in their quest for athletic parity; they were not, however, completely victorious in their quest for equity. Thus it was the women who brought home the gold medals from the 1992 Summer Olympics, but most intercollegiate athletic programs in American colleges and universities continue to grant more scholarship aid to male athletes than to female athletes, and more money is spent on men's sports than on women's sports.

There was a lot of very active opposition to the 1972 Education Amendments. The National Collegiate Athletic Association (NCAA) as well as the leadership of many prominent universities were in the forefront of the opposition. In 1984, the Supreme Court in its decision in *Grove City* v. *Bell* (104 S.Ct. 1211) narrowed the scope of Title IX when the majority wrote that the government does not have broad, institution-wide authority to enforce Title IX whenever educational institutions receive federal money. Immediately thereafter, legislation was introduced into Congress to reinstate the broader federal authority assumed by the 1972 Education Amendments. It was not until 1991 that Congress finally passed the Civil Rights Act of 1991, which did reestablish the broad scope of Title IX.

Women's groups worked together and in coalition with African-American rights organizations and groups representing the aged and the disabled on the campaign to enact this civil rights law. Women, the aged, the disabled, and racial minorities are all population groups that were effected by the Supreme Court's narrow interpretation of Title IX because federal laws and regulations that addressed equality of opportunity for these population cohorts all have wording similar to that in the 1972 Education Amendments.

C. The Special Case of Freedom of Choice Regarding Abortion

Although the successes of the African-American and women's groups in the areas of employment and education may be questioned as reflecting the bias of upper-class and middle-class interests often to the exclusion of the concerns of the less affluent, these groups nonetheless have been reasonably successful in achieving some of their goals. When discussing free choice regarding abortion (Gelb and Palley, 1987; Mohr, 1978), the discussion must turn from considerations of success to considerations of failure. In 1973, the Supreme Court handed down its decision in *Roe* v. *Wade*, which denied states the right to deny a woman the right to terminate a pregnancy during the first trimester. Since 1976, however, this right has been whittled away by Congress and by the Supreme Court. There has been a congressional ban against the use of Medicaid funds to pay for most abortions (the Hyde Amendment), which was upheld by the Supreme Court in *Harris* v. *McRae* (100 S.Ct. 2671). Also, Congress enacted legislation that prohibited the use of federal funds for abortions for military women, military dependents, and Peace Corps volunteers. Funds were also denied to clinics that provide abortions; and federally funded birth control clinics were not permitted to even counsel women about the availability of abortion as an option to carrying a fetus to term. The "gag rule" that was imposed during the Bush administration was reversed by Bill Clinton when he assumed the presidency in 1993.

In 1992, the Supreme Court in a five to four decision, decided in *Planned Parenthood* v. *Casey* that states could impose some constraints on women seeking abortions if these constraints do not impose an "undo burden" on the woman. To date, the term *undo burden* has not bee defined—although parental consent and 24-hour waiting periods are not deemed to be an undo burden. Since such policies produce delays, they are viewed by women's groups as particularly burdensome for rural and poor women.

Why have women's groups that engineered a well-managed mass-based mobilization, which peaked in the spring of 1992 with a March on Washington that drew upward of one million participants from all over the nation, often failed in this area during the 1980s? First, this is an issue that divides women themselves. Thus there are women in the countermovement to free choice. Also, this is an emotionally charged issue and the anti-choice movement—that is, the Right to Life movement—has built its support on the emotionality of the issue. The anti-choice groups discuss dead babies and the murder of babies. Fundamental values—oftentimes rooted in religious beliefs—are being challenged by feminist organizations when they support freedom of choice. Moreover, this is an issue on which compromise is very difficult. True believers on both sides of the abortion debate cannot budge in their adherence to their positions. Finally, the Right to Life adherents saw their support in the courts blossom in the 1980s and early 1990s. During the Reagan and Bush administration, many judges were appointed to federal district courts and the courts of appeal who were opposed to abortion rights. The justices appointed to the Supreme Court were generally against freedom of choice too. In fact, the Bush administration was accused of using an abortion rights "litmus test" in selecting judges to serve in the federal judiciary.

Abortion rights is an issue, as just noted, where compromise is very difficult to achieve. Wereas stages can be developed to expand job opportunities or athletic facilities, decisions regarding motherhood cannot be phased in gradually to American women.

D. Assessment

Briefly consider the pluralist theorems introduced earlier in this chapter. Even if one finds it difficult to quantify success or finds success to have a middle- and upper-class bias, one can impressionistically note achievements in the areas of both employment and education for African-Americans and women. In both of these areas, coalitions were built to provide broad-based support. For example, in the case of school desegregation, many groups have provided *amicus curia* briefs when desegregation cases have been in the courts. Similarly, women's groups have garnered support from education and religious and labor groups as well as from the traditional women's organizations in their drive for educational and athletic equity.

In addition, the employment and education issues that have been selected by African-Americans and women have been both defined in their scope and limited in their potential for dividing group members into competing groups. Thus all African-Americans and women want to receive equal pay for equal work, regardless of their relative class status, or in the case of women, their current out-of-home employment status.

Even though they have not been addressed in this chapter because of the limitations of space, policy networks have been established by African-Americans and women, although women have been more diligent in the administrative monitoring stages of the policy process. This was especially true of Title IX, where much of the detail of implementation was worked out by bureaucratic agencies. In conjunction with this observation, it is significant to note that both African-Americans and women have been most willing to provide technical and informational resources to government agencies. The Urban League and the NAACP both maintain ongoing data analysis that are provided to public decision officials. Similarly in education, it was a women's monitoring efforts that provided the data about the limited compliance checks by the Office of Civil Rights on Title IX that led to an investigation of that office's compliance reviews.

Certainly, it must be clear that in the areas of employment and education, both African-Americans and women have compromised. Neither movement has been able to achieve optimum conditions for their group, but some progress has been made for members of both groups. Finally, inasmuch as women and African-Americans have defined their success in terms of increments of change rather than in terms of total victory, they have been able to achieve some successes and, over time, some significant changes that have benefitted women and African-Americans. Regarding abortion rights, as noted previously, this is an issue that has not surfaced as a success story for the women's movement because of a variety of interrelated factors.

IV. CONCLUSIONS

Certainly, conditions for some African-Americans and for some women have improved in the last decade. Also, expectations have changed, at least for middle-class and upper-class African-Americans and women. Working-class and poor African-Americans and women have not experienced great changes in their lives, and their expectations have not been significantly altered during the past 10 years. The groups that have been influential in representing African-Americans and women have operated very much within the constraints of pluralist politics and, perhaps ironically sometimes, the criticisms leveled against these movements is in the form of the charge that they have become too much a "part of the system."

Both the scholarly critics and the more popular social critics who appeal to the broad base of society tend to generalize about groups and their members. Thus African-Americans are perceived by many Americans to share more than racial characteristics and women are assumed to share more than sexual characteristics. Variations in education, income, occupation, and more generally social class identification are thus glossed over. Most of the successes for both African-Americans and women have not been for the majority of African-Americans and women. Most of the achievements have benefitted the upper- and middle-class members of these cohorts. In part, it is these people who have the skills to succeed if they are given the opportunities. However, often the rights communities that are dominated by the middle- and upper-class interests and that have represented African-Americans and women have not focused their attentions on the issues that more directly affect the less fortunate members of their group cohorts. In the quest for improved life chances for African-Americans and women, there seems to be an element of social class politics that sometimes overrides concerns for the problems of the poor and the working class.

REFERENCES

Barker, L., and McCoy (1976). *Black Americans and the Political System*. Winthrop, Boston, Chap. 7.

Barringer, F. (1992). White-Black Disparity in Income Narrowed in 80's Census Shows. *The New York Times* July 24: A1 and A16.

Blau, F. (1992). *The Economics of Women, Men and Work*, 2nd ed. Prentice-Hall, Englewood Cliffs, NJ.

Costain, A. (1975). A social movement lobbies: Women's liberation and pressure politics. Paper presented at the Southwest Political Science Association. San Francisco, CA. Sept. 2–5.

Evans, S. M., and Nelson, B. J. (1989). *Wage Justice*. University of Chicago Press, Chicago.

Friedman, M. (1980). The new black intellectuals. *Commentary* 69: 51.

Gelb, J., and Palley, M. L. (1987). *Women and Public Policies*. Princeton University Press, Princeton, NJ.

Gordon, G. J. (1991). *Public Administration in America*, 4th ed. St. Martins Press, New York.

Greenhouse, L. (1992). Justices ease court controls in school desegregation case. *The New York Times* April 1: A1 and B9.

Hacker, A. (1992). *Two Nations: Black and White, Separate and Unequal*. Scribners, New York.

Jencks, C. (1991). "Is the American Underclass Growing?," in *The Urban Underclass*, C. Jencks and P. Peterson (Eds.). Brookings Institution, Washington, D.C.

Mohr, J. (1978). *Abortion in America*. Oxford University Press, New York.

The New York Times (1980). August 12: B1, B6.

Palley, M. L. (1976). "Women and the Study of Public Policy." *Policy Studies Journal*.

Palley, M. L. (1978). Women as academic administrators in the age of affirmative action. *Journal of the National Association of Women Dean, Administrators and Counselors* 42: 3–9.

—— (1987). Political and legal rights. In *The Trapped Woman*. J. Figueira-McDonough and R. Sarri (Eds.). Sage, Beverly Hills, CA., Chap. 14.

Palley, M. L., and Preston, M. B. (1979). *Race, Sex and Policy Problems*. Lexington-Heath, Lexington, MA.

Reuther, R. R. (Ed.) (1974). *Religion and Sexism*. Simon & Schuster, New York.

Schiller, B. (1989). *The Economics of Poverty and Discrimination*, 5th ed. Prentice-Hall, Englewood Cliffs, NJ.

Stanfield, R. (1992). Black frustration. *The National Journal* 24: 1162–1166.

U.S. Bureau of Labor Statistics (1991). *Employment and Earnings*, 38, 1. January.

Urban League (1992). *The State of Black America, 1992*.

Walton, H. (1972). *Black Politics*. Lippincott, Philadelphia.

Wilson, W. J. (1987). *The Truly Disadvantaged: The Inner City, the Underclass and Public Policy*. University of Chicago Press, Chicago.

—— (1991). Research and the truly disadvantaged. In *The Urban Underclass*, C. Jencks and P. Peterson (Eds.). Brookings Institution, Washington, D.C.

The Washington Post National Edition (1992). "Who we are." June 8–14: 32–33.

24
Criminal Justice Policy

Ralph Baker and Fred Meyer
Ball State University, Muncie, Indiana

The problem of social order has been a fundamental one in the course of human affairs. The variety of activities known as crime constantly challenges our notions of order and tranquility. Yet no society has ever completely solved the problem of crime (Wilson and Herrnstein, 1985). This is as true for societies that have studied crime for years as for those without developed academic criminology departments (Igbinovia, 1989). The crime problem is particularly acute in democracies because it has the potential of alienating the masses from the political system and making them susceptible to the demagogic rhetoric of those who would destroy the very freedoms enjoyed by the people (Kornhauser, 1959).

The crime issue is a staple in United States' elections all the way from the race for county sheriff to the race for the White House. In large part, George Bush won the presidency in 1988 on the crime issue. The now infamous Willie Horton commercial was successful in portraying presidential candidate Michael Dukakis as "soft" on crime because of the Massachusetts prison furlough program. In addition, the Massachusetts governor was attacked for his American Civil Liberties Union (ACLU) membership and his opposition to the death penalty. The 1992 Democratic candidate for president, Bill Clinton, did not forget this lesson. He reminded audiences that not only did he favor the death penalty but that he was the only candidate who had been chief executive while the death penalty had been administered in Arkansas.

Despite the rhetoric and the actions of politicians, however, crime continues to plague the lives of everyday citizens. After a multimillion dollar effort to control crime began in 1970, violent crime has continued to soar in the United States to far surpass all other industrial nations (Curtis, 1985). This country's high crime rates more closely resemble Third World Countries than other developed societies even though we have adopted a conservative experiment in crime control based on the premise that the political state has been too lenient on criminals (Currie, 1985). Owing to that conservative experiment, the United States in the

1990s has a conservative Supreme Court, an increasingly used death penalty, an expanded prison system, an increased privatization of the criminal justice system, and the aforementioned law and order rhetoric dominating public debate. At the same time, the Reagan-Bush agenda has left the country with still high levels of street crime, difficulty in funding prison expansion, and extreme prison overcrowding (see Hudzik, 1987; Platt, 1987). Where is it all leading? Some see crime in this country remaining at high levels but with certain changes for the future: poor, young and uneducated male criminals being displaced by older, more affluent offenders; the increase in crime by women; and the legalization of some crimes like prostitution, gambling, and drug abuse (Bennett, 1987).

Our task in this chapter is not to prognosticate but rather to acquaint the reader with the most recent research in the area of criminal justice policy since the first edition of the *Encyclopedia of Policy Studies*. This chapter is divided into the following sections: criminology and policy, crime and offenders, the police, the legal actors, the corrections actors, and the media.

I. CRIMINOLOGY AND POLICY

As the crime problem continues to vex society, reformers call for different solutions. Some argue the criminal justice system is too intent on finding reasons to let guilty criminals go and thus leaving the streets unsafe and law-abiding citizens surrounded by predators (Fine, 1986). Others argue that improvements in the criminal justice system cannot guarantee success in controlling street crime but rather basic changes in the country's economic and social system are needed (Conrad, 1987; Gordon, 1990). These differences represent a dichotomy in solutions based on contradictory belief systems (see Edelman, 1977; Scheingold, 1991). Rather than representing a new trend, this dichotomy phenomenon can be traced back to the origins of criminology. The classic school believed that individuals choose to engage in criminal activities based on their own calculation of pain and pleasure (Beccaria, 1963). Since crime is based on rational behavior, the state must institute a swift and certain punishment policy that will measure the severity of punishment by the gravity of the crime. By the middle of the 19th century, the positivist scientific approach to discover the causes of crime came into vogue believing that punishment should fit the criminal not the crime. Biological, psychological, or sociological explanations for crime were sought. Lombroso (1876) believed criminals were born with physical characteristics different from other persons; Maudsley (1974) argued that criminals suffered from psychological deficiencies that made them morally insane. Like the classic adherents, however, these positivists looked for the causes of crime within the make-up of the offender. The sociological positivists were different. They looked to the offender's social environment to explain his or her criminal activity. The Chicago school of the 1920s, for instance, looked to such problems in society as inadequate housing, poverty, and broken families to explain urban crime. As a result, a dichotomy emerges. Is the cause of crime and thus its solution to be found in the individual or in the society where the criminal behavior occurs? Are we dealing with flawed individuals or a flawed society?

Today, criminologists continue to search for the causes of crime. Although mainstream criminology has been dominated by the sociological perspective, data now being generated from behavioral genetics, physiological psychology, psychopharmacology, and endocrinology indicate biological factors play a significant role in the development of antisocial behavior (Fishbein, 1990; Marsh and Katz, 1985). Such findings are often met with suspicion by policy makers because of negative associations with Social Darwinism and Hitler's master race rhetoric and resultant extermination policy (Mednick et al., 1987). Others argue that biological positivism has produced little in the way of meaningful reseach (Gottfredson and Hirschi, 1990).

Two of the more mainstream avenues of criminological research today are structural criminology on the one hand and several opportunity-based theories known as routine activities, lifestyle, and rational choice models (Miethe et al., 1991). Structural studies look at such factors as poverty (Patterson, 1991), economic and family stress (Linsky and Strauss, 1986), and unemployment (Walker, 1989). The relationship between unemployment and crime has been a particularly popular and controversial topic of research. One work has found high correlations between the unemployment rate among adult minority males and both motor vehicle theft and commercial robbery and between the unemployment rate for all males and commercial robbery (Vanagunas, 1989). Another concluded that the high rate of crime among urban black males stems from the structural linkages among unemployment, economic deprivation, and family disruption (Sampson, 1987). An additional study calculates that changes in the unemployment rate for urban settings would have major effect on crime (Kohfeld Sprague, 1988). However, this finding differs from earlier works (Freeman, 1983; Jenks, 1987). In addition, an earlier comprehensive review of 25 studies using aggregate data concluded that there is no firm evidence that lack of employment is linked to crime (Freeman, 1982). This finding confirmed the conclusions of other studies (Kvalseth, 1977; Williams and Drake, 1980; Wilson and Boland, 1978).

Opportunity theory also has been practiced with mixed results. Such efforts have either assumed a specific social structure and then investigated the effect of routine activities on risk of victimization (Garofalo, 1987; Lynch, 1987; Maxfield, 1987) or investigated the empirical victimization while assuming intervening routine activities or opportunities (Cantor and Land, 1985; Cohen and Felson, 1979). According to one scholar, the opportunity theory appears to be crime specific, explaining property crime better than personal crime and not very useful for societies that are not highly industrialized with a high level of inequality (Bennett, 1991a). In another cross-national study, the opportunity theory did not explain much of the change in crime rates (Bennett, 1991b). For this reason, many researchers are now using the approach theory in conjunction with other approaches (Cohen and Land, 1987).

The conflicting results of criminological research produce interesting options for public policy. They allow the dichotomy in criminal justice belief systems to persist. In fact, true believers can always blame the other position when policies fail (Edelman, 1977). No one really understands what causes crime; therefore, crime policies are reduced to competing visions of the good society and human nature (Scheingold, 1991). The politics take on symbolic value. Crime policies that blame the individual offender are closer to the cultural roots of the United States and are cheaper to implement. Ambitious politicians would dare not be considered weak on crime by blaming society for an offender's crimes. This in spite of the fact that the politics of law and order has not resulted in a meaningful reduction of the crime rate (Scheingold, 1984). Some scholars are left to remind us of the myths that drive our crime policy (Pepinsky and Jesilow, 1984; Wright, 1985). Others remind us of the "knowledge gap" about criminal behavior (Farrington et al., 1986). Some swim counter to the political tides by arguing that the only real solution lies in long-term economic policy that will provide real economic opportunities for people (Gordon, 1990). Still others like Wilson (1983a) counsel us that the possibilities of making major changes in crime rates are very limited. More radical changes, he argues, would be riskier because they would involve our conceptions of liberty, childrearing methods, and popular values (Wilson, 1975b). As a result, since we know many of the correlates associated with offenders, policy makers should concentrate on predatory street crimes by increasing neighborhood patrols, concentrating police efforts on career criminals, and maintaining well-staffed prosecutor and public defender offices in each community (Wilson, 1975b, 1983a). The answer to the question, Who is right? may depend on our knowledge of crime and the persons who commit crimes.

II. CRIME AND OFFENDERS

Although criminologists are often criticized for not having the definitive answer to the question, Why do some individuals commit crimes and others do not?, they make a valid point in arguing that their discipline has no control in the defining of the dependent variable (Gottfredson and Hirschi, 1990). Crime is defined by a political and legal process. Legislative bodies throughout the federal system define criminal behavior. Those persons who engage in such behavior are known as criminals. There are a great variety of criminals from Mafia bosses to shoplifters. Wilson argued that the criminal justice system ought to concentrate on career criminals. But who are they? Career criminals are those persons whose activities may be measured by the rate of their criminal activity, the seriousness of their offenses, and the length of time they are active (Blumstein et al., 1986). Career criminals or chronic offenders commit serious offenses with high frequency over extended periods of time. Data for different demographical subgroups defined in terms of age, sex, and race are available for career criminals (Adler, 1975; Berger and Simon, 1974; Hirschi and Gottfredson, 1984; Steffensmeier, 1989; Wilson and Herrnstein, 1985). In particular, the age-crime curve reflects variations in the proportion of persons who are offenders rather than the rate of offending. As a result, it really does not track career criminals. The major implication for criminal justice policy is that the greatest potential in selective incaputation is for offenders between the ages of 30 and 40 and not teens (Farrington, 1986).

Identifying the career criminal would seem to be an important step in reducing crime in the United States. First, the policy maker has to understand the differences in crime statistics presented by the Uniform Crime Reports (UCR) and National Crime Surveys (NCS) (see Biderman and Lynch, 1991) and then consider the ethical questions surrounding selective incarceration of persons who fit the career criminal. The most stable predictor is the Greenwood scale (see Greenwood, 1983). The seven variable scale includes prior conviction for the same offense as charged; incarceration for more than half of the preceding 2 years; a conviction prior to age 16; a commitment to a state juvenile authority; use of narcotics 2 years prior to present commitment; use of narcotics as a juvenile; and unemployment for more than half the time in the preceding 2 years. The Greenwood scale is not without its critics (see von Hirsch and Gottfredson, 1984). Recent research has found its predictive value in individual cases to be highly inaccurate (Decker and Salert, 1986).

Since it is impossible to identify the career offender accurately, criminals are often defined by the crimes they commit. Burglars and robbers commit property crimes and some of them are career offenders. Burglary is the most prevalent street crime in the United States and in cities with large minority populations, high population mobility, and high income inequality. It occurs most often in neighborhoods inhabited by young people, minorities, and renters. Burglaries are committed primarily by young males who are unskilled with respect to the work force (Shover, 1991). Burglary is a crime that is susceptible to situational crime prevention (Bennett and Wright, 1984). In robbery, the offender enjoys the momentary control over his or her victim (Katz, 1991). Both of these types of property offenders often abuse drugs or alcohol, do not consider the negative consequences of their acts, and specialize as they become older (Tunnell, 1992). Other criminals provide a great contrast to these property offenders. They include such a diverse group as drunk drivers (Foley, 1986; Jacobs, 1989); computer criminals (Francis, 1987; Kusserow, 1986; Parker, 1983); arsonists (Pettiway, 1987);

parental kidnappers (Strickland, 1983); shoplifters (Kallis and Vanier, 1985; Ray, 1987); and subway vigilantes (Rubin, 1986), just to name a few.

The most violent and irreversible of all crimes is murder. Murder rates vary greatly across different cultures. The murder rate in Iceland, for instance, is 0.5 homicides per million persons per year, 10 in most European countries, 25 in Canada, over 100 in the United States and Brazil, and several times higher than that in some central American countries (Daly and Wilson, 1988). Amazingly, the murder rate in New Guinea ranges from 5000 to 8000 deaths per million persons per year (Knauft, 1985). Scholars search for the psychological motivations of the crime of murder (Daly and Wilson, 1988), the psychobiology of this type of violent offender (Volavka et al., 1992), and probe the cycles of violence that often began with child abuse (Athens, 1989; Widom, 1989). Particularly frightening to the public are the serial killers (Egger, 1990; Holmes and DeBurger, 1988; Jenkins, 1989) and mass murderers (see Levin and Fox, 1985; Newton, 1988).

Research has shown that violent crimes are more likely to take place in years when temperatures are higher and in the hottest months of the year (Anderson, 1987). No relationship seems to exist, however, between the involvement of the United States in a war and the domestic homicide rate (Kleck, 19878). The homicide rate in U.S. metropolitan areas is strongly associated with ethnic inequality (Balkwell, 1990) and with racial residential segregation in suburban communities (Logan and Messner, 1987). More apparent is the link between homicide and violent crime in general with guns and drugs. Both have elicited many calls for new policies and some defense of the status quo (see Belenko, Blumstein and Goldstein, 1990; Fagan and Chin, 1991; Inciardi, 1991; Kaplan, 1986; Kleck, 1986; Kraus and Lazear, 1991; McDowall, 1991; Miller, 1991; Robin, 1991; Tonry, 1990; Zimring, 1985).

Citizens of the United States are both frightened and fascinated with organized crime. Many literary accounts of mob life became best sellers (see Anastasia, 1991; Carpenter, 1992; Lacey, 1991; Pileggi, 1985). Stereotypes of organized crime may be inaccurate (Byrum, 1987). It is not all run by a highly structured Mafia. Organized crime is also not just limited to the United States. It exists in Japan (Kaplan and Dubro, 1986), Poland (Marek, 1986), and China (Booth, 1990). The annual take of organized crime in the United States is somewhere between 42 and 106 billion dollars (Fishman et al., 1986). The average member's income in 1986 was estimated to be $296,699. Such figures necessarily lead to inquiries concerning the impact of organized crime on the political and economic system of the United States (see Alexander and Caiden, 1985) and methods to control its influence (Mastrofski and Potter, 1986). One study suggests that organized crime cannot be controlled as long as policy makers adhere to the alien conspiracy theory that depicts this type of crime as an underworld corporate enterprise made up of a distinct ethnic and cultural group. They argue that organized crime is made up of loosely structured businesses that are highly responsive to illicit market forces (Mastrofski and Potter, 1987).

Many argue, however, that white-collar criminals perpetrate more harm on society than career criminals, violent criminals, or organized crime (see Conklin, 1977; Katz, 1980). Also known today as business crime or occupational crime, such criminals may benefit through their occupations or professions or indirectly through employer organizational systems (Green, 1990). Examples of such crime are the recent savings and loan scandal (Calavita and Pontell, 1990; Pilzer, 1989), hazardous waste crime (Rebovich, 1986), Wall Street insider trading (Frantz, 1987), the Ford Pinto case (Cullen et al., 1987), medical criminals (Jesilow et al., 1985), auto repair fraud (Jesilow et al., 1985), and Love Canal (Frank, 1985). Business crime is different in nature because it is often private; there is no discernible violation of public order and often the criminal law plays only a limited role (Clarke, 1990). Stronger enforcement is obviously needed, with some analysts calling for an emphasis on negotiation rather than criminal law (see Benson, 1989; Clarke, 1990; Frank and Lambness, 1988).

The feminist movement has sensitized scholars to the special roles played by women in the criminal justice system (see Baron and Straus, 1989; Berger, 1991; Price and Sokoloff, 1982). Today, more women are delaying marriage, heading households, and joining the workforce full time but are not gaining on men with respect to salaries. Against this backdrop, they are also committing more crimes (Simon and Landis, 1991). In addition to traditional crimes like prostitution (Carmen and Moody, 1985; Miller, 1986; Hobson, 1987; Reynolds, 1986), battered women are fighting back and some are killing their abusive mates (see Browne, 1987; Faigman, 1986; Walker, 1984). Such occurrences signal to policy makers the need to investigate the causes and patterns of family violence (see Besharov, 1990; Blackman, 1989; Geotting, 1989; Hamberger and Hastings, 1986; Shupe et al., 1987). The role of pornography in setting up such violent confrontations has also been explored by scholars with mixed conclusions (see Malamuth and Donnerstein, 1984; Scott and Schwalm, 1988; and Zillmann and Bryant, 1989). Overall, there seem to be problems with applying traditional crime theories to women because such theories were written originally for men (Worrall, 1990).

III. THE POLICE

Police in their paramilitary uniforms represent important symbols in the criminal justice system. They serve as the visual embodiment of the state in its attempt to deter crime. They instill feelings of security in those citizens fearful of crime. Some of the early police research, in fact, suggested that much of the work of the police was little more than symbolic in nature. Kelling and his associates (1974) did a study in Kansas City, Missouri, to see how patrol techniques affected the crime rate. One part of Kansas City was divided into 15 beats that were further broken down into five groupings of 3 matched beats each. The neighborhoods in each grouping were alike in terms of basic demographical characteristics, crime incidence, and calls for the police. One of three patrol techniques was used in the three beats. One technique involved no preventive patrol, with cars entering only to answer specific calls. Another technique involved customary levels of service. The last technique involved intensified patrol, with cars cruising the area two or three times as much as normal. The duration of the experiment was 1 year. Crime rates and feelings of safety on the part of the citizens were not found to be related to the level of patrol. In essence, the Kansas City study suggested that much of the time spent by police officers could more profitably be expended elsewhere.

Two additional early studies suggested that another activity of police departments—investigation—was primarily of symbolic value. Greenwood and his associates (1977) as well as Greenberg and his associates (1975) did major studies of the process of investigation as carried out by police departments. They discovered that the process of investigation was relatively insignificant in the resolution of a crime.

Since these early studies there has been a wealth of studies suggesting that the work of the police is more than symbolic. Police activities can have an impact on the reduction of crime. Also, much of the empirical research has allowed administrators to deploy scarce resources in the most efficient way to achieve goals.

Much policy-based research has been supported by the Police Foundation, which originally was started with a Ford Foundation grant. Also, the Police Executive Research Forum has supported policy research. The research has brought some major changes in the delivery of police services.

It was discovered that concern by police departments over response time was really not necessary. The major factor that determines whether an arrest will take place at the scene of the crime is the time it takes a citizen to report the event. The rapidity with which the police get to the scene of the crime had little impact on the ability to bring about an arrest (Van Kirk, 1978). As a result of the response time study, departments began to respond to calls in different ways. In 1981, a study sponsored by the National Institute of Justice and carried out by the Police Executive Research Forum investigated differential response practices in three cities (Petersilia, 1987). Only 15% of calls required immediate response, whereas 30% could be handled by some other method than police response. The remaining 55% were classified as routine and thus not requiring immediate patrol response. Cahn and Tien (1981) did an evaluation of "management of demand" system of response, and it was funded by the National Institute of Justice. Noncritical calls to the police were handled by a variety of methods, including a 30-minute delayed response to the scene, telephone reporting, scheduled appointments, and walk-in reporting by the complainant. There was no increase in crime as a result of the use of these diverse response techniques. The police were able to use personnel more efficiently in responding to citizen calls.

Some studies suggest that the time the police free up for themselves through differential response to citizen calls can profitably be used on alternative patrol techniques. Cordner (1981) points out that directed patrol can be used to reduce certain targeted crimes in an area. Patrol officers will be expected to spend their time in a certain part of the city and to look for certain types of wrongdoing. While directed patrol reduces crime in one part of the city, it may displace into other areas.

Aggressive patrol by police involves frequently stopping drivers and questioning individuals who look suspicious. Field interrogation was found to lead to a reduction in the crime rate in a San Diego, California, study (Boydstun, 1975). Wilson and Boland (1976, 1979) found that lower robbery rates resulted when aggressive patrol techniques were employed. Often crackdowns on specific types of crime will involve intensive patrolling techniques in combination with extensive publicity surrounding the crackdown (Sherman, 1990). These campaigns involve a reduction in the targeted activity and have potential deterrent value. Thus policing when combined with intensive publicity can bring a reduction in specifically targeted criminal activity.

Other varieties of patrol have been found to have positive effects from the perspective of the police. Foot patrol, for example, was found to be associated with a reduction in the fear of crime in Newark, New Jersey, even though the foot patrol did not result in a reduced crime rate (Police Foundation, 1981). In Flint, Michigan, foot patrol resulted in a reduction of the fear of crime as well as a reduction in the crime rate (Trojanowicz, 1982).

The favorable reaction of citizens to foot patrol ultimately resulted in increased support for the concept of community policing. In fact, Skolnick and Bayley (1988) indicate that they found community policing to be popular in various parts of the world. They indicate the following common elements in community policing: crime prevention that is founded in local communities; the stress on the nonemergency service aspect of patrol; an increased level of responsibility to the public; and a decentralization of the command structure of the department. It has been asserted that community policing presents hope for a lessening of drug problems in communities (Moore and Kleiman, 1989).

Problem-oriented policing has developed in an attempt to make policing more responsive to the community. The approach involves gathering extensive information about significant community crime problems and then identifying potential solutions to the problems. This approach varies considerably from business as usual that involves reacting to crises as they occur (Cordner and Hale, 1992). In Newport News, Virginia, there was a reduction of some significant problems using problem-oriented policing (Eck and Spelman, 1987).

One area in which there is some question about the effectiveness of police intervention is that of domestic violence. Sherman and Berk (1984) carried out an experimental investigation of the impact of various sanctions on domestic violence. Officers were given forms with three different treatment options, including arrest. Some of the offenders were told to vacate the premises for 8 hours. A third group was "advised" by the police, which means that essentially nothing was done. The arrest option was found to be most effective in stopping repeat incidents during the 6-month period after the initial incident. As a result of the Minneapolis, Minnesota, study, police departments throughout the United States started prescribing arrest as a deterrent for further domestic violence (Petersilia, 1987). In their analysis of the experiment, Sherman and Berk (1984) were careful to stress the importance of replication of the Minneapolis study. The prescriptions from the study were publicized extensively and applied in police departments across the country. However, some of the actual replications of the Minneapolis study raised serious doubts about the deterrent effect of the arrest mandates that were being implemented in many departments. In Omaha, Nebraska, a replication of the Minneapolis study found that the arrest option did not serve to deter further violence. In fact, there was really not any difference between the three treatment options (Dunford et al., 1990). In the Minneapolis study, the police had been called to the address of domestic homicides at least once in the 2 years preceding the killing in 90% of the cases. However, in a replication of the study in Milwaukee, Wisconsin (Sherman et al., 1991), there was quite a different situation. Of the 33 domestic homicide victims during that period, only one had involved a prior call to the police. Thus the police did not have an advance warning system that would appear in all cities. The findings of these studies indicate the difficulty involved in generalizing from one city to another. This is particularly difficult in the area of domestic violence.

The inclusion of women and minority group members in policing has presented some difficulty to police departments. This problem of inclusion is found in police department in numerous cultures. In India, for example, women joined police forces as early as 1938. However, their progress through the steps of promotion has been slow. They have been used to carry out social work functions rather than policing duties (Aleem, 1989). Because of the stress on affirmative action in the United States, there has been continued concern with the extent to which women are showing up in policing. Although the numbers of women in policing in the United States has been on the increase, by 1986 only 3% of supervisory positions in cities in excess of 50,000 were held by women (Martin, 1990).

The inclusion of minorities in policing has been considered important by many civil rights groups since African-American officers, in particular, are considered to have better communication skills in dealing with ghetto neighborhoods. African-American officers have been found to have value patterns more similar to African-American citizens than do white officers on the police force (Walker, 1983). In Los Angeles, California, African-Americans were more likely to be shot for not obeying a command to halt than were whites. Also, police officers in Los Angeles were less likely to be disciplined when they shot African-Americans than when they shot whites. The Rodney King beatings in Los Angeles and the ensuing riots when the officers involved were initially acquitted of criminal charges suggests the severity of the problem. The attitudinal chasm between the African-American community and police departments continues to be quite large.

The nature of administrative leadership in police departments has been identified as an extremely important factor in the success of women in policing. Warner et al. (1989) found the most important factor associated with the hiring of women to be the existence of an affirmative action plan that included goals and guidelines. The policy priorities of the leadership of police departments appears to be an important factor in determining how women and minorities are treated in policing in the United States.

IV. THE LEGAL ACTORS

Prosecutors, defense attorneys, and judges are the legal actors in the criminal justice system. The trial courts in which they work have many similarities nationwide because of the existence of a national legal culture (Eisenstein et al., 1988). Defendants enjoy a series of rights guaranteed by the U.S. Constitution, and the national legal culture also dictates a common cast of participants: the legal actors. The trial courts do exhibit differences; however, they are political in nature and adapt to their own set of community norms (Eisenstein et al., 1988). The lower criminal courts in the United States, with an emphasis on assembly-line justice, are depressing institutions in comparison to the general trial courts. They have been described as crowded, dingy, and depressing sites that tend to bore the judges, dull the prosecutors, and depress the defense attorneys—all to the detriment of the defendants (Feeley, 1979).

The role of the local prosecutor is still one of major gatekeeper in the criminal justice system. Although the U.S. Attorney General, the U.S. Attorneys, and State Attorneys General may have more prestige, it is the elected local prosecutor that exerts the most discretionary power in the system (see McDonald, 1979; Stewart, 1987). In making their charging decisions, they exhibit different political styles and formulate different policies. The political styles of local prosecutors may vary from confrontational or subtle change agents to protector of the status quo (Flemming, 1990); their policies from emphasizing charging in all cases in which the necessary legal elements are present to charging in only those cases they are absolutely confident of winning to being most concerned with the resources management of the prosecutor's office or the well-being of the defendant (see Jacoby, 1980).

One question that arises in the use of prosecutorial discretion is that of fairness. In other words, are racial, ethnic, or gender factors taken into consideration in the charging decision? The answer in some cases appears to be yes. The race of the victim has been found to be important in decisions concerning whether to ask for the death penalty (see Paternoster, 1984). Prosecutors are more likely to request the death penalty if the victim in the case is white. Other studies have shown the influence of ethnicity and gender as well. One probe found that both Hispanics and blacks are at a disadvantage in the felony charging process as well as males (Spohn et al., 1987).

The term *general trial courts* used above is somewhat of a misnomer. The norm in the United States is negotiated justice. Prosecution and defense agree to the charge and sentence recommendation and a trial is bypassed. Most of the interactions that prosecutors have with defense attorneys and judges is through the practice of plea bargaining (see Mather, 1979). Through plea bargaining, the prosecutor holds the power in local criminal courts (Heumann, 1978). The judges primarily play a passive role. One of the considerations made by prosecutors in the process is their assessment of the defense attorney in the case and sometimes their friendship (Champion, 1987). Owing to its prevalence, plea bargaining has generated a great deal of controversy (Smith, 1986) and some call for its demise (Schulhofer, 1986).

Defense attorneys in the criminal justice system live a kind of dual existence. They are the personification of the important right to counsel and yet they are often outcasts in their own profession (see McDonald, 1983; McIntyre, 1987). Further, there are a variety of factors that create tension for defense attorneys. They must possess both the skills of an extroverted courtroom advocate and careful legal researcher; they must be both an adversary of the prosecutor and an amiable negotiator; they must earn their living and yet the cases that are most lucrative—white-collar crimes and organized crime—they find least desirable; and they have the problem of trying to maintain their professional reputation while practicing in virtual isolation from other members of the bar (Wice, 1978). In spite of these problems, the role of defense counsel is still considered crucial in the United States as well as in other countries such as Japan and Zimbabwe (George, 1990; Hatchard, 1987).

In most jurisdictions in the United States, defendants are represented by either privately retained counsel or public defenders. There also can be overlaps in these two roles. In some states, an attorney may be both a part-time public defender and a private defense attorney. Where that is not the case, friction may develop between the two types of defense lawyers. Although the rights of the accused cases decided by the Warren Court created more criminal defense work for lawyers, most of the defendants who have benefitted are indigent and cannot afford to pay for representation (see Wice, 1978). Public defenders also carry the additional burden of functioning as legal anomalies. They are paid by the state to defend individuals against criminal charges brought by the state (see McIntyre, 1987). Finally, most studies indicate that public defenders do nearly as well in their bargaining with prosecutors as private attorneys (Sterling, 1983).

Judges in the United States work in a dual court system. There is a separate system of national courts and state courts. The two systems operate relatively independent of one another and have different selection procedures. Federal judges are nominated by the president and confirmed by a majority vote of the Senate. This procedure only is reexamined after particularly bitter nomination contests are waged, as in the unsuccessful attempt to confirm Robert Bork and the successful effort to confirm Clarence Thomas for the U.S. Supreme Court. States use partisan elections, nonpartisan elections, appointment systems, and combinations of initial appointment and later retention elections. A 20-year study of judicial retention elections from 1964 to 1984 revealed that three of every four voters cast their ballot to retain an incumbent judge and that only 1% of these judges were ever defeated (Hall and Aspin, 1987). Three state supreme court judges were defeated at the same time in California, however, because they all opposed the death penalty (Wold and Culver, 1987). Elections create another set of problems. A study of Chicago judicial elections revealed the great amounts of money that were raised for the campaigns and the appearance of impropriety that is evoked when attorneys and litigants give money to judicial candidates (Nicholson and Weiss, 1986). Whether such campaigns influenced the type of corruption uncovered in Operation Greylord is purely speculative (Bensinger, 1988).

Judges in the United States also differ on the basis of whether their duties are primarily appellate or trial in nature. The most prestigious appellate judges are the nine members of the U.S. Supreme Court. Through the power of judicial review, they have the ability to make policy in the area of the rights of the accused. Many of their policies and policy modifications regarding such issues as the right to counsel, the death penalty, and the exclusionary rule continue to be debated in the law journals and other scholarly publications across the country (Cohen, 1990; Green, 1990; Haas and Inciardi, 1988; Jackson and Riddlesperger, 1986; Keating, 1985; White, 1991; Zimring and Hawkins, 1986). A recent article argues that using a neoinstitutional model composed of the variables of political composition, the generally stable attitudes of its members, its policy-making priorities, and the political environment; the Supreme Court's policy outputs in criminal justice disputes can be predicted (Epstein et al., 1989).

By way of contrast, trial judges would seem to be losing power in an era of bargain justice. Yet they still play an important role in court management and sentencing. Many trial courts still suffer from the problem of court delay, but policy analysts have provided solutions for this problem (see Nagel, 1986). At the federal level, a multiple intervention time-series model has reduced the amount of delay from seven months to less than three months (Garner, 1987). General trial court reform can best be accomplished by an administrative approach (Feeley, 1983), which depends on a variety of organizational factors like size of jurisdiction and a number of individual factors such as the length of time the judge has sat on the bench (Ryan et al., 1980). Judges' sentencing authority has been reduced by plea bargaining and the movement toward determinate sentencing (see Goodstein, 1985; Griset, 1991). Trial judges are not left without power in this area, however, and today have the assistance of computer software packages (Simon et al., 1991). Yet, the question of fairness still arises. Studies continue to show that defendants who opt for a jury trial and are found guilty receive substantially harsher sentences than defendants who plead guilty (Uhlman and Walker, 1980).

V. THE CORRECTIONS ACTORS

Prisoners pass through the corrections system in the United States in ever-increasing numbers. The total number of inmates in 1991 was 823,414, with 71,608 being incarcerated in federal facilities and the remainder in state institutions. This represented a 6.5% increase from the previous year. The number of prisoners in local jails in 1991 was up over 5% from 1990, with a total of 426,479 such persons (Bureau of Justice Statistics, 1992). Blacks tend to be overrepresented in corrections facilities (Fax, 1982; Nelson, 1991), as are aborigines in Australian prisons (Gorta and Hunter, 1985). Today successful coping involves dealing with overcrowding (Koneazny and Schwartz, 1983–1984), sexual violence (Lockwood, 1980), inmate subcultures and the effects of long-term incarceration (Garfolo and Clark, 1985; MacKenzie and Goodstein, 1985), loss of freedom (Harris, 1986), loss of children (Baunach, 1985; Hairston, 1989), and AIDS (Lambrou, 1989; Skoler and Dargar, 1990). The whole process of coping may lead to maladaptation in prison (Toch et al., 1989), with little hope for positive change in the prisoner (Zamble and Porporino, 1988).

In the 1970s, the picture for corrections appeared particularly bleak. The incarceration rate for the baby-boom generation was starting to reach its peak. The public was particularly concerned with this explosion of prison populations (Petersilia, 1987). In addition, Martinson (1974) published an article that purported to show that nothing works in corrections. As a result, correctional activity was frequently portrayed as the warehousing of difficult people the society did not know how to treat. The projections were particularly dire in terms of overcrowding. Even a recent survey of top-level correctional officials indicated that most states will still not be able to build themselves out of the correctional dilemma (Cox, 1990). In addition, recidivism was at a high level, which places additional pressures on the correctional systems. There was no significant difference in rearrest rates of those released for "good time," meritorious conduct plus good time, court order, or parole (Delaware, Executive Department, 1984).

The fiscal implications of imprisonment have caused correctional researchers to evaluate the feasibility of continued prison construction as the desired goal in correctional policy (Clear and Harris, 1987). It is increasingly argued that imprisonment does not bring about crime reduction. In addition, more cost effective alternatives are being identified as better alternatives. Clear and Harris (1987) suggest that proactive approaches to offenders be taken at three points: the entry point, the prison location point with a consideration of alternative types of prison, and the exit point. There are increasing indicators in the research that support the rationality of a more cost-effective approach to imprisonment (New Jersey, The Governors Management Improvement Plan, 1983).

The Manhattan Bail Project carried out by the Vera Institute of Justice found that individuals with roots in the community could be released on their own recognizance and not have to pay a bail bondsperson or be incarcerated while awaiting trial (Freed and Wald, 1964). This reform has been adopted in many cities. At least 30 states changed their rules of criminal procedure to allow judges to consider the likelihood of appearance at trial by the defendant (Petersilia, 1987). This research has helped to reduce the cost of jail for many municipalities by simply removing some from incarceration.

The prisons are increasingly being reserved only for those who are most likely to be violent and to be chronic offenders. Because of cost considerations and the intensity of behavior exhibited by this population, incapacitating this segment of the criminal population will, it is argued, reduce the level of crime (Piper, 1985).

Intensive-supervision probation (ISP) and parole have been identified as very promising alternatives to prison (DiIulio, 1991). Unlike the unstructured probation and parole programs in operation throughout the country, these programs involve extensive supervision of the offender. Also, the programs involve mandated work and education. In addition, drug and alcohol testing occurs on a random basis. The offenders usually live in a center with strict rules governing most aspects of life. If the program lacks residential centers, there will be regular and frequent contact with the staff. Frequent checks of arrest records occur. Financial responsibility is built into the program. Offenders are usually expected to make restitution to victims. Also, offenders are expected to contribute to the costs of supervision. There have been several studies confirming the success of intensive supervision. In a program in Georgia (Erwin and Bennett, 1987) the recidivism rate for probationers in the ISP program was around 25%, whereas the comparable rate for imprisoned offenders was over 40%. In addition, the $14,000 per year cost of a prison bed was saved, and the participant contributed over 90% of the cost of the program. In an ISP program in New Jersey, the recidivism rate was about 10%. Pearson (1985) also estimated that the state saved about $7000 per year as compared with the cost of incarceration.

Increasingly, the literature indicates that rehabilitation can be effective with select segments of the prison population (DiIulio, 1991). Gendreau and Ross (1987) have made a major contribution to rekindling interest in the pursuit of rehabilitation in the context of prison. Generally, the new rehabilitation programs provide prisoners with role models who are not criminals. Also, programs provide problem-solving skills to the criminal so that prisoners link action to their consequences. Successful programs use financial and human resources that are available in the community. An attempt is made to build interpersonal relationships that strengthen empathy. Also, an attempt is made to strengthen respect for authority that is legitimate. Successful programs also provide support services after the prisoner returns to the community (DiIulio, 1991). Generally, any rehabilitative program has not been found to work with the violent, repeat offender. The evidence supporting existing rehabilitation still requires extensive replication to confirm the viability of rehabilitation with select populations. Questions still remain about the methodology that has been employed to study rehabilitation in the contemporary prison.

VI. THE MEDIA

The media are considered to be important influences on criminal justice policy for a variety of reasons. Graber (1979) indicated that as much as 95% of the general public identify the mass media to be their chief sources of crime information. In addition, the media are often cited as significant sources of attitudes regarding crime—particularly attitudes supportive of crime control and retributive justice (Lewis, 1984; Stroman and Seltzer, 1985).

The extent of media stress on crime has been cited as a source of the fear of fictimization among members of the public. In addition, the media stress on crime makes crime an important factor on the public agenda (Gordon and Heath, 1981). Originally, the literature on the public agenda function of the media indicated that media stress on certain topics will translate into important topics for members of the public. In addition, public agenda literature suggested that the media will influence public policy through a linear process. In this process, the initial stimulus is the appearance of a particular story. The existence of the story increases the importance of the issue among members of the public, who in turn mobilize interest groups who encourage policy makers to respond (Rogers and Dearing, 1988). Recent studies suggest the media have an impact on the public agenda but not in a linear fashion (Doppelt and Manikas, 1990). There is conjecture that members of the public with attitudes that match the media agenda regarding crime select media coverage that confirms their pre-existing views (Surette, 1992). The public agenda research indicates that the impact of the media is greater for television than for newspapers. Also, the effects of the media appear to increase with subjection to the stimulus, particularly if the individual lacks direct experience with crime. The effects of the media are often characterized as interactive with individual and social variables (Rogers and Deering, 1988; Weaver, 1980).

An additional link between the media and criminal justice policy is being established by those doing research into agenda building as opposed to agenda setting. Agenda building involves an examination of the relationship between the media and the policy agenda of decision makers. The interaction between the media and decision makers appears to play a significant role in making crime issues salient on the agendas of decision makers (Doppelt and Manikas, 1990; Graber, 1989; Lang and Lang, 1983). For example, the relation between the media and local decision makers in investigative reporting stories is the most important factor in bringing an issue to the agenda of decision makers (Cook et al., 1983; Leff et al., 1986; Protess et al., 1987). Fishman (1978) documented the creation of new enforcement squads as well as the introduction of legislation to deal with the problem of a wave of crime against the elderly. The topic had received extensive coverage in the media. In Great Britain, media coverage of muggings elicited significant response from policy makers (Hall et al., 1981). Snow (1984) identified the media coverage of the Hinckley shooting of President Reagan as a precipitant in the campaign for changing the insanity plea. In a study of prosecutors in Indiana, the prosecution of pornography cases was related to a prosecutor's perception that pornography was an important item on the media's agenda (Pritchard et al., 1987). The relationship between the media, the policy makers, and the public requires additional research. Greater specifity is required to understand the way in which crime ultimately comes to be part of the public policy agenda (Surette, 1992).

There is some indication in the research that the media can generate certain types of crime. Of particular concern has been the impact of media pornography and violence on the criminal behavior of individuals. The media have been established as one of many variables that have an impact on the genesis of crime (Surette, 1990). Specifically, media portrayals of sexual violence have been found to produce antisocial attitudes about females and particularly about rape (Surette, 1992). The depiction of violent sexual material is mediated by the dispositions of individual viewers (Malamuth and Briere, 1986). Hypermasculine males are likely to be influenced by violent pornography in the media (Gray, 1982). However, there is a significant gap in existing knowledge. Limiting violent pornography has not been empirically linked to a reduction in sexual crime (Imrich et al., 1990). It may be that hypermasculine males simply seek out sexually aggressive media portrayals to reinforce their hostile attitudes. Thus the causal link between the media portrayal of aggressive pornography and sex crimes remains problematic at this point (Surette, 1992). The link between hostile attitudes and sex crimes has not been confirmed empirically (Surette, 1992).

VII. CONCLUSIONS

Criminal justice policy research is a relatively new field. Nonetheless, it has provided significant knowledge to those working in the area. For example, more efficient patterns of policing have developed from the study of police patrol. Cost-effective service delivery is increasingly being stressed in departments that are aware of what works. Similarly, in corrections, the research has indicated that programs such as intensive supervision probation and parole save jurisdictions considerable amounts of money and produce significantly lower recidivism rates than found among comparably violent populations that are imprisoned. Generally, the literature reviewed for this chapter reflects the development of middle-level theory. There still are some extremely important questions that remain to be answered in the research. One of the most significant of these questions is what types of policies are conducive to a reduction in the crime rate. Most of the work reviewed for this chapter leaves this central question with answers that require extensive replication or studies with more extensive methodological sophistication.

Also, the area of criminal justice policy research presents the very difficult problem of generalizability. As was evident in the replications of the Minneapolis domestic violence response study, arrest did not work to reduce the level of violence in the other cities. Additional variables might be used by researchers in constructing their research design so conclusions could be drawn about the strength of relationships with hypothesized causative factors. This is particularly important in highly conflictual and sensitive areas such as domestic violence. A variety of factors—cultural, organizational, and biological—may be helpful in the study of what works to reduce the crime rate. The next generation of research in criminal justice policy has the potential for extensive contributions to knowledge. The criminal justice system with its exceedingly high recidivism rate could change very markedly as the results of research now in progress are translated into practice.

REFERENCES

Adler, F. (1975). *Sisters in Crime*. McGraw-Hill, New York.

Aleem, S. Women in policing in India. *Police Studies* 12(3): 97–103.

Alexander, H. E., and Caiden, G. E. (Eds.) (1985). *The Politics and Economics of Organized Crime*. D.C. Heath, Lexington, MA.

Anastasia, G. (1991). *Blood and Honor: Inside the Scarfo Mob—The Mafia's Most Violent Family*. Morrow, New York.

Anderson, C. A. (1987). Temperature and aggression effects on quarterly, yearly, and city rates of violent and nonviolent crime. *Journal of Personality and Social Psychology* 52(6): 1161–1173.

Athens, L. H. (1989). *The Creation of Dangerous Violent Criminals*. Routledge, London and New York.

Balkwell, J. W. (1990). Ethnic inequality and the rate of homicide. *Social Forces* 69(1): 53–70.

Baron, L., and Straus, M. A. (1989). *Four Theories of Rape in American Society*. Yale University Press, New Haven, CT.

Baunach, P. J. (1985). *Mothers in Prison*. Transaction Books, New Brunswick, Oxford, England.

Beccaria, C. (1963). *Essay on Crimes and Punishments.* Bobbs-Merrill, Indianapolis, IN.

Belenko, S., Fagan, J., and Chin, K. (1991). Criminal justice responses to crack. *Journal of Research in Crime and Delinquency* 28(1): 55–74.

Bennett, G. (1987). *Crimewarps: The Future of Crime in America.* Anchor Books, Garden City, NY.

Bennett, R. R. (1991a). Routine activities: a cross-national assessment of a criminological perspective. *Social Forces* 70(1): 147–163.

—— (1991b). Development and crime: a cross-national, time-series analysis of competing models. *Sociological Quarterly* 32(3): 343–363.

Bennett, T., and Wright, R. (1984). *Burglars on Burglary.* Gower: Brookfield, VT.

Bensinger, G. J. (1988). Operation Greylord and its aftermath. *International Journal of Comparative and Applied Criminal Justice* 12(1, 2): 111–118.

Benson, J. L. (1989). The influence of class position on the formal and informal sanctioning of white-collar offenders. *The Sociological Quarterly* 30(3): 465–479.

Berger, A. S., and Simon, W. (1974). Black families and the Moynihan report: A research evaluation. *Social Problems* 22: 145–161.

Berger, R. J., Neuman, W. L., and Searles, P. (1991). The social and political context of rape law reform: an aggregated analysis. *Social Science Quarterly* 72(2): 221–238.

Besharov, D. J. (Ed.) (1990). *Family Violence: Research and Public Policy Issues.* The American Enterprise Institute, Washington, D.C.

Biderman, A. D., and Lynch, J. P. (1991). *Understanding Crime Incidence Statistics: Why the UCR Diverges From the NCS.* Springer-Verlag, New York.

Blackman, J. (1989). *Intimate Violence.* Columbia University Press, New York.

Blumstein, A., Cohen, J., Roth, J. A., and Visher, C. A. (Eds.) (1986). *Criminal Careers and Career Criminals*, Vol 1. National Academy Press, Washington, D.C.

Booth, M. (1990). *The Triads: The Chinese Criminal Fraternity.* Grafton Books, London.

Boydstun, J. E. (1975). *San Diego Field Interrogation: Final Report.* Police Foundation, Washington, D.C.

Browne, A. (1987). *When Battered Women Kill.* Free Press, New York.

Brownstein, H. H., and Goldstein, P. J. (1990). Research and development of public policy: the case of drugs and violent crime. Journal of Applied Sociology 7: 77–89.

Bureau of Justice Statistics. (1992). *National Update.* U.S. Department of Justice, Washington, D.C.

Bynum, T. S. (Ed.) (1987). *Organized Crime in America: Concepts and Controversies.* Criminal Justice Press, Monsey, NY.

Cahn, M. F., and Tien, J. (1981). *An Alternative Approach in Police Response: Wilmington Management of Demand Program.* U.S. Department of Justice, National Institute of Justice, Washington, D.C.

Calavita, K., and Pontell, H. N. (1990). Heads I win, tails you lost: Deregulation, crime and crisis in the savings and loan industry. Crime and Delinquency 36(3): 309–341.

Cantor, D., and Land, K. C. (1985). Unemployment and crime rates in post-World War II United States: A theoretical and empirical analysis. *American Sociological Review* 50: 317–332.

Carmen, A., and Moody, H. (1985). *Working Women: the Subterranean World of Street Prostitution.* Harper & Row, New York.

Carpenter, T. (1992). *Mobgirl: a Woman's Life in the Underworld.* Simon & Schuster, New York.

Champion, D. J. (1987). District attorneys and plea bargaining: An analysis of the prosecutorial priorities influencing negotiated guilty pleas. *Prosecutor* 20(4): 25–32.

Clarke, M. (1990). *Business Crime.* St. Martin's Press, New York.

Clear, T., and Harris, P. M. (1987). The costs of Incarceration. In *America's Correctional Crisis.* S. D. Gottfredson and S. McConville (Eds.). Greenwood Press, New York.

Cohen, F. (1990). Miranda and police deception in interrogation: Comment on Illinois v. Perkins. *Criminal Law Bulletin* 26(6): 534–546.

Cohen, L. E., and Felson, M. (1979). Social change and crime rate trends: A routine activity approach. *American Sociological Review* 44: 588–608.

Cohen, L. E., and Land, K. C. (1987). Sociological positivism and the explanation of criminality. In *Positive Criminology*. M. R. Gottfredson and T. Hirschi (Eds.). Sage, Newbury Park, CA.

Conklin, J. E. (1977). *Illegal But Not Criminal: Business Crimes in America*. Prentice-Hall, Englewood Cliffs, NJ.

Conrad, J. P. (1987). Dealing with crime on the streets. In *Handbook on Crime and Delinquency Prevention*. E. H. Johnson (Ed.). Greenwood Press, Westport, CT.

Cook, F., Tyler, T., Goetz, E., Gordon, M., Protess, D., Leff, D., and Molotch, H. (1983). Media and agenda setting effects on the public interest group leaders, policy makers, and policy. *Public Opinion Quarterly* 47(1): 16–35.

Cordner, G. (1981). The Effects of Directed Patrol: A Natural Quasi-Experiment in Pontiac. In *Contemporary Issues in Law Enforcement*. J. J. Fyfe (Ed.). Sage, Beverly Hills, CA.

Cordner, G. W., and Hale, D. C. (Eds.) (1992). *What Works in Policing?* Anderson, Cincinnati, OH.

Cox, G. H., and Rhodes, S. L. (1990). Managing Overcrowding: Corrections Administrators and the Prison Crisis. *Criminal Justice Policy Review* 4(2): 115–143.

Cullen, F. T., Maakestad, W. J., and Cavender, G. (1987). *Corporate Crime Under Attack: the Ford Pinto Case and Beyond*. Anderson, Cincinnati, OH.

Currie, E. (1985). *Confronting Crime: An American Challenge*. Pantheon, New York.

Curtis, L. A. (Ed.) (1985). *American Violence and Public Policy: An Update of the National Commission on the Causes and Prevention of Violence*. Yale University Press, New Haven, CT.

Daly, M., and Wilson, M. (1988). *Homicide*. Aldine De Gruyter, New York.

Decker, S. H., and Salert, B. (1986). Predicting the career criminal: An empirical test of the Greenwood scale. *Journal of Criminal Law and Criminology* 77(1): 215–236.

Delaware, Executive Department (1984). *Recidivism in Delaware: A Study of Rearrest After Release From Incarceration*. Statistical Center, Dover, DE.

DiIulio, J. (1991). *No Escape*. Basic Books, New York.

Doppelt, J., and Manikas, P. (1990). Mass Media and Criminal Justice Decision Making. In *The Media and Criminal Justice Policy*. R. Surette (Ed.). Thomas, Springfield, IL, pp. 129–142.

Dunford, F. W., Huizinga, D., and Elliott, D. S. (1990). The role of arrest in domestic assault: The Omaha police experiment. *Criminology* 28: 183–206.

Eck, J. E., and Spelman, W. (1987). *Problem Solving: Problem-Oriented Policing in Newport News*. Police Executive Research Forum, Washington, D.C.

Edelman, M. (1977). *Political Language*. Academic Press, New York.

Egger, S. A. (Ed.) (1990). *Serial Murder: An Elusive Phenomenon*. Praeger, New York.

Eisenstein, J., Flemming, R. B., and Nardulli, P. F. (1988). *The Contours of Justice*. Little, Brown, Boston.

Epstein, L., Walker, T. G., and Dixon, W. J. (1989). The Supreme Court and criminal justice disputes: A neoinstitutional perspective. *American Journal of Political Science* 33(4): 825–841.

Erwin, B., and Bennett, L. (1987). New Dimensions in Probation: Georgia's Experience with Intensive Probation Supervision (IPS). *Research in Brief*, National Institute of Justice, Washington, D.C.

Faigman, D. L. (1986). Battered woman syndrome and self defense: A legal and empirical dissent. *Virginia Law Review* 72(3): 619–647.

Farrington, D. P. (1986). Age and crime. In *Crime and Justice: An Annual Review of Research*, vol. 7. M. Tonry and N. Morris (Eds.). University of Chicago Press, Chicago.

Farrington, D. P., Ohlin, L. E., and Wilson, J. Q. (1986). *Understanding and Controlling Crime*. Springer-Verlag, New York.

Feeley, M. M. (1979). *The Process is the Punishment*. Russell Sage Foundation, New York.

—— (1983). *Court Reform on Trial*. Basic Books, New York.

Fine, R. A. (1986). *Escape of the Guilty*. Dodd, Mead, New York.

Fishbein, D. H. (1990). Biological perspectives in criminology. *Criminology* 28(1): 27–72.

Fishman, M. (1978). Crime waves as ideology. *Social Problems* 25(5): 531–543.

Fishman, S., Rodenrys, K., and Schink, G. (1986). *The Income of Organized Crime*. Wharton Econometric Forecasting Associates, Philadelphia.

Flemming, R. B. (1990). The political styles and organizational strategies of American prosecutors: Examples from nine courthouse communities. *Law and Policy* 12(1): 25–50.

Foley, D. (1986). Case study in DWI countermeasures. In *Stop DWI: Successful Responses to Drunk Driving*. D. Foley (Ed.). Lexington Books, Boston.

Fox, J. G. (1982). *Organizational and Racial Conflict in Maximum-Security Prisons*. Lexington Books, Lexington, MA.

Frank, N. (1985). *Crimes Against Health and Safety*. Harrow and Heston, Albany, NY.

Frank, N., and Lombness, M. (1988). *Controlling Corporate Illegality: the Regulatory Justice System*. Anderson, Cincinnati, OH.

Francis, D. B. (1987). *Computer Crime*. E.P. Dutton, New York.

Frantz, D. (1987). *Levine and Company: Wall Street's Insider Trading Scandal*. Henry HOlt, New York.

Freed, D., and Wald, P. (1964). Working Paper. National Conference on Bail and Criminal Justice.

Freeman, R. (1982). Crime and the labor market. *NBCR Working Paper* No. 1031. National Bureau on Economic Research, Cambridge, MA.

—— (1983). Crime and unemployment. In *Crime and Public Policy*. J. Q. Wilson (Ed.). Institute for Contemporary Studies, San Francisco, pp. 89–106.

Garofalo, J., and Clark, R. D. (1985). The inmate subculture in jails. *Criminal Justice and Behavior* 12(4): 415–434.

Garofalo, J. (1987). Reassessing the lifestyle model of criminal victimization. In *Positive Criminology*. M. R. Gottfredson and T. Hirschi (Eds.). Sage, Beverly Hills, CA, pp. 23–42.

Garner, J. H. (1987). Delay reduction in federal courts: Rule 50(b) and the Federal Speedy Trial Act of 1974. *Journal of Quantitative Criminology* 3(3): 229–250.

Gendreau, P., and Ross, R. P. (1987). Revivification of Rehabilitation: Evidence from the 1980s. *Justice Quarterly* 4(3): 349–408.

George, B. J., Jr. (1990). Rights of the criminally accused. *Law and Contemporary Problems* 53(1, 2): 71–107.

Goetting, A. (1989). Patterns of marital homicide: A comparison of husbands and wives. *Journal of Comparative Family Studies* 20(3): 341–354.

Goodstein, L., and Hepburn, J. (1985). *Determinate Sentencing and Imprisonment*. Anderson, Cincinnati, OH.

Gordon, D. R. (1990). *The Justice Juggernaut*. Rutgers University Press, New Brunswick, NJ.

Gordon, M., and Heath, L. (1981). The news business, crime and fear. In *Reaction to Crime*. D. Lewis (Ed.). Sage, Newbury Park, CA, pp. 227–250.

Gorta, A., and Hunter, R. (1985). Aborigines in NSW prisons. *Australian and New Zealand Journal of Criminology* 18(1): 26–40.

Gottfredson, M. R., and Hirschi, T. (1990). *A General Theory of Crime*. Stanford University Press, Stanford, CA.

Graber, D. (1979). Evaluating Crime-Fighting Policies. In *Evaluating Alternative Law Enforcement Policies*. R. Baker and F. Meyer (Eds.). Lexington Books, Lexington, MA, pp. 179–200.

Graber, D. (1989). *Mass Media and American Politics*. CQ Press, Washington, D.C.

Gray, S. (1982). Exposure to pornography and aggression toward women: The case of the angry male. *Social Problems* 29(4): 387–398.

Green, B. A. (1990). The good faith exception to the fruit of the poisonous tree doctrine. *Criminal Law Bulletin* 26(6): 509–533.

Green, G. S. (1990). *Occupational Crime*. Nelson-Hall, Chicago.

Greenberg, B., Elliott, C. V., Kraft, L. P., and Procter, H. S. (1975). *Felony Investigation Decision Model—An Analysis of Investigative Elements of Information*. Stanford Research Institute. Menlo Park, CA.

Greenwood, P. W. (1983). Controlling the crime rate through imprisonment. In *Crime and Public Policy*. J. Q. Wilson (Ed.). Institute for Contemporary Stalin, San Francisco, pp. 251–269.

Greenwood, P., Chaiken, J., and Petersilia, J. (1977). *The Investigation Process*. Lexington Books, Lexington, MA.

Griset, P. L. (1991). *Determinate Sentencing: the Promise and the Reality of Retributive Justice*. State University of New York Press, Albany, NY.

Haas, K. C., and Inciardi, J. A. (Eds.) (1988). *Challenging Capital Punishment*. Sage, Newbury Park, CA.

Hairston, C. F. (1989). Men in prison: Family characteristics and parenting views. *Journal of Offender Counseling, Services and Rehabilitation* 14(1): 23–30.

Hall, S., Critcher, C., Jefferson, T., Clarke, J., and Roberts, B. (1981). The social production of news: mugging in the media. In *The Manufacture of News*. S. Cohen and J. Young (Eds.). Sage, Newbury Park, CA.

Hall, W. K., and Aspin, L. T. (1987). What twenty years of judicial retention elections have told us. *Judicature* 70(6): 340–347.

Hamberger, L. K., and Hastings, J. E. (1986). Characteristics of spouse abusers: Predictors of treatment acceptance. *Journal of Interpersonal Violence* 1(3): 363–373.

Harris, J. (1986). *Stranger in Two Worlds*. Macmillan, New York.

Hatchard, J. (1987). Judicial attitudes towards the right to legal representation in Zimbabwe. *International Journal of Comparative and Applied Criminal Justice* 11(1): 23–31.

Heumann, M. (1978). *Plea Bargaining*. University of Chicago Press, Chicago.

Hirschi, T., and Gottfredson, M. (1984). Age and the exploration of crime. *American Journal of Sociology* 89: 552–584.

Hobson, B. M. (1987). *Uneasy Virtue: the Politics of Prostitution and the American Reform Tradition*. Basic Books, New York.

Holmes, R. M., and DeBurger, J. (1988). *Serial Murder*. Sage, Newbury Park, CA.

Hudzik, J. K. (1987). Surviving the loss of federal dollars and mandate: The case of state planning agencies. *Journal of Criminal Justice* 15(2): 105–120.

Igbinovia, P. E. (1989). Criminology in America. *International Journal of Offender Therapy and Comparative Criminology* 33(2): v–x.

Imrich, D., Mullin, C., and Linz, D. (1990). Sexually Violent Media and Criminal Justice Policy. In *The Media and Criminal Justice Policy*. R. Surette (Ed.). Thomas, Springfield, IL, pp. 103–123.

Inciardi, J. A. (Ed.) (1991). *The Drug Legalization Debate*. Sage, Newbury Park, CA.

Jackson, D. W., and Riddlesperger, J. W. (1986). Whatever happened to the exclusionary rule, The Burger Court and the Fourth amendment? *Criminal Justice Policy Review* 1(2): 156–168.

Jacobs, J. B. (1989). *Drunk Driving*. The University of Chicago Press, Chicago.

Jacoby, J. E. (1980). *The American Prosecutor: A Search for Identity*. Lexington Books, Lexington, MA.

Jenkins, P. (1989). Serial murder in the United States 1940–1990: A historical perspective. *Journal of Criminal Justice* 17(5): 377–392.

Jenks, C. (1987). Genes and crime: an exchange. *New York Review of Books* 34: 50–52.

Jesilow, P., Geis, G., and O'Brien, M. J. (1985). Is my battery any good? A field test of fraud in the auto repair business. *Journal of Crime and Justice* 8: 1–20.

Jesilow, P. D., Pontell, H. N., and Geis, G. (1985). Medical criminals: Physicians and white collar offenses. *Justice Quarterly* 2(2): 149–165.

Kallisa, M. J., and Vanier, D. J. (1985). Consumer shoplifting: Orientations and deterrents. *Journal of Criminal Justice* 13(5): 459–473.

Kaplan, D. E., and Dubro, A. (1986). *Yakuza: the Explosive Account of Japan's Criminal Underworld*. Addison-Wesley, Reading, MA.

Kaplan, J., Jr. (Ed.) (1986). Gun control. *Law and Contemporary Problems* 49(1): 1–267.

Katz, J. (1980). The social movement against white collar crime. In *Criminology Review Yearbook* 2. E. Bittner and S. Messinger (Eds.). Sage, Beverly Hills, CA.

—— (1991). The motivation of the persistent robber. *In Crime and Justice: A Review of Research*, Vol 14. M. Tonry (Ed.). University of Chicago Press, Chicago.

Keating, M. M. (1985). New York v. Quarles: The dissolution of Miranda. *Villanova Law Review* 30(2): 441–461.

Kelling, G. L., Pate, T., Dieckman, D., and Brown, C. (1974). *The Kansas City Preventive Patrol Experiment: A Summary Report.* The Police Foundation, Washington, D.C.

Kleck, G. (1986). Policy lessons from recent gun control research. *Law and Contemporary Problems* 49(1): 35-62.

—— (1987). America's foreign wars and the legitimization of domestic violence. *Sociological Inquiry* 57(3): 237-250.

Kohfeld, C. W., and Sprague, J. (1988). Urban unemployment drives urban crime. *Urban Affairs Quarterly* 24(2): 215-241.

Koneazny, P. M., and Schwartz, K. D. (Eds.) (1984). Colloquium: The prison overcrowding crisis. *New York University Review of Law and Social Change* 12(1): 1-356.

Kornhauser, W. (1959). *The Politics of Mass Society.* Free Press, Glencoe, IL.

Krauft, B. M. (1985). *Good Company and Violence Sorcery and Social Control in a Lowland New Guinea Society.* University of California Press, Berkeley, CA.

Kraus, M. B., and Lazear, E. P. (Eds.) (1991). *Searching for Alternatives: Drug Control Policy in the United States.* Hoover Institution Press, Stanford, CA.

Kusserow, R. P. (1986). An inside look at federal computer crime. *Security Management* 30(5): 74-77.

Kvalseth, T. O. (1977). A note on the effects of population density and unemployment on urban crime. *Criminology* 15(1): 105-110.

Lacey, R. (1991). *Little Man: Meyer Lansky and the Gangster Life.* Little, Brown, Boston.

Lambrou, I. (1989). AIDS behind bars: Prison responses and judicial deference. *Temple Law Review* 62(1): 327-354.

Lang, D., and Lang, K. (1983). *The Battle for Public Opinion.* Columbia University Press, New York.

Leff, D., Protess, D., and Brooks, S. (1986). Crusading journalism: Changing public attitudes and policy-making agendas. *Public Opinion Quarterly* 50(3): 300-315.

Levin, J., and Fox, J. A. (1985). *Mass Murder: America's Growing Menace.* Plenum, New York.

Lewis, R. (1984). The media, violence and criminal behavior. In *Justice and the Media.* R. Surette (Ed.). Thomas, Springfield, IL, pp. 51-69.

Linsky, A. S., and Strauss, M. A. (1986). *Social Stress in the United States: Links to Regional Patterns of Crime and Illness.* Amburn House, Duver, MA.

Lockwood, D. (1980). *Prison Sexual Violence.* Elsevier, New York.

Logan, J. R., and Messner, S. F. (1987). Racial residential segregation and suburban violent crime. *Social Science Quarterly* 68(3): 510-527.

Lynch, J. P. (1987). Routine activity and victimization at work. *Journal of Quantitative Criminology* 3: 283-300.

Mackenzie, D. L., and Goodstein, L. (1985). Long-term incarceration impacts and characteristics of long-term offenders: An empirical analysis. *Criminal Justice and Behavior* 12(4): 395-412.

Malamuth, N., and Briere, J. (1986). Sexual Violence in the Media: Indirect Effects on Aggression Against Women. *Journal of Social Issues* 42(3): 75-92.

Malamuth, N. M., and Donnerstein, E. (Eds.) (1984). *Pornography and Sexual Aggression.* Academic Press, Orlando, FL.

Marek, A. E. (1986). Organized crime in Poland. In *Organized Crime: A Global Perspective.* R. J. Kelly (Ed.). Rowman and Littlefield, Totowa, NJ, pp. 159-171.

Martin, S. E. (1990). *On The Move: The Status of Women in Policing.* Police Foundation, Washington, D.C.

Martinson, R. (1974). What Works? Questions and answers about prison reform. *Public Interest* 35: 22-54.

Marsh, F. H., and Katz, J. (Eds.) (1985). *Biology, Crime and Ethics: A Study of Biological Explanations for Criminal Behavior.* Anderson, Cincinnati, OH.

Mastrofsky, S., and Potter, G. (1986). Evaluating law enforcement efforts to control organized crime: The Pennsylvania Crime Commission as a case study. *Policy Studies Review* 6(1): 160-170.

—— (1987). Controlling organized crime: A critique of law enforcement policy. *Criminal Justice Policy Review* 2(3): 269-301.

Mather, L. M. (1979). *Plea Bargaining or Trial?* Lexington Books, Lexington, MA.

Maudsley, H. (1874). *Responsibility in Mental Disease.* Macmillan, London.

Maxfield, M. G. (1987). Lifestyle and routine activity review of crime: Empirical studies of victimization, delinquency, and offender decision-making. *Journal Quantitative Criminology* 3: 275-282.

McDonald, W. F. (Ed.) (1983). *The Defense Counsel.* Sage, Beverly Hills, CA.

McDowall, D. (1991). Firearm availability and homicide rates in Detroit, 1951-1981. *Social Forces* 69(4): 1085-1101.

McIntyre, L. J. (1987). *The Public Defender.* University of Chicago Press, Chicago.

Mednick, S. A., Moffit, T. E., and Stack, S. A. (1987). *The Causes of Crime.* Cambridge University Press, Cambridge.

Miethe, T. D., Hughes, M., and McDowall, D. (1991). Social change and crime rates: And evaluation of alternative theoretical approaches. *Social Forces* 70(1): 165-185.

Miller, E. M. (1986). *Street Woman.* Temple University Press, Philadelphia.

Miller, R. L. (1991). *The Case for Legalizing Drugs.* Praeger, New York.

Moore, M. M., and Kleiman, M. A. R. (1989). The police and drugs. In *Perspectives on Policing.* National Institute of Justice, Washington, D.C.

Nagel, S. S. (1986). *Law, Policy, and Optimizing Analysis.* Quorum Books, New York.

Nelson, J. F. (1991). *The Incarceration of Minority Defendants: an Identification of Disparity in New York State, 1985-1986.* New York State Division of Criminal Justice Services, Albany, NY.

New Jersey, The Governor's Management Improvement Plan (1983). *Department of Corrections: The Correctional System, Strategic Issues and Alternatives.* Trenton, NJ.

Newton, M. (1988). *Mass Murder: on Annotated Bibliography.* Garland, New York.

Nicholson, M. A., and Weiss, B. S. (1986). Funding judicial campaigns in the Circuit Court of Cook County. *Judicature* 70(1): 17-25.

Parker, D. B. (1983). *Fighting Computer Crime.* Scribner's Sons, NY.

Paternoster, R. (1984). Prosecutorial discretion in requesting the death penalty: A case of victim-based racial discrimination. *Law and Society Review* 18(3): 437-478.

Patterson, E. B. (1991). Poverty, income, inequality, and community crime rates. *Criminology* 29(4): 755-776.

Pearson, F. (1985). New Jersey's Intensive Supervision Program: A Progress Report. *Crime and Delinquency* 31(3): 393-410.

Pepinsky, H. E., and Jesilow, P. (1984). *Myths That Cause Crime.* Seven Locks Press, Cabin John, MD. and Washington, D.C.

Petersilia, J. (1987). *The Influence of Criminal Justice Research.* Rand Corporation, Santa Monica, CA.

Pettiway, L. E. (1987). Arson for revenge: The role of environmental situation, age, sex and race. *Journal of Quantitative Criminology* 3(2): 169-184.

Pileggi, N. (1985). *Wiseguy: Life in a Mafia Family.* Simon & Schuster, New York.

Pilzer, P. Z. (1989). *Other People's Money.* Simon & Schuster, New York.

Piper, E. (1985). Violent recidivism and chronicity in the 1958 cohort. *Journal of Quantitative Criminology* 1(4): 319-344.

Platt, T. (1987). U.S. criminal justice in the Reagan era: An assessment. *Crime and Social Justice* 29: 58-69.

Police Foundation (1981). *The Newark Foot Patrol Experiment.* Police Foundation, Washington, D.C.

Price, B. R., and Sokoloff, N. J. (Eds.) (1982). *The Criminal Justice System and Women.* Clark Boardman, New York.

Pritchard, D., Dilts, J., and Berkowitz, D. (1987). Prosecutors use of external agenda in prosecuting pornography cases. *Journalism Quarterly* 64(2): 392-398.

Protess, D., Cook, F., Curtin, T., Gordon, M., Leff, D., McCombs, M., and Miller, P. (1987). The impact of investigative reporting on public opinion and policymaking: Targeting toxic waste. *Public Opinion Quarterly* 51(2): 166-185.

Ray, J. (1987). Every twelfth shopper: Who shoplifts and why? *Social Casework* 68(4): 234–239.

Revbovich, D. (1987). *Understanding Hazardous Waste Crime: A Multistate Examination of the Offense and Offender Characteristics in the Northeast*. New Jersey Division of Criminal Justice, Trenton, NJ.

Reynolds, H. (1986). *The Economics of Prostitution*. Thomas, Springfield, IL.

Robin, G. D. (1991). *Violent Crime and Gun Control*. Anderson, Cincinnati, OH.

Rogers, E., and Dearing, J. (1988). Agenda-setting research: Where has it been, where is it going? In *Communication Yearbook II*. J. Anderson (Ed.). Sage, Newbury Park, CA, pp. 555–594.

Rubin, L. B. (1986). *Quiet Rage: Bernie Goetz in a Time of Madness*. Farrar, Straus and Girous, New York.

Ryan, J. P., Ashman, A., Sales, B. D., and Shane-DuBow, S. (1980). *American Trial Judges*. The Free Press, New York.

Sampson, R. J. (1987). Urban black violence: The effect of male joblessness and family disruption. *American Journal of Sociology* 93(2): 348–382.

Scheingold, S. A. (1984). *The Politics of Law and Order*. Longman, New York and London.

—— (1991). *The Politics of Street Crime*. Temple University Press, Philadelphia.

Schulhofer, S. J. (1986). The future of the adversary system. *Justice Quarterly* 3(1): 83–93.

—— (1987). Reconsidering Miranda. *University of Chicago Law Review* 54(2): 435–461.

Scott, J. E., and Schwalm, L. A. Pornography and rape: An examination of adult theater rates and rape rates by state. In *Controversial Issues in Crime and Justice*. J. E. Scott and T. Hirschi (Eds.). Sage, Newbury Park, CA.

Sherman, L. (1990). Police crackdowns. *NIJ Reports* (March/April): 2–6.

Sherman, L., and Berk, R. (1984). The specific deterrent effects of arrest for domestic assault. *American Sociological Review* 49( ): 261–272.

Sherman, L., Schmidt, J. D., Rogan, D., and De Riso, C. (1991). Predicting domestic homicide: Prior police contact and gun threats. In *Woman Battering: Policy Responses*. M. Steinman (Ed.). Anderson, Cincinnati, OH.

Shover, N. (1991). Burglary. *In Crime and Justice: A Review of Research*, Vol 14. M. Tonry (Ed.). University of Chicago Press, Chicago.

Shupe, A., Stacey, W. A., and Hazlewood, L. R. (1987). *Violent Men, Violent Couples*. Lexington Books, Lexington, MA.

Simon, E., Gaes, G., and Rhodes, W. (1991). ASSYST—The design and implementation of computer-assisted sentencing. *Federal Probation* 55(3): 45–55.

Simon, R. J., and Landis, J. (1991). *The Crimes Women Commit, The Punishments They Receive*. Lexington Books, Lexington, MA.

Skolnick, J. H., and Bayley, D. H. (1988). Theme and variation in community policing. In *Crime and Justice*, Vol 10. M. Tonry and N. Morris (Eds.). University of Chicago Press, Chicago, pp. 1–37.

Skuler, D. L., and Dargar, R. L. (1990). AIDS in prison—Administrator policies, inmate protests, and reactions from the federal bench. *Federal Probation* 54(2): 27–32.

Smith, D. A. (1986). The plea bargaining controversy. *Journal of Criminal Law and Criminology* 77(3): 949–967.

Snow, R. (1984). Crime and justice in prime-time news: The John Hinckley, Jr. case. In *Justice and the Media*. R. Surette (Ed.). Thomas, Springfield, IL, pp. 212–232.

Spohn, C., Gruhl, J., and Welch, S. (1987). The impact of the ethnicity and gender of defendants on the decision to reject or dismiss felony charges. *Criminology* 25(1): 175–191.

Steffensmeir, D. J., Allan, E. A., Harer, M. D., and Streifel, C. (1989). Age and the distribution of crime. *American Journal of Sociology* 94(4): 803–831.

Sterling, J. S. (1983). Retained counsel versus the public defender. In *The Defense Counsel*. W. F. McDonald (Ed.). Sage, Beverly Hills, CA, pp. 151–170.

Stewart, J. B. (1987). *The Prosecutors*. Simon & Schuster, New York.

Strickland, M. (1983). *How to Deal with Parental Kidnapping*. Rainbow Books, Moore Haven, FL.

Stroman, C., and Seltzer, R. (1985). Media use and perceptions of crime. *Journalism Quarterly* 62(2): 340–345.

Surette, R. (1990). The media and criminal justice policy—Future prospects. In *The Media and Criminal Justice Policy*. R. Surette (Ed.). Thomas, Springfield, IL, pp. 299–312.

Surette, R. (1992). *Media, Crime and Criminal Justice*. Brooks/Cole, Pacific Grove, CA.

Toch, H., Adams, K., and Grant, J. D. (1989). *Coping*. Transaction Publishers, New Brunswick, NJ.

Tonry, M. (1990). Research on drugs and crime. In *Drugs and Crime*. M. Tonry, J. Q. Wilson (Eds.). University of Chicago Press, Chicago.

Trojanowicz, R. (1982). *An Evaluation of the Neighborhood Foot Patrol Program in Flint, Michigan*. National Center for Community Policing, Michigan State University, East Lansing, MI.

Tunnell, K. D. (1992). *Choosing Crime: The Criminal Calculus of Property Offenders*. Nelson Hall, Chicago.

Uhlman, T. M., and Walker, N. D. (1980). He takes some of my time; I take some of his: An analysis of judicial sentencing patterns in jury cases. *Law and Society* 14(4): 323–341.

Van Kirk, M. (1978). *Response Time Analysis: Executive Summary*. National Institute of Law Enforcement and Criminal Justice, Law Enforcement Assistance Administration, Washington, D.C.

Vanagunas, S. (1984). Crime and unemployment: Another look. *Journal of Behavioral Economics* 13(1): 101–112.

Volavka, J., Martell, D., and Convit, A. (1992). Psychobiology of the violent offender. *Journal of Forensic Sciences* 37(1): 237–251.

VonHirsch, A., and Gottfredson, D. (1984). Selective incapacitation: Some queries on research design and equity. *New York University Review of Law and Social Change* 12(1): 11–51.

Walker, D. B. Black police values and the black community. *Police Studies* 5(4): 20–28.

Walker, L. E. (1984). *The Battered Women Syndrome*. Springer, New York.

Walker, S. (1989). *Sense and Nonsense About Crime*. Brooks Cole, Pacific Grove, CA.

Warner, R., Steel, B., and Lovrich, N. (1989). Conditions associated with the advent of representative bureaucracy: The case of women in policing. *Social Science Quarterly* 70(3): 562–578.

Weaver, D. (1980). Audience needs for orientation and media effects. *Communications Research* 7: 361–376.

White, W. S. (1991). *The Death Penalty in the Nineties*. University of Michigan Press, Ann Arbor, MI.

Wice, P. B. (1978). *Criminal Lawyers*. Sage, Beverly Hills, CA.

Widom, C. S. (1989). The cycle of violence. *Science* 244: 160–166.

Williams, K. R., and Drake, S. (1980). Social structure, crime and criminalization: An empirical examination of the conflict perspective. *Sociological Quarterly* 21(Autumn): 563–575.

Wilson, J. Q. (1975). *Thinking About Crime*. Basic Books, New York.

—— (1983). *Crime and Public Policy*. Institute for Contemporary Studies, San Francisco, CA.

Wilson, J. Q., and Boland, B. (1979). *The Effect of the Police on Crime*. U.S. Government Printing Office, Washington, D.C.

Wilson, J. Q., and Bolard, B. (1978). The effect of the police in crime. *Law and Society Review* 12(3): 367–390.

Wilson, J. Q., and Boland, B. (1976). Crime. In *The Urban Predicament*. W. Gorham and N Glazer (Eds.). The Urban Institute, Washington, D.C.

Wold, J. T., and Culver, J. H. (1987). The defeat of the California justices: The campaign, the electorate, and the issue of judicial accountability. *Judicature* 70(6): 348–355.

Worrall, A. (1990). *Offending Women*. Routledge, London and New York.

Wright, K. N. (1985). *The Great American Crime Myth*. Greenwood Press, Westport, CT.

Zamble, E., and Porporino, F. J. (1988). *Coping, Behavior, and Adaptation in Prison Inmates*. Springer-Verlag, New York.

Zillman, D., and Bryant, J. (1989). *Pornography: Research Advances and Policy Considerations*. Lawrence Erlbaum, Hillsdale, NJ.

Zimring, F. E. (1985). Violence and firearms policy. In *American Violence and Public Policy*. L. A. Curtis (Ed.). Yale University Press, New Haven, CT.

Zimring, F. E., and Hawkins, G. (1986). *Capital Punishment and the American Agenda*. Cambridge University Press, Cambridge, New York.

25
Education Policy

Fred S. Coombs

University of Illinois, Urbana-Champaign, Illinois

Education policy is a relative newcomer to policy studies. Only since the 1960s have educational issues intruded with any regularity in Congress or the U.S. Supreme Court. State governments routinely considered funding levels and school recognition issues but left most questions of how to run schools to local district authorities. What treatments there were of policy questions tended to come from the field of educational administration. In the last 30 years, other students of the policy process discovered this sleeping giant that had been all but invisible for so long.

In the 1990 to 1991 school year, about $393 billion (7.2% of our gross national product) was spent on some 3.5 million teachers, 300,000 school administrators, and 115,000 school buildings, as well as books, equipment, and transportation, all committed to the education of our nation's youth. Those teachers taught 60.2 million youngsters; many of the administrators served in one or another of the 15,400 local public school districts that comprise a unique and fascinating part of our national political culture. In all, almost 3 out of every 10 Americans are engaged in a direct way with the U.S. educational system (Grant and Eiden, 1980). This chapter is about the policy side of that huge enterprise: how the resources are sought and allocated and how the interests of the many people involved are expressed in, and shaped by, education policy.

The declaration that there exists a politics of education worthy of systematic study came in Eliot's (1959) article in the *American Political Science Review*. In what Sroufe (1980) characterized as a "modest article, modestly titled," Eliot called attention to the apolitical mystique that had served to render education immune from political inquiry. He then went on to identify several inviting lines of research, including resource procurement, the coping strategies of school administrators, and the tension between lay and professional control of the curriculum.

Two decades later, despite the presence of a growing band of scholars who specialize in the politics of education, one may still question whether there is anything so distinctive about their work as to warrant the designation of a separate field. Peterson (1974) identified the central tenet of much of the politics of education literature ("School policy-formation is conducted autonomously by specialists in the field who are virtually impervious to pressures from external forces.") and suggests that the appeal of this field for many political scientists is the very isolation and autonomy that seems to make it different (p. 350). He goes on, however, to argue that education policy making, when compared with other policy areas, is probably no more autonomous than many others. "In fact," he concludes, "there is no convincing theoretical reason for claiming that educational politics have such a distinctive character that their study requires special analytical, conceptual, and/or methodological tools" (p. 349).

Although it is still difficult to cite compelling theoretical reasons for the emergence of the field, there are more practical incentives for specialization, some of which ultimately may affect the development of theory. First, educational policy making is characterized by extraordinary *complexity*, with thousands of participants working in a staggering array of structural settings. It is laden with its own cultural history, its own legal precedents, its own financial and political arrangements, and its own jargon. It is, in short, a field so vast and varied that attempting to develop some understanding of its nature taxes the abilities of most scholars.

A second characteristic of educational policy is the *visibility* of the educational system and most policy deliberations. By virtue of the simple fact that almost all citizens have been to school and many also have children in school, most believe they have special insight into the realm of education policy. Whereas large segments of the population escape direct contact with the national defense establishment or the public welfare system, relatively few avoid an intimate experience with schooling at some point.

Citizens' exposure to schools, and that of their progeny, heightens their awareness of educational issues (although, in most cases, their knowledge remains limited), and their own experiences color their orientations toward educational policy. The adage in educational circles is that everyone is an "expert" about school policy. There is an underlying distrust of professional expertise that contradicts conventional wisdom and a possessiveness about the operation of public schools that obtains in few other policy sectors.

Third, education, perhaps more than any other policy field, is marked by a *dispersion of authority* (Halperin, 1978). Policy is not only formulated and implemented at multiple levels, but there is also an intricate distribution of authority within levels. U.S. elementary and secondary education policy is made and carried out in a system remarkably disjointed from the policy system for postsecondary education. Different local administrators and boards, different state bureaucracies, and different legislative committees typically govern the two realms.[1]

Even within the elementary and secondary system, one may study educational policy at the classroom, school building, local district, county or regional, state, and federal levels. Each of these strata find well-socialized actors often counterpoised in complex relationship to one another. Whether we examine the interaction of students, parents, teachers, and principals at the building level; superintendents, members of the board of education, and teacher organization leaders at the local school district level; members of the state school board, the governor, legislators, judges, and interest group leaders at the state level; or members of Congress, Supreme Court justices, the Secretary of Education, White House staff, and a powerful education lobby at the federal level; authority is diffuse and decentralized, and accountability is difficult. There is frequent overlap of function both within and between levels of government and duplication of programs is not uncommon.

Fourth, the study of education policy is further complicated by the fact that the educational process itself is marked by multiple objectives and *ambiguity about goals* in most institutional settings. For example, a significant portion of the public believes that our educational system should be more selective, whereas many others believe students should never fail in the ideal system. Similarly, the most important objective for many is the academic preparation of youngsters for college, whereas others put the priority on preparing students for the world of work. This state of affairs, coupled with our primitive knowledge of how to reach even clearly stated goals and the inherent difficulty of evaluating educational outcomes, has kept the study of education policy more descriptive, more historical, and more normative than policy study in some other areas such as health care, agriculture, or public transit.

Educational patterns and priorities differ from one school to the next, in part, because communities differ. Schools in this system of dispersed authority tend to reflect the dominant characteristics of their neighborhoods and communities. This is so because teachers, administrators, board members, and especially students bend the school to the shape of the community. The variety of urban, suburban, and rural neighborhoods across this land has resulted in remarkable variation in our schools (Metz, 1990).

Fifth, education is a *labor intensive* process. Outlays for school buildings, bus transportation, and textbooks are not insigificant expenditures, but personnel costs—for teachers, administrators, and support staff—account for approximately 70% of the budget of most school districts (Grant and Eiden, 1980). Given the prevalence of negotiated reduction-in-force clauses in teacher contracts that protect faculty with seniority, and legal constraints in terminating tenured teachers and administrators, fixed costs are relatively high. Whereas a governor may contemplate cutting highway construction by 40% in a lean fiscal year, cuts of that magnitude are seldom politically feasible in education. Rapidly expanding school enrollments in the 1960s and corresponding enrollment decline in the 1970s and 1980s strongly affected the character of education policy making, but school budgets did not, in general, decline proportionately to enrollment (Odden, 1976: 25–27).

I. EMERGENCE OF THE FIELD OF EDUCATION POLICY STUDIES

In attempting to explain the emergence of the politics of education as a field, Scribner and Englert (1977: 6) trace the development of political science through stages of moral philosophy, legalism, realism, and behavioralism. As they suggest, behavioralism, with its emphasis on theory building, comparison across political systems, and integration among the social sciences, set the stage nicely for the advent of the politics of education as a field of study. By 1980, however, the erstwhile enthusiasm for exploring individual orientation and behavior had turned sharply toward a reexamination of the policy process itself.[2] The advent of a sweeping educational reform in 1983, heralded by a remarkable federal report entitled *A Nation at Risk*, riveted the attention of educational policy researchers on the nature and effects of educational reform. Unflattering comparisons with other nations, most often Japan, in that and subsequent reports induced a spate of new cross-national studies comparing input variables (such as expenditures per pupil, length of the school day or school year, class size, and teacher salaries) and output variables (such as educational attainment or academic achievement) across countries (Stevenson et al., 1986).

The theoretical lineage of educational policy studies comprises several distinct blood-lines. Before political science discovered the field, students of educational administration were doing occasional work which today would qualify as a politics of education (Carter, 1960; Charters, 1953; Counts, 1927). The scientific management orientation of the early 1900s, with its emphasis on finding the "one best way" (Bobbett, 1913; Taylor, 1911) had yielded to bureaucratic models stressing efficiency (Callahan, 1962; Weber, 1946), and then to human relations approaches (Baldridge, 1971) and modern organization theory assuming limited rationality (Cohen et al., 1972; March and Simon, 1958; Weick, 1969). A major component of work in politics of education is still devoted to the analysis of organizations (e.g., schools, classrooms, local school districts, state agencies, or even legislatures) using concepts and propositions from organization theory.

Political scientists, on the other hand, have for the most part eschewed organization theory in favor of theoretical approaches that emphasize the interplay of interests in the allocation process. Among the patron saints, Lasswell (1936) receives more acknowledgments than any other political scientist, but his work is most often cited simply to frame the key question: Who gets what, when, how? Two other aspects of Lasswell's work, the value configuration approach (Lasswell and Kaplan, 1950) and his description of political man rationalizing private motives in terms of the public interest (Lasswell, 1930) have seldom found their way into the politics of education literature. Robert Dahl's pluralist democracy also resonates with much of the research in politics of education. Some scholars conclude that their observations fit a pluralist model, whereas others lament the existence of an alleged monolithic professional elite that does not. Although the section of *Who Governs*? (1960) that deals with the education issue area is somewhat at variance with most other case studies (Peterson, 1974), the framework established by Dahl, with shifting coalitions of competing elites in each issue area, is still a congenial one for many studying the politics of education. The incrementalists (Braybrooke and Lindblom, 1963; Lindblom, 1959, 1965; Wildavsky, 1964) have also been well represented in the politics of education literature, particularly when attention turns to analysis of budgetary processes.

In the background, although now infrequently cited, one can detect the influence of Bentley (1908) in his path-breaking volume that called attention to the role of groups in the governmental process and of Truman (1951), who led the resurgence of group theory in the postwar era. The analysis of the action of interest groups in the development of education policy has served as the basic organizing rubric for scores of case studies (Bailey and Mosher, 1968; Gittel, 1968; Lannaccone and Lutz, 1970; Munger and Fenno, 1962; and Thomas, 1975). The relative influence various interest groups exercised, the strategies they employed, the coalitions they formed, and the manner in which they attempted to maintain their own vitality in the process—these are the topics most politics of education researchers turned to in their attempts to explain why some proposals become policy and others do not.

There has been, however, a loyal opposition. Almond and Coleman's (1960) *The Politics of the Developing Areas* provided the discipline a functional perspective that ultimately influenced much more than comparative politics. Of their functional categories of behavior, interest aggregation and interest articulation still occasionally appear in treatises on politics of education. In the same vein, Easton's (1965) development of systems analysis, building on the work of sociologist Parsons (1951, 1964), provided a perspective quite different from the group theorists. Attention was drawn to the demands being placed on the educational system, the level and source of diffuse support, the conversion process by which inputs (demands and support) become outputs (usually conceived of as policies), feedback from outputs to inputs, and the relationship of the educational system to its environment.

One almost immediate consequence of systems analysis was the rapid accumulation of studies of political socialization during the 1960s. In the early, generally positive socializing experiences of children, political scientists found the source of the diffuse support for the political system that enables it to withstand the particularistic demands of various interests. Attempts to link that socialization process to the policy process through the mediating concept of participation have appeared in political science (Milbrath, 1965; Verba and Nie, 1972). We still know very little, however, about how individuals develop their basic beliefs and values about education, and we know even less about how those basic orientations relate to policy preferences or participation in the formation of education policy.

We should not leave Easton's (1953) name without acknowledging one additional contribution: In *The Political System*, he offered a definition of politics ("the authoritative allocation of values") that most political scientists could rally around. Given such an expansive charge, it was only a matter of time until some of Easton's colleagues began to seek out nonconventional arenas where values are authoritatively allocated. The educational system was almost virgin territory.

The most explicit use of systems analysis in educational policy studies appears in a volume by Wirt and Kirst (1972). Chapter headings ("Schools and System Support," "The Origins and Agents of Demand Inputs," and "The Local Conversion Process: Boards and Subsystems") indicate the manner in which these authors used the framework of systems analysis to organize their survey of the field. With the exception of political socialization research, however, few researchers have gone beyond using the language of systems theory as a means of classifying actions and identifying processes. To date, there has been little work that generates hypotheses suggested by a systems viewpoint or attempts to test them. As Wirt (1977: 401) acknowledges: "Quite frankly, the best theory we now have is only descriptive, i.e., the heuristic framework of 'systems analysis'." Using school policy as a case in point, Wirt provides what he hopes will be a "more dynamic aspect to research" with his observation that "policy originates in the gap between two differing distributions in the society, that of existing resources and that of existing needs" (p. 403). Focus on the disjunction between needs and resources in American schools might, in Wirt's view, illuminate many aspects of the policy-making process.

Policy output analyses (where "output" is defined as expenditures per pupil by state or local governments) using multiple regression techniques were well represented in the educational politics literature of the 1960s and 1970s (Dye, 1966; 1967; Sharkansky, 1968; Zeigler and Johnson, 1972). The prevalent finding from these studies was that "political" variables (e.g., interparty competition, voter turnout, degree of malapportionment of the state legislature, or partisan control of the legislature) have markedly less effect than "economic" variables (e.g., state per capita income, urbanization, or industrialization) on expenditures per pupil.[3] A less discussed finding is that wealthier communities and states tend to spend a smaller portion of their resources for education than their less fortunate counterparts (Bloomberg and Sunshine, 1963; Dye, 1966, 1967).

One far-reaching contribution to theory on policy implementation suggests that the traditional "top-down" model of the implementation process may be dysfunctional in some kinds of policy making (Mazmanian and Sabatier, 1983: Chapters 1 and 2). Current reform proposals often insist on "bottom-up" planning or policy making (see Sizer, 1984). The related concept of "backward mapping" presented by Elmore (1980) has been used often in the education policy literature.

Other themes from political science have made their way into the politics of education field more recently. In his frontal challenge to liberal democracy, *Strong Democracy: Partic-*

ipatory Politics for a New Age, Barber (1984) considers the potential contribution of education vouchers to the participation oriented "strong democracy" he advocates. He suggests some limited experimentation with vouchers because of the need to galvanize citizens with some kind of participation. He warns, however, "Incentives privatize: vouchers transform what ought to be a public question ('What is a good system of public education for *our* children?') into a personal question ('What kind of school do I want for *my* children?')" (pp. 293–297).

Although few researchers have attempted to represent any aspect of the educational policy system by formal models or even by tightly reasoned economic theory such as Downs (1957) provided the field of electoral politics, an important new link with economic theory of the marketplace has developed. The most thorough exposition of this new direction is *Politics, Markets, and America's Schools* (Chubb et al., 1990), in which the authors argue that current attempts at educational reform will fail because they do not address the traditional system of democratic governance in education. Chubb et al. propose a market-based system of parent choice that would create competition between schools for students. This competition would, in their theory, promote greater school autonomy leading to higher-quality schools with increased academic achievement.

The educational policy process and its products has also received strong criticism from the left. The most persistent theme—that public schooling in developed countries reinforces the existing social order—has come largely from sociology (Bourdieu and Passeron, 1970) or economics (Bowles and Gintis, 1976; Carnoy and Levin, 1976) rather than from political science. Criticism of recent education policy and the processes by which it is fashioned may also be found in the work of curriculum theorists (Apple, 1990), critical theorists, and libertarians.

Even more diverse than the theoretical legacy of educational policy research are the methodologies employed. Information gained from traditional case studies, ethnographies, participant observation, cross-sectional surveys, census data, government reports, depth interviewing, and experiments has contributed to what we know about education policy, and analysis has ranged from historical interpretation to statistical testing of hypotheses, multiple regression techniques, and on occasion, time-series analysis and causal modeling. Although a growing band of scholars from both political science and education has converged on education policy in recent years, an interesting contrast exists in the modal research style in each field. Most political scientists, after witnessing decades of case studies that yielded little in the way of cumulative theory, have turned to more systematic, more theoretical studies of the policy process. Many educational researchers, sometimes charged with having provided an embarassingly small and fragile knowledge base and too little practical help for schools despite decades of testing and experimenting, have abandoned the "normal science" tradition in favor of ethnographic or case-study approaches. In their studies, they attempt to impart an intuitive understanding of observed phenomena by describing events in a way the reader can relate to his or her own experience. Exceptions exist, of course, on both sides.

II. FOCUS ON POLICY ANALYSIS

After years of relative neglect, the renewal of attention to policy within the discipline of political science has strongly affected work in the politics of education over the last decade. In fact, Peterson's (1974) identification of policy analysis as the unifying theme in a disparate literature may have been prescient. Yet, policy analysis means different things in different contexts. For most political scientists, policy analysis is any analysis of the process by which policy is made or implemented. In their quest to understand the policy process, analysis that leads to generalizations, then theory, about that process is the goal.

For policy makers in the U.S. Education Department, however, policy analysis is likely to mean identification of the major problems and needs in education that require corrective action—and the establishment of priorities in addressing those problems within the limits of available resources. For a policy analyst working in a state education agency or on the staff of a legislative committee, policy analysis more probably means analysis of a specific policy alternative that has been proposed (perhaps in draft bill form), identifying other viable alternatives, and attempting to foresee the consequences of those alternatives. Although these three kinds of endeavors require some of the same skills and perspectives, they are not the same thing. The unseemly confusion about just what policy analysis is stems from three quite legitimate but different uses of the term.

Note that in the first interpretation, where the primary objective is explanation of the policy process, policy is often viewed as a dependent variable and the search will be for independent variables that bring it about. Thus a finding that variation in expenditures per pupil by state and local governments (viewed as ''policy'') is best accounted for by such variables as per capita income, urbanization, or industrialization (Dye, 1966; 1967) help us better understand the process by which policy is generated, even though educational policy makers are virtually powerless to change any of the independent variables.

In the second and third kinds of policy analyses, however, policy makers are searching for ways to change policy that will, in turn, affect the dependent ''outcome'' variables in desirable ways. If, for example, a state legislator wants to know how to raise the reading comprehension scores of graduating seniors in an urban school district, it may help in understanding the problem to know that economically disadvantaged children generally score lower in reading comprehension, but it will not resolve the problem. He or she still needs to know what can be changed through legislation or school policy that will raise reading scores in that district. Tougher teacher certification laws? Continual assessment programs? More money for remedial programs? Better reading materials and facilities? A more stringent grade promotion policy? These are the kinds of variables that can be manipulated through the policy process, and someone will have to estimate the effects of each to determine which is most likely to bring about the desired change in reading scores.

Better assessment of the extent to which policy at any level affects the amount and nature of student learning is badly needed. As Hawley (1977: 320) puts it, we need more attention ''to issues that go beyond questions of who governs and how governors behave to the straightforward question, 'So what?' '' There is substantial evidence that, in general, the nature of the school one attends has less effect on many educational outcomes, including academic achievement, than the nature of the family one grows up in (Coleman et al., 1966). This is not to suggest that schools do not matter, but it does suggest that the kind of school one attends (at least within the range of those available) may not make as much difference as once thought. Most available studies of the impact of variables such as class size, school facilities, the experience, academic qualifications, or salary of teachers, racial desegregation, or even expenditure per pupil, provide little reassurance that those things have major effect on academic achievement or other desired educational outcomes.

Although many of these studies are flawed, the difficulty of conducting valid impact studies is considerable, in part because such studies inherently require the attribution of the cause of an observed effect to a policy. When outcomes are as difficult to measure as many educational outcomes, all of the familiar problems of causal inference are compounded. Yet the importance of impact studies to the policy analysis enterprise is clear, and they represent one of the most promising areas of research in coming years.

Educational policy analysis has a strong ally in this imposing task. The field of educational evaluation is a relatively mature, sophisticated area that can contribute measurably to the work of the policy analyst. Program evaluation in education has profited from years of experience in the extremely difficult task of measuring educational outcomes. Yet, in his list of 11 factors influencing federal education legislation, based on the judgment of congressional staff members in education, Andringa (1976) ranked program analysis eleventh, two places behind policy research studies and reports. Evaluations may be heeded more often as their authors become better aware of the political context of their assessments. By the same token, it is difficult to imagine any very informative policy analysis that does not address the predicted effects of proposed courses of action on such educational outcomes as academic achievement, school leaving, self-esteem, or employability. Educational program evaluators can contribute in major ways to policy analysis on the impact side.

III. TYPES OF EDUCATION ISSUES

One indication that theory has been slow to develop in education policy studies is the absence of any widely accepted comprehensive typology of education issues. With emerging awareness of the importance of better understanding the kinds of issues likely to arise under specific conditions (Bachrack and Baratz, 1962) and the likelihood and the nature of the political game changes from one type of issue to another (Dahl, 1961), the classification, the categories of financial, curricular, access, personnel, school organization, and governance issues suggest themselves.

Most prevalent among research in education policy are studies of *financial issues* that attempt to answer the question: Who pays, how much, for what? A challenge to the inequities of the real property tax as a major revenue component in funding elementary and secondary education, based on the "equal protection" clause of the Fourteenth Amendment, is one such issue (*Rodriguez* v. *San Antonio School Dist.*, 1973; *Serrano* v. *Priest*, 1971; Wise, 1967).

Because most policy issues have implications for funding, financial considerations will play some part in their political resolution. Proponents of voucher plans in the Bush administration were demanding a radical change in school funding but based their campaign on the premise that parent choice of the school their child attends would serve ultimately to improve the curriculum, pedagogy, and organization of all schools. Other perennial issues are more purely financial in nature. Studies of budgeting, referenda, tax and expenditure limitations, and collective bargaining are examples of research bearing on financial issues. An excellent introduction to educational finance issues is Monk's (1990) *Educational Finance: An Economic Approach*.

A secondary category, *curricular issues*, revolves around the question: What should be taught? Classic among these confrontations over content has been the still-continuing battle between creationists and the scientific community over the treatment of evolution in biology textbooks (Nelkin, 1978). But the genre is broad enough to include skirmishes in many local school districts over the appropriateness of sex education, driver training, or so-called "frills" like art, music, and drama. School boards contemplating graduation requirements or debating the wisdom of adding more vocational courses at the expense of the foreign languages are further examples of curriculum decisions. Studies are now beginning to appear that explore the manner in which curricula are established and the role various institutions such as educational foundations, the business community, and the commercial textbook industry have played in shaping it.

The fuller form of the question might well read What should be taught to whom?, and those last two words point toward a set of what we shall call *access issues*. As industrialized countries have moved inexorably toward universal education, compulsory education laws (usually through age 16) have become the norm. Yet, even these educational systems are faced with selecting certain students for certain kinds of educational experiences.[4] How severe this selection should be, at what age it should take place, and on what basis it should be made are inescapable policy issues in the U.S. system as well as others. Some systems defer selection as long as possible and permit substantial student or parental choice in the matter. Others select students for certain programs relatively early and base the decision on "objective" criteria, such as examinations or grades, rather than the interest or self-assessment of the students. Tracking, ability grouping or streaming, grade repeating, and bilingual programs at the elementary and secondary level as well as admission requirements at the postsecondary level typify issues arising from questions of access.

The most celebrated educational policy decision of our time, the 1954 U.S. Supreme Court school desegregation decision grew out of an access issue. The failure of certain states and school districts to grant children of color admission to historically white schools was deemed unconstitutional because, in denying those children access, they were denied equal protection under the law (Crain, 1968; Orfield, 1978).

A third category of questions may be termed *pedagogical issues*. These issues focus not on the substance of what students should be taught, but on how they should be taught. Most obviously, pedagogical issues arise around the way reading, social studies, or other subjects are taught. Teachers often enjoy considerable latitude with respect to issues of this kind and their resolution may be considered a matter of classroom policy in those cases. But pedagogical issues frequently surface at the school, district, or state level as well. For example, about half of the states have passed legislation that governs the use of corporal punishment in schools. Other aspects of student discipline, such as student suspension policy and student dress codes, will also be codified at either the state or local level. More general questions of school organization will often be argued in terms of how they affect the way students learn. Which schools need to be built and where? Which ones can be closed? Should there be separate middle schools? Should two existing school districts be consolidated? How can students and faculty be racially integrated? These and a raft of other pedagogical problems, including class size, curricular tracking, homogeneous grouping, multiage classrooms, grading, and inclusion of handicapped students into the regular classroom may become public issues to be resolved by the policy process.

The question Who should teach and administer the schools? embraces yet another set of issues. These *personnel issues* have spawned complex certification requirements and tenure laws in every state. Teacher competency tests in many states and attempts to develop and implement a national teacher examination are personnel policy issues that may dramatically affect the nature of the teaching corps. Even the manner in which teachers and administrators are identified and recruited from the pool of qualified candidates and the preparation they receive in our schools of education are important personnel policy questions that shape the teachers and administrators of our nation's schools.

Finally, *governance issues* address the question: Who should make policy and who is accountable for the performance of the educational system? The struggle between those who would centralize the school system and those who would decentralize it has flared sporadically since the late 1960s (Gittell, 1968). Authorities at each level of policy making tend to try to maximize their own discretion and resent incursions by officials at other levels. A fair amount of attention has been given to questions of this order (Cronin, 1976; Hill, 1976; Kirst, 1989), including proposals for new and stronger governance responsibilities for the school site (Guthrie, 1978). Other recurring governance issues have included the question of whether or not state boards of education or Chief State School Officers (CSSOs) should be appointed or elected and the legitimacy of teacher strikes during negotiation.

By 1990, two related governance issues had moved to the forefront of the education reform movement. The first of these, site-based management, would transfer authority for some school policy from the local district to the "site" or school. School councils with parents, residents, teachers, administrators, and sometimes students were the bodies most often endowed with the new responsibilities of governance. The growth of site-based management was, in part, a response to a new wave of effective schools research that emphasized the role of the school principal as an educational leader (rather than manager) who must establish clear academic goals and a school climate conducive to learning in order to raise the academic achievement of students.

The second emerging governance issue, high on the agenda of both national teacher organizations, was teacher empowerment. U.S. teachers had already achieved a fair amount of control over their own salaries, tenure, working conditions, and other "labor" questions through collective bargaining. The teacher empowerment movement pushed for more teacher involvement in important educational policy questions as well—hiring of new teachers, the design of the curriculum, and the selection of textbooks, among others.

IV. THE STRUCTURE OF INTERESTS IN EDUCATION

One way or another, almost everyone is involved in education. Students, teachers, and school administrators are engaged daily in the schooling process. Compulsory education commits most children to at least 10 or 11 years of interaction with teachers and other children—approximately 6 hours a day for 180 days—in a school setting. Many others, including parents, employees, realtors, and taxpayers, have less direct but still important interests in the way that schooling is conducted.

At the root of the erstwhile fiction that education is nonpolitical was the assumption that all actors in the enterprise have the same basic interest: the proper education and welfare of children (Tyack, 1974). Student protests, teacher strikes, and a sharp upturn in voter rejections of school tax increases have disabused us of this notion. We also recognize today that differences among youngsters in their interests, abilities, experiences, motivation, and needs make it likely that a proper education for one will be improper for another. By its very nature, public education is a series of guesses about what would be optimal for a given student and compromises as that student's claim on scarce resources competes with the claims of other students. Teachers, administrators, business, and taxpayers, to name just a few, also have their legitimate claims on the system. The political task, performed at many levels by many people, is to identify these competing claims as accurately as possible and resolve them in ways that leave no significant interest alienated.

If we adopt the simplifying expedient of assuming that people's preferences on issues are identical to their interests,[5] it is not difficult to identify several more or less coherent interest groups in the education realm. Some of these interests are not politically effective, either because they lack consensus, organizational talent, or other political resources. Parents, for example, act like an interest group on only a few kinds of issues, such as expansion or cutting of student aid programs at the college level. On most educational questions they are hopelessly divided. Parent teacher organizations have waged effective campaigns at the national level against sex and violence in television programming and have generally been among the advocates of increased funding of education at the state level. Where general support for schools, administrators, or funds is needed, the local Parent Teacher Association (PTA) can be counted on, but many controversial issues find members of the PTA on both sides in about equal numbers. It has not been an organization that took the lead in demanding changes in school policy (Campbell et al., 1970; Wirt and Kirst, 1972; Zeigler and Jennings, 1974). Recently, parent advocacy groups — most notably the National Committee for Citizens in Education — have organized parents to bring pressure to bear on the education establishment in somewhat more specific ways. The impact of such groups on education policy has been marginal, at best.

One area where parents have demonstrated their effectiveness beyond all doubt is in special education programs. Parents of the handicapped have the incentive to commit necessary time and resources to bring about improvements in special education programs and make them more accessible. In most states, the special education lobby is a force to be reckoned with.

Students, of course, have even more severe problems than parents in operating as an effective interest. There are few issues on which students display strong agreement, and in cases where some consensus does exist, lack of resources hampers effective political action. Even in postsecondary institutions, the experience, political expertise, and resource base of students is in such short supply that long-term influence on institutional policy is rare.

Teachers are a different matter. Their two major organizations, the National Education Association (NEA) and the American Federation of Teachers (AFT) possess all of the attributes of effective interest groups. They enjoy a large, committed membership, organizational talent, ample financial resources, and a clear sense of purpose across a wide range of issues. They have the ability to shape public opinion on some questions and the power to invoke a variety of sanctions, including the strike, when demands are not met. The emergence of these organizations as influential advocates of the interests of teachers at the local, state, and federal levels is one of the most consequential shifts that has taken place in the interest structure of American education since World War II.

To be sure, teachers had some liabilities that historically dampened their impact on education policy. The NEA, heavily influenced by school administrators then in its ranks, ignored many issues that might have benefited teachers in favor of broader professional issues (Iannaccone, 1967; Masters et al., 1964). And the prevailing myth that education was beyond politics weakened the commitment of both men and women teachers to pursue vigorously their own welfare (Rosenthal, 1969; Zeigler and Peak, 1970). In the future, however, the size and resources of American teacher organizations places them among the most influential interests in the policy process. More generally, it is difficult to imagine the implementation of any fundamental reform in American schools without the support of American teachers.

A host of other school-related interests bear on the policy process as well. School administrators formulate and implement policy, but they also have their own interests that are articulated by several professional associations.[6] Similarly, school board members have their own association at the state and federal levels that advise members how to bargain more effectively with teachers on the one hand, even while lobbying hard on numerous issues in legislative circles on the other. Textbook publishers, teacher colleges, athletic booster clubs, and education research foundations are examples of other parts of the diverse education establishment with discernible interests of their own. The interests of minority children in the educational process are represented not only by old-line civil rights organizations, but by an effective array of groups that have grown up around the categorical programs of the Johnson and Carter presidencies.

The local community has its own interest in school policy. Growth-oriented business interests look to the salutary reputation of local schools, coupled with low tax rates, to attract new residents and corporate investments. The construction industry profits from new school building programs and realtors have long recognized the intimate relationship between school location and residential housing patterns, including the social class and racial composition of neighborhoods.

Finally, we must acknowledge the broadest interest of all in terms of numbers of people affected. Schools cost money, and the revenues slated for education are a significant proportion of that paid by taxpayers in all states. Despite the argument by some professional educators that if something is sound educationally it should not matter how much it costs, taxpayers have an understandable interest in the education budget. They may mobilize episodically, during bond or tax increase referenda, or perhaps in support of particularly frugal candidates for the school board. Taxpayer associations are among the most potent lobbying groups in many state capitals and can be counted on to challenge major new educational programs on grounds of fiscal responsibility.

V. COMPETING EDUCATIONAL VALUES: QUALITY, EQUITY, AND EFFICIENCY

One objective of policy studies is to elucidate the relationship between policy alternatives and underlying values (Wirt, 1977). The values served by education policies are many and varied, but in political discourse that attempts to justify a preference for one alternative over another, three values stand out among the others.

The first value perceived to be at stake in many educational issues is *quality* or excellence. Of course, quality is even harder to define and measure in education than in many other policy fields, since a quality program for one student may not be a quality program for another. The term is not entirely devoid of meaning, however. In general usage, "quality" connotes educational programs that emphasize academic achievement, highly qualified teachers and administrators, and restricted access to weed out students ill-suited to a course or program while allowing the most able to realize their full potential.

Other education policies, including many introduced at the state and federal level in the 1960s, are justified primarily on the basis of *equity*. American educators have always prided themselves on the promotion of "equality of educational opportunity" in this society. It is clear, however, that geographical disparities—between states and between local districts within states—in the kind of education provided are greater in American education than in many of the economically developed nations of the world. Much of this inequality is traceable to the reliance of elementary and secondary education on the real property tax that may yield many times the revenue per pupil in the wealthiest districts as in the poorest districts (Wise, 1967). State (and, to a lesser extent, federal) contributions have gone some appreciable distance toward equalizing revenue per pupil, but the gap between the amounts spent on pupils in wealthy districts and pupils in poor districts remains large.

Many educational programs and policies have been devised to alleviate such inequities. School aid formulas in most states provide proportionately more assistance to poorer districts. By far the largest federal education program, in terms of dollars expended, was Title I of the Elementary and Secondary Education Act of 1965 (reauthorized as Chapter 1 of the Education Consolidation and Improvement Act) that provides supplemental assistance to schools with a high proportion of economically and educationally disadvantaged pupils. Head Start, Follow Through, the Education for All Handicapped Children Act, Title IX, school desegregation, and the Bilingual Education Act are just a few of the other major programs that have been justified primarily on grounds of equality. In higher education, Pell grants (formerly Basic Educational Opportunity Grants) and the guaranteed student loan program provided many students who might otherwise have been denied the chance an opportunity for postsecondary education.

The value of *efficiency* injects the element of cost into policy deliberations. Cost, it should be pointed out, is a consideration that runs against the grain for a good part of the education community. As already suggested, teachers, administrators, and parents often take the position that if a program has been shown to be good for the education of children, it should be pursued, irrespective of the cost. Yet, the implementation of most education policies requires money, and there are trade-offs to be considered both within local districts, where the allocation of finite resources requires a judgment about which programs will yield greater benefits for the money, and at the state and federal levels, where education competes with other sectors, such as public health, social welfare, and energy conservation, for a larger share of the budget.

A precise definition of efficiency would focus on the ratio of a program's benefits to its costs (McMahon, 1980; Nagel, 1980). Interests that invoke the value of efficiency, however, tend to emphasize the costs. The usual instinct of efficiency-minded individuals is to "cut the fat out" of education budgets, rather than to attempt to improve efficiency by increasing the output at little or no additional cost. In actual practice, such program cuts often involve trimming back art and music from the curriculum or extracurricular activities.

At the federal level, fraught with budget deficits and sluggish growth, "efficiency" concerns vied with "quality" in the period from 1980 through 1992. During this era, the value of efficiency was even more evident at the state and local levels, as state after state experienced tax rebellions fueled by the rising unpopularity of local property taxes. The ultimate effect of many of these skirmishes was to shift responsibility for primary funding of education from the local district to the state.

One could easily suggest other values—"community" (Peshkin, 1978), "liberty" (Guthrie, 1980), or "local control" (Wirt, 1977)—for our list, but most issues are debated with reference to "quality," "equity," or "efficiency." Sometimes the question is which of two or more alternatives will provide the greatest benefits in one of these value areas (i.e., which will improve the quality of schooling more: reducing class size or giving teachers more released time?). At other times, the issue pits one value against another. Court desegregation orders, based on the principle of equity, are attacked for lowering the quality of education provided or for raising its costs through expensive (i.e., inefficient) busing plans (Crain, 1968; Orfield, 1978). School closings, proposed by boards and administrators as a way to lower costs during periods of enrollment decline (efficiency), are opposed for the alleged damage wrought to quality programs in existing neighborhood schools. State or national testing programs, proposed with an eye toward improving academic standards (quality), are criticized for discriminating against minority students (equity). Why and how these three values, or others, are used in the justification of policy positions in education has received very little empirical attention. There is a need for policy research, in education as in other fields, to clarify and elaborate the linkages between values and policy (Guthrie, 1980; McMahon, 1980; Merritt and Coombs, 1977; Wirt, 1977).

VI. LOCAL EDUCATION POLICY

By dint of omission, the U.S. Constitution leaves education to the states. State legislatures, however, have typically passed much of their constitutional authority on to local school boards, and there are few places in the U.S. political system where the norm of local control has been as strong. School officials in local school districts continue to make a wide range of policy decisions affecting in important ways the nature and quality of a child's educational experience as he or she moves through that community's public schools. Although it is true that the discretion of local education authorities has in recent years been narrowed by state and federal intervention, it is also the case that local boards and administrators continue to exercise substantial control over the nature of the teaching staff, the number, size, and location of schools, the list of courses offered, textbooks used in those courses, extracurricular activities offered, student discipline, grading, graduation and promotion requirements, and a host of other policy concerns (Sergiovanni et al., 1980).

The typical structural arrangement is a local school district, delegated authority by the state, and governed by an elective lay board of education.[7] That board appoints a superintendent of schools to provide leadership in the day-to-day operation of the district. In point of fact, many superintendents exercise substantial policy influence simply by bringing certain questions to the board while skirting other potential issues.

Much of the policy studies literature in education at the local level addresses the "who governs" question. Particularly intriguing to scholars in this area has been the relationship between school boards and superintendents. Zeigler and Jennings (1974) list an assortment of useful political resources available to each camp but find a general tendency for boards to remain overly passive, even on clearly political questions, when confronted with the professional expertise of the superintendent. "School boards should govern or be abolished," they contend, in a system that cherishes lay control but often supports a professional elite characterized as relatively impervious to outside pressures (p. 254).

Iannaccone and Lutz (1970) point to a mechanism that, over time, gives the community some measure of control even though the policy process may appear to be closed at any given point in time. The pattern, known as incumbent defeat, begins with some significant change in the socioeconomic composition of the community that leads to heightened conflict in school board elections, and finally to defeat of an incumbent board member. A change in the control of the board follows, followed by the resignation or dismissal of the superintendent and replacement by a new one better attuned to the values of the new board. Such a process reintroduces the possibility of system responsiveness to strong public dissatisfaction, even without citizens monitoring the board's every move and providing input before each meeting.

Another useful concept in assessing the relative influence of boards, superintendents, and publics is what McGivney and Moynihan (1972) call the zone of tolerance. This is a range of activity that will be tolerated by the dominant elements of the public. It is possible that both boards and superintendents jockey for position within this zone (or their perception of the zone) but attempt not to stray outside it to avoid loss of public confidence and, perhaps, the incumbent defeat syndrome.

Closely related to the zone of tolerance notion is another concept that political scientists may recognize as one introduced by Friedrich (1946) some years ago—the law of anticipated reaction. This dictum, when applied to education, says that boards and superintendents attempt to anticipate the reactions of the lay pubilc to contemplated policy alternatives, pursuing only those for which the anticipated reaction is favorable, or at least not too threatening. Similarly, superintendents may attempt to anticipate the reactions of board members before structuring agendas or making recommendations to the board. The significance of this is that publics may exercise power over boards, and boards over superintendents, simply by virtue of their reputations, and in a manner that a researcher attempting to observe influence attempts might miss entirely (Boyd, 1976).

Although some researchers believe the school system is capable of responding (albeit in rather ponderous fashion) to shifts in majority sentiment of the laity, less can be said about its responsiveness to minority interests (Boyd, 1976). The demand for local control of schools, pressed most strenuously by African-Americans during the late 1960s and early 1970s, has met resistance from entrenched administrators, incumbent board members, and teacher organizations alike (Fantini et al., 1970; Gittell and Hollander, 1968). The irony is that minority interests historically have been best served in U.S. education by higher levels of authority. Local school districts have seldom placed equity concerns at the top of their list, and recent advances in school desegregation, compensatory education for the disadvantaged, bilingual education, and special education have usually come at the instigation of federal or state government.

When one incorporates the public into our consideration of "who governs," still other questions are raised. Mann (1977: 71) points out that citizens may control either through participation or through representation. But how representative are school boards (usually elected in low information, low turnout, and often uncontested elections) of their constituents? To what extent do school board members agree with constituents on their role as trustee or delegate, the importance of issues, or on referred resolutions to those issues (Zeigler, 1974)? Although a community unhappy with the performance of its public schools can still bring about policy changes, Wirt (1975) suggests several trends that have reduced the responsiveness of local school boards to public demand, including increased state and federal intervention, increased competition among interest groups, greater differention of political cultures, and the intensification of professionalism. But how can elected board members in ever larger school districts know what is valued by their constituents? In recent years, we have begun to accumulate more systematic data bearing on the public's educational values, their beliefs about education, and their preferences on certain current issues (see the annual Gallup survey of the public's stance on educational issues published each September since 1978 in *Phi Delta Kappan*). Our understanding of how these citizen orientations develop, change, relate to each other, and ultimately affect the policy process is still inadequate.

One special case of citizen input that has received sustained scholarly attention is the school referendum. As indicated above, the U.S. school system has relied heavily on a locally assessed real property tax for revenue. The importance to school districts of passing tax increases and bond referenda has made the maintenance of general public support for school programs a high priority for both professional administrators and school board members. Research on the question of why referenda pass or fail has yielded somewhat mixed findings (Drachler, 1977: 205–209). Voters of lower socioeconomic status are less likely to vote in school referenda but, in general, the poor, less educated, older voter, and the voter with no children in public school, is less likely to support the referenda when they do vote (Elam, 1973). Furthermore, school referenda are seldom pure tests of public support for local schools. The specifics of the proposal, prevailing economic conditions, and the public mood with respect to the overall tax burden are inextricably entwined with general support for schools.

The most prominent change in the power structure of many districts has been the emergence of teacher organizations as effective political forces. Much of their influence is exercised through the medium of collective bargaining, which provides a means of pressing their demands across an array of perennial issues, including salary and fringe benefits, class size, work conditions, and discipline policy. The rapid growth of the AFT and its success in organizing new districts forced the NEA to adopt a more militant posture with respect to collective bargaining and work actions. In those districts that bargain collectively, the power equation now finds board members and administrators on one side of the bargaining table and teachers on the other.

Precisely who has benefited more from the advent of collective bargaining is still a matter of some dispute (Odden, 1977). Whereas early studies showed that collective bargaining had minimal influence on teachers salaries, a report by Chambers (1976) indicates that collective bargaining can increase mean teacher salaries by as much as 15%. Bargaining has reduced the traditional discretion of superintendents and board members in certain key policy areas (Shedd, 1990). School board associations, including the parent National School Board Association (NSBA), have strenuously opposed collective bargaining. In many districts that have adopted collective bargaining, the role of the superintendent has changed from advocate of the rights and interests of teachers before the board of education to representative of the board in day-to-day contacts with teachers. Although it seems reasonable to assume that collective bargaining may have brought about subtle shifts in the way teachers are perceived by the public, there has not yet been adequate assessment of the manner in which bargaining has affected diffuse public support for teachers, schools, or the character of the policy process at the local level.

VII. EDUCATION POLICY AT THE STATE LEVEL

Nowhere in the entire spectrum of education policy are things changing more rapidly than at the state level. Although the most recent reform is associated with the publication of *A Nation at Risk* (National Commission on Excellence in Education, 1983), the leadership for that reform came from the states. Governor after governor pushed reform legislation through usually enthusiastic state legislatures as education reform became not only politically acceptable but politically indispensable. At the same time, most states assumed a larger share of the funding burden from local districts. Federal aid was increasingly channeled to schools through the state administrative apparatus. "Flow-through" funds of this sort offer little additional discretion to state officials but have bolstered the state education bureaucracy significantly.

State legislatures have long been center stage in the formulation of education policy at this level, and the transformation in the composition and operation of the legislative branch of state government since World War II has been profound. Even as reapportionment during the 1960s made them more representative, the workload expanded in many state legislatures to make legislating a more or less full-time job. As the number of bills each session increased, specialization was fostered, with some legislators becoming education specialists. Professional staff support for major education committees and political parties became available in many states.

On the executive side, governorships have moved toward 4-year terms and more authority in fiscal matters. The education bureaucracy has expanded rapidly. Chief State School Officers are increasingly appointed from the ranks of the profession rather than elected, and the agencies they administer have been among the fastest growing in many state capitals.

State boards of education, elected in some states but more generally appointed, initiate more legislation and exercise control over a wide range of lesser policy matters that do not require legislative action.

Iannaccone (1967) drew from the works of Bailey (1962), Masters (1964), and Usdan (1963) to construct a typology of prevailing linkages between education structures at the state level. Looking specifically at the political activities of school administrators, professional education groups, and school board associations as they influenced the decision making of legislatures in 11 previously studied states, Iannaccone concluded that four types of relationship were observable. The first pattern, found in New England and labeled "disparate," was characterized by provincialism, localism, and defense of the home district against outsiders and central government. The second pattern, "state-wide monolithic," was found in New York, New Jersey, and Rhode Island. This product of closed-system politics, presumed to be the modal type, finds compromise taking place among the education interest groups rather than in the legislature. When cracks occur within the education establishment, as happened in Michigan and California, a "fragmented" pattern may emerge, with education interest groups forming coalitions and aligning with kindred political parties while the legislature assumes a more critical stance. The "syndical" pattern, found only in Illinois, employed a special governmental body, with legislators among its members, to plan, sift, compromise, and recommend education policy to the legislature (p. 41).

The dominant education issue at the state level is the amount of funding to be made available for education in the next fiscal year and the way that sum is to be divided among the various parts of the education establishment. Education issues involving money get the most attention, and those who hold the purse strings tend to make the decisions on education in the states (Rosenthal and Furman, 1980). Particularly important in recent years have been controversies over the shape of the school aid formula, the division of funds between K–12 schools and higher education, and the extent of state support for private education. Meanwhile, legislators in many states, alarmed by sharp increases in property taxes at the local level and sales and income taxes at the state level, have considered and sometimes imposed tax limitations designed to check the burgeoning costs of education. California led the movement some have characterized as a tax revolt with Proposition 13, and several other states have followed suit. More recently, attention has turned to expenditure limitations where constitutional or statutory provisions are passed capping education budgets.

Aside from performing the function of resource allocation, state governments also perform a regulatory function (deciding the standards by which teachers may be certified, for example) and provide numerous services to local districts. In the larger states, each major area of the curriculum is represented by consultants and other service people at the state level available to provide support to local teachers and administrators.

Fiscal issues were not the only ones surfacing at the state level, however. In nonurban areas of the country, there was a consolidation of local districts, stimulated by the desire for greater efficiency and the provision of higher-quality education in larger schools that could assemble a critical mass of students facilities and staff. Only occasionally has a case been made for the latent functions of the small rural school in the community it serves (Peshkin, 1978). The most visible current issue in many states are the growing demands for accountability in the educational process. Proposals for raising academic standards range from systematic assessment of student progress, to standardized state-imposed graduation tests that must be passed by a student before he or she can graduate from high school.

The current reform movement is only one reason that momentum has moved toward the states in the interplay of local, state, and federal authorities. Local dissatisfaction with high taxes has had the effect of increasing the state's contribution in some states. One consequence of that trend has been the assumption of more control for those states over new facets of education policy. At the same time, federal programs have been cut severely and the new philosophy in Washington favors block grants that give increased discretion to state authorities over categorical programs targeted for specific uses or populations. Several social changes, including increased within-state and between-state migration and communication, argue for an augmented state role in the educational enterprise.

VIII. THE FEDERAL ROLE

Although the quantum leap in federal education activity did not come until the mid-1960s, several pieces of legislation prior to World War II served as major stimulis to the development of state and local efforts (Thomas, 1975). The passage of the Lanham Act in 1940 authorizing the construction, maintenance, and operation of schools in federally "impacted" areas and the Serviceman's Readjustment Act (GI Bill of Rights) in 1944 both signaled a new federal willingness to aid education as a means of attacking other problems. The soaring birth rates following the end of the war, coupled with the precedent of 7.8 million veterans being directly assisted by the federal government, placed a strain on the educational system from preschool through graduate school and virtually guaranteed the continued involvement of the federal government in what had previously been an almost exclusively state and local preserve (p. 20).

The National Science Foundation Act (1950) established a precedent for federal support for educational research while P.L. 81-815 (for school construction) and P.L. 81-874 (for operating expenses) extended categorical aid to impacted areas in a continuation of the principle of the Lanham Act. The U.S. Supreme Court ruling in Brown v. *The Board of Education* (1954) was destined to involve the federal courts and the Department of Justice in hundreds of local school desegregation cases across the country. By 1958, the national preoccupation was with Sputnik I, and Congress responded with the National Defense Education Act (P.L. 85-864) designed to enhance the national security through better education. The Cooperative Research Act (P.L. 83-531) of 1954, the Higher Education Facilities Act (1958), the Vocational Education Act (1963), and the Library Construction and Services Act (1954) were other instances of legislation that set the stage for the massive Elementary and Secondary Education Act (ESEA) and the Higher Education Act (HEA) in 1965.

In an insightful paper summarizing a number of characteristics of educational policy making at the federal level, Halperin (1978) points out that federal initiates in education are almost never justified as aid to improve education, per se, but are usually attempts to accomplish some noneducation goal through educational means. Most federal programs, in fact, owe their existence to external social forces rather than the efforts of educators, and many of the most influential programs have come from noneducation congressional committees and noneducation agencies in the executive branch.

Much education policy in Washington is arrived at in relatively nonpartisan fashion; in fact, most congressmen pay relatively little attention to it, and only a handful have emerged as specialists in this policy area. Even presidents who have included educational themes in their campaigns devote little attention to the topic once in the White House. Over 500 educational programs are scattered so widely that no one speaks for education. One could defend the claim, in fact, that there is very little federal education policy, in the broader sense, but rather hundreds of uncoordinated programs and policies.

A major shift in the federal role did occur with the Reagan and Bush administrations with the explicit disavowal of the large, relatively expensive federal programs of their predecessors and their attempts to exercise national "leadership" in educational matters by using the "bloody pulpit" available to the president or the secretary of education (Boyd, 1990: 45). A reluctant Democratic Congress refused to eviscerate most of the programs, but diminished funding tipped the balance even further away from Washington. Of the two central themes that emerged from the federal attempt at leadership, one resonated and one did not. The quest for higher curricular standards appears to have taken root with state leaders and a sympathetic public, and by 1992, the reform had turned sharply in this direction. Proposals for parent choice among both public and private schools, on the other hand, face a much less certain future during the Clinton administration.

Education interests are well-represented in Washington, and much of the lobbying centers around the quest for more munificent funding of programs rather than questions of educational philosophy. A loosely structured coalition of interests called the Committee for Educational Funding meets periodically to coordinate their individual assaults on Congress and the national treasury.

Mention of the role of the courts is, of course, most appropriate when discussing federal policy, although judicial intervention in education has also taken place at the state and local levels. A series of cases, including *Brown* v. *The Board of Education* (racial desegregation), *Lau* v. *Nichols* (bilingual education), and Pennsylvania Association for Retarded Children (special education) have dramatically shaped the educational issues of our lifetimes. In education, as in other areas, the U.S. Supreme Court has given new meaning to the term *judicial activism*. It remains to be seen whether an era of judicial restraint is on the horizon (Van Geel, 1977).

The relationship between federal education programs and their state counterparts is not always an easy one. At the time of the passage of the Elementary and Secondary Education Act in 1965, there was general acknowledgment that most states did not have the administrative wherewithall to implement large new federal programs. As a consequence, much federal aid was channeled directly to local districts, even while an attempt was made to bolster the capacity of states to administer such programs in the future. At present, it appears that the tide may have turned. State-initiated reform, especially in school finance and special education domains, was the rule rather than the exception in the 1970s (Odden et al., 1976: 27-28). This shift created a compelling need for greater attention to intergovernmental relationships to assure that categorical aid from the federal government complemented the various forms of equalizing formulas enacted by the states. It can be argued that federal initiatives like impact aid (P. L. 874), Title I of ESEA, and The Education of All Handicapped Children (P.L. 94-142), actually had unintended disequalizing effects (Odden et al., 1976: 28-29) because they served as a disincentive to states to build equity considerations into their own programs.

The Reagan years saw a rapid increase in expenditures for elementary and secondary education from state and local sources but a decrease in federal expenditures. Between 1981 and 1988, the budget of the Department of Education decreased from 0.6% of the gross national product (GNP) to 0.4%, and the federal share of all expenditures for elementary and secondary education dropped from 8.7 to 6.2% (Clark and Astuto, 1990: 11). Even more significant was a dramatic shift in the federal policy agenda toward programs that attempted to foster competition both between schools (e.g., by publicizing student achievement scores by school, school districts, and states) and between individuals (e.g., by individual awards and recognition to encourage excellence). Other elements of the Reagan education program included an emphasis on performance standards for teachers and students, emphasis on traditional academic areas of the curriculum, parental choice, and character development to strengthen traditional values (Clark and Astuto, 1990: 14–15).

Despite the fact that George Bush laid claim to the title of "education president" during the presidential campaign of 1988, his administration essentially continued the policies of the Reagan administration in both their budgetary and ideological aspects. The chasm between a Democratic Congress and Republican administrations continued to grow, with the Congress intent on salvaging the heart of the categorical programs and both administrations pushing to cut those programs or let them devolve to the states. If attacks by the secretary of education on existing policies and practices became somewhat less strident, the sponsoring of an Education 2000 initiative to develop "break the mold" schools across the country and the president's erratic drumbeat in support of public and private school choice continued along the new course the Reagan operatives had charted.

IX. THE ROAD AHEAD IN EDUCATION POLICY STUDIES

As of this writing, the U.S. education system is experiencing sharp discontinuities that may significantly alter the nature of education policy making and even public schooling itself. As has been the case throughout our history, these changes are responses by the education system to broader changes in the social and economic orders. The most recent challenge has been to educate future generations in ways that will ensure the competitiveness of the United States in a quickly changing global economy. If the argument of human capital theorists that investments in human resources will pay dividends in economic productivity went virtually unheard for decades, it now seems to fuel the reform. The Clinton administration is not only reinforcing the movement of its Republican predecessors toward more rigorous academic standards, but it plans to invest heavily in the vocational training and retraining of underemployed workers.

Demography itself plays a seminal role in shaping school policy. The rapid decline in the birth rate during the mid-1960s and early 1970s reversed the precipitous growth in school enrollments that had been in progress since World War II. Suddenly the teacher shortage became a teacher surplus. Almost as quickly, school boards were faced with closing buildings proudly built a mere decade before. School districts whose local tax sources were supplemented by enrollment-sensitive state formulas found state aid declining. Scholars of school finance who had assumed growth was the normal condition turned to studies of retrenchment. Business managers accustomed to thinking in terms of incremental budgeting now worried about budget decrements. Legislatures and school boards who had been practicing distributive politics now were faced with the more difficult task of redistributive politics (Lowi, 1964).

As enrollments began a slow expansion again in the 1980s and early 1990s, the policy agenda changed again. New patterns of teacher education were proposed (Holmes Group, 1986) as college students returned to teacher preparation programs. Whatever the future may hold for birth rates, the demographical certainty is that the U.S. population in the 1990s will be proportionately older. This shift has implications for the structure of the educational establishment, with relatively more resources going to education beyond the traditional schooling years. It may also portend an increasingly difficult competition with other policy sectors for local, state, and federal dollars. The demands of older citizens will be for more security, better health care, and an assortment of services other than education. Their greater numbers may translate fairly readily into greater political influence.

Enrollments were not the only thing that had grown during the boom years since World War II. Even after discounting inflation, educational expenditures per pupil increased five-fold between 1950 and 1975 (Guthrie, 1980: 46) and continued their ascent right through the Reagan and Bush years. Class size has been reduced and many educational programs and specializations have been added. Tens of thousands of school buildings were constructed. Yet, one can document no dramatic improvement in educational outcomes over this period; in fact, if one accepts standardized test scores as valid indicators of school performance, we may have lost ground (Flanagan, 1976; Munday, 1980).

The combination of demographical shifts, skyrocketing costs, educational reform, and meager evidence of improving quality of education in our schools has created a volatile political climate for education. The costs of certain equity-based policies of the 1960s, including busing for racial desegregation and the development of state equalization formulas, has been high in terms of the support of many middle-class citizens. The promise of higher quality through educational reform has yet to bear demonstrable fruit. A public and political leaders increasingly disenchanted with the performance of their public schools are casting about for alternatives.

One last change in the environment in which educational policy changes takes place should be noted. Over much of our national history, we have looked to education as the solution to all social and economic and political problems. As noted earlier, federal programs have almost always been instrumental in character—attempting to use education to eradicate poverty, banish racial prejudice, develop a better space program, or restore U.S. economic competitiveness in the world marketplace. Repeated disillusionments have led to a more guarded, and doubtless more realistic, assessment of the role of education in creating basic social and economic reform (Carnoy and Levin, 1976).

The implications of all of this for the study of education policy are several. First, if things change so rapidly, it is doubtful that much that we think we know about how education policy is formulated will be true 20 years from now. Tensions between the profession and the lay public will change in character as both the profession and the orientations of the public change. Relationships between the various levels of educational policy making may change dramatically. It is difficult to identify laws, propositions, or even common knowledge that we confidently believe will survive these changes.

The need, first of all, is for more basic research on education policy. Impatience with the limited payoff of basic research in education to date has prompted some to suggest that research efforts should be redirected toward applied research that would yield immediate dividends in the improvement of schools. There is, however, no certain way to improve educational outcomes without improving our knowledge of the policy process.

The problem is not that we have had too little basic research but that it has not usually been policy relevant. Basic research probing the linkages between the preferences of constituents and the policy process (Tucker and Zeigler, 1980) is needed, as is research that establishes better the link between educational policy and changes in educational outcomes (Hawley, 1977).

For basic research to be policy relevant, it is necessary to identify variables that are alterable through policy change and that will also bring about the kind of educational outcomes we seek. Until we have a much better idea of how interventions are likely to affect a student's academic achievement, conduct, attitudes (including educational aspirations), or access to continued schooling, for example, policy analysis is likely to continue to be a sometimes futile exercise.

There is also a need for research that is more theoretical if we are to better understand the conditions under which certain of our findings no longer obtain (Burlingame and Geske, 1979). One consequence of the school improvement focus of most educational research has been an almost total neglect of the theories which may, ironically, ultimately provide the best hope for school improvement.

Methodologically, there is a lacuna between shelves of single case studies on the one hand and a smaller number of policy output studies using all 50 states to determine the correlates of educational expenditures. Multiple case studies (Burlingame and Geske, 1979) and even larger studies comparing schools, districts, or states on selected policy-relevant variables are badly needed at this point to elaborate and test our prototheory.

One implication of these observations is that students of educational policy will probably not be able to do the job alone. Attention to the demographic, social, or economic changes that precipitate changes in education policy will require expertise from specialists in those areas. Closer examination of the impact of education policy on students will require methodological sophistication and intuition about schooling more likely to be found among educational researchers. Knowledge of the policy process alone leaves us far short of the capability to foresee changes in the environment that will stimulate new policy proposals, to predict the educational outcomes of proposed alternatives with confidence, and to make timely adjustments. Education policy analysis will have come of age when its theories and its methods are equal to that task.

ACKNOWLEDGMENTS

The author is indebted to Marcia K. Chicoine for bibliographical assistance and constructive comments on the first edition of this chapter, and to Catherine E. Wycoff for similar assistance on the second edition.

NOTES

1. See Peterson (1974) for an excellent discussion of the political aspects of higher education.
2. We should note that the behavior movement was largely directed at explaining relatively discreet behavior, like voting, by invoking other individual attributes (e.g., demographic variables) or psychological orientations (e.g., attitudes, beliefs, or values). Ironically, the conceptual elaboration of these "explanatory" variables far outstripped our still rudimentary classificatory schemes for political behavior itself (Milbrath, 1965). More useful ways of conceptualizing political behavior are still needed before we can proceed very far in our current attempts to explain policy output.
3. See Peterson (1974) for thoughtful critique of examples of comparative policy output analysis in the education area.
4. Selection in Europe historically has been earlier and more severe than in the United States, but reforms in many countries have virtually eliminated England's "11 plus" examination and its functional equivalents in other countries. Access issues also include the existence of courses or curricula to which some students are not admitted for reason of ability, age, or sex.
5. Although Truman (1953) defined interests as attitudes, it would seem more straightforward in relating them to the policy process if we focused on specific preference on a given issue; that is, all individuals who favor granting tuition tax credits share an interest on that issue. This notion of subjective interest will be of greater utility in policy studies than the concept of objective interest.
6. The American Association of School Administrators (AASA) is the most influential, with some 18,000 members, many of them superintendents. Other groups are the National Association of Secondary School Principals (NASSP) and the National Elementary School Principals Association (NESPA).

7. School boards in a number of our largest cities are appointed by the mayor. In many of these cities, the separation of city governance and educational governance typical of most localities is much less absolute.

REFERENCES

Almond, G. A., and Coleman, J. S. (Eds.) (1960). *The Politics of the Developing Areas*. Princeton University Press, Princeton, NJ.

Allison, G. T. (1969). Conceptual models and the Cuban missile crisis. *The American Political Science Review* 63: 689–718.

Andringa, R. C. (1976). Eleven factors influencing federal education legislation. In *Federalism at the Crossroads*: *Improving Educational Policymaking*. George Washington University, Washington, D.C., pp. 79–80.

—— (1976). The view from the hill. In *Federalism at the Crossroads*: *Improving Educational Policymaking*. George Washington University, Washington, D.C., pp. 71–78.

Apple, M. W. (1990). What reform talk does: Creating new inequalities in education. In *Education Reform*: *Making Sense of It All*. S. B. Bacharach (Ed.). Allyn and Bacon, Boston.

Bacharach, S. B. (Ed.) (1990). *Education Reform*: *Making Sense of It All*. Allyn and Bacon, Boston.

Bachrack, P., and Morton, S. B. (1962). Two faces of power. *American Political Science Review* 56 (December): 947–952.

Bailey, S. K., and Mosher, E. K. (1966). *ESEA*: *The Office of Education Act of 1965*. Inter-University Case Program #100. Bobbs-Merrill, Indianapolis, IN.

Baldridge, J. V. (1971). The analysis of organizational change: A human relations strategy versus a political system strategy. R & D memo ~75, Stanford Center for R & D in Teaching, Stanford University.

Barber, B. R. (1984). *Strong Democracy*: *Participatory Politics for a New Age*. University of California Press, Berkeley, CA.

Bentley, A. R. (1908). *The Process of Government*. University of Chicago Press, Chicago.

Berke, J. S., and Kirst, M. W. (1972). *Federal Aid to Education*. Lexington Books, Lexington, MA.

Bloomberg, W., Jr., and Sunshine, M. (1963). *Suburban Power Structures and Public Education*. Syracuse University Press, Syracuse, NY.

Bobbitt, F. (1913). The supervision of city schools: Some general principles of management applied to the problems of city school systems. In *Twelfth Yearbook of the National Society for the Study of Education*. National Society for the Study of Education, Bloomington, IL.

Bourdieu, P., and Passeron, J. C. (1970). *La Reproduction*: *Elements pour une Theorie du Systeme d'Enseinement*. Editions de pour Minuit, Paris.

Bowles, S., and Gintis, H. (1976). *Schooling in Capitalist America*: *Educational Reform and the Contradictions of Economic Life*. Basic Books, New York.

Boyd, W. L. (1976). The public, the professionals, and educational policy making: Who governs? *Teachers College Record* 77 (May): 539–577.

—— (1990). How to reform schools without half trying: Secrets of the Reagan administration. In *Education Reform*: *Making Sense of It All*. S. B. Bacharach (Ed.). Allyn and Bacon, Boston.

Braybrooke, D., and Lindbloom, C. E. (1963). *A Strategy of Decision*. Free Press, New York.

Broudy, H. S. (1965). Conflict in values. In *Educational Administration—Philosophy in Action*. R. Ohm and W. Monohan (Eds.). University of Oklahoma, College of Education, Norman, Oklahoma.

Burlingame, M., and Geske, T. G. (1979). State politics and education: An examination of selected multiple-state case studies. *Educational Administration Quarterly* 15 (Spring): 50–75.

Burnsed, B., Rep. (1980). Higher education: Legislative issues in the 80's. State Legislatures. 6 (September): 21–25.

Callahan, R. (1962). *Education and the Cult of Efficiency*. University of Chicago Press, Chicago.

Campbell, R. F., and Mazzoni, T. L., Jr. (1976). *State Policy Making for the Public Schools.* McCutchen, Berkeley, CA.

Campbell, R., Cunningham, L., McPhee, R. F., and Nystrand, R. (1970). *The Organization and Control of American Schools.* Merrill, Columbus, Ohio.

Carnoy, M., and Levin, H. M. (1976). *The Limits of Educational Reform.* David McKay, New York.

Carter, R. F. (1960). *Voters and Their Schools.* Institute for Communication Research, Stanford, CA.

Chambers, J. G. (1976). The impact of bargaining on the earnings of teachers: A report on California and Missouri. Paper presented to the U.K.-U.S. Conference on Teacher Markets, University of Chicago, December.

Charters, W. W. (1953). Social class analysis and the control of public education. *Harvard Educational Review* 23: 268-283.

Chubb, J. E., and Moe, Terry M. (1990). *Politics, Markets, and America's Schools.* Brookings Institution, Washington, D.C.

Clark, D. L., and Astuto, T. A. (1990). The disjunction of federal education policy and educational needs in the 1990s. In *Education Politics for the New Century.* D. E. Mitchell and M. E. Goertz (Eds.). Falmer, London.

Cobb, R. W., and Elder, C. D. (1972). *Participation in American Politics: The Dynamics of Agenda-Building.* Allyn and Bacon, Boston.

Cohen, D. M., March, J. G., and Olsen, J. P. (1972). A garbage can model of organizational choice. *Administrative Science Quarterly* 17: 1-25.

Coleman, J. S., Campbell, E. Q., Jobson, C. J., McPartland, J., Mood, A. M., Weinfield, F. D., and York, R. L. (1966). *Equality of Educational Opportunity.* U.S. Government Printing Office, Washington, D.C.

Coombs, F. S. (1977). Who participates in educational change—How? In *Reorganizing Education: Management and Participation for Change,* Vol I. Sage, London.

—— (1980a). Bases of non-compliance with policy. *Policy Studies Journal* 8 (Summer): 885-891.

—— (1980b). Opportunities in the comparison of state education policy systems. Stanford University: Institute for Research on Educational Finance and Governance, Project Report No. 80-A16.

Coons, J. E., and Sugarman, S. D. (1978). *Education by Choice: A Case for Family Control.* University of California Press, Berkeley, CA.

Counts, G. S. (1927). The social composition of boards of education: A study in the social control of public education. *Supplementary Education Monographs* 30.

Crain, R. (1968). *The Politics of School Desegregation.* Aldine, Chicago.

Cronin, J. M. (1976). The federal takeover: Should the junior partner run the firm? In *Federalism at the Crossroads: Improving Educational Policymaking.* George Washington University, Washington, D.C., pp. 1-5.

Dahl, R. (1961). *Who Governs? Democracy and Power in an American City.* Yale University Press, New Haven, CT.

Dearman, N. B., and Plisko, V. W. (1980). *The Condition of Education 1980 Edition.* National Center for Education Statistics, Washington, D.C.

Downs, A. (1957). *An Economic Theory of Democracy.* Harper & Row, New York.

Drachler, N. Education and politics in large cities, 1950-1970. In *The Politics of Education: The Seventy-sixth Yearbook of the National Society for the Study of Education, Part 11.* National Society for the Study of Education, Chicago.

Dye, T. R. (1966). *Politics, Economics, and the Public: Policy Outcomes in the American States.* Rand McNally, Chicago.

—— (1967). Governmental structure, urban environment, and educational policy. *Midwest Journal of Political Science* 11: 353-380.

Easton, D. (1953). *The Political System: An Inquiry into the State of Political Science.* Knopf, New York.

—— (1965). *A System Analysis of Political Life.* Wiley, New York.

Easton, D., and Dennis, J. (1965). *Children in the Political System.* Wiley, New York.

Elam, S. (Ed.) (1973). *The Gallup Polls of Attitudes Toward Education, 1969–1973.* Phi Delta Kappa, Bloomington, IN.

Eliot, T. H. (1959). Toward an understanding of public school politics. *American Political Science Review* 53: 1032–1051.

Elmore, R. (1980). Backward mapping: Implementation research and policy decisions. *Political Science Quarterly* 94: 601–16.

Fantini, M. M., Gittell, M., and Magat, R. (1970). *Community Control and the Urban School.* Praeger, New York.

Flanasan, J. C. (1976). Changes in school levels of achievement: Project TALENT ten and fifteen year retest. *Educational Researcher* 5: 9–11.

Friedrich, C. J. (1946). *Constitutional Government and Democracy.* Ginn and Company, Boston.

Froman, L. A. (1968). The categorization of policy contents. In *Political Science and Public Policy.* Markham, Chicago, pp. 41–52.

Gallup, G. H. The 10th annual Gallup poll of the public attitudes toward the public schools. *Phi Delta Kappan* September: 35.

Garms, W. L., Guthrie, J. W., and Pierce, L. C. (1978). *School Finance: The Economics and Politics of Public Education.* Prentice-Hall, Englewood Cliffs, NJ.

Gittell, M. (1968). *Participants and Participation: A Study of School Policy in New York City.* Praeger, New York.

Gittell, M., and Hollander, T. E. (1968). *Six Urban School Districts: A Comparative Study of Institutional Response.* Praeger, New York.

Grant, W. V., and Eiden, L. J. (1980). *Digest of Education Statistics 1980.* National Center for Education Statistics, Washington, D.C.

Grumm, J. G., and Wasby, S. L. (Eds.) (1981). *The Analysis of Policy Impact.* Lexington Books, D. C. Heath, Lexington, MA.

Guthrie, J. (1978). Proposition 13 and the future of California's schools. *Phi Delta Kappan* September: 12.

Guthrie, J. W. (1980). An assessment of educational policy research. *Educational Evaluation and Policy Analysis* (September–October): 41–55.

Halperin, S. (1976a). Block grants or categorical aids? What do we really want—Consolidation, simplification, decentralization? In *Federalism at the Crossroads: Improving Educational Policymaking.* George Washington University, Washington, D.C., pp. 67–70.

—— (1976b). Federal takeover, state default, or a family problem? In *Federalism at the Crossroads: Improving Educational Policymaking.* George Washington University, Washington, D.C., pp. 19–22.

—— (1976c). Is the federal government taking over education? *Compact* (Summer): 2–4.

—— (1978). The political world of Washington policymakers in education. Institute for Educational Leadership, Washington, D.C.; unpublished manuscript.

Hawley, W. D. (1977). If schools are for learning, the study of the politics of education is just beginning. In *The Politics of Education: The Seventy-sixth Yearbook of the National Society for the Study of Education: Part II,* J. D. Schribner (Ed.). The National Society for the Study of Education, Chicago.

Hess, R. D., and Torney, J. V. (1967). *The Development of Political Attitudes in Children.* Aldine, Chicago.

Hill, W. G. (1976). The role of the State in education. In *Federalism at the Crossroads: Improving Educational Policymaking.* George Washington University, Washington, D.C., pp. 27–34.

Iannaccone, L., and Cistone, P. J. (1974). *The Politics of Education.* ERIC Clearinghouse on Educational Management, University of Oregon, Eugene, OR.

Iannaccone, L., and Lutz, F. (1970). *Politics, Power and Policy: The Governing of Local School Districts.* Merrill, Columbus, OH.

Iannaccone, L. (1967). *Politics in Education.* Center for Applied Research in Education, New York.

Institute for Educational Leadership (1976). *Federalism at the Crossroads: Improving Educational Policymaking.* George Washington University, Washington, D.C.

Kirst, M. (1979). The new politics of state education finance. *Phi Delta Kappan* February: 427.

—— (1989). Who should control the schools? Reassessing current policies. In *Schooling for Tomorrow*: *Directing Reforms to Issues that Count*. J. T. Sergiovanni and J. H. Moore (Eds.). Allyn and Bacon, Boston.

Kirst, M. W., and Garms, W. I. (1980). The demographic, fiscal, and political environment of public school finance in the 1980s. Paper delivered at the annual meeting of the American Educational Finance Association (AEFA), San Diego, March, 1980.

Kirst, M. W., and Mosher, E. K. (1969). Politics of education. *Review of Educational Research* 39 (December): 623–640.

Kissick, S. (1980). The changing look of school finance reform. State Legislatures. 6 (September): 15–19.

Knickman, J. R., and Reschovsky, A. (1980). The implementation of school finance reform. *Policy Sciences* 12 (October): 301–314.

Lanone, G. R., and Smith, B. L. R. (1973). *The Politics of School Decentralization*. D. C. Heath, Lexington, MA.

Lasswell, H. D. (1930). *Psychopathology and Politics*. Viking Press, New York, pp. 261–262.

—— (1936). *Politics*: *Who Gets What, When and How?* McGraw-Hill, New York.

Lasswell, H. D., and Kaplan, A. (1950). *Power and Society*: *A Framework for Political Inquiry*. Yale University Press, New Haven, CT.

Lehne, R. (1978). *The Quest for Justice*: *The Politics of School Finance Reform*. Longman, New York.

Levin, H. M. (Ed.) (1972). *Community Control of Schools*. Brookings Institution, Washington, D.C.

Lindblom, C. E. (1959). The science of "muddling through." *Public Administration Review* 18: 79–88.

—— (1965). *The Intelligence of Democracy*. Free Press, New York.

Lowi, T. (1964). American business, public policy, case-studies, and political theory. *World Politics* 6: 677–715.

Mann, D. (1976). *The Politics of Administrative Representation*: *School Administration and Local Democracy*. D. C. Heath, Lexington, MA.

—— (1977). Participation, representation, and control. In *The Politics of Education*: *The Seventy-sixth Yearbook of the National Society for the Study of Education*: *Part 11*, J. D. Schribner (Ed.). National Society for the Study of Education, Chicago.

March, J., and Simon, H. (1958). *Organizations*. Wiley, New York.

Masters, N. A., Salisbury, R., and Eliot, T. H. (1964). *State Politics and the Public Schools*. Knopf, New York.

Mazmanian, D. A., and Sabatier, P. A. (1983). *Implementation and Public Policy*. Scott, Foresman, Glenview, IL.

Mazzoni, T. L., and Campbell, R. F. (1976). Influentials in state policy-making for the public schools. *Educational Administration Quarterly* 12 (Winter): 1–26.

McGivney, J. H., and Moynihan, W. (1972). School and community. *Teachers College Record* 74 (December): 317–356.

McMahon, W. W. (1980). Efficiency and equity criteria for educational budgeting and finance. College of Commerce and Business Administration, University of Illinois at Urbana-Champaign, Faculty Working Paper #733.

Merritt, R. L., and Coombs, F. S. (1977). Politics and educational reform. *Comparative Education Review* 21 (June/October): 247–273.

Metz, M. H. (1990). Real school: a universal drama amid disparate experience. In *Education Politics for the New Century*. D. E. Mitchell and M. E. Goertz (Eds.). Falmer, London.

Milbrath, L. (1965). *Political Participation*: *How and Why Do People Get Involved in Politics?* Rand McNally, Chicago.

Minar, D. (1966). Community basis of conflict in school system politics. *American Sociological Review* 31: 822–835.

Mitchell, D. E., and Goertz, M. E. (Eds.) (1990). *Education Politics for the New Century*. Falmer, London.

Mitchell, D. E., and Iannaccone, L. (1979). The impact of legislative policy on the performance of public school organization. Paper prepared for the California Policy Seminar.

Monk, D. H. (1990). *Educational Finance: An Economic Approach.* McGraw-Hill, New York.

Munday, L. A. (1980). Changing test scores: Basic skills development in 1977 compared with 1970. *Phi Delta Kappan* 60: 670–671.

Munger, F. J., and Fenno, R. F. (1962). *National Politics and Federa Aid to Education.* Syracuse University Press, Syracuse, NY.

Murphy, J. T. (1974). *State Education Agencies and Discretionary Funds.* Lexington Books, Lexington, MA.

—— (Ed.) (1980). *State Leadership in Education: On Being a Chief State School Officer.* Institute for Educational Leadership, George Washington University, Washington, D.C.

Nagel, S. S. (1980). What is efficiency in policy education? Paper presented at the 1980 Education Network Conference.

National Commission on Excellence in Education (1983). *A Nation at Risk: The Imperative for Education Reform.* Government Printing Office, Washington, D.C.

Nelkin, D. (1977). *Science Textbook Controversies and the Politics of Equal Time.* The MIT Press, Cambridge, MA.

Odden, A., Augenblick, J., and Vincent, P. E. (1976). *School Finance Reform in the States 1976–77: An Overview of Legislative Actions, Judicial Decisions and Public Policy Research.* Education Commission of the States, Denver, CO.

Orfield, G. (1969). *The Reconstruction of Southern Education.* Wiley, New York.

—— (1978). *Must We Bus? Segregated Schools and National Policy.* The Brookings Institution, Washington, D.C.

Parsons, T. (1951). *The Social System.* The Free Press, New York.

—— (1969). *Politics and Social Structure.* The Free Press, New York.

Peshkin, A. (1978). *Growing up American: Schooling and the Survival of Community.* University of Chicago Press, Chicago.

Peterson, M. W. (1974). Administration in higher education: Sociological and social-psychological perspectives. In *Review of Research in Education.* F. Kerlinger and J. B. Carroll (Eds.). Peacock, Itasca, IL.

Peterson, P. E. (1974). The politics of American education. In *Review of Research in Education,* Vol. 2. F. N. and J. B. Carrol (Eds.). Peacock, Itasca, IL.

—— (1976). *School Politics, Chicago Style.* The University of Chicago Press, Chicago.

Rich, J. M. (1974). *New Directions in Educational Policy.* Professional Educators Publications, Lincoln, NE.

Rodriguez v. San Antonio Independent School District (1971). 337 F. Supp. 280 (W.W. Texas, 1971), rev'd. 441 U.S. 1.

Rosenthal, A., and Fuhrman, S. (1980). Education policy: Money is the name of the game. *State Legislatures* 6 (September): 7–10.

Salisbury, R. H. (1965). State politics and education. In *Politics in the American States.* H. Jacobs and K. Vines (Eds.). Little, Brown, Boston, pp. 331–370.

—— (1968). The analysis of public policy: A search for theories and roles. In *Political Science and Public Policy.* A. Ranney (Ed.). Markham, Chicago, pp. 151–175.

Scribner, J. D., and Englert, R. M. (1977). The politics of education: An introduction. In *The Politics of Education: The Seventy-sixth Yearbook of the National Society for the Study of Education. Part 11.* J. D. Scribner (Ed.). The National Society for the Study of Education, Chicago.

Sergiovanni, T. J., Burlingame, M., Coombs, F. S., and Thurston, P. W. (1980). *Educational Governance and Administration.* Prentice-Hall, Englewood Cliffs, NJ.

Sergiovanni, T. J., and Moore, J. H. (Ed.) (1989). *Schooling for Tomorrow: Directing Reforms to Issues that Count.* Allyn and Bacon, Boston.

Serrano v. Priest (1971). 5 Cal. 3rd 584, 487 p. 2nd 1241.

Sharkansky, L. (1968). *Spending in the American States.* Rand McNally, Chicago.

Shedd, J. B. (1990). Collective bargaining, school reform, and the management of school systems. In *Education Reform: Making Sense of It All.* S. B. Bacharach (Ed.). Allyn and Bacon, Boston.

Simon, H. J. (1945). *Administrative Behavior.* Macmillan, New York.

Sizer, T. R. (1984). *Horace's Compromise: The Dilemma of the American High School.* Houghton Mifflin, Boston.

Sroufe, G. E. (1980). The very last word about politics of education research. *Politics of Education Bulletin* 9 (Fall): 1-6.

Stevenson, H. W., Lee, S. Y., and Stigler, J. W. (1986). Mathematics achievement of Chinese, Japanese and American children. *Science* 231 (February): 693-699.

Taylor, F. (1911). *The Principles of Scientific Management.* Harper & Row, New York, Reprinted by Harper & Row in 1945.

Thomas, N. C. (1975). *Education in National Politics.* David McKay, New York.

Thompson, J. T. (1976). *Policymaking in American Public Education.* Prentice-Hall, Englewood Cliffs, NJ.

Time for Results: The Governors' 1991 Report on Education (1986). National Governors' Association, Washington, D.C.

Timpane, M. (1976). Into the Maw: The uses of policy in Washington. *Phi Delta Kappan* October: 177-178.

Truman, D. (1951). *The Governmental Process: Political Interests and Public Opinion.* Knopf, New York.

Tucker, H. J., and Zeigler, L. H. (1980). *Professionals Versus the Public: Attitudes, Communication, and Response in School Districts.* Longman, New York.

Tyack, D. (1974). *The One Best System.* Harvard University Press, Cambridge, MA.

U.S. Department of Education, National Center for Education Statistics (1992). *The Condition of Education, 1992.* Washington, D.C.

VanGeel, T. (1977). Two models of the Supreme Court in school politics. In *The Politics of Education: The Seventy-sixth Yearbook of the National Society for the Study of Education, Part II.* J. D. Scribner (Ed.). National Society for the Study of Education, Chicago.

Verba, S., and Nie, N. H. (1972). *Participation in America: Political Democracy and Social Equality.* Harper & Row, New York.

Walter, R. L. (1975). *The Teacher and Collective Bargaining.* Professional Education Publications, Lincoln, NE.

Weber, M. (1946). *Essays in Sociology.* Translated and edited by H. H. Gerth and C. W. Mills. Oxford University Press, New York.

Weick, K. E. (1969). *The Social Psychology of Organizing.* Addison Wesley, Reading, MA.

Wildavsky, A. (1964). *The Politics of the Budgetary Process.* Little, Brown, Boston.

Wiley, D. K. (1979). State level educational politics: Old problems and new research directions. Paper presented at the 1979 Annual American Education Research Association (AERA) Meeting, San Francisco, April 6-10.

Wirt, F. M. (1975). Social diversity and school board responsiveness in urban schools. In *Understanding School Boards.* P. L. Cistone (Ed.). D.C. Heath, Lexington, MA.

—— (1977a). School policy culture and state decentralization. *The Politics of Education.* The National Society for the Study of Education, Chicago.

—— (1977b). Reassessment needs in the study of the politics of education. *Teachers College Record* 78 (May): 401-412.

—— (1980a). Comparing educational policies: Theory, units of analysis, and research strategies. *Comparative Education Review* 24 (June): 174-191.

—— (1980b). Is the prince listening? Politics of education and the policymaker. Paper delivered at 1980 Annual Meeting of the American Political Science Association (APSA), Washington, D.C., August 28-31.

Wirt, F. M., and Kirst, K. W. (1972). *The Political Web of American Schools.* Little, Brown, Boston.

Wise, A. E. (1967). *Rich Schools, Poor Schools: The Promise of Equal Educational Opportunity.* University of Chicago Press, Chicago.

Wolanin, T. R. (1976). Congress, information and policymaking for postsecondary education: Don't trouble me with the facts. In *Federalism at the Crossroads: Improving Educational Policymaking.* George Washington University, Washington, D.C., pp. 81-98.

Yudof, M. G. (1979). Law-and-education research: Past and future. *New York University Education Quarterly* Fall: 10–15.

Zeigler, L. H., and Johnson, K. F. (1972). *The Politics of Education in the States.* Bobbs-Merrill, New York.

Zeigler, L. H., Jennings, M. K., and Peak, G. W. (1974). *Governing American Schools.* Duxbury Press, North Scituate, MA.

26
Population Policy

Michael E. Kraft
University of Wisconsin, Green Bay, Wisconsin

Changes in the characteristics of a nation's population usually occur slowly, are little noticed in the short run, and are treated as either insignificant or beyond the reach of governmental policy. Yet slight changes in the birth, death, and growth rates of a population, or modest changes in its composition or distribution, may have great effects on the type and level of demands citizens make on government, the capacity of government to respond to those demands, and the distribution of political power. Thus, population changes are among the most important factors affecting public policy and the quality of life in a nation.

This chapter focuses on the United States. I examine recent population trends, major policy developments of the last several decades, the politics of population policy, and contemporary policy challenges. Attention is given as well to world population conditions and trends, both in the less developed countries (LDCs) and the developed nations, and their policy consequences.

Because several other chapters in this book deal with selected aspects of population trends in the United States, I make no attempt to cover them here. These include migration, land use, housing, and (in any detail) the environmental and natural resources implications of population change. Many public policies have some effect on the kinds of population trends under consideration here, and population changes have a reciprocal effect on a wide variety of public policies. Partly for this reason, most of this chapter emphasizes explicit and direct population policies rather than implicit and indirect policy actions that affect human population change.

I. POPULATION POLICY DEFINED

Population policy is not easily defined or categorized. To some extent, the reasons are not specific to population policy, but can be found in the complexity of public policy in general.

Lasswell and Kaplan (1950) define policy concisely as a "projected program of goals, values, and practices." However, as Jones (1984) notes, public policy is used in a variety of ways. It may refer to goals to be achieved, plans or proposals (means) to achieve them, formal or authorized programs and their effects, or specific decisions or actions taken in setting goals, formulating plans, and implementing programs. Moreover, public policy in a given area may not be self-evident; it must be specified by the analyst, making use of policy makers' stated intentions, the formal language of statutes and administrative regulations, and the observable policy decisions of government officials.

Aside from the difficulty of defining policy precisely, there are problems unique to the subject of population. For present purposes, a rigorous definition of population policy is not essential, nor need we review the full range of definitional issues that students of population policy have raised. After a search of 34 authors writing between 1940 and 1975, Corsa and Oakley (1979) found consensus on the following elements: Some demographic effect is intended or produced, governments participate in some way, indirect as well as direct means are included, and the concern is population-influencing rather than population-responsive policies. Taking into account the varying usage and these common elements, they offer the following definition: Population policy consists of "those actions of government that affect or attempt to affect the balance between births, deaths, and migration of human beings" (p. 156).

This a fairly inclusive definition. It allows for unintended consequences of government action and indirect policy impact on components of a nation's population and does not specify how purposive, sustained, or coherent the actions of government need be. Miller and Godwin (1977) expand the scope of population policy further. It should include, they argue, "something a government chooses to do or not to do" about population problems. Thus "nondecisions," decisions not to take action, are considered important. By not taking action on population, governments allow other influences (e.g., private decision making) to determine population events.

Such broad definitions are needed to capture much of what the United States and other nations have done (and not done) about population problems. At the same time, for many purposes one needs to differentiate between *explicit* population policies having as their major goal the achievement of particular demographic effects (e.g., lower fertility) and other policies, such as the regulation of abortion, that have only indirect and/or unintended population impacts. The United States has never adopted an explicit or comprehensive national population policy, but a variety of more limited policies affecting population trends have been enacted in the last several decades.

II. WORLD POPULATION TRENDS AND POLICY IMPLICATIONS

Prior to examining U.S. population trends and policy actions, an overview of demographic developments on a worldwide basis—in developing as well as developed nations—is useful. The exercise helps to place U.S. population policy issues into the broader context in which they must be assessed.

The major population trend is one of rapid growth. The extraordinary modern acceleration of growth began around 1750. Prior to that time, human history was characterized by a relatively stable or very slowly growing population. By 1800, however, the world population rose to 1 billion people, by 1900 to 1.7 billion, and by 1950 to 2.5 billion (Coale, 1974). In October 1992, it stood at 5.5 billion, or more than twice as large as it was only 40 years earlier (United Nations, 1992).

With an estimated 1992 crude birth rate of 26 per 1000 population and a death rate of 9 per 1000 population, world population is growing at an annual rate of 1.7% (Population Reference Bureau, 1992). At this rate, population size increases by 93 million per year, or over 250,000 per day. World fertility rates have been declining for the last two decades, and continued decline is expected. Even so, the United Nations medium, or most likely, projection, for the year 2000 is 6.3 billion and for 2025, 8.25 billion. With a striking difference in the growth rate between developed nations (0.5%) and the less developed (2.0%), 95% of the growth over the next several decades is expected to occur in the LDCs.

Stabilization of the world's population is unlikely this side of 8 to 10 billion. Writing in 1978, Tsui and Bogue predicted a rapid slowdown to a zero rate of growth, and they estimated that a peak global population of 8.1 billion would be reached by 2050. Their estimate and those of similar forecasts assumed that family planning programs in the developing world would be vigorously supported and that social and economic development would continue to reinforce the tendency toward lower fertility. Other forecasts are less optimistic about such assumptions. In 1992, the United Nations reported that its medium projection indicated that the world's population would reach 10 billion by the middle of the next century, and that growth would continue for another 100 years until 2150, where it would be about 11.6 billion. Its high projection scenario put the figure at 12.5 billion in 2050 and an astonishing 20.7 billion a century later. Under the most *optimistic* assumptions, the U.N. forecasts a world population peaking at 8.5 billion by 2050 and declining thereafter (Sadik, 1992; United Nations, 1992).[1]

All of these projections depend on assumptions of a declining fertility rate and of no substantial increase in mortality rates due to famine, disease, exhaustion of natural resources, or war. With nearly 40% of the developing world's population (excluding China) under the age of 15, however, there is a built-in momentum that will result in continued population growth even if replacement-level fertility is achieved in the next few decades. The later replacement-level fertility is reached, the larger the eventual size of the population.

In addition to high rates of growth, the world's population is undergoing rapid urbanization. The LDCs quadrupled the size of their urban populations between 1950 and 1985 (a 4% rate of growth), and the trend continues. Only 17% of the population in the LDCs was urban in 1950, but about 45% is expected to be urban by 2000 in comparison with 75% in developed nations (Keyfitz, 1990). The United Nations estimates that by the year 2025, over 60% of the LDC population will be urban.

The effects can be seen in the size of the world's largest cities. By the year 2000, the five largest are expected to be Mexico City, with a projected population of 26 million; São Paulo, with 22 million; Tokyo, with 19 million; Shanghai, with 17 million; and New York, with close to 17 million. The next five largest metropolitan areas (in order) will be Calcutta, Bombay, Beijing, Los Angeles, and Jakarta, all between 14 and 16 million. More than half the urban growth rate in recent years is attributable to natural population increase, not migration, although migration is clearly a major factor (Demeny, 1986). As a consequence of such growth, the world's cities are likely to exhibit a range of urban and environmental ills, from severe air pollution to woefully inadequate infrastructures for transportation, water, and waste disposal.

These aggregate rates obscure important differences among nations and regions of the world, particularly related to fertility and growth prospects. The fertility decline has been greatest in Asia and Latin America, and especially in China, Taiwan, Indonesia, Singapore, South Korea, the Philippines, Thailand, Sri Lanka, Cuba, and Mexico. These declines have occurred where couples have information about birth control and access to contraceptives, and often where government support for family planning programs is strong. In most of these cases, the nations are undergoing rapid industrialization, and thus perhaps entering a demographic transition that may imitate the fertility decline of developed nations. In contrast, sub-Saharan Africa has shown almost no fertility decline, and some Asian nations (particular Muslim regions) are making little progress toward lower fertility despite national family planning programs of long standing (Horiuchi, 1992). In some nations, the pronatalist culture is strong enough to limit sharply the acceptability and effectiveness of family planning (e.g., in Nepal, Pakistan, and Kenya) (Keyfitz, 1990).

In sharp contrast to the general picture of rapid growth in the LDCs, fertility is at or below replacement level in some 40 developed nations, including the United States, Canada, Australia, New Zealand, and most of Western and Northern Europe (Population Reference Bureau, 1992). A number of European countries are at or slightly below zero growth rates, with birth and death rates at about the same level. In 1992, Germany, Hungary, and Bulgaria had small negative rates of growth. Austria, Denmark, Belgium, Greece, Sweden, Great Britain, Luxembourg, Italy, and Russia are at or close to zero, and the United Kingdom and Sweden are not far above that level. The average growth rate for Europe is only 0.2% per year. Although population in the developed nations is still growing by an average of 0.5% per year, most demographers expect a continuation of present low fertility rates and stabilization at a relatively early date, in Europe by the year 2000 and perhaps in the United States by the mid-21st century, depending on immigration rates (see below).

A range of policy challenges face nations with a slowing rate of growth, most especially those derived from a changing age structure and perceptions of declining national power or possible adverse effects on economic growth (Davis et al., 1986; Kraft, 1984; McIntosh, 1983; Teitelbaum and Winter, 1985). Yet, one also needs to consider the impact of even low rates of growth in the developed nations on the world's supplies of food, energy, and natural resources, and on the global environment. For example, with only 5% of the world's population, the United States consumes 30% of its commercial energy and produces 18% of greenhouse gases. The richest one quarter of the world's nations consume 60% of the food, 70% of the metals and energy, and 85% of the wood; generate 90% of industrial and hazardous wastes; and use 80% of ozone-depleting chlorofluorocarbons (CFCs). From this perspective, low rates of growth, nongrowth, or even population decline may have positive effects on natural resources and environmental quality.

Despite such common arguments over the nature of population problems in the industrial nations, the situation faced in the LDCs is more grave and immediate. Each day nearly 40,000 children under age 5 in the poor nations die from diseases that rarely kill Americans who have access to modern health care services. Those nations with a 2% annual rate of growth (the average for the LDCs in 1992) may be expected to double in size in 35 years. To maintain even the present low standard of living, these nations must double their supply of food, raw materials, and energy in a little over three decades. That would be a monumental task for much of the developing world, even with appreciably higher levels of external economic aid. Because the growth rate in some regions is considerably higher than the 2% average (it is 2.6% for Northern Africa, 3.2% in Eastern Africa, 2.8% in Western Asia, and 2.5% in Central America), the future in some nations may be even more bleak.

There are, of course, varying estimates of the possibility of compensating for such rapid population growth with increases in food, energy, use of natural resources, public services, and employment (Davis and Bernstam, 1991; Demeny, 1986; Ehrlich and Ehrlich, 1990; Keyfitz, 1990; Repetto, 1987; Simon, 1989). Economists, demographers, and ecologists, among others, tend to disagree in part because of different assumptions about the capacity of economic, social, and natural systems to support such large and growing populations. The widely read and influential Brundtland Commission report, *Our Common Future* (World Commission on Environment and Development, 1987), emphasized instead an interdisciplinary and integrated approach the subject would seem to require. The commission concluded that continued economic growth was imperative to meet human needs, but that environmental effects could be minimized if a path of "sustainable development" were followed. However, it also estimated that to meet basic human needs and minimal aspirations for development with the expected doubling of the world's population over the next four decades would require a 5- to 10-fold increase in economic activity. Hence, the conclusion of most serious observers of the interrelationships of population, environment, and development that the next several years will be a critical time for formulating appropriate policy actions (MacNeill et al., 1991).

Demographers have long debated the relative importance of population policy (chiefly family planning programs) and economic and social development in reducing fertility rates in the LDCs. In the 1970s, Tsui and Bogue (1978) and Mauldin and Berelson (1978) argued that family planning programs had a significant, independent effect in reducing fertility, whereas Demeny and others disputed the evidence supporting such conclusions (Demeny, 1979). A recent World Bank study that examined 19 developing nations calculated that family planning programs accounted for 39% of the decline in fertility rates and socioeconomic development for 54% (Keyfitz, 1990). Increasingly there is consensus that only a combination of population policy and social and economic development will lower fertility sufficiently to allow economic progress in the developing nations (Johnson, 1988; Keyfitz, 1990; Menken, 1986). However, critics continue to fault the population or family planning establishment for emphasizing aggressive policies, giving insufficient attention to the impact on women's health, and contributing to abuses of human rights (Hartmann, 1987).

The implication of the consensus position is that emphasis should be given to those development policies likely to enhance a couple's motivation to keep family size small. These include reduction of infant and child mortality rates through improved health services, improvement in agricultural productivity and nutrition, provisions for old age security, expansion of education, and especially enhancement of the economic and social status of women (Demeny, 1974; Keyfitz, 1990; Rich, 1973). Access to the information and means to achieve desired family size is also essential, and thus effective family planning programs play a key role.

To judge from the number of nations adopting such policies in recent years, there is some basis for modest optimism. In 1960, only India and Pakistan supported organized family planning programs for the purpose of reducing birth rates. By 1978, 35 developing nations—with 77% of the developing world's population—had such official policies for reducing population growth (van der Tak et al., 1979). The policies adopted, the politics of policy making and implementation, and the impacts of these programs vary widely (Corsa and Oakley, 1979; Keyfitz, 1990; Godwin, 1975; Norman and Hofstatter, 1978; Simmons, 1986).

On a more pessimistic note, a good many studies and arguments point to poor prospects for successful economic and social development and population limitation in a world increasingly subject to ecological constraints (Meadows et al., 1992; Ophuls and Boyan, 1992; Tobin, 1993). The more insightful analyses emphasize the necessity of significant changes in political institutions and public policies to achieve population stabilization and sustainable economic growth (CEQ and Department of State, 1980; MacNeill et al., 1991; Mathews, 1991).

III. POPULATION TRENDS IN THE UNITED STATES AND POLICY IMPLICATIONS

In most respects, population trends in the United States are similar to those of other developed nations: The fertility rate declined appreciably after the "baby-boom" years of 1945 to 1959 and remained low until recently, when it rose again. It is now very close to the so-called re-placement-level total fertility rate (TFR) of 2.1.[2] There are some distinctive features of U.S. demographic changes as well, including a high level of both legal and illegal immigration and population redistribution among regions and between metropolitan and nonmetropolitan areas.

The population of the United States in late 1992 stood at approximately 256 million, with a natural rate of increase of 0.8%. With a TFR of 2.0 (up from 1.8 a decade ago), the U.S. population is still growing, and will continue to do so for at least another six decades, even if the fertility rate remains below the replacement level. That growth is a factor of a high level of immigration and recent increases in the fertility rate.

Estimates of future fertility dramatically affect projections of population size and the date of arrival of a stable or stationary population. Some demographers have argued, as Westoff (1978) did a more than a decade ago, that "nothing on the horizon suggests that fertility will not remain low. All the recent evidence on trends in marriage and reproductive behavior en-courages a presumption that it will remain low" (p. 54; see also Westoff, 1986). As a result of later marriages, higher divorce rates, an increase in the number of women in the labor force, the popularity of smaller families, and child-free lifestyles, some expect a decline in the TFR, possibly to 1.5 children per woman. Others, most notably Easterlin (1980), have suggested that fertility rates are likely to rise in the future as a consequence of the less restric-tive social and economic conditions under which today's younger cohorts are being raised—less competition due to fewer numbers in each cohort in comparison to the baby-boom cohorts.

The fertility rate *has* risen significantly in the past few years, as noted. But the major reason seems to be far higher immigration rates than expected, with higher fertility rates among immigrants, particularly Hispanics. In late 1992, the Census Bureau reported the U.S. popu-lation was growing much faster than its earlier estimate. As recently as 1988, the bureau be-lieved that U.S. population would stabilize by the year 2038 at some 301 million. Now it esti-mates that the nation will reach 275 million by the year 2000 and 383 million by 2050, a 50% increase in six decades (Pear, 1992).

The major uncertainties in these projections are fluctuations in the fertility rate and the level of immigration. Immigration has accounted for between 25 and 50% of recent growth. During the 1980s, the United States admitted 500,000 to 600,000 legal immigrants a year, a significant increase over the 400,000 per year that prevailed in the 1970s (Teitelbaum, 1986). Despite concern among many economists and environmentalists over the adverse impacts of such high levels of immigration, in 1990, the U.S. Congress further liberalized immigration policy. Under the new rules, legal immigration is likely to rise to 700,000 per year. Estimates of illegal immigrants vary from about 150,000 to 1 million annually, and are unreliable. Nev-ertheless, it is significant that the Census Bureau estimated in 1992 that 200,000 illegal immi-grants will arrive each year for the next 60 years, or twice the number it had estimated earlier (Pear, 1992).

With a continuation of these fertility and immigration rates, the composition of the popu-lation will change in many respects. There will be a rapid growth in both the Hispanic and Asian-American populations, and a sizable increase in the African-American population. Hispanic Americans will likely account for about 40% of U.S. population growth over the next 60 years. The non-Hispanic white population will decline to about 53% of the total popu-lation from 75% in 1992. The population will also get older. The median age (28 in 1970 and 33 in 1992) is expected to increase by the year 2035 to 39. The percentage of the population over age 65 is likely to rise from 12% in the late 1980s to between 14 and 22% by 2030, depend-ing on prevailing fertility rates. At current fertility levels, the consensus estimate is that those over age 65 will increase to about 19% of the population. The number of people older than age 85 will increase dramatically, from 3.3 million in 1992 to nearly 7 million by 2020 and 18 million by 2050. At the same time, the proportion of the population under age 18 will decline.

These changes in the age structure have some obvious and much discussed, although not entirely predictable, effects on the demand for public services (e.g., education, social security, and health care) and on politics and the economy (Fosler et al., 1990; Kraft, 1984). The impact of the baby-boom cohort as it moves through the life cycle has also been much noted, and because its size is known, its impact in the future can be projected with some confidence (Bouvier and De Vita, 1991; Light, 1988). However, the exact form of future generational conflicts between young and old cohorts, the severity of them, and the actual long-term effects of the population and age structure on economic and social conditions and policies are still matters of much debate.

A review of the aggregate population changes experienced in recent years and projected for the future tends to overlook existing population distribution among regions and between metropolitan and nonmetropolitan areas. It also ignores trends in redistribution that pose vastly different policy problems for regions, states, and cities. Space limitations require that I leave a discussion of these trends and policy implications to others.[3]

These population trends in the world and the United States suggest a number of policy issues:

1. Should the United States and other developed nations welcome sustained low fertility and continue to support programs and practices that will keep fertility low—or attempt at some point to raise fertility and slow the decline in the growth rate through pronatalist policies? What policy options are available for either course of action, and by what standards should they be evaluated? For example, should environmental and resource implications of a large and growing population take precedence over the effect of growth on the labor market or other economic conditions?
2. What might governments and other organizations do to plan for and adapt to the demographic changes associated with present fertility levels and with present and expected patterns of internal migration and immigration? What policy alternatives are available to affect population distribution and immigration directly? What are the appropriate criteria to assess possible courses of action, such as local or regional growth management policies (Stein, 1993) or more restrictive policies on both legal and illegal immigration?
3. How should the United States and other nations respond to the world population situation and the need for sustainable economic development? Should current policies of international population assistance be greatly expanded? Altered in some way? By what standards should such policies be evaluated?

The rest of this chapter addresses a selected set of these issues. I focus on how the U.S. government has dealt with population trends, especially over the previous two decades. Emphasis is given to characteristics of the policy-making process and to the political and institutional constraints on population policy making. Finally, I ask about additional policy needs and the contribution that might be made by political scientists and policy analysts to clarification of population issues and policy alternatives.

IV. EVOLUTION OF U.S. POPULATION POLICY

A. Population Policy Before 1960: A Nonissue

For most of U.S. history, population trends have been nonissues and few policies have been adopted. That is somewhat surprising given the impressive rates of growth and migration of

the U.S. population over the past 200 years. Yet, national policies develop only when population change is perceived to be a societal problem and when governmental intervention is considered legitimate. With few exceptions, population changes throughout U.S. history have
not been perceived as a problem necessitating governmental action.

Concern for the composition and distribution of the nation's population dates back to at
least 1790, when the first census was taken. Yet, aside from a variety of laws dealing with
births, marriages, divorces, contraception, and abortion—adopted for moral or medical rather
than demographic purposes—there was little population policy activity on a national scale.
The policies that were adopted, at both the state and federal level, generally were pronatalist.
For example, the Comstock Act of 1873 defined contraceptives as obscene material and prohibited interstate distribution of them; it was not formally repealed until 1971. Abortion was
illegal from the middle of the 19th century except to save the life of the mother (Stetson, 1973).

The first national concern for a broader population policy arose in the late 1930s in the
context of extremely low fertility rates during the Depression and fears about economic stagnation. In 1938, the subcommittee on population problems of the National Resources Committee presented a report to President Roosevelt entitled Problems of a Changing Population. The committee concluded that the "transition from an increasing to a stationary or
decreasing population may on the whole be beneficial to the life of the Nation." This view
was similar to one offered by the Commission on Population Growth and the American Future in 1972. The committee also recommended a conservative immigration policy to limit
competition from unskilled workers, expressed concern over the relationship between high
fertility levels and poverty, urged expanded programs for equality of opportunity in education, health, and cultural development, favored strengthening of research agencies concerned
with population studies, and recommended the institution of a 5-year census rather than the
constitutionally prescribed decennial census (Westoff, 1974).

Sharing the fate of future population commissions, the committee's report received little
attention from the president or the nation, partly because of the rapidly changing environment of the late 1930s and early 1940s. A concern for low fertility in the 1930s would later
become a concern over high fertility in the late 1960s and early 1970s, which in turn faded
with declining fertility rates. As Westoff (1974) observed, after World War II, "the main focus
of professional interest in population policy turned toward the underdeveloped world."

Even by the late 1950s, with increasing evidence of the adverse impacts of a rapidly growing world population, population issues had barely begun to achieve visibility and legitimacy
in U.S. politics. As one measure of the low agenda status of population during this period,
The New York Times index entries for population and vital statistics increased only from
1 inch in 1950 to a little more than 2 inches in 1958 (Piotrow, 1973). The low salience of the
issues and the controversiality of birth control deterred most public officials from taking
leadership roles. The climate at the time is illustrated by President Dwight Eisenhower's remarks during a press conference in December 1959:

> I cannot imagine anything more emphatically a subject that is not a proper political or
> governmental activity or function or responsibility. . . . This government will not, as
> long as I am here, have a positive political doctrine in its program that has to do with
> the problem of birth control. That's not our business (Piotrow, 1973: 45).

The political sensitivity of birth control in part reflected the influence of the Catholic
Church. Catholic opposition to governmental efforts on birth control was evident throughout
the 1950s and 1960s. For example, the American Catholic bishops had opposed a recommendation in 1959 by the Committee to Study the Military Assistance Program (also called

the Draper committee after its chairman, William Draper) that the U.S. government "assist those countries with which it is cooperating in economic aid programs, on request, in the formulation of their plans designed to deal with the problem of rapid population growth" (Westoff, 1974). The Draper committee failed to impress President Eisenhower with its recommendation. It also had little apparent impact outside the White House. The opposition to proposals of U.S. assistance and the lack of sustained media coverage were soon to be reversed. In the late 1950s and early 1960s, population activists were organizing and lobbying on the issues, gaining press coverage, and creating a constituency for policy change.

B. Population Policy, 1960 to 1969: A Peripheral Issue Matures

Breaking with President Eisenhower's declaration of nonpolicy, initially with considerable reluctance, President John Kennedy supported population activities of the United Nations, and in 1963, he established the National Institute of Child Health and Human Development (NICHD) within the Department of Health, Education and Welfare (HEW) (later Health and Human Services [HHS]). It included a research program on human reproduction. In 1963, Congress included in the foreign aid bill authorization to support population research, and the U.S. Public Health Service contributed $500,000 to the World Health Organization to be used for research on human reproduction. By 1965, President Lyndon Johnson completed the transition from the Eisenhower era. In a State of the Union message, he pledged that he would "seek new ways to use our knowledge to help deal with the explosion in world population and the growing scarcity in world resources." The contrast to the earlier period is notable. A political consensus was emerging on the importance of population growth and on public policy to deal with it.

In 1966, Congress amended two statutes, the Foreign Assistance Act and the Food for Peace Act, to authorize additional support for international population programs. For fiscal 1968, Congress earmarked $35 million of appropriated funds for population assistance, which was increased to $50 million for fiscal 1969 (Population Reference Bureau, 1971). Other actions followed in the executive branch. In 1966, the Department of State, the Agency for International Development (AID), the Peace Corps, and the U.S. Information Agency announced jointly their support for programs aimed at limiting population growth in developing nations. In 1967, AID made funds available for these purposes. By 1967, then, one part of the federal government's population policy was set in place.[4]

Most of the credit for the impressive changes in U.S. population assistance policy during the 1960s goes to policy entrepreneurs in Congress rather than to Presidents Kennedy and Johnson. Piotrow (1973) explains:

> Congress—both individual legislators and specific committees—set the agenda for public discussion of the population problem, defined the issue in ever more acceptable terms, reiterated the relevance and feasibility of action, drew up specific proposals to establish priority in funds as well as in words, and enacted these proposals into binding legislation, largely against the opposition of the executive agencies.

The actions of several policy leaders on the Hill stand in sharp contrast to presidential timidity during this period. For example, from 1965 to 1968, Senator Ernest Gruening (D., Alaska) chaired 31 days of hearings on world population problems, with testimony by 120 witnesses. The Gruening hearings helped to frame the issues and legitimize later policy action.

On the domestic front, in 1968, President Johnson created a Committee on Population and Family Planning, jointly chaired by John D. Rockefeller III, and Wilbur Cohen, the Secretary of HEW (later HHS). The committee recommended rapid expansion of the foreign assistance program; expansion of the Center for Population Research, which was established in the summer of 1968 in NICHD; establishment of a Commission on Population to be appointed by the president; rapid expansion of the federal government's family planning programs for the poor; and expansion of federal support for population studies centers. The committee's immediate impact was slight, although its long-term effect was greater. The Johnson administration released the report in early January, just before the president's departure from office. Johnson also refused to support the committee's recommendations on funding in the fiscal 1970 budget. As far as population issues had come since 1959, then, they remained controversial, held only a tenuous grip on the nation's attention, and received low priority on the institutional agenda.

C. U.S. Population Policy Formation: 1969 to 1974

The political climate shifted significantly in the late 1960s. Following a presidential message on population in 1969, Congress in 1970 created the commission that had been advocated by the Johnson committee 2 years previously. It also approved major legislation on family planning and population research. Despite such impressive actions in 1969 and 1970, however, population remained something of a nonissue in U.S. politics, and public policy development failed to keep pace with the flurry of recommendations handed down by various commissions, select committees, and independent study groups in the 1970s and 1980s.

On July 18, 1969, President Richard Nixon sent to Congress the first presidential message ever on population. It dealt primarily with domestic population growth, and its major recommendation was to establish a Commission on Population Growth and the American Future to study the impact of continued population growth in the United States. Nixon also urged an increase in funding levels for population research and establishment of a family planning office in HEW (now HHS), and called for a national goal of providing "adequate family planning services within the next 5 years to all who want them but cannot afford them." The last request was essentially an increase in federal support for family planning assistance rather than a fundamental change in the type of program the government had instituted as early as 1967 (as part of the Economic Opportunity Act and the Child Health Act of 1967).

In light of the historical neglect of population issues, the tone of Nixon's message was gratifying to population activists. He referred to population growth as "one of the most serious challenges to human destiny in the last third of this century," and focused on growth of the U.S. population. Nixon asked Congress to authorize inquiry by the commission in three specific areas: (1) the probable course of population growth, internal migration, and related demographic developments through the year 2000; (2) the resources in the public sector required to deal with anticipated growth in population; and (3) ways in which population growth might affect the activities of federal, state, and local governments. Congress added two areas of concern that were rising rapidly on the nation's agenda in 1970 as legislators began dealing with environmental protection policy: the impact of population growth on resources and the environment, and "the various means appropriate to the ethical values and principles of this society by which our nation can achieve a population level properly suited for its environmental, natural resources, and other needs." This last mandate allowed the commission "to regard its mission as 'interventionist' rather than 'accommodationist' " (Westoff, 1973).

In March 1970, Congress enacted legislation creating the commission. After 2 years of extensive hearings in Washington and around the nation, the commission issued its recommendations in a report entitled *Population and the American Future*, backed up by six sizable volumes of research findings. Its major conclusion was stated boldly:

[N]o substantial benefits will result from further growth of the Nation's population, rather that the gradual stabilization of our population through voluntary means would contribute significantly to the Nation's ability to solve its problems. We have looked for, and have not found, any convincing economic argument for continued population growth. The health of our country does not depend on it, nor does the vitality of business nor the welfare of the average person.

The commission was the most significant attempt in the recent history of the United States to treat population issues in a comprehensive and systematic manner. Yet, its activities and recommendations drew a very mixed reaction from several quarters. Bachrach and Bergman (1973) attacked the operation of the commission as an "opportunity forfeited." They argued that the commission's final report remained "within familiar bounds and dealt with issues in a familiar range." Indeed, the commission emphasized the reduction of unwanted fertility, perhaps the most consensual possible policy option for limiting population growth. The executive director of the commission, Charles Westoff, explained this conventional approach as "having everything":

It implied helping people to achieve what they want; it did not imply any radical solutions to the problem of population growth . . . it was singularly unobjectionable; it was theoretically easy to do; and its costs were low! It was difficult to imagine a policy with more political promise (Westoff, 1973).

From a different perspective, as staff director of political research for the commission, Nash (1978) argued that the policy actions recommended by the commission could be traced to some pure elements of chance in the appointments process and in its internal deliberations. In effect, Nash suggested that the recommendations resulted from a process falling short of a model of rational policy analysis.

The reaction of the Nixon White House to the final report was not unexpected given a sharply declining birth rate at the time, a reduced concern for environmental problems, and the upcoming 1972 election. Two months after its release, Nixon criticized recommendations on abortion and on the provision of contraceptive information and services for minors and ignored the rest of the report. His statement made no mention of the effects of population growth or the commission's conclusion on the desirability of population stabilization.

Congress was responsive to one major population policy concern. In 1970, it adopted the Family Planning Services and Population Research Act, Title X of the Public Health Service Act (also known as the Tydings Act after its sponsor, Senator Joseph Tydings). It provided for an Office of Population Affairs in HEW (now HHS) to help coordinate government population activities, and for grants for voluntary family planning projects and to state health departments for family planning services; for research and training in reproduction, contraceptive development, and behavioral sciences related to family planning and population; and for population and family planning education. The major goal of the Act was the extension of family planning services to all in need of them, with special attention to the needs of low-income individuals.

As notable as the 1970 Act was, it was mainly a consolidation of previously established family planning program that included some expansion of authorization in that area as well as in research, training, and education. As such, it represented no break with the dominant U.S. approach to population policy: voluntary family planning without any explicit demographic goals or government-wide coordination of objectives and programs having some demographic consequences. Some critics see a preference for such a policy as reflecting the influence of a "population establishment" that included, among others, the Population Council, Planned

Parenthood/World Population, the Ford Foundation, the Rockefeller Foundation, and certain prominent individuals identified with federal population activities since the early 1960s (Bachrach and Bergman, 1973). Other factors identified as major influences on policy choice included the belief in professional demographic circles that elimination of unwanted fertility would be sufficient to deal with U.S. population problems (Westoff, 1973); the limits or constraints imposed by the prevailing U.S. ideology on population issues (Nash, 1972); and the inability of critics of this policy perspective to build a large enough constituency to change policy direction.

Nearly all other policy proposals introduced in the Congress throughout the 1970s and 1980s fared poorly. As fertility continued to decline, so did enthusiasm for other recommendations of the population commission, such as creation of a National Institute of Population Sciences, an Office of Population Growth and Distribution in the Executive Office of the President, and a Joint Committee on Population in Congress, and strengthening of the Office of Population Affairs in HHS (Commission on Population Growth and the American Future, 1972).

One deviation from the usual inattention to these issues was a hearing held in the Senate in August 1971 on a Population Stabilization Resolution. Introduced in both houses of Congress, and sponsored by 36 senators and 25 representatives, the resolution had been endorsed by the Population Commission, and in many respects was politically safe. It authorized no new spending or offices, and it referred specifically only to voluntary means to reach stabilization. However, it did state boldly and for the first time a specific demographic goal for the nation: stabilization of the population (U.S. Congress, 1971).

Although it was not, strictly speaking, a population policy, the decision of the U.S. Supreme Court in *Roe* v. *Wade* (1973) legalizing abortion must stand as one of the more significant policy developments of the early 1970s. Rather than resolving conflict on the subject, however, the Roe decision contributed to continuing public debate over the morality of abortion, women's rights, and the effects of abortion access on social services and health care (Rubin, 1987). Rarely did public discussion include its impact on demographic trends, which would have been difficult to determine in any event. The causal relationship between abortion and birth rates is not fully understood, but restrictions on abortions (and elimination of virtually all federal funding of them) that continued throughout the 1970s and 1980s may have pushed up fertility rates—even if the exact number of additional births cannot be estimated.

D. Policy Recommendations and Conflicts: 1975 to 1992

The major population policy issues in the United States in the late 1960s and early 1970s focused on the implications of continued growth on the quality of life—both within the United States and worldwide. Thus, this set of issues was explored comprehensively, if not exhaustively, in the reports of the Commission on Population Growth and the American Future. On the whole, little policy change resulted from the commission's work and related efforts to study or promote this set of issues.

In the late 1970s and 1980s, with the arrival of lower fertility rates in the United States and with a decline in fertility rates in the developing nations, population concerns rarely occupied center stage on the political agenda. Reports of declining fertility received prominent coverage and were often taken to mean the "population problem" was a thing of the past. Even the release of President Jimmy Carter's *Global 2000 Report* in 1980 (CEQ and Department of State, 1980), which projected sharp increases in the world's population and consequent future environmental and resource crises, had little effect. With Ronald Reagan's election as president, U.S. policy on population shifted dramatically to the right. The administration strongly supported new conservative perspectives on population that largely dismissed the consequences of continued growth (Simon, 1981, 1989; Wattenberg, 1987). These changes were most visible in a Heritage Foundation–funded rebuttal to *Global 2000* (Simon and Kahn, 1984) and at the United Nations Conference on Population in Mexico City in 1984. The new views remained influential throughout President George Bush's 4 years in office.

Population issues in this period changed in other respects as well. Attention shifted from national growth to questions of population distribution and the local impact of growth rates. Other new issues in the late 1970s and 1980s included immigration policy and the effects of a changing age structure on public policy. Some issues prominent in the early 1970s, most notably abortion, remained high on the nation's agenda throughout the period. New immigration policies were approved in the United States, but the only other major change made in population policy concerned international assistance, and even here the effect was largely symbolic. Some of the most important developments in this period merit brief discussion.

1. Select Committee on Population

In the fall of 1977, the U.S. House of Representatives established a Select Committee on Population, which mounted a major study of population issues that continued through the 95th Congress. The broad scope of the committee's inquiry was rivaled only by that of the Population Commission of 1970–1972. House Resolution 70, creating the committee, directed it to conduct a full and complete investigation of the causes of changing population conditions and their consequences for the United States and the world; national, regional, and global population characteristics relative to the demands on limited resources and the ability of nations to feed, clothe, house, employ, and govern their citizens; various approaches to population planning to ascertain those policies and programs, within the United States as well as other nations, that would be most effective in coping with unplanned population change; and the means by which the U.S. government can most effectively cooperate with and assist nations and international agencies in addressing successfully population-related issues (U.S. Congress, 1978a).

The committee assembled a sizable staff (30 to 40) and conducted 37 days of hearings between February and August of 1978. Its final reports on those hearings and other staff work were released in some 10 volumes in four major areas: population and development, domestic consequences of U.S. population change, legal and illegal immigration to the United States, and fertility and contraception in the United States.

The committee recommended substantial increases in funding for and diversification of population research, especially in the social sciences; substantial expansion of funding for family planning services under Title X of the Public Health Service Act and more aggressive promotion of those programs by HHS; increased attention to adolescent fertility and contraceptive needs of adolescents; increased support for contraceptive research and development; a comprehensive review of the Immigration and Naturalization Act of 1965 and its implementation; expanded research on immigration and its consequences for the United States; expansion of U.S. foreign assistance programs, and especially a stronger commitment to activities at the highest levels of government; expanded research on the consequences of the changing composition of the U.S. population (especially aging of the population); and increased attention to methods of planning for the consequences of population change (U.S. Congress, 1978a, 1978b).

Two recommendations, those dealing with planning for the consequences of a changing population and the use of demographic data in policy making, were of special importance because the problems are so often ignored. On the former, the committee called for Congress to undertake a thorough investigation to identify all population-sensitive programs and policies, to assess their impact on population, and to consider alternative mechanisms for improving the ability of the federal government to (1) conduct continuing analysis of the interrelationships of demographic change and federal programs and policies; (2) coordinate programs and policies that will be affected by changes in the size, composition, and geographical distribution of the population or that may affect population; and (3) to develop alternative policies and programs to plan for future population change and assess the costs and benefits of each course of action (U.S. Congress, 1978a). The failure to have developed institutional mechanisms for such population policy analysis and decision making is one of the major omissions in U.S. population policy.

With respect to the use of demographic data in policy making, the committee was concerned with (1) the accuracy, timeliness, and policy relevance of the statistical data produced by federal agencies, and (2) its incorporation into all major presidential, executive agency, and congressional reports. In particular, the committee pointed to the need to use extensive *demographic* analysis in all such reports, and the need to develop clear guidelines for the preparation and use of population projections for states and local areas in federal funding allocation formulas where they are already used.

Although many of these recommendations merely reflected long-standing concerns among professional demographers and public officials, their restatement by the select committee may have served, as Chairman James Scheuer (D., N.Y.) put it, a "consciousness-raising" function, particularly for the 16 members of the committee who took those concerns back to their respective standing committees. The committee's work received virtually no coverage in the mass media or even in public policy journals. However, much like the population commission in the early 1970s, the committee can be said to have contributed to both the problem and policy streams, to use John Kingdon's (1984) terms for agenda setting.

Shortly after the committee's demise, the Population Association of America (the leading professional association of demographers) formed a Committee on Public Affairs to help call attention to the same kinds of population problems and to provide "objective and scientific briefings on population change for policy makers in the Congress and the Executive Branch" (PAA Affairs, 1979). In late 1979 and 1980, these included briefings for several congressional committees on the implications of demographic change for welfare programs and the foreign assistance programs of AID and on legal and illegal immigration. The Public Affairs Committee later assisted the Congressional Research Service (which at that time included no professional demographers on its staff) and the congressional Office of Technology Assessment, which was studying birth-control technology and possible changes in U.S. policy on contraceptive development, distribution, and financing in the LDCs.

2. Immigration and Refugee Policy

A second major national investigation of population issues took place in the late 1970s under the auspices of the Select Commission on Immigration and Refugee Policy. The impact of both legal and illegal immigration on the nation and the failure of existing policies had become acutely evident (Keeley, 1979; North, 1978). The 16-member commission, chaired by the Rev. Theodore M. Hesburgh, was created by Congress in 1978 to provide the first comprehensive review of immigration policies and laws since 1911, to assess past and present migration and its consequences, and to recommend policy changes. That work was begun in August 1979 and was completed with publication of its final report in February 1981. Although the commission enjoyed the services of a staff of 25, and held 12 hearings around the country, it did not compile extensive research reports in the fashion of the Population Commission and the House Select Committee on Population. Its final report was, however, equally controversial.

There was a good deal more agreement among the commissioners on the scope of the problems of immigration than there was on the most effective and acceptable solutions. Reports by the commission's staff, and voting by the commissioners themselves, pointed to the difficulty of building policy consensus. Agreement was reached easily on recommendations such as providing additional funds and staff for enforcement of immigration laws, particularly along the United States–Mexican border, and instituting administrative reforms in the Immigration and Naturalization Service. Yet, a deeply divided commission barely reached agreement on other issues, including measures to discourage continued illegal immigration. The commission's key proposal, however, included the establishment of civil and criminal penalties against employers who hire illegal aliens; an amnesty for most illegal aliens already in the United States; a sizable increase in the level of numerically limited immigration—from 270,000 a year to 350,000 a year (not counting refugees); and the adoption of stricter enforcement methods along U.S. borders (U.S. Congress, 1981a; *The New York Times*, 1981). The commission did not consider immigration within the context of population policy, a peculiar stance given the very heavy contribution immigration makes to overall growth of the U.S. population.

The Reagan White House endorsed many of the Hesburg Commission's recommendations, and during the 1980s, Congress considered a range of policy proposals on both legal and illegal immigration. It enacted two major changes in immigration law that incorporated much of what the commission had recommended. Congress took 5 years to resolve sharp disagreements over the politically sensitive issue of illegal immigration, with the House having a more difficult time of it than the Senate. In late 1986, the 99th Congress enacted the Immigration Reform and Control Act. Its major provisions included prohibition of the hiring of illegal aliens, to be enforced with tough employer sanctions, and the granting of amnesty to illegal aliens who had established residency in the United States prior to 1982. By 1992, however, the Census Bureau reported there was no evidence of any reduction in illegal immigration (Pear, 1992).

In 1990, after 4 years of effort, the 101st Congress approved the most sweeping revision of U.S. immigration policy in 25 years with passage of the Immigration Act. The Act revised the visa allocation system, keeping preferences for immediate relatives of U.S. citizens but boosting job-related visas for those with special work skills. Legal immigration is expected to climb to about 700,000 annually for the first 3 years and then decrease slightly to 675,000 per year. Total annual immigration was estimated by the Census Bureau in 1992 to be 880,000 a year over the next six decades. Refugees and those fleeing political persecution at home (some 131,000 in 1991) are in addition to these totals.

3. The Mexico City Policy and U.S. Bilateral Aid Programs

Amid much conflict between developed nations and LDCs, in 1974, the United Nations adopted a sweeping World Population Plan of Action at a meeting in Bucharest, Rumania, that helped to legitimize government involvement in population policy and build international cooperation (Finkle and Crane, 1975). The U.S. government was fully committed to international population policy, was by far the largest donor to assistance programs, and played a leadership role in these efforts (NSC Ad Hoc Group on Population, 1980).

In 1984, representatives from 149 nations met in Mexico City at the International Conference on Population to adapt the Bucharest plan to new social, political, and economic conditions and to revise its recommendations. Although fertility rates had declined modestly in the 10-year interval (from 2.03 to 1.67), the conference noted continuing reasons for concern. Chief among these was the perpetuation of high rates of growth in the LDCs, widening economic disparities between developed nations and the LDCs, rapid urbanization, and environmental and resource impacts that constrained future economic development. The conference endorsed the basic premise that population policies must be part of an overall strategy of development, as must improvement in the status of women in society. It also urged governments to adopt national population policies that could help achieve such goals while respecting (as the United Nations had always emphasized in population policy) "human rights, the religious beliefs, philosophical convictions, cultural values, and fundamental rights of each individual and couple to determine the size of its own family."

The United States representative, former Senator James L. Buckley, added a twist to U.S. policy that has come to be called the Mexico City Policy. Reflecting a new Reagan administration population policy that was widely attributed to the strongly pronatalist economist Julian Simon, Buckley said that "population growth is, of itself, neither good nor bad," but rather its effect depends upon the circumstances. He asserted that development of free-market economies was "the natural mechanism for slowing population growth," and hence should be the preferred policy path. He also announced a "sharpening of focus" of U.S. population assistance policy to be more responsive to "human dignity and family values" (Buckley, 1984; see also U.S. AID, 1983).

The direct impact of the Mexico City Policy was clear even if indirect effects are difficult to assess. The United States said it would no longer contribute money to the U.N. Fund for Population Activities, the major multilateral funding agency for international family planning programs, because it believed such funds were used by China and other nations in violation of these principles. At that time, the United States was the largest contributor to the U.N. program, pledging about $38 million a year (27% of its budget). Support also was ended for nongovernmental organizations that "perform or actively promote abortion," whether or not U.S. funds are used directly for those purposes (direct use having been barred by Congress since 1974).

Despite the U.N. fund cutoff, the United States maintained its bilateral population assistance programs, which for fiscal 1985 involved about $290 million (approximately 44% of all international population aid). By fiscal 1993, the foreign aid bill funded international population assistance at $430 million, the largest in the history of the program. Most of the funding supports family planning services and contraceptives, research, and demographic surveys, and the United States remains the principal donor to family planning programs worldwide. To put the U.S. program in perspective, in 1992, the U.N. Population Fund's budget was about $225 million a year. It is also important to note that population program officials argue the funds are insufficient to achieve world needs. The U.N. has said that to stabilize world population at 10 to 11 billion by the year 2100 would require doubling current budgets, among other actions to lower fertility.

Those goals of meeting world family planning needs were written into the U.N. Amsterdam Declaration on world stabilization strategy, developed in late 1989 at a U.N. conference and signed by the United States and 78 other nations. It calls for each developed nation to contribute 4% of its foreign aid budget to international population programs, which would provide $9 billion annually. That amount was thought to be enough to provide every woman in the world with access to family planning services. By the early 1990s, a Congressional Coalition on Population and Development, endorsed by 89 members of Congress, pressed for that level of funding. The Bush administration favored increased spending on international population programs, although not as high as the 4% level, in part because of studies (including one by the National Academy of Sciences) calling population "the biggest single driver of atmospheric pollution" and global warming (Alper, 1991).

Despite increased funding of U.S. bilateral aid programs, critics of the Mexico City Policy were unappeased. They considered it poorly designed, unworkable, and inappropriate (some called it "voodoo demographics"), and they fought it over the next 8 years in Congress and the courts, without much success. Both the House and Senate voted to overturn the Mexico City Policy and restore funding to the U.N. program ($20 million worth in opposition to any funding. As late as summer 1992, President Bush threatened to veto the foreign assistance appropriation bill if the provision was left in. Thus, between 1986 and 1992, the United States eliminated all U.S. contributions to the U.N. population program. Underlying the Reagan and Bush defense of the Mexico City position was pressure from right-Underlying the Reagan and Bush defense of the Mexico City position was pressure from right-wing groups convinced that China's population policy involved widespread use of coercive abortions or involuntary sterilizations. The political pressure continued even though China denied the charges, and no evidence supporting the allegations was found by a congressional investigating team that visited China in 1987 or in separate studies by AID. Aside from the loss of funds for the U.N. population program, perhaps the greatest effect of the Mexico City Policy was to signal the withdrawal of the United States from a position of world leadership on population issues (Donaldson, 1990; Finkle and Crane, 1986; Johnson, 1988). Indeed, nothing that occurred through 1992 indicated a return to the nation's earlier role of world leader on population.

As one sign of the continuing controversy surrounding international population policy, the United Nations Conference on Environment and Development (the Earth Summit), held in June 1992, was timid on the subject. Official documents substituted for the standard term *family planning* the more innocuous *appropriate demographic policies*. The conference itself was divided on population issues. Conference Secretary-General Maurice Strong and several heads of state favored putting population at the center of environmental policy recommendations. But nongovernmental organizations (including feminists, some environmentalists, and poverty activists) and representatives of many LDCs rejected that position. They did so in part to protest the refusal of industrialized nations to give equal consideration to their own "overconsumption" of resources as a fundamental cause of global environmental problems.

Despite these disagreements, the summit's key action document, Agenda 21, which the United States supported, included a full chapter on population (Demographic Dynamics and Sustainability). It called for adoption by every nation of a national population policy, an incorporation of population issues into environmental planning, more research on environmental carrying capacity, a strengthening of population-related institutions, and greater inclusion of women and local communities in population program management. The next U.N. International Conference on Population and Development, scheduled for summer 1994 in Cairo, seems likely to revisit many of these issues.

4. *Controversies Over Family Planning and Abortion*

For much of the 20 years of its existence, the U.S. family planning program (especially that part under Title X) has been controversial. At the peak of the program, more than 2500 agencies were operating clinics in some 5000 sites that provided services to nearly 5 million patients (low-income women and teen-agers). By 1992, the number of clinics and patients had declined by about 20% and annual federal spending stood at $180 million. Title X represented more than half of all federal expenditures for family planning through the mid-1970s and a little over a third by the late 1980s. The decline in funding is particularly notable in light of studies showing that every dollar of public funds spent to provide contraceptive services saved $4.40 in costs that otherwise would have been incurred in health care, welfare, and nutritional services (Forrest and Singh, 1990).

In recent years, political conflict has centered on provision of services to unmarried teenagers and the availability of abortion counseling and services. Strongly organized antiabortion forces kept Congress from renewing family planning programs and putting their funding on a regular basis. From 1984 to 1992, often bitter battles over abortion services created a legislative gridlock that forced Congress to put Title X on an emergency funding basis. In another instance reflecting the same forces, in 1988, HHS reinterpreted the 1970 family planning act to approve a "gag rule" that prohibited staff of federally funded family planning clinics from providing any information to patients about abortion; in a five to four decision in 1991 (*Rust* v. *Sullivan*), the Supreme Court upheld the prohibition on abortion counseling. That decision mobilized supporters of these programs, and in 1992, both houses of Congress voted to reverse the HHS interpretation of Title X. President Bush vetoed the legislation, and Congress lacked the votes to override his veto. However, two days after taking office, President Bill Clinton overturned the HHS rule by executive order.

The courts were active on abortion issues in other ways during the 1970s and 1980s. Antiabortion forces had long hoped the Supreme Court would overturn the 1973 *Roe* v. *Wade* decision legalizing abortion, opening the gates to restrictive state abortion laws. With new justices appointed by Presidents Reagan and Bush, many supporters of family planning and abortion rights feared the Court would reverse the Roe decision in 1992. However, in a five to four ruling in *Planned Parenthood* v. *Casey*, the Court took a middle ground, with five separate opinions running to 156 pages. It reaffirmed a woman's right to terminate a pregnancy in the early stages and indicated a total ban on abortions would be unconstitutional. The justices backed away from the position that abortion is a fundamental right, and four of them indicated they favored overturning the Roe decision. It is certain the Court will be forced to clarify abortion rights further.

E. U.S. Population Policy and Politics: An Overview

As this review of policy development makes clear, governmental actions directed at components of U.S. population problems have evolved slowly over a considerable time, and for varying purposes. To summarize, since the mid-1960s, the federal government has adopted direct and indirect policies on international population assistance, domestic family planning information and services, population research, and immigration. Population agencies have been established in the Department of Health and Human Services (the Office of Population Affairs and NICHD's Center for Population Research) and in the State Department (AID and the Office of Population). A National Security Council Ad Hoc Group on Population was established in 1975 to help coordinate foreign policy aspects of the work of 18 U.S. departments and agencies (NSC Ad Hoc Group on Population Policy, 1980).

This collection of policies, although impressive from some perspectives, is neither an explicit nor comprehensive national population policy, a goal that was endorsed for all nations at the 1992 Earth Summit. The United States has no national growth policy and no population distribution policy. Despite the administrative changes of the past 25 years, it also lacks the institutional capacity to plan for and adapt to population changes.

Critics have elaborated on the costs of such omissions in U.S. policy (Corsa, 1979; Oosterbaan, 1980; Sundquist, 1975). For example, the U.S. government urges other nations to curtail population growth that exacerbates global environmental and resource problems, yet the nation has no policy to limit its own prodigious growth rate. The Select Committee on Population in 1978 addressed one critical element in the U.S. nonpolicy:

> The Federal Government has no capacity to plan systematically for population change; yet changes in the size, age, composition and geographical distribution of the population can, and often do, have profound effects on Federal policies and Federal policies and programs often influence the direction of population change unintentionally (U.S. Congress, 1978b).

Congress has held hearings periodically on population growth policy as well as policies for planning for population change (U.S. Congress, 1981b, 1981c). These were an outgrowth of the *Global 2000 Report* and the efforts of national environmental groups, particularly the Global Tomorrow Coalition. The political climate generally has not been conducive to serious consideration of these proposals. However, following the reemergence of population issues on the agenda in the late 1980s, environmental groups have become far more aggressive in urging congressional consideration of population pressures in responding to global environmental threats such as climate change and loss of biological diversity. In addition to the long-standing population groups such as Zero Population Growth, the Population Crisis Committee, and the Population Institute, the Sierra Club and the Audubon Society have taken up the population cause. The Sierra Club, for example, has an international population program with a Washington director. In 1991, some 100 environmental organizations began a campaign to persuade Congress and the White House to restore U.S. leadership on global population issues (Alper, 1991).

The limited character of U.S. population policy is not a puzzle. It can be explained by the nature of population trends, the characteristics of the U.S. political system, and the politics of population policy making. The impact of trends such as a slowly growing population—or even maldistribution of the population—is often uncertain, long-range, and diffuse rather than clearly predictable, immediate, and specific. Thus, except for controversial issues such as abortion or intense local growth pressures (e.g., in southern California), population issues have not occupied a prominent position on the systemic or institutional agendas. Moreover, neither the U.S. public nor policy makers tend to be well informed about population trends and their consequences (Hetrick et al., 1972). To the extent population issues are associated with sensitive matters of human reproduction, religion, and individual rights, population policies may be viewed as politically hazardous and best avoided (Bachrach and Bergman, 1973; Littlewood, 1977).

Even when population issues do reach governmental agendas, institutional fragmentation tends to inhibit policy development. Sundquist (1978) compared the capacity of the United States for policy making on population distribution to that of five European countries and concluded that the pluralistic American political system made the building of consensus and policy adoption inordinately difficult even when agreement existed in the executive branch on desirable policy change. Congress itself suffers from certain institutional incapacities. Michael Teitlebaum, staff director of the select committee in 1977 to 1978, calculated that between 30 and 100 committees in Congress dealt with population issues. Congress, he said was characterized by "chaos": "Much that happens is accidental or not understood by those that make it happen" (Population Reference Bureau, 1979). Understandably, members of Congress tend not to accord population issues a high priority. There is little political incentive to do so. Policy making is most successful when proposals are supported by large, well-organized interest groups, when there is a strong constituency for policy change, and when leadership in the White House and Congress is able to overcome institutional fragmentation. There has been no constituency for population policy and little sustained policy leadership over the past two decades. However, the recent efforts of environmental groups to promote population issues may alter the political climate and incentives.

V. POLICY CHOICES AND POPULATION POLICY ANALYSIS

What new population policies are needed in the United States? The answer, of course, depends on how one assesses population trends and their consequences—both worldwide and in the United States, the capacity of current policies to deal satisfactorily with those problems, and the effectiveness of additional or revised population policies. The kinds of questions that might be asked can be noted for five areas of population policy: growth, distribution, population planning, population research, and international assistance.

1. *Population Growth Policy.* Should the United States adopt a formal policy on population growth, setting a particular goal for the "optimum" size of the U.S. population or for a rate of growth consistent with other national goals (e.g., on the environment, energy use, economic growth, and human rights)? In particular, should there be a population stabilization policy clearly setting a goal of a stationary or nongrowing population and providing a variety of means to achieve that goal? What role should immigration policy play within this context? Should net immigration (both legal and illegal) be maintained at the present level, allowed to increase, or reduced? What costs, benefits, and risks are associated with major policy alternatives, including a continuation of present policy? How effective are such policies likely to be? What criteria should govern decision making on growth and immigration policies (e.g., concern for individual freedom, social justice or equity, maternal and child health, environmental quality, or economic well-being)?

2. *Population Distribution Policy.* How do present federal, state, and local policies influence the distribution of population and economic growth? Should the United States adopt an explicit national policy to influence the distribution of the population? What type of policy will best minimize the undesirable economic and social effects of migration and changing patterns of regional growth and economic development? What costs and benefits are associated with the major policy alternatives?

3. *Population Planning.* Should federal, state, and local governments adopt policies to facilitate demographic data analysis and planning for changes in the size, age composition, and geographical distribution of the population? What improvements in data gathering and analysis are needed? What kinds of institutional arrangements are best suited for long-range population planning?

4. *Population Research.* What kind of research is most directly pertinent to the current and anticipated needs of policy makers? Should research in health-related aspects of population sciences and in basic demography be emphasized over the more applied social sciences and policy analysis, as has long been the case?

5. *International Assistance.* What changes, if any, are desirable in U.S. international economic and population assistance? Should present emphasis on family planning programs be changed? Should aid be channeled through multilateral agencies rather than through AID? How might population assistance programs be more fully integrated with overall U.S. foreign policy objectives, and should they play a greater role in foreign policy decisions?

As many of these questions indicate, development of population policy involves analysis of complex and intensely controversial issues such as immigration, family planning, and abortion. Policy analysis of demographic changes contributes to the making of policy choices by clarifying policy alternatives and their consequences and by explicating criteria of policy evaluation and choice (Miller and Godwin, 1977). However, such analysis is not easy. Despite the growth of an enormous literature on population (well over 100,000 books and articles have been indexed by *Population Index* since 1950), fertility and migration decision making is complex and knowledge of causal relationships is limited and imprecise. Knowledge of the consequences of population change is similarly limited. Thus, considerable uncertainty surrounds any population policy analysis, and policy recommendations often lack a firm grounding in scientific knowledge. These limitations flow partly from inherent methodological weaknesses in the study of population dynamics and their effects—including the uncertainty of long-range population projections. But they also reflect the still modest degree of research on population trends and consequences and on policy alternatives. During the 1970s, only 3 to 4% of all citations in the *Population Index* dealt with policy issues, and many of these were only marginally related to public policy choice; the situation is much the same in the early 1990s.

One consequence of such a weak policy literature is the absence of clear guidelines for policy makers, evident, for example, in the conclusions of a National Academy of Sciences conference on population and development in 1974:

> In the absence of hard data on the effectiveness (and on the secondary and tertiary effects) of most population policies, the seminar participants necessarily relied on common sense, empirical observations, philosophical predilections, ideological biases, and practical political considerations (Stycos, 1977).

The response to these conditions should not be a general call for "more research," but a specific enumeration of the type of policy-relevant inquiries that offer the greatest promise. A number of such research agendas have been prepared for social scientists, and perusal of them would be a useful starting point for those entering the field (Berelson, 1976; Demeny, 1988; Ilchman, 1975).

Political scientists who do not embrace policy analysis can nevertheless contribute to policy evaluation and development by improving our understanding of the political and institutional constraints on population policy making and the impact of population change on governmental institutions and political processes. There is no shortage of suggestions for additional research in these areas. Over a decade ago, the Center for Population Research in NICHD distributed an extensive list of topics on "Political Aspects of Population, Family Planning, Reproduction Research: Research Problem Areas and Research Ideas." Other research ideas can be found in literature from the 1970s (e.g., Clinton, 1973; Godwin, 1975; Nash, 1972; Weiner, 1971) as well as more contemporary work.

Improved knowledge of the determinants and consequences of population change and of policy alternatives should be helpful in clarifying the issues. Population policy analysis cannot, of course, replace political interaction and choice. As made clear by numerous governmental studies and independent assessments in recent years (MacNeill et al., 1991; World Commission on Environment and Development, 1987), the next several decades will be a critical time in human history. Population and environmental changes are occurring on a vast scale worldwide and have enormous implications for human welfare and the natural systems that sustain life. These developments provide the best reason to give population trends the serious consideration they so obviously merit and to illuminate the policy choices that can help to bring about a more sustainable human future than otherwise likely to occur.

NOTES

1. There are, of course, significant uncertainties in estimating present population sizes and in projecting rates and sizes for the future. A good review of some of these uncertainties can be found in Demeny (1979) and Haub (1987). Demeny sums up the problem of diverse forecasts:

   > In an age of national planning bureaus, world plans of action, and global targets, predicting
   > the future population is apt to be a thriving industry. Indeed, population projections have pro-
   > liferated in the last decade or two, well beyond the degree that would be reasonably explained
   > by ordinary human curiosity, increased scientific ability to fathom the future, or the require-
   > ments of old-fashioned social policymaking. . . . The interested customer nowadays can choose
   > among an impressive variety of population forecasts, national, regional, and global, and the
   > number of such forecasts seems to increase from year to year (p. 141).

2. The total fertility rate (TFR) refers to the average number of children that would be born to each
   woman in a population if each were to live through her child-bearing years (15 to 49) bearing children at the same rate as women of those ages actually did in a given year. In simple terms, the TFR
   answers the question: How many children are women having at present: In developed nations with
   low mortality rates, a TFR of 2.1 indicates "replacement-level" fertility or the level at which the nation's population would stop growing eventually. Migration is not considered in calculating the TFR.
3. Relatively recent works on population distribution policy include National Academy of Sciences
   (1980), Sundquist (1975, 1978), Berry and Dahmann (1977), Frey (1990), and Fosler et al. (1990).
4. An extensive review of U.S. international population policy, including a history of population assistance
   programs, budgetary allocations, international conferences held, and current policy issues can be
   found in NSC Ad Hoc Group on Population Policy (1980). See also Donaldson (1990), Johnson
   (1988), and Piotrow (1973).

REFERENCES

Alper, J. (1991). Environmentalists: Ban the (population) bomb. *Science* 252 (May 31): 1247.

Bachrach, P., and Bergman, E. (1973). *Power and Choice: The Formulation of American Population
   Policy*. Lexington Books, Lexington, MA.

Berelson, B. (1976). Social science research on population: A review. *Population and Development
   Review* 2 (June): 219–266.

Berry, B. J. L., and Dahmann, D. C. (1977). Population redistribution in the United in the 1970s. *Population and Development Review* 3 (December): 443–472.

Bogue, D. J., and Tsui, A. O. (1979). A reply to Paul Demeny's "On the End of the Population Explosion." *Population and Development Review* 5 (September): 479–493.

Bouvier, L. F., and De Vita, C. J. (1991). The baby boom—Entering midlife. *Population Bulletin* 46
   (November): 1–34.

Buckley, J. L. (1984). Statement delivered at the United Nations International Conference on Population, Mexico City. Reprinted in *The New York Times*, August 8, p. 4.

Clinton, R. L. (1973). Population, politics, and political science. In *Population and Politics*. R. L. Clinton (Ed.). Lexington Books, Lexington, MA, pp. 51–57.

Coale, A. J. (1974). The history of the human population. In *The Human Population*. Scientific American (Ed.). Freeman, San Francisco, pp. 15–25.

Commission on Population Growth and the American Future (1972). *Population and American Future*.
   U.S. Government Printing Office, Washington, D.C.

Corsa, L. (1979). Population policy in the United States. *Sierra*, May/June: 12–13, 62–63.

Corsa, L., and Oakley, D. (1979). *Population Planning*. University of Michigan Press, Ann Arbor, MI.

Council on Environmental Quality and Department of State (1980). *The Global 2000 Report to the
   President: Entering the Twenty-First Century*. U.S. Government Printing Office, Washington,
   D.C.

Davis, K., and Bernstam, M. S. (Eds.) (1991). *Resources, Environment, and Population: Present Knowledge, Future Options.* Oxford University Press, New York.

Davis, K., Bernstam, M. S., and Ricardo-Campbell, R. (Eds.) (1986). Below-replacement fertility in industrial societies: Causes, consequences, policies. *Population and Development Review* 12 (Suppl.): 1–36.

Demeny, P. (1974). The populations of the underdeveloped countries. In *The Human Population.* Scientific American (Ed.). Freeman, San Francisco, pp. 105–115.

—— (1979). On the end of the population explosion. *Population and Development Review* 5 (March): 141–162.

—— (1986). The world demographic situation. In *World Population and U.S. Policy.* J. Menken (Ed.). W. W. Norton, New York, pp. 27–66.

—— (1988). Social science and population policy. *Population and Development Review* 14 (September): 451–479.

Donaldson, P. J. (1990). *Nature Against Us: The United States and the World Population Crisis, 1965·1980.* University of North Carolina Press, Chapel Hill, NC.

Easterlin, R. A. (1980). *Birth and Fortune: The Impact of Numbers on Personal Welfare.* Basic Books, New York.

Ehrlich, P. R., and Ehrlich, A. H. (1990). *The Population Explosion.* Simon & Schuster, New York.

Finkle, J. L., and Crane, B. A. (1975). The politics of Bucharest: Population, development, and the new international economic order. *Population and Development Review* 1 (September): 87–114.

—— (1985). Ideology and politics at Mexico City: The United States at the International Conference on Population. *Population and Development Review* 11: 1–28.

Forrest, J. D., and Singh, S. (1990). Public-sector savings resulting from expenditures for contraceptive services. *Family Planning Perspectives* 22 (January/February): 6–15.

Fosler, R. S., Alonso, W., Meyer, J. A., and Kern, R. (1990). *Demographic Change and the American Future.* University of Pittsburgh Press, Pittsburgh, PA.

Frey, W. H. (1990). Metropolitan America: Beyond the transition. *Population Bulletin* 45 (July): 1–49.

Godwin, R. K. (Ed.) (1975). *Comparative Policy Analysis: The Study of Population Policy Determinants in Developing Countries.* Lexington Books, Lexington, MA.

Hartmann, B. (1987). *Reproductive Rights and Wrongs: The Global Politics of Population Control and Contraceptive Choice.* HarperCollins, New York.

Haub, C. (1987). Understanding population projections. *Population Bulletin* 42 (December): 1–43.

Hetrick, C. C., Nash, A. E. K., and Wyner, A. J. (1972). Population and politics: Information, concern, and policy support among the American public. In *Governance and Population.* A. E. K. Nash (Ed.). U.S. Government Printing Office, Washington, D.C., pp. 301–331.

Horiuchi, S. (1992). Stagnation in the decline of the world population growth rate during the 1980s. *Science* 257 (7 August): 761–765.

Ilchman, W. F. (1975). Population knowledge and population policies. In *Comparative Policy Analysis.* R. K. Godwin (Ed.). Lexington Books, Lexington, MA, pp. 217–265.

Johnson, S. P. (1988). *World Population and the United Nations.* Cambridge University Press, New York.

Jones, C. O. (1984). *An Introduction to the Study of Public Policy*, 3rd ed. Duxbury Press, North Scituate, MA.

Keeley, C. B. (1979). *U. S. Immigration: A Policy Analysis.* Population Council, New York.

Keyfitz, N. (1989). The growing human population. In *Managing Planet Earth.* W. Clark (Ed.). Freeman, New York, pp. 61–72.

Kingdon, J. W. (1984). *Agendas, Alternatives, and Public Policies.* Little, Brown, Boston.

Kraft, M. E. (1984). Political responses to population stabilization and decline in the United States and Western Europe: Implications for population policy. In *Public Policy and Social Institutions.* H. Rodgers (Ed.). JAI Press, Greenwich, CT, pp. 219–255.

Lasswell, H. D., and Kaplan, A. (1950). *Power and Society.* Yale University Press, New Haven, CT.

Light, P. C. (1988). *Baby Boomers.* Norton, New York.

Littlewood, T. B. (1977). *The Politics of Population Control.* University of Notre Dame Press, Notre Dame, IN.

Mathews, J. T. (Ed.) (1991). *Preserving the Global Environment*: *The Challenge of Shared Leadership*. Norton, New York.

Mauldin, W. P., and Berelson, B. (1978). Conditions of fertility decline in developing countries, 1965–1975. *Studies in Family Planning* 9 (May): 89–147.

MacNeill, J., Winsemius, P., and Yakushiji, T. (1991). *Beyond Interdependence*: *The Meshing of the World's Economy and the Earth's Ecology*. Oxford University Press, New York.

McIntosh, C. A. (1983). *Population Policy in Western Europe*: *Responses to Low Fertility in France, Sweden, and West Germany*. Sharpe, New York.

Meadows, D. H., Meadows, D. L., and Randers, J. (1992). *Beyond the Limits*: *Confronting Global Collapse, Envisioning a Sustainable Future*. Chelsea Green, Post Mills, VT.

Menken, J. (Ed.) (1986). *World Population and U.S. Policy*: *The Choices Ahead*. Norton, New York.

Miller, W. B., and Godwin, R. K. (1977). *Psyche and Demos*: *Individual Psychology and the Issues of Population*. Oxford University Press, New York.

Nash, A. E. K. (Ed.) (1972). *Governance and Population*: *The Governmental Implications of Population Change*. U.S. Government Printing Offices, Washington, D.C.

—— (1978). Procedural and substantive unorthodoxies on the population commission's agenda. In *Population Policy Analysis*. M. E. Kraft and M. Schneider (Eds.). Lexington Books, Lexington, MA, pp. 55-65.

National Academy of Sciences (1980). *Population Redistribution and Public Policy*. National Academy Press, Washington, D.C.

NSC Ad Hoc Group on Population Policy (1980). *U.S. International Population Policy*: *Fourth Annual Report of the NSC Ad Hoc Group on Population Policy*. U.S. Department of State, Washington, D.C.

The New York Times (1981). Panel asks rise in immigration, with tighter law enforcement. February 27, pp. 1, B5.

North, D. S. (1978). The growing importance of immigration to population policy. In *Population Policy Analysis*. M. E. Kraft and M. Schneider (Eds.). Lexington Books, Lexington, MA, pp. 81-91.

Nortman, D. L., and Hofstatter, E. (1978). *Population and Family Planning Programs*, 9th ed. Population Council, New York.

Oosterbaan, J. (1980). *Population Dispersal*: *A National Imperative*. Lexington Books, Lexington, MA.

Ophuls, W., and Boyan, A. S., Jr. (1992). *Ecology and the Politics of Scarcity Revisited*: *The Unraveling of the American Dream*. Freeman, San Francisco.

PAA Affairs (1979). Population Association of America, Washington, D.C. (Summer).

Pear, R. (1992). New look at the U.S. in 2050: Bigger, older and less white. *The New York Times*, December 4, pp. 1, 10.

Piotrow, P. T. (1973). *World Population Crisis*: *The United States Response*. Praeger, New York.

Population Reference Bureau (1971). Population activities of the United States government. *Population Bulletin* 27 (August): 2-27.

—— (1979). Intercom, May, p. 12.

—— (1992). 1992 World Population Data Sheet. Population Reference Bureau, Washington, D.C.

Repetto, R. (1987). Population, resources, environment: An uncertain future. *Population Bulletin* 42 (July): 1-43.

Rich, W. (1973). *Smaller Families through Social and Economic Progress*. Overseas Development Council, Washington, D.C.

Rubin, E. R. (1987). *Abortion, Politics, and the Courts*: *Roe v. Wade and Its Aftermath*, rev. ed. Greenwood Press, New York.

Sadik, N. (1992). *The State of World Population 1992*: *A World in Balance*. United Nations Population Fund, New York.

Simons, G. B. (1986). Family planning programs. In *World Population and U.S. Policy*. J. Menken (Ed.). Norton, New York, pp. 175-206.

Simon, J. L. (1981). *The Ultimate Resource*. Princeton University Press, Princeton, NJ.

—— (1989). *Population Matters*: *People, Resources, Environment and Immigration*. Transaction Books, New Brunswick, NJ.

Simon, J. L., and Kahn, H. (Ed.) (1984). *The Resourceful Earth*: *A Response to Global 2000*. Basil Blackwell, New York.

Stein, J. M. (Ed.) (1993). *Growth Management*: *The Planning Challenge of the 1990s*. Sage, Newbury Park, CA.

Stetson, D. M. (1973). Population policy and the limits of government capability in the United States. In *Population and Politics*. R. L. Clinton (Ed.). Lexington Books, Lexington, MA, pp. 247–271.

—— (1978). Family policy and fertility in the United States. In *Population Policy Analysis*. M. E. Kraft and M. Schneider (Eds.). Lexington Books, Lexington, MA, pp. 103–114.

Stycos, J. M. (1977). Population policy and development. *Population and Development Review* 3 (March/June): 103–112.

Sundquist, J. L. (1975). *Dispersing Population*: *What America Can Learn from Europe*. Brookings Institution, Washington, D.C.

—— (1978). A comparison of policy-making capacity in the United States and five European countries: The case of population distribution. In *Population Policy Analysis*. M. E. Kraft and M. Schneider (Eds.). Lexington, MA, pp. 67–80.

Teitelbaum, M. S. (1986). Intersections: Immigration and demographic change and their impact on the United States. In *World Population and U.S. Policy*. J. Menken (Ed.). Norton, New York, pp. 133–174.

Teitelbaum, M. S., and Winter, J. M. (1985). *The Fear of Population Decline*. Academic Press, New York.

Tobin, R. J. (1993). Environment, population, and economic development. In *Environmental Policy in the 1990s*, 2nd ed. N. J. Vig and M. E. Kraft (Eds.). Congressional Quarterly Press, Washington, D.C., pp. 275–297.

Tsui, A. O., and Bogue, D. J. (1978). Declining world fertility: Trends, causes, implications. *Population Bulletin* 33 (October): 1–55.

U.S. AID (1983). U.S. AID Policy Paper on Population Assistance [excerpt]. *Population and Development Review* 9 (March): 185–192.

U.S. Congress (1971). Declaration of U.S. Policy of Population Stabilization by Voluntary Means. Special Subcommittee on Human Resources of the Committee on Labor and Public Welfare, U.S. Senate, 92nd Cong., 1st Sess.

—— (1978a). Final Report of the Select Committee on Population. U.S. House of Representatives, 95th Cong., 2nd Sess.

—— (1978b). Domestic Consequences of United States Population Change. Select Committee on Population, U.S. House of Representatives, 95th Cong., 2nd Sess.

—— (1981a). U.S. Immigration Policy and the National Interest. Committee on the Judiciary, U.S. House of Representatives and Committee on the Judiciary, U.S. Senate, 97th Cong., 1st Sess.

—— (1981b). A bill to establish a national population policy and to establish an Office of Population Policy. H.R. 907, 97th Congress, 1st Sess.

—— (1981c). A bill to establish in the Federal Government a global foresight capability with respect to natural resources, the environment, and population. S. 1771, 97th Cong., 1st Sess.

United Nations (1992). *World Population Prospects*: *The 1992 Revision*. United Nations Population Division, New York.

van der Tak, J., Haub, C., and Murphy, E. (1979). Our population predicament: A new look. *Population Bulletin* 34 (December): 1–41.

Wattenberg, B. J. (1987). *The Birth Dearth*: *What Happens When People in Free Countries Don't Have Enough Babies?* Pharos Books, New York.

Weiner, M. (1971). Political demography: An inquiry into the political consequences of population change. In *Rapid Population Growth*: *Consequences and Policy Implications*. National Academy of Sciences (Ed.). Johns Hopkins Press, Baltimore, pp. 567–617.

Westoff, C. F. (1973). The Commission on Population Growth and the American Future: Its origins, operations, and aftermath. *Population Index* 39: 491–502.

—— (1974). United States. In *Population Policy in Developed Nations*. B. Berelson (Ed.). McGraw-Hill, New York, pp. 731–759.

—— (1978). Marriage and fertility in the developed countries. *Scientific American* 239(December): 51–57.

—— (1986). Fertility in the United States. *Science* 234 (October 31): 554–559.

World Commission on Environment and Development (1987). *Our Common Future*. Oxford University Press, New York.

SUGGESTED READINGS

Bibliographies

Driver, E. D. (1972). *World Population Policies*: *An Annotated Bibliography*. Lexington Books, Lexington, MA.

Kraft, M. E., and Schneider, M. (1984). Population Policy. In *Basic Literature in Policy Studies*: *A Comprehensive Bibliography*. S. Nagel (Ed.). JAI Press, Greenwich, CN, pp. 305–316.

Population Index. Office of Population Research, Princeton University, Princeton, NJ (quarterly annotated bibliography).

Sourcebook on Population: *1970–1976*. Population Reference Bureau, Washington, D.C., 1976.

U.S. Immigration and Naturalization Service (1979). *Immigration Literature*: *Abstracts of Demographic, Economic, and Policy Studies*. U.S. Government Printing Office, Washington, D.C.

Data Sources, Newsletters, and Periodicals

American Demographics. American Demographics, Ithaca, NY (monthly).

Current Population Reports. U.S. Bureau of the Census, Washington, D.C.

Demographic Yearbook. United Nations, New York.

Demography. Population Association of America, Washington, D.C.

Family Planning Perspectives. Planned Parenthood Federation of America, New York.

Journal of Population. Human Sciences Press, New York.

PAA Affairs. Population Association of America, Washington, D.C.

Population Bulletin. Population Reference Bureau, Washington, D.C.

Population and Development Review. Center for Policy Studies, Population Council, New York.

Population and Family Planning Programs: *A Compendium of Data Through 1983*, 12th ed. (1985). Population Council, New York.

Population Reports. Population Information Program, Johns Hopkins, Baltimore.

Population Studies. University Press, London.

Population Today. Population Reference Bureau, Washington, D.C. (11 times a year).

Population Research and Policy Review. Elsevier Scientific, Amsterdam.

U.S. Census of Population. U.S. Bureau of the Census, Washington, D.C.

World Population Prospects. United Nations, New York.

The ZPG Reporter. Zero Population Growth, Washington, D.C.

Part H
PROBLEMS WITH AN URBAN AND REGIONAL PLANNING EMPHASIS

27
Land Use Policy

Norman Wengert
Colorado State University, Fort Collins, Colorado

Land use policy in the United States originated in the initial settlement of the American colonies after 1507, a major issue having been the occupation, ownership, and distribution of the land resource for use. After independence, the new government announced fundamental land use policies in the ordinances of 1785 and 1787. In 1862, the Homestead Act was a further expression of basic land use policy. The flood of population throughout American history created the urban land use policy issues and gave rise to urban land use controls toward the end of the 19th century continuing to the present. Zoning (in many variations), subdivision controls, and urban planning institutions became the tools of U.S. land use policies, with all levels of government playing particular roles. Emerging as a crucial land use policy issue appears to be that of providing "affordable housing" for the poor and disposed (often minorities). In this respect, the development of policies and administrative methods concerning affordable housing in the Mount Laurel (NJ) litigation and subsequent legislative action may have begun a new policy approach for meeting housing needs for low-income and impoverished citizens in highly urbanized metropolitan regions. The various techniques for implementing land use policies are described in this chapter.

I. TWO FOCI FOR U.S. LAND USE POLICY

Public policy for land use has two major foci: one concerns privately owned land and the other concerns publicly owned land. The principal category of public land is the so-called "public domain" owned and managed by the national government and still constituting about one third of the total U.S. land area. Other publicly owned lands, relatively small, pose many specialized policy issues not discussed in this chapter.

From a jurisdictional point of view, local governments (cities, towns, counties) have major responsibility for private lands pursuant to state constitutions, statutes, and state-administered common law. State and local governments are, of course, under the U.S. Constitution. In recent years, both state and federal governments have been expanding their roles with respect to private lands (Wright and Wright, 1985).

In those states created from the public domain, federal policies were the beginning of land use policy. In lands acquired from Mexico in 1848, Spanish and Mexican laws and traditions influenced land use policies. In an indirect way public domain problems and their policy resolution impacted land use policy even in nonpublic domain states.

Viewed from a different perspective, land use policy was shaped by two dominant forces: (1) the tremendous quantity of land in the public domain (regarded as vacant) and (2) the unprecedented increases in the U.S. population and its rapid, although uneven, spread throughout the land.

This chapter seeks to describe and explain public land use policy and its application in the context of (1) land ownership by private individuals; (2) the public domain and how it was dealt with; (3) the tremendous amount of land available; and (4) the growth, movement, and location of the U.S. population.

Some land use policies in the United States have been deliberately formulated in order to achieve particular results. Other policies have evolved, being the cumulative results of human social, political, and economic actions, practices, customs, and traditions. In the several centuries that white citizens have been dealing with land use in the United States, the situation changed from almost complete laissez-faire before the American Revolution to the present extensive system of governmental control shaped by a myriad of private interests and influences (Young, 1991).

II. THE PUBLIC DOMAIN

Until the beginning of this present century it was never doubted that America's destiny was to occupy the land from sea to shining sea, with farming (agriculture) being the major economic activity and the land in private ownership. Thomas Jefferson's hostilities to cities and urban life and his belief that yeoman farmers were essential to the achievement of democracy were widely shared. It was not anticipated that after 200 years, the federal government would still own one third of the land in the United States or that urban population would far exceed rural.

In colonial times, towns were established with minimal planning as service centers for surrounding farms. Commercial facilities were built to accommodate trade and commerce. In the 19th century, manufacturing and mining were developed, but few great issues were raised about their location or manner of land use.

The major instrument for land use decisions was the private deed or contract that could restrict how land was to be used (restrictive covenants). The location of streets, roads, the town square, the church, and perhaps the school probably were discussed in town meetings. Local governments also were involved in the development of infrastructure, but land use policies were largely the by-products of other decisions. The city of Philadelphia, for example, required the planting of shade trees along some sidewalks to protect pedestrians in the heat of summer. Transport modes and routes were significant influences; after 1830, railroads became increasingly important determinants of where people worked and lived.

After independence, the new government struggled with how best to privatize millions of acres of what came to be known as the public domain; settlement could not be controlled. One of the charges in the Declaration of Independence was that the king had tried to restrain movements west (The Quebec Act). It is important to note that from the beginning of white settlement, squatting on land presumed to be vacant was common. Timber and minerals were considered to be there for the taking without permits or constraints. Even in the 1890s, Congress continued to allow "bona fide" settlers to take wood without charge for fences, housing, barns, and so forth. First come, first served was a part of the frontier ethic. To suggest the need for title to land from which minerals or timber were being taken was considered an imposition. Later historians would complain about the theft of natural resources, but most "pioneers" were not bothered by legal technicalities of securing title to the land being exploited, and the U.S. government had neither the institutions nor the manpower nor the will to define or protect the national interest.

The "taking" approach shaped western mineral and water law. Title was not required to "stake a claim," and western water rights were established under the slogans "first in time, first in right" and "use it or lose it." The first general statute concerning mining on the public domain was enacted in 1872. The first forest preservation legislation was enacted in 1891 authorizing presidential withdrawal from entry under the land laws of areas designated by him as forest reservations (now National Forests). Until the Forest Service (1905) was able to put rangers on patrol in the reservations, millions of board feet of lumber were taken, as needed, and burning to clear land was not unusual!

In the early 1800s, the national government began selling small tracts to individual settlers. The hope (which persisted until 1862) was to finance the costs of government from the sale of land, but prices were so low and squatting so common that receipts were never very large. In addition, during most of the 19th century, Congress used land grants as a kind of currency to achieve a variety of objectives.

As additions to the national domain occurred (Louisiana Purchase, 1803; Florida, 1810; the Southwest, including California, as ceded by Mexico in the Treaty of Guadaloupe Hidalgo, 1848; Alaska, 1867; and a few smaller additions), the issues of what to do with the public domain loomed ever larger. The body of public land legislation was considerable, but various policy problems continued to plague policy makers. Table 1 records the gross distribution of public domain lands; and it suggests the extent to which Congress used land grants to achieve developmental, educational, and other social objectives (Gates, 1968; Hibbard, 1924, 1965; Peffer, 1951).

A few additional statistics (from the same source) complete the broad picture. The total area of the 50 states is 2,263,587,200 acres. Of this area, the original public domain totaled 1,837,770,240 acres. The present acreage "owned" by the federal government is 741,508,662 acres, of which 330,846,881 are in Alaska. Much of the balance is desert, rangeland, and mountain land. The public domain managed by the Bureau of Land Management totals 450,195,000 acres. The acreage managed by the U.S. Forest Service (withdrawals and purchases) totals 187,547,493 acres. The National Park Service is responsible for about 25 million acres. Thus, the land in private, state, and local government ownership totals about 1.5 billion acres. In passing, it might be noted that the lands controlled by the Bureau of Land Management, the U.S. Forest Service, and the National Park Service today pose many environmental and management policy issues. The land in private ownership is the primary focus of this chapter, however.

III. TWO POLICY ORDINANCES

Before the present U.S. Constitution was adopted (1789), the Continental Congress enacted two ordinances that established policies of lasting importance for public domain lands. The *first* was the Land Ordinance of 1785 and the *second* was the Northwest Ordinance of 1787 (Commager, 1934).

Table 1. Disposition of Public Lands, 1781–1977

Type	Acres
Disposition by methods not elsewhere classified	303,500,000
Granted or sold to homesteaders	287,500,000
Granted to states	
Support of common schools	77,600,000
Reclamation of swampland	64,900,000
Construction of railroads	37,100,000
Support of miscellaneous institutions	21,700,000
Purposes not classified elsewhere	117,500,000
Canals and rivers	6,100,000
Construction of wagon roads	3,400,000
Total granted to states	328,300,000
Granted to railroad corporations	94,300,000
Granted to veterans as military bounties	61,000,000
Confirmed as private land claims	34,000,000
Sold under timber and stone law	13,900,000
Granted or sold under timber culture law	10,900,000
Sold under desert land law	10,700,000
Grand Total	1,144,100,000

Modified from *Public Land Statistics*, U.S. Department of the Interior, Bureau of Land Management, 1977, Table 3. This is an annual publication, but the gross data have not changed significantly since 1977.

In its stress on order, the Ordinance of 1785 was typical of "The Age of Reason." It authorized a cadastral survey of the entire public domain. The survey was to be based on latitude and longitude, dividing the land into *townships* generally 6 miles square. Each township, in turn, was divided into 36 sections, each being 640 acres or 1 square mile. The sections could be and often were divided into tracts of 320, 160, 80, 40, and 20 acres. Units of varying sizes, of course, were not prohibited. The Ordinance provided that section 16, approximately in the center of each township, was reserved for the support of public schools. Sections 8, 11, 26, and 29 were reserved for the national government. The secretary of war was authorized to implement congressional land grants to veterans of the Revolutionary War.

The second major land use enactment of the Continental Congress was the Northwest Ordinance of 1787 establishing guidelines for the settlement and governance of the "Northwest Territory," which became Ohio, Indiana, Illinois, Wisconsin, and Michigan. This ordinance, in effect, set policy for the creation of new states out of the public domain lands. It recognized elements of English property law. It authorized the subdivision of the entire territory and provided for interim territorial governments (legislatures, governors, judges). It also guaranteed certain civil rights, and after such "grand" provisions, the ordinance established the per acre price of land at $1.50! Sale of public domain lands continued until the enactment of the Homestead Act in 1862.

Regrettably, Native American rights and interests were generally ignored or dealt with in a cavalier and cruel fashion. Nevertheless, the Northwest Ordinance of 1787 did provide:

> Article 3. . . . The utmost good faith shall always be observed towards the Indians; their lands and property shall never be taken from them without their consent; and in their property rights and liberty they shall never be invaded or disturbed, unless in just

and lawful wars authorized by Congress; but laws founded in justice and humanity shall from time to time be made for preventing wrongs being done them, and for preserving peace and friendship with them.

Most Indian tribes had limited concepts of property rights in land. Because of the superior force of the white settlers, Indian claims frequently were ignored even when based on treaty terms that were made the "law of the land" by the Constitution. Indian tribes pledged to live on reservations giving up rights to lands outside the reservations and agreeing not to roam freely as in the past. The implications of some of these treaties for water rights are today beginning to be litigated in some western states and could have drastic impact on present water allocations and uses.

Together, the ordinances of 1785 and 1787 opened up the Northwest Territory to settlement and promoted the establishment of privately owned, relatively small farms. The ordinances anticipated state governments with the same power and authority over land use possessed by the original 13 states. The national government was clearly regarded as the temporary custodian of the public domain pending its total privatization.

When the Constitution was adopted and well into the 19th century, citizens and leaders were abysmally ignorant of the "western" lands. For a long period it was believed that rainfall in the plains followed the plow! Therefore, settlement proceeded westward. The Reclamation Act of 1902 (32 Stat. 388) illustrates this commitment to private farm ownership even under arid conditions. It says, in effect, if the land is too arid to farm, the federal government will build dams and other structures to "make the desert bloom."

IV. THE HOMESTEAD ACT

The most important legislation of the 19th century with respect to the public domain and its settlement for farming was the Homestead Act of 1862 (12 Stat. 392), under which a person might acquire 160 acres (more under later special conditions) by living on it and working it as a farm. To settlers coming from the seaboard states or from Europe, 160 acres was a large farm, often more than one man and his family could handle (Peffer, 1951). The idea of settling the continent continued to be accepted as America's "manifest destiny" by most leaders (Gates, 1968; Peffer, 1951).

Although fraught with fraud and deception in implementation, the Homestead Act resulted in 250 million acres being converted to farms, mostly so-called "family farms," as Jefferson had hoped. The extent to which small farms still dominate American agriculture is indicated by data on the number and average size of farms.

In 1935, when the number of farms peaked and the average size of U.S. farms reached its lowest point, the number of farms was about 6.5 million and the average size was under 300 acres. There was considerable variation in size reflecting both economic and environmental factors. Wisconsin, even today, has numerous dairy farms of 60 acres or less. In 1990, the number of farms totaled about 2.1 million and the average size had increased to about 475 acres. Although the situation in each state and in each county is different, these data suggest some of the changes in land use planning and control for farm lands.

V. CHANGING PUBLIC INTERESTS

After the Civil War, pressures began to build for policies to protect the nation's remaining forest resources that were being wantonly wasted. These pressures culminated in the Withdrawal Act of 1891 (26 Stat. 1095). It took another 15 years before the U.S. Forest Service was created to administer the forest reserves. National Parks were established on a case-by-case basis beginning with Yellowstone Park in 1872. The National Park Service was created in 1916 to administer the parks.

The balance of the public domain was in a kind of limbo after World War I; some policy makers were still hoping to privatize these lands. This policy issue was not resolved until the enactment of the Taylor Grazing Act in 1934 (48 Stat. 1269) and the creation of the Bureau of Land Management in 1946, after which massive privatization ceased (Gates, 1968).

In any case, land use planning and the control of private lands in the United States have been primarily a 20th century phenomenon—usually a belated response to problems of urban growth and in small part to an awareness of better farm management. There was some local planning before 1900, but it hardly rated as major policy (Meck and Netter, 1983).

It is probably a coincidence that government concern for both rural and urban land use policy crystallized in the second decade of the 20th century. In 1914, Congress enacted the Smith-Lever Agricultural Extension Act, and in 1916 New York City began the first zoning program!

Both actions involved an implicit rejection of traditional laissez-faire approaches by government. Although each of these programs was very different in method and motivation, they both purported to seek wiser, better use of land. Through the Extension Act, farmers were to be taught how to apply Agricultural Experiment Station research. New York City, similarly, sought to rationalize urban land uses by grouping more or less homogeneous activities and structures on particular streets and in identified sections. An ultimate objective of both programs was "prosperity" for the farmer through more efficient production and for the urban property owner by fending off "undesirable" developments and structures.

In contrast to the Extension Act, which stressed the need to educate its farmer constituents, New York City and most others that adopted zoning relied on "police power"—regulations—to accomplish zoning goals. The idea that zoning should be "in accordance with a comprehensive master plan" did not become a part of the emphasis on urban land use control until the late 1920s (Haar, 1955). Properly used as vehicles for debate and discussion, comprehensive master plans could have served important educational functions concerning land use alternatives and issues. However, in most jurisdictions, the educational function of comprehensive planning has never been stressed. There is perhaps some hope that present-day environmental planning with its emphasis on "impact analyses" and its concerns for long-range consequences will improve the quality of local participation in planning and public understanding thereof.

Farm land use planning and control was, if not a major objective, nevertheless an important by-product of the New Deal and subsequent farm programs. Payments for conservation farming practices used economic incentives, rather than regulation, to achieve land use planning and control goals. The Soil Conservation Service, a New Deal program begun in 1935, promoted Soil Conservation Districts for farm and community planning. In recent years, with drought and dust blowing, there has been renewed interest in regulating agricultural land uses, especially "sod busting" on lands that should be kept in grass cover. However, there is little doubt that education and financial incentives (government payments), and group persuasion, not regulation, remain the chief techniques for influencing farm land use practices.

Public interest in urban land use planning and control seems to be cyclical, being roughly correlated with the ups and downs of the economy and especially of the real estate and housing markets. When urban land transactions are booming, public interests in controlling development, with some lag, also intensify. Thus, the widespread support for zoning in the

1920s coincided with a booming real estate market. After World War II, a similar boom occurred and with it a growing interest in better land use controls. More recently, in the 1970s and early 1980s (when the first edition of this book was written), there was growing attention to both local and state land use planning and control. Many states considered and some enacted laws giving municipalities and counties greater land use control authority. As the boom faltered and idle subdivisions began to show up outside of cities, this interest declined.

VI. PATTERNS OF URBAN GROWTH

Some have suggested that the elaborate structure of legal/constitutional protection of property in federal and state constitutions was a scheme of the rich to protect their interests, using the power of government to this end. Such economic determinist views (Marxian) overlook two ideological factors of substantial importance to American concepts of freedom and liberty. The *first* of these principles recognizes the relationship of land ownership to civil liberties and to resistance to autocratic governments. The *second* is the belief that widely held land ownership is essential for effective democracy.

It was not just rhetoric that led the people of Virginia (1776) and Massachusetts (1780) to link property ownership with life and liberty in their respective Bills of Rights. Two hundred years of English history had well established that possession of property was essential to the ability to resist tyranny. John Locke's justification of the "Glorious Revolution" of 1688 was familiar to many Colonial leaders if not by direct exposure then through Blackstone's *Commentary on the Laws of England* published in the 1760s. The supremacy of Parliament, as well as the importance of property in land, was clearly set forth by Blackstone; from whom, incidentally, Jefferson borrowed some choice phrases of the Declaration of Independence.

For Jefferson and many of his peers, the empty continent held the prospect of widespread land ownership, which, in turn, was regarded as essential to the kind of yeomen farmers felt necessary as a foundation of democracy. Although Virginia did not adopt Jefferson's proposal that every male citizen be granted 40 acres, that state led in abolishing primogeniture and feudal dues, and fee-simple ownership was stressed. Blackstone defined "ownership" in the way many Americans thought of the subject then and still do today. Ownership, Sir William Blackstone wrote, is ". . . that sole and despotic dominion which one man exercises over the external things of this world, in total exclusion of the right of any other individual in the universe" (Ehrlich, 1959: 113). This dominion, according to Blackstone, extended to the center of the earth and up into the sky.

VII. THE CHICAGO EXPERIENCE—REALITIES OF METROPOLITAN GROWTH

Incorporated as a city in 1837 with a population of 4470, Chicago grew sevenfold in 13 years to almost 30,000 in 1850. Twenty years later (1870), its population approached 300,000. The Great Fire of October 7–9, 1871, destroyed a third of the city—17,450 buildings—leaving 100,000 homeless. However, within a few years, the city was substantially rebuilt, and by 1900, Chicago's population topped 1.6 million. Chicago (within its city limits) reached 3.6 million in 1950. The city itself declined to 2.7 million in 1990, but the metropolitan region totaled over 8 million.

No one could say that Chicago was either beautiful or distinctive—except perhaps for the way in which the lake front and its park system were developed in the 1890s reflecting to some degree the "city beautiful" movement of the late 19th century.

In the Chicago real estate boom of the 1920s, open areas around Chicago were platted for miles in all directions. Boosters claimed that in due course Chicago would absorb Milwaukee 90 miles away. The collapse of the real estate market in 1927 ended such expectations and impoverished many speculators and promoters. Still today, "boom or bust" continues to characterize large segments of urban development and land use (Reilly, 1973)!

VIII. INCREASING INTEREST IN LAND USE CONTROLS

Land use planning and control of private lands are primarily a 20th century phenomenon. In prior centuries, a kind of control was achieved by conditions and restrictions written into deeds transferring or encumbering real property. However, such restrictions were only incidentally designed to achieve public purposes. Enforcement, for example, required a private suit by one of the parties in interest. Today in Houston, where zoning is not used, such restrictions are the basis for controlling urban land development. In that case, the municipal government has been given the authority to enforce deed restrictions (Siegan, 1972).

At the turn of the century, most houses were constructed one by one as individual units. During World War I, acute housing shortages stimulated construction of row housing, including the boxlike triplexes still standing in some New England cities. In the 1920s, lower-priced houses began to be built in a more or less uniform style, so that entire neighborhoods often consisted of look-alike houses. Narrow lots of 25 or 30 feet were common, because at that time, before mass ownership of automobiles, being able to walk short distances to streetcar lines was necessary. The 50- or 150-foot lot was one response to automobile transportation.

Most Americans only vaguely appreciated the meaning of the shift from dominantly rural to dominantly urban. In 1900, rural and urban populations were just about even. By 1920, urban population exceeded rural, and by 1990, rural population was about 4.5 million and urban population was about 245 million. Much of the urban growth since 1920 has been concentrated in what the U.S. Census Bureau came to call metropolitan statistical areas, pointing to the fact that the population increases were occurring in suburban communities adjacent or close to central cities. The automobile was, of course, a major factor in making this pattern of growth viable.

During the Great Depression (1930–1941), little land development had taken place, so land use planning and control became irrelevant. There was some housing construction under generous financial arrangements made possible by various New Deal programs, but the housing and home construction market in the 1930s was no comparison to that which had existed prior to 1927 and would occur again in the 1980s. Housing construction during World War II used up much subdivided land.

After 1945 (as noted), political interest in land use planning and control again responded to cyclical factors as the real estate market improved and demand for housing increased. The postwar era, with pent-up consumer demands backed by substantial personal savings and easy financing, saw the beginning of a housing boom that with some ups and downs continued through the 1980s. Population increases, plus prosperity and ease of financing, contributed to the continued high demand for housing (Listokin, 1974). When the economy began to slump in the mid 1980s, an oversupply of housing became evident with wide regional variations despite growing homelessness.

The so-called "flight to the suburbs" is criticized as being racially motivated, but it must be emphasized that by no stretch of the imagination could the central cities have absorbed population growth since 1945. Suburban growth was absolutely necessary if the populace was to be housed. The issue of suburban political independence is a different question, as is the lack of affordable housing in many suburbs.

It often is overlooked that the real impact of the automobile on land use was not felt until after World War II, because the Depression had brought an end to the automobile boom. prior to 1928, the automobile, the truck, and the bus were not up to supporting suburban growth. One must have lived at the time to realize fully how primitive automobile technology was before 1928. Highways were only beginning to be built as the Depression hit. They were really not completed until the 1956 Interstate program.

Americans owned 23 million automobiles in 1929 and used 14 million gallons of gasoline. In 1941, these figures were 29.6 million cars and 24 million gallons of gas, with 18 million gallons being used in passenger vehicles. By 1950, only 5 years after the war, the number of vehicles reached 40 million and gas consumption 35.6 million gallons, of which 25 million gallons were used in passenger cars. In 1970, Americans owned 89 million cars and used 92 million gallons of gas, with 66.7 million gallons for passenger vehicles. Just incidentally, the decline in mass transit mileage did not begin until 1950, although the peak was reached in 1921.

IX. AFTER WORLD WAR II

Again in the 1970s, the real estate and housing markets were very active. However, another significant shift in the pattern of growth had occurred. In the 1920s, subdivision development focused on the land, with the developer generally selling individual lots to prospective homeowners. After World War II, it was common for the developer to build houses on the lots sold. Levittown, New York, was a model for this type of development, and the pattern was widely followed in metropolitan regions throughout the nation. Developers sought large tracts, combining several farms in one development. This meant that new subdivisions often had to be located some distance from existing housing. The result was leap-frogging, with smaller tracts of vacant land scattered among the developments. Another consequence was that city planning agencies, in effect, lost control over where housing (urbanization) would occur, since it usually was beyond city limits. Sometimes the pattern of land use and types of development within the tract may have been negotiated between the developer and county planners. Control was limited, since county planners often were less assertive than their city colleagues.

It was not unexpected that this pattern of growth involving many acres and millions of dollars required complex political decisions about the allocations of burdens and benefits. In most cases, too, these types of developments required substantial financing involving savings and loan associations, banks, insurance companies, and the like. Few anticipated what in the 1990s became the "S & L scandal." In earlier times, individuals usually secured loans on a house-by-house basis. Now savings institutions became involved whose depositors were insured by the U.S. government. When the economy slumped, the government became the owner of empty and unsold properties.

As in the collapse of the real estate market in 1927, so in the late 1980s and early 1990s a surplus of housing, apartments, and office buildings was evidence of overdevelopment. There were many subdivisions but relatively little construction. There were some indicators in the summer of 1992 that real estate sales and home construction was picking up in some markets.

At the same time, one of the country's major problems, that of homelessness (or perhaps more accurately described as the lack of affordable housing), is posing difficult problems in many metropolitan areas. However, the active interest in land use planning and control evidenced in the 1970s does not seem to have revived in the 1990s. This may reflect the fact that many of those who had sought land use regulation and control in the 1970s have shifted their interests and activities to environmental problems.

X. CONTROL TECHNIQUES

As concern increased for the ways in which land was being developed and used, particularly urban or suburban land on the fringes of towns and cities, two basic control techniques evolved. The *first* was *zoning* and the *second* was control of the *subdivision process*. Both were responses to the magnitude and rapidity of land use changes; i.e., mostly urban growth. A *third* and often later development—organizational or institutional in character—was the recognition of a local government land use planning function and the creation of planning agencies to discharge that function. In some states, the emphasis was on increasing the state government role.

For many local governments, planning meant simply establishing a planning committee or commission, generally made up of citizens. Professional staffing, even in the larger municipalities, lagged. In fact, especially in smaller towns and cities, planning agencies have no staff even today. Some states require municipalities and counties to have planning organizations, but such statutes may not be enforced, and funding may not be provided. In many cases, regulation is minimal. Planning commissions prefer negotiation with developers.

A. Zoning

Zoning of an urban area was begun by New York City in 1916. After discussion and involvement of many businesses and community groups, zoning was initially applied to midtown Fifth Avenue. Its purpose was to preserve the exclusivity of the avenue above 34th Street. Support, as has been the case in many zoning situations, was organized by influential interests seeking to control by regulation what seemed impossible to control by ordinary market forces (Makielski, 1966).

As originally intended, zoning was designed to segregate various types of urban development, seeking a kind of neighborhood homogeneity by favoring some uses and keeping undesirable developments and uses out. The objective was, by grouping similar economic activities, to protect property values, minimize neighborhood changes and deterioration, and establish stability in certain amenity values (Babcock, 1969).

As zoning spread, three basic zones were standard: residential, commercial, and industrial. However, very soon, as restrictive benefits began to be realized, the number of zones increased substantially. Today residential zones may distinguish between single-family and multifamily housing. Some ordinances establish additional categories. Commercial zones may distinguish between small neighborhood ventures and shopping malls. Supermarkets, gasoline stations, and professional offices may be separated. Industrial zones usually distinguish between light and heavy industry, but they also may segregate other activities such as warehousing and truck terminals.

Zoning in Manhattan was originally political. In most jurisdictions it remains political with the beneficiaries (developers, promoters, real estate dealers) dominating the process. One reason for this is that the people who will live on the properties and who will conduct business on the properties usually are not identified at the time zoning decisions are made.

Some of the literature presents zoning as a rational way of achieving logical plans. Where a professional planning staff makes zoning recommendations, community benefits often may be secured, but the basic premises of zoning—neighborhood homogeneity—are rarely challenged. The hidden agenda involved in zoning decisions comes to light when subdivisions are zoned for high-cost upper-class housing. The "not in my neighborhood" syndrome is very evident (Babcock and Bosselman, 1973)!

1. Affordable Housing—The Mount Laurel Litigation

As the pattern of large-scale development of land and housing came to dominate the market, especially in highly urbanized areas, a new type of issue began to emerge; namely, the issue of affordable (usually minority) housing. Earlier, when construction was primarily an individual choice, the type and cost of any particular house meeting general requirements was not challenged, although restrictive covenants in deeds and some zoning set quality standards favoring "upper-class" housing!

Historically, the fact that zoning was enacted by the city council led many courts to regard the zoning function as legislative and not subject to substantive challenge in litigation. The courts asserted that to go behind the legislative judgment would be to substitute their views for those of the legislative body.

The factual situation began to change as large-scale projects, comprising a part of the city Master Plan, became the format for review and approval. In a precedent-setting case, the Master Plan of Mount Laurel, a new Jersey town in a highly urbanized portion of the state, was challenged, with the plaintiffs arguing that the Master Plan did not provide for low-income, minority, affordable housing. Housing for the poor and minorities had been that vacated by lower- and middle-class families as they moved up the housing ladder to new and perhaps more luxurious homes. However, in densely populated areas, growth exceeded the supply of secondhand housing, and many poor and minority families could not find homes. In large cities (Detroit; St. Louis; Washington, DC; and others), the high-rise solution, begun in the 1930s, had been rejected as undesirable. Thus, the shortage of housing for the poor and for minorities was intensified. This shortage was particularly apparent in urban areas found in parts of New Jersey where dozens of small towns contiguous to each other all strive to develop the richest tax base with the lowest commitments to potential government costs (e.g., schools).

The New Jersey town of Mount Laurel developed a Master Plan that provided, on remaining vacant land within the town, for additional upper-class homes. No provision was made for areas in which affordable housing for low-income residents might be built. This lack was challenged by the NAACP. Ultimately, the New Jersey Supreme Court ruled that the Mount Laurel plan violated substantive due process provisions of the New Jersey Constitution. After considerable additional litigation and general turmoil among planners and land developers, the New Jersey Supreme Court required affirmative steps for affordable housing in communities across the state. Every community in the state was required to enact land use regulations that would assume a "fair share" of low-income housing and provide a realistic opportunity for decent housing for at least some part of its lower-income residents (Steinberg, 1989). The court rationalized its decision stating, ". . . the constitutional obligation is simple. The State controls the use of land, all of the land. In exercising that control it cannot favor rich over poor" (Steinberg, 1989: 10).

Responding to the Mount Laurel situation and to the clamor of those affected by the Mount Laurel decision, in 1985, the New Jersey Legislature enacted a Fair Housing Act. The act confirmed the importance of providing "affordable housing" for low-income and impoverished families. Interestingly, it allowed the allocation of up to one-half of a community's "fair share" of low-income housing to another nearby community willing to accept it. This adjustment was partly a matter of land availability and partly of entrepreneurship. The Act also established a nine-member Council on Affordable Housing that took from the courts the responsibility for determining each community's fair share of such housing. Ultimately, the adequacy of the plans of every New Jersey community will be reviewed.[1]

Economic (and racial) segregation by means of zoning and the Master Plan was the negative issue in the Mount Laurel litigation. Where an area is blanketed with small, contiguous municipalities, the segregation and discrimination of zoning and master planning are likely to become evident. Also, where a half dozen small cities butting up against each other have unlimited authority to zone, it is not surprising that they will likely seek high-value housing (high ratables), small commercial development, and clean industry (if any industry at all). This describes a fairly common suburban situation, but now in New Jersey, first under court orders and now under the Affordable Housing Council, cities must take on their fair share of low-income housing. Yet traditionally, courts have required challengers of land use decisions to have a demonstrable economic interest in the area involved. Thus, it is not clear to what extent other state courts may decide to follow New Jersey in Mount Laurel situations. To move in this direction, courts will need to tackle the substantive due process issue. It is well to stress that the New Jersey court relied on the due process language of the New Jersey Constitution, a document adopted since World War II. Also, it seems clear that the substantive record in the New Jersey urban areas almost speaks for itself. In not too many regions is the factual situation duplicated.

One issue that New Jersey has not solved and that seemed less important, when real estate markets were booming and funds for development seemed readily available, is the need to *construct* affordable housing. Merely designating areas on maps as places where affordable housing "may" be built does not *provide* tangible housing, and with state and federal budgets strapped, the needed subsidized housing may not be built! Another issue not dealt with is the relationship of affordable housing to where employment opportunities may be found. To avoid this issue may be to ghetto-ize affordable housing.

The situation is not static, and once the real estate market revives, one may expect further development of affordable housing issues. The Oregon Supreme Court has held, for instance, that whereas the initial zoning decision is legislative in character, rezoning decisions are quasi-judicial and must meet procedural and evidentiary requirements of the judicial process (*Fasano* v. *Board of County Comm. of Washington County*, 507 P.2d 23. Oregon, 1972). Under its state land use control system, Oregon places considerable stress on basing decisions on evidence laid out in a challengeable record. Other courts have achieved a somewhat similar effect by once again insisting that zoning must be in accordance with the Master Plan. However, obviously, the urban problems in Oregon are not comparable to those of New Jersey. It may be that issues of affordable housing might arise in cities such as Los Angeles, but the problems of raising capital for building such housing are formidable!

Zoning often stirs up considerable political controversy among those who expect to benefit. As indicated, the goal of the Fifth Avenue merchants who initiated zoning was simple and explicit: Keep Fifth Avenue for upper-class shoppers and upper-class businesses. All zoning allocates benefits and burdens, but the initiative still lies with real estate developers and promoters in most jurisdictions.

2. Constitutional Challenges

Constitutional challenges to zoning have been frequent. In an early case (*Village of Euclid* v. *Ambler Realty Co.,* 272 U.S. 365, 1926), Justice George Sutherland, writing for the Court, sustained the use of the "police power" to achieve neighborhood homogeneity. Although the validity of zoning in general was thus sustained, many specific zoning decisions continue to be challenged, frequently as "takings" of property requiring compensation. In *Pennsylvania Coal Company* v. *Mahon* (260 U.S. 393, 1922), Justice Oliver Wendell Holmes stated the doctrine that land use regulation which went too far could involve a "taking" of property requiring compensation or alternately cancellation of the regulations. This decision has been the basis for frequent challenges of land use regulations, since by its terms the criteria for valid or invalid regulations must be formulated situation by situation. In June 1992, the Supreme Court said that beach erosion regulations that frustrated development were a "taking" of property requiring compensation (*Lucas* v. *South Carolina*, 112 Sup. Ct. Reporter 2886, June 29, 1992).

Zoning spread rapidly during the 1920s, in part because Secretary of Commerce Herbert Hoover promoted a model zoning statute for state adoption authorizing municipalities to issue zoning regulations.

Toward the end of the 1920s, the Department of Commerce also promoted a Model Planning Act for municipalities, but this model was less popular than the Model Zoning Act (Hagman, 1971). Logically and technically, zoning should be based on a Master Plan and the Model Zoning Act so provided, but most jurisdictions felt unable to implement such a requirement (Haar, 1955). When zoning was challenged as not conforming to nonexisting Master Plans, many courts were willing to accept the zoning ordinance as itself part of the plan. Thus, when fully zoned, a city was considered fully planned.

3. A Critique of Zoning

After more than 75 years, zoning has been accepted as a modest land use planning and control technique, and the literature contains numerous criticisms, including:

1. Zoning often is regarded as a kind of game manipulated by developers and financial interests for their gain. Rezoning, variances, and other loopholes favoring growth and development allow powerful interests to achieve the land use patterns and profits they seek (Babcock, 1969; Hinds et al., 1979).
2. Zoning is used as a device for discrimination to keep out undesired development and encourage desired growth. By controlling the size, quality, and style of housing, it assures a degree of uniformity and may tend to control family size. Thus, it serves as an indirect means of controlling school and other service costs with the objective of keeping property taxes low.
3. Zoning rarely has been used as a dynamic control technique and may not be suited to such use. Thus, Houston, without zoning, presents land use patterns not significantly different from cities of similar size with zoning (Siegan, 1972).
4. Once the requirement that zoning must be in accordance with a Master Plan was weakened or even abrogated, zoning failed to provide for integrated growth (Haar, 1955).

In contrast to urban zoning that was designed to limit the ultimate occupant of the subdivided land, rural zoning was perceived as a means for controlling present occupiers of farm land restricting their uses and methods of farming. Where land use changes were occurring (as in the recreation lake regions of northern Wisconsin) rural zoning was proposed to influence and control development. However, in general, the dynamic possibilities of rural zoning to guide land uses and farming practices was never realized. One reason for this failure was resistance of farmers to government control. There also is some question whether the knowledge of soils and farm management was adequate for sensible controls, which should be based on entire farm planning (Rowlands et al., 1948; USDA 1952, 1972).

B. Subdivision Control

Subdivision controls became significant after World War II, largely in response to changes in development practices: large subdivisions with many of the houses built under the direction of the developer with financing and other details arranged in advance. This approach reflected sophisticated financial arrangements as well as high-tech design and construction methods.

Three types of subdivision control may be distinguished. The first and oldest type focused on roads and streets, on mapping, and plat approval. It was primarily reactive to what the developer may have submitted. A second and newer approach (more typical of large cities) seeks to shape subdivision development to achieve desired patterns for the larger community. It may include such factors as schools and environmental concerns. This approach requires a professional planning staff with which the developer negotiates. The extent to which this type of control is exercised by local governments varies, probably reflecting population densities, rates of growth, and political alignments in particular communities. The third type of control, one only beginning to be important, involves state government review and intervention (Reilly, 1973).

In all types of subdivision control, decisions are likely to be highly political, as in the case of zoning. The regulating governments usually are not capable of dealing with the wisdom of particular subdivision proposals. Rarely is the appropriateness of a location or possible alternatives considered; neither is the community need for additional development reviewed.

Increasingly, some consideration may be given to environmental factors such as open space (parks and green areas). Lot size, house bulk, setback, and similar physical criteria may be specified. Streets, sidewalks, sewers, water lines, and some other capital facilities may be mandated.

1. Planned Unit Development

''Planned unit development,'' is a special type of subdivision control that has found favor in many communities. In a PUD, the developers bargain with local authorities to develop a piece of land in rather specific ways. The local community usually will have a PUD ordinance that gives instructions as to how and what should be included in the PUD. Among the frequent requirements are open space and mixed single-family and multifamily units; the latter usually being double or quadruple condos. Sometimes a low-rise apartment complex may be included. Thus, the pattern of total development is more or less fully elaborated before approval is given. All units, including open spaces, are agreed on; hence, the name ''planned unit development.'' In some cases, the PUD may include development of community facilities or in lieu thereof cash payments to the local authorities.

The massive construction of housing units (single-family and multifamily) after 1945 was in large part a free-market response to pent-up demands reflecting population increases, postwar prosperity, and easy mortgage financing. Much of the increase would have been impossible without a variety of governmental financial aids to potential homeowners, developers, and builders. However, at that time, the fact of government interest usually did not involve extensive land use controls. At times, the pace of development was very rapid and the number of units constructed overwhelming. Under these circumstances, prudent action often gave way to urgent population pressures and to profit motives. In the 1950s, complaints began to be voiced in the media, in magazines, and in books. Vocal critics looked at the growth around them and were appalled. Ticky-tacky construction (Keats, 1820, 1957), urban sprawl, strip cities, fragmented development with massive destruction of farm lands, and decay of central cities disturbed many. Yet the cacophony of complaints did not add up to a remedial program.

There is little doubt that the Interstate Highway Program, begun in 1956, hastened the unplanned spread of urbanization. It seems clear that the public would not have abandoned the highway program. It also is clear that few highway planners foresaw the problems that massive highway construction, including metropolitan circumferential bypasses, triggered. Just as in the case of river and harbor expenditures, so with respect to highways, the sellers of cement, asphalt, earth movers, and line paint joined with the driving public to see the program to its conclusion.

Many of the communities in which extensive growth occurred were ill equipped to deal with it. Growth was a new experience; the previous growth era of the 1920s was outside the experience of most decision makers, and institutions for channeling growth forces did not exist. In any case, the factors contributing to growth in the 1950s were new and different. One of these was technological change.

Diesel-powered earth movers were available only after World War II, and the heavy trucks, now taken for granted, did not exist prior to 1945. Mobile cement mixers, power hand tools, and new materials (such as plywood and chip board) changed the character of construction. These technological changes (and others), together with the easy availability of mortgage money (Federal Housing Administration [FHA] and Veterans Administration [VA] loans), all contributed to the pace of housing development and made the large-scale housing project a reality with 40, 80, or several hundred acres being developed at one time.

For much of the period after World War II, homes could be purchased with little or no down payment, with mortgages running for 25, 30, or more years. As a result, the individually built custom house became the symbol of upper-class housing. Middle- and low-income families moved into used housing or into newly built project houses marked by considerable uniformity in design, style, and appearance. As large acreages became necessary, these often were some distance from existing urbanized areas with smaller parcels of vacant land in between; hence, the problems of sprawl, fragmentation, and strip developments.

A contributing factor to the sometimes chaotic patterns of development was the fact that zoning was a municipal function, and in most states, city jurisdiction did not extend beyond city boundaries. In most states, too, county governments had limited zoning authority, and even when counties exercised such authority, their views tended to be less restrictive than those of the affected cities. In many cases, county governing bodies reflected rural attitudes favoring unbridled growth and the hope for profits from the sale of farm lands for subdivisions. Even where counties were required to have planning commissions, these often were token concessions to growth management. In Colorado, for example, county planning was mandated in the 1960s, but by 1980, less than half of the 63 counties had adopted comprehensive plans, and many had citizen commissions but no technical staffs. Once the pace of real estate development declined, interest in county planning also declined.

2. Idle Subdivisions

Yet undeveloped lands already platted and subdivided, often with paving and utilities, within existing municipalities or on the fringes of existing municipalities could provide housing for many millions! Colorado alone is said to have sufficient land platted for an additional 15 million people. However, at present, institutional devices are inadequate either to assure development or to require that lands presently designated for urban purposes be utilized before developing additional subdivisions.

XI. INNOVATIONS

Although zoning continues to be an important land use control technique, with subdivision regulation equally important where growth is occurring, some new and amended techniques are being tried as devices for realizing public interests in land use control. In addition, the focus of interest seems to be shifting to broader issues of housing needs (affordable housing) and to more complex issues of environmental impact (DiMento, 1990; Frieden, 1979).

A. Growth Management

Much growth management in the United States has focused on the very local town or city, which raises serious questions as to whether, where, and how growth occurs and whether growth management is within the competence of municipal and county governments. Many of the factors that stimulate growth have been left to free-market decisions, with communities often competing with each other for job-producing investments. Although state and local governments have had economic promotional agencies, little attention has been paid to the issues of where new activities should be located. Few attempts at rational decisions in the context of general welfare have been recorded. A national perspective generally is absent. The decisions most often are political in the harshest terms of pork-barrel politics and political favors.

Logically, one might assume that growth decisions would be made in a carefully analyzed policy framework, but in fact, growth management, where practiced, is not a comprehensive technique but rather the application of a variety of local controls favoring locally defined objectives. However, so long as the U.S. population continues to increase and population characteristics change, increased housing (i.e., land development) obviously is needed. The hard questions are: Where should such additions to the housing supply be made, what types are needed, and how should they be related to employment opportunities? Unfortunately, "the not in my backyard" syndrome is all too often the guiding principle of local land use decisions.

Frequently, opponents of growth seek to preserve the present character of their communities; e.g., to retain a rural, small-town setting and low taxes. In the case of large cities (Boulder, CO), the goal is to protect certain amenities associated with a particular lifestyle. Population caps, fixing maximum population or limiting annual growth to a definite number of new dwellings, are among the devices used (Urban Land Institute, 1975, 1978, 1980).

The constitutionality of growth controls, as a general police-power purpose, remains unsettled partly because most controls contain loopholes (Godschalk et al., 1977). However, if courts dealing with densely settled areas follow the New Jersey precedents (discussed above) established in the Mount Laurel litigation, the needs for low-income housing may well result in an expansion of the "fair share" doctrine requiring communities to provide for low-income, minority housing.

Where purposes other than exclusion have been sought (e.g., historic preservation; capital investment phasing in relation to fiscal capacity; containment of growth costs at reasonable levels; and provision of adequate service, environmental protection, and quality of life considerations for the general population), some courts have been willing to accept growth controls as a proper exercise of the police power. Development timing and limited moratoria (e.g., on sewer and water line extensions) have been accepted where the record indicates that the growth control was not merely to exclude new development but to rationalize and systematize growth.

The simple fact that dollar costs of providing service to new housing will increase probably is not sufficient as a basis for limiting growth. However, problems associated with providing infrastructure may justify delay or timing control. Yet some courts have used utility analogies in requiring municipalities to serve new residents.

Closely related to the problems of providing service is the doctrine of "the right to travel," usually interpreted as the right to live and work where one may choose. Although not yet articulated by courts reviewing growth management attempts, it ultimately could have a far-reaching impact on such controls when simply seeking to keep people out. Although municipal corporations may not be confronted with these arguments, county governments do have an obligation to serve all residents. School districts face similar requirements. The implications of combining the "requirement to serve" with the concept of "fair share" of low-income, minority housing could be far reaching!

B. State Governments and Land Use Control

For various reasons, including the locus of political power, it has been suggested that states should "take back" powers delegated to local governments with respect to land use planning and control (Healy, 1976). The American Law Institute has proposed a model code that seeks to reassert state responsibilities over certain aspects of land use control. A few states have moved in this direction but not without vehement opposition from organized local governments, real estate developers, and farmers. Some of the opposition arguments have been ideological; others have focused on the bald recognition of political power (Levin et al., 1974). A few states have enacted state controls over industrial and power plant siting decisions. Under federal pressure, states have been enacting strip mining regulation statutes. Some 30 states, also because of federal requirements, have passed coastal zone planning statutes. As a result of indirect pressure, states and local governments also have enacted flood plain zoning to comply with the terms of the Flood Insurance Act.

C. Federal Land Use Controls

Several indirect controls over land use, as a result of federal actions, have been described. Today the federal role is more limited, one of the more significant policy roles being that of the Federal Reserve lowering the prime interest rate in order to increase individual home mortgages and stimulate the real estate market.

In the context of a generally shrinking role of the federal government and the evident need for additional housing, the late 1970s and early 1980s saw a variety of legislative proposals introduced into the Congress to expand the federal role in land use planning and control; however, such legislation was not enacted. In many respects, the developing role of the federal government today may well be its interest in and concern for the environment. It is not a big step from a concern for the human environment to a concern for a fair share of low-income housing, including that which the homeless, poor, and minorities may require. Focus on the environment, however, does not necessarily mean that the federal government will have a unified, integrated, and coordinated approach to land use controls. The field will remain that of local and state governments.

D. Local Controls of Development

Zoning will continue to be a major local land use control, and questions of exclusionary zoning will continue to be litigated. Some confusion has been introduced into these questions of exclusion by a sweeping statement by Justice William Douglas in the 1974 decision in *Village of Belle Terre* v. *Boraas* (416 U.S. 1, 1974). Justice Douglas wrote with respect to the goals of zoning:

> . . . [we favor] a quiet place where yards are wide, people few, and motor vehicles restricted. . . . The police power is not confined to elimination of filth, stench, and unhealthy places. It is ample to lay out zones where family values, youth values, and the blessings of quiet seclusion and clean air make the area a sanctuary for people.

This idyllic statement clearly avoids the kind of "fair share" issues raised in the New Jersey Mount Laurel litigation. It seems unlikely that the present (1992) U.S. Supreme Court would attempt to reconcile the Douglas image of zoning with the fair share image of Mount Laurel. Zoning and constitutional tests of particular zoning decisions thus very likely will remain state issues. This means, among other things, that considerable variation among the states will continue, in part reflecting population density and poverty differences and in part different attitudes among state courts. It might be predicted that less urbanized states may continue in the direction outlined by Justice Douglas.

In any case, local zoning will remain important in land use control. Zoning restricting churches, schools, and social club facilities has been sustained in some jurisdictions, the factual situation being a critical variable. On the positive side, zoning has been approved where it seeks to provide scenic vistas, play areas, green zones, and similar amenities. The test of "going too far" (as Justice Holmes suggested) is the extent to which all value and use is taken from the owner.

Some flexibility has been introduced into zoning (in some jurisdictions) by a number of adaptations that reflect the change in purpose behind zoning. In a few jurisdictions "floating zones" are permitted. These serve as a kind of advance notice to a zoned area that when circumstances develop and the need is clear, predetermined zoning changes will be made.

1. Incentive Zoning

Incentive zoning and compensatory zoning are devices by which positive motivations are given to persuade a developer to fulfill comprehensive plan objectives. In a number of European countries, various positive incentives, including subsidies, are used to accomplish community goals and direct the pace and location of development (Wengert, 1979a). Two variants involving use of incentives should be mentioned. One is the PUD, previously discussed, under which higher density and housing diversity on one part of a tract is allowed if the remaining area is left in open space for recreation and similar community uses.

The second device based on economic motivation involves the purchase by the government of *developmental rights*, leaving in the property owner only those residual rights approved for use of land in a particular area. Purchase of development rights has been much discussed as a means for preserving prime agricultural lands and preventing their conversion to nonagricultural uses. However, it is a technique not used much.

A variant of the purchase of development rights is the largely untried device of "transferable development rights" (TDRs), where costs of controls limiting certain types of development are converted into a kind of scrip that the restricted owner can then transfer (i.e., sell) to developers who are required to secure additional rights to develop their own lands to levels deemed economically attractive. Without purchasing TDRs from restricted owners, developers themselves would be prevented from full development. TDR systems seek to compensate owners for development foregone and at the same time to permit transfer of the foregone development to another piece of property, usually in the vicinity. The TDR system assumes marketlike transactions between private parties, with government establishing the rules under which the market would operate (Wengert, 1979b). The TDR system was proposed for historic preservation (Costonis, 1974; Rose, 1975) but since has been urged in other contexts, including preservation of farm lands.

2. Fiscal Zoning

Both law and policy on fiscal zoning is unclear. If the "right to travel" is stressed, then the fact that locational choices may increase government costs must, like the costs of school desegregation, be borne by whatever government operates in the area.

Most growth is not without some additional costs to the community and by inference places a burden on existing residents. To illustrate, 60-year-old water mains (they have a normal life of 80 to 100 years) were laid when costs of pipe and labor were at an all-time low for this century. Clearly, water mains of the same size and quality put in today to serve a new subdivision will cost many times more, but water rates within the boundaries of a particular jurisdiction do not vary as between old and new users. Capital improvements, such as new mains, are paid for by the entire system. Hence, those served by the 60-year-old mains will be absorbing a greater share of the new capital costs than residents served by new mains. Construction of new schools to serve new subdivisions also follow similar principles. In fact, where rates are uniform, most capital facilities, except those charged directly to abutting property owners, will show a similar disproportionate allocation of cost burdens.

The costs of new infrastructure facilities will be higher than those for older areas, and many such costs are capitalized in the price of housing. The requirement that land (or in lieu payments) be dedicated for parks, schools, and other facilities similarly places the burden directly on the new developments. Increased operating costs (e.g., a larger police force, more patrol cars), where economies of scale do not apply, can mean that old residents pay for a part of the costs of growth, but in some cases, they also may get increased economic benefits.

Any discussion of the costs of sprawl must deal with the fundamental inequities of the property tax system and particularly the inefficiencies, inequities, and political manipulation in assessment procedures. Many of the complaints about the costs of growth may be minimized through more effective administration of the property tax.

Fiscal zoning seeks to prevent developments that are likely to add to the property tax burden and/or more positively are likely to produce additional, perhaps disproportionate, tax benefits.

Large-lot zoning; control of bedroom space, particularly in apartments, so that families with children cannot be accommodated; and a variety of other devices are used to minimize costs to the local government. Where motives are clearly negative and the evidence of discrimination is unequivocal, many courts will strike down fiscal zoning. However, the evidence is not always clear, and as indicated above, some courts accept zoning designed to preserve a quiet, suburban way of life, even when the principal beneficiaries seem to be middle- and upper-class residents.

E. Land Banking

The term *land banking* suggests a variety of techniques with differing goals and objectives. One form of land banking used in Saskatchewan, Canada, assists young farmers in acquiring farms. Another form occurs in Australia, Sweden, and several other European countries where it is tied closely to land use controls providing a holding device for keeping lands out of the speculative market and directing their ultimate use to desired ends (Strong, 1979). In all its various forms, land banking involves a government agency or public corporation that acquired land by purchase, gift, or otherwise to consolidate holdings and establish tracts for particular controlled uses. In Holland, for example, municipalities regularly have been acquiring land in advance of development. When the land is needed for development, it is sold or leased with land needed for public purposes being retained. In new towns in Germany, a quasi-public corporation acquires the land needed and then leases or sells parcels back to developers subject to specified controls. In most of these situations, land banking is a vital part of land use plan implementation.

NOTE

1. Note on Mount Laurel sources. There were three Mount Laurel cases: 1975, 1983, and 1986. The citations are: Mount Laurel I (1975), *South Burlington County NAACP* v. *The Township of Mount Laurel*, 67 N.J. 151; Mount Laurel II (1983), *South Burlington County NAACP* v. *The Township of Mount Laurel*, 92 N.J. 151; and Mount Laurel III (1986), *The Hills Development Company* v. *The Township of Bernards*, 105 N.J. 1.

   There is a tremendous literature on the Mount Laurel issues, especially in various law reviews. An excellent summary of the subject may be found in Steinberg, M. K. (1989), *Adaptations to an Activist Court Ruling: Aftermath of the Mount Laurel II Decision for Lower-Income Housing*, Lincoln Institute of Land Policy, Cambridge, MA.

REFERENCES

American Law Institute (1975). *A Model Land Development Code: Complete Text and Commentary.* American Law Institute, Philadelphia.

American Planning Association (1989). *The Best of Planning: Two Decades of Articles from the Magazine of the American Planning Association.* APSA, Chicago.

Babcock, R. F. (1969). *The Zoning Game.* University of Wisconsin Press, Madison.

Babcock, R. F., and Bosselman, F. P. (1973). *Exclusionary Zoning.* Praeger, New York.

Blaesser, B., and Weinstein, A. C. (Eds.) (1989). *Land Use and the Constitution: Principles for Planning Practice.* Planners Press, American Planning Association, Chicago.

Burchell, R. W., and Listokin, D. (1975). *Future Land Use.* Center for Urban Policy Research, Rutgers University, New Brunswick, NJ.

Burrows, L. B. (1978). *Growth Management.* Center for Urban Policy Research, Rutgers University, New Brunswick, NJ.

Commager, H. S. (Ed.) (1934). *Documents of American History.* F. S. Crofts, New York. Document #78, Land Ordinance of 1785, p. 123. Document #82, The Northwest Ordinance, July 13, 1787, p. 128.

Costonis, J. J. (1974). *Space Adrift.* University of Illinois Press, Urbana.

DiMento, J. (Ed.) (1990). *Wipeouts and Their Mitigation: The Changing Context for Land Use and Environmental Law.* Lincoln Institute of Land Policy, Cambridge, MA.

Ehrlich, J. W. (1959). *Ehrlich's Blackstone.* Capricorn, New York.

Feldman, E. J., and Goldberg, M. A. (Ed.) (1987). *Land Rights and Wrongs, The Management, Regulation and Use of Land in Canada and the United States.* The Lincoln Institute of Land Policy, Cambridge, MA.

Frieden, B. J. (1979). *The Environmental Protection Hustle.* M.I.T. Press, Cambridge, MA.

Friedmann, J. (1987). *Planning in the Public Domain.* Princeton University Press, Princeton, NJ.

Gates, P. W. (1968). *History of Public Land Law Development.* Public Land Law Review Commission, U.S. Government Printing Office, Washington, DC.

Godschalk, D. R., Brower, D. J., McBennett, I. D., and Vestal, B. A. (1977). *Constitutional Issues of Growth Management.* ASPO Press, American Society of Planning Officials, Chicago.

Haar, C. M. (1955). In accordance with a comprehensive plan. *Harvard Law Review* 68: 1154.

Hagman, D. C. (1971). *Urban Planning and Land Development Control Law.* West, St. Paul, MN.

Healy, R. G. (1976). *Land Use and the States.* Johns Hopkins University Press, Baltimore.

Hibbard, B. H. (1924, 1965). *A History of the Public Land Policies.* University of Wisconsin Press, Madison.

Hinds, D. S., Carn, N. G., and Ordway, N. (1979). *Winning at Zoning.* McGraw-Hill, New York.

Jacobs, H. M. (1992). Planning the use of land in the 21st century. *Journal of Soil and Water Conservation* 47: 32.

Keats, J. (1820, 1957) *The Crack in the Picture Window,* Houghton-Mifflin, Boston.

Land use controls (1990). Special Issue, *Land Economics* 66: 229–355.

Levin, M. R., Rose, J. G., and Slavet, J. S. (1974). *New Approaches to State Land-Use Policies.* Lexington-Heath, Lexington, MA.

Listokin, D. (Ed.) (1974). *Land Use Controls: Present Problems and Future Reform.* Center for Urban Policy Research, Rutgers University, New Brunswick, NJ.

Makielski, S. J., Jr. (1966). *The Politics of Zoning: The New York Experience.* Columbia University Press, New York.

Marcus, N., and Groves, M. W. (Eds.) (1970). *The New Zoning.* Praeger, New York.

Meck, S., and Netter, E. M. (Ed.) (1983). *A Planner's Guide to Land Use Law.* Planners Press, American Planning Association, Chicago.

Nelson, R. H. (1977). *Zoning and Property Rights.* M.I.T. Press, Cambridge, MA.

Peffer, E. L. (1951). *The Closing of the Public Domain.* Stanford University Press, Stanford, CA.

Reilly, W. K. (Ed.) (1973). *The Use of Land: A Citizen's Guide to Urban Growth, A Task Force Report Sponsored by the Rockefeller Brothers Fund.* Thomas Y. Crowell, New York.

Roddewig, R. J., and Duerksen, C. J. (1989). *Takings: Responding to the Takings Challenge.* American Planning Association, Chicago.

Rose, J. G. (Ed.) (1975). *Transfer of Development Rights.* Center for Urban Policy Research, Rutgers University, New Brunswick, NJ.

Rose, J. G., and Rothman, R. E. (Eds.) (1977). *After Mount Laurel: The New Suburban Zoning.* Center for Urban Policy Research, Rutgers University, New Brunswick, NJ.

Rowlands, W., Trenk, F., and Penn, R. (1948). *Rural Zoning in Wisconsin.* University of Wisconsin, Agricultural Experiment Station, Bulletin 479, Madison.

Siegen, B. H. (1972). *Land Use Without Zoning.* Lexington-Heath, Lexington, MA.

Slater, D. C. (1984). *Management of Local Planning.* International City Management Association, Washington, DC.

Steinberg, M. K. (1989). *Adaptations to An Activist Court Ruling, Aftermath of the Mount Laurel II Decision for Lower-Income Housing.* Lincoln Institute of Land Policy, Cambridge, MA.

Strong, A. L. (1979). *Land Banking: European Reality, American Prospect.* Johns Hopkins University Press, Baltimore.

Urban Land Institute (1975, 1978, 1980). *Management and Control of Growth,* vols 1–3 (1975), vol. 4 (1978), vol. 5 (1980) (various eds.). Urban Land Institute, Washington, DC.

U.S. Census Bureau (1976). *The Statistical History of the United States.* Basic Books, New York.

U.S. Council on Environmental Quality (1971). *The Quiet Revolution in Land Use Control.* Prepared by F. Bosselman and D. Callies, U.S. Government Printing Office, Washington, DC.

—— (1973). *The Taking Issue.* Prepared by F. Bosselman, D. Callies, and J. Banta. U.S. Government Printing Office, Washington, DC.

—— (1974). *The Costs of Sprawl.* Prepared by Real Estate Research Corporation, U.S. Government Printing Office, Washington, DC.

U.S. Department of Agriculture, Bureau of Agricultural Economics (1952). *Rural Zoning in the United States.* By E. D. Solberg. Agricultural Information Bulletin No. 59, U.S. Government Printing Office, Washington, DC.

U.S. Department of Agriculture, Economic Research Service (1972). *Rural Zoning in the United States: Analysis of Enabling Legislation, Misc.* Pub. No. 1232, U.S. Government Printing Office, Washington, DC.

U.S. Department of the Interior, Bureau of Land Management (1977). *Public Land Statistics, 1977.* U.S. Government Printing Office, Washington, DC.

Weaver, C. L., and Babcock, R. F. (1979). *City Zoning: The Once and Future Frontier.* Planners Press, American Planning Association, Chicago.

Wengert, N. (1979a). National and state experiences with land use planning. In *Planning the Uses and Management of Land.* Agronomy Society of America, Crop Science of America, and Soil Science Society of America, Madison, WI, pp. 27–45.

—— (1979b). Constitutional principles applied to land use planning and regulation: A tentative restatement. *Natural Resources Journal* 19: 1–20, University of New Mexico School of Law, Albuquerque.

Williams, N., Jr. (1974, with updates). *American Planning Law: Land Use and the Police Power.* Callaghan, Chicago.

Wright, R. R., and Wright, S. W. (1985). *Land Use in a Nutshell,* 2nd ed. West, St. Paul, MN.

Young, K. H. (Ed.) (1991). *1991 Zoning and Planning Law Handbook.* Clark, Bordman, New York.

28
Transportation Policy

James A. Dunn, Jr.
Rutgers University, Camden, New Jersey

I. TRANSPORTATION AS A POLICY AREA

Transportation policy, more than most policy areas, operates on the frontier between markets and politics. Because transportation policy decisions are closely linked to so many private investment, employment, residential, and recreational decisions, it is impossible and undesirable for government alone, in a democratic society, to shape all the important aspects of the transportation system. Because transportation is so vital to modern society, because it is so obtrusive, and because it is so expensive, it is inevitable that governments will intervene in the transportation system.

Governments perform four key functions related to the development and operation of transportation systems:

Promotion: establishing conditions and incentives that make private investment in a transportation mode profitable (e.g., land grants to western railroads) and making public investments that make it possible for private investment to succeed (e.g., construction of airports and air traffic control systems)
Regulation: assuring fair and equitable treatment to customers and stability of income to operators (e.g., Interstate Commerce Commission (ICC) rate regulation)
Coordination: planning the interaction of the different modes so that maximal benefits are derived from each (e.g., making sure that there is easy access to the airport from center city)
Rationalization: coping with the externalities and social burdens imposed by transportation operations on third parties and maximizing the efficiency of the system from a social accounting standpoint (e.g., imposing vehicle exhaust standards to combat air pollution)

Transportation policy studies should therefore be "political economy" in the truest sense of the term. They require a close partnership between economics and political science, with important contributions from disciplines such as geography, planning, law, and engineering. It has not always been easy to establish this productive dialog. There are two principal difficulties to be overcome. First, transportation policy making tends to be fragmented along modal lines. Each mode (e.g., railways, airlines, buses, highways, subways) is based on a different technology, serves different needs, and involves a different set of actors, interests, and institutions. Transportation policy decisions are made by a bewildering array of bureaucratic, legislative, judicial, independent regulatory, quasi-public, state, and local agencies. It is difficult to formulate a common intellectual paradigm for all of these diverse arenas. What does airline deregulation have in common with a ride sharing promotion program or a freeway revolt?

Second, economics and political science tended to view any policy problem through their own disciplinary prism. This can reduce their ability to communicate. A brash young economist once began an analysis of transportation investments and land values with this scenario:

> A city (conceived for simplicity as a single point) is located in the center of an undifferentiated, uniformly fertile plain. Land on the plain is useless except to produce food for sale in the city. . . . Transportation can take place in straight line in any direction. The cost of shipping a unit of food one mile is initially $t. (Mohring, 1976)

Needless to say, this model provides little help to policy makers grappling with politically difficult decisions about the route of a controversial interstate highway, how to find new sources of funds for an urban mass transit system, or the impact of regulatory changes on regional freight rail systems.

For their part, political scientists, when they took an interest in transportation policy at all, would often examine a particular decision or issue as a case study of one of their discipline's pet concepts (e.g., "interest group politics," "agenda setting," "organizational behavior") and ignore the need for a rigorous analysis of the opportunity costs of the policy and the possibility for recommendations on how to achieve optimal outcomes.

Fortunately, economists have learned that to be heard in the policy debate, they must pay much more attention to the political and organizational pressures. In addition to exposing hidden inefficiencies and calculating the "true costs" that public policies impose on transportation systems, economists have become adept at designing realistic institutional reforms that could be politically acceptable solutions (Lave, 1986). Political scientists, for their part, have become much more conversant with the microeconomic tools and the general economic approach to problems. Rather than attempting to reverse the thrust of market forces, political scientists increasingly recognize the need to adapt policy recommendations to encourage and take advantage of market processes (Lindblom, 1977).

Transportation policy studies have moved closer to a true political economy approach, one that considers institutions and stakeholders, in addition to supply and demand, and political processes in addition to costs and benefits. This is not to say that a complete and coherent new framework for integrating transportation policy has been achieved. As two informed observers recently noted, "the concept of a national transportation policy seems to escape scholars and the public despite the existence of . . . [official] statement[s] on national transportation policy" (McKenna and Anderson, 1990). But there has been clear progress in applying tools and concepts from different disciplines in a more integrated way to specific policy problems.

This chapter examines how the growth of a political economy focus to transportation policy studies has interacted with the evolution of public policies relating to transportation in the United States. It begins by summarizing the notable policy successes of the late 1970s and early 1980s involving the deregulation of the common carrier transportation industries. It follows the way in which the policy debates from the 1950s to the 1990s have attempted to discover politically and economically feasible ways of managing the explosion of personal mobility in metropolitan areas. The efforts made to regulate the characteristics of the automobile in areas such as air pollution reduction, safety, and energy efficiency are reviewed. Finally, this chapter briefly draws some international comparisons and contrasts with Western Europe and the developing world and points to some issues that may have worldwide relevance in the future.

II. THE POLITICAL ECONOMY OF DEREGULATION

Deregulation of common carrier transportation industries is perhaps the premier example of how the political economy approach to transportation policy studies has contributed to improving U.S. transportation policy. Over many years, political scientists and historians documented how public regulatory bodies were often "captured" by self-interested stakeholders (Huntington, 1952). Economists showed how regulatory policy gave too much weight to existing (often inefficient) carriers by restricting entry of competitors into service and by establishing minimum as well as maximum rates and fares. Regulatory procedures were too slow and costly and tended to prevent mergers and consolidations that could have led to lower operating costs (MacAvoy, 1979). Regulatory officials and the legislative committees that oversaw their activities had little notion of how best to coordinate the several modes of transportation. Attempts to plan coherent long-term strategies foundered because of the conflicting and contradictory goals embodied in the regulatory system. On the one hand, regulation was supposed to protect the public from overcharging and other abuses by the carriers; on the other hand, it was also supposed to ensure the overall health of the industry being regulated so that service would continue to be provided. In the airline and trucking modes, regulation was apparently failing in the former responsibility (Douglas and Miller, 1974) and in railroads it was failing in the latter (Moore, 1972).

The remedy prescribed was initially called "regulatory reform," but it soon became known as "deregulation." Its goal was to reduce regulatory distortion and permit the return of competitive market forces. This "deregulation paradigm" has had a major impact on commercial airlines, railroads, trucking, and intercity bus lines in the United States. Beginning in the mid 1970s, the Ford administration made it a priority item. Conservatives had long preached the need to reduce government regulations, and liberals were glad to confront big businesses that were overcharging the public.

Deregulation was pushed first and farthest in the newest common carrier mode, the air transport industry. Experimental fare deregulation was begun in the mid 1970s by the Civil Aeronautics Board (CAB). There followed the Airline Deregulation Act of 1978, which expanded the scope of price competition through discount fares, made it easier for existing airlines to add new routes, and for new airlines to enter the industry. It also stipulated that the CAB, which had regulated the economics of the industry since 1938, would be completely abolished in 1985.

What has been the impact of deregulation on the U.S. air transport industry since 1978? Early studies completed in the mid 1980s (Bailey et al., 1985; Morrison and Winston, 1986) showed that competition increased substantially immediately following deregulation, as new low-cost, often nonunion carriers jumped into the market. Ticket prices fell on long-haul routes between major cities stimulating a great increase in passenger demand but rose on short-haul routes requiring continuation of federal subsidies for service to small communities. No studies have been able to demonstrate that deregulation has reduced airline safety. In fact, the fatal accident rate has declined steadily since deregulation.

The most recent comprehensive review of deregulation's impact (National Research Council, 1992) confirms these early trends but takes note of continuing problems. If competition has increased, so has concentration. There are fewer major trunk carriers, but they have increased their share of the total passenger market. They have adopted a hub-and-spoke route structure, reducing the number of non-stop flights, and increasing the frequency of flights overall. But it is increasingly expensive for more than one airline to compete in a given hub, which threatens to reduce competition in the long run. The international dimension has become increasingly important because some carriers have substantial earnings from international business, which grew faster than the domestic market and is more profitable because many international markets remained regulated.

Congestion and lack of capacity at airports and in the air traffic control system has emerged as a significant problem. Airport facilities are provided by local authorities, who need more revenue if they are to keep up with demand for new runways, terminals, and gates. Economists recommended congestion pricing to shift traffic from the busiest hours. But nearby residents, community groups, and politicians resist such an approach, fearing more noise at night and during early morning hours. Congress' response was to authorize airport authorities to collect a passenger facility charge (PFC) of $3 per departure that can be applied toward approved capital improvements. No such new source of revenue has been earmarked for the Federal Aviation Administration, which has been affected by the overall federal budget difficulties, and which will likely be a crucial bottleneck hindering future growth if its financial resources are not augmented.

The early success and the strong public approval of airline deregulation gave impetus to the push for deregulation in other modes. In the trucking industry, the major motor carrier firms and the major truckers union were strongly opposed to deregulation (Robyn, 1987). Nevertheless, the ICC began pursuing regulatory reform policies in trucking hoping to duplicate the success of the CAB. This pushed Congress into action. The Motor Carrier Act of 1980 did not go as far as complete deregulation of the trucking industry, but it did promote a substantial amount of regulatory reform. The law eased restrictions on entry into service by shifting the burden of proof from the applicant to the opponent of a new service. It reduced operating restrictions that required circuitous routing and empty backhauls, and it granted some rate-making flexibility within a zone of reasonableness and set up a commission to study further rate liberalization.

Airline and trucking deregulation were aimed at thriving industries and were intended to lower rates to customers by increasing competition among firms in the same mode. Regulatory reform was applied to an industry in serious financial difficulty by the Staggers Rail Act of 1980. This bill aimed to increase railroads' revenues by directing the ICC to allow them greater freedom to raise their rates. At the same time, it sought to retain some protection for "captive" shippers (e.g., utility companies dependent on coal shipped by rail), who feared that in a situation of "market dominance" their rates would be increased unfairly (Keeler, 1983). In the 1980s, the U.S. freight rail industry improved its earnings and increased its capital investment while shedding thousands of miles of light-density branch lines. Instead of simply abandoning these lines, class I railroads have found it more profitable to sell or lease them to short-haul or regional railroads, which continue to operate them with lower cost labor and subsidies from state or local governments (Watt, 1988).

The Bus Regulatory Reform Act of 1982 introduced similar flexibility vis-à-vis the ICC for the bus industry. It did not completely abolish regulation but liberalized entry requirements and freed bus companies of rigidly regulated fairs. The Act also allowed them to drop unprofitable service, and it even permitted the ICC to overrule state regulatory agencies on exit applications if the state ruling caused an undue burden on interstate commerce. Since 1982 the bus industry has had to weather a serious national strike brought on by pressure on wages. It has also seen consolidation among the numerous smaller communities (Meyer and Oster, 1987).

The progress made toward reintroducing competition in common carrier transportation industries is a monument to the power of the political economy approach to transportation policy analysis. It shows that sustained and detailed criticism of ineffective public policies can, under the right conditions, help bring about policy reform. What were the conditions that enabled the deregulation movement to score its successes? First, there was a shift in the hierarchy of problem priorities. Satisfying organized producer groups in the transportation sector came to be seen as less urgent than finding ways of dealing with the highly salient problem of inflation, which was approaching double digits by the end of the 1970s. This led the executive branch to make a strong commitment to deregulation as an inflation-fighting tool, and to push it strongly in the legislative arena. Second, the deregulators were able to find allies within the transport sector (railroad companies, airline passenger groups, highway shippers) who strongly supported the reforms because it was in their interest. This prevented the opposition from forming a united front and helped in lobbying the bills through Congress. Third, the spillover effects of the early successes helped rally informed public opinion behind the process by giving concrete evidence of its benefits. A 5% reduction in trucking rates is unlikely to excite the general public, but a 50% discount from regular air fares does (Derthick and Quirk, 1985).

Occasionally, one hears calls for "reregulation" in one or another of the modes. Some worry about foreign airlines buying equity in a U.S. airline and thereby getting access to all of its U.S. markets without reciprocal advantages for the U.S. carrier. Coal and utility shippers push new regulations on granting "competitive access" to one railroad on lines owned by another on petition by a shipper, receiver, or a rival railroad. But such pressures simply reflect the fact that the deregulation was never total and comprehensive in any mode. Adjustments will continue to be needed from time to time, but deregulation (or regulatory reform) counts as a notable policy success.

III. AUTOMOBILITY AND ITS DISCONTENTS

The automobile (including its cousins, the truck and the bus), has been the central factor shaping transportation development since the 1920s. Virtually all the economic difficulties and most of the policy changes made toward other modes of land transportation have been made in response to the impact of motor vehicles on their markets, balance sheets, or physical operating environment. The policy problems involved in coping with the ever-more dominant position of the motor vehicle go well beyond the transportation policy arena. They touch on some of the most basic questions of U.S. society (Flick, 1975). In what sense is Charles Wilson's celebrated dictum ("What's good for GM is good for the country") still true, if it ever was? How far must railroads, public transit systems, community and transportation planners, land developers, business enterprises, tax systems, pedestrians, bicyclists, and everyone else adjust their priorities to the insistent priorities of the motor vehicle? This article will address only two of the most central policy issues posed by the automobile: how to manage problems brought on by ever-increasing automobile travel in decentralizing metropolitan areas, and how to modify directly some of the external effects of mass automobility to achieve important environmental and energy policy goals.

A. Managing Metropolitan Mobility

The automobile is a magnificent machine for enhancing individual mobility. Given even a rudimentary road and street network, the auto adds dimensions of privacy, convenience, and comfort that collective means of transport are very hard put to match. The motor car's biggest disadvantage is its very attractiveness. Virtually everyone who can afford one soon has one. An automobile-dominated metropolitan area is one in which efficient operation of other modes of transportation becomes more difficult. The auto requires massive investments in highway infrastructure and leads to increasingly decentralized, low-density growth. In addition, the auto is a voracious consumer of resources—oil, land, public infrastructure investment, human lives, clean air, and so forth. These costs are cumulatively quite important, and efforts to deal with them have dominated metropolitan transportation policy for the past four decades (Dunn, 1981).

The definition of what the main problem is in the urban transport system and the policy prescriptions for dealing with it have gone through several distinct phases in recent decades (Altshuler, 1979). The phases may be identified by their principal policy thrust.

1. Highway Capacity Expansion

In the mid 1950s, the key problem of urban mobility was perceived as being congestion; there were too many automobiles clogging major arteries at peak hours and too few parking spaces. Central cities were losing shoppers and jobs because it was inconvenient to travel there. Major road improvements were needed to keep up with the growth of traffic by car. Although state and local highway departments were making some efforts to expand urban road capacity, it was only with the passage of the Federal Aid Highway Act and the Highway Finance Act of 1956 that a federal program and a financing mechanism were created that permitted an extraordinary era of urban highway building. The new laws created the federal highway trust fund to receive the receipts from motor fuel and tire taxes and fund 90% of the cost of constructing new interstate superhighways, including urban expressways. With their federal (and state) trust fund revenues, highways were virtually self-financing. The more gasoline and rubber automobiles consumed, the more roads could be built (Rose, 1979; Schwartz, 1976).

For a while, the addition of new road capacity seemed to be outpacing the addition of new traffic. The new expressways relieved rush-hour congestion on older arterials and began to create some reverse commuting as businesses located in newly developed suburbs. But critics soon charged that the lack of "balance" in urban transportation was hurting the cities worse than congestion (Mowbray, 1969; Mumford, 1963). The new urban expressways encouraged middle-class migration to the suburbs. They disrupted neighborhoods and destroyed urban amenity. By making auto commuting easier and fostering growth of low-density settlement in the suburbs, they hurt public transportation financially and socially. Soon only the poor, minorities, and people who could not drive such as the handicapped and elderly would be left riding transit.

2. Revival of Urban Public Transportation

In the late 1960s and 1970s, an important countercurrent to auto dominance developed. Freeway revolts broke out in many cities. Mayors, planners, transit equipment manufacturers, and transport workers' unions formed a transit lobby to push for more federal funding for capital equipment and operating expenses. Federal spending for public transportation rose from $39 million in 1964 to over $3 billion by 1979. States and cities were permitted to "swap" their interstate highway funds for transit funds, and the federal matching share for transit was raised to 80%. Showcase rapid rail systems were built in a number of cities, including Washington, DC. Medium and smaller towns received new buses and support facilities. The trend toward declining ridership was reversed, and the quality of service improved notably. An industry that had been on its way to extinction in all but a few of the country's largest cities was saved. It was transformed into a sector dominated by publicly owned enterprises and given a new, public service–oriented sense of mission (Smerk, 1991).

Yet, among some transport policy analysts there soon arose a skepticism about whether this expansion was really worth the cost. They pointed out that federal aid had increased 3000% between 1970 and 1978. Projecting this trend into the next decade, they announced that this constituted a fiscal crisis of transit. Second, they pointed out that, even with rising ridership, transit's share of the overall urban passenger miles traveled was quite small (less than 3%) and likely to get smaller. Such a small proportion of total urban travel could not be expected to bring about major improvement in the problems generated by auto domination of metropolitan transportation (Altshuler, 1979). Third, public funds seemed actually to be making things worse in a number of key areas. The productivity of transit organizations was declining. Wages, salaries, and benefits were incrasing much faster than inflation and so was cost per passenger mile produced. Political pressures led transit authorities to extend service into low-density areas where deficits were even higher. Studies showed that promised energy savings would materialize only over very long pay-back periods, perhaps centuries. Expensive new rapid rail systems were used for long-distance commuting rather than in-town trips, in effect subsidizing affluent suburbanites rather than poorer inner city residents.

3. Retrenchment and Privatization of Public Transit

The Reagan administration took office in 1981 with what it perceived as a mandate to cut domestic spending. It proclaimed a policy of no new starts for major capital projects and attempted to eliminate federal operating assistance for transit programs (as well as for Amtrak passenger rail service). Congress, responding to the concerns of urban representatives and the transit lobby, prevented the Reagan administration from abolishing federal transit aid. Nevertheless, federal spending from transit stagnated in constant dollars and declined in real terms (Smerk, 1991).

Frustrated in direct political confrontation, the Reagan administration developed a "flank attack" on subsidies to big public transit systems. This was the privatization thrust of the mid 1980s. It showcased the work of economists and analysts who recommended privatization as the way out of the politico-financial impasse of public transit. Intellectually, the privatization theorists made two novel points. First, they suggested that the best, perhaps the only, way to stop the hemorrhage of subsidy dollars to large public transportation organizations was to reduce their size sharply. The quickest way to shrink them was to turn their "profitable" rush-hour routes over to private bus companies. Although these routes may generate a lot of revenue, they are not really profitable for public transit companies, because they require too much investment in excess equipment and labor. Far from creaming the profit from public transit, contracting out these lines to private enterprise would be "creaming the deficit" (Cervero, 1988). Other services ranging from payroll and accounting to bus maintenance should also be contracted out.

Second, the privatizers suggested that the function of deciding what public transit services were so essential that they must continue to be produced on a subsidized basis should be separated institutionally from the function of actually producing the service. This would enable public authorities to put public and private enterprises on an equal footing in competing for the contract to deliver the services and force many productivity improvements in the public enterprise (Lave, 1985).

Beginning in 1984, under a new Urban Mass Transit Administrator, the Reagan administration attempted to administratively compel public transit agencies to adopt these changes, especially the contracting out of bus routes. Many public transit agencies were reluctant to dismantle their service networks in wholesale fashion, and they resisted the administration's initiative by bureaucratic foot dragging and political counterpressure. Congressional hearings warned the administration not to go beyond the law in linking disbursement of local funding to compliance with the executive privatization initiative (Guskind, 1987).

4. More Flexible Funding and Better Capacity Management

The Bush administration wanted to avoid confrontation with Congress but still sought to keep federal funding for transit at a low level. In transit, and also in highways, it sought to shift more of the burden of financing infrastructure investment to state and local governments (U.S. Department of Transportation, 1989). But Congress asserted its own version of transportation policy in the Intermodal Surface Transportation Efficiency Act of 1991 (ISTEA), which authorized substantially more money than the Bush administration wanted, as well an unprecedented number of local-interest "demonstration projects." ISTEA set the framework for surface transportation policy through 1996 and authorized a total of $151 billion through its 6-year period. But because of the spending restrictions imposed by the Budget Enforcement Act of 1990, and the fact that many of the "pork barrel" demonstration projects are given priority over programmatic and formula-based spending, the ISTEA funding will not be as much of a bonanza as it might have seemed.

This gives added importance to the Act's major policy initiative, which is that it authorized greater flexibility on the part of state and local officials to shift funds between highways and mass transit to achieve the mix of facilities and management systems most appropriate for their area. Thus, rather than encouraging the building new lanes of highway or new transit lines, the stringent budgetary situation and the new federal aid flexibility points to making more efficient use of existing capacity. State and local officials will have more discretion, but they will also have to take more responsibility for making hard choices to impose intrusive, mobility-restricting regulatory measures. In local politics, anything that physically restricts access or mobility has proven politically unpopular indeed. U.S. metropolitan areas are not well served institutionally to be able to do anything but cater to travel demand.

5. The Future: Regulation or Innovation?

The titles of several recent studies of transportation and decentralization in U.S. metropolitan areas indicate that the problem of congestion is once again back at the top of the policy agenda. They suggest that U.S. commuters are *Stuck in Traffic* (Downs, 1992) and experiencing *Suburban Gridlock* (Cervero, 1986) in *Edge City* (Garreau, 1991). Decentralization has not eliminated congestion, it has simply spread it out. Downs (1992) examined 23 congestion-reducing policy options available under present institutional and political conditions. He concluded that the policies that are most politically acceptable are the least likely to make significant reductions in peak-hour traffic congestion. Those few options that are most likely to reduce the amount of rush-hour traffic are also the most politically unpalatable. Relatively acceptable but ineffective policies include encouraging the formation of transportation management associations (TMAs) linking employers and planners, encouraging employees to ride public transit or form carpools, designating expressway space for high-occupancy vehicle (HOV) lanes, and so forth. Even where individual traffic abatement programs may seem successful, what typically happens is that any new road space resulting from a drop in rush-hour congestion is quickly filled by new drivers who shift their routes or leave public transport or carpools.

Two policies that, in principle, could make a major difference in peak-hour congestion, have very high political costs. The first is the economists' venerable scheme of congestion pricing. By charging drivers tolls for the use of scarce peak-hour road space, it should be possible to eliminate a significant portion of single-occupant vehicle rush-hour trips. Drivers would either form carpools to share the cost of tolls (which might be discounted for HOVs) and other operating expenses, or they would time-shift their strips outside of the peak period. A second strategy is to eliminate free parking for employees and impose a surcharge on commercial long-term parking. This too should stimulate ride sharing among commuters. It has the additional advantage of permitting access for shopping, recreation, and other trips that do not require long-term parking.

Both options are certain to meet with strong resistance from commuters, employers, and politicians, who fear that they may cause companies to relocate to areas not covered by the higher tolls and parking restrictions. In addition, both options focus on peak-period trips and would do little to address the growing problem of off-peak congestion. Indeed, by providing drivers with an incentive to time shift their commuting trips, they might make it worse.

Cervero (1987) emphasizes the importance of better regional coordination between land use decisions and transportation planning. In particular, he stresses the need for balanced growth and mixed use land development that minimizes the need for long commutes between home, work, shopping, and entertainment. One can cite numerous examples of efforts being made in the direction of better planning, and further help may soon be at hand. The 1990 Clean Air Act Amendments stipulate that by 1994 metropolitan regions that do not comply with clean air standards must develop plans whereby employers with more than 100 workers have ride-sharing programs to reduce rush-hour commuting trips. Whether this will be enough to make major inroads in auto use remains to be seen, especially in the light of past exemptions and postponements of clear air mandates affecting businesses. The classic U.S. policy-development pattern is that increased public regulatory and planning powers are fiercely resisted until the situation has reached a crisis that is so serious that an emergency response is needed.

Americans would much prefer to rely on a technological fix. Some observers see a new one in the offing: Intelligent Vehicle and Highway Systems (IVHS). This is a set of disparate and still-developing techniques, including systems for advanced traffic management, advanced travel information, automatic vehicle identification and location, automatic vehicle control, and collision avoidance. One simulation of the congestion-reduction effects of IVHS predicted that a full-blown deployment of an automated system could increase highway capacity by as much as 103% (Bender, 1982). But the individual technologies need a great deal of further development; and IVHS, as an integrated system, is still at the drawing-board stage. Federal spending for research in the area was only $2.3 million in 1990. It will rise to over $100 million annually before the middle of the decade. The costs of developing and deploying a national IVHS system have been estimated as high as $34 billion through the year 2010 (GAO, 1991). The question of how to allocate shares of this cost between levels of government and between the public and private sectors is still to be resolved, as are the problems of establishing national technical standards for IVHS systems and how to handle the problem of liability for accidents caused by system failures. There is, of course, no guarantee that capacity improvements brought about by IVHS will not simply induce more traffic onto the road until even the "smart" highway is again congested.

B. Regulating the Automobile Industry and Its Products

Attempting to restrict mobility enough to make major improvements in congestion reduction, let alone air pollution and energy consumption, is a very inefficient regulatory strategy. The tremendous fragmentation of jurisdictions provides an insuperable obstacle to "cracking down" on drivers hard enough to make a significant difference in these "external" costs of the automobile. The obvious alternative is to use the federal government's national powers to regulate the producers of automobiles, not the owners. By setting standards for vehicle performance in areas such as safety, emissions, and energy, Washington can act directly on Detroit, thereby avoiding jurisdictional clashes with states and unpopularity with voters.

The political feasibility of this strategy emerged almost by chance out of the imbroglio between Ralph Nader and General Motors (GM) over auto safety in the mid 1960s. Nader's book *Unsafe at Any Speed* (1965) charged that GM made things worse by ignoring design defects in its Corvair model. A Senate subcommittee hearing exploded into headlines when Nader revealed that General Motors had hired private investigators to uncover evidence to discredit his book and his testimony.

This led to landmark legislation, the National Traffic and Motor Vehicle Safety Act and the Highway Safety Act of 1966. It also established a pattern of adversarialism in relations between Detroit and Washington that proved to be unfortunate, resulting in acrimony, litigation, and long delays in introducing new standards. The administrative agency created by this legislation, the National Highway Traffic Safety Administration (NHTSA) became the focal point for federal auto safety regulatory policy. For the first 10 years of its existence, NHTSA pressed Detroit hard to modify the design of its products to integrate greater occupant crash protection measures. It stressed so-called "passive" safety devices that would operate automatically to protect occupants in a crash rather than unpopular "active" devices, such as the ignition interlock system requiring drivers to buckle safety belts before their car would start. In 1970, NHTSA issued Standard 208, which required car manufacturers to install automatic air bags for passenger collision protection. It was estimated that the device could save up to 9000 lives per year. But the implementation of the regulation was delayed for over 20 years by complex court actions and political maneuvers. Only in the 1990s did manufacturers "voluntarily" begin to make driver's side airbags widely available (Mashaw and Harst, 1990).

In the meantime, other auto regulatory initiatives aimed at improving air quality and energy efficiency had been taken. The Clean Air Act amendments of 1970 set auto emissions standards for hydrocarbons, carbon monoxide, and nitrogen oxide and directed the Environmental Protection Agency to enforce them on the nation's auto manufacturers. Although delayed four times in the 1970s, by 1981 the automakers did begin to meet the standards set over a decade previously.

A similar path was followed for fuel-efficiency regulation. The Arab oil embargo of 1973 to 1974 put energy conservation on the national political agenda. As part of the Energy

Policy and Conservation Act of 1975, Congress established a schedule of Corporate Average Fuel Economy (CAFE) standards for new cars, rising from 18 miles per gallon in 1978 to 27.5 miles per gallon (mpg) in 1985. The Big Three auto companies initially resisted the standards, then grudgingly seemed to accept them in the wake of the second energy crisis brought on by the Iranian revolution. In the energy glut years of the mid 1980s, GM and Ford fell back into petitioning for exemptions and rollbacks of the CAFE standards. There is no disputing the fact that the fuel efficiency of new cars in the United States improved dramatically over the years when the CAFE standards were taking effect (1978 to 1985). One study estimated that some 35 billion fewer gallons of gasoline were purchased in 1987 because of the regulations. It estimated the cumulative savings through 1987 at around $260 billion (Greene et al., 1988). Some economists wonder whether to attribute all the progress to the CAFE standards or to give some credit to increased fuel costs (Crandall, 1986). In the early 1980s, motor fuel prices were indeed rising and this reinforced the message that CAFE sent manufacturers and consumers. By the middle of the decade, gasoline prices began to fall sharply, and the continued fuel efficiency of the U.S. new car fleet can only be attributed to the CAFE standards.

The Reagan administration, sympathetic to Detroit's complaints about regulatory overkill, moved to "roll back" many existing and proposed regulations in the safety and energy areas, and opposed efforts to reduce auto emissions further. The Bush administration compromised on the Clean Air Act Amendments of 1990, with requirements for cleaner burning motor fuels and the 1994 employer ride-sharing requirements, but the executive branch and lobbyists for the auto industry successfully resisted efforts all legislative efforts to raise CAFE standards beyond 27.5 mpg.

One of the most intriguing policy arguments of the late 1980s concerned the interaction effects of automobile regulations in different areas. Some pollution control devices may have slightly reduced fuel efficiency. More important, some researchers charged that the CAFE standards were contributing to an increase in deaths and injuries in auto accidents. They argued that there was a direct correlation between a vehicle's weight and its ability to protect its occupants in a crash. The main way manufacturers met the 27.5-mpg fuel efficiency standard was to make cars lighter. They concluded that CAFE standards were killing people (Crandall and Graham, 1989). Safety advocates countered that this was all the more reason to press ahead with more stringent safety standards.

The Reagan years not only ended the politics of acrimony between Detroit and the executive branch, but also saw a bipartisan push to grant trade protection against Japanese imports. The Reagan administration, responding to intense pressure from the auto companies, the auto workers' union, and the congressional delegations from the major auto manufacturing states, maneuvered Japan into a so-called "voluntary" restraint agreement (VRA). The initial terms of the VRA terms called for the Japanese to limit exports to 1.68 million for the period 1981 to 1983. In subsequent years, the VRA was extended, and had a more generous 2.3 million vehicle limit. Virtually all mainstream U.S. economists pointed out that this form of protecting auto companies profits and workers jobs was both costly and clumsy. It drove up the price of all vehicles, not just Japanese imports. It encouraged Japanese manufacturers to move into upscale market niches and to open "transplant" assembly facilities in the United States to get around the import quota (Dunn, 1987). The Big 3 U.S. auto makers flourished financially during the 1980s boom even while producing fewer vehicles and providing fewer jobs. When recession struck in 1990, however, they plunged into financial crisis again.

The balance sheet of both the automobile industry and the fabled U.S. "car culture" looked more mixed in 1992 than in any recent decade. Despite its many problems, loudly decried by social critics, the automobile had always seemed to represent a dynamic, independent, and rising force in U.S. society. Its power required other socioeconomic institutions, from transit companies and retail department stores to the restaurant industry, to adjust to its imperatives. The automobile may have been disruptive, but it always seemed to be strengthening the economic and industrial fabric of the nation. It is the image of the automobile as a source of strength that is changing. After the experience of the Chrysler "bailout" and a decade of costly trade protection, foreign imports held over one-third of the U.S. market. The U.S. auto manufacturers, especially the once-mighty General Motors, were experiencing financial difficulties even worse than in the 1980 to 1982 period. The combination of automobile imports and oil imports accounted for the majority of the growing U.S. trade deficit. The United States and its allies had to fight a war to protect access to Persian Gulf oil. Automobile exhaust emissions were still the major source of several of the most noxious air pollutants. The automobile/highway coalition's dogged resistance to increasing federal motor fuel taxes and "diverting" the receipts to the general treasury contributed substantially to the persistence of the federal budget deficit (Dunn, 1992).

None of these problems were new. None could be blamed on excessive federal regulation during the Reagan-Bush years. They all have resisted the policy solutions that have been attempted over the years. They are inherent in the trajectory that the automobile has described in U.S. society and culture. Once incredibly attractive and dynamic, the automobile has become a prosaic necessity and a source of perennial problems for public policy. Barring an ecological catastrophe, the auto will remain a very important factor on the U.S. transportation scene. But it is likely that the United States' other problems and policy imperatives (e.g., trade and budget deficits, the economy, the environment) will impinge on the automobile's former dominance and require it to adjust to the nation's other priorities more than it has in the past.

IV. COMPARATIVE PERSPECTIVES AND CONCLUSIONS

A. The European Experience: Assuring Alternatives to the Auto

Western European transportation policy has always had a stronger component of governmental *dirigisme* than American policy (Dunn, 1981). Particularly on the continent, European policy has been less unconditionally accommodating to the imperious demands of the automobile. In the first instance, European governments made sure that the automobile more than pays its own way fiscally. European taxes on auto sales, ownership, and motor fuel are much higher than in the United States. In nations such as France and Italy, the majority of the national superhighway system has been financed by tolls, with motor fuel taxes going into the general treasury and not a special highway fund. In all European countries, public revenues generated by the automobile make a substantial net positive contribution to public budgets, after deductions for infrastructure are taken into account. In the United States, by contrast, automobile-generated revenues only cover about 55% of highway infrastructure spending (Dunn, 1992; International Road Federation, 1991).

Second, most European cities and metropolitan areas have drawn back from the brink of permitting the degree of auto dominance and dispersed development found in the United States. They have acted to preserve the compact cores of their urban areas and channeled suburban development into denser, more transit-friendly clusters of mixed use and more self-contained developments. Public transit networks have been modernized, expanded, integrated, subsidized, and promoted. Transit preservation has been a costly effort, but it has been carried out with far less ideological backlash than the United States experienced in the 1980s (Pucher, 1988).

Third, measures to restrain automobile traffic have been widely implemented and successfully adopted in European cities of all sizes. Germany, perhaps the world leader in well-planned pedestrianization of city centers, has shown skeptical shopkeepers that pedestrianization can actually help business. The Netherlands is undoubtedly the leader in retaining a major share of urban travel for the bicycle. Other nations have begun to work hard to restore two-wheel traffic. Germany's Federal Environmental Agency made a major effort with a "bicycle-friendly town" project in the 1980s that went well beyond just providing bike paths. Bike shelters at train stations and tram stops, bike rental centers, low auto speed limits, repainting of streets for bike-turning lanes, and a public relations campaigns to create a bicycle-friendly climate were all included (Tolley, 1990).

European transportation and urban planners have implemented a variety of other traffic-restraint measures aimed at reducing the speed of autos in cities and discouraging their access to certain areas. In German cities, the practice of *Verkehrsberuhigung* (traffic calming) has as its object to slow down automobile speeds substantially so that motorized and nonmotorized traffic becomes compatible. This is done by narrowing roads, by slightly elevating road surfaces, or by installing green areas, tree planters, and so forth (Keller, 1986: 46). In the Netherlands, planners have used similar measures to rebuild streets completely so that they serve as *Woonerfen* (living areas) where bicyclists, pedestrians, children, and a few slow-moving local autos can coexist in harmony. Gothenburg, Sweden, has installed a successful traffic cell system that has reduced traffic between cells in the central city by up to 50%. A number of Italian cities, with Bologna being the first, now restrict entry into their historic old city centers to vehicles belonging to residents or local businesses. Jones and Hervik (1992: 144) conclude that ". . . traffic restraint will become an active ingredient of urban transport policy in many European cities. . . ."

European rail policy has evolved in almost the opposite direction of that of the United States. Privately owned railroads in the United States shed passenger traffic and concentrated on low-speed trainload shipments of bulk freight. Publicly owned railways in Western Europe reduced the relative importance of freight and invested in modernizing their passenger train network. In the 1960s and 1970s, this entailed the unpopular closure on many lightly traveled branch lines serving small towns and villages. By the 1980s, however, the policy of concentrating infrastructural investment on main lines between major urban centers began to pay off. The most celebrated success was the French *train à grande vitesse* (TGV), which began service in 1981 with a new roadbed and new rolling stock on the Paris to Lyons route. TGV lines have begun to shoot out from Paris in all directions, including one to connect with the new tunnel under the English Channel (Révue générale des chemins de fer, 1993). Other European nations also have their own fast train program. The Germans opened the first stretches of their Inter-City Express (ICE) in 1991. Italy and Britain are developing high-speed trains, and Sweden and Switzerland are cooperating on a train project. The European Community is attempting to coordinate and supplement national rail efforts toward the creation of a network of high-speed trains spanning the whole 12-nation community. Although the current generation of European rail projects makes use of conventional steel wheel on rail, the Europeans, and Germany in particular, are pressing on with research and demonstration projects based on magnetic levitation (maglev) technology. Europe should be well positioned to exploit, deploy, and export maglev technology commercially if and when it becomes financially feasible (Vranich, 1991).

B. Developing Nations: Overcoming the Mobility Deficit

Mobility is closely associated with economic prosperity. Cross-national data show that the most economically developed nations also have the greatest mobility of goods and, even more so, of people. One important dimension of the chasm between the rich nations and the poor nations has been called the "mobility gap." For example, Africa, Asia (excluding Japan), and Latin America have approximately 77% of the planet's population, but they have only 17% of the world's rail freight shipments, 10% of the paved roads, and 5% of the motor vehicles. The U.S. state of Kentucky, with a population of 3.6 million, has more trucks than the vast subcontinent of India—population 750 million! The mobility gap leaves 2 billion people virtually disconnected from the rest of the world (Owen, 1987).

Transportation, then, is a very important factor contributing to economic growth. The policy challenge for developing countries is to increase the amount of mobility in their societies in a way that does not divert scarce resources from other vital development needs. There is little doubt that better roads and more motor vehicles are desperately needed in the countryside of Third World countries. Rural roads must be given all-weather paving so that feed and fertilizer can reach farmers and agricultural products can be marketed to customers beyond the local region. Famine more often results from breakdowns in transportation and distribution than crop failure. More buses must be made available so that village children can attend high school and rural families can visit health clinics. The list of rural mobility needs is very long.

Equally important, developing nations must provide means of urban mobility for the many millions migrating to the cities. Here there is vigorous debate among planners over the relative merits of road-based modes such as (usually private) automobiles, jitneys, and buses versus usually public rail-based modes, including subways. Some worry that governments will waste scarce capital on expensive, inflexible rail systems for prestige or be persuaded by consultants and equipment vendors that rail is more "modern." The World Bank's economists believe that bus systems on a properly managed right of way (e.g., HOV lanes during peak hours) can serve the needs of rapidly growing urban areas with large numbers of low-income residents on the periphery. They maintain that the scarce capital needed to construct an expensive urban rail system would be better invested in housing, sewers, schools, and other badly needed facilities for mushrooming urban populations in the developing world (Rimmer, 1986).

The issue of the role of the automobile in world economic development is also fraught with controversy. Few doubt that the tremendous growth of the automobile industry, with its millions of good production jobs and its democratization of car ownership was, on balance, a beneficial development in the West. The success of its motor industry was an important factor in Japan's postwar economic boom, and South Korea has made auto production one of its key development strategies. Taiwan, Thailand, and Malaysia may also try to follow this path. But what happens to world levels of oil consumption and atmospheric pollution when India and China launch major motorization efforts? Could the planet's ecosystem survive if auto ownership levels in Asia, Africa, and Latin America reached U.S. or West European levels? The other side of the question is whether it is equitable to consign two thirds of the world's population to mobility based on the bicycle and rickshaw? For most Third World inhabitants, even the bicycle is a luxury, and the automobile is reserved to the privileged elite. Providing the resources and financing for the automobile system may actually be hurting development. In Haiti, for example, only one half of 1% of the population owns an auto, but one third of the country's imports are devoted to fuel and transport equipment (Renner, 1988).

Transportation policy is thus closely linked to much broader issues of global equity and ecological survival. These meta-issues challenge transportation policy makers and analysts in both the advanced industrial countries and the developing world to rework their policy agendas toward achieving common goals. Policies in both these worlds ought to be aimed at pre-venting transportation systems, particularly the auto/highway system, from continuing to overconsume scarce energy resources and arable land, pollute the environment, and kill and maim hundreds of thousands of human beings each year.

In the developed countries, especially the United States, it is not just traffic that needs to be "tamed," but also the tendency for social evolution and economic growth to require ever-more intensive inputs of transportation to sustain themselves. It is feckless and futile to speak of reducing the "mobility gap" between the developed and the developing world with the motorization rate in the United States having surpassed one vehicle for every adult in-habitant and still rising. Transportation policy making needs to find ways to incorporate con-cern for the long-term interests of humankind as well as the short-term interests of present populations, entrepreneurs, and developers.

That kind of thinking has not been prominent in transportation policy studies, but it has not been totally absent. Far more needs to be done, of course, before a "new paradigm" emerges that can achieve this balance. Americans are not going to join carpools out of fervor to help Haiti or Djibouti (formerly Somaliland). But if the logic of policy evolution in U.S. metropolitan areas makes greater ride sharing inevitable, it may make the changes more palat-able to know that there is some logical connections between the change in their "lifestyle" and the possibility of improvement in the developing nations. At the present time, it would be fallacious to think that such a connection exists or must exist. It is quite possible that it could work out that an unfavorable turn of events results in mobility restrictions in the United States and even worse conditions in many developing nations. All that one can say now is that such a connection may be possible, and that it is worthwhile devoting a greater portion of the ingenuity and analytical prowess of future transportation policy studies to see if it can be realized.

REFERENCES

Akaha, T. (1990). *International Handbook of Transportation Policy.* Greenwood Press, Westport, CT.

Bailey, E. E., Graham, D. R., and Kaplan, D. P. (1985). *Deregulating the Airlines.* M.I.T. Press, Cam-bridge, MA.

Bender, J. G., et al. (1982). *Systems Study of Automated Highway Systems, Final Report.* General Motors Corporation GM Transportation Systems Center, and Federal Highway Administration, Washington, DC.

Brown, A. E. (1987). *The Politics of Airline Deregulation.* The University of Tennessee Press, Knox-ville, TN.

Cervero, R. (1988). *Transit Service Contracting: Cream-Skimming or Deficit Skimming?* U.S. Depart-ment of Transportation, Washington, DC.

—— (1986). *Suburban Gridlock.* Rutgers University, Center for Urban Policy Research, New Bruns-wick, NJ.

Crandall, R., and Graham, J. D. (1989). The effect of fuel economy standards on automobile safety. *Journal of Law and Economics* 32: 97.

Crandell, R., et al. (1986). *Regulating the Automobile.* The Brookings Institution, Washington, DC.

Derthick, M., and Quirk, P. J. (1985). *The Politics of Deregulation.* The Brookings Institution, Wash-ington, DC.

Douglas, G. W., and Miller, J. C., III (1974). *Economic Regulation of Domestic Air Transport: Theory and Policy.* The Brookings Institution, Washington, DC.

Downs, A. (1992). *Stuck in Traffic: Coping with Peak-Hour Traffic Congestion.* The Brookings In-stitution, Washington, DC.

Dunn, J. A. (1992). The Politics of Motor Fuel Taxes and Infrastructure Funds in France and the United States. Paper presented at the annual meeting of the American Political Science Association.

—— (1987). Automobiles in international trade: Regime change or persistence. *International Organization* 41(2): 225–252.

—— (1981). *Miles to Go: European and American Transportation Policies*. M.I.T. Press, Cambridge, MA.

European Conference of Ministers of Transport (1992). *Investment in Transport Infrastructure in the 1980s*. OECD Publications Service, Paris.

Felton, J. R., and Anderson, D. G. (Eds.) (1989). *Regulation and Deregulation of the Motor Carrier Industry*. Iowa State University Press, Ames.

Flink, J. J. (1975). *The Car Culture*. M.I.T. Press, Cambridge, MA.

Garreau, J. (1991). *Edge City*. Doubleday, New York.

Guskind, R. (1987). Leave the driving to us. *Planning* July, 6–10.

International Road Federation (1991). *World Road Statistics 1986–1990*. International Road Federation, Washington, DC, and Geneva.

Jones, P., and Hervik, A. (1992). Restraining car traffic in European cities: An emerging role for road pricing. *Transportation Research* 26A(2): 133–145.

Keeler, T. E. (1983). *Railroads, Freight, and Public Policy*. The Brookings Institution, Washington, DC.

Keller, H. (1986). Environmental traffic restraints on major roads in the Federal Republic of Germany. *Built Environment* 12(1/2): 44.

Lave, C. A. (Ed.) (1985). *Urban Transit: The Private Challenge to Public Transportation*. Ballinger, Cambridge, MA.

Lindblom, C. E. (1977). *Politics and Markets: The World's Political-Economic Systems*. Basic Books, New York.

MacAvoy, P. W. (1979). *The Regulated Industries and the Economy*. W. W. Norton, New York.

Mashaw, J. L., and Harfst, D. L. (1990). *The Struggle for Auto Safety*. Harvard University Press, Cambridge, MA.

Meyer, J. R., and Oster, C. V. (1987). *Deregulation and the Future of Intercity Passenger Travel*. M.I.T. Press, Cambridge, MA.

Mohring, H. (1976). *Transportation Economics*. Ballinger, Cambridge, MA.

Moore, T. G. (1972). *Freight Transportation Regulation*. The Brookings Institution, Washington, DC.

Morrison, S., and Winston, C. (1986). *The Economic Effects of Airline Deregulation*. The Brookings Institution, Washington, DC.

Mowbray, A. Q. (1969). *Road to Ruin*. J.B. Lippincott, Philadelphia.

Mumford, L. (1963). *The Highway and the City*. Harcourt, Brace, New York.

Nader, R. (1965). *Unsafe at Any Speed*. Bantam Books, New York.

National Research Council. (1992). *Winds of Change: Domestic Air Transport Since Deregulation*. Transportation Research Board, Washington, DC.

Owen, W. (1987). *Transportation and World Development*. Johns Hopkins University Press, Baltimore.

Pucher, J. (1988). Urban travel behavior as the outcome of public policy: The example of modal-split in Western Europe and North America. *APA Journal* 509.

Organization for Economic Cooperation and Development (1988). *Deregulation and Airline Competition*. OECD, Paris.

Renner, M. (1988). *Rethinking the Role of the Automobile*. Worldwatch Institute, Washington, DC.

Revue générale des chemins de fer (1992). A decade of TGV operation, Special Issue of the *Revue générale des chemins de fer*.

Reynolds-Feighan, A. J. (1992). *The Effects of Deregulation on U.S. Air Networks*. Springer-Verlag, Berlin.

Rimmer, P. J. (1986). *Rikisha to Rapid Transit: Urban Public Transport Systems and Policy in Southeast Asia*. Pergamon Press, Sidney.

Robyn, D. (1987). *Braking the Special Interests*: *Trucking Deregulation and the Politics of Policy Reform*. University of Chicago Press, Chicago.

Rose, M. (1979). *Interstate*: *Express Highway Politics 1941–1956*. Regents Press of Kansas, Lawrence, KA.

Schwartz, G. T. (1976). Urban freeways and the interstate system. *Southern California Law Review* 49: 406.

Smerk, G. M. (1991). *The Federal Role in Mass Transportation*. Indiana University Press, Bloomington, IN.

Sperling, D. (1988). *New Transportation Fuels*: *A Strategic Approach to Technological Change*. University of California Press, Berkeley.

Tolley, R. (Ed.) (1990). *The Greening of Urban Transport*: *Planning for Walking and Cycling in Western Cities*. Belhaven Press, London.

Thompson, S. J. (1984). *Deregulation of Transportation*. Congressional Research Service, Washington, DC.

U.S. Department of Transportation (1989). *Moving America*: *New Directions, New Opportunities*. U.S. Department of Transportation, Washington, DC.

U.S. General Accounting Office (1991). *Smart Highways*: *An Assessment of Their Potential to Improve Travel*. U.S. General Accounting Office, Washington, DC.

Vranich, J. R. (1991). *Supertrains*: *Solutions to America's Transportation Gridlock*. St. Martin's Press, New York.

Watt, W. J. (1988). *The Future of Freight Railroads in the Northeast and Midwest*. Northeast-Midwest Institute, Washington, DC.

Wright, C. L. (1992). *Fast Wheels, Slow Traffic*: *Urban Transport Choices*. Temple University Press, Philadelphia.

Zuckermann, W. (1991). *End of the Road*: *The World Car Crisis and How We Can Solve It*. Chelsea Green, Post Mills, VT.

29
Environmental Protection Policy

Geoffrey Wandesforde-Smith
University of California, Davis, California

I. INTRODUCTION: INTO THE MAINSTREAM

In the first edition of this encyclopedia, the chapter on environmental policy by Helen Ingram and Dean Mann neatly encapsulates almost a decade and a half of previous thinking and research by a variety of mainstream scholars in the United States (Ingram and Mann, 1983). The chapter frankly acknowledges that there is more than one way to approach an understanding of how politics and policy are associated with each other in the nation's recognition and treatment of its environmental problems. The differences in approach are so marked that priority attaches in some new accounts to reconciling alternative ways of thinking about environmental problems and solutions (Norton, 1991).

Not all of the approaches now in use see politics or government playing a major and constructive role in environmental problem solving. The merits of different perspectives in these terms are still hotly debated; perhaps even more so now in the wake of the Reagan revolution than when the first edition of this book was published (Greve and Smith, 1992; Harris and Milkis, 1989; Ophuls and Boyan, 1992; Paehlke, 1989; Smith, 1992).

Accepting that vigorous exchanges occur over the question of how to gauge the relationship between politics and policy, on the one hand, and environmental problem solving, on the other hand, Ingram and Mann incline to the view, nevertheless, that politics can and does and should make a positive contribution. History teaches us several specific and important lessons about the nature of this contribution.

II. CURRENTS IN THE MAINSTREAM

One lesson is that progress in solving problems through public policy instruments is always uncertain and usually slow (cf. Smith, 1992: ch. 4; Rosenbaum, 1991: ch. 3). Policy itself, the stuff that makes up the outputs of political processes aimed at influencing government decisions, can sometimes change quite dramatically over a short time. Getting problems solved, however, which means changing the outcomes policies produce in society and in the economy, as well as changing the outputs of the political system, is a process that typically advances incrementally. And it may move so slowly, or so imperceptibly, that policy comes to be associated with failure, possibly even superfailure (Mazmanian and Morrell, 1992).

At both levels, outputs and outcomes, Ingram and Mann (1983) see that change is largely driven by the peak associations of the environmental movement. The groups at the top of the movement, in other words, supply most of the effective political demand that shapes the broad outlines of environmental policy change. Public opinion about and media coverage of environmental issues also have an important influence. But these variables need an agency to translate them into effective inputs to the political system—perhaps in the first instance by deliberately inflaming opinion or otherwise attracting media attention. And it is the top groups that perform this function, often with exquisite skill, but also largely without much assistance from, or interaction with, grassroots groups, according to the standard accounts (Freudenberg and Steinsapir, 1991; Lowe and Morrison, 1984; LaMay and Dennis, 1991; Mitchell, 1990; Mitchell et al., 1991).

These groups are more or less unified at different points in time, and their tactics and strategies may be more or less coordinated depending on what issues are at stake and what broader political circumstances prevail (Adams et al., 1985). What they accomplish, singly and together, however, is generally far less than what is needed *really* to solve environmental problems, if the evidence about deteriorating conditions and trends, and the more positive evidence about the prospects for pollution prevention and sustainable development, is fully credited.

The implication is clearly that the diversity of the movement, which might in some ways be considered a strength, is also a cause of shortfalls in problem solving, as well as a contributory factor in the reluctance of policy makers, for all sorts of reasons, to buy wholesale into the environmental movement's agenda.

On balance, however, history shows Ingram and Mann that, with all its imperfections, American-style representative democracy has the great advantage that it can be a learning process. Politics is, in this sense, an important and functional, although not perfect, mechanism for social adaptation to changing environmental conditions, as well as a mechanism for the generation of perceptions about what problems exist and how serious they are.

Most importantly, environmental politics in the context of a pluralistic and representative democracy, such as obtains in the United States and is guaranteed by the Constitution, is open. It is not completely open to everyone. It is open enough, however, to allow alternative and competing hypotheses about how and why the environment is changing, and what, if anything, therefore, policy makers should do about it, to be aired and to be challenged.

The improvement of both public policy and environmental conditions can be anchored, therefore, directly to the structure of the political system (Ingram and Ullery, 1980; Ingram and Mann, 1983: 700–710; Mann, 1986). It could and probably should be tied closely to the entrepreneurial strategic uses political actors make of the opportunities for change they can leverage within the interstices of this structure, although because entrepreneurial explanations focus on individuals as units of analysis rather than aggregate constructs, such as groups or policy networks, they have never found the favor they deserve (see e.g., Petracca, 1992; but also see Doig and Hargrove, 1987; Kingdon, 1984). In any event, policy progress need not be thought to depend on less reliable and less durable factors, such as the changing electoral fortunes of political parties, or the waxing and waning in mass public or elite consciousness of political paradigms and ideologies (Inglehart, 1977, 1990; Milbrath, 1984).

Thus, Ingram and Mann (1983) could adopt, a decade ago, a critical stance that is at once blunt and appealing. It allows them to say not only that environmental politics works in the United States but also that it does not work as well as it should. At the same time, they can hold out the hope, for the long-term future, that environmental politics can be made more powerful and effective, as experience and research provide evaluation and feedback, to fuel the political learning process.

One can readily imagine why this positive and forward-looking assessment gets a warm welcome among environmental policy researchers. Political science and policy analysis both receive strong endorsement from Ingram and Mann (1983), as disciplines making material contributions to efforts not just to comprehend but also to deal with the environmental crisis.

On this count, Ingram and Mann (1983) respond directly to the disciplinary challenges Jones (1972) outlines in an even earlier essay. In this aggressively mainstream and truly formative statement, Jones lays it down very clearly that unless students of environmental politics and policy go out of their way to bring their work into the disciplinary mainstream, they run the risk of making both their subject and their research seem marginal and poorly grounded.

Now, of course, 10 more years have passed since Ingram and Mann wrote their essay, and the question of whether the mainstream account is still tenable needs to be asked. In some respects, the answer is that it has done more than hold its own. It has been expressly codified (Ingram and Mann, 1989: 135; and generally Lester, 1989a).

III. CUTS ACROSS THE CURRENT?

However, as we shall see, in other respects there are developments that cut across the current of the mainstream and raise questions about the mainstream account that are, at the very least, intriguing and that in some respects challenge both the empirical assessment and the normative evaluation the mainstream offers for what can be expected in the way of policy change.

And it is of more than passing interest that this opportunity to reappraise the mainstream account and evaluation of environmental politics arises at the beginning of the Clinton presidency. There is always a question about the extent to which electoral outcomes and presidential leadership can realign the multitudinous and multifarious political factors that seem in the past to have constrained the ability of the U.S. political system to deal more forthrightly and decisively with the nation's environmental ills (Kraft, 1984; Vig, 1990, 1993).

Clearly, if there is a tendency to incrementalism built into the functioning of the system, at least with respect to policy outputs, it can be overcome, as it was recently in relation to some parts at least of the 1990 Clean Air Act Amendments, the only major environmental policy accomplishment of the Bush administration (Bryner, 1993; Cohen, 1992). In their essay of 10 years ago, Ingram and Mann (1983: 688) are more forthright in their acknowledgment of the frequency with which this can happen than most other authors, who tend to be deeply suspicious of the idea that the United States can make, and has made in the past, bold leaps forward in environmental policy.

In fact, the evidence is that, in addition to election results and entrepreneurial leadership initiatives, shifts in public opinion and in mass media treatment of environmental issues, which are themselves interrelated, can also contribute to the creation of moments of rapid change in environmental policy. And the question of whether the Clinton presidency will prove to be one of these defining moments, when all the major and potentially favorable factors come into alignment, is both unavoidable and fascinating (Vig and Kraft, 1993).

On the face of it, the Clinton presidency offers only the second chance in more than 20 years, since the beginning of the environmental era, in 1970, to test whether election returns, translated into congressional majorities, together with presidential leadership and other favorable factors, can overcome the inertial incrementalism of the system. Indeed, in some respects, such as the inclusion of former Senator Albert Gore in the administration, as vice president, the chances of significant forward progress have never been better (Gore, 1993).

This is not to say that only Democratic presidencies, such as those of Carter and Clinton, can be used to test the association between difficult and divided political circumstances, on the one hand, and incremental policy accomplishments, on the other hand, presented by the mainstream version of how we understand and evaluate environmental politics in the United States. It is true, however, that present expectations of what can normally be accomplished by way of environmental policy change and problem solving are the product of a period in which political control of the major institutions of U.S. government has been divided, and in which the Republicans have controlled the presidency, and latterly, in effect, the Supreme Court, but not the Congress (Fiorina, 1992). In the mainstream text, this is a recipe for policy gridlock (Kraft, 1993).

The question of whether more decisive and effective action on environmental problems than we are used to seeing is possible will, thus, next arise on a Democratic watch and during President Clinton's tenure, which is just now beginning. Such action has been demanded, and is expected (Gore, 1993: xi–xx). If it materializes, the normalcy of incrementalism in environmental policy change, as it has developed under the divided government conditions of the last 20 years, will need reconsideration, as will the prospects for nonincremental changes in environmental conditions.

IV. ESSENTIALS OF THE MAINSTREAM VIEW

Ingram and Mann, acknowledged leaders in the study of U.S. environmental politics for more than 20 years, have refined and polished the mainstream view to the point that they consider it codified (Ingram and Mann, 1989; Mann, 1986, 1991). They have reached this point at the cost of some wavering and misgivings, however, both about theory and about practice (Fairfax and Ingram, 1990; Ingram, 1990).

This is in part because there is not, as already noted, unanimity among students of environmental policy about what theoretical premises to adopt for the analysis and understanding of environmental politics and policy. It is also because so much of the evidence about the positive impact policy has had on society, on the economy, and on environmental conditions appears to be equivocal (Burtraw and Portney, 1991; Rosenbaum, 1991; Tietenberg, 1992).

In addition, there is doubt in some quarters about whether the study of environmental politics and policy has shown itself to be appropriately self-conscious about theory, and method, over the last 20 years (Francis, 1990; Symposium, 1991a). And there is doubt too about whether a coalescence around a single, over-arching or dominant theoretical paradigm is possible or necessary or desirable (Fairfax and Ingram, 1990).

In this scholarly and analytical climate, the codification of a mainstream account has to be undertaken with some trepidation, and can only be made at a price. The choice and decision of an analyst to understand the world one way inevitably means that the analytical purchase and understanding available from alternative frameworks are discounted or are traded off for conclusions that fit with familiar and comfortable constructs. In the end, the question everyone has to ask is whether this price is worth paying (Minow and Spelman, 1990). Ingram and Mann, and others, believe that the price for delineating and subscribing to a mainstream account is right.

In addition to coming at a price, however, this bold (and we should also say courageous) delineation of a mainstream account over the last several years comes amid troubling times. In its favor, it does come after two decades of sustained research effort on many aspects of environmental policy in the United States. At the end of such a period, one might argue, it is time to consolidate and take stock—to ask, as Piasecki and Asmus (1990) did, whether our politics and politics are helping us achieve excellent results.

It also comes though at a time when old orders are collapsing. It is a time when new ideas and much new information about environmental problems and policies are flooding into the analyst's computer, if you will, from around a changing world. The very idea of a mainstream theoretical account of environmental politics and policy, especially if it is based almost entirely on the analysis of American experience, is bound to seem antediluvian and on the verge of being overwhelmed.

It is an old adage of policy research, indeed of all research, that absent some pretense about how to make a changing world and its people stand still, in effect, and stand still long enough for struggles over theory to be framed and to be resolved, no progress is possible (Putt and Springer, 1989). So one has to cast about somewhere for an anchor. This simple truth about the necessity for theoretical choice should not itself be sufficient, however, to make us throw in our lot with Ingram and Mann, attach an anchor to their craft, and float along with them in the mainstream view of life.

To achieve the analytical purchase on the world that they seek, it might look as if those in the mainstream have followed the simple necessity for choice to a simple conclusion. They seem to have opted for the view that environmental politics is indistinguishable from politics in general, and that analysis of the former is just one among many devices for illuminating the latter. The choices made are more complex and disputatious than this.

Strange to say, however, that despite one or two vigorous and imaginative examinations of the roots of mainstream thinking (Bosso, 1987; Lowe and Rudig, 1986), mainstream theory choices for the study of environmental policy have in most important respects gone largely unexamined. In a post–cold war world, changing so fast it seems less likely than ever to stand still, this lack of critical attention to foundational assumptions is unacceptable.

Where then are the foundational assumptions of the mainstream view? What are they? And what are some of the things that might be said about the price they exact?

A. Foundational Assumptions

More than in any other single place, the codification of the mainstream view takes shape in Ingram and Mann's essay for, as well as in the many other excellent contributions to, a recent and in some respects tremendously useful landmark volume, *Environmental Politics and Policy: Theories and Evidence*, released to mark the 20th anniversary of Earth Day, 1970 (Lester, 1989a). By most accounts, the original Earth Day is a date that marks the advent of the modern environmental era in U.S. political life (Cahn and Cahn, 1990).

In this collection of essays, even more clearly than in some other, recent, broadly gauged surveys that also swim in the mainstream (Vig and Kraft, 1990; McKee, 1991; Portney, 1992; Rosenbaum, 1991; Scheffer, 1991; Smith, 1992), attention is riveted on how the political system works. The first and chiefly empirical concern is whether and how the system works to produce environmental policies. In addition and above all, however, explanation is premised on, and securely fastened to, a normative conception of policy that is almost unrelievedly instrumental. The key intellectual obsession goes beyond, therefore, creating an understanding of how environmental policies are initially produced and later modified through the political system.

The instrumental conception of policy also demands that at every stage, from setting the agenda of policy makers to policy enforcement and on to policy reformulation, explanation must be framed and results must be judged in terms of whether the environmental public policies that exist, and those that are proposed, are or will be successful. Do they or will they solve perceived environmental problems as defined by environmentalists with the support of environmental science?

The idea that except by accident, neglect, or a surfeit of irrationality, the political system entertains policies for reasons other than problem solving, or that among its most important products are rhetorical reformulations and cultural redefinitions of problems, is sometimes grudgingly acknowledged but is generally considered an anathema (Dwyer, 1990; but see, e.g., Gusfield, 1981; Killingsworth and Palmer, 1992; Pildes, 1991; Pildes and Anderson, 1990; Stone, 1988; Torgerson, 1990; Vining and Schroeder, 1987; Yeager, 1991).

Around its most basic instrumental premise, the mainstream code constructs itself largely as follows. There is an assumption that it makes sense to approach the study of environmental politics and policy by focusing on the political system, and more particularly on the formal and informal institutions that make up that system—Congress (Kraft, 1989), the executive branch (Rosenbaum, 1989), and the courts (Wenner, 1989) at the federal level, for example, as well as interest groups (Ingram and Mann, 1989), political parties (Calvert, 1989), elites (Rushefsky, 1989), and the mass public (Dunlap, 1989).

The system can be assumed to have an interest in solving perceived environmental problems through public policy instruments (although other devices, like markets, can also be brought into the picture [Dryzek and Lester, 1989]), because that is a rational stance. In addition, it puts a premium on policy success, which, if it is forthcoming, in turn confers legitimacy on the system and on the actors who work through it. Policies may be treated as if they were hypotheses and the political system as if it were a testing device.

The dynamics of the system can be understood by imagining that policy instruments work their way through successive and recursive policy cycles (Jones, 1970, 1975), a view recently recodified and rigidly applied by Portney (1992). Ideally, the steps between definition of a problem and its solution by efficient and effective policy follow each other in order.

The lessons of experience in testing policy ideas are fed back into policy reformulation, and the cyclical recursions are, therefore, progressive. When this cyclical progression does not occur, perhaps because it is diverted or interrupted by politics aimed at something other than "getting the job done," there is a sense that all is not normal. The orderliness and stability and, therefore, the predictability of environmental policy processes are threatened (Rosenbaum, 1991: 69).

Further it can be assumed, that the political system's cyclical efforts to produce policies to solve problems are shaped by a funnel of causation (Lester, 1989b, following Hofferbert, 1974; Ostrom, 1990). At the wide end of the funnel are essentially stable or slowly changing variables, such as the environment itself (nature, or, more accurately, Nature [FitzSimmons, 1989]), geography, history, and the social and economic structure of society. At the narrow end, closer to the point at which policy outputs emerge from formal policy conversion routines, like the legislative process, there are variables to account for more malleable influences on policy, such as governmental institutions and the behavior of elites.

Within the dynamics set up by this funnel of causation, it can be still further assumed that the political system's efforts to produce policies to solve problems are chiefly goaded and guided by the environmental movement. In other words, it is safe to assume that there is a movement, although the environmental policy literature contains no agreed on or widely shared statement of what it is or where it came from (see, however, Bosso, 1991; Eyerman and Jamison, 1991; McCann, 1986).

Further, the movement for all practical political intents and purposes consists of and works through interest groups and associated policy communities or networks (Salisbury et al., 1992), especially a rather small number of top groups and their networks (Mitchell et al., 1991), even though most of the organizational base of the movement lies, and has always lain, below this elevated surface. Observation and close analysis of the interaction between the movement, its groups, and policy networks, on the one hand, and the major institutions of government, on the other hand, tells us most of what we want and need to know about why environmental politics and policy work the way they do (Ingram and Mann, 1989).

The basic building blocks of comprehension then are variations on ideas about politics as a cyclical system, about policy as instrumental problem solving, and about civil society as a polyarchy of group-dominated subsystems that have been with us since soon after the end of World War II (Wengert, 1955).

Employing all of these assumptions, what does *Environmental Politics and Policy: Theories and Evidence* (Lester, 1989a) have to say about the state of environmental politics 20 years after the original Earth Day? The answer is essentially the same as the one given by Ingram and Mann (1983) when they made their own, preliminary survey, almost a decade previously.

The system works but not very well. Environmental problems remain serious and are in important respects underattended by governments. But there is hope for improvement. We must all keep working, most especially to improve our understanding of the political system itself, but also to see that the system gets better quality environmental information to process in its efforts at problem solving.

The other distinguishing general feature of this overall assessment of where we are with contemporary environmental policy, and in our efforts to understand what role policy can play in problem solving, is that it stands on an almost exclusively American base. There is only one chapter in *Environmental Politics and Policy: Theories and Evidence* that glances briefly at environmental politics outside the United States (Stevis et al., 1989).

Since this understates the relevance of a recent explosion of new comparative and international literature on environmental policy, (see, e.g., Caldwell, 1990; Carroll, 1988; Dahlberg, 1985; Hurrell and Kingsbury, 1992; Kakonen, 1992; Kay and Jacobson, 1983; Mathews, 1991; McCormick, 1989; Pearson, 1987; Porter and Brown, 1992; Soroos, 1986; Vogel, 1986; Young, 1989), this issue is addressed first in the remainder of this chapter. Some brief critical comments on the challenge at home end the essay.

V. THE CHALLENGE FROM ABROAD

It has always made sense to think of the United States as the rule rather than the exception. Founding a general understanding of U.S. environmental politics on universal assumptions seems to have merit, for example, because modern environmentalism as an indelible, central feature of post-war political life first took root in the United States (Hays, 1987). Comparativists see differences between the United States and other countries in the way political systems recognize and deal with environmental issues. But the organization of the analysis of these differences usually follows American norms and reflects American preoccupations (Dierkes et al., 1987; Enloe, 1975; Kelley et al., 1977; Lundquist, 1980; Vogel, 1992).

The purpose of learning about successful environmental policy ideas and practice in the United States, at least in part, and certainly by implication if not explicitly, has always been understood to involve laying a base or foundation from which to project successful ideas to the rest of the world. This takes for granted the interest of the rest of the world in learning from American experience, and assumes too that no great obstacles stand in the way of those who want to follow the American way.

Hence, there has never been any serious attention to or discussion of American exceptionalism in the literature on environmental politics and policy that has developed in the United States (but see Coates, 1989; Morris, 1988, 1989; Wrobel, 1993). Phenomena of environmental politics that exist in the United States but are out of the mainstream attract little scholarly interest in the United States, even though, in a larger, global context, understanding environmental politics requires attention both to the phenomena themselves and to the fact that they are underrepresented in U.S. political experience (Eckersley, 1992; Hay and Haward, 1988; Rudig, 1990).

This state of affairs needs some adjustment. Everyone probably concedes that the adaptation of successful U.S. policy ideas, like environmental impact assessment, to local political conditions abroad requires some modification of the ideas themselves. But because American analysts have tied the improvement of environmental public policy and of environmental conditions so directly to structural variables that are not replicated abroad, no one seems ready to acknowledge that the projection of American lessons about what works and what does not, and why, needs major reconsideration. Impact assessment is an excellent case in point (Taylor, 1984).

Given the political conditions that prevail in many parts of the Third World and the political dynamics of international regimes (Symposium, 1992), the root, instrumental American assumption and belief—that environmental public policy best solves problems when it is the product of structural pluralism—looks very tenuous. Indeed, in many cases, and despite what appears to be a wild proliferation of structural overlap and redundancy in the international political communities that deal with environmental issues, the tight coupling between policy and problem solving that analysts are schooled to look for, on the basis of American experience, is neither detectable now nor, apparently, anticipated in the future (Haas et al., 1992; Levy et al., 1992).

At the most, and when it is at its best, the international politics of the environment yields not so much solutions to problems but rather a very wide variety of ongoing processes for the diagnosis, discussion, negotiation, and reconsideration of environmental issues (Haas, 1990; Young, 1989; and, e.g., Adler and Crawford, 1991; Rosenau and Czempiel, 1992). Within these processes, political actors agree to keep talking about what they think their problems are and how together they might tackle them. And the maintenance of these continuing relationships is at least as important for the expression it gives to diverse environmental values as for the opportunity it affords to converge on problem solutions. Modern means of global communication are already facilitating, and will likely intensify, these relationships (Frederick, 1993).

This is plainly visible, for example, in assessments of the most recent, large-scale manifestation of international environmental politics, the Rio Summit, more formally known as the United Nations Conference on Environment and Development (UNCED), held in June 1992. The assessments of UNCED differ. None of them can be read seriously to suggest, however, either that the politics leading up to Rio, or the politics occurring at Rio, or the politics that will now ensue are going to lead any time soon to solving any of the great many problems aired and debated both at the Earth Summit and at the parallel summit of nongovernmental organizations (Grubb et al., 1993; Haas et al., 1992).

What one can say about the Rio Summit is that, at the very least, it throws into high relief the noninstrumental or expressive contributions politics can be expected to make on an ongoing basis to defining environmental problems, to apportioning blame for their existence, and to incorporating into solutions a direct and explicit consideration of justice, as well as efficiency (Choucri, 1993a, 1993b; Stone, 1993). It is then also very tempting to say that the actors in international environmental politics would have better things to do with their time and energy than engage each other in chronically indeterminate processes and relationships if the structural and institutional pluralism of the context in which they conduct their affairs was better developed, more orderly, and in short more American.

But taking this tack simply brings analysts back to asserting the centrality of structural variables and structured relationships as preconditions for environmental policy success (Kitschelt, 1986). And it thus avoids any careful look at the other major possibility; i.e., environmental problems do not have solutions, certainly none that the world's political system, if there were such a thing, could agree on and implement. Political exchanges and interactions in the international system rather quickly take initial problem definitions and reframe and redefine them. They rather obviously create, display, and sustain multiple ideas about what nature means, and about what it means to save nature. And these ideas coexist. They exhibit little convergence even over very long periods of time. One does not vanquish the others in order that right answers to problems may be found and so that universally agreed and acceptable solutions may succeed.

So even if the simple project of exporting U.S. environmental policy ideas abroad were to be amended by requiring as a (probably infeasible) precondition that the rest of the world replicate the exceptionally convergent structural pluralism that, by most accounts, sustains whatever environmental policy success is apparent in the United States the salvation of the world's environment would still look very uncertain.

VI. THE CHALLENGE AT HOME

The challenge from abroad, then, quickly points us back to home. We think we have come a long way, as analysts, as policy makers, and as citizens by working under the pretense that U.S. environmental problems have solutions. It is an article of mainstream faith, in fact, that it makes sense to treat the political system and its efforts to address environmental issues as if it were driven by a relative handful of central actors who puzzle over problems and who want the correct answers for them. The currents of mainstream inquiry flow fast toward calculating the instrumental probabilities of success for these actors. And so there is little room either for the cultural roots of expressive politics or for the cultural consequences of public policy whether these occur at the center or out on the fringe.

This is surprising. A good number of the environmental policy initiatives that eventually find their way into mainstream public policy and, therefore, into mainstream accounts of that policy have their origins on the fringes of political life and do not start out looking like the right answer. They are often grown and nurtured in grassroots groups and organizations or perhaps in state associations that exist largely on altruism, the efforts of volunteers, and gifts from charitable foundations (Freudenberg and Steinsapir, 1991; Lester, 1993; Palmer, 1993).

This neglect of the fringes supposedly concentrates attention on policies and politics that are realistic. But as economists, who are far from being the fringiest of those on the fringes of environmental politics, can testify, this concern for political realism leaves out an awful lot. After more than 20 years, economic policies for the environment are still having trouble getting the realistic consideration they deserve (Anderson et al., 1977; Helm, 1991; Kelman, 1981; Symposium, 1990). Economists make, in fact, an excellent case in point, as do a variety of public interest law groups. Their contributions to transforming policy for water, wildlife, and pesticides, for example (Hundley, 1992; MacIntyre, 1987; Tober, 1989; Tobin, 1990), have been enormous.

Indeed, by focusing so intently on what the right answers are to policy problems and on the variables at the center of the nation's political life that determine their success, mainstream analysts have almost certainly overdetermined the ability of politics and policy to deliver a progressive agenda (Rose-Ackerman, 1992). And they have surely overestimated the ability of environmental science and scientists, especially ecologists, to supply protective cover for this operation (Bramwell, 1989).

Certainly, if the narrowly instrumental question of how to find solutions to the problems of the U.S. environment as they are presented to policy makers has a right answer, or a set of right answers, we would like to know what it is. And we would like to know how the political system can contribute to bringing about this solution. The trick, it seems, is to effect a neat conjunction between the best possible understanding of the environment and the best possible understanding of the political system so that those who are working within the system can be smarter and "get it right" (Ingram and Schneider, 1991).

But for this trick first to seem intellectually attractive and then for it to play itself out in politics, there has to be a fixed, or at least theoretically fixable, point of reference, a baseline of truth about the real world that separates right answers from wrong ones or, at least, the clearly better from the clearly worse. This is why the environmental policy process is almost invariably portrayed as a process that involves using public programs to act with Nature or, in a stronger form, to act by or only in accordance with the law of Nature (Hinchman and Hinchman, 1989; but see also Cheney, 1989).

Good environmental policy, under this rubric, means doing right by Nature. "Saving the Earth" means going back to Nature, or, if it is too late for that, it means "listening to the Earth," at least, as a prelude to good-faith efforts at environmental restoration (Berger, 1985; Chiras, 1992; Horwitz, 1991; Koppes, 1988; Matless, 1990; McEvoy, 1986; Merchant, 1987; Miller, 1992: Chapters 1, 25, 26).

The seemingly fixed idea of Nature at work here, however, is just one variety of nature (Worster, 1977). It is a Nature that is imagined to exist outside of and to be antecedent to the cultural forms we know as politics and policy. Politics can affect this Nature, and it can and should respect it. But according to mainstream orthodoxy, politics cannot make Nature. Nature, therefore, can be acted on but it cannot be an actor (but see Cronon, 1987; McEvoy, 1988).

In this quintessentially historicist view of environmental policy, the only thing that really matters about the relationship culture (politics and policy) establishes with Nature (the environment) is its instrumentalism—its ability to improve the end-state effectiveness of the relationships society seeks to establish with Nature. Thus, successful policy improves the quality of the environments people encounter every day, whether in a wilderness landscape or in the heart of a city, by making them more natural. It improves human health by removing risks that occur when Nature is polluted. It makes resource management and allocation more sound by respecting the knowledge we have of how Nature works. In short, success inheres in bringing culture and Nature into closer and more harmonious alignment (Lowenthal, 1990).

If, on the other hand, much and perhaps most of what happens in environmental politics has to do with the social creation and recreation of Nature (Evernden, 1992), a great deal of what is now ignored or treated as inexplicable by mainstream accounts of environmental policy change begins to seem vital and relevant. If Nature can be a dependent variable in the great funnel of political causation, there can clearly be shifting cultural understandings, or ideologies, of Nature (Burgess, 1990; Olwig, 1984). There can be a dynamic and politically influential environmental pluralism (Albanese, 1990). And neither the existence nor the political influence of this pluralism can be dismissed as the manifestation of error (Schiff, 1962).

Changing ideas about Nature need to be treated, then, as more than epiphenomena chiefly of interest to intellectual historians (Huth, 1990; Nash, 1982; Oelschlaeger, 1991; Runte, 1987, 1991; Strong, 1988). The cultural redefinition and reevaluation of Nature is a form of political problem solving, and it is one that can have profound consequences for the meaning we attach to the world in which we find ourselves (Cronon, 1991; Kelley, 1989; Walton, 1992). Indeed, the fleeting moments (Barth, 1990) in which Nature and culture redefine each other through politics shape the outlines of environmental policy evolution.

In this respect, the emergence of the modern environmental movement has to rank as one of the most important fleeting moments in modern political history. The mainstream account of environmental politics and policy still proceeds, however, almost 25 years after Earth Day without the benefit of a plausible and generally accepted explanation for this development. This is no place to remedy that deficiency. But let me close with a few observations I hope will be both provocative and helpful.

Some of the roots of what is now often referred to, without any real precision, as the modern environmental movement go back to the 19th century. They go back, for example, to a science-based conservation ideology that was seized on with great vigor and given a number of important, concrete, institutional expressions in the United States by progressive politicians (Hays, 1959; Keller, 1990; Pisani, 1984). They go back too to the intense, emotion-laden religiosity about Nature preservation that was fueled most notably by John Muir but also by a variety of other Nature lovers (Fox, 1981; Stegner, 1990).

After World War II, various interpretations of the findings of a newly burgeoning biological science fed a perception that the economic and social structures supporting life in the advanced industrial states were corrupt (Fleming, 1972; Rubin, 1989). These structures tolerated pollution, which adversely affected human health and degraded environmental resources. Despite steadily rising affluence, the perception took hold that the quality of life might actually be declining.

More generally, the economic and social structures that supported postwar expansion might very well turn out to be unsustainable according to the laws of Nature. The costs of failing to transform or to replace them accrued, therefore, not just in a diminished quality of life for particular individuals, groups, and nations but also in a loss of the life-support systems for civilization as a whole (Caldwell, 1970, 1990). The concerns could, thus, be pushed beyond very practical and material issues having to do with human health and happiness into the realms of morality and ethics (Des Jardins, 1993).

It has never been clear exactly how or when or by what human agency this more modern, science-based but also intensely moralistic account of the world's environmental predicament was grafted onto earlier 19th century views, and was then forged into the contemporary environmental movement in the United States. Given that the modern depiction of a nation and a world in environmental crisis moved quickly from being the preoccupation of an elite to capturing the imagination of the mass media and the general public, perhaps the obvious and remarkably sustained popularity of modern environmentalism among the mass public has made it seem redundant to ask these questions.

Among other things, however, the emergence of environmentalism as a political force to be reckoned with in the United States was probably the result of the enterprising emulation by a relatively small number of activists of the strategies and tactics of the civil rights and anti–Vietnam War movements (Epstein, 1991; McCann, 1986). The clever deployment and exploitation of modern methods of political communication and mobilization played a role too by helping to capture the attention of policy makers and to evoke responses from them (McFarland, 1976).

At which point, as far as the mainstream account goes, small but important footholds in the institutional interstices of the U.S. political system were secured. And as a consequence of its dogged and diligent exploitation of these, the environmental movement has now settled down to a rather comfortable middle-age of interest group politics as usual (Ingram and Mann, 1989).

This is a politics in which the peak associations dominate and in which all eyes are on the prize of influencing public policy. In the beginning, concerns understandably focus on policy formulation. But with greater institutionalization and maturity, this gives way to concerns about implementation, which is the stage of evolution Ingram and Mann (1983) describe for the environmental movement in their encyclopedic survey 10 years ago.

At all of the stages that occur once the influence of the movement as a form of mass mobilization politics and direct political action has crested, however, influence depends on effective leadership, sustained membership, the deployment of appropriate strategies, and the building of political coalitions. There is no going back to the old ways. These older methods are, by definition, unnecessary and run too great a risk of public and elite alienation. They threaten instability, which is a condition in which interest group pluralism loses its effectiveness.

This account is shot through with difficulties, however. Leaving aside the lack of an explanation of where the modern U.S. environmental movement came from, and whether pre-existing and established interest groups had a role in its genesis, the most difficult idea is the one that says that the movement phase of contemporary environmentalism has passed to be replaced with a more conventional interest group politics.

On the face of it, this account is contradicted by several instances since the early 1970s when environmental groups in the United States have shown an ability to coalesce into a movement that is something greater than the sum of their parts and then to dissolve or disassemble into their constituent elements. It is as if, in Costain's (1992) felicitous phrase, we should be prepared more often to think of social movements as interest groups and perhaps vice versa. Moreover, instrumental concerns, the obsession with influencing public policy, although present, do not appear to have been the predominant or exclusive concerns in these florescences of movement politics.

On the contrary, ideas and emotions, together with some very vigorous outbursts of moral outrage, appear not only to have been present but also to have been deliberately and very successfully mobilized. In fact, the evidence is that both environmentalists and their chief political opponents have learned how to tap moral outrage as a political resource and how to use it to produce something that is more powerful than a single group, or even a coalition of groups, but perhaps does not quite metamorphose into a full-fledged social movement (Epstein, 1991; Short, 1989).

The environmental groups that give the clearest and most persistent expression to this outrage and keep it alive are generally labeled radical fringe elements and are marginalized in mainstream accounts. But at some moments in political time, at least, and not once but repeatedly, they appear to play a very important part in the overall unfolding of the political drama that is environmental politics in the United States. And for that reason, if for no other, the recent increase in attention to such groups, and to the radicalism of all environmental groups, is most welcome (Lewis, 1992; List, 1993; Manes, 1990).

There are, in other words, serious grounds for questioning whether the standard, pluralist, interest group model that now stands at the center of the mainstream account of environmental politics and policy in the United States is adequate, in any of its variants, to explain and to understand environmentalism or to explain the relationship environmentalism has to policy change. This is especially true if interest group pluralism is embedded in a larger set of narrowly instrumental assumptions about policy as problem solving. A range of new work on interest groups underscores these doubts about old models (Petracca, 1992).

Environmental policy processes do far more than repair or restore a ravaged Nature according to a single, progressive design; a design that is collectively arrived at only after considerable political struggle but is then widely perceived to be legitimate because it is "in the public interest" and is, therefore, widely subscribed. Environmental policy processes are also vital mechanisms for human interactions that create and assign meaning and significance to a plurality of understandings and interpretations of Nature. They may and often do raise questions less about the workings of Nature and more about its human value that seem to have no answer' and which can even be considered to be unanswerable, but that nevertheless deserve consideration (Stone, 1987). They are processes that may now be starting to grapple with the end of Nature; at least that form of Nature that the environmental movement and students of it have usually had in mind (McKibben, 1989; Strathern, 1992).

These questions about the meaning and value of Nature arise from and tap a pluralism that runs to much deeper structures in U.S. society than those represented at any one point in time by the structural pluralism of the environmental movement's peak associations and its policy networks. And in the light of this social and cultural pluralism, we can bring a critical perspective to the study of environmental politics and policy that is now notable for its absence in the mainstream account, where the treatment of politics as if it were problem solving cannot find a place either for the cultural roots of political life or for its cultural contributions.

At home, as well as abroad, then, and even as mainstream thinking seems to be coming into its own with a code of understanding that may have broad appeal, there are crosscurrents stirring up new and disturbing thoughts about environmental politics and policy. It seems these new thoughts are fully able to carry the vigorous analysis of this most fascinating subject well into the 21st century and with some surprising twists and turns along the way.

REFERENCES

Adams, J., et al. (1985). *An Environmental Agenda for the Future.* Island Press, Washington, DC.

Adler, E., and Crawford, B. (1991). *Progress in International Relations.* Columbia University Press, New York.

Anderson, F., et al. (1977). *Environmental Improvement Through Economic Incentives.* Johns Hopkins University Press, Baltimore.

Barth, G. (1990). *Fleeting Moments: Nature and Culture in American History.* Oxford University Press, Oxford, England.

Berger, J. (1985). *Restoring the Earth.* Alfred Knopf, New York.

Bosso, C. (1987). *Pesticides and Politics: The Life Cycle of a Public Issue.* University of Pittsburgh Press, Pittsburgh, PA.

—— (1991). Adaptation and change in the environmental movement. In *Interest Group Politics*. A. Cigler and B. Loomis, Eds. CQ Press, Washington, DC, pp. 151–176.

Bramwell, A. (1989). *Ecology in the 20th Century: A History*. Yale University Press, New Haven, CT.

Bryner, G. (1993). *Blue Skies, Green Politics: The Clean Air Act of 1990*. CQ Press, Washington, DC.

Burgess, J. (1990). The production and consumption of environmental meanings in the mass media: A research agenda for the 1990s. *Transactions, Institute of British Geographers* (New Series), 15: 139–161.

Burtraw, D., and Portney, P. (1992). Environmental policy in the United States. In *Economic Policy Towards the Environment*. D. Helm, Ed. Blackwell, Oxford, England.

Cahn, R., and Cahn, P. (1990). Did Earth Day change the world? *Environment* 32: 16–20, 36–43.

Caldwell, L. (1970). *Environment: A Challenge to Modern Society*. Natural History Press, New York.

—— (1990a). *Between Two Worlds: Science, The Environmental Movement, and Policy Choice*. Cambridge University Press, Cambridge, England.

—— (1990b). *International Environmental Policy: Emergence and Dimensions*, 2nd ed. Duke University Press, Durham, NC.

Calvert, J. (1989). Party politics and environmental policy. In *Environmental Politics and Policy: Theories and Evidence*. J. Lester, Ed. Duke University Press, Durham, NC, pp. 158–178.

Carroll, J. (Ed.). (1988). *International Environmental Diplomacy: The Management and Resolution of Transfrontier Environmental Problems*. Cambridge University Press, Cambridge, England.

Cheney, J. (1989). The neo-stoicism of radical environmentalism. *Environmental Ethics* 11: 293–325.

Chiras, D. (1992). *Lessons from Nature: Learning to Live Sustainably on the Earth*. Island Press, Washington, DC.

Choucri, N. (1993a). Global Accords at UNCED: What Next? *Environment MIT, 7*: 11–15.

—— (Ed.) (1993b) *Global Accords: Environmental Challenges and International Responses*. MIT Press, Cambridge, MA. In publication.

Coates, P. (1989). "Support your right to arm bears (and pecadillos)": The higher ground and further shores of American environmentalism. *Journal of American Studies* 23: 439–446.

Cohen, E. (1988). *Ideology, Interest Group Formation, and the New Left: The Case of the Clamshell Alliance*. Garland, New York.

Cohen, R. (1992). *Washington at Work: Back Rooms and Clean Air*. Macmillan, New York.

Costain, A. (1992). Social movements as interest groups: The case of the women's movement. In *The Politics of Interests: Interest Groups Transformed*. M. Petracca, ed. Westview Press, Boulder, CO, pp. 285–307.

Cronon, W. (1991). *Nature's Metropolis: Chicago and the Great West*. W. W. Norton, New York.

Cronon, W. (1987). Revisiting the vanishing frontier: The legacy of Frederick Jackson Turner. *Western Historical Quarterly* 18: 157–176.

Dahlberg, K., et al. (1985). *Environment and the Global Arena: Actors, Values, Policies, and Futures*. Duke University Press, Durham, NC.

Des Jardins, J. (1993). *Environmental Ethics*. Wadsworth, Belmont, CA.

Dierkes, M., Weiler, H., and Antal, A. (1987). *Comparative Policy Research: Learning from Experience*. Gower, Aldershot, England.

Doig, J., and Hargrove, E. (Eds.) (1987). *Leadership and Innovation: A Biographical Perspective on Entrepreneurs in Government*. Johns Hopkins University Press, Baltimore, MD.

Dryzek, J., and Lester, J. (1989). Alternative views of the environmental problematic. In *Environmental Politics and Policy: Theories and Evidence*. J. Lester, Ed. Duke University Press, Durham, NC, pp. 314–330.

Dunlap, R. (1989). Public Opinion and Environmental Policy. In *Environmental Politics and Policy: Theories and Evidence*. J. Lester, ed. Duke University Press, Durham, NC, pp. 87–134.

Dwyer, J. (1990). The pathology of symbolic legislation. *Ecology Law Quarterly* 17: 233–316.

Eckersley, R. (1992). *Environmentalism and Political Theory*. State University of New York Press, Albany, NY.

Enloe, C. (1972). *The Politics of Pollution in Comparative Perspective*. David McKay, New York.

Epstein, B. (1991). *Political Protest and Cultural Revolution: Nonviolent Direct Action in the 1970s and 1980s.* University of California Press, Berkeley, CA.

Evernden, N. (1992). *The Social Creation of Nature.* Johns Hopkins University Press, Baltimore, MD.

Eyerman, R., and Jamison, A. (1991). *Social Movements: A Cognitive Approach.* Pennsylvania State University Press, University Park, PA.

Fairfax, S., and Ingram, H. (1990). No theory, no apology: A brief comment on the state of the art in natural resources policy and the articles herein. *Natural Resources Journal* 30: 259–262.

Fiorina, M. (1992). *Divided Government.* Macmillan, New York.

FitzSimmons, M. (1989). The matter of nature. *Antipode* 21: 121–132.

Fleming, D. (1972). Roots of the new conservation movement. *Perspectives in American History* 6: 7–91.

Fox, S. (1981). *John Muir and His Legacy: The American Conservation Movement.* Little, Brown, Boston.

Francis, J. (1990). Natural resources, contending theoretical perspectives, and the problem of prescription: An essay. *Natural Resources Journal* 30: 263–282.

Frederick, H. (1993). *Global Communication and International Relations.* Wadsworth, Belmont, CA.

Freudenberg, N., and Steinsapir, C. (1991). Not in our backyards: The grassroots environmental movement. *Society and Natural Resources* 4: 235–245.

Gore, A. (1993). *Earth in the Balance: Ecology and the Human Spirit.* Plume edition, Penguin Books, New York.

Greve, M., and Smith, F. (Eds.). (1992). *Environmental Politics: Public Costs and Private Rewards.* Praeger, New York.

Grubb, M., et al. (1993). *The Earth Summit Agreements: A Guide and Assessment.* Earthscan Publications Ltd. (for the Royal Institute of International Affairs), London.

Gusfield, J. (1981). *The Culture of Public Problems.* University of Chicago Press, Chicago.

Haas, P. (1990). *Saving the Mediterranean: The Politics of International Environmental Cooperation.* Columbia University Press, New York.

Haas, P., Levy, M, and Parson, E. (1992). Appraising the Earth Summit: How should we judge UNCED's success? *Environment* 34: 6–11, 26–33.

Hays, S. (1959). *Conservation and the Gospel of Efficiency: The Progressive Conservation Movement.* Harvard University Press, Cambridge, MA.

—— (1987). *Beauty, Health, and Permanence: Environmental Politics in the United States, 1955–1985.* Cambridge University Press, Cambridge, England.

Helm, D. (1991). *Economic Policy Towards the Environment.* Blackwell, Oxford, England.

Hinchman, L., and Hinchman, S. (1989). "Deep ecology" and the revival of natural right. *Western Political Quarterly* 42: 201–228.

Hofferbert, R. (1974). *The Study of Public Policy.* Bobbs-Merrill, Indianapolis, IN.

Horwitz, H. (1991). *By the Law of Nature: Form and Value in Nineteenth Century America.* Oxford University Press, Oxford, England.

Hundley, N. (1992). *The Great Thirst: Californians and Water, 1770s–1990s.* University of California Press, Berkeley, CA.

Hurrell, A., and Kingsbury, B. (Eds.) (1992). *The International Politics of the Environment.* Clarendon Press, Oxford, England.

Huth, H. (1990). *Nature and the American Mind: Three Centuries of Changing Attitudes.* New edition. University of Nebraska Press, Lincoln, NE.

Inglehart, R. (1977). *The Silent Revolution: Changing Values and Political Styles Among Western Publics.* Princeton University Press, Princeton, NJ.

—— (1990). *Culture Shift in Advanced Industrial Society.* Princeton University Press, Princeton, NJ.

Ingram, H. (1990). *Water Politics: Continuity and Change.* University of New Mexico Press, Albuquerque, NM.

Ingram, H., and Mann, D. (1983). Environmental protection policy. In *Encyclopedia of Policy Studies.* S. Nagel, ed. Marcel Dekker, New York, pp. 687–725.

—— (1989). Interest groups and environmental policy. In *Environmental Politics and Policy*: *Theories and Evidence*. J. Lester, Ed. Duke University Press, Durham, NC, pp. 135–157.

Ingram, H., and Schneider, A. (1991). Improving implementation through framing smarter statutes. *Journal of Public Policy* 10: 67–88.

Ingram, H., and Ullery, S. (1980). Policy innovation and institutional fragmentation. *Policy Studies Journal*, 8: 664–682.

Jones, C. (1970). *An Introduction to the Study of Public Policy*. Wadsworth, Belmont, CA.

—— (1975). *Clean Air*: *The Policies and Politics of Pollution Control*. University of Pittsburgh Press, Pittsburgh, PA.

—— (1972). From gold to garbage: A bibliographic essay on politics and the environment. *American Political Science Review* 66: 588–595.

Kakonen, J. (Ed.). (1992). *Perspectives on Environmental Conflict and International Relations*. Pinter, London.

Kay, D., and Jacobson, H. (Eds.). (1983). *Environmental Protection*: *The International Dimension*. Allanheld, Osmun, Totawa, NJ.

Keller, M. (1990). *Regulating a New Economy*: *Public Policy and Economic Change in America, 1900–1933*. Harvard University Press, Cambridge, MA.

Kelley, D., Stunkel, K., and Wescott, R. (1976). *The Economic Superpowers and the Environment*: *The United States, the Soviet Union, and Japan*. W. H. Freeman, San Francisco.

Kelman, S. (1981). *What Price Incentives? Economists and the Environment*. Auburn House, Auburn, MA.

Killingsworth, M., and Palmer, J. (1992). *Ecospeak*: *Rhetoric and Environmental Politics in America*. Southern Illinois University Press, Carbondale, IL.

Kingdon, J. (1984). *Agendas, Alternatives, and Public Policies*. Little, Brown, Boston.

Kitschelt, H. (1986). Political opportunity structures and political protest: Anti-nuclear movements in four democracies. *British Journal of Political Science* 16: 57–85.

Koppes, C. (1988). Efficiency, equity, esthetics: Shifting themes in American conservation. In *The Ends of the Earth*: *Perspectives on Modern Environmental History*. D. Worster, Ed. Cambridge University Press, Cambridge, England.

Kraft, M. (1984). A new environmental policy agenda: The 1980 presidential campaign and its aftermath. In *Environmental Policy in the 1980s*: *Reagan's New Agenda*. N. Vig and M. Kraft, Eds. CQ Press, Washington DC, pp. 29–50.

—— (1989). Congress and environmental policy. In *Environmental Politics and Policy*: *Theories, and Evidence*. J. Lester, Ed. Duke University Press, Durham, NC, pp. 179–211.

—— (1993). Environmental gridlock: Searching for consensus in Congress. In *Environmental Policy in the 1990s*, 2nd ed. CQ Press, Washington, DC. In publication.

LaMay, C., and Dennis, E. (1991). *Media and the Environment*. Island Press, Washington, DC.

Lester, J. (Ed.). (1989a). *Environmental Politics and Policy*: *Theories and Evidence*. Duke University Press, Durham, NC.

—— (1989b). Introduction. In *Environmental Politics and Policy*: *Theories and Evidence*. J. Lester, Ed. Duke University Press, Durham, NC, pp. 1–9.

—— (1993). A new federalism? Environmental policy in the states. In *Environmental Policy in the 1990s*, 2nd ed. N. Vig and M. Kraft, Eds. CQ Press, Washington, DC. In publication.

Levy, M., Haas, P., and Keohane, R. (1992). Institutions for the earth: Promoting international environmental protection. *Environment* 34: 12–17, 29–36.

Lewis, M. (1992). *Green Delusions*: *An Environmentalist Critique of Radical Environmentalism*. Duke University Press, Durham, NC.

List, P. (1993). *Radical Environmentalism*: *Philosophy and Tactics*. Wadsworth, Belmont, CA.

Lowe, P., and Morrison, D. (1984). Bad news or good news: Environmental politics and the mass media. *Sociological Review* 32: 75–90.

Lowe, P., and Rudig, W. (1986). Review article: Political ecology and the social sciences—The State of the Art. *British Journal of Political Science* 16: 513–550.

Lowenthal, D. (1990). Awareness of human impacts: Changing attitudes and emphases. In *The Earth as Transformed by Human Action*. B. Turner, Ed. Cambridge University Press, Cambridge, England, pp. 121–135.

Lowi, T. (1986). The welfare state, the new regulation, and the rule of law. In *Distributional Conflicts in Environmental-Resource Policy* A. Schnaiber, N. Watts, and K. Zimmerman, Eds. Gower, Aldershot, England, pp. 109–149.

MacIntyre, A. (1987). Why pesticides received extensive use in America: A political economy of agricultural pest management to 1970. *Natural Resources Journal* 27: 533–578.

Manes, C. (1990). *Green Rage: Radical Environmentalism and the Unmaking of Civilization*. Little, Brown, Boston.

Mann, D. (1986). Democratic politics and environmental policy. In *Controversies in Environmental Policy*. S. Kamieniecki, R. O'Brien, and M. Clarke, Eds. State University of New York Press, Albany, NY, pp. 3–34.

—— (1991). Environmental learning in a decentralized political world. *Journal of International Affairs* 44: 301–337.

Mathews, J. (Ed.). (1991). *Preserving the Global Environment: The Challenge of Shared Leadership*. W. W. Norton, New York.

Matless, D. (1990). Definitions of England, 1928–89: Preservation, modernism, and the nature of the nation. *Built Environment* 16: 179–191.

Mazmanian, D., and Morrell, D. (1992). *Beyond Superfailure: America's Toxics Policy for the 1990s*. Westview Press, Boulder, CO.

McCann, M. (1986). *Taking Reform Seriously: Perspectives on Public Interest Liberalism*. Cornell University Press, Ithaca, NY.

McCool, D. (1987). *Command of the Waters: Iron Triangles, Federal Water Development, and Indian Water*. University of California Press, Berkeley, CA.

McCormick, J. (1989). *Reclaiming Paradise: The Global Environmental Movement*. Indiana University Press, Bloomington, IN.

McEvoy, A. (1986). *The Fisherman's Problem: Ecology and Law in the History of California's Fisheries, 1850–1980*. Cambridge University Press, Cambridge, England.

—— (1987). Toward an interactive theory of nature and culture: Ecology, production, and cognition in the California fishing industry. *Environmental Review* 11: 289–305.

McFarland, A. (1976). *Public Interest Lobbies*. The American Enterprise Institute, Washington, DC.

McKee, D. (Ed.). (1991). *Energy, the Environment, and Public Policy: Issues for the 1990s*. Praeger, New York.

McKibben, B. (1989). *The End of Nature*. Random House, New York.

Merchant, C. (1987). The theoretical structure of ecological revolutions. *Environmental Review* 11: 265–274.

Milbrath, L. (1984). *Environmentalists: Vanguard for a New Society*. State University of New York Press, Albany, NY.

Miller, G. (1992). *Living in the Environment*, 7th ed. Wadsworth, Belmont, CA.

Minow, M., and Spelman, E. (1990). In context. *Southern California Law Review* 63: 1597–1652.

Mitchell, R. (1990). Public opinion and the green lobby: Poised for the 1990s? In *Environmental Policy in the 1990s*. N. Vig and M. Kraft, Eds. CQ Press, Washington, DC, pp. 81–99.

Mitchell, R., Mertig, A., and Dunlap, R. (1991). Twenty years of environmental mobilization: Trends amongnational environmental organizations. *Society and Natural Resources* 4: 219–234.

Morris, D. (1988). "Help keep the pecadillo alive": American environmental politics. *Journal of American Studies* 22: 447–455.

—— (1989). "Help keep the pecadillo alive": American environmental politics: A rejoinder. *Journal of American Studies* 23: 446.

Nash, R. (1982). *Wilderness and the American Mind*, 2nd ed. Yale University Press, New Haven, CT.

Norton, B. (1991). *Toward Unity Among Environmentalists*. Oxford University Press, New York.

Oelschlaeger, M. (1991). *The Idea of Wilderness: From Prehistory to the Age of Ecology.* Yale University Press, New Haven, CT.

Ophuls, W., and Boyan, S. (1992). *Ecology and the Politics of Scarcity Revisited.* W. H. Freeman, New York.

Paehlke, R. (1989). *Environmentalism and the Future of Progressive Politics.* Yale University Press, New Haven, CT.

Palmer, T. (Ed.). (1993). *California's Threatened Environment: Restoring the Dream.* Island Press, Washington, DC.

Pearson, C. (Ed.). (1987). *Multinational Corporations, Environment, and the Third World.* Duke University Press, Durham, NC.

Petracca, M. (Ed.). (1992). *The Politics of Interests: Interest Groups Transformed.* Westview Press, Boulder, CO.

Piasecki, B., and Asmus, P. (1990). *In Search of Environmental Excellence: Moving Beyond Blame.* Simon & Schuster, New York.

Pildes, R. (1991). The unintended cultural consequences of public policy: A comment on the symposium. *Michigan Law Review* 89: 936–978.

Pildes, R., and Anderson, E. (1990). Slinging arrows at democracy: Social choice theory, value pluralism, and democratic politics. *Columbia Law Review* 90: 2121–2214.

Pisani, D. (1984). *From Family Farm to Agribusiness: The Irrigation Crusade in California and the West, 1850–1931.* University of California Press, Berkeley, CA.

Porter, G., and Brown, J. (1992). *Global Environmental Politics.* Westview Press, Boulder, CO.

Portney, K. (1992). *Controversial Issues in Environmental Policy: Science vs. Economics vs. Politics.* Sage, Newbury Park, CA.

Putt, A., and Springer, F. (1989). *Policy Research: Concepts, Methods, and Applications.* Prentice-Hall, Englewood Cliffs, NJ.

Rose-Ackerman, S. (1992). *Rethinking the Progressive Agenda: The Reform of the American Regulatory State.* Macmillan, New York.

Rosenau, J, and Czempiel, E-O. (1992). *Governance without Government: Order and Change in World Politics.* Cambridge University Press, Cambridge, England.

Rosenbaum, W. (1989). The bureaucracy and environmental policy. In *Environmental Politics and Policy: Theories and Evidence.* J. Lester, Ed. Duke University Press, Durham, NC, pp. 212–237.

—— W. (1991). *Environmental Politics and Policy,* 2nd ed. CQ Press, Washington, DC.

Rubin, C. (1989). Environmental policy and environmental thought: Ruckleshaus and Commoner. *Environmental Ethics* 11: 27–51.

Rudig, W. (Ed.). (1990). *Green Politics, One.* Edinburgh University Press, Edinburgh.

Runte, A. (1987). *National Parks: The American Experience,* 2nd rev. ed. University of Nebraska Press, Lincoln, NE.

—— (1991). *Public Lands, Public Heritage: The National Forest Idea.* Roberts Rinehart, Niwot, CO.

Rushefsky, M. (1989). Elites and environmental policy. In *Environmental Politics and Policy: Theories and Evidence.* J. Lester, Ed. Duke University Press, Durham, NC, pp. 261–286.

Sagoff, M. (1988). *The Economy of the Earth.* Cambridge University Press, New York.

Salisbury, R., Heinz, J., Nelson, R., and Lauman, E. (1992). Triangles, networks, and hollow cores: The complex geometry of Washington interest representation. In *The Politics of Interests: Interest Groups Transformed.* M. Petracca, Ed. Westview Press, Boulder, CO, pp. 130–149.

Scarce, R. (1990). *Eco- Warriors: Understanding the Radical Environmental Movement.* Noble Press, Chicago.

Scheffer, V. (1991). *The Shaping of Environmentalism in America.* University of Washington Press, Seattle, WA.

Schiff, A. (1962). *Fire and Water: Scientific Heresy in the Forest Service.* Harvard University Press, Cambridge, MA.

Short, C. (1989). *Ronald Reagan and the Public Lands: America's Conservation Debate, 1979–1984.* Texas A&M University Press, College Station, TX.

Smith, Z. (1992). *The Environmental Policy Paradox.* Prentice-Hall, Englewood Cliffs, NJ.

Soroos, M. (1986). *Beyond Sovereignty: The Challenge of Global Policy.* University of South Carolina Press, Columbia, SC.

Stegner, W. (1990). It all began with conservation. *Smithsonian* 21: 35–43.

Stevis, D., Assetto, V., and Mumme, S. (1989). International Environmental Politics: A Theoretical Review of the Literature. In *Environmental Politics and Policy: Theories and Evidence.* J. Lester, ed. Duke University Press, Durham, NC, pp. 289–313.

Stone, C. (1987). *Earth and Other Ethics: The Case for Moral Pluralism.* Harper & Row, New York.

—— (1993). *The Gnat is Older than Man: Global Environment and Human Agenda.* Princeton University Press, Princeton, NJ.

Strathern, M. (1992). *After Nature: English Kinship in the Late Twentieth Century.* Cambridge University Press, Cambridge, England.

Strong, D. (1988). *Dreamers and Defenders: American Conservationists.* University of Nebraska Press, Lincoln, NE.

Symposium (1990). Since Earth Day 1970. *Resources* 99: 1–17.

—— (1991a). Toward better theories of the policy process. *P.S.: Political Science and Politics* 24: 144–173.

—— (1991b). The politics of the global environment. *Journal of International Affairs* 44: 287–493.

—— (1992). Knowledge, power, and international policy coordination. *International Organization* 46: 1–390.

Taylor, S. (1984). *Making Bureaucracies Think: The Environmental Impact Statement Strategy of Administrative Reform.* Stanford University Press, Stanford, CA.

Tietenberg, T. (1992). *Innovation in Environmental Policy: Economic and Legal Aspects of Recent Developments in Environmental Enforcement and Liability.* Edward Elgar, Aldershot, England.

Tober, J. (1989). *Wildlife and the Public Interest: Nonprofit Organizations and Federal Wildlife Policy.* Praeger, New York.

Tobin, R. (1990). *The Expendable Future: U.S. Politics and the Protection of Biological Diversity.* Duke University Press, Durham, NC.

Torgerson, D. (1990). Limits of the administrative mind: The problem of defining environmental problems. In *Managing Leviathan: Environmental Politics and the Administrative State* R. Paehlke and D. Torgerson, Eds. Bellhaven, London. pp. 115–161.

Vig, N. (1990). Presidential leadership: From the Reagan to the Bush administration. In *Environmental Policy in the 1990s: Toward a New Agenda.* N. Vig and M. Kraft, Eds. CQ Press, Washington, DC, pp. 33–58.

—— (1993). Presidential leadership and the environment: From Reagan and Bush to Clinton. In *Environmental Policy in the 1990s,* 2nd ed. CQ Press, Washington, DC. In publication.

Vig, N., and Kraft, M. (Eds.). (1990). *Environmental Policy in the 1990s: Toward a New Agenda.* CQ Press, Washington, DC.

—— (Eds.). (1993). Environmental Policy in the 1990s, 2nd ed. CQ Press, Washington, DC. In publication.

Vining, J., and Schroeder, H. (1987). *Emotions in environmental decision making: Rational planning versus the passionate public. In Social Science in Natural Resource Management Systems.* M. Miller, R. Gale, and P. Brown, Eds. Westview Press, Boulder, CO, pp. 181–192.

Vogel, D. (1986). *National Styles of Regulation: Environmental Policy in Great Britain and the United States.* Cornell University Press, Ithaca, NY.

—— (1992). The public interest movement and American trade policy. In *Environmental Politics: Public Costs and Private Rewards.* M. Greve and F. Smith, Eds. Praeger, New York, pp. 155–175.

Wengert, N. (1955). *Natural Resources and the Political Struggle.* Random House, New York.

Wenner, L. (1989). The courts and environmental policy. In *Environmental Politics and Policy: Theories and Evidence.* J. Lester, Ed. Duke University Press, Durham, NC, pp. 238–260.

Worster, D. (1977). *Nature's Economy: A History of Ecological Ideas.* Cambridge University Press, Cambridge, England.

Wrobel, D. (1993). *The End of American Exceptionalism*: *Frontier Anxiety from the Old West to the New Deal*. University of Kansas Press, Lawrence, KS.

Yeager, P. (1991). *The Limits of Law*: *The Public Regulation of Private Pollution*. Cambridge University Press, Cambridge, England.

Young, O. (1989). *International Cooperation*: *Building Regimes for Natural Resources and the Environment*. Cornell University Press, Ithaca, NY.

PART I:
PROBLEMS WITH A NATURAL SCIENCE OR ENGINEERING EMPHASIS

30
Technology: Innovation and Consequences

Frederick A. Rossini
George Mason University, Fairfax, Virginia

Alan L. Porter
Georgia Institute of Technology, Atlanta, Georgia

I. TECHNOLOGY

Technology is a reproducible way of doing something that may be embodied in entities such as physical matter, instructions, living organisms, or groups of organisms. This is really an arbitrary description of a pervasive phenomenon. Indeed the accelerating human romance with technology has produced a civilization, committed to the primacy of economics, that places human beings into a symbiotic relationship with technology, a relationship that has become progressively more intimate over time. Symbolically, it is the transition from the peg leg to the pacemaker, from the external and merely auxiliary, to the internal and perceived necessity, to a total technological environment. There is apparently no alternative available to technology in the developed world.

Thus, how to deal with technology becomes a major concern of economic and political institutions, whether they face it explicitly or as part of some other category of concern. It may sound extreme to say that all policy is technology policy, but all policy at least involves a technological component. Why? Because technology is linked intimately to a social system; that is, to people and their formal and informal relationships. No social system is without its embedded technologies. As Mel Kranzberg has put it on so many occasions: "Technology is people." For better or worse, Ellul's (1964) concept of the pervasive dominance of technique (technology) has a true ring in our society. We have made our decision: the direction is set, now the task is to deal with it.

In the broadest sense, technology policy deals with how to implement "desirable" novelty on a broadly sustainable scale and how to deal with its "desirable" and "undesirable" consequences. These are the issues of technological innovation and impact assessment. The first is driving us to leap; the second is holding us to look before we leap and adjust the leap accordingly. This is reminiscent of the classic split between promoters and regulators. Yet in most cases, the promoters have the actual power and the regulators have only influence.

For the purposes of this chapter, the focal unit of analysis is the innovation itself. Policy making depends critically on how the innovation is embedded into economic, political, and social institutions. These are addressed. Decisions affecting technology depend on understanding the nature of innovation, how it actually takes place, and how it interacts with societal institutions to produce impacts.

II. SETTING THE SCENE

This section offers some distinctions and explanations basic to understanding and dealing with innovation and its consequences.

Innovation is sometimes confused with invention (Kelly et al., 1978). Understanding this distinction is fundamental to understanding technology policy issues. Invention is not a societal policy issue, but innovation is. Invention is demonstrating for the first time anywhere that something exists or works. It can be a scientific discovery or the packaging of existing technologies to form a novel system. Innovation is embedding the invention in a stable context in which it is widely or significantly implemented, thereby causing societal impacts. Innovation involves an organized context in which the invention is adapted into a stable form. In invention, this organized context is common but not necessary. Not every invention becomes an innovation. Innovation requires a wide range of skills beyond creating novelty. These include developing the invention into a stable manufacturable product or useful process, adapting the invention to particular contexts, creating societal interest in the innovation, and delivering the innovation to its potential users.

Contemporary industrial societies are committed to economic growth as a major goal. Innovation drives economic growth. There may be other related societal goals such as sustainable growth and environmental protection, but here too innovation plays a major role. For these goals depend on such innovations as energy conservation technology and environmental monitoring and control systems. They also depend on understanding the impacts of major innovations.

A simple, straightforward conceptual approach to focusing on the congeries of an innovation and its consequences is the technology delivery system (TDS) developed by Wenk and Kuehn (1977). This is a conceptual model, expressed by a boxes and arrows map, of an innovation and the societal institutions involved in its development and implementation, both on the small scale of direct development and the larger scale of societal support, regulation, and impact. Figure 1 provides an example of a generic TDS. An actual TDS would be much more specific and focused.

The TDS of each innovation is unique. An innovation may have many TDSs representing different emphases or times. Each is a snapshot of part of a larger process. The underlying dynamics are conceptually straightforward, if often empirically complex. Societal resources, institutions, and values influence the development of a certain innovation in a particular institutional context. This development produces an innovation that is introduced broadly or significantly. This introduction produces consequences that modify the societal context that influenced the development of the innovation in the first place. This process iterates, forming what could be considered a continuous spiral of innovation, since the institutions and innovations involved never return to their earlier states. The split between the issues of how to promote successful innovation and how to deal with its consequences can be reflected in the construction of the TDS for any innovation. The next two sections reflect that split as both practice and the literature deal with these issues separately, which in our judgment is not the most appropriate approach.

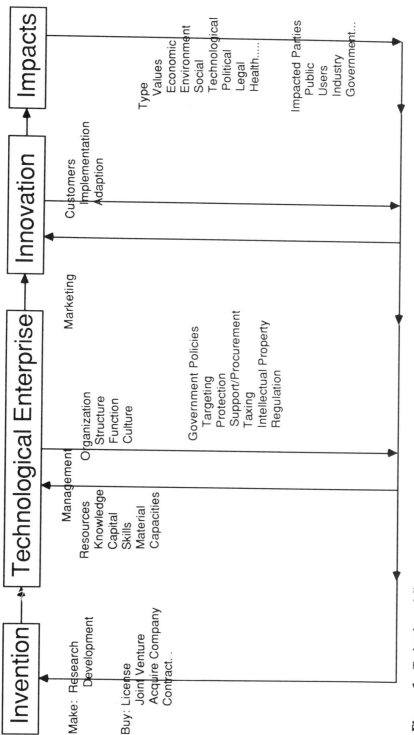

Figure 1 Technology delivery system.

III. TECHNOLOGICAL INNOVATION

A. Models of Innovation

Technological innovation has been viewed as a process with component stages or elements. (Two important sources on innovation are Kelly et al., 1978, and Tornatzky and Fleischer, 1990). Innovation is a life-cycle process; that is, it extends from first concept to obsolescence. Two major types of innovation models have been commonly proposed. The linear model is an attempt to portray the process as a connected series of stages through which an innovation progresses in a linear, unidirectional order. A typical list is:

Basic Research
Applied Research
Development/Engineering
Manufacturing
Market Introduction
Wide Dissemination
Maturity
Obsolescence

The alternative approach is the ecological model. In the ecological model, the stages remain, but they are not mandatory, nor does the innovation proceed in anything like a linear path. Stages may be omitted or truncated. There may be feedback/feedforward loops among the stages or functions of the innovation process. The linear order of the stages is seen as a logical rather than as a functional priority.

The linear model is most popular among those who wish to show the importance of scientific knowledge to technological innovation. This relationship is often indicated to be causal in order to support the policy that society needs to support basic science in order that technological innovations may be developed.

However, the history of innovation does not support the linear model. Technological innovation was common long before modern science came into being. Moreover, many innovations made in modern times, for example, the machinery that drove the industrial revolution, were made by persons not learned in the science of the times. Such machinery was visible to the naked eye, and a skilled mechanic could construct useful machines on a trial and error basis. Only in the case of phenomena related to such areas as chemistry and electricity, where what was happening was not visible and thus required conceptual models, did a scientific background become useful for innovation. Furthermore, there has not been the least pretense of a scientific basis in the innovation of social technologies (outside of economics). Yet social technological innovations, such as representative government and the social security system, have been important in the development of modern society.

Overall, the ecological view of innovation is a more satisfactory way of representing the process. It considers innovation as a process of phases that has a life cycle. At the same time, it allows for the real complexities and convolutions that are part of that cycle. It neither requires nor excludes basic science. Yet if basic science enters the innovation process, it may do so at the beginning, middle, and/or toward the end of the process. Each innovation has its own environment, so that the ecology of innovation is not uniform across all sectors and developments.

The next sections discuss some important issues in the ecology of innovation.

B. Basic Research

Basic research is the term most commonly used in the literature to describe research that is not directed to a specific sort of outcome. Most often it refers to scientific research, but it may also involve fundamental studies in technology. Scientific research is directed at knowing, whereas technological research is focused on ways of doing things that are ultimately useful.

Because of its focus, basic research does not usually lead immediately to technological innovation. Yet science provides the intellectual underpinnings of most contemporary innovations other than in social technologies. The scientific environment is a remote breeding ground for technological innovation. It is the case that the existence of the science of chemistry made it easier for a chemical industry to develop, and that the scientific discovery of the matter-energy equivalence made it possible for the nuclear weapons and power industries to exist. Yet because of its distance from innovation and the uncertainty of its results, basic research is a chancy investment for organizations that must show an annual profit. Since World War II in the United States there has been an ideology of scientific research, enacted into national policy, that posits that investment by the society in basic research is desirable both for its economic development and its security. Similar beliefs exist in many other industrial nations.

One consequence of this ideology is that the persons and organizations that perform basic research are generally different from those that participate in any other phases or functions of innovation. In the United States, much basic research is done in universities—almost 50% in 1991 (National Science Board, 1991)—with some being performed in government, industrial, and nonprofit laboratories. Even where basic research is performed in an industrial laboratory, the personnel engaged in basic research are often physically, organizationally, and functionally removed from those engaged in other phases of the innovation process. Most applied research and development in the United States is performed by industry—over 70% in 1991 (National Science Board, 1991). The personal, institutional, and ideological disconnects between basic research and other phases of innovation in the United States and other countries have had significant implications for innovation. In particular, preeminence and success in basic research do not necessarily transfer into success in technological innovation. Since the results of much basic research are essentially free goods, the ability to access and utilize basic research is more important in innovation than the ability to produce basic research. Thus, the issue of the linkage between basic research and innovation includes the issue of technology transfer.

Traditionally, basic research is performed by persons who identify themselves with intellectual disciplines and are organized along disciplinary lines. The university department is the paradigm case of this arrangement. Yet traditionally organized government and national laboratories, as well as some major industrial basic research laboratories, also have used disciplinary organization. More recently, project funding by the government and a more functional orientation by many corporations have led to a cross-disciplinary focus. In the university, this has been manifested by the rise of cross-disciplinary centers and institutes. Although these organizations do not have the power of the traditional departments over the career fate of faculty members, they often have substantial monetary and equipment resources, thereby providing a strong incentive for departments to engage in constructive dialogue to promote win-win situations.

In the United States, interinstitutional technology transfer from universities, government laboratories, and national laboratories to industry has received attention. The National

Aeronautics and Space Administration (NASA) and the national laboratories have technology transfer offices, as do a number of research universities. States, such as Virginia, have established nonprofit corporations to transfer state university research to the private sector. Many research universities have established industry-university cooperative research centers, with or without government support. Industrial firms have addressed the issue of intrainstitutional transfer of the results of basic research. A principal mechanism for technology transfer has always been "on the hoof," the movement of knowledgeable individuals from one organization to another. Industry's hiring of university graduates is the prototype of this mechanism.

The post–World War II ideology that fostered large-scale support for basic research because of its long-term benefits for society is being reevaluated in the context of the end of the cold war, the lack of a clear connection between basic research and innovation, and, at least in the United States, large debts and a shortness of readily available funds.

Major issues involving basic research and innovation include obtaining a clearer understanding of their relationship, and thus of an appropriate scheme for society's support for basic research; understanding alternative intellectual and institutional approaches for organizing basic research; and devising institutional mechanisms for fostering interorganizational and intraorganizational technology transfer.

C. Applied Research, Development, and Engineering

In the United States, industry is the principal funder and performer of applied research and development (R&D)—51.5% compared with the government's 43.5% (National Science Board, 1991). In 1991, the Department of Defense supported 56% of the government-sponsored R&D, including 78% of development. Most of this R&D is performed by industry.

International comparisons are illuminating. For 1989, the most recent year for which comparative figures are available, industry in Japan and Germany paid for a greater proportion of the nation's research and development than in the United States. The U.S. government spent 65.5% of its R&D budget on defense. Japan spent 9.0% of its governmental R&D budget on defense, whereas Germany spent 19.0%. The figures for industrial development offer stark contrast: the U.S. government spends 0.2% of its R&D budget here versus Japan's 8.1% and Germany's 19.0% (National Science Board, 1991).

The most important policy issues in this area focus on strategy to make effective use of R&D for innovation. Strategy can be considered at two principal levels of aggregation— the nation and the individual firm. These levels represent the nature of innovation, which, from our perspective, is primarily an organizational problem and only secondarily an intellectual problem. The national level centers on the role of government in innovation. Innovation is what is driving the world economy. As Kash (1989) points out, the degree to which a national economy is organized for innovation in the commercial sector determines its success in the present and future world marketplace.

The firm level keys on the contribution of private organizations. The first essential is for the firm to accept that it is an innovating organization. This requires a self-understanding of its character and culture as an organization, as well as the core technological capabilities it wishes to cultivate. This understanding is extended to those components of its external environment—customers, competitors, suppliers, government entities—that impact its ability to innovate. Within this focus, technology is viewed as a component of organizational strategy. The primary issue is getting the technology into the organization and deploying it for both product and organizational improvement. The next issue is to structure the organization so that this occurs on a continuous basis.

There are two generic options for bringing new technology into an organization—make or buy. The term *buy* masks a large number of distinct alternatives. Rubenstein (1985) has made an extensive list that includes licensing; joint ventures; buying minority interests in firms; contracting for research services from other companies, research institutes, or universities; cooperative R&D ventures; acquiring small high-technology companies; hiring specialists; and working on innovation with suppliers and customers.

These approaches are not mutually exclusive, nor do they exclude performing R&D internally. Yet each has its own characteristic strengths and weaknesses that make it desirable in some circumstances and not useful in others.

Licensing provides the technology but does not guarantee any internal capability for adaptation. Joint venturing is useful when two or more firms have complementary technical capabilities that may lead to a profitable synthesis. This may be a sound approach provided the organizational cultures and technical capacities can be synthesized into a new and effective organization. Corning has used this approach repeatedly over the years. Two companies, IBM and Apple, are trying it now. The purchase of a minority interest may give a firm access to a technology it needs and a position in a desirable section of an industry. AT&T had this in mind for the workstation sector of the computer industry when it bought 20% of Sun Microsystems, a move that it has since reversed. Contracting for services elsewhere may be used as an exclusive approach in an area or to supplement an internal program. However, contractors have their own agendas. For example, university faculty members look toward publication in refereed journals and so, in many cases, are not centrally focused on the need to develop economically useful property. Cooperative research ventures involving corporations often do not get the best people a corporation has to offer. In the case of industry-university consortia, there is the tendency by many university groups to focus on problems of academic, rather than industrial, interest. When a company acquires a small, high-technology firm to bolster its innovative capabilities in a particular area, a culture clash may occur between the more bureaucratic culture of the larger firm and the more free-flowing approach of the smaller firm. The challenge in cases like this is to preserve the innovative spirit of the smaller group while integrating it into the overall focus and strategy of the larger firm.

The "make" option involves an internal R&D capability for the firm. The strategic decision as to what areas characterize the core or central technological capabilities of the firm gives focus to the overall R&D effort. Internally performed R&D includes at least those areas that are central to the firm's business. There are a number of explicit and implicit strategies that can drive a firm's R&D efforts.

Technological leadership requires that a firm be the first or among the first in its industry to market with technologically innovative products or the first to use new and innovative processes in its operations. This strategy involves an aggressively innovative R&D component in its organization. In the microcomputer industry, Apple has taken this position.

A "second to market" strategy generally involves R&D within the organization. In this case, at least a substantial component of the R&D is defensive or imitative in character. It may involve a market-driven approach to product introduction and emphasize the solution to customers' problems rather than an aggressive emphasis on technology. IBM has taken this position in the microcomputer industry.

Cost-minimization strategy involves adapting or innovating in process and product redesign areas where the goal is to produce an adequate product for the least cost. In the microcomputer industry, the clone makers exemplify this position. This approach does not require an internal product R&D capability. Indeed cost minimization involves appropriating others' work as much as possible.

A niche market approach to an industry is one that may depend heavily on R&D but in a restricted area. In this case, a firm commits itself to only selected niches in an industry where it intends to be a technical leader and significant force. Tektronix, with its substantial role in color printers and graphics terminals, is a good example of a niche firm in information technology.

Government policy decisions impacting innovation both direct the overall innovative capacity of the economy and impact the individual firm's ability to innovate and style of innovation. In this discussion, the United States will be emphasized, but it is clear that other countries, especially Japan, are of considerable interest at this time. Areas of significance include intellectual property policy, tax policy as it impacts R&D and innovation, anti-trust policy (in the United States), procurement, regulation, and direct incentives to develop and adopt innovations (an approach rejected by U.S. administrations from 1980 to date but practiced by major industrial powers such as Japan).

Patent protection in the United States is most valuable in the pharmaceutical industry where patenting is a serious issue because of the long Food and Drug Administration (FDA) approval times. In many industries, the practice of inventing around a patent and the locus of burden of defending the patent on the patent holder make it less essential. Of particular current interest is the case of software. Copyright will protect manuals and codes, but concepts underlying particular software may be patented. Since there is a no long-term body of law affecting software, it remains the most interesting and fluid intellectual property areas at this time.

Tax credits for R&D are a policy tool that the U.S. government has used to stimulate increased R&D by U.S. industry. The approach taken is for firms to deduct from their taxes 25% of R&D spending above the average of expenses of the 3 preceding years. This has been enacted temporarily and renewed as it expires.

Historically, the United States used anti-trust laws to discourage collaborative R&D by industrial firms that were competitors in the market because of the government's concern for competition in the marketplace. The National Cooperative Research Act of 1984 changed this situation for precompetitive R&D. This allowed the formation of a number of industrial R&D consortia, such as the Microelectronics and Computer Corporation (MCC) to take place. The other major industrial nations do not have the history of trust busting that led in the United States to anti-trust legislation. Japan has used such consortia, with government sponsorship and involvement, to develop areas of interest to the national economy.

Government procurement has been a stimulus for innovation in the U.S. defense sector. This pattern began with World War II and has continued through the cold war. It is not yet clear how this long-term relationship between the Department of Defense (DOD) and the industrial sector will work out in the post–cold war world. Yet over decades, DOD organizations, especially the Advanced Research Projects Agency (ARPA), have seeded the development of many commercially significant high-technology innovations. The development of computing capabilities is especially significant. The list of some of these capabilities is illustrative to indicate the extent of influence of defense procurement on high-technology development. Areas of significant start-up funding include high-performance computer architectures, networking, artificial intelligence and expert systems, the use of computer-aided design (CAD) in chip development, graphics, and programming languages (COBOL, ADA).

As Kash (1989) notes, U.S. government procurement in the defense, agriculture, and health areas has played a major role in bringing about the country's eminence in these technological areas. Areas where this procurement has not occurred, especially those targeted by Japan, such as consumer electronics and automobiles, have not flourished. Aeronautics, an area of traditional U.S. preeminence, has been targeted both by Japan (through collaborations with U.S. firms such as Boeing) and European Economic Community (EEC) nations (through Airbus). It will be interesting to see how the world market in this area changes over the next decade.

Regulation substantially impacts innovation. A chilling example is the impact of building codes on innovation in the construction sector, especially residential construction. By requiring specific technologies, innovation is almost a liability. The slow development and implementation of modern electric buses in residential construction, despite perceived advantage, illustrates the limited role innovation has played in this industry. Utility regulation provides a rate of return on an asset base. Where R&D spending is viewed as an investment in an asset base, regulation provides an incentive to spend relatively more on R&D than if it were considered as an operating expense. Meeting environmental or other performance standards, for example, in the automobile industry, stimulates innovation where the technology to meet the standards is not specified. Yet these innovative efforts often detract from efforts to improve the product being subjected to the performance standards and the processes for manufacturing it.

U.S. administrations have diligently avoided direct incentives to innovate since 1980. Indeed efforts prior to that date, except for procurement, were limited and largely ineffective. The argument is often given that the marketplace, and not government, should determine what areas are ripe for innovation. Japan and France pick areas for government involvement, France to the level of the firm. Areas targeted by "Japan, Inc." include consumer electronics, automobiles, and, most recently, aerospace. Their success in capturing worldwide market share in the first two has been little short of awesome.

Two opportunities now present themselves for U.S. industry to stage a comeback in these industries. The first opportunity, in automobiles, is the result of innovation by General Motors. Its innovative venture in automobile development and marketing for the U.S. market, the Saturn Corporation, has been a resounding success. Can the U.S. automobile industry transfer the lessons learned here in quality production and successful marketing to its floundering sectors? The second opportunity is the establishment of a standard for high-definition television (HDTV) for the United States in 1993 by the Federal Communications Commission. Since the competitors are from the United States, this offers a window of opportunity to bring back television production in the United States. Will U.S. industry seize the opportunity?

D. Technology Transfer and Deployment

Technology transfer, diffusion, implementation of innovations, and *deployment* are terms that refer to the process of moving a technology—at whatever stage in its development—to the next stage and ultimately to broad societal usage. Areas involved include transfer of concepts and prototypes from academic and government laboratories to industry; transfer of concepts and prototypes from industrial R&D laboratories to other parts of the firm such as development, engineering, and manufacturing; transfer of process innovations to manufacturing organizations; widespread adoption of innovations; and modification of organizations to achieve organizational goals.

This movement of concepts, products, and processes is, however, not one way. Adopters of innovations feed back their needs to developers through market and other channels, including intraorganizational communications. In the U.S. agricultural sector, the extension agent has historically provided feedback between the agricultural research station and the farmer. Some products are designed with substantial input from customers. When Hewlett-Packard wished to improve its successful Laser-Jet II line of printers incrementally, it asked its most significant customers what about the printer needed improvement. Taking this input seriously, it produced the equally successful Laser-Jet III line.

Although it is generally conceded that U.S. R&D—academic, governmental, and industrial—is at the forefront of many areas, the record of producing this R&D is far better than that of transferring it into commercial products, processes, and services. This problem not only exists between institutions in various sectors but also within industrial firms. In the mid-1980s, the Industrial Research Institute, a professional organization made up of R&D vice presidents and directors from firms performing about 85% of industrial R&D in the United States, held a seminar for its members entitled "How to Talk to Your CEO." Regulation and anti-trust concerns hindered AT&T from transferring much interesting technology from its internal operations to commercial products. It was reported to the authors by an AT&T employee attending a Technology Forecasting Short Course they conducted in 1981 that AT&T had internally at that time a 32-bit microprocessor and a 256-Kbyte RAM chip. These would not be commercially available until years later.

Often R&D functions are isolated from other functions in a firm. The culture of R&D organizations is different from other parts of the firm in that it espouses such values as knowledge and technical excellence that are not commonly held by other parts of the organization. It is no secret that in many, if not most, U.S. firms, it is not possible for an R&D executive to become CEO. Linear handoffs from research to development to engineering to manufacturing divisions are often less than smooth; time and information are too often lost. An approach to integrate the various subcultures within an organization is to use development teams composed of persons from every relevant organization from research to marketing. For large-scale innovations, especially those that are potentially disruptive of the organization or its markets, this project team approach has real merit.

Intersectoral transfers have their own unique problems. Although NASA and the National Laboratories have set up their own technology transfer organizations, their impact has been minor. In addition to technology transfer offices, universities have developed industry-university research consortia focused on interdisciplinary problem areas, such as manufacturing and microelectronics, of interest to industry. These consortia allow industrial input into the scope and direction of the university research being funded. Problems in transferring the results of the research include the lack of direct involvement of industrial researchers with their university colleagues, the low salience of the technical reports produced to industrial firms due to their academic character, and the lack of familiarity of most university researchers with industry and its needs.

"Relative advantage" to the adopter is the foremost factor that promotes the adoption of innovations, whether product, process, or service. Relative advantage is most immediately economic advantage—more profit—but it also involves social and psychological components. These include the perception of advantage, the ease with which the innovation can be adopted through its perceived complexity and amount of disruption to existing operations, and the rate at which initial uncertainty about the innovation can be reduced.

The adopting organization's character is critical for adoption. First, information about the innovation needs to enter the organization. Thus, boundary management to achieve rapid and comprehensive information flow is important. This usually takes place informally through the gatekeeper function (Allen and Cohen, 1969). The gatekeeper is an informal information gatherer and transmitter dealing with information both from within and without the organization. This function was first observed in R&D laboratories, but it is involved in almost every part of an organization. Then there is the process of decision making within the organization. By involving in the decision process those who will be impacted by the innovation, relevant information about the appropriateness of the innovation for the organization may surface; problems and pitfalls in implementation may be made clear; and the support of the people who will actually implement the innovation may be attained. This support is critical for effective implementation, as without it the innovation may be nothing but a financial and organizational burden to the firm.

The importance of transferring and implementing innovations cannot be overemphasized, because without implementation the most promising innovation will never achieve its potential. Those organizations that fail to take advantage of innovations that can move them forward and keep them competitive in a rapidly changing world economy may imitate the producers of steam locomotives in the United States who disappeared during the 1950s, never comprehending the changes in product and process technologies that led to the dieselization of the U.S. railroads.

E. Policy for Innovation and Technology

With the end of the cold war, the "realities" on which public policy is based have disappeared. No clear-cut set of replacements has yet emerged. This is of substantial significance for technology and innovation because in the United States the driver for high technology innovation has been the defense sector. The ideological position of no governmental interference in the private sector could be maintained while the "noninterfering" government acted as a monopsonist in the defense industry driving the cutting edge of technology forward. The shift away from this situation is already underway, and there is no transfer of the government's role occurring yet.

The conclusion appears to be that a comprehensive review of technology and science policy is badly needed at this time to provide a framework for the future in the same way that the post–World War II consensus provided a framework for the past 40 plus years. There are old ideas that need revisiting, such as the creation of a single governmental department for science and technology. There are newer ideas that need exploring, such as government proactively involved in the selection of areas in technology and science for national targeting. The planet has too few resources to deal with the overwhelming redundancy involved in maintaining a worldwide market, with nations duplicating one another at every turn. There is certainly no reason for nationally based projects in big science. At the same time, the maintenance of a viable economy based on technology requires some degree of national reflection on the need to pick and choose sectors of excellence (not firms or specific technologies) at a time when the nation's competitors are successfully doing just that. Fundamental research in important technology areas that can be transferred to outcomes that are economically beneficial is a process issue. Government creates the playing field on which the nation's industry operates. The old field was fraught with ideology that denied the reality of what was happening. Hopefully, an informed national discusion will lead to the development of an environment that can develop the formulation of a new view of the role of technology and science in human societies by taking into account economic and environmental issues. Such a new view will enable the nation and the world to take advantage of changing conditions to use technology as a tool for human development.

IV. TECHNOLOGY IMPACT ASSESSMENT

The treatment of technology impact assessment that follows is based on the work of Porter et al. (1991), and Porter et al. (1980).

A. Assessing the Consequences of Technologies

Beginning in the 1960s, attempts were made to understand the consequences of technological change before it occurred—looking before leaping. These attempts were undertaken because of the importance of technological change in society and the difficulty of understanding its impacts, especially long-term, indirect, and unintended impacts. The attempt was bedeviled by the lack of any adequate descriptive or predictive theory of sociotechnical change that related to data of any kind. Because of the pressing societal need, this deficiency did not stop the attempt to assess the consequences of technologies; it only shifted the locus from theory to technique. In its earlier incarnations in the 1960s and early and mid 1970s, many of the techniques used were quantitative in nature and subject to the truism "garbage in, garbage out." During the subsequent period, quantitative techniques, except in areas of analysis, such as cost-benefit analysis and environmental modeling, where well-founded approaches existed, gave way to qualitative techniques and approaches based on judgment.

Institutions developed around impact assessment. The Office of Technology Assessment of the U.S. Congress is a good example. Professional communities engaged in impact assessment developed. Their focuses ranged across environmental impact, social impact, technology, and risk assessment. Professional organizations, such as the International Association for Impact Assessment, were formed. Analytical and political frameworks mixed. Public concern for impact assessment rose throughout the world during the 1980s. The glaring exception was the United States, where the government showed little interest in future-oriented policy studies.

Intellectually, impact assessment is a focus of interest rather than a body of accepted knowledge or a well-defined collection of methods. Its practitioners come from a wide range of intellectual backgrounds and organizational affiliations. The driving theme is the management of sociotechnical change by anticipating outcomes. Since these outcomes will occur in the future, and there is no body of predictive theory to guide impact assessment practitioners, assessment lays out the range of likely consequences, not what will specifically occur.

Impact assessments are interdisciplinary in character, since the range of likely consequences of a technology knows no disciplinary boundaries. For example, the development of the microcomputer has had dramatic economic and organizational consequences that have altered most productive sectors. For instance, networking is shifting the computer from a stand-alone tool to an active component in an all-encompassing information environment that, in turn, triggers profound economic, technological, social, and environmental consequences.

B. Performance of Impact Assessment

Impact assessment involves a number of component tasks. We distinguish 10 such components. The emphasis on each component will vary according to the focus of the study, policy interest, and level of effort. The term *components* designates a set of tasks that do not follow a single linear order. Table 1 lists these tasks, which will be described briefly (Porter et al., 1980, 1991).

1. Problem Definition/Bounding

The first activity is to determine the nature and scope of the study. This is one task that should never be omitted. Indeed, as "scoping," it is required in the preparation of all environmental impact statements in the United States. The policy objectives and available resources must be considered and matched to the issue in question to determine the coverage of the study.

Table 1. Component Tasks of an Impact Assessment

1. Problem Definition/Bounding
2. Technology Description
3. Technology Forecast
4. Societal Description
5. Societal Forecast
6. Impact Identification
7. Impact Analysis
8. Impact Evaluation
9. Policy Analysis
10. Communication of Results

Berg (1975) has usefully delineated six areas that should be bounded. These are: time horizons, spatial extent, institutional interests, detail on the subject of the assessment, impact areas, and policy options. It should be clear that it is essential to know from the beginning who are to be the users of the study and to direct the form and media of the output to them. This means, for example, that information directed to politicians should not be in the form of a thick technical report with two volumes of appendices. The study resources and time available for the work should be carefully considered in determining the depth and sequencing of the tasks to be performed. The parties at interest in the assessment should be considered and their different world views, priorities, and cognitive styles investigated to determine the various perspectives that could be taken in the assessment. Finally, it is essential to remember that boundaries remain provisional with the expectation that some will be revised during the course of the study as new information is uncovered and different perspectives emerge. In impact assessment, bounding is a continuous process, the importance of which cannot be overstated.

2. Technology Description

Technology (or project or program) description is the first of a cluster of tasks that include technology forecast, societal description, and societal context forecast, as indicated in Table 1. These component tasks prepare for the work of dealing with the impacts. Technology description is an empirical task that uses the current state of the art knowledge from technical and trade literature and from experts in the field. The importance of this task is in clearly understanding the subject matter of the assessment. For futuristic technologies that have not yet been implemented, such as space colonies, technology description may blend into technology forecast. Indeed the character of the description of a technology is determined by its stage in the innovation process. Mature technologies, such as dams and power plants, are widely understood. Newer technologies, such as nanotechnology and genetic engineering, are more uncertain and speculative in character. There is often a good deal of uncertainty and fluidity in their characterization representing their fluid and uncertain state at any time. In any case, the first essential for the technology assessment is the best physical and functional description of the technology available. Then it is pertinent to consider supporting technologies and scientific areas. Areas where breakthroughs are required to move the state of the art forward are quite relevant, as are competing technologies. The earlier in the innovation process a technology is, fewer are the parties at interest, the more closely held the knowledge about it, and the less the significance of institutional and political considerations. The depth to which a technology should be grasped in a study is determined by the purpose of the study, the users of the study, and the time and resources available.

3. Technology Forecast

Technology forecasting attempts to anticipate the character, intensity, and timing of changes in technologies (Bright, 1978). This task obviously rests heavily on the technology description, but it also relies on the societal description and forecast as well. For instance, the establishment of a space colony depends to a great extent on economic, political, and social factors in addition to the technology. High-quality forecasts rest on using the best available data, understanding the relationships involved in the development of technology, including institutional relationships, and making sound core assumptions. Core assumptions are the basic presuppositions underlying the forecast. Ascher (1978) offers three general principles of forecasting that we have found to be extremely sound guidelines.

1. A short time frame for a forecast is strongly associated with increased accuracy.
2. Methodological sophistication contributes little.
3. The core assumptions are critical to the quality of the forecast.

Sound judgment is the most critical requisite for a successful forecast. Various data and judgment-based forecasting techniques supplement and help structure judgment to yield credible forecasts.

The most significant of these techniques (though strictly speaking it is not a forecasting technique but a means to supply the information base for forecasting) is monitoring. "Monitoring is to watch, observe, check, and keep up with developments, usually in a well defined area of interest with a specific purpose" (Coates et al., 1986). Monitoring is scanning relevant environments—literature, people, data bases, physical environments—for pertinent information. The following steps are generally useful in monitoring.

1. Determine the monitoring objectives and focus.
2. Describe the subject of monitoring and map its pertinent context.
3. Adapt an appropriate monitoring strategy (i.e., what to monitor, when, how long, how to structure the output, and so forth).
4. Implement the monitoring strategy.
5. Interpret, evaluate, and communicate results.

Monitoring's strength is that it can sweep in a large volume of relevant information. Its weakness is that this informaton may not be filtered and structured. Monitoring can be readily grasped by almost anyone. Yet it is important and useful to almost every forecasting effort. For example, it is central to Naisbitt's best-selling books dealing with the future.

An extremely commonly used technique, and one that some analysts believe is synonymous with forecasting, is trend analysis. Trend analysis consists of using mathematical and statistical techniques to extend quantitative time series into the future. Trend extrapolation requires that the area being forecast have significant quantitative parameters for which good-quality data are available over a reasonable period of time. How much data and how good depends on the needs of the forecast. Many sophisticated techniques for trend analysis have been developed that require good data over long periods of time. Although useful and instructive, these techniques do not address the common situation of the impact assessor who has little data, covering a relatively short period of time, and who needs to project it over a long time. Trend analysis assumes that the future will continue about the same as the past without major discontinuities. Its strength is that it offers substantial, data-based forecasts of important parameters that are especially accurate over short time frames. Its weaknesses are that it is vulnerable to cataclysms and discontinuities, and it forecasts only parameters that can be quantified. Although trend analysis does not explicitly require a causal model or a quasicausal model to determine the form of change over time of the parameter being projected, understanding the causal relationships involved is more useful than simply trying to find the curve that best fits the available data. Two very commonly used models are the line and the s-curve. The line is the simplest curve form and can fit any data set. When no other model is available, one can always start with the line. The s-curve has successfully represented in many cases processes of interest to impact assessors, such as the adoption of a technology, the substitution of one technology for another technology, and the changes in a technology over its life cycle. A more detailed treatment of trend analysis is given by Porter et al. (1991).

Expert opinion is a widely used approach that rests on the assumption that there are experts—persons who know substantially more about an area being forecast than the average individual. It is not always easy to identify experts. Some indicators include having worked in a technological area for a long period of time; holding patents in that area; authoring books, articles, and technical reports about the technology; and being identified as an expert by persons involved in that area. It is important to remember that technology experts include not only researchers and developers of the technology, but also persons involved in product development and commercialization and in transferring the technology from one sector to another, as well as within organizations, as well as parties at interest who have significant experience with the technology. Involving experts who are nontechnologists may break the groupthink that is common among groups that work in the same area. There are various approaches to extracting the opinion of experts. Three significant activities involved in extracting expert opinion are *estimating* the answer to questions, giving and receiving *feedback* on the answers of other experts, and *talking* among experts to understand the bases of others' positions. The survey is a commonly used technique in which experts are asked to estimate their answers to a set of questions. These responses are then analyzed. Whenever specific questions are used, it is an excellent idea to pretest them on a small number of persons similar to those to whom the questions are going to be asked. Almost invariably a set of questions yields some ambiguities that need to be resolved before the questions can be asked meaningfully. (The authors are prepared to testify to the accuracy of this statement!) Committees add talking to estimating. They are vulnerable to social and psychological impacts of group process. These include dominance effects in which verbal and articulate persons may intimidate those who are less self-assured and in which subordinates may hesitate to contradict the wisdom of their superiors. The Delphi technique eliminates talk while adding feedback. In its most common form (and there are many), Delphi consists in giving a survey to a group of experts, feeding the analyzed results back to them, and then asking them to answer the survey again. This process is iterated until the overall pattern of responses is stable. Almost always the responses converge. Adding face-to-face interaction for discussing the questions to Delphi gives EFTE (Nelms and Porter, 1985). There are many other variations of expert opinion gathering.

The generation of scenarios in forecasts provides a technique that has a number of advantages over other approaches. Scenarios may be cast as snapshots of a subject at some time in the future; future histories, or timelines, by which the subject goes from its present state to some future condition; and combinations of snapshots and future histories. Scenarios are often presented in groups. In cases of emphasis on a single factor, groups of three are common, representing optimistic, pessimistic, and baseline scenarios. Scenarios may take advantage of literary devices in their presentation and may use multimedia to make the forecast results accessible to a wide range of users. Some of the best scenarios of the past have been the great works of science fiction. Scenarios are excellent communication devices. They may integrate information from different sources and in diverse forms into a single coherent presentation. Quantitative and qualitative forecasts can be interrelated in the scenario format. The following steps constitute a checklist for scenario construction.

1. Identify the dimensions of the topic of interest.
2. Identify users' interests and the appropriate style of information presentation.
3. Specify time frame.
4. Specify societal and technological assumptions.
5. Set out the important dimensions to be included in the scenarios.
6. Decide on the number of scenarios and their emphases.
7. Construct and present the scenarios.

In addition to the techniques presented briefly above, there are a number of modeling techniques, both quantitative and judgmental, that may prove useful. It is important to remember that there are no facts about the future, so it is often helpful to approach the same forecasting task with a number of different approaches and techniques. Convergence of results builds confidence in their validity and utility.

4. Societal Description

Those aspects of the state of society that may potentially interact with the technology or other subject of the assessment should be described accurately. The technology delivery system—TDS—discussed earlier and illustrated in Figure 1, is a useful tool for conceptualizing the societal environment of a technology. The emphasis here is on the points of contact between the technology and its societal context where interactions leading to impacts may occur. The TDS will be different depending on the purposes and users of the study. Components important in societal description include the demographics of potentially impacted populations, economic drivers and impediments, institutional environments in which development takes place, societal values driving or inhibiting the technology (such as in the case of genetic engineering), political and legal conditions, and aspects of the physical environment with which interaction is likely. The level of depth and form of description depend on the users' interests.

5. Societal Forecast

This is perhaps the trickiest task involved in impact assessment because it involves the projection of the societal context without interaction with the subject of the assessment. It should not be confused, as it often is, with social impact assessment. Moreover, outside of demography and economics, social forecasting is poorly developed intellectually and is suspect in many quarters. As in the case of any forecast, the result is a range of likely outcomes, often in the form of scenarios, rather than one particular future. The TDS developed in societal context description is a useful starting point. The techniques discussed in the section on technology forecasting may prove useful here as well. Monitoring remains the technique of choice to develop the baseline information from which a forecast can be constructed. For demographic and economic trends, trend analysis is appropriate. For other dimensions, we suggest a mixture of expert opinion and scenarios, emphasizing expert opinion for matters near in time and scenarios for more distant issues. These techniques can be augmented by judgmental modeling as is appropriate. Scenarios make good integrators of societal futures.

6. Impact Identification

In our context, impacts refer to the products of the interaction between a technology or other development and its societal context. Although, as Table 1 indicates, the assessment tasks associated with impacts can be logically distinguished from those involved in describing and forecasting technology and its societal context, in practice these aspects may become completely intertwined. In particular, if one is trying to assess the impacts of a long-range technological development of grand scope, the technology is so apt to affect its societal context in a substantial way that technological and societal forecasting will be linked with impact analysis. Thus, a useful distinction can be drawn between the direct or immediate impacts of a technology (those resulting from the development per se) and the higher-order impacts (those effects resulting from the continued interaction of the technology with a context modified by the direct impacts and impacts of the direct, and ultimately higher-order, impacts). These effects may overwhelm the analyst—imagine trying to untwine all the higher-order environmental impacts of the automobile, which were largely unanticipated when the technology was first introduced. Consider technologies with major impact potential such as nanotechnology, nuclear fusion energy, and virtual reality whose future impacts may be overwhelming, or nil if the technology is not developed or widely adopted.

There are basically two approaches to identifying impacts—scanning and tracing. Scanning techniques identify potential impacts by investigating the full range of candidate impacts in a single, direct step. Tracing techniques construct structural relationships between development actions and impacts, and among impacts, creating a causal trail in which impacts become causes of higher-order effects. Either or both approaches can be useful depending on the characteristics of the task.

Scanning methods search the impact field to minimize the probability that significant impacts will be overlooked. The simplest approach is to use a checklist—an a priori listing of all candidate impacts. The list may be relatively brief at a high level of abstraction, or it may be highly detailed and relatively concrete. One widely used approach is to classify impacts by the disciplines used to analyze them, such as economic, environmental, social, and political. An alternative approach is to list all parties potentially affected by the development and how they may be impacted. This list is scanned and the ways in which the development could affect each party are identified. The matrix takes the checklist one dimension further. Crossing a list of affected parties with a list of possible impacts creates one approach to scanning in two dimensions.

Tracing methods emphasize structural relations that may be expressed as a formal model or as a chain of causes and effects. The relevance tree, considered qualitatively, graphically depicts the linkages between various members of sets of elements, moving from level to level by some causal relationship. To construct such a tree, a series of "what if" questions must be answered for each node at each level. Yet this exercise needs to be kept in bound so that a relevant and manageable output results.

Scanning and tracing techniques can be combined effectively to assay potential impacts. When the potential impacts are identified, another step is necessary to identify those that will be significant within the scope of the study for further analysis. This is often done through expert judgment considering the magnitude of effects, probability of occurrence, timing, and the importance of the impact from the perspective of the analysis.

7. Impact Analysis

Impact analysis links the identification of significant impacts to their evaluation in the formulation of effective policy to deal with them. It is here that serious analysis of magnitudes and likelihoods of occurrence are made. In this task, disciplinary expertise and quantitative skills, such as cost-benefit analysis and environmental modeling, are most useful. Considered here are both impacts of a technology on its societal context and impacts of that societal context on a technology. Such areas as law, regulation, and values provide good examples of the latter, whereas environmental and economic impacts illustrate the former in many cases. This treatment briefly reviews some of the major categories broken out by discipline.

One of the most significant categories of impacts is economic. As Mansfield (1989) noted: "the rate of technological change is perhaps the most important single determinant of a nation's rate of economic growth." Yet technological change that benefits the economy must be embedded in economically usable products, processes, and services. On the macro-level, techniques, such as input-output analysis, that track economic flows across industry lines may sometimes be useful. A most common technique used on the micro-level is cost-benefit analysis in its various forms. Substantial treatises (e.g., see Sassone and Schaffer, 1978) have been written on this subject. Conceptually it appears very simple. An innovation costs so much money. It produces so much in benefits. If the benefits exceed the cost, then the innovation is financially successful; if the costs exceed the benefits, then it is not. Yet this procedure is fraught with perils. First, in many cases, the future costs and benefits of an innovation can only be estimated with a substantial degree of uncertainty. Thus, from one perspective, costs could substantially exceed benefits; from another, the contrary would be the case. Beyond the mere estimates, this issue turns on where the boundaries of the innovation are drawn, with everything outside being considered external and thus not counted as a cost or benefit. Costs to distant locations from pollution are thus often ignored. Then there is the time value of money that also requires an estimate, since the forecasting of interest or discount rates is not particularly accurate. Furthermore, there may need to be different discount rates for the private and public sectors. Then the time frame of the analysis needs to be considered. Sometimes extending the time frame will turn an unprofitable innovation into a profitable one; sometimes the opposite will be true. Short payback periods required by management before an innovation can be developed as a product have created grief with many corporate R&D directors by preferring the short term to the long. The serious application of cost-benefit analysis requires sound judgment, careful analysis, and a clear understanding of why and how judgments were made.

Environmental impact analysis is an important field in its own right owing to the requirements in the United States and other nations for environmental impact statements (EISs) or their equivalents. The subject of environmental assessment and policy is vast. This treatment will limit itself to pointing out major categories of environmental impacts. These include ecosystems, land use, water quantity and quality, air quality, noise, and radiation. There are legal requirements in many of these areas. Some technology developments have major environmental impact potential, such as nuclear power plants. Some, such as the computer, appear to have few. Yet the manufacture of microprocessors may create significant environmental impacts owing to the residues of the process. Ecosystem assessment depends on baseline data. This implies the use of some form of survey (as quantitative as possible) to project the differences attributable to the technological development being assessed. Major land impacts include land use, solid waste, erosion, and pollution (e.g., pesticides or other chemicals). Water quality concerns include hydrologic characteristics, physical properties, chemical constituents, and biological constituents. Water quantity and quality analysis often involves the use of computer-based models. Air quality considerations cross national borders, as in the case of acid rain. Five primary pollutants are hydrocarbons, carbon monoxide, nitrogen oxides, sulfur oxides, and particulates. These may combine to generate secondary pollutants, such as smog. Other hazardous toxicants such as asbestos, arsenic, lead, and mercury may be present in the air. Modeling is extensively used to analyze air quality. Noise is associated with human activity such as transportation, construction, and industry. Noise impacts relate to community annoyance as well as to physiological and structural damage. Radiation is an area of high public sensitivity in the nuclear power sector as well as with microwave devices and video display terminals. The perception of risk and negative impacts on the one hand, and the scientific evidence on the other, are sometimes at odds in this area in which great uncertainties exist.

Social impacts range from changes in community institutions, demography, and support services due to large projects, to lifestyle changes associated with such developments as the birth control pill, to values-related issues involving genetic engineering. Although demographical changes and community development impacts have relatively stable methodologies (see, e.g., Leistritz and Murdoch, 1981), the study of lifestyle, psychological, and values changes is largely qualitative in character.

Political and legal impact analysis relies heavily on institutional and legal analysis. In these cases, the study of "impacts on" and "impacts of" are both important in understanding the influences of, and on, technological change.

The final category of impact mentioned here is technological. Technological impacts refer to the changes in technologies caused by technological development. These include vertical, horizontal, and systemic impacts. Vertical changes relate to the natural development and succession processes within a given family of technologies; for example, the technological developments involved in the progressively greater integration of silicon chips. Horizontal impacts result when developments in one technology drive those in another. The greater and greater integration of chips has driven the development of optical technology for interconnections within computers, since the number of interconnections has increased dramatically while their size has been reduced substantially. Systemic impact result from technological developments that lead to the ability to develop systems going far beyond the original technological breakthrough. These may be technological system or sociotechnical systems.

8. Impact Evaluation

Impact evaluation integrates the impact analyses with the perspectives on which the study was based to enable comparison of alternatives and to assist in the process of policy analysis. Both impact assessment and policy analysis grapple with values. The effort to assign values to impacts and alternative implementations is not straightforward. In a typical assessment, the parties at interest have differing perspectives that result in different valuations of impacts and alternatives. Basic questions in impact evaluation include:

What is to be evaluated?
Who are to be involved in the evaluation and what roles do they play?
How are evaluation criteria to be determined?
What are the criteria; how are they to be weighted and measured?

There are two basic approaches. Where the perspective from which the evaluation is being undertaken is relatively unambiguous, one can use quantitative or structured techniques as noted by Porter et al. (1991). Where it is important to consider the divergent perspectives of various parties at interest, a participatory process can be used, such as that involved in environmental mediation to arrive, if possible, at an acceptable consensus of valuation.

9. Policy Analysis

Policy analysis involves systematically understanding the conditions and factors on which policy decisions are based. It provides analytic support to all phases of the policy-making process. Impact assessment is a form of policy analysis. Policy analysis, in a far more restricted sense, is a component of impact assessment. In this last role, policy analysis considers the evaluated impacts and determines the institutions and individuals that have the ability to deal with the impacts, either positively or negatively, and the range of actions they are capable of taking. Despite the fact that it appears toward the end of the list of impact assessment tasks, policy analysis should be begun at the beginning of the assessment process by determining the communities and institutions that can influence the technological development—the parties at interest and the roles that they may play. The involvement of these communities with the study should enhance both the realism and acceptance of the study. The policy analysis task in impact assessment is typically qualitative in character. Recommendations from a study are almost always desirable unless the ground rules of the study preclude them. The involvement of parties at interest, or at least their awareness, may enhance the credibility of the study and its recommendations. Most recommendations are ignored unless those who can implement them are involved to the point where they hold a stake in the recommendations being implemented.

10. Communication of Results

Effective communication requires focusing on the users of the study and on the purposes for which they will use the study. Thus content and form need to be tailored to the users and their purposes. As noted in the section on policy analysis above, it is desirable for these users to be in contact with the study throughout its performance and to feel that in some sense it is "theirs." This sense of proprietary interest makes the transition from study to action easier. Communication can be oral, as with briefings, roundtables, or panels. It can also be in either the traditional print media or the newer multimedia. Communication needs to be pointed to getting the parties at interest to do what needs to be done. Impact assessment is not an intellectual exercise of knowledge for the sake of knowledge. It is knowledge for the sake of action, for progressive sociotechnical change.

C. Directions for Impact Assessment

At present, the role of impact assessment is limited largely to environmental and related issues. Its practice has been largely in the industrialized First World where the negative impacts of technological development have been felt the longest. Impact assessment is an activity that should be seen as a critical component of the innovation process, taken in a very broad sense. In particular, the process of technological innovation and the activity of impact assessment should be joined at the very beginning—when the innovation emerges in concept. The question at that time, which can be answered in general terms, is where the innovation could lead, not only for the innovating organization, but also for all the institutions and communities with which the innovation will come in contact. At first, this process is little more than speculatively sketching out the technology's developmental trajectory along with perceived impacts and the parties at interest. As the innovation takes form and reaches the point where it will have a broad impact, the level of effort should increase along with the clarity with which the innovation is seen. The assessment process should continue to the obsolescence of the technology, having already begun to assess its successor technologies. Just as the modern corporation now sees technology as a strategic element, so the modern society should view technology as a strategic component of its development. It would be highly desirable for impact assessment to be written into the fabric of modern society as a necessary component of sociotechnical change in which all institutions are engaged.

V. IMPLICATIONS FOR THE POLICY PROCESS

The present role of technology in society and its public and private institutions leads us to propose three principles for understanding and dealing with the technological component of contemporary society.

1. Technology is a central component of contemporary society that could not exist without it. It is integral to all social change, which is really sociotechnical change. Technology needs to be treated by society in a manner commensurate with its importance.
2. Because of the rapid and increasing rate of sociotechnical change, the present needs to be viewed from the future, not as an extension of the past or with the short-term view of the present.
3. Because of the importance and rate of sociotechnical change, technology needs to be dealt with proactively rather than reactively.

These principles will be discussed in order.

The centrality of technology crept up on society. Over the centuries, technology shifted from a collection of useful, but isolated, tools to an environment in which human society is inseparably intertwined. This "environmental" role of technology is illustrated by today's networked information technology that provides a surrogate nervous system for society. Because until World War II the engineer and scientist were seen as persons whose roles were useful but not central to society, the illusion of technology as an entity separable from the human matrix in which it is embedded was fostered. With today's information technology, that perspective is obsolete; with tomorrow's genetic and nanotechnology, it will be gone. It is not an exaggeration to say that every major public policy issue today is deeply involved with technology. Areas such as health, national security, labor, communications, agriculture, and transportation are technologically intensive. Areas that appear to be oriented toward people, such as economic and labor policy, are dependent on the state of technology. Even governmental processes, such as elections and the operations of the various branches of government, can be altered by changes in technology. In international affairs, technology underlies both the economic and military power of nations. For too long technology has been an exogenous variable in analyzing these areas, explicitly so in economics. Persons involved in these areas as actors or students in most cases lack a basic understanding of technology, since, unlike science, it is not part of the basic K–12 curriculum. There is not an adequate effort underway to understand from theoretical and empirical perspectives the issues involved in sociotechnical change. This imbalance between reality on the one hand, and perceived reality and education on the other, is one of the most unfortunate features of contemporary society.

It is now apparent that one crucial difference between the "haves" and "have nots" in the not too distant future, if not now, will be their familiarity and comfort with computerized information systems. These constitute the "nervous system" of the work environment, a nervous system that is not even beginning to be mature, but that is beginning to extend to the home and to the individual person, so that shortly it will be ubiquitous. Proposals to develop a single focus within government for technology and science should be carefully considered as they address a common, dominant theme.

The concept of dealing with the present from the perspective of the future or "managing the present from the future" was developed by Smits et al. (1987). The underlying analysis is that the rate of quantitative and qualitative sociotechnical change is so rapid that using the past as a model for dealing with the present is inadequate in much the same way that it is for rearing children in an environment where the life experience of parents does not encompass that of their children. The past is certainly no guide to international relationships at a time when the cold war assumptions that dominated since the end of World War II no longer hold. Likewise, a present-oriented approach forgoes the possibility of consciously developing a stable world order that can endure. The decade of the 1980s has demonstrated that a near-term orientation to profit does not strengthen the technological position of an organization, and that the maintenance of a national lifestyle of immediate gratification on credit weakens the long-term position of a society by driving up debt, eroding the trade balance, and maintaining a low savings rate. The alternative to these perspectives is to use likely or realistically desirable futures to drive today's decision-making process. As has been discussed earlier, the study of the future serves to narrow the uncertainty of the possible and to analyze feasible paths to desirable states. The extrapolative case is used where the perspective is an area where the sponsors of the analysis have little control. Here the question is what is possible and then what is likely. The users of the forecast are poised to take advantage of this information. Both future states and paths to those states should result from the analysis. In the case of normative analysis, a desired future state is posited and then paths to that state are developed. Depending of the character and likelihood of the paths, the desired state may be revised to reflect what is likely to be achieved. Coupling sound analysis with intuition may produce a vision of the future. As used here, a vision is not a clear, unchanging view, but rather an ever changing panorama of the main features of interest. Every component of a vision is continually being revised. The vision is focused and guided by a conceptual framework for analyzing the future, the observations that underlie the analysis, and the intuition that performs the synthesis that turns discrete elements into a coherent whole.

There is no cookbook recipe for creation of visions of the future. Yet there are tools, and hopefully there is the will that is required to make the effort to shift our orientation from the present and the past to the future. This implies that foresight becomes a major part of the policy process. Rigid global planning, as practiced in the former Soviet Union, is an obvious disaster. Yet looking before leaping remains sound common sense. Both extrapolative and normative analysis and planning activities are part of any sound organization, including a government.

Finally, the importance of dealing with technology proactively cannot be overemphasized. To start, there are simply not enough resources available for a single nation to be unilaterally at the cutting edge of science and technology in every area where this knowledge will prove useful for technological development. Japan has proven this by tilting the playing field to encourage and support areas of technological development deemed to be of importance to the nation. This policy approach has enabled the Japanese economy to make fantastic progress during the last two decades. The United States, which followed a hands-off policy during the same period, saw its economy recede, at least in relative terms. Decisions come hard to professional, industrial, and governmental communities programmed to believe that decisions about relative emphasis on areas of science and technology are to be made by market forces, not policy makers. All decisions are unpopular with some of the impacted groups. Yet analytically supported decisions, with attention to and involvement of the parties at interest, are surely preferable to decision by ideology and default.

These principles offer the conceptual outlines to a realistic approach to understanding and managing technological change. Innovation is uncertain; the future is never known definitively. Yet the bottom line is that technology is presently so important to human beings that it needs to be actively managed by human beings. Taking advantage of the character of technology and human capabilities, this is possible but by no means easy.

REFERENCES

Allen, T. J., and Cohen, S. I. (1969). Information flow in research and development laboratories. *Administrative Sciences Quarterly* 14: 12–19.

Ascher, W. (1978). *Forecasting: An Appraisal for Policy Makers and Planners*. Johns Hopkins University Press, Baltimore.

Berg, M. R. (1975). Methodology. In *Perspectives on Technology Assessment*. S. R. Arnstein and A. Christakis (Ed.). Science and Technology Publishers, Jerusalem, pp. 63–72.

Bright, J. R. (1978). *Practical Technology Forecasting*. The Industrial Management Center, Austin, TX.

Coates, J. F., Coates, V. T., Jarratt, J., and Heinz, L. (1986). *Issues Management*. Lomond, Mt. Airy, MD.

Ellul, J. (1964). *The Technological Society*. J. Wilkenson, Translator, Vintage, New York.

Kash, D. E. (1989). *Perpetual innovation*. Basic Books, New York.

Kelly, P., Kranzberg, M., Rossini, F. A., Baker, N. R., Tarpley, F. A., Jr., and Mitzner, M. (1978). *Technological Innovation: A Critical Review of Current Knowledge*. San Francisco Press, San Francisco.

Leistritz, F. L., and Murdoch, S. H. (1981). *The Socioeconomic Impact of Resource Development: Methods for Assessment*. Westview Press, Boulder, CO.

Mansfield, E. (1989), *Economics: Principles, Problems and Decisions*. W. W. Norton, New York.

National Science Board (1991). *Science and Engineering Indicators—1991*. U.S. Government Printing Office, Washington, DC.

Nelms, K. R., and Porter, A. L. (1985), EFTE: An interactive delphi method, *Technological Forecasting and Social Change* 28: 43–61.

Porter, A. L., Rossini, F. A., Carpenter, S. R., and Roper, A. T. (1980). *A Guidebook for Technology Assessment and Impact Analysis*. North Holland, New York.

Porter, A. L., Roper, A. T., Mason, T. M., Rossini, F. A., and Banks, J. (1991). *Forecasting and Management of Technology*. John Wiley & Sons, New York.

Rubenstein, A. H. (1985). Make or buy decisions in research and development. Paper Presented at the Institute of Management Sciences Meeting, Boston.

Sassone, P. G., and Schaffer, W. A. (1978). *Cost-Benefit Analysis: A Handbook*. Academic Press, New York.

Smits, S. J., Rossini, F. A., and Davis, L. M. (1987). Managing the present from the future: The challenge of preparing for technology in rehabilitation. *Journal of Rehabilitation Administration* 11 (4): 121–130.

Tornatzky, L. G., and Fleischer, M. (1990). *The Process of Technological Innovation*. Lexington Books, Lexington, MA.

Wenk, E., Jr., and Kuehn, T. J. (1977). Interinstitutional networks in technological delivery systems. In *Science and Technology Policy*. J. Haberer (Ed.). Lexington Books, Lexington, MA, pp. 153–175.

31
U.S. Health Policy in Developmental and Cross-National Perspective

David Falcone and Robert Broyles
University of Oklahoma, Oklahoma City, Oklahoma

Steven R. Smith
Duke University, Durham, North Carolina

This chapter examines U.S. health policy and health system performance in cross-national perspective with regard to the goals of cost containment, access expansion, and maintenance of quality of care. That performance has been less than impressive, and virtually all principal actors in the health policy arena agree that substantial reform is necessary.

Yet the system has been resistant to change. The factors behind this resistance are examined in a review of the development of U.S. health policy from an emphasis on health care as a public good, to a largely symbolic expression of health care as a right, to a recent focus on health care as a limited resource. It is shown that the means by which government has attempted to influence the allocation of this resource have been regulation in lieu of policy, couched in the rubric of planning in the 1970s, competition in the 1980s, and now increasingly in terms of managed competition.

We suggest that a rational approach to reform would be the adoption of a social insurance model. The major barrier to such a reform is the difficulty the distinctive U.S. political structure imposes on the expression of political will, a difficulty often mistakenly attributed to contemporary ideological preferences or "American exceptionalism."

Since the publication of the first edition of *The Encyclopedia of Policy Studies* U.S. health policy developments have continued to exhibit what Alford (1975) referred to as "dynamics without change." In lieu of a major shift in policy or a clear articulation of existing policy, regulations "governing" U.S. health institutions have proliferated in the form of buoys to guide a health services ship that is increasing in size and speed. This course is unlikely to remain steady; even representatives of the insurance industry now have joined in the call for major changes that will have substantial impacts on how that course is to be charted and how health services are to be financed and delivered. In deciding how to chart the course, there is a growing recognition that maps are more affordable and expeditious than buoys.

Using a typology of numerous reform proposals, this chapter examines the forms the changes in health policy direction might take. We suggest that a rational approach to reform would be the adoption of a social insurance model. The major barrier to such a reform is the difficulty imposed by the distinctive political structure of the United States on the expression of political will, a difficulty often mistakenly attributed to contemporary ideological preferences. But first we examine where U.S. health policy stands in cross-national perspective with regard to the pursuit of ensuring the broadest possible access to high-quality health services at bearable societal cost.

After locating the U.S. health care system in space, as it were, we place it in time by presenting an overview of major developments in U.S. health policy. In so doing, we take up the issue of why assurance of the provision of health services became a governmental concern and how that concern has been justified by an expansion of the types of health services that are perceived to be public goods. We show that ideological debate about health care as a right has given way to preoccupations about the most effective means of allocating health services in order to protect government budgets and control costs.

In the prevailing view, it now matters less *why* government is involved in health services financing and delivery than *how* government can most efficiently discharge the responsibilities that it has assumed. In deciding that issue, the ability of the United States to learn from other countries has been hampered by a prescriptive incrementalism, a belief that U.S. political culture cannot accommodate systemic reform. However, it has become evident that several states' political cultures are not anethma to foreign health program models. In this regard, the U.S. states may be partners in a worldwide devolution of government responsibility for health services, as there is an increasing perception that the optimal locations of health programs, i.e., where public demand for the services most nearly equals public willingness to supply them, are at subnational levels.

Before proceeding to the comparative analysis, let us clear up some definitional underbrush. How is health policy distinctive? What, for present purposes, is meant by policy, health policy, and health?

I. POLICY

The problem of deriving a useful working definition of health policy obviously requires some specification of the meaning of policy. This is an imposing task, not because of the scarcity of meanings with some currency, but because of the lack of commonly accepted conceptions. If the latter have an underlying dimension, it would be that of an orientation that forms the basis for decision rules, whether the decisions are what Etzioni (1967) has called "bit" or "contextuating." In this view, a given policy may virtually preordain that all legislative, bureaucratic, judicial, and administrative actions would be regarded as of the "bit" variety— that is, serially incremental but part of a shifting policy context. The evolution of the welfare state—at least up until the mid 1970s—is an example of this pattern. The policy toward societal (via government) responsibility for the equality of opportunity and maintenance of a minimally acceptable standard of living has been loosely formulated so as not to collide with the shibboleths of classic liberalism. Therefore, U.S. health policies, such as the Maternal and Child Health/Crippled Children Services Program under the Social Security Act, the Kerr-Mills federal-state conditional grants to provide care for the elderly poor, and the Comprehensive Health Planning Program, Regional Medical Program, Medicare, and Medicaid have been targeted to specific beneficiaries or problem areas as resources have permitted and groups have demanded action.

When we think of policy as an orientation, however, we usually think of a "contextuating" government action; namely, one that explicitly initiates a new government strategy for attacking a problem and sets the stage for further predictable actions. The Social Security Act is a prime example, although even its original set of provisions can be viewed as a pragmatic, episodic response to a perceived crisis. The distinction between contextuating and bit policy is drawn here not so much to set forth a rudimentary typology as to indicate that what we really are distinguishing are explicit and implicit policies. There has been little in the way of definitive contextuating health policy in the United States, although some have so regarded the 1946 Hospital Survey and Construction (Hill-Burton) Act, because it marked the legitimacy of at least a measure of government-induced health planning, and Medicare, because it was a "health" as opposed to welfare (i.e., not a means-tested) program.

For this reason, there is a reigning claim that we have no national health policy. (Related to this is the claim that we have no health system but rather a collage of modes of health services delivery.) In the perspective suggested in the foregoing discussion, this claim turns into one that holds that the financing and organization of health care is not yet a government priority, that the United States has not decided to launch an articulated, coordinated movement toward the assumption of societal responsibility for the financing of health services in an attempt to make health services universally available and accessible.

II. HEALTH POLICY

Several types of policies directly affect or seek to affect health. Those that come readily to mind are primarily legislative, but also judicial and public administrative decisions dealing with the rates of production, geographical and specialty distribution of health manpower; health care financing; assurance of the quality of health personnel, institutions, and services; occupational safety and environmental protection; and attempts to limit the consumption of presumably destructive substances such as alcohol, tobacco, and synthetic carcinogens. As we will discuss later, in some instances, the seemingly indirect effects on health of education, housing, income maintenance, or other policies may be even more consequential than the direct effects of policies that deal patently with health. Nevertheless, for analytic purposes, it is useful to limit the conception of health policy to the conventional notion; i.e., public decisions that seek primarily to affect health or the behavior of principal actors—professional and institutional—in their roles in the health arena. Indeed, employing this restriction allows one to make statements such as the one above that posits some other policies may ultimately have a more telling impact on health than more strictly health policies, or that there is a need for integrating different policy areas. In this regard, health and welfare are perhaps those policy areas most frequently cited (e.g., see DeJong, 1977).

III. HEALTH AND HEALTH CARE

If health policy analysis is bounded by its subject matter, then the question arises as to what is meant by health and health care. That there is no dearth of literature on this topic is understandable in light of the fact that the societal meaning of health at any given time obviously has profound consequences for policy. For the Greeks, health was a state of harmony, and some commentators such as Sigerist (1970) think, "this is still the best general explanation we have." To some extent, this conception is beginning to be institutionalized in the form of the holistic health movement.

A less romantic view is that health is freedom from disease. In either conception, however, as Banta (1990) has put it, "health care could become a tyranny" if defined too broadly, particularly in the case of mental illness and chronic disease (e.g., in some ways, aging at a certain point could be viewed as an illness). Currently, the most widely cited definition of health is the one posited by the World Health Organization that, if implemented, might invite the tyranny that concerns Banta. According to this definition, health is a "state of complete physical, mental and social well-being and not merely the absence of disease or infirmity." When one takes into consideration the perceptual (e.g., what is "pain") and social (e.g., what is "disability") factors involved in the determination of what constitutes health and disease, there is almost no limit to the scope of health care.

A new issue has been raised by the quantification of health status indices, incorporating social as well as biological factors, which would seem to require some decision about composite cutoff points to designate a threshold of health. The activism of one's orientation then would determine where one would make the cut.

Related to the activism-passivism continuum on which health, and thus health care, can be conceived is the differentiation between personal health and public health services. This distinction is more marked in the United States than in other countries, but it is ubiquitous. Briefly, the public health perspective evisions health in terms of populations or groups, whereas, in the extreme, personal health services are delivered in a mythically unique doctor (or presumably some other health professional)–patient relationship. This distinction is shaded in particular instances (e.g., family practitioners attempt to view their patients in the context of the patients' families and communities, and the public health service does deliver health care to individuals), but it exists in reality and motivates profound differences in attitudes toward policy. For example, the American Public Health Association has traditionally supported comprehensive universal and publicly administered national health insurance programs in opposition to representatives of the personal health care sector, such as the American Medical Association and, to a lesser extent, the American Hospital Association.

Generally speaking, those with a public health orientation also tend to take a relatively more active stance on sumptuary policies such as those relating to tobacco and alcohol. With some reservations, one could say that when the inevitable clashes between individual liberty and perceived public good occur, the public health persuasion tends to emphasize the latter.

Health and health care obviously are portmanteau terms, as illustrated by the foregoing catalogue of conceptions. They all are within the ambit of health policy analysis and often underlie scholarly and public debate—for example, whether the "health" care of the elderly is becoming "overmedicalized." This point will be elaborated in a later section on the evolution of U.S. health policy.

IV. THE DISTINCTIVENESS OF HEALTH POLICY: HEALTH POLICY ANALYSIS AS AN AREA STUDY

The division of labor in compiling this encyclopedia rests on the assumption that there is some utility in categorizing policy studies by subject matter area, institutions, and actors with which they are chiefly concerned. Health policy formation and implementation excite a number of interrelated issues involving principal actors and institutions that warrant differentiating it from other area studies if only because of pedagogical and information management considerations.

The major issues in health policy to some extent coincide with those that form the basis of traditional ideological divisions regarding the allocation, regulation, and distribution of resources, but they can be isolated for analytic purposes and, in fact, are often contested by advocates whose socioeconomic political and "health" positions might appear inconsistent or, at least, multidimensional. For example, a prototypical conservative (classic liberal), who would normally oppose government intervention in the private sector, nevertheless might hold that market aberrations in the delivery of health services justify an unusual degree of public regulation in this area. The issues overlap with themselves as well as with general questions regarding individual liberty versus social welfare and equality of opportunity versus equilitarianism. Their relationship with such broader questions need only be remarked once the issues are explicated. The prototypical health issues are characterized by differential emphases on:

1. Public versus personal health services
2. Health versus medical care
3. Prevention versus cure
4. Social versus individual responsibility for health

If there is anything approaching a left-right continuum in health policy, the above contrasting positions would probably form the chief components and would be, for the most part, properly arrayed. As mentioned previously, at one pole would be the advocates of close regulation of "demerit" goods such as tobacco, alcohol, and inappropriately used drugs; promotion of health education; less reliance on medical care and more attention to such factors in health as environmental hazards and housing. At the opposite end of the continuum would be arguments with a ring familiar to students of other policy areas—that is, an equation of "need" with "demand" and, in general, the view that government should treat most health services as it should any other good that can be divisibly consumed. In between these extremes, scaleability would be frustrated by the same variations in salience and inherent noncardinality that characterize other social, psychological, economic, and political policy cleavage patterns. For example, it is tenable that proponents of seat belt requirements might oppose increases in taxes on the sale of manufactured tobacco products because of perceptions about the price or income elasticity of cigarette consumption or sentiments against regressive taxation. Or, self-interest aside, proponents of a compulsory universal and comprehensive national health insurance might take issue with attempts to increase the supply of physicians on the grounds that the latter would unduly generate demand, whereas the former would meet demand with existing resources and, through the concentration of financing, enable effective cost containment. In short, issues in the health policy arena, no less than in others, are multidimensional. As Converse (1964) observed some time ago of left-right "belief systems" in general, positions on health policy tend to cluster more among the "elite" than the "mass public." In health policy, even among those who are most constrained ideologically, there likely are strong crosscurrents of opinion. Systematic explanations of these attitudinal questions has scarcely begun.

With regard to process variables, there obviously also are institutional actors distinctive to the health field—the four health subcommittees of Congress, for example, or health agencies of the Department of Health and Human Services. In addition, there are myriad interest groups with an overriding interest in health policy—such as the American Medical Association, the American Hospital Association, the Federation of American Hospitals (representing proprietary hospitals), the American Health Care Association (representing proprietary nursing homes), the American Nursing Association, the National League for Nursing—that can be expected to exert influence on all major issues. However, this is a relatively trivial distinction because, as was the case with major issues, the same could be said for any policy area. In fact, focusing health policy analysis on characteristics of such institutions because they are putatively health policy centered might obscure generalizations about administrative behavior.

In short, health policy studies are open to the same criticisms as those leveled against area studies in comparative politics.

Area studies have been defended in this regard on the basis of the special knowledge that accrues from an intensive interdisciplinary understanding of a country or region. The same grounds could be used to justify health policy analysis if a lietmotiv for health policy can be demonstrated. One may be found in that, until recently, health policy has been unique in defying the liberal democratic tradition that has been the mainstream of development for other types of policies. The specific form this has taken has been the appropriation of the authority of the state to sanction medical, professional dominance, and autonomy. It is true that the presence of disproportionate power relations characterizes political struggles in all policy areas. Nevertheless, the degree to which this is the case in the health field and the fact that it has been explicit marks a deviation from the norm. Granted that this is a distinctive trait, does it justify a policy area approach? Not logically, because, in fact, it is a trans-area perspective that highlights it. However, taking a trans-area policy approach toward health without the intensified focus might not let us see that what we have termed professional dominance is a significant aberration that touches the roots of democracy in the United States.

V. THE U.S. HEALTH SYSTEM IN CROSS-NATIONAL PERSPECTIVE: COST, ACCESS, QUALITY

Health policy analysis has caught up with, perhaps even surpassed, other areas of policy analysis in regard to the development of a literature with an international perspective. There are, of course, conceptual, methodological reasons for this development but it also is due, in part, to the recognition that other countries with attitudes toward health and levels of economic development that are similar to the United States have greatly expanded access to health services and have done so at bearable cost. In fact, a cross-national perspective suggests that universal access may very well be a prerequisite for cost control.

In addition to improving access to health services and controlling their cost, countries also strive to maintain an acceptable level of *quality* of care. The latter is the most elusive of the aforementioned goals to define and measure, so the reasonably systematic literature on comparative health policy is all but silent on the subject. Nevertheless, there are bits and pieces of evidence that bear on comparative levels of quality. This evidence will be examined after a consideration of the Janus goals of improved access and controlled cost.

The discussion of access will be restricted to financial barriers to receipt of services. Admittedly, all countries face other limitations to access, particularly with respect to supply of services. For example, constrictions on the supply of high-technology services in Canada and the United Kingdom mean that there are queues for these services (Enthoven, 1991; Maylor, 1991). And, the financial implications of these barriers to access are not trivial given the opportunity costs of time or, in some cases, the direct costs of jumping the queues.

The geographical distribution of services also affects access, and some countries, such as Sweden, are more highly regionalized, or planned, than others; e.g., one large tertiary care hospital per defined geographical area fed with referrals by several smaller hospitals that in turn are fed by polyclinics. The geographical distribution of health care facilities and personnel has not been the subject of much comparative research, probably because comparative maldistribution is so closely tied to comparative population density and, therefore, is largely intractable. Suffice it to say that the distribution problem is perceived to be ubiquitous but, as one would expect, it is a particularly pressing concern in geographically large countries such as Canada and the United States.

A. Access and Cost

It has become commonplace to refer to the United States as the only developed, industrialized nation, except for South Africa, that does not have a national health insurance (NHI) program (the term should be "government-mandated" health insurance program, since not all countries' universal programs are "national," but here we defer to convention and use NHI). The United States does have both government-provided and government-financed health services, but they do not combine to form a purposeful, integrated program. Examples of health service *provided* by the U.S. government are those of the Veterans Administration and Indian Health Service. Government *financed* services include Medicare, Medicaid, the Civilian Hospital and Medical Services Administration for the Uniform Services, and a growing number of state-sponsored health insurance plans. Further, and less widely recognized, the government sponsors the purchase of employer-provided health insurance through tax exemptions, referred to as "tax expenditures," the revenue that governments forego by not taxing otherwise "normal" areas of taxation (Falcone and Warren, 1988).

Still, as Table 1 indicates, in regard to the proportion of health expenditures that are public and the percentage of the population covered by government health programs, the United States is by far the lowest among the "Big Seven" Organization for Economic Cooperation and Development (OECD) nations; i.e., those with the largest gross domestic products (GDPs). Adding in tax expenditures raises the U.S. public expenditure function (government health expenditure/GDP) somewhat, perhaps by as much as 5%, but not nearly enough to approach the corresponding figure for the next lowest country, Japan (72%).

In interpreting public expenditures as public involvement, at least two qualifications are in order. First, many U.S. expenditures are public in the sense they are made through the collective action represented by government-regulated insurance companies. The OECD definition refers only to expenses directly incurred by governments. That is why analysts of these countries' expenditures on health use "reprivatization" to refer to the 1980 to 1990 decline

Table 1. Health Expenditures in "Big-Seven" Organization for Economic Cooperation and Development (OECD) Nations

Country	Total health expenditure as percent of gross domestic product: 1990 (%)	Per capita health expenditure: 1990 ($)	Public health expenditures as percent of total health expenditures: 1990 (%)	Percentage of public covered: 1987		Compound growth of health expenditure rate as percent of gross domestic product 1980–1990
				Inpatient	Outpatient	
Canada	9.3	1770	73	100.0	100.0	2.3
France	8.8	1532	74	98.0	99.0	1.6
Germany	8.1	1486	73	92.2	92.0	−0.4
Italy	7.7	1236	76	100.0	100.0	1.2
Japan	6.5	1171	72	100.0	100.0	0.1
United Kingdom	6.2	972	84	100.0	100.0	0.7
United States	12.1	2566	42	43.0	43.0	2.7

Currencies are measured in purchasing power parities.

Sources: Excerpted from Tables 1 and 2 in Schieber et al. (1992) and OECD (1990).

in the proportions of expenditures that are public in Canada, France, Germany, Italy, and the United Kingdom even though the percentage of the population covered in these countries has not changed. Second, private enterprises in the U.S. health industry—e.g., voluntary not-for-profit and for-profit hospitals, physician practices—are beleaguered by government regulations, perhaps even more so than are institutions and actors in the British National Health Service (Leichter, 1992).

And this is not to be entirely unexpected: Without a directive policy about what institutions and actors should do in a state committed to assurance of equality of opportunity (see below), there must be numerous sanctions on what governments perceive to be untoward behavior. These sanctions give raise to a byzantine array of administration interactions that may add as much as $100 billion annually to overall U.S. direct expenditures on health services, both public and private.

In addition to generating administrative costs (Barer and Evans, 1992; Evans, 1990; Woolhandler and Himmelstein, 1991), the absence of a government-mandated health insurance program in the United States leaves from 35 to 40 million Americans, mostly working persons or their dependents, uninsured at some time during the year. This compromise in access, unmatched by other Big Seven nations, is dynamically interrelated to the high levels of U.S. expenditure on health care: Health insurance becomes unaffordable to employers and employees because uncompensated care is relatively expensive; e.g., emergency room versus physician's office services as a site for primary care.

Partly as a consequence of its asystemic approach to health services financing and delivery, the United States spends far more on health care, measured in purchasing power parties, than any other nation (see Table 1). This observation holds whether one examines expenditures as a percentage of GDP or per capita: Either way, the U.S. "lead" is considerable. To dramatize the fact that the U.S. case is an "outlier," Figure 1 displays the well-known positive linear relationship between per capita health spending and per capita GDP for 24 OECD countries. The goodness of fit overall is remarkable; the United States clearly is a deviant case. The fact of the deviance is of less concern than its extent: The nearest country to the United States in regard to health expenditures as a percent of GDP, Canada, is almost 3 percentage points behind the United States.

The reason for the deviance cannot be found in any obvious indicator of Americans' exceptional need or demand for medical care. The United States has the smallest proportion of population who are elderly (65 years of age or older), about 0.12, of the OECD Big Seven (Schieber et al., 1992) and, in all countries, the elderly consume medical services at three times the rate of the nonelderly. Further, as is obvious from the data in Table 2, the average number of annual physician visits or hospital days per person in the United States are not abnormally high; in fact, they are relatively low. And, based on cross-national comparisons of gross lifestyle measures such as per capita alcohol and tobacco consumption, it does not appear that Americans lead unusually threatening lives (U.S. Department of Commerce, Bureau of The Census, Tables Nos. 1451 and 1452, 1991), so one would not expect them to be unusually high users of health services.

Why, then, the U.S. deviance in health care expenditures? Answers to this question have focused on a number of interrelated factors (Rice, 1992), including (1) U.S. investment in "flat of the curve medical technology" (i.e., the use of services whose marginal benefit is very small in relation to their marginal cost); (2) a tort system that fosters litigation and, hence, expensive defensive medicine; (3) fee-for-service medicine that encourages overutilization; and (4) multiple payers for services so that there is not one or only a few funders who bear

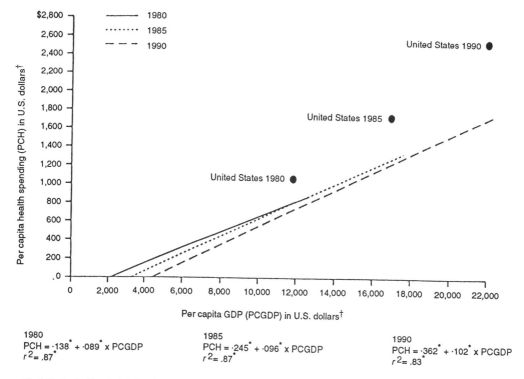

1980
$$PCH = \cdot138^* + \cdot089^* \times PCGDP$$
$$r^2 = .87^*$$

1985
$$PCH = \cdot245^* + \cdot096^* \times PCGDP$$
$$r^2 = .87^*$$

1990
$$PCH = \cdot362^* + \cdot102^* \times PCGDP$$
$$r^2 = .83^*$$

*Statistically significant at .01 level.
†Calculated in purchasing power parities.
NOTE: GDP is gross domestic product.
SOURCE: Tables 1, 28, 33, and 36 of the Appendix to Schieber, Poulier and Greenwald (1992).

Figure 1. Per capita health spending and per capita GDP for the United States and other Organization for Economic Cooperation and Development countries: 1980, 1985, and 1990.

Table 2. Use of Physician and Hospital Services in Big Seven OECD Countries: 1988

Country	Physician contacts per capita	Inpatient days per capita
Canada	6.6	2.0
France	7.1	3.0
Germany	11.5	3.5
Italy	11.0	1.9
Japan	12.9	4.1
United Kingdom	4.5 (1986)	2.0
United States	5.3	1.3

Source: Excerpted from Exhibits 4 and 5 in Schieber et al. (1991).

the brunt of expenditures. Let us examine these explanations for the U.S. health expenditure performance in turn to see how well they hold up in comparative perspective.

The first explanation is entirely plausible. With the exception of extracorporeal shock wave lithotripsy units, with which Germany is most generously supplied, the United States has far more high-technology services—magnetic resonance imagers, open-heart surgery, cardiac catheterization, organ transplantation, and radiation therapy units—than any of the other Big Seven countries (Jonsson, 1990; Roublee, 1989). And, it is plausible, albeit not empirically demonstrated, that supply of these services causes demand and that utilization, in the aggregate, does not markedly affect health outcomes, most commonly measured in the form of life expectancy/mortality rates. (Of course, there are other, far less frequently measured outcomes, such as disability, anxiety reduction, comparative invasiveness and discomfort of procedures, that may be affected by ready availability of state of the art technologies.) There is little doubt that these technologies often are inefficiently distributed because hospitals compete for patients, hence physicians, not on the basis of price (except, perhaps, where managed care plans have heavy market penetration), but on the basis of the availability of income-generating/labor-saving technologies (Farley, 1985; Hadley and Swartz, 1989; Robinson and Luft, 1987).

We will take up these incentives below in discussing explanation 4 (multiple payers for services). First, let us dispense with explanations 2 (malpractice) and 3 (fee-for-service). The extent to which medical malpractice is used as a means of redress of grievance in the United States far surpasses that in any other country, for a number of interrelated reasons, among them: American litigiousness generally; relatively open citizen access to court hearings in the United States; the fact that compensatory damages can be relatively high, since, unlike the other Big Seven countries, the United States does not provide its citizens comprehensive health insurance at no cost at the point of purchase; and, some would say, the widespread use of contingency fees by U.S. attorneys. Whatever the case, malpractice claims are a trivial proportion of health care costs. However, the defensive medicine that malpractice induces does carry significant, albeit unknown, costs (Lewin-VHI, 1993). It is problematic whether defensive medicine is necessary, since most malpractice involves acts of commission rather than omission, but it does not matter: Defensive medicine either (or both) (1) is perceived to be necessary (Lawthers et al., 1992) or (2) offers a justification for practicing medicine in a way physicians prefer. Consequently, tort reform is on several state agendas (Bovberg, 1991). It is generally acknowledged, nevertheless, that tort reform will hardly solve the expenditure inflation problem.

With regard to the prevalence of fee-for-service medicine, there are at least two reasons why this practice cannot explain comparatively high U.S. expenditures. First, the prevalence is declining while medical care relative expenditure inflation (the amount by which the rate of increase in the medical care price index exceeds that of the consumer price index) is not. Second, fee-for-service hardly is uniquely American, whereas having the highest level of health care spending patently is.

Turning to a more plausible, if somewhat flawed, explanation for U.S. health care expenditure performance, multiple sources of funding, we encounter the "concentrated interest hypothesis," (which albeit perhaps sometimes tacit) has led to fascination with single-payer plans for government health insurance (Falcone, 1992). With some oversimplification, the hypothesis can be stated briefly as follows. If the effects of a program's costs are concentrated and the effects of its benefits are diffused, then the pain of the costs will be more acutely felt by major political actors than the pleasure of the benefits. If a program's benefits are concentrated, as they are on providers under fee-for-service reimbursement, and the program's costs are diffuse—say among governments and private insurers—there will be a more intense political force for expansion of benefits than for curtailing costs. (Obviously, the fee-for-service variable that was discounted above as an explanatory *single* factor does come into play when *combined* with the multiple-sources-of-funding variable.)

Regarding national health care systems, the extreme case of cost concentration is the British National Health Service wherein the overwhelming majority of the direct costs of providing care (i.e., excluding opportunity costs such as the lack of productivity incurred because of queues for elective surgery) are the responsibility of the national government. In each budget cycle, health programs compete for limited public funding with other categories of expenditure such as education, highways, and defense. The benefits, however, basic health services with no fees at the point of service delivery, are spread across a large unorganized population. Providers in the United Kingdom do not directly benefit from demand; in fact, they lose in terms of time and effort expended, since general practitioners are paid on the basis of the numbers of patients in their "panels" rather than per service, and specialist ("consultants") are salaried. Of course, there is a growing, but still small, fee-for-service reimbursed sphere of private practice.

On the other hand, in the United States, where there are multiple sources of funding, often referred to as "pluralistic" funding, the impact of costs is spread among payers, whereas the predominantly fee-for-service reimbursed providers derive large marginal benefit from each unit of utilization. In Canada, fee-for-service reimbursement for physicians prevails and, therefore, the marginal benefit to providers and consumers of utilization of any and all services resembles that of the U.S. system. But, in each Canadian province, virtually all the marginal costs are incurred by a central source: the treasury (Barer and Evans, 1992). Most empirical analyses of the concentration of interest hypothesis have examined the above continuum and, as is well-known by now, health care costs in the countries mentioned, measured in terms of purchasing power parities, either as percent of GDP or per capita, are highest in the United Kingdom, lowest in the United States, with Canada in between and closer to the United States (see Table 1).

The concentration of interest hypothesis seems to make sense, not only in cross-national perspective (Culyer, 1990) but also on examination of trends in U.S. government health programs (Marmor et al., 1976). In this country, the most imposing budget-restraining efforts have been exercised by Medicare. The program's costs are concentrated in the Health Care Financing Administration (HCFA) and a small (albeit rapidly growing) number of older adults. Medicare has applied prospective capitated budgeting to hospital expenditures and is extending the method to physician reimbursement. Attempts to expand benefits, e.g., via "catastrophic" coverage legislated in the late 1980s, were daunted by the bearers of the attendant costs, older Americans, once this relatively narrow and politically powerful group became aware of the price tag.

As was mentioned and will be further discussed in looking at U.S. trends, policy proposals in the United States have relied on the validity of the concentration of interest hypothesis. However, as is the case with many intuitively appealing hypotheses based on examples, this one is flawed. For one thing, the cost experience of prepaid plans in the United States is not consonant with the hypothesis (Miller and Luft, 1993). Of course, this may be because, in most plans, providers are not at risk financially and, therefore, the concentration of interest does not take effect.

But the hypothesis also fails where it started—in the international arena. Two examples should be sufficient to make this point. First, Germany and Japan have comparatively low health care expenditure levels—Japan's is the lowest among all OECD member nations—and they have multiple sources of funding. Japan also has fee-for-service medicine, unsafe lifestyles, very highly paid physicians, most of whom are specialists, and very high physician and hospital utilization rates. Second, returning closer to home, despite the fact that each of Canada's provincial health insurance plans is funded by a fixed, global operating budget, that country is second only to the United States in health care spending, even if it still is far behind.

In short, monopsony, concentrated interest in budget control, a single-payer, is neither a necessary nor a sufficient condition for cost containment. Rather concentrated interest fortifies *public will* to control costs. This political will is more and more evident in the United States as large employers are assuming, via hospital cost-shifting, more of the burden of underfinanced (Medicaid) and uncompensated care. The question remains as to whether distinctively U.S. political structures and processes, which were built on and have sustained purposive irresponsibility, can be adapted so that the political will can be effectively expressed. This point will be elaborated in the historical perspective section.

B. Quality of Care

In Donabedian's (1980) now classic construct, quality can be measured in terms of inputs, structures/processes, or outcomes. Inputs refer to resources used in the health production function; e.g., personnel, physical plant, and equipment. Structures/processes are how the inputs are combined to produce health; e.g., for hospitals, whether they regularly and diligently monitor patient care. Of course, by their very definition, the quality of inputs and structures/processes cannot be accurately determined until one has a measure of the quality of what is being produced. As noted at the outset of this chapter, there is hardly consensus on what health is. Even when there is agreement in what health is *not*, e.g., infant mortality figures, there are formidable measurement problems (Liu et al., 1992). Still it may be instructive to look at U.S. performance on two generally used indicators, age-specific mortality rates and life expentancy, and one set of attitudinal variables, citizens' satisfaction with the health care system.

The mortality and life expectancy data are displayed in Table 3. Reminded that none of these indicators is an unambiguous measure of quality, it nevertheless is noticeable that the United States certainly does not clearly excel on any. By a slight margin the United States leads in life expectancy at age 80 for both men and women. This could be due to our relative willingness to invest heavily in life-sustaining measures at later stages of life or to an inherent survivability of persons who did not succumb to infant mortality in a nation where the probability of doing so was comparatively high. U.S. infant mortality is still high, as the ranking in Table 3 indicates, but it has come down markedly in recent years. Admittedly, infant mortality is subject to multiple causes, many of which are beyond the immediate control of public or personal health care delivery modes. But, again, the point here is not that the United States does not match up with other developed countries on outcome indicators but rather that this country is not demonstrably better off for all it spends.

Nor does it appear that high spending produces satisfaction with the system. The Blendon et al. (1990) data presented in Table 4, which indicate that U.S. public opinion favors major reform of the health system, are consistent with those derived in other surveys conducted since 1988 (Blendon et al., 1991; Blendon and Taylor, 1989). Of course, public opinion about health services is not a definitive measure of their quality, particularly based on results of the Blendon et al. questionnaire that asks respondents about their views of the "health care system." However, the extent of the disaffection evinced by respondents in repeated

Table 3. Infant Mortality Rate and Life Expectancy at Selected Ages, Big Seven OECD Nations: 1989

	Life expectancy at						
	birth		age 60		age 80		Infant mortality
Country	female	male	female	male	female	male	
Canada	79.7(1986)	73.0	23.2	18.4	8.9	6.9	.71
France	80.6	72.5	24.0	18.8	8.4(1987)	6.8(1988)	.75
Germany	79.0	72.6	22.2	17.8	7.6(1987)	6.1(1987)	.75
Italy	80.0	73.5	22.9	18.3	8.0	6.4	.86
Japan	81.8	75.9	24.3	20.0	8.7	6.9	.46
United Kingdom	78.4	72.8	21.7	17.4	8.2	6.2	.79
United States	78.6	71.8	22.7	18.6	9.0	7.1	.91

Source: Computed from tables in OECD (1990).

surveys does call into question the appropriateness of existing U.S. arrangements for financing and organizing health services delivery. In the ensuing sections, we examine how those arrangements developed and what might be done to alter them.

VI. THE HISTORY OF U.S. HEALTH POLICY: AN OVERVIEW

The evolution of health policy in the United States can be divided into three stages. Vestiges of the past and primordia of the future are evident in each, but the developments seem to follow an historical pattern that has parelleled the relative dominance of classic versus social or reform liberalism in U.S. political culture. In fact, with a tolerable degree of over-simplification, milestones in health policy (Flock and Sanazaro, 1973; Littman, 1991) can be seen as "caused" by different shades of emphasis in the liberal tradition (Jaeger, 1974). This is not to say that the underlying factors in the shaping of health policy were not primarily economic or episodic—no one would discount the effects of the Depression, for example—only that

Table 4. The Public's View of Their Health Care System in Big Seven OECD: 1990

	Minor changes needed[a] (%)	Fundamental changes needed[b] (%)	Completely rebuild system[c] (%)
Canada	56	38	5
France	41	42	10
West Germany	41	35	13
Italy	12	46	40
Japan	29	47	6
United Kingdom	27	52	17
United States	10	60	29

On the survey, the question was worded as follows: [a]"On the whole, the health care system works pretty well, and only minor changes are necessary to make it work better"; [b]"There are some good things in our health care system, but fundamental changes are needed to make it work better"; [c]"Our health care system has so much wrong with it that we need to completely rebuild it."
Source: Harvard-Harris-ITF, 1990 Ten-Nation Survey. Adapted from Blendon et al. (1990).

the justification for them has been couched in rubrics drawn from two major strains in liberalism: one that stresses the policy goal of equality of opportunity versus another that pursues absolute equalitarianism.

The three stages, the last of which is still emerging and may be regarded as a synthesis of (or compromise between) the first two, can be delineated according to the prevailing societal conception of health in each; that is, whether health care is viewed as (1) a public good, (2) a basic right, or (3) a limited resource. The latter can be further divided into a period wherein allocation of the limited resource was attempted by planning and one wherein allocation ostensibly is being sought through management and control (Anderson, 1991).

A. Health Care as a Public Good

This is not the place, and it is probably unnecessary, to outline the construct of a public good. In the context of this discussion, suffice it to say that from the late 19th century until the Great Depression, the dominant view was that society at large derived a collective benefit from the provision of a minimum level of health care to all, that it was in each individual's best interest for government to impose a measure of health care on everyone. As Jaeger (1974) has put it, the primary basis for early U.S. health policy was "economic protectionism." Therefore, quarantine policy was enforced because of the severe economic consequences stemming from the spread of communicable diseases, a threat exacerbated by the urbanization accompanying the Industrial Revolution. Similarly, marine hospitals were established to limit the potential harm to the community from the disease-carrying, often homeless derelicts who plied the sea trade on which the United States was heavily dependent. Later, in a decidedly more positive vein, the Progressives argued that our industry, productivity, and national security were undermined by illness, absenteeism, and disability and that these losses were unnecessarily left largely to chance. Variations on this theme were echoed by Franklin Roosevelt (Office of the Federal Register, 1939), Harry Truman (President's Commission on the Health Needs of the Nation, 1952), and Dwight Eisenhower (Office of the Federal Register, 1960) among others.

At first, even some of the most limited, essentially negative or defensive policies were criticized by extreme market determinists such as Herbert Spencer; for example, public provision of care for the insane was not consonant with "social Darwinism" (Girvetz, 1950, cited in Jaeger, 1974). Although this stance was not necessarily characteristic of the dlimate of opinion about health policy (or any other type of policy, for that matter) during the late 19th century, it was sufficiently legitimate to be the explicit basis for President Pierce's veto of a bill authorizing federal land grants for mental hospitals (Richardson, 1897, cited in Jaeger, 1974).

Coupled with economic protectionism in the development of U.S. policy, but certainly not as important and less distinctive to this country, has been a limited paternalism, as reflected in Herbert Hoover's contention that social and health insurance should rest on the notion "that the responsibility of the people as a whole is to provide only a reasonable subsistence . . . and not destroy private institutions and efforts" (Hoover, 1946, cited in Jaeger, 1974). It is safe to say that paternalism never has been as pronounced in the United States as has been the poor-law mentality in the United Kingdom. However, it was a necessary concession to the decline of philanthropy and to the emergence of reform liberalism with a stress on derived as well as natural rights. The U.S. compromise resulting from the tension between classic liberalism's focus on the preservation of individual autonomy and the expression of free choice and reform liberalism's (including pragmatism's) emphasis on the need to alter social conditions so as to lessen the impact of adversity was the view that the state could take steps to encourage equality of opportunity; that is, to provide individuals the chance to manifest their inherent or acquired inequalities.

Partly as a result of the prevalence of this view, relative to other nations, the assumption of governmental responsibility for the provision of health services in the United States has lagged behind public education but, in some respects, has outpaced more direct welfare measures (Heidenheimer, 1973). The first policies of this type were targeted at the blind and disabled, the elderly poor, needy mothers and children, and crippled children.

B. The Right to Health

Gradually the legitimacy of government activity to ameliorate misfortune that was largely beyond the control of the afflicted began to be expanded to include a duty to provide—or ensure the provision—of health care because of individuals' social "right to health." This notion has not been embodied in policy, but it has been mentioned in the rhetoric supporting authoritative proposals dating at least as far back as a 1929 address by Franklin Roosevelt. In 1944, this right became a keystone of national policy—FDR's "second Bill of Rights." It was enunciated in his State of the Union message (*Congressional Record*, 1944, cited in Jaeger, 1974) as:

> regardless of station, race or creed. . . . The right to adequate medical care and the opportunity to achieve and enjoy good health; The right to adequate protection from the economic fears of old age, sickness, unemployment. . . .

Jaeger (1974) notes that by 1952 this statement of rights had been expanded by a presidential commission "to include more than just freedom from disease, pain and untimely death, for health now was interpreted to mean 'optional physical, mental and social efficiency and well-being.' "

The right to health has been reasserted by succeeding presidents and has become a rallying phrase in congressional debate on a variety of national health insurance proposals. It also was a force in the Office of Economic Opportunity Neighborhood Health Centers movement of the 1960s. However, as a rationale for policy, the right to health has been overshadowed somewhat by a preoccupation with cost control and by the perceived need to restructure the health care delivery system in order to achieve a higher overall marginal productivity of resources. In short, one could say that the focus now is on the optimum mentioned in the 1952 commission's statement, and that term is being used in its economic sense.

C. Health Care as a Limited Resource: Allocation by Planning and Regulation

The shift in emphasis from the right to health care can be attributed to trends outside the ideological mainstream highlighted in the foregoing discussion. Of course, even the most politically voluntaristic observer would concede that traditional ideological concerns fluctuate with varying economic circumstances or, at least, that the availability of resources is an enabling factor in the translation of proposals into policy. Another significant conditioning factor in the development of health (as well as other) policy has been the shifting power of the federal versus subnational governments which, in turn, has been the result of cataclysmic environmental changes such as those surrounding World War II and the Great Depression. The former gave rise to titles dealing with health in the Social Security Act, which has been the framework for subsequent redistributive policy such as Titles XVIII (Medicare), XIX (Medicaid), and XX (special services). Although it was not the first legislation to do so, the Social Security Act used the conditional grant to obviate possible constitutional impediments. By 1937, the Supreme Court acknowledged that federal spending power sanctioned this device.

Some portray the New Deal as the thin edge of the wedge in government intrusion into the personal health services sector. Others point in this regard to what was first seen as a more benign conditional grant program to encourage "planned" hospital construction and renovation—the Hill-Burton Act of 1946. The Act was an amendment to the Public Health Service Act, as have been other major manpower and planning acts. Hill-Burton was part of the federal program that used "displaced" wartime expenditures in an attempt to revive the hospital industry and reduce the geographical maldistribution of services. In part, the Act accomplished this, but it also established (what now seem to be) limited controls (e.g., the requirement that a recipient hospital render a given portion of free care) and legitimized large-scale government activity at the core of the health system.

By the late 1970s, the government's role, particularly that of the federal government, had expanded greatly (some would say hypertrophically). In 1965, 25% of all national health expenditures were public; the corresponding figure for 1980 was 41.1%, which, as we have seen, is about today's level. Of all public expenditures, approximately 70% were made by the federal government in 1990 (Congressional Budget Office, 1992) versus 52% in 1965 (Freeland et al., 1980), and not only had programs covering specific segments of the population grown in number and scope, the numbers of beneficiaries had increased and health costs had spiraled. This made the health care industry oligopsonistic at least, and some components (e.g., nursing homes) in most states are near monopsonies. As suggested by cross-national comparisons, as well as by common sense, this concentration of resources resulted in a sharpened, if somewhat ineffectual, cost consciousness (Culyer, 1990; Leu, 1986). The concentration has been heightened by the federalization of financing and, because a significant proportion of state and local expenditures are federally stimulated (e.g., Medicaid and Title XX are conditional grant programs), the effect has perhaps been even more marked than the intergovernmental shift in expenditures would lead one to expect.

Cost consciousness during the 1970s was expressed at the federal level in the form of what has been termed, some would say euphemistically, planning policy. Initially, "representative" advisory agencies (comprehensive health planning agencies) were formed at the state and local levels to review the purchase of facilities and equipment and new construction. Probably the summary verdict on the effectiveness of these agencies in restraining "unneeded" expansion of the health services delivery network would be that they failed from a process evaluation perspective in providing effective consumer representation and, with respect to outputs, they did not really prevent an unnecessary proliferation of services (Altman, 1978).

To correct these deficiencies, health systems agencies (HSAs) were set up under the legislative authority of Public Law 93-641 with more specific representation mandates and more substantial enforcement powers over resource allocation decisions. Criticism of the functioning of CHPs and HSAs (along with agencies such as Professional Standards Review Organizations [PSROs], which were charged with, in effect, cost-benefit review of health professionals' decisions) centered on the fact that (although this might not have been the way the indictments were explicitly phrased) these agencies were making regulations in lieu of policy. The combined activities of these agencies have been described as constituting a patchwork quilt of regulatory decisions that did not add up to a basic framework for resource allocation. This caused some influential policy actors to look to national health insurance as a mechanism for regulating resource allocations and delivery modes; thus, vindicating the claims of the medical establishment that government financing implies government control.

The emphasis on "rationalization" of the allocation of health resources—reorganization; substitution of paramedical personnel for physicians, ambulatory for inpatient care, family practice for specialist and subspecialist care; shared services versus pure competition among hospitals; an emphasis on prevention or, at least, palliation versus curative strategies; foreshortened versus prolonged, heroic treatment of the terminally ill—was not solely the result of more starkly visible economic factors, although in specific instances (e.g., euthanasia), financial constraints have been viewed as the prime motivating factors behind the new emphasis in health policy (Slaby and Tancredi, 1977). Rather the shrinking of resources has been accompanied by demonstrations that the benefit-to-cost ratios of some medical care modalities are not particularly impressive, especially in the case of technologically advanced care with frequently undesirable side effects (Cochrane, 1972; Thorpe, 1992) or with no positive effect on quality of life (Riley et al., 1986; Scitovsky, 1984). The fact that accelerated expenditures have been accompanied by virtually constant (or time linear) morbidity and mortality rates has engendered suspicion or cynicism about the efficacy of medical care.

When these doubts were combined with an increasing sensitivity to iatrogenesis (treatment-induced illness), the result was a general attitude downplaying the supervening efficacy of medical services in health (David, 1990; Feldstein, 1992; Phelps, 1992); and, at the extreme, an anti-interventionist stance that regarded therapeutic modalities as not only ineffective but despiritualizing or dependency inducing. The seminal works expressing this view predated modern supertechnology (Beard, 1936; Dubos, 1959), but their vogue was enhanced by popularist authors such as Illich (1976). The "antimedicalists" are a decided minority among health care activists (if that is an appropriate term in this particular instance), but they have had a leavening influence on expectations about the susceptibility to medical care of leading causes of mortality, morbidity, and disability or quality of life.

The rising costs and dampened expectations about the efficacy of health care have diminished the force of the right-to-health movement, if only because it is difficult to posit that one has a right to something that often is beyond human control, and because it is clear that, even if it were feasible, government assurance of a right to health care would preclude public attention to other priorities. In the wake of this realization, there have been several attempts to avert a tempting nihilism. One such attempt has been health promotion. An institutionalization of the promotion strategy that has been the object of unusually favorable federal attention in a period of restricted budgets has been the health maintenance organization (HMO) (Miller and Luft, 1993). This model can be seen as an effort on the part of decision makers to avoid a trade-off between cost and quality because it promises an optimum by making it economically advantageous for these providers (thus, their salaried physicians) to forego hospitalizing their patients whenever possible. Because HMO enrollees prepay a fixed sum for the entire spectrum of health services, it also is in the institution's best interest to prevent catastrophic illness among its patient population, thus fending off the potential criticism that HMOs have built-in incentives toward undercare.

As appealing as the HMO or other models with similar incentive structures may be in concept, however, their ability to side step quality-cost trade-offs rests ultimately on the effectiveness of the type of health promotion they practice. Such effectiveness has not been demonstrated (Davies et al., 1986; Manning et al., 1984; Miller and Luft, 1993); therefore, implicit decisions about how much the existing demand or need for health care can be accommodated may have to be explicated, as uncomfortable as this may be in this patently vital policy-making area. If the experience of other countries is instructive, it seems that some kind of rationing of health care services must be resorted to if costs are to be contained (Schwartz and Mendelson, 1992).

D. Health Care as a Limited Resource: Allocation by Management and Control

Anderson (1990) has described the health policy orientation of the 1980s as one of "management and control." In light of the perceived ineffectiveness of policy *explicitly* focused on planning and regulation to achieve an expansion of access or cost containment, governments during this period have imposed even more dracionian controls on health services. The Health Planning and Resources Development Act was repealed in 1986 at the crest of a wave of federal measures that focused on competition, which was improperly construed as antithetical to planning. Capitation, for example, the hospital prospective payment system (PPS) with reimbursement based on diagnosis-related groups), was used to effect budget containment (often erroneously referred to as cost containment). The actual *costs* of PPS and other budget-protecting maneuvers were obscured as they were passed on from hospitals to third parties to major purchasers of insurance and, finally, to the insured. Physicians' fees were frozen by Medicare.

The rhetorical demise of "regulation" and its companion "planning" was reflected in the fact that course titles in graduate programs in health and public administration that formerly had included "planning" now replaced this designation with "management." These courses' clothes were in a new fashion but they clad the old contents. Planning had signaled optimal allocation of resources, within political as well as socioeconomic constraints, with publicly responsible direction. Competition sought to retain the aura of public responsibility—for example, recipients of government-subsidized services increasingly were termed "consumers"—but also attempted to obviate the need for a persistent, regulatory government presence. However, the planning "duck" survived and gradually policy analysts and policy makers are recognizing that competition and regulation and competition and planning are false dichotomies (Kinzer, 1988). "Planning" may have lost its allure but its necessity is increasingly being recognized, albeit in a new rubric (Brown, 1992).

As this book is going through the process of publication, we await the policy initiative of a president who clearly is committed to comprehensive health care reform. The general shape of the reform is entirely predictable on the basis of the review of trends presented in the chapter on health policy in the first edition of the *Encyclopedia of Policy Studies*; i.e., that optimization on three objectives—cost containment, access enhancement (with attendant requirements for availability of primary care services)—and high-quality (typically defined by health professionals as high technology) services—requires a pragmatic approach to issue resolution. The ideological flirtation with an attempt to establish monopolistic competition in health care during the Reagan administration turned into an attempt to cope with the results during the Bush administration. The decidedly pragmatic coping had to recognize that competition requires regulation (Kinzer, 1988, 1990). In the rhetoric of that recognition, the "R" word has taken on the euphemism "managed competition," a phrase that also is intended to obviate the need to use the term *rationing* in polite conversations about health policy imperatives (albeit the term is more and more common in discussions at the state level, particularly in the health policy bellweather state of Oregon).

Managed competition now represents a conceptual convergence of capitation, competition, and case management, "buzzwords" of the 1980s (Spitz and Abramson, 1987) that are juggled around reform proposals in the 1990s. Pitted against them now are terms such as *global budgeting*, and *single-payer system*, well-known in other countries such as Canada and Germany, that less subtly than *managed competition* connote the thrust of federal government policy. Again, that thrust is that health care is a limited resource, not totally unlike others, and, absent a price mechanism that we seem unlikely to invoke, must be subject to ersatz prices. The latter take the form of opportunity costs, such as relinquishing the freedom to choose how much medical care one can receive and, relatedly, from whom, or foregoing "moral hazard," the liberty that indemnity insurance allows to purchase services beyond the point where marginal cost equals marginal benefit (Pauly, 1978, 1988).

One predictable policy direction has been to focus responsibility on the states, or "devolution" as this maneuver traditionally is called in other political systems where subnational units retain some measure of discretion over health policy. Devolution has an ideological resonance for some anticentrists; it also has a management cachet: as productive firms some countries have become too large to be efficient. Whatever the justificatory rhetoric, devolution could be seen as an abdication of a national responsibility to provide a public good: hence, the emphasis the devolvers put on a "minimal benefits" package of health services that must be provided in order for devolvees to receive the devolver's funds. And there are enough federal funds to make the federal condition for receipt a mandate for their provision. So, in all likelihood, states will be given the opportunity to come up with means of providing a basic benefit package with considerable decision latitude as to *how* that provision is to be accomplished.

There already is considerable evidence about the variation in state policy that may ensue (U.S. Government Accounting Office, 1992). For conceptual clarity, we have organized the major policy options in terms of three "models" drawn from international comparisons, congressional proposals, and suggested incremental adjustments to the status quo. These models are outlined below, with no attempt to disguise our biases about their relative effectiveness in optimizing cost and access. The issue of quality, typically couched in terms of quantity (either in units or their aggregate price) by economists, cannot possibly be addressed without much more conceptual refinement and societal agreement. For present purposes, we assume an acceptable level of quality to be a constant.

VII. WHITHER?[1]

As pointed out at the beginning of this chapter, there seems to be a virtual consensus of opinion among policy analysts and major players in the health policy arena that the U.S. health industry is in disarray. Among the problems most resistant to incremental reform are inflationary pressures, the attendant growth in health insurance premiums, and distributional inequities in access to services. Recently, a chorus of voices has recommended national health insurance as a mechanism that promises to control spending and reduce inequities in access to care. But the proliferation of NHI proposals so complicates the process of rational choice that the voice of the chorus has been less than resonant. Not since the mid 1970s has the health policy window opened on such a broad landscape.

Here we present a synthetic review of the state of the debate concerning NHI, integrating previous studies in an evaluation of the basic features of three types of proposals for reducing distributional inequities and controlling inflationary pressures. On the basis of this review, a social insurance scheme resembling Canada's NHI program appears to be the optimal approach. This is not an earth-shattering observation. More unexpected, perhaps, is a tentative suggestion about why the social insurance approach has not been pursued; a suggestion based on a review of three interrelated explanations for stasis in U.S. health policy.

The first explanation is based on the putatively distinctive embrace by the United States of the tenets of classic liberalism such as individualism, freedom of choice, and antipathy toward government encroachment in what are regarded as properly private spheres of activity. The second explanation focuses on professional dominance in the health policy arena. Both the first and second explanations foster prescriptive incrementalism, or to borrow from Evans (1985), an "illusion of necessity."

A third explanation is that the United States' almost unique political structure, infused at the outset by laissez faire principles, is primarily responsible for the apparent direct effects of ideological constraints. In fact, however, it can be argued that ideological variables may only appear to affect policy because of their vestigial force now exerted through the structures these variables helped put in place. Still, the subscription to ideological determinism on the part of policy analysts may engender a self-fulfilling prophesy.

It is, therefore, understandable that certain political elites would want the illusion maintained. On the other hand, it is seemingly ironic that reform-oriented policy analysts would subscribe to the illusion. Although it would be overly heroic to assume that policy analysts' recognition of the illusion for what it is will further reforms, such a recognition may be a *necessary* condition for changing the conversation about limits of the possible in formulating and implementing an optimal NHI program. If the barrier to reform represented by the illusion is removed, analysts and activists can begin to work on the problem of how to achieve needed policy reform within the context of a constraining political structure.

The assessment of NHI proposals requires a clear definition of concepts and a specification of the forces that are likely to influence inflationary pressures in the U.S. health industry. The distinction between costs or expenses and expenditures is somewhat ambiguous, whereas, until recently, the pressures that influence spending on health care were not articulated with clarity. We now turn to these fundamental issues before presenting our taxonomy of NHI proposals.

A. Basic Definitions

For present purposes, the term *expenditure* refers to the actual or anticipated payments from patients or private and public insurers to providers of care. Conversely, the term *operating cost* (or *expense*) refers to the monetary value of labor supplies and other items that are used to provide direct patient care and, in the case of hospitals, general support services. Our evaluation of NHI proposals also will consider the costs of performing administrative functions and acquiring capital in the health industry.

The problem of controlling costs and expenditures is confounded by essentially three sets of pressures. First, as Evans (1991) argues, expenditures simultaneously represent the dominant source of patient revenue to hospitals and physicians, whereas costs constitute the source of income to those who supply resources to the health industry. Accordingly, providers and suppliers of resources are motivated to stimulate use, costs, expenditures and, hence, professional income.

The second pressure stems from the fact that the growing burden of financing health care motivates governmental authorities, members of the business community, and others who assume the ultimate responsibility for financing health care, to restrain or compress inflationary pressures. Finally, in response to pressures that restrain or reduce spending, providers of health care and health insurance may adopt a politically expedient solution and engage in practices designed to transfer costs or expenditures to other entities. Hence, the ability of a NHI program to reduce inflationary pressures depends on (1) a mechanism for reducing or eliminating the potential to transfer costs and expenditures and (2) restraints on the volume of care, costs, and the professional income of providers.

B. A Taxonomy of Plans

An intellectual organization of the NHI debate requires a classification scheme that captures the basic features of the most prominent recommendations. The taxonomy adopted here consists of the three prototypes described in Table 5. As defined by the OECD (1987), the dominant features of the social insurance (SI) model are universal coverage, a comprehensive range of benefits, public sponsorship, and private ownership of resources. The SI model also assumes that the administrative infrastructure, funding responsibility, and locus of control for the plan reside with a single authority or agency. Consistent with the proposals advanced by Himmelstein et al. (1989), Terris (1988), and Fein (1991), the funding agent employs a system of prepayment based on an approved operating budget to finance hospital care and relies on salaries or a capitation system to compensate physicians.

By contrast, the mixed insurance (MI) model assumes that the responsibility for sponsoring coverage is shared by the public and private sector. In proposals advanced by the National Leadership Commission on Health care (1989), Nutter et al. (1991), Rockefeller (1991), and, to a lesser extent, Ethoven and Kronick (1991), the private component of the MI model is characterized by the requirement that employers provide coverage for employees and their dependents. The public component comprises programs such as Medicare, Medicaid, or a risk pool to cover the elderly, the disabled, and those who are without an attachment to the labor force. Retaining current methods of financing care in the private sector, proponents of the MI model recommend that the public programs rely on a prospective pricing system, based on Diagnosis Related Groups (DRGs), and the fee-for-service system, adjusted for the relative resource consumption associated with each procedure, to compensate hospitals and physicians, respectively.

The private insurance (PI), or consumer sovereignty model, is characterized by employer sponsorship or the individual purchase of insurance, a dependence on private sources of financing health care, and private ownership of health resources (OECD, 1987). The PI envisions little, if any, direct participation of governmental authorities in the process of financing

Table 5. Basic Features of the Social, Mixed and Private Insurance Models

	Insurance Models		
Feature	Social	Mixed	Private
Source of funding	Single agent	Public agency Private insurers	Private sources
Method of hospital compensation	Prepayment	Public: rate regulation Private: current methods	Current methods
Unit of hospital payment	Approved budget	Public: DRGs Private: current units	Current units
Method of physician payment	Salary capitation	Fee-for-service RBRVS	Current methods
Method of financing capital	Capital grants	Public: rate regulation Private: current methods	Current methods

health care. Consistent with the basic features of the PI model, proposals advanced by Butler (1991), Enthoven (1981), Butler and Haislmaier (1989), Pauly et al. (1991), and, to a lesser extent, Enthoven and Kronick (1991) recommend (1) a system of vouchers or tax credits that enable the individual to purchase insurance coverage, (2) a mandated set of minimum health benefits, and (3) little or no change in the current system of compensating providers.

C. Controlling Hospital Operating Costs and Expenditures

The basic features of the three prototypes are by no means uniform, and each creates a distinctive set of incentives that materially influence the potential for NHI to control inflationary pressures in the hospital sector. The elimination of multiple sources of funding, an application of a unified method of compensating providers, and the adoption of a single unit of payment are dominant attributes of the SI model. As suggested by Himmelstein et al. (1989), the annual level of compensation should be determined by the anticipated operating expenses reported in the global budget of the hospital. Once approved, the institution would receive the authorized funding in the form of periodic installments intended to finance operating activity on a current basis.

The basic features of the SI model have several advantages. One is that the fiscal responsibility of the funding agent is limited to the authorized level of compensation, a feature that controls expenditures on hospital care. Further, if funding is restricted to a set of periodic installments, the hospital is induced to ensure that operating expenses are less than the predetermined rate or level of prepayment. Recognizing that the basic features of the SI model are similar to the Canadian method of financing hospital care, the weight of evidence clearly indicates that a system of prepayment, based on the budget, would control operating costs, reduce distributional inequities, and maintain or improve the quality of a care (Barer and Evans, 1989; Detsky et al., 1983; Evans, 1982, 1990; Fuchs and Hahn, 1990; Iglehart, 1986; Pfaff, 1990; Roos et al., 1990, 1992). Accordingly, the adoption of the SI model as a prototype of a national health plan that is characterized by the universal application of a unified system of prepayment would restrain expenditures and exert uncompromised fiscal pressure on hospitals to reduce costs.

Of course, counterarguments have been expressed. Some can be discounted because of the patent self-interestedness of their proponents. Others, such as those advanced by Shiels et al. (1992) and Danzon (1992) have been addressed effectively by Barer and Evans (1992).

The basic features of the SI model may result in unintended and undesired outcomes. To ensure that operating costs are less than or equal to the periodic installment, the hospital might reduce the volume of care by lowering admissions, treating less severe cases, compressing the length of stay, and minimizing the amount of ancillary care provided to the patient population. The potential undesirable outcomes might be avoided by supplementing the periodic installments with an end-of-period adjustment that would motivate the hospital to improve efficiency and provide the care required to satisfy the health needs of the patient population.

As demonstrated by Broyles and Rosko (1990, 1987) and by Broyles and Reilly (1984), it is possible to partition the difference between actual expenses and expected costs or annual compensation into portions that are attributable to:

1. The provision of more or less required care than planned
2. The provision of unnecessary services

3. The use of resources more or less efficiently than anticipated
4. A set of higher or lower factor prices than expected
5. A set of joint effects resulting from differences in volume, efficiency, and factor prices

If actual operating expenses exceed the amount of annual compensation, the end-of-period adjustment should compensate the hospital for unanticipated increases in factor prices that are clearly attributable to market forces and for any additional units of care required to satisfy the health needs of the patient population. In addition, the hospital should be permitted to retain, for discretionary use, all or a portion of the savings that result from the use of resources more efficiently than planned.

On the other hand, the additional costs resulting from the relatively inefficient use of resources should be excluded from the expenses that are recovered as an end-of-period adjustment. In a similar fashion, the additional expenses generated by the provision of unnecessary care should be excluded from the allowable costs that are recovered as an adjustment to compensation. The identification of unnecessary use would be among the most difficult problems in the administration of a national health program that adopts the SI model as a prototype. However, a system of threshold values, similar to those that currently identify Medicare outliers, might be adopted initially. If implemented aggressively, the set of periodic installments and the end-of-period adjustment are policy instruments that encourage the hospital to benefit from improved efficiency and to provide the care required by the health needs of the patient population.

If a U.S. NHI program were based on the MI model, the potential to control inflation would be diluted by a partial application of rate regulation and the concurrent dependence on multiple sources of funding. There are persuasive arguments that multiple sources of funds for financing the use of care would enable the hospital to transfer costs from one group of patients or payers to another and thereby avoid the rigors of rate regulation (Danzon, 1982; Detsky et al., 1983; Evans, 1982; Hsiao and Dunn, 1987; Inglehart, 1986; Lewis and Associates, 1981; Manga and Broyles, 1986; Miller and Byrne, 1977; Sloan and Becker, 1984). Hadley and Swartz (1989) concluded that, when compared with the rate of inflation expected to occur in the absence of prospective payment, a partial application of rate regulation reduced expenses by only 11% and a universal application by 13 to 15%. Similarly, results reported by Broyles (1990), Rosko and Broyles (1986, 1987), Rosko (1989a and b), Blair (1987), and Thorpe (1987) indicate that a partial application of prospective payment exerts less fiscal pressure on hospitals to reduce price differentials and control operating costs than does a universal application of rate regulation.

The proposed reliance on case mix or DRGs to establish prospective prices also mitigates the potential of the MI model to control expenditures and costs. If rates of payment include a uniform profit margin, providers of hospital care are induced to increase expenditures and improve the net surplus by stimulating the number of admissions, the volume of service, and, to the extent that expenses depend on output, the costs of care. The incentive to increase the number of cases to which fixed costs are assigned lowers the expense per patient and, holding prices constant, improves profitability. Although hospitals would be induced to ensure that operating expenses per case were less than or equal to the predetermined rate of payment, previous assessments of prospective payment systems, based on DRGs, indicate that the resulting cost savings would be attenuated by an increase in admissions (Rosko and Broyles, 1986, 1987; Salkever et al., 1986).

The adoption of the MI model as a prototype for a national health care system might also exacerbate the problem of distributional equality and perhaps compromise the quality of care. For example, the hospital may lower the length of stay and reduce the amount of ancillary care per patient in order to ensure that operating expenses per case are less than the corresponding prospective price (Broyles and Rosko, 1985; Hsiao and Dunn, 1987; Long et al., 1987; Rosko, 1989; Rosko and Broyles, 1986, 1987; Schramm et al., 1987; Zuckerman, 1987). In addition to the potentially adverse effects that might result from a decline in the length of stay and the use of ancillary care, differential profit margins per case may reduce the dependence of access on medical need. If the net profit per discharge were to differ among diagnostic categories, the hospital might increase the portion of the patient population for which a high net surplus is anticipated and reduce the number of cases that are expected to result in a loss or a low net surplus. Similarly, the adoption of a stringent set of prospective prices would lower the net surplus or increase the net loss per case and thereby reduce the rate of admitting patients whose care is publicly financed. Although the potential decline in admissions might lower costs and expenditures, it is likely that the adoption of a stringent set of prospective prices would reduce the access of public beneficiaries to inpatient care or force the hospital to transfer costs to the private sector.

It is also possible that a national health program with the basic features of the MI model would induce hospitals to improve profitability by admitting patients whose conditions require a less intensive or costly course of treatment. Although a decline in case severity may lower operating costs, it is possible that, with other factors held constant, the diagnostic mix would remain stable and result in little, if any, effect on expenditures in the short term. Accordingly, the reliance on DRGs to establish prospective prices would mean that the admission decision and the course of treatment might depend more on financial incentives that are specific to the hospital than on the health needs of the patient.

The private insurance approach is based on the assumption that market forces induce providers of care and private insurers to lower costs, reduce prices, attract patients from less-efficient sources, and thereby control inflationary prressures. The PI model also assumes that insurance coverage insulates the patient and provider from the economic effects of consuming health care and that the cost consciousness of both is enhanced by higher deductibles, coinsurance rates, and effective premium payments. Further, proponents of the PI model contend that the typical patient is tempted to consume health services for which marginal costs exceed marginal benefits, but the effects of moral hazard are reduced or eliminated by market pressures.

It is problematic whether market pressures induce providers of hospital care to lower costs and reduce prices to attract patients. A review of the literature by Broyles and Rosko (1988) indicates that the demand for care is price inelastic. Since revenues are stimulated by an increase rather than a decline in price, it is difficult to conclude that hospitals will compete for patients by reducing charges, lowering expenditures, decreasing patient revenues, thereby compromising their fiscal performance. Conversely, a growing body of evidence indicates that greater market pressures induce providers to engage in nonprice competition for patients by improving quality or offering more amenities. Hospitals appear to compete for physicians by acquiring sophisticated equipment, providing space, or offering more amenities, practices that increase rather than reduce costs (Hadley and Swartz, 1989; Farley, 1985; Robinson and Luft, 1987).

The PI model also assumes that market pressures induce providers of insurance coverage to control the cost of care and attract consumers from less-efficient sources by lowering premiums, offering a more comprehensive set of insured benefits, or reducing the deductible and the coinsurance rate. However, there are at least three factors that vitiate the willingness and ability of private insurers to lower the costs of care, expenditures, and hence effective premiums. First, most analysts recognize that as the cost of health and hospital care increases the demand for health insurance grows, which suggests that the effective control of cost may reduce or limit the demand for coverage. Second, the fact that the demand for health insurance is inelastic (Broyles and Rosko, 1988) means that a decrease in premiums would probably reduce the revenues generated by the insurance industry. Third, unless insurers adopt a uniform payment policy, the reliance on multiple sources of funding encourages providers of service to transfer costs from stringent to less stringent insurers and prevents a comprehensive approach to the problem of reducing the costs of hospital care.

Among the most questionable elements of the PI model and, to a lesser extent the MI model, is the role assigned to the consumer. In the model, legislation requiring firms to offer employees multiple options or a system of tax credits enables consumers to select the plan that is most congruent with their preferences. However, an informed assessment of alternate sources of insurance requires the consumer to evaluate his or her current and future health status in relation to (1) the potential use of service, (2) the benefit structure, (3) the effectiveness of care, and (4) its relative costliness as the first three factors are translated into effective premium payments, deductibles, and coinsurance rates. The ability of consumers to conduct such an assessment is confounded by multiple factors. As suggested by Arrow (1963), the need for health services is irregular and unpredictable. Arrow also contends that uncertainty concerning quality and outcome is more pervasive in the health industry than in other sectors of the economy and that "recovery from disease is as unpredictable as its incidence." Uncertainties surrounding the incidence of disease or injury, the potential need for service, and the efficacy of treatment impair the ability of the individual to evaluate alternatives, to select the plan that offers the preferred benefit structure at least cost, and to ensure that only efficient plans survive and flourish.

Proponents of the PI and the MI approach also contend that a higher effective price for care increases the cost consciousness of consumers, reduces use, contains costs, and lowers expenditures. The reliance on high effective prices to reduce use is based on the normative economic proposition that, given the budget constraint and a well-defined preference function, the consumer, rather than the supplier, selects the mix of goods or services that maximizes utility or satisfaction. Recognizing the complexity of medical knowledge and technology, however, the physician occupies a superordinate position in the provider-patient relationship and is a more important determinant of use, costs, and expenditures than the consumer. With the exception of utilization initiated by the patient, supply and demand decisions are neither independent nor separable, implying that the ability to control use, cost, and expenditures resides more with the physician and other providers than with the patient. Although higher effective prices or direct charges might lower initial patient-provider contacts, the adoption of the PI model as the prototype for a national health plan would create few, if any, incentives that induces the provider to reduce use, costs, expenditures, and hence professional income. It is overly optimistic to expect the physician to act as a perfect agent for the patient regarding costs and prices.

D. Controlling Administrative Costs

Among the most important features of the SI model is the potential to control or reduce administrative costs. As reported by Woolhandler and Himmelstein (1991), a substantial and growing proportion of hospital expenses is related to the performance of billing and administrative functions. Recent estimates indicate that approximately $80 billion, or 1.5%, of the GNP is committed to the performance of administrative functions by physicians, hospitals, providers of long-term care, and 1500 private insurers (Feinglass and Holloway, 1991; Herzlinger, 1991). That the dependence on multiple sources of funding has contributed to substantial and increasing administrative costs has also been documented by Evans (1990) and by Harrington et al. (1991). Recent estimates derived by these authors indicate that the adoption of the SI model as a prototype for a NHI program, characterized by a single source of funding, would result in savings of $50 to $100 billion.

By contrast, the MI model and the PI model are characterized by a dependence on multiple sources of funding and few, if any, mechanisms that promise to reduce spending on marketing, advertising, billing, and processing claims. Relman (1991) and Harrington et al. (1991) suggest that administrative costs represent 15 to 20% of the premium payments to private insurers. Since the MI and the PI models are characterized by a reliance on multiple sources of insurance, it is unlikely that the adoption of these approaches would alter the application of premium payments or retard the rate of increase in administrative costs.

E. Controlling Capital Costs

A desirable attribute of the SI model is the potential for separating the mechanism of financing operating costs from the process of funding capital acquisitions. As indicated, the SI model enables the funding authority to rely on the principles of prepayment and the approved budget to finance operating costs, excluding the expenses associated with acquiring plant assets, performing medical research, and operating educational programs. To compensate for these exclusions, the summary presented in Table 1 suggests that a reliance on a system of capital grants to finance investment activity in the health industry is a basic feature of the SI model.

Viewed from the perspective of the provider, Broyles and Reilly (1984) contend that a system of capital grants would reduce or eliminate the dependence of health organizations on depreciation charges as a method of recovering the costs of capital and would mitigate the problems caused by disparities between historic and replacement costs. It is also likely that a system of capital grants would reduce the institution's reliance on internally generated funds to finance the acquisition of plant assets, establish a dependence of funding decisions on capital needs, and diminish the debt burden of many health organizations.

Viewed from a societal perspective, the problem of controlling the amount of spending on capital consists of three interrelated components. The first two involve the problems of determining the additional investment required to satisfy the health needs of the population and the total amount of funds available for capital acquisition. Since it is neither possible nor desirable to fund all proposals, the third involves an assessment of capital proposals and the allocation of available resources among potential recipients.

The control exerted by existing regulatory agencies in the health industry is usually limited to a local area or a single state. This limitation creates an environment in which it is difficult, if not impossible, to restrict the total amount of capital spending (Manga and Broyles, 1986). The policy option of assigning the responsibility for determining the total among of investable funds, approving capital proposals, and financing approved projects to central or regional authorities enhances the ability of society to control aggregate expenditures on plant and equipment. In addition, a central or regional agency that is responsible for evaluating, approving, and financing capital projects represents a mechanism for resolving conflicts among political jurisdictions, increasing the priority assigned to the planning function, enhancing the commitment to the review process, and ensuring that the allocation of available funds contributes maximum benefits to the population at risk. A centralized review process would also enable the fiscal agent to accumulate relevant information, assemble the resources required to evaluate capital projects, and employ a uniform set of standards to allocate available funds (Detsky et al., 1983; Evans, 1982; Inglehart, 1986).

Consistent with the basic features of the MI model, and perhaps the PI model, public or private providers of coverage might adopt a system of capital grants or rely on a system of prospective prices to finance capital acquisitions. However, Boles (1989) argues that the incorporation of capital expenses in prospective rates of compensation would increase the cost of future debt issues or restrict the access of health institutions to capital markets. The incorporation of capital expenses in prospective prices would establish a direct relation between the amount of compensation and the flow of patients or the volume of care. Since both exhibit volatility, the resulting variation in revenue and cash flows would increase the risk assigned to debt issues of health organizations. Given that investors require a higher rate of return to compensate for greater risk, the potential incorporation of capital expenses in prospective prices would increase the relative costliness of long-term debt issues and impair the ability of health organizations to acquire equipment in which recent technological innovations are embodied.

It is also likely that the distribution of risks imposed on hospitals would not be uniform. The fiscal performance and ability to support the costs of debt, to include higher interest charges, are frequently determined more by the characteristics of the service area than by the efficiency of operations. As a consequence, it is likely that the adverse effects of incorporating the costs of capital in prospective rates of payment would be greater among inner-city and urban hospitals than among their suburban counterparts.

When combined with the adoption of the PI or the MI model as the prototype for a national health program, the inclusion of capital expenses in rates of payment would influence the mix of projects that might be approved and funded by many health institutions. Consistent with the need to preserve the fiscal viability of their organizations, health administrators would be motivated to approve only those projects that would improve profitability and to reject capital proposals that serve no marketing functions, contribute to community service, or are required to provide services that result in losses.

F. Controlling Physician Expenditures

As indicated by Table 5, the SI model is characterized by a reliance on salaries or a capitation method to compensate physicians. Capitation has at least two advantages. First, if adjustments in the rate of compensation are independent of previous practice patterns, the capitation method severs the traditional dependence of the physician's professional income on the volume of care he or she renders. Second, the use of per capita rates transfers fiscal risk from the funding agent to the provider, which might motivate physicians to increase net income by improving efficiency or acquiring resources at lower prices.

On the other hand, a reliance on per capita rates might result in undesirable outcomes. For example, if the rate of payment were to reflect prior practice patterns, physicians might prescribe additional units so as to increase the capitation rate in a future period resulting in inflationary pressures similar to those stimulated by the reliance on costs to compensate hospitals. Further, in the absence of provisions that reduce or eliminate the effects of biased selection, physicians would be induced to augment net income by enrolling patients who are expected to require relatively few diagnostic and therapeutic services, a practice that might jeopardize the access of those in greatest need of care (Hornbrook et al., 1989; Rossiter et al., 1988; Thomas et al., 1983). As suggested by findings reported by Anderson et al. (1990), the effects of these outcomes might be mitigated by basing per capita rates on the input costs of the provider and the health status of patients, as measured by age, sex, and disability. Finally, the incentive to improve efficiency that was identified earlier as an advantage of capitation might lead to an inappropriately low volume of service and exacerbate inequities in the distribution of care.

A national health program that is based on the SI model and relies on salaries to compensate physicians would also sever the dependence of income on the volume of care and the case load of the provider, features that are likely to restrict spending more than those associated with the capitation method. However, a reliance on annual salaries would induce physicians to restrict the case load, commit less time to market activity, and lower the volume of service per hour or per patient (Glaser, 1970; Rosko and Broyles, 1988). In addition to the potentially adverse effects on quality, access, and productivity, a reliance on salaries to compensate physicians requires the establishment of an income structure that accurately reflects the relative value of the services provided by the various specialties, which is a requirement fraught with political difficulties.

Unlike the SI model, the multiple sources of funding that characterize the MI and PI models require primary reliance on the fee-for-service system of compensating physicians. Unfortunately, the fee-for-service mechanism enables physicians to augment their professional income and increase expenditures by prescribing additional units of service (Glaser, 1970; Langwell and Nelson, 1986; Wilensky and Rossiter, 1986). Further, since profit margins differ among components of care, the provider is induced to prescribe those services for which the net surplus is greatest, an incentive that distorts the course of treatment in relation to the medical needs of the patient.

The potentially undesirable effects of differential profit margins might be reduced by basing the fee schedule on a relative value scale that reflects not only the time requirements and complexity of various services but also the practice costs of the physician. Although findings reported by Maloney (1991) suggest that a relative value scale may fail to capture the relative costliness of service with precision, adjusted fees might reduce the dependence of practice patterns on differences in the profit margins of various components of care. In addition, a reliance on resource consumption to develop the fee schedule should address inequities in the charges for cognitive and technical procedures (Hsaio, 1988). However, in the absence of a mechanism that imposes limits on expenditures or volume, a national health insurance program that is based on the MI or the PI model and features the fee-for-service mechanism would induce the physician to augment income by providing additional units of service. As a consequence, the adoption of the MI or the PI model is unlikely to control pressures exerted by physicians to stimulate expenditures and increase professional earnings (Lee et al., 1990).

VIII. THE POLITICS OF ACTION AND INACTION

The economic assessment suggests a reasonably clear structure for a national health plan that would control costs, limit expenditures, improve access, and increase the dependence of utilization behavior on medical need. In addition, adoption of the SI model would favorably affect most Americans by providing universal, portable, and comprehensive coverage. Certainly, the 35 to 40 million Americans who at any given time are uninsured would benefit from the adoption of the SI model. A social insurance program would also benefit those with preexisting health conditions, those who might lose their coverage if they change jobs or become unemployed, and those who might experience a financial disaster as a result of a catastrophic illness.

The failure of the United States to implement such a SI plan could be viewed as an enigma. As pointed out in the previous section of this chapter, social insurance for health services has been on the federal agenda for some time. As someone once remarked, "national health insurance is an idea whose time has come and come and come."

Several factors, in isolation or combination, have been cited as reasonable explanations for the failure of SI plan proposals. Viewed from a cross-national perspective, Heidenheimer (1973) cleverly argues that, in contrast to U.S. recalcitrance in health policy, U.S. progressivism in educational policy can be attributed, in part, to the fact that the socioeconomic status of teachers and civil servants is similar but below that of physicians. Because of this status differential, policy makers have been reluctant to place physician behavior under public control. Heidenheimer's argument may have once had some credibility but, given the regulations that have been imposed on physician behavior during the last decade, it is no longer valid as an explanation for the lack of progress toward a social insurance model for NHI.

Recently, a comparative perspective has been used, albeit with varying degrees of explicitness, to highlight U.S. ideological exceptionalism as the cause of inaction on a SI plan for health services. Reduced to its simplest terms, the exceptionalism argument asserts that Americans have what they want in the way of health policy because they so highly value individualism, unfettered competition, free choice, and the absence of government interference in their daily lives. However, the argument rests on a shaky empirical foundation (Alford, 1963; Lipset, 1990; Marmor and Mashau, 1990), fails to comport with our acceptance of government programs in other policy areas, represents an inadequate explanation of the SI programs that dominate the health environment of Australia or Canada, and flies in the face of the fact that, as we have argued, in lieu of policy, the U.S. health industry is rife with regulation (Leichter, 1992; Manga and Broyles, 1986). If Americans were so averse to the imposition of government on personal freedoms and were so enamored of unfettered competition, they would not wear seat belts and would still be receiving medical care from providers trained at barber colleges rather than from physicians who benefit from a government-sanctioned monopoly. Finally, even if Americans were as ideologically exceptional as they are romanticized to be, there is no reason to believe that political culture *determines* public policy.

Another argument for the absence of SI for health services is the pressure group dominance model. This argument not only comes close to begging the question, it also is not consonant with the fact that, although providers and physicians are *everywhere* powerful, the United States is *unique* among Western developed nations in regard to SI for health services (Glasser, 1990; Marmor, 1991; Saltman, 1992).

So much for what does not work as an explanation for American uniqueness. What does work? The status of the United States as an "outlier" can be explained, in large part, by the interplay of political will and political structure. Political will refers to public opinion mobilized in support of policy and sustained vigilance in ensuring the implementation of programs derived from policy. It is what Key (1965) termed a "consensus of decision" as opposed to a consensus that merely is supportive of a given course of governmental action. In the absence of a crisis, such a consensus is triggered by political elites; it does not spring phoenixlike from otherwise latent public opinion.

Political structure refers to the institutional arrangements for public decision making that are necessary to activate and express political will. Political structure and political will are so dynamically related that the latter is subsumed by the former in conceptualizing determinants of policy. Parliamentary, responsible governments are viewed as having the political will to stimulate and forcefully act on a consensus or "widespread agreement" when, in fact, it is the political structure that gives the public realistic confidence that its preferences will be registered on an action agenda.

The importance of political structure was obscured for some time by the fact that an informal, aconstitutional veneer, a party system with vigorous leadership, masked to some extent the effects of institutionally implanted deadlocks of democracy, to use Burns' (1967) phrase. But now, with less powerful legislative parties (Falcone and Hartwig, 1990), the purposely nondecision-biased effects of political structure are unmasked. Political reform per se and the need for structural change, once the clarion call of Marxists, Marxians, and easy-to-dismiss utopians, now are resonantly articulated by mainstream political thinkers such as Morone (1990a,b) and Osborne and Goebler (1992). No doubt in recognition of the fact that policy change cannot await political change, health policy proposals are seeking ways to obviate traditional political institutions.

The importance of political institutions also was once discounted because of a methodological inadequacy of policy analysis. Social and economic variables, when used in conjunction with available political variables such as party competition, electoral participation, indicators of the professionalism of legislatures, and the institutionalization of bureaucracies, seemed paramount as determinants of policy (Falcone and Mishler, 1977). No wonder: the most important political variable, the structuring of governmental responsibility and accountability, was a virtual constant in these analyses.

Thus, we return to traditional political science for an unraveling of the enigma posed by the demonstrated inability of the U.S. political system to convert needs and demands into legislation and related programs. The United States is unique among Western polities in regard to SI for health services; among these polities, the United States also has unique structures for making public decisions at both state and national levels. There is a compelling, albeit necessarily unscientific, inclination to conclude that the content of policy and the structure of the decision-making process that produces the policy are causally related.

One more impediment to recognizing the power of political structure as a determinant of policy is the fact that the structure originally was, in fact, an explicit expression of a laissez faire ideology. It is safe to say that the U.S. political structure has outlived classic liberalism. Yet the structure gives rise to inaction that comports with this ideological persuasion and so reinforces the myth that the pervasiveness of laissez faire precepts dictate policy, a remarkable self-fulfilling prophesy akin to one of Evans' (1985) "illusions of necessity."

Given the widely perceived urgency of the need for health system reform and the demonstrated cost effectiveness of the social insurance model, and given the nearly intractable nature of political structure, what are the options open to health policy entrepreneurs? The answer is not obvious, but our brief review of explanations for past inaction suggests what approaches *not* to take. Further laments about feasibility constraints, such as interest group dominance and ideological antipathy to governmental action, will only lead to further laments. A more productive approach would include two strategies. One would emphasize the strains of communitarianism in the U.S. political culture (Dionne, 1991; Reich, 1987). Another would be to seek ways to obviate the political structural bias that now breeds inaction by insulating from political forces, to the extent possible, responsibility for financing and regulating health services.

IX. CONCLUSIONS

After presenting a working definition of health policy, this chapter reviewed U.S. health system functioning in cross-national perspective with regard to cost containment, expansiveness of access, and quality. It was argued that, on each of these interrelated dimensions, most definitely the first two, the performance of the United States has not been overly impressive. Yet the system has been resistant to change.

Factors behind this resistance were examined in reviewing the development of U.S. health policy from one centered on a concept of health care as a public good, to a largely symbolic expression of health care as a right, to a recent emphasis on the fact that health care is a limited resource. It was shown that the means by which government has influenced the allocation of this limited resource have been regulations in lieu of policy, couched in the rubric of planning in the 1970s, then competition in the 1980s, and now increasingly in terms of managed competition.

Whatever the terminology in which it is expressed, there is virtual consensus among principal actors in the health policy arena that substantial change is necessary. In the final section of this chapter, we have suggested that the adoption of the social insurance model as a prototype for a NHI program is the most effective approach to the problem of redressing inequities in the distribution of care, controlling operating expenses, limiting capital costs, and withstanding pressures from providers to increase expenditures on health care. In particular, a reliance on the approved operating budget as the unit of compensation, the principles of prepayment, an end-of-period adjustment, and a system of capital grants are of fundamental importance to the problem of controlling inflationary pressures in the hospital sector. The discussion also suggests that a reliance on salaries or a capitation method represents an effective means of controlling costs and expenditures in the market for physician services.

As numerous references in this review indicate, our analysis is hardly the first to come to the above conclusion. All the more ironic, then, even to those inured to the irrationalities of the U.S. policy process, is the fact that, as noted at the outset of this chapter, the "dynamics without change" description of health politics posed by Alford (1975) continues to typify progress toward a social insurance model for NHI. Two avenues of inquiry into reasons for the comparative lack of progress the United States has made in this regard lead to interest group dominance and the distinctive adherence by the United States to the precepts of classic liberalism. We hope to have effectively challenged the validity of these explanations as well as their utility for advancing the cause of acceptance of a social insurance model for NHI. In fact, these explanations risk becoming self-fulfilling prophesies—"illusions of necessity."

Instead of these explanations, we posit another reason for the glacial pace of the social insurance model: the structure of the U.S. government and its bias toward nondecisions. A problem this explanation shares with the ideological explanation is its obviously low "cash value." That is, what does one do with knowledge of the fact that power relations are structured by U.S. institutions in such a way as to make macroscopic redistributive policies extremely difficult to formulate? Gainsaying the likelihood of significant structural change, we suggest considering ways to insulate the funding mechanism and regulation of health services from the political process. This suggestion is far easier to make in general than in specifics.

NOTE

1. This section borrows from Bryoles, R., Falcone, D., Goldsteen, R., and Reilly, B. (1993). The state of the debate on national health insurance. *Journal of Health, Politics, Policy and Law*, forthcoming.

REFERENCES

Alford, R. (1975). *Health Care Politics*: *Ideological and Interest Group Barriers to Reform*. University of Chicago Press, Chicago.

—— (1963). *Party and Society*. Rand Mcnally, Chicago.

Altman, D. (1978). The politics of health care regulation. *Journal of Health Politics, Policy and Law* 2: 560–580.

Anderson, O. (1991). Health services in the United States: A growth enterprise for a hundred years. In *Health Politics and Policy*, 2nd ed. T. Littman and L. Robins (Eds.). Delmar Press, Albany, NY, pp. 38–52.

Anderson, G., Steinberg, E., Powe, N., et al. (1990). Setting payments rates for capitated systems: A comparison of various alternatives. *Inquiry* 27: 225.

Arrow, K. (1963). Uncertainty and the welfare economics of medical care. *American Economic Review* 53: 941.

Banta, D. (1990). What is health care? In *Health Care Delivery In The United States*. A. Kovner (Ed.). Springer, New York, p. 9.

Barber, B. (1984). *Strong Democracy*: *Participatory Politics for a New Age*. University of California Press, Berkeley, CA.

Barer, M., and Evans, R. (1992). Interpreting Canada; models, mind-sets and myths. *Health Affairs* 11(1): 44.

—— (1986). Riding north on a south-bound horse? Expenditures, prices, utilization and incomes in the Canadian health care system. In *Medicare at Maturity*: *Achievements, Lessons and Challenges*. R. Evans and G. Stoddard (Eds.). University of Alberta Press, Calgary, Canada.

—— (1992). The meeting of the Twain: Managing health care capital, capacity and cost in Canada. In *Technology and Health Care in An Era of Limits*. A. Gelijns (Ed.). National Academy Press, Washington, DC, pp. 97–119.

Beard, J. (1936). The contribution of Cholera to public health. *Scientific Monthly* 43: 206–220.

Blair, B. (1987). *Maryland Hospital Financial Trends: 1977 Through 1986*. Maryland Chapter of the Hospital Financial Association, Baltimore.

Blendon, R., Leitman, R., Morrison, I., and Donelan, K. (1990). Satisfaction with health systems in ten nations. *Health Affairs* 9: 185–192.

Blendon, R., and Taylor, H. (1991). Views on health care: Public opinion in three nations. *Health Affairs* 8: 149–157.

Blendon, R., Donelan, K., Jovell, A., Pellise, L., Costas, and Lombardia, E. (1991). Spain's citizens assess their health care system. *Health Affairs* 10: 216–228.

Boles, K. (1989). Implications of the method of capital cost payment on the weighted average cost of capital. *Health Services Research* 21: 189.

Bovberg, R. (1991). Lessons for tort reform from Indiana. *Journal of Health Politics, Policy and Law* 16: 465–441.

Brown, L. (1992). Political education of federal health care regulation. *Health Affairs* 11: 17–37.

Broyles, R. (1990). Efficiency, costs and quality: The New Jersey experience revisited. *Inquiry* 27: 86.

Broyles, R., and Reilly, B. (1984). National health insurance: A new imperative. *Journal of Medical Systems* 8: 331.

Broyles, R., and Rosko, M. (1988). The demand for health care and health insurance: A review of the empirical literature. *Medical Care Review* 45: 291.

—— (1990). *Fiscal Management of Healthcare Institutions*. National Health Publishing, Owings Mills, MD.

—— (1987). The Medicare payment system: a conceptual approach to the problem of controlling profitability. *Health Care Management Review* 12: 35.

—— (1985). A qualitative assessment of the Medicare prospective payment system. *Social Science and Medicine* 10: 1185.

Broyles, R., Falcone, D., Goldsteen, R., and Reilly, B. (1993). The state of the debate on national health insurance. *Journal of Health Politics, Policy and Law*, forthcoming.

Butler, S. A tax reform strategy to deal with the uninsured. *Journal of the American Medical Association* 265: 2541.

Butler, S., and Haislmaier, E. (1989). *A National Health System for America*. The Heritage Foundation, Washington, DC.

Burns, J. M. (1967). *The Deadlock of Democracy: Four Party Politics in America*, rev. ed. Prentice-Hall, Englewood Cliffs, NJ.

Cochrane, A. (1972). *Effectiveness and Efficiency: Random Reflections on Health Services*. Nuffield Provincial Hospitals Trust, London.

Converse, P. (1964). The nature of belief systems in mass publics. In *Ideology and Discontent*. D. Apter (Ed.). Free Press, Glencoe, IL, pp. 206–261.

Congress of The United States, 78th (1944). *Congressional Record, 2nd Session,* United States Government Printing Office, Washington, DC.

Congressional Budget Office (CBO) (1992). *Projection's of National Health Expenditures, By Type of Spending and Source of Funds*. CBO, Washington, DC, Table 1.

Culyer, A. (1990). Cost containment in Europe. In *Health Care Systems in Transition*. Organization for Economic Cooperation and Development (OECD) (Ed.). OECD, Paris, pp. 29–40.

Davies, A., Ware, J., Brook, R., Peterson, J., and Newhouse, J. (1986). Consumer acceptance of prepaid and fee-for-service care: Results from a randomized trial. *Health Services Research* 21: 429–452.

Davis, K. (1989). Comment on "What can Americans learn from Europeans?" In *Health Care Systems In Transition*. Organization for Economic Cooperation and Development (Ed.). p. 87.

Davis, K. et al. (1990). *Health Care Cost Containment*. The Johns Hopkins University Press, Baltimore.

Danzon, P. (1992). Hidden overhead costs: Is Canada's system less expensive? *Health Affairs* 11(1): 21.

Danzon, P. (1982). Hospital profits: The effects of reimbursement policy. *Journal of Health Economics* 1: 29.

De Jong, G. (1977). Interfacing national health insurance and income maintenance. *Journal of Health Politics, Policy and Law* 1: 405–432.

Detsky, A., Stacey, S., and Bombardier, C. (1983). The effectiveness of a regulatory strategy in containing hospital costs. *New England Journal of Medicine* 309: 151.

Donabedian, A. (1980). *The Definition of Quality and Approaches to its Assessment*. Health Administration Press, Ann Arbor, MI.

Dubes, R. (1959). *Mirage of Health*. Doubleday, Garden City, NY.

Enthoven, A. (1981). *Health Plan*. Addison-Wesley, Reading, PA.

Enthoven, A., and Kronick, R. (1991). Universal health insurance through incentives reform. *Journal of the American Medical Association* 19: 2532.

Etzioni, A. (1967). Mixed-scanning: A "third" approach to decision-making. *Public Administration Review* 27: 385–392.

Evans, R. (1982). Health care in Canada: Patterns of funding and regulation. In *The Public/Private Mix for Health*. G. Mclachlan and A. Maynard (Eds.). Nuffield Provincial Hospital Trust, London.

—— (1983). *Strained Mercy: The Economics of Canadian Health Care*. Butterworth, Toronto.

—— (1985). Illusions of necessity: Evading responsibility for choice in health care. *Journal of Health Politics, Policy and Law* 10(3): 439.

Evans, R. (1990). Tension, compression and shear: direction, stresses and outcomes of health care cost control. *Journal of Health Politics, Policy and Law* 15: 101.

Falcone, D. (1992). The state of the art of state health policy reform. *Journal of The Oklahoma Medical Association*.

Falcone, D. and Hartwig, L. (1990). Congress and health policy: The legacy of reform and retrenchment. In *Health Politics and Policy, 2nd Ed*. T. Litman and L. Robins (Eds.). Delmar Publishers, Albany, NY, pp. 117–134.

Falcone, D., and Warren, D. (1988). The shadow price of pluralism. *Journal of Health Politics, Policy and Law* 13: 735–752.

Farley, P. (1985). Competition among hospitals-market structure and its relation to utilization, costs and financial position, DHHS No. PHS 85-3353, Department of Health and Human Services, Washington, DC.

Fein, R. (1991). The health security partnership. *JAMA* 19: 2555.

Feinglass, J., and Holloway, J. (1991). The initial impact of the Medicare prospective payment system on United States health care: A review of the literature. *Medical Care Review* 48: 91.

Feldstein, P. (1992). *Health Economics*, 4th ed. Delmar Press, Albany, NY, pp. 15 ff.

Flook, E., and Sanazaro, P. (1973). Health services research: Origins and milestones. In *Health Services Research and Research and Development in Perspective*. Flook and Sanazaro (Eds.). Health Administration Press, Ann Arbor, MI.

Freeland, M., Caht, G., and Schendler, C. (1980). Projections of national health expenditures: 1985–1990. *Health Care Financing Review* 1: 68–77.

Fuchs, V., and Hahn, J. (1990). How does Canada do it? A comparison of expenditures for physicians' services in the United States and Canada. *New England Journal of Medicine* 323: 884.

Gabel, J., DiCarlo, S., Sullivan, C., and Rice, T. (1990). Employer sponsored health insurance, 1989. *Health Affairs* 9: 161.

Girvetz, H. (1950). *From Wealth to Welfare*. Stanford University Press, Stanford, CA, p. 53–54.

Glaser, W. (1970). *Paying the Doctor*. Johns Hopkins University Press, Baltimore.

—— (1990). Designing fee schedules by formulae, politics and negotiations. *American Journal of Public Health* 80: 804.

Hadley, J., and Swartz, K. (1989). The impact on hospital costs between 1980 and 1984 of hospital rate regulation, competition and changes in health insurance coverage. *Inquiry* 26: 35.

Harrington, D., Cassel, C., Estes, C., Woolhandler, S., and Himmelstein, D. (1991). A national long-term care program for the U.S.: A caring vision. *Journal of the American Medical Society* 226: 3023.

Heidenheimer, A. (1973). The politics of public education, health and welfare in the U.S.A. and western Europe: How growth and reform potentials have differed. *British Journal of Political Science* 3: 315.

Herzlinger, R. (1991). The simplest, best cure for our health care crisis. *Medical Economics* 18: 135.

Himmelstein, D., Woolhandler, S., et al. (1989). A national health program for the United States: A physician's proposal. *New England Journal of Medicine* 320: 102.

Holahan, J., et al. (1991). *Balancing Access, Cost and Politics: The American Context for Health Systems Reform*. Urban Institute, Washington, DC.

Hoover, H. (1946). *Addresses on the American Road*. Van Nostrand, New York, p. 225.

Hornbrook, M., Bennet, M., and Greenlick, M. (1989). Adjusting the AAPCC for selectivity and selection bias under Medicare risk contracts. In *Advances in Health Economics and Health Services Research*. R. Scheffler and L. Rossiter (Eds.). JAI Press, Greenwich, CT.

Hsiao, W., and Dunn, D. (1987). The impact of DRGs payment on New Jersey hospitals. *Inquiry* 24: 203.

Hsiao, W., Braun, P., Yntema, D., and Becker, E. (1988). Estimating physicians' work for a resource-based relative value scale. *New England Journal of Medicine* 319: 835.

Iglehart, J. (1986). Canada's health care system. *New England Journal of Medicine* 315: 202–208, 778–784.

Illich, I. (1976). *Medical Nemesis*. Pantheon, New York.

Jaeger, B. J. (1974). The normative bases of American health policy, unpublished paper. Duke University, Durham, NC.

Jonsson, B. (1990). What can Americans learn from Europeans? In *Health Care Systems in Transition*. Organization for Economics Cooperation and Development (OECD) (Ed.). OECD, Paris.

Key, V. O. (1965). *Public Opinion and American Democracy*. Knopf, New York.

Kinzer, D. (1988). The decline and fall of deregulation. *New England Journal of Medicine* 388: 112–116.

—— (1990). Entitlement to health care: Can we get there from here? *New England Journal of Medicine* 322: 467–470.

Langwell, K., and Nelson, L. (1986). Physician payment systems: A review of history, alternatives and evidence. Medical Care 43: 5.

Lawthers, A., Localio, A., Laird, N., Lipsitz, S., Hebert, L., and Brennan, T. (1992). Physicians perceptions of the risk of being sued. *Journal of Health Politics, Policy and Law* 17: 443–482.

Lee, P., Le Roy, L., Ginsberg, P., and Hammons, G. (1990). Physician payment reform: An idea whose time has come. Medical Care Review 47: 137.

Leichter, H. (1992). *Free to Be Foolish*: *Politics and Health Promotion in the United States and Great Britain*. Princeton University Press, Princeton, NJ.

Leu, R. (1986). The public-private mix and international health care costs. In *Public and Private Health Services*: *Complementaritics and Conflicts*. A. Culyer and B. Jonsson (Eds.). Basil Blackwell, Oxford, England.

Lewin and Associates Inc. (1981). Differential reimbursement of hospitals, final report to HCFA, no 600-77-0073, HCFA, Washington, DC.

Lewin-Vitl, Inc. (1993). Estimating the costs of defensive medicine. Prepared for MMI Companies, Inc., presented at the February meeting of the National Medical Liability Reform Coalition, Washington, DC.

Lipset, S. M. (1990). *Continental Divide*: *The Values and Institutions of the United States and Canada*. Routledge, New York.

Littman, T. (1991). Appendix: Chronology and capsule highlights of the major historical and political milestones in the evolutionary involvement of government in health in the United States. In *Health Politics and Policy*, 2nd ed. T. Littman and L. Robins (Eds.). Delmar Press, Albany, NY, pp. 395–411.

Liu, K., Moon, M., Sulvetta, M., and Chawla, J. (1992). International infant mortality rankings: A look behind the numbers. *Health Care Financing Review* 13: 105–118.

Long, M., Chesney, J., Ament, R., et al. (1987). The effect of PPS on hospital product and productivity. *Medical Care* 25: 524.

Maloney, J. (1991). A critical analysis of the resource-based relative value scale. *JAMA* 266: 3453.

Manga, P., and Broyles, R. (1986). Evaluating and explaining U.S.-Canada health policy. In *Research in Public Policy Analysis and Management*. S. Nagel (Ed.). JAI Press, Greenwich, CT.

Manning, W., Leibowitz, S., Goldberg, G., et al. (1984). A controlled trial of the effects of a prepaid group practice on use of services. *New England Journal of Medicine* 310: 1505–1510.

Marmor, T. (1991). Commentary on Canadian health insurance: Lessons for the United States, U.S. Government Printing Office. *Report to the Committee on Government Operations*, Washington, DC.

Marmor, T., and Mashau, J. (1990). Canada's health insurance and ours: the real lessons, the big choices. *The American Prospect* Fall:

Marmor, T., Wittman, D., and Heagy, T. (1976). The politics of medical inflation. *Journal of Health Politics, Policy and Law* 1: 69–84.

Morone, J. (1990a). *The Democratic Wish*: *The Limits of American Government*. Basic Books, New York.

—— (1990b). American Political culture and the search for lessons from abroad. *Journal of Health Politics, Policy and Law* 15: 129.

Miller and Byrne Inc. (1977). *Cost Differential Study*: *State of Connecticut*. Final Report to the Connecticut Hospital Association.

Miller, R., and Luft, H. (1993). Managed care: Past evidence and potential trends. *Frontiers of Health Services Management* 10: in publication.

Morris, J. (1985). *Searching for a Cure*: *National Health Policy Considered*. Berkley-Morgan, Washington, DC.

National Leadership Commission on Health Care (1989). *For the Health of a Nation*. Health Association Press, Ann Arbor, MI.

Nozick, R. (1974). *Anarchy, State and Utopia*. Basic Books, New York.

Nutter, D., Helms, C., et al. (1991). Restructuring health care in the United States. *JAMA* 19: 2516.

Office of the Federal Register (1939). *The Public Papers and Addresses of Franklin D. Roosevelt, 1939*. Macmillan, New York, pp. 97 ff.

Office of the Federal Register (1960). *Public Papers of the Presidents of the United States*: *Dwight D. Eisenhower*. National Archives and Records Service, Washington, DC, p. 77.

Organization for Economic Cooperation and Development (1987). *Financing and Delivering Health Care*. OECD, Paris.

Osborne, D., and Gaebler, T. (1991). *Reinvesting Government*. Addison-Wesley, Reading, MA.

Pauly, M. (1970). *Medical Care at Public Expense*. Praeger, New York.

—— (1988). Is medical care different? *Journal of Health Politics, Policy and Law* 13: 227–237.

Pauly, M., Danzon, P., Feldstein, P., and Hoff, J. (1991). A plan for responsible health insurance. *Health Affairs* 10: 5.

Pfaff, M. (1991). Differences in health and spending across countries: Statistical evidence. *Journal of Health Politics, Policy and Law* 15: 1.

Phelps, C. (1992). *Health Economics*. Harper Collins, New York, pp. 505–508.

The President's Commission on the Health Needs of the Nation (1952). *Building America's Health*. Government Printing Office, Washington, DC, p. 1.

Relman, A. (1991). Where does all that money go? *Health Management Quarterly* 13: 2.

Rice, T. (1992). Containing health care in the United States. *Medical Care Review* 49: 19–66.

Richardson, J. (Ed.) (1987). *A Compilation of the Messages and Papers of Presidents, 1789–1989*. Bureau of National Literature, New York, pp. 2782–2784.

Riley, G., Cubits, J., Prihoda, R., and Stevenson, M. (1986). Changes in distribution of Medicare expenditures among aged enrollees, 1969–82. *Health Care Financing Review* 7: 53–64.

Robinson, J., and Luft, H. (1987). Competition and the cost of health care, 1971–1982. *JAMA* (June 19): 3241.

Rockefeller, J. (1991). The Pepper Commission's blue print for health care reform. *JAMA* 19: 2507.

Roos, L., et al. (1990). Post-surgical mortality in Manitoba and New England. *JAMA* 263: 2453.

—— (1992). Health and surgical outcomes in Canada and the U.S. *Health Affairs* 11(2): 56.

Rosko, M. (1989a). A comparison of hospital performance under the partial Medicare PPS and state all-payer rate setting systems. *Inquiry* 26: 48.

Rosko, M. (1989b). Impact of the New Jersey all-payer rate setting system: An analysis of financial ratios. *Hospital and Health Services Administration* 34: 53.

Rosko, M., and Broyles, R. (1986). Impact of the New Jersey all-payer DRG system. *Inquiry* 23: 67.

—— (1987). Short-term responses to the DRG Prospective pricing mechanism in New Jersey. Medical Care 25: 88.

—— (1988). *The Economics of Health Care*: *A Reference Handbook*. Greenwood Press, New York.

Rossiter, L., Nelson, M., and Adamache, K. (1988). Service use and costs for Medicare beneficiaries in risk-based HMOs and CMPs. *American Journal of Public Health* 78: 937.

Roublee, D. (1989). Medical technology in Canada, German and the United States. *Health Affairs* 8: 178.

Roybal, E. (1991). The US health act. *JAMA* 19: 2545.

Salkever, D., Steinwachs, D., and Rupp, A. (1986). Hospital cost and efficiency under per service and per case payment in Maryland. *Inquiry* 23: 56.

Saltman, R. (1992). Single-source financing systems: A solution for the United States? *JAMA* 6: 774.

Schieber, G., Poullier, J. P., and Greenwald, L. (1992). An international comparison and data update. *Health Care Financing Review* 13: 1–88.

Schwartz, W., and Mendelson, D. (1992). Why managed care cannot contain hospital costs—without rationing. *Health Affairs* 11: 100–107.

Scitovsky, A. (1984). The high cost of dying: What do the data show? *Milbank Memorial Fund Quarterly/Health and Society* 62: 591–608.

Schiels, J., Young, G., and Rubin, R. (1992). Canada: Do we expect too much from its health system. *Health Affairs* 11(1): 7.

Sigerist, H. (1970). *Medicine and Human Welfare*. McGrath, College Park, MD, p. 57. Cited in Banta, 1990.

Slaby, A., and Tanoredi, L. (1977). The politics of moral values: Policy implications. *Journal of Health Politics, Policy and Law* 2: 20–31.

Sloan, F., and Becker, E. (1984). Cross subsidies and payment for hospital care. *Journal of Health Politics, Policy and Law* 8: 660.

Spitz, B., and Abramson, J. (1987). Competition, capitation and care management: Barriers to strategic reform. *The Milbank Quarterly* 65: 3.

Terris, M. (1991). Global budgeting and the control of hospital costs. *Journal of Public Health Policy* 12: 61.

Thorpe, K. (1987). Does all-payer rate setting work? The case of the New York prospective reimbursement methodology. Journal of Health Politics, Policy and Law 12: 391.

—— (1992). Health care cost containment: Results and lessons from the past 20 years. In *Improving Health Policy and Management*. S. Shortell and U. Reinhardt (Eds.). Health Administration Press, Ann Arbor, MI, pp. 227–274.

U.S. Department of Commerce, Bureau of the Census (1991). *Statistical Abstract of The United States*. U.S. Government Printing Office, Washington, DC, Table Nos. 1451–1542.

U.S. Department of Commerce (1990). Health and Medical Services. *U.S. Industrial Outlook*, Washington, DC.

U.S. Government Accounting Office/USGAO (1992). *Health Care Spending: Nonpolicy Factors Account for Most State Differences*. USGAO, Washington, DC.

Wilensky, G. (1988). Filling the gaps in Health insurance: Impact on competition. *Health Affairs* 7: 133.

Wilensky, G., and Rossiter, L. (1986). Alternative units of payment for physician services. *Medical Care Review* 43: 133.

Woolhandler, S., and Himmelstein, D. (1991). The deteriorating administrative efficiency of the U.S. health care system. *New England Journal of Medicine* 324: 1253.

Zuckerman, S. (1987). Rate setting and cost containment: All-payer versus partial payer approaches. *Health Services Research* 22: 307.5–84.

32
Energy Policy

Robert M. Lawrence
Colorado State University, Fort Collins, Colorado

It was in the 1970s that the United States awoke to the fact it did not have a national energy policy. The "wake-up call" came in the form of politically caused dislocations in the flow of oil to the United States and its allies from the Middle East arising out of the periodic wars between the state of Israel and various Arab neighbors. The "oil weapon," as it was called in those days, was an effort by Arab oil-exporting nations to pressure the United States and some of the Western European states to cease their support of Israel or face the cutoff of Middle Eastern oil. The oil weapon failed in the sense that it galvanized the Nixon administration and subsequent administrations to think about energy in terms of national policy and to organize an effort for achieving energy independence. By 1993, neither the national energy policy nor the correlative organizational efforts required to implement it were fully complete, but President George Bush did sign into law a National Energy Act in October of 1992, and President Bill Clinton did inherit an articulated national energy strategy.

A complicating and confusing factor in the formulation of the nation's energy policy was the lack of hard evidence regarding the impact on the world's climate that could be expected from the continued burning of fossil fuels. The near certainty among scientific spokespersons of a few years ago had by 1993 given way to some scepticism regarding the actual effects resulting from the burning of petroleum products, coal, and wood.

Energy independence has not been achieved, and given the political, economic, environmental, and supply problems, probably could not have been. However, the realization born of the 1970 problems, compounded by pressure from environmental groups to adopt clean-energy alternatives, led to the creation of a Department of Energy and several efforts to create a national energy plan. Like many national policies in the United States, the one for energy fluctuates somewhat according to which political party occupies the White House. The party most often in office since Lyndon Johnson decided not to run for reelection in 1968 has been the Republican Party. Republicans typically view energy as a production and distribution problem and rely on market forces to produce efficient solutions. Republicans, especially Ronald Reagan and his followers, are wary of moving too fast in imposing controls on energy production and use before the allegations of environmental damage are fully demonstrated. The Democrats typically believe in tempering market forces with government action designed to protect both the interests of their poor and middle-class constituents and of the environment.

In 1991, the Persian Gulf War between Iraq and the United Nations Coalition led by the United States, appeared to many to be a war about who would control the oil-rich lands on either side of the Persian Gulf. Although Kuwait was freed of Iraqi domination, and gasoline prices in the United States stabilized between $1.25 and $1.50 a gallon, the Middle East situation remained volatile, with Israel, which has little oil, and Iraq and Iran, which have huge oil supplies, remaining as potential belligerents in a future war. The largest Mideast producer of oil, Saudi Arabia, continues as a conservative monarchy in a region seething with religious and political upheaval, and experts debate how long the Saudi ruling family will continue to control the country.

Even as Iraq was held in check by the United Nations sanctions voted into place during the Gulf War, Iran was embarked on a $2 billion a year arms build-up. In response to Western criticism of their arming, Iran's Deputy Foreign Minister Ali Mohammad Besharati noted that Iran was surrounded by potentially hostile neighbors and thus was warranted in replacing the equipment lost in the 8-year Iran-Iraq war. Intelligence experts at the Central Intelligence and Department of State are divided about whether and how soon the Iranians could develop nuclear weapons. Because of the unresolved political problems in the Middle East, U.S. energy policy will continue to be held hostage to some extent to events in that troubled part of the world.

The good news about the Middle East was that the dissolution of the Soviet Union and the independence of Eastern Europe meant the United States would no longer need fear Soviet efforts to influence the supply of Mideast oil in order to advance the interests of Communism. Additionally, the demise of the Soviet Union meant that less emphasis would be needed to produce an array of nuclear weapons to counter the U.S.S.R., and thus there was talk of sharply reducing the activities of the national nuclear weapons laboratories and production centers, with the possibility that some money thus saved could be invested in new energy technologies.

On the home front, environmentalists claimed that certain energy practices substantially endangered the Earth's environment, and in some cases directly threatened human life. Of greatest concern was the greenhouse effect, and the question of where radioactive wastes from nuclear power plants and the nation's nuclear weapons programs could be safely stored for centuries.

Regardless of the swings in energy policy based on differing views of what it is proper for government to do and which constituencies have the most influence on different administrations, certain characteristics of energy policy appear to endure both the passage of time and changes in the national political leadership. For example, there are the physical properties and geographical location of various energy sources; the economic costs of energy production and distribution; environmental concerns; and the interface of energy policy with foreign and defense priorities (Yergin, 1991).

I. CREATION OF THE DEPARTMENT OF ENERGY

In 1977, the Congress passed the Department of Energy Organization Act (Public Law 95-91), and the Department was activated by President Jimmy Carter on October 1, under its first

Secretary, James R. Schlesinger. According to its own public information statement, the Department of Energy is responsible for

> . . . long-term, high-risk research and development of energy technology; the marketing of federal power; energy conservation; the nuclear weapons program; energy regulatory programs; and a central energy data collection and analysis program (Department of Energy, 1991: 1)

Prior to its establishment, there were a number of precursor agencies to the Department of Energy, each one of which held responsibilities that encompassed bits and pieces of the nation's energy activities. For example, prior to World War II, the Tennessee Valley Authority and the Department of Interior (the Bonneville Power Administration, Southwest Power Administration) had built large hydroelectric dams on river systems such as the Tennessee, Columbia, and Colorado. The rates for the electricity from such projects crossing state boundaries are regulated by the Federal Power Authority and the Interstate Commerce Commission. Beginning in the 1930s, the Rural Electrification Administration made loans to construct electric lines to farm families, and in some cases, it assisted in building power plants to provide electricity to rural Americans.

In terms of technological research and development, the antecedents to the Department of Energy can be traced back to 1942 when the Manhattan Engineer District of the US Army was created to develop the atomic bomb. Following World War II, Congress debated whether the new form of energy obtained from splitting uranium and plutonium atoms should be placed under military or civilian control. President Harry Truman favored the latter, and in January 1947, the Atomic Energy Commission (AEC) was established and headed by a civilian chair, with four other civilian commissioners. The AEC was charged with the development of additional nuclear weapons, including in 1949 thermonuclear bombs; with the design of nuclear reactors to propel naval vessels, particularly submarines; and with the task of modifying the wartime nuclear reactors designed to produce the artificial element plutonium for bombs to civilian reactors operated to produce electricity for domestic and industrial uses. As civilian nuclear power reactors came on-line, the AEC was made responsible for their regulation, with special emphasis on safety concerns.

Responding to the energy crisis of the early 1970s, President Nixon established the Federal Energy Office in the Executive Office of the White House in 1973. The next year, the Federal Energy Administration was created as a temporary but independent agency, whose responsibilities included the development of a petroleum products allocation plan together with energy conservation policies, establishment of the strategic petroleum reserve, and the collection of energy information and its analysis.

By 1975, political pressure built to have the civilian nuclear power reactors regulated by an independent agency rather than the AEC. The consequence was that the AEC was dissolved and two new agencies were established. The Nuclear Regulatory Commission (NRC) was empowered to regulate civilian nuclear power reactors, whereas the Energy Research and Development Administration (ERDA) was created to manage the programs in regard to nuclear weapons, naval reactors, and energy development.

The philosophical differences between Republican and Democratic perspectives can be seen in the difference between the Carter and Ford administrations. For example, in his 1976 energy message, President Gerald Ford supported ideas such as the deregulation of natural gas, increased funding for nuclear power, authorization for the private enrichment of uranium, amendment of the Clean Air Act to ease automobile emission standards, encouragement for the greater use of coal, and the extraction of oil from the Naval Petroleum Reserves.

In contrast, President Jimmy Carter's national energy perspective urged the nation to reduce its consumption of energy, adopt energy-conservation measures, and develop energy alternatives to the heavy reliance on oil and coal. These themes were advanced in the National Energy Conservation Policy Act, the Powerplant and Industrial Fuel Use Act, the Public Utilities Regulatory Policy Act, the Energy Tax Act, the Natural Gas Policy Act, and finally by the creation of the Synthetic Fuels Corporation. President Carter was not successful in persuading the Congress to pass the crude oil equalization tax that was intended to increase the price of domestically produced crude oil to world levels in order to stimulate conservation.

During the Carter administration, the sense of concern about energy policy was heightened by the hostage crisis with Iran and the accident at the Three Mile Island nuclear power plant in Pennsylvania.

Reflecting Republican philosophy, the Reagan administration changed the national energy plan to implement a different set of values than those in place during the Carter years. The new national energy plan was designed to control federal spending, reduce inflation, and stimulate growth in the economy by eliminating government regulations and price controls that were believed by the Reagan administration to discourage domestic energy production. The Reagan national energy plan emphasized privatization where possible and looked for market forces to stimulate energy exploration and development. As with other functions of the federal government except for national defense activities, President Reagan attempted to restore the government to what he conceived was its proper role, which was a more limited role than previously was the case. Initially this thrust included the suggestion that the Department of Energy be disassembled.

Congress, particularly the Democrats, disagreed, and the Department of Energy continued to function—with special emphasis on nuclear weapons development and modernization, including an effort to use lasers and particle beams to devise a defense against incoming ballistic missiles; filling the Strategic Petroleum Reserve with oil; eliminating or modifying federal energy regulations perceived as barriers to private enterprise; and attempting to stimulate the development of synthetic fuels in the private sector.

In the middle years of the Reagan administration, the original thrust toward reducing the government's role in energy activities ran up against the fact that certain energy research and development initiatives are too large, too costly, and too risky for the private investment sector to support. Facing this reality, Department of Energy Secretary Donald P. Hodel sought more privatization of energy research and development activities where possible, but he also supported federal investment in expensive basic research areas. These included supercomputers, the Superconducting Super-Collider project in Texas, high-energy physics, new nuclear reactors, and advanced solar energy systems.

In President Reagan's last term, John S. Herrington served as the Secretary of the Department of Energy. Secretary Hodel's themes were continued and the Department responded to increased public concern over the safety and environmental protection at the nation's aging nuclear weapons production facilities and laboratories, including production and research nuclear reactors. This concern was heightened by the 1986 accident at the Chernobyl nuclear reactor near Kiev, in what would become the independent nation of Ukraine by 1992.

Retired Navy Admiral James D. Watkins was appointed the Secretary of the Department of Energy by President Bush. Watkins and the Bush administration were less intense than the Reagan administration regarding the reduction of governmental activity and the corresponding increase in the private sector; still that Republican theme continued in a more muted form.

II. THE BUSH ADMINISTRATION'S NATIONAL ENERGY PLAN

On February 20, 1991, the Bush administration unveiled another national energy plan—this time it was titled the National Energy Strategy. The plan may be analyzed in terms of its four constituent parts: increasing energy and economic efficiency, securing future energy supplies, enhancing environmental quality, and fortifying foundations.

A. Increasing Energy and Economic Efficiency

Realizing that 36% of the energy currently consumed in the United States is used to generate electricity, the National Energy Strategy seeks to harmonize the extensive federal, state, and local oversight of the electric power industry so that electric producers will have fewer rules and regulations confronting them.

Both taxes and government fiscal incentives are seen as tools to be used for stimulating more efficient energy operations. For example, a favorite incentive of President Bush was the Alternative Minimum Tax (ATM) relief plan. This is an arrangement whereby independent oil and natural gas producers are provided more than $1 billion in tax relief in the period 1992 to 1997. Further, the government itself will seek to serve as a model for more efficient energy use as for example in the construction of government buildings. Additional evaluation of the CAFE (Corporate Average Fuel Economy) program is designed to further the energy efficiency of the government's extensive fleet of vehicles.

Another stimulus for the natural gas industry is the deregulation of natural gas pipeline rates as well as the reform of pipeline rate structures.

Efficiency is not only the concern of the federal government. Both environmentalists and those supporting the sustainable growth perspective place energy efficiency high on their list of "must" changes in how the nation utilizes energy. Why that is so is demonstrated by the following quotation from Meadows et al. (1932) in *Beyond the Limits*:

It [energy efficiency] means the same or better material quality of life, usually at less cost—not only less direct energy cost, but also less pollution, less drawdown of domestic energy sources, less conflict over siting facilities, and, for many countries, less foreign debt and less military cost to maintain access to or control over foreign resources.

Further

On the conservative end of the range, it seems certain that the North American economy could do everything it now does, with currently available technologies and at current or lower costs, using half as much energy (Meadows et al., 1932: 75).

B. Securing Future Energy Supplies

1. Oil

Forty percent of the nation's primary energy use is in the form of oil, and 97% of the energy used in the United States for transportation comes from oil. During the early 1990s, the nation consumed nearly 17 million gallons of oil a day, of which slightly over 7 million barrels per day (MBD) came from domestic production leaving approximately 10 MBD to be imported. In terms of total usage, the United States accounts for about 25% of world consumption.

The problems with oil are that (1) much of the oil obtained from overseas comes from the politically volatile Middle East, and (2) when oil is burned, there are environmental impacts, the exact character of which has not yet been fully determined.

Until recently, the political volatility of the Middle East was a result of the hostility between the state of Israel and various Arab nations, with the latter using the oil weapon to punish Western countries providing support for Israel or using the artificially high price of oil to purchase an array of high-technology weapons, some of which could be used against Israel. Sometimes Arab oil nations would share oil revenues with terrorist groups, including the Palestine Liberation Organization. Now, additional destabilizing factors in the Middle East political equation include the political ambitions of Saddam Hussein of Iraq, and the rising political clout of the fundamentalist Islamic perspective seen most dramatically in Iran but with adherents in other nations such as Egypt.

In terms of U.S. energy dependence on foreign sources, it is unfortunate that some 65% of the world's known oil reserves are found in the Persian Gulf area, principally in the nations of Saudi Arabia, Iran, Iraq, Kuwait, and lesser principalities. Given assumptions about the continued growth in oil consumption by the United States and its industrialized allies, plus the growth in the use of oil by the developing nations, there appears no feasible means by which either the world or the United States can insulate itself from substantial reliance on Persian Gulf oil. Instead of oil independence, which was in fact the announced policy of Washington for a short period during the Nixon administration, the United States has adopted, and is expanding, a number of policies designed to absorb and deflect the deleterious impacts of dependence on Middle East oil.

Collectively, these policies are called energy security activities. They include economic support for a diversified and increased supply of oil outside the Middle East; greater energy efficiency and flexibility in all sectors of the U.S. economy, particularly in transportation where more reliance on alternative fuels is the stated goal. The National Energy Strategy calls for improved contingency planning with the expansion of correlative mechanisms such as larger international stockpiles of oil and the development of additional "excess" production capacity, both of which can be utilized in crisis periods to moderate the pressure for higher prices and to offset the political gains of nations using oil for their national purposes. Emergency preparedness plans to respond to emergencies are heightened by support for the plan to enlarge the nation's Strategic Petroleum Reserve up to 1 billion barrels, and the development of advanced recovery techniques for increasingly harder to obtain oil that remains in existing domestic oil fields.

The search for increased and diversified oil reserves is made difficult by a variety of factors. Within the United States, developers of additional oil and gas supplies must contend with the political fact of life that access to the oil and gas under federal lands is contested by environmental groups. Examples of this difference of opinion has developed in regard to the coastal plain of the Arctic National Wildlife Refuge (ANWR) in Alaska and the Outer Continental Shelf off the nation's ocean coast lines. Proponents of the development of the ANWR point to the surge in domestic oil production occasioned by the development of the Prudhoe Bay region in Alaska. Further, supporters of the ANWR development state that tapping the 8% of the refuge that is coastal plain could dramatically increase the domestic oil production of the nation. One estimate is that the ANWR could provide an additional 870,000 barrels per day of oil by 2005 (Department of Energy, 1991/1992: 79). New oil production in the ANWR would also carry the advantage of ensuring that the Alaska oil pipeline will continue to be used at full capacity as the North Slope production declines in the future. And in a proposal that bothers some environmentalists, potential ANWR developers point out that oil discoveries in the area could contribute to additional development of other North Slope and Beaufort Sea areas. Opponents prefer alternative energy sources, and they note the environmental damage done to the Prince William Sound area of Alaska when an oil tanker ran aground and its tanks spilled oil into the Sound.

In Alaska, but outside the boundaries of the ANWR, are five major oil and gas fields that have not been developed. These are West Sak, Point Thompson, Seal Island/North Star, Gwydyr Bay, and Sandpiper Island. At the current time, regulatory and technical barriers prevent the development of these fields.

In 1990, President Bush deferred the leasing of Outer Continental Shelf areas off the coasts of Washington, Oregon, California, and parts of the north Atlantic seaboard and eastern Gulf of Mexico areas until the year 2000. The basic argument for development of these deferred areas is the estimate that there is a good chance they will contain 3.1 billion barrels of recoverable oil and 9.4 trillion cubic feet of natural gas.

At the current time, states off whose coasts oil and natural gas development takes place receive 100% of the revenues from leases within 3 miles of shore, except for Florida and Texas whose state waters extend outward about 10 miles. Otherwise revenues from leases between 3 and more than 6 miles beyond state waters are divided 73% to the federal government and 27% to the state governments. Revenues from leases beyond 6 miles of shore go entirely to the federal government. Prodevelopment interests within the Bush administration pointed out that changing the allocation of lease funds to benefit coastal communities more would add an incentive for such development.

In an effort to stimulate recovery from depleted oil fields, and to encourage independent producers, in 1990, President Bush proposed and the Congress adopted a package of tax incentives. Nevertheless, the costs to producers of recovering oil left in older fields is hampered by the increasing costs of advanced recovery techniques.

New external oil reserves beyond the Middle East are made difficult to develop because oil-prosperous nations are understandably hesitant to permit extensive U.S. investment and control of new and modern drilling operations; thus oil production remains somewhat outdated and inefficient. To encourage non–Middle East nations to exploit their oil reserves, the United States is exploring new arrangements that would preserve the oil-prosperous nations' sovereignty but permit U.S. development investments. Much American interest has been shown in Russia since the demise of Communism.

2. Natural Gas

Natural gas furnishes about 20% of the energy used in the United States. Its use is especially important for home heating, where it supplies approximately half of the energy consumed in U.S. homes. Attractive aspects of natural gas include the fact that only about 8% is imported from abroad, and almost all of that is from Canada; thus largely freeing Washington from concerns regarding the potential cutoff of supplies due to political instability. The cost of natural gas is reasonable in comparison with other fuels, and natural gas is considered a "clean" source of energy. By that it is meant the burning of natural gas produces hardly any sulfur oxides, essentially no particulate matter (smoke), and considerably less nitrogen and carbon oxides than other fossil fuels. In particular, the consumption of natural gas results in much less carbon dioxide than coal or oil.

Given these attractive characteristics of natural gas, it comes as a surprise to learn that its use has fallen by more than 10% since 1970. The explanation provided by the Bush administration's Department of Energy is that federal and state regulations have accumulated in such a way as to create:

> . . . an atmosphere that is not conducive to the investment decision necessary for producers, transporters, and consumers of natural gas to expand the market. Indeed, our

analysis suggests that current statutory and regulatory impediments may be decreasing natural gas use by about 1 trillion cubic feet each year (Department of Energy, 1991/1992: 86–87).

Therefore, the National Energy Strategy contains language that mandates efforts to streamline the Environmental Impact Statement (EIS) process required by the Environmental Protection Agency in regard to the construction of new gas pipelines that involve "major federal actions." Instead of all federal agencies involved in the pipeline construction, preparing EIS papers, only one agency, the Federal Energy Regulatory Commission, will be required to file an EIS. In response to chronic supply shortages in the wellhead-regulated interstate natural gas market, compared with abundant supplies in the unregulated intrastate markets, the Wellhead Decontrol Act of 1989 was passed into law. Accordingly, wellhead price controls were eliminated by January 1993. Also, the Omnibus Budget Reconciliation Act of 1990 contained several energy tax incentives that will benefit natural gas producers with the intended result of spurring production.

3. Coal

Most abundant of the nation's fossil fuels, coal now provides 24% of the primary energy used in the United States. Further, coal is a valuable export earning foreign exchange credits with shipments to Europe, South America, and Japan. The dimensions of the U.S. coal wealth are impressive. More than a quarter of the world's coal is in the United States, and this supply represents 90% of all the energy resources in the nation. Eight-six percent of the coal is used in the generation of electricity, with about 55% of the nation's electricity being produced by the burning of coal to convert water to steam and thence to electricity.

Coal is extremely attractive as a national fuel because the entire supply is beyond the reach of any foreign political action, thus guaranteeing the security of supply, and the size of the U.S. coal supply means the price is reasonable. On the other hand, however, both the mining of coal and its burning result in significant human safety and environmental problems, with some of the latter not yet thoroughly understood.

This interface of attractive economic and supply characteristics of coal with safety and environmental concerns frames the problems to which the Department of Energy and associated entities must respond. According to the National Energy Strategy Plan, the effort to resolve this set of circumstances contains a number of initiatives.

The safety of miners working the underground deposits of coal, primarily in the eastern half of the United States, was legislated into law with the Federal Coal Mine Health and Safety Act of 1969. This legislation is enforced by the U.S. Bureau of Mines.

The immediate environmental concerns about coal mining, both strip mining on the surface and underground mining, are surface subsidence resulting from the collapse of underground mines, dust caused by surface mining, acid water runoff, and land reclamation. In general, these concerns are addressed in the Surface Mining Control and Reclamation Act, whose implementing agency is the Department of the Interior. The U.S. Bureau of Mines within the Interior Department and the Environmental Protection Agency, an independent entity, also are involved in the environmental aspects of coal mining. The position of the Bush administration regarding environmental problems associated with coal mining is seen in official language on the subject.

The Administration's policy goal is to protect the environment, but also ensure that regulations are effective, timely, and economical. Reducing uncertainty over the content of new regulations is a critical element of this policy (Department of Energy, 1991/1992: 101).

Perhaps more formidable, because they are less well understood, and therefore more controversial, are the potential impacts of coal burning upon the Earth's climate. The problem is defined by the term *greenhouse effect*. It is contended by many scientists that the carbon dioxide released when coal is burned accumulates in the atmosphere where it traps heat from the sun, thus leading to a warming of the Earth's temperature with allegedly deleterious effects.

In analyzing the potential for damage from a greenhouse effect, it should first be noted that some amount of greenhouse effect, like that present during the evolution of humans, is useful because a modest amount of heat entrapment ensures the kind of climate that has been conducive to both plant and animal development. In comparison to Earth, the atmosphere on Mars is thin and lacking in carbon dioxide, thus too cold for life as we know it. In fact, there is a proposal, called terra forming, that would increase the greenhouse effect on Mars 100 years from now by artificially introducing carbon dioxide to the point where enough heat is retained to make the planet habitable. The opposite to Mars in Venus. There it appears too much carbon dioxide traps heat to the extent that life is not possible.

Thus, the argument about the contemporary greenhouse effect is that, on the one hand, the Earth needs more carbon dioxide than Mars but not nearly as much as Venus. Or, to put it another way, the contemporary amount of carbon dioxide in the Earth's atmosphere is about right and care should be taken not to increase it dramatically. Then the "64-dollar" question is whether, and to what extent, continued and increased burning of coal and other industrial and agricultural activities contributes to an increase in the greenhouse effect and the resulting rise in temperatures that would be harmful. An associated environmental concern regarding the burning of coal is acid rain. This problem is believed to result from the combination of oxides of sulfur, released by combustion of fossil fuels, gasoline and coal, with water to produce very weak sulfuric acid that is deposited as rain or snow, with harmful effects on structures made of stone and marble and on plant life.

In the 1980s, vocal scientists and politicians raised the concern about global warming. A prime example was a high-profile scientist at the National Center for Atmospheric Research (NCAR) named Stephen Schneider. Schneider wrote and spoke about the greenhouse effect, appeared before congressional committees, and eventually wrote a book about his concerns. *Global Warming* was published by the Sierra Club in 1989, and it represents an environmental perspective about the relationship of coal use and the Earth's climate.

Politicians, such as Tim Wirth, former Democratic Senator from Colorado, and the Vice President of the United States, former Democratic Senator Albert Gore from Tennessee, were early adherents of Schneider's concern. On the dust jacket of *Global Warming*, the Vice President wrote

Global warming will be the greatest environmental challenge of the 21st century. Stephen Schneider has become a principal source of expertise for policymakers concerned about the potential consequences of climate change. His *Global Warming* is one of the most concise and authoritative accounts of the science and policy issues surrounding this most important debate.

And in his own book, *Earth in the Balance*, Vice President Gore (1992: 96) wrote

Given the apparent close relationship between CO2 and temperatures in the past, it hardly seems reasonable—or even ethical—to assume that it is it is probably all right to keep driving up CO2 levels. In fact, it is almost certainly not all right. Isn't it reasonable to assume that this environmental equilibrium could have sudden and disastrous effects?

Prominent lay environmentalists such as Robert Redford lent their names to support Schneider's work. Also on the dust jacket of *Global Warming* appeared this statement from Redford:

Climate change could well be the biggest challenge now facing the world. All of us will need to understand climate change in order to learn how we can slow it down and adapt to that which cannot be avoided. Stephen Schneider is masterful at translating enormously complex scientific principles into a language that we can all comprehend.

In his book, and it is representative of the thinking done by many others, Schneider attempts to assess the probabilities that modern industrial practices like, but not limited to, increased burning of fossil fuels such as oil and coal, will increase the greenhouse effect in ways that will be harmful. Although carefully employing caveats which reflect scientific unknowns, Schnelder (1989: 284) nevertheless ends the book with this concluding statement:

"Are we entering the Greenhouse Century?" I asked in the subtitle of this book. It should be clear by now that I believe we've been in it for a while already, but admit that it will take a decade or so more of record heat, forest fires, intense hurricanes or droughts to convince the substantial number of sceptics that still abound. Unfortunately, while the antagonists debate, the greenhouse gases keep building up in the atmosphere. I wonder what we will say to our children when they eventually ask what we did—or didn't do— to create the Greenhouse Century they will inherit.

Schneider and others, including former Senator Tim Wirth and Vice President Gore, moved from the scientific perspectives in which they believed to the political arena of actions to be taken in response to the problems associated with an increasing greenhouse effect. What Schneider proposed in his book, what Wirth suggested before the Senate, and what Gore wrote in his book were collectively a series of technological improvements to reduce the emission of carbon dioxide and other gases from the combustion of coal and finding energy alternatives to coal which produce less greenhouse gases, or, in the case of solar energy, no greenhouse gases.

Persons such as Schneider, the scientist, and Wirth and Gore, the politicians, are generally mindful of the economic impact on industry and labor when dramatic changes are mandated for environmental purposes. After suggesting that electric-generating plants switch from coal to natural gas in order to reduce acid rain and carbon dioxide, Schneider writes (1989: 264–265)

I realize that such a switch would be a staggering blow to the coal mining industry. . . . To be sure, a fair-minded society would not expect one industry or group of workers to absorb such an economic shock without major financial assistance. I am happy to have my taxes on energy services increased for the purposes of job retraining, worker relocation, developing alternative industry in the region, and so on.

Taking a different view to that of the Schneiders, Wirths, and Gores of this world are the Reagans and Bushs. Their philosophical position is that government should not move to modify or dislocate business and industry until such time as hard evidence exists that certain practices are indeed harmful to the environment and then action can be taken. As the Bush administration's Department of Energy put it:

> The overriding theme behind these goals is to reduce the *scientific uncertainty* [emphasis added] associated with climate change and to develop cost-effective, long-term strategies that will balance energy and environmental needs (Department of Energy, 1991/1992: 172–173).

On page 174 of the same report, the statement is found:

> In virtually all these issues, the salient feature is the *significant scientific uncertainty* [emphasis added] associated with predicting the behavior of the coupled ocean-atmosphere-land Earth system.

The principal component of the Bush administration's effort to establish the true situation regarding the greenhouse effect is the U.S. Global Change Research Program. Thus, President Bush could claim that he was "the environmental President" even as environmentalists asserted he was merely protecting business interests at the expense of the environment.

The argument between the Bush administration and the United States and other governments and environmentalists regarding appropriate responses to the greenhouse effect came to a head in June of 1992 at the United Nations Earth Summit held in Rio de Janeiro, Brazil. On the one hand, the U.S. industrial allies favored a treaty that would contain timetables and elimination rates for the reduction of greenhouse gases, most notable of which was carbon dioxide. On the other hand, President Bush, backed by business groups, objected to including strict performance standards regarding the burning of fossil fuels into an international treaty binding on the United States. Instead, the president and his allies preferred energy conservation to mandated standards.

In an interesting juxtaposition of U.S. leadership, the Democratically controlled Senate sent Albert Gore, then a senator from Tennessee, to represent that body at the Earth Summit. During the ensuing presidential election campaign, the senator who would become the vice president sharply criticized President Bush for his lack of environmental responsibility, including that at the Rio meetings. For his part, President Bush cynically referred to then Senator Gore as "Mr. Ozone" during the closing days of the 1992 presidential campaign.

The Earth Summit involved more than arguments between U.S. politicians. It also symbolized a clash of interests between the developed world, which to date has created most of the world's pollution, including the production of greenhouse gases, and the developing world, which is being asked to develop in ways that preserve the environment and retard global warming, all at considerable economic cost.

In a sense, China is representative of the developing nations that cannot visualize themselves making economic sacrifices in response to requests by developed nations sitting atop a standard of living made possible by ignoring the environment. The particular problem the developed world has with China is in regard to Beijing's plans to expand industrialization dramatically by burning an increasing amount of its extensive coal reserves. According to some western observers, this will make China the number one emitter of carbon dioxide after the year 2000 and thus a major contributor to the presumed warming of the Earth. To date, the Chinese have shown little interest in curbing their industrialization in order to lessen what may or may not be a global warming problem.

Both former President Bush and the Chinese government can cite a growing number, but still a minority, of scientists who urge a go-slow approach to changing industrial habits out of concern for the greenhouse effect. Their perspective is that too many variables that are not well understood are involved in the physics of the Earth's climate to make definitive predictions about global warning. The doubting scientists also noted that increased carbon dioxide should be absorbed by the oceans and that some warming and increased CO_2 would be beneficial to plant life.

Because of the complexity of the situation and the intensity of opposing views, the scientific argumentation on the relationship of fossil fuel burning to global warming, and resultant political activity, will probably continue on for some time. Arguments about exactly how the dispute should be viewed and what to do about global warming could wax and wane in accord with the data base that is accumulated and various interpretations of it.

For its part, the Department of Energy in the Bush administration stated it would work with the standards established by the Clean Air Act Amendments of 1990, which is intended to reduce sulfur dioxide and nitrogen oxides, but warned that switching to low-sulfur coal would

> . . .disrupt local economies and create unemployment in some regions that produce high-sulfur coal. Reducing the use of coal would hurt coal-producing regions in general (Department of Energy, 1991/1992: 102).

At the time, Schneider (1989) published his book, when many other articles and speeches were also emanating from the scientific community on the increase in the greenhouse effect, the weather in the United States seemed to be adding support for the global warming hypothesis. The last several years of the 1980s and the first of the 1990s were hotter than usual. But then the summers of 1991 and 1992 were cooler, and discordant voices were raised in the scientific community casting doubt upon the analyses of Schneider and others.

However, some scientists suggested that the cooling was the result of the 1991 eruption of Mt. Penatubo in the Philippines, which hurled tons of very small particulate matter into the upper atmosphere. Their thesis was that as the fine ash circulated high above the Earth, it reflected energy from the sun; thus perhaps compensating for the warming caused by the greenhouse effect.

While Bush adherents, on the one hand and environmentalists, on the other hand, argue about global warming, both sides generally agree that a number of technical improvements in the combustion of coal that are touted to improve efficiency and reduce the harmful oxides should be pursued. Of course with the change in presidential administrations, and in particular with former Senator Gore as the vice president, one may expect to see an acceleration in the efforts to find alternatives to coal, as well as in the efforts to clean up the burning of coal.

4. Nuclear Power

There are 111 nuclear plants in the United States. Approximately 20% of the nation's electricity is produced by nuclear power. Nuclear power plants produce no greenhouse gases and no acid rain. The uranium fuel for such plants is indigenous to the United States, which ensures the energy security of nuclear power.

In spite of these advantages, no new nuclear reactor has been ordered in the United States since 1978. The reason is the widespread perception by many Americans that nuclear reactors are not safe and the correlative concern that the wastes from nuclear reactors is difficult, if not impossible, to dispose of safely. These worries stem in part from remembrances of the accident at the Three Mile Island nuclear power station in Pennsylvania, and the much more serious accident at the Chernobyl nuclear facility near Kiev, in what is now Ukraine.

The situation with nuclear reactors is a good example of the NIMBY syndrome, wherein residents living near to a proposed nuclear power plant location say in effect "not in my back yard." This perspective means that electric utility company executives who propose to construct nuclear plants must contemplate a long, arduous, and expensive fight in the media, in various political contexts, and in the courts before their investments pay off. The prospect of having construction delayed and funds tied up during the process of obtaining the necessary siting permits is obviously unattractive to the utilities' management when compared with the quicker, easier, and less costly construction of a plant fueled by oil or coal. In fact, a Department of Energy study states that the long-lead times necessary to build a nuclear power plant mean that the cost of the resulting electricity will be priced slightly higher than that from a coal-fired generating plant (Department of Energy, 1991/1992: 109).

Considering the future, the Bush administration, joined by some electric utilities, voiced concern about what is claimed will be a shortfall in electricity by the late 1990s and into the next century if nuclear power plant construction is not commenced soon. Environmental groups answer that the projected shortfall can be met by alternative energy sources, conservation, and greater energy efficiency.

The strategy of the Bush administration to resolve the estimated electricity shortfall was comprised of four objectives—the maintenance of exacting safety standards for currently operating reactors and the development of even safer ones; reducing the economic risk for utilities desiring to build nuclear power plants; reducing the regulatory risk for utilities desiring to build nuclear power plants; and the establishment of a safe and politically acceptable nuclear waste disposal program. Concerning the attainment of these goals, the Department of Energy (1991/1992: 108) statement is a reaffirmation of the economic philosophy of the Reagan and Bush administrations:

> An overriding theme behind these goals is to remove undue regulatory and institutional barriers to the use of nuclear power for generating electricity in the United States. These include some barriers to constructing new nuclear powerplants, to extending the life of existing generating units, and to disposing of powerplant radioactive waste.

To meet the requirement for new and safer nuclear power reactors, the Department of Energy is cooperating with commercial reactor manufacturers to develop two new Advanced Light Water Reactors and two Advanced Light Water Reactors with passive safety features. The passive safety designs are intended to operate automatically, without reliance on human operators and their possibility of mistaken action and to remove heat in an emergency, thus cooling down the reactor to prevent an accident. Th announced objective of the Department of Energy is to have the first of these new reactors operating by the year 2000.

Looking further ahead, the Department of Energy is funding research and development on two more advanced reactors, the Advanced Liquid-Metal Reactor and the Modular High-Temperature Gas Reactor. A highly regarded proposed advantage of the Advanced Liquid-Metal Reactor is that it is designed to consume long-lived radioactive elements such as americium, plutonium, and neptunium, thus obviating the need to find long-term and safe disposal sites for them. The Modular High-Temperature Gas Reactor, like the Advanced Liquid-Metal Reactor, is being advertised as being particularly efficient.

The Department of Energy supports efforts to reform and streamline the activities of the U.S. Nuclear Regulatory Commission. This is the entity that is responsible for issuing licenses for the construction of new nuclear power plants. The idea is to reduce the amount of lead time for obtaining the necessary licenses, and thus the attendant financial risk, for electric utilities contemplating the construction of nuclear reactors. Another plan to reduce the financial risk in nuclear power plant planning is the standardization in the design of nuclear reactors. Heretofore most reactors have been custom designed for a particular utility, which means their licensing requires more time than would be the case with standardized and uniform designs.

In a further effort to reduce financial risks, the Department of Energy is supporting the design of a midsize nuclear reactor that would be more attractive to some utilities than the very large reactors that require so much more capital and that may be too large for certain utility operations.

In a move to ensure reasonably priced uranium fuel for the electric utilities, the 1992 National Energy Act contains a provision for converting the government's uranium-enrichment program into what is hoped will be a more competitive organization. A halfway step toward privatizing the uranium fuel business was the creation of an interim government enrichment enterprise. However, the development of nuclear weapons will remain the sole responsibility of the Department of Energy and of the Department of Defense.

Currently, the licensing process for nuclear power plants allows several important decisions to be rendered after construction of the facility. This means that after huge investments have been made in a particular plant, the license necessary to operate the plant can be denied. Although the Nuclear Regulatory Commission acted in 1989 to reform the postconstruction licensing requirement, the United States Circuit Court of Appeals for the District of Columbia observed that "such reforms lie not with the NRC, but with Congress." The matter awaits congressional action (Department of Energy, 1991/1992: 113).

An aspect of the U.S. federal system is the fact that states have the right, along with the central government, to regulate radioactive materials emanating from nuclear reactors. Since the states may enact regulations that are stricter than those of the federal government, there exists the potential for dual regulation. This situation also is subject for review and possible streamlining.

Almost since the beginning of commercial nuclear reactor use, environmental groups have voiced concern about the safe storage for very long periods of time of highly radioactive wastes produced by nuclear power plants. So far, the electric utilities have successfully stored the radioactive wastes, but some of their storage capacity is nearly full. Therefore, the Department of Energy has implemented two waste disposal programs for spent fuel and other wastes from nuclear power plants.

The first is to prepare a permanent, for at least 10,000 years, geological repository for high-level commercial nuclear wastes beginning in 2010; and a repository for similar wastes produced by national defense facilities in 2015. The candidate repository site is Yucca Mountain, Nevada.

The second program is the development of Monitored Retrievable Storage facilities that could hold wastes for up to 40 years. Such sites are intended to begin operations by 1998 to relieve the burden of nuclear wastes storage at onsite storage facilities at nuclear power plants. Most of the interest in having a Monitored Retrievable Storage site nearby has come from Native American tribes for two basic reasons. Native American tribes have considerable flexibility to negotiate directly with the federal government even if the state in which they are located is opposed. Further, these tribes are looking for means to bolster their depressed economies with the addition of jobs and with the enhancement of reservation infastructure such as roads and other facilities that would accompany site construction. Tribal members are not unanimous about receiving nuclear wastes under their lands, with a few stating the arrangement would be the second instance of the white man's policy of genocide.

Because communities and states showed little interest in having a Monitored Retrievable Storage site located nearby, the Congress, in an unusual move, created the position of U.S. Nuclear Waste Negotiator. The office is located in Bosie, Idaho. In the years ahead, the U.S. Nuclear Waste Negotiator will be responsible for arranging the siting of several nuclear waste storage sites.

Before the presidential election in the fall of 1992, Congress passed and President Bush signed into law a controversial plan to open the $1 billion Waste Isolation Pilot Plant, near Carlsbad, New Mexico. The purpose of the facility, carved into salt deposits a half mile below the surface, is to test procedures for storing transuranic wastes from nuclear weapons plants in 10 states. In contrast to the spent nuclear fuel from power plants, transuranic wastes consist of rubber gloves, laboratory coats, plastic bags, and tools that have become contaminated with plutonium particles during the manufacture of nuclear weapons.

An ironic twist to the development of additional nuclear power plants is the relationship of that possibility to the growth or demise in concern regarding the greenhouse effect and global warming. Should concern increase among environmentalists about global warming, and should that concern spread to the general public, almost irresistible pressures will ensue for expansion of the nuclear power base. However, if the greenhouse effect and global warming turn out to be much less serious than postulated in the late 1980s and early 1990s, then the affordability and flexibility of coal will ensure that much of the new electric-generating capacity will be fossil fuel fired, not nuclear.

Much further into the future there is the possibility that some type of fusion reactor will be developed that will produce immense amounts of electricity. Such a reactor would replicate the physical process that fuels the sun and other stars. To date, achieving this result without using an atomic bomb to provide the necessary heat, as is the case with a thermonuclear bomb, has proved to be beyond the grasp of this nation's and other nation's scientists. However, because of the immense potential of fusion power, the Department of Energy is pursuing two fusion research programs (Department of Energy, 1990).

The oldest of the two programs is the effort to develop what is called magnetic confinement fusion. In this process, hot, ionized gas, called a plasma, is confined by a strong magnetic field and heated until the fusion reaction thus begun can be self-sustaining. The U.S. Magnetic Fusion Energy Program is endeavoring to confine burning plasma in a doughnut-shaped magnetic container called a *Tokamak*. This Russian word is used by Americans to recognize the pioneering work on this concept done in the former Soviet Union.

The immediate Magnetic Fusion Energy effort is directed toward building the International Thermonuclear Experimental Reactor (ITER). This international activity is composed of scientists from the United States, the European Community, Japan, and the Russian Federation. Current plans are for the construction of a full-scale demonstration plant by the year 2005.

The second fusion development effort is called the Inertial Fusion Energy Program. In this process, small fuel pellets are bombarded by high-intensity laser or particle beams to produce plasma that is confined by its own inertia. Because some of the inertia fusion work is linked to national security purposes, it could be a while before international cooperation on this process will be extensive.

The promise of fusion is impressive. Because the fuel, isotopes of hydrogen, is plentiful, development of fusion would assist the nation work toward energy security. Fusion would not contribute to either global warming or acid rain problems as does the burning of the fossil fuels. A new, reliable, and reasonably priced source of electricity would be a boon to the nation's 21st century economy. As foreseen now, the evolving fusion energy program will be gradually integrated into the private sector for ultimate management. That of course is years into the future and the precise plans are therefore hazy.

One of the potential fuels for an advanced fusion reactor is helium 3, a remarkable isotope of helium that is not found on the Earth but is found on the moon, although the amount of the substance is subject to speculation. Thus, one of the reasons to return to the moon on a permanent basis, as set forth in NASA's currently shelved Space Exploration Initiative, is to investigate the amount of, and access to, the moon's helium 3.

5. The Special Problem of the Breeder Reactor

The Japanese government continued to take action in 1992 that kept open a heated debate between advocates of growth in the nuclear power supply, on the one hand, and environmentalists plus non-nuclear proponents, on the other hand. The problem began in the 1980s when decision makers at the Nuclear Fuels Division of the Japanese Science and Technology Agency announced a long-term plan to move toward what is called the plutonium fuel cycle.

This energy process involves extracting the artificial element plutonium from the spent fuel left from the operation of an ordinary uranium-fueled nuclear power plant, whose purpose is to produce electricity. In such a plant, uranium fuel in the reactor core is bombarded by neutrons that convert part of the uranium into the artificial element plutonium. The plutonium can then be removed by a chemical separations procedure and is either stored, or, as has been the case with a major nuclear weapons power like the United States, it can be fabricated into the sophisticated atomic triggers used to detonate thermonuclear weapons. Third, the plutonium can be used to make crude atomic bombs. A fourth option for using plutonium is what interests the Japanese government. Short on fossil fuels, Tokyo wants to upgrade the plutonium extracted from the spent fuel from its currently operating uranium reactors to "reactor-grade" plutonium. This would then be used in a special nuclear power plant termed a breeder reactor. In such a reactor, the plutonium would be fissioned, which would produce heat that would be converted into electricity. Additionally, some of the neutrons from the fission process would be focused on uranium and convert it into more plutonium than the original loading of the reactor—in other words, the device would "breed" more fuel than it consumed, which is seen by the Japanese as a potential boon for a nation short on conventional sources of energy. The first Japanese prototype breeder reactor is the $4.5 billion Monju Nuclear Power Plant.

There are two problems with the plutonium fuel cycle as seen by opponents, particulary the Washington-based Nuclear Control Institute, which led the worldwide opposition to the Japanese plan. One cause for concern is that plutonium is extremely toxic. A single speck in the lungs can cause cancer. Further, in comparison with uranium, plutonium is more difficult to handle and to machine into fuel rods or pellets for nuclear reactors. Last, there is the problem suggested by the fact that plutonium is often called the "poor man's bomb material" because it can be made into atomic weapons.

Despite widespread international objections, a Japanese freighter carrying casks containing 1.7 tons of plutonium that has been processed in Europe from spent fuel received from Japanese power reactors sailed from Cherbourg, France, to Japan in November 1992. Because of fears about a highjacking during the long ocean voyage, the *Akatsuki Maru* was escorted by a lightly armed vessel and kept under surveillance by U.S. satellites. The 1992 sailing was the first of a series of shipments planned over the next several decades that would total 30 tons of plutonium. The reactor-grade plutonium is not scheduled for use in the Monju plant until 1995 or thereafter. Whether or not the Japanese breeder plan will actually reach fruition was the subject of considerable debate within the Japanese government, a debate whose intensity was heightened by the external criticism leveled at Japan.

The debate in which the Japanese government became involved had been argued out before, most notably in the United States in the late 1970s. Then the Carter administration made the decision that a plutonium-fueled breeder reactor should not be built owing to the toxicity of the substance and because of the ease with which it can be made into atomic bombs by rogue nations, subnational groups, or potentially even by terrorists.

The concerns felt in the United States more than a decade ago were shared by a number of nations that protested the Japanese plan. The protests resulted from worries about the safety of the Japanese transporting plutonium on the high seas and, more importantly, concerns about what Japan was really planning to do with such attractive bomb-making material.

Japan is recognized worldwide as a competent industrial giant. However, fears remain from the days of Japanese imperialism before and during World War II regarding whether Tokyo can be trusted with plutonium. In their own defense, Japanese officials stated that their nation among all others, the single recepient of nuclear bombing attack, could be trusted not to build such weapons. Further, Japanese spokesmen pointed out that Japan needed the breeder technology in order to expand the energy potential of uranium that was needed by a nation short on fossil fuels such as natural gas, coal, and petroleum.

6. Uranium and Plutonium from Weapons

The end of the cold war produced a strange new source of uranium for use in U.S. nuclear power plants. In a kind of "swords into plowshares" arrangement, President Bush announced late in 1992 that the United States would purchase weapons-grade uranium from the former Soviet Union's dismantled nuclear weapons. The highly enriched uranium would be blended with stocks of less-enriched uranium to produce reactor-grade fuel. The deal called for Washington to buy, using hard currency, 10 tons of the weapons-grade uranium a year for 5 years and then at least 30 tons a year after that.

The agreement appeared to benefit both nations. The former Soviets badly need dollars as they attempt to convert to a market economy. The United States can save money by buying their uranium and thus decrease the production of reactor-grade uranium at its own aging and thus inefficient production plants. Both nations are interested in reducing their nuclear weapons arsenals in the aftermath of the cold war confrontation. President Bush hailed the arrangement in this way:

> This agreement will help ensure that nuclear weapons-grade material does not fall into the wrong hands, while providing funds to economy. . . At home, this agreement will secure long-term supplies of less expensive fuel for U.S. nuclear power stations to the benefit of American consumers, with no adverse impact on American jobs.

Although the uranium purchase was generally applauded as both a wise economic move and an acceptable way to disarm, there were objections voiced in the United States. The primary concern was about whether the highly enriched uranium, prime bomb-building material, could be safely transported from Russia to the United States.

For its part, the U.S. Department of Energy, in accordance with bilateral international agreements on disarmament and unilateral actions taken by the president, is significantly reducing the U.S. nuclear weapons stockpile by taking bombs and warheads out of the active inventory and dismantling them. The work, which is expected to continue during most of the 1990s, is being accomplished at the Pantex nuclear weapons facility near Amarillo, Texas.

The chemical explosives from the weapons are destroyed by burning at the Pantex plant. The uranium components are sent for storage to the Y-12 plant at Oak Ridge, Tennessee, as are the lithium 6 deuteride materials. Tritium is shipped to the Savanah River Plant in South Carolina. The plutonium "pits," whose implosion provides the fission reaction that triggers the fusion process of thermonuclear weapons, are stored in bunkers at the Pantex facility. Exactly what will eventually be done with the nuclear components of dissembled U.S. weapons, other than storage, is something of an open question. Unlike Japan, the Department of Energy has no plans to use the plutonium to begin a plutonium fuel cycle using breeder reactors. Of course, should international conditions substantially change, some of the stored nuclear materials could be refabricated into new weapons. (Norris and Arkin, 1992).

As the overall manager of the nation's sprawling nuclear weapons production complex, the Department of Energy came under increasing pressure in the late 1980s to modernize, make safer, and environmentally clean up its facilities. Part of the interest in such activity was spurred by the decline and then the end of the cold war confrontation with the Soviet Union that had fueled the nuclear weapons program after World War II. Interest in the safety and environmental consequences of the nuclear production facilities also was stimulated by the fact many of the plants were old and therefore in need of repair or retirement. For example, the Los Alamos Laboratory dates back to 1943 and the initial effort to develop an atomic bomb. In response to the concern about the nuclear weapons facilities, the Department of Energy is engaged in a long-run operation to modernize, consolidate, and clean up its nuclear weapons activities.

7. Hydropower

A little over 9% of the electricity produced in the United States comes from hydropower; i.e., impounded water flowing through a turbine or from pumped-storage hydropower. The latter involves pumping water up to a higher elevation when there is an excess of electricity and then releasing it to flow back down through a turbine during periods of peak electric demand.

Most federal hydropower projects, dams, are built and operated by either the Army Corps of Engineers or the Bureau of Reclamation, which is within the Department of the Interior. The electricity produced by these projects is marketed by the five regional federal power marketing administrations. These are Bonneville, Southwestern, Southeastern, Western Area, and Alaska. The relatively small proportion of electricity produced by private enterprise is regulated by the Federal Energy Regulatory Commission.

Although some increase in small private hydropower operations may occur here and there, the days of the large federal dams built on major rivers in the western United States are probably over. This is because the environmental movement, both the national organizations and their localized extensions, are so politically strong that building a dam to flood a large canyon in the western United States would be an extremely difficult accomplishment. Even the small private enterprises are made difficult by a complex set of license requirements involving a number of federal and state agencies. So difficult is the red tape for acquiring all the necessary licenses, the Department of Energy has adopted as one of its goals the streamlining of the process. Nonfederal hydropower projects with a capacity of 5 megawatts or less would be exempted from regulation by the Federal Energy Regulatory Commission.

8. The Nonhydro Renewable Energy Sources

Despite the claims of some environmentalists, the five nonhydro renewables do not at this time offer much hope of making large-scale contributions to the nation's basic energy requirements. The problem is cost. In only a few specialized areas can biomass, geothermal, photovoltaics, solar thermal, or wind energy be economically competitive to the standard energy sources. This situation is unfortunate because the five nonhydro renewables rank at the top of the scale in terms of energy security, and for the most part, they are far less polluting than oil, coal, or nuclear power.

Biomass can be converted to heat, as in the burning of municipal solid wastes, or converted to liquid fuel in the form of ethanol fermented from corn and other grains or methanol produced by gasifying biomass. When solid wastes are burned, concerns are heard about the toxicity of air emissions and ash byproducts. Currently, only ethanol made from corn is produced in commercial quantities. The nearly 900 million gallons of ethanol is blended with gasoline in concentrations of 10% and is sold as gasohol, which then makes up 8% of the gasoline used in the United States. Such fuel burns cleaner than regular gasoline.

Solar energy remains the darling of the environmentalists, as they compare the lack of environmental damage from that energy source to the fossil fuels and to nuclear power. But as with other nonhydro renewables, the cost factor has kept solar energy for heating and lighting purposes in check. Still, the Department of Energy estimates there are more than 1 million solar space- and water-heating systems currently in use. And it is estimated that some 300,000 to 350,000 homes use some type of passive solar design such as facing the home toward the sun (Department of Energy, 1991/1992, 127). Solar thermal energy is found as parabolic trough collectors in southern California. Photovoltaics, the direct conversion of sunlight into electricity, is technically feasible for remote locations far removed from electric lines and for use on satellites, but it is not price competitive in most markets yet.

Wind energy has been used since humans harnessed it to turn windmills and sail across the seas. However, until turbines for converting the wind into electricity are improved, wind energy will not normally be competitive to the large fossil fuel or nuclear-powered plants. However, there are some wind-power "farms" in California.

Geothermal power comes from tapping water or stream that has been heated deep underground. A problem is finding areas where the Earth's crust is sufficiently thin to permit drilling or where geothermal heat is naturally available through geologic circumstances. One such place in the United States is the Geysers dry steam field in northern California. Because of environmental concerns, the geothermal activity in Yellowstone National Park is not available for commercial exploitation.

The position of the Department of Energy regarding the nonhydro renewables is that the steady advancement of technology, assisted by government-funded research and development, various tax incentives, and bureaucratic reforms, will make these sources of energy more attractive in the future in terms of price.

> However, photovoltaics, wind, solar thermal, and some biomass and geothermal technologies have not yet reached a level of performance and cost that permit their diverse, widespread use. Because these technologies are still developing, they are not yet cost competitive with conventional energy sources, except in certain markets (Department of Energy, 1991/1992: 124).

9. Synthetic Fuels

As noted earlier, the United States is blessed with one of the world's largest reserves of coal. In addition, some of the world's finest supplies of oil shale are found in sparsely inhabited regions of Colorado, Utah, and Wyoming.

The technology exists to convert both coal and oil shale into synthetic gasoline or other synthetic liquid fuels. However, at the current time, the cost of converting coal is unattractive, as the estimated price per barrel of synthetic oil would be $35 to $40 and for oil shale even more, which is far above the $17 to $20 a barrel price of West Texas Crude. Nevertheless, the Department of Energy continues to pursue research on the liquefaction of coal striving to reduce the costs per barrel to $30. Less interest is focused on oil shale because the economics are less attractive at the current time.

Another problem with synthetic fuels derived from coal is the release of carbon dioxide when they are burned. Currently, the use of such fuels would release more carbon dioxide than the direct use of petroleum fuels or the burning of coal.

10. *Advanced Energy Technologies*

As is stated in the *National Energy Strategy*, "One of the keys to ensuring future energy security is reducing U.S. oil vulnerability" (Department of Energy, 1991/1992: 136). The report goes on to conclude one of the best ways to achieve this is, ". . . increasing investments for technology research and development (R & D) in areas with the greatest potential for reducing oil vulnerability" (p. 136). The stated means for encouraging the desired R & D will be "Government-industry-university cost-shared efforts and by offering prizes and awards for inventive technical approaches" (p. 136). To the reader who remembers President Eisenhower's warning about the "military-industrial complex," the call for an energy-industry complex rings a small cautionary reflex. The descriptive word *small* is used because at this point it does not appear the energy complex will have available to it the several hundreds of billions of dollars provided to the Pentagon and the military contractors by the Congress during the recent cold war.

A number of advanced energy technologies are on the Department of Energy's agenda for financial support. Advanced Oil Recovery Technologies will focus on extracting the two thirds of the known U.S. oil not now recoverable. The effort to develop new industrial technologies will concentrate on more energy-efficient industrial processes, the development of high-temperature materials, and the cogeneration of electricity and space heating from power plants. Vehicle propulsion research features work on advanced concepts such as automotive gas turbines, which might replace the internal combustion engines currently in use, and improvements in internal combustion engines to permit the burning of alternative fuels. The electric vehicle initiative will endeavor to improve the current generation of electric cars whose range is now limited by battery capabilities. The Advanced Transportation Fuels from Biomass program is an effort to move the extraction of ethanol from corn and sugar cane to include trees and grasses. The Aeronautical and Air Systems research will seek to improve the fuel efficiency in the U.S. commercial air fleets. Research on telecommuting is designed to enhance this new mode of working at home while being connected electronically with a central workplace, thus saving both time and transportation energy use.

High-speed rail and magnetic levitation could lead to high-speed transportation in the range of 200 to 600 miles, which would save on gasoline use in heavily populated areas. The Intelligent Vehicle–Highway Systems program is designed to improve traffic efficiency on crowded highways by means of electronic communications and computer technology.

Although the work on the various new technologies will be coordinated by the Department of Energy, many federal entities will also be involved.

C. Enhancing Environmental Quality

As can be seen from the above examination of the various energy sources, a constant concern by both environmental groups and government agencies is environmental quality. Although the concern about environmental impacts caused by energy use is universal, agreement about which abatement and mitigation strategies should be adopted is hotly debated. An important piece of legislation representing the diverse perceptions of environmental protection is the Clean Air Act Amendments of 1990. The Bush administration hailed the amendments in this fashion;

> The 1990 Clean Air Act Amendments, which are an integral component of the National Energy Strategy, will limit the major air pollutants from powerplants, vehicles, and industry. In many cases, pollutants will be reduced from current levels—despite economic growth and increase use of energy (Department of Energy, 1991/1992: 17).

A week before the 1992 presidential election, but a full 2 years after President Bush signed the Act, the Bush administration announced plans to implement the legislation. According to the former Environmental Protection Agency administrator in the Bush administration, William Reilly, the law was a "ground-breaking step in environmental improvement" that features the following major initiatives.

In an attack on acid rain, the Clean Air Amendments of 1990 state that by the year 1995, the nation's 110 largest and highest-emitting power plants must reduce their sulfur dioxide emissions by means of new technologies, the use of scrubbers in the smoke stacks, or with whatever else they choose to do. In the year 2000, emission standards will be increased for the original 110 plants and will be set for an additional 800 smaller plants. By the year 2010, all plants must have reduced their combined emissions of sulfur dioxide to 9 million tons. Further, power plants that produce less sulfur dioxide than they are allowed to do under the law may "trade" the difference with another utility on the Chicago Board of Trade.

D. Fortifying Foundations

The Secretary of the Department of Energy in the Bush administration, Admiral Watkins, felt strongly about the need to spur basic research in science and engineering that could lead to technical solutions to energy problems. To that end, the fourth major objective of the Department of Energy outlined in the *National Energy Strategy* document, is to underwrite and encourage basic research.

Recognizing that the private sector ". . . is primarily responsible for developing and commercializing technology . . .", the *National Energy Strategy* contains the statement:

> . . . but the Federal Government has a critical role in basic and applied scientific research. The extensive system of national research laboratories and Federal support of academic and private research can profoundly influence the focus, scope, and pace of energy technology development (Department of Energy, 1991/1992: 20).

Therefore, the Department of Energy supports fundamental science and engineering research estimated to be more than $11 billion annually across 10 federal agencies and energy-related applied research of approximately $3 billion annually across 7 federal agencies. Further, the Department of Energy is on the record in support for using financial incentives to stimulate private industrial research; helping to fund university research; maintaining research facilities that are available to both the private sector and universities; and pursuing bilateral and multilateral international agreements to construct and operate high-cost, long-term experimental research centers. In addition, the argument is made in the *National Energy Strategy* that the Department of Energy strengthen technology transfer from government and university research facilities to the private sector, including adequate protection for the intellectual property developed in the government-funded programs.

Last, in a policy position similar to that taken by the Aeronautics and Space Administration (NASA), the Department of Energy supports the idea that the federal government ought to make a modest contribution, 6% of the total funding, to improving precollege education in mathematics, science, technology, and engineering and that

> Special emphasis must be placed on recruiting women and underrepresented minorities into the technical work force, to recruiting and preparing qualified math and science teachers for our schools, and to broadening the base of "science literacy" among the U.S. public (Department of Energy, 1991/1992: 22).

Late in the fall of 1992, President Bush signed into law the Energy Policy Act of 1992. It generally followed the outline set forth previously in the *National Energy Strategy*.

Almost immediately after President Bush announced the National Energy Strategy various groups were making criticisms. Typical of the concerns that were voiced are the below referenced articles in The *Bulletin of the Atomic Scientists* and *The Environmental Magazine*. Writing in the former journal, Joseph Romm criticized the Bush plan as doing too little to reduce U.S. dependence on Middle East oil. By his calculations, oil imported from the Middle East in 1985 was priced at $200 a barrel when the cost of keeping the Persian Gulf shipping lanes open is added to the normal production costs. Obviously, the price of Middle East oil in the mid 1990s will be much higher when the cost of the Gulf War and the cost of keeping U.S. forces in the Middle East after the Gulf War are added up. Critics suggest that instead of spending the money necessary to support the military presence of the United States in the Gulf area, it would make better sense to aggressively start moving energy-efficient technologies into the private sector. The one area that generally receives the most attention from those critical of the Bush energy plan is the use of petroleum by cars. Many critics support Romm's calculations that

> The average car in the United States gets only about 20 miles per gallon. If new-car fuel economy were raised from 27 to 40 gallons, U.S. oil consumption would be reduced by 2.8 million barrels per day by the year 2005. This is a million barrels per day more than we now import from the Persian Gulf, and it is almost 10 times the oil production rate likely from the Arctic National Wildlife Refuge (Romm, 1992: 34).

Environmentalists and others suggested the Bush energy plan erred by not including a tax on gasoline, which they argued would lead to greater efficiency warranted by economics. This subject was made part of the 1992 presidential debates when independent candidate Ross Perot called for a new 50ᶜ a gallon tax for American motorists. He and others pointed out that the Europeans and the Japanese pay much more in gasoline taxes than do Americans with minimal adverse impact on their economies. Nearly a year after the 1992 presidential election, and after a bruising fight in the Congress where many interest groups were arrayed against him, President Clinton was only able to secure a tax increase of 4.3¢ on a gallon of gas.

Will Nixon, writing in *The Environmental Magazine*, suggested an alternative to Bush's energy plan similar to proposals from other environmental groups. It called for improving energy efficiency by 2 to 3% a year; increasing car fuel efficiency up to 45 miles per gallon for cars and 35 miles per gallon for light trucks by 2001; increasing the gasoline tax by 50ᶜ a gallon; increasing research and development spending on renewable energy up to a level equal with the spending on nuclear power; and creating a tax credit for renewable energy and a carbon tax on fossil fuels (Nixon, 1991: 33).

1. Then and Now

There is a noticeable contrast between the energy situation facing the United States in the early 1970s and that before the nation in the early 1990s. Then, the country and its major allies were being buffeted by the oil shocks from the Middle East. Then, the nation was correctly described by President Nixon as being "profligate" in its use and misuse of energy resources. Then the nation had no Department of Energy and no central theme to orchestrate its energy future. Then the nation was generally not aware of potential environmental impacts from the burning of fossil fuels.

Now much has changed except for the continued potential of oil disruptions or artificially high oil prices from the Middle East. Thus, although it is not carried out by the Department of Energy, American foreign policy that works toward peace in the Middle East and the correlative objective of continued oil flow at reasonable prices is a most vital aspect of the overall American energy policy. In contrast to the 1970s, however, the political calculus is more complex with the rise of Islamic fundamentalism and the presence of Saddam Hussein in Iraq.

The increases in oil prices occasioned by actions of Middle East nations actually have worked to the advantage of the United States. In traditional economic fashion, an increase in prices and temporary scarcities forced the government and the buying public to mend their wasteful ways in a fashion no amount of preaching from political leaders or academics could have done.

The results are now everywhere to seen—much more fuel-efficient automobiles; new construction of both commercial buildings and private dwellings built with an eye on thermal energy efficiency; research on a wide spectrum of new technologies designed to provide additional efficiencies in energy consumption; an effort to remove bureaucratic and fiscal barriers to the discovery of new finds of traditional energy sources and the development of new energy sources; the development and, more importantly, the acceptance of a conservation ethic; and the awareness that energy use worldwide can impact on the global climate and general environment.

To paraphrase a common saying, the United States today, in comparison to the early 1970s, is leaner in regard to energy use but less mean in regard to the impact of energy use on the environment. Of course, not everyone is happy, because that is in the nature of things. Some of the entrepreneurs and developers are miffed at what they see as unnecessary restrictions on their God-given right to make a profit by using the Earth's resources as they see fit. On the other side, some of the environmentalists are worried that too few restrictions have been adopted. Both groups should look at where we have come. Money, lots of it, can still be made at entrepreneurship and development, and the world has not come to an environment end; in fact, none of the environmental catastrophes so grimly predicted 20 years ago have occurred. And therein lies the danger.

Having been shocked out of its energy complacent ways 20 years ago, the nation buckled down to make reasonable adjustments. Now that those adjustments are paying off, there is the danger that a complacent perspective will again dull American perceptions of the need for continued efforts at conservation, technical innovation, and adjusting lifestyles. It may be a long while yet before the promise of the fusion research provides "unlimited" amounts of clean electricity and eases some current energy concerns.

Beyond our borders, the energy situation is not so promising, but of course that statement can be made about most comparisons between activity in the United States and that in the developing parts of the world. In an era when internationalism is quite the proper perspective, the international interrelationship of all countries in environmental terms is certainly evident. No where is that more obvious than in the external effects on parts of Europe of the Chernobyl reactor accident and the potential worldwide effects of acid rain and the greenhouse effect, assuming those two problems do exist at the levels many believe.

If fossil fuel use, particularly coal, is as harmful as often portrayed, then the world must gird for problems stemming from the fact that large portions of the Earth's peoples want the good life that they see in industrialization, which is based heavily on greater oil use and, particularly, coal use.

If the world does follow in the U.S. energy-using footsteps, we Americans bear some responsibility, and there should be some self-interest motivation to transfer our "have it both ways" technology to others. That it is a reference to the American view that one can enjoy a higher standard of living and a healthy environment.

The demise of the Soviet Union is creating a unique energy/environment situation. After more than 70 years of ideologically sanctioned neglect, the regions formerly under Communist rule are facing some extraordinarily bad environmental situations that ought to be cleaned up and repaired for the sake of local peoples and to some extent for the sake of the world. Money can be made at environmental cleanup, and the money formerly spent in the buying of immense stockpiles of weapons could be spent usefully in such enterprises.

In the early 1970s, the Gaia hypothesis had not yet been set forth. That came later in the decade when British scientist James Lovelock (1979) wrote *Ages of Gaia*. According to this hopeful perspective, the planet may have a self-healing and nurturing character that could appropriately be named after the Greek mother Earth goddess Gaia. This perspective holds that nature, or life itself, when taken as a whole, has the capability to offset potentially damaging events such as global climate change. Thus, it is pointed out that the increased temperatures from the greenhouse effect could be countered by increased clouds to cool the Earth that would arise from increased evaporation from the oceans.

Whether or not the Gaia hypothesis is correct, and whether or not the burning of fossil fuels is quite dangerous, will have to await both the passage of time and the intense investigations of scientists. How much time we can spend in study will remain a matter of some debate among entrepreneurs, on the one hand, and environmentalists, on the other, and both will try to enlist the powers of government for their particular purposes.

Last, the concern of some persons 20 years ago that civilization was running out of energy does not appear to be as urgent a problem in the early 1990s. There is a great deal of energy, although much of it, like the fusion of hydrogen atoms, is not yet tapped. The problems are not so much in regard to the supply of energy but the location of energy reserves, political impediments to their distribution, and potentially negative consequences to the use of some energy forms. The fact that the United States created the Department of Energy in 1977 and passed the National Energy Act of 1992, with numerous pieces of energy legislation in between, suggests that at least this society can adjust to energy problems. Of course, that adjustment does not occur as fast as some would like, and it occurs too fast and in the wrong direction for others. But the adjustments and the coping does happen!

2. The Clinton-Gore Election

The election of Bill Clinton, formerly the governor of Arkansas, to the presidency, and of Al Gore, a former senator from Tennessee to the vice presidency, portend changes for the nation's energy policy. As noted above, the vice president has been a vocal advocate of assessing energy activities in the context of environmental concerns. Shortly after the November election results were tabulated, President-Elect Clinton indicated that the Department of Energy would play a major role in meeting his campaign promise to reinvigorate the economy while protecting the environment.

Even before the Clinton inauguration, the broad outlines of the new administration's energy perspectives had appeared in the press. Basically, the Clinton plan would move further and faster in the general directions laid out in the Energy Act of 1992. According to the new president, the nation should be weaned more quickly from coal and oil by the introduction of cleaner and less costly energy alternatives such as domestically produced natural gas. Further, Clinton said he would use tax incentives and research funds to support and encourage expansion in the use of renewable energy sources and to enlarge the U.S. share of the world market in pollution control and mitigation equipment and technologies. A longer-run objective of the Clinton energy plan was stated as making the United States more industrially competitive with other nations by making the country's manufacturing more efficient by making energy utilization more efficient.

It appeared the new president might not wait for Congress to enact his energy perspectives; he could start the process of energy change by issuing executive orders. Examples were said to include dramatically enlarging the Bush administration's plan to convert hundreds of thousands of government vehicles to compressed natural gas that burns more cleanly than gasoline and could be cheaper; accelerating the delayed program to require more energy-efficient buildings and appliances; and placing more emphasis on developing renewable energy sources instead of coal and nuclear. The Clinton energy plan also was thought to include making available to private industry the advanced technology being developed by the Department of Energy to clean up the environmental consequences resulting from the operation of the nation's nuclear weapons production plants.

REFERENCES

Bush, G. (1992). *Statement by the President upon Final Passage of* H.R. 776, Washington, DC.

Department of Energy, Fusion Policy Advisory Committee (1990). *The Nation's Fusion Program.* U.S. Government Printing Office, Washington, DC.

Department of Energy (1991). *The Department of Energy's Heritage.* U.S. Government Printing Office, Washington, DC.

Department of Energy (1991/1992). *National Energy Strategy.* U.S. Government Printing Office, Washington, DC.

Department of Energy (1992). *National Energy Strategy—One Year Later.* U.S. Government Printing Office, Washington, DC.

House of Representatives, 102d Congress, 2d Session (1992). *Energy Policy Act of 1992.* U.S. Government Printing Office, Washington, DC.

Gore, Al (1992). *Earth In the Balance.* Houghton Mifflin, Boston.

Lovelock, J. (1979). *The Ages of Gaia.* Oxford, London.

Mathews, J., and Tuchman, E. (1991). *Preserving The Global Environment.* The American Assembly, New York.

Meadows, D., Meadows, D., and Randers, J. (1992). *Beyond the Limits.* Chelsea Green, Post Mills, Vermont.

Nixon, W. (1991). Energy for the next century. *The Environmental Magazine* May/June:

Norris, R. S., and Arkin, W. M. (1992). Pantex lays nukes to rest. *Bulletin of the Atomic Scientists* October:

Rhodes, R. (1986). *The Making of the Atomic Bomb.* Simon & Schuster, New York.

Romm, J. (1991). Needed—A no-regrets energy policy. *Bulletin of the Atomic Scientists* July/August:

Schneider, S. (1989). *Global Warming.* Sierra Club, San Francisco.

Silver, C. S., and DeFries, R. S. (1990). *One Earth—One Future.* National Academy of Sciences Press, Washington, DC.

U.S. Congress (1977). *Department of Energy Organization Act.* Government Printing Office, Washington, DC.

Yergin, D. (1991). *The Prize.* Simon & Schuster, New York.

33
Biomedical Policy

Robert H. Blank
University of Canterbury, Christchurch, New Zealand

Unlike many other policy areas, biomedical policy is not highly developed on the political agenda. However, the issues surrounding biomedical technologies are bound to become increasingly sensitive areas of policy as they continue to move onto the public agenda in the 1990s (Blank and Bonnicksen, 1992; Blank and Mills, 1989). Biomedical issues promise to be among the most difficult because the stakes are so high—in many instances, the decisions made make the difference between life and death of identifiable persons. A basic question is how much of our resources are we willing and able to put into these highly intensive and expensive medical interventions? Increasingly, policy makers at the national, state, and local levels must make difficult choices regarding the use of these revolutionary, and frequently controversial, technologies.

Although biomedical policy is in reality inseparable from health policy, and they share much in common, conceptually it is useful to distinguish the two areas. Health policy is primarily concerned with broader questions of health care delivery and funding. The allocation priorities made in health policy help define the boundaries of biomedical policy and affect how these technologies are perceived. For instance, although the decision whether to fund organ transplants or prenatal care is a matter of health policy, it has a direct impact on the development and use of transplantation technologies through the incentive structure it creates by setting health care priorities.

The focus of this chapter is on the emerging policy issues that accompany the proliferation of technological innovations in biomedicine. To a large extent, however, the growing health care funding crisis is tied to the diffusion of biomedical interventions in the last decade. Although there is disagreement as to the extent to which technologies have contributed to the health care crisis, few persons discount their role in increasing costs. Furthermore, as public expectations for access to these highly promising technologies have heightened and interest groups demanding such access have multiplied, biomedical technologies have moved to the center of the health policy agenda (Riegelman, 1991).

In their broadest sense, biomedical technologies encompass much of what today is termed medicine. From new biologicals and drugs, to sophisticated diagnostic machines such as magnetic resonance imaging (MRI) and computed tomography (CT) (formerly called computerized axial tomography [CAT]), to life-support systems used to extend life, biomedical technologies have a tremendous influence over the way we define health care in the 1990s. This chapter focuses on policy developments and issues in a few of the most dramatic applications of biomedical technology, including human genetics, reproduction, neonatal intensive care, and organ transplantation. It also examines new issues surrounding the concept of death that follow the rapid developments in our capacity to intervene technologically in the dying process. Current policy and assessment initiatives and literature are analyzed for each of these issue areas.

I. BIOMEDICAL TECHNOLOGY AND BIOMEDICAL POLICY

At their base, all biomedical technologies focus on the question of the extent to which we ought to intervene directly in the human condition. They differ only in the stage of intervention (gametes, fertilized egg, developing embryo, fetus, newborn, within life cycle, end of life) and in the means of accomplishing the intervention. Although each innovation raises a unique set of opportunities and problems, it shares broader social and political ramifications that must be evaluated in a systematic and timely fashion.

Although there is a historical tie between the recent interest in biomedical ethics and the emerging interest in biomedical policy, and the two approaches overlap, the emphasis in policy analysis is critically different from that in bioethics. There are three policy levels that are crucial in health care issues. First, decisions must be made concerning the research and development of the technologies. Because a substantial proportion of medical research is funded either directly or indirectly with public funds, it is logical that public input should be required at this stage. The growing, although still limited, interest in forecasting and assessing the social as well as technical consequences of medical technologies early in research and development represents one attempt to facilitate a broader public input.

The second policy level relates to the individual use of technologies once they are available. Although direct government instrusion into individual decision making in health care ought to be limited, the government does have at its disposal an array of more or less implicit devices to encourage or discourage individual use. These include tax incentives, provision of free services, and education programs. Whether or not explicit rationing of health care resources will be a necessary future policy option remains to be seen (Blank, 1988; Califano, 1992; Lamm, 1992). However, some observers feel that as the social costs of certain forms of treatment become high, we must reassess our notion that physicians ought to act primarily as agents of the patients, and we must give consideration to the role of physicians as trustees of scarce medical resources (Knaus, 1986).

The third, and perhaps most critical, level of health care policy centers on the aggregate societal consequences of widespread application of a technology. For instance, what impact would wide diffusion of artificial heart transplants have on the provision of health care? Adequate policy making here requires a clear conception of national goals, extensive data to predict the consequences of each possible course of action, an accurate means of monitoring these consequences, and mechanisms to cope with the consequences if they are deemed undesirable. Moreover, the government has a responsibility in ensuring quality control standards and fair marketing of all medical applications. As technologies become widely available that allow for sex preselection, collaborative conception, neural grafting, and extended life spans, social patterns will be affected. Observers question the impact of such capabilities on the family, on demographical patterns, and on the structure and size of the population. Policy planners must account for these potential pressures on the basic structures and patterns of society and decide whether provision of such choices is desirable.

The need for integrated and clearly articulated policy objectives to deal with the expanding array of high-cost technologies is clear. However, it must be acknowledged that the attainment of these objectives is difficult given the inextricably complex cultural, social, and political context of biomedical decision making. In a pluralist society, there are many conceivably legitimate but contradictory goals, especially concerning issues as fundamental as those that relate to human life and death. Moreover, because these issues are not amenable to bargaining and compromise techniques, it is a formidable task to attain a rational balance among the competing goals.

At its foundation, much of the controversy surrounding the development and application of biomedical technologies centers on conflicting goal criteria. Some of the competing goal orientations that frame public policy to varying degrees are the maximization of (1) individual freedom and choice, (2) social or public good, (3) scientific and technological progress, (4) positive quality of life, (5) human dignity, (6) efficiency, (7) social stability, and (8) consideration of alternative concepts of justice. Reactions to specific innovations, as well as to science and technology in general, varies depending on the predominant social values.

One barrier to the creation of effective biomedical policy is that both consumers and providers have expectations of unlimited availability of medical technology. These expectations fuel unrealistic public demands, which, in turn, are encouraged by many providers of health services (Mechanic, 1986: 215). The suppliers of high-technology goods and services have a large stake in the continued growth of the health care industry. Furthermore, the infusion of corporate medicine and for-profit hospitals into the health care community heightens the stakes.

All political decisions involve tradeoffs as goods and services are distributed across a population. Whatever allocation scheme is applied, some elements of society will benefit and others will be deprived. The philosophical debate has long centered on what criteria ought to be used to determine whether or not a particular policy is just or fair. Since Plato first argued that health resources should not be wasted on the sickly and unproductive, the distribution of these limited resources (money, technologies, skilled personnel, time) potentially has been part of a public policy debate. Although until recently the dominant strategy in the United States was to minimize direct governmental intervention in the allocation of medical resources, this policy perspective is rapidly changing.

To date, there has been a tendency in the United States to avoid making the difficult decisions regarding the distribution of scarce medical resources. Most often, the "solutions" merely shift costs from the individual to the government or from one agency to another. Aaron and Schwartz (1984), for instance, see a pattern toward reliance by policy makers on prospective reimbursement schemes to solve health cost problems. Although this approach gives the appearance of resolving the problem, these shifts only delay the need to make the hard choices at a later date. Brandon (1982) argues, however, that we are running out of easy options and purported panaceas. Despite these interim shifts in the burden of payment, the prevailing approach fails to address the critical issues relating to the need to establish policy priorities and set limits on the use of high-cost medical technologies.

Another problem in attempts to constrain unchecked proliferation of biomedical technologies is that American culture is preoccupied toward progress through technological means. This heavy dependence on technology to fix our health problems, at the exclusion of non-technological solutions or prevention, is also tied to a tendency of Americans to look always for the easiest solutions. In the words of Mechanic (1986: 207), "As a culture, we do far better in the application of a 'technological fix' than in building complex social arrangements that must be sustained over time in coping with expressive, frustrating, and often intractable problems." The quest for increasingly higher levels of technologies in order to avoid more difficult changes in lifestyle is strong even when it is obvious that technologies cannot provide the sought-after panaceas.

Because of their threat to traditional individualistic values, decisions concerning the use and priorities of biomedical research and technology will be made within a highly politicized context. The politically sensitive nature of these technologies, as well as recent trends in funding and increased public awareness, demonstrates that technical decisions are no longer made apart from politics. The 1970s saw a growing public role in biomedical research as a result of a combination of inflation, multiplying health care costs, and the general freedom-of-information climate. As the costs of biomedicine swell and an increasing proportion of the funding comes from public monies, public debate over priorities will intensify.

The first policy question surrounding biomedical technology is, What level of technological intervention is appropriate for a given problem? Otherwise stated, How far should we go in controlling our own destiny in our quest for a technological fix to extend life? These issues will heighten as we apply gene therapy to enhance human capabilities, develop neural grafting and other brain-intervention capabilities, and begin to understand the genetics of aging. Despite potential drawbacks, the momentum for expanded technological intervention in all the areas introduced here is powerful.

The second policy question flows from the first. Who should determine whether a particular technology is developed, funded, or applied in a specific case? Pressures for governmental controls threaten the traditional physician-patient relationship and personal autonomy, but they will increase because of economic constraints. In this era of scarce resources, in part brought on by high-cost technologies, we can no longer assume that just because a technology is available, we can or should use it. Although some persons still argue that these decisions should be made exclusively in the private sector, the government must be intimately involved in setting priorities for use of these technologies.

The role of the government becomes even more crucial regarding the question of allocation and distribution of biomedicine. Should these technologies be available to all persons on an equal basis? The traditional market-oriented, third-party payer system leaves out many people. The debate over whether or not the government has a responsibility to pay when the individual cannot will intensify as the scope of technological intervention broadens. Congressional action regarding catastrophic insurance, the ongoing policy battle over the funding of liver transplants, and the emerging demands for government funding of reproduction-aiding technologies are but three examples of the difficulty of this issue within our value system. Can we as a society fail to save the life of an individual who needs a liver transplant when the technology is available? What if that person's abuse of alcohol directly caused his or her condition? What criteria do we use to determine who gets scarce resources? Although in one way these allocation decisions are prototypical policy questions, their direct life-death implications make them unique.

The last policy question that society must address is, What are the impacts on society of the use of each new technology? Once a technology is widely diffused, it is unlikely that efforts to limit its use because of negative long-term social consequences will succeed. Technology assessment must be anticipatory and broad based. Although assessment efforts of the government have increased substantially in the last decade (Office of Technology Assessment, 1982, 1987a, 1987b, 1988a, 1988b, 1990), they are constrained by a value system that largely favors technological progress. As a result, the difficult choices of rejecting specific technologies because of their negative social consequences are rarely made.

In summary, the rapid diffusion of biomedical technologies, in conjunction with demographical trends, is leading to the need for increasingly arduous decisions as to how best to use them. As we come to realize that we cannot afford to do everything for everybody, we are thrust into policy dilemmas that deal directly with human life and death. Ironically, these dilemmas are all the more difficult because we are now at the brink of developing remarkable capacities to intervene directly in the human condition from preconception to life extension. Just when we have the technical capacity to do things we only recently could imagine, rising expectations and scarce resources combine to limit the availability. The resulting need to allocate biomedical technologies, in turn, raises critical concerns over whose needs take precedence, what individual rights and responsibilities entail (see e.g., Blank, 1992), and when societal good justifies restricting individual good. Although by no means new, these policy issues take on renewed importance within the context of the emerging conflicts accentuated by our technological successes in biomedicine.

II. HUMAN GENETIC TECHNOLOGIES

The United States is now pursuing a national goal to map and sequence the human genome. According to James Watson (1990: 44), the first director of the National Center for Human Genome Research, the money required to determine the sequence of the 3 billion base pairs will be an order of magnitude smaller than the money needed to send a person to the moon, but "the implications of the Human Genome Project for human life are likely to be far greater".

The Human Genome Initiative (HGI) has become an international research effort with the goal of analyzing the structure of human DNA and determining the location of the estimated 100,000 human genes. The information generated by HGI will serve as a source book for biology and medicine in the next century and will "help us to understand and eventually treat many of the more than 4000 genetic diseases in which genetic predisposition plays an important role" (NCHGR, 1990: vii). This initiative is being coordinated by the National Institutes of Health (NIH) and the Department of Energy (DOE).

In anticipation of its lead role in the HGI, NIH established the Office of Human Genome Research in 1988. In 1989, after the fiscal 1990 budget proposal designated $100 million for human genome research, thus justifying an independent program, the office became the National Center for Human Genome Research (NCHGR). The eagerness to fund HGI and the quick approval of center status reflect the strong support for this research both within the administration and Congress.

In addition to the U.S. commitment, Britain, Japan, Italy, the former Soviet Union, France, the European Economic Community, Australia, and Canada have either announced national HGI programs or are expected to do so. Furthermore, a group of international molecular biologists and human geneticists established the Human Genome Organization (HUGO) in 1988 (McKusick, 1989: 913). The HGI is certain to stimulate the organization of other large genome projects in the private sector on animals and plants of commercial importance (Cantor, 1990: 51).

A. Genetic Diagnosis and Testing

At present, two types of tests are being performed on the DNA of cells taken from blood samples. For conditions where the responsible gene has been identified, the tests use a DNA probe, or labeled segment of DNA, that binds directly to the defective gene if it is present. For those conditions where the specific gene is not yet known, genetic markers are identified that are close enough to the gene to be inherited with it. These restriction fragment length polymorphisms (RFLPs) indicate the approximate chromosome location of an unknown gene. By using overlapping RFLPs related to a gene disorder, the actual gene can eventually be isolated. Through the use of increasingly sophisticated cloning and sequencing techniques, tests to uncover these markers in individuals are being developed. These techniques will be used prenatally or neonatally or to identify adults who are carriers.

Following the discovery of such a molecular probe for the Huntington's disease gene in 1983, efforts have been initiated to identify genetic markers for Alzheimer's disease, sickle cell anemia, manic depression, malignant melanoma, and a host of other conditions. Out of this research, a gene for cystic fibrosis was found in 1989 (Marx, 1989). The identification of the retinoblastoma gene on chromosome 13 in 1986 and the discovery of its linkage to breast cancer in 1988 have led to considerable enthusiasm over the genetic bases of cancer.

In addition, research is now underway to identify genetic factors that might predispose a person to be alcoholic. Although no single gene or gene complement has yet been found, "researchers are accumulating a great deal of information associating genetic factors with alcohol abuse" (Barnes, 1988: 415). In 1991, the National Institute on Alcohol Abuse and Alcoholism launched a major study on the genetics of alcoholism. The $25 million budget for the first 5 years will provide funding for the first systematic, multilevel study of the subject (Holden, 1991). Similar research on cocaine abuse is in the preliminary stages.

As new diagnostic tests and genetic probes emerge, public expectations will rise and the demand for access to information derived from such efforts will intensify. Once the tests become accepted by policy makers as legitimate, it is likely that legislatures and courts will recognize professional standards of care that incorporate them. Even though there is considerable phenotypic variance in the expression of genes, many people are likely to perceive a positive gene probe test as an indicator of a person's biological destiny (Nelkin and Tancredi, 1989).

Sensitive policy dilemmas emerge in genetic screening as more precise and inclusive tests give us the capacity to identify people who are at high risk for a disease or condition. Increasingly, policy makers will face pressures from employers and insurance companies for access to information obtained from these tests (Blank, 1990: 40). The potential use of DNA probes to identify persons at risk for poor health accentuates the issue of how much information should be made available to employers. When, if ever, is the patient's right to privacy to be sacrificed for the interests of the employer? Under what circumstances does the genetic counselor's or physician's responsibility to society outweigh his or her responsibility to the patient? As more knowledge is gained about specific susceptibilities related to genetic traits, and as more accurate tests are found for a wide variety of these traits, debate on workplace screening will grow.

B. Human Gene Therapy

Although routine human gene therapy is not imminent, many research centers in the United States are working to develop techniques that will permit such treatment. These techniques would correct genetic defects, not by environmental manipulations, but instead by acting directly on the DNA in the affected person's cells. Gene therapy attempts to introduce normal genes into chromosomes of cells that contain defective genes in the hope that the manipulated cells will express themselves and ultimately replace the defective ones, thus curing the patient (Selden et al., 1987).

The first attempt at gene therapy was conducted at NIH in September 1990, when doctors treated a 4-year-old girl who suffered from a grave immune deficiency because she lacked the enzyme adenosine deaminase. The doctors took the girl's own white blood cells, altered them by inserting a gene from the missing enzyme, and transplanted the altered cells back into her. Two months after this test, the Food and Drug Administration (FDA) gave approval for a test using genetically modified tumor-infiltrating lymphocytes in 10 patients with advanced melanoma. This strategy of introducing a cancer-fighting substance into the DNA of the blood cells of patients with melanoma represents another approach that has wide implications for treatment of many diseases.

Although applications for new tests of gene therapy proliferate, some observers already see us entering a "second-generation" of gene therapy (Merz, 1989). The recent melanoma test evidences a shift away from the initial strategy of replacing defective genes with normal ones throughout the body and toward the use of transplanted genes as drug-delivery systems to supply proteins only to the organs that need them. This development means that gene therapy is about to be extended to nongenetic diseases such as emphysema, cardiovascular disease, liver failure, acquired immunodeficiency syndrome (AIDS), malignant tumors, and blood and immune diseases. The implications for the practice of medicine are staggering. This move from diagnosis to therapy raises many policy issues regarding the role that government ought to play in encouraging or discouraging such research and application. It also raises ethical questions concerning parental responsibilities to children, societal perceptions of children, the distribution of social benefits, and the definition of what it means to be a human being.

III. HUMAN REPRODUCTION

We are currently undergoing the second phase of a revolution in human reproduction that began in the 1960s with the separation of procreation from sexual intercourse made possible by the availability of the contraceptive pill. Although that part of the revolution continues with the emergence of long-term subdermal contraceptive implants such as NORPLANT and abortifacients such as RU 486 (Blank, 1991), the second stage of the revolution promises to be accompanied by alterations in social attitudes and behavior that exceed the changes still reverberating from the contraceptive revolution. Precipitating the second phase is the aggregation of techniques that effectively remove the need for sexual intercourse from reproduction.

Donor insemination of sperm, ova donation, in vitro fertilization, and embryo transfer are but the first of many innovations that allow for an unlimited combination of germ materials. The ability to store human semen, ova, and embryos indefinitely through cryopreservation, along with new techniques to separate sperm so as to preselect the sex of one's offspring, give us the capacity to exert considerable technological control over the characteristics of future generations in addition to overcoming infertility for many men and women. Recent innovative procedures such as gamete intrafallopian transfer (GIFT), embryo lavage, egg fusion, micromanipulation of sperm, and twinning of embryos are likely to heighten reproductive intervention possibilities dramatically (Blank, 1990).

The ability to carry out fertilization under the microscope in the laboratory opens up the likelihood of using gene testing and therapy techniques on the embryo before it is transferred for implantation. The process of creating identical twins by dividing two-cell embryos could permit extensive genetic testing on one twin—the other would be transferred to the womb only if its "twin" passed the tests. Moreover, the transfer of an embryo produced via in vitro fertilization into the abdominal cavity of a male might allow male "motherhood" in the near future. In contrast, the fusion of two eggs might well eliminate the need for the male contribution to procreation and allow two women to each contribute an egg and thus produce a daughter with two mothers and no father. Questions also arise over the use of "spare embryos" that are left after in vitro fertilization and over the possible production of embryos to be used specifically for research.

Policy issues that accompany this new revolution are numerous and highly volatile. To what extent should the government encourage, regulate, mandate, or prohibit their development and specific applications? Demand for new applications is likely to heighten, particularly from infertile couples and parents who want more control over the characteristics of their progeny or access to techniques that permit unconventional families, such as two lesbian women who want a daughter through egg fusion. The rapid commercialization of these services raises concern as to how best to protect the interests of often vulnerable consumers. Furthermore, as resources become more scarce, issues are raised concerning how high a priority should be placed on these techniques as compared, for example, with research aimed at preventing infertility. Difficult questions of equity in access to reproductive technologies also are critical because the Supreme Court has declared procreation a fundamental right. Should Medicaid pay for in vitro fertilization if that is the only possibility of a poor woman becoming pregnant so that she might exercise her right?

Despite many congressional hearings, as yet there is no national policy regarding these new technologies. Moreover, state policy where it exists is often inadequate and contradictory (Blank, 1990). Even an uncontroversial area such as screening potential sperm donors to assure the health of the child of donor insemination has been ignored by all but several states. Thus far, the states have failed to provide any legal controls on the delivery of reproductive services even though they have the authority to do so through licensing. More importantly, their appears to be little inclination for proactive policy making in this area—When states have acted it is usually in response to a sensational case. For example, when the New Jersey Supreme Court invalidated surrogate motherhood contracts in *In re Baby M* (577A. 2d 1227, 1988), over 70 bills were introduced in state legislatures to forbid or regulate this practice. In the end, only a few states acted. Likewise, few states have legislated insurance coverage for reproductive-aiding technologies, including in vitro fertilization, in response to an effective lobbying effort for groups such as Resolve, Inc., of Belmont, Massachusetts.

By and large, any standards that exist in this area are self-imposed by professional associations such as the American Fertility Society and the American Association of Tissue Banks (Bonnicksen, 1989: 82 ff). Although the standards promulgated by these organizations are valuable and provide some control over the use of reproductive technologies, the problem with guidelines as opposed to regulation is that there is no authority behind the guidelines to ensure compliance. Instead of the force of law, association guidelines rely on creditation privileges and ethical sanctions. There is, however, little to stop the establishment of nonaccredited or nonsanctioned cryobanks, fertility clinics, or other services. Although lack of compliance with the guidelines by nonmember businesses carries some risk, in the emerging highly lucrative commercial fertility industry, voluntary guidelines might not be a strong enough form of self-enforcement or policing of such activities.

Not surprisingly response to these controversial technologies has been considerably more visible in many other countries, particularly most of the European nations, Canada, and

Australia. Despite the wide variation in the mode and comprehensiveness of the responses of these countries to the issues surrounding reproductive technologies, several international patterns are emerging. Basically, donor insemination (DI) has gained widespread acceptance by policy makers and ethics committees. In most countries, the child of DI with a married woman and her husband's consent is considered irrefutably a legitimate offspring of the husband. Similarly, in vitro fertilization (IVF) is widely accepted if it is conducted on married (or stable) couples and donor eggs are not used. In vitro fertilization has less support when donor gametes are used, however, and almost none for use by single individuals. Most countries also realize the need for some type of regulation of DI and IVF facilities, although action to that end is fragmented to date.

In contrast, surrogate motherhood, especially commercial surrogacy, has been rejected by virtually every country that has considered it. With only several exceptions, surrogacy contracts are either unenforceable or illegal. There is considerable sympathy for the imposition of criminal penalties on agencies that practice surrogacy for a profit. Interestingly, there has been very little debate in these countries over the issue of payment to surrogate mothers, which has monopolized much of the discussion in the United States.

The most important contribution of the myriad of comparative policy activity on reproductive technologies, however, is to illustrate the range of mechanisms available to deal with the issues they raise. It is striking that the United States did not have any single body on the scale of the Warnock Committee in Britain. In part, this neglect is a function of our pluralist, federal system and the lack of a clear agenda-setting role of the government that is present in a parliamentary system. It also reflects the fact that these technologies have largely been placed in an individual rights context in the United States where governmental involvement is viewed as a threat, not protection, of the individual. In combination with the tendency of the Reagan and Bush administrations and Congress to steer clear of the issues for political reasons, this has retarded the national dialogue.

IV. TREATMENT OF SERIOUSLY ILL NEWBORNS

In a press conference held to announce guidelines for infant bioethics committees (IBCs), Robert J. Haggerty, then vice-president of the American Academy of Pediatrics, asserted that the question of who decides how to treat newborns with severe disabilities and how those decisions are made "has become the moral issue of our time" (American Academic of Pediatrics, 1984: 1). Ironically, it is medicine's new-found capacity to intervene and save severely ill infants that has produced these controversial moral and public-policy dilemmas. Until very recently, nature decided which infants would survive and which would die. Today, however, increasingly sophisticated neonatal treatment has put nature on the defensive and saves infants from a variety of physical conditions that in the near past would have certainly been fatal. In some cases, the patients go on to lead fulfilling lives. In many others, though, the surviving infant's quality of life is so low as to raise doubts about the use of the life-saving treatment. The result, according to the President's Commission for the Study of Ethical Problems in Medicine and Biomedical and Behavioral Research (1983: 198), is that

> medicine's increased ability to forestall death in seriously ill newborns has magnified the already difficult task of physicians and parents who must attempt to assess which infants will benefit from various medical interventions and which will not. Not only does this test the limits of medical certainty in diagnosis and prognosis, it also raises profound ethical issues.

Moreover, these ethical issues soon become policy issues because a large proportion are paid for by public funds, and neonatal care is extremely expensive in comparison to its frequently marginal long-term benefit.

A. Neonatal Intensive Care

1. Premature Infants

There are two categories of seriously ill newborns. The first comprises those infants born prematurely with very low birth weight (VLBW), which is usually defined as less than 1500 grams. By 1985, over \$2 billion was spent on neonatal care for some 200,000 infants (Gustaitis and Young, 1986). Although VLBW babies represent only 1% of all live births, they account for 50% of all neonatal deaths (Lantos et al., 1988). Their relative risk of neonatal death is almost 200 times greater than normal birth weight infants (McCormick, 1985). Moreover, 30 to 40% of surviving VLBW babies require rehospitalization and many suffer long-term disabilities because of their low birth weight (Shankaran et al., 1988). Despite rapid advances in neonatal technology, mortality and long-term morbidity of infants born weighing less than 750 grams were not improved between the early and late 1980s (Hack and Fanaroff, 1989).

2. Infants with Congenital Abnormalities

The second category of seriously ill infants includes those inflicted with congenital abnormalities requiring major medical attention if the infant is to live. About 4% of the infants born in the United States have one or more detectable congenital abnormalities. Although these situations account for only a small fraction of the neonatal intensive care cases, they dominate the discussion in the media. Most common among these abnormalities are neural tube defects, such as spina bifida and anencephaly, and the Down syndrome. The fact that spina bifida exhibits such a wide variation in severity makes decisions as to whether or not aggressive surgical treatment is warranted—and if so, what treatment is most appropriate—exceedingly difficult.

Similarly, although all individuals born with the Down syndrome are mentally retarded, the degree of retardation varies widely and cannot be determined in early infancy, when the decision to treat or not treat the patient is crucial. Further fueling the debate over treatment of affected infants, a significant minority of children with the Down syndrome are born with a gastrointestinal blockage, congenital heart defects, or both. Although surgical treatment in these cases often is routine, many parents and physicians reject intervention efforts that preserve this type of life.

3. Long-Term Treatment

The dependence on highly sophisticated and expensive neonatal intensive care illustrates our society's tendency to stress curative medicine and ignore prevention. A large proportion of the low-weight pregnancies are precipitated by controllable environmental factors, yet "efforts to treat the problem have gained support far in excess of efforts to prevent it" (Miller, 1984: 553). Instead of spending relatively small amounts of money to educate pregnant women and to provide adequate prenatal care and nutrition, we continue to emphasize after-the-fact treatments that exact a very high toll on society, especially on those individuals directly affected. This point is critical, because many of the neonatal survivors have life-long diseases or handicaps that require a long-term, exhausting commitment to these infants after they leave the hospital. This less dramatic but crucial follow-up care never seems to attract the support from the medical community and public officials that neonatal intensive care units (NICUs) have received.

B. Government Involvement in Treating Critically Ill Infants

Events of the last decade have brought a new player into these life-death decisions, beginning with the Reagan administration's "Baby Doe" regulations. These regulations were a reaction to the well-publicized case of an infant with the Down syndrome infant with an incomplete esophagus who was denied lifesaving surgery and allowed to die with parental consent. Issued in 1983 by the Department of Health and Human Services (HHS) under a federal law banning discrimination against the disabled (Section 504 of the Rehabilitation Act of 1973), they ensured that treatment would not be deliberately withheld from handicapped infants. A "hot line" was set up on which hospital staff and others were urged to report potential violations. The courts, however, struck down the original regulations and a modified version in May 1984.

In September 1984, after months of emotional hearings and difficult negotiation, Congress passed a child-abuse act (HR 1904, PL 98-457) that included controversial Baby Doe provisions. The law required states, as a condition of receiving federal child-abuse aid, to have procedures for responding, through existing state child-protection agencies, to reports of medical neglect of handicapped infants in life-threatening situations. Hospitals were encouraged, although not required, to establish committees to review such cases. Most controversial, the Act created a new category of criminal neglect. Failure to initiate aggressive action to save a baby was defined as a criminal offence unless treatment is "virtually futile" in saving the infant's life, the infant is "irreversibly comatose," or the treatment itself is "inhumane." Obviously, the wording of these exceptions and the Act's references to "reasonable medical judgment" were ambiguous and open to a variety of interpretations (Rhoden and Arras, 1985).

The Baby Doe provisions were backed by a coalition of medical, handicapped, and right-to-life groups and had strong support from the Reagan administration. In contrast to the American Hospital Association (AHA) and the American Academy of Pediatrics (AAP), the American Medical Association (AMA) did not support the infant-care provisions, because it felt they left no room for consideration of the quality of life severely disabled infants would face if kept alive indefinitely. The AHA would have preferred to see the federal government stay out of this area, but they accepted the final, compromise version of the bill over previous ones.

May 1985 brought further "Baby Doe" regulations in the form of the HHS's final rule implementing the Child Abuse Amendments. The wording of the regulations showed clearly that the Reagan administration intended to interpret the provisions of the Act as narrowly as the courts would allow. The HHS regulations rigidly interpreted the Act's "medical indications" policy; again rejecting any consideration of subjective quality-of-life judgments.

On June 9, 1986, the Supreme Court struck down the administration's 1983 Baby Doe rules (*Bowen* v. *American Hospital Association*). In a 5 to 3 vote, the Court ruled that the federal law prohibiting discrimination against handicapped individuals in activities receiving financial assistance does not give the Secretary of Health and Human Services the right to intervene in decisions regarding medical treatment of handicapped infants. Justice Stevens, writing the plurality opinion (Justice Berger concurred with the judgment but disagreed with the reasoning), stated: "Section 504 does not authorize the secretary to give unsolicited advice either to parents, to hospitals, or to state officials who are faced with difficult treatment decisions concerning handicapped children." Opponents of the Baby Doe rules hailed the decision as a return of discretion to parents and physicians, whereas proponents viewed it as undermining the newborn's right to be treated aggressively. But, especially since state laws regulating intervention in cases of medical neglect were not affected by the decision, the extent to which it affects the treatment of severely ill newborns is questionable (Caplan et al., 1992).

V. ORGAN TRANSPLANTATION

Perhaps the most dramatic area of biomedical technology, and the most expensive on a per-case basis, is organ transplantation of major organs. Recent forays into artificial heart transplants, partial liver transplants, transplantation of baboon organs into humans, and grafting of fetal neural tissue into the brains of patients with Parkinson's disease are natural extensions of the desire to replace diseased or worn-out organs. In the last decade, advances in surgical procedure, organ preservation techniques, tissue matching, and drug treatment have combined to accelerate the use and magnitude of organ transplantation. As survival rates have improved, the demand for transplant surgery has multiplied.

In November 1987, 3-year-old Tabatha Foster received a new liver, pancreas, small intestine, and parts of a stomach and colon at Children's Hospital in Pittsburgh after her system failed. Multiple transplants of this scope will increase as more transplant centers develop the capabilities. The demand for transplant surgery is potentially unlimited in a population willing to go to any expense to prolong life. Transplant availability has already expanded rapidly to keep up with this demand. The number of medical centers doing liver transplants climbed from 3 to 36 in 4 years, and the number of heart transplant centers multiplied from 5 in 1982 to 71 in 1987. More than 180 medical centers are now performing some type of transplant surgery.

Table 1 presents data on transplant procedures in the United States. By far the most common transplant is the kidney. Its moderately low cost, its reimbursement through Medicare, and the relative availability of donor organs ensures continued expansion of that program. Kidney transplants are clearly the most routine, although even here, up to 20% of the transplant patients die within one year and about 40% die within 3 years. The policy problems of other major organ transplants exceed those of the kidney program; primarily because of the large initial cost of these procedures and the significantly lower survival rates. Although liver transplant survival rates have continually risen, they are especially problematic because of the nature of the organ and the difficulty of obtaining suitable donor organs.

A. Issues in Organ Transplantation

The development that has substantially improved the survival rate of patients receiving transplants is the introduction of the drug cyclosporine, one of the most potent and specific immunosuppresants discovered so far. Approved by the Food and Drug Administration in 1983 for routine use, it suppresses the body's natural immunity system and keeps it from rejecting the transplanted organ. Cyclosporine is unique in that although it suppresses production of the white blood cells responsible for organ rejection, it does not grossly interfere with the activation of those cells that destroy bacteria.

Cyclosporine has dramatically reduced the incidence of organ rejection and roughly doubled the overall 1-year survival rate of each type of organ transplant. It has also accelerated rehabilitation and reduced hospital costs (Austen and Cosimi, 1984: 1437). Despite its effectiveness in suppressing the immune system and in markedly improving survival rates, cyclosporine, like all medical innovations, has its disadvantages. For one thing, it is expen-

Table 1. Organ Transplantation in the United States

	Kidney	Pancreas	Liver	Heart	Heart/Lung
First Transplant	1954	•	1963	1967	1981
Number performed in 1987	8976	87(1985)	724	1368	37
Cost	$25,000·$30,000	$35,000·$60,000	$135,000·$250,000	$60,000·$110,000	$100,000·$300,000
1-year survival rate/ cyclosporine	80·95	35·40	60·70	75·80	
Approximate number of centers (1987)	120	21	36	71	9
Estimated number who could benefit per year	7000	5000	10,000	50,000	

Source: American Council on Transplantation.

sive. Maintenance doses for patients with transplants cost anywhere from $6,000 to $10,000 per year: Although this cost may be reduced somewhat in the future, it will remain high. More important, however, are the drug's severe side effects. The major toxic effect of cyclosporine is impaired kidney function in virtually all patients who have used it (Strom and Loertscher, 1984: 728). It has also been linked to liver damage, hypertension, and an increased risk of the cancer lymphoma (Austen and Cosimi, 1984: 1437).

In addition to the issues surrounding cyclosporine, organ transplantation raises many other serious policy questions. One prominent problem concerns ensuring a sufficient supply of organs, especially those (such as the heart, pancreas, and liver) that require a brain-dead donor. The donor problem is complicated by the fact that the organs of only about 10 to 15% of persons who suffer brain death each year are available for transplant; in part because the Uniform Act for the Donation of Organs requires the documentation of consent before organs can be transplanted. Although the rate of donations may rise through education campaigns, the overall size of the pool might actually shrink as medicine learns to save more potential donors (Wehr, 1984: 458). This has led to calls for "passage of presumed consent laws in all of the fifty states" where organs could be used in the absence of specific written objections from the person (Cwiek, 1984: 99). Furthermore, because some organ transplantations require over 100 units of blood, concern has been expressed over the distribution of this potentially scarce resource.

In spite of all the technical advances, it is still unclear how many lives are usefully extended by new organs. Even under optimal circumstances, 30 or 40% of liver transplants will fail within a month, and during that month the patient endures considerable pain. Even if the patient survives for 1 or 2 years or more, post-transplant existence can be excruciating for the patient and family. Hale (1984) describes the postsurgical ordeals of patients who have undergone transplant surgery and must now live "tethered to medical treatment for life." She cites the high suicide rates among patients who have received kidney transplants as well as less extreme forms of revulsion against the loss of control over their lives following the surgery.

Organ transplants, like all expensive lifesaving treatments, raise innumerable questions of social priorities. Do they represent the efficient use of health-care resources? Do they justify the tradeoffs required to provide the requisite amount of resources? Does the state have authority to redistribute financial resources—or the organs themselves—so as to enable transplant surgery for all those who would benefit? Finally, in a liberal society, does a dying person have a right to a new organ? How far does this right extend when it conflicts with the rights of others to more basic health-care needs? These difficult questions of fairness, equity, efficiency, and cost are inescapable (Mathieu, 1988).

B. Government Involvement in Transplantation

In 1972, Congress passed the End Stage Renal Disease (ESRD) Act that extended Medicare coverage for dialysis and transplantation to all patients with kidney disease. The ESRD program is often cited as an example of short-sighted decision making. Because original estimates severely underestimated the number of eligible patients, the first-year costs of $241 million far exceeded the estimate of $135 million. By 1983, the cost of the ESRD program exceeded $2 billion per year for approximately 70,000 patients. As a result, these patients, who represent about 0.25% of all Medicare beneficiaries, account for 13% of total Medicare expenditures for outpatient care and almost 10% of all Medicare B (inpatient) costs. The advent of federal funding made the dialysis population not only considerably larger but also sicker and older. In 1967, only 7% of patients receiving dialysis were over age 55; by 1983, this had climbed to 45%. In the United States, many patients on dialysis suffer from other diseases or are past the age that would exclude them from treatment in Britain and other countries that have a national health service.

Annas (1985: 187) notes that the ESRD decision "simply served to postpone the time when identical decisions will have to be made about candidates for heart and liver transplantation." That time has now arrived, and the ESRD experience has made Congress wary of rushing in to support federal funding of liver and heart transplantations. On the other hand, policy makers face significant political pressures to guarantee access to organs to those persons who need it. Just as the ESRD program was the result of emotional lobbying efforts, so today's office holders increasingly are becoming the targets of constituents who appeal for public aid in obtaining and paying for expensive transplant surgeries. Especially difficult to resist are the pleas for lifesaving transplants from parents on behalf of young children.

In order to ease the difficulties of patients and their families in seeking organ transplant surgery and take these decisions out of the realm of public relations, Congress passed the Organ Transplant Act in 1984. Interestingly, a provision that would have financed cyclosporine for patients who could not afford it was omitted in the final version. The act (PL 98-507) authorized the expenditure of $2 million annually to support a national computerized system for matching patients with donors of these scarce organs and up to $12 million in 1987 for grants to create or upgrade local and regional agencies that produce human organs for transplantation and that participate in the computerized matching network. The Act also established a national registry of transplant patients to facilitate scientific evaluations of transplant procedures and directed the Secretary of Health and Human Services to assign responsibility for administering organ transplant programs to the Public Health Service or another appropriate body. Finally, it prohibited the purchase or sale of human organs for transplantation and authorized jail terms of up to 5 years for deliberate violations of this provision.

The Organ Transplant Act also created a task force to study and report on the ethical, legal, and financial aspects of organ transplants. In July 1986, the National Task Force on Organ Transplantation issued its final report. Among its many recommendations was a call for federal financing of heart and liver transplantations. In order to provide equitable access to these "gifts of life," the task force recommended that patient selection for transplantation be based on "publicly stated and fairly applied" medical criteria, including the need and the probability of success. It also recommended that the government should provide immunosuppressive medication to all patients who could not afford it.

Furthermore, the task force recommended creation of a national network to coordinate all organ recovery and distribution. In order to ensure an adequate supply of organs to meet the increased demands government funding would unleash, the task force urged all states to enact the Uniform Definition of Death Act and Congress to adopt "routine inquiry/required request" legislation. The former action would make brain-dead bodies available for transplantation, whereas the latter would require hospitals routinely to ask all potential donors (or next of kin) if they wish to donate their organs.

Just before the task force issued its final report, HHS Secretary Otis Bowen announced the government's decision to start funding heart transplantations for qualified Medicare patients. Under this action, heart transplant programs approved by the Health Care Financing Administration (HCFA) would be reimbursed. The criteria specify that, to be approved, a facility must have performed 12 or more heart transplants in each of the previous 2 years and 12 transplants before that. It must also have an average survival rate of at least 73%. Despite HHS projections of a maximum of 10 centers, by 1987 this number was exceeded.

In separate actions since 1986, the government has moved toward funding cyclosporine for all transplant patients and has established a national policy of required request for potential organ donors. Under the fiscal 1987 budget legislation (PL 99-509), hospitals that fail to establish required-request procedures will lose eligibility for participation in Medicare and Medicaid programs. Also, HHS has allocated over $5 million in grants for organ-procurement programs to coordinate recovery and distribution. Both of these actions have been taken to increase substantially the supply of organs, which, in view of the rapid movement toward governmental sanctioning and public funding of organ transplants, is the only factor holding back transplant programs. These steps by the government have accelerated the number of heart and liver transplantations performed, much as occurred with kidney transplantations in the 1970s. As in the case of treatment of severely ill newborns, the current response of policy makers to transplantation demonstrates the powerful momentum behind high-cost technological intervention in the United States.

VI. DEATH-RELATED ISSUES

The tremendous advances in technology's capacity to keep the human body biologically alive have also, ironically, deepened some groups' commitment to defend the patient's right to die. As mechanical respirators, artificial organs, and invasive life-prolonging treatments permit the almost indefinite extension of biological existence, many persons are questioning of the ethics of keeping the patient alive at all costs. Increasingly, the use of artificial support systems is quietly rejected, particularly for chronically ill elderly patients. Do not resuscitate (DNR) orders that set limits on the use of lifesaving treatment are commonplace in hospitals. The desire to die with dignity, free from tubes and machines, reflects a disenchantment with technological prolongation of life and raises demands for euthanasia policies.

What role should the government take in decisions to forego life-sustaining treatment? The President's Commission (1983: 1) argued that because death today is a much less private matter than it once was, usually occurring in a hospital or nursing home with many people involved, the "resolution of disagreements among them is more likely to require formal rules and means of adjudication.'' Furthermore, because biomedical developments have made death more a matter of deliberate decision, what once was the province of fate now becomes a matter of human choice. Although the commission concluded that the major responsibility for ensuring ''morally justified processes of decision making'' lies with physicians, it called for institutional safeguards to protect the best interests of patients.

A. Euthanasia

Within the past decade, the legal landscape concerning euthanasia has changed dramatically. Although there remain inconsistent court rulings over the right to die, in large part the courts have accepted the right of patients and in some cases their families or friends to authorize termination of livesaving treatment, including feeding and hydration tubes. For instance, in *Delio* v. *Westchester County Medical Center* (1987), a New York appellate court found that the patient alone has the right to make the ''ultimate decision'' to refuse treatment and that there could be no countervailing interest in prolonging life by force feeding that the patient would have found to be ''demeaning and degrading to his humanity.''

More recently, attention has been shifted from this ''passive'' type of euthanasia to questions of the legality of ''active'' types in which lethal injections are used to bring on the death of willing patients. The failed 1991 Washington state initiative that would have allowed physician-assisted death is certain to be followed by similar attempts in other states. Interest groups such as the Hemlock Society and Choice in Dying (previously the Society for the Right to Die) are active in lobbying for legislation that permits death with dignity. The widespread sales of Derek Humphrey's *The Final Exit*, and support among some groups for Dr. Kevorkian's suicide-assisting machine indicate growing concern for individuals to take control over the circumstances surrounding their deaths.

Although public opinion surveys demonstrate an ambivalence toward active euthanasia, there is considerable support for allowing individuals to discontinue life-support systems where there is no hope of recovery. A Gallup Poll conducted for *Hospitals* magazine in December 1986 found that 70% of the respondents were ''very willing'' to have life-support systems discontinued and 12% were ''somewhat willing,'' whereas only 18% were unwilling. Likewise, in a nonrandom poll by the magazine *Ladies Home Journal* in April 1987, 97% felt that terminally ill people have the ''right to euthanasia.'' In the Gallup survey, 72% said they would be willing (46% ''very willing'') to disconnect artificial support systems on behalf of a relative. The proportion of the population opposed to passive voluntary euthanasia appears relatively small, although many of those opposed are very committed in their opposition.

As of 1987, 39 states had living-will laws. Of these, 18 had been enacted in the 2 previous years. Increasingly, these statues are becoming standardized along the lines of the Uniform Rights of the Terminally Ill Act recommended by the National Conference of Commissioners on Uniform State Laws. Some states have replaced earlier living-will statutes with new, broadened laws. The Arkansas Rights of the Terminally Ill or Permanently Unconscious Act, for instance, authorizes appointment of a health-care proxy to act on the patient's behalf when necessary and expands coverage to include permanently comatose patients as well as the terminally ill. (For an excellent summary of state living-will statutes, see Society for the Right to Die, 1987.) In addition, many states are passing durable power of attorney legislation that gives an individual(s) designated by the terminally ill person decision-making power should that person lose the capacity to make medical decisions.

In a related matter of policy, the Joint Commission on Accreditation of Hospitals required all hospitals in the United States to establish, by January 1988, formal policies regarding resuscitation of terminally ill patients. Although many hospitals had formal DNR policies, many other facilities had instead depended on a confusing array of information "no-code," "slow code," and "partial code" categories, generally with no provision for patient consent. The failure by many hospitals to acknowledge their actions, often on grounds of potential liability, has acquired increasing policy importance because of the large number of potential candidates; now estimated at over 1.5 million per year.

B. Redefining Death

Another issue with similar roots as euthanasia is the need to redefine death within the context of the new capacities to extend biological existence indefinitely. The President's Commission concluded that "in light of ever increasing powers of biomedical science and practice, a statute is needed to provide a clear and socially-accepted basis for making definitions of death" (1981: i). Although the Commission acknowledged the linkage of this issue to euthanasia, it concluded that, as matters of public policy, the two can be treated separately, and thereby avoiding much of the emotional sensitivity that euthanasia arouses.

The traditional medical definition of death has been the permanent cessation of respiration and circulation. In the near past, this was unambiguous, because once these functions ceased, they could not be restored. But advances in medical techniques, which now permit machine-regulated breathing and heartbeat even when the capacity to breathe spontaneously is irreversibly lost, have made the traditional determination of death inadequate. The emphasis has shifted to brain function as the critical criterion. Because the brain cannot regenerate neural cells, once the entire brain has been seriously damaged, spontaneous respiration can never return even though breathing may be sustained by respirators or ventilators. The machines can maintain certain organic processes in the body, but they cannot restore consciousness.

Like most matters of public health, the determination of death traditionally has been within the province of each state's common law. This dependence on the courts to determine and apply criteria for death has resulted in considerable uncertainty and a lack of consistency across jurisdictions and potential for abuse. Two efforts to resolve these problems have resulted: (1) many state legislatures have enacted statutory standards, and (2) a national standard has been proposed.

In 1970, the Kansas state legislature became the first to recognize brain-based criteria for determination of death. Within several years, four states passed laws patterned on the Kansas model. The Capron-Kass proposal (1972) offered the states a more succinct substitute that eliminated some of the Kansas model's ambiguity. To date, seven states have adopted the Capron-Kass model with minor modifications, whereas three others have done so with more substantial changes. Two other model statutes (American Bar Association, 1975; National Conference of Commissioners on Uniform State Laws, 1978) have been enacted by five and two states, respectively. The American Medical Association's 1979 proposal, which includes extensive provisions to limit liability for persons taking actions under the proposal, has not been adopted in any state. About 10 states have nonstandard statutes that often include parts of one or more of these models, whereas about 10 states have no statutory determinations of death.

The debate in the late 1980s shifted to the distinction between "total brain death" (including the brain stem) and partial brain death (the cessation of selected functions). Can a person be considered dead even though some parts of the brain remain alive? The brain stem can maintain the respiratory system even if the higher brain is not functioning, and the Commission contends that to declare dead a person who is spontaneously breathing yet has no higher brain functions would too radically change our definition of death. If, however, it is our higher brain functions that define us as humans, then partial brain death could be a more appropriate standard. As knowledge about the functioning of the brain increases, this issue may either dissipate or intensify. Currently, whole brain death has consensual support among most experts and the public. Although a few short years have powerfully transformed the meaning of death, many questions remain. Our very conception of what it means to be human are challenged by these rapid advances in medical technology.

VII. CONCLUSIONS

Although biomedical issues are recent additions to the policy agenda and are currently undergoing severe stress as they move from private to public matters, they promise to become acrimonious and challenging problems in the 1990s. Because they entail high personal stakes, including in many instances the difference between life and death, and because they potentially affect every individual in society, they represent a set of politically explosive issues. This brief review of selected areas of developments in biomedical policy demonstrates the complexity and political sensitivity of the issues that accompany these often remarkable interventions in the human experience.

As biomedical issues move into the public agenda and through the policy process at an accelerating rate, they will force elected officials to make excruciating decisions that they to date have preferred to avoid. Considerable effort is required to analyze where we as a society wish to go with biomedicine and what place it should play in the allocation of increasingly scarce resources. More rigorous and critical assessment of these technologies is necessary before they are widely diffused. As difficult as it might be to preclude or at least redirect certain technological advances, choices must be made as to the priorities assigned to each. This in turn necessitates an expanded public dialogue and debate over the range of issues illustrated in this chapter.

REFERENCES

Aaron, H. J., and Schwartz, W. B. (1984). *The Painful Prescription: Rationing Hospital Care.* The Brookings Institution, Washington, DC.

American Academy of Pediatrics (1984). Guidelines announced for infant bioethics committees. *News and Comment* 35: 1.

Annas, G. J. (1985). The prostitute, the playboy, and the poet: Rationing schemes for organ transplantation. *American Journal of Public Health* 75: 187–189.

Austen, W. G., and Cosimi, A. B. (1984). Editorial retrospective: Heart transplantation after sixteen years. *New England Journal of Medicine* 311: 1436–1438.

Barnes, D. M. (1988). The biological tangle of drug addiction. *Science* 241: 415–417.

Blank, R. H. (1988). *Rationing Medicine.* Columbia University Press, New York.

—— (1990). *Regulating Reproduction.* Columbia University Press, New York.

—— (1991). *Fertility Control: New Techniques, New Issues.* Greenwood Press, Westport, CT.

—— (1992). *Mother and Fetus: Changing Notions of Maternal Responsibility.* Greenwood Press, Westport, CT.

Blank, R. H., and Bonnicksen, A. L. (Eds.) (1992). *Emerging Issues in Biomedical Policy*, vol I. Columbia University Press, New York.

Blank, R. H., and Mills, M. K. (Eds.) (1989). *Biomedical Technology and Public Policy.* Greenwood Press, Westport, CT.

Bonnicksen, A. L. (1989). *In Vitro Fertilization: Building Policy From Laboratories to Legislatures.* Columbia University Press, New York.

Brandon, W. P. (1982). Health-related tax subsidies: Government handouts for the affluent. *New England Journal of Medicine* 307: 947–950.

Califano, J. A. Jr. (1992). Rationing health care: The unnecessary solution. *University of Pennsylvania Law Review* 140: 1525–1538.

Caplan, A. L., Blank, R. H., and Merrick, J. C. (Eds.) (1992). *Compelled Compassion: Government Intervention in the Treatment of Critically Ill Newborns.* Humana Press, Totowa, NJ.

Canter, C. R. (1990). Orchestrating the human genome project. *Science* 248: 49–51.

Cwiek, M. A. (1984). Presumed consent as a solution to the organ shortfall problem. *Public Law Forum* 4: 81–99.

Gustaitis, R., and Young, E. W. D. (1986). *A Time to be Born, A Time to Die.* Addison-Wesley, Reading, MA.

Hack, M., and Fanaroff, A. A. (1989). Outcomes of extremely low-birthweight infants between 1982 and 1985. *New England Journal of Medicine* 321: 1642–1647.

Holden, C. (1991). Probing the complex genetics of alcoholism. *Science* 251: 163–164.

Knaus, W. A. (1986). Rationing, justice, and the American physician. *JAMA* 255: 1176–1177.

Lamm, R. D. (1992). Rationing of health care: Inevitable and desirable. *University of Pennsylvania Law Review* 140: 1511–1524.

Lantos, J. D., Miles, S. H., Silverstein, M. D., and Stocking, C. B. (1988). Survival after cardiopulmonary resuscitation in babies of very-low-birth weight: Is CPR futile therapy? *New England Journal of Medicine* 318: 91–95.

Marx, J. L. (1989). The cystic fibrosis gene is found. *Science* 245: 923–925.

Mathieu, D. (Ed.) (1988). *Organ Substitution Technology: Ethical, Legal, and Public Policy Issues.* Westview Press, Boulder, CO.

McCormick, M. C. (1985). The contribution of low birth weight to infant mortality and childhood morbidity. *New England Journal of Medicine* 312: 82–89.

McKusick, V. A. (1989). Mapping and sequencing the human genome. *New England Journal of Medicine* 320: 910–915.

Mechanic, D. (1986). *From Advocacy to Allocation: The Evolving American Health Care System.* Free Press, New York.

Merz, B. (1989). Gene therapy enters 'second generation.' *American Medical News* 22(29): 3, 11.

Miller, C. A. (1984). The health of children, a crisis in ethics. *Pediatrics* 73: 550–558.

National Center for Human Genome Research (NCHGR) (1990). *Understanding Our Genetic Heritage.* National Technical Information Service, Springfield, VA.

Nelkin, D., and Tancredi, L. (1989). *Dangerous Diagnostics: The Social Power of Biological Information.* Basic Books, New York.

Office of Technology Assessment (1982). *Strategies for Medical Technology Assessment.* U.S. Government Printing Office, Washington, DC.

—— (1987a). *Life-sustaining Technologies and the Elderly.* U.S. Government Printing Office, Washington, DC.

—— (1987b). *Neonatal Intensive Care for Low Birthweight Infants.* U.S. Government Printing Office, Washington, DC.

—— (1988a). *Infertility: Medical and Social Choices.* U.S. Government Printing Office, Washington, DC.

—— (1988b). *Mapping Our Genes: Genome Projects—How Big, How Fast?* U.S. Government Printing Office, Washington, DC.

—— (1990). *Neural Grafting: Repairing the Brain and Spinal Cord.* U.S. Government Printing Office, Washington, DC.

President's Commission for the Study of Ethical Issues in Medicine and Biomedical and Behavioral Research (1981). *Defining Death*. U.S. Government Printing Office, Washington, DC.

—— (1983). *Securing Access to Health Care*. U.S. Government Printing Office, Washington, DC.

Rhoden, N. K., and Arras, J. D. (1985). Withholding treatment from Baby Doe: From discrimination to child abuse. *Milbank Memorial Fund Quarterly* 63: 18–51.

Riegelman, R. H. (1991). Taming medical technology. In *Paying The Doctor: Health Policy and Physician Reimbursement*. J. D. Moreno (Ed.). Auburn House, Westport, CT.

Selden, R. F., Skoskiewicz, M. J., Russell, P. S., and Goodman, H. M. (1987). Regulation of insulin-gene expression: Implications for gene therapy. *New England Journal of Medicine* 317: 1067–1075.

Shankaran, S., Cohen, S. N., Linver, M., and Zonia, A. (1988). Medical care costs of high-risk infants after neonatal intensive care. *Pediatrics* 81: 372–378.

Strom, T. B., and Loertscher, R. (1984). Cyclosporine-induced nephrotoxicity: inevitable and intractable. *New England Journal of Medicine* 311: 728–729.

Watson, J. D. (1990). The human genome project: Past, present, and future. *Science* 248: 44–48.

Wehr, E. (1984). National health policy sought for organ transplant surgery. *Congressional Quarterly Weekly Report* 25: 453–458.

34
Space Policy

Robert M. Lawrence
Colorado State University, Fort Collins, Colorado

In a scientific sense, contemporary U.S. space policy can be traced back to Sir Isaac Newton's third law of motion, which states, "To every action there is always opposed an equal reaction: or the mutual actions of two bodies upon each other are always equal, and directed to contrary parts." In this way, Newton explained why rockets would eventually work. The early rocket scientists, K. E. Tsiolkovsky in Russia, Robert H. Goddard, in the United States, and Hermann Oberth in Germany, came to understand that Newton's observation meant the hot gases expelled from the back, or nozzle, of a rocket would thrust the rocket forward. They also knew it would make no difference whether the rocket operated in the Earth's atmosphere or in the void of space; in either case the rocket would be propelled forward.

The dreams of actually using Newton's law to carry humans beyond the hold of Earth's gravitational field were prefaced by science fiction writers who plied their trade in the latter 1800s. There was Edward Everett Hale, who penned the "Brick Moon," which was published in the *Atlantic Monthly*; Jules Verne, who wrote *Journey from the Earth to the Moon*; and H. G. Wells, who wrote *The War of the Worlds*. The writings of all three authors captured many imaginations, including those with the nascent technical skills to set in motion events that in fact would lead to the moon. As civilization nears the 21st century, years after the deaths of the early science fiction authors and of the rocket scientists, the observation Charles A. Lindbergh made more than a quarter of a century ago remains appropriate:

> Year by year, time keeps turning pages of fiction over into the preface of fact. Satellites are now orbiting our earth; missiles have struck the surface of the moon; space probes have hurtled out beyond the gravitation that we humans feel (Lehman, 1988: xx).

In a political and bureaucratic sense U.S. space policy owes its beginnings to the realization, forced by the necessity of World War II, that enormous strides in science and technology can be made rapidly when governmental assets and direction are invested in large-scale research and development. Hitherto such activity had mainly occurred in the ivory tower aloofness of the universities and according to the proprietary and entrepreneurial independence of private enterprise. Fighting for its life, the U.S. could no longer live as it had. The most impressive example of the World War II use of science and technology by the government was the development of the atomic bomb. After 1947, the marriage of big government to big science received a second impetus that is still clearly obvious today. That stimulus came from the belief government-sponsored science was necessary for a successful defense against the widely perceived threat from communism in general and from the Soviet Union in particular. The influence of the cold war on scientific research and development is not the only area of American life dramatically impacted by the fear of communism, but what happened in the other areas is beyond the scope of this chapter. What is of specific interest in the context of U.S. space policy is the fact that first the military and then the civilian space programs have been the most impressive example of government-induced research and development since the end of World War II. The down side of such governmental expansion of power was noted by President Eisenhower and will be examined later.

In all three of the nations that most pioneered rocket development in the 20th century—the Soviet Union, Nazi Germany, and the United States—the major governmental interest in rockets was not fueled by scientific curiosity but in the utility seen for missiles by the military. The purely scientific interests had to remain hidden deep within the minds of some German scientists, had to relinguish primacy to the military in the Soviet Union, and shared importance with the military in the United States. Thus, much of this chapter will trace, describe, and analyze the impetus supplied by national defense concerns to U.S. space policy and the constant interface between national defense–oriented space policies and civil space policies. Even today, with the cold war proclaimed over by both former President George Bush, and his successor President Bill Clinton, the military motivation remains strong, if not dominant, in the space efforts of the United States.

I. THE YEARS OF POLICY PAUCITY

In the beginning, there was no U.S. government space policy. There was only physics professor Robert H. Goddard of Clark University, Worchester, Massachusetts, his enthusiastic and supportive wife Esther, and a small band of dedicated assistants (Lehman, 1988). Goddard launched the world's first liquid-fuel rocket on March 16, 1926. The place was a few miles from Worchester, at Auburn, Massachusetts. It is recorded that the rocket weighed 9 pounds. It ascended to the height of 41 feet and fell to the ground 184 feet away (Lehman, 1988: ix). This unimpressive start to U.S. rocket programs is put into perspective when it is recalled that in 1903 the Wright brothers' airplane flew for 120 feet at Kitty Hawk, North Carolina.

Scholarly research indicates that Goddard cherished deep within himself the belief that in time, and he thought it would be a long time after his demise, humans would sit atop giant rockets and hurl themselves up to the moon, and beyond, possibly to Mars (Lehman, 1988: 40–61). However, Goddard was a private person, not often given to voicing what then would have been wild speculations. Thus, he generally covered his secret and personal mission with the stolidly scientific objective suggested in the title of a piece published in 1919 by the Smithsonian Institution, "A Method of Researching Extreme Altitudes" (Lehman, 1988: 83). During most of his subsequent life, except when working on World War I and World War II applications of his rocket research, Goddard publicly projected the image of a scientist developing rockets in order to carry instruments to high altitudes for scientific sampling of the upper atmosphere. Further, Goddard's personality was such that he did not readily share his research with others. Thus, what might have been an earlier formation of a critical mass of talent and interest in U.S. rocketry led by Goddard did not occur.

In fact, there was no sustained U.S. space policy until after World War II when the American military finally saw utility in Goddard's previous work and that of others.

During the interwar years, the U.S. government slept in regard to both rocket research and the development and other aspects of national defense. It was markedly different in Europe. There both Stalin and Hitler marshalled their respective governmental assets to support concentrated efforts to develop rockets for military purposes.

In the United States, Goddard was experimenting with rockets that he fired a few thousand feet into the skies near Roswell, New Mexico. When the war began he had designed a rocket 22 feet long that weighed 500 pounds when fully fueled by a mixture of gasoline and liquid oxygen.

In the newly born Soviet Union, Lenin expressed what the Americans would later learn about the necessity of mating government assets with scientific talent—"The war taught us much, not only that people suffered, but especially the fact those who have the best technology, organization, and discipline, and the best machines emerge on top. . . . It is necessary to master the highest technology or be crushed" (McDougall, 1985: 24). In 1924, there was created within the Soviet state the Central Bureau for the Study of the Problems of Rockets.

Stalin succeeded Lenin and carried on the theme that industrial and scientific prowess must be sought as national priorities to defend the revolution. His words in 1931 were:

> The backward are beaten. But we do not wish to be beaten! No, we do not! The history of Old Russia consisted of being constantly beaten for her backwardness. The Mongol Khans beat her. The Turkish beys beat her. The Swedish feudalists beat her. The Polish-Lithuanian nobles beat her. The Anglo-French capitalists beat her. Everyone beat her—for her backwardness (McDougall, 1985: 29).

Largely out of sight of the West and with no concern for Soviet citizens, Stalin converted flesh, bones, and blood into an industrial and scientific base that supported, among other projects, an impressive rocket program. While lagging behind the Germans in the size and range of their rockets, the Russians developed and used extensively the battlefield rocket called *Katiusha* (meaning Kathy). It was fired in terrifying bursts of multiple launches with devastating effect against German troops. And the Soviets established before and during World War II the scientific foundation that after the war would propel the U.S.S.R. into direct space competition with the United States.

Several years before Hitler came to power, the German Army's Ordnance Ballistic Section set about to build a long-range liquid-fuel rocket. The choice to lead a secret scientific team was Walter Dornberger. He in turn selected a brilliant younger scientist named Wernher von Braun as an assistant. They and their rocket group proved what could be accomplished by a large scientific and engineering team backed by the financial assets of a powerful central government. In 1934, the Germans first successfully fired a liquid-fueled rocket. At the rocket research facilities at Peenemunde, and elsewhere, the Germans developed the wonder weapons Hitler hoped would win the war. These were given the designations of V-1 and V-2. The V stood for Vergeltungswaffe, or vengeance weapon. The first was a pilotless airplane propelled by an air-breathing jet engine similar to one designed by Goddard and patented in 1934. First launched on a destructive mission in June of 1944, it could carry a high-explosive bomb several hundred miles across the English Channel to explode somewhat aimlessly in England. In September 1944, the V-2, a 12-ton pure rocket, was also fired against England, and targets in Western Europe that had been recently freed of Nazi occupation. The V-2 was similar in design to Goddard's 1939 rocket except that it was 46-feet high, and could climb to an altitude of nearly 70 miles before descending on a ballistic path to its target.

During the interwar years, Goddard and his small team lived a scientific hand-to-mouth existence, wondering each year if the small grants to fund their research and experimentation from the Smithsonian Institution and the Daniel Guggenheim Fund for the Measurement and Investigation of High Altitudes, together with various kinds of support from Clark University, would be renewed. In 1932, the decline in stock values caused the Guggenheim support to fall short of requirements. The professor was forced to close down his Roswell facility and returned to Clark University to resume his teaching duties.

However, several years later with the enthusiastic backing of Charles Lindbergh and others, the Danial and Florence Guggenheim Foundation resumed full support for Goddard's research. The professor's team moved back to Roswell in 1934 and again conducted high-altitude rocket research until Goddard signed a contract with the Army Air Force and the Navy in late 1941 for military research and development. Then, for the sake of the war effort, Goddard exchanged his work on rockets that fired straight up for the development of rockets to lift heavily laden military planes quickly into the air. The device was called JATO for Jet Assisted Take Off. At the request of the military, the Goddard team moved to the Navy's Engineering Experiment Station at Annapolis, Maryland, in 1942 and spent the rest of the war there.

Professor Goddard died on August 10, 1945. The previous month, the Army had established, across a mountain range from Roswell, a rocket testing area at White Sands, New Mexico. The U.S. Government had finally decided to establish the first phase of its space policy. Like the Germans and Russians before, the initial U.S. space policy would be military in character. But unlike the totalitarian nations, U.S. military space policy would evolve in a different way.

It should be noted that as the Goddard machine shop and launching tower stood idle in Roswell, New Mexico, with its pioneering scientist in Washington working on the rather mundane JATO units, the U.S. government invested some 2 billion dollars in its primary effort to win the war by means of advanced science—Professor Robert Oppenheimer's atomic bomb program—which was centered several hundred miles to the northwest at Los Alamos, New Mexico. In Germany, the reverse was true, as Hitler lavishly supported the V-1 and V-2 efforts, the Nazi atomic bomb project directed by the Nobel Laureate in physics, Werner Heisenberg, was poorly funded, and in the end failed to produce either a uranium or plutonium weapon.

By the 1930s, other rocket and space enthusiasts could be identified in the United States. For example, in New York, there was G. Edward Pendray, one of the founders of the American Interplanetary Society, which later became the American Rocket Society. In Washington, Dr. Charles G. Abbot, Secretary of the Smithsonia Institution, viewed rockets as realistic possibilities to help explore the upper atmosphere. On the west coast, California Institute of Technology President Robert A. Millikan supported the European refugee Theodore von Karman in establishing a rocket research program at the institute's Guggenheim Aeronautical Laboratory. In 1939, the laboratory started receiving government funds for rocket development, and by 1944 had been renamed the Jet Propulsion Laboratory, or JPL, of contemporary times.

However, these sporadic efforts, like Goddard's, were not part of a unified government space policy. That did not start to emerge until after World War II when the results of the German activity were known; when many of the German scientists, including von Braun, had emigrated to the United States; and when the new menace of the Soviet Union was perceived.

II. THE EARLY COLD WAR PERIOD

It is frequently believed in the United States that the cold war with the Communist world in general, and with the Soviet Union in particular, began with Sir Winston Churchill's "iron curtain" speech of March 5, 1946. Speaking at Westminster College in Fulton, Missouri, the former wartime Prime Minister of Great Britain called on the United States to take the lead in standing up against the Communist tide believed to be lapping at Western Europe (Broad, 1963: 512–516). Momentum was added to Churchill's call for defensive action by the July 1947 *Foreign Affairs* article titled "The Sources of Soviet Conduct" (Kennan, 1947: 566–582). Although not identified as such at the time, the State Department's foremost Kremlinologist George F. Kennan later acknowledged himself the author of the seminal piece. As the Truman administration started to make the containment policy the centerpiece of its foreign policy, the U.S. Army was testing two-stage rockets comprised of a captured German V-2 as the first stage and a U.S. built rocket as the second stage.

During World War II, Americans learned about the amazing physical results that could be expected when the taxing power of a modern central government is used to support scientific research and development. Soon after the war, this marriage of science and the government was utilized to provide the United States with an array of impressive military missiles. The theory about how to utilize the new weapons, some of which were soon to be equipped with nuclear warheads, came later. And in time, President Eisenhower would identify a new problem that has not yet been fully resolved—how politically to absorb into a democracy the consequences of combining science and technology in the process of weapons development and production, the combination that was called by Eisenhower the military-industrial complex.

Immediately after World War II, the Army and Navy experimented with captured V-2 rockets in a variety of settings. However, plans by Convair to build a new large rocket, an intercontinental range ballistic missile (ICBM) were not funded because of budget restrictions. Although concerns about Soviet expansionism were growing in the mid and late 1940s, military missiles to cross the Atlantic were not deemed necessary because the newly created Air Force (National Security Act of 1947) had B-29s and B-50s and soon would be receiving B-36s, a huge bomber powered by both jets and reciprocating engines, the pure jet B-47 bombers, and later the much larger pure jet B-52s. The logic for building the large fleet of bombers to replace the aging B-29s and B-50s was nuclear deterrence.

According to this theory, the United States could counter the Soviet manpower advantage with aircraft-delivered atomic bombs. After the Soviet acquisition of the atomic bomb in 1949, President Truman ordered the development of the hydrogen bomb, which was also for bomber delivery. With the 1952 election of President Eisenhower and his appointment of John Foster Dulles as Secretary of State, the policy of deterrence was extended. Concerned that U.S. economic and human resources would be drained away by recurrences of Korea-type wars on the periphery of the Soviet empire, Dulles sought to contain communism in a way he contended would be cheaper in blood and dollars. His deterrent plan was called massive retaliation.

The initial postwar enthusiasm for military missiles was mirrored by considerable interest in peaceful rockets for scientific exploration. In particular, the Navy sat a small second-stage U.S. built rocket on V-2s and called the successful result the Viking program. Viking launches were used to explore the upper atmosphere. At the White Sands test range, the Army placed

American-made second-stage rockets on modified V-2s and reached the height of 250 miles. The next logical step was to place into earth orbit a small satellite to make scientific observation, and the military started that work. The new Air Force think tank, the RAND Corporation, located in Santa Monica, California, explained how a satellite would work. At the speed of 17,000 miles an hour, the final stage of a multistage rocket would enter orbit around the Earth as its centrifugal force matched the pull of gravity. At orbiting speed, the satellite would then circumvent the Earth every 90 minutes. If placed in a polar orbit, a satellite could observe the Earth rotating slowly below.

The RAND report was bullish on the potential of satellites, not only for military purposes but as unparalleled vehicles for scientific research. Among the tasks the RAND authors envisioned for satellites were a secure observation platform, communications relay vehicle, and as the initial step leading to journeys to the nearest planets. In an unplanned anticipation of the coming Soviet Sputnik, the RAND report stated that the first satellite launch, "would inflame the imagination of mankind, and would probably produce repercussions in the world comparable to the explosion of the atomic bomb" (McDougall, 1985: 102). The major historian of the nation's first four decades of space activity, Walter A. McDougall, suggests that the policy and bureaucratic upheavals caused by the National Security Act of 1947, which created a unified Department of Defense, resulted in the cancellation of the first U.S. satellite project in 1948. But the reversal would be temporary because of the impetus for space development provided by perception of the Soviet threat.

As was to be the case time after time, the perception that the Soviet Union poised a dramatic threat to the United States and its allies soon reversed official policy regarding satellites. Three back-to-back shocks combined to refocus U.S. attention on the Communist threat and secondarily on the need to develop large rockets for various military purposes. In 1949, the anti-Communist government of Chiang Kai-shek was defeated by Mao Tse-tung, who then established the Peoples Republic of China; even worse, the Soviet Union detonated its first atomic bomb years before many U.S. scientists expected it; then in the early summer of 1950, using Soviet military equipment, North Korea invaded South Korea.

III. AN INTENSIFIED COLD WAR RIVALRY

The immediate consequence of the Soviet atomic bomb explosion was a reevaluation by the Department of State and the Department of Defense of U.S. foreign and national security policy. Secretary of State Dean Acheson and a senior State Department official, Paul Nitze, played primary roles in shaping the 1950 document that became known as NSC-68 (National Security Council No. 68). Acheson described the document in his memoirs thus:

> So our analysis of the threat combined the ideology of communist doctrine and the power of the Russian state into an aggressive expansionist drive, which found its chief opponent and, therefore, target in the antithetic ideas and power of our own country (Acheson, 1969: 375).

Acheson noted that, "It takes more than bare hands and a desire for peace to turn back this threat" (Acheson, 1969: 375). The conclusion of NSC-68 was that the United States should lead the free world toward a rapid and sustained build-up in political, economic, and military capability. The June 1950 invasion of South Korea by the North Korean Army, using Soviet weapons, was "the straw that broke the camel's back" regarding whether the United States should take a more or less aggressive stand against communism. Thereafter, and for years to follow, the general thesis of NSC-68—that the Communists are coming—formed the principal point of departure for much U.S. public policy.

What the Communist world appeared to be doing, and what the United States proposed to do as a response, set the stage for renewed interest in an U.S. ICBM, followed by a submarine-launched ballistic missile (SLBM), both of which could carry the new thermonuclear warheads. In November 1952, the United States detonated a hydrogen device; in August 1953, the Soviets exploded a deliverable hydrogen bomb; followed in March 1954 by the test of a large U.S. deliverable thermonuclear weapon that destroyed a Pacific atoll and left a crater in the bottom of the lagoon. Furthermore, the incoming Eisenhower administration had a secretary of state who was interested in weaving thermonuclear weapons into U.S. foreign policy.

Writing 5 months before the national elections of 1952, John Foster Dulles asked how could the United States help defend the 20,000 mile–long line that separated the "free world" from the Communist bloc? In answering his own question, Dulles ruled out the construction of a 20,000 mile–long Maginot Line or the maintenance of a standing U.S. army capable of matching the Red (as they were called in those days) Armies, "man for man, gun for gun and tank for tank at any particular time or place their general staff selects" (Dulles, 1952: 150). Dulles asserted to do so would "mean real strength nowhere and bankruptcy everywhere" (Dulles, 1952: 150). The solution proposed by Dulles was, ". . . for the free world to develop the will and organize the means to retaliate instantly against open aggression by Red armies, so that, if it occurred anywhere, we could and would strike back where it hurts, by means of our choosing" (Dulles, 1952: 150). Dulles explained his solution to the problem of containing Communist hordes by using an analogy:

> The principle involved is as simple as that of our municipal police forces. We do not station armed guards at every house to stop aggressors—that would be economic suicide—but we deter potential aggressors by making it probable that if they aggress, they will lose in punishment more than they can gain by aggression (Dulles, 1952: 150).

To carry out his proposal, Dulles advised what he described as a "community punishing power." He urged that the "free world" should obtain the capability to "hit with shattering effectiveness the sources of power and lines of communication" of the Communist block whenever Red forces crossed national boundaries. After the Eisenhower administration had been in Washington a year, Dulles had the opportunity of turning his preelection proposal into public policy. In a prepared speech the secretary of state announced that the president and his advisers in the National Security Council had decided to make a basic change in U.S. foreign and defense policy. The change, said Dulles, was that henceforth the United States would face the Communist bloc on the free world boundary line by depending "primarily upon a great capacity to retaliate instantly by means and at places of our choosing" ("Text of Dulles' Statement on Foreign Policy of Eisenhower Administration," *New York Times*, January 13, 1954). Dulles said that not only did this decision afford the best method to protect the free world from Communist aggression but that it permitted ". . . a selection of military means instead of a multiplication of means. And as a result it is now possible to get, and to share, more security at less cost" ("Text of Dulles' Statement on Foreign Policy of Eisenhower Administration," *New York Times*, January 13, 1954).

Six months before Dulles' speech, the von Braun team, now installed at the new Ordnance Guided Missile Center at Redstone Arsenal, Huntsville, Alabama, had launched a new U.S. rocket. It was the 500-mile range Redstone IRBM (Intermediate Range Ballistic Missile).

Commenting on the administration's decision, James Reston (1954) wrote:

The President and the Secretary of State did not say, as President Truman had said in the Truman Doctrine, that the United States must be prepared to oppose Communist aggression where it occurred. They went beyond that. They said that the United States must be free to retaliate 'instantly,' not necessarily against the Communist troops in the field but anywhere we chose with any weapons we chose.

In other words they told Moscow and Peiping, as clearly as governments ever say these things, that, in the event of another proxy or brushfire war in Korea, Indo-China, Iran or anywhere else the United States might retaliate instantly with atomic weapons against the U.S.S.R. or Red China.

Several months after Dulles' announcement of the new policy of massive retaliation, Vice President Richard Nixon reaffirmed the administration's position when he made the following reply to a critical speech given by the defeated Democratic presidential candidate Adlai Stevenson:

Rather than let the Communists nibble us to death all over the world in little wars we would rely in the future primarily on our massive mobile retaliatory power which we could use at our discretion against the major source of aggression at times and places that we chose. ("Text of Nixon Reply to Stevenson Attack on the Administration," *New York Times*, March 14, 1954).

Even more so than during the Truman administration, the policy of massive retaliation required an increasing number of nuclear weapons, and eventually a more effective means of delivering them than airplanes. Soon the Department of Defense turned to rockets—ICBMs and SLBMs.

In the summer of 1954, the previous warnings about the Soviet Union contained in NSC-68 was expanded in the Killian Report, named after its chairman, James R. Killian, the president of the Massachusetts Institute of Technology. This accumulation of warnings, plus the massive retaliation perspective of Secretary Dulles, combined with the technical possibilities associated with thermonuclear warheads to give birth to the first U.S. ICBM program. The missile was named Atlas. The responsibility to integrate all the complex systems necessary to hurl a nuclear warhead from the continental United States against targets in the U.S.S.R. was given to an Air Force Brigadier General Bernard A. Schriever.

The concern about the Soviet threat caused the Atlas program to receive a top-priority ranking within the Air Force. That designation, plus the integrative genius of General Schriever and those he selected to assist him, moved the Atlas program rapidly toward fruition. Realizing that the first-generation of almost anything can be improved, the Air Force authorized a second, improved ICBM called Titan.

While the Air Force worked on its ICBMs in the mid 1950s, the Army, in the form of Major General John B. Medaris, and the Navy in the form of the Navy Special Projects Office, cooperated on an IRBM (intermediate-range ballistic missile) that was upgraded from von Braun's Redstone rocket. The Army Ballistic Missile Agency at Huntsville, Alabama, was the site for development of the new missile that was called Jupiter. As Jupiter was being developed, it became obvious that it would be difficult to launch a liquid-fuel missile from a submerged submarine. Out of that problem was born the Navy's solid-fuel SLBM, the first generation of which was called Polaris. It would be carried on another of America's amazing inventions—Admiral Hyman Rickover's nuclear-propelled submarine fleet. Concurrently, the Air Force decided it needed an IRBM and development started on the Thor.

A negative factor in regard to the Atlas, Titan, Jupiter, and Thor was that liquid-fuel missiles take a long time to be readied for launch. This was seen as becoming a problem if the time arrived when danger of Soviet attack required a rapid launch. The Air Force moved to correct this problem with Atlas and Titan by commencing work on a solid-fuel ICBM, which would become the long-range version of the Polaris, the first of which would be called Minuteman after the quick-reacting American patriots of 1776. As the solid-fuel missiles moved to the fore in the 1960s, the older liquid-fuel rockets were used for scientific launches.

In time, much of the rationale for building solid-fuel ICBMs and SLBMs was derived from the belief U.S. security rested on maintenance of pre- and postlaunch invulnerability. This concept held that the deterrent value of missiles was linked to their ability to survive a Soviet attack and then to be used in retaliation. Liquid-fuel missiles were difficult to place underground or in submarines, and they could not be easily moved about on land. Thus, they would in time become vulnerable to Soviet first-strike missile attacks. On the contrary, solid-fuel missiles, like cartridges in a revolver, could be stored deep underground or in submarines from whence they could be launched nearly instantaneously.

IV. A FURTHER INCENTIVE FOR MISSILE DEVELOPMENT— THE TRIAD CONCEPT

It can be argued the idea that three separate nuclear weapons delivery systems, two of which were missiles, were needed to target the Communist world came originally from interservice rivalry (Beckman, 1992: 91). However the TRIAD concept came to stand on its own strategic merits.

During the late 1950s analysts at RAND and elsewhere began to worry about the vulnerability of U.S. bombers and slow-reacting liquid-fuel missiles sitting atop the ground should the Soviets develop missiles to attack them in a first strike. The fear was that the bombers and missiles would have little warning of a pending missile attack and would be caught on the ground and destroyed in a missile "Pearl Harbor." The answer settled on for this problem was the TRIAD. According to this view, the United States should maintain three separate means of delivering nuclear weapons. One "leg" would be land-based bombers, the second leg would be land-based ICBMs, and the third leg submarine carried SLBMs. Gradually, the idea took hold that such a deployment would make it difficult, probably impossible, for the Soviets to target three separate delivery systems simultaneously, each of which had very different characteristics. Further, to defend against a TRIAD of three kinds of delivery systems would place heavy burdens on Soviet defensive capabilities. For example, the Soviets would have to prepare to shoot down jet bombers flying at low altitude while intercepting ICBM warheads approaching over the North Pole, and they also would have to intercept SLBM warheads following trajectories from any of the world's oceans. In particular, the Kennedy administration championed the TRIAD.

V. SATELLITES

Parallel to the increased impetus placed on military missile development in the 1950s was the interest in satellites, particularly spy vehicles. And the motivation was the same, the threat perceived to emanate from the Communist world led by the Soviet Union.

The analysts at RAND supplied the national defense rationale for the first U.S. satellite program. According to McDougall (1985: 108), who has an entire chapter on early U.S. satellite policy, "The RAND document of October 1950, more than any other, deserves to be considered the birth certificate of American space policy."

The RAND document set out to establish both the peacetime and the wartime utility of satellites. At that time, satellites were not viewed as weapons, although this would change as technology advanced. However, satellites could contribute to the use of other weapons with their unique ability to provide constant surveillance of the enemy, as well as timely weather information. Both capabilities had been assets sought by military commanders using other less-effective means since war became an instrument of national policy. Moreover, the RAND analysts realized the political and psychological value of satellites that would be perceived by allies, enemies, and the neutrals as conferring special advantages to the United States based on the demonstration of superior technology. Although this enhanced capability could be reassuring to allies, it was expected to have the reverse effect on the Communists, particularly the Soviet Union. For this reason, the RAND thinkers suggested that the announcement of U.S. satellites be set in a context which emphasized their peaceful and scientific characteristics rather than their military ones.

Wrestling with the political problem of how to announce U.S. satellites to the world, then in defending their actual use for reconnaissance purposes, constituted the core problem with which the RAND report dealt. As McDougall (1985: 109–110) points out, surveillance satellites pointed directly to basic differences between an open society, accustomed because of the First Amendment freedom of the press to inquire into all kinds of government activity; and the closed society where government activity was either heavily shrouded in secrecy or blacked out entirely. Such a threat to Soviet security concerns would likely be highly provocative according to the RAND authors; it would certainly be viewed by the Kremlin as illegal and possibly as an aggressive act.

What to do? Resort to international law suggested that the overflight of a nation's airspace in an airplane was generally illegal without consent. Could this principle be applied to satellites passing several hundred miles overhead? The problem then, according to the RAND report, was whether there is a dividing line between airspace and space, and did the legal principles governing the former apply to the latter. It was clear that the Soviet's took a very protective position about their airspace, and it followed they would extend their vertical sovereignty upward into the void of space. Evaluating the work of the RAND analysts McDougall (1985: 109) writes:

> In these few pages the RAND Corporation spelled out the central political problem attending the birth of the Space Age. The new Superpowers were locked in Cold War. One of the contestants was an open society, the other secret and closed. A great premium was thus attached to reliable surveillance techniques by the open society. Reconnaissance satellites offered such a technique. But just as important as developing such technology was establishing the legal right to use it.

The solution suggested by the RAND report was for the United States to first launch an innocuous scientific satellite that would not pass over the Soviet Union to test Moscow's and international reaction. This could be followed by a more intrusive satellite. So it was that in 1955 the Air Force secretly informed military contractors of the requirements for the first U.S. satellite.

McDougall (1985: 111) has described the technical parameters:

> They included the ability to attain a precise, predicted orbit; to be stabilized on three axes with a 'high-pointing accuracy', to maintain a given attitude for disturbing torques;

to receive and execute commands sent from the ground; and to transmit information to ground stations. This was no 'quick and dirty' orbiting beeper, (a reference to Sputnik) but a large, sophisticated spacecraft integrating the most advanced technology from a dozen fields of American industry.

In this way began what would become an enormous, expensive, and continuing, U.S. space reconnaissance effort generally referred to as the "Deep Black" programs (Burrows, 1986; Krass, 1989). In 1992, bowing to congressional pressure to open up information long classified because of cold war justifications, the Department of Defense announced the existence of a hitherto secret organization dedicated to operating the nation's spy satellites and planes. The government agency is called the National Reconnaissance Office (NRO). According to the Department of Defense, the NRO mission is "to ensure that the U.S. has the technology and space borne and airborne assets needed to acquire intelligence worldwide" (Department of Defense Press Release, September 18, 1992).

It should be noted that before the United States became competent in the satellite surveillance business, a complementary program was initiated based on aircraft reconnaissance. A secret aircraft research center in California operated by Lockheed and run by an aeronautical genius, Kelly Johnson, called the Skunk Works, produced the U-2 spy plane. Such planes began flying high over Communist lands in the mid 1950s to provide the Eisenhower administration photographic details of the adversary. A U-2 piloted by Francis Gary Powers was shot down by the Soviets in May 1960 causing an understandable rift between Washington and Moscow. Several years later, during the Cuban missile crisis of 1962, a similar plane was shot down over Cuba killing its pilot, Air Force Major Rudolf Anderson, Jr., the only U.S. casualty of that confrontation. Subsequently, the U-2s were constrained in their operations. However, the U.S. requirement for reconnaissance continued unabated, and the aeronautic capability that built the U-2 next produced the SR-71. This extremely high-performance spy plane was never shot down. It was retired from active duty in 1990. Currently, there are rumors circulating around Edwards Air Force Base, California, that a successor to the SR-71 that has even more spectacular performance characteristics is being tested at night.

NSC-68 defined for the Truman administration a growing Soviet threat that it was thought could be answered in part by increased U.S. military capability based on advanced science and technology. Similarly, in the Eisenhower administration, the Kilian Report noted the growing Soviet missile capability was going far beyond the V-2s captured from the Germans after World War II. The thrust of the Killian report was that the United States had no choice but to emphasize building its own military missiles and to simultaneously pursue the means of monitoring Soviet military activities from space.

While the Pentagon, Central Intelligence Agency (CIA), and Eisenhower's White House worried about the mounting Soviet threat, civilian scientists suggested using the nation's growing rocket capability to further high-altitude research. The civilian community pressured the government that the United States should participate in an upcoming, 1957, International Geophysical Year by launching small earth satellites to make scientific observations. The program was called Vanguard, and perhaps understandably, it took a back seat in terms of funding to the military missile development programs.

VI. SPUTNIK

On the evening of October 3, 1957, neither John F. Kennedy nor Lyndon B. Johnson could have known the opportunity that the Soviet Union would hand them and the Democratic party the next day. For it was on October 4 that the Soviets orbited a small earth satellite called Sputnik. In terms of the kind of advanced science that the Americans were planning for their satellites, Sputnik was not impressive. Nor did Sputnik undermine the security of the United States, which was already building its first nuclear-tipped ICBMs. Sputnik's impact was political. It was the first human craft to orbit the Earth and that is what counted in the political context. The launching of the second Soviet satellite on November 3, a 6-ton orbiting object with the little dog Liaka on board, did nothing to factually change the military relationship between the United States and the U.S.S.R., but it added to the public's concern, the media's shrillness, and the Democrats' prospects for success.

With the Soviet Union dissolved and economically prostrate, it is difficult for contemporary Americans to look backward and remember the fear, verging at times on paranoia, that gripped much of the country in 1957 as a result of the Soviet space feat. Led by the president himself, the Eisenhower administration tried to explain to the public nothing had changed; that the United States was embarked on an orderly plan to build both military missiles and scientific satellites; that it would be dangerous to subordinate the values of a free society for the kind of central governmental control necessary to duplicate the Soviet action immediately. Nevertheless, the administration did implement some recommendations of the next national security study, the Gaither Report, that warned about Soviet capabilities and intentions. U.S. missile research and development subsequently increased.

Sputnik became a partisan political issue. The Democratic attack was led by Lyndon Johnson, who chaired the hearings before the Preparedness Investigation Subcommittee of the U.S. Senate Armed Services Committee. Officially titled the "Inquiry into Satellite and Missile Programs," the hearings could more honestly have been called "What Happened Because the Republicans Were Asleep and Stingy with the Budget."

There is a saying in the United States that "what goes around, comes around." Recalling the bashing of Democrats on defense policy by Presidents Reagan and Bush, one cannot help but observe that what Johnson and Kennedy did to the Republicans following Sputnik was similar to what the Republicans did to the Democrats in the 1980s.

In 1952, Wernher von Braun had written a series of articles for *Colliers* magazine in which he outlined a futuristic plan for rocketing humans to the moon and beyond (von Braun, 1952: issues dating from January–February through November–December). In testimony before Johnson's Preparedness Subcommittee, von Braun returned to the subject and suggested that the United States create some kind of centralized government space agency. Still today, "space cadets" are amazed at reading von Braun's 1952 articles and realizing the foresightedness of the transplanted German scientist.

Senator Johnson concluded the subcommittee's investigation, and the report of its work was added to the litany of reports that urged Americans to work harder, study harder, and invest more in the life and death struggle with communism, including space competition.

Following a philosophy that would appear again in his farewell address, President Eisenhowever was not pressured by public fear after Sputnik into creating an immediate and massive centralized government complex to combat communism. His approach was more deliberate. Some reorganization here, some increase in funding there, but no crash program that would lead the United States toward a centralized scientific, bureaucratic, totalitarian state such as had first launched a satellite but that had lost so much in human freedom since 1917. Many savvy interests around the country sensed that if they could associate their purpose with the fear of the U.S.S.R., they could obtain federal funding. Education was only one of the national programs that cashed in.

In fact the author, who entered graduate school a month before Sputnik, owes part of his doctorate to the National Defense Education Act of 1958, which provided funds for his graduate education. And if the reader will accept another personal note that makes a point about national research and the communist threat—Up until 1992 when the USSR collapsed, the author would suggest to his American government classes that if AIDS could be linked in the public mind to the Soviet danger, money for research on the disease would be no problem.

VII. THE INITIAL SPACE RACE WITH THE SOVIETS

The first U.S. satellite launch was on December 6, 1957. The Vanguard rocket exploded in disaster. However, a rival to Vanguard, the Jupiter launch vehicle developed by the Army and the von Braun team at Huntsville, Alabama, put the first U.S. satellite, Explorer, into orbit January 31, 1958. Vanguard I achieved orbit on March 17, 1958, and the space race with the Soviets was on. The question before the government, industry, the science community, and the taxpayers was how to organize U.S. participation.

Obviously the ICBMs, SLBMs, and IRBMs, plus military satellites, ought to be controlled by the Department of Defense, with care taken to prevent ruinous rivalry between the three armed services. But what of the nonmilitary satellites and the rockets to place them in orbit? There were many contenders for the role of civilian space czar such as the Atomic Energy Commission, the National Science Foundation, and the National Advisory Committee on Aeronautics. Each had its advocates and a typical Washington scenario ensued that was composed of sincere concern about the nation's interest mixed with the quest for personal and bureaucratic power.

The result was that within a year of Sputnik's appearance, the Congress passed and Eisenhowever signed a bill creating the National Aeuronautics and Space Administration (NASA) on October 1, 1958. Congress also created two new standing committees, the Senate Committee on Aeronautical and Space Sciences and the House Committee on Science and Astroneutics. Thus began a bureaucratic and policy struggle that continues to this day. The major components of the struggle are questions about the relative merits and weighting of military versus civilian space objectives; the extent to which the United States participates in international space efforts, including implementation of the idea that space exists for all mankind, and the use of space for arms control and disarmament.

In NASA's formative years, the plans were laid for placing Americans into space, the Mercury/Gemini programs; and for sending them to the moon; the Apollo program. The question the Eisenhower administration had to deal with was whether these efforts justified a space race with the Soviet Union or a slower-paced more deliberate approach to space exploration. Eisenhower's perspective was that it need not be a race that would be financially wasteful and contributory to the military-industrial complex he feared would erode freedom and individualism. On the other hand, the president acknowledged U.S. civil and scientific space programs should move forward to counter the image of superiority portrayed by Soviet space activities. Eisenhower's purpose was too little, too late for his Democratic challengers, and the alleged slowness of the Republicans in responding to the Soviet space challenge became a principal facet of the developing Kennedy-Johnson campaign. The Democrats also threw in the fallacious missile gap that they alleged the Republicans had permitted to occur in regard to the military relations with the U.S.S.R. The political furor after Sputnik again demonstrated the political logic that in order to move prescriptions for government activity into announced and funded public policies the Soviet card should be played.

As an aside, it should be noted that for the first time in decades the 1992 quest for the White House was not fought out over the question as to which candidates would be best suited to defend the nation from the Soviet Union or which political party was perceived as the most patriotic and dedicated to national security.

VIII. EISENHOWER'S LEGACY

A political scientist, Malcolm Moos, who was working as a speech writer for the president wrote it, but a retired five-star general and two-time Republican President of the United States Dwight D. Eisenhower, said it:

> This conjunction of an immense military establishment and a large arms industry is new in American experience. The total influence—economic, political, even spiritual—is felt in every city, every state house, every office of the Federal Government. We recognize the imperative need for this development. Yet we must not fail to comprehend its grave implications. Our toil, resources, and livelihood are all involved; so is the very structure of our society (Office of the Federal Register, 1961: 1038).

Then in an oft-quoted passage, somewhat reminiscent of Washington's farewell address, President Eisenhower issued this warning in his farewell address:

> In the councils of government we must guard against the acquisition of unwarranted influence, whether sought or unsought, by the *military-industrial complex* [emphasis added]. The potential for the disastrous rise of misplaced power exists and will persist.
> We must never let the weight of this combination endanger our liberties or demo-cratic processes. We should take nothing for granted. Only an alert and knowledgeable citizenry can compel the proper meshing of the huge industrial and military machinery of defense with our peaceful methods and goals, so that security and liberty may prosper together (Office of the Federal Register, 1961: 1038).

Eisenhower then explained what in his view was happening:

> Akin to, and largely responsible for the sweeping changes in our military-industrial pos-ture, has been the technological revolution during recent decades.
> In this revolution, research has become critical; it also becomes more formalized, complex, and costly. A steadily increasing share is conducted by, for, or at the direction of the Federal government.
> Today, the solitary inventor tinkering in his shop, has been overshadowed by task forces of scientists in laboratories and testing fields. In the same fashion the free uni-versity, historically the fountainhead of free ideas and scientific discovery, has experienced a revolution in the conduct of research. Partly because of the huge costs involved, a gov-ernment contract becomes virtually a substitute for intellectual curiosity. For every old blackboard there are now hundreds of new electronic computers.
> The prospect of domination of the nation's scholars by Federal employment, proj-ect allocations, and the power of money is ever present—and is gravely to be regarded.
> Yet in holding scientific research and discovery in respect, as we should, we must also be alert to the equal and opposite danger that public policy could itself become the captive of a *scientific-technological elite* [emphasis added] (Office of the Federal Register, 1961: 1038).

The retiring president could not have foreseen the extent nor exact dimensions of governmental space programs involving the military-industrial complex and the scientific-technological elite such as the Strategic Defense Initiative or the Space Exploration Initiative. But his warning would echo with resonance through out the cold war years, into the era of President Bush's New World Order, and beyond to the New Covenant times declared by President Bill Clinton.

IX. KENNEDY VERSUS KHRUSCHEV— B-52s, ICBMs, and SLBMs

On November 9, 1960, John F. Kennedy became the President-Elect and thus inherited the fruition of the military research and development undertaken since the cold war began. His response was to order a speed-up in military procurement, including rockets. Specifically he would soon be the Commander-in-Chief of the TRIAD configuration of bombers, land-based missiles, and sea-based missiles that many believed was a major deterrent to Soviet attack. Air Force General Curtis LeMay's Strategic Air Command operated a fleet of what was perhaps the best strategic bomber ever built, the Boeing B-52. Its range would be extended worldwide by KC-135 jet tanker planes from which the B-52s could refuel while in flight on their way to drop thermonuclear bombs anywhere. The first American ICBMs were deployed as the second leg of the TRIAD. Being subject to the limitations of liquid-fuel missiles, the Kennedy administration would replace them by ordering Minuteman I ICBMs that would be protected against Soviet attack by being buried in underground steel and concrete silos in the thinly populated areas of the American west. Eventually 1000 were deployed. The third leg of the TRIAD was the Polaris SLBM, of which 16 could be carried aboard the projected 41 U.S. nuclear-powered submarines, making for a total of 656 missiles based under the oceans.

Kennedy and Secretary of Defense Robert McNamara moved swiftly to amass the largest amount of U.S. firepower to date, much of it being nuclear warhead–carrying missiles. Part of the rationale for expanded numbers of missiles was McNamara's "city avoidance" strategy. This plan called for a counterforce capability capable of destroying Soviet military forces as well as cities if necessary. Far behind with his TRIAD, it is no wonder Khrushchev tried to redress the nuclear imbalance by attempting the Cuban missile gamble and then hastily withdrew rather than challenge U.S. superiority. Kennedy also enjoyed the advantage provided by the burgeoning successes of two U.S. photographic spy satellite programs, part of the Deep Black effort, the Discoverer, and SAMOS series. Further, the new president also was the beneficiary of the MIDAS satellite program designed to use infrared sensors to detect Soviet missile tests.

Parts of Kennedy's inaugural address offered the prospect for negotiated settlements of outstanding problems with the U.S.S.R. But the new president also stated:

Let every nation know, whether it wishes us well or ill, that we shall pay any price, bear any burden, meet any hardship, support any friend, oppose any foe to assure the survival and the success of liberty (Sorensen, 1965: 246).

And

We dare not tempt them [adversary nations] with weakness. For only when our arms are sufficient beyond doubt can we be certain beyond doubt that they will never be employed (Sorensen, 1965: 247).

In association with the Kennedy military missile build-up came the creation of Kennedy's Arms Control and Disarmament Agency (ACDA) in 1961. The new agency's charter was suggested in its name. For some hardliners, the ACDA appeared counterproductive, but the Kennedy administration claimed it would contribute to strategic nuclear stability, and the growing idea that space could be used as the medium through which the deterrent weapons would travel, but not a place where nuclear weapons should be permanently stationed. In 1963, a treaty was negotiated with the Soviets banning nuclear weapon tests in space (U.S. Arms Control and Disarmament Agency, 1990: 45–48). Called the Partial Nuclear Weapons Test Ban Treaty, this was the first of what would be a succession of agreements implementing the U.S. view that the permanent militarization of space, i.e., deploying weapons systems therein, should be avoided.

A concept associated with arms control and disarmament was the Kennedy ideal of cooperating with the Soviets in certain space activities such as scientific data collection and sharing the costs of the more expensive missions. At the time, this space policy thrust was mostly rhetoric with little of substance to show the world.

X. KENNEDY VERSUS KHRUSCHEV— THE YURI GAGARIN WILD CARD

The new president did not hold the lead in the man-in-space competition with the Soviets. What he did have was Vice President Lyndon Johnson, and his Texas-sized enthusiasm for space activities, newly installed in the chairman's role of the National Space Council; and the advice from the National Academy of Sciences that space exploration would be a great inspirational venture. Then came a shock similar to that administered by Sputnik. On April 12, 1961, the Soviets announced that Yuri Gagarin had orbited the earth, and for the second time in half a decade, the Soviets appeared to many as the technologically superior society. (Wolfe, 1979: 198). Moscow crowed that the Socialist state was better designed than haphazard free-enterprise systems to bring technology to its peoples and, by implication, to the world's citizens not yet committed to either means of social organization.

As with the Sputnik launch, Congress and the media wanted to know why the United States continued to be second. Kennedy's friend and biographer Theodore C. Sorensen records that after the Soviet feat the president requested a briefing on what the United States could do in space, and he was told by scientists the best chance of beating the Soviets was to place an American on the moon. According to Sorensen:

> The President was more convinced than any of his advisers that a second-rate, second-place space effort was inconsistent with this country's security, with its role as world leader and with the New Frontier spirit of discovery. Consequently he asked the Vice President as Chairman of the Space Council to seek answers to all the fundamental questions concerning the steps we could or must take to achieve pre-eminence in space. . . .'' (Sorensen, 1965: 525)

The next month, Kennedy delivered a special second State of the Union Message to the Congress. In it the President pledged to land a man on the moon and return him safely to earth ''before this decade is out.'' The Congress was almost unanimous in supporting Kennedy's new space initiative and the dollars flowed to NASA; thanks again to the perceived threat from the Soviet Union. The fact that several weeks before Kennedy's speech Navy Commander Alan Sheppard became the first American in space, but not yet in orbit, probably helped with the Congress.

Kennedy viewed the moon effort as a means to test and thereby improve the American spirit of adventure and the nation's leadership. He voiced his views in a September 1962 speech at Houston's Rice University:

> But why, some say, the moon? . . . And they may well ask, why climb the highest mountain? Why, thirty-five years ago, fly the Atlantic? Why does Rice play Texas [A traditional, but almost inevitably more powerful, football rival]. . . . We choose to go to the moon in this decade, and do the other things, not because they are easy but because they are hard; because that goal will serve to organize and measure the best of our energies and skills. . . . Many years ago the great British explorer George Mallory, who was to die on Mount Everest, was asked why did he want to climb it, and he said, 'Because it is there.' Well, space is there, and . . . the moon and the planets are there, and new hopes for knowledge and peace are there (Sorensen, 1965: 528).

Thus, the United States embarked on a journey to the moon, largely for political reasons relating to the worth of the United States and competition with the Soviet Union. But there were also other reasons such as strengthening the scientific and technical base of the country.

A successful way station to the moon was Marine Colonel John Glenn's Earth orbit in February, 1962, 10 months after the Gagarin orbit. The year before President Kennedy was assassinated, the space race gap started to close.

Although cooperation with the Soviets in the Kennedy era was sparse, cooperative ventures with U.S. industrial allies began. The general pattern was for foreign scientific satellites to be launched by U.S. rockets. But a problem soon arose over collaboration with U.S. allies. It was the obvious one that sooner or later the Europeans would become competitors more than partners in space, particularly in regard to communications satellites. McDougall (1985: 352) observes that, "In the end, U.S. policy toward Europe came to resemble that toward the USSR: cooperation in science, decided aloofness in engineering."

XI. PROFITS AND LOSSES IN SPACE

At an altitude of 22,238 miles (35,786 kilometers), a satellite's revolutions about the Earth are synchronized with the revolutions of the Earth; hence the satellite maintains a fixed position in relation to a point on the Earth below. A satellite in such a geosynchronous orbit has a line-of-sight view of about 30% of the Earth. Thus, it is a unique platform from which to relay communications signals downward. From these facts arose a complicated problem for the Kennedy administration involving the proper relationship between public funding and private profits.

The problem was that private communications companies did not have Air Force nor NASA launch rockets at their command, and the latter government agencies were not in the civilian communications business. The resulting question was to what extent should the government space program subsidize the potentially lucrative private communications market. The arguments ran the gamut from proposals that communications satellites should constitute some sort of government monopoly to suggestions that obviously favored the large and established companies like AT&T and ITT. After acrimonious congressional debate a compromise was struck between the most extreme positions on either end of the spectrum. Despite some grumping by liberals about government giveaways, the Communications Satellite Act of 1962 was passed and signed by the president. The Act created the COMSAT Corporation, which became the single U.S. operator of international satellite communications and the U.S. member of the international satellite communication system (INTELSAT). This was also the year the world's first active repeater communications satellite was launched. Built by Bell Telephone Laboratories, Telstar I proved the feasibility of commercial satellite communications.

COMSAT is a private company that has a considerable interface with the federal government. In addition to the three members of the 15-person governing board appointed by the president, COMSATs commercial activities are reviewed by the Federal Communications Commission. NASA is responsible for research and development and for launching COMSAT satellites on a reimbursable schedule. Fifty percent of COMSAT stock was offered to authorized international common carriers and the rest to private investors.

The basic international theme for the U.S. venture into the commercial communications field was stated by President Kennedy while requesting additional congressional support when he invited, ". . . all nations to participate in a communication satellite system in the interests of the world peace and closer brotherhood among peoples throughout the world." The contrast between the U.S. perspective and the secret character of Soviet activity was evident and intended (Statement by the President on Communication Satellite Policy, July 24, 1961).

Section 102 of the 1962 Communications Act fills in the details of U.S. policy:

(a) The Congress hereby declares that it is the policy of the United States to establish, in conjunction and in cooperation with other countries, as expeditiously as practicable, a commercial communications satellite system, as part of an improved global communications network, which will be responsible to public needs and national objectives, which will serve the communications needs of the United States and other countries, and which will contribute to world peace and understanding.

(b) The new and expanded telecommunication services are to be made available as promptly as possible and are to be extended to provide global coverage at the earliest possible date. In effectuating this program, care and attention will be directed towards providing such services to economically less developed countries and areas as well as those more highly developed, toward efficient and economical use of the electromagnetic frequency spectrum, and toward the reflection of the benefits of this new technology in both quality or services and charges for such services.

Within 2 years, U.S. policy was imparted to the fledging International Telecommunications Satellite Organizations and its original charter, the Agreement Establishing Interim Agreements for a Global Communications Satellite System. Signatory states were Canada, the United States, United Kingdom, and friendly Western European nations. Since only the United States had the technical capacity necessary to create the system COMSAT held 61% of the ownership in INTELSAT. Although the charter called for substantive issues to be decided by voting, a scholar of satellite communications developments, George Codding (1990: 40), writes, "As it turned out, most decisions were made without resorting to a vote, a tradition of consensus that remains very much alive to this day." The Interim Agreement was replaced by a permanent accord in 1973.

The diffusion of scientific and technological power predicted by W. W. Rostow (1971) in *The Stages of Economic Growth* has impacted on the international satellite communication field with the result INTELSAT is no longer alone. The Soviets created INTERSPUTNIK for their satellite nations. Then came INMARSAT for nations with extensive maritime operations, EUTELSAT for Europe exclusive of the Soviet zone, ARABSAT for members of the League of Arab States, and the Palapa System operated by Indonesia and used by its neighbors, the Philippines, Malaysia, and Thailand. About the competition that arose for INTELSAT, Codding (1990: 65) has written:

The United States plan of the 1960s was to create a single global system providing satellite communications for the world at large. The American plan, however, was doomed from the start. It was wishful thinking to believe that all other countries would voluntarily join a system in which the United States held a dominant position.

Codding also observes that it was wishful thinking to believe other nations would not catch up to the U.S. in technology.

As technical capabilities increased, the more advanced nations began operating their own domestic communications satellite systems. In the United States, the emphasis on deregulation begun in the Carter administration, complemented by the privatization thrust of the Reagan and Bush administrations, served to spur competitive domestic satellite operations in which the Federal Communication Commission assisted with a series of rulings. It is of course the hope in the United States that the nations in the former Soviet zone of Europe plus those comprising the former Soviet Union will adopt a free market approach to communications satellites.

Both the international and the domestic communications satellite systems now face a new competitive challenge from fiberoptics cables. Which system will be most competitive in the future or how the two systems may complement each other is not clear at this time.

As was earlier the case with radio, communications satellites need to operate in a context wherein the distribution of radio band frequencies for the uplinks and downlinks, and geosynchronous orbiting positions, is done in a way to avoid interference. For international systems, this requirement leads naturally to international cooperation. In the case of international communication satellites, the a priori assignment of orbital positions and radio frequencies to specific countries is done by the International Telecommunication Union. Regarding domestic U.S. satellite communications, the allocation decisions are made for government users by the National Telecommunications and Information Administration, a division within the Department of Commerce, and for private companies by the Federal Communication Commission.

XII. APOLLO

President Kennedy did not live to see Americans land on the moon; and Vice President Lyndon Johnson was retired in Texas, forced there by the hostility of his own party about the Vietnam War. On July 20, 1969, Neil A. Armstrong and Edwin "Buzz" Aldrin took the first human steps on the moon. The moon adventure was savored by Richard Nixon, the man Kennedy had defeated in 1960 partly by asserting the Republicans had been slow to move the country ahead in both military and civil space. Neither cosmonauts from the Soviet Union nor those from the new Russia have set foot on the moon. So it was that the United States demonstrated twice in 25 years that government investment in, and control of, big science and engineering could produce (1) the atomic bomb and (2) a flight to the moon.

XIII. POST-APOLLO—ARMS CONTROL

The public's post-Apollo glow was dimmed because of the disintegrative forces set in motion by the debate on the Vietnam War, the political trauma of the Watergate scandal, and the nation's focus on the civil rights movement. However, somewhat out of public view, several thrusts begun earlier gathered momentum. There was United Nations action on a space treaty, U.S.-U.S.S.R. agreement on missile arms control, and technological advances in both military and civil missiles and space vehicles.

In London, Washington, and Moscow, the second international effort at regulating national activity in space was signed on January 27, 1967. Officially designated the Treaty on Principles Governing the Activities of States in the Exploration and Use of Outer Space, Including the Moon and other Celestial Bodies, the simplified title is The Outer Space Treaty (U.S. Arms Control and Disarmament Agency, 1990: 55–60). This document is much broader in regard to the scope of covered activities than the 1963 Partial Nuclear Weapons Test Ban Treaty.

The Outer Space Treaty had been in "gestation" since shortly before the first Soviet ICBM tests and the orbiting of Sputnik in 1957. The initial suggestion was to implement the U.S. position that there should be international monitoring of space vehicle tests. On the verge of their space spectaculars, the Soviets showed little interest. Broader Western proposals followed that called for the prohibition of weapons of mass destruction in orbit and space. Speaking before the United Nations General Assembly on September 22, 1960, President Eisenhower proposed adoption of the anticolonial and disarmament principles earlier incorporated in the Antarctic Treaty (1959) for the space environment. The Soviet counter was for "general and complete disarmament," including the space environment. However, Moscow insisted on a provision unacceptable to Washington. It was the linkage of space disarmament to the removal of U.S. overseas bases that housed missiles threatening to the Soviet Union.

After signing the Partial Nuclear Weapons Test Ban Treaty, Soviet Foreign Minister Gromyko dropped the offending linkage matter and indicated willingness to ban mass destruction weapons in orbit. U.S. United Nations Ambassador Adali Stevenson said Washington had no plans to place such weapons in space. The next month, the U.N. General Assembly unanimously welcomed the Soviet and American statements and called for all nations to refrain from introducing weapons of mass destruction into space. By 1966, both the United States and the U.S.S.R. had submitted draft space treaties, with the Soviet version being inclusive of both a ban on such weapons stationed on celestial bodies and in the rest of space. The United States concurred and the long-standing U.S. interest in making space a kind of sanctuary where earthly military rivalries would be excluded entered into the international legal regime with the commendation of the General Assembly.

The rivalries excluded from space by the Outer Space Treaty fall into two categories. In regard to weapons, there are two provisions. The first prohibits the stationing of nuclear weapons or other mass destruction weapons in earth orbit, on the moon or other celestial bodies, or elsewhere in space. Second, the treaty limits the use of the moon and other celestial bodies exclusively to peaceful purposes, with military activities being expressly banned.

Potential colonial rivalry was also excluded by the Treaty. For example Article I reads as follows:

> The exploration and use of outer space, including the moon and other celestial bodies, shall be carried out for the benefit and in the interest of all countries, irrespective of their degree of economic or scientific development, and shall be the province of all mankind.
>
>   Outer space, including the moon and other celestial bodies, shall be free for exploration and use by all States without discrimination of any kind, on a basis of equality and in accordance with international law, and there shall be free access to all areas of celestial bodies.
>
>   There shall be freedom of scientific investigation in outer space, including the moon and other celestial bodies, and States shall facilitate and encourage international cooperation in such investigations (U.S. Arms Control and Disarmament Agency, 1990: 55–56).

According to Article II:

> Outer space, including the moon and other celestial bodies, is not subject to national appropriation by claim of sovereignty, by means of use or occupation, or by any other means (U.S. Arms Control and Disarmament Agency, 1990: 56).

One way to appreciate the potential policy importance of the Outer Space Treaty is to compare it to the historical record on Earth. That record, including the great discoveries of Columbus that were recalled in 1992 with the Quincentenary, is one of conflict over territorial rights to lands, waters, underground minerals, and peoples. The Outer Space Treaty seeks to exclude these forms of human confrontation from all celestial bodies and to "develop," if that is the right word, those bodies in the broad interests of all mankind. Such a departure from the human experience could probably be made only in regard to territories which are so hard to reach and apparently so difficult and expensive to economically exploit. What will happen when the moon and Mars are more frequently visited, and what will happen should economic assets such as helium 3 be discovered there that are worth more than their cost of extraction and use in situ or their shipment back to Earth is not now clear.

Cynics also can note that it is not as difficult to exclude weapons of mass destruction from space places that are far less convenient and much more expensive for their placement than from strategically favorable spots on earth. On the other hand, the Outer Space Treaty does seem to include substantial international thinking that reflects the interconnectedness of earthlings and the need felt by some nations to start acting differently toward one another.

On May 26, 1972, the Soviet Union and the United States signed an executive agreement to place upper limits on the numbers of their ICBMs and SLBMs; and a Treaty to limit severely the numbers of antiballistic missiles (ABMs) (U.S. Arms Control and Disarmament Agency, 1990: 157–173). Collectively, the two arrangements were called the SALT I Accords, the acronym standing for Strategic Arms Limitation Talks. The Interim Agreement Between the United States of America and the Union of Soviet Socialist Republics on Certain Measures with Respect to the Limitation of Strategic Offensive Arms set ceilings on the big land-based and sea-based missiles. In this way, the United States slowed down the growing Soviet nuclear arsenal and preserved nuclear weapons stability embraced by the concept of MAD—mutual assured destruction. The ABM Treaty was seen to contribute to strategic nuclear weapons stability by severely limiting the introduction of antiballistic missiles into the defensive systems of the United States and the Soviet Union. Coupled with the second-strike deployment configuration both nations were adopting, the two arrangements meant that in practice neither of the nuclear superpowers could hope to attack the other and survive.

The second-strike configuration involved both antagonists deploying hardened ICBMs and undersea SLBMs that would be difficult to destroy in a first strike, thus assuring unacceptable retaliation in a second strike and presumably the deterrence of nuclear war.

To the dismay of many, the Interim Agreement did not halt the deployment on existing missiles of additional warheads called MIRVs (multiple individually targeted re-entry vehicles). Thus, both nations increased their firepower even though the numbers of their delivery systems were constrained.

Article V of the Interim Agreement established an important precedent concerning a point that had worried the United States since it first developed reconnaissance satellites. The concern was about the legal status of spy satellites that orbit across the territory of another sovereign nation, such as the U.S.S.R. In Article V, the two signatories agreed to permit the other to use "national technical means of verification," i.e., surveillance satellites, to assure compliance with the provisions of the agreement (U.S. Arms Control and Disarmament Agency,

1990: 170). They further agreed not to interfere with the operation of the other's satellites nor to fool them with "deliberate concealment measures which impede verification." These few words in 1972 have been expanded since to provide one of several basic means whereby successor arms control and disarmament treaties can be verified. Thus, the original RAND perspective that space would be vitally important in terms of observations made from orbit was, and still is, correct.

Although the ABM Treaty, and amendments thereto, permit the United States to deploy 100 ABMs, such deployment has not taken place to date. That is because the Democratically controlled Congress never appropriated the necessary funding. The reason for that is found in congressional skepticism regarding the capability of ABMs. In 1972 and thereafter, many believed scientific opinion that suggested no ABM system would be effective against a few thousand incoming Soviet warheads accompanied by many thousands of decoys. The problem was that since one thermonuclear warhead could destroy much of a city, a defensive scheme had to have effectiveness rates higher than engineering could promise. The Soviets did exercise their option to deply primitive ABMs around Moscow. These were deemed in the United States to be ineffective against an U.S. strike but perhaps somewhat useful against a Chinese attack.

The effect of the SALT I Accords was to start codifying the American belief, which was apparently shared by the Soviets, that peace was the product of certain and unacceptable nuclear retaliation should either military superpower attack the other—mutual assured destruction was now established by treaty.

XIV. POST-APOLLO—NASA

After the stunning success of Apollo, NASA tried to conceive of equally impressive follow-on programs. This was difficult for several reasons. As noted before, the Vietnam War followed by Watergate, compounded by civil rights unrest, combined to focus attention on the many earthly problems facing the country, none of which were resolvable by application of space technology. Furthermore, while the Soviet Union continued to appear fearsome in a military space context, the immediate scientific race with Moscow seemed to have been won as the Soviets were not going to the moon.

Before the Watergate storm began, Nixon in his first term reviewed the shopping list of "big ticket" NASA possibilities, which included a manned mission to Mars, orbiting space stations around the moon and the Earth, and an Earth to low Earth orbit shuttle. He selected the shuttle, officially called the Space Transportation System, and postponed the Earth space station, which in time came to be called Space Station Freedom. Neither had the glamor nor the urgency of Apollo because times had changed, so development and funding proceeded at a more deliberate pace. The official rationale for the shuttle was that it would provide more efficient access to Earth orbit than would expendable rockets. The space historian Walter McDougall (1985: 422) cynically comments that, ". . . the periodic problem of an ailing aerospace industry gave the space program back a future. By 1971 the NASA administrator feared the industry could not survive another year of diminished space work." McDougall (1985: 423) continues to note that the next year,

> . . . the White House became sensitive to the electoral logic of aerospace depression in states like California, Texas, and Florida. After North American Rockwell provided exaggerated estimates of the employment it would stimulate, Nixon and his adviser John Ehrlichman approved of the STS.

The space station was justified, but not yet built, as a place to test human and manufacturing techniques in a zero-gravity environment, as an observation platform, and as a potential way station on the road back to the moon and eventually perhaps to Mars. As Congress reorganized itself, the prestigious space committees fell by the wayside. Space matters were to be handled in the Senate Commerce Committee and in the House by the Science and Technology subcommittees. The shuttle was inherited by successive one-term Presidents Gerald Ford and Jimmy Carter. Then Ronald Reagan decided to complement his Strategic Defense Initiative with the civilian equivalent of seizing the high ground, the Space Station Freedom.

XV. POST-APOLLO—MILITARY

Worries of a potential Soviet first strike on U.S. land-based missile silos started to take on more substance in the 1970s. What particularly bothered the Pentagon was the increased accuracies of Soviet missiles, which enabled them to achieve a greater kill rate against their targets; and the emergence of a giant Soviet ICBM capable of carrying 10 or more warheads, called the SS-18. So the search was begun by the Pentagon to reinstate the prelaunch invulnerability of Minuteman III ICBMs, the 1980s iteration of the land-based missile. The Carter administration announced a counter in the form of the Multiple Protective Shelter (MPS) plan for a new and larger missile, the 10-warhead MX. There was talk that the SS-18 might give the Soviets a decapitation capability by literally cutting off the political and military head of the U.S. government with first strikes on command and control centers and underground bunkers. Part of the rationale for the MX was to give the United States the same ability.

The MPS was a Rube-Goldberg arrangement whereby several hundred MXs would be secretly shuttled between several thousand shelters scattered around Nevada and Utah in a kind of Dr. Strangelove shell game. The idea was that the Soviets would not know in which shelters the missiles were hidden; in order to assure success of a first-strike they would have to target all of the shelters and thus waste most of their warheads.

Political, economic, and environmental problems caused Carter's successor, Ronald Reagan, to scrap the MPS plan and instead install 50 MXs, renamed the Peace Keeper, into retrofitted former Minuteman III silos in Wyoming.

XVI. REAGAN AND "STAR WARS"

On the evening of March 23, 1983, President Reagan surprised the country, including some of his own advisers, by suggesting before a national TV audience that advances in science and engineering might enable the nation physically to defend itself against ballistic missile attack. The plan was officially called the Strategic Defense Initiative (SDI), but it was almost immediately dubbed Star Wars because of its Hollywood-like wonder weapons that suggested the movie with the same title.

In his address, the president noted that Mutual Assured Destruction had worked well. However, he said it would be preferable in the future to defend the U.S. population against nuclear missile attack by shooting down incoming warheads rather than by threatening terrible retaliation against the Soviet population, a strategy the president noted was, ". . . a sad commentary on the human condition." He continued:

Are we not capable of demonstrating our peaceful intentions by applying all our abilities and our ingenuity to achieving a truly lasting stability? I think we are. Indeed, we must.

After careful consultation with my advisers, including the Joint Chiefs of Staff, I believe there is a way. Let me share with you a vision of the future which offers hope.

It is that we embark on a program to counter the awesome Soviet missile threat with measures that are defensive. Let us turn to the very strengths in technology that spawned our great industrial base and that have given us the quality of life we enjoy today.

What if free people could live secure in the knowledge that their security did not rest upon the threat of instant U.S. retaliation to deter a Soviet attack, that we could intercept and destroy strategic ballistic missiles before they reached our own soil or that of our allies? (*Weekly Compilation of* Presidential Documents, July 22, 1983).

The president acknowledged that coupling an effective missile defense to the existing offensive capability of the United States would ". . . raise certain problems and ambiguities . . . and could be viewed as fostering an aggressive policy, and no one wants that" (Weekly Compilation of Presidential Documents, 1983).

The President then made his appeal:

". . . I call upon the scientific community in our country, those who gave us nuclear weapons, to turn their great talents now to the cause of mankind and world pace, to give us the means *of rendering these nuclear weapons impotent and obsolete*" [emphasis added] (*Weekly Compilation of Presidental Documents*, July 22, 1983).

The speech concluded:

My fellow Americans, tonight we're launching an effort which holds the promise of changing the course of human history. There will be risks, and results take time. But I believe we can do it. As we cross the threshold, I ask for your prayers and your support. Thank you, good night, and God bless you (*Weekly Compilations of Presidential Documents*, July 22, 1983).

For a second time a President held forth the possibility that space would be the place where the United States could achieve amazing feats. So far, however, the Reagan hope has not been realized.

From its inception, the SDI has been the most controversial of any U.S. space program, military or civil. The original critique of SDI featured three concerns. It was argued that some of the "gee whiz" weapons were simply too difficult to build; that the weapons that could be deployed would be neutralized by a determined Soviet opponent; and that SDI would threaten the existing system of deterrence and pressure the Soviet Union to respond in ways that would exacerbate the arms competition. Proponents denied the first two arguments, and they claimed that if SDI pressured the Soviets to do anything, it would be to make Moscow more amenable to U.S. initiatives as the alternative to running another technological race with the United States.

Had it been successful, the Reagan initiative would have moved the United States beyond the atomic bomb program and Apollo to new levels of accomplishment involving big government, big science, and big engineering, all in the name of national security in space. A successful SDI would have meant U.S. military mastery of the atmosphere and near space more dramatic than anything done yet on Earth-bound battle fields. To date, many of the technical obstacles have proved insoluble, which does not mean, however, that they will never be solved. But for now the centerpieces of the SDI, the nuclear pumped x-ray laser, other types of lasers, particle beam weapons, and the electromagnetic rail gun have not been demonstrated as deployable weapons. Additionally, it is not clear whether the computer hardware and software can be developed to manage space battles. In 1992, the Department of Energy announced that further testing of the x-ray laser would be canceled.

As the technical intractability of certain components of the SDI became apparent, the program was scaled down. Instead of protecting the U.S. population against ballistic missile attack, the plan was redesigned to protect hardened ICBM silos from attack, a much easier task than protecting "soft" cities. Proponents claimed the new posture would add sufficient uncertainty to an attacker's plans to dissuade him from launching an attack. Later, as the concern about massive missile attack from the former Soviet Union decreased the SDI underwent another significant modification, and received a new name. It is currently called GPALS, which stands for Global Positioning Against Limited Attack.

The rationale for GPALS is that the contemporary nuclear missile threat to the United States is more to be found in the potential capability of nations like Iraq, Iran, North Korea, and China; or in accidents among the four former Soviet republics — Russia, Ukraine, Byelo-Rus, and Kazakhstan—which inherited the former U.S.S.R.'s large nuclear missiles. In scenarios dealing with the later nations, the projected attack would be small and probably accidental; and in the case of the former group of nations, it would be small and technically unsophisticated. Thus, it is argued by enthusiasts that in response to either attack mode, GPALS can be less technically advanced than the original SDI because the attacks would be substantially less than a full Soviet attack would have been. GPALS as currently constituted would involve two types of satellites. "Brilliant Eyes" would be surveillance craft designed to provide warning of a ballistic missile launch. "Brilliant Pebbles" would be a fleet of interceptor missiles orbiting the Earth. These would be fired against enemy warheads, presumably destroying them in flight. The system might be augmented by ground-based interceptors to kill warheads the Brilliant Pebbles line of defense missed.

Russian President Boris Yeltsin has expressed an interest in possibly collaborating with the United States in the deployment and operation of GPALS, which was renamed Global Protection System (GPS) in the Russian-American context (Joint U.S.-Russian Statement on A Global Protection System, June 17, 1992). The Russian interest is not surprising given the fact that most of the nations that appear moving toward acquisition of both ballistic missile technology and nuclear weapons are located near Russia. The eventual deployment of either GPALS or the GPS will require Moscow and Washington to make alterations in the AMB treaty of 1972. Specifically, changes would be required in regard to the prohibition contained in Article V that, "Each Party undertakes not to develop, test, or deploy ABM systems or components which are sea-based, air-based, space-based, or mobile land-based" (U.S. Arms Control and Disarmament Agency, 1990: 158).

The effort to defend against ballistic missile attack with ground based interceptors received an initial boost during the Persian Gulf War. The public viewed TV film of U.S. built Patriot antimissiles apparently destroying incoming warheads carried by SCUD battlefield missiles. Controversy still surrounds exactly how successful the Patriots were, and whether the success they had against primitive SCUD warheads can be extrapolated into an effective defense against more sophisticated IRBM and ICBM warheads.

There were signs in 1993 that the Congress was becoming disenchanged with GPALS and therefore funding for missile defense would be increasingly earmarked for battlefield defenses against SCUD and Super-SCUD type missiles.

In 1992 and 1993, charges of fraud were made about the SDI program that, if proved, would more than vindicate President Eisenhower for issuing the warning about the military-industrial complex in his farewell address. The allegations, made by whistleblowers, are that SDI officials falsified the performance of some SDI components, thus covering up failures in order to maintain funding for the program (Weiner, 1993).

XVII. SPACE IMPERIALISM?

Looking to the future, there is a collection of military-oriented space enthusiasts who suggest that the United States is in a technical position realistically to consider adopting a policy that would exclude threatening nations from entering space. For some, this would be a logical extension of the original SDI concept that could justify transferring some assets from NASA to the Strategic Defense Initiative Office within the Department of Defense. For others, it would be a corruption of the SDI concept and an a debasement of U.S. science and technology; to say nothing about being alien to the traditional U.S. opposition to imperialism.

Advocates of U.S. military space dominance use the analogy of army troops seeking the high ground so that fire can be brought down on the enemy below. From this perspective, space is the new high ground and the United States should develop further the capability not only to seize the area for national security proposes but to deny space to others. Although this view is not an announced policy of the government, bits and pieces of it have appeared in nongovernmental quarters. For instance, a recent Heritage Foundation paper carries the suggestion that the United States issue a warning to other nations that they do not have a guaranteed right to enter space. Baker Spring (1992) writes, "If Third World leaders realize the U.S. and its allies will destroy their satellites or render them useless in case of war, they will be less likely to make the investment in the first place" (*Space Weapon Systems: A Looming Proliferation Threat*, 1992: 13).

A related thesis is suggested in an article titled "Principles of Space Warfare."

> The expansion of American and allied military power in space will create a supremacy of military power for the West. It will mean dominate power by those who regard peace as the ultimate winning strategy, who believe in the absence of any ideology but human liberty, and who believe in rule by force of law and majority vote rather than terror. The balance of terror will be but a memory. Therefore the United States should continue its efforts to develop and deploy a space based Strategic Defense System as the first step to creating space power. The United States should also embark on a program to build true military power and warfighting ability in space as the best guarantee of true peace (Brandeburg, 1992: 45).

Both Edward Teller, one of the principal designers of the H bomb, and a long-time advocate of military preparedness, and his protege at the Lawrence Livermore Laboratory, Lowell Wood, have discussed the projection of U.S. military capability into space. Teller has spoken of a "space blockade" that would prevent any other nation from placing into space either civil or military satellites. According to retired Air Force General Danny Graham, the founder of the High Frontier Organization that supports space defense, Brilliant Pebbles would provide ". . . the kind of control the British once had on the high seas" (Klein and Stober, Denver Post, August 2, 1992).

Herein may be one of the hotly debated aspects of future U.S. space policy—to what extent and for what purposes should the nation's space assets be utilized to extend U.S. military power into the space environment, possibly at the cost of reduced support for scientific endeavors, and in contravention of the ABM Treaty's prohibitions against space-based ABMs. Here also may be found the next example of President Eisenhower's concern about the military-industrial complex. As the world's remaining military and space superpower, the United States will have to wrestle with how its immense space-based capabilities should be melded to its public purposes.

XVIII. REAGAN AND SPACE-RELATED DISARMAMENT

The president who referred to the Soviet Union as the "Evil Empire," Ronald Reagan, left office after concluding the first real disarmament treaty with Moscow, in contrast with arms control agreements; and establishing the framework for a second disarmament agreement. The Intermediate Nuclear Forces Treaty (INF) was signed in December 1987. Its objective, now completed, called for the destruction of U.S. and Soviet ground-launched ballistic missiles and cruise missiles in the 500- to 5500-kilometer range. This treaty followed a period of missile deployment in Eastern Europe by the Soviets and counterdeployment by the United States in Western Europe (U.S. Arms Control and Disarmament Agency, 1990: 350–362). In time, the examination of Soviet documents that has been promised by Russian President Boris Yeltsin may validate this claim as fact. But for now, it can only be hypothesized that the Soviet willingness to sign the INF was a function of Reagan's spirited counterdeployment of GLCMs and Pershing IRBMs plus Mikhail Gorbachev's interest in "new thinking for a new world" (Gorbachev, 1987: 17).

The Strategic Arms Reduction Treaty (START) aimed at eliminating parts of each nation's strategic TRIAD. The negotiations begun during the Reagan administration reached fruition when Presidents Bush and Gorbachev signed the agreement during their July 1991 summit meeting in Moscow. The agreement to reduce the Strategic Nuclear Delivery Vehicles (SNDVs) by approximately 30% was speedily overtaken by events in the Soviet Union, including the resignation of Mikhail Gorbachev, and subsequent dissolution of the U.S.S.R. on Christmas 1991.

Even more sweeping agreements to reduce strategic nuclear weapons were accomplished during the June 1992 summit in Washington between Bush and Yeltsin (*Arms Control-Related Material from the Summit Meeting Between US President Bush and Russian Federation President Yeltsin*, June 16–17, 1992). These were preceded in the fall of 1991 by a unilateral announcement by President Bush that tactical nuclear weapons would be withdrawn from deployment assuming reciprocity on the part of the former Soviet Union. The two presidents agreed that both nations would reduce their number of warheads down to between 3800 and 4250 during the 7-year life of the Treaty. It was also agreed to further reduce the number of warheads down to between 3000 and 3500 by the year 2003, or the end of 2000 if the United States contributes to financing the destruction of the Russian strategic arms. As part of this arrangement it was agreed to eliminate all MIRVed ICMBs and limit SLBM warheads to no more than 1700 to 1750.

Unless Russia and the other three former Soviet republics possessing long-range nuclear missiles renege for some reason, the United States and Russia could enter a stable and finite nuclear-deterrent position. In time, their relationship may go beyond that to replicate the long-standing relationship between the United States, England, and France—a situation in which the nuclear weapons possessed by those nations are not politically significant to each other.

During the cold war period, the missiles that would have traveled through space and the surveillance satellites that watched from space probably contributed to the deterrence of war between the two military superpowers because neither side wanted to pay the horrible price of a nuclear conflict. This utilization of space may thus have accomplished what military balances on land and sea have generally failed to do.

Some first steps have been taken to limit the acquisition of ICBMs by nations thought in the West to be rogue and immature countries. For example, the United States and the other industrial states have entered into an arrangement to constrain the acquisition of ballistic missile technology. The arrangement to achieve this result is called the Missile Technology Control Regime (MTCR). Adherents are supposed to regulate the provision of ballistic missiles and components with which to make ballistic missiles to other nations and subnational groups.

The problem with the MTCR is the effectiveness of monitoring compliance against greed and the need to include all nations capable of making such technology available. At the current time, the potential manufacture and distribution of SCUD missiles by Iraq, Rodong-1 missiles by North Korea, and IRBMs and ICBMs by China remains a problem. Further, as revelations unfold about sales of high technology to Iraq, it is clear there are always firms and individuals, and sometimes governments, who will make an illegal sale simply for the impressive profits to be made or in the pursuit of personal or national interest. Whether or not the United Nations inspections of Iraq will evolve into the kind of precedent with "teeth" that could be applied worldwide to the spread of missile technology is not yet clear.

A possible consequence of the cold war's termination, which involved the United States and Russian cooperation in space was suggested in 1992. It is for the two nations to combine their impressive Deep Black satellite surveillance and reconnaissance assets for international observation (Lawrence et al., 1992). It has been suggested that the photographs and other data thus obtained be published by the United Nations on a regular basis to alert the world community to nefarious and aggressive activities. The rationale for this proposal is an extension of Niels Bohr's suggestion that a more open world is a more peaceful world.

Any way one views civilization's move into the 21st century, it appears that space can provide finite deterrence between the large powers if it is required, serve as a check against challengers of the international regime favored by the large powers, and as a place from which general surveillance can be made.

XIX. NEITHER OUT OF FEAR NOR FOR PROFIT

The Russian Tsiolkovsky dreamed of space colonies and Goddard and von Braun of going to the moon. But most of the emphasis in the U.S. space program has come from real or imagined military necessity, particularly the fear of the Soviet Union. Related to that is the need to spy on the world for the sake of national security or to verify treaties with potential cheats. There also was the need to prove in space that American society was superior to that of the Soviet Union. Some impetus also has come from the logic of Adam Smith—that money can be made in space. The best example of that to date is the communications satellite systems. However, originally submerged among these other motivations is a reason that dates back to when the first human, or perhaps humanoid, wondered about his or her origin and of that of the Earth and of the sky. Human curiosity, either purely scientific, theological, or a mixture of both, has fluctuated as a reason for space activity.

Given the end of the cold war, and until the next threat to national security thought capable of being countered by space occurs, the United States and others can pursue the scientific exploration of space using men and women and robotics. Relative to what is out there to be explored and understood, the effort has barely begun. But there is an initial track record.

The U.S. scientific venture into space began with a 10.5-pound satellite launched on January 31, 1958. This diminutive device gave early evidence of the differences that would characterize the nonmilitary space programs of the United States and the U.S.S.R. Although small, Explorer I carried sophisticated miniaturized instruments that discovered the Van Allen radiation belt above the Earth. Typically, the Soviet satellites won the weight-lifting competition, whereas the American ones were more advanced scientifically.

In April 1960, the first of a long series of weather satellites was launched. Tiros I orbited the Earth at 450 miles and established the policy that U.S. weather satellites would share the data they collected with the world. Later the Nimbus and ESSA (Environmental Science Services Administration) satellites would follow Tiros. Today's TV viewer takes for granted the satellite photos of developing weather phenomenon that illustrate the evening news.

The Apollo missions were preceded by a series of precursor space craft that reconnoitered the moon. The first was Pioneer I, which missed the moon in the fall of 1958, but traveled 71,000 miles from Earth. Next were the Rangers, which photographed the moon in 1964 and 1965. They were followed in 1966 by Lunar Orbiter I, which took additional photographs. In the same year, Surveyor I made the first of several robotic American soft landings on the moon. The Apollo program itself extended from July 20, 1969, when the first Americans walked on the moon, to the sixth and last visit of Apollo 17 in December 1972.

Nonpiloted exploration of the nearby planets began with the Mariner series, the first of which flew by Venus in 1967. Later Mariners flew by Mars and Mercury. Viking I and Viking 2 soft landed on Mars in 1976 and were unable to establish whether primitive life existed. Pioneer 10 was launched on the successful 5-year journey to Jupiter in 1972. The Voyager series of spacecraft was first launched in 1976 to fly by Jupiter, Saturn, and Uranus and reached the later planet 10 years later.

As the planets were being explored, NASA launched a number of scientific craft in the 1960s to observe the Earth and other parts of our solar system. Included in these missions were the Orbiting Geophysical Observatory to study the Earth; Orbiting Astronomical Observatory; the Passive Geodetic Satellite for mapping the Earth; the Applications Technology Satellite to test satellite performance; the Biosatellite to examine the effect of weightlessness on primitive life forms; and the Orbiting Solar Observatory. It was and continues to be U.S. policy to share the scientific information obtained from these and similar satellites and spacecraft with the world.

In the 1970s, the United States continued its policy of supporting scientific launches with a number of satellites designed to study the Earth and the solar system. There was the Earth Resources Technology Satellite I, NOAA I, Landsat I, and the Laser Geodynamics Satellite. Later came the Helios spacecraft, the International Ultraviolet Explorer, the International Sun Earth Explorer, and the High Energy Astronomical Observatory. In 1981, the Solar Maximum Mission Observatory was launched. The importance of the esoteric data obtained by these craft may have been lost on many of the taxpayers who funded the projects; however, a check of the scientific space literature is a testament to the valuable information obtained. Another example of U.S. internationalism in space was demonstrated in 1975 when the Apollo craft rendezvoused with the Soviet Soyuz.

Skylab was launched May 14, 1973. The purpose was to obtain data on human performance in a zero-gravity environment. The Soviets did their experimenting with humans in space for a prolonged period of time with their space station MIR, which is still in orbit around the Earth.

To a large extent, the 1980s were the years of the U.S. shuttle that was built as a transport vehicle to low earth orbit, a laboratory to test humans and materials in microgravity, and as a launching platform for a variety of satellites and space probes. Although not yet used in this way, the shuttle was designed to ferry materials up to construct, and later supply, Space Station Freedom. The first shuttle, Columbia was launched April 12, 1981. On January 28, 1986, the shuttle Challenger was lost in an explosion shortly after launch.

The Challenger disaster profoundly impacted American space policy. President Reagan commissioned a 12-person panel headed by former Secretary of State William Rogers and including astronaut Sally Ride to determine what had happened. The Rogers Commission concluded there were several reasons for the tragedy. First, engineers at Morton Thiokol and NASA's Marshall Space Flight Center had incorrectly designed seals known as "O-rings" used to join sections of the solid-rocket boosters to the shuttle. Second, launch officials were not informed that some engineers had warned that the launch should not be attempted in 36-degree (Fahrenheit) weather, because the unusual cold could adversely effect the seals. Last, general blame was placed on NASA for attempting to accomplish too much in too short a period of time, with too little resources, thus reducing the emphasis on safety.

Recently revealed information from former Soviet sources indicates that the Soviets also tried to accomplish too much without proper preparations. Khruchchev is reported to have ordered hurried launches to celebrate state anniversaries. Some of these ended in disaster (30th American Astronomical Society Goddard Memorial Symposium, 1992).

As a result of the Rogers Commission findings, President Reagan ordered NASA to cut back on its work load; in particular to cease trying to be a business for launching commercial satellites with the shuttle. Consequently, commercial firms that had planned on the shuttle to launch their satellites were forced to look elsewhere for launch vehicles, particularly to the Europeans.

Another policy impact of the Challenger loss was renewed interest in the long-standing argument over which is best—satellites and spacecraft with humans aboard or those without them. Obviously the latter cost less because no life-support systems are needed, and there is less public confidence loss when there is an accident. On the other hand, the craft carrying humans have a better chance of being fixed when there is a nonlethal malfunction of some equipment component. The current NASA policy is a kind of compromise. There is the Space Exploration Initiative designed for human exploration projected at a cost of 3 to 4 billion dollars a year for some years. There is also the new Small Planetary Mission program involving nonpiloted scientific probes costing less than 150 million dollars each. Examples are NEAR (Near Earth Asteroid Rendezvous) fly along and MESUR (Mars Environmental Survey).

In what some would consider a rather off-beat activity, NASA is conducting an experiment to discern whether life exists beyond the solar system. Termed SETI (Search for Extra Terrestrial Intelligence), this effort is composed of two distinct activities. The high-sensitivity target search seeks signals originating near stars like our sun, which conceivably might have life-cradling planets circling them that are within 100 light years of Earth. The second effort is called the sky survey. As its name suggests, this program consists of radio telescopes that search the entire sky for signal evidence of advanced societies elsewhere.

After the loss of Challenger, there was some expectation in the United States that private launch firms would arise to handle the backlog of satellite launches. This did not happen and the U.S. shuttles resumed flying in 1988.

With the return of the shuttles, including a replacement for Challenger, named Endeavour, the launching of U.S. scientific craft resumed. The Magellan spacecraft was launched from the shuttle Atlantis and mapped Venus in 1990; the Galileo spacecraft was launched from Atlantis and will arrive near Jupiter in 1995; the Ulysses spacecraft was launched from the Discovery shuttle and will near the sun in 1994.

A major disappointment occurred in regard to the Hubble Space Telescope that was launched from Discovery on April 24, 1990. At 13 tons, and costing 1.5 billion dollars, the Hubble was the heaviest and most expensive scientific spacecraft launched up to that time (in 1991 an even heavier craft, the 17-ton Gamma-ray Observatory was launched by the Atlantis shuttle). Designed to peer into the universe from 381 miles (614 km) above the haze and distortions of the Earth's surface, the Hubble's images have not been as sharp as intended owing to its main mirror having been ground to the wrong specifications. The spacecraft also wiggles part of the time, because its solar cell "wings" flex when the craft goes into or out of the sunlight. Attempts at repearing the Hubble are set for 1993.

The Hubble Space Telescope and the Gamma-ray Observatory are the first two parts of the four-component Great Observatories program. The program design is to provide observation of the universe at all wavelengths except radio. The partially completed Advanced X-ray Astrophysics Facility is scheduled to be launched in 1997, and the Space Infrared Telescope Facility is still under study.

In September 1992, NASA used a Titan III rocket to successfully launch the Mars Observer spacecraft to the "red planet." Costing 980 million dollars, the mission involves an 11-month flight to Mars, and then several years will be spent in mapping and studying the planet's geology and climate as a prelude to the possible landing of humans on Mars in the second decade of the next century. The 2.5-ton craft will operate in a near-polar orbit at 235 miles above the Martian surface. The launch of the Mars Observer opened an era of expanded international cooperation in space with the participation of 11 Russians.

XX. AFTER THE COLD WAR—
THE SPACE EXPLORATION INITIATIVE

In November 1989, the Berlin Wall was breached. This physical event legitimated the political unraveling of the Soviet Empire in Eastern Europe and later of the Soviet Union itself. For the first time, NASA and its political advocates would have to justify the civil space program without reference to the competition with, or fear of, the "Evil Empire." Four months earlier, President Bush noted the changing relations with the Soviet Union and the impact those changes would have upon the U.S. space program in a speech he gave while standing on the steps of the Smithsonian Institution in Washington. On July 20, 1989, the President announced the next major U.S. space effort in this way:

> In 1961, it took a crisis—the space race—to speed things up. Today we do not have a crisis. We have an opportunity.
>
> To seize this opportunity, I am not proposing a 10-year plan like Apollo. I am proposing a long range, continuing commitment.
>
> First, for the coming decade—for the 1990s—Space Station Freedom—our critical next step in all our space endeavors.
>
> And next—for the new century—back to the Moon. Back to the future. And this time, back to stay.
>
> And then,—a journey into tomorrow—a journey to another planet—a manned mission to Mars (America at the Threshold, 1991: iv).

Going to the moon and Mars were dreams shared by both the youthful Robert Goddard in Massachusetts and the young Werhner von Braun in Germany, and the idea had been discussed in NASA for years. The dream became national policy for a while because the president said it was. Work began to integrate the moon-Mars vision, officially known as the Space Exploration Initiative, into a coherent policy context that would give requisite guidance to NASA and inform the Congress and the public what the overall plan is.

Some of the conceptualizing had already been done in the aftermath of the Challenger accident. Astronaut Sally Ride, a member of the Rogers Commission, suggested that civil space activities logically should consist of two different but complementary kinds of activity—

Mission to Planet Earth (MTPE) and Mission From Planet Earth (MFPE). The former would involve the use of space assets to collect information regarding how the Earth physically functions, including the dynamics of global climate change and the impact of humans on the Earth's environment. The latter would use space assets, including human pioneers, to study and explore the relationship of the Earth to the solar system, and the relation of the solar system to the universe.

Somewhat concurrently with the formulation of the MTPE and MFPE perspectives there developed considerable criticism of NASA. The unhappiness with the space agency was based on more than just the Challenger accident. There had been problems with hydrogen leaks on later shuttles, there was the spherical aberration difficulty with the Hubble Space Telescope, and various launch processing errors such as a work platform left in a shuttle engine compartment. The criticism also included an alleged institutional bias against new ideas, bureaucratic inertia, and failure to develop an overall plan for civil space activities.

Such concerns led to the creation of the Advisory Committee on the Future of the U.S. Space Program, generally called the Augustine Committee after its chairman, Norman R. Augustine, Chairman and CEO of the Martin Marietta Corporation. After hearing testimony from over 375 persons, many of whom are prominent in the space community, the Augustine Committee completed its work in December 1990 and reported to the NASA Administrator, Richard A. Truely, and through him to Vice President Dan Quayle, Chairman of the National Space Council.

Although the Augustine Committee supported the general parameters of the MTPE and MFPE, it added considerable specificity and structure to the overall NASA context in which these two mission-oriented programs would be carried out (*Summary and Principal Recommendations of the Advisory Committee on the Future of the U.S. Space Program*, 1990). Further, it was the Committee's belief that greater direction had to be provided the space program or it would drift through the 1990s.

> In defining a space agenda we believe it is not sufficient merely to list a collection of projects to be undertaken in space, no matter how meritorious each may be. It is essential to provide a logical basis for the structure of the program, including a sense of priorities (*Summary and Principal Recommendations of the Advisory Committee on the Future of the U.S. Space Program*, 1990: 5).

Of the two missions, the Augustine Committee suggested that

> ". . . some degree of urgency" be attached to MTPE because it ". . . is the undertaking that in fact brings space down to earth—addressing critical, everyday problems which affect all the earth's peoples," which, ". . . will provide us with a much better understanding of our environment, how we may be affecting it, and what might be done to restore it. (*Summary and Principal Recommendations of the Advisory Committee on the Future of the U.S. Space Program*, 1990: 5).

The Augustine Committee held that augmenting space science on which all else is based warranted the highest priority, above space stations, manned missions to the planets, and other higher-visibility activities.

> It is this endeavor in science that enables basic discovery and understanding, that uncovers the fundamental knowledge of our own planet to improve the quality of life for all people on earth, and that stimulates the education of the scientists needed for the future. Science gives vision, imagination, and direction to the space program, and as

such should be vigorously protected and permitted to grow, holding at or somewhat above its present fraction of NASA's budget even as the overall space budget grows (*Summary and Principal Recommendations of the Advisory Committee on the Future of the U.S. Space Program*, 1990: 5).

The Augustine Committee identified the manned space program as being the source of considerable controversy concerning the nation's civil space program. They noted that robotic space craft can perform many tasks at lower costs in dollars and lower risks to life than humans and therefore should be extensively utilized. Nevertheless, part of the Committee's Report emphasized that humans are an indispensable part of U.S. space activity.

Mars, specifically the human exploration of the red planet called for by President Bush in the Space Exploration Initiative was held out by the Committee as being the long-range "... magnet for the manned space program." The Committee's justification for paying the higher dollar costs and running the risk to lives associated with humans journeying to Mars is a candid statement of the basic rationale for human exploration of space.

It needs to be stated straightforwardly that such an undertaking probably must be justified largely on the basis of intangibles—the desire to explore, to learn about one's surroundings, to challenge the unknown and to find what is to be found (*Summary and Principal Recommendations of the Advisory Committee on the Future of the U.S. Space Program*, 1990: 6).

In the context of the SEI, the Augustine Committee suggested a new management approach. It is to tailor the long-term moon-Mars project to available funding, rather than was the case with Apollo, to attempt to follow a specific schedule and live with the pressures that procedure generates. It was suggested that such a pay as you go approach would better endure the vagaries of changing presidential administrations, the potential changing makeup of the Congress, and unpredictable economic circumstances. Also, it was noted that linking the SEI to funding availability would mean it would bear unforeseen fiscal problems rather than bleeding away money from other important, but less visible, scientific activities.

In structuring a cumulative, or building block, approach to the SEI program, the Augustine Committee suggested that the next step is to build a less complex, more practical Space Station Freedom. The Earth-orbiting craft is deemed necessary to provide a life sciences laboratory to prepare astronauts for the rigors of long space flights and to enable microgravity experiments to be conducted. Thereafter a return to the moon as another stepping stone to Mars is recommended.

To sustain a reinvigorated space program focused on the MTPE and MFPE, the Augustine Committee emphasized two crucial components of the physical infrastructure it believed was necessary for both missions. Noting that the United States has not developed a new main rocket engine for two decades, the Committee called for such an endeavor. Noting that routine "trucking" into space does not require the expensive shuttle, the Committee suggested the development of a new, unmanned, heavy-lift vehicle, which would be potentially "man-rateable." From this type of research and development the Committee felt would evolve the engine and spacecraft suitable for the return voyages to the moon.

The Augustine Committee recognized the initial role played by NASA in stimulating other national space programs and approved of the international flavor of many NASA projects, and then a cautionary note with a nationalistic flavor was added. The warning was that international agreements by their very nature involve additional levels of bureaucracy that can delay decisions. Further, the Committee suggested the United States, "... retain management control for critical inline program elements in certain long-term undertakings such as human space exploration," and that Washington remain "fully competitive" in regard to the development of launch vehicles which broadly impact on the, ". . . fundamental viability of America's civil and commercial space programs" (*Summary and Principal Recommendations of the Advisory Committee on the Future of the U.S. Space Program*, 1990: 8).

Currently, and for some time into the future, the U.S. international activity with the highest visibility, and the greatest overall cost, is Space Station Freedom. The European Space Agency (ESA) is providing an attached laboratory, a free-flying polar platform, and a co-orbiting man-tended free flyer. Japan will build an attached laboratory. Canada is building a Mobile Servicing System and a robotic arm for assisting in assembly of the space station. From Italy will come a minipressurized logistics module and possibly a life sciences laboratory. The United States is contributing the basic infrastructure for the manned base and the polar orbiting platforms plus a laboratory module and a habitation module. The assured Crew Return Vehicle might be purchased from Russia, from a U.S. corporation, or from the ESA.

The evolution of Space Station Freedom should provide a number of lessons to the United States and its space partners regarding long-term international space cooperation. For now, NASA's Deputy Director of International Relations has noted some initial lessons (Cline, 1992). These are the observations that—It is useful to involve partners at an early stage of program development, but not so early that U.S. concepts are not clear; and negotiation of a space partnership means the United States and others will have to compromise and at times be willing to give up positions taken for domestic political reasons in order to achieve international accord. This may apply to the United States regarding Washington's tendency to define leadership of the project as meaning U.S. domination.

Other observations are that the United States should strike the right balance between autonomy and interdependence; and that once a deal is made, the United States ought to live by it. Regarding the latter point, many have noted that the U.S. performance in the Space Station Freedom program will go a long way toward demonstrating Washington's trustworthiness, or the lack thereof, and either type of behavior will impact significantly on future international efforts.

It is obvious that if the United States is to meet its international space commitments, the Congress must understand the crucial nature of sustained, and reliable funding over time.

In regard to funding, the Augustine Committee suggested NASA's budget be slimmed by canceling the projected purchase of an additional shuttle, by streamlining Space Station Freedom, and by replacing some future shuttle launches with the use of a new, unmanned, heavy-lift vehicle, presumably less costly. With an eye toward the Congress, the Committee stated the civil space program would benefit enormously from the ". . . provision of predictable and stable funding" (*Summary and Principal Recommendations of the Advisory Committee on the Future of the U.S. Space Program*, 1990: 8).

Fifteen months after the release of the Augustine Committee's report, a document was published that focused directly on the most glamorous, costly, and dangerous in terms of human life, component of the nation's future space policy—the Space Exploration Initiative. Titled *America at the Threshold*, this document was produced by an unusual group of 23 senior space professionals called The Synthesis Group, who executed an unusual charge (*America at the Threshold: The Synthesis Group Report*, 1991). It was to review and then synthesize ideas and suggestions, some of which were "pretty far out" using one official's description, about the SEI that had been previously gathered by NASA using an Outreach Program involving personal letters of solicitation from the NASA Administrator Richard H. Truely and public announcements. The chairman of The Synthesis Group was Lieutenant General Thomas P. Stafford, USAF (Ret.), a Gemini and Apollo astronaut and Commander of the Apollo-Soyuz Test Project.

The Synthesis Group provided justification for the SEI by citing the following reasons—increase knowledge of the solar system and what is beyond; rejuvenate interest in mathematics, science, and engineering; re-establish U.S. world leadership; develop technology with terrestrial applications; facilitate additional space exploration and commercialization with the development of a heavy-lift vehicle; and provide a boost to the U.S. economy. Such space boosterism and the accompanying rationale is not surprising given the composition of the Synthesis Group, which included men with ties to NASA, the Air Force, the Strategic Defense Initiative Office, and such private aerospace companies as McDonnel Douglas, Space Industries, Grumman, Rockwell International, and Raytheon.

The reasons provided in 1991 by the Synthesis Group for returning on a permanent basis to the moon and venturing on to Mars are similar to the reasons set forth to support the original visits to the moon, with the exception that the basic political motivation for Apollo, competition with and fear of the Soviet Union, is missing. And therein may be the soft spot in U.S. civil space policy for some time. No matter how ugly and threatening Iraq, Iran, North Korea, or similar states are and no matter how bloody the ethnic violence in the Balkins, nothing can focus the attention of the American public on space competition or on national defense as did the Soviet Union under Stalin, Khrushchev, and Brezhnev. Of course, if Russia turns toward Fascist and Nationalist expansionism, or if China or Japan become militarily threatening, some future president may again have the "ammunition" to link space policy to national survival.

Only time will tell if the necessary political leadership will exist to rally the taxpaying American public to support space efforts based on the kind of intangibles noted in the Augustine Committee Report and repackaged by the Synthesis Group in their report, *America at the Threshold*. Actually time did run out in 1992, at least temporarily, on the Space Exploration Initiative's bold plan to return humans to the moon and from there on to Mars. Two reasons account for putting the SEI on an indefinite hold. The originator of the plan, President George Bush, failed in his bid for reelection in November. Further, concern about the federal budget deficit drained away much appeal from the multibillion dollar space project.

Somewhat the same point can be made in regard to U.S. military space policy. With the demise of the U.S.S.R., the justification for 300 billion dollar defense budgets, including a portion for ICBMs, SLBMs, and related hardware, has also decreased. However, in a strange reversal of affairs, the need for space-based surveillance may increase because the world is less orderly now than during the cold war.

Since history teaches that humankind periodically has a rendezvous with great endeavors, it is likely that the Space Exploration Initiative will resurface when the fiscal and political times are right. It may then have a new name, and be championed by a different national administration, but the focus will again be on human visitation to, if not habitation of, the moon and Mars. When that happens much of the "homework" done in the past few years by the Synthesis Group should prove useful, and therefore it is reviewed here.

The bulk of the Synthesis Report explains the four "menus," or architectures, available for selection as the focus of the SEI. Each architecture is an alternative space mission, together with the sequential building blocks thought to be needed in order to achieve the specific mission objectives. Many of the building blocks are fundamental and therefore common to all four architectures just as in a restaurant, eating utensils, plates, glasses, and a table are basic requirements regardless of what is being eaten.

All four architectures contribute in different ways to the three goals postulated for the SEI—exploration and science, human presence in space, and space resource development. The four architectures, or options, that can be pursued under the rubric of the SEI are:

1. *Mars exploration.* In this architecture, the emphasis is on Mars and those activities absolutely required to prepare for a journal to Mars. Thus, a return to the moon is viewed as a step to Mars and not as a final goal.
2. *Science emphasis for the moon and Mars.* This plan calls for both the moon and Mars to be explored, with the former being used as an observing platform. Both robotic and human exploratory activities are specified.
3. *The moon to stay and Mars Exploration.* The emphasis here is on establishing a permanent human presence on the moon that will support substantial exploration and observation, with smaller exploration teams venturing on to Mars.
4. *Space resource utilization.* The focus of this plan is the development of lunar resources, followed by use of Martian resources. Examples of the former would be to provide potential energy for the Earth in the form of helium 3, which might be the fuel for fusion reactors on Earth; the collection of solar energy; the extraction of propellants from the moon's regolith such as hydrogen and oxygen; and the extraction of ceramics and metals to aid in moon construction.

In undertaking any of the four architectures, the Synthesis Group advised a set of priorities different from those present during the Apollo program. In recognition of the changing political times, the contemporary set of priorities are safety, cost, performance, and schedule. These should be contrasted with the Apollo program priorities, which were safety, schedule, performance, and cost. Regarding the health and safety of the astronauts, rated the top priority in both priority sets, the Synthesis Group identified three particular hazards for SEI astronauts. These are the effect of prolonged zero gravity on the human body, galactic cosmic radiation, and radiation ensuing from solar flare activity. Although it may not be an immediate health factor, confinement in a small space capsule for extended periods of time could negatively impact mental health.

The new technology most obviously common to all four architectures is a heavy-lift launch vehicle capable of placing 250 metric tons in low Earth orbit. By comparison, the Saturn V rocket used to launch the Apollo moon craft had a lift capability of 140 metric tons. Common to the first three architectures will be a new propulsion system for travel to Mars, a nuclear thermal rocket. This new engine is needed to reduce the time Mars-bound astronauts are exposed to zero gravity and galactic radiation. Thus, the SEI policy is captive to successful research on, and the development of, major new propulsion units.

In regard both to the moon and Mars, the Synthesis Group proposed the sequence of flights be (1) precursor reconnaissance missions, (2) cargo missions, and (3) piloted missions. The earliest humans could be expected on Mars is 2012, or the trip might be as late as 2018. This time frame means the SEI represents the longest projected period of sustained operations for a particular objective ever attempted by the U.S. government. By contrast, when Washington accepted George Kennan's proposal for the "containment" of communism, there was no realization the task would last until the early 1990s. In fact, Kennan, writing in the "X" article, suggested a time frame of 10 to 15 years (Kennan, 1947: 576).

Synthesis Committee members, and NASA itself, claim to see in the SEI and other space activities a powerful tool to help cure what is widely held to be the decline in science, mathematics, and technological interest among young Americans. Thus, the nation's space policy is being harnessed to advance education policy. The theory is that the glamor and glitz of returning to the moon and going on to Mars will help kindle an interest in young persons about the sciences and mathematics, which is needed if the nation is to remain scientifically competitive. In the Synthesis Report, the perspective is put in this fashion:

The excitement of space exploration continues to capture the imagination of young people, as it did during the Apollo era. The Space Exploration Initiative provides a way to excite the minds of the nation's students, attracting them to the study of mathematics and science; it also provides a vision for the future, giving focus and application for mathematics and science studies. Additionally, the new discoveries from the Space Exploration Initiative will lead to new developments in science. In much the same way, the technical requirements of the Space Exploration Initiative will spur new engineering and technology developments. Finally, the Space Exploration Initiative will foster new information management and communications technologies which will bring the excitement of discovery and exploration directly to the classroom (*America at the Threshold*, 1991: 105).

Obviously the techniques differ, but the hope of spurring the interest of young people in mathematics and science extends from kindergarten through graduate training.

The end of the cold war provided several immediate benefits to the U.S. space program. One is the increased cooperation with the Russian MIR program whose cosmonauts hold the records on the amount of time for humans living in zero gravity. The other is the availability of some former Soviet space equipment, such as large rocket engines like the Energiya, for purchase or lease by the United States. In this regard, suggestions have been made for leasing the MIR, thus obviating the need to build Space Station Freedom. To date, this suggestion has received little official endorsement, because of the argument that space station Freedom would offer so much more state of the art advantages. However, plans were announced in late 1992 for an U.S. space shuttle to dock with the Russian MIR to demonstrate the new spirit of cooperation in the post-cold war world. On September 2, 1993 the United States and Russia signed a space accord which envisions future cooperation in piloted space exploration between Moscow and Washington, including the latter's space station partners, Canada, Japan, and several European nations. The lofty cooperative goals set in the accord are of course tied to the question of whether Russia will survive as a reliable political and economic entity.

Recognizing the contributions to be made from the fields of energy and defense, the Synthesis Report recommended that the implementing agency for the SEI be NASA, with the Department of Energy and Department of Defense being major contributors in terms of technology development and concept definition. The need for extensive interfacing by NASA with other government agencies, industry, and the universities was also recognized.

In the late summer of 1993 the apparent loss of the $1 billion Mars Observer to unknown causes added to public and governmental concerns over the effectiveness of NASA. The likely consequence of these worries will be yet another study, or studies. The focus will center upon answering questions about what should be the mission objectives, and the management style, for NASA in the post-Cold War world, a world with different national priorities and different budgetary constraints than those previously experienced.

XXI. CONCLUSIONS

Americans going to the moon, which began as the secret dreams of a solitary professor of physics in the 1920s, has been accomplished. Going back to the moon and on to Mars was, during the Bush administration, the announced policy of the U.S. government. Now it is on hold. What began as a research effort receiving an intermittent supply of a few thousand dollars from the Smithsonian Institution for building a small rocket is now a 14.5 billion dollar enterprise spread among some of the most powerful agencies in the executive branch, with special interest groups supporting increased funding for this or that missile/satellite project. What began as one professor and several assistants testing rockets on a ranch in New Mexico grew, in the case of the Apollo program, to some 400,000 people in some 20,000 locations, spending billions of dollars.

The very success of the U.S. space program up to the mid 1990s now constitutes one of the challenges to public policy on space. Having done so much, and succeeded so well, the current question is what should be done for an encore. Bigger programs, costing greater sums, to even more exotic space places, may be on a future national agenda. How these will be managed, paid for in competition with many other public programs, will constitute a public policy problem to be solved in the future.

Just like the most recent lottery winner inundated with schemers who have plans for the winner's bonanza, the allure of the space program has attracted all kinds of groups and individuals who want to use the success of space to further their particular mission. One of the most powerful of the groups wanting to use space, possibly more for their purposes than those of the nation as a whole, is the military-industrial-scientific complex. How to separate the true uses of space for national purposes from the debased uses President Eisenhower warned about will be difficult.

U.S. space prowess, both military and civil, will tempt the United States to undertake activities that are either not required for the nation's best interests or are antithetical to the nation's best traditions. On the other hand, space could provide the United States new opportunities to make unique contributions to a better world for all humanity. Distinguishing between the two categories of national policy will be a true test of the nation's maturity in the third century of its life.

In the final analysis, future U.S. space policy will depend more on solving the tough problems associated with politics, economics, leadership, and followship than technological difficulties.

BIBLIOGRAPHY

Acheson, D. (1969). *Present at the Creation*. Norton, New York.

American Astronautical Society (1992). *30th AAS Goddard Memorial Symposium*. April.

Beckman, P., et al. (1992). *The Nuclear Predicament*, 2d ed. Prentice-Hall, Englewood Cliffs, NJ.

Brandenburg, J. E. (1992). Principles of space warfare and power. *Space* Winter: 33–47.

Broad, L. (1963). *Winston Churchill*. Hawthorn, New York.

Burrows, W. E. (1988). *Deep Black*. Berkley, New York.

Cassidy, D. C. (1992). Uncertainty — *The Life and Science of Werner Heisenberg*. Freeman, New York.

Cline, L. F. H. (1992). Cooperation on Space Station Freedom: An American Perspective. Paper presented before the Third International Conference on Engineering, Construction and Operations in Space, June 1992. Denver, Colorado.

Codding, G. A., Jr. (1990). *The Future of Satellite Communications*. Westview Press, Boulder, CO.

Dulles, J. F. (1952). A policy of boldness. *LIFE*, May 19.

Encyclopedia Americana Annuals, Space Exploration, 1966–1992.

Gorbachev, Mikhail. (1987). *Perestroika*. Harper & Row, New York.

Kennan, G. F. (1947). ("X") The sources of Soviet conduct. *Foreign Affairs*. July: 566–582.

Klein, J., and Stober, D. (1992, Aug. 2). "SDI: D stands for Domination." *Denver Post*.

Krass, A. (1989). *The Verification Revolution.* Union of Concerned Scientists, Boston.

Lawrence, R. M. (1987). *The Strategic Defense Initiative.* Westview Press, Boulder, CO.

Lawrence, R. M., and Piontkowsky, A. (1993). UNSATS: Merging Classical Political Theory with Advanced Space Surveillance Technology for the Post Cold War World. 11th High Frontier Conference, Space Studies Institute, Princeton, New Jersey, May, 1993.

Lehman, M. (1988). *Robert H. Goddard.* Da Capo, New York.

McDougall, W. A. (1985). *. . . the Heavens and the Earth.* Basic Books, New York.

Rhodes, R. (1986). *The Making of the Atomic Bomb.* Simon & Schuster, New York.

Reston, J. (1954, Jan. 17). " 'Massive Atomic Retaliation' and the Constitution." *New York Times.*

Rostow, W. W. (1971). *The Stages of Economic Growth.* Cambridge University Press, Cambridge, England.

Spring, B. (1992). *Space Weapon Systems: A Looming Proliferation Threat.* Heritage Foundation.

Sorensen, T. C. (1965). *Kennedy.* Harper & Row, New York.

Tirman, J. (Ed.) (1986). *Empty Promise — The Growing Case Against Star Wars.* Beacon Press, Boston.

von Braun, W. (1952). Human travel to the moon. *Colliers,* a series of articles from January–February through November – December.

von Karman, T. (1967). *The Wind and Beyond.* Little, Brown, Boston.

U.S. Government. *Summary and Principal Recommendations of the Advisory Committee on the Future of the U.S. Space Program,* December, 1990.

U.S. Government (National Aeronautics and Space Administration). *Search for Extra-Terrestrial Intelligence,* June, 1990.

U.S. Government (Arms Control and Disarmament Agency). *Arms Control and Disarmament Agreements,* 6th ed. 1990.

U.S. Government (The Synthesis Group Report). *America at the Threshold.* May, 1991.

U.S. Government (National Aeronautics and Space Administration). *Advanced Technology for America's Future in Space,* 1991.

U.S. Government (National Aeronautics and Space Administration). *Integrated Technology Plan for the Civil Space Program,* 1991.

U.S. Government (White House). *National Security Strategy of the United States.* August 1991.

U.S. Government (White House). *Joint US–Russian Statement on a Global Protection System,* 1992.

Weiner, T. (1993, Aug. 19). "Congress Duped on 'Star Wars'?" *Denver Post.*

Wolfe, T. (1979). *The Right Stuff.* Bantam Books, New York.

Part J
CONCLUDING THOUGHTS

35
Values, Ethics, and Standards in Policy Analysis

Louise G. White
George Mason University, Fairfax, Virginia

The closing decade of the 20th century finds political systems engulfed in making difficult policy choices amid growing conflict and declining public resources. The field of policy studies has responded with substantive policy studies and recommendations, many of which are summarized in this book. There has also been an outpouring of critical writings about the theory and practice of policy studies itself and its assumptions, norms, and practices. This second body of literature challenges many of the basic assumptions and contributions of the field. It charges that substantive policy studies take a narrow and technocratic approach to policy choices and that they diminish the meaning of politics and the work of democratic institutions. Although their arguments are often presented in very academic and inaccessible terms, the critics are making very serious charges. The purpose of this chapter is to examine these debates and describe recent modifications in the study and practice of public policy.

Policy studies encompasses two broad subjects: policy analysis and the policy process (cf. Sabatier, 1991). Analysis expanded in the United States during the 1960s out of a belief that the political process was unable to deal creatively with pressing policy problems and that it was inordinately influenced by special interests and was wedded to the status quo.[1] In order to insulate policy analyses from a debilitating process, those concerned with improving public policy launched "the rationality project," which is an effort to use reason to intervene in public affairs (Stone, 1988). The lack of involvement by political scientists in this project left a void readily filled by operations research and economics, with the result that analytic prescriptions have emphasized technical approaches to relatively narrow problems (deLeon, 1988: 24).

An increasingly vocal group of critics wants to reverse this relationship between analysis and policy. Professional analysis needs to be a much more overtly political and participatory process. Instead of defining rational analysis solely in instrumental terms, as selecting means to ends, rational analysis should involve the public more broadly and should include reasoned reflection about political values. In spite of a broad consensus among the critics, it is not always clear how to translate their proposals into practice making their alternative model relatively easy to dismiss. In the meantime, however, the original theories on which both analysis and process were based are being modified, with the result that some, but not all, of the critics' concerns are being addressed.

This chapter reviews these developments. After a brief summary of the dominant theories of analysis and process (Sect. I), it describes the critics' concerns and their alternative approach to policy studies (Sect. II). They come at a time when many are questioning the actual effectiveness of policy studies—they lack a compelling theoretical base, they are largely underutilized, and their recommendations are undermined during implementation. After examining the model of the critics, the chapter looks at revisions in the theories of analysis and process that have partially addressed problems raised by the critics (Sect. III). By recognizing multiple perspectives and discourse among concerned parties, the revisions link analysis to a more open policy process. Ideas and information and political persuasion all have a prominent role to play and can lead to changes in beliefs and policies. These dynamics, however, are largely confined to discourse within the community of policy professionals and do not include reasoned debate among the broader public. A concluding section summarizes the implications of these theoretical developments for the practice of policy studies (IV).

I. DOMINANT THEORIES OF POLICY ANALYSIS AND PROCESS

A. Theories of Policy Analysis

Policy analysis applies rationality, control, and predictability to an often messy and frustrating policy process (Meehan, 1972). This "rationality project" relies on three assumptions: (1) It is possible objectively to analyze information about alternatives through scientific research methods. (2) Policy goals and values are set in the policy arena and the task of analysis is to formulate means to achieve them. (3) Satisfaction of individual preferences is the appropriate normative criterion for choosing among the alternatives.

The first assumption, based on positivism, states that there is an objective world that exists outside of the mind. Since it is lawfully ordered, we can come to understand it through research methods that encourage neutrality and objectivity. With the proper procedures the mind can describe this order and the causal relations that give rise to it either through deduction from theory or from observed correlations. In one version, operationalism, a thing is defined by the way we measure it; intelligence quotient is what IQ tests measure rather than a set of cognitive skills (Dallmayr, 1986). And poverty is defined in terms of specific income figures rather than as a social condition. Analysts use well-developed research techniques of observation and measurement to propose and test relations or predictions and to control extraneous variables. By thinking logically about how to accomplish policy goals, developing appropriate models and concepts, and carrying out relevant empirical research, they assume they can produce sound policy recommendations. The standard model includes clarifying goals, laying out alternative ways of reaching them, comparing the costs and benefits of the alternatives, and selecting the one that will best achieve the goals given limited resources (Brewer and deLeon, 1983; Quade, 1975; Stokey and Zeckhauser, 1978).

The second feature is grounded in the positivist argument that the only knowledge we can be certain of is empirically based, and that scientific reasoning and analysis cannot decide among different value positions. Therefore, it is important to separate facts and values and to focus analysis and research on the facts or means to given ends. This limitation is not too troubling, since values or policy goals are appropriately given to analysts through the political process.

The third aspect of the policy analysis paradigm, in spite of the claim that analysis eschews values, is a strong normative claim drawn from economics. Economic analysis is grounded in methodological individualism. Objectively, the theory assumes that analysts can make propositions about the content of individual preferences, and these in turn provide a basis for policy recommendations. Normatively the theory affirms the basic integrity of individuals as the legitimate interpreter of preferred policies. Preference satisfaction takes the place of other criteria such as individual welfare or needs or rights.[2]

Objective statements about preferences are based on two other assumptions. First, individuals rationally prefer whatever they perceive to be in their self-interest, and second, by defining self-interest as maximizing ones position, it is possible to deduce the content of interests. These assumptions are important. Economists appreciate that individuals act from a mixture of self-interest and altruism. Unless analysts can state ahead what factors go into a person's utility function, however, they end up with a tautology; namely, that peoples' behavior simply reflects whatever they prefer, making testable predictions impossible.[3] Also since self-interest is a common feature of behavior, and other interestedness is presumably less reliable, it is helpful to reduce the necessity of relying on altruism and see how far one can go in basing policies solely on a more reliable self-interest (Buchanan, 1986; Schultz, 1977).

The purpose of public policy is to maximize these preferences subject to the constraints of limited resources and conflicting preferences. Since not all preferences can be satisfied, some mechanism or set of rules needs to be developed to maximize these. The ideal criterion, the Pareto criterion, simply states that a policy is preferred if it makes at least one person better off and none worse off. The theory then turns its attention to examining rules or institutional arrangements for coming as close as possible to this criterion. Options include the market and cost-benefit analysis as a second-best replacement (White, 1989).

In a market where individuals have sufficient information about alternatives and where they can freely engage in exchange, they will trade back and forth until none can be better off, and everyone's marginal rates of substitution are the same. In this way, markets provide a process for determining policy and they enable decision makers to avoid interpersonal comparisons among preferences; comparing, for example, the utilities of the rich and poor. Perfectly functioning markets therefore meet the Pareto criterion and come closest to satisfying individual preferences. Even when markets are imperfect, which is frequently the case, they are less imperfect than the alternative of the public sector with its high transaction costs and opportunities for rent-seeking behavior. If one does rely on the government to provide public policies, then one should look for ways to incorporate incentives, choice, and competition (Wolf, 1979).

Cost-benefit analysis is an alternative that simulates the market by assuming that individuals trade back and forth and that the beneficiaries pay the losers. Whether or not such compensation actually takes place is a political decision. Like the theory of the market, cost-benefit analysis tries to establish an equilibrium rather than introduce change. Although it relies on analytic judgments rather than market processes, in practice, cost-benefit analysis is very compatible with market mechanisms. Analysts using this technique typically argue that one way to reduce transaction costs is to rely on market incentives wherever possible (Bobrow and Dryzek, 1983; Schultz, 1977).

Cost-benefit analysis is second best to a market solution for several reasons. First, since the unit of comparison is invariably money, it is difficult to price and include preferences for qualitative items even though economists try to use a variety of shadow prices for quality of life variables (Haveman and Weisbrod, 1975; Tribe, 1973: 627). Second, because they typically have to make assumptions about preferences, economists deal with average tastes rather than marginal ones (Mishan, 1969). Third, cost-benefit tradeoffs always depend on the spread of the net used to determine which factors should be counted as a cost or benefit and the extent to which indirect costs (externalities) are included. Do the costs of suburban zoning policies, for example, include effects on nonresidents who would like the option of moving there (White, 1979)?

Although methodological individualism has many critics, it makes several theoretically important contributions. First, the emphasis on results corrects earlier models that based policy prescriptions on professional judgments and led to what one publication wryly describes as "doing good," well-meaning efforts that clearly were often not good for recipients. Second, cost-benefit analysis can compensate for social and economic inequities by treating all individuals as equal whether or not they are active in the market or the political system. The fact that it does this on the basis of a relatively narrow range of preferences rather than on insubstantial and undependable motives such as altruism and public spiritedness is considered a strength by proponents and a major failing by critics[2] (White, 1979). Third, it is an important reminder that the poor and inarticulate members of society have their own view of their preferences and that their responses often make sense to them and are not simply a function of irrationality or ignorance. Fourth, and perhaps most important of all, economic analysis offers an important tool for diagnosing the dynamics of the policy process. It predicts what will occur insofar as people do act in their self-interest. At the same time, for those interested in change, it includes a narrow range of preferences and limited opportunities for promoting change (White, 1976).

B. Theories of the Policy Process

A second branch of policy studies deals with the policy process. One view conceptualizes the process as a series of stages such as formulation, implementation, and evaluation. Since this stages model does not have a causal understanding of behavior, however, it is not really a theory (Sabatier, 1991). Conceptually, process theories emphasize that cognitive limits on individuals make analysis difficult and that politics governs nearly every policy decision. In these respects, process theory has been antagonistic to analysis (Garson, 1980–1981). Some add that in reality there is little evidence that analysis has had much influence on the outcomes of the process. Descriptively, they report that policies are determined by the policy process and add that in any case, given the uncertain basis of analysis, it is preferable to rely on the policy process.

The dominant theory of the process is incrementalism as developed by theorists such as Charles Lindblom (1968) and Aaron Wildavsky (1979). It is impossible to anticipate the effects of policies ahead of time or to anticipate future reactions to new policies and therefore social interaction provides a better basis for public policy. Robert Goodin, a critic, distinguishes among three variants of incrementalism: (1) "Muddle through," a form of decision theory that argues that since we do not know how policy inputs translate into outputs, we settle for what is satisfactory. Hence, we continue to do whatever seems to work satisfactorily. (2) "Learn by doing," in which incrementalism becomes a research strategy for learning by doing and produces small adjustments in a policy or program based on experience with the policy. (3) "Adaptation," a strategy for correcting mistakes by making modest changes. The more modest they are the less likely one is to foreclose future options (Goodin, 1983: Chap. 2).

Policy analysis has an uneasy role in this incremental process. Most of the proponents worry about the excesses of rationality and expertise and professional analysis (Lindblom,

1968; Wildavsky, 1979) or they note that analysis is often largely irrelevant to policy outcomes (e.g., Goldstein et al., 1978). This charge has led to a large number of studies describing the functions that analysis does play in a largely incremental process (see review in Jenkins-Smith, 1990: 47–55). One of the most interesting has been Weiss' (1977) claim that analysis has an indirect effect on policy by gradually enlightening officials about issues and alternatives. Analysis in this perspective "provides the intellectual background of concepts, orientations, and empirical generalizations that inform policy. As new concepts and data emerge, their gradual cumulative effect can be to change the conventions policymakers abide by and to reorder the goals and priorities of the practical policy world" (p. 544).

Incrementalism is often criticized as essentially conservative because it provides no basis for dealing with major social problems or designing policy interventions. According to Paris and Reynolds (1983), it assumes that public problems are intractable and that policy learning comes from personal learning rather than from analysis, and thus offers an inadequate and reactive response. "The neoconservative reaction is a council of despair . . . guided by so few criteria of adequacy that it amounts to the proposal that essentially irrational ideologies be the inputs to the decisionmaking process . . ." (p. 259). And Goodin (1983: 34) adds that without a theory, incrementalists have no way to decide when they should intervene or how to interpret results.

II. A CRITICAL PERSPECTIVE ON POLICY STUDIES

A number of observers take a very different approach to public policy and offer a critique of the dominant theories and practices described in the last section. The critique is consistent with an increasingly widespread world view that challenges many of the tenets of positivism and traditional social science. Two researchers at the Stanford Research Institute reviewed recent developments in a variety of disciplines from biology to political science to linguistics and list seven ways in which the map of reality is changing significantly within these disciplines[4]:

1. From a simple probabilistic world to a complex and diverse one
2. From a single hierarchy to several interacting orders
3. From a machine like universe to one in which everything is interconnected, and each part can tell us something about the whole
4. From a determinate to an indeterminate universe, in which prediction and control are impossible
5. From direct to mutual causality making causal influences difficult to specify
6. From systems built on simple units to a system created in unpredictable ways
7. From objectivity to an appreciation that there are multiple pespectives (Schwartz and Ogilvy, 1979)[5]

Intellectually stimulated by this new paradigm and troubled by the discouraging record of policy research (Cook, 1985: 29–38), criticism of traditional approaches to policy studies has been growing. Although there are some differences among the critics, there is a broad agreement that the dominant theories—both analysis and process theories—are deeply flawed because they demean the political process and separate empirical studies from value discussions. First, positive methodology is deeply flawed in assuming there is an objective reality that we can learn about through proper methods of research. Second, policy raises value questions and discussions of values needs to be part of any policy analysis or policy process. Third, since one cannot objectively prove that one set of values is desirable, it is necessary to arrange for a reasoned discourse about policy alternatives, including value positions. Ideally, such a discourse will take place in a broad participatory process where people are encouraged to explore their common life and perspectives on the public interest.

A. Methodological Concerns

Critics begin by challenging the content and methodology of the dominant economic paradigm and its assumption that there is an objective and knowable basis for public policy. There is no objective reality that we can know independently; rather there are multiple views of social reality and policy problems and no definitive way to adjudicate among them. There are several reasons for accepting a plurality of views. Most obviously, social relations are so complex and multicausal that it is difficult if not impossible to describe and explain events fully. More importantly, individuals try to understand their world and in doing so they construct meanings and then respond to these social constructions rather than to the world itself (Berger and Luckmann, 1967). Observers operate within their own understandings of reality and subjective knowledge and cannot know reality apart from their assumptions (Cook, 1985: 24–25; Popper, 1959). These understandings change as individuals adapt their behavior on the basis of their experiences, and therefore generalizations and predictions about the future are not reliable. Since interests are subjectively based and people can be mistaken about what is in their interests, there is no justification for using preferences as a basis for public policy.

This methodological point—policy problems and issue can be defined in different ways— is crucial to the critics' case. Further the most important policy debates are those among different social constructions and policy definitions (Reich, 1988; Stone, 1988). For example, explanations for poverty will differ according to assumptions about the relationship between individuals and society and the relative importance of such values as equality, efficiency, and individual rights (Hawkesworth, 1987). And policy elites frequently trace policy problems to a narrow band of offenders rather than define them as general public problems. Thus, drinking has been defined as a problem for alcoholics, which allows officials to focus the blame on a few people and ignore the social problem of normal drinkers (Moore, 1988).

It follows that all policy arguments, like all facts in general, are "theory laden," which means that each set of facts assumes a distinctive world view about what is important and what causes what. There is no independent or objective reference point for deciding among them (Allison, 1969; Kuhn, 1962). This lack of objectivity and the reality of a pluralism of meanings is the central characteristic of what is often termed the postpositivist era. According to Reich (1988), in a postpositivist world, analysts should not simply try to solve problems and propose means. Their challenge is "also to offer alternative ways of understanding public problems and possible solutions and thus to expose underlying norms to critical examination" (p. 6). Instead of satisfying existing preferences, analysts should clarify them and pose alternatives.

An important group among the critics propose that "interpretive research" be used in place of a positivist approach to research.[6] Since humans have intentions and try to act meaningfully, research methods drawn from the natural sciences are inappropriate. It is less important to know how many hold a particular opinion, and it is more important to explore the meaning that people attribute to this opinion. Thus, research should seek to understand and interpret what people mean by their preferences and actions. We need to understand the meaning that the poor ascribe to their situation and the interpretation they give to policy options. If we do not, and they view a policy as externally imposed, they will resist it (Jennings, 1987: 150).

Because meanings depend on their context, they have to be both observed and interpreted. First-level observations describe what subjects are doing, how they understand what they are doing, and the meaning they attach to their actions. Second-level findings interpret what people do, which is referred to as bracketing. They ask about the norms and values people hold, how they arose, how they are maintained, and how they can be changed (Paris and Reynolds, 1983: 172; Rabinow and Sullivan, 1979).

Interpretive research is often used to critique those in authority. Researchers ask how those in charge of a situation understand the people they oversee and then interpret how that understanding affects the recipients of the policy. For example, an interpretive study of juvenile justice showed that data on delinquency do not represent objective facts. Rather they were created by those coping with delinquency and thus serve the needs of these officials (Cicourel, 1965). Understanding how citizens view issues is important to avoid results such as the "white flight" response to busing policy. Understanding how policy makers view citizens is important to determine whether the facts they work with are ideologically based. "Information on the understandings of both policy maker and citizen may be important to obtaining sound, relevant empirical premises for policy arguments, and this is precisely what such participant observation attempts to offer" (Paris and Reynolds, 1983: 183–184).

The observer is no longer a neutral analyst but is part of this world of meaning and interpretation; "there is no outside, detached standpoint from which we gather and present brute data. When we try to understand the cultural world, we are dealing with interpretations and interpretations of interpretations" (Rabinow and Sullivan, 1979: 7). We have to be engaged in a situation in order to understand it. A problem can arise if the subject does not agree with an interpretation of his or her behavior. Who is correct? Interpretivists argue that an interpretation has to be consistent with an actor's view and has to be intelligible to them, but this is not wholly satisfactory. Policy designers may want to challenge a subject's view of their behavior or they may want to point to macrostructural conditions in the society that a subject may be blind to (Paris and Reynolds, 1983: 185–190).[7] Some avoid this problem by promoting "reasoned discourse" as described below rather than offering interpretations.

B. Value Choices and Public Policy

Policy is inherently about value choices and those in the policy studies community need to deal explicitly with value statements. Normative debate is impossible within the traditional framework of policy analysis because it separates facts from values. Although it is true that facts cannot be used to establish certain values on an objective basis, facts and values are integrally related. First, as noted above, all sets of facts are based on theories that assume certain values rather than others. The meaning of the facts depends on these values that need to be discussed openly. Second, facts can be used to think about values, examine their impacts, and select among them (Hawkesworth, 1987). Current discussions of health care policy implicitly involve debates over the values of equity and efficiency. Each of these values makes a different set of facts relevant, but these facts in turn can help examine how appropriate the values are (Smith and Jennings, 1977).

C. Reasoned Discourse

Since policy choices based on values cannot be empirically proven, how does one avoid relativism and select among policy alternatives? It is important to be aware of assumptions and value positions implicit in different choices. It is necessary to go further, however, and explore them critically. Any set of assumptions overlooks opportunities for change that were not anticipated by the model making it easy to conclude that the situation assumed in the model is impossible to change (Hirschman, 1979). The only recourse is to design a reasoned and critical discourse among different perspectives or policy options using the discourse to both pose alternatives and critique the options.

Reasoned discourse is very different from the usual view of policy making. Market institutions and cost-benefit analysis are designed to aggregate interests. They ignore political processes for informing and persuading and developing new preferences.[8] Similarly, process theories rely on political knowledge to describe how individuals and groups interact according to their preferences, how they bargain and negotiate a compromise, or how they revise their views through trial and error. However, they do not try to explain the reasons for their views or look for occasions where individuals or groups may reflect on their views and change them as they interact with others. According to the critics both traditions—analysis and process—are flawed. They uncritically accept existing preferences and assume that values are outside of their scope of concern (Hawkesworth, 1988: 24–25). Preferences are unreliable guides for two reasons. First, individuals' rational assessments of their preferences are frequently unreliable guides to what individuals would prefer if they were better informed or took a longer view. Second, people construct their own meanings about the world, none of which are generally and objectively true. For both reasons, it is useful to try to understand preferences, where they come from, and how they can be changed.

These writers turn to an older tradition of rationalism as reasoned reflection. Rationality changes from an instrumental search for appropriate means to accomplish policy goals to reflection on assumptions and choices. One influential source for the approach is Habermas (1971, 1975), who argues that preferences are heavily influenced by prevailing social norms. The only way to avoid being constrained by these is to reflect on them critically. By means of such reflection, citizens can arrive at a rational (reasoned, thoughtful) consensus. It is not sufficient, however, simply to have individuals negotiate among themselves for that will only produce a distorted result. Instead they need to come together as a community and through fully open communication, critically examine several perspectives and the obstacles that keep them from arriving at a rational consensus. In such a community with open and voluntary discourse, members can test the validity of different norms and agree on which are "right."[9]

The critics offer several versions of such a decision process, although none of them assume with Habermas that participants will actually arrive at a rational consensus. Paris and Reynolds (1983), for example, describe a policy inquiry process that encourages citizens and analysts to subject their views or ideologies to empirical evidence and normative critique. Policy theories and proposals differ from scientific statements because they can never be conclusively established. In this sense, they are "underdetermined" by evidence. However, they can be *rationally* established if they are supported by good, albeit inconclusive evidence and reasons (p. 204). A rational research strategy would, "First, construct a set of alternative policy generalizations. Second, eliminate from this set those which can be falsified. Third, assess the comparative empirical warrant and policy relevance of the remaining members of the set" (pp. 210–220). Later they add, "the intellectual attitude of a person who wants a rational ideology must be one of openmindedness. In a sense he adopts the attitude of a scientist, *seeking* consistent knowledge proved by the data, *knowing* all the while that the best he can attain is an ideology defensible by good but not conclusive reasons." Therefore we need political institutions that provide an occasion for analysts to inform peoples' preferences as well as aggregate them (p. 261).

Sagoff (1988) explores how this approach would influence social regulation in general and environmental policy in particular. He rejects the common practice of treating all goods and preferences as economic terms. Instead he offers four distinctions:

1. *Citizen interests* which deal with public interests *versus consumer interests* that deal with private interests.
2. Values that are considered *judgments* about the *good versus motives*, which can include both self-interests and public values.
3. *Public versus private interests*, both of which can be shaped by government actions and public policy.
4. Careful *attention to detail* and openmindedness *versus* use of a particular research *methodology*.

The second item in each of these pairs is consistent with the dominant model of policy analysis based on economic reasoning. Instead of relying on these narrow concepts, social regulation should be decided through public debate and based on moral, cultural, and political reasons. For example, instead of basing regulation on economic efficiency, we should base it on such values as public concerns for health and safety. There is no methodology that we can use to determine these: "we have to rely on the virtues of deliberation—openmindedness, attention to detail, humor, and good sense" (Sagoff, 1988: 17).

Another version of reasoned discourse is presented by Hawkesworth (1988), who is particularly concerned that such discourse address both empirical and value issues. He worries that others separate these by accepting empirical evidence at face value and focus solely on value differences. Empirical statements are only meaningful in the context of specific value positions, and therefore both have to be examined carefully. Values and theories are always "contestable" and "must be judged in terms of the world they envision and the life they make possible" (pp. 86–87). He describes a reasoned discourse about workfare that integrates values and evidence. First, examine the theoretical assumptions on which workfare proposals are based. What assumptions do they make about the poor, the reasons for poverty, and their attitudes toward work and welfare. How well do these assumptions fit empirical evidence about attitudes and the number of poor who would be able to work? Second, determine the consistency of policy proposals. He observes that the two goals of workfare policy are inconsistent. On the one hand, workfare tries to make work experiences interesting enough to transmit work skills; on the other hand, it tries to make the workfare experiences sufficiently unattractive that people will choose to stay off workfare. Third, ask if the policy can be implemented as designed. He notes that past experiences with workfare are not reassuring. People are typically placed in such low-level jobs that they cannot find comparable jobs later. Fourth, ask about the results if workfare were enacted. Hawkesworth (1989: 169–182) proposes that on the basis of evidence at hand, the results of workfare would be highly negative, would impose a lot of control over people, and foreclose debate about the meaning and role of work.

The central thrust of all these strategies is that reasoned discourse involves more than simply opening political debate to more participation. The more basic problem is that experts dominate the process in such a way as to close off discourse and stifle the kind of inquiry that needs to take place. According to Heclo (1978), the official policy community, which is composed of a broad array of different groups and officials, tends to "complexify" policy issues that separate them from the issues dealt with in public discourse. He worries that policy expertise easily becomes disconnected from public concerns. This bias occurs in three ways: (1) Technocrats dominate the process and citizens cannot follow what goes on. (2) Analysts distort policy differences by focusing on utility rather than encouraging reasoned deliberation. (3) Analysis tends to lift up so many uncertainties that it is hard to know how to respond (see summary in Jenkins-Smith, 1990, Chap. 3).

These dynamics are illustrated by a case study of a decision among economists, scientists, and citizen groups about whether to build a dam on the Delaware River. The analysts, relying primarily on cost-benefit analysis, failed to speak to the issues that were most important to the public and political leaders—preventing flooding and providing recreation. Technical studies did not deal with the values at stake and the debate was cloaked in formalities that shut out those who cared most about the issue. The ecologists were intimidated by engineers and economists, who tended to converse with each other in a technical language. As a result, the technical analyses failed to inform political decisions. In reflecting on what could have made a difference, Socolow (1976) makes several recommendations: Submit the proposals of experts to evidence and reasoned reflection; make data more available to all parties; make better use of the hard sciences to establish at least some body of facts; and rely on institutions that are not parties to the dispute but are in a position to collect and disseminate information about the environment.

The critics are assuming that policy studies have the potential to correct technocratic bias if other interests and explanations are fed into the discourse. "The policy sciences, one might reasonably suggest, meet their social responsibilities effectively when they articulate public problems understood only vaguely by those affected and when they formulate strategies to attack the structural sources of those problems before they realize crisis proportions" (Best and Connolly, 1975). The authors of this quotation go on to illustrate how the policy sciences have failed to perform this function with environmental policy. Observers remained wedded to market solutions and failed to analyze the structural problems and the ways in which capitalism leads to a deterioration of the environment. For example, analysts failed to show that corporate oil interests undermined rapid transit on the West Coast and limited the range of products available to the public. Instead of analyzing these dynamics and pointing to social results, the policy community focused on incentives for individuals to pursue their independent interests.

To open up policy formulation, analysts and experts need to engage with citizens in a broader political debate. The model proposes four ways to encourage such a process: (1) Include multiple observers and sources of information; (2) ensure that all have access to needed information and analysis; (3) encourage active participation by everyone; and (4) design institutions to encourage information sharing and learning (Bobrow and Dryzek, 1987: 177–179). It opens the process to a variety of interests and combines analysis and process in a single interactive discourse. On the one hand, professionals need to have their assumptions open to analysis and criticism. At the same time, they have useful information that can inform and perhaps alter the preferences of others. Preferences can change and be informed not only by technical studies but also by ideas and reflections on value positions. The policy community has no purchase on the truth and its technical competence should not be allowed to overwhelm or bias the discussions. Individuals respond to ideas and arguments and political persuasion and are not just creatures of their narrowly defined political interests; rather political actors can bring about change by evoking community and appealing to the public and community interests.

The critics want to encourage far-reaching changes and refuse to be limited by present realities. As a result they have not grounded their comments in a very realistic analysis of the public's capacity or interest in such a discourse. They are correct that the public has a greater capacity for political reasoning than is assumed in traditional models of policy analysis and process, but they also tend to be overly optimistic about that capacity, to link it too closely to public spiritedness, and to overlook the problems in making informed decisions about complex problems. Because their proposals are not very realistic, they have been easy to dismiss.

Even proponents are not very sanguine about their prospects. Fischer (1990), for example, notes that the kind of reasoned debate about norms that he has in mind probably has to wait until society evolves to become more community oriented. And Bobrow and Dryzek (1987) worry that the model's "pursuit of rational normative consensus is inconsistent with the dominant political tradition in the Western world—liberalism" (pp. 181–182).

III. REVISIONS IN POLICY STUDIES

A. Revisions in Theory and Practice of Analysis

In the meantime, those active in policy studies have been making major revisions. In part, they are responding to disappointments with the effectiveness and utilization of analysis and the capacity of the policy process. In part, they have been caught up in the same intellectual shifts in perspective as the critics. Although many of their revisions echo the concerns of the critics, it has been difficult for those involved in policy studies to live with the claim that there is no objectively valid knowledge or comprehensive theory and that analysts cannot play the role of the neutral, objective observer or researcher. Even those who are willing to modify the theory and practice of policy studies are eager to avoid a relativism that accommodates to whatever result comes out of an analysis or out of the policy process. An open-ended reasoned discourse comes uncomfortably close to this outcome. Therefore, most of the revisions in traditional policy studies accept the value of a discourse proposed by the critics but are more interested in using the process to arrive at a defensible position than in maintaining an ongoing process of discourse.

The revisions described here all link analysis and process in some way. Analysis is valuable because it frees the policy process from being held hostage to prevailing opinions and interests or to incremental changes in the status quo. Alternatively, a process that compares and interprets analyses can legitimize one policy choice over another. According to Cook (1985: 21–22), the common element in all of these revisions is multiplism, an appreciation that there are different perspectives on an issue and different ways to approach it. The only way to address these is to incorporate multiplism into ones analysis or research—to take different perspectives, different sets of data, different research methods, or different measures into account. He lists the following types of multiplism:

1. Multiple definitions of concepts
2. Multiple research methods
3. Careful plans to carry out several studies on a single subject
4. More informal synthesis of loosely related studies relevant to a subject
5. Models with multiple causes
6. Testing of several rival hypotheses
7. Involvement by a variety of stakeholders
8. Use of several theories or value frameworks
9. Advocacy by multiple analysts
10. Research with multiple targets

Specific examples include sampling across multiple groups and contexts, placing greater emphasis on literature reviews because they explicitly take other studies into account, using qualitative data to raise research questions beyond those suggested by specific theories, consulting with different groups of stakeholdes, and taking into account the experiences of several implementors (Cook, 1985: 38–44).[10]

Multiplism can be carried out through research by testing multiple hypotheses or using different data sources. Such efforts not only improve the quality of the analysis but also ensure that analysis is more apt to be used. Or it can be conducted through structured discourses such as involving multiple stakeholders or asking advisory boards to monitor an analysis. Cook (1985: 47–49) concludes that multiplism "promises to make policy research more intellectual, value conscious, and debate-centered." He adds an important warning, however. Since biases in research may be socially shared by several groups and interests, multiplism does not necessarily produce different perspectives and may only end by dulling our critical faculties.

Even with multiplism, however, once one acknowledges there is no single objective truth to be found, it is still necessary to establish some criterion for formulating policy choices. According to Bozeman and Landsbergen (1989), credibility offers a more reasonable criterion than objective truth. Credibility refers to the subjective believability of results and means that acceptable results do not depend only on logic and data but also on the credibility structure of the user. In reality, policy makers actually use a credibility approach. Instead of looking for generalities, policy makers are much more apt to rely on history, analogies, and metaphors when they think about problems and formulate policy choices. Most policy choices concern specific local problems where policy makers cannot rely on large numbers of cases or statistical controls. Credibility as a standard allows them to focus on specific problems without worrying about establishing scientific generalities.

Credibility refers to the way in which individuals assess the believability of an argument. It depends on a mix of cues—the experience of particular individuals, the nature of the evidence, and the structure of the argument. It ". . . shifts the focus from the methodological character of policy analysis to the decision process" (Bozeman and Landsbergen, 1989: 365). Further, it suggests that formal analysis is not superior to ordinary knowledge but has to compete with ordinary knowledge. Credibility forces analysts to examine the assumptions they make about their criteria for formulating policy responses, it encourages people to change their minds, and it allows experts and nonexperts to communicate with each other.

It is still necessary to determine which views or perspectives should be included in policy discourse. Several authors propose a framework that specifically incorporates a variety of views. Dunn (1981, 1986) proposes that policy analyses follow a stipulated logical structure that highlights different perspectives and the assumptions behind them. Using Toulmin's analysis of rational argumentation, his framework facilitates critical thinking even though participants may have a hard time looking at what they are doing from a critical perspective. It has two purposes—to ensure that there will be a debate and to introduce new information and ideas. The point is to let different actors into the arena, ensure that participants will focus on different variables, and guarantee critical reflection. This forensic framework is similar to a legal debate. Both sides try to persuade a neutral observer in an adversarial process that is highly structured to assure fairness. By evaluating evidence according to specific rules of evidence, such a process presumably leads to a correct decision (Bozeman and Landsbergen, 1989; see also Foster, 1980).

A second example of discourse among multiple perspectives is Bobrow and Dryzek's (1987) more openended contingency theory. They begin by defining a number of paradigms for approaching policy studies, each containing a set of assumptions about how to define policy problems, what data to focus on, and the appropriate values. Their paradigms include welfare economics, public choice, structural analysis, information processing, and political philosophy. Based on an analysis of the paradigms, they conclude that each can be useful under some conditions, depending on such factors as the amount of conflict in the situation and the tractability of the problem. An approach they call policy design draws on the paradigms according to the goals of a particular policy, its context, and a reading about what could be changed in the situation. They lay out a series of steps to address relevant value questions, to capture the context, and to establish criteria for selecting an approach appropriate to these (see also Smith and Jennings, 1977; Fischer and Forrester, 1987).

B. Revisions in Policy Process Theory

Just as the concepts of multiplism and credibility have opened up the content of analysis, recent developments in the theory of the policy process emphasize its openness and fluidity. The new model is variously described as garbage can theory, revisionism, or organized anarchy theory. It challenges both the rational analysis model—it assumes that policies are driven by goals and incrementalism—it assumes too much predictability in what is in reality a very incoherent process. Instead the policy process is often random and unpredictable. Problems, solutions, participants, and choice opportunities are all present, but they typically exist independently of each other, and may have little relationship to each other. A policy solution designed through analysis will not necessarily address salient problems; those most invested in it may get diverted onto another issue, and it may not be timed to coincide with an opportunity to enact it. And indeed there may be no resolution at all (Cohen et al., 1972).

Writing some years later, March and Olsen (1984, 1989), two of the original formulators of the model, observed that although garbage can theory is very appealing in capturing the reality in the policy process, it has failed to point to opportunities for change, to include a role for intentions, or provide means to resolve conflicts. Sabatier (1991) adds that the model downplays the political role of analysts and policy ideas. A number of other theorists concur and have been making some important amendments to the theory. In general, their versions of the policy process find more opportunities for introducing ideas and change into the process than the original versions of garbage can theory acknowledged.

Heclo (1978), for example, finds that although the policy process is indeed loosely organized, ideas and policy expertise play an important role. As the government has taken on increased policy responsibilities, organized and concerned interests have multipled, each concerned with a specialized policy arena, and sharing a "common base of information and understanding." Policy is made in a severely fragmented governing system linked by loosely organized "issue networks," the members of which share knowledge about a particular policy arena and interact in formal and informal ways. In this version, specialized expertise can play a formative role as experts puzzle over policy problems and promote different ideas and solutions. Viewing policy making at the local level, Springer (1985) found a similarly loose and dynamic process in which problem solving and analysis play an important role. If we are willing to define analysis as ad hoc problem solving rather than the use of a strict methodology, it is clear that analysis is conducted under many different guises throughout organizations and often by individuals who are challenged by particular policy problems.

Kingdon (1984) amends the model by focusing on problems, proposals, and politics, each of which contributes to a "policy soup." "Proposals are generated whether or not they are solving a problem, problems are recognized whether or not there is a solution, and political events move along according to their own dynamics" (1992: 4). Although there may be policy goals as well as program strategies, these do not necessarily relate to each other. In fact, goals are often developed in retrospect to justify policies carried out for other reasons. And yet change does occur and ideas do make a difference.

Picture a community of specialists in health, transportation, or any other area: researchers, congressional staffers, bureaucrats in planning and evaluation offices, academics and analysts working for interest groups. Ideas float around in such communities. Specialists have their notions of future directions and their specific proposals. They try out and revise their ideas by going to lunch, attending conferences, circulating papers, holding hearings, presenting testimony, publishing articles, and drafting legislative proposals. Many, many ideas are considered at some point along the way. I have been struck by how much the process by which proposals are selected from this very large set of ideas resembles biological natural selection. . . . [N]ew elements are sometimes introduced (mutation), and others are formed from previously existing elements (recombination) (Kingdon, 1992).

This revised process theory has important implications for policy studies. We can anticipate these by examining the meanings the theory gives to preferences, ideas, the policy process, and institutions.

Research on individual preferences shows they are complex and are grounded in immediate experiences and weakly connected to policy preferences. They are a complex mixture of private and public concerns; concerns that cannot be analytically separated in any meaningful way (Kingdon, 1988). Nor are they clearly connected to policy preferences. A growing body of research shows that "tangible personal interests are seldom correlated with policy opinions" and "personal costs and benefits are poor predictors of how people wish government to act" (Green, 1992: 128). Moreover, people appear to behave differently in the political arena than they do in the economic marketplace. Whereas individuals respond to price changes of economic goods as economists would predict, that is, they want less as the price rises, when they think about public goods, their preferences do not always vary according to the price of the good or the amount being spent on it. Examples include tax money for environmental protection and shelter for the homeless (Green, 1992: 139).

Thus, preferences are complex and not easily defined as either self-interested or public interested. Instead of characterizing preferences, it is more useful to ask how they are formulated, and by extension how they can be changed. The point is that people are not clear about what their interests are and what would be in their self-interest. They use ideas and new information to reflect on their interests and frequently revise them as they receive new information and as they experience the results of past decisions (Kingdon, 1988). According to Stone (1992), preferences are largely shaped by immediate experiences and a fairly narrow set of circumstances. Constrained by bounded rationality, preferences can be either self-interested or publicly oriented. The important point is that they are formed out of ones immediate situation. "Narrow cognition allows for complex motivation, including moral agency. It suggests that the foundation for group politics is less a matter of individual pursuit of material self-interest than it is of identification limited mainly to others in one's immediate orbit of contacts and activities" (p. 21).

March and Olsen (1989: 160–161) agree. Preferences are not driven by purposes or goals but rather by cues in ones social setting. Individuals are intentional, which means that instead of being motivated by the anticipated consequences of their actions, they respond to cues in their organizations or situations. Instead of always pursuing a rationally defined self-interest, they want to do what is appropriate and fitting. And it can be misleading to try to sort out self- and public-interestedness, since these may or may not coincide. Simon (1985) paints a similar picture. His theory of cognitive rationality proposes that individuals select actions or express preferences that are appropriate to their situation, meaning that they usually have reasons for what they do. But because their knowledge and experience are limited, individuals select satisfactory, not optimal responses and we cannot posit ahead of time or predict what these will be. To do so we need empirical evidence about the ways in which people view their situations. One of the most important and useful kinds of research is to try to understand more fully how people view their situation and what their preferences are. "The study of the mechanisms of attention direction, situation defining, and evoking are among the most promising targets of political research" (p. 303).

The assumption that preferences are always being interpreted and that they can and do change influences the nature of the policy process. According to this revised theory, change comes about when a policy entrepreneur is able to take advantage of opportunities and link problems and solutions. Intentions and purposiveness can make a difference. Further entrepreneurs are not limited to traditional brokering roles. They can and do trade in the currency of ideas and problem-solving strategies to build coalitions and promote change. Political conflict is less about negotiating clear interests, and more about different ways to frame policy issues. Ideas in the form of problem definitions become an important strategy in mobilizing new groups into the process as Schattschneider (1961) suggested years ago.

Leaders looking for opportunities to appeal to new groups for support provides the dynamic for the process. Since individuals form and change their views on the basis of immediate circumstances and group identities, leaders have more success engaging people around such experiences than in making appeals based on abstract ideals and principles. According to Baumgartner and Jones (1991), policy is affected by its institutional setting. When the institutions change, new groups are able to express their beliefs.[11] They describe how policy entrepreneurs explore which set of institutions will help them develop a supporting coalition. For example, if environmental policy is handled through the courts it will mobilize a different set of interests than if it is handled through the private sector. Their research matches other studies showing that learning and change is most apt to occur as people are caught up in solving immediate problems (Mucciaroni, 1989; Springer, 1985).

Learning and change are also mediated through institutions. Whereas economists view institutions as instruments, as ways to improve efficiency and register preferences more accurately, this perspective on institutions views them as ways to bring order to a complex situation and to enable people to learn and communicate new roles. Individuals try to make sense out of their lives, and institutions can provide such meaning, especially when there is a great deal of ambiguity and complexity (March and Olsen, 1989: 27–48). They give people cues about what is expected of them by focusing their attention and telling them what is appropriate.

Sabatier (1988, 1991) and Jenkins-Smith (1990) propose an advocacy coalition model that tracks the conditions under which learning among different interests actually takes place. The model consists first of the policy environment. It includes stable properties such as cultural values that are least likely to change and external events such as new technologies that are more likely to introduce change into a system. The second element in the model are the beliefs of policy makers. These include core beliefs, such as views on equity that are very unlikely to change and secondary beliefs, such as opinions about employment policy, that are more accessible to change. The third element in the model includes occasions for formulating policies. How does one structure these events to encourage participants to reflect on alternative policies? Change is most likely when different views are included, all parties have the technical resources to analyze issues, and there is an apolitical occasion for a dialogue. "The purpose is to force debate among professionals from different belief systems in which their points of view must be aired before peers . . . [The result is] a greater convergency of views over time concerning the nature of the problem and the consequences of various policy alternatives" (Sabatier, 1988: 155–56). Jenkins-Smith reviews a number of policy decisions where such a strategy has been used, and concludes that it works far better than the critics contend, since it does not eliminate political debate or defer unduly to experts (1990).

There are common elements in all of these proposals. First, they assume that there are different perspectives on problems and that ideas are socially constructed. Second, they provide a structure for discourse out of a desire to avoid relativism and arrive at a reasonably defensible policy proposal. They share Cook's (1985) concern to avoid what he calls "mindless relativism," an unwillingness to make any distinctions among different methods. Some methods are still better than others, and some questions are still more pertinent than others. In Cook's version, there is a real world, which we can only know imperfectly, and we can critically choose a desirable alternative only after considering multiple perspectives and sources of information (pp. 57–59).[12]

This revised view of the policy-making process amends the traditional pluralist model of interest-group bargaining by focusing on the ways in which preferences and views emerge and the ways in which policy makers and analysts influence preferences. It amends the traditional view of analysis by paying less attention to finding a warrant for one policy over another and more attention to infusing new information into the policy process. In both respects it fits with the model of the critics.

In other respects, this revised model does not address the critics' concerns. The proposed process does not stress broad public participation and it does not presume that those in power have their own elite interests to protect. In fact, Baumgartner and Jones (1991) found that policy elites were responsible for all of the instances of policy change they describe, whereas the public only became involved after the fact. There are also structural biases according to Stone (1983, 1991). The fragmentation of the U.S. political system means that leaders look for support among those who are apt to give them the most help and this often means business elites. This bias in favor of relatively narrow interests is not due to the power of elites. The reason is more indirect; political leaders rely on those who have the greatest chance of helping them succeed. Heclo (1978) adds a related worry. Although a policy process composed of loosely organized issue networks allows new ideas to circulate, the resulting complexity and specialization make it more difficult to govern. Administrators focus their attention on members of the relevant issue network and on the technical aspects of issues. As a result, they are less apt to spend time developing broad policy positions or explaining policies to a broad public or mobilizing a broad constituency.

IV. POLICY STUDIES THEORY RECONSIDERED

Policy studies as a field provides an interesting challenge. It includes descriptive and explanatory theories of the policy process on the one hand and also prescriptive theories about how to intervene in that process to make it more effective. By and large these two strains of theory have developed separately from each other and even counter to each other. Theories of rational analysis do not take into account the realities of the policy process or organizational decision making and implementation. It is easy to find evidence they are not widely used or used only indirectly to enlighten policy makers "over the long run." Similarly, theories of the policy process overlook opportunities for intervening in that process and bringing about change, and the only way for rational intentions and ideas to play a role has been to override that incremental process of trial and error and adjustment. Theories of analysis and process are therefore linked in an uneasy tension in which each presumably counteracts the weaknesses in the other.

In response to this stalemate, a sizeable body of criticism has emerged within the field that has focused on the technocratic bias in analysis and the conservatism of the process model and their mutual inability to explain or point to possibilities for significant political, value-oriented change. The critics recognize a plurality of theories that shape how we view policy problems and interventions and insist that policy studies should deal overtly with value issues. Although some urge a new approach to research that focuses on interpreting reality rather than demonstrating truth, most of their prescriptions involve broad public discourse among different value positions and an emphasis on defining a public interest.

In the meantime, some important revisions are making their way into the field of policy studies both in theories about analysis and the policy process. These revisions are interesting because they link analysis and process theories and potentially can address their respective weaknesses. They could make analysis more "usable" in the broadest sense of that term and harness it to encourage change through the policy process. Revised views of analysis adopt some of the arguments of the critics and write about mediating among different views. Revised views of the policy process take ideas and belief systems more seriously and open the way for a more creative and less insulated role for analysis. By stressing multiple methods and discourse, they open up the process to involve interaction rather than aggregation. Participants in that process need to be more self-conscious about their views and modest about their conclusions.

Analysis can play several roles in this interactive process:

1. Analysis can facilitate change by introducing new ideas, but it will be more effective if it does so as part of a political debate rather than in the form of abstract ideas or methodologically valid arguments. As Kingdon (1992) observes, "ideas don't drive changes by themselves, since they must be coupled with more conventional political forces, but ideas do have a considerable independent impact on policy outcomes." This observation leads him to call for more research on the ways in which policy elites use analysis and ideas to persuade others. It also means that policy analysts are not neutral contributors to the policy process and largely outside of it but students of that process and participants in it.

2. It is more important for analysis to generate different perspectives on problems and introduce information into the process than to offer solutions to problems. Because people change their views, and because definition of interests are socially constructed, analysis in the form of research into policy alternatives and their probable impacts can help policy actors define what is in their interest. Such redefinitions can have an important impact on the policy process.

3. Insofar as analysis and policy research are directed to the public, it will have most impact by contributing to discussions around issues of immediate concern to them rather than by appealing to more remote public interests. Analysts need to understand the reasons for peoples' preferences and biases and then join in a discourse in which participants reconsider and enlarge their preferences. Discourse about immediate concerns can deal with both self-interests and publicly oriented interests, and there is a greater chance of arriving at a credible policy response in the context of immediate concerns than through appeals to public interests. Evoking public interests is not impossible, however. For example, the deficit could become increasingly salient to the public and they in turn could force the issue networks to deal with this cross-cutting public issue.

4. Institutions can bring some useful order and structure into this process. The fluid, open-ended process described in the revised theory can be very complex and confusing, which in turn can make it hard for unorganized interests to find an entree into the process. This

same complexity makes it easier for well-defined interests to be more involved in the process and for governing officials to pay more attention to them. Simpler and more predictable institutions can make it easier for political entrepreneurs to mobilize and inform less powerful groups and can insure those groups get the information they need to contribute to debates.[13]

One last caveat is in order. The revised theory of the policy process rejects the equilibrium assumptions associated with both traditional policy analysis and incremental policy processes. Although real change is possible, there is no guarantee that it will come about or that entrepreneurs will mobilize multiple perspectives or look for new ways to define policies (e.g., March and Olsen, 1985: 54–57). Because of its complexity, there are biases in the system operating against such changes. Thus, it is very possible that the critics' fears will not be assuaged, that policy analysis will continue to be technocratic and separate from a broader public debate over values, and that this insulation will make it difficult to deal creatively with policy issues. This continuing concern is very real and timely according to Vaclav Havel, a dissident playwright, leader of the Czechoslovakian revolution, and former president of that country.

> Man's attitude to the world must be radically changed. We have to abandon the arrogant belief that the world is merely a puzzle to be solved, a machine with instructions for use waiting to be discovered, a body of information to be fed into a computer in the hope that, sooner or later, it will spit out a universal solution. . . . A politician must become a person again, someone who trusts not only a scientific representation and analysis of the world, but also the world itself. He must believe not only in sociological statistics, but also in real people. He must trust not only an objective interpretation of reality, but also his own soul; not only the summary reports he receives each morning, but also his own feeling (Speech at World Economic Forum, Davos, Switzerland, February 4, 1992).

NOTES

1. It is often hard to remember now, given frequent charges that policy analysis has become a conservatizing force, but originally policy studies developed as a challenge to the conservatizing tendencies of behavioralism and its uncritical stance towards the policy process (Easton, 1969; Surkin and Wolfe, 1970).

2. An evenhanded description of the economic model by a political scientist is found in Rhoads (1985). Analyses of its assumptions can be found in Bobrow and Dryzek (1987) and Jenkins-Smith (1990).

3. Ostrom (1982) reminds us that this assumption is not as limiting as it might seem at first. Inductive models, which begin by describing peoples' actual preferences are limited to actual behavior. Methodological individualism, by virtue of its narrower assumptions, can ask how individuals would behave under different policies or institutional rules.

4. Lincoln (1985) discusses this work in more detail in her own recent edited collection of essays describing the new paradigm as it affects research and organization studies.

5. For similar descriptions of an emerging paradigm see Palumbo (1985), Lincoln (1985), and Mason and Mitroff (1981).

6. The approach is described by proponents in Schutz (1977), Rabinow and Sullivan (1979), Bernstein (1977), Healy (1986), Torgerson (1986), and Jennings (1987). It is sympathetically analyzed in Paris and Reynolds (1983: 166ff) and Dallmayr and McCarthy (1977).

7. Bergmann (1985) illustrates how a labor economist could use interpretive theory. Economists are famous, she observes, for making unwarranted assumptions about individual preferences deduced from their theories and not based on observations. As an example, she cites a well-known economic argument that unemployed persons could have taken another job at a lower wage or in a different

location but have chosen not to, and by inference have a preference for leisure over work in their situation. Economists are assuming that people select jobs on the basis of wages and that opportunities for lower-paying jobs are present but typically offer no empirical support. This research poses some important questions:

> What are the options that laid-off people think they face? What are their attitudes and behaviors when faced with such options? . . . [S]omeone seriously interested in the purely factual issues . . . might try to interview a few dozen or a few hundred laid-off workers. The workers could be asked about how they explore their options, what they think their options are, and what their attitudes toward those options are'' (pp. 34–35).

8. The studies that specifically critique economic thinking for public policy is voluminous. Some of the sources include Bergmann (1989), Best and Connolly (1975), Bobrow and Dryzek (1987), Fischer (1990), Goodin (1982), Hawkesworth (1987), MacRae (1973, 1976), Nelson (1977), Rhoads (1985), Sagoff (1988), Schneider and Ingram (1990), Stone (1980, 1983), and Tribe (1972).
9. For a review of meanings of rationality, see Cahill and Overman (1990). For reviews of this approach, see Paris and Reynolds (1983), Dallmayr (1986), and Hawkesworth (1987). Brunner (1991) places the approach in the context of Lasswell's early formulation. Kelman (1987) applies it to policy-making process.
10. For similar discussions of analytic developments, see Kelly (19868), Palumbo and Nachmias (1983), and MacRae (1976).
11. There is a growing literature on institutions. See, e.g., Brandl (1988), Hirschman (1970), Nelson (1977, 1987), Wildavsky (1987), Huff (1985), Berman (1980), and Palumbo (1985).
12. This reasoning fits with those social scientists who write about the ''thereness'' of reality. Even though we view reality through partial perspectives, those models still have to confront an external reality which, however imperfectly, can amend and alter the models (e.g., Kaplan, 1965).
13. March and Olsen (1989: 27), R. Nelson (1977), Palumbo (1985), Huff (1985), Berman (1980).

REFERENCES

Allison, G. (1969). Conceptual models and the Cuban missile crisis. *American Political Science Review* 63(3): 689–718.

Baumgartner, F. R., and Jones, B. D. (1991). Agenda dynamics and policy subsystems. *Journal of Politics* 53: 1044–1074.

Berger, P., and Luckmann, T. (1967). *The Social Construction of Reality.* Doubleday, Garden City, NY.

Bergmann, B. R. (1989). Why do economists know so little about the economy? In *Unconventional Wisdom.* S. Bowles, R. Edwards, and W. Shepherd (Eds.). Houghton Mifflin, Boston.

Berman, P. (1980). Thinking about programmed and adaptive implementation: Matching strategies to situations. In *Why Policies Succeed or Fail.* H. Ingram and D. Mann (Eds.). Sage, Beverly Hills, CA.

Bernstein, R. (1977). *The Restructuring of Social and Political Theory.* Harcourt Brace, New York.

Best, M., and Connolly, W. (1975). Market images and corporate power: Beyond the 'economics of environmental management.' In *Public Policy Evaluation.* K. Dolbeare (Ed.). Sage, Beverly Hills, CA.

Bobrow, D., and Dryzek, J. (1987). *Policy Analysis By Design.* University of Pittsburgh, Pittsburgh, PA.

Bozeman, B., and Landsbergen, D. (1989). Truth and credibility in sincere policy analysis. *Evaluation Review* 13(4): 355–379.

Brandl, J. (1988). On politics and policy analysis as the design and assessment of institutions. *Journal of Policy Analysis and Management* ;7: 419–424.

Brewer, G., and deLeon, P. (1983). *The Foundations of Policy Analysis.* Dorsey, Homewood, IL.

Brunner, R. (1991). The policy movement as a policy problem. *Policy Sciences* 24: 65–98.

Buchanan, J. (1987). The constitution of economic policy. *American Economic Review* 77: 243–250.

Cahill, A. G., and Overman, E. S. (1990). The evolution of rationality in policy analysis. In *Policy Theory and Policy Evaluation*. S. Nagel (Ed.). Greenwood, New York.

Cicourel, A. (1965). *The Social Organization of Juvenile Justice*. Wiley, New York.

Cohen, M. D., March, J. G., and Olsen, J. P. (1972). A garbage can model of organizational choice. *Administrative Science Quarterly* 25: 89–101.

Cook, T. D. (1985). Postpositivist critical multiplism. In *Social Science and Social Policy*. R. Shotland and M. Mark (Eds.). Sage, Beverly Hills, CA, pp. 21–62.

Dallmayr, F. R. (1986). Critical theory and public policy. In *Policy Analysis: Perspectives, Concepts, and Methods*. S. Nagel (Ed.). JAI Press, Greenwich, CN.

Dallmayr, F., and McCarthy, T. (1977). *Understanding and Social Inquiry*. University of Notre Dame Press, Notre Dame, IN.

deLeon, P. (1988). *Advice and Consent: The Development of the Policy Sciences*. University of Pittsburgh Press, Pittsburgh, PA.

Dunn, W. N. (1981). *Public Policy Analysis*. Prentice-Hall, Englewood Cliffs, NJ.

—— (1986). *Policy Analysis: Perspectives, Concepts, and Methods*. JAI Press, Greenwich, CT.

Easton, D. (1969). The new revolution in political science. *American Political Science Review* 63: 1051–1061.

Fischer, F. (1990). *Technocracy and the Politics of Expertise*. Sage, Beverly Hills, CA.

Fischer, F., and Forester, J. (Eds.) (1987). *Confronting Values in Policy Analysis*. Sage, Beverly Hills, CA.

Foster, J. L. (1980). An advocate role model for policy analysis. *Policy Studies Journal* 8: 958–964.

Garson, G. D. (1980–1981). From policy science to policy analysis: A quarter century of progress? *Policy Studies Journal*, Special Issues No. 2: 534–44.

Goldstein, M. S., Marcus, A., and Rausch, N. (1978). The nonutilization of evaluation research. *Pacific Sociological Review* 21: 21–44.

Goodin, R. E. (1982). *Political Theory and Public Policy*. University of Chicago, Chicago.

Green, D. P. (1992). The price elasticity of mass preferences. *American Political Science Review* 86(1): 128–148.

Habermas, J. (1971). *Knowledge and Human Interests*. Translated by J. J. Shapiro, Beacon, Boston.

—— (1975). A postscript to *Knowledge and Human Interests*. *Philosophy of the Social Sciences* 3: 157–189.

Haveman, R., and Weisbrod, B. (1975). Defining benefits of public programs. *Policy Analysis* 1: 169–196.

Hawkesworth, M. (1987). *Theoretical Issues in Policy Analysis*. State University of New York Press, Albany, NY.

Healy, P. (1986). interpretive policy inquiry. *Policy Sciences* 19: 381–396.

Heclo, H. (1978). Issue networks and the executive establishment. In *The New American Political System*. A. King (Ed.). American Enterprise Institute, Washington, D.C.

Hirschman, A. E. (1970). *Exit, Voice and Loyalty*. Brookings Institution, Washington, D.C.

—— (1979). The search for paradigms as a hindrance to understanding. In *Interpretive Social Science*. P. Rabinow and W. Sullivan (Eds.). University of California, Berkeley, CA.

Huff, A. S. (1985). Managerial implications of the emerging paradigm. In *Organizational Theory and Inquiry: The Paradigm Revolution*. Y. S. Lincoln (Ed.). Sage, Beverly Hills, CA.

Jenkins-Smith, H. (1990). *Democratic Politics and Policy Analysis*. Brooks/Cole, Pacific Grove, CA.

Jennings, B. (1987). Interpretation and the practice of policy analysis. In *Confronting Values in Policy Analysis*. F. Fischer and J. Forrester (Eds.). Sage, Beverly Hills, CA.

Kaplan, A. (1965). *The Conduct of Inquiry*. Chandler, San Francisco, CA.

Kelly, R. (1986). Trends in the logic of policy inquiry. *Policy Studies Review* 5(3): 520–528.

Kelman, S. (1987). *Making Public Policy*. Basic Books, New York.

Kingdon, J. W. (1984). *Agendas, Alternatives, and Public Policies*. Little, Brown, Boston.

—— (1988). Ideas, politics, and public policies. Paper prepared for delivery at annual meeting of the American Political Science Association, Washington, D.C.

—— (1992). Agendas, ideas and policy change. Paper prepared for delivery at conference on ''The Dynamics of American Politics.'' University of Colorado, Boulder, CO.

Kuhn, T. S. (1962). *The Structure of Scientific Revolutions.* University of Chicago, Chicago.

Lincoln, Y. S. (Ed.) (1985). *Organizational Theory and Inquiry: The Paradigm Revolution.* Sage, Beverly Hills, CA.

Lindblom, C. (1968). *The Policy-Making Process.* Prentice-Hall, Englewood Cliffs, NJ.

MacRae, D., Jr. (1973). Normative assumptions in the study of public choice. *Public Choice* 16(Fall): 27–39.

—— (1976). *The Social Function of Social Science.* Yale University, New Haven, CT.

March, J. G., and Olsen, J. P. (1984). The new institutionalism: Organizational factors in political life. *American Political Science Review* 78: 734–749.

—— (1989). *Rediscovering Institutions.* Free Press, New York.

Mason, R., and Mitroff, I. (1981). *Challenging Strategic Planning Assumptions.* New York: John Wiley.

Meehan, E. J. (1972). What should political scientists be doing? *The Post-Behavioral Era: Perspectives on Political Science.* G. J. Graham, Jr., and G. W. Carey (Eds.). McKay, New York.

Miller, T. (1984). Conclusion: A design science perspective. In *Public Sector Performance: A Conceptual Turning Point.* T. Miller (Ed.). Johns Hopkins University, Baltimore.

Mishan, E. (1969). *Welfare Economics.* Random House, New York.

Moore, M. (1988). What sort of ideas become public ideas? In *Power of Public Ideas.* R. Reich (Ed.). Ballinger, Cambridge, MA.

Mucciaroni, G. (1989). Political learning and economic policy innovation: The United States and Sweden in the post–World War II era. *Journal of Policy History* 1: 391–418.

Nelson, R. (1977). *The Moon and the Ghetto.* W.W. Norton, New York.

—— (1987). Roles of government in a mixed economy. *Journal of Policy Analysis and Management* 6: 541–557.

Ostrom, E. (1982). Introduction. In *Strategies of Political Inquiry.* E. Ostrom (Ed.). Sage, Beverly Hills, CA.

Overman, E. S. (1988). Theory development in policy science. Book Review Essay. *Policy Sciences* 21: 109–115.

Palumbo, D. (1985). Foreword: Future directions for research in policy studies. In *Organizational Theory and Inquiry: The Paradigm Revolution.* Y. S. Lincoln (Ed.). Sage, Beverly Hills, CA, pp. 7–20.

Palumbo, D., and Nachmias, D. (1983). The preconditions for successful evaluations: Is there an ideal paradigm? *Policy Sciences* 16: 67–79.

Paris, J., and Reynolds, J. (1983). *The Logic of Policy Inquiry.* Longman, New York.

Popper, K. (1959). *The Logic of Scientific Discovery.* Basic Books, New York.

Quade, E. S. (1975). *Analysis for Public Decisions.* Elsevier, New York.

Rabinow, P., and Sullivan, W. (1979). *Interpretive Social Science.* University of California, Berkeley, CA.

Reich, Robert (Ed.) (1988). *Power of Public Ideas.* Ballinger, Cambridge, MA.

Rhoads, S. (1985). *The Economists' View of the World.* Cambridge University, New York.

Sabatier, P. A. (1988). An advocacy coalition framework of policy change and the role of policy oriented learning therein. *Policy Sciences* 21: 129–168.

—— (1991). Toward better theories of the policy process. *PS* 24(2): 147–156.

Sagoff, M. (1988). *The Economy of the Earth.* Cambridge University, Cambridge, England.

Schattschneider, E. E. (1961). *The Semi-Sovereign People.* Holt, Rinehard & Winston, New York.

Schneider, A., and Ingram, H. (1990). Policy design: Elements, premises and strategies. *Policy Theory and Policy Evaluation.* S. Nagel (Ed.). Greenwood, New York, p. 77.

Schultz, C. (1977). *The Public Use of Private Interests.* Brookings Institution, Washington, D.C.

Schutz, A. (1977). Concept and theory formation in the social sciences. In *Understanding and Social Inquiry.* F. Dallmayr and T. McCarthy (Eds.). University of Notre Dame Press, Notre Dame, IN.

Schwartz, P., and Ogilvy, J. (1979). *The Emergent Paradigm: Changing Patterns of Thought and Belief.* Analytic Report 7, Values and Lifestyles Program. SRI International, Menlo Park, CA.

Simon, H. A. (1985). Human nature in politics. *American Political Science Review* 79: 293–304.

Smith, M. P., and Jennings, E. T., Jr. (1977). *Distribution, Utilization and Innovation in Health Care.* American Political Science Association, Washington, D.C.

Socolow, R. (1976). Failures of discourse. In *When Values Conflict*. L. Tribe (Ed.). Ballinger, Cambridge, MA.

Springer, J. F. (1985). Policy analysis and organizational decisions: Toward a conceptual revision. *Administration and Society* 16(4): 475–508.

Stokey, E., and Zeckhauser, R. (1978). *A Primer of Policy Analysis*. Norton, New York.

Stone, C. (1980). The implementation of social programs: Two perspectives. *Journal of Social Issues* 36: 13–33.

—— (1983). Whither the welfare state? Professionalization, bureaucracy, the market alternative. *Ethics* 93: 594–610.

—— (1992). Group politics reexamined: From pluralism to political economy. Paper prepared for presentation at Center for the Study of American Politics. University of Colorado, Boulder, CO.

Stone, D. (1988). *Policy Paradox and Political Reason*. Scott, Foresman, Glenview, IL.

Surkin, M., and Wolfe, A. (Eds.) (1970). *An End to Political Science*. Basic Books, New York.

Torgerson, D. (1986). Between knowledge and politics. *Policy Sciences* 19: 33–59.

Tribe, L. (1972). Policy science: Analysis or ideology? *Philosophy and Public Affairs* 2(Fall): 66–110.

Weiss, C. (1977). Research for policy's sake: The enlightenment function of social research. *Policy Analysis* 3: 531–545.

White, L. G. (1976). Rational theories of participation. *Journal of Conflict Resolution* 20 (2): 255–278.

—— (1979). Approaches to land use policy. *Journal of the American Planning Association* 45: 62–71.

—— (1989). Public management in a pluralistic arena. *Public Administration Review* 49(6): 522–532.

Wildavsky, A. (1979). *Speaking Truth to Power*. Little, Brown, Boston.

Wildavsky, A. (1987). Choosing preferences by constructing institutions. *American Political Science Review* 81: 3–21.

Wolf, C. (1979). A theory of non-market failure. *Journal of Law and Economics* 22: 107–139.

Epilog: Projecting Trends in Public Policy

Stuart S. Nagel
University of Illinois, Urbana-Champaign, Illinois

The purpose of this Epilog is to discuss recent trends in about four different fields of public policy and ideas that cut across those trends.

The fields of public policy consist of:

1. Economic issues, including unemployment-inflation, consumer-business relations, agriculture, and labor policy
2. Social issues, including poverty, discrimination, and criminal justice
3. Urban-regional planning and science policy, including environmental protection, housing-land use, energy policy, and health policy
4. Political issues, including freedom of communication and international peace

The cross-cutting issues consist of:

1. The division of labor between the public and private sectors on these issues
2. The division of labor between branches and levels of government
3. The use of incentives to encourage socially desired behavior
4. The application of meaningful evaluative methods to these issues
5. Deciding on the goals to be achieved, especially at a high level of generality that cuts across these issues

I. THE FIELDS OF PUBLIC POLICY

This section is concerned with describing some of the major changes that have occurred in the main fields of public policy since 1900. Those changes have generally occurred during three time periods. The first period was the era of Woodrow Wilson, partly continuing the public policy program of Theodore Roosevelt. The second period was the era of Franklin Delano Roosevelt, partly continued by Harry Truman. The third time period was the 1960s during the presidencies of John F. Kennedy and Lyndon Johnson. The intermediate time periods tended to legitimize the policy changes that had occurred during the 1910s, 1930s, and 1960s. Thus, the subsequent nonrepeal of (1) the Wilson legislation later in the 1920s, (2) the FDR legislation later in the 1950s, and (3) the Kennedy-Johnson legislation later in the 1980s has served to make those changes less controversial and more accepted.

Another way of thinking in terms of cycles in policy change is by periods that promote greater equality or sharing of productivity advances as contrasted to periods that concentrate on technological improvements for increasing national productivity. Thus, the 1910s, 1930s, and 1960s were periods emphasizing more rights to consumers, workers, minorities, and other nondominant groups. The 1920s, 1950s, and 1980s were periods with a relative emphasis on economic growth rather than equalizing of previous gains.

In discussing each specific policy field, one can ask what happened in that field in the 1910s, 1930s, and 1960s in order to see better how things have changed, although important changes may have also occurred in the intermediate periods. Some subject matters have been undergoing substantial change as early as the 1910s or 1930s, such as consumer and labor matters. Others have not shown much activity until the 1960s or later, such as poverty-discrimination and environment-energy.

A. Economic Issues (Especially Unemployment-Inflation, Consumers, and Labor)

On unemployment, inflation, and regulating the business cycle, the big contribution of the 1910s was the establishment of the Federal Reserve System. That system allows for stimulating the economy to reduce unemployment by lowering interest rates and by lowering the cash requirements banks need to keep on reserve. The opposite is to be done in time of inflation to dampen the economy. It is interesting to note that this kind of monetary policy that had been a radical proposal in the Wilson administration is now conservative economics, especially that associated with Milton Friedman.

The contribution of the 1930s was the explicit establishment of Keynesian economic policy. It involves stimulating the economy to reduce unemployment by decreasing taxes and increasing government spending. The opposite is to be done in time of inflation to dampen the economy. Keynesian economics largely replaced Federal Reserve monetary policy for dealing with the depression, because no matter how low the interest rates are and how much lending money is available, business firms are unwilling to borrow to expand their plants if they are currently operating at substantially less than 100% of capacity.

The contribution of the 1960s and later to the handling of unemployment and inflation is the increasing adoption of a more focused incentives approach. Keynesian policy did not work well for dealing with inflation of the 1960s or later because it is politically unfeasible to increase taxes and decrease government spending sufficiently. Worse is the fact that in the 1970s, we were faced with increased unemployment and increased inflation simultaneously due to the ability of businesses and unions to keep prices and wages high even though demand had fallen off. Monetary and Keynesian approaches advocate stimulating the economy to deal with unemployment and dampening the economy to deal with inflation, but both cannot be done simultaneously.

The more contemporary Reagan and Carter administrations increasingly looked toward using a system of incentives to stimulate potential employers to hire the unemployed and to stimulate unemployed people to obtain jobs and training. The incentives system can also help stimulate new technology and increased income, thereby expanding the need to hire people. The incentives system can also be used to reduce inflation. In that regard, tax breaks can be given to business firms and labor unions for not raising prices or wages. This has been discussed in the economic policy literature but not yet implemented. The inflation of the early 1980s was mainly dealt with by raising interest rates, but that may be too costly an approach in terms of hurting economic growth.

Prior to about 1910, consumer-business relations in the United States were controlled almost completely by the marketplace and a pro-business legal system. As of the Woodrow Wilson years, the Clayton Anti-Trust Act was passed. It was slightly more consumer-oriented than the previous Sherman Anti-Trust Act, which emphasized protecting business firms from monopolies, although business firms are important consumers from other businesses. More important was the establishment of the Federal Trade Commission and the Pure Food and Drug Administration that had a definite consumer orientation. In the field of common law, Justice Cardozo of the New York Court of Appeals established the principle that consumers could sue manufacturers for defective products even if the consumer had not dealt directly with the manufacturer and even if the consumer could not prove the manufacturer was negligently responsible for the defect except by circumstantial evidence. That was the beginning of effective products liability litigation. Consumer rights were strengthened in the 1960s as a result of congressional legislation establishing the Products Safety Commission. The common law courts also established the idea that a consumer contract could be too unconscionable to be enforced, and that consumers must be given minimum due process before they can be subjected to product repossession or a lien on their wages or property.

Prior to about 1910, labor-management relations in the United States were controlled almost completely by the marketplace and a pro-management legal system. Some gains were made during World War I in essential industries like railway labor where strikes could be highly effective. The really important legislation, though, did not come until the 1930s partly because the Supreme Court found wage, hour, and child labor legislation to be unconstitutional. The key 1930s legislation was the National Labor Relations Act (NLRA). It allowed workers to petition for a secret ballot election to determine whether they wanted to be represented by a union, and it prohibited management from firing workers simply because they wanted to join a union. Also highly important was the Fair Labor Standards Act that provided for minimum wages, overtime pay, and a prohibition on child labor. There have been amendments to the NLRA in subsequent years, but the extremely emotional and sometimes lethal battles between labor and management in the 1930s are now relatively noncontroversial.

B. Social Issues (Especially Poverty, Discrimination, and Crime)

In the development of public policy, the have-not groups who have relatively greater power are more likely to achieve their policy goals first. Thus, the consumers succeeded in obtaining important legislation and judicial precedents in the 1910s. Most people considered themselves consumers. Labor succeeded in obtaining important policy changes in the 1930s. Labor has less political influence than consumers collectively do. It was not until the 1960s, however, that poor people and race-sex minorities succeeded in obtaining important policy changes, since they have the least power of those three sets of interest groups.

The war on poverty was an important policy activity of the 1960s. Perhaps its greatest gains were in the form of judicial precedents which held (1) welfare recipients were entitled to at least minimum due process and nonarbitrary classification before they could be terminated, (2) indigent defendants were entitled to court-appointed counsel in felony and misdemeanor cases, (3) delinquents, illegitimate children, and neglected children were entitled to hearings with at least minimum due process and no arbitrary denial of equal protection, and (4) tenants could withhold rent if landlords failed to satisfy minimum implied warranties of habitability. Also important was the beginning of work incentive programs that provided for (1) being allowed to keep a portion of one's earning without losing welfare benefits, (2) being provided with day-care facilities so that mothers of preschool children could work, and (3) being provided with meaningful training. Also important was legislation for rent supplements to rent economic housing in the marketplace and for food stamps to buy food in the marketplace rather than rely on federal commodities or food handouts. The Reagan administration added an increased emphasis on the importance of economic prosperity and growth for dealing with poverty, as contrasted to specific antipoverty programs, and also the importance of incentives to business to provide on-the-job training and to hire welfare recipients.

In the realm of race discrimination, the gains have been mainly at the Supreme Court and congressional levels during the 1960s in such areas as (1) voting rights, by abolishing the poll tax and racial malapportionment; (2) criminal justice, by abolishing discrimination in becoming a juror, lawyer, or a judge; (3) education, by prohibiting legally required segregation and providing federal aid to education that stimulates compliance with desegregation guidelines; and (4) housing, by prohibiting race and sex discrimination in job activities. Any judicial precedent or legislation that benefits the poor is likely to benefit blacks, and vice versa, given the correlation between those two policy fields.

On the matter of criminal justice, the early 1900s first saw the Supreme Court say that something in the Bill of Rights was applicable to the states starting with the principle against double jeopardy. In the 1930s, right to counsel was established but only for capital and serious felony cases. The 1960s saw the important right to counsel extended to misdemeanor cases, pretrial interrogation, and post-trial appeal. The 1960s also saw the establishment of the rule excluding illegally seized evidence on a nationwide basis. That was also a time for bail reform that involved more releasing of defendants prior to trial accompanied by screening, periodic reporting, notification, and prosecution for failing to appear for trial. There were also increased experiments and concern for reducing delay in the criminal and civil justice process. The Supreme Court established minimum rights for people on parole, probation, or in prison.

C. Science Policy (Especially Environment and Health)

The end of the 1960s saw an increased concern for two sets of policy problems that had not previously been salient. The first was environmental protection. Prior to about 1970, people tended to think of air, water, and landfills as virtually unlimited goods unless they lived in an area where there was a water shortage. As of about 1970, people became much more concerned with the public health aspects of air pollution, water pollution, and solid waste disposal. Federal legislation was passed providing for standard setting, permits, inspections, hearing procedures, and other rules designed to protect the environment. Along related lines, prior to 1970, energy was also thought of as an almost unlimited inexpensive product. Since 1975, however, there has been increased legislation designed to stimulate energy conservation and regulate new forms of energy production such as nuclear energy.

Prior to the 1960s, health policy was largely left to the marketplace and private charity. Probably the first big breakthrough with regard to government responsibility was the establishment of Medicare for the aged and Medicaid for the poor. Such programs might have been established sooner, but they required mustering sufficient public support to overcome the power of the American Medical Association. As the elderly have increased in absolute and percentage terms, increased pressure has been placed on Medicare funds. The idea of federal funding is now well accepted, and even the Reagan administration proposed federally funded catastrophic health insurance. Someday there may be government salaried doctors for Medicaid and Medicare patients, as there are government salaried lawyers under the Legal Services Corporation. Doing so is substantially less expensive to the taxpayer than reimbursing the private health care providers.

D. Political Policy (Especially Free Speech, World Peace, and Government Reform)

The previous issues tend to have a chronological relation in the order of consumer, labor, poverty-discrimination, and environment-elderly. The political issues tend to be a more constant concern like the economic issue of unemployment-inflation. One can argue that free speech is the most important public policy issue, because all the other policy problems would be poorly handled if there were no free speech to communicate the existence and possible remedies for the other problems. Free speech, however, was not recognized as a national right in the sense of being applicable to the states by way of the first and the fourteenth amendment until the 1930s. At that time, the Supreme Court first declared the states had an obligation to respect first amendment free speech. The early cases though involved blatent forms of government censorship and suppression of ideas, including criticism of the mayors of Minneapolis, Minnesota, and Jersey City, New Jersey. In the 1960s, the Supreme Court declared unconstitutional less severe nonpolitical activities such as (1) restrictions on most pornography, (2) allowing ordinary libel suits by public figures instead of requiring intentional libel or gross negligence, and (3) restrictions on commercial speech such as lawyer advertising.

On the matter of world peace, the same time periods of expansion in public policy were also time periods when the United States became involved in World War I in the 1910s, World War II in the late 1930s, and the Vietnam War in the 1960s. Part of the explanation might be that the liberal Democrats of the 1910s and the 1930s were more prone to go to war with the reactionary governments of Kaiser Wilhelm, Adolf Hitler, and Hideki Tojo. In the 1960s, the liberal Democrats may have been trying to avoid appearing to be soft on communism more than the Republicans would have to be, which could have been a factor leading to the Vietnam War. More important in terms of current trends is the fact that there has been no international war comparable to World War I or II in the second half of the 20th century, and the likelihood of such a war may be decreasing as a result of recent changes in the Soviet Union and agreements between the former U.S.S.R. and the United States. That trend could be very desirable in terms of making funds available for economic growth that would otherwise be wasted on armament.

The third subfield under political policy is government reform. It can be subdivided into legislative, judicial, and administrative reform. Government reform refers to changes in the structures and procedures of those institutions so as to make them more effective in achieving their purposes and more efficient in doing so with less time and expense. Effective and efficient functioning of government structures affects all public policies. During the 20th century in the United States, there have been significant changes in all three sets of institutions.

At the congressional and state legislative level, the reforms include (1) redrawing legislative districts so as to provide for equal population per district, (2) the lessening of the filibuster whereby a minority bloc of the U.S. Senate could prevent a bill from coming to a vote, (3) an overemphasis on the power of seniority in choosing committee chairs as contrasted to merit or a vote by the committee members, (4) less power to the house speaker and committee chairs to make binding agenda decisions, (5) more voting rights for women, blacks, poor people, and young people, (6) more technical competence available through legislative staffs, and (7) more open disclosure of activities of interest groups and income of legislators. An especially important reform for the future that relates to legislative representation is the idea of expanding representation and participation to provide for voter registration by way of being on the census and vote-casting at any polling place in the country on election day.

At the judicial level or branch, the reforms include (1) free counsel for the poor in criminal and civil cases, (2) encouraging out-of-court settlements through pretrial procedures, (3) shifting cases away from the courts to administrative agencies, (4) the computerizing of court records for increased efficiency, (5) encouraging alternative dispute resolution through ad hoc arbitration, (6) clearer guidelines for more objective sentencing and the determination of damages, and (7) higher standards for admission to the bar and the bench with more emphasis on professional responsibility. An important reform for the future that relates to the judicial process is the idea of selecting judges on the basis of having been specially trained and tested for the bench in law school like high-level civil servants rather than through a system of political appointment or election.

At the administrative level or branch, the reforms include (1) more emphasis on hiring on the basis of merit rather than political considerations; (2) more performance measurement and evaluation of government programs; (3) more professional training, especially in schools of public affairs and administration; (4) a lessening of elected department heads in state government, so as to have better coordinated control in the hands of state governors; (5) more use of professional city managers to supplement mayors at the municipal level; (6) improved grievance procedures, collective bargaining, and working conditions; (7) the development of the field of administrative law for clarifying due process in administrative adjudications, rule making, and judicial review; (8) better coordination of administrative agencies across different levels of government; and (9) more freedom of information for the public to be able to obtain access to administrative records.

E. Mutually Beneficial Results

Table 1 summarizes some of the trends in specific policy fields. The overall idea is that there have been increased benefits for people who had few rights as of the base years of 1910, 1930, or 1950. These people have been the immediate beneficiaries of the policy changes. It is, however, unduly narrow to limit the analysis to those immediate effects. The longer-term and broader effects have generally been to benefit the dominant groups as well, or the total society.

This is shown, for example, on the top row of Table 1. Labor has benefitted from better wages, shorter hours, better working conditions, the ending of child labor, and the lessening of race and sex discrimination. Also highly important is the stimulus those labor policies have had on encouraging the development and adoption of labor-saving technology. The United States as of 1990 might still be using relatively cheap labor and be a lower technology country if it had not been for the successful efforts of labor unions and working-class people to increase the cost of their labor. A third-level result is that the labor-saving technology has made labor more productive and more skilled. This has the effect of increasing wages still further, thereby stimulating greater consumption and the creation of new jobs, especially in service fields.

Likewise, one can go through each of the 11 policy fields and see that the initial policy changes have tended in a direction of increasing the rights of the have-nots. Those increases

Table 1. Some Trends in Specific Policy Fields

Policy fields	Benefits for the have-nots	Benefits for the haves or all
Economic policy		
Labor	Better wages, hours, working conditions. No child labor. Less discrimination.	Stimulus to labor-saving technology. Happier and more productive workers.
Consumer	More rights concerning product liability.	Stimulus to providing better products and greater sales.
Political-legal policy		
Free speech	More rights in politics, art, and commerce	Stimulus to creativity.
Due process and criminal justice	More rights to counsel, notice, hearings.	More respect for the law.
Equal treatment	More rights to blacks, women, and the poor on voting, criminal justice, schools, employment, housing, and consumer.	More equality of opportunity and allocation on the basis of merit.
Government reform	Less corruption, intimidation, and incompetence.	More effectiveness and efficiency.
World peace and trade	Increased standards of living for developing countries.	Uplifted countries become good trading partners.
Social policy		
Poverty	More rights as employees, consumers, tenants, welfare recipients, and family members.	The same rights apply to middle-class employees, consumers, tenants, and family members.
Education	More access to more education.	More efficient economy from better training. Less welfare.
Science policy		
Environment	More rights to cleaner air, water, solid waste, noise, radiation, and conservation.	The same rights are important to all people.
Health	More access to medical help.	That includes catastrophic help from which even the rich benefit.

have in turn stimulated benefits for the total society, regardless whether one is talking about consumer rights, free speech, criminal justice, equal treatment, government reform, world peace-trade, poverty, education, environment, or health.[1]

II. THE DIVISION OF LABOR BETWEEN THE PUBLIC AND PRIVATE SECTORS

A. The General Public-Private Controversy

The long-term trends are toward defining more activities as worthy of public involvement, including government involvement. Explanations for those long-term trends include (1) growth of big business, accompanied by the loss of face-to-face consumer-manufacturer relations and sometimes the growth of monopoly power; (2) growth of big labor and other pressure groups promoting government activities; (3) increasing severity of war and defense needs;

and (4) increasing severity and complexity of large-scale unemployment, inflation, and international trade problems; and (5) urbanization and the resulting loss of self-sufficiency, including the loss of the extended family caring for a variety of relatives.

The form of government involvement has been changing in recent years away from regulation and the threat of punishment for wrongdoing toward more use of incentives to encourage rightdoing such as subsidies, tax breaks, and low interest loans. There is also a trend toward more contracting out of government activities and the use of market supplements or vouchers as contrasted to the activities being provided for by government employees. There is still a trend toward an overall increase in the percentage of the labor force that is employed by government and the percentage of the gross national income that is paid by government.

As for trends among the levels of government, there is a trend toward the national government having an increasing percentage of the total government labor force and government revenues. When it comes to government ownership, however, there may be a trend toward more municipalization. This manifests itself in the public power field where in the 1930s the cry was for nationalization of the power industry. In the 1980s, there was more talk about cities operating their own power companies, partly because new technologies make that more feasible. There is also increased talk about having competing power companies. Thus, this area, like so many others, illustrates the state of flux of the public-private controversy.

An especially important and interesting trend is the fact that government involvement and privatization are increasing simultaneously. Government involvement in the economy and the general society is increasing for reasons mentioned above. Privatization is increasing because the government is finding that some of its increased activities can be more effectively, efficiently, and possibly equitably handled by contracting to the private sector. Thus, indicators of government involvement are increasing, such as government employment and tax revenues-expenditures. At the same time, there is more government contracting even for activities that have traditionally been solely government activities, such as the operating of prisons. In recent years, more government personnel and money has gone into federal, state, and local prisons as a result of baby boom crimes, court orders requiring improved prison conditions, and determinate sentencing that requires fixed terms that are higher than previous average sentences. At the same time, a number of states are contracting with private firms for the operation of prisons and various forms of community-based corrections.

B. The Socialism-Capitalism Controversy

The public-private controversy should be distinguished from the socialism-capitalism controversy.

1. One distinction is that the public-private controversy covers all public functions, whereas the socialism-capitalism controversy is mainly concerned with the major means of production and distribution. Thus, the public-private controversy might refer to the contracting of watchman services by a government agency that now uses government employees or the takeover of garbage collection services by a city that has now become too large for private scavengers. The socialism-capitalism controversy is more likely to argue over whether a government should take over the steel mills or the coal mines from the private sector or return them to the private sector.
2. Another distinction is that the public-private controversy tends to be more pragmatic in looking to the individual circumstances of the activity that is proposed for takeover or privatization. The socialism-capitalism controversy tends to react more on ideological

grounds and to favor taking over virtually everything from a socialistic perspective or to favor privatizing virtually everything from a capitalistic perspective.
3. A further distinction relates to the criteria for choosing among the alternatives. The public-private alternatives tend to be decided by talking in terms of effectiveness, efficiency, equity, public participation, predictability, procedural due process, and feasibility. The socialism-capitalism alternatives tend to be decided by talking in terms of which alternative will achieve more gross national product, freedom, popular control, opportunity, security, and initiative, as is done in the classic and contemporary literature debating those alternatives.
4. The public-private controversy tends to accept a positive role for the government, especially with regard to funding various activities. The controversy is not over government involvement versus no involvement but more over the form that government involvement should take. That often means talking in terms of subsidies, liability rules, regulation, contracting, but not necessarily ownership. On the other hand, public versus private ownership is the key concept in the socialism-capitalism controversy, or at least it has been in the past.

On the matter of trends concerning the distinctions between these two controversies, the trend is toward blurring the distinctions as indicated by the following:
1. Socialists in government have become more concerned with routine governmental matters than they were when they were out of government writing Communist manifestos about taking over the major means of production and distribution.
2. Socialists have become more pragmatic and less ideological, as indicated by the party platforms of the German Social Democrats, the British Labor Party, and both the Soviet and Chinese Communist parties.
3. Socialists are increasingly using concepts like effectiveness, efficiency, and equity, which are associated with public policy evaluation. Systematic program evaluation is increasingly occurring in both socialistic and capitalistic countries.
4. Ownership is lessening in importance in socialistic thinking. This is indicated by the recognition that ownership of the steel mills in Poland and elsewhere in Eastern Europe has possibly not been as oriented toward the interests of workers and consumers as private ownership of the steel mills in West Germany, Japan, and elsewhere in the Western world. Who controls (and for what interest) may be more important than who owns the title to the property.[2]

C. More Pragmatism, Less Ideology

Table 2 summarizes some of the trends concerning various public-private sector activities. The overall idea is that we are moving away from the more extreme activities toward more pragmatic intermediate approaches. That can be seen at both ends of the five-point continuum. The pure marketplace as an approach for dealing with public policy matters has greatly lessened. If one looks at the 11 policy fields in Table 1, none of them are being handled from a pure marketplace perspective, even though the marketplace was substantially more important a generation or two ago. Thus, there is more government regulation, litigation, and use of subsidies and tax breaks in all 11 fields.

For example, in Table 2, the top row concerning labor was almost completely a marketplace matter until the 1930s. The Supreme Court had held that minimum wage laws were unconstitutional and also maximum hour laws and child labor laws. There were no laws yet for

Table 2. Trends in Public-Private Sector Activities

Activities	Trends	Advantages
Pure marketplace	Decreasing except where competition benefits consumers or where government contracts out government functions.	Good for prices, quality, and safety where competition present.
Subsidies and tax breaks	Increasing to encourage socially desired behavior.	Good where politically feasible and where discretion is allowable.
Litigation	Increasing as injured persons acquire more rights and relations become more anonymous.	Good for compensating injured persons, especially if on a no-fault basis.
Government regulation	Plateauing after previous increases.	
Government ownership	Decreasing in advocacy.	Good for activities that private enterprise does not want to conduct.

the Supreme Court to hold unconstitutional regarding race or sex discrimination. The year 1938 brought the Fair Labor Standards Act governing wages, hours, and child labor. The year 1964 brought the Civil Rights Act, which contained prohibitions against race and sex discrimination. The year 1980 brought the Reagan administration with its Enterprise Zones designed to provide subsidies and tax breaks for business firms that reduce unemployment in the inner city.

At the opposite end of the continuum, one should note the reduced advocacy of government ownership even by those associated with socialist politics. The Socialist Party of Eugene Debs in the early 1900s and of Norman Thomas in the 1930s received many votes when advocating government ownership and operation of the basic means of production and distribution in the United States. Many people say that the Democratic party destroyed the Socialist party by adopting socialist ideas concerning social security and labor legislation, but the Democratic party never pushed the idea of government ownership with the possible exception of the Tennessee Valley Authority. That lessening of advocacy of government ownership is not peculiar to the United States. The idea has substantially decreased in the program of the British Labor party, the German Social Democrats, and the French Socialists. It has lessened in various aspects of agriculture and retail sales within eastern Europe and China. Even traditional government functions are now sometimes being contracted out to private enterprise, such as the operating of some prisons, although the government retains control and responsibility.

III. THE DIVISION OF LABOR AMONG GOVERNMENT STRUCTURES

Here we are primarily concerned with how the division of labor among government structures facilitates or hinders the development of solutions to the ideas for dealing with the public policy issues. U.S. government structures both facilitate and hinder such developments.

A. Federalism

Federalism facilitates the development of public policy ideas in various ways. One way is by providing a testing ground for trying out new ideas. Good examples include the contrived experiments of the 1970s, including the housing experiments conducted by the Department of Housing and Urban Development (HUD). In one such experiment, HUD arranged for rent supplements for the poor in a number of communities. In some of the communities, landlords were informed as to what maximum would be tolerated by HUD in order to protect poor people and the taxpayers from being overcharged. In other communities, landlords were not informed as to what maximum would be tolerated. In accordance with true experimentation, the communities were randomly allocated to each of these two alternative policies. It was interestingly found that the communities that in effect had rent control standards tended to charge higher rents under the rent supplement program than communities with no rent control standards. The explanation was that the landlords interpreted the standards as allowing or even encouraging them to raise their rents to the maximum without risking any loss of rent supplement tenants. In the other communities, landlords were reluctant to raise their rents for fear they would lose tenants who reliably paid the rent as a result of the rent supplements and who tended to take reasonably good care of the property as a result of the selection criteria for determining who gets rent supplements. Other examples include the attempts by the Law Enforcement Assistance Administration to fund special pretrial release projects in various communities and then to make comparisons across communities with different types of projects or with no projects at all. One could point out that federalism is not essential for such interplace experiments, since unitary governments also have diverse cities that can be the basis of such experiments. A federal form of government, however, does encourage diversity and an experimental tradition across both states and cities more so than a unitary government is likely to do.

Federalism provides multiple policy-formation places for generating new ideas. In the U.S. context, that means 50 state governors and 50 state legislatures. They are more likely to generate new innovation concerning public policy than if they were just employees in 50 field offices of a national government department. The semiautonomy of the 50 states generates independence that leads to innovation. Innovation in turn leads to increased productivity, although only a small portion of innovative ideas may be productivity successes. Examples include new technological and management science developments in dealing with crime, firefighting, pollution, transportation, and other urban policy problems. State highway departments, for example, do sometimes develop new ideas relevant to road building, and state universities certainly are a source of a great deal of innovation. One might, however, point out that state government agencies as contrasted to state universities have not been as innovative in developing new technologies as private contractors have been. That may reflect a lack of adequate incentives in state bureaucracies, but they are more likely to be innovative under a federal system than under a unitary system.

One of the main ways in which federalism encourages societal productivity is by the healthy competition among the states for attracting business firms and population. The competition is healthy when it is based on offering better governmental services. It is not so healthy in terms of societal benefits and costs if it is based on allowing business firms to operate with child labor, racially discriminatory practices, or unsafe working conditions. Those socially undesirable forms of competition though tend to be eliminated or lessened by federal legislation that provides more uniform standards where they seem to be socially desirable. To a considerable extent, people move from one state to another for reasons of economic opportunities, educational opportunities, and climate/scenery. State governments can definitely influence educational opportunities by how much money they choose to allocate to schools. They can also influence economic opportunities by offering business firms legitimate tax breaks for locating in their respective states, especially where the business firm and the state have mutually beneficial interests. States can even influence the scenery factor by how much money they choose to devote to improving their recreational environment.

On the other hand, federalism can interfere with societal productivity by generating some wasteful duplicative effort and conflicting governmental regulations. The duplicative effort of maintaining 50 state governments may not involve very much incremental cost over the governmental presence that would otherwise have to be maintained if there were 50 or even 10 national government regions or subregions. More important, the costs of excessive duplication may be substantially less than the costs of not obtaining the opportunities for innovation that come from 50 heads rather than one. As for conflicting interstate regulations, the Supreme Court attempts to deal with that by declaring them in violation of the free flow of interstate commerce. When business firms object to so-called conflicting state regulations, they are generally objecting to the idea of being subject to economic regulation regardless whether it is uniform or nonuniform regulation.

B. Separation of Powers

Just as 50 state governments plus one national government are likely to lead to innovative ideas than just one national government with or without 50 regional offices, so also is innovation likely to be increased by having executive and legislative branches of government that are independent of each other, with both separately seeking to appeal to voters. Separation of powers was originally defended as a conservative check-and-balance idea. It could also be defended as a way of increasing innovation. However, requiring that new ideas be adopted by two branches of government and two legislative houses can delay the implementation of new ideas.

There is clearly a healthy competition between federal executive agencies and Congress in seeking to develop technically competent units that can evaluate and propose new policies for achieving given goals. Within the 1970s, four congressional agencies greatly improved their competence in that regard; namely, the General Accounting Office, the Congressional Budget Office, the Office of Technology Assessment, and the Congressional Research Service. The competence of congressional staffs for doing policy analysis has also improved. On the executive side, more systematic policy evaluation is now being done, for example, by the Office of Management and Budget, the White House Domestic Staff, and specialized evaluation units within HUD, and the Departments of Health and Human Services, Energy, Labor, and Defense. Those developments are partly attributable to executive agencies taking the lead and Congress feeling the need to keep up by improving its own policy-evaluation competence. If the chief executive were an extension of the legislature by way of being a parliamentary prime minister, there would be less likelihood of those developments, which are conducive to better governmental policies and societal productivity.

Many recent concrete examples can be given of the development of diverse ideas between Congress and the White House. For example, since 1965, there have been substantial differences between the branches of government concerning foreign policy in Vietnam and Latin America. There have been substantial differences on how to deal with energy problems, inflation-unemployment, and social welfare matters. That has been true when Congress and the president have been dominated by different political parties as in the Nixon, Ford, and Bush administrations. It has also been true when the Democrats have controlled both branches of government, as in the Johnson and Carter administrations. It was also true in the Reagan administration, when the White House and the Senate were under Republican control and the House of Representatives was under Democratic control. The key question is whether the productivity benefit of multiple sources of ideas outweighs the productivity detriment of slowness in getting the new ideas adopted. The system in effect represents a compromise between innovation and stability with innovation especially coming in times of the domestic crises of a depression-recession or a period of upheaval in the demands of relatively worse off groups within society, as indicated by the innovative policy periods of the 1930s and the 1960s.[3]

C. Trends Within Trends

Table 3 summarizes some of the trends in the roles of different levels and branches of government regarding the formation and implementation of public policy. The overall trend is toward increasing activity at all levels and branches of government for reasons mentioned in discussing the general public-private controversy. Within that overall trend, the national government has especially increased its role largely as a result of the increased geographical broadness, complexity, and expensiveness of public policy problems. Also within the overall trend, the executive branch of government has especially increased, largely as a result of the need for speed, technical specialization, and a broader constituency.

Table 3. Trends in the Roles of Levels and Branches of Government

Levels or branches	Trends	Advantages
Level		
National	Increasing, especially on unemployment-inflation, foreign-defense policy, and civil liberties.	Coordination and uniformity across states.
States	Increasing but not as much with an emphasis on criminal justice, property rights, and family relations.	Coordinated across cities and counties plus being closer to where programs are implemented.
Cities	Increasing, especially on zoning, sanitation, police, fire, and schools.	Closer to where programs are implemented.
Branches		
Executive	Increasing, especially on foreign-defense policy and unemployment-inflation.	Speed, unity, and possibly decisiveness.
Legislative	Increasing, but not as much, with an emphasis on taxing-spending policy.	Debate and diversity of viewpoints.
Judicial	Plateauing after previous increases especially in civil liberties & liability.	Relative immunity from the pressures of reelection.
Political units		
Parties	Same as national; more in states.	Candidates
Interest groups	More via PACs.	Organized information and education.
Public opinion	More via surveys and demonstrations.	Feedback

Saying there has been an increase at the national level and in the executive branch may tend to oversimplify, since the policy-making role of states, cities, legislatures, and courts has also increased. It is also an oversimplification because it does not adequately recognize that some public policy fields are very much in the domain of (1) the states, such as policies that relate to contracts, property, torts, and family law; (2) the cities or other local governments, such as zoning, sanitation, police, and schools; (3) the legislatures, such as taxing-spending policy; and (4) the courts, such as free speech, criminal justice, and equal protection under the law.

IV. INCENTIVES TO ENCOURAGE SOCIALLY DESIRED BEHAVIOR

Public policy has the potential for encouraging socially desired behavior by working through five different approaches that can be collectively referred to as an incentives approach to public policy. Those five approaches are:

1. Increasing the benefits of doing right
2. Decreasing the costs of doing right
3. Increasing the costs of doing wrong
4. Decreasing the benefits of doing wrong
5. Increasing the probability that the benefits and costs will occur

That checklist logically leads to such questions as who are the doers and what benefits and costs are involved. The answers depend on the specific subject matters to which we now turn.

A. Some Examples

Perhaps the most basic problem for a developing country or area is to encourage good government in the sense of competent, dedicated people and in the sense of stimulating innovative, useful ideas for dealing with social problems. Using the five-part checklist, public policy can encourage competency and diversity by such means as:

1. Increasing the compensation of meritorious government workers
2. Decreasing the communication costs of people with innovative ideas by providing them with access to mass media
3. Increasing the possibility of removal or demotion from government for those who do not satisfy competency standards
4. Confiscating the gains of people in government who corruptly benefit from wrongdoing
5. Decreasing the risks of whistleblowers who report wrongdoing and providing bonuses for those who report rightdoing.

The realm of political science is sometimes divided into internal and external government problems. External or foreign policy tends to be dominated by problems of how to encourage peaceful interaction on the part of other countries, especially neighboring countries. Relevant public policy incentives in that regard might include:

1. Increasing the benefits of mutual trade by developing agreements to benefit from each others specialties
2. Decreasing the costs of mutual trade by lowering barriers in the form of tariffs, quotas, complicated customs arrangements, and other restrictions
3. Increasing the cost of wrongdoing by developing internationally imposed penalties

4. Decreasing the benefits of wrongdoing by emphasizing that aggressive interaction will result in the acquisition of nothing of value by virtue of policies that provide for destruction of oil wells and other resources if necessary
5. Detection systems to determine that wrongdoing is occurring or is being prepared for

At the macroeconomics level, public policy is primarily concerned with decreasing unemployment and inflation or increasing employment opportunities and price stability. Devices such as manipulation of the money supply or taxing-spending differences are not so meaningful if unemployment and inflation are increasing simultaneously. An economy also can become distorted by trying to order business firms not to justifiably raise prices or by trying to order unemployed workers into certain jobs. An incentives approach might include such devices as:

1. Tax incentives to business firms and labor unions for keeping prices and wages down and also monetary incentives to employers to hire the unemployed and monetary incentives to the unemployed to accept training and jobs
2. Decreasing the costs of finding jobs and workers through better information systems
3. Increasing the costs of violating price-wage guidelines and work incentives by withdrawing benefits and (in rare cases) by fines and other negative penalties
4. Confiscating the benefits of price-wage violations by special taxes on the gains
5. More accurate information on prices, wages, and unemployment in order to allocate the benefits and costs more effectively

The problem of encouraging technological innovation is an especially important problem because technological innovation has large multiplier effects by virtue of its spillover into providing job opportunities, better products and workplaces, less expensive housing, antipollution devices, and other high-technology ways of dealing with social problems. Applying the checklist here might involve noting:

1. Government subsidies may be especially important for technological innovation because private capital may not be available in sufficient quantities and may not be so willing to wait for risky returns.
2. There are wasteful costs in reinventing the wheel, which means public policy should strive to inform those who can benefit from new technologies as to what is available.
3. Penalties can be imposed on firms that do not modernize such as automobile manufacturers or steel mills. The penalties can at least consist of not being provided with bail-out money or tariffs if they are threatened by more modern competition.
4. As for decreasing the benefits of doing wrong by not adopting new innovations, there are few benefits with the exception of not having to adapt or retool.
5. There is a need for more coordination in the allocation of subsidy benefits and tax incentives for technological innovation that may necessitate having a coordinating agency like the Japanese Ministry for International Trade and Investment.

B. General Aspects of Incentives

The incentives approach to public policy should be supplemented by a structures approach whereby public policy is viewed as also providing social structures that encourage socially desired behavior. For example, one can decrease crime through the above-mentioned incentives that cause people to choose right from wrong when faced with a decision dilemma. It would, however, be better to structure social relations so that people are seldom faced with such decision dilemmas. Gun control is an example of such structuring. If gun control does effectively remove a large quantity of guns from circulation, then the likelihood is less that an individual will be faced with deciding whether or not to shoot someone. On a broader level of structuring, one might note that if people have been socialized into considering killing other people as a virtually unthinkable activity, then they will also seldom, if ever, face a decision dilemma of whether or not to kill someone. It would not enter their minds to even entertain the dilemma, let alone decide in favor of the wrongdoing position. One can also appropriately structure relations in dealing with other social problems, as well as crime.

The incentives approach to public policy is as applicable to a socialist government as to a capitalist government. The key difference is that under a socialist government, the incentives are generally directed toward government managers rather than private entrepreneurs. In the field of environmental protection, for example, the Soviet Union was just as faced with how to get factory managers to adopt antipollution devices as the United States is. Under either system, factory managers have been traditionally rewarded in terms of the demand for their products and the lowness of their production costs. Adopting antipollution devices does not increase demand-income or reduce expenses. In fact, it increases expenses. Thus, either economic system requires public policy incentives to get relevant decision makers to operate contrary to the traditional reward system by adopting expensive antipollution equipment.

The incentives approach is applicable to developing areas in either developing or developed countries. The essence of the incentives approach is manipulating the benefits and costs of rightdoing and wrongdoing in order to encourage socially desired behavior. That includes the kinds of changes that are needed in order to develop a developing area desirably. The development of such areas may especially mean providing incentives for internal or external capital and innovators. It also generally or often means providing for good government, foreign policy, unemployment/inflation, economic regulation, crime control, ethnic relations, housing, environmental protection, and energy.

If public policy is important in providing these kinds of developmental incentives, then public policy studies also is important. Policy studies is largely the study of how to make public policy more effective and efficient. Thus, the question of how can policy studies be useful to developing areas is closely related to questions of how can public policy be useful. One can perhaps conclude that policy studies can be most useful by further exploring the ways in which public policy can provide incentives for societal development and improvement.[4]

C. A Bigger Package of Incentives

Table 4 summarizes some of the trends regarding incentives for encouraging socially desired behavior. One overall trend is an increasing reliance on rewarding the rightdoer as contrasted to punishing the wrongdoer. The emphasis on rightdoing manifests itself more in decreasing the costs of rightdoing (such as tax deductions) rather than in increasing the benefits of rightdoing (such as reward subsidies), since tax deductions are more politically feasible. Within the concern for wrongdoers, there is an increasing emphasis on penalties other than traditional jail and fines, such as confiscating profits-property, reimbursement of victims, and penalties by way of missed opportunities that might otherwise be meaningfully available.

The administration of incentives programs may be improving toward a higher probability of the benefits and costs occurring. On the other hand, the role of socialization to make various kinds of wrongdoing unthinkable has lessened with the decreased impact of

Table 4. Trends in Incentives for Encouraging Socially Desired Behavior

Incentives	Examples	Trends	Advantages
Increase benefits of rightdoing	Reward subsidies	Increase	Can buy cooperation but expensive and politically unpopular.
Decrease costs of rightdoing	Tax deductions	Bigger increase	Buys less cooperation but politically more feasible.
Decrease benefits of wrongdoing	Confiscate profits	Increase but only in criminal activities	Could change behavior but difficult to apply.
Increase costs of wrongdoing	Big penalties	Increase	Penalties tend to be absorbed as an expense and hemmed in by due process.
Increase probability of benefits and costs occurring	Better monitoring and bounties	Increase through improved personnel	Essential for benefits and costs to be meaningful, but worthless if benefits are not substantial.
Socialization to make wrongdoing unthinkable	Street crimes among middle class people	Decrease in the importance of conscience	May require special upbringing.
Physical structuring make wrongdoing difficult	Gun prohibition or control	Mild increase	Effective but may not be politically feasible.

the family and the school. There is a trend toward more physical structuring to make wrongdoing difficult, such as better street lighting to discourage mugging and rapes, more areas within the control and responsibility of individual apartments, and more gun control to reduce the availability of lethal weapons. The biggest overall trend is the compositing of an increased variety of approaches for dealing with wrongdoing across all policy problems, including pollution, discrimination, business relations, and not just traditional criminal behavior.

V. METHODS OF EVALUATING ALTERNATIVE POLICIES

The key trend in methods for evaluating alternative policies is a movement toward multi-criteria decision making and the use of microcomputer software for facilitating that kind of evaluation. The essence of multi-criteria decision making is the processing of a set of goals to be achieved, alternatives available for achieving them, and relations between goals and alternatives in order to choose the best alternative, allocation, or predictive decision rule.

The key microcomputer software in this context is Policy/Goal Percentaging (abbreviated P/G%). It involves the analyzing of public policy problems by:

1. Listing available alternatives on the rows of a two-dimensional matrix
2. Listing criteria for judging the alternatives on the columns of the matrix
3. Inserting scores in the cells showing how each alternative relates to each criterion
4. Transforming the scores if necessary to consider that the goals may be measured on different dimensions
5. Aggregating the transformed scores across each alternative in order to arrive at a summation score for each alternative
6. Drawing a conclusion as to which alternative or combination should be adopted

The forms of traditional optimizing that the above analysis can supplement or improve upon include:

1. Payoff matrices, which show alternatives on the rows, contingent events on the columns, and payoffs in the cells from each alternative given the occurrence or nonoccurrence of the contingent event
2. Decision trees, which represent a combination of arrow diagrams and payoff matrices by showing a set of decision forks, probability forks, and other paths leading to a set of payoffs
3. Optimum level curves, which show that too much or too little of a policy produces a hill-shaped or valley-shaped relation with benefits, costs, or benefits minus costs
4. Indifference curves and functional curves, which are considered useful for allocating scarce resources

There are a number of methodological problems involved in systematically evaluating alternative public policies. They include how to deal with (1) multiple dimensions on multiple goals, (2) multiple and possibly conflicting constraints, (3) multiple alternatives that are too many to determine the effects of each one, (4) complicated relations between goals and alternatives, (5) missing or imprecise information concerning such inputs as the weights of the goals or the relations between goals and alternatives, and (6) simplicity of analysis and presentation in spite of the above multiplicity and complexity. On each of those six methodological problems there are trends away from traditional optimizing toward variations on multi-criteria decision making, with P/G% as an illustrative example.

A. Multiple Dimensions on Multiple Goals

The P/G% approach has a relatively distinct way of handling each of those problems that can be contrasted with traditional optimizing. Multi-dimensional criteria are handled by P/G% mainly by weighting the raw scores on different criteria in terms of the relative importance of the criteria and in light of the measurement units used. P/G% also handles multi-dimensional criteria by converting the raw scores into weighted part/whole percentages, which makes them into dimensionless numbers. That is especially useful when the criteria are abstract and measured on scales like 1–5 scales rather than measured in concrete units like dollars, miles, years, pounds, and so forth.

Traditional optimizing, on the other hand, tends to deal with multi-dimensionality problem by working with a single objective function or a composite goal. Multi-objective programming and arrow diagrams are exceptions, since they do preserve the separate goals. Working with a composite goal moves the multi-dimensionality problem back to a process that is separate from the optimizing process. That compositing process often emphasizes measuring all the subgoals in terms of dollars or some other common measurement unit rather than preserving the distinctive measurement of each separate goal.

B. Multiple Constraints

Multiple constraints are handled by P/G% by optimizing without taking constraints into consideration and then making adjustments if the optimizing solution does not satisfy all the constraints. Traditional optimizing tries to satisfy the constraints first and then to optimize within those constraints or to do both simultaneously. Under such a system, one may satisfy equity constraints by giving to each person, group, or place whatever minimum they are entitled to. The sum of those minimums is then subtracted from the grand total available to be allocated. By satisfying constraints before optimizing, the solution reached is likely to deviate more from the unconstrained optimum than by satisfying the constraints after optimizing. This is so because any person, group, or place that scores low on the criteria will receive minimum allocation plus a proportionate share of the residue of the grand total available to be allocated. Thus, any persons who would otherwise be entitled to only the bare equity minimums would unnecessarily receive more than the minimum contrary to the optimizing criteria.

On the matter of conflicting constraints, the P/G% approach emphasizes handling such conflicts through a combination of prioritizing, compromising, and expanding the resources, alternatives, or criteria. Suppose there are minimum equity constraints which say Place 1 should receive $400 as a minimum and Place 2 should receive $200. Suppose further that the total budget only provides for $500. Most traditional optimizing would deal with the above problem of conflicting constraints by reporting that the problem is unsolvable given those constraints. There is, for example, nothing inherent in decision theory, calculus optimizing, or mathematical programming as to how conflicting constraints are to be handled.

C. Multiple Alternatives

Multiple alternatives may be so many that one cannot determine the effects of all of them. This is especially true in an allocation problem where the number of ways of allocating scarce monetary resources to three or more persons may be virtually astronomical. The P/G% approach handles such situations by converting the raw scores into part/whole percentages. Those part/whole percentages are used as allocation percentages to multiply against the grand total in order to determine the allocation for each person, group, or place.

Traditional optimizing is often not concerned with allocations matters because the alternatives are discrete rather than continuous alternatives. By definition, a discrete or lump-sum alternative is either chosen or not chosen, whereas a continuum alternative allows for degrees. Where allocation or degrees are involved, traditional optimizing tends to use a classic calculus optimization approach if one can obtain true derivatives or elasticity coefficients. In most policy evaluation problems, however, valid elasticity coefficients are virtually impossible to obtain because of reciprocal causation, spurious causation, interaction, and unsatisfactory data. As a result, P/G% uses part/whole percentages as proxies for elasticity coefficients. Traditional optimizing may also allocate via the reiterative guessing of mathematical programming. That approach may be unrealistic if it makes linear assumptions. Where nonlinear programming is involved, the computer may get stuck in nonoptimum solutions.

D. Relations Between Goals and Alternatives

The P/G% approach tends to determine relations between alternatives and goals by relying on the perceptions of knowledgeable insiders. Traditional optimizing prefers statistical or behavioral data analysis on the theory that such analysis is less biased than asking interested persons. Statistical analysis, however, often has the serious defects of not being able to deal with reciprocal causation, spurious causation, and interactions, as mentioned above. A typical time-series, for example, may show a positive relation between anticrime expenditures and crime occurrence, not because the expenditures cause crime but because crime occurrence causes expenditures. Even if the statistical analysis can get the direction of the relations correct, one cannot trust the magnitude of the relations regardless how accurate the original raw data is.

The P/G% approach also tends to rely more on deduced relations than statistical relations. This enables one to evaluate alternatives before they are adopted. That is also generally true of payoff matrices, decision trees, and multiobjective programming but not statistical curves for optimum level, indifference, or functional analysis. By deducing relations from known facts or reasonable premises, one thereby avoids such problems in empirical analysis as a lack of sufficient experimental or control group and lack of sufficient before or after data. Preadoption deductive modeling also avoids the problem of policies being adopted to the unnecessary detriment of people and the problem of bureaucratic inertia and newly vested interests interfering with changes if one has to rely on postadoption evaluation.

E. Missing Information

Missing information is often handled under the P/G% approach by changing the questions. Asking for the exact value of an input item can be changed to asking whether the input item is above or below a threshold value. Threshold values are at a point where a higher or lower score will affect the alternative that is considered best. Most people find it easier to deal with questions that ask, for example, whether a probability is more or less than .70 rather than ask what is a probability.

Traditional optimizing tends to deal with missing information by finding the information that is missing. That can be needlessly expensive and it can paralyze decision making. Sometimes missing or imprecise information is dealt with by eliminating cases or variables. That can result in research overemphasizing variables that are easily measured even though they may be relatively unimportant.

F. Simplicity of Analysis and Presentation

On simplicity of drawing conclusions, that is promoted by having a user-friendly microcomputer program that requires virtually no technical knowledge in order to use the program even though the program is based on principles of classic optimization. The P/G% program is like that, but that is not so with programs available for drawing conclusions in decision theory, calculus optimization, or mathematical programming.

On simplicity of presentation, the P/G% approach or the PG table presents results in terms of alternatives on the rows, criteria on the columns, and relations in the cells, with an aggregate total across each row. That approach is in conformity with Lotus 1-2-3 analysis, which is the best-selling software in the world. It is also in conformity with common sense as contrasted to the more difficult presentation formats in traditional optimizing.

G. Conclusions Concerning Multi-Criteria Decision Making

In light of the above considerations, one can conclude that P/G% and related MCDM analysis may have much to offer as supplements to traditional optimizing. MCDM approaches are relatively new compared with the more traditional methods. They are, however, catching on fast largely as a result of new microcomputer software. Programs with names like LightYear, Expert Choice, and PrefCalc are selling well and being widely used. P/G% is relatively new among the MCDM approaches.

In comparison to the other MCDM approaches, P/G% emphasizes:

1. Part/whole percentaging for dealing with multi-dimensionality rather than forcing common measurement units on the goals
2. Postoptimizing constraint adjustments rather than trying to build into the program all possible constraint situations

3. Part/whole percentaging allocations rather than have a program that only deals with discrete or lump-sum alternatives
4. Relations determined by the user's knowledge often on 1–5 attitude scales rather than emphasize relations that provide for more complicated measurement which tend to leave out important relations
5. Sensitivity analysis for dealing with missing information rather than requiring that missing information be filled in
6. Simplicity in drawing conclusions by way of the user-friendly P/G% program and simplicity in presenting results by way of the PG table

It is important to emphasize that P/G% seeks to be simple in order to encourage use of the program and the results, but being simple does not mean being simplistic. Being simplistic refers to being simple by leaving out important considerations. That is contrary to the way in which P/G% and most other MCDM programs work. Along with their simplicity, they actually provide greater detail by (1) separating out the subgoals of the overall objective function, (2) allowing for more goals and alternatives, and (3) being explicit in stating constraints, relative weights of the goals, and the nature of the relations.

One might also emphasize that the P/G% and MCDM software are in a state of rapid development, with new improvements being adopted as a result of new experiences. Microcomputer software does lend itself to experimentation and creative change, thereby stimulating further insights as to how the new software can be made even more valid, versatile, and user-friendly. Such software can thus become even more of a contribution to the development of better decision making in government, law, business, and elsewhere.[5]

H. Methodological Review

Table 5 summarizes some of the trends regarding methods of public policy evaluation. The key overall trend is toward new ideas that combine both simplicity and validity. There is a trend toward the use of microcomputer software that facilitates systematic trial-and-error experimentation. There is also a trend toward an expert systems perspective that seeks to de-

Table 5. Trends in Methods of Public Policy Evaluation

Methods	Examples	Trends	Advantages
Multiple dimensions on multiple goals	Multi-criteria decision making	Increase	Can deal with nonmonetary benefits and monetary costs and multiple goals.
Missing information	Breakeven analysis, best-worst scenarios, and graphics	Increase	Can deal with missing info without having to gather the information.
Allocation analysis	Part/whole percentaging	Increase	Avoids assumptions and measurement needs of OR/MS.
Multiple and conflicting constraints	Prioritizing, compromising, or expanding the constraints	Increase	The expanding approach encourages growth where everyone comes out ahead.
Multiple prediction	If-then analysis	Increase	Fits what good decision makers actually do.
Simplicity	Spreadsheet analysis	Increase	Easy to manipulate including what-if analysis.

velop methods by analyzing how good decision makers implicitly decide rather than trying to deduce how they should decide in light of unrealistic and/or unfeasible premises that relate to calculus optimization or mathematical programming.

More specific trends relate to how to deal with each of the six major obstacles to systematic evaluation mentioned in the methods column of Table 5. Those separate trends involve moving toward (1) multi-criteria decision making rather than single objective functions, (2) variations on breakeven analysis to determine critical values of missing information rather than trying to devise expensive ways of not having missing information, (3) the use of percentaging methods to deal with allocation problems, (4) an expansionist philosophy to deal with conflicting constraints, (5) variations on if-then analysis for multiple prediction, and (6) spreadsheet analysis as the most popular decision-aiding software.

VI. DEVELOPMENT OF HIGHER GOALS

A. General Aspects

One of President Carter's mottos was, "Why not the best?" President Kennedy used to say when people would question his high goals that it was better to aim higher and only get half-way there than to aim not so high and get all the way there. Achieving the optimum is considered to be a high goal, although that partly depends on how the optimum is defined. The optimum may, however, not be high enough, or at least what is customarily considered to be the optimum.

The purpose here is to pursue that thought in the context of public policy problems, especially policy problems that are as fundamental as unemployment and inflation. If unemployment and inflation can both be reduced to close to 0%, then the economy almost by definition is in a state of high prosperity. Such prosperity leads to improvements in all other problems such as reduced poverty, discrimination, crime, and health problems. It can also have positive effects on conditions of consumers, farmers, labor, the environment, housing, and education, as well as civil liberties and international peace.

A society operating at the optimum or above it on various policy problems can thus be defined as a society that distributes benefits and costs in such a way to encourage socially desired behavior regarding optimum unemployment, inflation, crime, and other social problems, but that also does as much as possible to make undesirable behavior impossible and unthinkable.

Achievement brings both personal happiness and societal happiness, and achievement is encouraged by having high but realistically obtainable goals. No goals are too high so long as they are physically possible. Even what is physically possible may be subject to change. It is thus socially desirable for a society to be an optimizing society or one that is seeking to achieve the optimum or the super-optimum on various social indicators. That is true with regard to public policies concerning unemployment, inflation, crime, world peace, free speech, poverty, discrimination, health, environment, education, consumers, and government structures/procedures.

All policy problems are capable of being conceived as having a level of achievement that would traditionally be considered optimum. They also have a level of achievement that can be considered as doing better than the optimum. Table 6 summarizes some of the possibilities. The arrangement is roughly random order. It is difficult and unnecessary to try to arrange major policy problems in order of importance. One could offer something in favor of every problem being the most important problem. They are all essential to the smooth functioning of a society and to general societal happiness.

Table 6. Some Trends in Specific Policy Fields

Policy problem	An optimum society	A better than optimum society
Economic problems		
Unemployment	Zero unemployment	That plus a higher percent of adults in the labor force and fully employed
Inflation	Zero inflation	That plus increased benefits for prices paid
Consumer	Zero fraud	That plus giving useful information
Political problems		
World peace	Zero casualties	That plus world cooperation
Free speech	Zero interference	That plus providing a supportive atmosphere for innovative ideas
Government	Zero waste and corruption	That plus creativity, popular participation, equity, and due process
Social problems		
Crime	Zero crime	That plus zero civil wrongdoing and job wrongdoing
Poverty and discrimination	Zero poverty and discrimination	That plus productive job satisfaction
Education	Zero functional illiteracy	That plus rising to one's maximum, with broadness and inquisitiveness in education
Science problems		
Health	Zero non-aging diseases	That plus health robustness and greater longevity
Environment	Zero pollution	That plus reclamation and renewal

B. Economic Problems

On the subject of unemployment policy, the goal in the Reagan administration was to at least avoid double-digit unemployment, meaning unemployment at 10% or greater. The goal of the Carter administration, as indicated in the Humphrey-Hawkins legislation, was to get unemployment below 6%. A goal of about 3% unemployment is often considered ideal in that anything less than 3% would mean that people are not sufficiently moving upward from one job to another. The problem of goals in this context is not the number, whether it be 10%, 6%, or 3%. The problem is the base to which the percentage is applied. That base is frequently referred to as the labor force, which is generally defined as people who are actively looking for employment. That constitutes about 110 million people as of 1990. An expanded base that might bring the figure up to 200 million people would include the following:

1. All people over age 65 who would be interested in working if they could be provided with job opportunities that are appropriate to the skills that they often have but that they are discouraged from using because (1) there is a lack of public policy stimuli encouraging employers to hire older people, and (2) public policy discourages older people from seeking jobs by decreasing or removing the social security allotments that they would otherwise receive.

2. People with various kinds of disabilities who could also be provided with appropriate job opportunities.

3. Mothers of preschool children who would be working if they not only had job opportunities but also meaningful day care programs and no disincentive loss of various welfare benefits.
4. People who only have seasonal jobs but who would like to have year-round jobs.
5. People who only have part-time jobs but who would like to have full-time jobs.
6. People who have full-time jobs who would like to do some additional work.
7. People who have all the work quantitatively that they can handle but the quality of what they do is substantially beneath their skills.

By adding those last few categories, one can say that the U.S. population is about 95% un-employed or underemployed. The goal should not be to have low employment but on a labor base that does not exclude about half or more of all the people and people-hours that could be included.

On the subject of inflation, the initial goal of the Reagan administration was to get in-flation below double digits, meaning below 10%. One could argue that if 6% unemployment is a desirable goal, then so is 6% inflation on the theory that an increase in one is as bad as an increase in the other in accordance with the misery index put forth by Reagan in running against Carter. One could also argue that 3% inflation is a more desirable goal on a theory of symmetry with 3% unemployment. That implies a slight upward movement in prices and wages stimulates business development and worker productivity. The problem here is also not the number, whether it be 10%, 6%, or 3%. It is the base or formula that is used in cal-culating inflation percentages. The standard procedure is to only look to price changes, not to changes in the quantity or quality of what the consumer is receiving. It is quite possible in an increasingly productive society for a product to double in price and yet for inflation to drop below zero on that product because the quality of what the consumer receives has more than doubled. For example, if a car selling for $3000 almost doubles in price to $5000 but now lasts 15 years when it formerly lasted 6 years, then the cost-benefit ratio has gone from $3/6 down to $5/15 or from 50 to 33%. That is a 17% drop in the cost-benefit ratio, which is roughly like saying that inflation has gone down below 0 to a −17%. This is instead of wrongly overemphasizing that the price has gone up from $3 to $5 or up $2 on a base of $3, which would be an inflation rate of 67%. In other words, we should get our priorities straight; namely, that getting prices down is less important than getting up the quality and quantity of what consumers receive. That is especially true since there is a lot more realistic room for in-creased quality and quantity than there is for substantial price decreases.

Consumer policy is closely related to inflation policy, just as labor policy is closely re-lated to unemployment, poverty, and discrimination. Consumer policy though also illustrates well the distinction between traditional optimums that emphasize removing obvious wrongs, whereas neglecting the less obvious. The obvious wrongs tend to be sins of commission like consumer fraud, which involves active deception. The less obvious wrongs tend to be sins of omission or failures to take affirmative action, such as failing to supply consumers with use-ful information that could enable them to be more rational consumers.

C. Political Problems

Having world peace as measured by zero war casualties would be wonderful. That is true of the achievement level in the middle column labeled ''An Optimum Society'' for every policy problem in Table 6. If, however, there are two time periods and both have zero war casual-ties, the better time period would be the one that has more world cooperation. That includes cooperation regarding unemployment, inflation, crime, free speech, poverty, discrimination, health, environment, education, consumer policy, and government institutions. The specialized agencies of the United Nations strive to achieve those cooperation goals, such as the World Health Organization, the International Labor Organization, and the United Nations Economic, Social, and Cultural Organization.

The United States has a reasonably good record on not interfering with freedom of speech. The main exceptions are where another constitutional right is in conflict, such as (1) due process in criminal proceedings requiring avoidance of prejudicial pretrial newspaper publicity, (2) equal treatment under the law requiring some restrictions on campaign expenditures, and (3) the right to privacy requiring restrained newspaper reporting on the private lives of non-public figures. One could measure the degree of free speech by looking to the number of people held in jail for activities that are critical of the government or other institutions. Getting a score of zero on such interference may, however, not be enough. A society deserves a higher score on free speech if in addition to noninterference, it provides a supportive atmosphere for innovative ideas. That can include (1) requiring radio, TV, and other mass media to be willing to sell time to groups critical of society's institutions, (2) requiring the mass media to give free time to all major candidates if they give free time to any one candidate for office, and (3) making inexpensive cable TV time available to fringe groups who would otherwise not be able to buy time to communicate their ideas.

An important policy problem is the problem of improvements needed in the structures and procedures for policy formation and implementation. That can be considered a meta-problem, since it cuts across all the specific problems, although so does free speech, education, unemployment, poverty, and still other problems. The Reagan administration and others conducted strong campaigns against waste and corruption in government. It would be fine if all waste, corruption, and other forms of inefficiency were eliminated. Again, however, that ignores the sins of omission whereby the government operates wastefully and ineffectively because it is not encouraging creativity with regard to developing new ideas for dealing better with public policy problems. One could also say that if two societies are equally devoid of waste and corruption, the second society is the better one if it stimulates more popular participation in government activities, more equity/fairness in the distribution of benefits and costs, and more due process in enabling those who have been wrongly denied benefits or subjected to costs to be able to defend themselves with witnesses, cross-examination, and counsel.

D. Social Problems

On the subject of crime policy, the Reagan administration and most administrations seemed happy with having no increase in major crimes from one year to the next. The idea of major decreases is considered almost unrealistic. In reality, however, one could make an argument for going beyond major decreases. The "beyond" does not mean somehow having negative crime but rather like the unemployment index, talking in terms of broadening the base on which the calculations are made. The base in this context means what is included as wrong-doing. The usual crime calculations involve adding various felonies like murder, robbery, and rape together and then dividing by the population of the city, state, or nation to obtain crimes per capita or a specific crime per capita. This involves totally leaving out forms of wrongdoing that can be far more harmful than what is included. For example, all forms of negligent behavior that result in death, total disability, and great pain and suffering are not counted as part of a broader wrongdoing index if the defendant's behavior did not violate a criminal statute. This is true even though the behavior violates a statute or precedent relating to intentional torts, gross negligence, or other forms of civil liability. A broad wrong-doing index might also include on-the-job wrongdoing that does not qualify as grounds for imprisonment or damages but does quality as grounds for being fired. A horrible place to live might have no murders but lots of killings through negligence or worker malfeasance that result in life-jeopardizing product defects. Likewise, a society might be a great place in which to live even if it has some murders and other felonies but virtually no negligence or worker malfeasance. There is a need for a more meaningful crime index or wrongdoing index that will consider more forms of wrongdoing, although not necessarily giving them all equal weight. As of now, many very serious forms of wrongdoing are given virtually no weight at all in our goal for reducing individual wrongdoing.

in the 1960s, there was talk about eliminating the poverty gap by spending 15 billion dollars to bring every poor family up to the line separating being poor from not being poor. That line was roughly figured at $4000 a year for a family of four as of 1965. The price now is much higher. The important point though is that poverty means more than just being below an annual income level. If poor families were brought up to that level, they would be better off. If, however, they still have high unemployment, low education, and dead-end jobs, they are not likely to have the happiness that goes with having middle-class employment opportunities. Thus going beyond the optimum of zero poverty means having an economy and education system whereby everyone can have access to a job that provides productive job satisfaction. In a superideal world, everyone would enjoy their productive jobs so much that they would continue at their jobs even if they were to become independently wealthy and would no longer need to work for the income.

Closely related to poverty is the policy problem of discrimination. In the 1960s, legislation was passed at the national, state, and local levels providing for fair employment, open housing, public accommodations, and other rights against discriminatory treatment. If there were 100% compliance, we would then have a form of zero discrimination. The absence of such racial and related discrimination in the housing field, for example, does not sufficiently help blacks if their incomes are so low that they cannot afford decent nondiscriminatory housing. What is needed to make nondiscrimination more meaningful is the economic ability and education to be able to take advantage of fair opportunities in employment, consumer rights, and other activities.

On the matter of goals for educational policy, the United States and most countries would be pleased to achieve 100% functional literacy or zero functional illiteracy. Literacy means being able to read and write at a bare minimum level. Functional literacy means being able to read and write sufficiently to be able to complete job applications and to carry on the reading and writing aspects of a normal job. A goal that is better than that optimum would be to have zero functional illiteracy and have everyone rise to their maximum educational achievement level. One could also seek to achieve higher quality standards in education. The standards might include the kind of broadness that is tested for in the National Educational Assessment Program. Educational quality could also include stimulating a high level of inquisitiveness as contrasted to rote learning of facts and doctrines.

E. Science Policy Problems

On the matter of health policy, a society might be considered operating at the optimum if governmental programs have succeeded in stimulating the development and distribution of cures and vaccines for all nonaging or nondegenerative diseases. Merely not having diseases is an excellent societal condition. It is even better though to have a society without diseases plus a high degree of robust health or wellness. That manifests itself in people being energetic and mentally healthy, which may also involve productive job satisfaction. Also on the matter of health, we may be reaching the point where there will be no need to tolerate even disproportionately aging diseases like cancer, heart disease, and diabetes. The time may come when modern genetics will make it possible to change the genes of people not yet conceived so as to adjust their biological clocks. Doing so will mean growing to adulthood but not into old age. People would still die as a result of accidents, although a super-optimum society would have a minimum of accidents as a form of civil wrongdoing. Many people now say they would not want to live indefinitely, but that is probably a sour-grapes attitude, since living indefinitely is not currently available. People are probably no more likely to commit suicide at age 300 than they would be now at age 30.

As for environmental protection, one might consider conditions as being optimum if there were no pollution regarding air, water, solid waste, noise, radiation, or other forms of pollution. That would be fine. The absence of air pollution, however, might make urban and rural slums more visible. What also is needed is more reclamation and conservation of land that has been ruined or damaged from strip mining, erosion, overgrazing, and other forms of bad land use. What also is needed is more urban and rural renewal of buildings and other man-made structures but in such a way as to minimize the disruption to the present occupants.[6]

F. Predicting and Prescribing Future Public Policy

Table 6 summarizes the ideas presented with regard to doing better than the optimum. It shows how that kind of thinking can apply to all policy problems, including (1) economic problems like unemployment, inflation, and consumer rights; (2) political problems like world peace, free speech, and government reform; (3) social problems like crime, poverty, discrimination, and education; and (4) science policy problems like health policy and environmental policy.

Table 6 does not indicate what the trend is in defining goals for each policy problem. The implication, however, is that if one goal is better than another, there would eventually be a trend toward the better goal. "Better" in this sense brings us to a high level of generality such as the standard of the greatest happiness for the greatest number. There is a trend toward higher goals, although that varies depending on the policy field. Goals in civil liberties, education, and health are frequently being raised. Other fields may involve some reduction in goals in order to accommodate problems that have become more severe, such as the problems of pollution and drug-related crime.

Table 6 fits this essay on "Projecting Trends in Public Policy," not so much because the table tells what will be but because it implies what ought to be. One can make a case for saying that the world is getting better on many important dimensions. That is a key idea of Table 1 on some trends in specific policy fields. One can make a case even easier for the idea that the world should be getting better. Both optimists and pessimists are likely to agree that there is room for improvement. Optimists believe that the improvement can occur more readily than pessimists do. Table 6 could be interpreted from an optimistic perspective as at least a partial projection of future trends in public policy. Table 6 can be more easily interpreted from either perspective as a worthy agenda for the future of public policy. Either interpretation fits the title of this essay on "Projecting Trends in Public Policy" regardless whether the trends are predictive or normative trends.

It is hoped that this essay will stimulate further ideas about what will be and why. It is even more hoped that it will stimulate further ideas about what should be and how.

VII. THE FUTURE OF PUBLIC POLICY

Looking back over the 20th century and especially over the past 40 years from 1950 to 1990, one can observe various trends in public policy substance and the study of public policy.

A. Goals to Be Achieved

There is a trend toward higher goals for society in economic, social, political, and science policy. This can be seen in the redefining of concepts like poverty, equality, fair procedure, free speech, good government, adequate education, adequate health, and a clean environment.

There have been major changes in almost all fields of public policy. Those changes have resulted in increased benefits for the less privileged groups in society but also increased benefits simultaneously for the more privileged groups. In the field of labor policy and consumer policy, for example, there are now more rights to workers and consumers, but those rights have provided a stimulus to labor-saving technology and a stimulus to generating better products. Those effects have promoted greater productivity, sales, and profits.

B. Means for Achieving Policy Goals

There is a trend toward the use of positive incentives like subsidies, tax breaks, and low-interest loans for encouraging socially desired behavior. This can be contrasted with an emphasis on negative incentives associated with jail, fines, and injunctions.

There is a trend toward more policy making on the part of the national government relative to the states and cities and more policy making on the part of the executive branch relative to the legislative and judicial. One should, however, note that policy making is increasing among all levels and branches as governments are given more responsibility to deal with various social problems.

There is a trend toward a more pragmatic, mixed approach in dividing responsibility between the public and private sectors for public functions. This can be contrasted with a more ideological approach that allocates between the public and private sectors by determining what would be capitalistic or socialistic.

C. Methods for Analyzing Alternative Public Policies

There is a trend toward evaluation methods which emphasize multi-criteria decision making and spreadsheet analysis. This can be contrasted with an emphasis on single objective functions, decision trees, regression analysis, and linear programming.

D. Institutions for Conducting and Communicating Public Policy Analysis

There has been a substantial growth and now a plateauing out at a high level of activity with regard to policy evaluation training programs, research centers, funding sources, publishing outlets, scholarly associations, and other policy evaluation institutions. See Table 7 for a partial listing of policy analysis institutions. Table 8 shows the elements of policy analysis in an historical perspective.

Table 7. Policy Analysis Institutions

Training programs
John F. Kennedy School of Public Policy at Harvard University
Woodrow Wilson School of Public Policy at Princeton University
Graduate School of Public Policy at the University of California at Berkeley
Institute of Policy Studies at the University of Michigan
Research centers
Brookings Institution, Washington, D.C.
American Enterprise Institute, Washington, D.C.
Government Accounting Office, Washington, D.C.
Abt Associates, Cambridge, Massachusetts
Funding sources
Ford Foundation
National Science Foundation
Rockefeller Foundation
National Institute of Justice
Publishing outlets
Policy Studies Journal and Policy Studies Review
Journal of Public Policy Analysis and Management
Policy Sciences
Lexington-Heath Publishers
Scholarly associations
Policy Studies Organization
Association for Public Policy Analysis and Management
American Political Science Association
American Society for Public Administration

For further details concerning the examples, see Nagel, S. (1980). *The Policy Studies Handbook*. Lexington-Heath. Lexington, Mass.

E. Some Overall Trends

The post-1985 time period can be characterized as one in which (1) there are higher goals for public policy, including the goal of satisfying both liberals and conservatives; (2) there are more positive incentives, more sources of ideas among government levels and branches, and more pragmatic relations between the public and private sectors for achieving those goals; and (3) there is a trend toward multi-criteria decision making and spreadsheet analysis.[7]

Table 8. The Elements of Policy Analysis in Four Recent Time Periods

Time period	Goals	Means	Methods	Institutions
Pre-1960	Good government	Describing policies	Journalism, history, and philosophy	The APSA and the APSR
1960–1975	Goals as being unscientific	Correlating policies	Statistical analysis	Behavioral and regional journals
1975–1985	Goals as variables	Feasible and interdisciplinary policies	Benefit-cost analysis	Policy journals and courses
Post-1985	Questioning goals	Incentives, multiple government foci, and pragmatism	MCDM spreadsheet analysis	Design science

Table 9. The Generic SOS Solution from a Spreadsheet Perspective

4A. The alternatives
   Alternative
   1 CONSERVATIVE ALT.
   2 COMPROMISE
   3 LIBERAL ALT.
   4 SOS1 (Dominating SOS)
   5 SOS2 (Non-Dominating SOS)
   6 SOS3 (New-Goal SOS)

4B. The criteria

Criterion	Meas. Unit	Conserv. Weights	Liberal Weights
1*CONSERVATIVE GOAL	1–5 Scale	3.00	1.00
2*LIBERAL GOAL		1.00	3.00
3 NEUTRAL GOAL		2.00	2.00

4C. Scores of alternatives on criteria

	CONS.GOAL	LIB.GOAL	NEUT.GOAL
CONSERVATIVE ALT.	5.00	1.00	3.00
COMPROMISE	3.10	3.10	3.00
LIBERAL ALT.	1.00	5.00	3.00
SOS1	5.10	5.10	3.10
SOS2	4.50	4.50	2.90
SOS3	4.00	4.00	4.00

4D. Initial analyses

Alternative	Conserv. Combined Rawscores	Liberal Combined Rawscores
1 CONSERVATIVE ALT.	16.00	8.00
2 COMPROMISE	12.40	12.40
3 LIBERAL ALT.	8.00	16.00
4 SOS1	20.40	20.40
5 SOS2	18.00	18.00
6 SOS3	16.00	16.00

Notes to the alternatives:

1. The conservative alternative is shown first because it tends to be the current alternative on which we would like to improve. The conservative alternative or set of alternatives in a policy problem tends to differ from the liberal alternatives in the relative extent to which it favors those who are relatively well off in a society, whereas the liberal alternative tends to favor those who are not so relatively well off.

2. The first super-optimum solution (and the most difficult to achieve) is to find an alternative that is better than the conservative, liberal, and compromise alternatives on *all* the goals. The second super-optimum solution is an alternative that is not better on all the goals than the other alternatives, but it is better on the overall or combined score adding across the goals. The third super-optimum solution is not better on all the goals and is not better on the overall score with the initial goals, but it is better on the overall score than the non-SOS alternatives when another goal is added.

Notes to the criteria:

3. The conservative goal or goals in this context are by definition goals that conservatives disproportionately favor, as indicated by the fact that those goals are given relatively high weight by conservatives. The liberal goals are likewise given relatively high weight by liberals. Note however that in a typical policy problem, conservatives tend to give positive weight to liberal goals (although relatively less weight than to conservative goals), and vice versa with liberals.

4. The scores of the alternatives on the criteria are based on a 1–5 scale for the sake of simplicity, although that does not have to be. Under a 1–5 scale, 5 means highly conducive to the goal, 4 means mildly conducive, 3 means neither conducive nor adverse, 2 means mildly adverse, and 1 means the alternative is highly adverse to the goal.

VIII. POLICY STUDIES, FUTURES RESEARCH, AND SUPER-OPTIMUM SOLUTIONS

Studying trends in public policy is an especially appropriate subject for combining skills that relate to public policy studies and futures research. The field of policy studies is relevant to understanding the substance. The field of futures research is relevant to understanding the methodology of projecting trends.

The analysis that has been presented implies that trends in public policy proceed through a series of time periods that alternate between a push for greater societal productivity and then a push for greater equalitarian division of the results of the increased productivity. That may imply productivity precedes equalitarianism, which is partly true. It is difficult to be equalitarian if societal resources are especially scarce as in times of recession, famine, or losing a war. On the other hand, equal opportunity is essential to fully realizing societal productivity. The productivity of many countries of the world has increased substantially in recent years as a result of providing greater job opportunities to women, ethnic minorities, the elderly, the disabled, and others who have been qualified for more productive jobs than they were previously in.

Another defect in the implications of the analysis is the idea that those alternating periods can continue indefinitely. That may be so regarding increased productivity. New technologies do generate other new technologies at an expanding rate rather than with diminishing regurns. There may be diminishing returns or plateauing out in a given technology (such as automobiles) but not in a broad field (such as transportation) or in technology in general. On the other hand, equality of opportunity can eventually reach the point where there is al-

---

Notes to the relation scores:

5. The conservative alternatives logically score high on the conservative goals and low on the liberal goals, and vice versa for the liberal alternatives. The compromise alternative scores slightly above the middle on each goal. That avoids ties in this analysis, and that is the general nature of compromises.

6. The scores of the super-optimum solutions on the conservative, liberal, and neutral goals are consistent with their definitions. Likewise the scores of the alternatives on the neutral goal are consistent with the definition of the neutral goal as being between the conservative goal and the liberal goal in its normative direction.

Notes to the initial analyses:

7. The combined raw scores are determined by adding the weighted relation scores together. For example, the conservative alternative receives 16 points using the conservative weights by adding (3 times 5) to (1 times 1). Using the liberal weights, the conservative alternative receives only 8 points by adding (1 times 5) to (3 times 1). For the sake of simplicity in this generic analysis, only the conservative goal and the liberal goal are used. The neutral goal has to be activated to enable the "New Goal SOS" to be a super-optimum solution.

8. Using the conservative weights, the conservative alternative logically comes out ahead of the liberal alternative, and vice versa using the liberal weights. The compromise alternative is the winner among those three alternatives with an aggregate score of 24.80 versus 24.00 for either the conservative or the liberal alternative, but the compromise alternative is only the second choice of both groups.

9. The three super-optimum alternatives all do better than the traditional compromise. What is more important, the three super-optimum alternatives all simultaneously do better than the conservative alternative using the conservative weights and they do better than the liberal alternative using the liberal weights. That is the essential characteristics of a super-optimum alternative. It is the *new* first choice of both groups.

10. Even the worst of the three super-optimum solutions comes out so far ahead of the traditional compromise that the only way the traditional compromise could be a winner is (1) if one or more of the goals were to be given a negative weight, or (2) if one or more of the relation scores were to go above 5, below 1, or otherwise be unreasonable.

most no major discrimination against groups of people. We do seem to be approaching that desirable limit, whereas not approaching a technological saturation.

One result of the continuing concern for productivity growth and decreasing need for concern about nonmerit discrimination is a changing of ideological divisions. The past divisions have mainly related to conservatives (who tend to emphasize the interests of those who are relatively well off in a society) versus liberals (who tend to emphasize the interests of those who are not so relatively well off). The present and future divisions are increasingly related to (1) those who seek to expand the total societal product through industrial policy and supply-side economics versus (2) those who still think in terms of fixed pies, zero-sum games, and the idea that the main way to benefit the poor is to take from the rich. The new expansionist philosophy emphasizes solutions to public policy problems that benefit categories of rich-poor, whites-blacks, males-females, urban-rural, north-south, and other groups that were formerly considered inherently in conflict over scarce resources.

Some policy analysts are even advocating and predicting the idea of super-optimum solutions where all sides in traditional policy conflicts can come out ahead of their original best expectations (see Table 9). An example is the U.S. national debt. Traditional conservatives argue the need to cut domestic spending. Traditional liberals argue to need to cut defense spending. They may reluctantly compromise by cutting both and even by raising some taxes. The new expansionist thinkers look for ways to increase the gross national product so there can be increased revenue even with a constant tax rate and without cutting needed expenditures.

If there is going to be more emphasis on super-optimum solutions that can simultaneously achieve otherwise conflicting goals or tradeoffs, then we are in for an exciting future in the development of public policy substance and methods. It is trite to say that these are exciting times. It has not yet become trite to say that we may be entering into super-optimum times. That does not mean that the solutions reached will necessarily be super-optimum. It does mean that policy makers and policy analysts may be expanding their thinking away from tradeoffs and split-the-difference compromises toward thinking about ways in which we can have our expanded pie and eat it too. The future looks good for creative thinkers, systematic policy analysts, and insightful futures researchers.[8]

APPENDIX: THE CLINTON ADMINISTRATION

At the time this brief appendix is being written, Bill Clinton's administration has only been in office for about four months. It may therefore be premature to try to indicate where the Clinton administration fits into an analysis of public policy trends for the 20th century. There are, however, some things that can be said by projecting past and recent occurrences independent of current news events.

Prior to the 1990s or at least the 1980s, public policy has developed in the United States in a pattern of cycles. The cycles have involved alternating between (1) periods emphasizing increased national productivity and (2) periods emphasizing increased equity in the distribution of the previous productivity benefits. The post-Civil War period through the McKinley administration was a prime time of rapid growth in American industry, transportation, population, urbanization, and westward movement. The administrations of Theodore Roosevelt and Woodrow Wilson showed a new concern for equity toward consumers, as manifested in such legislation as the Clayton Anti-Trust Act and the Pure Food and Drug Act.

The 1920s were a boom period for increased productivity after World War I. The 1930s involved a great deal of concern for equity toward workers, as indicated by such legislation as the National Labor Relations Act and the Fair Labor Standards Act. They provided for rights regarding collective bargaining and better working conditions. The late 1940s and the 1950s involved another boom period of increased productivity after World War II. The 1960s were marked by an increased concern for equity toward African-Americans, low-income people, and women, as indicated by the civil rights legislation of 1964, 1965, and 1968, as well as the Great Society programs. The 1970s and 1980s involved a renewed emphasis on productivity subsequent to the distracting Vietnam War.

Moving into the 1990s, one might anticipate a renewed emphasis on some aspects of equity. There comes a time, however, when equity tends to plateau out because groups decrease that were formerly not receiving their fair share of the productivity benefits. As of 1990, the Supreme Court has broadened the concept of equal treatment under law to include ethnic groups, religions, gender, sexual orientation, age, disability, and other criteria that do not relate to individual merit. Congress has also passed legislation designed to implement nondiscrimination. Productivity can continue to improve on into the future. As new technologies develop, the gross national product can continue to expand.

The programs of the Clinton administration (as expounded during the campaign and to a lesser extent during the first few months in office) seem to provide a synthesis of both productivity and equity concerns. That shows in the health-care proposals which President Clinton considers to be an especially important part of his program. In discussing the proposals, he shows concern for productivity in documenting how American business is hurt in international competition by high medical-care costs and overly frequent absenteeism. In discussing the proposals, he also shows concern for equity by documenting how middle-class people are unable to afford adequate medical care, especially if expensive hospitalization or procedures are involved. The middle-class health-care consumer in that regard may be worse off then the low-income person who can draw upon Medicaid or Medicare.

It might also be noted that both President Clinton and President Reagan have endorsed programs for dealing with policy problems and the national debt by emphasizing economic growth. That is in contrast to the more traditional conflict between Democrats and Republicans over how to raise money for public programs and for making payments on the national debt. The Democrats in the past have emphasized cuts in defense spending and increases in income taxes, especially on higher incomes. The Republicans have emphasized cuts in domestic spending and the possibility of starting a federal consumption tax like the value-added tax. As of 1993, the Democrats in Congress talk in terms of substantial tax increases and less substantial spending decreases, whereas the Republicans talk in terms of substantial spending decreases and less substantial tax increases.

The perspective that emphasizes economic growth takes the position that what is needed is better quality spending and tax incentives to stimulate the adoption of new technologies and the upgrading of worker skills in order to increase national productivity. Doing so means increasing the gross national product and thus the tax base, which allows for greater tax revenue at a constant or reduced tax rate. The greater revenue provides additional funds for further stimulating productivity and especially for dealing with various policy problems and national debt reduction. That is expansionist thinking directed toward super-optimum solutions, whereby all major groups can come out ahead of their best initial expectations simultaneously.

That is the kind of new public policy which may be especially emphasized at the end of the 20th century and the beginning of the 21st. Such win-win solutions to public policy problems involve combining productivity and equity simultaneously, rather than sequentially in a cyclical pattern. Economic growth by definition means increased productivity. It also facilitates larger slices of the total economic pie for all major groups.[9]

The first few months of the Clinton administration have been distracted by short-term concerns with 1993 summer employment, new appointments to federal positions, and issues that relate to sex and relatively gossipy matters, rather than long-term economic growth. It is, however, anticipated that the Clinton administration will regain the broader visions that were expressed in the campaign. This is likely to occur not so much due to the personality of President Clinton, but due more to the social, economic, political, and technological forces that have been developing throughout the 20th century in the United States and elsewhere.

NOTES

1. For further details on the recent history of developments in the fields of public policy, see Theodore J. Lowi and Alan Stone (eds.), *Nationalizing Government: Public Policies in America* (Sage, Beverly Hills, CA, 1978); John Schwarz, *America's Hidden Success: A Reassessment of Public Policy from Kennedy to Reagan* (Norton, New York, 1988); Robert Bremmer, et al. (eds.), *American Choices: Social Dilemmas and Public Policy since 1960* (Ohio State University Press, Columbus, 1986); and David Rothman and Stanton Wheeler (eds.), *Social History and Social Policy* (Academic Press, San Diego, Calif. 1981).
2. For further details on trends in the division of labor between the public and private sectors, see Martin Rein and Lee Rainwater (eds.), *Public/Private Interplay in Social Protection: A Comparative Study* (M. E. Sharpe, Armonk, N.Y., 1986); David Linowes (ed.), *Privatization: Toward More Effective Government* (Government Printing Office, Washington, D.C., 1988); and Dennis Thompson (ed.), *The Private Exercise of Public Functions* (Associated Faculty Press, New York, 1985).
3. For further details on trends in the division of labor among levels and branches of government, see James Sundquist, *Constitutional Reform and Effective Government* (Brookings Institution, Washington, D.C., 1985); David Walker, *Toward a Functioning Federalism* (Winthrop, San Francisco, 1981); and Michael Reagan and John Sanzone, *The New Federalism* (Oxford University Press, New York, 1981).
4. For further details on trends regarding incentives to encourage socially desired behavior, see Barry Mitnick, *The Political Economy of Regulation: Creating, Designing, and Removing Regulatory Forms* (Columbia University Press, New York, 1980); William Hamilton, Larry Ledebur, and Deborah Matz, *Industrial Incentives: Public Promotion of Private Enterprise* (Aslan Press, Washington, D.C., 1984); and Alfred Blumstein (ed.), *Deterrence and Incapacitation* (National Academy of Sciences, Washington, D.C., 1978).
5. For further details on trends regarding methods of public policy evaluation, one can compare relevant books from the 1950s, 1960s, 1970s, and so on, such as Daniel Lerner and Harold Lasswell (eds.), *The Policy Sciences* (Stanford University Press, Palo Alto, CA, 1951); Raymond Bauer and Kenneth Gergen (eds.), *The Study of Policy Formation* (Free Press, New York, 1968); Irving Horowitz and James katz, *Social Science and Public Policy in the United States* (Praeger, New York, 1975); Nick Smith (ed.), *New Techniques for Evaluation* (Sage, Beverly Hills, CA, 1981); and S. Nagel, *Evaluation Analysis with Microcomputers* (JAI Press, Greenwich, CT, 1988).
6. For further details on trends regarding the development of higher goals for America and elsewhere, one can compare relevant books from the 1960s, 1970s, and 1980s such as Henry Wriston (ed.), *Goals for Americans: The Report of the President's Commission on National Goals* (American Assembly, Prentice-Hall, Englewood Cliffs, NJ, 1960); Kermit Gordon (ed.), *Agenda for the Nation* (Brookings Institution, Doubleday, New York, 1968); Henry Owen and Charles Schultze (eds.), *Setting National Priorities: The Next Ten Years* (Brookings Institution, Washington, D.C., 1976); and Isabel Sawhill (ed.), *Challenge to Leadership: Economic and Social Issues for the Next Decade* (Urban Institute, Washington, DC, 1988).

7. For further details on relations between policy studies and futures research, see Albert Somit, *Political Science and the Study of the Future* (Dryden, Fort Worth, TX, 1974); Franklin Tugwell, *Public Policy and the Study of the Future* (Winthrop, San Francisco, 1973); Wayne Boucher (ed.), *The Study of the Future: An Agenda for Research* (National Science Foundation, Washington, D.C. 1977); Edward Cornish, *The Study of the Future: An Introduction to the Arts and Science of Understanding and Shaping Tomorrow's World* (World Future Society, Bethesda, MD, 1977); and S. Nagel, "Policy Studies and Futures Research," 14 *World Future Society Bulletin* 1·10 (1980).

8. For literature on super-optimum solutions, see Lawrence Susskind and Jeffrey Cruikshank, *Breaking the Impasse: Consensual Approaches to Resolving Disputes* (Basic Books, New York, 1987); S. Nagel, *Higher Goals for America: Doing Better than the Best* (University Press of America, Lanham, MD, 1989); and S. Nagel, *Evaluation Analysis with Microcomputers* (JAI Press, Greenwich, CT, 1989).

9. For further details on the plans of the Clinton Administration and commentaries regarding those plans, see Bill Clinton and Al Gore, *Putting People First: How We Can All Change America* (New York: Times Books, 1992), Henry Aaron and Charles Schultze (eds.), *Setting Domestic Priorities: What Can Government Do?* (Washington: Brookings, 1992), Robert Reich, *The Work of Nations: Preparing Ourselves for 21st Century Capitalism* (New York: Knopf, 1991), and David Osborne and Ted Gebler, *Reinventing Government: How the Entrepreneurial Spirit is Transforming the Public Sector from Schoolhouse to Statehouse, City Hall to the Pentagon* (Reading, Mass.: Addison-Wesley, 1992).

Author Index

Aaron, H., 88, 913, 812
Aberbach, J. D., 380
Abercrombie, N., 25
Abramowitz, A. I., 380
Abramson, J., 767
Achen, C. H., 325
Acheson, D., 852
Adamache, K., 766
Adams, C., 175
Adams, J., 697
Adams, K., 586
Addison, J. T., 450
Adler, E., 697
Adler, F., 578
Agarwala-Rogers, R., 88
Akaha, R., 681
Alber, J., 175
Alchian, A. A., 451
Aleem, S., 578
Alexander, H. E., 380, 578
Alford, R., 174, 762
Alison, G., 149
Alker, H., 298
Alkin, M., 88
Allan, E. A., 585
Allen, R. L., 273
Allen, T., 729
Alleyne, R. H., 450
Allison, G., 88, 298, 609, 875

Almond, G. A., 174, 609, 214
Almquist, P., 325
Alonso, W., 639
Alper, J., 477, 638
Altman, D., 762
Amacher, R., 214, 215
Ambrosius, M., 244
Ament, R., 765
Ames, B., 174, 504
Anastasia, G., 578
Anderson, C. A., 451, 578
Anderson, D. G., 682
Anderson, E., 702
Anderson, F., 697
Anderson, G., 762
Anderson, J., 450
Anderson, O., 762
Anderson, P., 298
Andringa, R. C., 609
Andriole, S. J., 298, 304
Annas, G. J., 812
Antal, A., 698
Anter, D., 763
Anton, T., 215, 244
Apple, M. W., 609
Argyris, C., 88
Arieff, I. B., 380
Arkes, H., 25
Arkin, W. M., 793

Subject Index